W9-BDB-823

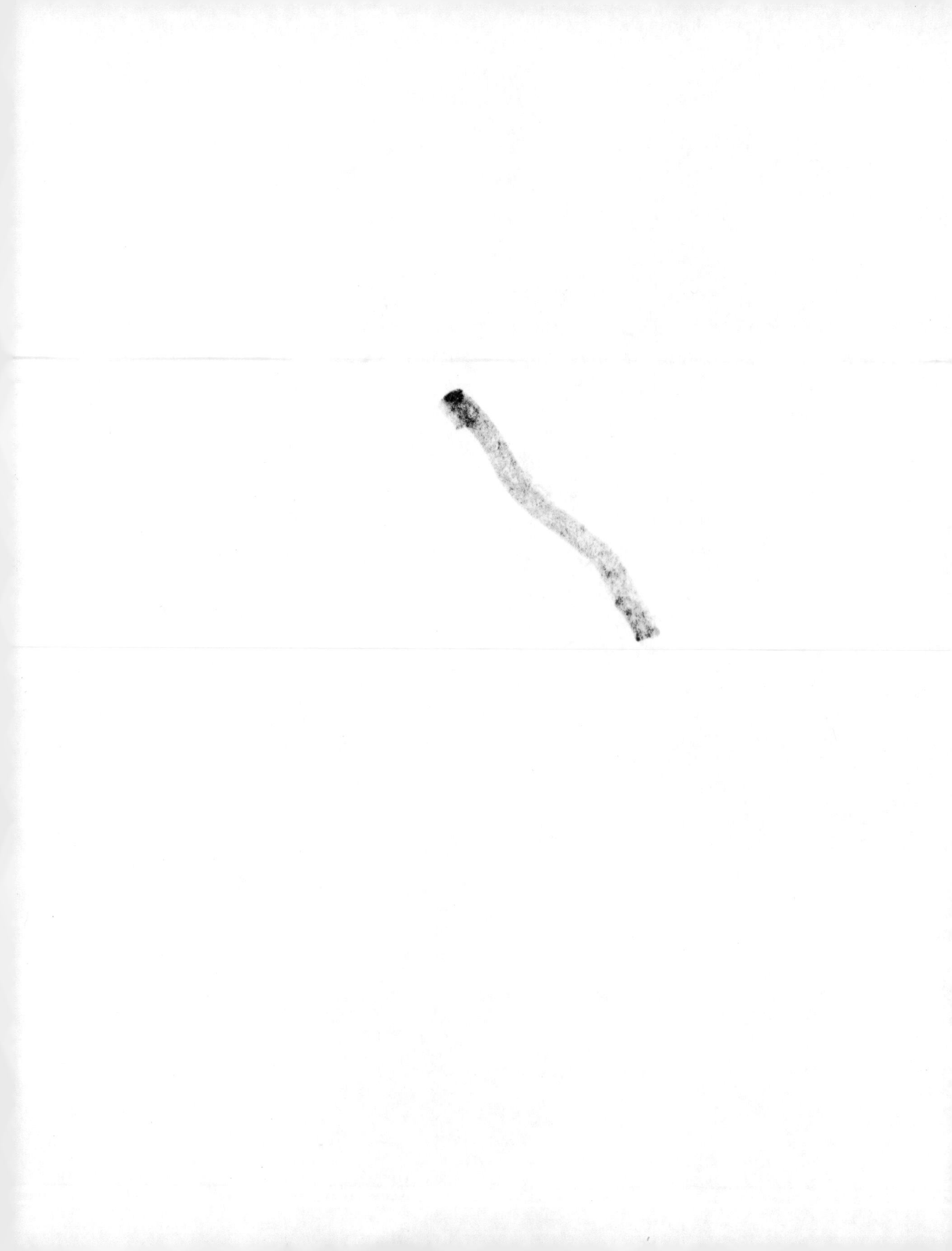

Principles of Operations Research for Management

Irwin Series in Quantitative Analysis for Business
Consulting Editor Robert B. Fetter Yale University

Principles of Operations Research for Management

FRANK S. BUDNICK

DENNIS McLEAVEY

RICHARD MOJENA
All of the University of Rhode Island
In collaboration with Thomas E. Vollmann

1988 Second Edition

Homewood, Illinois 60430

Acquisitions editor: Richard T. Hercher
Project editor: Lynne Basler
Copyediting coordinator: Jean Roberts
Production manager: Bette Ittersagen
Designer: Jeanne Feldman
Compositor: Beacon Graphics
Typeface: 10/12 Times Roman
Printer: R. R. Donnelley & Sons Company

ISBN 0-256-02643-2

Library of Congress Catalog Card No. 87–81435

Printed in the United States of America

1 2 3 4 5 6 7 8 9 0 DO 5 4 3 2 1 0 9 8

To

My Family, Friends, and Students

F. S. B.

Janet, Christie, and Andy
Dad and Marge
Rob, Pam, Craig, and Megan

D. W. M.

All Who Care

R. M.

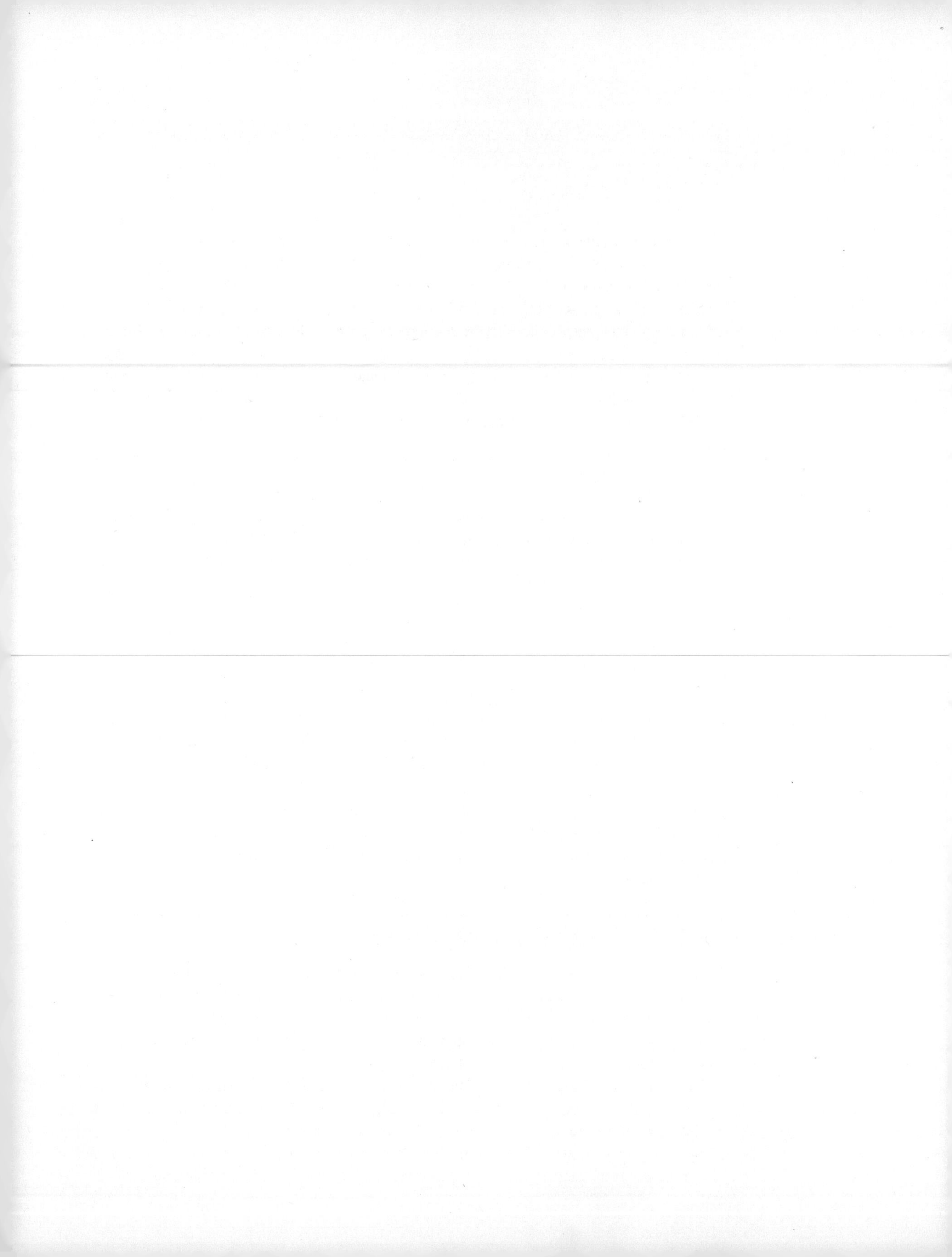

PREFACE

This textbook is primarily intended for use in a one-semester course in management science, operations research, or quantitative methods in schools of management or business administration. Specifically, it is designed for the frequently required course in OR/MS at the junior-senior and MBA levels. The textbook is also suitable for OR/MS courses designed for majors in economics, public administration, and health administration. Additionally, it may be appropriate as a primary or supplementary source in a two-semester course for undergraduate majors in OR/MS. Feedback from the more than 200 universities and colleges that adopted the first edition indicates that the book has been utilized in the ways it was intended.

OBJECTIVES AND ORIENTATION

Our primary objective in this book is to demonstrate the contribution OR/MS can make in support of effective decision making. To accomplish this we present a comprehensive and (we hope) lucid survey of OR/MS techniques, illustrating their applicability in decision-making settings.

An important aspect of our decision-making orientation is reflected in the design of Chapter 1. An eight-step *decision paradigm,* which includes the scientific method, is developed in depth. The paradigm is a framework that outlines a process for applying OR/MS in problem-solving, decision-making situations.

Our emphasis on managerial decision making is reflected by a strong applications orientation; however, this does not imply a superficial or "cookbook" treatment of the models and their solutions. We are convinced that a reasonable amount of theoretical foundation is required to avoid misapplication and incorrect decision implications. We have attempted to suppress mathematical rigor without sacrificing conceptual rigor. For the most part, proofs and other mathematical developments that are of interest to the quantitatively inclined have either been relegated to appendices or identified as advanced (optional) sections and starred (**) exercises that can be omitted without loss of continuity.

IMPORTANT ASPECTS OF THE SECOND EDITION

Our apologies to those of you who have waited so long for the promised second edition of this text. Although it is long overdue, we hope you will be pleased with the changes we have made. In discussing these changes, we will first overview general changes that are reflected throughout the book. We follow with a discussion of specific changes associated with different chapters.

Generally, the organization of chapters within this edition is such that models can be discussed without focusing on solution algorithms. The organization allows for coverage of the models, their assumptions, and applications. For those who wish to delve into the specifics of solution algorithms, such material is available. In many chapters, solution algorithms are overviewed and computer-based implementation is illustrated using a variety of software packages. The greater emphasis on computer-based solutions is also reflected by a significant increase in the number of exercises having computer requirements. Exercises with computer requirements are designated by the symbol 🖳 .

Other additions to the text include:

Selected articles that make significant contributions to the understanding of a topic.

End-of-chapter cases, which provide applications that are larger scale and more complex than those found in the exercise sets.

"Selected Application Reviews," which offer evidence of the successful implementation of operations research/management science.

Answers to selected odd-numbered exercises.

Tables of e^x, e^{-x}, $ln\ x$, and normal probability distribution values.

Regarding specific changes on a chapter-by-chapter basis, a *problem-solving framework* is presented in Chapter 1 to provide students with guidance in solving exercises within the text. This framework is illustrated in a variety of examples throughout the text. The material on *classical optimization* has been reorganized in this edition. Rather than the original two chapters, Chapter 2 focuses on the application of the calculus to unconstrained and constrained optimization problems. Appendix B at the end of the text reviews *differentiation* and *the methodology of classical optimization*. This reorganization reflects the concensus that most students using this book have had at least one course in differential calculus.

The material on *linear programming* has been reorganized. Chapter 3 introduces the LP model, its assumptions, applications, and special issues. Chapter 4, a new chapter, focuses on *geometric and computer-based solution methods*. Chapter 5 allows instructors to examine *postoptimality analysis* and the *dual problem* without understanding the mechanics of the simplex. Chapter 6 presents the *simplex method*, including simplex-based sensitivity analysis. Also discussed in this chapter are the simplex analysis of primal and dual problems as well as an overview of other LP algorithms including the "Ellipsoid algorithm." This reorganization should make it easier for professors to cover the linear programming material in a non-algorithmic manner.

Chapter 7 has been reorganized to focus first on the structure, assumptions, and applications of *transportation and assignment models*. Solution algorithms have been moved to the second half of the chapter. Two new sections have been added: one discusses the Hungarian solution algorithm for assignment models and the other presents computer-based analysis for both transportation and assignment models.

Chapter 8 presents a comprehensive treatment of *integer and zero-one programming*. New examples and applications have been added along with a new section on computer-based solution methods. Chapter 9 provides an expanded and more comprehensive treatment of *goal programming*. Along with illustrations of computer-based solution methods, Section 9.4 overviews extensions of goal programming into other areas of multicriteria math programming.

Chapter 10 is a new chapter on *network models*. It provides an expanded and more comprehensive treatment of network modeling and specialized network algorithms.

Also illustrated are computer-based solution methods. Chapter 12 represents a significant rewrite of the material on *dynamic programming*. More emphasis is placed on backward recursion solution methods.

In Chapter 14, we focused on improving the clarity of the presentation of *Markov processes*. The addition of "lily pad models" offers a nice visual model of these processes. The Chapter 15 discussion of *inventory models* includes a new section on aggregate inventory management. Another new section on multiechelon inventory management and scheduling includes a discussion of MRP and just-in-time (JIT) inventory systems.

Chapter 17 represents a significant rewrite of the material on *simulation*. More emphasis is given to the process of simulation. A new section on "manual simulation" introduces students to the process at an elementary level. The material on "System Dynamics" and "World Dynamics" has been eliminated in this edition.

Chapter 18 is a new wrap-up chapter that emphasizes the role of operations research/management science in problem solving and decision making. It covers the extent to which OR/MS has been implemented within organizations and discusses keys to successful implementation. The last section examines possible future directions for the field.

Examples and Exercises

Since the book is intended for users rather than designers of quantitative techniques, there is a strong emphasis on realistic scenarios through examples, exercises, and cases. Exercises are found both within the chapter (follow-up exercises) and at the end of the chapter (additional exercises). Follow-up exercises serve to reinforce, integrate, and extend immediately preceding material, whereas the chapter-end exercises offer an opportunity for review and new scenarios.

The portfolio of applications includes those in the traditional functional areas of business (e.g., finance, marketing, accounting, management, production); those that can be classified as "classic" OR (e.g., traveling salesman, trim loss, knapsack, caterer, reliability, replacement); and those that include the public sector (e.g., urban systems, environmental protection, health care delivery, emergency response systems). Because the management process transcends private enterprise, we have made a particular effort to provide meaningful applications in the public sector. In our years of teaching, we have found that diversity and richness of applications is appealing to students, better highlights the benefits of quantitative modeling, and reveals important similarities across decision-making environments. A convenient reference for locating page numbers for the applications in the book follows the contents.

Prerequisites

The only prerequisite assumed for the text is an understanding of basic algebra and basic statistics. Additional quantitative prerequisites are either reviewed in appendices or developed as necessary. For example, appendices review differentiation and the methodology of classical optimization as well as fundamentals of matrix algebra. Basic concepts in probability and statistics are reviewed in the chapter-length Appendix A. Many of our students have commented about how useful this appendix has been in providing a concise summary review, even for purposes unrelated to their course in operations research.

Except for Chapter 2 and some advanced materials, chapters in this text are written in such a manner that they do not require calculus.

We wish to express our deep appreciation to many who have contributed to this project, both explicitly and implicitly, and to those who provided valuable suggestions through their review of the manuscript. These include Jeffrey Baum (State University of New York, College at Oneonta); Graham Links (CSP Foods Corporate); Robert Haessler (University of Michigan); Clarence Jones (Duquesne University); Authella Bessent (University of Texas at Austin); James Fitzsimmons (University of Texas at Austin); Brent Bandy (University of Wisconsin-Oshkosh); S. K. Goyal (Concordia University); Bruce Woodworth (Oregon State University); and Richard Reid (University of New Mexico). A special thanks to Jim Fitzsimmons, University of Texas at Austin, for his conscientious efforts and insightful suggestions. In addition, we would like to thank Chon-Huat Goh for his efforts in developing solutions to exercises in the book. Thanks also to Deborah Ferrette for her assistance on many aspects of the project, to "Speedy" Ede Williams for her help in typing parts of the manuscript and instructor's manual, and to our students who suffered through the class testing of the manuscript, providing invaluable corrections and suggestions. We also wish to thank our families, who remained cheerfully (we think) supportive in spite of our long hours and frequent absences.

Frank S. Budnick
Dennis W. McLeavey
Richard Mojena

CONTENTS

TABLE OF APPLICATIONS

Private Sector

Accounting — Finance

Management

Marketing

Production

Classic OR

Public Sector

1

The Process of Operations Research/ Management Science

Chapter Outline

This text focuses on problem solving. Specifically, it addresses the process of managerial problem solving. This process begins with a mechanism for identifying, verifying, and defining potential problems. What follows is a systematic search for solution alternatives to present to the ultimate decision maker(s), the recommended decision, and implementation questions about the recommended solution. Successful implementation is the ultimate measure of whether the problem has been solved or still exists.

We will explain the particular orientation we bring to the process of problem solving in this chapter and reinforce it throughout the remainder of the text.

1.1 INTRODUCTION TO THE PROCESS

Orientation

Our orientation, as reflected by the book's title, is toward the use of **operations research (OR)** as an approach to managerial decision making. The field of operations research, or **management science (MS),** is concerned with the development and application of quantitative analyses to the solution of problems faced by managers of public and private organizations.[1] More specifically, theory and methodology (tools) in mathematics, probability, statistics, and computing are adapted and applied to the identification, formulation, solution, validation, implementation, and control of administrative or decision-making problems.

We believe that elements of a decision environment frequently lend themselves to quantification. To the extent that this is true, we believe that appropriate analysis of these quantitative elements can yield significant inputs for the purpose of decision making. We are not so self-assured as to suggest that a quantitatively derived decision input is superior to all other inputs. Nor would we suggest that all problems lend themselves to such analysis. We do believe that many problems are amenable to quantitative analysis and that such analysis holds the potential for more effective decision making.

Our philosophy is that, when a problem is conducive to quantitative analysis, the results and recommendations of such analysis should be viewed as one of possibly many inputs to the ultimate decision maker(s). Along with the quantitatively based input(s), there may be subjective as well as experientially based inputs. In some cases the quantitative input may be significant; in other cases it may be useless. From the perspective of the decision maker, the most important point is the ability to evaluate this input (as well as all others) and to utilize the inputs to make an effective decision.

Many of you will ultimately find yourselves in management positions. You may be faced with the task of evaluating quantitatively based decision inputs. After *conscientious* study with this text, you should be in a better position to evaluate these inputs and thus be a more effective decision maker.

Our commitment to applications in this book should not be interpreted as an avoidance of rigorous material. Although rigor will not be developed for rigor's sake alone,

[1] In schools of business administration or management, MS and OR are essentially synonymous. Where OR is housed in, say, schools of engineering, the emphasis tends to be on mathematical proofs and, of course, on nonbusiness applications.

FIGURE 1–1 The Role of Quantitative Analysis in the Decision-Making Process

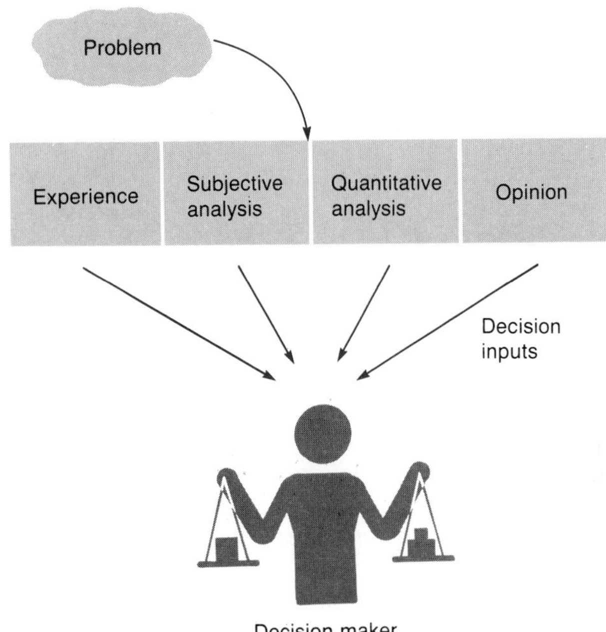

we maintain that a certain degree of quantitative sophistication is necessary to clearly understand the different modeling techniques and their assumptions, limitations, extensions, and reasons for success and failure. Our interest is in good applications, and good must be distinguished from bad on a technical as well as on an applied basis.

An applications orientation results in the presentation of many techniques by example. We have attempted to make the examples realistic, rich, and varied. Because there are many ways of looking at the same problem, several examples will be revisited in subsequent chapters. Since management is a general process, the examples will be based on public as well as private sectors, on large as well as small firms. Furthermore, we will try to show how problem structure in one decision-making situation is very similar to problem structure in other kinds of decision-making situations.

A Framework

There is general acceptance of what is involved in the process of integrating operations research/management science (OR/MS) into the decision-making, problem-solving effort. The process is described differently (i.e., the words and steps) by various authors and practitioners. For example, Green, Lee, and Newsom classify the problem-solving process according to three major stages: (1) **the premodeling function,** (2) **the modeling function,** and (3) **the implementation function.**[2] Emphasiz-

[2]Thad B. Green, Sang M. Lee, and Walter B. Newsom, *The Decision Science Process* (New York: Petrocelli Books, 1978), pp. 3–22.

ing the behavioral aspects of the process, the premodeling function (stage) focuses on developing an understanding of the user (the person[s] with the problem) and developing good relationships with the user and within the user's organization. The modeling function (stage) emphasizes the vital role of the user in developing a quantitative model of the decision environment. Finally, the implementation function (stage) emphasizes the importance of the modeler/user partnership, communication, and organizational relationships in implementing the problem solution.

We organize the process as an **eight-step paradigm,** or framework for decision making:

Premodeling
1. **Recognition of a Need.** (The perception that some action needs to be taken, or perhaps taken better.)
2. **Problem Formulation.** (Translation of the perceived need into an explicit statement of both the need and the criteria by which problem solution is to be judged.)

Modeling
3. **Model Construction.** (Construction of a mathematical replica or representation of the problem.)
4. **Data Collection.** (Gathering the specific inputs to the model which reflect actual problem conditions.)
5. **Model Solution.** (Manipulation of the input data to produce results.)
6. **Model Validation and Sensitivity Analysis.** (Testing model results to ensure validity and determining the implications of errors in estimating input data.)

Postmodeling
7. **Interpretation of Results and Implications.** (Broad reexamination of problem criteria in light of model results.)
8. **Decision Making, Implementation, and Control.** (Behavioral and technical change requirements estimation in both short-run and long-run conditions.)

Notice that we have adapted the Green classification scheme identifying steps 1 and 2 as premodeling phases, steps 3–6 as modeling phases, and steps 7–8 as postmodeling.

Figure 1–2 is a schematic diagram of the eight-step process. We want to make it clear that this paradigm is not to be regarded as a rigid set of steps that one enters at one end and proceeds through on a direct course to the other end. On the contrary, a great deal of cycling back and forth through the steps in any particular problem should be expected. The ideas included in the eight-step paradigm will be utilized and reemphasized in subsequent chapters. We will not, however, subject you to the drill of squeezing each problem through all eight steps of the following paradigm. In Sections 1.2 thru 1.4, we will overview the different steps in the process, highlighting the significant aspects of each.

The User-Designer Partnership

When integrating OR/MS into the problem-solving, decision-making effort, we strongly advocate forming a partnership between those who perceive they have a problem (the **users**) and those who have the specialized knowledge or skills in problem solving (the **designers**). The user has ultimate decision-making responsibility, and the designer is assumed to have the expertise in operations research.

FIGURE 1–2 The Decision-Making Process

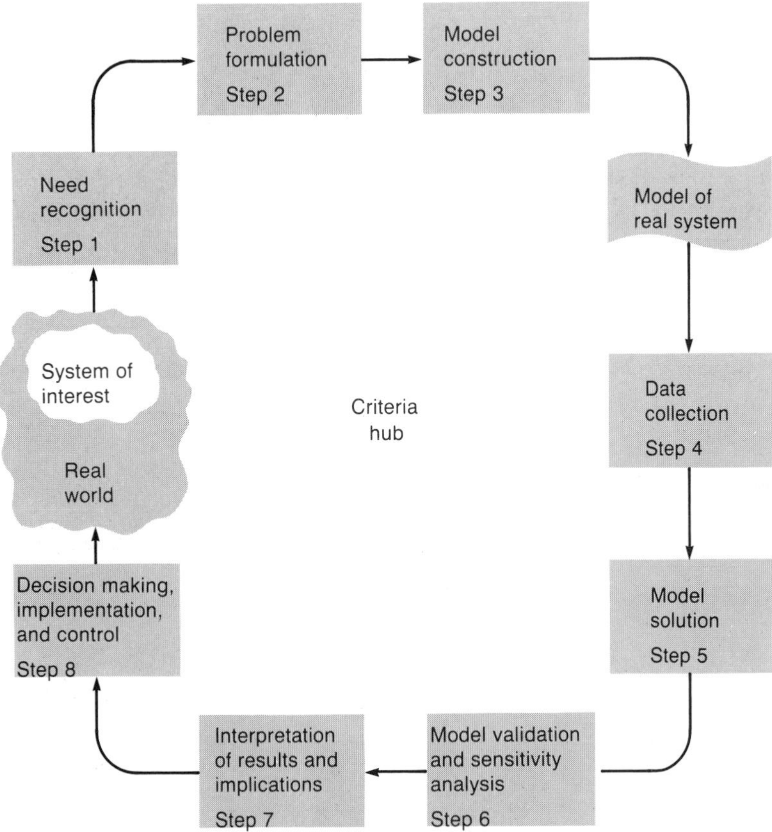

We describe the **user-designer concept** as a style of problem investigation that more thoroughly involves the user in the analysis. The user brings knowledge of and experience with the problem setting, understanding of organizational relationships, and an ability to identify key players who are likely to be impacted by the problem or its solution. The user's participation will also enhance his or her understanding of the decision input derived from an OR/MS analysis.

The user-designer partnership should result in better communication and mutual understanding between the (often, nontechnical, nonquantitative) user and the designer. The expected result is an accelerated evolution in problem formulation, model building, and problem solution, as well as an increased likelihood of successful resolution of the problem.

1.2 PREMODELING

Step 1 — Need Recognition

The decision-making process is triggered by the perception that a decision needs to be made — that some action needs to be taken, or perhaps taken better. The perception of a need for a decision may be *subjective* or *objective*. Experienced managers may have a sixth sense that alerts them to a problem. On the other hand, bed utilization rates in an obstetrical unit of a hospital may provide hard evidence of either declining birth rates or reduced admissions due to competition. The observations may be precursors to the prospect of losing accreditation for the hospital's obstetrical unit.

The key elements in detecting a perceived need are the measures of performance used by the organization. The signal of a potential need is usually based on an unfavorable comparison between actual performance and desired performance, as shown in Figure 1–3. Thus implicit in this is an ability to identify the objectives or criteria for an organization or other measures that accurately reflect them.

FIGURE 1–3

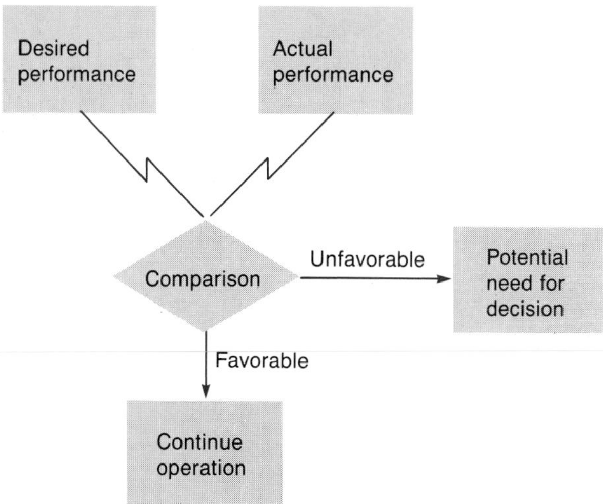

Criteria or Objectives. In any decision-making environment, goals, objectives, or criteria are used to assess the status quo. When the assessment is negative, the decision-making process has been started. Some people like to think of goals as being more broad in orientation than objectives, which in turn are less specific than criteria. We will not make this distinction, since one person's criterion might be another person's goal; we will generally use the term *criterion* as somewhat all-encompassing and at the same time will often use the management science term *objective function*. All of these terms have the same purpose in decision making: *criteria dictate, direct, or drive the decision-making process.*

Criteria are possessed by individuals as well as by organizational entities, such as departments, companies, hospitals, or city governments. For example, a manager in an industrial firm has personal aspirations, and the company has profit, growth, and other objectives. A medical doctor has personal as well as professional objectives, such as income and experience, and the hospital has such objectives as care, reputation, fiduciary responsibility, cost minimization, and so forth. The town mayor might be interested in political patronage and getting reelected in addition to being a good representative of the people; and the town has objectives of providing community services, minimizing the tax burden, or providing a healthy environment in which to bring up children.

One of the critical problems in decision making stems from the fact that there are many criteria involved in any decision; in fact, it is probably fair to say that there are *too* many. The decision maker has many objectives, and those objectives have to be balanced with the criteria of other individuals and organizational subunits. What we have, then, is a set or system of criteria that operates throughout the decision-making process. Need might be recognized in terms of only one criterion, or the perception may take place in terms of several criteria.

One of the primary problems in decision making within a multicriteria environment is **goal congruence.** Criteria sets or systems need to be established so that they are consistent: Achievement of the company manager's goals should be consistent with company criteria; the doctor's goals must not be realized at the expense of the goals of the patient or hospital; and the town mayor's objectives should not be at the expense of the constituents. In step 7 of our decision-making paradigm, we will see that, laudable as goal congruency may be, it will never be achieved perfectly. Suboptimization within organizational units is a fact of life.

Surrogates. All high-level (ultimate or universal) criteria tend to be vague. The manager of a company might want "fulfillment from life." How does the company know when it is maximizing profits? What is professional status for a doctor? How do we maximize community services?

In any decision-making environment, ultimate criteria will often be nebulous, and it is necessary to establish **surrogates**, or stand-ins, by which we can judge particular actions. The purpose of a surrogate criterion is to reduce a nebulous, though terribly important, objective into some less nebulous objective—one that can be measured. For example, a surrogate for a person's standard of living (ultimate criterion) might be personal income or annual percentage growth in personal income. A company's performance (ultimate criterion) is often measured in terms of surrogate criteria, such as profit as a percentage of sales, return on stockholders' equity, market share, or percentage growth in sales. Hospitals are continually evaluated by accrediting agencies as well as by boards of directors in terms of such measures as the number of patient-days spent in the hospital per death, percentage occupancy in the maternity section, and so forth. Even successful politicians are concerned with the margin by which they have won. Professional plant location specialists evaluate towns in terms of such measures as tax rate, assessed evaluation, and student-faculty ratios in schools.

Surrogate criteria are always necessary, but they are simultaneously dangerous. The danger in using these surrogates is that they are not "the ultimate criteria." It is always possible to improve performance in terms of a surrogate, while performance in terms of ultimate criteria is degraded.

▶ Example 1.1 Metropolitan Boston Transit Authority—MBTA

An increasing number of complaints, unfavorable newspaper editorials, and statements by politicians about the subway service in Boston caused the governing board of the

MBTA to question present operations. The board asked the subway operations manager to identify ways to improve service.

What are the criteria for a problem like this? Who has the criteria? Clearly, there are criteria for the taxpayers of Massachusetts who subsidize metropolitan mass transportation. There are also subway-user criteria, as well as criteria possessed by individuals and organizational entities concerned with transportation issues (subways, buses, trains, expressways, toll bridges, and so on). Other criteria that well may be important include those possessed by politicians, newspapers, lobbying groups, or other power sources that can exert pressure on subway operations.

The use of surrogates is obviously needed in this problem. Examples might include net profit or loss from operations, number of passengers, passenger-miles traveled, passenger waiting times, passenger travel times, ticket price per ride, breakdown frequency, equipment utilization, number of robberies in subway stations, wages of personnel, percentage of minority persons employed, automobile gasoline consumption, expressway traffic counts, and bonded debt levels.

Some of these surrogates conflict with others; for example, reducing the price per ride might reduce the net profit from operations. Others are more consistent, such as reducing both breakdown frequencies and passenger waiting. Moreover, potential conflicts exist: All trains could spend more time undergoing preventive maintenance, which would leave fewer trains in service. Finally, as noted in the discussion of surrogates, improvement in terms of these stand-ins may work to the detriment of the ultimate goals. For example, subway commuters might want to reach work in less time (passenger travel time minimization becomes the surrogate); the act of closing every other subway station will reduce travel time but might increase the time between leaving the house and arriving at the job.

To illustrate how the user-designer interaction *might* occur for this MBTA example, assume that the user is the operations manager, that equipment utilization and net return from operations are the major surrogate criteria, and that the problem has evolved to the stage of making a decision about reduced fares during nonpeak hours in order to stimulate subway travel.

In Chapter 2 you will see one model for dealing with this problem. In using the model it will be necessary to ascertain whether or not the model is valid and whether or not correct decision implications can be drawn from it. Of much more fundamental importance, however, is whether or not this model can be used at all: Is it compatible with the MBTA operations manager's style of thinking? Can the manager understand the model, both in its present formulation and in its logical extensions? Are the initial decision implications consonant with the operations manager's perceived decision alternatives? How robust is the model? That is, to what extent can the model permit open-ended evolution in problem delineation?

Example 1.2 Gotham City Hospital—GCH

The complexities of administering the operations of hospitals have fostered an increasing number of OR applications for improving operations.[3] For example, the arrival and departure of patients have been treated in the context of queuing models; the management of medical supplies has relied on inventory models; and the scheduling of beds and nonemergency surgery have benefited from mathematical programming.

[3]See David H. Stimson and Ruth H. Stimson, *Operations Research in Hospitals: Diagnosis and Prognosis* (Chicago: Hospital Research and Educational Trust, 1972).

GCH is a medium-size hospital experiencing "growing pains." In recent weeks a large number of complaints have suggested that the waiting times of patients in the emergency room have been too long.

FOLLOW-UP EXERCISES

1. What is a reasonable set of ultimate goals for GCH? List surrogate criteria that might reflect these goals. Illustrate the user-designer concept with yourself in the role of "expert" consultant on some system or procedure that could be used to reduce the long waiting times. Make any assumptions you need to, but explicitly state them. Particularly note conflicting surrogate criteria and how these conflicts can be resolved.
2. An individual has stated that her overall goal in life is to "be successful." What surrogate criteria might be appropriate? Identify any potential conflict among the surrogate criteria.

Step 2—Problem Formulation

The perceived problem may reflect a tactical (short-run) need or a strategic (long-term) need. There may be a perception that the actions taken today may be inappropriate tomorrow. On the other hand, the perception may be that current organizational policies and strategies might not lead to desired levels of organizational performance five years from now. Whether the problem is tactical or strategic, we must be able to define it to solve it.

Like a medical doctor, the user-designer team is usually presented with symptoms rather than a diagnosis. To define the nature of the problem, the symptoms must be examined, and other symptoms should be sought. A **systems** orientation is frequently taken in examining the symptoms.[4] The **systems approach**[5] views the organization as consisting of a group of subsystems integrated to accomplish specific objectives. Subsystems within an organization may be defined along traditional functional lines (marketing, finance, production, etc.) or in other less obvious ways. The power of the systems orientation is its recognition of the integrated whole—that actions in one subsystem can impact on other subsystems. A typical result of applying the systems orientation in the problem formulation phase is an expansion in the scope of the problem compared with the preliminary diagnosis. Close examination often reveals that the impact of the perceived problem goes well beyond the place where the original symptoms appeared.

The problem formulation step should generate some very specific outputs, which will become basic building blocks for a quantitative representation of the problem. These products include the definition of **variables, parameters, constraints,** and the **objective function.**

Variables are measurable factors that bear on the problem of interest. Generally a distinction is made between **controllable variables** and **uncontrollable variables.** The former are those under the direct control of the decision maker and are often termed **decision variables.** Conversely, uncontrollable variables affect the criteria for

---

[4]A good, readable reference on the application of systems theory to organizations is Richard A. Johnson, Fremont E. Kast, and James E. Rosenzweig, *The Theory and Management of Systems* (New York: McGraw-Hill, 1967).

[5]C. West Churchman, *The Systems Approach* (New York: Dell Publishing, 1968).

decision making but are *exogenous,* or not subject to direct manipulation by the decision maker. For example, a controllable variable in an inventory problem is the level at which to restock inventory, and an uncontrollable variable might be the demand for the item being inventoried.

Parameters are measurable conditions inherent in the structure of the problem. In mathematical terms, they are typically identified as **constants**. The cost of stocking (carrying) a unit of a product over some period of time and the cost of ordering or the start-up cost of producing a batch of items are examples of parameters for an inventory problem.

Constraints represent restrictions placed on the controllable and uncontrollable variables. In actual practice very few problems can be considered unconstrained. For the inventory example, constraints might be placed on the amount of capital invested in inventory or on the amount of space allocated to inventory.

The **objective function** is the representation of the criterion or criteria in the problem. Ideally, the criteria can be redefined structurally as a single measurable surrogate criterion, or objective function, the value of which is influenced by the controllable and uncontrollable variables, parameters, and constraints.

In *multiple criteria* problems, it is either not feasible or not desirable to redefine criteria into a single measurable criterion. For example, a decision as to the number of servers to include in a queuing (waiting line) system might be based on such criteria as average number of customers in line, average waiting time per customer, or utilization of the service facility. In this case, a composite criterion function (Figure 1–4a) or a trade-off function (Figure 1–4b) between surrogate criteria may resolve conflicts. If appropriate costs can be assigned to a customer waiting, then the composite criterion function in Figure 1–4a becomes a total cost function. (Do you agree with the indicated conflict in Figure 1–4a?) Chapter 9 discusses more direct approaches to multiple criteria problems.

FOLLOW-UP EXERCISES

3. For Example 1.1 (MBTA) identify examples of controllable variables, uncontrollable variables, parameters, and constraints.
4. **Partially Controllable Variables.** When trying to identify the controllable and uncontrollable variables in a problem setting, some variables do not fit neatly into one of the two categories. Although their values are not entirely controllable, a possibility exists of influencing their values. An example is raw material price. Although some might consider this to be uncontrollable, negotiation and discount structures might result in partial control of these prices. Identify other examples of partially controllable variables.
5. **Time-Dependent Categorizations.** The time frame for a problem setting can influence how a problem element is classified. For example, plant capacity might be classified as a "given" or parameter over the short run. Over the longer run, plant capacity could be considered a controllable variable. Give examples where the time frame for solving the MBTA example might influence the classification of problem elements.
6. **Air Hijacking and Terrorism.** Because of recent terrorist activities, a major airline that flies international routes is examining different ways of reducing the likelihood of such incidents. (*a*) Assuming the need for prevention measures is immediate, identify examples of controllable, uncontrollable, and partially controllable variables, parameters, constraints, and criteria. (*b*) Do the same assuming the development of longer run strategies.

FIGURE 1–4 Criteria and Trade-Offs for a Queuing Problem

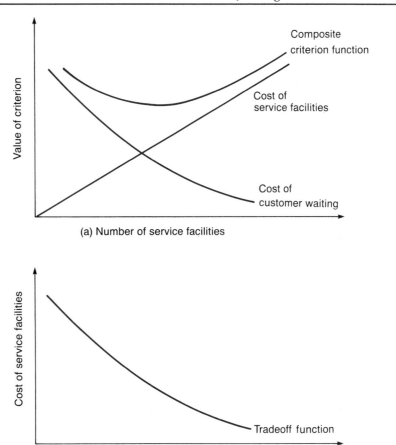

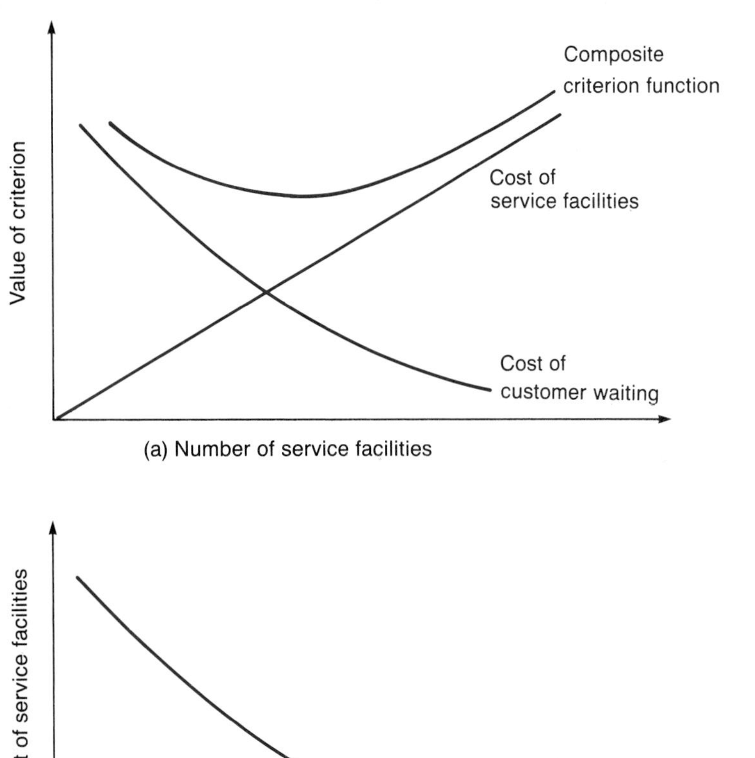

1.3 MODELING

We now discuss what might be considered the modeling phase of the problem-solving, decision-making process.

Step 3—Model Construction

Once an explicit formulation of the problem has been achieved, the next step is to construct a replica or representation of the problem, that is, a mathematical model.

Mathematical Models. A **mathematical model** explicitly states the mathematical structure that relates the inputs (controllable and uncontrollable variables, constraints, and parameters) to the outputs (values for the criterion as expressed through the objective function).[6] Models are used in place of the real system for

[6]Mathematical models represent a subset of **symbolic models,** the latter including both mathematical and logical structures. **Iconic models** (e.g., sculpture, globe of the earth, wind tunnel airfoil) and **analogue models** (e.g., graphs, maps) are not of significant interest to OR.

many reasons—economy and range of experimentation being two important ones. Good models capture the essence of reality and are *robust;* they have the ability to remain appropriate as circumstances within the problem environment change.

The following illustrates a mathematical model (as developed in Example 2.3).

Minimize

$$\overline{T} = \frac{1}{3}\left(\frac{x}{v_x} + \frac{y}{v_y}\right) \tag{1.1}$$

subject to

$$x \cdot y = A \tag{1.2}$$

where the controllable variables x and y represent the dimensions of a rectangular police patrol sector; v_x and v_y denote the uncontrollable variables average travel velocities for a patrol vehicle in the x directions and y directions, respectively; $\overline{T}$ is the criterion, average response time of a patrol vehicle; and Equation 1.2 represents an area constraint for the sector (the parameter A represents area). Equation 1.1 is typically termed the objective function. The constant ⅓ represents a parameter that results from the development of the model.

The Model-Building Process. The use of quantitative representations of reality is the key feature that differentiates quantitatively-based decision making from decision making in general. Model building is essentially a process of deciding what features or aspects of a complex real-world problem are to be represented for analysis. In this process, all eight steps of the paradigm play a role.

We noted in the introduction to the eight-step paradigm that it should not be regarded as a rigid set of steps to be completed mechanistically. Figure 1–5 shows this graphically. On the left side of the figure, the real world has been depicted as a large system or set. Within that set is a smaller system of interest, such as the MBTA. Based on the recognition of a need, the clockwise flow leads to a model of the real system, back to implemented changes in the real system, back to problem formulation, and so forth.

The Role of Criteria. Figure 1–5, compared with Figure 1–2, depicts a *criteria hub* or center to the decision-making process. Earlier in this chapter the notion of a set of criteria that drives, directs, or dictates the decision-making process was presented. Similarly, criteria drive, direct, or dictate the model-building process. Put very simply, models are built for particular purposes.

The above paragraph may seem repetitious or intuitively obvious, but is worth emphasizing that in this process an abstract statement and actual practice can be dramatically separated. Experience indicates that the greatest deficiency in model-building efforts may be the lack of a clearly delineated set of criteria. It can virtually be *guaranteed* that you will fall into this trap during your quantitative analysis course, as well as in other endeavors. Indeed, one of the most important lessons for you to learn from this course is how to fall into the trap less frequently and how to recognize the condition sooner when it occurs.

Suppose you are asked to construct a diagrammatic or flowchart model of a bank teller's operation. To make the task even simpler, suppose that the bank teller only

FIGURE 1–5 The Decision-Making Process with Criteria Hub

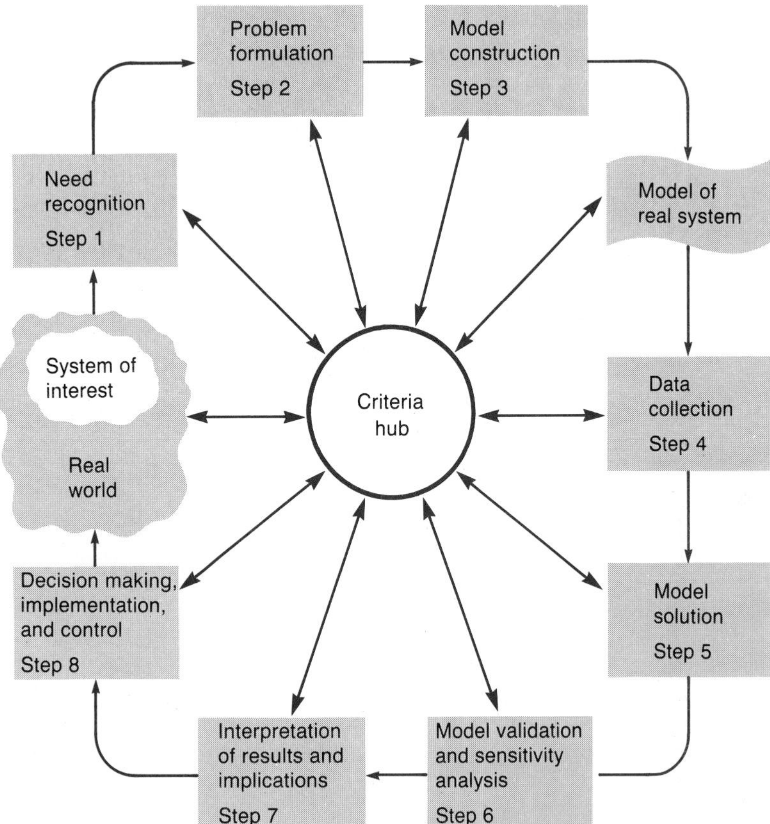

cashes checks. How would you construct such a model? What features or aspects of the teller's job would you include? How would you relate the model features? Does the teller always count out the paper money before the silver? Is it necessary to include the counting of silver separately from that of paper money? Is it necessary to include the process of counting money separately from the process of account verification?

The only way one can adequately answer such questions is to consult the criteria system. That is, *why* is this model being built, and what questions are to be examined with the model? If one were interested in knowing how to improve the teller's efficiency or speed, a reasonable approach might be to break the task into very small details such as studying the individual hand motions involved in counting silver and paper money. If, however, one were willing to accept the present job methods but were concerned with how many teller stations to have open at various times during the day, then selection of model entities (and the concomitant data collection process) would be quite different.

Level of Aggregation. The criteria system not only dictates the appropriate entities to be represented in a model, but also the *way* they are to be represented. The necessary degree of detail, or what is often called the appropriate **level of aggregation,** can be determined only by falling back on the criteria system. As stated above, the major reason for using a model is economy; a model is an abstract that contains the essence of the real—but only the essence—for a particular set of criteria. It therefore follows that the essence implies a necessary level of detail, and the necessary level will vary for different problems.

One of the authors once had a very interesting experience with the level-of-aggregation question. The issue was the subject of classroom discussion and assigned reading, but in an abstract way. At the end of one class day, students were asked to prepare an initial design proposal for a digital simulation model of beef production. During the next class session, two students were asked to put their design on the blackboard, and other students added relevant features. As the session progressed, the model became more and more detailed and complicated (that is, it had a *low* level of aggregation). Typical additions included provision for meat products that were canned, institutional uses, TV dinners, the corn-hog cycle, the inventory of beef held on the hoof at slaughterhouses, and meat substitutes. After about two hours, all blackboards in the classroom were covered, and it was difficult to make any sense out of the total model. Finally, the students suggested that perhaps they were getting too complex in their approach. A lively discussion ensued in which it became abundantly clear that no objectives had been explicitly stated for the model-building exercise. At that point, the students stated objectives and constructed a relatively simple, highly aggregated model.

Striking the appropriate balance of detail in a model involves an evaluation of trade-offs between the accuracy of representation and the complexity of the model (and therefore its manipulation). Normally, the greater the level of detail, the greater the degree of representation but the less the ease of manipulation of the model (Figure 1–6). With less detail, the degree of representation is less, and ease of manipulation is greater. Choosing the appropriate level of detail for a model is an art

FIGURE 1–6 Level of Aggregation Trade-Offs

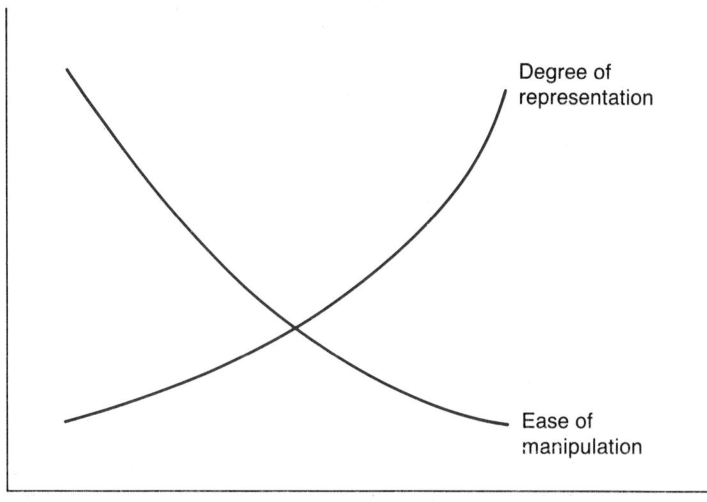

form. The key is identifying and *including* significant interrelationships and excluding insignificant ones.

FOLLOW-UP EXERCISE

7. Gotham City Hospital (GCH) is contemplating the expansion of its emergency room facilities. GCH estimates that during the busiest two-hour period of the day, one to six patients will arrive every five minutes. Patients require between 10 and 60 minutes for treatment; it can be assumed that arrivals and departures take place only at 5 minute intervals (for example, a patient will stay for 20 or 25 minutes but not 23 minutes). A crap-shooting friend observed that the number of patients arriving in a five-minute period can be "simulated" by the throw of a die and that treatment time can be "simulated" by two dice with the value of the dice multiplied by five. List controllable and uncontrollable variables, parameters, constraints, and surrogate criteria that seem relevant. Formulate the problem at a high level of aggregation; then formulate the problem at a more disaggregated level. Can you formulate and operationalize a model to help GCH? What data would you need?

Step 4 — Data Collection

Once the structure of a model has been determined, it is usually necessary to collect data for the modeling process. Data gathering has usually begun before this point, but this is the point where data collection must be completed.

Management Information Systems. To the extent that an organization has well-developed **management information systems (MIS),** the data collection step will be facilitated. This is certainly a direction in which organizations have been moving. Computerized **databases** permit *robust* data collection by allowing more data to be held in a basic disaggregated form. **Database management systems** and their user-friendly query languages allow decision makers great flexibility in accessing or manipulating data. Combining or accumulating can be done without destroying the original identity of the basic data. Disaggregated data can be assembled or combined in many different forms depending on user-oriented inquiries, assumptions, or hypotheses.

It follows that augmenting such a computerized databank with a group of computerized models provides an opportunity for *human-machine interaction* leading to rapid evolution in problem delineation — model formulation — problem solution. This is the type of capability offered through **decision support systems (DSS).** Whereas management information systems tend to support structured (more routine) decision making, decision support systems offer potential to assist with unstructured or ill-structured problems (i.e., those that occur infrequently or those for which the problem setting is changing constantly). Because of the potential of integrating computerized databases, modeling techniques, and decision makers in an interactive environment, we will continue to expand on the DDS concept as we move through the text.

Systems of Measurement and Scales. The collection of data implies a system of measurement. For example, if an aerospace engineer is considering the lift characteristics of various airfoil configurations, a unit of measurement is needed for lift (pounds); a study of refinery capacity requires a unit of measurement for flows through various processing units, say, cubic feet per minute or barrels per day; and an

OR model for production scheduling needs cost data in units of dollars per item and technological data in units of labor hours per item.

The unit of measurement in turn implies one of the following scales of measurement: nominal, ordinal, interval, or ratio. A **nominal scale** is simply a scale with mutually exclusive categories, for example, colors and makes of automobiles. An **ordinal scale** consists of mutually exclusive catagories that have rank order; the magnitudes of numbers have relative but not absolute meaning. For example, suppose that some commodity is graded excellent, good, or fair. The numbers three, two, and one can be associated with these grades, but one would not want to conclude that the absolute difference between excellent and good is the same as that between good and fair or that excellent is three times as desirable as fair.

An **interval scale** has the additional property that equal differences between numbers represent equal differences in the attribute those numbers measure. Interval scales set the origin or zero point arbitrarily, such as 0°C or noon and midnight for clocks.

Finally, a **ratio scale,** in addition to the properties of the interval scale, has the properties that the numbers are proportional to the attribute they represent and the zero point is meaningful. For example, suppose a Volkswagen is priced at $8,000 and a Porsche at $32,000. If the attribute is costliness, then the Porsche is four times as costly as the Volkswagen.

The upshot of the preceding discussion is that very close attention must be paid to the relationship between the global criterion (attribute), the unit of measurement (scale) for the surrogate criterion, and the form of the mathematical or statistical analysis. This latter item is of special importance because the simple mathematical operation of summation requires the assumption of at least the interval scale. (Can you explain why?)

Estimation and Forecasting. Typically, problem formulation and model selection require the analyst to estimate and forecast parameters and values for uncontrollable variables. Both of these procedures can be accomplished either statistically or subjectively.

Statistical estimation requires the ability to access data available in objective form **(hard data)** either through sampling from primary and secondary documents or through sample surveys. In either case, these procedures require sound sample designs in order to (1) avoid biases and misinterpretations and (2) obtain probabilistic estimates of the variability of the sample statistics.

In time-dependent applications, parameters and uncontrollable variables must be estimated using **statistical forecasting models.** For example, the demands for blood types in a blood-bank inventory model exhibit both seasonal and trend patterns that can be estimated by **exponential smoothing models** or **regression models.** Appendix A, at the end of the book, presents statistical estimation and forecasting in greater detail.

An important part of model development is **statistical hypothesis testing.** It may be hypothesized, for example, that the distribution of interarrival times at an emergency room is of a specific theoretical form (e.g., exponential). Goodness-of-fit tests such as **chi-square**, provide a means of testing the hypothesis that an empirical distribution represents a sample from some theoretical distribution. Further discussion of this appears in Section A.4 of Appendix A.

In many cases, statistical estimation and forecasting may be impossible, too costly, or unwarranted—so we turn to **subjective estimation.** For example, historical demand or cost data for the introduction of a totally new product are unavailable, and market testing may be too costly. It is possible, however, to generate so-called **soft data** by polling individuals with expertise. In some cases, the estimates can be as accurate as (or more accurate than) those obtained using statistical estimation procedures.

The term *soft data* can also include the measurement of attributes that are inherently difficult to quantify, for example, preferences (as in Example 1.3), opinions, and "quality." If these aspects are important to the problem being analyzed, their lack of "hardness" should not discourage their use in a quantitative model. Use of sensitivity analysis (as described later in Step 6) and careful attention to scaling can go a long way toward compensating for their lack of explicitness.

When misapplied, statistical estimation and forecasting give the illusion of accuracy by providing precision (Think about it!); if the data you use are "dirty" and biased (*G*arbage *I*n), then your model results may be quite unusable (*G*arbage *O*ut). As you might expect GIGO presents a formidable real-world problem to the OR analyst which can be devastating if ignored.

▶ Example 1.3 Committee Assignments

Fifty members of a college faculty are to be assigned to eight standing committees according to their preferences. Two numbering schemes for assessing committee preferences are being considered.

1. Each faculty member ranks the committees in order of preference from one to eight.
2. Each faculty member assigns a weight on a scale of zero to one indicating dispreference for each committee; a weight of zero means highest preference.

FOLLOW-UP EXERCISES

8. What is the attribute being measured here? What type of scale is 1? Is 2 more nearly an interval scale than 1? Why isn't 2 a true interval scale? If the criterion is to minimize overall faculty dispreference, then which scale would you recommend? Why? Are these "hard" or "soft" data? (We will return to this problem in Chapter 7.)
9. For the police patrol sector problem, indicate units of measurement and scale considerations for the surrogate criteria, variables, and parameters either given in Equations 1.1 and 1.2 or identified in Exercise 2. Identify and discuss the issues involved in estimating or forecasting these values. What source(s) would you use for data collection? Can you think of other considerations that might require special attention?
10. Consider the same issues for GCH (Example 1.2 and Exercise 7).

Step 5—Model Solution

Model solution is obviously an important aspect of operations research; indeed, the major part of this book is devoted to a careful development of solution procedures. In many ways, however, it is the most straightforward aspect of the decision-making process. This can be attributed largely to the wide body of mathematical algorithms and solution techniques developed during the past 40 years, enhancements of these methods for the purpose of more efficient implementation, and the ever-growing power and availability of computers. Great skill in this part of the process, however, does not by itself ensure superior decisions.

Solution Procedures. In a general sense, the solution of a model consists of finding those values for the controllable variables that result in outcomes that are judged superior in terms of criteria. Because there is great variety in the solution procedures for models in operations research, we have adopted the concept of taxonomic structure from the biological sciences in an attempt to categorize quantitative techniques and to provide you with a "road map" to the materials covered in the text. Figure 1–7 presents our taxonomy of OR models. For ease of reference, the chapters that treat these models are parenthetically inserted in the blocks.

Taxonomy of OR Models. Models are dichotomized as either **deterministic** (nonprobabilistic) or **stochastic** (probabilistic). Some models, however, are treated more appropriately as **hybrids** of these two categories. Deterministic models, as opposed to stochastic models, assume that values for all uncontrollable variables and parameters are known with certainty and are fixed. As we all know, however, the real world is probabilistic. So why bother with deterministic models? First, mathematical modeling is more tractable under deterministic assumptions than under probabilistic assumptions (as you will come to realize). In other words, certain complex processes can be feasibly modeled and solved deterministically but not probabilistically. Second, some real-world systems are stable enough to be modeled effectively by deterministic approaches. Finally, a feature of all deterministic modeling allows for consideration of the effects of uncertainties: sensitivity analysis (step 6 of the paradigm).

Most of the deterministic models can be characterized as those that optimize (maximize or minimize) some objective function (surrogate criterion expressed in terms of variables and parameters) usually subject to a set of constraints; that is,

Optimize

$$z = f(\mathbf{X}, \mathbf{Y})$$

subject to (1.3)

$$\mathbf{G}(\mathbf{X}, \mathbf{Y}) \begin{pmatrix} \leq \\ = \\ \geq \end{pmatrix} \mathbf{B}$$

where z is the criterion of interest expressed as a function of **X**, the set of controllable variables, and **Y**, the set of uncontrollable variables; **G(X, Y)** is the set of constraints expressed as functions of the controllable and uncontrollable variables; and **B** represents the set of right-hand–side constants associated with the set of constraints. Note that the constraint set can consist of inequality as well as equality relationships. Procedures for solving models of the type given by Equation 1.3 are collectively called **mathematical programming.**

FIGURE 1–7 Taxonomy of OR Models

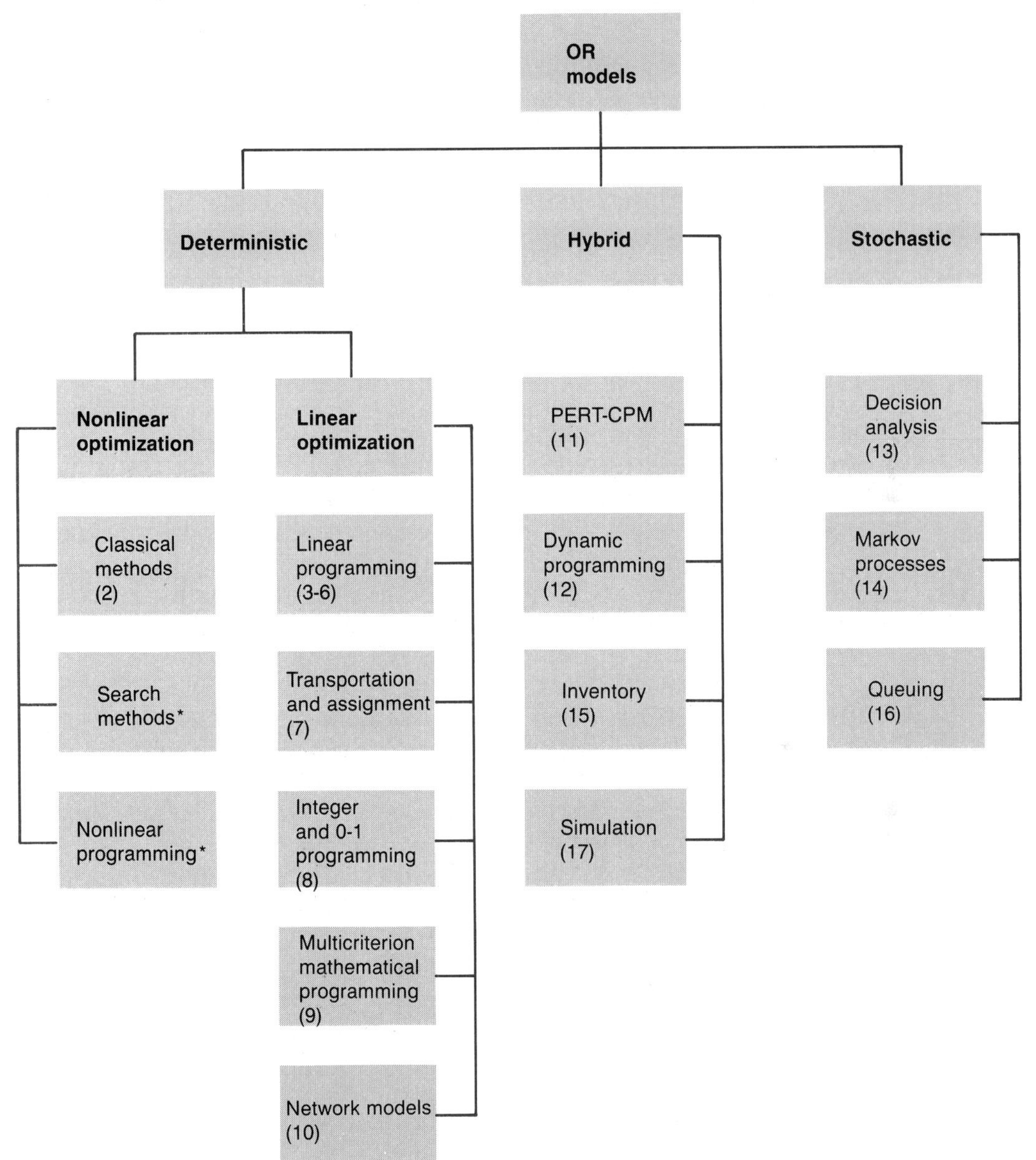

*Not covered in this text.

The distinction between **linear** and **nonlinear optimization models** is based on the nature of the objective function and/or constraints; for example, **linear programming** models are characterized by a linear objective function and linear constraints. **Transportation** and **assignment models** can be viewed as special cases of linear programming, whereby certain efficiencies can be realized in the solution procedures.

When the decision variables in linear optimization models are restricted to either integer or 0–1 values, so-called **integer** and **0–1 programming models** are appropriate. **Network models** represent these types of problems in terms of flow diagrams. Capitalizing on the special structure of certain linear programming problems, these models are impressive in their flexibility of modeling and efficiency of solution. **Multicriteria linear programming models** optimize a multiple criteria objective function that is linear subject to a set of linear constraints.

For each of these linear models, the solution procedure is based on a specific iterative algorithm. An **iterative algorithm** is a solution procedure that starts with some solution (complete or partial) and then proceeds to better or more complete solutions by a set of rules. The procedure is repeatedly applied until no further improvement in the objective function is achieved or until some stopping condition is met.

Nonlinear optimization models are classified more by the method of solution than by the structure of the model: **Classical methods** apply differential calculus; **search methods** use gradient and hill-climbing techniques, and **nonlinear programming methods** apply special **algorithms** (solution procedures) to exploit certain mathematical structures in the functional relationships.

Queuing (waiting line) models (as do inventory and competitive models) occupy a special category in that they have been developed specifically for a given area of application. Queuing models essentially attempt to predict the operating characteristics (e.g., average length of queue and utilization of service facilities) of queuing systems. In some cases, these models can be formulated in terms of a surrogate cost criterion and solved by an optimization procedure.

Models of **Markov processes** attempt to characterize the behavior of certain probabilistic processes by systems of mathematical equations. Attention is usually focused on the ability to predict the behavior of the system (including surrogate criteria) rather than on the need to optimize some objective function. For example, these models have predicted market shares of specific products, have been applied to equipment replacement and reliability problems, and have characterized certain equipment failure and queuing phenomena.

Decision analysis represents a formalized approach to decision making under uncertainty, which incorporates and integrates concepts from utility theory, probability distribution theory, and Bayesian probability theory.

Dynamic programming is an approach to optimization that is uniquely suited to many deterministic and probabilistic problems; several models include deterministic and probabilistic representations: **PERT-CPM** is an approach to planning, scheduling, and controlling complex projects that can be characterized as networks; **inventory models,** both deterministic and stochastic, specify inventory policies that minimize expected cost.

Simulation is an important form of deterministic and stochastic modeling that represents the behavior of complex systems by computerized mathematical or logical models. By properly representing the uncertainties, relationships, and interactions of individual components in a system, it is possible to reproduce that system artificially. As opposed to the physical simulation of systems (e.g., space flight simulators, wind tunnel models, and planetariums) OR simulation models represent the system with mathematical approaches especially suited to manipulation by digital computers. Simulation is particularly valuable for the investigation of problems too complex to be analyzed by other OR procedures.

In concluding this section, we might note that Figure 1–7 omits "cross fertilization." For example, certain inventory models, decision theory models, and stochastic processes can be characterized as probabilistic dynamic programming models; queuing models can be treated as stochastic processes; and simulations of inventory and queuing systems are common. There are also many situations in which the overall modeling effort integrates more than one of these models to address various subsystems of the overall problem setting.

Step 6 — Model Validation and Sensitivity Analysis

Once a solution to the model is generated, there is a critical need for postsolution analysis. This analysis should focus on the validity of the model as well as the validity of the solution.

Model Validation. Model validation is concerned with whether or not the model accurately represents the problem environment. Although we treat it as step 6 in our paradigm, do not assume that validation necessarily follows solution. Validation is a continuous procedure that begins in the model construction phase and ends only when the environmental conditions from which the original problem was identified no longer exist.

The validation process needs to be both objective and subjective. Although in this text we will emphasize objective validation tests, in the last analysis the decision maker has to believe in the model. A good deal of this belief is a natural by-product of the user-designer concept; the inclusion of inputs and opinions from independent, unbiased sources also fosters belief.

Models may contain structural limitations that do not accurately represent the way in which variables are actually related to one another. For example, many models assume that production output is linearly proportionate to the level of production input. This may not be a valid assumption when the effects of economies of scale are significant and it illustrates the importance of intimately understanding the structural assumptions made in the statement or derivation of the model.

The model validation process can also indicate that certain variables included are either not significant or that their influence runs counter to the anticipated effect. For instance, in Forrester's *Urban Dynamics* models,[7] such decision variables as expenditures on low-cost housing and job retraining produce results that are either insignificant or counterintuitive. In contrast, models often exclude significant variables. The exclusion of the industrial sector in a pollution model would be a gross logical error.

Determining the significance of variables and models can often be done by using such statistical tools as correlation and regression analyses, hypothesis testing (such as chi-square), and the analysis of variance and covariance. For example, an analysis of variance can be used to test for significant differences in mean criterion values between the models and reality for various levels of the variables.

The expression "The proof of the pudding is in the taste" applies to model development and validation. Although scientists (including operations researchers) always strive to predict and explain through causal relationships, there are occasions when causal explanation is not the over-riding objective. If prediction is the ultimate objective, the bottom-line test of the validity of a model is how well it predicts.

[7]See J. W. Forrester, *Urban Dynamics* (Cambridge, Mass.: MIT Press, 1969).

Solution Validation. Once a solution has been found, decision makers should be concerned with (*a*) whether or not the solution is better than other alternatives and (*b*) the degree of stability in the results.

The most common benchmark for evaluating a solution is the level of performance of the existing system. The comparision can be based on historical levels of performance, using actual data gathered in the past, or on projected performance. Obviously, a favorable comparison is essential if the solution is to be considered further. Moreover, any increase in the cost of implementing the new solution should be more than offset by projected benefits.

Decision makers also need to be concerned about the stability of model results. Stability, in this instance, refers to the sensitivity of the recommended decisions and the projected measures of system performance to changes in model parameters. In most models, the degree of accuracy of the parameters depends on the appropriateness of the data available and the validity of the procedures used in analyzing the data. **Sensitivity analysis** is concerned with determining the amount by which these parameter estimates can be in error before the generated decision alternative will no longer be superior to others.

1.4 POSTMODELING

In the postmodeling phase of the problem-solving, decision-making process, we want to test the results against reality and determine whether or not they are worthy of further consideration. If they are, we want to convey them in an effective manner to the ultimate decision maker. If we have maintained the user-designer partnership throughout, and have not had our heads buried in the sand, there should be less likelihood of our results failing the next test of reality.

Step 7—Interpretation of Results and Implications

This step is concerned with a critical examination of user objectives or criteria and the evaluation of those criteria in light of model results. For example, are the trade-offs and criteria valid for the ranges implied in the solution? That is, do the explicit surrogate criteria still hold, or must other objectives be considered? What are the solution's implications for other systems not included in the model? An important part of this step is an understanding of the term *optimum*.

Satisficing. The word *optimum* has a particular meaning in management science. An optimal solution is the best and can be mathematically *proved* to be the best. The optimal solution, however, is always relative to a carefully stated criteria set, and the criteria will almost always be surrogate criteria.

We have noted several times that real-world problems tend to have many nebulous criteria. It is extremely difficult, if not impossible, to find a truly optimal solution (within the tight definition given above). An alternative to achieving "optimal" solutions is achieving "satisfactory" solutions; "satisficing" becomes the goal instead of "optimizing," and the decision maker accepts decisions that are satisfactory or "good" instead of "best." To arrive at a decision that results in satisfactory levels of all criteria, the decision maker must be concerned with the trade-offs between them. (Remember the trade-off concept as presented in Figure 1–3?)

An obvious problem with satisficing is the determination of what represents a good or satisfactory solution. It is much easier to specify the absolute best than to settle for something less—particularly when the decision maker does not *know* how far away from optimal a given solution lies.

Suboptimization. The concept of "suboptimization" refers to the penalty one pays for less than perfect overall system design or global decision making. It *always* exists, and occurs for many reasons, including noncongruency of criteria, poor choices of surrogate criteria, omitted criteria, and poor trade-offs between the criteria. The analytical process almost assures suboptimization, since usually a small subset of the entire system is chosen for analysis.

To illustrate suboptimization, consider a firm structured along functional lines. Marketing would like to maximize customer service by never being out of products (implying high inventories). Finance would like to minimize the cost of inventory holding and replenishment. Clearly, these surrogate criteria are in conflict, and the global criteria for the firm, such as profits and long-term growth, may be suboptimized.

It is almost impossible to accurately assess the degree of suboptimization at the highest system level. Who knows how much more profit a company might have been able to make with better decisions? Even if it were possible to determine the ultimate profit potential, profit is only one surrogate. One possible way to cope with this dilemma is to make comparisons of companies within an industry, metropolitan hospitals of similar size, mass transit systems for different cities, and so forth. Useful as these comparisons may be, the goals or objectives derived from them are suboptimal rather than optimal.

Although the management science models in this text will always address less than the "total system," the results of the analysis will often force better total-system thinking. If an optimum-producing model indicates one decision, and the decision makers choose another, there are natural tendencies to ask why. The resultant analysis should lead to an improvement in suboptimization.

Step 8—Decision Making, Implementation, and Control

One Input to the Decision Process. A decision maker often has access to a great deal of information at the time the final decision is made. This information constitutes a set of *inputs* for consideration. These inputs range from purely subjective ones (such as one's "gut feelings") to inputs derived through quantitative analysis, to those relating to other issues (such as political, ethical, or behavioral considerations). Implicitly, the decision maker assigns a subjective weight to each input, which expresses its significance.

It should be clear that the recommendation based on an OR study constitutes *one* input to the decision process. In some cases it may be the primary input; in others it may be one of many. In some cases it may be a highly significant input; in others, it may be of little value. In some cases its monetary benefit exceeds its cost of implementation; in other cases it does not. Thus decision makers who are receiving quantitatively derived inputs must be capable of assessing their significance.

Several factors can facilitate one's ability to assess the "significance" of quantitatively derived inputs. A person with a technical educational background is more likely to understand the key aspects of quantitative solution procedures and scientific methodology. In addition, this person is in a better position to bridge the communications gap that often exists between technical specialists and nontechnical decision makers. Upon completing this book, *you* should find yourself in a position to be a more effective user of quantitative inputs. *You* should be able to ask the "right" questions of OR analysts, to critique assumptions that have been made in the analysis and to be generally familiar with the types of quantitative tools employed.

Participating "in the evolutionary process" is another way of improving one's ability to assess inputs. This is the user-designer concept.

Use of Management Science/Operations Research. MS/OR modeling can be effective in "capturing the essence" of reality, clarifying complex relationships, and providing a "laboratory" for exploring policy implications and answering "What if?" types of questions. The primary justification for the use of MS/OR, however, is *cost effectiveness*. The difference between the benefits of using MS/OR and the costs of developing and implementing MS/OR solutions can exceed that of any other approach. This is particularly true for one-time major projects (e.g., construction of the Superdome or selection of major capital investments) and ongoing projects (e.g., production and inventory control systems).

Conversely, MS/OR should not be used when it is not cost effective. (For example, the cost of collecting data for the model may exceed any potential monetary benefits from using the model, or an alternative approach may be more cost effective, or decisions need to be made within a time span that is too short for a legitimate MS/OR analysis.) To illustrate, consider the franchised outlets for a national food chain. The development of a computerized inventory control system exclusively for one outlet would probably result in adverse cost effectiveness because of high developmental costs; however, the development of this system by the national organization for use by all outlets may result in substantial net benefits for the entire organization.

Implementation

Operations research survived the "honeymoon" period during the 1950s and 60s in which a number of our OR forefathers were preoccupied with the glories of the newly developed quantitative techniques. Exquisite mathematical models were painstakingly constructed at huge expense to organizations, and top management patiently waited for the "word" to come down that would lead their firms to the "promised land." Unfortunately, many firms never reached the promised land, and management's opinion of their prophets began to sour. The fault must be shared by both OR specialists and management. In some instances, the OR analysts developed solutions that were either inappropriate or incapable of being implemented. In other cases, technically valid solutions were developed, but management as well as OR personnel failed to properly prepare the organization for the change associated with implementation.

Both parties should now realize that implementation within organizations is not only a critical step in the process but is also a delicate and sensitive stage in which knowledge of the behavioral sciences can be an asset.

Preparing the Organization for Change. A major implication of decision making is change in the operating environment for at least one level of an organization. Major policy decisions can have far-reaching implications. Something as simple as deciding to buy raw materials more frequently may affect the purchasing, receiving, production, and accounting functions within the buyer's organization and the sales, shipping, purchasing, warehousing, and accounting functions of the seller's organization.

Dedication to a thorough program of education recognizes explicitly the "here to there" problem. It is simply too easy to expect an environment to change because management wishes it to change. Even if operating personnel agree with the proposed changes, they have to see how these changes are to be implemented and exactly what changes are required in their own decision making.

A very good way for this to be accomplished is to recognize a fundamental law of organization: All managers can see clearly the need for educating those *below* them organizationally; some can see the need for educating those *above* them; very few can see the need for educating themselves. By involving themselves intimately in the education of their subordinates, managers enhance their own education.

Planning for Change. During implementation the key people must stand up and be counted. It follows that it is crucial to identify these key people and *plan* how and by what means they *will* stand up to be counted. All of the prior stages in the decision-making paradigm are of no consequence if successful implementation does not occur, and the value of a solution cannot be tested unless implementation is achieved.

To a considerable degree, improving implementation success involves understanding the behavioral sciences. Individual and group decision-making processes, cognitive styles, reactions to uncertainties, educational requirements, and individual as well as organizational ability to change authority relationships are representative issues.

The user-designer concept attempts to deal with these issues by involving the key players deeply in the model-building and implementation process. Users will be more likely to produce decision alternatives that can be implemented and to plan timetables consistent with organizational realities.

Developing an implementation plan should involve all those who will be affected by the new solution (either directly or indirectly). Their participation induces a favorable environment, enables cooperative attitudes and relationships, and reduces misunderstanding, anxiety, and efforts to sabotage the new system. All plans for implementation must have timetables consistent with achieving these characteristics. The short article beginning on page 26 provides a humorous, yet insightful, account of a successful implementation.

On System Acceptance

GENE WOOLSEY

Mineral Economics Department
Colorado School of Mines
Golden, Colorado 80401

Common folklore among members of our profession holds that the only absolute requirement for system acceptance is "top management commitment." May I respectfully suggest that, in my experience, another requirement is equally absolute: user (bottom-level management) acceptance. I have now seen the spectacle, in a number of cultures, of splendid systems going down to defeat and taking the committed top management right along with them. The hard facts are these: if the people at the bottom of the managerial heap who will have the joy of facing the green screens every day don't see the new system as a help, they will slowly, and with malice, ignore it to death.

It is not, however, my purpose to discuss how system acceptance may be done wrong. On the contrary, I will now present a true story about a gentleman, now number two in his company, who did it stylishly right. He was hired as a systems czar by a large midwestern manufacturing company to design, build, and gain acceptance for a wall-to-wall production control and reporting system for the whole plant. He was given virtual carte blanche to do it any way he wanted, a munificent salary, all the subordinates he needed, a budget, expected results, and a deadline. Clearly, here was an opportunity to become famous or notorious, with his preference definitely for the former.

HOMEWORK

Now the first thing our paladin did was to study carefully why other large systems of this type had failed. Careful detective work showed that whatever the level of acceptance by top management, the nonacceptance by the troops that had to deal with the system on a day-to-day basis was the key. More study showed that invariably the CRT displays and the listing to be used by the grunts down below were presented to them as a big surprise with the (usually implied) understanding that they should take it because "mother knows best." Then there was the customary tap dancing that their inputs were earnestly solicited, so long as they understood that any desired changes were already impossible due to reprogramming costs. Based on this information, our systems czar took a slightly different approach.

He also took a careful look at exactly how this particular manufacturing plant operated. The plant was a building the length of a couple of football fields and roughly a field and a half wide. Raw material came, literally, into one end of the plant, and finished product was shipped out the other. For each of the various products made, flow sheets through different machine groups were easy to construct and follow. The machine groups were numbered from one through nine within the plant.

A machine group was under the absolute control of a floor supervisor; typically, his domain of power and influence stretched from one side of the plant to the other and was about 30 yards long for a major machine group. Each group was demarcated by bright-colored lines painted on the floor. Often floor supervisors were seen discussing production problems with each other, but interestingly, in most cases they were careful to stand only on their own sides of the line when doing so. Our hero sensed that the floor supers had rather powerful senses of territoriality, shared by their subordinates.

Finishing his homework, he discovered what appeared to be a common thread among the failed systems. In every case where failure resulted, when the customary exercise of "soliciting lower management commitment" was finished, only the sharpest or most open-to-change management was tapped. The reasons were obvious; (*a*) who wants to listen to dummies, and (*b*) it's always easier working with people who are ready for change. He had accurately observed that the subtraction of the above subsets from the set of management left those people most likely to sabotage the system to death, that is, (*a*) the dummies, and (*b*) the people who never wanted the damned thing in the first place.

(continued)

THE BEGINNING

He therefore requested for his test case two floor supervisors who met the following requirements:

a. Must be in adjoining machine groups.

b. Had already voiced violent opposition to *any* new system.

c. Were not exactly mental giants.

Top management reacted negatively to his initial request, quoting the reasons stated above. However, he persisted, finally stating his case as, "I want the Archie Bunkers." Top management, predicting disaster, took care to give him exactly what he had asked for: Virgil and JoeBob. Now these two gentlemen can best be described by their bowling trophies, smokeless tobacco, mesomorphic builds, lifetime NRA memberships, and the bumper stickers on their identical big-wheeled pickups that said, "They Can Take My Gun When They Peel My Cold Dead Fingers From Around It." Declining the offer to have them meet in his office, our winner made an appointment with them on neutral ground, the canteen that their two machine groups shared in the plant. To say that suspicion was rife was a massive understatement. Both JoeBob and Virgil started off telling our hero exactly what they thought of the whole idea of computerizing the plant in general and the idea of starting with them in particular.

They discoursed with feeling about having things shoved down their throats, with strong implications of assured sabotage of anything they didn't like. After giving them sufficient time to complete the requisite spleen venting, our hero asked them what information they would like to make their jobs easier. Stunned silence resulted from both supervisors, until JoeBob broke it with the comment that the reason they didn't have a quick answer was simply because they had never been asked that question before. It took some time to convince them that this particular systems man didn't have a form ready for them to comment on that he would then ignore, as had happened before. The discussion continued over lunch during which JoeBob and Virgil discovered that the systems type was a dove hunter of ability and also an NRA member.

The openness of discussion that afternoon was in considerable contrast to that of the morning. JoeBob and Virgil revealed that what they would really like to have was a list of all the jobs coming at them at least two machine groups away. It seems that for over 20 years they had been coming to work an hour early and sitting down over coffee and scheduling their two machine groups to try to minimize both setups and hassle to themselves. The systems type asked them how they would like these jobs sorted, anticipating something like due date, priority, machining requirements, or size of job. He was rather startled to discover that their primary interest was by metallurgy, because that dictated more than anything else the setup time for the particular kinds of machine groups managed by our two supervisors. He then spent considerable time laying out a report format exactly as JoeBob and Virgil wanted. After about three tries, he presented them with a computer-generated form in precisely the format that they could mark up in the most effective way for their scheduling. He also spent many late hours modifying the existing reporting system to generate this form.

After about three weeks of tinkering, the systems man appeared in the canteen at 7:00 A.M. to present Virgil and JoeBob with the information they wanted, in the form that they wanted. He watched happily as Virgil and JoeBob really went to work, and by 7:18 or so, they had essentially scheduled their two machine groups for the day. They also generated some changes they wanted in the form, which generated a few more wee hours of programming by our hero and his minions to get it back to them. Suffice it to say that, within a week, the form seemed to stabilize, and a week later it was dove season, so JoeBob and Virgil took off a few days for their annual hunting trip.

While they were gone, our hero was summoned to tell his boss of progress on the supersystem to come. The boss was not pleased to hear that the only result of some weeks' work was that a new report was now being generated at great cost for two floor supervisors. "Why good heavens man, they aren't even middle management." The biggy was told to have faith; our man knew what he was doing.

The routine was this: the DP department generated the form the previous night, and it was delivered to the desks of Virgil and JoeBob *no later than* 7 A.M. Our hero emphasized the importance of the

(continued)

delivery time to the head of ADP, who was not particularly thrilled at the whole idea of this process. Strange events, however, began to happen down on the shop floor during the next few weeks.

THE MIDDLE

Virgil and JoeBob began to really get off on the use of their new toy. Our hero knew that it was all over when Virgil and JoeBob asked for one more small change to be made in the report. JoeBob said, "Could the top line say, 'MACHINE GROUP REPORT FOR MR. JOEBOB STUCKER,' for me and for Virgil's, the same except for 'MR. VIRGIL UPCHURCH.'" This was quickly done, and our protagonist sat back to watch what he knew would soon occur.

We must remember that there was a certain spirit of territoriality (and competition) between the floor supervisors. If Virgil (who supplies JoeBob) suddenly can load his machines to near optimality, and JoeBob is fitting his schedule to Virgil's supply to do the same, funny things start to happen. The machine group supervisor who supplies Virgil's group suddenly finds Virgil (standing on his own side of the line) loudly asking "When are you going to get off your rear and give me some more material to work with?" After all, Virgil is all caught up and is just waiting for him and his crew to get with it. In short, Virgil is sucking harder than his supplier can blow.

Meanwhile, the poor supervisor supplied by JoeBob suddenly finds that he is unable to see his machines behind the mounting inventory supplied daily through the incredible productivity of JoeBob's group. He is not amused by JoeBob (standing on his own side of the line, of course) loudly wondering when he and his crew are going to get their stuff together and get some work done. We now have JoeBob blowing harder than his receiver can suck. It does not take long for the macho men, JoeBob and Virgil, to become royal pains in the rear to any floor supervisor who supplies them or receives work from them. They receive monthly productivity awards three months running and for maximizing quarterly productivity to undreamed-of heights, are presented (appropriately) with a pair of matching Parker shotguns, suitably engraved.

The next day the two supervisors who have been most abused by Virgil and JoeBob come in, roll over, and ask to be let in on the secret. Graciously, JoeBob and Virgil suggest a talk with our hero, who is delighted to oblige. Suitable product lines are chosen to make these two converts also look like the winners JoeBob and Virgil already are, and at this point the conversion is clearly sure to spread (eventually) to both doors of the plant.

THE END

At this point in the exercise, the head of ADP, still unconvinced that these reports are the right way to go (could be the "not invented here" syndrome), gets rather behind in his work. On his way out the door one evening, he is faced with dropping some task to be done overnight in order to cover himself with his superiors. There is just too much work and too little time. As he scans the list of possible jobs, his eye lights on the reports generated for our (now) four supervisors. He instructs one of his troops to "call those guys in the morning and tell them they will have the reports by nine," and he leaves.

The next morning Virgil, JoeBob, BillyJim, and BobbyGene show up at 7 A.M. only to get phone calls from ADP informing them that they (might) get their reports by 9. Upon receiving this information, after a council of war, they call back and casually inquire as to when the ADP manager gets to work and would the subordinate happen to know "where he parks?" It so happens that our hero happens to be in the computer center that morning on other business and overhears the conversation. He requests clarification from the subordinate and realizes, in a blinding flash of insight, what is about to happen.

He runs for the door and is sprinting across the parking lot as our story plays itself out. He sees the ADP head zip into his designated, nameplated parking place in the executive parking lot in his Porsche Targa. He also sees two massive pickup trucks with-loaded window gunracks immediately pull in behind the Porsche and two large, angry southerners alight. By the time he reaches the scene, badly out of breath, Virgil and JobBob have the miscreant spread-eagled against his Porsche, and both are screaming: *"Where's my form?"*

This, ladies and gentlemen, is *system acceptance*.

Reprinted by permission of Gene Woolsey, "The Fifth Column: On System Acceptance," *Interfaces* 16, no. 3 (May–June 1986), Copyright 1986, The Institute of Management Sciences.

It is essential that OR personnel follow through on projects and be involved in the implementation stages. Most projects will need minor adjustments in the solution at the time of implementation. Since OR personnel possess the greatest understanding of the technical aspects of the solution, they are the logical persons to make judgments regarding technical modifications.

Whenever possible, the implementation plan should allow for pretesting the solution. This is especially important when the solution involves widespread changes in an organization. Pretesting on a small scale allows one to work out the "bugs" prior to a complete program of implementation. Marketing researchers utilize this approach regularly by selecting test markets in which to experiment with new products or promotion strategies.

The implementation plan should also provide "manual override capability"; the user should be able to make a decision without the use of the MS/OR system. This is particularly helpful in the initial stages of implementation if the user is not fully "comfortable" with the new system. Experience indicates that the frequency of manual overrides declines over time.[8]

Manual overrides and pretesting not only facilitate implementation procedures but also provide performance feedback. Actual benefits can be compared with expected benefits to determine the relative success of the new program. If actual benefits are not as great as expected, then reasons must be sought.

Control

The final concept we want to emphasize is control, or system monitoring, after an ongoing solution has been implemented. In this section we discuss why control systems are necessary, the nature of a feedback control system, and the importance of management information systems in this stage.

It's a Dynamic Environment! The most significant reasons for control systems are to make sure that the implemented system is living up to expectations and that the solution remains valid over time. Once the new system is in place and is performing satisfactorily, controls are needed to keep the system functioning in a changing environment: Unexpected combinations of factors occur (such as high inventories simultaneously with stockouts), and even the conditions leading to the original decision change *because* of the decision. Changes which can occur in a system or model may be classified as changes in:

1. The importance of criteria.
2. The degree of control over decision variables.
3. The values of parameters and uncontrollable variables.
4. The constraints on the system.
5. The structure of the system.

The first classification of change simply recognizes that the measures of performance used in developing the new solution may not always retain the same level of

---

[8]See J. L. Bishop, Jr., "Experience with a Successful System for Forecasting and Inventory Control," *Operations Research* 22, no. 6 (1974), pp. 1224–31; and R. E. D. Woolsey, "On Doing Good Things and Dumb Things in Production and Inventory Control," *Interfaces* 5, no. 3 (1975), pp. 65–67.

importance. Lower-level criteria may, over time, replace those originally deemed most important, or new criteria may be identified and supplant those in the original criterion set. During the gasoline shortage of 1974, the normal criteria used by firms or individuals in selecting and purchasing gasoline (minimize cost, maximize quality of gasoline, maximize level of customer service, and so forth) were supplanted in most instances by a criterion of maximizing gasoline availability. This was true for both customers and suppliers.

The second category of change simply suggests that internal and external factors may indeed change over time. A firm that operates within a regulated industry, such as the utility industry, may find that its ability to make certain types of decisions changes as the degree of industry regulation changes. An example of this is the price that a firm charges for its goods or services. Collective bargaining may dramatically change the discretion management has in making decisions about its employees. Similarly, the general state of the economy can have a widespread influence over what is controllable. For example, the ability to float a bond issue and the expected yield from the financial program are subject, in part, to economic conditions.

Third, the values of parameters and uncontrollable variables are very likely to change, even over the short run. A good example of this is the effect of a changing technology. The technology in manufacturing microcomputers underwent a rapid change in which unit-cost parameters, and consequently price decision variables, decreased significantly over a short period. The costs of a firm's factors of production may change, causing modifications in objective function and/or constraint relationships.

Fourth, the constraints on a system are likely to change over time. Constraints in the original problem may disappear in the future. As an example, the discovery of new and cheaper energy sources might eliminate an energy constraint, or at least reduce the extent to which energy is a constraint. On the other hand, conditions that were not constraining originally may later become significant.

Finally, the structure of the system itself may change. A merger with another firm — say, a major supplier — may generate significant changes in both the structure and operation of the two component firms. Federal legislation instituting a new payment system for Medicare/Medicaid patients has caused significant changes in the health care delivery system.

Feedback Control Systems. The existence of a dynamic environment raises the need for an effective control system; otherwise, the implemented solution will degrade over time. In effect, a control system will detect the previously discussed changes and make appropriate adjustments in the solution. Notice that the act of making decisions in itself *causes* conditions to change. For example, if inventories are too high, it would be common to put pressure on the sales force, who in turn might increase sales efforts, which could increase sales, which could decrease inventories.

What we have just described is **feedback control.** In a general sense, an ongoing view of the decision-making process can be diagrammed as in Figure 1–8. At the left-hand side is the decision-making process, as described by the eight-step paradigm. This process yields a decision or set of decision outputs, which in turn leads to results. Information channels are used to gain knowledge of the results, which are transformed into a set of perceptions about the actual results, which act as an input to further decision making. Notice that this process interacts continuously with the real world; the real-world influences affect every aspect of the process.

FIGURE 1–8 Decision Making as a Feedback Control Process

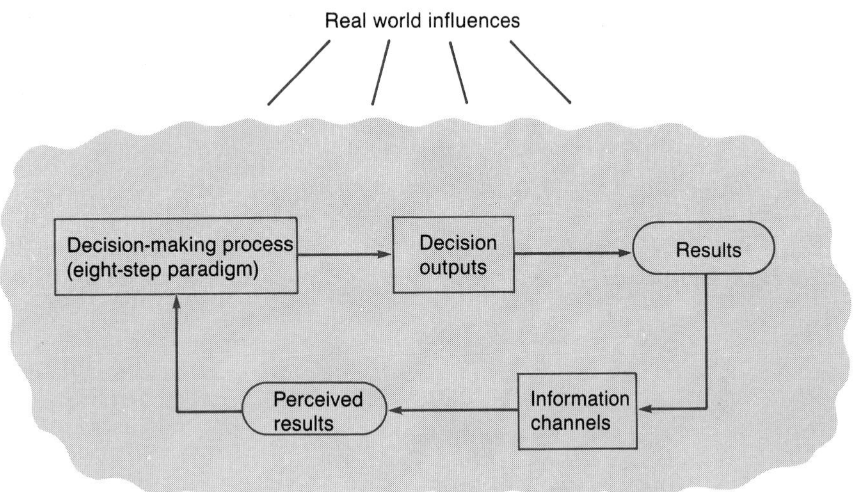

In order to have an effective feedback control system, certain elements are essential. There is a need for both a system and a method of measurement. There is also a need for a method of comparison between planned and actual results. In addition, there must exist an activating mechanism that responds to comparisons outside of predetermined performance tolerances. This mechanism signals to the decision-making authority that the process is out of control and that there is need for corrective action.

1.5 IMPACT OF OPERATIONS RESEARCH/MANAGEMENT SCIENCE

The impact of OR/MS in its less than four decades of existence as a formal field of study has been nothing short of remarkable. Although we have already indicated reasons for various shortcomings in the field, the fact remains that the quantitative analysis of managerial, economic, and social problems has proliferated, has become entrenched, and is maturing. To wit: Numerous graduate programs of study offer OR/MS degrees; many corporations, consulting companies, and universities put on nationally based seminars on specific modeling procedures; OR/MS departments are well-established in relatively large corporations and governmental agencies; management consulting groups provide OR/MS services to small and medium-size organizations; and several personnel placement companies specialize in searching for and placing individuals with OR/MS expertise.

To give you an idea of the areas and scope of OR/MS applications, we have compiled a partial list of real-world applications in Table 1–1. Subsequent chapters will provide greater detail in relating specific applications to specific models. In Chapter 18 we will provide additional evidence of the impact of OR/MS.

TABLE 1–1 OR/MS APPLICATIONS

Public Sector

Urban-Social
- City planning
- Courtroom congestion and scheduling
- Income maintenance and family assistance
- Air-water pollution control
- Solid waste disposal
- Educational planning and schoolbus scheduling
- Personnel planning
- Air and highway traffic patterns
- Mass transit systems
- Regional and world development
- Public utilities regulation
- Population planning
- National resources planning and allocation
- Municipal zoning
- Emergency response systems
- Law enforcement
- Political campaign strategies

Health
- Health indices construction
- Health care delivery system evaluation
- Blood inventory policies
- Hospital admissions
- Diagnostics
- Disease control
- Dietary planning
- Hospital utilization and scheduling

Aerospace-Military
- Inventory, distribution, maintenance of equipment
- Reliability of space vehicles
- Satellite queuing
- Missile defense and allocation
- Search and rescue efforts

Private Sector

Service
- Portfolio management
- Insurance and risk management
- Location of retail facilities
- Fleet scheduling
- Actuarial science
- Professional sports drafts
- Feedlot optimization
- Auditing strategies
- Advertising media mix
- Airplane scheduling
- Telephone switching
- Transportation scheduling
- Utilization of banking facilities

Industrial
- Food and chemical blending
- Production scheduling
- Optimal inventory policies
- Distribution of products
- Working capital management
- Capital budgeting
- Advertising strategies and market shares
- Product safety testing
- Assignment of facilities
- Planning, scheduling, and controlling complex projects
- New product introduction
- Plant layouts
- Quality control
- Replacement and servicing policies
- Queuing analysis of facilities

1.6 USING THE BOOK

Although this book will expose you to the premodeling, modeling, and postmodeling phases of the process, much attention will be focused on the modeling phase. We will examine various modeling techniques—their assumptions, applications, strengths, and limitations—and will reinforce concepts with applied exercises and several cases. The exercises will typically require one or more of the steps in Figure 1–9. First, there is a translation from the verbal description of a problem to the mathematical representation. After the mathematical model has been developed, a solution must be generated either manually or using the computer. Once a mathematically derived solution is generated, it must be interpreted within the context of the original problem.

FIGURE 1–9

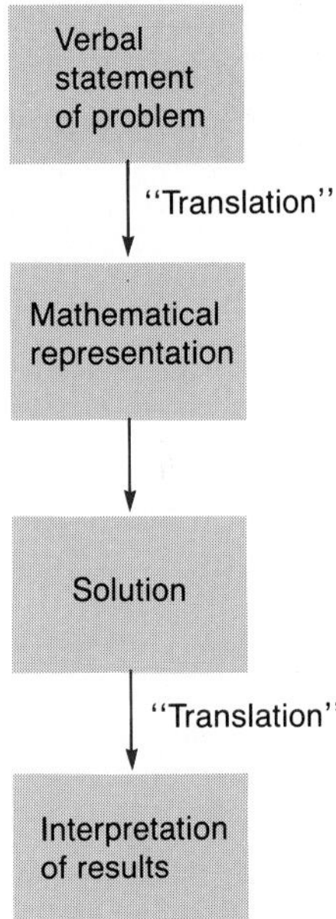

Our experiences indicate that students typically have difficulty translating from the verbal description to the mathematical and then from the mathematical solution to the verbal interpretation of results. It is the classic "word problem" (or "story problem") dilemma we have all faced since elementary school. Your skills in this area will improve as you work through the text. To provide some guidance in this process, the following section suggests a problem-solving framework. It will have some resemblance to the decision-making paradigm, although it is directed at helping you with exercises and cases.

Problem-Solving Framework

For any given exercise or case, you need only a subset of the following steps. We will reinforce the framework periodically in the book, illustrating its use in example problems.

PROBLEM-SOLVING FRAMEWORK

1. **Verbal Statement of the Problem.**
2. **Decisions.**
   a. **Verbal Statement.**
   b. **Mathematical Definition.**

3. **Criteria.**
   a. **Verbal Statement.**
   b. **Mathematical Definition.**
4. **Constraining Conditions.**
   a. **Verbal Statement.**
   b. **Mathematical Statement.**
5. **Mathematical Model.**
6. **Model Outcomes.**
7. **Interpretation of Results.**

To illustrate the use of the framework, consider the following simple example.

Example 1.4 In-House Computer versus Service Bureau Decision

A large medical group practice has 30 full-time physicians. Currently, all billing of patients is done manually by clerks. Due to the heavy volume of billing, the business manager believes it is time to convert from manual to computerized patient billing. Two options are being considered: (1) the group practice can lease its own computer and software and do the billing itself (the *make* option), or (2) the group can contract with a computer service bureau that would do the patient billing (the *buy* option).

The costs of each alternative are a function of the number of patient bills. The lowest bid submitted by a service bureau would result in an annual flat fee of $3,000 plus 95 cents per bill processed. With the help of a computer consultant, the business manager has estimated that the group can lease a small business computer system and the required software at a cost of $15,000 per year. Variable costs of doing the billing in this manner are estimated at 65 cents per bill.

It is apparent from the cost data that the service bureau option would be less costly than the lease option up to a particular volume of patient bills. Beyond this, the lower variable cost per bill would more than offset the higher fixed cost for the lease option. The medical group wants to know the critical patient volume beyond which leasing is less costly.

1. **Verbal Statement of Problem**
   Determine the number of patient bills beyond which the lease option is less costly.
2. **Decisions**
   a. **Verbal Statement**
      Number of patient bills per year.
   b. **Mathematical Definition**
      Let x = Number of patient bills per year.
3. **Criteria**
   There are no criteria in this problem that require optimizing (maximizing or minimizing).
4. **Constraining Conditions**
   The critical point beyond which the lease option is less costly is the *break-even point* for the two options.
   a. **Verbal Statement**
      Total annual cost of service bureau equals total annual cost of leasing.

b. Mathematical Statement
If $S(x)$ = Annual billing cost using a service bureau,
$S(x) = 3{,}000 + 0.95x$.
If $L(x)$ = Annual billing cost of leasing,
$L(x) = 15{,}000 + 0.65x$.
Therefore, we wish to determine the value of x such that $S(x) = L(x)$.

5. **Model**
Determine value(s) of x such that $S(x) = L(x)$, or

$$3{,}000 + 0.95x = 15{,}000 + 0.65x$$

6. **Model Outcomes**

$$S(x) = L(x)$$

when

$$\begin{aligned} 3{,}000 + 0.95x &= 15{,}000 + 0.65x \\ 0.30x &= 12{,}000 \\ x &= 40{,}000 \end{aligned}$$

7. **Interpretation of Results**
The number of patient bills per year that will result in annual billing costs being equal for the service bureau and leasing options is 40,000. At a billing volume *less than* 40,000, the service bureau option is less costly. For a billing volume *greater than* 40,000, the leasing option is less costly.

SELECTED REFERENCES

Ackoff, Russell L., and Maurice W. Sasieni. *Fundamentals of Operations Research*. New York: John Wiley & Sons, 1968.

Anthony, R. N. *Planning and Control Systems, A Framework for Analysis*. Cambridge, Mass.: Harvard University Press, 1965.

Beer, Stafford. *Decision and Control*. New York: John Wiley & Sons, 1966.

Churchman, C. West; Russell L. Ackoff; and E. L. Arnoff. *Introduction to Operations Research*. New York: John Wiley & Sons, 1957.

Green, Thad B.; Sang M. Lee; and Walter B. Newsom. *The Decision Science Process*. New York: Petrocelli Books, 1978.

Huysmans, J. *The Implementation of Operations Research*. New York: John Wiley & Sons, 1970.

Miller, David W., and Martin K. Starr. *Executive Decisions and Operations Research*. 2nd ed., Englewood Cliffs, N.J.: Prentice-Hall, 1969.

Mockler, Robert J. *The Management Control Process*. New York: Appleton-Century-Crofts, 1971.

Newman, W. H. *Constructive Control Design and Use of Control Systems*. Englewood Cliffs, N.J.: Prentice-Hall, 1975.

Senn, James A. *Informations Systems in Management*. Belmont, Calif.: Wadsworth Publishing, 1982.

Tannenbaum, A. S. *Control in Organizations*. New York: McGraw-Hill, 1968.

Thierauf, R. J. *Decision Support Systems for Effective Planning and Control*. Englewood Cliffs, N.J.: Prentice-Hall, 1982.

CASE Diet Planning

Consider the decision area of diet or menu planning for an institution such as a school, hospital, or nursing home. You are asked to prepare a report that explores the suitability of OR/MS methods in assisting with diet planning. No explicit boundaries are placed on your discussion except that this report for management will be one input in the decision of whether or not to incorporate an OR approach. Your report should include your recommendations.

Many issues could be addressed. Although not intended to be exhaustive, the following list suggests issues to consider.

Time frame for decision making (single meal, weekly menu, etc.).

Goals or objectives.

Appropriate surrogate criteria.

Controllable variables.

Uncontrollable variables.

Deterministic versus stochastic elements.

Functional form of significant relationships
(linear, nonlinear, discrete, continuous, etc.).

Constraints (restrictions/requirements).

Sources of data.

Difficulties in estimating parameters.

As you discuss various issues, you should comment on those which lend themselves to mathematical representation and those which do not. Also address the issue of who should be involved in the process of conducting the study and address possible implementation obstacles if a new system of menu planning is introduced.

Since we all have some level of interest in eating (some of us more than others), draw on your own interests and preferences in preparing your report.

2

Classical Deterministic Models

Chapter Outline

We assume throughout this text that some of the criteria on which decisions are made are quantifiable and can be represented by mathematical functions. The mathematical relationships used to represent these criteria are called *objective functions,* as defined in Chapter 1. We believe aspects of many problems are quantifiable. We also contend that analysis of these quantifiable factors can yield special insights that can assist in making decisions.

This chapter focuses on problem structures represented mathematically by so-called *classical deterministic models,* as opposed to probabilistic models. When problems are represented accurately by such models, we show that solutions are generated rather easily through the use of *the calculus*. The purpose of this chapter is to demonstrate the applicability of calculus to *unconstrained* classical deterministic models and to *constrained* classical deterministic models.

Since the solution techniques involve differential calculus, we assume that you are familiar with elementary rules for finding derivatives. If you are unfamiliar with the concepts and techniques of differential calculus, carefully study Appendix B. These fundamentals can be mastered if you have a rudimentary knowledge of algebra and you make a commitment. If you are familiar with calculus, a reading of Appendix B should serve to clear the "cobwebs."

2.1 MATHEMATICAL REPRESENTATION OF RELATIONSHIPS

Before discussing the mathematical representation of objective functions, we review functional notation.

Functional Notation

A **function** is a mathematical relationship for which the value of a particular variable is determined from the values of one or more other variables. For example, the relationship

$$y = f(x) \tag{2.1}$$

implies an association between the variables x and y. Specifically, Equation 2.1 indicates that the value of the variable y is a function of, or depends on the value of the variable x. In this context, y is the **dependent (criterion) variable** and x the **independent (predictor) variable.** Equation 2.1 is read "y is a function of x" where the expression $f(x)$ can be verbalized as "f of x." Also, $f(x)$ is the value of the algebraic function f at x. Each value of x is associated with one and only one value of y, but the same y value may be associated with more than one x value. A function from a set A to a set B can then be considered a rule of correspondence assigning a uniquely determined element $f(x)$ to each x in a prescribed subset of A.

▶ Example 2.1 Salary Function

Starting salaries of truck drivers for the Humorous Ice Cream Company are based on an incentive system. Salaries depend on the sales generated by each driver. This salary-sales relationship might be expressed symbolically as

$$y = f(x)$$

or

$$\text{Salary} = f(\text{dollar sales})$$

where "salary" is the criterion variable and "dollar sales" is the independent variable. The precise relationship between the two variables might be expressed as

$$y = 50 + 0.25x$$

where y = Weekly salary in dollars and x = Weekly sales in dollars. Suppose this function determines *your* weekly salary. Can you interpret the way in which you are being compensated? You should conclude that drivers are paid a base weekly salary of $50 and receive a commission of $0.25 on every dollar of sales. For example, if a driver were to generate $250 in sales during a given week, the salary of $112.50 could be determined easily by substituting 250 for x in the above *linear function.* (Note also that we can infer weekly sales from the salary figure. If salary were $300, you could solve for the weekly sales figure of $1,000.)

In many instances, the criterion variable depends on more than one variable. Consequently, a more general functional representation of the association between some criterion variable, y, and a set of n independent variables is

$$\begin{aligned} y &= f(x_1, x_2, x_3, \ldots, x_n). \\ &= f(\mathbf{x}) \end{aligned} \tag{2.2}$$

where $\mathbf{x}$ represents the vector of n independent variables.

Representation through Continuous Mathematical Functions

A significant number of models in economics and management utilize discrete or integer variables. Units of a product, number of employees, and dollars and cents are all examples of variables characterized by discrete values. In most cases, functions that are based on variables that are continuous—time, length, volume—are treated more readily than discrete functions. Indeed, differential calculus rests on the premise that the function being treated is continuous. A function is continuous if there are no kinks or discontinuities in it. A kink or corner in the graph and a discontinuity or break in the curve both mean that no tangent can be drawn at the point in question. Fortunately, discrete functional relationships often are approximated quite well by continuous mathematical functions, as the subsequent example illustrates.

▶ Example 2.2 Sales Function

A certain company is interested in studying how sales revenue for a district responds to different levels of assigned sales personnel per district. Figure 2–1 reflects empirical data gathered within a representative sales district where the number of personnel assigned ranged from one to eight. Each data point reflects the number of personnel in the district and the associated level of sales for the district. The data seem to indicate *diminishing returns* beyond three people. Note that the function is discrete since both sales and personnel, assuming the latter cannot be split among districts, are discrete

FIGURE 2–1 Empirical Data for Example 2.2

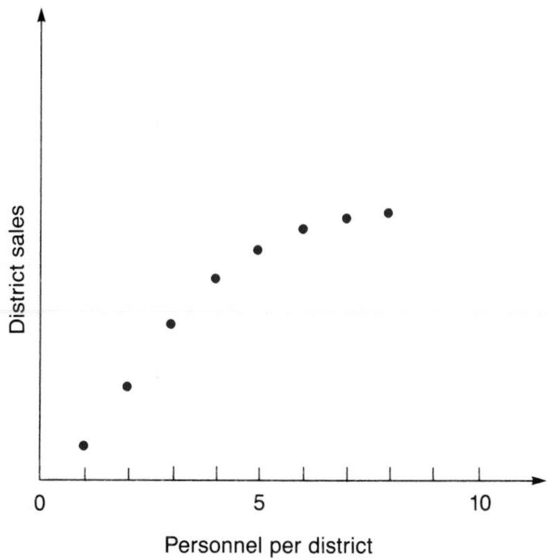

variables. As Figure 2–2 indicates, however, a continuous function is approximated by fitting a smooth curve to the plotted data. Although the curve extrapolates between integer values of the variable, the important feature is that it provides a fairly accurate portrayal of the relationship between district sales and number of personnel assigned per sales district.

FIGURE 2–2 Continuous Function Approximation for Example 2.2

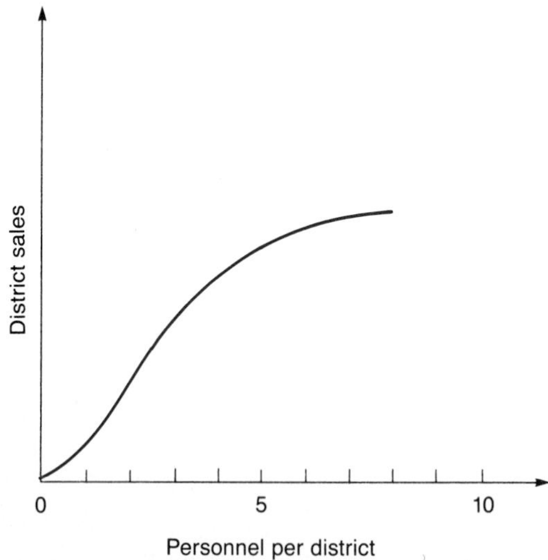

You will find in this chapter that where criterion relationships or objective functions are represented by continuous mathematical functions, the methods of differential calculus provide a convenient search procedure for identifying conditions of optimality.

The Concept of Optimality

In the introduction to this chapter, we presumed that the criteria on which decisions are made are often quantifiable and capable of representation by mathematical functions called objective functions. The ultimate purpose for making a decision is to try to influence the objective function in a favorable direction. **Optimization** is the state of either minimization or maximization of the chosen measure of effectiveness. For example, the objective in a hospital emergency room might be to minimize the average waiting time between arrival at the hospital and attendance by medical personnel. In Example 2.2, the company might be interested in determining the number of personnel it should assign to a particular district in order to maximize district profits.

FIGURE 2–3 Minima and Maxima

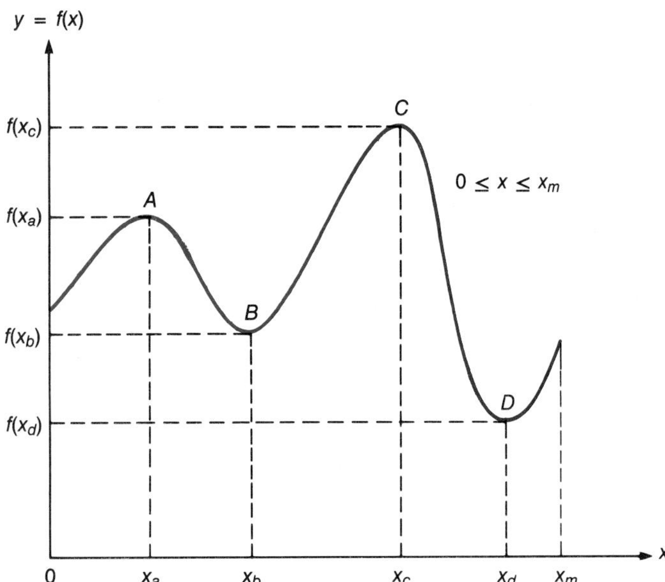

Consider Figure 2–3, where the criterion variable depends on one independent variable. This continuous objective function is rather strange looking, but it is useful in demonstrating some concepts of optimality. Assume that the independent variable x has values ranging between $x = 0$ and $x = x_m$.

Given that variable x represents the independent variable, a function is said to reach a **relative** or **local maximum** at a point $x = a$ if $f(a)$ is greater than the value of $f(x)$ for any adjacent value of x. Similarly, a function is said to reach a **relative** or **local minimum** at a point $x = a$ if $f(a)$ is less than the value of $f(x)$ for any adjacent value of x. (Note that we are confining our attention to continuous functions). For example, in Figure 2–3 relative maxima occur at points A and C as well as when

$x = x_m$ on the curve. If you select a point adjacent to x_a, the value of the criterion variable is less than $f(x_a)$. The same argument applies to adjacent points surrounding $x = x_c$. Following the definition of a relative minimum, one would conclude that relative *minima* occur at points B and D and when $x = 0$. For values of the independent variable adjacent to either $x = x_b$ or $x = x_d$, the value of the criterion variable is greater than $f(x_b)$ or $f(x_d)$, respectively.

A function is said to have an **absolute maximum** at a point $x = a$ if $f(a)$ is greater than $f(x)$ for any other allowable value of x. The absolute maximum in Figure 2–3 occurs at point C where $x = x_c$. The value of the function at x_c is $f(x_c)$, and it is larger than that for any other value of x within the region $0 \leq x \leq x_m$. Similarly, a function is said to have an **absolute minimum** at point $x = a$ if $f(a)$ is less than $f(x)$ for any other allowable value of x. In Figure 2–3, the absolute minimum occurs at $x = x_d$. $f(x_d)$ is less than $f(x)$ for any other value of x, where $0 \leq x \leq x_m$. A local maximum or minimum can also be an absolute maximum or minimum.

FIGURE 2–4 Absolute Minimum and Maximum (End points)

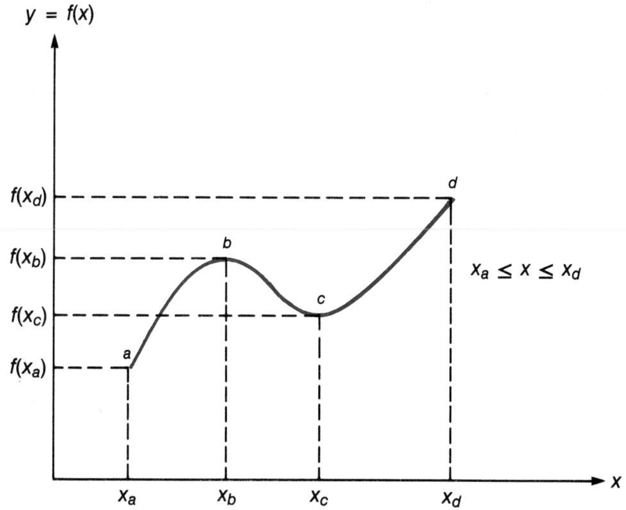

End points on a function must be evaluated when identifying optimal values for a criterion variable. Consider Figure 2–4 as an example. In this situation, the allowable values of x range from $x = x_a$ to $x = x_d$. A quick glance at this figure indicates that the absolute maximum for the criterion variable occurs not at $f(x_b)$, the local maximum, but when $x = x_d$; the absolute minimum occurs when $x = x_a$, not at the local minimum $f(x_c)$. Notice that these are the end points on the allowable range for the independent variable.

Other points that must be considered as candidates for absolute maxima and minima are points of discontinuity on a function. This is illustrated in Figure 2–5. The absolute minimum occurs at the end point x_a, and the absolute maximum occurs at the point of discontinuity x_c. Consequently, in examining for absolute maxima and minima one should evaluate the function not only at the local maxima and minima but also at the end values of the allowable range for the independent variable and at points of discontinuity.

FIGURE 2–5 Absolute Maximum at Point of Discontinuity

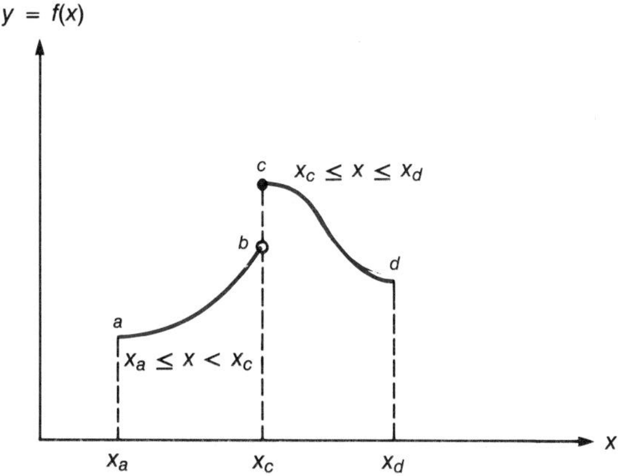

Selecting Values for Decision Variables

Ideally decision makers would like complete control of the criterion variable. Although such powers are rare (monopolistic conditions might approximate this situation), most decision makers are capable of partially controlling the relative achievement of their objectives. They do so by making decisions concerning the variables over which they have control. Such **decision variables** might include the level of personnel resources to hire, the amount of money to allocate to advertising, the number and timing of daily runs of a mass transit system, the hours of operation of a bank, the number of sections of a required college mathematics course to offer during a semester, and so forth. Note that decision variables are represented as independent variables. For example, if the objective function looks like that in Figure 2–6, and if the goal is to maximize the value of the criterion variable, then we would like to manipulate the value of x as close to x^* as possible.

If the functional relationship $y = f(x)$ is known and no restrictions or constraints are placed on the decision variables, then we can search for the optimal set of decision variables $\mathbf{x}^*$ using **unconstrained optimization** techniques as demonstrated in this chapter.

Realistically, there may be practical, competitive, or legal restrictions on the values independent variables can assume. For example, budget considerations could set restrictions on the number of persons who can be hired or on the allowable amounts of money that can be expended for advertising. Within these limits of control the decision maker hopes to influence the value of the objective function in the most favorable direction.

If $y = f(x)$ is known and subject to a set of constraints on the decision variables, then we can search for the optimal set $\mathbf{x}^*$ by one of the constrained optimization techniques in the following chapters. In two variable problems with one equality constraint, often the problem can be formulated as *unconstrained*.

In many cases we may not know the functional relationship between the criterion variable and the decision variables. Only through a trial-and-error procedure might

FIGURE 2–6 Manipulation for Achieving Optimization

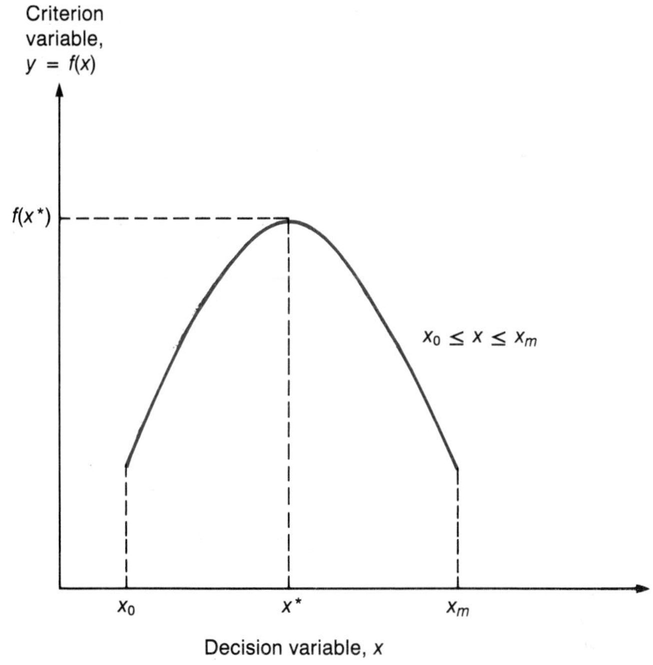

we realize the best values to assign the decision variables. The greater the degree of uncertainty about the relationship among the relevant variables, the greater the likelihood that a systematic and efficient search procedure can be identified.

2.2 WHERE DO THE RELATIONSHIPS COME FROM?

This book details many of the solution techniques for quantitative models of decision processes. In doing so, however, we do not want you to lose sight of the importance and the pitfalls associated with the *formulation* of quantitative models. One of the traditional areas of neglect in discussing classical optimization theory is the question of the source of a model. As a systems analyst or management scientist, chances are slim that a decision maker will come to you and lay a quadratic profit equation on your desk to be solved. And yet, many calculus texts would lead the student to believe that the extent of one's interest should simply be to solve *predetermined* systems of equations.

This section attempts to create greater awareness of the source of these criterion equations or objective functions. The discussion will focus on those situations wherein the logical structure of the relationships between variables is *well-defined* and those wherein the logical structure is *ill-defined*.

Functional Relationship Well-Defined

There are a variety of problem situations in which the logical structure of the way variables interrelate is well-defined. This generally means that a systematic observation of the variables of interest leads to an exact mathematical representation of the relationship between variables. A classic example of this situation is the determination of total revenue for a firm. If the firm sells each unit at the same price, p, total revenue from selling q units is simply found by multiplying price per unit times the number of units sold, or

$$TR = p \cdot q$$

where TR represents total revenue. Under the assumption of a constant selling price, this model logically and deterministically represents the total revenue function.

The following example illustrates a decision situation in which the interrelationships between variables are well-defined either by their obvious structure or by assumptions made about the structure.

▶ Example 2.3 Police Patrol Sectors[1]

Management scientists have examined urban service systems with special interest in improving the effectiveness of emergency-response systems: police response, ambulance response, and fire department response. How might cities go about the process of deciding on optimal dimensions of patrol sectors for any emergency-response unit? We will cast this example within the framework of police patrol sector design, but the analysis can be extended to include any of the other types of response systems.

Suppose a rectangular patrol sector is to be designed for a police patrol car so as to minimize the average travel time to incidents. Assume that a patrol car responds only to the calls in its patrol sector and that a call for assistance is equally likely to originate from any point in the patrol sector. In addition, assume that at the instant a call occurs, the patrol car is equally likely to be at any point within the patrol sector. Statistically, assume that the positions of the patrol car and the calls for service are independent variables and that their values are uniformly distributed over the patrol sector.

Figure 2–7 illustrates some of the other aspects of the problem. The figure portrays a system of city blocks. The patrol sector in this application is rectangular with dimensions x by y (the decision variables). In addition, the directions of travel are parallel to the boundaries of the patrol area. This means that travel distances are computed on a "city-block" or "right-angle" basis. If a call is received at the location (x_2, y_2) and the patrol unit is currently located at (x_1, y_1), the patrol unit must follow the existing pattern of streets, combining an easterly movement with one in a northerly direction.

Travel speeds within a city vary according to direction of travel, time of day, and section of the city. This model assumes that *effective* speeds can be determined. Effective travel speeds in the x and y directions, respectively, are defined by v_x and v_y.

---

[1]The motivation for this example came from the work of Richard C. Larson, *Urban Police Patrol Analysis* (Cambridge, Mass.: MIT Press, 1972). Recently, Vincent Mabert developed a short-interval forecasting system for the 911 daily emergency calls to the Indianapolis Police Department. Vincent A. Mabert, "Short-Interval Forecasting of Emergency Phone Call Work Loads," *The Fifth International Symposium on Forecasting,* June 9–12, 1985.

FIGURE 2–7 Rectangular Patrol Sector

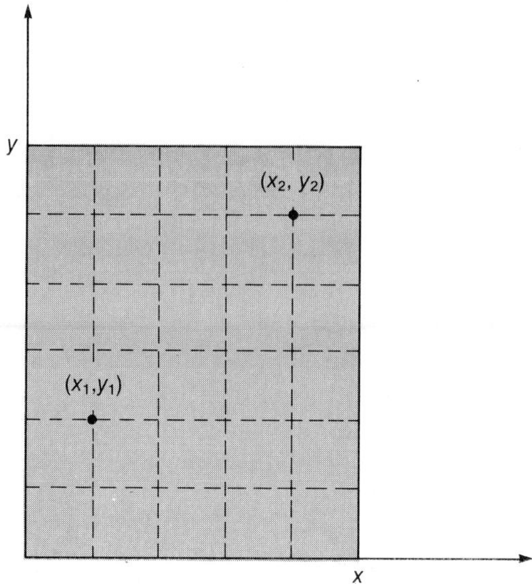

Let us begin to utilize the problem-solving framework outlined in Chapter 1. For this example, we will only formulate the mathematical model. The next section returns to the problem and develops a solution.

1. **Verbal Statement of Problem**
   Determine the dimensions of a rectangular patrol sector that minimizes average travel time to incidents.
2. **Decisions**
   a. **Verbal Statement**
      Dimensions of rectangular patrol sector.
   b. **Mathematical Definition**
      x = Width of patrol sector, stated in miles.
      y = Length of patrol sector, stated in miles.
3. **Criteria**
   a. **Verbal Statement**
      Average travel time to incidents.
   b. **Mathematical Definition**
      For the incident-patrol locations in Figure 2–7, the distances traveled in the x and y directions are given by

$$d_x = |x_2 - x_1|$$

and

$$d_y = |y_2 - y_1| .$$

Total travel time (T) is

$$T = t_x + t_y$$

where t_x = Travel time in the x direction, and t_y = Travel time in the y direction; or, since travel time is the distance traveled divided by the travel speed,

$$T = \frac{d_x}{v_x} + \frac{d_y}{v_y}.$$

The overall objective for the police administrator in this example is to determine the dimensions of the rectangular patrol sector that would minimize the criterion variable "average travel time" ($\overline{T}$) for responding to calls for service. (If we assume that there is no delay between receiving a call and dispatching a car, then the objective translates into one of minimizing average *response* time to a call for assistance.)

It can be shown that the *average* distance traveled in the x and y directions for uniformly distributed incidence and patrol car locations are, respectively,

$$\overline{d_x} = \frac{x}{3} \text{ and } \overline{d_y} = \frac{y}{3}$$

where x and y are the dimensions of the sector. If locations were recorded and the travel distances were noted in both the x and y directions for a large number of crimes, the *average* travel distances in the x and y directions would statistically tend toward the $\overline{d_x}$ and $\overline{d_y}$ values as indicated above. Consequently, the objective function in this problem becomes

$$\overline{T} = \frac{x}{3v_x} + \frac{y}{3v_y}$$

$$= \frac{1}{3}\left(\frac{x}{v_x} + \frac{y}{v_y}\right)$$

where $\overline{T}$ is the average travel time.

4. **Constraining Conditions**
Given that the objective is to minimize $\overline{T}$, this would occur when $x = y = 0$. It should be apparent that this *mathematical* result is unrealistic. The mathematical model is missing one important element.
   a. **Verbal Statement**
   One condition police planners often attempt to create is equal workloads for patrol cars. A way of approximating this condition is to assume that the number of calls received is proportional to the area of the sector patrolled. Thus another condition in the model is that the area of each sector must be predetermined.
   b. **Mathematical Statement**
   If the area of each sector is denoted as A, then we can state the constraining condition

$$x \cdot y = A$$

5. **Mathematical Model**
The final statement of the model is to minimize

$$\overline{T} = \frac{1}{3}\left(\frac{x}{v_x} + \frac{y}{v_y}\right) \tag{2.3}$$

such that

$$x \cdot y = A. \tag{2.4}$$

This can easily be restated in terms of one variable with no constraints. Do this before solving the problem in the next paragraph.

Suppose that major roads run in the north/south direction (y) and consequently police cars travel twice as fast in that direction (i.e., $v_y = 2v_x$. Further, suppose that $A = 10$ square miles. Convince yourself that $x^* = 2.236$ miles and $y^* = 4.472$ miles.

Functional Relationship Estimated

Many situations exist wherein the logical interrelationships among variables are not known exactly. Consequently it is more difficult to mathematically formulate an objective function. In such cases, we often collect relevant data through sampling to determine whether or not any regular pattern of behavior is apparent. If a pattern does seem to exist, then a curve-fitting procedure may be employed to quantitatively model the relationship. The means of fitting the curve might range from simply "eyeballing" to more rigorous procedures, such as regression analysis.

The following example illustrates a situation in which the logical structure is not defined sufficiently to simply write down the relevant functional relationship.

▶ Example 2.4 Single Product Pricing Problem

The Massachusetts Bay Transit Authority (MBTA) wishes to smooth its demand for subway services. The subway system operates at capacity during the early morning and late afternoon rush hours, and it operates far below capacity during the late morning and early afternoon hours. The MBTA wants to stimulate greater demand during off-peak hours and to encourage riders who do not need to travel during peak hours to travel at other times. Homemakers shopping in the city during the day are examples of this category of riders.

The MBTA has been experimenting with off-peak fares in order to determine the effects on demand. Currently, a program allows passengers to travel for \$0.30 rather than the normal \$0.75 between the hours of 10 A.M. and 1 P.M. Data have been gathered showing demand under other fares as depicted in Figure 2–8.

The data, when graphed, offer strong evidence of a linear demand function during off-peak hours. Since this demand function was not available initially, it is necessary to approximate it from collected data. Fitting a least-squares regression[2] line to the data, we estimate the demand equation as

$$q = 45 - \frac{1}{2}p$$

or

$$p = -2q + 90 \tag{2.5}$$

[2]Regression analysis is reviewed in Appendix A.

FIGURE 2–8 MBTA Demand Data

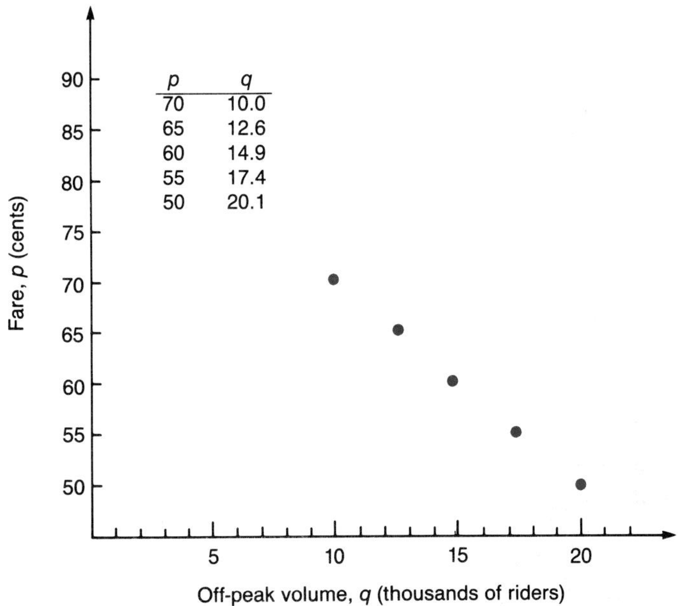

where p = Off-peak fare (cents), and q = Off-peak demand (thousands of riders).

If the objective is to maximize the demand for off-peak service, observation of Figure 2–8 would suggest that fares be eliminated, resulting in an estimated 45,000 passengers during these hours.

2.3 SINGLE-VARIABLE APPLICATIONS[3]

This section presents a set of applications involving optimization of functions in one variable. The examples include those formulated earlier in the chapter.

▶ Example 2.5 MBTA Continued

Example 2.4 showed how a functional relationship was estimated relating quantity demanded to price. Now suppose the objective is to maximize total revenue during this period. Using the problem-solving framework:

1. **Verbal Statement of Problem**
   Determine the price to charge per ride in order to maximize total revenue during off-peak daylight hours.
2. **Decisions**
   a. **Verbal Statement**
      Fare to charge for each ride.
   b. **Mathematical Definition**
      p = Off-peak fare (cents).

[3]Knowledge of Section B.1 in Appendix B is assumed.

3. **Criteria**
   a. **Verbal Statement**
   Total revenue.
   b. **Mathematical Statement**
   As stated earlier, total revenue is price per unit times number of units sold, or

$$TR = p \cdot q. \tag{2.6}$$

In its current form, total revenue is stated as a function of two independent variables. If quantity were to be expressed in terms of price, total revenue could be written as a function of only one independent variable, p. This is accomplished easily by solving Equation 2.5 for q and substituting in Equation 2.6. The resulting objective function is

$$TR = 45p - \frac{p^2}{2}.$$

4. **Constraints**
   None.
5. **Model**
   With no constraints, the model for this problem consists of the objective function

$$TR = f(p) = 45p - \frac{p^2}{2} \tag{2.7}$$

6. **Model Outcomes**
   Equation 2.7 is quadratic in form and graphs as a parabola, concave downward. To determine whether any relative maxima or minima exist, *stationary points* are first identified. As mentioned in Appendix B, stationary points are those whose tangent slope equals zero. Taking the first derivative of the revenue function with respect to the variable p,

$$f'(p) = 45 - 2\frac{p}{2}$$
$$= 45 - p.$$

Setting this equal to zero in order to identify points of zero slope, we get

$$f'(p) = 45 - p = 0$$

or

$$p^* = 45.$$

Testing the stationary point by means of the second derivative yields

$$f''(p) = -1.$$

Thus a relative maximum exists for $f(p)$ when $p = 45$.

7. **Interpretation of Results**
   Since the value of the second derivative is negative throughout the range of p, we conclude that there exists an absolute maximum for total revenue when a fare of 45 cents is charged. The revenue function is sketched in Figure 2–9.

FIGURE 2–9 Total Revenue Function for MBTA

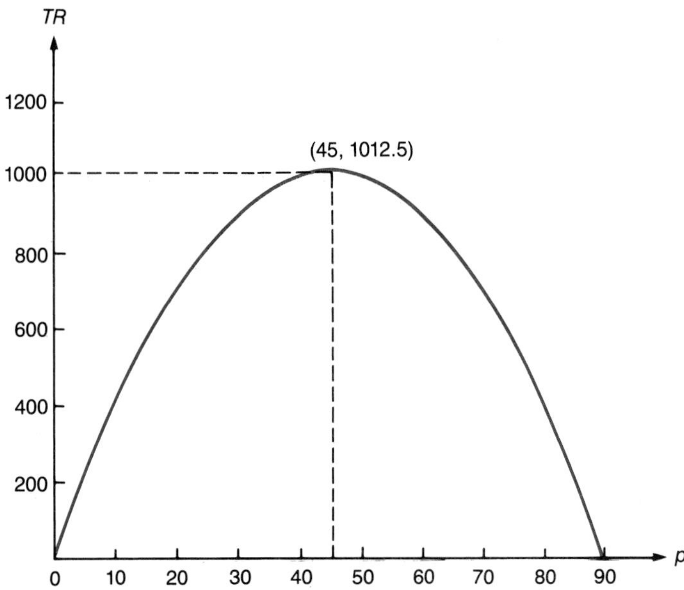

Maximum total revenue is found by substituting $p^* = 45$ into the revenue function:

$$TR^* = 45(45) - \frac{(45)^2}{2}$$

$$= 1{,}012.5$$

Based on the way we defined variables, can you verify that the maximum total revenue is $10,125? We determine expected demand during the off-peak hours with a fare of 45 cents by substituting this value of p into the demand equation:

$$q^* = 45 - \frac{p^*}{2}$$

$$= 45 - \frac{45}{2}$$

$$= 22.5 \text{ (thousand passengers)}.$$

The current demand is $q = 45 - 30/2 = 30$ (thousand passengers). Thus total revenue each day for the off-peak period would equal $9,000. The suggested fare policy would result in a daily increase of $1,125 in revenues over the current policy with a fare of 30 cents.

FOLLOW-UP EXERCISES

1. Thoroughly investigate the implications of the solution just derived. Show total revenue at prices of 30 cents, 40 cents, 45 cents, and 50 cents.
2. Develop an equation to show how sensitive total revenue is to changes in price. Does the sensitivity depend on the price level?

▶ Example 2.6 Optimal Advertising Period

Mow-Down Records, Inc. has recently recorded its latest "fad" album: *Love That OR.* "Fad" albums are those advertised on local television and are sold by direct mail only. Mow-Down uses a number of test cities as pilot areas for new releases. A medium-size western city has been selected to test market the latest album, and Mow-Down wishes to determine for how many days the advertising campaign should be conducted in order to maximize total profits. From the many campaigns conducted within this city, the company has determined that the proportion of target customers purchasing an album depends on the length of the promotional campaign. The proportion has been observed to behave empirically according to the function $(1 - e^{-0.02t})$, where t equals the number of days of the campaign.[4] The target market is estimated at 100,000 people and the profit margin for each album is $2, exclusive of advertising expenditures. Current costs for spot advertising on local television are $2,000 per day. Fixed expenses associated with initiating the promotion campaign are $2,500.

1. **Verbal Statement of Problem**
   Determine the number of days Mow-Down should advertise in order to maximize total profit.
2. **Decisions**
   a. **Verbal Statement**
      Number of days to conduct advertising campaign.
   b. **Mathematical Definition**
      t = Number of days of advertising campaign.
3. **Criteria**
   a. **Verbal Statement**
      Total profit.
   b. **Mathematical Statement**
      Profit is estimated by computing the gross profit margin less promotion expenses. A necessary component in determining gross profit margin is the number of albums sold. This is stated in terms of the target market size and response function as

$$\text{Number of albums sold} = 100{,}000(1 - e^{-0.02t}).$$

Thus

$$\text{Gross profit margin (dollars)} = (2)(100{,}000)(1 - e^{-0.02t})$$

or

$$G(t) = 200{,}000(1 - e^{-0.02t}).$$

Promotion costs are easily stated as

$$C(t) = 2{,}000t + 2{,}500.$$

Now, the net profit function is formulated as

$$\begin{aligned} P(t) &= G(t) - C(t) \\ &= 200{,}000(1 - e^{-0.02t}) - 2{,}000t - 2{,}500 \\ &= 197{,}500 - 200{,}000e^{-0.02t} - 2{,}000t. \end{aligned}$$

[4]Recall that $e = 2.718\ldots$ is the base of natural logarithms. The given function and all estimates can be determined by the estimation methods of Appendix A.

4. **Constraints**
   None.

5. **Mathematical Model**
   The model for this problem consists of the net profit function

$$P(t) = 197{,}500 - 200{,}000e^{-0.02t} - 2{,}000t$$

6. **Model Outcomes**
   The derivative of the profit function is found to be

$$P'(t) = -200{,}000(-0.02)e^{-0.02t} - 2{,}000$$
$$= 4{,}000e^{-0.02t} - 2{,}000\,.$$

   Setting this to zero, we get

$$e^{-0.02t} = \frac{2{,}000}{4{,}000} = \frac{1}{2}\,.$$

   To determine the value of t that satisfies the equation, we find the natural logarithm of both sides of the equation, or

$$-0.02t = -0.6932$$
$$t = \frac{-0.6932}{(-0.02)}$$

   or,

$$t^* = 34.66\,.$$

   You should verify by the second derivative test that $P(t)$ is maximized when $t = 34.66$.

7. **Interpretation of Results**
   Net profit is maximized if the advertising campaign is conducted for 34.66 days. Verify that if the campaign is conducted for this period that net profit will be approximately \$28,185 and that approximately 50 percent of the target market is expected to purchase the album. Figure 2–10 graphically portrays the firm's profit function.

FOLLOW-UP EXERCISES

3. If Mow-Down can purchase only whole days of advertising, how many should they purchase and what is the maximum profit?
4. Show that a small (+0.005) change in the −0.02 coefficient has a large impact on profit. What are the implications for the decision maker?
5. How sensitive are (*a*) the maximum profit and (*b*) the optimal length of the promotion campaign to a 100 percent increase in the daily advertising rate? What are the implications of this result for the decision maker?
6. Letting T = Market size, v = Variable advertising expenditure, c = Fixed expense of promotion campaign, m = Profit margin per album, $(1 - e^{-at})$ = Market response function over time, a = Constant, and t = Length of promotion campaign, show (by derivation) that for a given city the optimal length of a promotion campaign by Mow-Down can be determined by solving for t in the equation

$$e^{-at} = \frac{v}{mTa}\,.$$

FIGURE 2–10 Profit Function for Mow-Down Records, Inc.

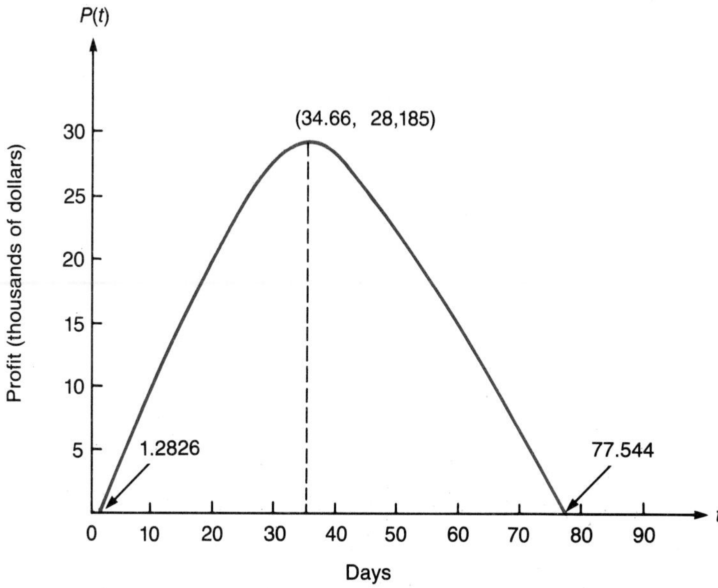

7. Sketch the market response function and interpret its behavior in the context of this application.

Example 2.7 Patrol Sector Design Continued

In Example 2.3 we discussed and formulated a model for the design of police patrol sectors. The problem was to define the dimensions of the rectangular patrol sector that would minimize the average travel time ($\overline{T}$) for responses to calls for service. Suppose police planners wish to assign each car to a patrol sector of 4 square miles and that effective travel speeds in the x and y directions are $v_x = 10$ mph and $v_y = 10$ mph. Substituting these values into Equations 2.3 and 2.4 yields

$$\overline{T} = \frac{1}{3}\left[\frac{x}{10} + \frac{y}{10}\right] \tag{2.8}$$

and

$$x \cdot y = 4. \tag{2.9}$$

In this section we will proceed to a solution using the problem solving framework.

6. **Model Outcomes**
Notice that the criterion variable is stated as a function of two independent variables (x and y) and that Equation 2.9 acts as a constraint on the decision variables. However, the dependence between x and y in 2.9 allows us to solve for one of the variables in terms of the other (it makes no difference which variable is solved in terms of the other), thereby reducing Equation 2.8 to one decision variable and eliminating 2.9 altogether. Solving for x in Equation 2.9 and substituting in Equation 2.8 allows us to express $\overline{T}$ in terms of one independent variable:

$$\bar{T} = \frac{1}{3}\left[\frac{(4/y)}{10} + \frac{y}{10}\right]$$

$$= \frac{4}{30y} + \frac{y}{30}.$$

Since the objective is to minimize average travel time, we take the first derivative to identify any stationary points for the function:

$$f'(y) = -\frac{4}{30y^2} + \frac{1}{30}.$$

Setting the first derivative equal to zero gives

$$\frac{1}{30} = \frac{4}{30y^2}.$$

Multiplying both sides by $30y^2$ and solving for the unknown gives $y^* = \pm 2$. Since a negative dimension is meaningless in this problem, the positive root is the only one of interest. To determine the nature of this stationary point, we take the second derivative

$$f''(y) = \frac{8}{30y^3}$$

$$f''(2) = \frac{1}{30} > 0.$$

Because this value is greater than zero (and will be for all $y > 0$), we conclude that an absolute minimum exists at $y = 2$. The corresponding value for x, from Equation 2.9, is also 2.

7. **Interpretation of Result**
   The average response time is minimized if the dimensions of the rectangular patrol sector are 2 miles by 2 miles. The optimal average travel time of 0.133 hour or 8 minutes is found by substituting the dimensions into Equation 2.8.

FOLLOW-UP EXERCISES

8. You should consider the assumptions underlying this model and the effects violations would have on the structure and solution. To wit: nonrectangular travel, heterogeneity of neighborhoods with regard to density, and the probabilistic nature of travel time. Did you find the assignment of 4 square miles to patrol sectors to be too arbitrary? What objectives, constraints, or other factors might be introduced in determining the area of a sector?
9. Determine the optimal grid dimensions and travel time for:
   a. $v_x = 10$ mph, $v_y = 20$ mph, and $A = 8$ square miles.
   b. $v_x = 10$ mph, $v_y = 10$ mph, and $A = 10$ square miles.

► Example 2.8 Replacement Model

The **machine** or **equipment replacement problem** is concerned with determining the optimal point in time at which to replace a capital asset that is characterized both by average capital cost (depreciation) that decreases over time and by operating cost that increases over time. For example, a new automobile is characterized by a depreciation cost that, although high initially, declines over time. As time goes on, however, the cost of operating (including maintaining) an automobile increases.

This trade-off in costs can be resolved by minimizing the criterion given by the sum of average capital cost and operating cost. If $K(t)$ represents the estimated *total* capital cost over the time period t, and $0(t)$ represents the estimated *average* cost of operation (and maintenance) per unit time period over the ownership period t, then

$$C(t) = \frac{K(t)}{t} + 0(t) \tag{2.10}$$

represents the *average cost per unit time period* of owning the asset over the length of time given by t.

To illustrate a simple case: Suppose the particular asset in question has an initial purchase price of P, a salvage value given by S *that is independent of age,* and an average operating and maintenance cost that increases linearly over time (with intercept "a" and slope "b"). Thus,

$$K(t) = P - S \tag{2.11}$$

and

$$0(t) = a + bt. \tag{2.12}$$

According to Equation 2.10,

$$C(t) = \frac{P - S}{t} + (a + bt). \tag{2.13}$$

The optimal point in time at which to replace this asset is determined by differentiating $C(t)$ with respect to t, setting $C'(t)$ to zero, and solving for t:

$$C'(t) = \frac{-(P - S)}{t^2} + b$$
$$= 0$$

or

$$t^* = \left(\frac{P - S}{b}\right)^{1/2}. \tag{2.14}$$

Since $C''(t) = 2(P - S)/t^3 > 0$ for all $t > 0$ and $P > S$, it follows that t^* represents an absolute minimum. For example, *if* $P = \$100{,}000$, $S = \$20{,}000$, $a = \$5{,}000$, and $b = \$1{,}000$ per year, then $t^* \doteq 8.94$ years and $C(t^*) \doteq \$22{,}889$ per year (see Figure 2–11). Note that the total cost over the ownership period is given by the product $t^* \cdot C(t^*)$, or \$204,628 in the present example.

The model given by Equation 2.10 represents one version among many. Replacement models have been solved that include the treatment of discrete periods, an infinite time horizon (sequence of machines), costs expressed as present values, and uncer-

FIGURE 2–11 Average Cost Curves for Replacement Model

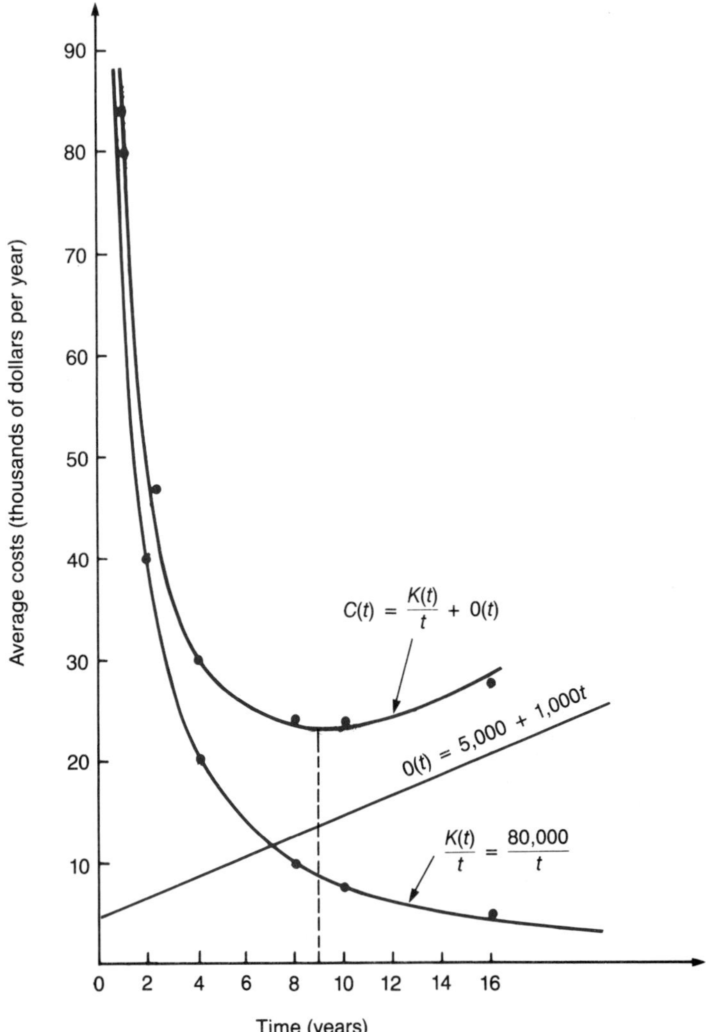

tainty with respect to failures and technological and economic obsolescence. A simple extension of Equation 2.11 would allow the salvage value S to be a function of the ownership period t.

FOLLOW-UP EXERCISES

10. Given the data in Example 2.8, find t^* and $C(t^*)$ for the following values of b: 600; 800; 1,200; 1,400. In your judgement, are t^* and $C(t^*)$ sensitive to this parameter?
11. Given the data in Example 2.8, find t^* and $C(t^*)$ for the following values of a: 1,000; 3,000; 7,000; 9,000. In your opinion, are t^* and $C(t^*)$ sensitive to this parameter?

12. Suppose you are given the following cost data for the operation and maintenance of a capital asset:

Year	Cost Each Year (dollars)	Cumulative Cost (dollars)	Average Cost (dollars per year)
1	6,000		
2	8,000		
3	10,000		
4	12,000		
5	14,000		

Fill in the last two columns and fit (by the "eyeball" method) a linear function to the last column to show that $0(t) = 5{,}000 + 1{,}000t$ (which you should recognize as the function used in the example). Why would it be logically wrong to fit a function to the first cost column?

**13. Suppose, instead of Equation 2.12, that

$$0(t) = at^b \tag{2.15}$$

where $a > 0$ and $b > 0$ are constants as before.

a. Determine $0'(t)$ and $0''(t)$ to show that $b > 1$ represents the case where operating costs increase at an increasing rate, and $0 < b < 1$ represents the case where operating costs increase at a decreasing rate. Plot $0(t)$ on a graph for the cases $b > 1$, $0 < b < 1$, and $b = 1$.
b. Derive an expression for t^* using Equations 2.11 and 2.15.
c. Find t^* using the same data as the example, except assume $0(t)$ to be of the form in Equation 2.15 with $a = 5{,}000$ and $b = 1.2$. Also try $b = 0.8$.

**14. State the expression for $C'(t) = 0$ for models that utilize Equation 2.15 and each of the following exponential capital cost functions:

$$K(t) = P(1 - d^t) \tag{2.16}$$

$$K(t) = P(1 - e^{-dt}) \tag{2.17}$$

where d represents the depreciation factor. For example, $d = 0.9$ would indicate that the salvage value in Equation 2.16, that is, $P(0.9)^t$, decreases by 90 percent per time period. How would you go about solving for t^*? Plot $K(t)$ and $K(t)/t$ for each case. Do the exponential cost functions make more sense than Equation 2.11?

**15. As you might recall from step six of the paradigm in Chapter 1, *sensitivity analysis* is concerned with the sensitivity of decisions and criteria to errors in estimating parameters and uncontrollable variables.[6] Suppose we were to define $b = \epsilon b'$ where b' represents the actual value of the estimated parameter b and ϵ denotes an error proportion. Using Equation 2.14, derive an expression for $t^*/(t^*)'$ in terms of ϵ where $(t^*)'$ represents the true optimum period. Evaluate and interpret these expressions for $\epsilon = 0.5$ and $\epsilon = 1.5$. Relate these results to your results in Exercise 10 by assuming $b' = 1{,}000$. Repeat the procedure for $a = \epsilon a'$.

[5]Double asterisks (**) designate examples and follow-up exercises that are more advanced than others. But don't be intimidated. We think you can handle many of these.

[6]Exercises 10 and 11 of this chapter treat this subject informally.

**16. Perform the sensitivity analysis described in Exercise 15 on the model you derived in Exercise 13.

**Example 2.9 Timing the Sale of an Asset

Suppose an investor has an opportunity to invest an amount of capital, C, in a project or asset. The project has the following characteristics: (1) The return on the investment or future selling price is estimated by a continuous function, $R(t)$; (2) disinvestment can occur at any time, at which time the investor receives the amount $R(t)$; (3) $R(t)$ is a *monotonically* increasing function, that is, $R'(t) \geq 0$; and (4) the rate of increase of $R(t)$ is decreasing, that is, $R''(t) < 0$, which identifies the function as *concave downward.*

The investor wishes to determine the optimal length of time, t^*, to hold the asset such that present net worth is maximized.

The **present value**[7] of the project, when disinvestment occurs at time t and the return $R(t)$ is discounted continuously at rate r, is given by

$$P(t) = R(t) \cdot e^{-rt}. \tag{2.18}$$

Since this project requires an investment of C, a more meaningful criterion is given by the **net present value:**

$$\begin{aligned} N(t) &= P(t) - C \\ &= R(t) \cdot e^{-rt} - C\,. \end{aligned}$$

Note that C need not be discounted because it represents an outlay in the present ($t = 0$). Given the objective of determining the value for t which maximizes $N(t)$, we derive the necessary condition that

$$\begin{aligned} N'(t^*) &= R'(t^*) \cdot e^{-rt^*} + R(t^*) \cdot e^{-rt^*} \cdot (-r) \\ &= 0\,. \end{aligned}$$

Simplifying gives

$$R'(t^*) - rR(t^*) = 0$$

or

$$R'(t^*) = rR(t^*) \tag{2.19}$$

as the necessary condition for an extreme point.

The second derivative is

$$N''(t) = [R'(t) - rR(t)] \cdot e^{-rt} \cdot (-r) + [R''(t) - rR'(t)] \cdot e^{-rt}.$$

Substituting Equation 2.19 for $R'(t)$ in the first bracket simplifies the expression to

$$N''(t) = [R''(t) - rR'(t)] \cdot e^{-rt}.$$

---

[7]Present value is a concept widely applied to financial criteria over time. The present value of receiving some amount $R(t)$ in t periods is that *present* amount which, when compounded at the investor's opportunity rate of interest, exactly yields $R(t)$ in t periods. For example, if you had \$100 to invest at 9 percent per year, in one year your investment would total \$109. Thus the present value to you of receiving \$109 one year from now is \$100. The act of converting future values to present values is called **discounting.**

Since $R''(t) < 0$, $r > 0$, $R'(t) \geq 0$, and $e^{-rt} > 0$, it follows that $N''(t^*) < 0$, which establishes the sufficient condition that t^* represents an absolute maximum. Note that if $N(t^*) < 0$, then the investment should not be undertaken.

Problems involving the sale of an appreciating asset with the above characteristics include investments in real estate, purchase of works of art, buying of wine from rare vintage years, and the aging of wines or distilled liquors.

To illustrate, suppose an oenologist has the opportunity to purchase a bottle of Chateau Lafite-Rothchild '59 for \$700. Historical analysis based on the sales of similar vintages coupled with an expert judgment of wine market trends results in the following estimate for the return function:

$$R(t) = 500(1 + t^{0.6}).$$

If the investor's opportunity cost (that is, minimum required rate of return including risk) is 15 percent per year based on continuous compounding, then the optimal time to sell can be estimated from Equation 2.19:

$$300t^{-0.4} = 0.15[500(1 + t^{0.6})]$$

$$300t^{-0.4} = 75 + 75t^{0.6}$$

$$300 = 75t^{0.4} + 75t$$

$$4 = t^{0.4} + t$$

or,

$$t + t^{0.4} - 4 = 0.$$

Using Newton's method, we get $t = 2.55$ years.[8] Thus approximately two and a half years from now the wine can be sold for $R(2.55) \doteq \$1{,}377$ giving a net present value of

$$N(2.55) = (1{,}377) \cdot e^{-0.15(2.55)} - 700$$

$$\doteq 939 - 700$$

$$\doteq \$239$$

In other words, the future sale price of \$1,377 has a present value of \$939 to the investor. The net worth of this investment is determined by subtracting the required outlay of \$700; hence, the investor would be \$239 richer based on today's dollar. We might note that \$1,377 for a bottle of wine is not unrealistic—a wine auction in New York City fetched more than \$18,000 for a single bottle!

FOLLOW-UP EXERCISES

17. Does the revenue function for the wine example satisfy the sufficient condition for maximization?
18. Solve the wine problem if $C = \$500$, $r = 0.15$, and $R(t) = 2{,}000(1.25 - 0.5^t)$. Determine the optimum period, sale price, and net present value.

**19. An alternative criterion, also theoretically pleasing, is the maximization of the *internal rate of return*. The internal rate of return is the value of r that satisfies

$$N(r, t) = R(t)e^{-rt} - C = 0.$$

[8]Newton's method of approximation is an iterative technique for finding the root(s) of an equation of the form $g(x) = 0$. If you need reminding, the root of an equation given by $g(x)$ is the value of x which satisfies $g(x) = 0$. The determination of roots is important primarily for sketching functions and identifying stationary points. The library of programs at your computer center should include various procedures for finding roots. Alternatively, a short program can be written to find roots by enumeration.

The following short program written using 1-2-3® from Lotus® was used to solve for t using Newton's method.

```
A1:  ^f(x1)          }
B1:  ^f'(x1)         } labels
C1:  ^x1             }
D1:  ^x2             }
A2:  +C2+C2^0.4-4        }
B2:  1+0.4*C2^(-0.6)     } formulae
C2:  0.5                 }
D2:  +C2-A2/B2           }
A3:  +C3+C3^0.4-4        }
B3:  1+0.4*C3^(-0.6)     } formulae repeated
C3:  +D2                 }
D3:  +C3-A3/B3           }
A4:  +C4+C4^0.4-4
B4:  1+0.4*C4^(-0.6)
C4:  +D3
D4:  +C4-A4/B4
A5:  +C5+C5^0.4-4
B5:  1+0.4*C5^(-0.6)
C5:  +D4
D5:  C5-A5/B5
```

Results:

f(x1)	f'(x1)	x1	x2
-2.74214	1.606286	0.5	2.207131
-0.42030	1.248750	2.207131	2.543715
-0.00354	1.228443	2.543715	2.546602
-0.00000	1.228288	2.546602	2.546602

Solving this equation for r gives

$$r = \frac{1}{t} \cdot \ln\left[\frac{R(t)}{C}\right].$$

Prove that the necessary condition for maximum r is

$$\frac{R'(t^*)}{R(t^*)} = \frac{1}{t^*} \cdot \ln\left[\frac{R(t^*)}{C}\right]. \tag{2.20}$$

**20. Solve the wine problem in Example 2.9 using the internal rate of return as the criterion in Equation 2.20. What is the optimal period? Optimal rate of return? Does it surprise you that the optimal period using internal rate of return is different from the optimal period using net present value?

2.4 TWO-VARIABLE APPLICATIONS[9]

Thus far we have treated models where a criterion variable is expressed as a function of one independent variable. It would be nice if objective function relationships were

[9]This section assumes knowledge of Section B.3 in Appendix B.

always that simple and uninvolved. In most situations, however, such an abstraction oversimplifies the problem. For example, if we were to determine the types of variables that influence the demand for products of a ski equipment manufacturer, a list of variables might include weather conditions, the quality of the equipment, the price and availability of gasoline, the price charged for equipment, and advertising expenditures of competing firms. In addition, realistic problems often include constraints on one or more variables. Thus advertising expenditures might be limited by a budget. This is not to imply that single-variable and unconstrained techniques are useless. Rather, the implication is that these techniques may not be adequate for certain situations. Accordingly, during the rest of this chapter we present methods of optimization for functions of more than one independent variable. This section presents examples of classical optimization where criterion variables are expressed as functions of two independent variables. Calculus-based methods of optimization with constraints are discussed in Section 2.6.

Because we are dealing with models consisting of one equation (the objective function), we will sometimes use the terms *model* and *objective function* interchangeably. Keep in mind, however, that more realistic and more complicated models will have several equations—whatever number needed to capture the essence of the problem.

Now we turn to a two-variable product-pricing problem.

Example 2.10 Two-Product Pricing Problem

A firm sells two products for which it has determined the demand functions $q_1 = 110 - 4p_1 - p_2$ and $q_2 = 90 - 2p_1 - 3p_2$, where q_i = demand (in units per day) for the *i*th product and p_i = price (dollars per unit) of the *i*th product. Note that the quantity demanded of one product depends on the price of that product as well as the price of the other product.

1. **Verbal Statement of Problem**
   Determine the prices that should be charged for each product in order to maximize total revenue per day from the two products.
2. **Decisions**
   a. **Verbal Statement**
      Price to charge for the two products.
   b. **Mathematical Definition**
      p_1 = Price (dollars/unit) for product 1.
      p_2 = Price (dollars/unit) for product 2.
3. **Criteria**
   a. **Verbal Statement**
      Total daily revenue from the sale of the two products.
   b. **Mathematical Statement**
      Total revenue for the two products is determined by

$$\begin{aligned} TR &= p_1q_1 + p_2q_2 \\ &= p_1(110 - 4p_1 - p_2) + p_2(90 - 2p_1 - 3p_2) \\ &= 110p_1 - 4p_1^2 - 3p_1p_2 + 90p_2 - 3p_2^2. \end{aligned}$$

4. **Constraints**
None.

5. **Mathematical Model**
The model for this problem consists of the total revenue function

$$TR = f(p_1, p_2) = 110p_1 - 4p_1^2 - 3p_1p_2 + 90p_2 - 3p_2^2. \quad (2.21)$$

6. **Model Outcomes**
To identify any stationary points on the revenue "surface," partial derivatives must be found with respect to p_1 and p_2 and set equal to zero (as described in Section B.3 of Appendix B):

$$f_{p_1} = 110 - 8p_1 - 3p_2 = 0$$

$$f_{p_2} = -3p_1 + 90 - 6p_2 = 0.$$

Solving the two equations simultaneously for p_1^* and p_2^*, we find that the only stationary point occurs when $p_1^* = p_2^* = 10$. In order to determine the nature of the stationary point, we find the second derivatives are found and $D(p_1^*, p_2^*)$ is evaluated:

$$f_{p_1p_1} = -8$$

$$f_{p_2p_2} = -6$$

$$f_{p_1p_2} = -3$$

$$D(10, 10) = (-8)(-6) - (-3)^2$$

$$= 39 > 0.$$

Since both pure partials are less than zero at $p_1^* = 10$ and $p_2^* = 10$, it is concluded that the stationary point is a relative maximum. In fact, the stationary point is an absolute maximum because D is greater than zero regardless of the values for p_1 and p_2.

7. **Interpretation of Results**
Our conclusion is that daily revenue will be maximized if the price of each product is set at \$10. The quantities demanded of each product—60 and 40 units per day, respectively—are found by substituting $p_1 = p_2 = 10$ into each of the original demand equations. Maximum revenue, as determined by substituting back into Equation 2.21 is \$1,000 per day.

FOLLOW-UP EXERCISES

21. Suppose total production cost (dollars per day) for two products is given by the function

$$c = 2q_1^2 + q_2^2 - 60q_1 - 100q_2 + 10{,}000. \quad (2.22)$$

Determine the quantities q_1 and q_2 that result in the minimization of total cost per day. Test the sufficiency condition for minimization. What is the minimum cost?

22. A firm sells two products. The demand functions for the two products are respectively $q_1 = 150 - 2p_1 - p_2$ and $q_2 = 200 - p_1 - 3p_2$, where q_i equals the annual demand (in hundreds of units) for product i and p_i equals the price (in dollars) per unit of product i. What price should be charged for each product if the objective is to maximize total revenue per year from the two products? How many units would be demanded of each product? What is the maximum total revenue?

▶ Example 2.11 Incinerator Location Model

A refuse incinerator is being planned to service four metropolitan areas. The relative locations of the metropolitan areas are shown in Figure 2–12, where coordinates are expressed in kilometers.

1. **Verbal Statement of Problem**
   Environmental management officials wish to determine the incinerator location that minimizes the sum of the squares of the distances from the incinerator to each metropolitan area.

FIGURE 2–12 Locations of Metropolitan Areas

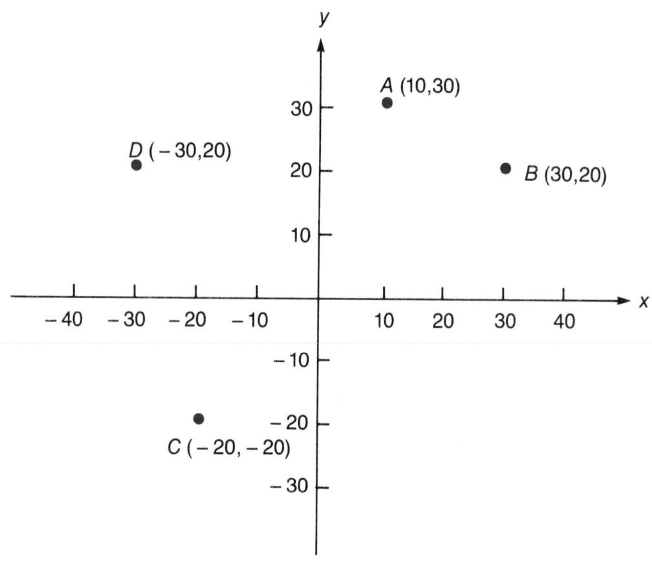

2. **Decisions**
   a. **Verbal Statement**
   Location of proposed incinerator.
   b. **Mathematical Definition**
   Referring to Figure 2–12, the unknowns are coordinates (x, y).
3. **Criteria**
   a. **Verbal Statement**
   Sum of squares of distances from the incinerator to each metropolitan area.
   b. **Mathematical Statement**
   First we need to determine an expression that represents the square of the distance separating the incinerator from each metropolitan area. Using the *Pythagorean Theorem,* we know that the distance d separating points (x_1, y_1) and (x_2, y_2) is represented by the equation

$$d = \sqrt{(x_2 - x_1)^2 + (y_2 - y_1)^2}.$$

To illustrate, the distance separating point *A* in Figure 2–12 and the incinerator (x, y) is

$$d_A = \sqrt{(x - 10)^2 + (y - 30)^2}.$$

As management scientists, we now return to the environmental officials with the following question: Would you accept a location close to three metropolitan areas but very far from the fourth? Or is it important to be close to all four metropolitan areas? With an answer that the officials do not want to be far from any one area, we jointly agree to revise the criterion to *squared distances* rather than simply distances.

To see the importance of this revision, consider only two metropolitan locations, *E* (10,0) and *F* (30,0). Locating the incinerator at L (20,0) would give a distance of 10 to *E* and *F* each for a total distance of 20. Locating the incinerator at *E* would give a distance of 0 to *E* and 20 to *F*, again for a total distance of 20. Squared distances, however, would give 200 in the first case and 400 in the second. Thus the squared distance criterion penalizes large distances more heavily.

Since we wish to minimize the sum of the squares of the distances separating the four areas and the incinerator, our criterion function is

$$S = d_A^2 + d_B^2 + d_C^2 + d_D^2$$

or

$$\begin{aligned} S &= f(x, y) \\ &= [(x - 10)^2 + (y - 30)^2] + [(x - 30)^2 + (y - 20)^2] \\ &\quad + \{[x - (-20)]^2 + [y - (-20)]^2\} + \{[x - (-30)]^2 + (y - 20)^2\}. \end{aligned}$$

4. **Constraints**
None.

5. **Mathematical Model**
The model for this problem consists of the criterion function

$$\begin{aligned} S = f(x, y) &= (x - 10)^2 + (y - 30)^2 + (x - 30)^2 + (y - 20)^2 \\ &\quad + [x - (-20)]^2 + [y - (-20)]^2 + [x - (-30)]^2 + (y - 20)^2. \end{aligned}$$

6. **Model Outcomes**
To determine the values of x and y that minimize S, we must first find the partial derivatives.

$$\begin{aligned} f_x &= 2(x - 10)(1) + 2(x - 30)(1) + 2(x + 20)(1) + 2(x + 30)(1) \\ &= 8x + 20 \\ f_y &= 2(y - 30)(1) + 2(y - 20)(1) + 2(y + 20)(1) + 2(y - 20)(1) \\ &= 8y - 100. \end{aligned}$$

If the two partial derivatives are set equal to zero, a stationary point occurs on the graph of $f(x, y)$ when $x^* = -2.5$ and $y^* = 12.5$.

The second partial derivatives are

$$\begin{aligned} f_{xx} &= 8 \qquad f_{xy} = 0 \\ f_{yy} &= 8 \qquad f_{yx} = 0. \end{aligned}$$

To test the nature of the stationary point we compute

$$D(-2.5, 12.5) = (8)(8) - (0)^2$$
$$= 64 > 0.$$

Since $D > 0$ and both f_{xx} and f_{yy} are positive, we can conclude that a relative minimum occurs on $f(x, y)$ when $x = -2.5$ and $y = 12.5$.

7. **Interpretation of Results**
The model outcome suggests that the sum of the squares of the distances from the incinerator to each metropolitan area will be minimized if the incinerator is located at coordinates $(-2.5, 12.5)$ in Figure 2–13.

FIGURE 2–13 Optimal Location of Incinerator

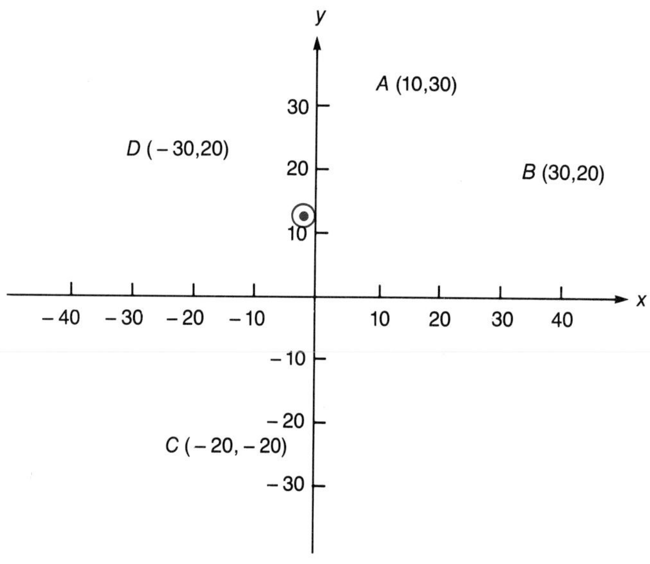

FOLLOW-UP EXERCISE

23. Suppose that in Example 2.11 the populations in areas *A* through *D* are 200,000, 500,000, 400,000, and 800,000, respectively. And assume that the size of an area's population is considered relevant in locating the incinerator. The criterion is to:

Minimize

$$S = \sum \text{population} \cdot (\text{distance})^2.$$

Determine the optimal location of the incinerator.

**2.5 UNCONSTRAINED *N*-VARIABLE OPTIMIZATION

The similarities between single and bivariate optimization also hold for **multivariate optimization,** or optimization with more than two independent variables. First it's necessary to identify all stationary points on the objective function. Such points are identified by setting all first partial derivatives equal to zero and solving the resulting system of simultaneous equations. Following the identification of all stationary points, a higher-ordered derivative test must be conducted to determine their nature. As the number of independent variables increases, the computational burden becomes greater and evaluation procedures may change slightly, but the conceptual basis for identifying extreme points is simply a logical extension of that used in the bivariate situation. This section generalizes the procedures of unconstrained classical optimization for the case of n independent variables.

Stationary Points

Given an objective function with n independent variables,

$$y = f(x_1, x_2, x_3, \ldots, x_n), \tag{2.23}$$

stationary points are identified by taking the first partial derivative of the function with respect to *each* independent variable. Each of these partial derivatives is set equal to zero and the group solved simultaneously to determine the coordinates of any stationary points. In other words, the following system of equations must be solved simultaneously:

$$\begin{aligned} \frac{\partial f}{\partial x_1} &= f_{x_1} = 0 \\ \frac{\partial f}{\partial x_2} &= f_{x_2} = 0 \\ &\vdots \\ \frac{\partial f}{\partial x_n} &= f_{x_n} = 0 \end{aligned} \tag{2.24}$$

We might note that the need to solve simultaneous equations can cause severe operational difficulties when the equations are nonlinear. In most instances, solutions by this method are not feasible.

Example 2.12

Given

$$\begin{aligned} y &= f(x_1, x_2, x_3) \\ &= x_1^2 - 2x_1x_2 + 2x_2^2 + 2x_1x_3 + 4x_3^2 - 2x_3, \end{aligned}$$

the conditions for the existence of any stationary points are that

$$\begin{aligned} f_{x_1} &= 2x_1 - 2x_2 + 2x_3 &&= 0 \\ f_{x_2} &= -2x_1 + 4x_2 &&= 0 \\ f_{x_3} &= 2x_1 \qquad\quad + 8x_3 - 2 &&= 0. \end{aligned}$$

Solving these three equations simultaneously, we see that the only stationary point has coordinates

$$x_1^* = -1, x_2^* = -1/2, x_3^* = 1/2.$$

FOLLOW-UP EXERCISES

24. Locate any stationary points for the function

$$y = x_1 - 4x_1x_2 - x_2^2 + 5x_3^2 - 2x_2x_3.$$

25. Determine the location of any stationary points on the function

$$y = 10x_1^2 + 15x_2^2 + 5x_3^2 - 60x_1 + 90x_2 - 40x_3 + 15{,}000.$$

26. Determine the location of any stationary points on the function

$$y = 8x_2^3 + 4x_1^2 + 12x_2^2 + 5x_3^2 + 3.5x_4^2 - 24x_1 + 20x_3 - 75{,}000.$$

Testing Stationary Points

As with single and bivariate optimization, we need to determine higher-ordered derivatives to examine the nature of a stationary point. In particular, one test requires the use of a matrix of second partial derivatives.[10] This matrix, called the **Hessian matrix**, has the form

$$\mathbf{H} = \begin{pmatrix} f_{x_1x_1} & f_{x_1x_2} & f_{x_1x_3} & \cdots & f_{x_1x_n} \\ f_{x_2x_1} & f_{x_2x_2} & f_{x_2x_3} & \cdots & f_{x_2x_n} \\ \vdots & \vdots & \vdots & \ddots & \vdots \\ f_{x_nx_1} & f_{x_nx_2} & f_{x_nx_3} & \cdots & f_{x_nx_n} \end{pmatrix}$$

The Hessian matrix is square, the principal diagonal contains the *pure* second partial derivatives, and the remaining elements are *cross* partial derivatives. The matrix is also symmetrical about the principal diagonal since the cross partial derivatives taken with respect to the same two variables are equal.

For an $(n \times n)$ Hessian matrix, a group of n submatrices can be identified. The first of these is the (1×1) matrix consisting of the element in position $(1, 1)$ of the Hessian. Denoting this matrix as $\mathbf{H}_1$, we see that

$$\mathbf{H}_1 = (f_{x_1x_1}).$$

The second submatrix is a (2×2) matrix consisting of the elements found in the upper left-hand corner of the Hessian, or

$$\mathbf{H}_2 = \begin{pmatrix} f_{x_1x_1} & f_{x_1x_2} \\ f_{x_2x_1} & f_{x_2x_2} \end{pmatrix}.$$

The third submatrix is a (3×3) matrix formed from the elements in the first three rows *and* first three columns of the Hessian, or

$$\mathbf{H}_3 = \begin{pmatrix} f_{x_1x_1} & f_{x_1x_2} & f_{x_1x_3} \\ f_{x_2x_1} & f_{x_2x_2} & f_{x_2x_3} \\ f_{x_3x_1} & f_{x_3x_2} & f_{x_3x_3} \end{pmatrix}.$$

[10] Appendix C presents a review of matrix notation.

Proceeding in the same manner, we see that the $(n \times n)$ submatrix is simply the Hessian itself.

The **principal minors** of the Hessian matrix are the **determinants** of the submatrices identified above.[11] These may be denoted by $|\mathbf{H}_i|$, where $\mathbf{H}_i$ represents the ith submatrix. If $(x_1^*, x_2^*, x_3^*, \ldots, x_n^*)$ represents the coordinates of a stationary point for a function involving n independent variables, then the test for extreme points is as follows:

1. Form the Hessian matrix with all partial derivatives evaluated at $(x_1^*, x_2^*, x_3^*, \ldots, x_n^*)$.
2. Evaluate each principal minor of the Hessian matrix.
3. a. If all principal minors are positive, then the Hessian matrix is termed **positive-definite** and the stationary point is a *relative minimum* on the original function.
   b. If the principal minors alternate in sign, with the odd-numbered minors negative and the even-numbered minors positive, then the Hessian is termed **negative-definite** and the stationary point is a *relative maximum* for the function.
   c. If neither of the above conditions exists, then the Hessian matrix is **semidefinite** and further analysis in the neighborhood of the stationary point is required to determine its nature.

Example 2.13

Continuing Example 2.12, the Hessian matrix of second partial derivatives is

$$\mathbf{H} = \begin{pmatrix} 2 & -2 & 2 \\ -2 & 4 & 0 \\ 2 & 0 & 8 \end{pmatrix}.$$

The submatrices and corresponding values of the principal minors are:

$$\mathbf{H}_1 = (2) \quad \text{and} \quad |\mathbf{H}_1| = 2;$$

$$\mathbf{H}_2 = \begin{pmatrix} 2 & -2 \\ -2 & 4 \end{pmatrix} \quad \text{and} \quad |\mathbf{H}_2| = 4;$$

$$\mathbf{H}_3 = \begin{pmatrix} 2 & -2 & 2 \\ -2 & 4 & 0 \\ 2 & 0 & 8 \end{pmatrix} \quad \text{and} \quad |\mathbf{H}_3| = 16.$$

Since $|\mathbf{H}_1|$, $|\mathbf{H}_2|$, and $|\mathbf{H}_3|$ are all > 0, we conclude that the stationary point is a relative minimum.

FOLLOW-UP EXERCISES

27. Verify that this procedure generalizes to include the single and bivariate optimization situations.
28. Determine the nature of all stationary points in Exercise 24.
29. Determine the nature of all stationary points in Exercise 25.

[11] Appendix C also presents a review of minors, cofactors, and determinants.

29. Determine the nature of all stationary points in Exercise 25.
30. Determine the nature of all stationary points in Exercise 26.

**2.6 OPTIMIZATION WITH CONSTRAINTS

Thus far discussion has focused on *unconstrained* optimization. This section introduces the subject of **constrained optimization** where an objective function is to be optimized subject to certain constraining or restricting conditions. This situation is the most typical in decision-making settings. Its use has become so widespread that an entire field called **mathematical programming** has evolved. To conceptually illustrate the nature of constrained optimization, we will present an example.

▶ Example 2.14 Product Line Model

A manufacturer of antipollution devices for smokestacks wishes to maximize the firm's profit. The objective function might take the form below, with a product line of n devices.

$$\text{Profit} = f(x_i)$$
$$= \sum_{i=1}^{n} (p_i - c_i)x_i - F$$

where p_i = selling price for ith item; c_i = Variable costs per unit for ith item; x_i = Number of units produced and sold of ith item; and F = Fixed expenses. Assuming an operational objective of determining the number of units of each item to produce in order to maximize profits, we see that the decision is fairly obvious. Produce an infinite number of each device so as to become infinitely wealthy. Fortunately, or unfortunately (depending on your point of view), the world of economics is not structured so ideally. Typically, the objective function is not so easy to formulate: Prices and quantities demanded can be related through demand functions, and costs of production and quantities produced can be related through production functions. Even if we assume that the objective function is an accurate representation of the profit relationship, there are usually restrictive conditions that have been neglected in this formulation: There will be limitations on the amounts of material, labor, and capital resources available for production; demand for the products of the firm will be limited; and items within the product line will compete with one another for input factors, restricting the way in which such resources can be allocated.

Solution by Substitution (Equality Constraints)

If an n-variable objective function is to be optimized subject to $n - 1$ equality constraints, it might be possible to solve for $n - 1$ of the variables in terms of the remaining variable. By a series of substitutions in this case, the objective function can be reduced to an unconstrained expression in one independent variable. Indeed, this is the exact procedure that was followed in solving the design for a police patrol sector (Example 2.7).

▶ Example 2.15 Pollution Control Model

An automobile manufacturer is considering the installation of two complementary antipollution devices (catalytic converters) in a new model automobile. Configurations of the two devices have been tested, in terms of installation cost. Exhaust quality tests and cost analyses uncovered a very strong relationship between each device. A least-squares fit to the data resulted in the criterion function

$$R(x_1, x_2) = -3x_1^2 - 2x_2^2 + 20x_1x_2$$

where $R(x_1, x_2)$ = Reduction in pollution particulates per cubic foot of exhaust; x_1 = Installation expenditure for the first converter (dollars); and x_2 = Installation expenditure for the second converter (dollars).

Prior analysis has established that any installation configuration will satisfy federal and state antipollution guidelines. An edict from "above," however, has established that exactly $100 is to be spent on the installation of either or both converters. At first, management was inclined to minimize installation expenditures subject to the satisfaction of pollution levels. Consumer pressures (and perhaps a social conscience), however, finalized the objective of maximizing

$$R(x_1, x_2) = -3x_1^2 - 2x_2^2 + 20x_1x_2$$

subject to

$$x_1 + x_2 = 100 .$$

Solving the constraint for x_1 and substituting this result in the objective function, we reduce the problem to maximizing

$$R(x_2) = -25x_2^2 + 2{,}600x_2 - 30{,}000 .$$

The original two-variable and one-constraint problem has been transformed to a problem stated in terms of one independent variable. Examining this function for stationary points, we see

$$R'(x_2) = -50x_2 + 2{,}600 = 0$$

or

$$x_2^* = 52 .$$

Testing the stationary point, we get

$$R''(x_2) = -50$$

which confirms that R is maximized when $x_2 = 52$. Thus, $48 and $52, respectively, should be expended for the installation of the two catalytic converters. This results in a reduction of 37,600 pollution particulates per cubic foot of exhaust.

**Lagrange Multiplier Method (Equality Constraints)

In many situations, it is either difficult or impossible to solve for one variable in terms of the others in an equality constraint as, for example, when there are three or more variables in the objective function. An alternative and powerful procedure widely used for solving constrained optimization problems is the **Lagrange multiplier technique.**

Assume a problem having the form:
Maximize (or minimize)

$$z = f(x, y)$$

subject to

$$g(x, y) = k \tag{2.25}$$

where k is a constant. The Lagrange multiplier method forms a new function composed of the objective function and a linear multiple of the constraint equation. This composite **Lagrangian function** has the form

$$L(x, y, \lambda) = f(x, y) - \lambda[g(x, y) - k]. \tag{2.26}$$

The variable λ (lambda) is called the **Lagrange multiplier.** Since the constraint function, $[g(x, y) - k]$, is required to equal zero, λ can equal any value, and the term $\lambda[g(x, y) - k]$ still equals zero. Consequently the value of the new Lagrangian function is the same as the value of the objective function, provided we assure that $g(x, y) - k = 0$ holds.

The creation of the Lagrangian function ingeniously transforms the original constrained problem into an unconstrained problem which can be solved by the procedures of n-variable optimization. That is, the determination of stationary points has been translated into the solution of the simultaneous equations

$$\frac{\partial L(x, y, \lambda)}{\partial x} = \frac{\partial f(x, y)}{\partial x} - \frac{\lambda \partial g(x, y)}{\partial x} = 0$$

$$\frac{\partial L(x, y, \lambda)}{\partial y} = \frac{\partial f(x, y)}{\partial y} - \frac{\lambda \partial g(x, y)}{\partial y} = 0$$

$$\frac{\partial L(x, y, \lambda)}{\partial \lambda} = g(x, y) - k = 0 \qquad \text{(but, voilà!)}.$$

(Note that the last equation represents the original constraint.)

Due to the dependence between x and y in the constraint, the test for determining the nature of the stationary point is somewhat more involved for the Lagrange multiplier method. The determinant of the following **bordered Hessian matrix** must be determined:

$$\mathbf{H}^B = \begin{pmatrix} 0 & g_x & g_y \\ g_x & L_{xx} & L_{xy} \\ g_y & L_{yx} & L_{yy} \end{pmatrix}$$

where g_x and g_y represent, respectively, the partial derivatives of the left-hand side of the constraint with respect to x and y; L_{xx} and L_{yy} represent the two pure partials of the Lagrangian function; and L_{xy} and L_{yx} represent the cross partials of the Lagrangian function.

By proof, it can be shown that: for $|\mathbf{H}^B| > 0$ the stationary point is a relative *maximum; for* $|\mathbf{H}^B| < 0$ the stationary point is a relative *minimum*.

▶ Example 2.16

Solve the previous problem by the Lagrange multiplier method. Rewriting the problem in the standard form of Equation 2.25, we get:

Maximize

$$R(x_1, x_2) = -3x_1^2 - 2x_2^2 + 20x_1x_2$$

subject to

$$x_1 + x_2 = 100\,.$$

The Lagrangian function is

$$L(x_1, x_2, \lambda) = -3x_1^2 - 2x_2^2 + 20x_1x_2 - \lambda[x_1 + x_2 - 100]$$

and the first partial derivatives are

$$\frac{\partial L}{\partial x_1} = -6x_1 + 20x_2 - \lambda = 0$$

$$\frac{\partial L}{\partial x_2} = -4x_2 + 20x_1 - \lambda = 0$$

$$\frac{\partial L}{\partial \lambda} = -x_1 - x_2 + 100 \quad = 0\,.$$

Solving these three equations simultaneously, we find a stationary point having coordinates $x_1^* = 48$, $x_2^* = 52$, and $\lambda^* = +752$. Testing the stationary point by forming the bordered Hessian matrix, we get

$$\mathbf{H}^B = \begin{pmatrix} 0 & 1 & 1 \\ 1 & -6 & 20 \\ 1 & 20 & -4 \end{pmatrix},$$

and $|\mathbf{H}^B| = 50 > 0$ which, as before, identifies the stationary point as a global maximum.

**Interpreting λ*

Lambda is much more than an artificial creation allowing for the solution of constrained optimization problems. It has an interpretation that can be very useful in applications. It can be shown for certain conditions that[12]

$$\frac{\partial L(x^*, y^*, \lambda^*)}{\partial k} = \lambda^*; \tag{2.27}$$

hence, λ^* represents the instantaneous rate of change in the optimal value of the objective function with respect to the constant while all other variables remain fixed. It follows that if λ^* is positive, an increase (decrease) in k results in an increase (decrease) in the optimal value of L according to Equation 2.27. Conversely, for negative λ^*, changes in optimal L move in the opposite direction from changes in k.

---

[12]Willard I. Zangwill, *Nonlinear Programming: A Unified Approach* (Englewood Cliffs, N.J.: Prentice-Hall, 1969), pp. 66–68.

In most managerial applications the right-hand–side constant, for practical reasons, is restricted to discrete changes. Therefore, lambda is often interpreted as the *approximate* change in the objective function when the constant in the constraint changes by *one* unit.

To illustrate, we substitute the appropriate values in the Lagrangian function in Example 2.15:

$$\begin{aligned} L(48, 52, +752) &= -3(48)^2 - 2(52)^2 + 20(48)(52) - (+752)(48 + 52 - 100) \\ &= 37{,}600 - 752(0)\,. \\ &= 37{,}600\,. \end{aligned}$$

If the 100 increases to 101 in the constraint, then the optimal value of L can be approximated by

$$\begin{aligned} L &= L(48, 52, +752) + \lambda^* \\ &= 37{,}600 + 752 \\ &= 38{,}352\,. \end{aligned}$$

Similarly, if the 100 in the constraint decreases to 99, then the optimal value of L can be approximated by

$$\begin{aligned} L &= L(48, 52, +752) - \lambda^* \\ &= 37{,}600 - 752 \\ &= 36{,}848\,. \end{aligned}$$

FOLLOW-UP EXERCISES

31. You should verify, by reworking the entire problem, that the optimal value of the objective function in Example 2.15 increases by 755.77 if the constraint becomes $x_1 + x_2 = 101$. (Note that this is close to the value of λ^*.)
32. Solve the police sector problem of Example 2.7 using the Lagrange multiplier method. Construct the bordered Hessian matrix and test the stationary point. Verbalize the meaning of λ^* in the context of this problem.

To reiterate a previous point, interpretation of the impact on the objective function depends on *both* the sign and the magnitude of λ^* *and* the direction of change of the constant in the constraint. Can you verify the characteristics of interpreting λ^* in Table 2–1?

TABLE 2–1 Interpreting λ^* for Equality Constraints Where $L(x, y, \lambda) = f(x, y) - \lambda[g(x, y) - k]$

Sign of λ^*	**Increase in Constant (k)**	**Decrease in Constant (k)**
Positive	Increase in optimal $f(x, y)$	Decrease in optimal $f(x, y)$
Negative	Decrease in optimal $f(x, y)$	Increase in optimal $f(x, y)$

**Generalization of the Lagrange Multiplier Method

The generalization of the technique to n variables and m equality constraints is a simple extension of the two-variable case.

Optimize

$$z = f(x_1, x_2, \ldots, x_n)$$

subject to

$$\begin{aligned} g_1(x_1, x_2, \ldots, x_n) &= k_1 \\ g_2(x_1, x_2, \ldots, x_n) &= k_2 \\ &\vdots \\ g_m(x_1, x_2, \ldots, x_n) &= k_m \end{aligned} \tag{2.28}$$

In this case, $(n + m)$ simultaneous equations are established from the first partial derivatives of the Lagrangian function

$$L(x_1, x_2, \ldots, x_n, \lambda_1, \lambda_2, \ldots, \lambda_m) = f(x_1, x_2, \ldots, x_n) - \sum_{i=1}^{m} \lambda_i[g_i(x_1, x_2, \ldots, x_n) - k_i] \tag{2.29}$$

The bordered Hessian is also a straightforward extension of the two-variable case, although the same cannot be said for the set of rules that determines the nature of the stationary point. For the case of three or more variables with only one constraint, the method involves only one lambda and is exactly the same as the two variable case.

**Inequality Constraints

The Lagrange multiplier method, although specifically designed for equality constraints, can be applied to the solution of problems characterized by inequality constraints (assuming global optima can be determined).

Consider this problem:

Maximize

$$z = f(\mathbf{X})$$

subject to

$$g(\mathbf{X}) \leq k \tag{2.30}$$

where **X** represents the set of independent variables $(x_1, x_2, \ldots, x_n)$. Treating Equation 2.30 as an equality, we form the Lagrangian function in the usual manner; that is:

Maximize

$$L(\mathbf{X}, \lambda) = f(\mathbf{X}) - \lambda[g(\mathbf{X}) - k].$$

From a previous section, we know that a *positive* λ^* implies that a *decrease* in k will *decrease* optimal L. Since the left-hand expression in Equation 2.30 *must be less than or equal to* k and the Lagrangian considers $g(\mathbf{X}) = k$, it follows that the *original* problem given by Equation 2.30 implies a *decrease* in k. A decrease in k, however, is undesirable because optimal L will decrease, which is contrary to our desire to *maximize*. Hence the constraint *binds* our solution; that is, maximum L will be achieved at $g(\mathbf{X}) = k$. The unconstrained stationary point would have $g(\mathbf{X}) > k$.

All of this leads us to conclude that, for a *maximization* problem characterized by a $\leq$ constraint, a *positive* λ^* implies that an increase in k (relaxation of the constraint) is *desirable*.

If λ^* were *negative*, then the decrease in k implied by Equation 2.30 would increase optimal L. This in turn implies that the constraint would *not be binding*. In other words, the problem should be solved by ignoring the constraint. In this case, the Lagrangian solution is termed **pseudo-optimal.**

Reasoning in a similar manner, we see that exactly opposite conclusions are reached for either minimization problems or $\geq$ constraints. Table 2–2 summarizes these conclusions. (To gain intuition, carefully study Example 2.17 and Figure 2–14 and solve Exercises 34 and 35. Then study the above logic once more.)

TABLE 2–2 Interpreting λ^* for Inequality Constraints Where $L(\mathbf{X}, \lambda) = f(\mathbf{X}) - \lambda[g(\mathbf{X}) - k]$

	Type of Constraint			
	($\leq$)		($\geq$)	
Optimization Objective	$\lambda^* < 0$	$\lambda^* > 0$	$\lambda^* < 0$	$\lambda^* > 0$
Maximize $f(\mathbf{X})$	(*a*) Ignore constraint (pseudo-optimal solution)	(*b*) Constraint binding; *increase k* if possible	(*c*) Constraint binding; *decrease k* if possible	(*d*) Ignore constraint (pseudo-optimal solution)
Minimize $f(\mathbf{X})$	(*e*) Constraint binding; *increase k* if possible	(*f*) Ignore constraint (pseudo-optimal solution)	(*g*) Ignore constraint (pseudo-optimal solution)	(*h*) Constraint binding: *decrease k* if possible

It is worth reiterating that the preceding discussion relates to optimization problems characterized by a single constraint. The conditions for testing the stationary points of problems having multiple inequality constraints are known as **Kuhn-Tucker conditions,** an advanced subject which will not be treated in this textbook, except for a brief application to linear programming in Chapter 5.[13]

▶ Example 2.17 Optimal Advertising Period

In the Mow-Down Records, Inc. problem of Example 2.6 the unconstrained objective function was derived as

$$P(t) = 197{,}500 - 200{,}000e^{-0.02t} - 2{,}000t$$

where $P(t)$ represented profits ($) and t was defined as the number of days in the advertising period. The optimal advertising period (t^*) was calculated as 34.66 days, yielding an expected profit of $28,180.

Now suppose that the original problem included the condition that no more than 30 days of advertising are to be considered. The problem now reads:

[13] Ibid.; Teichroew, *An Introduction to Management Science;* and Willard I. Zangwill, *Nonlinear Programming: A Unified Approach* (Englewood Cliffs, N.J.: Prentice-Hall, 1969).

Maximize

$$P(t) = 197{,}500 - 200{,}000e^{-0.02t} - 2{,}000t$$

subject to

$$t \leq 30 .$$

Optimizing by the Lagrange multiplier method, we have

$$L(t, \lambda) = 197{,}500 - 200{,}000e^{-0.02t} - 2{,}000t - \lambda(t - 30);$$

$$\frac{\partial L}{\partial t} = 4{,}000e^{-0.02t} - 2{,}000 - \lambda = 0;$$

$$\frac{\partial L}{\partial \lambda} = -t + 30 = 0 .$$

This gives an optimal solution of $t^* = 30$, $\lambda^* = 196$, and $P^* = \$27{,}740$. Noting that the problem is of the maximization type, that the constraint is of the $\leq$ type, and that $\lambda^* > 0$, we see that according to result *b* in Table 2–2 the constraint is binding. Hence *k* should be allowed above 30 days (if possible) to improve profits. Note that $\lambda^* = 196$ indicates that the instantaneous rate of *increase* in profits is \$196 in the direction of *increasing* days. Figure 2–14 graphically portrays this result.

If the constraint were $t \leq 50$, the Lagrangian optimal solution would be $t^* = 50$, $\lambda^* = -528$, $P^* = \$23{,}900$. (Can you verify this?) A negative λ^* gives us result *a* in Table 2–2, an indication that the constraint is *not* binding. Given this result, the unconstrained problem should be solved (that is, the Lagrangian solution is pseudo-optimal), which brings us back to $t^* \doteq 35$ and $P^* = \$28{,}180$.

Finally, for the constraint $t \geq 30$, we would have result *d* in Table 2–2; for $t \geq 50$, result *c* would apply.

FOLLOW-UP EXERCISES

33. With respect to the advertising problem, confirm that:
    a. The Lagrangian solution when $t \geq 30$ is pseudo-optimal, since $t = 35$ yields a higher profit *and* satisfies the constraint (result *d* in Table 2–2).
    b. The Lagrangian solution when $t \geq 50$ is optimal at $t = 50$, but t should be allowed to decrease if possible (result *c* in Table 2–2).34.By both the Lagrange multiplier method and by graph, analyze the following problems for *each* of the constraints separately:

    Minimize

$$Y = x^4$$

    subject to

$$a.\ x \leq 2$$
$$b.\ x \geq 2 .$$

Computer-Based Solution Methods

Computer software is available for performing nonlinear optimization. One such package is GINO (General Interactive Optimizer), a nonlinear programming package marketed by The Scientific Press in Palo Alto, California. This package is easy to use for the nontechnical person, and it is capable of solving unconstrained as well as constrained optimization problems. Figure 2–15 illustrates the model and solution to the

FIGURE 2–14 Solutions to Mow-Down Records, Inc.

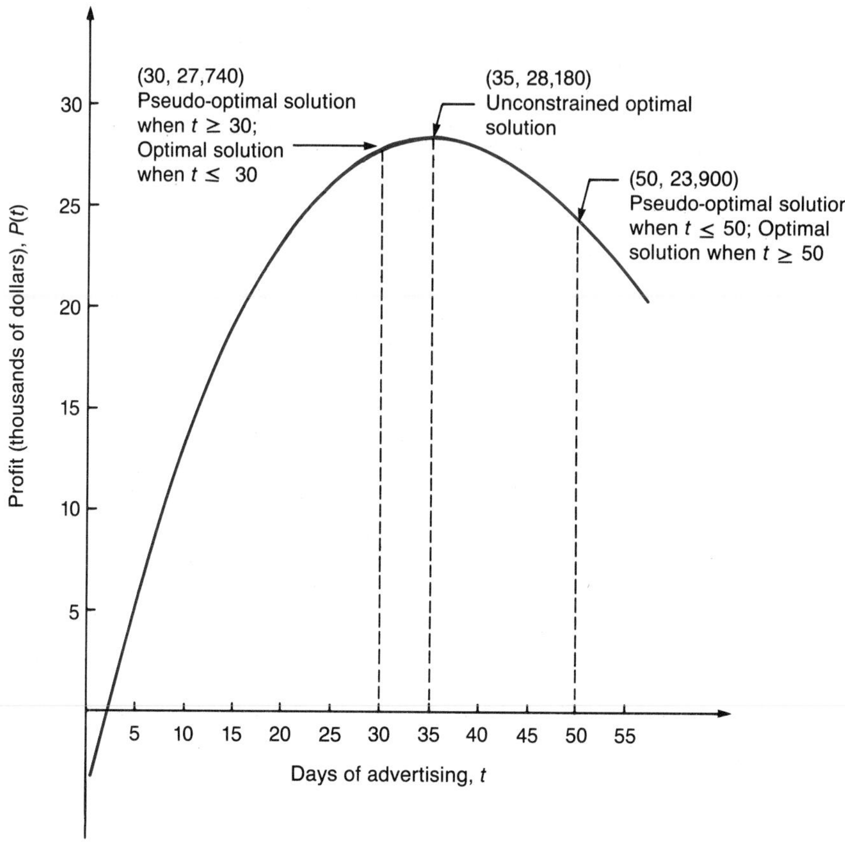

FIGURE 2–15 GINO Model and Results for Example 2.16

```
:  MODEL
?  MAX=-3*X1^2-2*X2^2+20*X1*X2;
?  X1+X2=100;
?  END
:  GO
SOLUTION STATUS: OPTIMAL TO TOLERANCES. DUAL CONDITIONS: SATISFIED.

                    OBJECTIVE FUNCTION VALUE
           (1)  37600.000000

       VARIABLE          VALUE              REDUCED COST
             X1          48.000000              .000000
             X2          52.000000              .000000

            ROW      SLACK OR SURPLUS              PRICE
            (2)           .000000             751.999878
```

problem solved in Example 2.16. The *model* part of Figure 2–15 is self-explanatory. Notice that the specification of the model is quite straightforward. The *go* command simply instructs the package to determine the solution. In the solution we see that the *objective function* is maximized at 37,600 when variable $X1 = 48$ and $X2 = 52$. The *reduced cost* section for this problem is not particularly meaningful for this problem; thus we will ignore it. The *row* section of the output provides an analysis of any constraints in the problem. The *slack or surplus* column indicates the extent to which a constraint is not satisfied as an equation.For a $\leq$ constraint, this measure is termed *slack;* for a $\geq$ constraint it is *surplus*. The constraint in this problem is an equation and it has been satisfied, yielding slack (surplus) of zero. The other part of the row analysis is the price column, which contains the value for lambda. Later in linear programming we will describe the information represented by lambda as a *shadow price*.

Figure 2–16 illustrates the model and solution for Example 2.17 (Optimal Advertising Period). Notice that the results are off slightly due to our rounding when solving the first derivative equations.

FIGURE 2–16 GINO Model and Results for Example 2.17

```
  MODEL:
     (1)  MAX=197500-200000 * EXP(-0.02 * T)-2000 * T;
     (2)  T < 30;
  END

: go
SOLUTION STATUS: OPTIMAL TO TOLERANCES. DUAL CONDITIONS: SATISFIED.

                    OBJECTIVE FUNCTION VALUE

              (1)  27737.671309

         VARIABLE          VALUE                REDUCED COST
                T          30.000000                 .000000

              ROW       SLACK OR SURPLUS               PRICE
              (2)              .000000            195.245865
```

2.7 CONCLUSION

This chapter has introduced the mathematical representation of functional relationships. Not only have we presented the notation of mathematical functions; we have also attempted to give you a sense of how analysts formulate these relationships. This chapter has also introduced the notion of optimality, a concept we will utilize throughout the book.

Calculus-based optimization methods have been a primary focus in the chapter. We have begun to illustrate the diversity of applications, first with unconstrained optimization models. The last section, discussing the Lagrange multiplier technique, provides a nice transition to constrained optimization models. These types of models are more realistic, and they will be the focus of much of the remainder of the book.

SELECTED APPLICATION REVIEW

In bond management, there is widespread use of measures of the sensitivity of bond prices to interest rate changes. An understanding of these measures requires knowledge of calculus, so we present bond price/interest sensitivity as a selected application.

Recall that a bond is an IOU whose face amount of $1,000 will be paid at maturity t, usually with biannual coupon payments. The *yield* or *return* will depend on the selling price of the bond. For example, a five-year $1,000 bond with no coupons might sell at $621. With a future value of $1,000, a five-year term, and a price of $621, such a bond yields 10 percent per year compounded (i.e., $621(1.10)^5 = 1{,}000$).

Letting P be the current price of the bond and r the *required* rate of return on the bond, we can determine the sensitivity of bond prices to changes in the required return. Changes in inflation expectations can lead to changes in required rates of return on bonds. These required rates of return can be thought of as interest rates.

Suppose we have

$$P = \frac{1{,}000}{(1 + r)^t} = 1{,}000(1 + r)^{-t}$$

then

$$\begin{aligned}\frac{dP}{dr} &= -t(1{,}000)\,(1 + r)^{-t-1} \\ &= \frac{-t}{(1 + r)}\,\frac{1{,}000}{(1 + r)^t} \\ &= \frac{-t}{(1 + r)}P\,.\end{aligned}$$

From this we see that bond prices decrease in response to interest rate increases with larger decreases for long maturities. To check this out, find two zero coupon bonds in *The Wall Street Journal* and follow them for the semester. Find New York Exchange bonds having the same starting price but different maturity. Try CATS (Certificates of Accrual on Treasury Certificates) if you can't find other bonds in the NYSE Bond Trading section of the newspaper. CATS zr 11-91 means the bond is a zero coupon (i.e., no intermediate coupons/payments) bond to pay $1,000 in the eleventh month of 1991, and you would pay ten times the quoted price stated as if it were a $100 bond (e.g., you might pay 10 × $66 = $660 for the $1,000 bond.)

In a recent *New York Times* article, Stephen J. Gould discusses the pandemic of AIDS and a simple growth model suggested by John Platt. Using limited data in 1984, John Platt suggested that AIDS was spreading in a simple exponential manner $(1, 2, 4, 8, 16, 32, \ldots)$.

Platt was criticized because exponential models are unrealistic and environmental factors should prevent simple exponential growth. That the bacterial cells will exhaust their supply of nutrients, that safe sexual practices can limit the spread of AIDS, and that an AIDS vaccine will be developed— these are the hopes in the race against this exponential enemy. Stephen J. Gould mentions that in 1987 the data still match Platt's extrapolated curve.

SOURCE: Adapted from the *New York Times* magazine, April 19, 1987.

SELECTED REFERENCES

Barnett, Raymond A. *College Mathematics for Management, Life, and Social Sciences*. 3rd ed. San Francisco: Dellen Publishing, 1981.

Budnick, Frank S. *Applied Mathematics for Business, Economics, and the Social Sciences*. 2nd ed. New York: McGraw-Hill, 1983.

Chiang, Alpha C. *Fundamental Methods of Mathematical Economics*. 3rd ed. New York: McGraw-Hill, 1985.

Childress, Robert L. *Mathematics for Managerial Decisions*. Englewood Cliffs, N.J.: Prentice-Hall, 1974.

Draper, Jean E. *Mathematical Analysis: Business and Economic Applications*. 4th ed. New York: Harper & Row, 1982.

Goldstein, Larry J.; David C. Lay; and David I. Schneider. *Mathematics for the Management, Life and Social Sciences*. 2nd ed. Englewood Cliffs, N.J.: Prentice-Hall, 1984.

Haeussler, Ernest F., Jr., and Richard S. Paul. *Introductory Mathematical Analysis*. 4th ed. Reston, Va.: Reston Publishing, 1983.

Richmond, S. B. *Operations Research for Management Decisions*. New York: The Ronald Press, 1968.

Riddle, Douglas F. *Calculus and Analytic Geometry*. 3rd ed. Belmont, Calif.: Wadsworth Publishing, 1979.

Schelin, Charles W., and David W. Bange. *Calculus for Business and Economics*. Boston: Prindle, Weber, and Schmidt, 1985.

Taylor, Claudia, and Lawrence Gilligan. *Applied Calculus*, Monterey, Calif.: Brooks/Cole Publishing, 1985.

Teichroew, D. *An Introduction to Management Science, Deterministic Models*. New York: John Wiley & Sons, 1964.

Theodore, Chris A. *Applied Mathematics: An Introduction*. 3rd ed. Homewood, Ill.: Richard D. Irwin, 1975.

ADDITIONAL EXERCISES

35. ***Breakeven on Options.*** A call option is the right to buy a given number of shares of stock at a given price on or before a specific date. The price at which the stock may be bought is called the *exercise* or *strike* price. The XYZ Company closed on Monday, June 18, at a price of $120\frac{1}{4}$ per share. At a strike price of 125, the option (to buy the one share) expiring in October closed at $\$3\frac{7}{8}$, almost \$4 for the right to speculate. Remembering that when one purchases a call option, one may or may not exercise that option, specify the function relating the option profit (loss) to prices of the XYZ stock just *before* the *expiration* or *maturity* date of the option. Clearly, at a stock price of \$125, there is a loss of \$3.875; and at a price of \$120, there is a loss of \$3.875. Do you see that one would not exercise the option at a price of \$120? At what price do we break even? What is the rate of change in profit relative to changes in the stock price above the break-even point (ignore commissions and taxes)? Sketch the graph of the function relating profit (loss) to prices of the stock. Hint: Profit will come only when the stock price exceeds the strike price and also covers the cost of purchasing the call option. You will want to specify the function when the stock price is below the strike price and when it is above. In this problem, the x-axis will have "stock price before October" and the y-axis will have "option profit." (Note that just before the expiration date, the option price will have virtually no speculative components.)

36. ***Sales Allocation Model.*** A book publisher estimates that its profits are directly related to the number of sales representatives ("reps") the company uses. Specifically, profit (p), in thousands of dollars, is related to number of reps (x) by the function

$$p = -20x^2 + 2{,}400x - 10{,}000 .$$

a. What number of reps will result in maximum profit?
b. What is the expected maximum profit?

37. ***Inventory Model.*** A pervasive problem among organizations is determining the appropriate quantities of inventory to keep on hand. A common decision relates to the quantities to order each time the firm replenishes its inventory (if the inventoried item is supplied by a vendor). These types of models are addressed specifically in Chapter 15. A firm has determined the following cost function, which expresses the annual cost of purchasing, owning, and maintaining its inventory as a function of the size of each order (q).

$$c = \frac{250{,}000}{q} + 400q + 50{,}000 .$$

a. Determine the order quantity, q^*, which results in minimum annual inventory cost.
b. What is the minimum cost?
c. Confirm the nature of the stationary point.

38. ***Import Tax Model.*** The government of a European country is trying to decide on the import tax it should charge on Japanese television sets. The government realizes that demand for these TVs will be affected by the tax. It has estimated demand (D) to be related to t, the import tax in dollars, according to the function

$$D(t) = 1{,}000{,}000 - 50{,}000t .$$

a. What tax will result in maximum tax revenues for the country? (Confirm the stationary point as a maximum.)
b. How many TVs will be expected to be sold at this tax rate?

c. What is the maximum revenue?

d. If the −50,000 in the demand equation could be in error by ±50 percent, what would be the effect on the optimal tax rate and maximum tax revenue?

39. ***Pricing Model.*** A company estimates the demand, q, for its product to be a function of the price, p, charged. Specifically, the demand function is

$$q = 10{,}000e^{-0.1p}.$$

Determine the price the firm should charge in order to maximize total revenue. What quantity will be demanded at this price? What is the maximum total revenue? Confirm the nature of the stationary point.

40. ***Sensitivity Analysis.*** In Exercise 39 perform a sensitivity analysis on the −0.1 coefficient. How sensitive are the optimal price, quantity demanded, and total revenue to changes in this coefficient if it can actually fluctuate between −0.05 and −0.5?

41. ***Charity Campaign Model.*** A well-known charity is interested in conducting a television campaign to solicit contributions. The campaign will be conducted in two metropolitan areas. Past experience indicates that the total contributions are a function of the amount of money expended for TV advertisements in each city. Specifically, the charity has determined approximate response functions that indicate the percentage of the population making a donation as a function of the dollars spent on TV advertising. The charity has $200,000 to allocate for advertising in the two cities. Letting x_1 and x_2 represent the number of dollars (in thousands) allocated, respectively, to cities 1 and 2, the charity wants to determine the values that maximize the total donations from the two cities.

	City 1	City 2
Response function	$(1 - e^{-0.06x_1})$	$(1 - e^{-0.04x_2})$
Population	750,000	600,000
Average donation per donor	$2.00	$1.50

(Hint: Take advantage of the fact that $x_1 + x_2 = 200$.) What are the maximum total donations? Confirm that the stationary point is a maximum.

42. ***Minimizing Average Cost Model.*** The total cost of producing q units of a certain product is described by the function

$$C = 200{,}000 + 2000q + 0.3q^2$$

where C is the total cost (in dollars). Determine the number of units q that should be produced in order to minimize the *average cost per unit*. What is the average cost per unit at this level of output? Total cost?

43. ***Public Utilities Model.*** A cable TV antenna company (CATV) is offering a special home entertainment package that provides extensive coverage of sports events and cultural events not normally seen on regular TV. In addition, subscribers can see new movies, available otherwise only in theaters. The company has determined that its profitability depends on the monthly fee it charges subscribers. Specifically, the relationship that describes annual profit P (in dollars) as a function of the monthly rental fee r (in dollars) is

$$P = -50{,}000r^2 + 2{,}250{,}000r - 5{,}000{,}000.$$

a. Determine the monthly rental fee r that should lead to maximum profit.

b. What is the expected maximum profit?

c. Assume that the local public utility commission has restricted the CATV company to a monthly fee not to exceed \$20. In light of this regulatory policy, what fee leads to a maximum profit?

d. What is the effect of the utility commission's ruling on the annual profitability of the firm?

44. ***Bill Collection Model.*** A financial institution offers a credit card that can be used in most countries. It has determined that the percentage P of accounts receivable (stated in dollars) collected t months after credit is issued is represented by the function

$$P = 0.8867(1 - e^{-0.6t}).$$

The average credit issued in any one month is \$125 million. The financial institution estimates that for *new credit* issued in any month, collection efforts cost \$1 million per month.

a. Determine the number of months t^* that collection efforts should be continued if the objective is to maximize the *net collections* N (dollars collected minus collection costs).

b. What is the maximum value for N?

c. What percentage of accounts receivable would not be collected?

45. ***Fire Equipment Replacement Model.*** A fire department wishes to determine an optimal policy for replacing its fire trucks. Each truck costs the department \$250,000. The department estimates average capital cost and average maintenance cost to be a function of x, the number of miles the vehicle is driven. The salvage value of the truck in dollars is expressed by the function

$$S(x) = 220{,}000 - 0.4x\,.$$

In other words, the value of the truck decreases by \$30,000 immediately and decreases additionally at a rate of \$0.40 per mile. The average maintenance cost (dollars per mile) is estimated by the function

$$0(x) = 0.0000025x + 0.30\,.$$

Determine the number of miles a truck should be driven prior to replacement if the objective is to minimize average cost per mile. Confirm that the stationary point is indeed a minimum.

46. For the replacement model described in the preceding exercise, derive an expression for x^* if $S(x) = s - rx$, $0(x) = mx + b$, and the purchase price is P. Compare this result to Equation 2.14. Comments?

47. ***Emergency Response Model.*** Three towns along a relatively straight coastline are located as indicated in Figure 2–17. The populations (in thousands) of towns A, B, and C are 8, 10, and 20, respectively. The three towns have agreed to support an emergency medical response facility (i.e., clinic with paramedics and one vehicle) that will service all three towns. Where should this facility be located if it is desired to minimize the sum of

$$(\text{Population}) \cdot (\text{Distance squared between town and facility})$$

for the three towns? (Hint: Let x = Location of facility according to above scale.) Confirm that your solution is an absolute minimum. Can you think of more desirable surrogate criteria for level of service?

48. ***Solid Waste Management Model.*** A community is planning to build a solid waste treatment facility. A major component of the facility is a solid waste agitation pool. The pool is to be circular in shape and is to have a volume capacity of 500,000 cubic feet.

FIGURE 2–17 Town Locations

Engineers estimate the construction costs as a function of the surface area of the base and wall of the pool. Costs are expected to be $20 per square foot for the base of the pool and $15 per square foot of wall surface. Figure 2–18 presents a sketch of the pool.

a. Determine the dimensions r and h (both in feet) that provide a capacity of 500,000 cubic feet at minimum cost. (Hint: volume of the pool is determined by $V = \pi r^2 h$ and circumference of a circle by $2\pi r$).

b. What are the minimum construction costs?

FIGURE 2–18 Agitation Pool

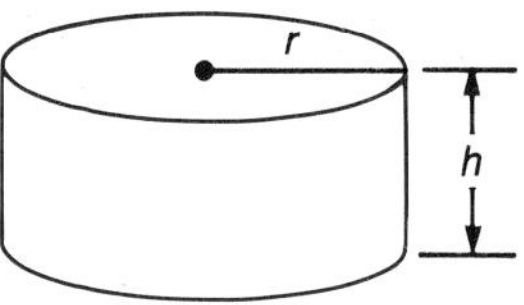

49. ***Pipeline Construction Model.* A natural gas company is planning to construct a pipeline that delivers natural gas between two cities. Figure 2–19 illustrates the relative locations of the originating city A and the destination city C. Points A and C are on opposite sides of a waterway, which is 15 kilometers wide. City C is 200 kilometers north of city A. The gas company is proposing a pipeline that will run north along the west side of the waterway, and at some point x will cross under the waterway to point C. Construction costs are $40,000 per kilometer along the bank of the waterway and $80,000 per kilometer for the section crossing the waterway.

a. Determine the crossing point that should result in the minimum cost of construction.

b. What is the minimum cost?

c. How long is the section of pipe crossing the waterway?

FIGURE 2–19 Pipeline Plan

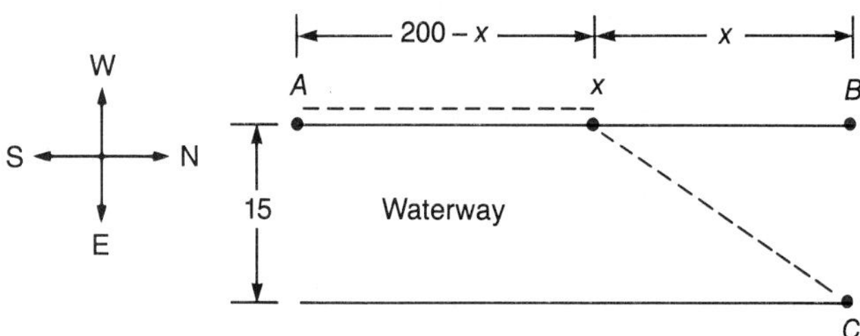

50. ***Media Mix Model.*** An advertising agency estimates that annual sales in units for one of its clients are a function of the expenditures made for TV and radio advertising. The estimating function is

$$z = 40{,}000x + 60{,}000y - 10x^2 - 20y^2 - 20xy$$

where z equals the number of units sold each year, x equals the amount spent for TV advertising, and y equals the amount spent for radio advertising (both in \$1,000s per year).

a. Determine how much should be expended for radio and TV in order to maximize the number of units sold each year. (Verify that you have found a maximum.)

b. What is the maximum number of units?

51. ***Least-Squares Model.*** The least-squares model is the most popular method for fitting a curve to a set of data points. With the *linear* least-squares model, the objective is to identify the "best" straight line that fits a set of data points. The line of best fit has the equation

$$y_c = ax + b$$

where y_c is the calculated value of y, a is the slope of the line, and b is the y-intercept. The least-squares method defines the line of "best" fit as the one that minimizes the sum of squared deviations between the *observed* values of y and the corresponding calculated y-values (those lying on the straight line). For the following data points, the "sum of squares" function is

x	5	10	15
y	50	30	20

$$S = \sum_{i=1}^{3} (d_i^2)$$

$$= \sum_{i=1}^{3} (y_i - y_{c_i})^2$$

or,

$$S = f(a, b)$$

$$= \sum [y_i - (ax_i + b)]^2$$

$$= [50 - (5a + b)]^2 + [30 - (10a + b)]^2 + [20 - (15a + b)]^2$$

a. Determine the values of a and b that minimize S.

b. What is the equation of the line of best fit?

52. Refer to the preceding exercise and determine the least-squares line of best fit to the following data points.

x	2	4	7
y	16	25	34

53. ***Least-Squares Continued.*** The least-squares regression model is not restricted to linear functional forms. Using the same approach as in Exercise 51, determine the quadratic function that minimizes the sum of the squares of deviations between actual and predicted values of y for the data below. Note that if we assume a quadratic function to have the form

$$y_c = ax^2 + bx + c,$$

then the criterion, S, becomes a function of a, b, and c.

Verify, using the Hessian matrix, that your values of a^*, b^*, and c^* do result in a minimum value for S. Also, verify that for this "contrived" example, $S^* = 0$.

x	1	−2	4	−1
y	9	−6	−30	5

54. ***Container Design Model.*** A rectangular container with top is to have a volume of 27,000 cubic centimeters. The objective is to minimize the amount of material used in constructing the container. Thus the surface area is to be minimized. Given the sketch in Figure 2–20, determine the dimensions that minimize the surface area. (Hint: $V = xyz$.)

FIGURE 2–20 Container Design

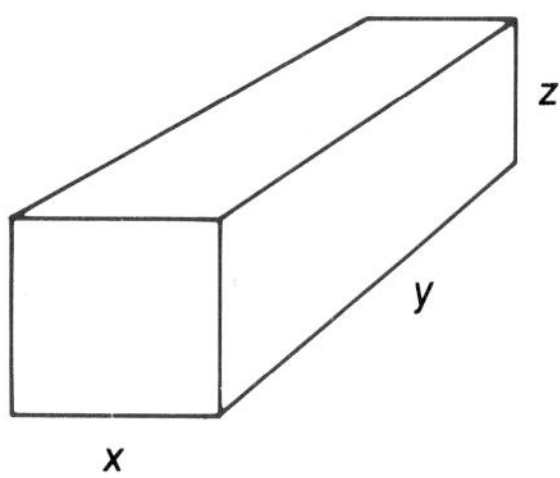

55. ***Fire Station Location Model.*** Three towns are located as indicated by the Cartesian coordinate system in Figure 2–21. Bond issues for constructing a new fire station that will service all three towns have passed in all three towns. It has been agreed that the station is to be located at a location that minimizes the sum of the squares of the distances separating each town center and the station. Determine the optimal location (x^*, y^*) of the fire station. Confirm that your stationary point is indeed a minimum. Does the surrogate criterion make sense? Why or why not? Can you think of better surrogate criteria?

56. In the preceding exercise, assume that the three towns have agreed that the station is to be located at a location that minimizes the sum of

(Tax revenue of town) · (Distance squared separating the town center and the station)

for all three towns. Determine the optimal location (x^*, y^*) if tax revenues in thousands of dollars are 800, 200, and 300, respectively, for towns A, B, and C.

57. ***Pricing Model.*** A firm manufactures three competing microcomputers. Demand functions for each of the three computers are expressed below as a function of the prices of the three computers.

FIGURE 2–21 Fire Station Map

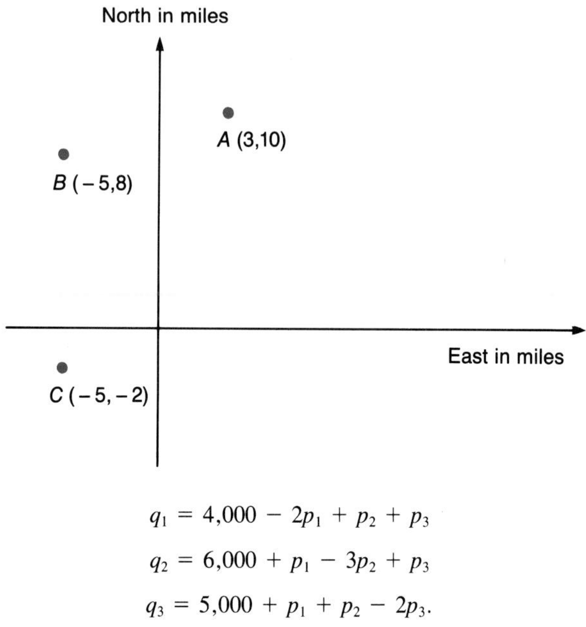

$$q_1 = 4{,}000 - 2p_1 + p_2 + p_3$$
$$q_2 = 6{,}000 + p_1 - 3p_2 + p_3$$
$$q_3 = 5{,}000 + p_1 + p_2 - 2p_3.$$

In this case q_i is the estimated demand (in units per year) for computer i, and p_i is the price of the ith computer (in dollars per unit).

a. Determine the prices that should be charged for the three computers so as to maximize total revenue (R) from the three computers. Verify that you have, in fact, identified a relative maximum.

b. What quantities should be produced if these prices are charged?

c. What is the maximum total revenue?

58. ***Joint Cost Model.*** A firm manufactures three products. The joint cost (production) function is

$$\begin{aligned} C &= f(q_1, q_2, q_3) \\ &= 10q_1^2 + 30q_2^2 + 20q_3^2 - 400q_1 - 900q_2 \\ &\quad - 1{,}000q_3 + 750{,}000 \end{aligned}$$

where C is the total cost (in dollars) of producing q_1, q_2, and q_3 units of products 1, 2, and 3, respectively.

a. Determine the quantities that result in a minimum total cost. Confirm that the stationary point is a relative minimum.

b. What is the expected minimum total cost?

c. Does your result in part *b* raise any questions?

59. Solve the following problems using the Lagrange multiplier technique. For each, interpret the Lagrange multiplier.

a. Maximize

$$f(x, y) = 10x^2y^8$$

subject to

$$100x + 100y = 50{,}000$$

b. Minimize

$$f(x, y, z) = 2x^2 + 5y^2 + z^2$$

subject to

$$2x + y - 4z = 10$$

c. Minimize

$$f(x, y, z) = x^2 + 5y^2 + 6z^2$$

subject to

$$z = 4x + 20y$$

60. A company produces three products. The profit function for the three products is

$$P = f(x_1, x_2, x_3) = Ax_1 + Bx_2 + Cx_3$$

where x_j = Number of units produced and sold of product j. The quantities produced are restricted such that the condition

$$x_1^2 + 2x_2^2 + 3x_3^2 = 40$$

is satisfied. Determine the quantities to produce that maximize P subject to the given constraint.

61. A company produces two types of products, A and B. The weekly cost function is estimated as:

$$C(x_A, x_B) = 504 + 20x_A - .05x_A^2 + 16x_B - .05x_B^2 + .01x_Ax_B$$

where $0 \le x_A \le 100$, and $0 \le x_B \le 100$. Because of cash flow restrictions, the company will spend only \$3,000 per week for production of the two products. If A sells for \$25 and B for \$20, determine the quantities to produce so as to maximize weekly revenue subject to the \$3,000 cost constraint.

3

Linear Programming: The Model and Its Applications

Chapter Outline

Chapter 2 treated the mathematical objective of maximizing or minimizing an objective function (criterion) in the classical manner, implementing the tools of differential calculus. This chapter introduces optimization models with multiple constraints. More specifically, we focus on models that are characterized by both *linear criteria* and *linear constraints*. Solution techniques developed for this class of problems fall under the heading of **linear programming.**

Models with linear objective functions and linear constraints are called **linear programming models.** Solution techniques to solve linear programming problems were not developed until 1947 by George Dantzig. This chapter presents problems that can be modeled as linear programming problems—and a problem or two that cannot be modeled as linear. We hope you will not apply the linear programming model indiscriminately but will appreciate the power and the limitations of the model. If you become too enthralled with the linear programming model, you might occasionally remind yourself that the world is not necessarily linear.

3.1 LINEAR OPTIMIZATION MODELS

Many linear optimization problems are characterized by the existence of two or more activities (variables) that compete for limited resources. The economist's problem is to determine the "best" allocation of scarce resources to the activities. The operational objective of linear programming is to determine the levels of activities (values for controllable variables) that optimize a linear criterion subject to resource limitations and other conditions expressed by linear constraints.

Economic applications of linear programming (LP) are prolific, diverse, and successful. The armed forces and the oil industry in particular have made extensive use of this technique. Besides such traditional manufacturing organizations as wood products, metals, automotive, and chemicals, the service and public sectors have increasingly utilized linear programming. The range of applications has been remarkable. For example, financial institutions have used LP for portfolio and cash management; industrial firms, for food and chemical blending; production departments, for scheduling and allocation; marketing departments, for media selection in advertising and the distribution of products; agricultural interests, for the production scheduling of farm products; and government agencies, for such varied uses as solid waste disposal, air and water pollution control, political redistricting, school bus scheduling, and natural resources planning. Of all the tools in operations research, with the possible exception of simulation, **mathematical programming** (of which linear programming is a subset) has found the most widespread use.

The two following examples introduce the formulation and conceptualization of linear optimization models. Next, come a generalized mathematical model for stating linear programming problems, a discussion of model characteristics, and a concluding set of examples on formulation. (Solution methods are deferred until the next chapter.)

▶ Example 3.1 Product Mix Problem with Two Products

The production manager for the Hastoy Children's Entertainment Company is scheduling hourly production levels for two of the company's most popular toys, an aircraft carrier and a farm set. In her own version of the economic choice between guns and butter, the production manager must decide how much of each product to produce weekly on the assumption that she can sell all she produces.

The carrier and the farm are both processed through two departments. The carrier requires four hours of production time per unit in department 1 and five hours per unit in department 2. The selling price of the carrier is $150; the labor cost per unit is $50; and the per-unit raw material cost is $15. The farm sells for $65, with labor costs of $30 per unit and raw material costs of $10 per unit. The farm requires three hours of production time per unit in department 1 and two hours in department 2. Weekly production capacity is 130 hours in department 1, and department 2 has unlimited capacity as it currently shows a lot of idle time.

From the above data, the production manager can see that the per-unit profit contributions are $85 on the carrier and $25 on the farm set. She simply subtracts the labor and material cost from the selling price and ignores overhead. Letting C be the number of carriers and F the number of farms, she comes up with the following model:

Maximize

$$85C + 25F$$

subject to

$$4C + 3F \leq 130 .$$

She excludes department 2 from the model because it does not present any constraint at all. Just as she gets ready to continue with her analysis, her department 2 supervisor informs her that one of the machines in the department has broken down. The supervisor estimates that the weekly production capacity will now be 300 hours in department 2. Believing his estimate, the production manager adds a second constraint to her model:

$$5C + 2F \leq 300 .$$

Her complete model now involves a linear objective function and two linear constraints.

A phone call from the marketing manager now informs her that at most 25 carriers should be produced each week. She adds the constraint

$$C \leq 25 .$$

FOLLOW-UP EXERCISE

1. Formulate a fourth constraint that results from the necessity of performing some finishing work in department 3. Department 3 has 100 hours of weekly capacity. The carrier requires three hours per unit in department 3, and the farm requires one hour per unit.

▶ Example 3.2 Single-Period, Product-Mix Model

The production manager for the Bonka Toy Manufacturing Company is scheduling hourly production levels for three of its more popular dump trucks: Bonka Junior, Mighty Bonka, and Super Bonka. Each truck is processed through three departments: fabrication, assembly, and packaging. Table 3–1 indicates the time required to process a unit in each department (in minutes per unit), the total production time available during each hour of operation (Are these figures possible? Explain!), and profit margins for each product.

TABLE 3–1 Product Mix Data

	Processing Time (minutes/unit)			Available Production Time (minutes/hour of operation)
Department	**Bonka Junior**	**Mighty Bonka**	**Super Bonka**	
Fabrication	1.00	1.20	1.25	1,200
Assembly	1.30	1.50	1.60	1,500
Packaging	0.80	0.75	0.90	950
Profit/unit	\$0.55	\$0.70	\$0.75	

Management has specified minimum hourly production levels for the Bonka Junior and Mighty Bonka trucks of 200 and 250 units, respectively. Also, no more than 225 units of the Super Bonka truck should be produced each hour.

The production manager wishes to determine the number of trucks to schedule each hour so as to maximize total contribution to profit while:

Using no more time in each department than available each hour.
Satisfying minimum production levels for Bonka Junior and Mighty Bonka.
Producing no more than the maximum specified for Super Bonka.

This problem can be formulated as a linear programming model. Let's return to our problem-solving framework.

1. **Verbal Statement of Problem**
   Determine the number of trucks of each type to schedule for production each hour so as to maximize total contribution to profit.
2. **Decisions**
   a. **Verbal Statement**
      Number of trucks of each type to schedule for production each hour.
   b. **Mathematical Definition**
      x_1 = Number of units produced per hour of Bonka Junior.
      x_2 = Number of units produced per hour of Mighty Bonka.
      x_3 = Number of units produced per hour of Super Bonka.
3. **Criteria**
   a. **Verbal Statement**
      Maximize total contribution to profit each hour.
   b. **Mathematical Statement**
      Given the profit/unit figures in Table 3–1, the linear objective function for this problem is

$$z = 0.55x_1 + 0.70x_2 + 0.75x_3.$$

4. **Constraining Conditions**
   a. **Verbal Statement**
      From the description of the problem, the following constraining conditions must be satisfied when deciding on values for the decision variables. During each hour of operation on any given day:
      (1) No more than 1,200 minutes may be scheduled in the fabrication department.
      (2) No more than 1,500 minutes may be scheduled in the assembly department.

(3) No more than 950 minutes may be scheduled in the packaging department.
(4) At least 200 units of the Bonka Junior model should be scheduled.
(5) At least 250 units of the Mighty Bonka model should be scheduled.
(6) No more than 225 units of the Super Bonka model should be scheduled. (In addition to these constraints, the nonnegativity condition requires that production quantities for the three models cannot be negative.)

b. Mathematical Statement

The first three constraints have a similar form. Using the data in Table 3–1, the constraint for the fabrication department is

$$1.00x_1 + 1.20x_2 + 1.25x_3 \leq 1{,}200\,.$$

The constraints for the other departments are developed in the same manner. The fourth constraint sets a minimum production level on the Bonka Junior model. The mathematical representation is

$$x_1 \geq 200\,.$$

Similarly, the fifth constraint is

$$x_2 \geq 250\,.$$

The mathematical representation of the last constraint is

$$x_3 \leq 225\,.$$

Finally, the nonnegativity condition states that $x_1 \geq 0$, $x_2 \geq 0$, and $x_3 \geq 0$.

5. Mathematical Model

The complete mathematical model for this problem is:

Maximize

$$z = 0.55x_1 + 0.70x_2 + 0.75x_3$$

subject to

Fabrication limit:	$1.00x_1 + 1.20x_2 + 1.25x_3 \leq 1200$	(1)
Assembly limit:	$1.30x_1 + 1.50x_2 + 1.60x_3 \leq 1500$	(2)
Packaging limit:	$0.80x_1 + 0.75x_2 + 0.90x_3 \leq 950$	(3)
Bonka Junior minimum:	$x_1 \geq 200$	(4)
Mighty Bonka minimum:	$x_2 \geq 250$	(5)
Super Bonka maximum:	$x_3 \leq 225$	(6)

and

$$x_1, x_2, x_3 \geq 0.$$

As with Example 3.1 the objective function and all constraints are linear.

FOLLOW-UP EXERCISE

2. Formulate the constraint that would represent the condition that:
   a. Total hourly production for the three models must exceed 600 units.
   b. Total hourly production for the three models must be no more than 850 units.
   c. Hourly production of the Mightly Bonka model should be at least 50 percent greater than that for the Super Bonka model.

d. Hourly production of the Bonka Junior model should be no more than 40 percent of total output of all three models.
e. In what way does the model differ from the reality described in the problem? Would the model allow fractional units to be produced? Is this likely to make the model inapplicable?

3.2 THE GENERALIZED LINEAR PROGRAMMING LP MODEL AND ITS ASSUMPTIONS

It's useful to generalize the statement of the LP model, as it increases our understanding of both its formulation and solution. In this section we state the characteristics of the LP model in a generalized form and analyze the underlying assumptions.

The **generalized linear programming model** is concerned with optimizing a **linear** objective function in n decision variables subject to two sets of conditions: (1) m **structural constraints** that are **linear**, and (2) n **nonnegativity conditions,** one for each decision variable.

The structural constraints are based on the decision variables and reflect the resource limitations and/or other conditions imposed on the problem. The nonnegativity conditions guarantee that each decision variable is nonnegative, a requirement in solution procedures. This condition does not pose an applied problem: First, almost all applications in economics and management treat variables that assume positive values exclusively; second, we can use an algebraic "sleight of hand" should we have a need for nonpositive variables (as illustrated in Section 3.4).

Mathematical Statement of the Generalized LP Model

Let us define the following symbols:

x_j = jth decision variable.
c_j = *Coefficient on* jth decision variable in the objective function.
a_{ij} = Coefficient in the ith constraint for the jth variable.
b_i = Right-hand–side constant for the ith constraint.
n = Number of decision variables.
m = Number of structural constraints.

Based on these definitions, the LP model can be stated as optimize (maximize or minimize)

$$z = c_1x_1 + c_2x_2 + \ldots + c_nx_n \tag{3.1}$$

subject to the structural constraints

$$\begin{array}{ll} a_{11}x_1 + a_{12}x_2 + \ldots + a_{1n}x_n\ (\leq, \geq, =)\ b_1 & (1) \\ a_{21}x_1 + a_{22}x_2 + \ldots + a_{2n}x_n\ (\leq, \geq, =)\ b_2 & (2) \\ \cdot & \cdot \\ \cdot & \cdot \\ \cdot & \cdot \\ a_{m1}x_1 + a_{m2}x_2 + \ldots + a_{mn}x_n\ (\leq, \geq, =)\ b_m & (m) \end{array} \tag{3.2}$$

and the nonnegativity conditions

$$
\begin{aligned}
x_1 &\geq 0 \\
x_2 &\geq 0 \\
&\cdot \\
&\cdot \\
&\cdot \\
x_n &\geq 0 .
\end{aligned}
\tag{3.3}
$$

Note that only one sign ($\leq, \geq, =$) would apply to each structural constraint. Also note that decision variables are placed on the left-hand sides of constraints, a convention consistent with solution procedures (as discussed in the next chapter).

A more efficient statement of the model is achieved by using *summation notation* as follows:

Optimize

$$z = \sum_{j=1}^{n} c_j x_j \tag{3.4}$$

subject to

$$\sum_{j=1}^{n} a_{ij} x_j (\leq, \geq, =) b_i, \qquad i = 1, 2, \ldots, m \tag{3.5}$$

and

$$x_j \geq 0, \qquad j = 1, 2, \ldots, n. \tag{3.6}$$

In the LP literature, 3.4 through 3.6 are often condensed as follows:

Optimize

$$\left\{ z = \sum_{j=1}^{n} c_j x_j \,\middle|\, a_{ij} x_j \leq, \geq, = b_i, \qquad i = 1, \ldots, m, \qquad x_j \geq 0 \right\} \tag{3.7}$$

where the symbol $|$ means "subject to" or "conditional upon."

Finally, another statement of the LP model utilizes matrix algebra.[1] If we define the row vector

$$\mathbf{c} = (c_1 \quad c_2 \quad \ldots \quad c_n) ,$$

the column vectors

$$\mathbf{x} = \begin{pmatrix} x_1 \\ x_2 \\ \cdot \\ \cdot \\ \cdot \\ x_n \end{pmatrix} \qquad \mathbf{b} = \begin{pmatrix} b_1 \\ b_2 \\ \cdot \\ \cdot \\ \cdot \\ b_m \end{pmatrix}$$

[1]Appendix C reviews operations in matrix algebra.

and the matrix

$$\mathbf{A} = \begin{pmatrix} a_{11} & a_{12} & \cdots & a_{1n} \\ a_{21} & a_{22} & \cdots & a_{2n} \\ \vdots & & & \\ a_{m1} & a_{m2} & \cdots & a_{mn} \end{pmatrix}$$

then 3.7 is simply stated as

Optimize

$$z = \{\underbrace{\mathbf{cx}}_{\text{same as 3.4}} \,|\, \underbrace{\mathbf{Ax} \leq, \geq, = \mathbf{b}}_{\text{same as 3.5}}, \quad \underbrace{\mathbf{x} \geq \mathbf{0}}_{\text{same as 3.6}}\} \tag{3.8}$$

where $\mathbf{0}$ is an n-element column vector with all elements zero.

Note in $\mathbf{A}$ that rows correspond to constraints, and columns correspond to variables. The version in 3.8 is a common expression of the LP model in the journal literature.

FOLLOW-UP EXERCISE

3. If the form in 3.4 and 3.5 disturbs you, now is the time to familiarize yourself with the use of subscripted variables and summation signs. Because meaningful problems in linear programming are characterized by extensive notation, shortcut symbols are commonly used. As the chapter unfolds, we rely more and more on the summation sign. On a separate sheet of paper, start with 3.4 and 3.5 and write them out in the long form, paying close attention to the values the subscripts assume. How many separate constraints are described in 3.5?

▶ Example 3.3 Multi-period Product Mix Model

This example is a *dynamic (time-dependent) variation* of the product mix problem. Suppose a firm has a contract to supply 500 units of product *A* and 700 units of product *B* at the end of two time periods, say, quarters. The objective is to determine how many units should be produced of each product in each period, subject to labor and raw materials constraints, such that the total of variable and inventory costs is minimized.

The variable costs of raw materials and labor vary from one period to the next, as given by Table 3–2.

TABLE 3–2 Variable Costs (*Dollars per unit*)

	Quarter	
Product	**1**	**2**
A	3	4
B	6	5

Units made in the first quarter must be stocked until delivery is made at the end of the second quarter. Without loss of generality, assume that carrying costs of inventory are incurred only for one period and are based on the units produced in the first quarter; that is, units produced in the second quarter do not incur inventory costs. A cost analysis indicates that it costs \$0.10 per unit per period to inventory product *A* and \$0.20 per unit per period for product *B*. Furthermore, leftover raw materials from one period to the next cost \$0.01 per kilo to store.

The technological data per product and the availability of raw material and labor are given in Table 3–3.

TABLE 3–3 Technological Data and Availabilities

	Per Unit of Product		Availability in Quarter	
	A	**B**	**1**	**2**
Labor (hours)	0.5	0.8	350	500
Raw materials (kilos)	10	7	6,000	4,000

For example, it takes 0.5 hour of labor and 10 kilos of raw material to produce each unit of product *A*. Note that the same raw material goes into both products and that excess raw material in the first quarter can be inventoried for use in the next quarter. Further assume that unused raw material at the end of the second quarter has been accounted for in the cost of products and that excess labor either has alternative uses or was not commissioned in the first place; that is, the availability figures in Table 3–3 are maxima, so the difference between the labor used and the labor available represents the amount not hired.

Let us formulate the LP model for this problem guided by the problem-solving framework.

1. **Verbal Statement of Problem**
   Determine the number of units of each product to produce in each period so as to minimize the sum of variable production costs and inventory costs.
2. **Decisions**
   a. **Verbal Statement**
      Number of units of products *A* and *B* manufactured in quarter 1 and quarter 2.
   b. **Mathematical Definition**
      x_1 = Units made of *A* in quarter 1.
      x_2 = Units made of *A* in quarter 2.
      x_3 = Units made of *B* in quarter 1.
      x_4 = Units made of *B* in quarter 2.
3. **Criteria**
   a. **Verbal Statement**
      Minimize the sum of variable production costs and inventory costs.
   b. **Mathematical Statement**

$$\begin{aligned} z = {} & 3x_1 + 4x_2 + 6x_3 + 5x_4 && \text{(variable production costs)} \\ & + 0.1x_1 + 0.2x_3 && \text{(product inventory costs)} \\ & + 0.01(6{,}000 - 10x_1 - 7x_3) && \text{(raw materials inventory costs)} \end{aligned}$$

or,

$$z = 60 + 3x_1 + 4x_2 + 6.13x_3 + 5x_4$$

Note that the appearance of a constant in the criterion is not part of the generalized LP formulation. In the actual solution to this problem, the constant would be ignored and added in as a "fixed charge" following the solution. Further note that the term $(6{,}000 - 10x_1 - 7x_3)$ represents unused raw material in the first quarter.

4. **Constraining Conditions**
   a. **Verbal Statement**
      (1) No more than 350 labor hours may be used during quarter 1.
      (2) No more than 500 labor hours may be used during quarter 2.
      (3) No more than 6,000 kilos of raw materials may be used during quarter 1.
      (4) Raw materials available for use during quarter 2 is limited to 4,000 kilos (not available during quarter 1) plus any leftover from the first quarter.
      (5) Total production of product *A* for the two quarters should equal 500 units.
      (6) Total production of product *B* for the two quarters should equal 700 units. (In addition to these constraints, the nonnegativity condition requires that production quantities cannot be negative.)
   b. **Mathematical Statement**
      The first four structural constraints are formulated using information in Table 3–3.

$$(1) \quad 0.5x_1 + 0.8x_3 \leq 350$$

$$(2) \quad 0.5x_2 + 0.8x_4 \leq 500$$

$$(3) \quad 10x_1 + 7x_3 \leq 6{,}000$$

$$(4) \quad 10x_2 + 7x_4 \leq 4{,}000 + (6{,}000 - 10x_1 - 7x_3)$$

$$\text{or,} \quad 10x_1 + 10x_2 + 7x_3 + 7x_4 \leq 10{,}000$$

The production requirement constraints are:

$$(5) \quad x_1 + x_2 = 500$$

$$(6) \quad x_3 + x_4 = 700$$

The nonnegativity condition is $x_j \geq 0,\ j = 1, 2, 3, 4$.

5. **Mathematical Model**
   The complete LP model for this problem is

   Minimize

$$z = 60 + 3x_1 + 4x_2 + 6.13x_3 + 5x_4$$

subject to

Labor availability for

Quarter 1: $\quad 0.5x_1 + 0.8x_3 \leq 350 \quad (1)$

Quarter 2: $\quad 0.5x_2 + 0.8x_4 \leq 500 \quad (2)$

Raw Material Availability for

Quarter 1: $\quad 10x_1 + 7x_3 \leq 6{,}000 \quad (3)$

Quarter 2: $\quad 10x_1 + 10x_2 + 7x_3 + 7x_4 \leq 10{,}000 \quad (4)$

Production requirements for

Product A:	$x_1 + x_2 = 500$	(5)
Product B:	$x_3 + x_4 = 700$	(6)

$$x_j \geq 0, \quad j = 1, 2, 3, 4$$

FOLLOW-UP EXERCISES

4. Write appropriate constraints for the following conditions:
   a. No more than 750 combined units of products A and B can be stored due to a shortage of available space in the warehouse.
   b. At least 250 units but no more than 450 units of product A are to be produced in the first quarter.
   c. The production of product A must not exceed the production of product B in any quarter.

**5. Can you reformulate the objective function such that inventory carrying costs are based on average inventories; that is, (beginning inventory + ending inventory)/2? Assume uniform (linear) buildup of product inventories and uniform depletion of the raw material inventory. Note that carrying costs are now incurred in both periods. Compare this new objective function to the previous objective function.

Underlying Assumptions

The deterministic (nonprobabilistic) nature of the LP model and the linearity assumptions make for certain tacit assumptions in applied problems. Although these assumptions are either met or closely approximated in many applications, users must be thoroughly familiar with their implications and limitations in order to avoid misusing the LP model. These assumptions, by the way, relate to the issue of validation in our paradigm of Chapter 1.

The following underlying assumptions are a direct result of the characteristics of the LP model:

1. The Model is Deterministic. This means that each coefficient (c_j, a_{ij}, b_i) is fixed and known with certainty. In many cases this is reasonable, as when parameters are set by administrative fiat, contractual obligations, or otherwise definitely known conditions. In many other cases, the parameters are random variables from either known or unknown probability distributions. In these cases, we should estimate parameters by sampling procedures, forecasting models, or probability models. For example, the costs in Table 3–2 and the technological data in Table 3–3 are, most probably, random variables from unknown probability distributions. They would have to be estimated by the arithmetic means of samples based on available (or subjective) data that had been projected into the quarters when production would take place. If you studied sampling theory in a basic statistics course, you should realize that the sample mean, used to estimate the population mean for some parameter in the LP model, is itself a random variable subject to fluctuations. In short, estimating parameters in the LP model requires great care. Fortunately, it is possible to evaluate the sensitivity of results to fluctuations in the parameters by **sen-**

sitivity analysis (Chapters 5 and 6) and by advanced programming models known as **parametric** (Chapter 5) and **stochastic linear programming** (Section 3.4).

2. The Model Is Proportional. This condition follows directly from the linearity assumptions for the objective function and constraints. This means that the criterion and the constraints expand or contract proportionally to the level of each activity. For example, doubling the number of units of product *B* produced in the second quarter (variable x_4) results in doubling its cost contribution and doubling its labor and material requirements. These conditions represent *constant returns to scale* rather than *economies or diseconomies of scale*. These conditions will not hold if, for instance, the cost coefficients in the objective function or the technological coefficients in the constraints vary as a function of the level for each activity; that is, if marginal costs decrease or production efficiency increases as the level of output increases. For such problems, linearity assumptions may hold over specific ranges of output, allowing the use of **piecewise linear programming procedures** (Section 3.4) in other special cases, **nonlinear programming algorithms** may be used.

3. The Model Is Additive. The assumption of proportionality guarantees linearity if and only if joint effects or interactions are nonexistent. This latter assumption implies that the total contribution of all activities (to the criterion or the constraints) is identical to the sum of the contributions for each activity individually. Put another way, "the whole is equal to the sum of its parts." This would not be true if, for example, a company produces two products that compete in the market; the resulting *cross elasticities* would cause interactions that would be reflected by multiplicative terms in the profit function; a change in demand for one will affect the demand for the other and the prices of both. With respect to Example 3.3, increasing the level of product *B* may affect the labor coefficient of product *A* (0.5 in Table 3–3) if, in so doing, skilled or experienced labor is diverted from product *A*. Should this be the case, the model would not be additive. If joint effects are minor, however, a practical solution might be obtained by assuming additivity.

4. The Decision Variables Are Divisible. This means that fractional levels for the decision variables are permissible; specifically, the objective function and constraints are continuous functions. Clearly, some problems require integer solutions; for example, how many tankers per month should be leased to transport crude oil from the Middle East to the United States? The decision variables in Example 3.3 are not necessarily restricted to integer values if one accounts for in-process products, products at various stages of production. If the standardized LP model is used for problems requiring *integer solutions,* then two obvious results are possible: Either the optimal solution will include all integer values for the activities or it will not. The former result is not uncommon and neatly circumvents the problem. The latter result can be treated by "fudging," that is, rounding each fractional answer to the nearest whole number. Doing so, however, may yield one of three possibilities: (*a*) The resulting solution may be the optimal integer solution; (*b*) The resulting solution may not be feasible; it may violate one or more of the structural constraints. (*c*) The resulting solution may not be the optimal *integer* solution. For the latter two cases, **integer programming models** (Chapter 8) may be warranted.

3.3 ADDITIONAL SCENARIOS AND FORMULATIONS

For the most part, the solution of linear programming models (Chapters 4–6) is standardized and readily available in commercial computer packages. Although such issues as large-scale problems and computationally efficient codes still present challenges to the operations researcher, the state of the art for the solution of such models is more than adequate. The recognition and correct formulation of problems in a linear optimization framework, however, still represent both a challenge and an opportunity for innovation. Of equal importance is the interpretation of results (Chapters 4 and 5), especially in light of the inherent assumptions of the model.

The following examples illustrate a wide variety of applications of linear programming. Careful study of these, coupled with your conscientious attack and review of the formulation exercises at the end of the chapter, can provide you with an excellent grounding in problem formulation. As indicated in Chapter 1, our problem-solving framework will be used only where we believe it will assist your understanding.

▶ Example 3.4 Capital Budgeting Model

In the static version of the capital budgeting (rationing) problem, the decision-making unit—be it a department in a private firm, nonprofit organization, or governmental agency—has various mutually exclusive projects it can undertake in a given period. Each project is characterized by a derived benefit and an associated cost. The objective is to determine which projects or portions of projects will maximize overall benefit subject to a budgetary constraint.

If we define the symbols

x_j = Proportion of the jth project undertaken.
c_j = Return (benefit) associated with the jth project.
a_j = Cost of the jth project.
b = Overall budgetary constraint (dollars available for investing).
n = Number of projects available.

the typical problem is formulated as

Maximize

$$z = \sum_{j=1}^{n} c_j x_j$$

subject to

$$\sum_{j=1}^{n} a_j x_j \leq b,$$

$$x_j \leq 1, \quad j = 1, \ldots, n,$$

$$x_j \geq 0, \quad j = 1, \ldots, n.$$

Thus z is a measure of total return, the first constraint represents the budgetary restriction, and the remaining constraints guarantee that the x_j's will be proportions between zero and one.

In many applications, the x_j's are not allowed to take on fractional values, and some projects may not be mutually exclusive.[2] Furthermore, in strictly financial applications, the c_j's are typically expressed in terms of *net present values.* Likewise, the a_j's and b are expressed in present dollars according to the concept of present value.[3]

The problem associated with the selection of projects need not be restricted to the firm. For example, the Department of Health and Human Services (HHS) and the Environmental Protection Agency (EPA) are both confronted with capital budgeting decisions: Which projects should be selected such that overall benefits are maximized and budgetary and other constraints are satisfied? As in all decisions relating to the public sector (on a benefit-cost basis), the most difficult part of the formulation is definition and quantitative determination of social benefits. Returns may be classified broadly as *direct and indirect benefits.* For example, EPA antipollution projects may have direct benefits in terms of cost savings to society (such as reduced maintenance of buildings and homes and dollar savings relating to the medical treatment of pollution-related illnesses) and indirect benefits as reflected by a better quality of life. Based on these comments and a moment's reflection, it is easy to appreciate the complexities of analyses and value judgments inherent in public welfare applications.

To illustrate, suppose that a team of management scientists, welfare economists, sociologists, and political scientists has analyzed a set of seven long-term projects for HHS as given by Table 3–4. The problem is to determine the proportions of each project to select so as to maximize the combined net benefit from the seven projects. Examine the calculation of *net benefit* for project 1. Its benefit-cost ratio is 1.1-1 or simply 1.10, so that

TABLE 3–4 Data for HHS Projects

Project	Benefit-Cost Ratio	Present Value of Cost (dollars in millions)
1	1.10	250
2	1.25	400
3	1.40	750
4	1.30	500
5	1.15	450
6	0.90	300
7	1.05	200

$$\frac{\text{Benefit}}{\text{Cost}} = 1.1$$

$$\text{Benefit} = 1.1 \times \text{Cost}$$

$$\begin{aligned}\text{Net benefit} &= \text{Benefit} - \text{Cost} \\ &= 1.1 \times \text{Cost} - \text{Cost} \\ &= .1 \times \text{Cost}\end{aligned}$$

For project 1, total cost can vary from \$0 to \$250 million, depending on the proportion of the project undertaken. If x_j = Proportion of the jth project undertaken, the cost incurred from project 1 equals $250x_1$ and the net benefit equals $(.1)(250x_1) = 25x_1$, both of which are stated in millions of dollars.

[2]We relax these assumptions in Chapter 8 (Example 8.11).

[3]See footnote on page 59 for a definition of present value.

If the total budget is \$2 billion (\$2,000 million), the complete LP formulation is:

Maximize

$$z = (0.1)(250)x_1 + (0.25)(400)x_2 + (0.40)(750)x_3 + (0.30)(500)x_4 + (0.15)(450)x_5 + (-0.10)(300)x_6 + (0.05)(200)x_7$$

$$= 25x_1 + 100x_2 + 300x_3 + 150x_4 + 67.5x_5 - 30x_6 + 10x_7$$

subject to

$$250x_1 + 400x_2 + 750x_3 + 500x_4 + 450x_5 + 300x_6 + 200x_7 \le 2{,}000 \quad (1)$$

$$x_1 \le 1 \quad (2)$$

$$x_2 \le 1 \quad (3)$$

$$x_3 \le 1 \quad (4)$$

$$x_4 \le 1 \quad (5)$$

$$x_5 \le 1 \quad (6)$$

$$x_6 \le 1 \quad (7)$$

$$x_7 \le 1 \quad (8)$$

$$x_j \ge 0, \quad j = 1, \ldots 7.$$

Now suppose that other "considerations" must be taken into account: The combined present value of expenses for projects 1 and 7 must exceed \$300 million; the combined present value of expenses for projects 3 and 4 must be less than \$700 million; and the present value of the amount expended on project 7 must be exactly 40 percent of the amount expended on project 3. These three additional constraints are expressed, respectively, as follows:

$$250x_1 + 200x_7 \ge 300 \quad (9)$$

$$750x_3 + 500x_4 \le 700 \quad (10)$$

$$200x_7 = (0.4)(750)x_3$$

or

$$-300x_3 + 200x_7 = 0. \quad (11)$$

FOLLOW-UP EXERCISES

6. Do you agree with the interpretation that a fractional value for a project means a smaller version of the project? Is this practical? What underlying assumption in the LP model necessitates the specification of fractional values? (In Chapter 8 we take up the capital budgeting problem with $x_j = 0$ or 1.)
7. In the context of this problem, what are the implications relating to the assumption of proportionality?

**8. Formulate the dynamic capital budgeting problem over m periods for n projects using the following symbols:

x_{ij} = Proportion of the jth project undertaken in the ith period.
c_{ij} = Return associated with the jth project in the ith period.
a_{ij} = Cost of the jth project in the ith period.
b_i = Budget for the ith period.

Make sure you stipulate the condition that no more than 100 percent of the *j*th project can be undertaken across all periods. Does this make $x_{ij} \leq 1$ for all *i* and *j* redundant? Explicitly state the model given the following: $m = 2$, $n = 3$, $c_{11} = 7$, $c_{21} = 4$, $c_{12} = 3$, $c_{22} = 9$, $c_{13} = 2$, $c_{23} = 10$, $a_{11} = 5$, $a_{21} = 2$, $a_{12} = 4$, $a_{22} = 7$, $a_{13} = 2$, $a_{23} = 6$, $b_1 = 9$, $b_2 = 12$.

▶ Example 3.5 Shift Scheduling Model

A local hospital administrator wishes to determine a work schedule for registered nurses (RNs). The union contract specifies that nurses work a normal day of six hours. The administrator has determined a daily work schedule in which the day is divided into eight three-hour shifts. Table 3–5 indicates the estimated minimum requirement for nurses per shift. Nurses will start work each day at the beginning of one of these shifts and end work at the end of the following shift.

TABLE 3–5 Requirements per Shift

	Period							
	1	**2**	**3**	**4**	**5**	**6**	**7**	**8**
Shift	12 midnight–3 A.M.	3–6 A.M.	6–9 A.M.	9 A.M.–12 noon	12 noon–3 P.M.	3–6 P.M.	6–9 P.M.	9 P.M.–12 midnight
Minimum number of required RNs	30	20	40	50	60	50	40	40

The administrator must specify the number of nurses that is to begin work each shift, so that the required number of nurses is available for each three-hour period. The objective is to minimize the total number of nurses employed.

Let x_j equal the number of nurses reporting to work *at the beginning* of period *j*. With this decision variable, the objective function is simply

Minimize

$$z = \sum_{j=i}^{8} x_j .$$

The structural constraints reflect the minimum staffing requirement for each period. These constraints are simple to formulate once you see the pattern. To illustrate, consider the staffing requirement of at least 30 nurses for period 1. Nurses on duty for this period would include those starting work at the beginning of this shift *plus* those who began work during the previous shift. Thus the constraint for period 1 is

$$x_1 + x_8 \geq 30 .$$

Similarly, the constraint for period 2 is

$$x_2 + x_1 \geq 20 .$$

The remaining six structural constraints follow the same pattern. The nonnegativity condition is

$$x_j \geq 0 \quad j = 1, \ldots, 8.$$

FOLLOW-UP EXERCISES

9. Completely formulate the hospital administration model.
10. Does the divisibility assumption create any difficulty in this problem? If it does, what recourse do you have?
11. Assume in Example 3.5 that RNs are paid an average of $12 per hour. Assume also that the objective is to minimize the total cost of meeting these staffing requirements. Modify the formulation to account for this.
12. In the preceding exercise, assume the union contract allows nurses to work an additional three hours on an overtime basis (at one and one half their hourly pay rate). The contract also specifies that any nurses requested to work overtime will receive full payment for three hours of overtime, even if they work less than three hours. Thus the administrator concludes that overtime, when assigned, will be for the maximum of three hours. The decisions for the administrator are: (a) How many nurses should start a regular six-hour day at the beginning of each shift? (b) How many should begin an overtime nine-hour day at the beginning of each shift? Assume that cost minimization is the objective. *Hint*: In addition to the definition of x_j as before, let y_j equal the number of nurses reporting to work in period j who will work an overtime shift.
13. In the preceding exercise, assume the union contract specifies that at least 10 percent of all nurses can expect overtime. Formulate the constraint(s) that guarantee this condition.

▶ Example 3.6 Blending Model

Linear programming is particularly useful in problems that combine ingredients to form a resultant end product. These *blending models* have been applied to a variety of problems including:

Blending of petroleum products.
Blending of feed mixes for agricultural use.
Blending of spirits.
Blending of fertilizers and grass seed.
Blending of metals to form alloy materials.
Blending of tobaccos.
Blending of teas and coffees.

The usual objective is to determine the optimal blend that minimizes cost. Typical constraining conditions include technological (recipe) requirements, limited availability of one or more input components, and production requirements related to the various final blends.

Consider the following illustration. A coffee manufacturer blends three component coffee beans into three final blends of coffee. Although the recipes for the three final blends are imprecise, certain restrictions must be satisfied when combining the three components:

Component 1 should constitute no more than 30 percent of final blend 1 by weight.
Component 2 should constitute at least 20 percent of final blend 3 by weight.
Components 2 and 3, combined, should constitute at least 80 percent of final blend 2 by weight.

In addition to the recipe restrictions, there is limited availability of the three components. The maximum weekly availabilities are 60,000, 25,000, and 50,000 pounds, respectively. Weekly capacity for the plant is 125,000 pounds. To satisfy the needs of a favored customer, weekly production should include at least 40,000 pounds of final blend 1.

Given that the three components currently cost the manufacturer $1, $1.20, and $1.35 per pound and that the three final blends are sold at wholesale prices of $1.75, $2, and $1.90 per pound, management wishes to **determine what number of pounds of each component should be used in each blend so as to maximize total weekly profit margin** (other weekly operating costs are excluded from consideration).

To formulate this problem as an LP model, define the double-subscripted decision variable

$$x_{ij} = \text{number of pounds of component } i \text{ used in final blend } j.$$

The objective is to maximize total weekly profit margin, as described by the following objective function.

Maximize

$$\begin{aligned} z &= \text{Total revenue from three final blends minus total cost of the three components} \\ &= 1.75(x_{11} + x_{21} + x_{31}) + 2(x_{12} + x_{22} + x_{32}) \\ &\quad + 1.90(x_{13} + x_{23} + x_{33}) - 1(x_{11} + x_{12} + x_{13}) \\ &\quad - 1.20(x_{21} + x_{22} + x_{23}) - 1.35(x_{31} + x_{32} + x_{33}) \end{aligned}$$

Note that $(x_{11} + x_{21} + x_{31})$ expresses the weight or amount produced of *final blend 1.* Similarly, the expression $(x_{11} + x_{12} + x_{13})$ gives the total weight used of *component 1* in the blending process. Further note the assumption implied by the structure of this function, that there are no material losses in the blending process. If 100 pounds of ingredients are combined, then 100 pounds of final product will result.

The simplified form of the objective function is

Maximize

$$\begin{aligned} z = {} & 0.75x_{11} + 1.00x_{12} + 0.90x_{13} + 0.55x_{21} + 0.80x_{22} + 0.70x_{23} \\ & + 0.40x_{31} + 0.65x_{32} + 0.55x_{33}. \end{aligned}$$

The recipe restrictions are represented by the following constraints:

$$x_{11} \le 0.30(x_{11} + x_{21} + x_{31})$$

or

$$0.70x_{11} - 0.30x_{21} - 0.30x_{31} \le 0 \qquad (1)$$

$$x_{23} \ge 0.20(x_{13} + x_{23} + x_{33})$$

or

$$-0.20x_{13} + 0.80x_{23} - 0.20x_{33} \geq 0 \tag{2}$$

$$x_{22} + x_{32} \geq 0.80(x_{12} + x_{22} + x_{32})$$

or

$$-0.80x_{12} + 0.20x_{22} + 0.20x_{32} \geq 0\,. \tag{3}$$

The component availability constraints are:

$$x_{11} + x_{12} + x_{13} \leq 60{,}000 \tag{4}$$

$$x_{21} + x_{22} + x_{23} \leq 25{,}000 \tag{5}$$

$$x_{31} + x_{32} + x_{33} \leq 50{,}000\,. \tag{6}$$

The plant capacity constraint is

$$x_{11} + x_{12} + x_{13} + x_{21} + x_{22} + x_{23} + x_{31} + x_{32} + x_{33} \leq 125{,}000\,. \tag{7}$$

The one production requirement for blend 1 is represented by the constraint

$$x_{11} + x_{21} + x_{31} \geq 40{,}000\,. \tag{8}$$

To complete the formulation, the nonnegativity condition is

$$x_{ij} \geq 0 \quad \text{for all } i \text{ and } j\,.$$

Note that double-subscripted variables simplify the conceptualization and statement of constraints for problems of this type. Alternatively, we could have defined the variables x_j, $j = 1, \ldots, 9$. This would simplify the subscripting but degrade the ease of formulation and interpretation, since it is more difficult to remember the meaning of subscripts within the context of the problem. To really see what we mean, try reformulating the constraints from scratch using x_j's.

FOLLOW-UP EXERCISES

14. With regard to the preceding example, formulate constraints that represent the following conditions:
    a. Component 2 should constitute exactly 40 percent of final blend 3.
    b. Total production of blends 1 and 3 should be no more than 70,000 pounds per week.
    c. Final blend 1 should have a composition of 20 percent component 1, 45 percent component 2, and 35 percent component 3. How many constraints are needed?
15. Restate constraints 4–8 in the blending example using summation notation.

**16. Suppose in the blending example that there is material loss in the blending process. Assume that the loss is a function of the particular component coffee bean. Modify the formulation to account for such losses if the loss percentages for the three components are 1 percent, 2 percent, and 0.5 percent. Assume that weekly capacity is stated in terms of number of pounds of input.

► Example 3.7 Media Mix Model

The media mix problem is concerned with allocating the advertising budget among media (television, radio, magazines, newspapers, and outdoor advertising) so that some criterion is maximized. Typical criteria include—in decreasing order of ease in formulation and increasing order of desirability or importance—total exposure, frequency (impact), reach (coverage), sales, and profits.[4] *Exposure per time period for a given medium* is defined as the product of (1) the number of members of the target group exposed to one insertion in the medium and (2) the number of advertisements in that medium. *Total exposure* then is the sum of exposures across media. *Frequency* is defined as the average number of advertisements seen by each potential consumer during one time period of interest. *Reach* is the total number of target-group consumers exposed to at least one advertisement in a given period.

Suppose a trade magazine reports the rated exposure (people per month per dollar of advertising outlay) for each of the above five media, respectively, as 22, 12, 15, 10, and 5. The advertising group of a company is to develop an optimal media mix restricted to the following conditions.

1. The total advertising budget is $1 million.
2. No more than 50 percent of the budget is to be expended on the airwaves (radio and television).
3. No more than 30 percent of the budget is to be expended on any one medium.
4. The rated exposure market segmentation targets indicated in Table 3–6 must be satisfied.

The problem is to determine the amounts of money to allocate for advertising in each medium each month so as to maximize total monthly exposures, while satisfying the above conditions.

TABLE 3–6 Rated Exposures by Market Segments

	Total Exposure Targets (100,000 people per month)		Rated Exposure by Medium* (people per month per dollar)				
Market Segment	**Minimum**	**Maximum**	**(1)**	**(2)**	**(3)**	**(4)**	**(5)**
Youth	25	35	10	5	1	0	1
Women	40	—	6	4	7	2	2
College educated	35	—	3	1	4	5	1

*(1) = Television.
(2) = Radio.
(3) = Magazines.
(4) = Newspapers.
(5) = Outdoor advertising.

Let us represent dollar expenditures (in units of $100,000 per month) by x_1 for television, x_2 for radio, x_3 for magazines, x_4 for newspapers, and x_5 for outdoor advertising. Note that the unit of measure for expenditures (hundred thousand) makes the divisibility assumption quite feasible.

If exposure is assumed to be deterministic, to be constant per dollar of advertising expenditure (proportionality), and to be free of media interaction effects (additivity), then the problem may be formulated as

Maximize

$$z = 22x_1 + 12x_2 + 15x_3 + 10x_4 + 5x_5$$

[4]For a more detailed presentation, see David B. Montgomery and Glen L. Urban, *Management Science in Marketing* (Englewood Cliffs, N.J.; Prentice-Hall, 1969).

subject to

$$\begin{aligned}
x_1 + x_2 + x_3 + x_4 + x_5 &\le 10 && (1)\\
x_1 + x_2 &\le 5 && (2)\\
x_1 &\le 3 && (3)\\
x_2 &\le 3 && (4)\\
x_3 &\le 3 && (5)\\
x_4 &\le 3 && (6)\\
x_5 &\le 3 && (7)\\
10x_1 + 5x_2 + x_3 + x_5 &\ge 25 && (8)\\
10x_1 + 5x_2 + x_3 + x_5 &\le 35 && (9)\\
6x_1 + 4x_2 + 7x_3 + 2x_4 + 2x_5 &\ge 40 && (10)\\
3x_1 + x_2 + 4x_3 + 5x_4 + x_5 &\ge 35 && (11)
\end{aligned}$$

and

$$x_j \ge 0, \quad j = 1, \ldots, 5.$$

Thus $22x_1$ is the exposure (in hundred thousands per month) provided by the television expenditures, $12x_2$ is the exposure generated by radio, and so on. Similarly, constraint 1 represents condition 1, constraint 2 reflects condition 2, constraints 3 through 7 meet condition 3, and constraints 8 through 11 satisfy condition 4.

FOLLOW-UP EXERCISES

17. Do the divisibility, proportionality, and additivity assumptions for this problem seem reasonable? Why or why not?
18. Describe how you would formulate the problem if *options* were available within media? As an example, assume that rated exposures are available for three television stations, four radio stations, five magazines, two newspapers, and six billboard locations. How many variables characterize this problem?
19. Describe how you would formulate the problem if *scheduling over time* were required? For example, suppose monthly allocations to the five media are required over a 12-month planning horizon and that exposures are affected by seasonal factors. How many variables would there be in this time-dependent (dynamic) media mix problem?

**20. Formulate a generalized LP model for the dynamic media mix problem using the following symbols:

x_{jkt} = Expenditure in the kth option of the jth medium in the tth period.
e_{jkt} = Effectiveness of the kth option of the jth medium in the tth period.
c_{jkt} = Monetary constraint for the kth option of the jth medium in the tth period.
b_{jt} = Monetary constraint for the jth medium in the tth period.
B_t = *Overall budgetary constraint in the* tth period.
E_{jktp} = Effectiveness of the kth option of the jth medium in the tth period for the pth market segment.
U_{tp} = Minimum target for the pth market segment in the tth period.
V_{tp} = Maximum target for the pth market segment in the tth period.

P = Number of market segments.
T = Number of periods.
M = Number of media.
n_j = Number of options in the jth medium.

Hint: Don't let multiple subscripting throw you; it's simply a convenience. For four periods ($T = 4$), five media ($M = 5$), and three options per medium ($n_1 = n_2 = n_3 = n_4 = n_5 = 3$), the total number of variables is 60 ($4 \times 5 \times 3$).

Example 3.8 Financial Mix Model

Another variation of the mix problem, besides product mix (Examples 3.2 and 3.3) and media mix (Example 3.7), is the financial mix problem.

Consider a company that must produce two products over a given production period which is, say, one quarter in length. The company can pay for materials and labor from two sources: company funds and borrowed funds.

The firm faces three decisions: **(1) How many units should it produce of product 1? (2) How many units should it produce of product 2? (3) How much money should it borrow to support the production of the two products?** In making these decisions, the firm wishes to maximize the profit contribution subject to the conditions stated below.

1. Since the company's products are enjoying a *seller's market,* it can sell as many units as it can produce. Furthermore, the amount the company can produce is small, relative to the overall market; so the amount produced has no effect on market prices. The company would therefore like to produce as many units as possible subject to production capacity and financial constraints. The capacity constraints, together with cost and price data, are given in Table 3–7.

TABLE 3–7 Capacity, Price, and Cost Data

			Required Hours per Unit in Department		
Product	**Selling Price (dollars per unit)**	**Cost of Production (dollars per unit)**	**A**	**B**	**C**
1	14	10	0.5	0.3	0.2
2	11	8	0.3	0.4	0.1
	Available hours per quarter		500	400	200

2. The available company funds during the production period amount to $30,000.
3. A bank will loan up to $20,000 per quarter at an interest rate of 5 percent (0.05) per quarter providing the company's *acid (quick) test ratio* is at least 3 to 1 while the loan is outstanding. A simplified acid-test ratio is given by the ratio of (1) cash on hand plus accounts receivable to (2) accounts payable.

According to Figure 3–1, payments for labor and materials are made at the end of the production period; hence any needed credit is obtained at that time. Shipments are made, on credit, at the end of the production period. Finally, sales revenue is received, and outstanding liabilities are paid off at the end of the next period.

Let us define:

x_1 = Number of units produced of product 1.
x_2 = Number of units produced of product 2.
x_3 = Number of dollars borrowed.

The profit contribution per unit of each product is given by the selling price less the variable cost of production. Total profit is computed by summing the profits from producing the two products *less* the cost associated with any borrowed funds. The objective function is stated as

Maximize

$$z = (14 - 10)x_1 + (11 - 8)x_2 - 0.05x_3$$
$$= 4x_1 + 3x_2 - 0.05x_3.$$

The production capacity constraints for each department, as given by Table 3–7, are

$$0.5x_1 + 0.3x_2 \leq 500 \quad (1)$$
$$0.3x_1 + 0.4x_2 \leq 400 \quad (2)$$
$$0.2x_1 + 0.1x_2 \leq 200 \quad (3)$$

The funds available for production include both the $30,000 cash that the firm now possesses and any borrowed funds. Consequently, production is limited to the extent that funds are available to pay for production costs. The constraint expressing this relationship is

FIGURE 3–1 Time-Dependent Financial Policies for Example

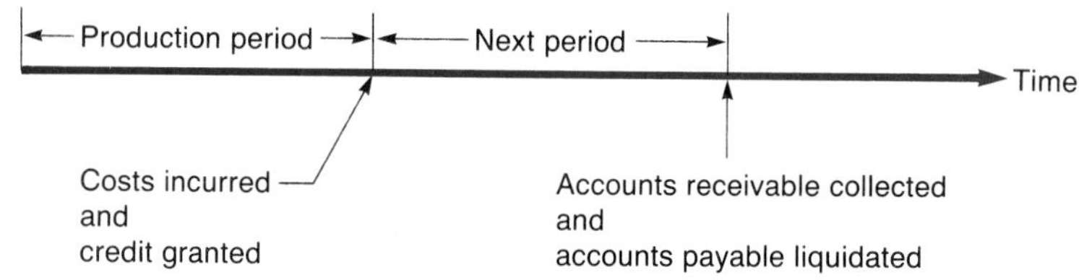

$$\text{funds used in production} \leq \text{funds available}$$
$$10x_1 + 8x_2 \leq 30{,}000 + x_3$$

or

$$10x_1 + 8x_2 - x_3 \leq 30{,}000. \quad (4)$$

The borrowed funds constraint, condition 3, is

$$x_3 \leq 20{,}000. \quad (5)$$

The constraint based on the acid-test condition is developed as follows:

$$\frac{\text{Cash on hand after production} + \text{Accounts receivable}}{\text{Accounts payable}} \geq 3$$

$$\frac{(30{,}000 + x_3 - 10x_1 - 8x_2) + 14x_1 + 11x_3}{x_3 + 0.05x_3} \geq 3$$

$$30{,}000 + x_3 + 4x_1 + 3x_2 \geq 3.15x_3$$

$$4x_1 + 3x_2 - 2.15x_3 \geq -30{,}000$$

$$-4x_1 - 3x_2 + 2.15x_3 \leq 30{,}000\,. \qquad (6)$$

Note that the first term in the denominator, x_3, represents the principal liability, and the second term represents the interest payable on that liability. Also note that constraint 6 was altered by multiplying the preceding line by -1 to express the right-hand-side constant as a positive number. Solution procedures generally require positive right-hand-side constants, as explained in Chapter 4.

Finally, the nonnegativity constraints are expressed as $x_j \geq 0$, $j = 1, 2, 3$.

FOLLOW-UP EXERCISES

21. Do the decision variables satisfy the divisibility assumptions? What recourse do you have if they do not?
22. What do the additivity and proportionality assumptions imply with regard to Table 3–7?
23. How would you handle the condition that, on the average, only 70 percent of the accounts receivable is collected by the company at the end of the next period?
24. Suppose that labor and material expenses were paid out on a weekly basis. Describe how this might modify the original problem.
25. Modify the example to include an opportunity cost of 3 percent per quarter with the use of company funds.

▶ **Example 3.9 Solid Waste Management Model—A Blending Problem[5]

In years past, the problems associated with the disposal of solid wastes (residues) from production processes were considered to be incidental to the problems associated with the production of the primary products. Recently, both the social and economic consequences of solid wastes have forced the explicit consideration of solid waste management. The following example clearly shows that decisions regarding the most efficient manner to produce a set of primary products completely interact with decisions pertaining to the efficient utilization of solid wastes.

A firm is involved in blending four final products as illustrated in Figure 3–2. The firm produces two primary products, each of which is manufactured through a chemical process that blends three raw materials. Table 3–8 shows how these materials must be blended in order to produce each of the two products. For example, it shows that at least 20 percent of the weight of product *A* must be accounted for by material 1, at least

[5]We are indebted to Albert J. Simone, College of Business Administration, University of Cincinnati for the orginal formulation of this model.

40 percent by material 2, and no more than 10 percent by material 3. Table 3–8 also shows the market prices for each product; assume that the firm, within its normal level of plant operations, can sell as many units of each product as it wants without affecting these prices.

FIGURE 3–2 Relationships for Solid Waste Management Problem

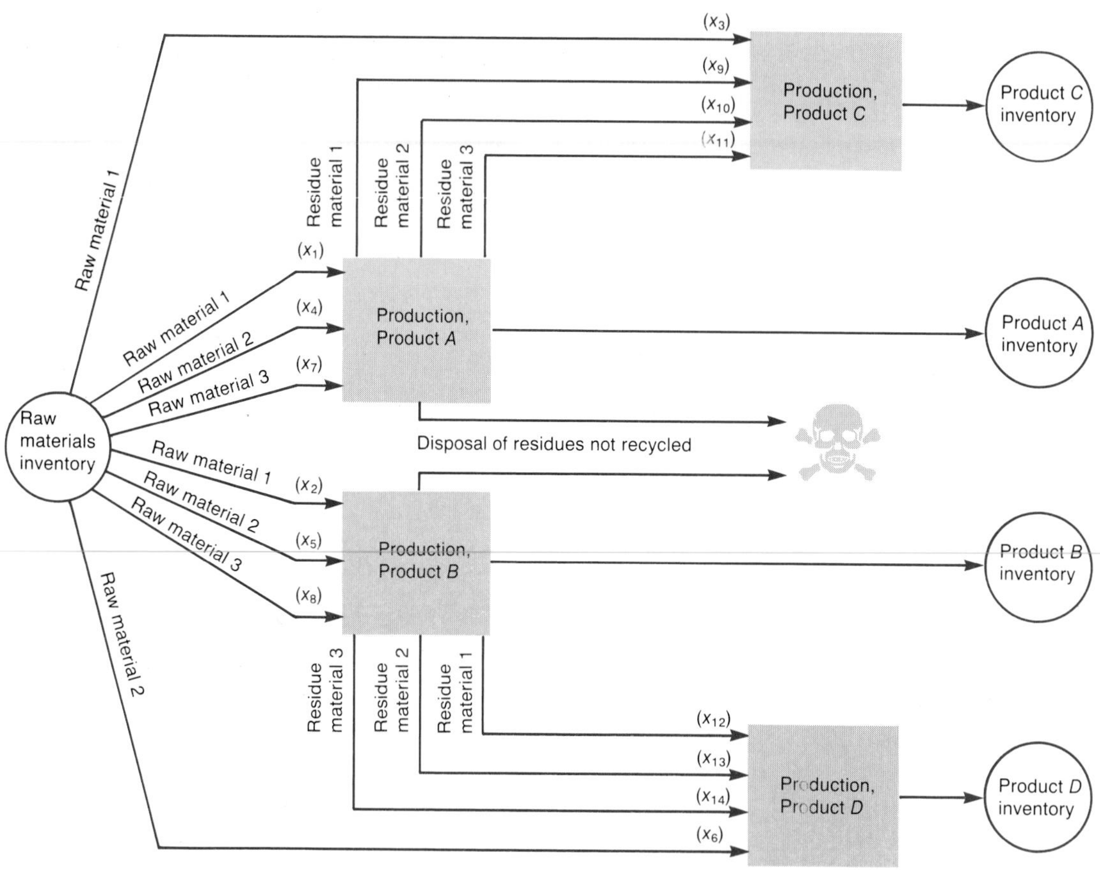

TABLE 3–8 Product and Price Specifications

Primary Product	Product Specifications	Unit Price
A	At least 20% of material 1 At least 40% of material 2 No more than 10% of material 3	$3.00
B	At least 10% of material 1 No more than 30% of material 3	2.50

In order to guarantee the ready supply of materials, the firm has agreed to purchase certain minimal amounts of each material during each planning period. Moreover, the physical capacities of the firm's manufacturing facilities limit the amount of each material it can handle during the planning period. The upper and lower bounds on the amount of each material that can be processed each period, along with the unit cost of each material, are shown in Table 3–9.

TABLE 3–9 Material Limits and Costs

Material	Minimum (lb.)	Maximum (lb.)	Unit Cost (per lb.)
1	2,000	6,000	$2.10
2	3,000	5,000	1.60
3	4,000	7,000	1.00

The nature of the manufacturing process is such that only a fraction of each material going into each product contributes directly to the primary products. The fraction not utilized in the primary products, known as the *coefficient of waste,* can be either (1) recycled (the material's chemical properties have changed as a result of the initial manufacturing operation) into a second related manufacturing process and turned into secondary products *C* and *D* or (2) disposed of in part or in total at a specific cost to the firm.

Table 3–10 shows the waste coefficients. For example, 10 percent of the amount of material 1 initially processed into product *A* is left over as a residue, and 20 percent of that processed into product *B* results in a residue.

TABLE 3–10 Waste Coefficients

	Product	
Material	A	B
1	0.1	0.2
2	0.2	0.2
3	0.4	0.5

Assume that secondary product *C* can be blended by mixing any amounts of the residues from materials 1, 2, and 3 derived from product *A* with the original (unprocessed) material 1, as long as the latter is exactly 20 percent of the mix by weight. Similarly, secondary product *D* can be blended by mixing any amounts of the residues from materials 1, 2, and 3 derived from product *B* with the original material 2, as long as the latter is exactly 30 percent by weight of the mix. No waste occurs in the manufacturing process associated with the production of these secondary products. The net revenue per pound (after all associated secondary production expenses) for products *C* and *D* are, respectively, $0.60 and $0.10.

Residue waste materials that are derived from the production of products *A* and *B* and that are not used to manufacture products *C* and *D* must be disposed of. Because the properties of the residue from different material-product combinations differ, the cost of disposing of each residue material not employed in a secondary product differs depending on the primary products from which it was derived. Table 3–11 shows these disposal costs.

TABLE 3–11 Disposal Costs

	Unit Costs ($/lb.)	
Material	**Product *A***	**Product *B***
1	$0.10	$0.05
2	0.10	0.05
3	0.20	0.40

The variable notation for the allocation of materials to products is given in Table 3–12. The notation for residues allocated to products *C* and *D* is given in Table 3–13. You may want to study Figure 3–2 to make sure you understand the product-raw material-residue relationships.

TABLE 3–12 Symbols for Material Allocation

	Allocated to Product			
Pounds of Material	***A***	***B***	***C***	***D***
1	x_1	x_2	x_3	—
2	x_4	x_5	—	x_6
3	x_7	x_8	—	—

TABLE 3–13 Symbols for Residue Allocation

	Allocated to Product	
Pounds of Residue from	***C***	***D***
Material 1—product *A*	x_9	—
Material 2—product *A*	x_{10}	—
Material 3—product *A*	x_{11}	—
Material 1—product *B*	—	x_{12}
Material 2—product *B*	—	x_{13}
Material 3—product *B*	—	x_{14}

The problem facing the firm then, is to decide:

1. **How many units of materials 1, 2, and 3 it should purchase.**
2. **How much of each material to allocate to primary products *A* and *B*.**
3. **How much of each material to allocate to secondary products *C* and *D*.**
4. **How much of each of the residue materials obtained from producing products *A* and *B* should be disposed of immediately rather than recycled into products *C* and *D*.**

The objective is to make these decisions in such a way that the resulting earnings (total revenue minus total cost) are maximized. This optimal amount of earnings must be obtained without violating the upper and lower limits on material purchases and without deviating from the product specifications on material content. At the same time, the firm must explicitly consider the various waste coefficients; the prices of products *A* and *B*; the unit costs of materials 1, 2, and 3; the net unit contribution to profit from products C and D; and the unit cost of disposing of each material-product residue combination. (Try solving this problem by other than analytic means!)

Note that the manufacture of secondary products C and D depends on an *initial commitment* of materials 1 and 2, respectively, to products C and D as well as on the residue from the production of primary products A and B. Thus secondary product and waste disposal decisions must be made when primary product decisions are made. From a total systems point of view, the optimal overall policy requires interdependence of these decisions; that is, the secondary product and/or waste disposal decisions must not be made after the primary product decision has been made.

Total profit (z) is defined as total revenue (r) minus total material costs (c) minus waste disposal costs (w); that is,

$$z = r - c - w .$$

Total revenue is determined by

$$r = 3.00(0.9x_1 + 0.8x_4 + 0.6x_7) + 2.50(0.8x_2 + 0.8x_5 + 0.5x_8) + 0.6(x_3 + x_9 + x_{10} + x_{11}) + 0.1(x_6 + x_{12} + x_{13} + x_{14})$$

where the first term represents the price of product A times the number of pounds of product A produced, the second term represents the price of product B times the number of pounds produced, the third term represents the net contribution of product C times the number of pounds of product C produced, and the last term the net contribution of product D times the number of pounds produced.[6] Total material cost is given by

$$c = 2.10(x_1 + x_2 + x_3) + 1.60(x_4 + x_5 + x_6) + 1.00(x_7 + x_8)$$

where the first, second, and third terms represent, respectively, the multiplication of the unit costs of materials 1, 2, and 3 (Table 3–9) and the quantities of materials 1, 2, and 3 purchased. The waste disposal cost is

$$w = 0.1(0.1x_1 - x_9) + 0.1(0.2x_4 - x_{10}) + 0.2(0.4x_7 - x_{11}) + 0.05(0.2x_2 - x_{12}) + 0.05(0.2x_5 - x_{13}) + 0.4(0.5x_8 - x_{14})$$

where each term represents the multiplication of the cost of disposing of a unit (pound) of a given material-product residue and the number of units of the material-product residue left over after all primary and secondary production have taken place.

Substituting the expressions for r, c, and w into the equation for z, multiplying all factors, and collecting all terms, we get the objective function to be maximized:

$$z = 0.59x_1 - 0.11x_2 - 1.5x_3 + 0.78x_4 + 0.39x_5 - 1.5x_6 + 0.72x_7 + 0.05x_8 + 0.70x_9 + 0.70x_{10} + 0.80x_{11} + 0.15x_{12} + 0.15x_{13} + 0.5x_{14} .$$

From Table 3–9 the linear inequalities that express the least and greatest amounts of each material that can be processed are:

$$x_1 + x_2 + x_3 \geq 2{,}000 \quad (1)$$

$$x_1 + x_2 + x_3 \leq 6{,}000 \quad (2)$$

$$x_4 + x_5 + x_6 \geq 3{,}000 \quad (3)$$

[6] Since the waste coefficients for material 1–product A, material 2–product A, and material 3–product A are, respectively, 0.1, 0.2, and 0.4, it follows that x_1 pounds of material 1, x_4 pounds of material 2, and x_7 pounds of material 3 will yield $(0.9x_1 + 0.8x_4 + 0.6x_7)$ pounds of product A. Right?

$$x_4 + x_5 + x_6 \leq 5{,}000 \tag{4}$$

$$x_7 + x_8 \geq 4{,}000 \tag{5}$$

$$x_7 + x_8 \leq 7{,}000\,. \tag{6}$$

For example, constraint 1 says that the number of pounds of material 1 allocated to products *A*, *B*, and *C* must be at least 2,000.

From Tables 3–8 and 3–10, the constraints that express the material content specifications for product *A* and *B* are

$$0.9x_1 \geq 0.2(0.9x_1 + 0.8x_4 + 0.6x_7)$$

or

$$0.72x_1 - 0.16x_4 - 0.12x_7 \geq 0 \tag{7}$$

$$0.8x_4 \geq 0.4(0.9x_1 + 0.8x_4 + 0.6x_7)$$

or

$$-0.36x_1 + 0.48x_4 - 0.24x_7 \geq 0 \tag{8}$$

$$0.6x_7 \leq 0.1(0.9x_1 + 0.8x_4 + 0.6x_7)$$

or

$$-0.09x_1 - 0.08x_4 + 0.54x_7 \leq 0 \tag{9}$$

$$0.8x_2 \geq 0.1(0.8x_2 + 0.8x_5 + 0.5x_8)$$

or

$$0.72x_2 - 0.80x_5 - 0.50x_8 \geq 0 \tag{10}$$

$$0.5x_8 \leq 0.3(0.8x_2 + 0.8x_5 + 0.5x_8)$$

or

$$-0.24x_2 - 0.24x_5 + 0.35x_8 \leq 0\,. \tag{11}$$

For example, from Table 3–10, since 10 percent of the amount of material 1 processed into product *A* results in a waste residue, only 90 percent of that amount of material 1 originally processed into product *A* is contained in primary product *A*. Thus if x_1 pounds are originally processed in this way, only $0.9x_1$ will appear in product *A*. In the same fashion, the contents of materials 2 and 3 in product *A* will be $0.8x_4$ and $0.6x_7$, respectively. From Table 3–8 it is specified that at least 20 percent of the total weight of product *A* must be accounted for by material 1. We also know that the total amount of product *A* produced is given by $0.9x_1 + 0.8x_4 + 0.6x_7$. Putting these facts together yields constraint 7. Constraints 8 through 11 are constructed in an analogous manner.

Table 3–10, together with the definition of variables $x_9, \ldots, x_{14}$, requires that the following constraints must also be satisfied:

$$x_9 \leq 0.1x_1 \quad \text{or} \quad x_9 - 0.1x_1 \leq 0 \tag{12}$$

$$x_{10} \leq 0.2x_4 \quad \text{or} \quad x_{10} - 0.2x_4 \leq 0 \tag{13}$$

$$x_{11} \leq 0.4x_7 \quad \text{or} \quad x_{11} - 0.4x_7 \leq 0 \tag{14}$$

$$x_{12} \leq 0.2x_2 \quad \text{or} \quad x_{12} - 0.2x_2 \leq 0 \tag{15}$$

$$x_{13} \leq 0.2x_5 \quad \text{or} \quad x_{13} - 0.2x_5 \leq 0 \tag{16}$$

$$x_{14} \leq 0.5x_8 \quad \text{or} \quad x_{14} - 0.5x_8 \leq 0\,. \tag{17}$$

For example constraint 12 states that x_9, the number of pounds of material 1–product *A* residue recycled back to secondary product *C*, cannot exceed the material 1–product *A* residue pounds ($0.1x_1$) generated by the production of product *A*.

The final two structural constraints give the material content specifications for secondary products *C* and *D*:

$$x_3 = 0.2(x_3 + x_9 + x_{10} + x_{11})$$

or

$$0.8x_3 - 0.2x_9 - 0.2x_{10} - 0.2x_{11} = 0 \tag{18}$$

$$x_6 = 0.3(x_6 + x_{12} + x_{13} + x_{14})$$

or

$$0.7x_6 - 0.3x_{12} - 0.3x_{13} - 0.3x_{14} = 0\,. \tag{19}$$

For example, constraint 18 says that exactly 20 percent of the total weight of product *C* (defined to be the sum of x_3, x_9, x_{10}, and x_{11}) must be accounted for by material 1.

Finally, the nonnegativity constraints must be satisfied;

$$x_j \geq 0, \qquad j = 1, \ldots, 14\,.$$

The solution to this rather formidable problem will be given in the next chapter.

FOLLOW-UP EXERCISES

**26. Appropriately modify the example if:
  a. All waste coefficients associated with material 2 are 0.4
  b. Thirty percent by weight of original material 2 must be present in product *C*.
  c. The maximum availability of material 2 is 15,000 pounds.
  d. The unit price of product *B* is $6.
  e. All disposal costs associated with material 1 are $1. per pound.

**27. Appropriately modify the example if the production of product *D* requires 20 percent by weight of raw material 1 in addition to the other ingredients previously specified. (Hint: Define a new variable in Figure 3–2).

**28. Assume that the production of products *C* and *D* results in 10 percent and 20 percent wastes, respectively, of all ingredients in the blends. All wastes of both products either can be combined to produce product *E* (which itself has no waste) or can be disposed of at a cost of $0.10 per pound. The net revenue per pound of product *E* is $0.40. Appropriately modify
  a. Figure 3–2.
  b. The formulation in the example.

**29. Modify the formulation to include variables that represent the weight of each product. Specifically, let x_{15} = Pounds produced of product *A*, x_{16} = Pounds produced of product *B*, x_{17} = Pounds produced of product *C*, and x_{18} = Pounds produced of product *D*.

3.4 SPECIAL ISSUES IN PROBLEM FORMULATION

Many applied problems have characteristics that would render them inconsistent with linear programming formulations. This section presents procedures for overcoming the problems associated with (1) nonnegative variables, (2) strict inequalities, and (3) deterministic assumptions.

Unrestricted and Nonpositive Variables

Section 3.2 mentioned that most applications of linear programming in management and economics require **nonnegative variables,** that is, variables restricted to either zero or positive values. We included this in the generalized LP model by specifying the *nonnegativity condition* ($x_j \geq 0$ for all j) and noted that solution methods require nonnegative variables.

Some problems, however, require different **sign conditions** on the variables. A **nonpositive variable** is not allowed to assume positive values according to the sign condition $x_j \leq 0$. An **unrestricted variable** is allowed to assume positive, zero, or negative values. For example, a variable that represents the percent change in the level of some activity is an unrestricted variable. Another example is the case where x_j represents the cash flow between a parent company and subsidiary company j.

Thus a problem having either nonpositive or unrestricted variables in its formulation would have to be modified to include only nonnegative variables before its submission to a solution algorithm. How do we do this? The answer is surprisingly simple. Replace any nonpositive variable x_j by the negative of a nonnegative variable $(-x_j)$; replace any unrestricted variable x_j by the difference between two nonnegative variables $(x_j' - x_j'')$.

▶ Example 3.10

Given the initial LP formulation:

Maximize

$$z = 5x_1 + 3x_2$$

subject to

$$x_1 + x_2 \leq 25 \quad (1)$$

$$3x_1 - 2x_2 \geq 5 \quad (2)$$

$$x_1 \geq 0$$

$$x_2 \text{ unrestricted,}$$

we express x_2 as $x_2 = x_2' - x_2''$ and substitute into the original formulation to give:

Maximize

$$\begin{aligned} z &= 5x_1 + 3(x_2' - x_2'') \\ &= 5x_1 + 3x_2' - 3x_2'' \end{aligned}$$

subject to

$$x_1 + (x_2' - x_2'') \le 25$$

or

$$x_1 + x_2' - x_2'' \le 25 \qquad (1)$$

$$3x_1 - 2(x_2' - x_2'') \ge 5$$

or

$$3x_1 - 2x_2' + 2x_2'' \ge 5 \qquad (2)$$

$$x_1, x_2', x_2'' \ge 0$$

In this case, the original problem with one nonnegative variable and one unrestricted variable is converted to a problem with three nonnegative variables. Wx_e should note that because of linear dependence between the variables x_2' and x_2'', only one of the variables can be positive for a given solution (the other will be zero). In the language of Chapters 4–6 only one of the two variables can appear in the *basis* for a given solution. Although a proof of this statement is beyond the scope of this text, you can see easily that at most one of the two variables needs to be positive to represent any value of the unrestricted variable. T0 illustrate, if $x_2 = 5$ in a solution, this would be represented by $x_2' = 5$ and $x_2'' = 0$. If $x_2 = -2$, then $x_2' = 0$ and $x_2'' = 2$.

Strict Inequality Constraints

You might have wondered how *strict* inequalities are handled in linear programming. For instance, what if the amount of money to be spent on television and radio in Example 3.7 is to be *less than* 50 percent of the budget? Constraint 2 would then be written $x_1 + x_2 < 5$ instead of $x_1 + x_2 \le 5$.

As you know, the standard form of a linear programming problem requires constraints as either *weak* inequalities ($\le$ or $\ge$) or equalities. To overcome this minor problem we simply substitute a value of the right-hand–side that is within an acceptable tolerance. For instance, the above constraint could be restated as $x_1 + x_2 \le 4.9999$.

FOLLOW-UP EXERCISES

30. Modify Example 3.10 if the sign condition on x_1 is nonpositive and both constraints are strict inequalities.
31. Express the following LP model as a generalized LP model.

Minimize

$$z = 6x_1 + 2x_2 - 3x_3$$

subject to

$$x_1 - 2x_3 \le 20 \qquad (1)$$

$$2x_1 + 3x_2 + 5x_3 > 40 \qquad (2)$$

$$x_1 - x_2 + x_3 < 25 \qquad (3)$$

$$x_1 \ge 0$$

$$x_2 \le 0$$

$$x_3 \text{ unrestricted}$$

Probabilistic Parameters

The specification of deterministic parameters is one of the key underlying assumptions of the generalized LP model. The *sensitivity analysis* developed in Chapter 5 is one way of acknowledging uncertainty in the estimation of parameters. *Dynamic programming* in Chapter 12 also considers this issue. Alternatively, if one or more parameters in an LP model are directly treated as random variables from specified probability distributions, then probabilistic or **stochastic programming** procedures are relevant.

A simple approach to solving LP models with random variables for parameters is the specification of expected values (means) for each probabilistic parameter, followed by the implementation of the usual (deterministic) solution. Unfortunately, it can be shown that this procedure will usually yield fallacious optimal solutions. For this reason, only stochastic programming procedures can guarantee the correct optimal solution (assuming, of course, that the data are correct).

Three approaches are common in stochastic programming: The first two seek an equivalent (but enlarged) deterministic version of the stochastic model, which is then solved either by the simplex method discussed in Chapters 4 and 6 (if the resulting model is linear) or by one of several nonlinear methods (if the resulting model is nonlinear); the third approach, termed **chance-constrained programming,** formulates a deterministic version of the stochastic model by incorporating what are called chance constraints (without enlarging the original problem). Significant increases in computational burden characterize the first two approaches, whereas conceptual problems in interpreting the optimal solution typify the third approach.

In general, as with all OR models, users must weigh the potential benefits associated with using more sophisticated models against the likely increase in costs that such models engender.

Later chapters discuss procedures that address other formulation issues. *Integer programming* (Chapter 8) addresses the divisibility assumption by guaranteeing integer values for decision variables. *Goal programming* (Chapter 9) allows multiple criteria in place of the single criterion in the LP objective function. *Dynamic programming* (Chapter 12) can be used for selected problems having integer variables, nonlinear objective functions and constraints, and probabilistic parameters.

3.5 SUMMARY

This chapter has examined the general structure of the LP model and discussed the underlying assumptions. It has illustrated the formulation of a diversity of applications, which will be reinforced in the following set of additional exercises.

The next six chapters will build on the foundation established in this chapter. Chapters 4–6 will emphasize methods of solving LP models as well as the important aspect of interpretation of results. Chapters 7–9 will examine special classes of LP models which broaden the scope of linear problem structures that can be addressed by mathematical programming models.

SELECTED APPLICATION REVIEW

The Chessie System in 1980 consisted of the Chesapeake and Ohio, Baltimore and Ohio, and Western Maryland railroads as well as subsidiaries. (Today, Chessie is a part of CSX Transportation, one of four major units of CSX Corp.) Chessie is a major freight operation, being the largest hauler of coal in the country. With a fleet of freight cars valued at more than $4 billion, annual expenditures for purchase, construction, and repair of their cars are extremely large. Chessie used linear programming to model fleet planning decisions. The model assists management in making decisions regarding the mix, timing, and quantity of freight cars to be repaired, built, or purchased. The model has also been extremely useful to Chessie for preparing annual budgets, planning labor stability in their Mechanical Department, developing a new policy of building cars for sale to other railroads, and planning the sale of cars in need of repair. First-year benefits included an increased contribution to profit and a $6 million reduction in the budget of the Mechanical Department. Continued use of the model (as of the time of the article) had resulted in a $2.5 million improvement in employee productivity and a $28 million increase in freight car sales.

Logo reproduced courtesy of CSX Transportation.

SOURCE: Lee C. Brosch, Richard J. Buck, William H. Sparrow, and James R. White, "Boxcars, Linear Programming, and the Sleeping Kitten," *Interfaces*, December 1980, pp. 53–61.

NORTH AMERICAN VAN LINES

Another example of linear programming being applied to fleet management is the decision support system developed for North American Van Lines. Helping management to determine the types and numbers of tractors to sell to owner/operators or to trade each week, the application has resulted in estimated savings of $600,000 per year along with other operating efficiencies.

SOURCE: Dan Avramovich, Thomas M. Cook, Gary D. Langston, and Frank Sutherland, "A Decision Support System for Fleet Management: A Linear Programming Approach," *Interfaces*, June 1982, pp. 1–9.

BancOhio
National Bank

Most large banks have centralized check-processing centers that process checks delivered from different branch offices. The timely processing of checks is important to minimize *float*—the amount of money represented by outstanding checks in the process of collection. The efficient processing of checks depends on the scheduling of encoder operators. The scheduling is complicated by the high variability of check volumes on a daily and hourly basis and by a fixed number of available encoding machines.

The BancOhio National Bank in Columbus, with assets exceeding $4 billion and with more than 130 branches, successfully applied linear programming in the development of a shift-scheduling system for its encoder operators. The model developed for the bank determines the number of full-time and part-time encoder clerks to assign to each of a set of predetermined shifts such that weekly wages (regular time and overtime) and float costs are minimized. Bank officials estimated first-year savings from the modified shift schedules to be $1 milllion.

Logo reproduced courtesy of BancOhio National Bank.

SOURCE: L. J. Krajewski and L. P. Ritzman, "Shift Scheduling in Banking Operations: A Case Application," *Interfaces*, April 1980, pp. 1–8.

DECISION SUPPORT SYSTEMS: PRODUCTION PLANNING FOR DAIRY MANAGEMENT

The Dairyman's Cooperative Creamery Association in Tulare, California, is the largest single milk processing plant in one location in the United States. Receiving approximately 5 million pounds of raw milk each day, a primary management concern is being able to move the milk through the plant in the production of the approximately 50 products that can be made at this location. A small optimization-based decision support system was developed for the Association and was implemented on a microcomputer. The milk-flow analysis program (MFAP) is an interactive, user-friendly software system used to plan daily production levels of all products and to forecast inventory levels. Imbedded within the planning system is a linear programming model that generates the daily schedules and forecasts.

The total cost of developing the system, including the cost of hardware, was less than $15,000. The results of implementation are that daily schedules are generated each morning in less than half an hour, compared with four hours per day before implementation. Daily plant throughput has

(continued)

increased by an estimated 150,000 pounds of milk per day. Annual profitability is estimated to have increased by $48,000 as a result of the increased throughput. As a result of the additional time freed up for supervisors, the overall explicit and implicit benefits are expected to contribute approximately $100,000 per year to annual profits.

SOURCE: Robert S. Sullivan and Stephen C. Secrest, "A Simple Optimization DSS for Production Planning at Dairyman's Cooperative Creamery Association," *Interfaces*, September–October, 1985, pp. 46–53.

SELECTED REFERENCES

Cook, Thomas M., and Robert A. Russell. *Introduction to Management Science*. 3rd ed. Englewood Cliffs, N.J.: Prentice-Hall, 1985.

Davis, K. Roscoe, and Patrick G. McKeown. *Quantitative Models for Management*. 2nd ed. Boston: Kent Publishing, 1984.

Hadley, G. *Linear Programming*. Reading, Mass.: Addison-Wesley Publishing, 1962.

Hillier, Frederick S., and Gerald J. Lieberman. *Introduction to Operations Research*. 4th ed. San Francisco: Holden-Day, 1987.

Lev, Benjamin, and Howard J. Weiss. *Introduction to Mathematical Programming*. New York: Elsevier North-Holland, 1982.

Taha, Hamdy A. *Operations Research: An Introduction*. 3rd ed. New York: Macmillan, 1982.

Thierauf, Robert J., Robert C. Klekamp, and Marcia L. Ruwe. *Management Science: A Model Formulation Approach with Computer Applications*. Columbus, Ohio: Charles E. Merrill Publishing, 1985.

ADDITIONAL EXERCISES

Note: For the following problems, we suggest that you utilize the problem-solving framework to guide you in your formulations.

32. ***Capital Expansion Model.*** A company wishes to purchase additional machinery in a capital expansion program. Three types of machines may be purchased: *A*, *B*, and *C*. Machine *A* costs $25,000 and requires 200 square feet of floor space for its operation. Machine *B* costs $30,000 and requires 250 square feet of floor space. Machine *C* costs $22,000 and requires 175 square feet of floor space. The total budget for this expansion program is $350,000. The maximum available floor space for the new machines is 4,000 square feet. The company also wishes to purchase at least one of each type of machine.

Given that machines A, B, and C can produce 250, 260, and 225 pieces per day, the company wants to determine how many machines of each type it should purchase so as to maximize daily output (in units) from the new machines.

a. Explicitly define your decision variables and formulate the LP model.

b. Assess the validity of the four underlying LP assumptions for this problem.

33. ***Agricultural Allocation Model.*** A university has offered a rent subsidy alternative to the families living in the graduate student housing complex. Near the complex are 20 acres that can be farmed. The university will allow the residents' organization to farm all or part of this land. Any derived profits can be apportioned to reducing the rent for the graduate families. Families may keep whatever produce they wish for their own use. The university has agreed to buy produce from the students, up to certain limits, for use within the dining services.

The students have agreed to plant lettuce, potatoes, tomatoes, and soybeans. Table 3–14 summarizes for each group over the growing season the projected yield per acre, the student demand, the maximum university demand, and estimated profit per unit. Note that there is no student or university demand for soybeans. Rather, this crop would be sold directly to a commodity broker for profit.

TABLE 3–14

Crop	Yield per Acre	Student Demand	Maximum University Demand	Profit
Lettuce	20,000 heads	8,000 heads	40,000 heads	$0.10 per head
Potatoes	20,000 lb.	10,000 lb.	100,000 lb.	$0.05 per lb.
Tomatoes	5,000 lb.	5,000 lb.	50,000 lb.	$0.20 per lb.
Soybeans	50 bu.	—	—	$3.60 per bu.

Formulate the LP model that would enable the students to determine the number of acres they should allocate to each crop so as to maximize total profit. Assume that student demands are to be satisfied exactly. Profit is earned on crops sold to the university (over and above student demands) and on the soybean crop.

34. Modify Exercise 33 to include the following conditions:

a. Lettuce, potatoes, tomatoes, and soybeans require 5,000, 2,500, 6,500 and 3,500 gallons of water per acre, respectively, over and above natural rainfall during the growing season. Available water is limited to 40,000 gallons.

b. Because of required crop rotation, the number of acres planted in soybeans can be no more than 50 percent of the combined total acres planted in the other three crops.

c. Composted manure is to be used for fertilizer. The requirements are 2,500 lb. per acre for lettuce, 1,000 lb. per acre for potatoes, 3,000 lb. per acre for tomatoes, and 900 lb. per acre for soybeans; however, only 40,000 lb. of fertilizer are available overall.

d. Much as the graduate students and their families enjoy working the farm, academic demands (and other pleasures) limit total available labor to 1,000 hours over the growing season. Lettuce requires 75 hours per acre, potatoes 35 hours per acre, tomatoes 60 hours per acre, and soybeans 90 hours per acre.

e. Discuss the extent to which you feel the four underlying LP assumptions satisfy this formulation.

35. ***Production-Vendor Model.*** Sniffy Smoke Sensers, Inc. is experiencing a tremendous growth in demand for its household smoke detectors. Sniffy produces both an AC model

and a battery-operated model. It has an opportunity to be the exclusive supplier for a major department store chain, The Seers Company. Seers wishes to receive at least 10,000 AC models and 8,000 battery-operated models each week.

Sniffy's unanticipated prosperity has left it short of sufficient capacity to satisfy the Seer's contract over the short run. However, there is a subcontractor who can assist Sniffy by supplying the same types of smoke detectors. Sniffy must decide how many units it will make of each detector and how many units it will buy from the subcontractor. Data in Table 3–15 summarize the production, price, and cost parameters.

TABLE 3–15

	Model (hours per unit)		
	AC	**Battery**	**Hours Available per Week**
Production Department	0.15	0.10	1,000
Assembly Department	0.20	0.20	1,000
Packaging Department	0.10	0.15	1,200
Total cost per unit	$7.00	$6.25	

The subcontractor has a weekly capacity of 15,000 units per week. However, it cannot produce more than 6,000 units per week of the AC model. For units supplied by the subcontractor, the cost per unit to Sniffy is $7.50 and $6.75, respectively, for the AC and battery models. The contractor has specified a minimum weekly order of 2,500 units.

The contract with Seers calls for Sniffy to receive $9 for each AC model and $10 for each battery model. Formulate the LP model that would allow Sniffy to determine the number of units of each type to produce and to buy so as to maximize total profit. Woule you say that divisibility poses a practical problem here? Explain. Do we know in advance that the subcontractor must be used?

36. ***Feed Mix Model.*** The manager of a feed lot operation is interested in blending a feed mix for the herd. The manager can purchase five different types of grain, each characterized by different nutritional contents. Table 3–16 indicates the nutritional contents (in ounces) per pound and the cost per pound of each grain type.

TABLE 3–16 Nutritional Content in Ounces per Pound of Grain

	Grain Type				
Nutritional Element	**1**	**2**	**3**	**4**	**5**
1	1.0	1.5	0.9	1.2	1.4
2	0.5	0.7	0.4	0.6	0.5
3	0.8	1.2	1.3	0.7	1.0
Dollar cost per pound	0.20	0.24	0.22	0.25	0.27

The manager wants the final feed mix to meet certain minimum nutritional requirements. Specifically, the final mix should have a composition such that:

1. Nutritional element 1 is at least 5 percent of the weight of the final mix.
2. Nutritional element 2 is at least 3 percent of the weight of the final mix.
3. Nutritional element 3 is at least 4 percent of the weight of the final mix.

The manager wishes to make 10,000 pounds of feed and to determine the number of pounds of each grain to include in the mix such that the nutritional specifications are satisfied.

a. If the objective is to minimize the cost of the feed mix, formulate the LP model for this problem.

b. How close might reality come to meeting the four underlying LP assumptions?

37. ***Capital Investment Model.*** A pension fund wishes to invest in one or more of six possible investments. Financial analysts have estimated the present value of effective annual rates of return for each alternative for the next three years. Table 3–17 illustrates these estimates. The data in this table indicate that the present value of investing \$10,000 in alternative 1 is the sum of \$1,200 (0.12 × \$10,000) for year 1, \$1,000 (0.10 × \$10,000) for year 2, and \$800 (0.08 × \$10,000) for year 3, for a total present value of \$3,000.

TABLE 3–17 Effective Annual Rate of Return

Investment	Year 1	Year 2	Year 3
1	0.12	0.10	0.08
2	0.14	0.10	0.10
3	0.15	0.12	0.08
4	0.10	0.12	0.15
5	0.08	0.12	0.18
6	0.25	0.15	0.05

Management has decided that \$300,000 will be invested. At least \$50,000 is to be invested in alternative 2 and no more than \$40,000 in alternative 5. Total investment in alternatives 4 and 6 should not exceed \$75,000, as these are risky investments.

a. If the objective is to maximize the present value of total dollar return for the three-year period, formulate the LP model for how much capital to invest in each alternative.

b. Can you comment on how relevant each underlying LP assumption is to this problem?

38. ***Rental Car Acquisition Model.*** A car rental agency wants to garner a share of the local car rental market. Having decided to capitalize on the public's inability to spell, the owner/manager of Hurts, Inc. now needs to purchase cars. Realizing that many travelers are not concerned about such frills as windows, hubcaps, radios, and heaters, the owner has decided to rent used cars rather than new cars.

Inez Tina (I. T.) Hurts has allocated \$50,000 for her initial purchases. She will purchase intermediate, compact, and subcompact cars. Average costs for these cars are \$1,000, \$1,200, and \$1,500, respectively. I. T. needs to decide how many cars of each type to purchase.

When making her decisions, I. T. must consider a number of factors. First, she estimates that gas availablity for her business will be limited to 30,000 gallons during the coming year. She estimates that initial fill-ups for her rentals will consume 800, 650, and 500 gallons per year, respectively, for each intermediate, compact, and subcompact car in her fleet. She also has 4,000 maintenance hours available during the year. The three models are expected to require 100, 85, and 75 hours of maintenance per year, respectively. An asssessment of the local demand for rental cars has concluded that I. T. should have no more than 10 intermediate cars in her fleet and no more than 30 compacts.

a. If annual receipts are expected to equal $2,500, $2,300, and $2,400, respectively, for each intermediate, compact, and subcompact car in the fleet, formulate the LP model that maximizes total annual revenue subject to appropriate constraints.

b. Can you comment on the relevancy of the LP assumptions to this problem?

39. ***Personnel Model.*** A new Federal Environmental Protection Organization is being formed, and 2,500 professional and 800 nonprofessional positions need to be filled. Recruiting costs average $1,000 for each professional position and $400 for each nonprofessional position. Typically, these costs are 10 percent higher than average for recruiting women and 25 percent higher for recruiting minorities (men and women). HHS has examined state employment records and has mandated that women should constitute at least 50 percent of new hirings in both professional and nonprofessional positions within the agency and minorities at least 40 percent of new hirings in each category. In addition, the number of minority men hired must be at least equal to the number of nonminority men. Let

x_1 = Number of nonminority women hired as professionals.
x_2 = Number of nonminority women hired as nonprofessionals.
x_3 = Number of minority women hired as professionals.
x_4 = Number of minority women hired as nonprofessionals.
x_5 = Number of nonminority men hired as professionals.
x_6 = Number of nonminority men hired as nonprofessionals.
x_7 = Number of minority men hired as professionals.
x_8 = Number of minority men hired as nonprofessionals.

Formulate the LP model that minimizes total recruiting costs in filling the agency's positions. Would you say that divisibility poses a practical problem here? Explain.

40. ***Contract Awards Model.*** An automobile manufacturer wants to award contracts for the supply of four different fuel injection system components. Four contractors have submitted bids on the components; Table 3–18 summarizes the prices bid per unit. Where no entry is made, the contractor submitted no bid.

TABLE 3–18

	Component			
Contractor	1	2	3	4
1	$25	—	$30	$40
2	$28	$80	$28	—
3	—	$75	$33	—
4	$30	$82	—	$42
Demand (units)	15,000	30,000	10,000	20,000

The demand for a component does not have to be supplied completely by one contractor. In fact, certain contractors have indicated maximum quantities that can be supplied at the bid price. Contractor 1 can supply no more than 18,000 of item 4, contractor 2 no more than 3,000 of item 1, contractor 4 no more than 15,000 units of item 2 and no more than 5,000 units of item 4.

There is no provision that awards must go to the low bidder. The automobile manufacturer wants to determine how many units of each item should be awarded to each contractor so as to minimize total costs for the four items. Contractor 4 has specified that it requires a minimum award of $500,000 if it is to supply any items at all. The automobile manufacturer wishes to avoid awarding over $1.2 million in awards to any one company. Formulate the LP model that can solve this problem if x_{ij} is the number of units awarded to contractor i for item j. Would you say that divisibility poses a practical problem here? Explain.

41. ***Transportation Model.*** Transportation models are perhaps the most extensively used linear models from an economic viewpoint. Oil companies alone literally spend millions of dollars annually to implement these models. This example introduces a simple version of the classical model. A more detailed presentation is left to Chapter 7.

    Suppose a chemical company manufactures liquid hydrogen at two different locations in the Northeast and must supply three storage depots in the same geographic region. Table 3–19 provides the relevant data for a given planning horizon. Assume that there are no differences in the product produced at the two plants and that each plant can supply each depot.

TABLE 3–19 Transportation Data: Shipping Costs *(Dollars per 1,000 gallons)*

	Depot			
Plant	**1**	**2**	**3**	**Supply (1,000 gallons)**
1	30	4	8	50
2	5	10	20	70
Demand (1,000 gallons)	40	60	20	120

The company wishes to determine the number of 1,000s of gallons to distribute from each plant to each depot. The objective is to minimize total transportation costs while assuring that the needs of each depot are satisfied and that each plant ships no more than its capacity. Formulate the LP model for this problem. *Hint*: Let x_{ij} equal the number of thousands of gallons shipped from plant i to depot j.

42. ***Blending Model I.*** A large distiller blends five bourbons into three final blends of whiskey. Table 3–20 summarizes the very precise recipes for the final blends of whiskey, the cost and availability information for the five component bourbons, and the wholesale price per gallon of each final blend. The numbers in the body of the table indicate the percentages each component bourbon contributes to the volume of each final blend. For example, Table 3–20 indicates that component 2 composes 15 percent of final blend 1.

TABLE 3–20 Bourbon Blending Data

	Final Blend (percent)				
Component	**1**	**2**	**3**	**Cost per Gallon**	**Maximum Availability per Week (gallons)**
1	20	10	30	$2.50	50,000
2	15	40	10	2.75	40,000
3	30	20	10	2.25	30,000
4	10	10	20	3.00	10,000
5	25	20	30	3.50	20,000
Wholesale price per gallon	$6.50	$7.50	$7.00		

Weekly processing capacity is 125,000 gallons, and the distiller wishes to operate at capacity. There is no problem selling the final blends, although minimum weekly production levels of 20,000, 20,000, and 10,000 gallons, respectively, have been established for the three final blends.

The manufacturer wishes to determine the number of gallons of each bourbon to use in each blend so as to maximize total weekly contribution to profit and overhead.

Formulate this as an LP model if the decision variable x_{ij} represents the number of gallons of component i used in blend j.

43. In the previous exercise, formulate the LP model if the decision variable x_j represents the number of gallons blended of final blend j.
44. ***Blending Model II.*** Assume in Exercise 42 that there are volume losses incurred in the blending process; that is, each gallon input results in less than a gallon of output. These losses are a function of the component used. The *loss coefficients* associated with the five component bourbons are 5 percent, 3 percent, 4 percent, 6 percent, and 2 percent, respectively. Further assume that the plant capacity of 125,000 gallons per week directly relates to components (the input) rather than to final blends (the output). Reformulate Exercise 42 using these assumptions.
45. ***Portfolio Model.*** Portfolio theory is an important specialization in the area of finance. Here we present a simplified scenario.

An endowment fund manager is attempting to determine a "best" investment portfolio and is considering six alternative investments. Table 3–21 indicates point estimates for the price per share, the annual growth rate in the price per share, the annual dividend per share, and a measure of the risk associated with each investment.

TABLE 3–21 Portfolio Data

	Alternative					
	1	2	3	4	5	6
Current price per share	\$80	\$100	\$160	\$120	\$150	\$200
Projected annual growth rate	0.08	0.07	0.10	0.12	0.09	0.15
Projected annual dividend per share	\$4.00	\$6.50	\$1.00	\$0.50	\$2.75	—
Projected risk	0.05	0.03	0.10	0.20	0.06	0.08

In this case risk is defined as the standard deviation in return. Dollar return per share of stock is defined as price per share one year hence less current price per share *plus* dividend per share. The fund has \$2.5 million to invest, and it wishes to satisfy the following conditions:

(1) The maximum dollar amount to be invested in alternative 6 is \$250,000.
(2) No more than \$500,000 should be invested in alternatives 1 and 2, combined.
(3) Total weighted risk should be no greater than 0.10, where

$$\text{Total weighted risk} = \frac{\sum_j [(\text{Dollars invested in alternative } j) \cdot (\text{Risk of alternative } j)]}{\text{Total dollars invested in all alternatives}}.$$

(4) For the sake of diversity, at least 100 shares of each stock should be purchased.
(5) At least 10 percent of the total investment should be in alternatives 1 and 2 combined.

(6) Dividends for the year should be at least $10,000.

If the objective is to maximize total dollar return (from both growth and dividends), formulate the LP model for determining the optimal number of shares to purchase of each investment alternative. (Assume that this is a one-year model and that fractional shares of securities may be purchased.)

46. ***Security Force Scheduling.*** The owner of a large industrial park wishes to determine the work schedule for security officers. The union contract specifies that officers are to work a normal shift of eight hours. They may work an additional four hours on an overtime basis with compensation at one and one half their hourly pay rate. Security officers are paid $6 per hour except for those working between midnight and 6 A.M. Any hours worked during this period are compensated for by a $1-per-hour shift differential.

The owner has determined a daily needs schedule that divides the day into 12 two-hour periods. Table 3–22 indicates the different periods and the minimum number of security officers required.

TABLE 3–22 Security Force Scheduling Data

	Period											
	1	2	3	4	5	6	7	8	9	10	11	12
From	Midnight	2 A.M.	4 A.M.	6 A.M.	8 A.M.	10 A.M.	Noon	2 P.M.	4 P.M.	6 P.M.	8 P.M.	10 P.M.
To	2 A.M.	4 A.M.	6 A.M.	8 A.M.	10 A.M.	Noon	2 P.M.	4 P.M.	6 P.M.	8 P.M.	10 P.M.	Midnight
Minimum number of security officers	26	28	30	25	20	18	16	16	18	20	24	24

Security officers always start work at the beginning of one of these time intervals. The owner wants to determine (*a*) the number of security officers to schedule for a normal eight-hour shift and (*b*) the number to schedule for 12-hour shifts which includes the regular eight-hour shift plus four hours of overtime. The objective is to minimize total daily wages while assuring the required coverage for each period. Carefully define your decision variables, and formulate the LP model for this problem. Does divisibility pose any particular problem?

47. ***Trim Loss (or Cutting Stock) Model.*** This classical LP scenario includes such applications as paper slitting and textile cutting, whereby jumbo reels are cut into smaller reels having various widths. Consider the following situation.

A paper mill produces jumbo reels of paper 60 inches wide. The company receives orders for reels 12 inches wide, 15 inches wide, 18 inches wide, and 25 inches wide. The manufacturer has received orders for 300, 250, 200, and 150 reels, respectively, of the 12-, 15-, 18-, and 25-inch reels. The firm wishes to determine how to meet these orders so as to minimize total waste.

Waste is defined as any leftover portions of a jumbo reel that cannot be used to meet demand. There are two sources of waste: *trim loss* and *surplus*. For example, if a jumbo reel is slit into two 25-inch reels, there will be leftover paper (trim loss) having a width of 10 inches. Since there is no use for 10-inch reels (insofar as the outstanding order is concerned), the 10 inches is a measure of waste. Note that this cutting pattern yields two 25-inch reels for each jumbo reel that is cut. Because different cutting patterns can create multiple reels out of jumbo reels, there is a likelihood that surplus or excess will be cut. For example, if 210 12-inch reels result from the cutting process and only 200 are required, then $(210 - 200) \times 12$ is a measure of surplus waste.

There are different ways (patterns) in which a 60-inch reel can be slit. (See Table 3–23.) The problem is to determine how many jumbo reels should be slit in each pattern so as to minimize total waste. As a start, determine the different patterns that can be used in slitting a jumbo reel, and note the attendant loss. Only consider patterns yielding waste less than the smallest required width. (There are 17 of these.) To help you along, we have filled in the relevant information for the first (arbitrarily selected) pattern. Pattern 1 specifies a jumbo reel is to be split into two 25-inch reels yielding a trim loss of 10 inches per jumbo reel.

TABLE 3–23 Patterns for Slitting 60-Inch Reels

Required Width (inches)	Pattern																
	1	2	3	4	5	6	7	8	9	10	11	12	13	14	15	16	17
12	0																
15	0																
18	0																
25	2																
Trim loss (inches)	10																

Define x_j as the number of jumbo reels to be slit according to pattern j and E_i as the excess (surplus) number of reels of required width i. Formulate the LP model for this problem. What are the implications of divisibility?

48. ***Cargo Loading Model.*** This class of models addresses decisions concerning the loading of cargo onto vessels, airplanes, trains, spacecraft, and so forth. Here we describe an LP scenario.

Consider a problem whereby limited quantities of four types of merchandise are available to be loaded into three holds of a freighter. These represent maximum quantities that can be shipped. Relevant data are given in Tables 3–24 and 3–25.

TABLE 3–24 Freighter Capacities

Hold (j)	Weight (tons)	Volume (cu. ft.)
1. Forward	100	6,000
2. Center	125	9,000
3. Aft	75	7,500

TABLE 3–25 Cargo Data

Merchandise (i)	Weight (tons)	Volume (cu. ft. per ton)	Revenue (dollars per ton)
1. Sugar	150	48.6	700
2. Rice	175	60.0	750
3. Ore	600	4.1	250
4. Soybeans	100	55.0	300

The captain needs to know how much weight of each type of merchandise is to be loaded in each hold such that total revenue is maximized without violating weight and volume constraints. Moreover, the merchandise must be loaded such that the "trim" of the ship is preserved. This means that the ratio of loaded weight in a hold to the weight capacity in that hold must be identical for all three holds. Formulate this problem as an LP model. (Hint: There are 12 variables and 12 structural constraints.)

CASE University Placement*

The placement office at State University coordinates the student interviewing process for about 1,500 students per academic year. Each student is seeking half-hour interview slots, but the placement office observes that each student typically wants inteviews with only 10 to 15 companies in which he or she is most interested. Because the placement office would like to ensure that all eligible students receive interviews if possible, the office limits the number of interviews to 20 during the original interview registration process. Each company specifies a number of interview slots, which may range from 11 to 168. Each student has a set of attributes (e.g., the student may or may not be a marketing major). The company specifies the minimum number of students it would like to interview who possess a particular attribute (e.g., it would like to interview at least three marketing majors). Students rank their first 20 choices and then allocate 1,000 utility points across the 20 choices. The placement officer then has clerical staff assign students to companies for interviews; but he thinks there must be a better way, particularly because of the number of complaints he is receiving from the students and clerical staff. You are offered a financial assistantship for the next academic year to provide a better way. Before awarding this assistantship, however, the placement officer has the good sense to ask you for a general description of your approach, detailed enough to be convincing but not necessarily completely fleshed out with every number. After finding out that the placement officer's objective is to maximize the utility of the interview schedule to the students, you study the problem and formulate a model. What is your presentation? If your decision variables are zero-one or yes-no, do they violate any linear programming assumption? If you solve a linear programming problem and ignore its integer restrictions, what does it mean if the solution involves no fractions? What model in Chapter 3 most resembles the model you present to the placement officer?

---

*This case is adapted from A. V. Hill, J. D. Naumann, and N. L. Chervany, "SCAT and SPAT: Large-Scale Computer-Based Optimization Systems for the Personnel Assignment Problem," *Decision Sciences*, April 1983, pp. 207–20.

4

Linear Programming: Geometric and Computerized Solutions

Chapter Outline

The previous chapter emphasized LP model formulation. This chapter introduces two types of solution processes for LP models: geometric solutions and computerized solutions.

4.1 OVERVIEW

This chapter and the next one take the perspective that most students using this book are potential users of LP models, rather than designer-technicians. We therefore provide an understanding of various solution procedures, giving special emphasis to the use and interpretation of computer-based solutions.

Our aim is to create an educated user: one who can formulate (or read) LP models, who understands underlying assumptions, who can implement a computer-based solution, and who can interpret the results. The preceding chapter focused on formulations and assumptions. This chapter and the next provide sufficient background material for you to feel comfortable with the results generated from a computerized "black box."

Geometric solutions are based on methods that make use of graphs in a two-dimensional coordinate system. This method is not used in actual practice; rather its purpose is to give a better understanding of the geometric properties of LP models and their solutions. "A picture is worth a thousand words" perhaps says it best for the user who does not need mathematical derivations.

In reality the system of linear inequalities that describes LP models requires a solution by one of many *algebraic methods,* the most popular being the *simplex method.* This chapter briefly overviews the simplex method, since most computerized procedures are based on this algorithm.

The next chapter continues our treatment of solutions by applying geometric and computerized methods to *postoptimality* or *sensitivity analysis.*

We *do* believe that a more thorough treatment of the "nuts and bolts" of the simplex method enhances one's technical understanding and ability to apply the technique. Thus Chapter 6 presents a detailed treatment of the simplex method. Those not requiring the level of detail in Chapter 6 can go on to Chapter 7 and beyond without loss of continuity.

4.2 SYSTEMS OF LINEAR INEQUALITIES

In LP formulations the set of constraints is represented by a **system of linear inequalities.** A first concern in solving LP problems is to identify the set of values for the decision variables that satisfy this system. Once these values are identified (if any exist), the next step is to search for the one(s) that maximize or minimize the objective function.

The Solution Space

In this section we consider graphical implications for systems of linear inequalities described by two decision variables x_1 and x_2. The presence of only two variables allows us to plot an inequality in **two-space**, a graph with two coordinate axes. This procedure makes possible the visualization of the **permissible half-space,** or the set of points (x_1, x_2) that satisfies the inequality.

To illustrate this concept, consider the following generalized inequality:

$$a_1x_1 + a_2x_2 \leq b\,, \tag{4.1}$$

where a_1, a_2, and b are assumed to be positive constants.

Let us solve Equation 4.1 for x_2 as a function of x_1. Subtracting a_1x_1 from both sides of the inequality and dividing both sides by a_2 we get[1]

$$x_2 \leq \left(\frac{b}{a_2}\right) - \left(\frac{a_1}{a_2}\right)x_1 \tag{4.2}$$

Focusing on the equality part (=) of Equation 4.2, we see that we have the *slope-intercept* form of a linear function, $y = mx + i$, where m and i represent the slope and y-intercept, respectively. Hence in this case b/a_2 represents the y-intercept, and $-a_1/a_2$ indicates the slope of the linear function as plotted in Figure 4–1.

Note that x_2 is on the vertical axis and x_1 is on the horizontal axis. Also we have

FIGURE 4–1 Permissible Half-Space

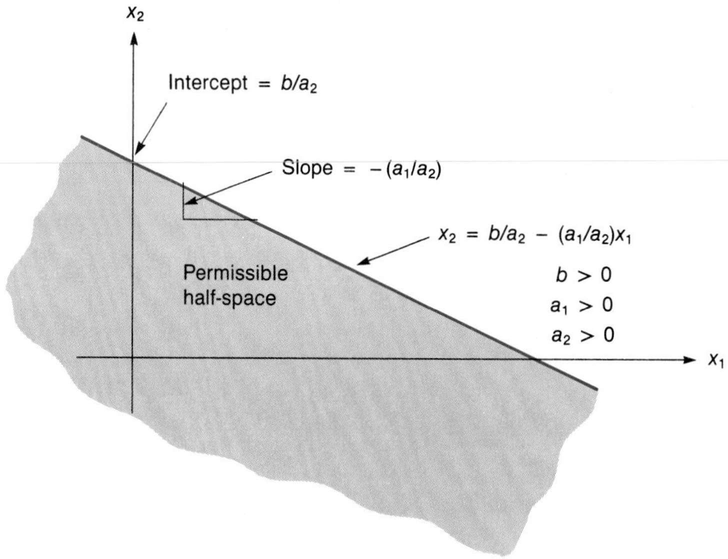

assumed that the parameters b, a_1, and a_2 are all positive, which gives us a *negatively*-sloped line with a *positive* intercept in Figure 4–1. In general, the signs of a_1 and a_2 determine whether the line has a positive or negative slope; the signs of b and a_2 establish either a positive, negative, or zero intercept. Figure 4–1 illustrates the most common case. We treat other cases later.

In Figure 4–1 the permissible half-space includes those points on the line and those points below and to the left of the line. Those on the line satisfy the equality (=) part of the inequality; those to the left satisfy the strict inequality (<) part. For an inequal-

[1]If a_2 were negative, the sense of the inequality would be reversed.

ity of the ($\geq$) type, the permissible half-space would include points on, above, and to the right of the line. If each inequality in a system of linear inequalities in two variables were graphed in a single diagram, the intersection of all of the permissible half-spaces would indicate the overall permissible region for the system. Typically, this is termed the **solution space** or **feasible region.**

▶ Example 4.1 Air Cargo Model

A Boston wholesaler has been caught in the middle of a strike by independent truckers. Meat is normally supplied from a packinghouse in Chicago by refrigerated trucks. The strike, however, has created a meat crisis that can be alleviated only by air freight. The wholesaler has chartered a plane and wishes to determine the amount of beef and pork to have shipped so that the profit contribution is maximized subject to weight and volume constraints of the cargo plane. Table 4–1 provides the relevant information for this problem.

TABLE 4–1 Data for Air Cargo Problem

Meat Type	**Profit Contribution ($100 per container)**	**Volume (cu. yd. per container)**	**Weight (1,000 lb. per container)**
Beef	7	5	2
Pork	10	4	5
Volume and weight availabilities		24	13

If x_1 and x_2 represent, respectively, the number of containers of beef and pork to be included in the shipment, the corresponding LP model is

Maximize

$$z = 7x_1 + 10x_2$$

subject to

$$\text{Volume constraint: } 5x_1 + 4x_2 \leq 24 \quad (1)$$

$$\text{Weight constraint: } 2x_1 + 5x_2 \leq 13 \quad (2)$$

$$x_1, x_2 \geq 0 .$$

(Here we ignore the integer restriction on containers and allow fractional containers. In Chapter 8 we will show how integer restrictions could be handled using integer programming.)

To determine the solution space for this problem, we must first graph the constraint set given by the structural constraints 1 and 2. Starting with the volume inequality, we first graph the equality portion

$$5x_1 + 4x_2 = 24$$

by finding two points on the line. The simplest procedure is to set $x_1 = 0$ and to solve for x_2, giving $x_2 = 6$, or the coordinate (0, 6). Next we let $x_2 = 0$ and solve for x_1, giving the point (4.8, 0). Connecting these two points on the graph gives us the equality portion of constraint 1, as illustrated in Figure 4–2.

FIGURE 4–2 Permissible Half-Space for Volume Constraint

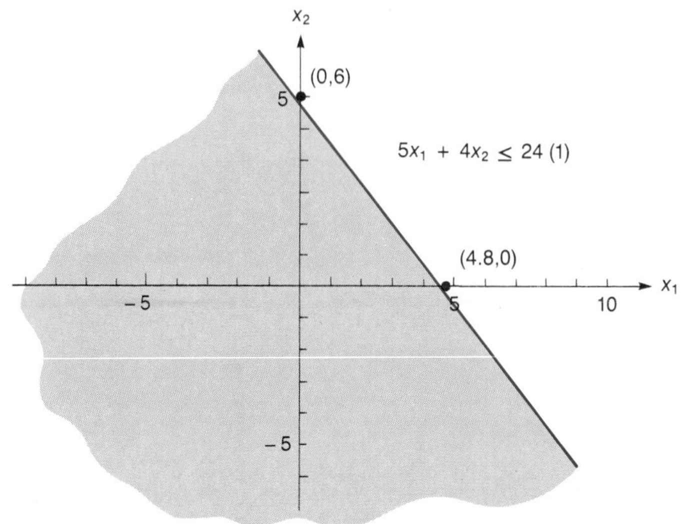

A simple procedure for determining the permissible half-space is to verify whether or not the origin (0, 0) satisfies the constraint. Substituting (0, 0) for (x_1, x_2) in constraint 1 suggests that the origin is permissible since $0 \leq 24$ satisfies the constraint. Thus all pairs of values (x_1, x_2) that satisfy the constraint are on, to the left of, or below the line, as shown in Figure 4–2.

The pairs of values (x_1, x_2) that lie on the line in Figure 4–2 represent the different quantities of beef and pork that would utilize all available volume on the cargo plane. Can you interpret the meaning of the pairs (x_1, x_2) that lie to the left and below the line?

The weight constraint is graphed in a similar manner, as illustrated in Figure 4–3. Interpret the meaning of the pairs (x_1, x_2) that lie on this line and the pairs that lie to the left and below the line.

The *solution space* for this problem consists of the pairs (x_1, x_2) that satisfy *all* constraints, including the nonnegativity restriction. The nonnegativity condition automatically restricts us to points within the first (northeast) quadrant. When we consider this and at the same time merge Figures 4–2 and 4–3, the resulting solution space for the air cargo problem appears in Figure 4–4.

Thus the solution space is the region given by the intersection of all permissible half-spaces, including that representing the nonnegativity condition. It follows that all points (x_1, x_2) within and on the boundary of the solution space simultaneously satisfy *all* constraints.

FOLLOW-UP EXERCISES

1. Answer the following regarding Example 4.1:
   a. Can we ship one container of beef and three of pork? Why or why not? Locate the corresponding point in Figure 4–4.
   b. Can we ship two containers of beef and one of pork? Why or why not? Locate the corresponding point in Figure 4–4.
   c. What are the coordinates of the point of intersection of the two structural constraints? What unique interpretation is associated with this pair of values?

FIGURE 4–3 Permissible Half-Space for Weight Constraint

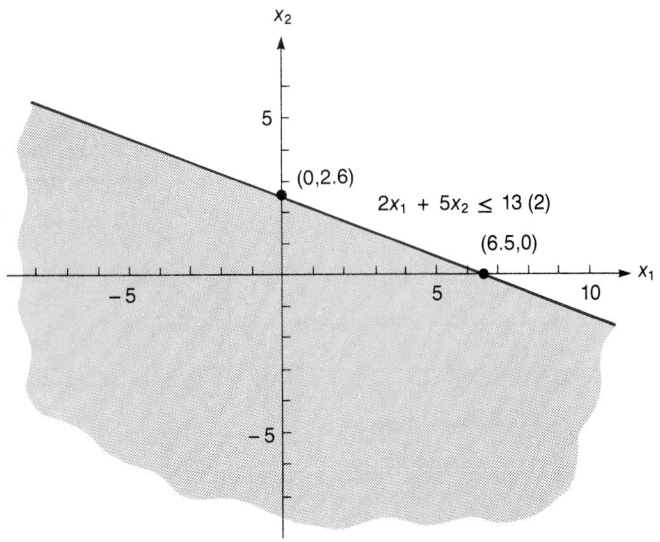

FIGURE 4–4 Solution Space for Air Cargo Model

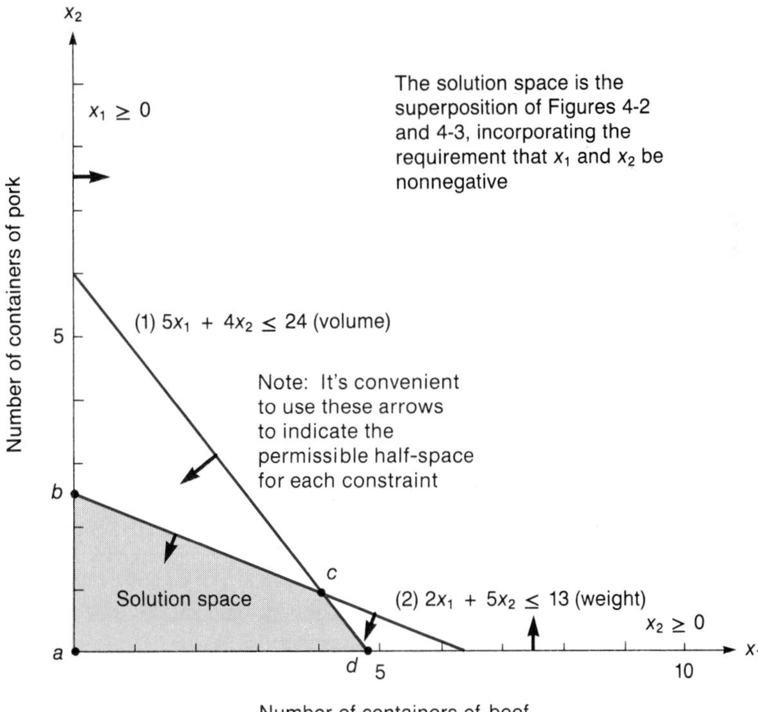

d. In Figure 4–4, interpret the shipping recommendations associated with points *b*, *c*, and *d*. Comment on the utilization of volume and weight capacities at these points.

Aberrations in the Solution Space

Certain abnormalities regarding solution spaces are "common" enough to warrant their recognition and an understanding of their implications. In this subsection we identify three such solution-space aberrations.

If there is no common intersection for the permissible half-spaces, no points satisfy *all* constraints, and there is no solution space. This is termed an empty or **null solution space,** as illustrated in Figure 4–5, where no points satisfy all three constraints. When this happens, the model is frequently said to have **no feasible solution.**

FIGURE 4–5 Null Solution Space *(No feasible solution)*

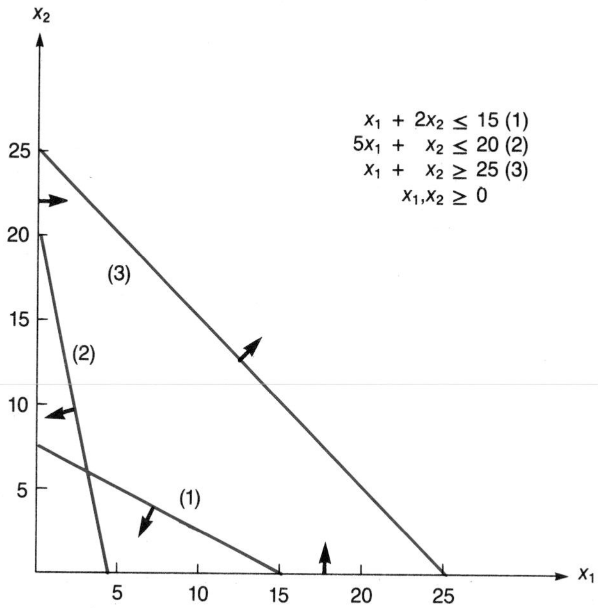

Several explanations are possible for the existence of a null solution space. Errors in formulating the constraints are highly likely, especially for real-world applications containing hundreds of constraints. Incorrect constraints are frequently attributable to errors in logic, errors in estimating the parameters (constants), and errors in assigning the correct sense to inequalities. Alternatively, the constraints might be formulated correctly, but the conditions are so restrictive that no values of the variables simultaneously satisfy all of the constraints. The inconsistency among the constraints may reflect the reality of the situation (e.g., require a minimum profit goal that cannot be achieved because of limited resources).

A second aberration is an **unbounded solution space.** As illustrated in Figure 4–6, an unbounded solution space extends without limit. In some LP models, this situation causes no problems and simply reflects the nature of the model constraints. In other models, an unbounded solution space may indicate the omission of one or more constraints that should have been included in the original model.

FIGURE 4–6 Unbounded Solution Space

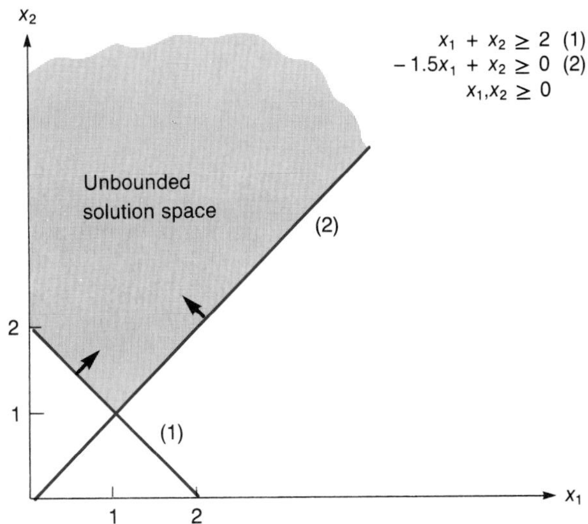

Redundancy is the third abnormality. Consider the solution space in Figure 4–4. Suppose we specify a third constraint that states "the total number of containers shipped must not exceed six." that is,

$$x_1 + x_2 \leq 6. \tag{3}$$

Adding this constraint to the system gives us Figure 4–7. Constraint 3 is said to be a **redundant constraint,** since its inclusion in the constraint set has no effect on the previous solution space, and its elimination has no effect. It is redundant if it contributes nothing to the definition of the solution space. Graphically, this means that the constraint does not define an edge on the area of feasible solutions. Stated differently, a redundant constraint is satisfied if all other constraints in the model are satisfied. In Figure 4–7 the points that satisfy constraints 1 and 2 automatically satisfy constraint 3.

What are the implications of the three aberrations? First, no optimal solution is possible with a null solution space. With an unbounded solution space, there *may* be an optimal solution in a bounded direction. Finally, redundant constraints do not preclude the existence of an optimal solution.

4.3 GEOMETRIC SOLUTIONS

Given the existence of a solution space, we are now ready to search for optimal values of the decision variables.

Feasible and Optimal Solutions

A **feasible solution** is a set of values for the decision variables (x_j's) that satisfies both the nonnegativity condition and all structural constraints in the problem. All points in a solution space or feasible region are termed **feasible solutions.**

FIGURE 4–7 Solution Space with Redundant Constraint

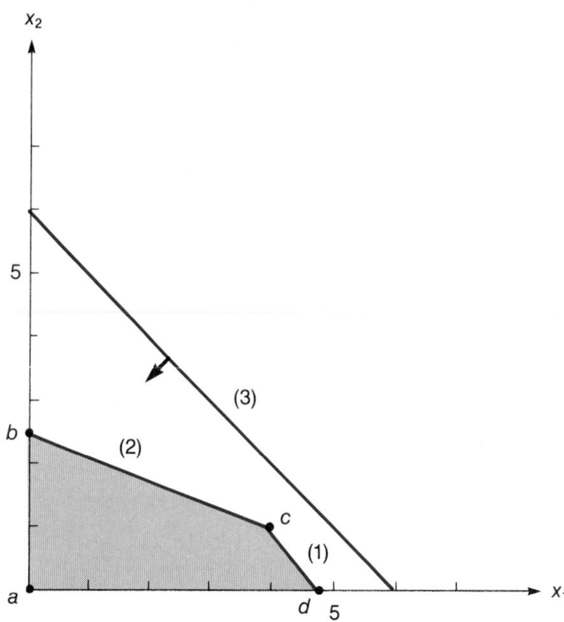

When a problem has a feasible region, *the number of feasible solutions is usually infinite.*[2] For example, the solution space for the air cargo model in Figure 4–7 is the **polygon** $\overline{abcd}$ that contains an infinite number of feasible solutions, as follows: (1) The infinite number of feasible solutions within the edges of the polygon; (2) the infinite number of feasible solutions along the edges of the polygon; and (3) the finite number of feasible solutions at the **corner points** or **vertices** or **extreme points** of the polygon, as given by points a, b, c, and d in Figure 4–7.

Our objective is to determine the **optimal solution,** that is, a feasible solution that yields the best or optimal value for the objective function z. In practice the task of identifying an optimal solution from an infinite number of feasible solutions is not as awesome as it sounds.[3]

Incorporating the Objective Function

For two-variable problems, a generalized objective function is represented by

$$z = c_1x_1 + c_2x_2 .$$

Notice that, as with the constraints, this function can be written in the form

$$x_2 = \left(\frac{z}{c_2}\right) - \left(\frac{c_1}{c_2}\right)x_1 \tag{4.3}$$

where z/c_2 is the y-intercept and $-c_1/c_2$ is the slope.

[2]The exception is a solution space defined by a single point.

[3]In some cases an infinite number of optimal solutions is possible, as we demonstrate later.

Plots of the function at different values of z are called **contours**. Figure 4–8 illustrates three contours for $z = z_1$, $z = z_2$, and $z = z_3$. The contours clearly show that greater intercepts are associated with greater values for the criterion (z) and vice versa; that is,

$$\frac{z_1}{c_2} > \frac{z_2}{c_2} > \frac{z_3}{c_2}$$

implies that $z_1 > z_2 > z_3$ for a constant $c_2 > 0$. Note that contours are parallel, since the slope $(-c_1/c_2)$ is the same for each contour. Moreover, by definition, all coordinates (x_1, x_2) along a given contour yield the same value of z.

FIGURE 4–8 Contours of Objective Function Given by Equation 4.3

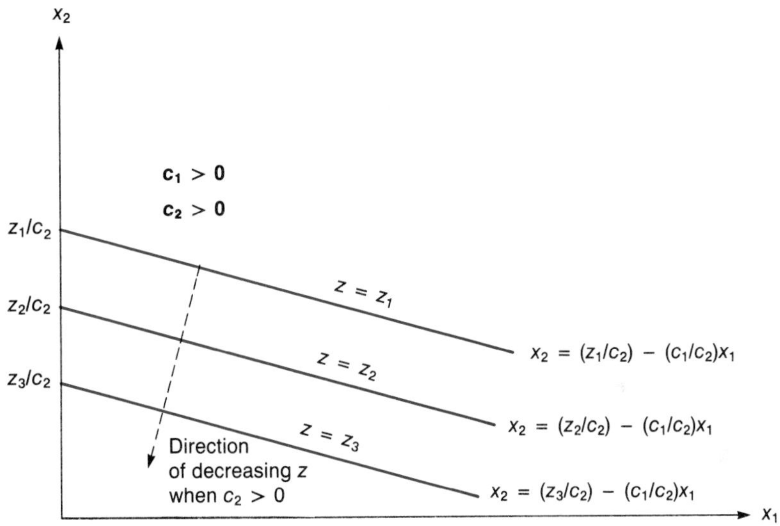

Since one is free, within the confines of the solution space, to choose values for x_1 and x_2 that optimize the function, the problem resolves itself into *superimposing a plot of the function 4.3 on the graph of the solution space and shifting the function parallel to itself in a direction that optimizes the criterion (downward for minimization problems and upward for maximization problems when* $c_2 > 0$*) until the solution space does not permit further shifting*. As demonstrated in the following example, the objective function ultimately passes through a corner point of the polygon; hence the optimal solution is determined by simultaneously solving the two constraints that form the optimal corner point.

▶ Example 4.2 Air Cargo Model Continued

In Example 4.1 we constructed the solution space for the air cargo model, but did not consider the objective of maximizing total profit contribution. Our objective is to find values for x_1 and x_2 that maximize the objective function

$$z = 7x_1 + 10x_2$$

without violating any of the constraints or nonnegativity conditions.

To accomplish our objective we must superimpose the objective function on the graph of the solution space given by Figure 4–4. First we express the objective function in its *slope-intercept* form, as follows:

$$x_2 = \left(\frac{z}{10}\right) - \left(\frac{7}{10}\right)x_1$$

or

$$x_2 = 0.1z - 0.7x_1 \tag{4.4}$$

This gives a slope of −0.7 and an intercept of 0.1z. To plot Equation 4.4 on the graph of the solution space, we must arbitrarily select a value for z. If we assign a value of, say, 14 to z, then Equation 4.4 becomes

$$x_2 = 1.4 - 0.7x_1. \tag{4.5}$$

We now have a line with intercept 1.4 and slope −0.7 that plots as the contour labeled $z = 14$ in Figure 4–9.

FIGURE 4–9 Solution to Air Cargo Model

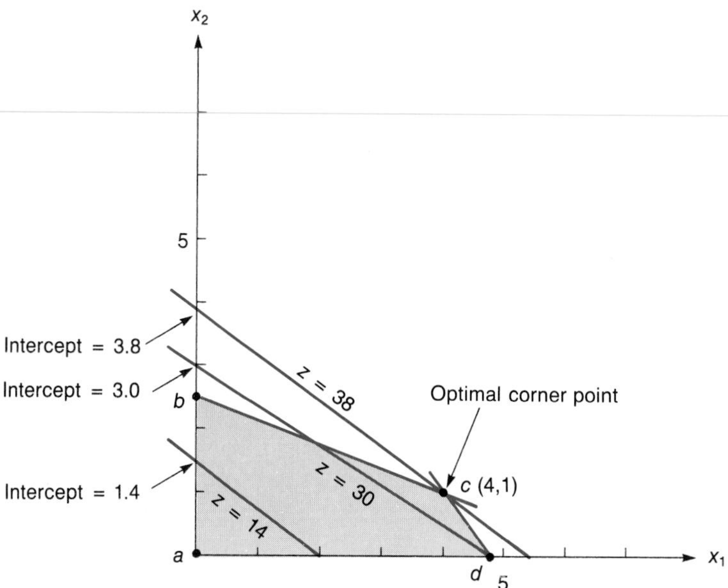

The pairs of (x_1, x_2) values along this contour represent the different quantities of beef and pork that can be shipped to yield a profit of 14 ($100s). Since both objective function coefficients are positive, we would expect that sliding this line parallel to itself, up and to the right, would yield higher values of z. To confirm this, we next sketched the contour $z = 30$. Note that a portion of this contour passes through the solution space. Thus there are feasible quantities of beef and pork that can be shipped and yield a profit of 30 ($100s). The points on this contour that *do not* lie within the solution space represent quantities that would generate the same profit; however, it is impossible to air freight these quantities, since they violate the weight constraint.

To maximize the value of z, we want to shift the objective function line up and to the right as far as possible while assuring that at least *one* point passes through the solution space. As seen in Figure 4–9, we can shift outward until the last point touched in the solution space is point c. If the line is shifted further, it represents higher values for z; however, the solution would not be feasible because none of the points on the line would be contained in the solution space. Thus the optimal solution is at corner point c.

In Figure 4–9 the coordinates of point c are (4, 1). Substituting these values into the objective function, the corresponding (and maximum) value for z is 38. Maximum profit of 38 ($100s) will be realized if four containers of beef and one container of pork are shipped. Note in Figure 4–9 that the contour $z = 38$ only touches extreme point c.

In our example we read the optimal values directly from the graph as (4, 1) at point c. The usual approach (which you should try in the exercises) is to sketch a rough graph of the solution space, superimpose and shift the objective function to determine the optimal corner point, and simultaneously solve the two equations that define the optimal corner point.

The Corner-Point Method

Because we know that an optimal solution will occur at one of the corner points on the solution space, graphical solutions can be generated easily using the following procedure.

Corner-Point Method

1. Graphically identify the solution space.
2. Determine the coordinates of each corner point on the solution space.
3. Substitute the coordinates of the corner points into the objective function to determine the corresponding value of the objective function.
4. An optimal solution occurs in a maximization problem at the corner point yielding the highest value of z and in a minimization problem at the corner point yielding the lowest value of z.

Table 4–2 illustrates the corner-point method for the air cargo model.

TABLE 4–2 Corner-Point Method: Air Cargo Model

	Corner Point	(x_1, x_2)	$z = 7x_1 + 10x_2$
	a	(0, 0)	$7(0) + 10(0) = 0$
	b	(0, 2.6)	$7(0) + 10(2.6) = 26$
Optimal corner point ⟶	c	(4, 1)	$7(4) + 10(1) = 38$
	d	(4.8, 0)	$7(4.8) + 10(0) = 33.6$

Since we are trying to maximize the value of the objective function, we identify point c (as before) as the optimal corner point.

FOLLOW-UP EXERCISES

2. Rework Example 4.2 if the profit contributions for beef and pork are, respectively, 20 ($100s) and 10 ($100s). Do we have a divisibility problem? Explain.
3. Modify the solution space for the air cargo model by adding two more constraints: "Ship no more than four containers in all" (note that this represents a "tightening" of the redundant constraint in Figure 4–7); and "ship at least two containers in all." Find the optimal solution and optimal value for z based on the objective function $7x_1 + 10x_2$.
4. Graphically solve the following LP problem.

   Maximize

$$z = 10x_1 + 3x_2$$

   subject to

$$\begin{aligned} 2x_1 + x_2 &\leq 10 && (1)\\ 2x_1 + 3x_2 &\leq 18 && (2)\\ x_1 &\geq 2 && (3)\\ x_2 &\geq 1 && (4)\\ x_1, x_2 &\geq 0 \end{aligned}$$

5. Modify the preceding exercise by adding:
   a. The fifth constraint $2x_1 + 3x_2 \leq 24$.
   b. The fifth constraint $2x_1 + 3x_2 \geq 24$.
6. Graphically solve the following LP problem.

   Minimize

$$z = 4x_1 + 3x_2$$

   subject to

$$\begin{aligned} x_1 + x_2 &\geq 8 && (1)\\ 2x_1 + x_2 &\geq 10 && (2)\\ 3x_1 + 5x_2 &\leq 45 && (3)\\ x_1, x_2 &\geq 0 \end{aligned}$$

7. Given the general objective function $z = c_1x_1 + c_1x_2$, verify the following characteristics. *Case 1:* $c_1 > 0$ and $c_2 > 0$ make for *negative* slope and *downward* shift for *minimization. Case 2:* $c_1 < 0$ and $c_2 > 0$ make for *positive* slope and *downward* shift for *minimization. Case 3:* $c_1 > 0$ and $c_2 < 0$ make for *positive* slope and *downward* shift for *maximization. Case 4:* $c_1 < 0$ and $c_2 < 0$ make for *negative* slope and *downward* shift for *maximization.* In general, does $c_2 > 0$ imply an upward shift of the objective function for maximization?

Alternative Optima

Alternative optimal solutions can exist if the objective function is *parallel* to a *binding* constraint. Figure 4–10 illustrates this for a *maximization* problem when $c_2 > 0$. Two points are worth remembering regarding alternative optimal solutions. First, the number of optimal solutions is infinite. In this particular instance, any point along the edge $\overline{bc}$ represents an optimal solution. Second, the constraint that is parallel to the objective function must be a *binding* constraint, one that prohibits further improvement in the objective function. For example, if we required minimization of the objective function in Figure 4–10, the optimal solution would occur at point *e*. With the minimization objective, the constraint represented by $\overline{bc}$ does not bind the movement of the objective function in the direction of minimization.

FIGURE 4–10 Alternative Optimal Solutions along $\overline{bc}$ for Maximization Objective ($c_2 > 0$)

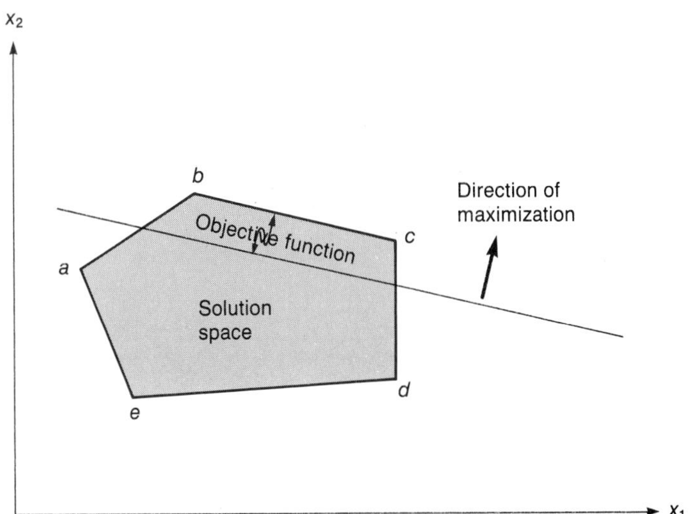

Alternative optimal solutions are signaled in the corner-point method when two corner points result in the same optimal value for z.

If alternative optima occur in actual practice, it simply means that more than one combination of values for the decision variables will result in the optimal value for the stated objective. The decision maker has choices, each of which generates the same optimal value for the stated criterion. Such a situation allows for consideration of other (perhaps qualitative) criteria not formally stated by the LP model. Related to this, see Exercise 11.

Unbounded Solutions

Earlier in the chapter we illustrated an *unbounded solution space*. When such a solution space exists, the value of the objective function may be either bounded or unbounded. In Figure 4–11, for example, the objective function would generate an **unbounded solution** if the objective is to *maximize* the criterion function; in other words, there is no upper limit on the value the objective function can assume because there are lower limits on (x_1, x_2) given by the line segment joining points *a* and *b* but no *upper* limits. For the same figure, if the objective were to *minimize* the criterion, then the optimal solution would be *bounded* at point *b*. Thus we must distinguish carefully between an unbounded solution space and an unbounded solution—the former is a necessary condition for the latter, but the latter will come about *only* if the solution space is unbounded in the direction of the optimal solution.

FIGURE 4–11 Bounded and Unbounded Solutions

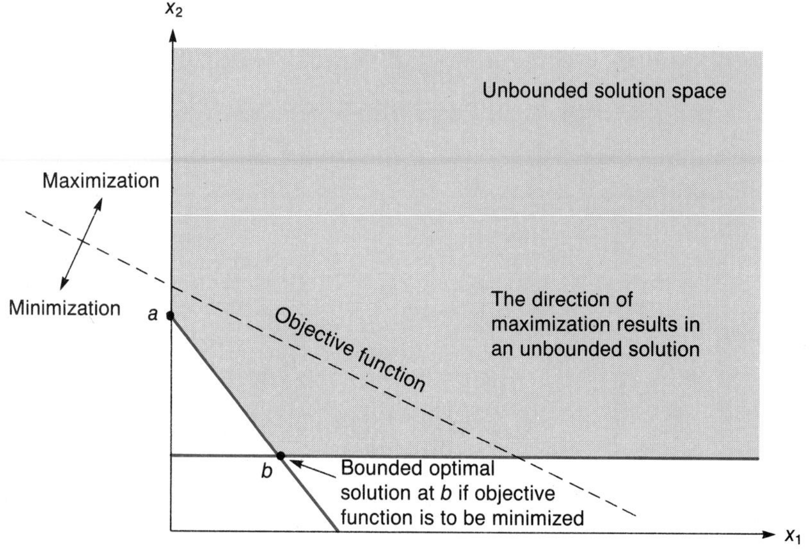

Unbounded solutions are typically the result of an error in the formulation of the problem. We challenge you to identify a real-world problem having no bound on the objective function. Thus evidence indicating an unbounded solution should give the analyst cause to review the formulation of the original problem.

Convex Sets

The solution spaces we have illustrated in Figure 4–12 are examples of **convex sets.** By definition, a convex set is an enclosure having the property that a straight line connecting any two arbitrarily selected points lies entirely within the set.

Figure 4–12 illustrates both convex (A, B, C) and nonconvex (D, E, F) sets. Putting on a nonconvex green can be frustrating; you might observe that 95 percent of all golf course greens are convex. Convex sets A and B are called **linear convex sets,** since all edges are linear.

The following statements play a fundamental role in the theory of linear programming.

> The solution space formed by linear inequalities is necessarily a linear convex set.

FIGURE 4–12 Convex (A, B, C) and Nonconvex (D, E, F) Sets

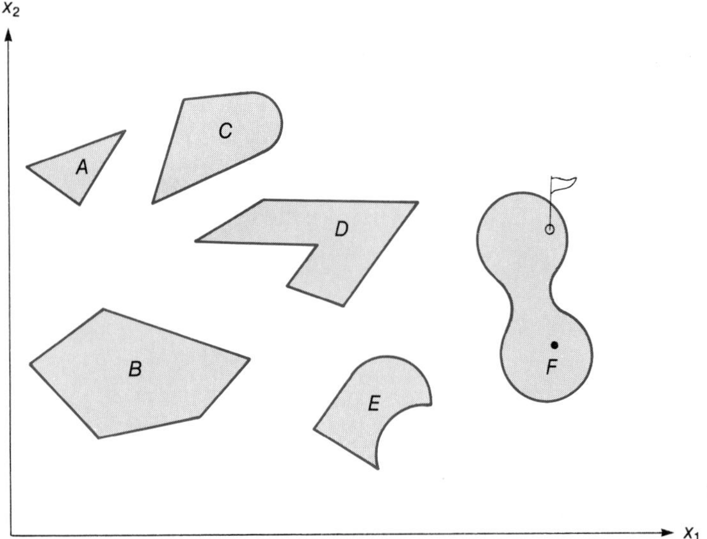

Sets A and B in Figure 4–12 illustrate this statement. You should verify by sketches that the nonconvex set D is an impossibility when constructed by linear inequalities.

> The optimal solution based on a linear objective function always includes a vertex in a linear convex set.

This statement is true regardless of the contour's inclination (slope) or direction of optimization. You should confirm this by determining maxima and minima for various objective functions in sets A and B of Figure 4–12. Before reading on, can you guess why this result is so important? *An optimum-seeking algorithm need only examine vertices in the solution space, thereby eliminating from consideration the infinite number of feasible solutions within and along the edges of the solution space.*

To conclude this section on geometric properties of the LP model, we might note that linear constraints in two variables are *lines* in **two-space** that form feasible regions *or* solution spaces called **convex polygons;** linear constraints are *planes* in **three-space** and *hyperplanes* in ***n*-space,** and form solution spaces called **convex polyhedrons.**

> Polyhedrons formed by hyperplanes are necessarily convex sets; the optimal hyperplane contour passes through a vertex (or vertices in the alternative optima case) of the convex polyhedron.

The above statement simply extends the results of the two-space case to the n-space case. Of course, proofs of these statements are based in mathematics, since we cannot visualize n-space polyhedrons when $n > 3$.

FOLLOW-UP EXERCISES

8. Consider the linear convex set below.

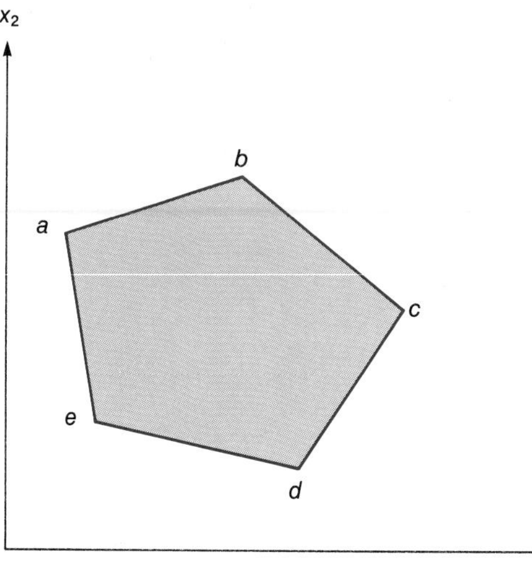

a. Take out your ruler (your pencil might do in a pinch) to represent the objective function and convince yourself that regardless of inclination and direction, the optimal solution always includes one or more of the extreme points a, b, c, d, e.
b. Why can't we guarantee that the optimal solution would include a vertex in convex set c of Figure 4–12?

9. Graphically solve the following LP problem:

Maximize

$$z = 9x_1 + 6x_2$$

subject to

$$3x_1 + 5x_2 \leq 45 \qquad (1)$$

$$6x_1 + 4x_2 \leq 48 \qquad (2)$$

$$x_1, x_2 \geq 0 .$$

10. Draw the solution space given by:

$$x_1 + x_2 \geq 4 \qquad (1)$$

$$4x_1 + x_2 \geq 8 \qquad (2)$$

$$x_1 \geq 1 \qquad (3)$$

$$x_2 \leq 6 \qquad (4)$$

$$x_1, x_2 \geq 0$$

and determine the optimal values of x_1, x_2, and z given each of the following objectives.

a. Maximize $z = 20x_1 + 10x_2$
b. Minimize $z = 20x_1 + 10x_2$
c. Minimize $z = 20x_1 + 5x_2$

11. The following LP model relates to a two-product, product mix decision where x_j = Number of units produced per week of product j. The objective function is one of profit maximization, and the two structural constraints reflect limited labor hours available each week in two departments.

    Maximize

    $$z = 8x_1 + 6x_2$$

    subject to

    $$2x_1 + 4x_2 \leq 160$$
    $$4x_1 + 3x_2 \leq 170$$
    $$x_1, x_2 \geq 0.$$

    a. Solve this problem using the corner-point method, and verify that alternative optimal solutions (product mixes) exist.
    b. Fully investigate incentives or disincentives for operating at the two different corner points that tied for maximum profit. Incorporate qualitative factors that might influence the decision.

12. Suppose the following coordinates have been calculated for a linear convex set.

Corner Point	Coordinates (x_1, x_2)
a	(60, 80)
b	(60, 70)
c	(50, 70)
d	(20, 100)
e	(20,120)

    Determine the optimal solution if we wish to:
    a. Maximize $z = 28{,}000 - 15x_1 - 10x_2$.
    b. Maximize $z = x_1 + x_2$.
    How do you know that your solution is an optimal solution?

4.4 OVERVIEW OF THE SIMPLEX METHOD

Solution Preliminaries

Consider the structural constraint set for the air cargo problem first described in Example 4.1

$$\text{Volume (cu. yds.): } 5x_1 + 4x_2 \leq 24 \quad (1)$$

$$\text{Weight (1,000 lbs.): } 2x_1 + 5x_2 \leq 13 \quad (2)$$

where x_1 = Number of containers of beef; x_2 = Number of containers of pork.

Because we know that the optimal solution is always at an extreme point, we could solve the air cargo problem by enumeration, using the corner-point method. We located the four vertices on the solution space, substituted their coordinates into the objective function, and concluded that the optimal solution occurred at (4, 1) with a maximum z-value of 38.

All LP problems could be solved this way except for the computational nightmare. With only two variables and two constraints, we had four vertices to examine. For problems with 100 variables and 100 constraints, complete enumeration would be out of the question. The following methods were developed to search the vertices efficiently. Because they are based on solving *systems of equations,* we must first convert from inequalities to equalities.

Real and Slack Variables

To convert a ($\leq$) constraint to an equation, we add a *nonnegative* **slack variable** S_i to the left-hand side. For example, constraints 1 and 2 are converted to equations as follows:

$$5x_1 + 4x_2 + S_1 \quad = 24$$
$$2x_1 + 5x_2 + S_2 \quad = 13\,.$$

Slack variables added to ($\leq$) constraints.
Note consistency of subscripts and equation numbers.

The reasoning for constraint 1 is as follows. Since the left-hand side ($5x_1 + 4x_2$) must be less than or equal to the right-hand side (24), it follows that by adding a nonnegative variable S_1 to the left-hand side, we can "balance" the two sides. In other words, S_1 picks up any "slack" in the left-hand side of constraint 1. Note that the subscript i on S_i is based on the constraint number. Thus S_1 is the slack variable for constraint 1, and S_2 is the slack variable for constraint 2. To distinguish between the decision variables (x_j's) and the slack variables (not to mention other variables we add later), the decision variables are often called **real variables.**

The introduction of the slack variables S_1 and S_2 allows the restatement of the original ($\leq$) constraints as equations. In addition to serving this algebraic function, the slack variable *can* have a meaning within the context of the problem. In this application S_1 and S_2 represent unused capacity in the airplane. In constraint 1, $5x_1 + 4x_2$ is the number of cubic yards of volume utilized by shipping x_1 containers of beef and x_2 containers of pork, and the right-hand side constant 24 is the volume capacity of each plane in cubic yards. Thus S_1 represents the unused or "slack" volume capacity. To illustrate, if $x_1 = 2$ and $x_2 = 3$, S_1 must equal 2 for constraint 1 to be satisfied. The interpretation is that shipping two containers of beef and three of pork will use 5(2) + 4(3) or 22 cubic yards of the volume capacity, leaving ($S_1 =$) 2 cubic yards of unused or slack capacity.

Consider an LP problem where the structural constraints have been converted to equations by adding slack variables. What we now have is an *augmented* LP model with a system of m simultaneous linear equations (that is, one equation for each structural constraint) in n variables (the total number of variables given by real plus slack variables). In this case an infinite number of solutions is possible since the system has more unknown variables than equations.[4]

---

[4]We *know* that the number of variables is greater than the number of equations ($n > m$) because we add one slack variable to *each* constraint. In Chapter 6 we demonstrate that such systems of equations potentially have an infinite number of solutions.

Now that we have added supplemental (slack) variables, we can redefine our LP model generally as;

Max or min

$$z = \mathbf{cx}$$

subject to

$$\mathbf{Ax} = \mathbf{b}$$

$$\mathbf{x} \geq 0$$

where

$$\mathbf{c} = (c_1, c_2, \ldots, c_n)$$

$$\mathbf{x} = \begin{pmatrix} x_1 \\ x_2 \\ \vdots \\ x_n \end{pmatrix}, \quad \mathbf{b} = \begin{pmatrix} b_1 \\ b_2 \\ \vdots \\ b_m \end{pmatrix}, \quad \text{and} \quad \mathbf{A} = \begin{bmatrix} a_{11} & a_{12} & \cdots & a_{1n} \\ a_{21} & a_{22} & \cdots & a_{2n} \\ \vdots & & \ddots & \vdots \\ a_{m1} & a_{m2} & \cdots & a_{mn} \end{bmatrix}.$$

Assuming there is a feasible solution, the task of a solution procedure is to reduce the number of solutions that need to be considered from an infinite number to a finite subset of solutions that contains the optimal solution(s) and then to find the optimal solution(s).

One way of looking at linear programming is this: If we only knew which m of our n variables were in the optimal solution, we could just solve the system of m variables in m equations and be done with it. For example, the air cargo problem gave us

$$5x_1 + 4x_2 + 1S_1 + 0S_2 = 24 \qquad (1)$$

$$2x_1 + 5x_2 + 0S_1 + 1S_2 = 13\,. \qquad (2)$$

If we knew the optimal solution involved x_1 and S_2, we could set $x_2 = 0$ and $S_1 = 0$ and solve the equations

$$5x_1 \qquad = 24$$

$$2x_1 + S_2 = 13\,.$$

Of course, the catch is that we do not know *which* variables will be in the optimal solution.

Basic Feasible Solutions

In order to describe our search for an optimal solution, let us start with some definitions. A **feasible solution** is any set of values for the n variables that satisfies both the structural and nonnegativity restrictions. A **basic solution** is a solution obtained by setting $n - m$ variables equal to zero and solving the system of equations for the values of the remaining m variables. These m variables are called **basic variables** and are said to constitute a **basis.** The remaining $n - m$ variables, or those that have been forced to a value of zero, are termed **nonbasic variables.**

Before we go any further, you should realize that for us to solve a system of equations where the number of variables (n) is greater than the number of equations (m), we must *first* create a balance between the number of variables and equations; that is, we reduce the number of variables to m by assigning values of zero to $(n - m)$ variables. Put another way, we generate a solution by selecting m variables from among n variables and assigning values of zero to the remaining $(n - m)$ variables. Suppose we have a system of ($m =$) two equations containing ($n =$) five variables. We could generate a solution by assigning values of zero to $(n - m)$ or $5 - 2 = 3$ variables, leaving us with two remaining variables and two equations. We could then solve the two equations for the remaining two variables.

The number of ways of selecting m variables from among n variables ($n > m$) is given by the combinatorial formula:

$$\binom{\text{Total number of variables}}{\text{Number of equations}} = \binom{n}{m} = \frac{n!}{m!\,(n - m)!} \tag{4.6}$$

Hence Equation 4.6 provides the maximum number of solutions that need to be considered, or the maximum number of *basic solutions*.[5]

This finite subset of basic solutions can be reduced further by considering strictly nonnegative basic solutions. A **basic feasible solution** is a basic solution that satisfies the nonnegativity restriction. The remarkable result is that *the optimal solution is contained within the subset of basic feasible solutions*. This is guaranteed by a theorem in linear programming that states:

> A closed linear convex set bounded from below has an optimal solution at an extreme point.

This theorem applies to our LP formulation because our system of linear inequalities forms a linear convex set, and this convex set is "bounded from below," as guaranteed by the nonnegativity restriction, $x_j \geq 0$.[6] Closed simply means that the set includes its boundaries.

[5]Note that, in general, we can generate an infinite number of solutions by assigning *arbitrary* values to the $(n - m)$ variables not chosen for solution. The fact that we assign values of zero to these variables gives rise to a finite subset of *basic* solutions.

[6]Another theorem in linear programming guarantees that linear inequalities form a linear convex set, a result we developed visually in our geometric solutions of Section 4.3. Also note from our geometric solutions that the axes for x_1 and x_2 serve to bound the solution space from "below." Moreover, the optimal contour line always passed through an extreme point.

To summarize all of this, we need only search for the optimal solution(s) from among the finite number of basic feasible solutions. *This is exactly equivalent to hopping around from one extreme (corner) point of the solution space to another, in search of the optimal extreme point(s).*

Solution by Enumeration

In theory any LP problem can be solved by **enumeration** as follows:

1. Add the appropriate supplemental variables to convert structural constraints into equation form.
2. Determine each *basic solution* by setting selected nonbasic variables to zero and solving the resulting system of linear equations. The number of basic solutions is given by Equation 4.6.
3. Identify the set of *basic feasible solutions* by eliminating all basic solutions having negative values for variables. (This is geometrically equivalent to identifying the extreme points in a solution space.)
4. Select the *optimal solution(s)* from those in the set of basic feasible solutions by evaluating the objective function (z) for each basic feasible solution. (This is geometrically equivalent to drawing a contour line through each extreme point and selecting the extreme point having the contour line with the best z-value.)

▶ Example 4.3 Solution of Air Cargo Model by Enumeration

Let us restate the air cargo LP model after the inclusion of supplemental variables. The augmented LP model is:

Maximize

$$z = 7x_1 + 10x_2$$

subject to

$$5x_1 + 4x_2 + S_1 \qquad = 24 \qquad (1)$$

$$2x_1 + 5x_2 \qquad + S_2 = 13 \qquad (2)$$

$$x_1, x_2, S_1, S_2 \geq 0 .$$

Figure 4–13 illustrates the geometric representation, where the linear convex solution space is given by the polygon $\overline{abcd}$, the optimal vertex is at point c ($x_1 = 4$ and $x_2 = 1$), and the optimal value for z is 38.

To solve this problem by enumeration, we first apply Equation 4.6. Noting that $n = 4$ (the four variables x_1, x_2, S_1, S_2) and $m = 2$ (two equations), we have a total of six basic solutions according to

$$\binom{4}{2} = \frac{4!}{2!2!} = \frac{4 \cdot 3 \cdot 2 \cdot 1}{(2 \cdot 1) \cdot (2 \cdot 1)} = 6 .$$

Table 4–3 shows the six basic solutions and their characteristics.

FIGURE 4–13 Geometric Representation of Air Cargo Solution

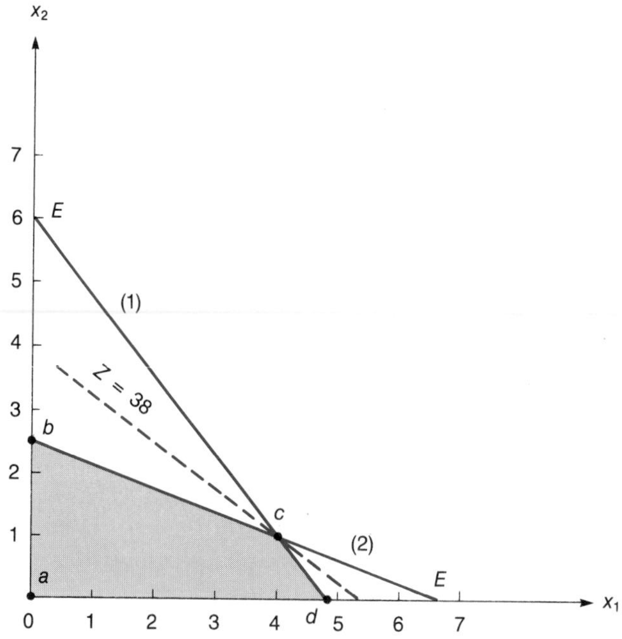

TABLE 4–3 Solution by Enumeration

(1) Basic Solution Number	(2) Basis	(3) Values of Basic Variables	(4) Vertex in Figure 4–13	(5) Feasible?	(6) Value of Objective Function
1	(S_1, S_2)	(24.0, 13.0)	*a*	Yes	0.0
2	(S_1, x_1)	(−8.5, 6.5)	*f*	No	—
3	(S_1, x_2)	(13.6, 2.6)	*b*	Yes	26.0
4	(S_2, x_1)	(3.4, 4.8)	*d*	Yes	33.6
5	(S_2, x_2)	(−17.0, 6.0)	*e*	No	—
6*	(x_1, x_2)	(4.0, 1.0)	*c*	Yes	38.0

*Optimal basic feasible solution.

Any one basic solution is generated by selecting $(m =)$ 2 basic variables and setting the remaining $(n - m =)$ 2 nonbasic variables to zero. This leaves a system of $(m =)$ 2 equations in $(m =)$ 2 unknown basic variables. For example, we generated solution number 4 by selecting S_2 and x_1 as the basis, setting S_1 and x_2 to zero, and solving for S_2 and x_1 in

$$5x_1 \qquad = 24 \tag{1}$$

$$2x_1 + S_2 = 13. \tag{2}$$

Thus—after some "blood, sweat, and tears"—we fill in columns 1–3 in Table 4–3.

Next we identify the set of basic feasible solutions by considering basic solutions that are feasible, or those having nonnegative values for basic variables. These are identified in column 5, which now leaves solution numbers 1, 3, 4, and 6 under consideration.

Finally we compute z for each of the four basic feasible solutions and select the optimal solution from among this set. This gives us column 6 in the table, and solution number 6 as the optimal basic feasible solution.

Note that the basic feasible solutions are in fact the extreme points a, b, c, d in Figure 4–13, and the infeasible solutions are the points e and f, which fall outside the solution space.

We might note that values taken on by slack and surplus variables indicate the role played by constraints in the solution. For example, constraints 1 and 2 are said to be **active constraints** at corner point c in Figure 4–13. This means that they are satisfied as equalities, or the solution $x_1 = 4$ and $x_2 = 1$ completely utilizes the available 24 cubic yards given by the constraint.

$$5x_1 + 4x_2 \leq 24 \tag{1}$$

and the available 13,000 pounds given by

$$2x_1 + 5x_2 \leq 13 . \tag{2}$$

Solution 6 in Table 4–3 specifies that $S_1 = 0$ and $S_2 = 0$, since these are nonbasic variables. Hence constraints 1 and 2 *must* be active constraints since each has a slack of zero.

Conversely, solution 3 in Table 4–3 shows that $S_1 = 13.6$ and $S_2 = 0$. In this case, constraint 2 is active, and constraint 1 is said to be an **inactive constraint.** That is to say, solution 3 with $x_1 = 0$ and $x_2 = 2.6$ utilizes all 13,000 pounds ($S_2 = 0$) of capacity in constraint 2 but does not use 13.6 cubic yards ($S_1 = 13.6$) of the available 24 cubic yards. Note that point b in Figure 4–13 shows slack relative to constraint 1 and no slack relative to constraint 2, which is consistent with the values taken on by slack variables in solution 3 of Table 4–3 (that is, $S_1 > 0$ and $S_2 = 0$).

In general, a solution yielding a value of zero for a slack variable (S_i) indicates that the corresponding constraint i is an *active* constraint; otherwise, the constraint is an inactive constraint.

A moment's reflection and calculations with Formula 4.6 should convince you that "brute force" solutions by enumeration are impractical; for example, the production mix problem of Example 3.3 would require the examination of 210 solutions, and the solid waste problem of Example 3.9 (which is small scale compared with actual applications) has more than 9 billion possible solutions. Assuming it takes a computer 0.1 second to generate each solution, we find 9 billion solutions would require more than nine years of continuous CPU time! As we discuss next, the simplex method usually converges rapidly on the optimal solution.

The Iterative Process

The **simplex method** is a clever algebraic procedure for solving systems of linear equations where a linear objective function is to be optimized. It is an iterative process that first identifies an initial basic feasible solution. The process then searches for a better solution. "Better" is evaluated according to whether or not the value of the objective function would be improved with another basic feasible solution. Is there another extreme point in the solution space that gives a better value for z? If a better solution exists, the simplex method generates it . The search continues until no further improvement in the objective function is possible.

better solution exists, the simplex method generates it. The search continues until no further improvement in the objective function is possible.

Alternatively, we can envision the iterative process in another way. At any point in the solution process we can imagine two pools of variables: m basic variables and $(n - m)$ nonbasic variables. By incremental analysis, the simplex method assesses whether or not the objective function can be improved by exchanging a basic variable for a nonbasic variable. If a particular exchange improves z, then the identified current basic variable is set to zero (which is equivalent to its *departure* from the basis), and the identified current nonbasic variable is given a solution value (which is equivalent to its *entry* in the basis). Each iteration results in an exchange of one variable from each of two pools, as indicated in Figure 4–14.

FIGURE 4–14 Simplex Exchange of Variables

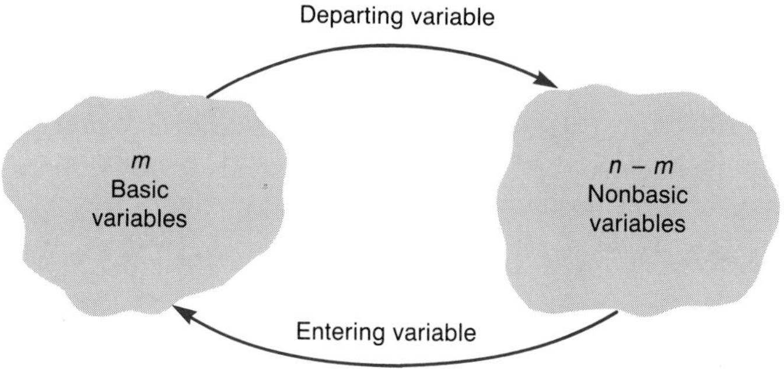

▶ Example 4.4 Solution of Air Cargo Model by Simplex Method

For the problem solved by enumeration in Example 4.3 the following sequence of solutions would occur when solving by the simplex method.

Solution (iteration)	Basic Variables and Values	Nonbasic Variables	z
1	$S_1 = 24.0$, (S_2) $= 13.0$	x_1, (x_2)	0
2	(S_1) $= 13.6$, (x_2) $= 2.6$	(x_1), (S_2)	26
3	(x_1) $= 4.0$, $x_2 = 1.0$	(S_1), S_2	38

Given the initial solution (iteration 1), an incremental analysis (implemented by the simplex method) reveals that the objective function can be improved by making x_2 a basic variable. In generating solution 2 from solution 1, S_2 is the departing variable, and x_2 is the entering variable. Given the second solution, analysis reveals that z can be improved by making x_1 a basic variable. In solution 3 we see that S_1 left the basis described in solution 2.

Once solution 3 is generated, the simplex algorithm determines that no exchange of variables would improve the current value of z. Hence solution 3 is optimal, which agrees with our result in Example 4.3. Note that the simplex method examined half the number of solutions required by the enumeration method. If we compare the simplex sequence of solutions with Figure 4–13, we see that the simplex method moved from an initial solution at extreme point *a*, to exterme point *b*, and finally to extreme point *c*.

> An important characteristic of the simplex method is its guarantee that each successive iteration is a basic feasible solution and that the value of the objective function is at least as good as the value in the previous iteration.

In practice, the simplex method is implemented by computer, as we demonstrate in Section 4.5. Our brief introduction to the simplex method in this section is meant only to give a superficial understanding of how most LP problems are solved. For a detailed understanding, study Chapter 6.

FOLLOW-UP EXERCISES

13. Determine *n*, *m*, and the number of basic solutions for Example 3.4.
14. Confirm solutions 2, 4, and 6 in Table 4–3 by solving the system of equations after setting nonbasic variables to zero.
15. By just looking at solution 4 in Table 4–3, identify active and inactive constraints. Are these consistent with the location of point *d* relative to constraints 1 and 2 in Figure 4–13? Explain.
16. Solve the following problem by enumeration.

    Maximize

    $$z = 3x_1 + 4x_2$$

    subject to

    $$2x_1 + 3x_2 \leq 300 \quad (1)$$

    $$4x_1 + x_2 \leq 350 \quad (2)$$

    $$x_1, x_2 \geq 0.$$

    Start by restating this problem in terms of supplemental variables. Verify your results by solving the problem graphically.

Surplus and Artificial Variables

Now that you have a general idea of the simplex formulation, you should be aware of some formulation details that you may encounter. When an LP problem contains ($\geq$) constraints, the left-hand side must be at least equal to the right-hand side constant; hence the inequality constraint can be forced into the form of an equation by *subtracting* a nonnegative excess or **surplus variable** *E*, from the left side. For example, suppose we specify the condition that "at least four containers of beef and pork must be shipped"; that is,

$$x_1 + x_2 \geq 4. \quad (3)$$

This inequality would be restated as the equation

$$x_1 + x_2 - E_3 = 4 . \qquad (3)$$

Surplus variable subtracted for (≥) constraint.
Note consistency of subscript and equation number.

Thus a surplus variable absorbs "surplus" on the left-hand side of a ≥ constraint. For example, if $x_1 = 3$ and $x_2 = 3$, then it follows from equation 3 that E_3 *must* equal 2 for the equation to hold. In words, if six containers are shipped and a minimum of four is required, then we have shipped two surplus containers according to constraint 3.

FIGURE 4–15 Air Cargo with New Constraint

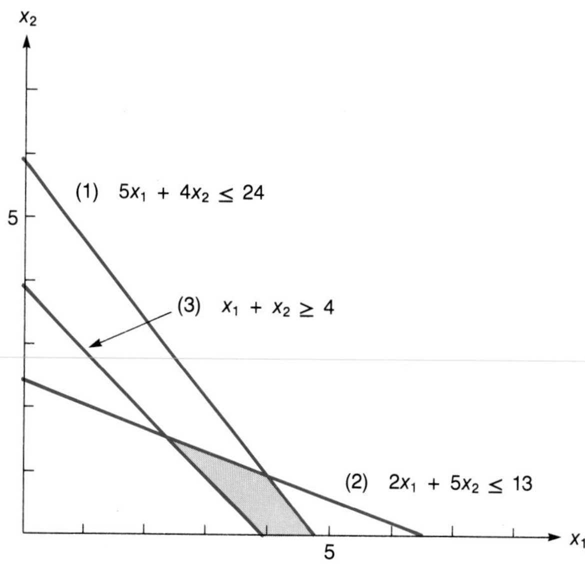

As we shall later see, the simplex procedure usually starts its search at the origin. When constraint 3 is added, we have an interesting difficulty that can be seen in Figure 4.15. The origin is not in the solution space! If we let $x_1 = x_2 = 0$, then E_3 would be negative as shown below.

$$x_1 + x_2 - E_3 = 4$$

$$0 + 0 - E_3 = 4$$

or,

$$E_3 = -4 .$$

But recall that all variables are constrained to be nonnegative. This requirement holds for any supplemental variables added, also. We've boxed ourselves into an algebraic problem. Suppose, though, that we add an *artificial variable,* A_3, to the left side of constraint 3. Then we have side-stepped the problem we created.

$$x_1 + x_2 - E_3 + A_3 = 4 . \tag{3}$$

Artificial variable added to $\geq$ constraint.
Note consistency of subscript and equation number.

Now, when $x_1 = x_2 = 0$, we could set $E_3 = 0$ and $A_3 = 4$, complying with the non-negativity requirement.

Can you determine why we would also add an artificial variable to each = constraint as well? For example, consider an original equality constraint given by

$$8x_1 + x_2 = 32 . \tag{4}$$

It would be restated as

$$8x_1 + x_2 + A_4 = 32 .$$

Artificial variable also added to = constraint.
Note consistency of subscript and equation number.

To reiterate, the simplex method requires that all constraints be restated as equations by introducing supplemental variables. Table 4–4 summarizes the treatment for each type of constraint.

TABLE 4–4

Constraint Type	Treatment
$\leq$	Add a **slack** variable (S_i) to the left side.
$\geq$	Subtract a **surplus** variable (E_i) and add an **artificial** variable (A_i) to the left side.
=	Add an **artificial** variable (A_i) to the left side.

Remember, *our convention* in this book is to assign a subscript to supplemental variables which corresponds to the constraint number.

Supplemental Variables and the Augmented LP Model

The slack, surplus, and artificial variables make up the set of **supplemental variables,** as described by the following schematic:

- Variables
  - Real (x_j's)
  - Supplemental
    - Slack (S_i's)
    - Surplus (E_i's)
    - Artificial (A_i's)

Remember that supplemental variables are added to an LP model in order to convert a constraint set into an equivalent system of equations. Let us call the resulting model the **augmented LP model.** A solution procedure then generates solutions using the augmented LP model.

In practice, we formulate an LP model as in Chapter 3 and then submit it to a simplex-based computer program. *We ourselves don't add supplemental variables,* since computerized algorithms are programmed to accomplish this step. So why have we intrigued you with the details? Simply because the output from computerized procedures usually includes such terminology as *real, slack, surplus,* and *artificial* variables. Moreover, a knowledge of the concepts in this section and the next gives you a better understanding of what's happening within our friend Hal.[7]

FOLLOW-UP EXERCISES

17. In words, state the meaning of values for S_1, S_2, and E_3 when $x_1 = 4$ and $x_2 = 1$ in the revised three-constraint air cargo problem.
18. Suppose $x_1 = 3$ and $x_2 = 5$ in the air cargo problem. What values must S_1 and S_2 equal? Explain why these values indicate a solution that's not feasible.
19. Modify the following constraints by adding supplemental variables:

$$5x_1 - 3x_2 + 4x_3 \geq 10 \quad (1)$$

$$x_1 + 2x_2 = 15 \quad (2)$$

$$x_2 + x_3 \leq 20. \quad (3)$$

20. Add the constraint

$$x_1 + x_2 \geq 4 \quad (3)$$

to the air cargo model in Example 4.3 and solve the new problem by enumeration. (Ignore artificial variables when solving by enumeration.)

21. ***Degenerate Solutions.*** If one or more basic variables has a value of zero, the solution or extreme point is said to be **degenerate**. Geometrically, this occurs if the number of lines passing through an extreme point is greater than the number of real variables. For example, in two dimensions, the coordinates of an extreme point are determined by the intersection of two lines. If a third line passes through this point, then the point is degenerate. In practice, degeneracy causes some problems with the postoptimality interpretations we discuss in the next chapter, but causes little problem with respect to the generation of a solution (which we talk about in Chapter 6).
    a. Add the constraint

    $$x_1 + x_2 \geq 5 \quad (3)$$

    to Figure 4–13. Which extreme point is degenerate?
    b. Solve the system of three equations that corresponds to the degenerate extreme point in part *a*. Let x_1 and x_2, and E_3 form the basis. Based on your result, how do you know that this solution is degenerate?
    c. Do you agree with the definition "A basis is the set of all positive variables in a solution"? Explain.
22. ***Solutions with A_i's in the Basis.*** Many simplex routines generate initial or starting solutions by setting each $x_j = 0$ and each $E_i = 0$. Thus only S_i's and A_i's appear in the initial basis. Geometrically, this is equivalent to starting the solution procedure at the origin of a coordinate system.
    a. Do you now see why we had to add artificial variables to $\geq$ and $=$ constraints? What would happen if an A_i were not added to a $\geq$ constraint? To an $=$ constraint?

[7]VCR aficionados might recognize Hal as the name of the computer-turned-malevolent in *2001: A Space Odyssey* and (reformed) in the movie *2010*.

b. If a basis contains any $A_i > 0$, do we have a feasible solution with respect to the original structural constraints? If not, why does the algorithm believe it to be a basic feasible solution?

c. How might a simplex algorithm encourage the departure of artificial variables from the basis? (Hint: It has to do with the treatment of A_i's in the objective function of the augmented LP model.)

d. If a starting basis contains three artificial variables, then how many solutions (iterations) must the algorithm examine before it finds the first "true" basic feasible solution?

4.5 COMPUTER-BASED SOLUTIONS

In actual applications, solving LP problems by hand calculation is unheard of, as the availability of efficient computer codes for the simplex method is widespread. Many computer manufacturers, or consulting firms, software makers, and commercial time-sharing vendors provide canned programs that solve LP problems. Generally, these programs are sophisticated simplex-based procedures that take advantage of certain computational and storage efficiencies.

The general user of LP, then, need not be concerned about the actual solution of a problem. Instead, users need "only" focus on the recognition of an LP problem, its formulation, its underlying assumptions, its preparation for submission to a computer, and the interpretation of output.

Model Formulation

First of all we assume that you have formulated an LP problem and that a computer code for its solution is available to you. If you don't have a computerized LP package, then read on anyway, since we demonstrate generally what would happen in practice.

LP computer routines usually assume that users have formulated a **generalized LP model** with n real variables and m structural constraints, according to the following structure:

Maximize (or minimize)

$$z = c_1x_1 + c_2x_2 + \cdots + c_nx_n$$

subject to

$$\begin{aligned}
a_{11}x_1 + a_{12}x_2 + \cdots + a_{1n}x_n(\le, \ge, =)b_1 \quad &(1)\\
a_{21}x_1 + a_{22}x_2 + \cdots + a_{2n}x_n(\le, \ge, =)b_2 \quad &(2)\\
\vdots \qquad\qquad\qquad\qquad &\ \vdots\\
a_{m1}x_1 + a_{m2}x_2 + \cdots + a_{mn}x_n(\le, \ge, =)b_m \quad &(m)
\end{aligned}$$

$$x_j \ge 0, \quad j = 1, \ldots n$$

where $(\leq, \geq, =)$ means *one* of the following: $\leq$, or $\geq$, or $=$.
Note that this structure requires us to:

1. Place all variables on the left-hand side of constraints.
2. Place all constants (excluding coefficients) on the right-hand side of constraints.

We might caution that *some routines require the use of nonnegative right-hand–side constants (b_i's)*. In practice this doesn't present a problem but it does require us to "massage" our formulation if we do have some negative b_i's. For example, if we have the constraint

$$3x_1 - 5x_2 + x_3 \geq -10$$

then we simply multiply both sides of the inequality by -1 to get

$$-3x_1 + 5x_2 - x_3 \leq 10 .$$

Note that the sense of the inequality is reversed as a result of multiplying an inequality by a negative number. *Does your LP package require nonnegative b_i's?*

We might further caution that *some routines require a specific ordering of constraints with respect to sense*. For example, several require ordering the m constraints by groups such that all $\leq$ constraints appear first, then all $\geq$ constraints appear next, and finally all $=$ constraints appear last. If this is a requirement on your system, then order and number your constraints accordingly. *Does your LP package require group ordering of constraints by sense?*

LP packages allow different degrees of flexibility in naming variables. Some require that variables be sequentially numbered (e.g., variable 1, variable 2, . . . or $x_1, x_2, \ldots$). If you formulated your problem using double subscripts (that is, x_{ij}'s), you might need to renumber the double-subscripted variables. For example, an original formulation using variables x_{11}, x_{12}, x_{21}, and x_{22} might require renaming the variables as x_1, x_2, x_3, and x_4, or variables 1, 2, 3, and 4. Other LP packages offer you some latitude in naming variables. In some, you might define variables with actual names or abbreviations (e.g., pork, beef, *x*11, *x*12).

Additionally, some packages enable the user to assign special names (or labels) to constraints. In the air cargo model we could label the constraints as *volume* and *weight* if we desired.

Preparing Input

Once the LP problem is properly formulated, we are ready for a computer-based solution. Specifics in this case vary from system to system, so you need details from either your instructor or the computer center. In particular you need to know exactly how to access and run the appropriate program.

Execution of the program then requires data input. Again, specifics vary depending on the program, but we must generally specify the following data input:

1. Whether the problem requires maximization or minimization.
2. The number of real variables (n).

3. The number of $\leq$, $\geq$, and $=$ constraints (or the total number of constraints, m, depending on how the package handles the specification of sense for each constraint).
4. Each right-hand–side constant (b_i's), each coefficient for the x_j's in the structural constraints (a_{ij}'s), and each coefficient for the x_j's in the objective function (c_j's).

Note that *the nonnegativity condition* ($x_j \geq 0$) *is not generally specified as input.* LP computer routines usually assume this condition.

Finally, note that the generalized LP model serves as input to almost all computer routines, not the augmented LP model discussed in Section 4.4. Computer routines generally convert the generalized LP model to the augmented LP form by adding the necessary supplemental variables.

Example 4.5

In this example, we will illustrate the use of an interactive LP package to solve the following problem.

Minimize

$$z = 3x_1 + 4x_2 + 6.13x_3 + 5x_4$$

subject to

$$0.5x_1 + 0.8x_3 \leq 350 \quad (1)$$

$$0.5x_2 + 0.8x_4 \leq 500 \quad (2)$$

$$10.0x_1 + 7.0x_3 \leq 6{,}000 \quad (3)$$

$$10.0x_1 + 10.0x_2 + 7.0x_3 + 7.0x_4 \leq 10{,}000 \quad (4)$$

$$x_1 + x_2 = 500 \quad (5)$$

$$x_3 + x_4 = 700 \quad (6)$$

$$x_j \geq 0, \quad j = 1, 2, 3, 4$$

You should realize that the input is specific to this computer package and will differ from any package you might run; however, the general principles are relevant.[8] Our particular computer routine

1. Allows negative b_i's (which this problem doesn't have anyway).
2. Requires the input of the number of constraints *by type* (4 of $\leq$ type, 0 of $\geq$ type, and 2 of $=$ type) and grouping of constraints by type for purposes of input (which is why we placed the $\leq$ type constraints before the $=$ constraints in the formulation).

[8]See Exercise xx for a description of IBM's popular MPSX package. Another popular, interactive, user-friendly package is called LINDO, developed by Linus Schrage at the Graduate School of Business, University of Chicago. An attractive feature of LINDO is its user friendliness. For example, the data input format for the LP model is nearly identical to the look of LP formulations. See Linus Schrage, *Linear, Integer, and Quadratic Programming with LINDO*, 3rd Ed., (Palo Alto, Calif.: Scientific Press, 1986).

3. Identifies variables using the standard x_j notation or allows user-specified names (we use the standard x_j notation).

Elements in color (or shaded) in Figure 4–16 identify portions typed by the user; nonshaded elements identify portions typed by the computer. You should refer to the generalized formulation above as you study the input; otherwise the illustration is self-explanatory.

FIGURE 4–16 Input for LP Problem in Example 4.5

```
Please supply the following information:
          Type of problem (MAX=1)  (MIN=2): 2
          Number of real variables        : 4
          Number of <= Constraints        : 4
          Number of >= Constraints        : 0
          Number of  = Constraints        : 2
------------------------------------------------------------
                  Input of constraints
------------------------------------------------------------
               CONSTRAINT No. 1 - <= Type
------------------------------------------------------------
X1 .5        X2 0        X3 .8        X4 0        RHS 350
------------------------------------------------------------
               CONSTRAINT No. 2 - <= Type
------------------------------------------------------------
X1 0         X2 .5       X3 0         X4 .8       RHS 500
------------------------------------------------------------
               CONSTRAINT No. 3 - <= Type
------------------------------------------------------------
X1 10        X2 0        X3 7         X4 0        RHS 6000
------------------------------------------------------------
               CONSTRAINT No. 4 - <= Type
------------------------------------------------------------
X1 10        X2 10       X3 7         X4 7        RHS 10000
------------------------------------------------------------
               CONSTRAINT No. 5 -  = Type
------------------------------------------------------------
X1 1         X2 1        X3 0         X4 0        RHS 500
------------------------------------------------------------
               CONSTRAINT No. 6 -  = Type
------------------------------------------------------------
X1 0         X2 0        X3 1         X4 1        RHS 700
------------------------------------------------------------
                Objective Function Input
                ------------------------
------------------------------------------------------------
X1 3         X2 4        X3 6.13      X4 5
```

Interpreting Output

This section illustrates computer output for two problems formulated earlier. The output format is specific to our LP package. In general, however, you should look for the following output from any LP program:

1. The optimal value of the objective function (z).
2. The optimal values for the real variables (x_j's).
3. The optimal values for supplemental variables (S_i's, E_i's, and A_i's).

In particular, you should relate the values of the supplemental variables to their respective constraints, since these have contextual meaning. Moreover, these give an indication of whether constraints are active or inactive.

You should also be aware that aberrations in solutions are possible, as discussed earlier in this chapter. For example, LP programs should identify the following abnormalities (should they occur) as part of the output:

1. **No feasible solution or null solution space.** In this case one or more artificial variables, *having positive values,* appear in the "optimal" basis.
2. **Unbounded solution space.** In this case the solution space is not closed.
3. **Redundant constraint.** In this case a *basic* variable (real or supplemental) will have a value of zero.
4. **Alternative optima.** In this case more than one extreme point is optimal, so that an infinite number of optimal bases are possible.
5. **Unbounded solution.** In this case it's theoretically possible to assign an infinite amount to one or more variables, ensuring that z approaches $+\infty$ in the maximization case and $-\infty$ in the minimization case.
6. **Degenerate optimal solution.** In this case one or more *basic* variables have values of zero in the optimal solution.

▶ Example 4.6 Computer Output for Example 4.5

The output in Figure 4–17 is a continuation of the computer run in Example 4.5. Note that the simplex algorithm required four iterations to find the optimal solution; that is, it examined just four basic solutions.

For the optimal solution, the objective function is minimized at a value of 5,084.75. The list of included variables represents the set of basic variables in the optimal basis. In this set, $x_1 = 500$, $x_3 = 75$, and $x_4 = 625$. Any variable not appearing in this list is a nonbasic variable with a corresponding value of zero. Thus the absence of x_2 suggests that $x_2 = 0$ in the optimal solution.

From the output, note that variable numbers beyond x_4 are the supplemental variables that have been introduced to each constraint by the computer package. For example, variable 5 has a value of 40, and it represents the slack variable added to constraint 1. Similarly, variable 7 represents the slack variable added to constraint 3; its value equals 475. The last basic variable is variable 8 (slack variable added to constraint 4), and its value is 100.

FIGURE 4–17

```
Objective function minimized at: 5084.75
4 iterations required
Included variables
-----------------
Variable     Quantity of       Variable      Associated with
 Number      this variable       Type        Constraint number
-------      ------------      ------        ----------------
  X1            500            REAL
  X3             75            REAL
  X4            625            REAL
  5              40            SLACK                1
  7             475            SLACK                3
  8             100            SLACK                4
```

Knowledge of the different types of supplemental variables added to each constraint is required to fully interpret the output. For our problem, four slack variables were added (one for each constraint) and two artificial variables were added (one for each = constraint). Thus a total of 10 variables (4 real and 6 supplemental) were part of the model when solved by the simplex. We know the values of the six basic variables. We have also noted that x_2 is nonbasic in the optimal solution. The remaining nonbasic variables must include a slack variable added to constraint 2 (and referred to as variable 6 by the package) and the two artificial variables added to constraints 5 and 6 (and referred to, respectively, as variables 9 and 10 by the package).

Aside from determining the values of all real and supplemental variables, the interpretation of output should also determine the extent to which constraints are satisfied. For our example, values of $x_1 = 500$, $x_2 = 0$, $x_3 = 75$, and $x_4 = 625$ result in constraints 1, 3, and 4 having slack of 40, 475, and 100, respectively. These three constraints are *inactive* in the optimal solution. Since the supplemental variables added to constraints 2, 5, and 6 all equal zero, these constraints are satisfied as equations and are *active* in the optimal solution.

Figure 4–18 illustrates the output for this problem when run on LINDO (see footnote 8). Notice that, in addition to the optimal value of the objective function, the Variable section summarizes the values of all decision variables, and the Row section summarizes the extent to which all constraints are satisfied. Values for slack and surplus variables are indicated in this section. Also notice that LINDO considers the objective function as row 1, constraint 1 corresponds to row 2, and so on. LINDO allows the user to specify unique names for variables as well as names or labels for constraints. We will defer discussion of the columns Reduced Cost and Dual Prices until Chapter 5.

FOLLOW-UP EXERCISES

23. The LP model presented in Example 4.5 and solved in Example 4.6 is (not by coincidence) the same as that formulated as the multiperiod, product mix model in Example 3.3. The only difference is the absence of the 60 in the objective function. Since the result in Example 4.6 is also the solution to the product mix example, fully interpret the solution to *that* problem. Carefully verbalize the *meaning* of *all* variables (real and supplemental), and *interpret* the extent to which constraints have been satisfied.

FIGURE 4–18 Sample of LINDO Output

```
LP OPTIMUM FOUND AT STEP 3
                    OBJECTIVE FUNCTION VALUE
1)                        5084.75000

     VARIABLE              VALUE              REDUCED COST
        X1              500.000000              .000000
        X2                 .000000             1.706250
        X3               75.000010              .000000
        X4              625.000000              .000000

        ROW          SLACK OR SURPLUS         DUAL PRICES
        2)               39.999990              .000000
        3)                 .000000             1.412500
        4)             1000.000000              .000000
        5)             3950.000000              .000000
        6)                 .000000            -3.000000
        7)                 .000000            -6.130000
```

24. Based on the output of x_j's in Figure 4–17 and the original formulation of z on page 99:
   a. Confirm the following cost breakdown.

Variable costs	\$5,075.00
Product inventory costs	65.00
Raw materials inventory costs	4.75
Total	\$5,144.75

   b. How important are the inventory costs relative to the variable costs of production? Do you think that the production decision (values for x's) would change if inventory costs were to be ignored in the formulation?
   c. Modify the LP formulation in Example 3.3 by defining

x_5 = Variable costs.

x_6 = Product inventory costs.

x_7 = Raw materials inventory costs.

x_8 = Total costs.

Hint: You need to modify the objective function and add some new constraints.
What's the advantage of this formulation?

25. Use an LP package to:
   a. Confirm our solution in Example 4.6.
   b. Answer Exercise 24*b* by altering the objective function.
   c. Solve the formulation in Exercise 24*c*.

4.6 SUMMARY

This chapter focused on the solution of linear programming models. We have explored the graphical analysis of LP models that can be stated in terms of two decision variables. The graphical perspective is very useful in illustrating various aspects of LP models as well as solving these models. To aid in LP computer package use, we overviewed the simplex method, including the way in which an LP model must be modified before solving using the simplex. We also discussed how the algorithm searches for the optimal solution(s). Our presentation of computer-based solution methods demonstrated one package, mentioned others, and attempted to prepare you for the types of features found in any package. Finally, this chapter discussed various phenomena that may occur when formulating and solving linear programming models, the reasons for these phenomena, and ways in which they evidence themselves. The included phenomena are *alternative optima, no feasible solution, redundant constraints, unbounded optimal solutions,* and *degenerate optimal solutions.*

Chapter 5 will examine *postoptimality analysis,* which provides a justification for using a deterministic modeling technique in an uncertain setting. Chapter 5 also discusses the *dual problem.* Those interested in more information about the simplex method are referred to Chapter 6. Understanding the workings of the simplex method will result in more effective use of linear programming.

SELECTED REFERENCES

See Chapter 3 references.

ADDITIONAL EXERCISES

26. Graphically solve the following problems:

a. Maximize

$$z = 6x_1 + 8x_2$$

subject to

$$x_1 \geq 2 \quad (1)$$

$$x_1 \leq 8 \quad (2)$$

$$x_2 \geq 2 \quad (3)$$

$$x_2 \leq 6 \quad (4)$$

$$2x_1 + 3x_2 \leq 21 \quad (5)$$

$$x_1, x_2 \geq 0.$$

b. Change the objective function to maximize $z = 6x_1 + 9x_2$.

c. Same as part *a* except change (5) to $2x_1 + 3x_2 \leq 8$.

d. Same as part *a* except change (5) to $2x_1 + 3x_2 \geq 8$.
e. Same as part *a* except change (5) to $2x_1 + 3x_2 \geq 21$ and eliminate (2).
f. Same as part *d* except minimize z.

27. Use the computer to solve each part in the immediately preceding exercise. Compare these results with the geometric results.
28. Graphically solve the following problems:

a. Minimize

$$z = 12x_1 + 9x_2$$

subject to

$$\begin{aligned} x_1 \quad\quad &\leq 10 & (1)\\ x_2 &\leq 8 & (2)\\ x_2 &\geq 3 & (3)\\ 2.5x_1 + x_2 &\geq 10 & (4)\\ 4x_1 + 3x_2 &\geq 18 & (5)\\ x_1, x_2 &\geq 0. \end{aligned}$$

b. Same as part *a* except minimize $z = 12x_1 + 3x_2$.
c. Same as part *a* except reverse inequality in (5).
d. Same as part *a* except eliminate 2.
e. Same as part *d* except maximize z.

29. Use the computer to solve each part in Exercise 28. Compare these results with the geometric results.
30. How many basic solutions are possible for the model in
    a. Exercise 26?
    b. Exercise 28?
31. ***Tour Planning.*** A local travel agent is planning a charter trip to a major Caribbean resort. The eight-day/seven-night package will include round-trip air transportation, surface transportation, hotel, meals, and selected tour options. The charter trip is restricted to 200 persons, and past experience indicates that there will be no problem finding 200 participants. What the travel agent must do is determine the number of *deluxe, standard,* and *economy* tour packages to offer for this charter. These three plans each differ according to seating and service for the air flight, quality of accommodations, meal plans, and tour options. Table 4–5 summarizes proposed prices for the three packages and corresponding expenses for the travel agent. The travel agent has chartered a jet airliner for the flat fee of $20,000.

TABLE 4–5 Prices and Costs of Tour Packages per Person

Tour Plan	Price	Hotel Costs	Meals and Other Expenses
Deluxe	$1,000	$300	$475
Standard	700	220	250
Economy	650	190	220

In planning the trip, certain considerations must be taken into account:

a. At least 10 percent of the packages must be of the deluxe type.
b. At least 35 percent but no more than 70 percent must be of the standard type.
c. At least 30 percent must be of the economy type.
d. The airliner allows for no more than 60 deluxe packages.
e. The hotel requests a guarantee that at least 120 of the tourists be on the deluxe or standard packages.

The travel agent wishes to determine the number of packages to offer of each type so as to maximize total profit.

a. Formulate the LP model for this problem.
b. Take advantage of the fact that 200 packages will be sold, and restate the LP model in terms of two decision variables.
c. Solve, graphically, for the optimal solution, and interpret your results.

32. Re-solve the problem in the last exercise for *each* of the following changes in assumptions.
    a. Hotel costs for the deluxe package are $295 per person rather than $300.
    b. An additional restriction in the original problem is that economy bookings are to be no more than 25 percent of total bookings for the other two packages (in order to increase the snob appeal of the tour).
    c. Assume that the hotel guarantee of at least 120 deluxe and standard packages is not required.
33. Given the constraint set and area of feasible solutions in Figure 4–19:

FIGURE 4–19

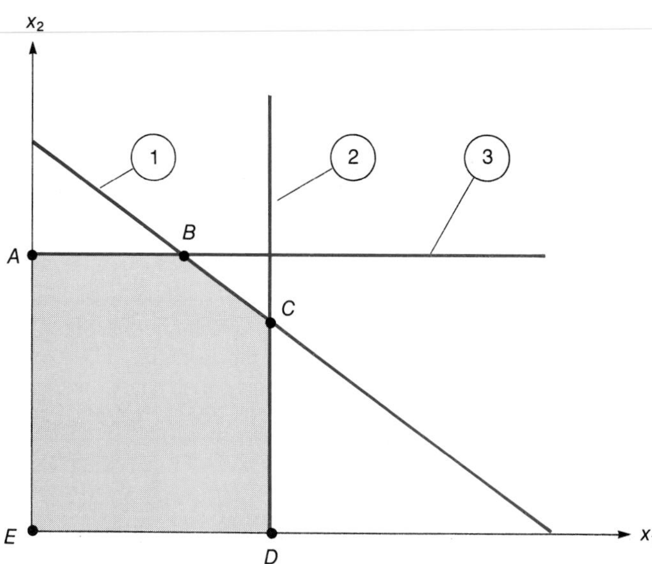

a. What *types* of constraints exist in this problem?
b. How many and what types of supplemental variables would be added to this problem if solving by the simplex method?
c. How many basic variables would there be if solving by the simplex?

d. What variables would be in the basis at corner point E?

e. What variables would be in the basis at corner point A? At corner point C?

34. Given the constraint set and area of feasible solutions in Figure 4–20:

FIGURE 4–20

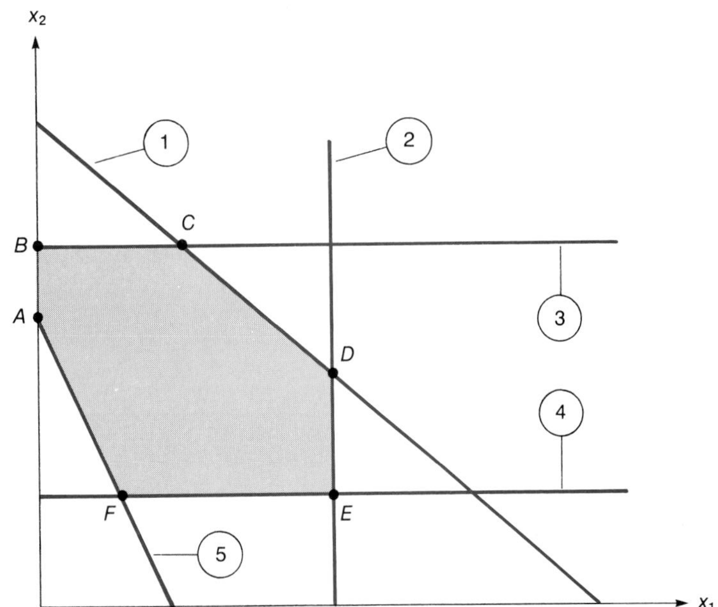

a. What *types* of constraints exist in this problem?

b. How many and what types of supplemental variables would be added to this problem if solving by the simplex method?

c. How many basic variables would there be if solving by the simplex?

d. What variables would be in the basis at corner point F? At corner point B? At corner point D?

35. An LP model contains 20 $\leq$ constraints, 25 $\geq$ constraints, and 10 = constraints. How many, and what types of, supplemental variables must be added if solving by the simplex? How many basic variables will there be?

36. An LP model contains 200 $\leq$ constraints, 150 $\geq$ constraints, and 75 = constraints. How many, and what types of, supplemental variables must be added if solving by the simplex? How many basic variables will there be?

37. ***Production-Vendor Model.*** The LP model for Sniffy Smoke Sensors, Inc. (Exercise 35, Chapter 3) is

Maximize

$$z = 2.00\text{ACPR} + 3.75\text{BAPR} + 1.50\text{ACSB} + 3.25\text{BASB}$$

subject to

$$.15\text{ACPR} + .10\text{BAPR} \leq 1{,}000 \quad \text{(production department)}$$

$$.20\text{ACPR} + .20\text{BAPR} \leq 1{,}800 \quad \text{(assembly department)}$$

$$
\begin{array}{lll}
.10\text{ACPR} + .15\text{BAPR} & \leq 1{,}200 & \text{(packaging department)} \\
\text{ACSB} + \text{BASB} & \leq 15{,}000 & \text{(sub capacity)} \\
\text{ACSB} & \leq 6{,}000 & \text{(sub AC capacity)} \\
\text{ACSB} + \text{BASB} & \geq 2{,}500 & \text{(sub min. order)} \\
\text{ACPR} + \text{ACSB} & \geq 10{,}000 & \text{(Seers min. AC)} \\
\text{BAPR} + \text{BASB} & \geq 8{,}000 & \text{(Seers min. Battery)} \\
\text{ACPR}, \text{BAPR}, \text{ACSB}, \text{BASB} & \geq 0 &
\end{array}
$$

(Note the departure from the usual x_j definition of variables. This is to illustrate that capability in some LP packages.)

Figure 4–21 presents the results of solving this problem using the same computer package illustrated in this chapter. Fully interpret the results of this solution by interpreting the values of all variables and analyzing the extent to which the constraints are satisfied. Which constraints are active?

FIGURE 4–21

```
Objective function maximized at:  61250
8 iterations required
Included variables
------------------
```

Variable Number	Quantity of this variable	Variable Type	Associated with Constraint number
ACPR	4000	REAL	
BAPR	4000	REAL	
ACSB	6000	REAL	
BASB	9000	REAL	
9	200.0001	SLACK	2
10	200	SLACK	3
5	12500	SURPLUS	6
7	5000	SURPLUS	8

38. ***Transportation Model.*** The LP model for the transportation model (Exercise 41, Chapter 3) is

Minimize

$$z = 30x_{11} + 4x_{12} + 8x_{13} + 5x_{21} + 10x_{22} + 20x_{23}$$

subject to

$$
\begin{array}{lll}
x_{11} + x_{12} + x_{13} & \leq 50 & \text{(plant 1 capacity)} \\
x_{21} + x_{22} + x_{23} & \leq 70 & \text{(plant 2 capacity)} \\
x_{11} + x_{21} & = 40 & \text{(depot 1 demand)} \\
x_{12} + x_{22} & = 60 & \text{(depot 2 demand)}
\end{array}
$$

$$x_{13} + x_{23} = 20 \qquad \text{(depot 3 demand)}$$

$$x_{ij} \geq 0$$

where x_{ij} = Number of thousands of gallons shipped from plant i to depot j.

Figure 4–22 presents the results of solving this problem using a computer package. Notice that this package allows for double-subscripted variable names. Fully interpret the results of this solution by interpreting the values of all variables and analyzing the extent to which the constraints are satisfied. Which constraints are active? Should we be concerned about the warning? How do you interpret this?

FIGURE 4–22

```
Objective function minimized at:  780
5 iterations required
Included variables
------------------
```

Variable Number	Quantity of this variable	Variable Type	Associated with Constraint number
x12	30	REAL	
x13	20	REAL	
x21	40	REAL	
x22	30	REAL	
11	0	ARTIFICIAL	5

Warning: All artificial variables have not been removed. If artificial variables are not at zero level, this problem set has no meaningful solution. If artificial variables are at zero level, then this problem may contain redundant constraints.

39. ***Blending Model I.*** The LP model for the blending model (Exercise 42, Chapter 3) is

Maximize

$$z = 3.7375x_1 + 4.70x_2 + 4.10x_3$$

subject to

$$.2x_1 + .1x_2 + .3x_3 \leq 50{,}000 \qquad \text{(availability comp. 1)}$$

$$.15x_1 + .4x_2 + .1x_3 \leq 40{,}000 \qquad \text{(availability comp. 2)}$$

$$.3x_1 + .2x_2 + .1x_3 \leq 30{,}000 \qquad \text{(availability comp. 3)}$$

$$.1x_1 + .1x_2 + .2x_3 \leq 10{,}000 \qquad \text{(availability comp. 4)}$$

$$.25x_1 + .2x_2 + .3x_3 \leq 20{,}000 \qquad \text{(availability comp. 5)}$$

$$x_1 + x_2 + x_3 \leq 125{,}000 \qquad \text{(plant capacity)}$$

$$x_1 \geq 20{,}000 \qquad \text{(min. production blend 1)}$$

$$x_2 \geq 20{,}000 \qquad \text{(min. production blend 2)}$$

$$x_3 \geq 10{,}000 \qquad \text{(min. production blend 3)}$$

$$x_1, x_2, x_3 \geq 0$$

where x_j = Number of gallons produced of final blend j.

Figure 4–23 presents the results of solving this problem using LINDO. Interpret the results of this solution by interpreting the values of all variables and analyzing the extent to which all constraints are satisfied. Determine the number of gallons of each component used in each blend, and break out the total revenue and total cost associated with each final blend.

FIGURE 4–23 LINDO Output

```
                 OBJECTIVE FUNCTION VALUE
 (1)       397750.000

 VARIABLE                 VALUE                    REDUCED COST
       X1            20000.000000                       .000000
       X2            60000.000000                       .000000
       X3            10000.000000                       .000000


      ROW           SLACK OR SURPLUS                DUAL PRICES
       2)            37000.000000                       .000000
       3)            12000.000000                       .000000
       4)            11000.000000                       .000000
       5)                 .000000                     47.000000
       6)                 .000000                       .000000
       7)            35000.000000                       .000000
       8)                 .000000                     -.962500
       9)            40000.000000                       .000000
      10)                 .000000                    -5.300000
```

40. ***Media Mix Model.*** The LP model formulated for the media mix problem in Example 3.7 is

Maximize

$$z = 22x_1 + 12x_2 + 15x_3 + 10x_4 + 5x_5$$

subject to

$x_1 + x_2 + x_3 + x_4 + x_5 \le 10$	(Total budget)
$x_1 + x_2 \le 5$	(Max for TV and radio)
$x_1 \le 3$	(Max TV)
$x_2 \le 3$	(Max radio)
$x_3 \le 3$	(Max magazines)
$x_4 \le 3$	(Max newspapers)
$x_5 \le 3$	(Max outdoor ads)
$10x_1 + 5x_2 + x_3 + x_5 \ge 25$	(Min exposures—youth)
$10x_1 + 5x_2 + x_3 + x_5 \le 35$	(Max exposures—youth)
$6x_1 + 4x_2 + 7x_3 + 2x_4 + 2x_5 \ge 40$	(Min exposures—women)

$$3x_1 + x_2 + 4x_3 + 5x_4 + x_5 \geq 35 \qquad \text{(Min exposures—col. ed.)}$$

$$x_j \geq 0, \qquad j = 1, 2, \ldots, 5$$

where x_j = Thousands of dollars allocated for advertising in medium j.

Figure 4–24 presents the results of solving this problem using LINDO. Interpret the results of this solution. Interpret the values of all variables, and analyze the extent to which all constraints are satisfied.

FIGURE 4–24 LINDO Output

```
                OBJECTIVE FUNCTION VALUE
 (1)       147.750000

 VARIABLE                 VALUE                  REDUCED COST
       X1               3.000000                    .000000
       X2                .250000                    .000000
       X3               3.000000                    .000000
       X4               3.000000                    .000000
       X5                .750000                    .000000

      ROW          SLACK OR SURPLUS                 DUAL PRICES
       2)                .000000                   3.250000
       3)               1.750000                    .000000
       4)                .000000                   1.250000
       5)               2.750000                    .000000
       6)                .000000                  10.000000
       7)                .000000                   6.750000
       8)               2.250000                    .000000
       9)              10.000000                    .000000
      10)                .000000                   1.750000
      11)               7.500000                    .000000
      12)               2.000000                    .000000
```

41. Solve and completely analyze the following problems using a computerized LP program:
    a. Hospital Administration Model, Example 3.5.
    b. Blending Model, Example 3.6
    c. Financial Mix Model, Example 3.8.

42. Solve and analyze one of the following models from Chapter 3 using a computerized LP package.
    a. Capital Expansion Model (Exercise 32).
    b. Agricultural Allocation Model (Exercise 33).
    c. Feed Mix Model (Exercise 36).
    d. Capital Investment Model (Exercise 37).
    e. Rental Car Acquisition Model (Exercise 38).
    f. Personnel Model (Exercise 39).
    g. Contract Awards Model (Exercise 40).
    h. Blending Model I (Exercise 42).
    i. Blending Model II (Exercise 44).
    j. Portfolio Model (Exercise 45).

k. Security Force Scheduling (Exercise 46).
l. Trim Loss (Cutting Stock) Model (Exercise 47).
m. Cargo Loading Model (Exercise 48).

43. ***The "Plain English" Solution.*** Analysts, students taking an MS/OR course, and various other people with technical inclinations usually communicate the results of their analyses by using technical terms, MS/OR jargon, and assorted buzzwords. This is fine when communicating among themselves. Often, however, the MS/OR user must translate analytic results into the language of action (i.e., plain English) understood by nontechnical implementers. This may not be as easy as it sounds. State one of your solutions to Exercise 41 or 42 in "plain English." (Not one technical term!)

CASE Solid Waste Management Model Revisited

Example 3.9 involved the formulation of a product blending/solid waste management model. Figure 4–25 presents the results of solving this problem using a computer package. Table 4–6 provides the complete model formulation.

FIGURE 4–25

```
Objective function maximized at:  6135.867
34 iterations required.
Included variables
------------------
```

Variable Number	Quantity of this variable	Variable Type	Associated with Constraint number
X1	3306.667	REAL	
X2	2362.667	REAL	
X3	330.667	REAL	
X4	2976.000	REAL	
X5	2024.000	REAL	
X6	0.000	REAL	
X7	992.000	REAL	
X8	3008.000	REAL	
X9	330.667	REAL	
X10	595.200	REAL	
X11	396.800	REAL	
15	4000.000	SURPLUS	1
17	2000.000	SURPLUS	3
20	3000.000	SLACK	6
21	1785.600	SURPLUS	7
24	1388.800	SURPLUS	10
29	472.533	SLACK	15
30	404.800	SLACK	16
31	1504.000	SLACK	17

Required:

1. After reviewing the problem in Example 3.9, provide a complete interpretation of the results of solving the model. Specifically, state in nontechnical terms the interpretation of:
   a. The values of all basic variables.
   b. The values of all nonbasic variables.
   c. The extent to which all constraints are satisfied.

TABLE 4–6 Solid Waste Management (Example 3.9) Model Formulation

$z = 0.59x_1 - 0.11x_2 - 1.5x_3 + 0.78x_4 + 0.39x_5 - 1.5x_6 + 0.72x_7 + 0.05x_8 + 0.70x_9 + 0.70x_{10} + 0.80x_{11} + 0.15x_{12} + 0.15x_{13} + 0.5x_{14}.$

$$x_1 + x_2 + x_3 \geq 2{,}000 \quad (1)$$

$$x_1 + x_2 + x_3 \leq 6{,}000 \quad (2)$$

$$x_4 + x_5 + x_6 \geq 3{,}000 \quad (3)$$

$$x_4 + x_5 + x_6 \leq 5{,}000 \quad (4)$$

$$x_7 + x_8 \geq 4{,}000 \quad (5)$$

$$x_7 + x_8 \leq 7{,}000. \quad (6)$$

$$0.72x_1 - 0.16x_4 - 0.12x_7 \geq 0 \quad (7)$$

$$-0.36x_1 + 0.48x_4 - 0.24x_7 \geq 0 \quad (8)$$

$$-0.09x_1 - 0.08x_4 + 0.54x_7 \leq 0 \quad (9)$$

$$0.72x_2 - 0.80x_5 - 0.50x_8 \geq 0 \quad (10)$$

$$-0.24x_2 - 0.24x_5 + 0.35x_8 \leq 0. \quad (11)$$

$$x_9 \leq 0.1x_1 \text{ or } x_9 - 0.1x_1 \leq 0 \quad (12)$$

$$x_{10} \leq 0.2x_4 \text{ or } x_{10} - 0.2x_4 \leq 0 \quad (13)$$

$$x_{11} \leq 0.4x_7 \text{ or } x_{11} - 0.4x_7 \leq 0 \quad (14)$$

$$x_{12} \leq 0.2x_2 \text{ or } x_{12} - 0.2x_2 \leq 0 \quad (15)$$

$$x_{13} \leq 0.2x_5 \text{ or } x_{13} - 0.2x_5 \leq 0 \quad (16)$$

$$x_{14} \leq 0.5x_8 \text{ or } x_{14} - 0.5x_8 \leq 0. \quad (17)$$

$$0.8x_3 - 0.2x_9 - 0.2x_{10} - 0.2x_{11} = 0 \quad (18)$$

$$0.7x_6 - 0.3x_{12} - 0.3x_{13} - 0.3x_{14} = 0. \quad (19)$$

$$x_j \geq 0 \quad j = 1, \ldots, 14$$

CASE Multiperiod Production/ Financial Mix

Refer to Example 3.8 (Financial Mix Model). Suppose we wish to formulate this problem with a one-year (four production-period) planning horizon. The decisions to be made are how many units of each product to produce in each of the four quarters and how much money to borrow (if any) *at the end* of each quarter. All of the data remain the same except for the number of hours available in departments A, B, and C each quarter. Table 4–7 contains these new figures.

TABLE 4–7

Quarter	Department A	Department B	Department C
1	2,000	2,400	1,200
2	1,600	1,800	800
3	2,000	2,200	1,000
4	2,400	2,600	1,400

Make the following assumptions:

a. Cash on hand at the end of a period is augmented by the cash inflows (accounts receivable collected) and depleted by the cash outflows (costs of production, principal repayment, and interest).

b. The company may borrow up to a maximum of $20,000 every three months; however, prior to issuance of a new loan, the principal and interest from any outstanding loan must be repaid.

c. All cash flows and all sales of products occur at the end of each quarter. For the latter, although production occurs uniformly during the quarter, the sale of all units occurs at the end of the quarter.

d. On average, 60 percent of accounts receivable are collected one period hence (one quarter after the sale of the units), 30 percent two periods hence, and 9 percent three periods hence (assumes a 1 percent default).

e. The acid-test condition must be satisfied during the period a loan is outstanding.

f. The objective is to maximize total profit contribution from production during the one-year period. For purposes of formulating the objective function, assume complete (99 percent) collection of receivables from sales made at the end of each of the four quarters (some of the collectibles will dribble in through the seventh quarter).

Required:

1. Formulate the LP model for this problem. (*Hint:* Define x_{ij} as the number of units of product i produced during period j and y_j as the number of dollars borrowed at the end of period j).

2. Solve for the optimal solution.
3. In nontechnical terms, write a report to management that summarizes your results.
4. Critique the assumptions made in the problem. What changes would make the model more realistic?

5

Linear Programming: Postoptimality Analysis and the Dual Problem

Chapter Outline

In discussing the decision-making paradigm in Chapter 1, we indicated that validation and interpretation are ongoing processes. Having formulated and solved an LP problem, we should next explore the sensitivity of our solution to changes in the values of parameters, a process called **postoptimality**, or **sensitivity analysis.** This chapter discusses sensitivity analysis, introduces the concept of a **shadow price,** and presents an alternative and useful approach to formulating and solving LP problems through the **dual problem.**

5.1 NATURE OF SENSITIVITY ANALYSIS

The Rationale

Rarely are the parameters (c_j's, a_{ij}'s, and b_i's) in any linear programming problem known with certainty. They are often, at best, estimates of the actual values of the relevant parameters. For example, rated exposures per dollar of advertising expenditure for media mix models (Example 3.7) usually are estimates of actual exposure rates determined by marketing research studies based on statistical sampling. The available labor hours per quarter in Example 3.8 (Financial Mix Model) are estimates that do not reflect the uncertainties associated with absenteeism or personnel transfers, and the required labor hours per unit are only point estimates of population averages. Likewise, profit contributions used in objective functions fail to portray the uncertainties associated with unit selling prices and variable expenses, such as wages, raw materials, and shipping. The point is that many of these parameters (constants) cannot be determined with certainty because of either measurement difficulties or probabilistic behavior (especially over time).

Even with such uncertainties, initial estimates must be made in order to solve the problem. In the typical business firm, accounting and marketing information systems often provide this type of information. Adherence to good sampling, estimating, and forecasting procedures tends to guarantee more viable and informative data. For example, we might estimate expected (mean) demand for a particular type of service using a mathematical forecasting model. If the forecasting procedure also provides information on the standard deviation and the associated probability distribution, then a meaningful lower and upper bound (confidence interval) for demand can be constructed.[1]

Once the problem has been solved using the "assumed" values, we should next question how the resulting LP solution (the optimal basis and value of the objective function) would be affected if the parameters took on values other than those used in the initial formulation. This type of postsolution analysis is called *postoptimality analysis* or *sensitivity analysis*. If postoptimality analysis reveals that the optimal basis and value of the objective function are only slightly affected by significant changes in the parameters, then the solution is judged to be *insensitive*. If, however, the basis and/or objective function do vary significantly with rather minor changes in the parameters, then the solution is characterized as *sensitive*.

[1]See Appendix A at the end of the text for a discussion of probability distributions and forecasting.

So how do we go about conducting sensitivity analysis? One obvious approach is the brute force approach: Change the value of a parameter and re-solve the entire LP model. This might be acceptable for small problems, but is clearly inefficient for problems where we wish to consider variations in many parameters. For example, brute force sensitivity analysis using three separate values for each of 20 objective functions coefficients requires 3^{20} or 3,486,784,401 separate solutions. Fortunately, efficient (and elegant) methods have been developed for generating sensitivity results without having to re-solve the entire problem. These methods are routinely implemented in most computer-based solutions.

Our presentation in this chapter is largely devoted to sensitivity analysis based on variation in one parameter at a time. Consideration of simultaneous variations in parameters is more realistic, but the methodology of such an analysis is beyond the scope fo this text.[2] In presenting sensitivity analysis, we first use an intuitive approach (where possible) to facilitate your anticipating the effects of changes in parameters; next we present graphical analysis. Finally, we illustrate the usual method of implementing sensitivity analysis: computer-generated sensitivity analysis. Those of you going on to Chapter 6 will learn to implement sensitivity analysis based on the simplex method.

The Linear Equation Revisited

Equation 5.1 is the equation for a straight line in two dimensions:

$$a_1x_1 + a_2x_2 = b. \tag{5.1}$$

If we write x_2 as a function of x_1, the slope of this line is given by the formula

$$m = \frac{-a_1}{a_2} \tag{5.2}$$

and the x_2-intercept is given by the formula

$$k_2 = \frac{b}{a_2}. \tag{5.3}$$

Figure 5–1 graphically portrays the situation when a_1, a_2, and b are all greater than zero.

Sensitivity analysis in linear programming deals with changes in the parameters of linear equations. To prepare you for later discussions, it's useful first to present the graphic responses of straight lines to changes in the constants. If, for example, the right-hand side (b) of Equation 5.1 *increases* to b', the slope of the line $(-a_1/a_2)$ is not influenced, but the x_2-intercept increases to (b'/a_2), and the x_1-intercept *increases* to (b'/a_1). Thus the line remains parallel to itself but moves outward from the origin as in line 2 of Figure 5–2. Can you verify what happens if b decreases?

If a_1 *increases* to a_1' (all other parameters remaining constant), the slope of our equation becomes more negative, the x_1-intercept decreases, and the x_2-intercept re-

[2]For simultaneous variations in parameters, see T. Gal, *Postoptimal Analyses, Parametric Programming and Related Topics* (New York: McGraw-Hill, 1979).

FIGURE 5–1 Linear Equation

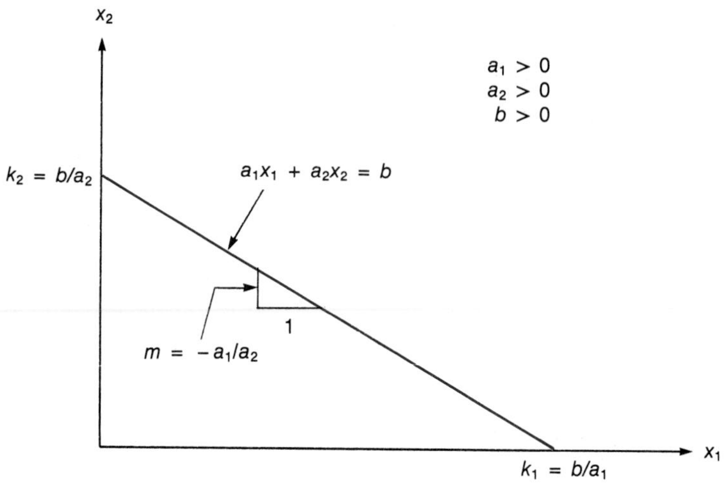

FIGURE 5–2 Response When b Increases to b'

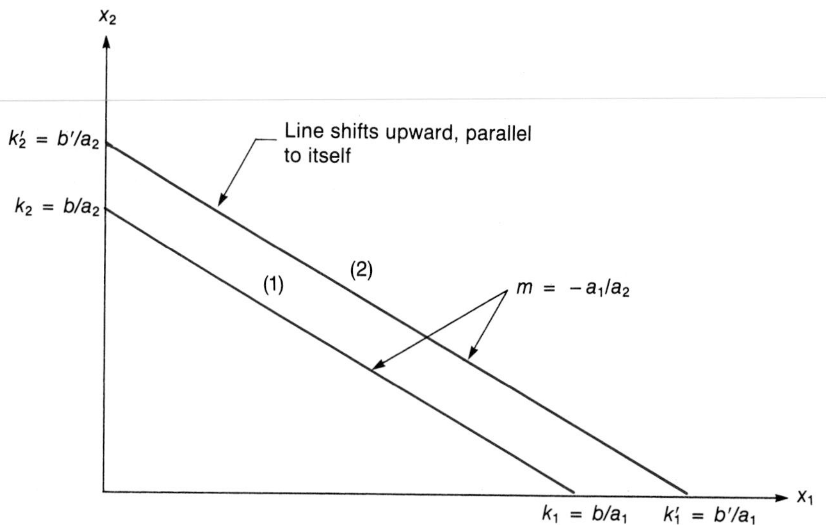

mains stationary. Line 2 in Figure 5–3 demonstrates this *clockwise* change in the orientation of line 1. A *decrease* in a_1 results in a less negative (or more positive) slope and no change in the x_2-intercept; that is, the line pivots *counterclockwise* about k_2. Digital watch owners please check with an old timer.

Finally, verify for yourself that if a_2 *increases,* the slope becomes less negative (a counterclockwise change), and the x_2-intercept decreases. Similarly, verify that the exact opposite changes occur if a_2 *decreases.*

FIGURE 5–3 Response When a_1 Increases to a_1'

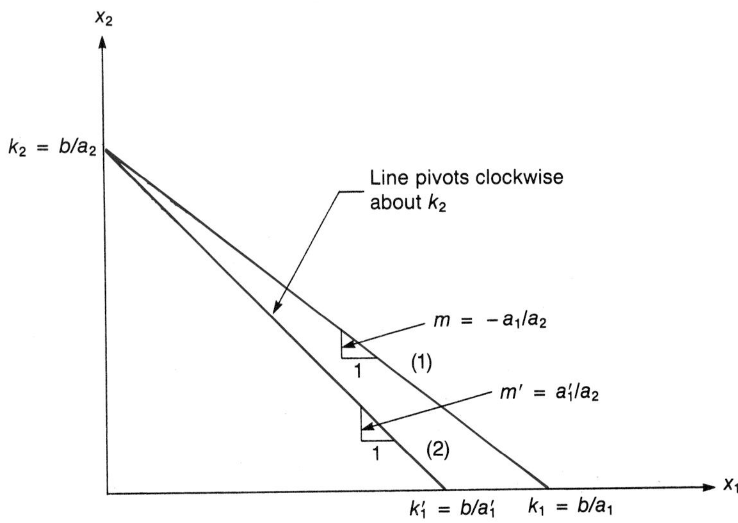

FOLLOW-UP EXERCISES

1. For the equation $4x_1 + 8x_2 = 24$, verify graphically the effects discussed in the last section by allowing each parameter to change by ±50 percent of its original value.
2. Do the effects described in the last section hold for negative a_j values? Change the equation in Exercise 1 to $-4x_1 + 8x_2 = 24$, and test the effects of ±50 percent changes in each parameter.

5.2 SENSITIVITY ANALYSIS—OBJECTIVE FUNCTION COEFFICIENTS (NONBASIC VARIABLES)

We first focus on the effects of variations in objective function coefficients (c_j's) corresponding to variables that do not appear in the optimal basis.

The Air Cargo Problem Revisited

Earlier we discussed the solution to the air cargo problem. In the current section we refer to this problem with one minor modification. Assume the profit contribution for beef is 20 ($100s) per container shipped instead of the original 7. The problem is reformulated below where x_1 and x_2 represent, respectively, the number of containers of beef and pork to be shipped.

Maximize

$$z = 20x_1 + 10x_2$$

subject to

$$\text{Volume capacity:} \quad 5x_1 + 4x_2 \leq 24 \qquad (1)$$

$$\text{Weight capacity:} \quad 2x_1 + 5x_2 \leq 13 \qquad (2)$$

$$x_1, x_2 \geq 0.$$

Figure 5–4 gives the geometric representation of the optimal solution (point c). The solution recommends the shipment of 4.8 containers of beef and no pork. The maximum profit for this shipment is 96 ($100s). Notice that with this shipment the volume capacity is totally utilized; however, the weight of the shipment falls 3.4 (1,000s) pounds short ($S_2 = 3.4$) of the plane's capacity. If solved by the simplex method, x_1 and S_2 would be in the optimal basis, and x_2 and S_1 would be nonbasic variables.

FIGURE 5–4 Air Cargo Optimal Solution

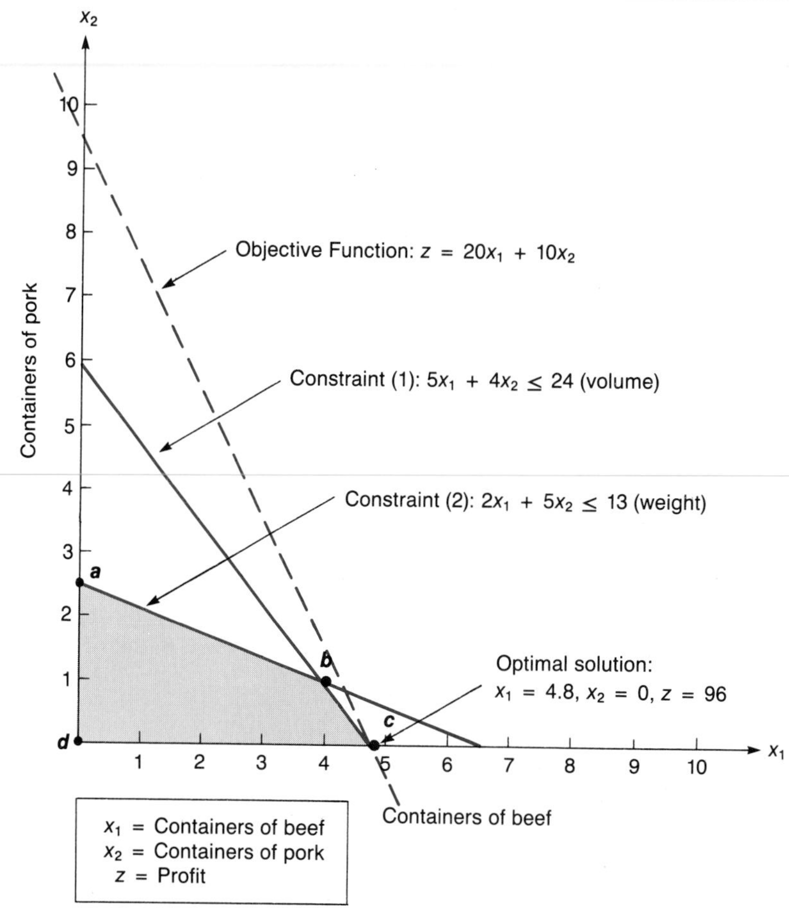

General sensitivity analysis for this problem is concerned with identifying the ranges over which parameters can fluctuate and still retain x_1 and S_2 in the basis. That is, what kinds of changes will cause a revision of the present decision to ship all beef? From a graphical perspective, we wish to determine the ranges of variation in the parameters within which the optimal solution remains at point c. In this section, the parameter of interest is the objective function coefficient for the nonbasic variable x_2 (that is, $c_2 = 10$).

Intuitive Approach

In a problem of this scale, intuition can be useful in anticipating expected effects. The nonbasic variables in the optimal solution to the present problem are S_1 and x_2. Since it is meaningless to consider a change in the profit associated with a slack variable (its objective function coefficient is almost always set equal to zero), our attention should be directed to the contribution from x_2 (pork). Relative to the profit contribution for beef ($c_1 = 20$), the contribution of 10 for pork is less attractive. We would expect that if the 10 were to decrease, pork would be even less desirable, and our decision to ship as much beef as possible would be reinforced; however, if the contribution were to increase for pork, we might expect that at some higher profit contribution pork would become a desirable commodity to ship. Thus, our intuition would suggest that the existing solution is *insensitive* to decreases in the contribution of pork but *sensitive* to an increase, beyond some point.

Geometric Approach

In this analysis we are questioning the effects on the slope of the objective function $(-c_1/c_2)$ given changes in c_2. The slope of the original objective function is $(-20/10)$ or -2. If c_2 decreases, the slope becomes more negative (the objective function rotates clockwise from z to z' in Figure 5–5*a*). This type of rotation provides even greater support for an optimal solution at point c and matches our intuitive statement that the solution is insensitive to decreases in the profit contribution of pork.

If, however, the contribution from pork (c_2) increases, the slope of the objective function becomes less negative (or reorients itself in a counterclockwise manner). If c_2 increases sufficiently, the objective function in Figure 5–5*b* becomes parallel to constraint 1, and we would have alternative optimal solutions along the edge $\overline{bc}$. If c_2 continues to increase, the slope of the objective function becomes less negative than that of constraint 1, and the optimal solution would occur at point b. Further increases in c_2 could eventually result in alternative optimal solutions along edge $\overline{ab}$ or an optimal solution at point a.

Note from Figure 5–5*b* that systematic increases in c_2 are equivalent to progressive counterclockwise rotations of the z profit line. The optimal extreme point or edge thus depends on the slope of the z-function relative to the slopes of constraints 1 and 2. To be more precise, let m_1, m_2, and m_z represent the slopes of constraint 1, constraint 2, and the objective function, respectively. See if you agree with the following slope relationships and conclusions.

If $m_z < m_1$, optimal solution at point c.

If $m_z = m_1$, alternative optimal solutions along $\overline{bc}$.

If $m_1 < m_z < m_2$, optimal solution at point b.

If $m_z = m_2$, alternative optimal solutions along $\overline{ab}$.

If $m_z > m_2$, optimal solution at point a.

FIGURE 5–5 Sensitivity to c_2

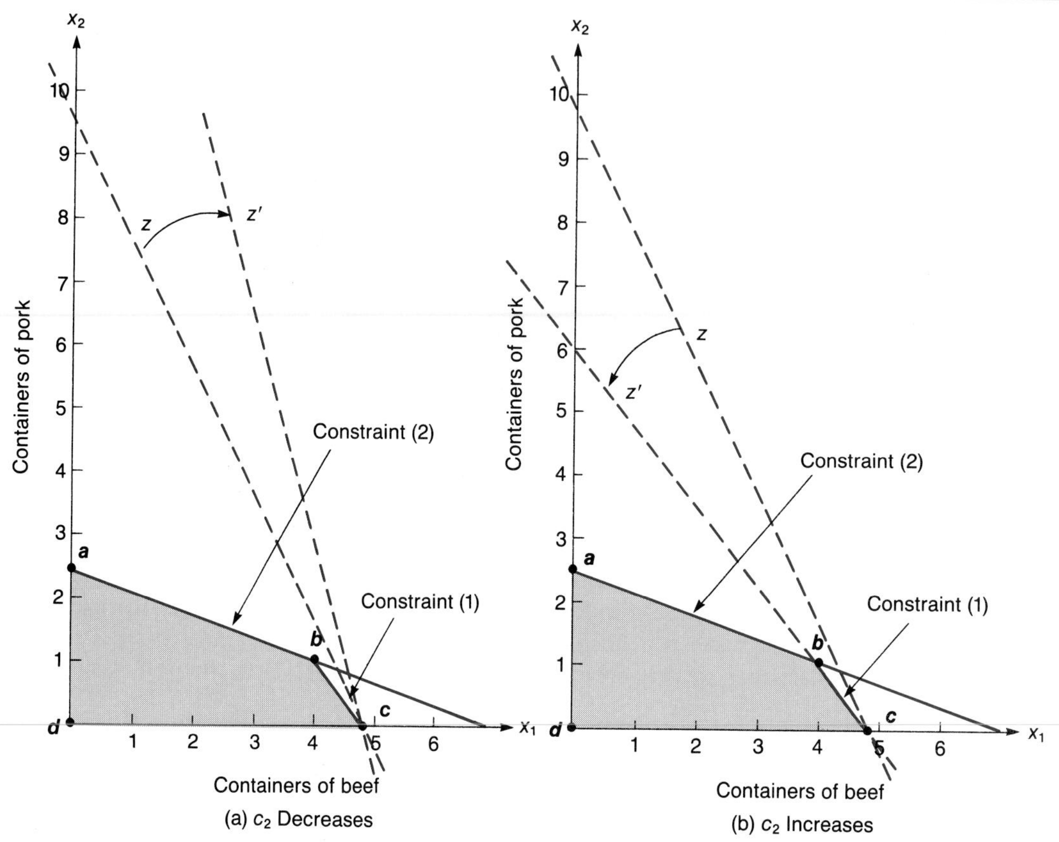

Example 5.1

Let us determine the value of c_2 that results in alternative optimal solutions along edge $\overline{bc}$. Since we assume that all parameters are held constant except for c_2, we have from Equation 5.2 and the equations given in Figure 5–4: $m_z = -20/c_2$ and $m_1 = -5/4$. The two slopes will be equal when

$$-\frac{5}{4} = -\frac{20}{c_2}$$

$$c_2 = -20\left(-\frac{4}{5}\right)$$

$$c_2 = 16\,.$$

Thus if c_2 *increases* by 6 from its assumed value of 10, alternative optimal solutions will exist along edge $\overline{bc}$.

Note that our analysis in this section agrees with our previous intuitive analysis: The optimal solution at point c is insensitive to decreases in c_2 but sensitive to increases.

As long as c_2 is in the range $-\infty < c_2 < 16$, and all other parameters remain fixed, the optimal solution is unaffected.

FOLLOW-UP EXERCISES

3. Would you conclude that the optimal solution at point *c* is relatively insensitive to changes in c_2? Explain.
4. By algebraic means determine the value(s) for c_2 that result in:
   a. A unique optimal solution at point *c*.
   b. A unique optimal solution at point *b*.
   c. Alternative optimal solutions along edge $\overline{ab}$.
   d. A unique optimal solution at point *a*.

5.3 SENSITIVITY ANALYSIS—OBJECTIVE FUNCTION COEFFICIENTS (BASIC VARIABLES)

We have separated the analysis for basic and nonbasic variables because the simplex-based analysis of objective function coefficients is slightly different for basic and nonbasic variables. As a result, many LP computer packages present the sensitivity results separately for the two types of variables (as we will see in Section 5.5).

Intuitive Approach

Continuing the air cargo example, the basic variables in the optimal solution are x_1 and S_2. As before, we ignore the slack variable and concern ourselves with the range over which the contribution on beef (c_1) can fluctuate before our decision of exclusive beef shipments changes. On an intuitive level we would expect that increases in the profit contribution for beef would reinforce the decision to ship beef only; however, we might expect that if the profit contribution were to decrease on beef, a point might be reached whereby beef becomes less attractive as a shippable commodity and we might consider the substitution of pork. Thus we would expect the optimal basis to be *insensitive* to increases but *sensitive* to decreases in c_1.

Geometric Approach

The slope of the objective function is $(-c_1/c_2)$ or $(-20/10)$. If c_1 increases and c_2 remains constant, then the slope becomes more negative or rotates in a clockwise direction. As seen in Figure 5–6, this reinforces point *c* as optimal. On the other hand, a decrease in c_1 results in a less negative slope or a counterclockwise rotation of the profit line. If c_1 decreases sufficiently, then the slope of the objective function will equal that of constraint 1, giving $\overline{bc}$ as the optimal edge. If c_1 decreases beyond this level, point *b* becomes the new optimal corner point. Further decreases result eventually in an optimal solution at point *a*.

Example 5.2

Let us determine the value(s) for c_1 that result in a unique optimal solution at point *c*. As stated before, point *c* is optimal when

$$m_z < m_1$$

FIGURE 5–6 Sensitivity to c_1

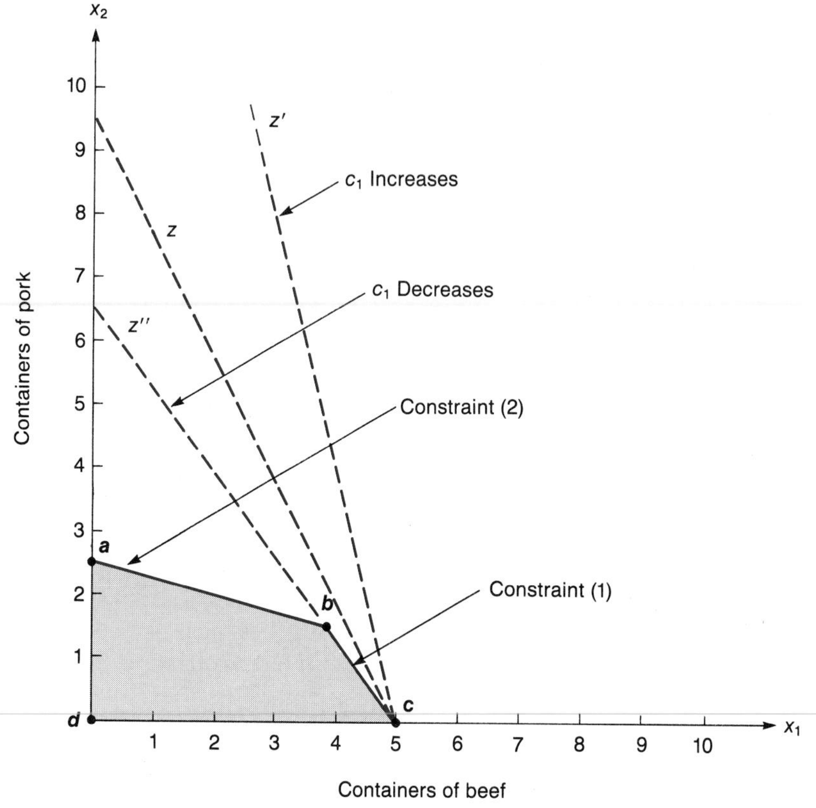

or when

$$-\frac{c_1}{c_2} < m_1$$

$$-\frac{c_1}{10} < -\frac{5}{4}.$$

Solving for c_1, we conclude that point c remains optimal as long as

$$c_1 > 12.5.$$

We can interpret this result by stating that it takes a decline in the profit contribution for beef of at least \$750 from its current value of \$2,000 to make the current decision of shipping all beef a nonoptimal decision. As long as the contribution of beef remains above \$1,250 and all other parameters remain constant, the decision to ship 4.8 containers of beef is optimal.

We should note that the *insensitivity* signal in the intuitive analysis for *this* example is correct; that is, the geometric analysis confirms that the optimal extreme point remains at point c, or is insensitive, should c_1 increase. More often than not, fluctuations in c_j both above some upper limit and below some lower limit will cause a change in the optimal extreme point. To illustrate why this is so, consider point b in Figure 5–6. If point b is optimal, then it follows that a sufficient clockwise rotation of the z function would establish point c as optimal. Similarly, a sufficient counterclockwise rotation of the z function would establish point a as optimal. Thus the c_j corresponding to a basic variable generally has upper and lower bounds within which the current optimal extreme point remains optimal.

> The essense of sensitivity analysis on the jth objective function coefficient addresses the question: By how much can c_j vary before the existing optimal extreme point is no longer optimal? Within the allowable range of variation for c_j:
>
> **1.** The current optimal extreme point remains optimal, which means that the same variables remain in the optimal basis and their values don't change.
>
> **2.** The optimal value of z changes if x_j is a basic variable and does not change if x_j is a nonbasic variable. A change in c_j outside its allowable range results in a new optimal extreme point.

FOLLOW-UP EXERCISES

5. By algebraic means, determine the bound(s) for c_1 that result in:
   a. A unique optimal solution at point b.
   b. Alternative optimal solutions along edge $\overline{ab}$.
   c. Alternative optimal solutions along edge $\overline{bc}$.
   d. A unique optimal solution at point a.
   e. Interpret these results within the context of the air cargo problem.
6. Suppose variable x_j is in the optimal basis, and sensitivity analysis for c_j yields a lower bound L_j and an upper bound U_j. Assuming all other parameters remain constant, can we conclude that a change in c_j such that $c_j < L_j$ or $c_j > U_j$ would necessarily result in the elimination of x_j from the optimal basis? Explain using Figure 5–6.
7. In Example 5.2:
   a. Specify the optimal solution (values for x_1, x_2, and z) if c_1 changes to 15, all other things equal.
   b. Let us define
      Δz^* = Optimal change in z.
      Δc_j = *Change in* c_j.
      x_j^* = Optimal value of *basic* variable x_j.
      Can you state an expression for Δz^* as a function of Δc_j? State a condition under which this expression for Δz^* is valid using the symbols c_j, Δc_j, L_j, and U_j, where the latter are defined in the preceding exercise. What must be true about Δx_j^*?
   c. Is the expression Δz^* in part b valid when x_j is a nonbasic variable? Explain.
   d. What can you conclude if $c_j + \Delta c_j = L_j$ or $c_j + \Delta c_j = U_j$?

5.4 SENSITIVITY ANALYSIS—RIGHT-HAND–SIDE CONSTANTS

This form of sensitivity analysis explores the range over which the right-hand–side (b_i) of a constraint can fluctuate so that the optimal solution remains *feasible*. Because intuition is only marginally helpful in this case, we proceed directly to a graphical analysis.

Geometric Approach

In the air cargo problem, the constraints represented volume and weight restrictions for the airplane. In the optimal solution at point c in Figure 5–7*a*, the volume constraint is binding (the available 24 cubic yards are used), there is slack in the weight constraint, variables x_1 and S_2 are in the optimal basis with respective values of 4.8 and 3.4, and $z = 96$.

Let us focus on changes for the right-hand–side constant of constraint 1, which is currently 24 cubic yards of volume. From Figure 5–2 we know that a change in the right-hand–side constant of a linear equation in the two variables causes changes in the x_1-intercept and x_2-intercept but no change in the slope of the line. Should the volume restriction ($b_1 = 24$) decrease, Figure 5–7*b* indicates that constraint 1 moves parallel to itself toward the origin, resulting in a contraction of the area of feasible solutions. Constraint 1′ reflects a decrease in b_1 to 16. With this change the feasible region contracts to the polygon $ab'c'd$, and the optimal solution occurs at c' with z' equaling 64.

If b_1 decreases sufficiently, constraint 1″ in Figure 5–7*c* indicates the point where *constraint 2 becomes redundant,* no longer forming an edge on the area of feasible solutions. As b_1 has decreased in value from the original 24 to 16 to 10.4, the variables x_1 and S_2 have remained basic at the optimal corner point (respectively, c, c', and c''), but their values have changed. That is, for any decrease in volume, x_1 decreases and S_2 increases. As the volume decreases, the recommendation is still "ship only beef," but less of it, and the amount of unused weight capacity increases. Another important observation is that as the volume capacity decreases, less beef is shipped and the maximum profit becomes smaller.

The big question still remains: How much can b_1 decrease such that the optimal basis consisting of x_1 and S_2 remains feasible? If we reexamine Figure 5–7, constraint 1 can be shifted inward until it intersects the origin at d (at which point $b_1 = 0$, or there is zero volume capacity). This represents the limit on decreases in b_1. Any further decrease violates the nonnegativity restriction for x_i (in addition to not making sense—negative volume capacity?).

Figure 5–8 illustrates the effects of increases in b_1. If the volume increases, constraint 1 moves away from the origin, resulting in an expansion of the feasible region. The optimal basis still contains x_1 and S_2—although x_1 is increasing, S_2 is decreasing, and z is increasing. When b_1 increases to a value of 32.5, represented by constraint 1‴, S_2 equals zero, and any further movement would lead to negative S_2 if the current basis remains intact. As you know, however, a negative value is not permissible for any variable, as an infeasible solution would result. Thus for values of b_1

FIGURE 5–7 Sensitivity to Decreases in b_1

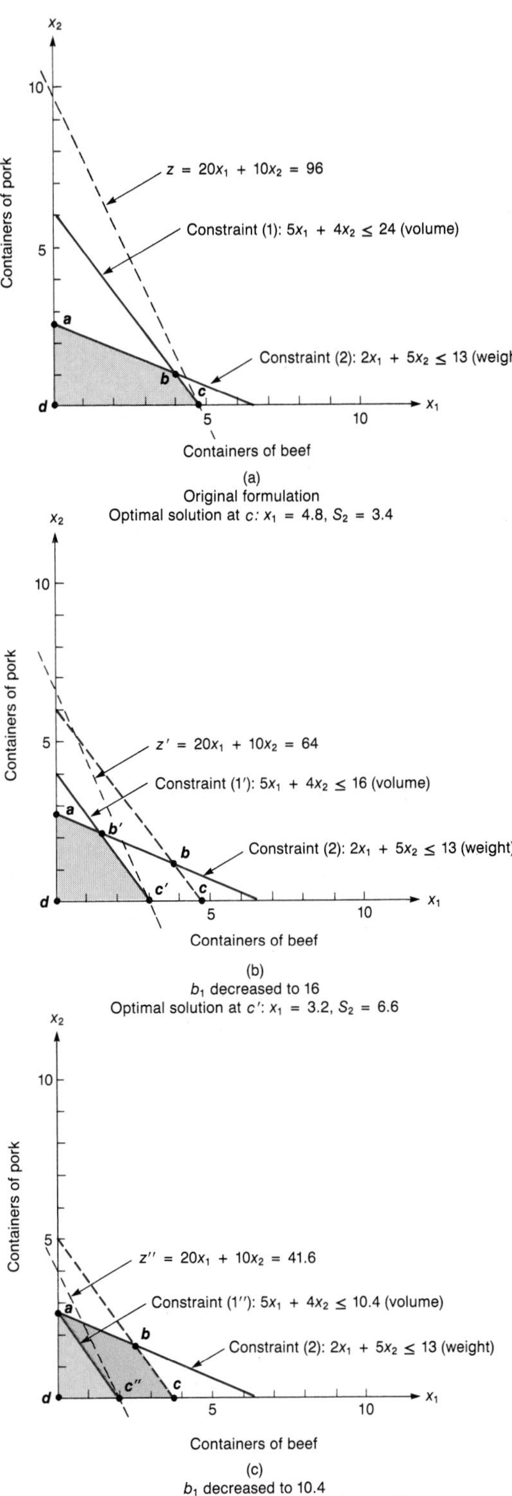

x2
10
5
Containers of pork
z = 20x1 + 10x2 = 96
Constraint (1): 5x1 + 4x2 ≤ 24 (volume)
Constraint (2): 2x1 + 5x2 ≤ 13 (weight)
a
b
c
d
5
10
x1
Containers of beef
(a)
Original formulation
Optimal solution at c: x1 = 4.8, S2 = 3.4
x2
10
5
Containers of pork
z' = 20x1 + 10x2 = 64
Constraint (1'): 5x1 + 4x2 ≤ 16 (volume)
Constraint (2): 2x1 + 5x2 ≤ 13 (weight)
a
b'
b
c'
c
d
5
10
x1
Containers of beef
(b)
b1 decreased to 16
Optimal solution at c': x1 = 3.2, S2 = 6.6
x2
10
5
Containers of pork
z'' = 20x1 + 10x2 = 41.6
Constraint (1''): 5x1 + 4x2 ≤ 10.4 (volume)
Constraint (2): 2x1 + 5x2 ≤ 13 (weight)
a
b
c''
c
d
5
10
x1
Containers of beef
(c)
b1 decreased to 10.4
Optimal solution at c'': x1 = 2.08, S2 = 8.84

greater than 32.5, constraint 2 becomes binding, constraint 1 is *redundant,* the optimal solution occurs at point b'', and the basis changes from x_1 and S_2 to x_1 and S_1. In essence, weight capacity becomes restrictive once volume capacity reaches 32.5 cubic yards. Additional increases in volume would go unused.

In summary, we conclude that the current optimal basis (x_1 and S_1) remains feasible for $0 \leq b_1 \leq 32.5$. Compared with the original value of 24, b_1 *may increase by as much as 8.5 units or decrease by as much as 24 units.*

> The essense of sensitivity analysis on the right-hand–side constant of the ith constraint (b_i) addresses the question: By how much can b_i vary before the existing optimal basis is no longer feasible? Within the allowable range of variation for b_i:
>
> 1. The mix of variables within the optimal basis remains the same.
> 2. The basis remains feasible.
> 3. The basis remains optimal.
> 4. Solution values change for one or more basic variables.
> 5. The optimal value of z changes if constraint i is active (S_i or E_i is zero); otherwise, optimal z is unaffected. A change in b_i outside its allowable range will result in either a new optimal basis or an infeasible solution (empty solution space).

FOLLOW-UP EXERCISE

8. What range of values can b_2 assume and still have the optimal basis remain feasible? Pick a value for b_2 within this range, and show that values for basic variables have changed, but not the value of optimal z.

Shadow Prices

A useful concept related to sensitivity analysis of right-hand–side (RHS) constants is the **shadow price.**

> The shadow price associated with constraint i, y_i, is the amount the optimal value of the objective function would change if the RHS constant of the ith constraint (b_i) were increased by one unit, providing the same variables remain in the optimal basis and all other parameters remain fixed. Alternatively, the shadow price y_i can be thought of as the rate of change in the optimal value of z as b_i is increased, providing the change in b_i is within the allowable range given by sensitivity analysis.

Since many $\leq$ constraints represent limited resources in LP problems, shadow prices are often thought of as representing the economic value of having an additional unit of a given resource. In effect, the shadow price is the "hidden price" (or opportunity cost) we pay for not having an additional unit of a resource. Alternatively, the

FIGURE 5–8 Sensitivity to Increases in b_1

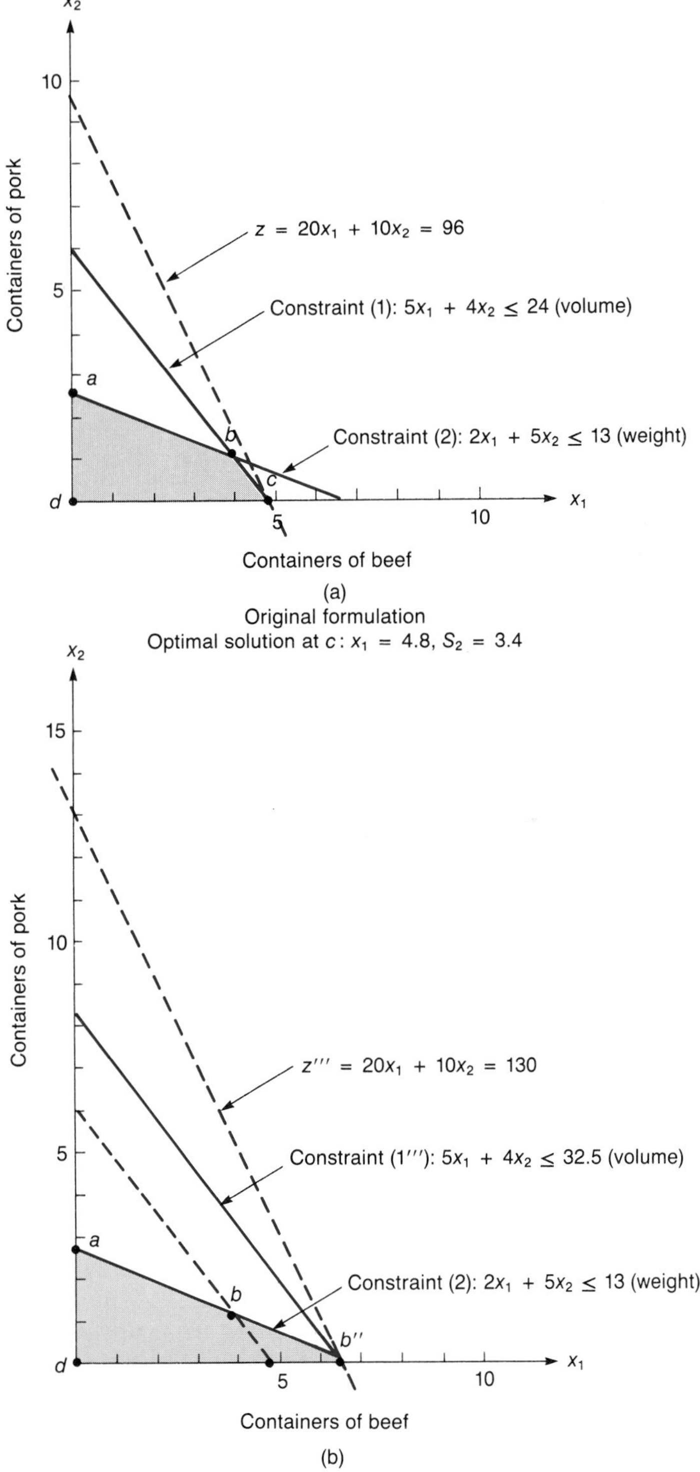

(a)
Original formulation
Optimal solution at c: $x_1 = 4.8$, $S_2 = 3.4$

(b)
b_1 increased to 32.5
Optimal solution at b'': $x_1 = 6.5$, $S_2 = 0$

shadow price is the maximum price we would willingly pay for an additional unit of the resource.[3]

▶ Example 5.3

Continuing with the air cargo example, the two structural constraints are both $\leq$ types representing volume and weight capacities. If we reflect for a moment on the definition of a shadow price, we might conclude that the value of an additional unit of a resource should depend in part on how much of the available resource is utilized in the optimal solution. If the current availability is not totally utilized (i.e., an inactive constraint) having additional units would be of no value; however, if the current availability is totally utilized (active constraint) there may be some economic value in having an additional unit.

In the optimal solution to the air cargo problem, all volume capacity is consumed by the 4.8 containers of beef. However, there is unused weight capacity of 3.4 (1,000s) pounds. We might expect that an additional cubic yard of volume capacity would improve our profit position. (In Figure 5–8 observe what happened to z when volume capacity increased from 24 to 32.5 cubic yards.) By contrast, we should expect that an additional unit of weight capacity would result in no change in profit.

To confirm our hypotheses we would need to re-solve the air cargo problem twice; once with $b_1 = 25$ and $b_2 = 13$, and a second time with $b_1 = 24$ and $b_2 = 14$. (You will be asked to do this in a follow-up exercise.)

When we solve with $b_1 = 25$, z is maximized at a value of 100 ($100s) at $(5, 0)$. Compared with the original solution value of 96, profit has increased by 4 ($100s) with the added cubic yard of space. Since $b_1 = 25$ is within the allowable sensitivity range of $0 \leq b_1 \leq 32.5$, it follows that $y_1 = 4$ is the shadow price associated with the volume constraint.

Note that the shadow price is forgone profit (the price we pay) for not having an extra cubic yard of space in the cargo hold. From a practical perspective, the shadow price is the maximum price we would willingly pay for an additional unit of volume. For example, if the shipping company offered an additional cubic yard of space for $300, then it pays to accept the offer, since expected profit contribution would increase by the value of the shadow price, or $400. Thus we would be better off by $100 ($400 – $300).

Now that we have established the shadow price $y_1 = 4$, we might ask "What's the expected optimal profit contribution if volume capacity were increased from the current 24 cubic yards to 27 cubic yards?" Since optimal $z = 96$ at $b_1 = 24$ and $y_1 = 4$ is valid in the range $0 \leq b_1 \leq 32.5$, we can say that an increase of 3 cubic yards (to $b_1 = 27$, which is within the allowable range for b_1) will improve optimal profit contribution by 4×3, or 12, to $z = 108$. Of course, if we have to pay more than 12 ($100s) for the extra 3 cubic yards, we're better off not accepting the offer.

> The change in the optimal value of the objective function is given by the product of the shadow price and the change in the RHS constant, providing the change in the RHS constant doesn't exceed its allowable bound.

[3] The shadow price is also called the **dual variable, dual activity, dual price,** or **imputed price.**

When the problem is re-solved with $b_1 = 24$ and $b_2 = 14$, the solution is identical to the original solution. Increasing the weight capacity results in no change in profit. Thus the shadow price associated with the weight constraint is zero, or $y_2 = 0$.

Finally, note that the unit of measurement for shadow prices in the air cargo problem is dollars per unit. For example, $y_1 = 4$ is actually $400 per cubic yard.

In practice shadow prices are determined routinely without completely re-solving the problem. (Chapter 6 will give procedures for computing shadow prices.) Also, most LP computer packages generate shadow prices (as does ours in Section 5.5).

Let us make some final points regarding shadow prices:

1. There is a range of validity for any shadow price that is established by the sensitivity analysis on the corresponding RHS constant. The shadow price of 4 for constraint 1 in Example 5.3 is valid for changes in b_1 within the range $0 \leq b_1 \leq 32.5$. The shadow price does not suggest that increasing the volume capacity of the cargo hold by 1,000 cubic yards will result in a 4,000 ($100s) increase in profit contribution. Changes in b_i outside the allowable range invalidate the definition of the shadow price.[4]
2. Shadow prices are usually associated with $\leq$ constraints, primarily because of economic interpretations; that is, a $\leq$ constraint frequently implies a resource limitation, which leads to the shadow price as the maximum price we would pay for an additional unit of that resource. However, our general definition of a shadow price as the rate of change in optimal z as b_i increases also is applied to $\geq$ and $=$ constraints.
3. The shadow price associated with a *binding* or *active* constraint—that is, an equality constraint, a $\leq$ constraint with $S_i = 0$, or a $\geq$ constraint with $E_i = 0$—is necessarily nonzero; the shadow price associated with an *inactive* constraint—where $S_i > 0$ or $E_i > 0$—is necessarily zero.[5] Rigorous mathematical proofs in the theory of LP confirm these statements, but for our purposes consider the air cargo problem again. In the optimal solution the volume constraint is active, which means that $b_1 = 24$ binds the optimal solution and $S_1 = 0$. We would expect that an increase in b_1 would increase optimal z, thereby implying a positive shadow price. The weight constraint with $b_2 = 13$ is inactive ($S_2 = 3.4$). We would expect that further increases in b_2 would have no effect on optimal z (since we would simply add more slack), thereby implying a shadow price of zero. Similar reasoning applies to $\geq$ constraints and their surplus variables (E_i's).
4. The behavior of optimal z with respect to the sign on the shadow price and the direction of change in b_i is summarized in Table 5–1. For example, a negative shadow price such as $y_5 = -10$ implies a decrease in optimal z for an increase (positive change) in b_5; a negative change in b_5 implies an increase in optimal z. Thus if the objective function is to be maximized, we would wish to decrease b_5; however, if the objective function is to be mini-

[4]If the change in b_i is on the boundary of the allowable range (for example, $b_i = 32.5$), then the optimal solution may be degenerate, and the shadow price definition may break down. See Exercise 11*d*. A degenerate solution has a *basic* variable with a zero value.

[5]There are some minor exceptions to these statements, which we mention in Section 5.7. See Table 5–4.

mized, we would wish to increase b_5. To see how a negative shadow price can arise, consider the following example of improving our position in a maximization problem by *decreasing* b_i: In a profit maximization problem, constraint i calls for at least b_i units to be invested in a low-profit activity. What change in b_i would result in higher levels of profit?

TABLE 5–1 Directional Effect on Optimal z

Change in b_i	Sign on Shadow Price Positive	Negative
Positive	Increase	Decrease
Negative	Decrease	Increase

5. Unfortunately, the definition of the shadow price with respect to its directional effect on optimal z is neither standardized in the literature nor (more important) in computer output. We have defined the shadow price as a marginal rate of change in optimal z based on a unit increase in b_i. Table 5–1 directly reflects this definition. A popular alternative defines the shadow price as a *marginal rate of improvement* in optimal z based on a unit increase in b_i. In this case a positive shadow price coupled with an increase in b_i increases optimal z in a max type problem and decreases optimal z in a min type problem. Thus positive shadow prices together with increases in b_i's are associated with improvements in optimal values of z. It is usually easy to decipher the convention used by a particular computer package when one examines the output.

FOLLOW-UP EXERCISES

9. Confirm the results of Example 5.3 by re-solving the air cargo problem with
   a. $b_1 = 25$ and $b_2 = 13$.
   b. $b_2 = 14$ and $b_1 = 24$.
10. Use the shadow price for the volume constraint to predict optimal profit if volume capacity is
    a. Increased to 30.
    b. Increased to 35.
    c. Decreased to 14.
11. Let us define

$$\Delta z^* = \text{Optimal change in } z.$$
$$\Delta b_i = \text{Change in } b_i.$$
$$y_i = \text{Shadow price for } i\text{th constraint.}$$
$$L_i = \text{Lower bound on } b_i \text{ from sensitivity analysis.}$$
$$U_i = \text{Upper bound on } b_i \text{ from sensitivity analysis.}$$

    a. State an expression for Δz^* as a function of Δb_i and y_i.
    b. State the condition under which this expression for Δz^* is valid.
    c. Apply the expression to the data in the preceding exercise.
    **d. What can you conclude if $b_i + \Delta b_i = L_i$ or $b_i + \Delta b_i = U_i$?

12. Suppose we have a solution where $y_1 = 5$, $y_2 = -3$, and $y_3 = 0$. What would you recommend with respect to independent changes in each b_i if the problem is of type:
    a. Maximization?
    b. Minimization?
13. How would your answers to the preceding exercise change if the shadow price were defined as a marginal rate of improvement? (See item 5 immediately preceding these exercises.)
14. Given the model:

    Maximize

    $$z = x_1 + x_2$$

    subject to

    $$x_1 \geq 3 \quad (1)$$

    $$x_1 \leq 7 \quad (2)$$

    $$x_2 \leq 4 \quad (3)$$

    $$x_1, x_2 \geq 0$$

    a. Determine shadow prices and their associated allowable ranges for b_i's. First specify the optimal basis and optimal solution values.
    b. Rework part *a* if the objective is to minimize $z = x_1 + x_2$.
    c. Rework part *a* if the objective is to maximize $z = -x_1 + x_2$.
    d. Suppose constraint 3 in part *a* is changed from type $\leq$ to type $=$. Rework part *b*.

5.5 COMPUTER-BASED ANALYSIS

In actual practice, sensitivity analysis is performed by the LP computer package used to solve the original problem. Example 5.4 illustrates and interprets the output from an LP package used in this text. Output from any package you might use will look different, but read on anyway, since it's the interpretation of these results that's important.

Example 5.4

Examples 4.5 and 4.6 illustrated the input and solution of the following LP problem using a computer package.

Minimize

$$z = 3x_1 + 4x_2 + 6.13x_3 + 5x_4$$

subject to

$$0.5x_1 + 0.8x_3 \leq 350 \quad (1)$$

$$0.5x_2 + 0.8x_4 \leq 500 \quad (2)$$

$$10.0x_1 + 7.0x_3 \leq 6{,}000 \quad (3)$$

$$10.0x_1 + 10.0x_2 + 7.0x_3 + 7.0x_4 \leq 10{,}000 \quad (4)$$

$$x_1 + x_2 = 500 \quad (5)$$

$$x_3 + x_4 = 700 \quad (6)$$

$$x_j \geq 0, \quad j = 1, 2, 3, 4$$

Figure 5–9 illustrates the complete output for this problem using LINDO. Reviewing the solution, the objective function is minimized at a value of 5084.75 when $x_1 = 500$, $x_2 = 0$, $x_3 = 75$, and $x_4 = 625$. Aside from x_1, x_3, and x_4, the other basic variables are S_1 (slack of 40 in constraint 1), S_3 (slack of 475 in constraint 3), and S_4 (slack of 100 in constraint 4).[6]

In Chapter 4 we delayed discussion of the Reduced Cost and Dual Prices columns. For LINDO, the reduced cost is the amount by which the objective function coefficient of a nonbasic (decision) variable must *improve* before that variable would be a candidate to enter the basis. Thus, as we examine Figure 5–9, the reduced costs for x_1, x_3, and x_4 are zero because they are in the basis. The reduced cost for x_2 (a nonbasic decision variable) is 1.706250. This variable was not included in the basis because its objective function coefficient was *too large* relative to the other variables. The reduced cost tells us that to improve its attractiveness, the objective function coefficient must be improved or *decreased* in value by 1.706250. Because the original coefficient was 4, we conclude that its value must decrease to 2.29375 before it will enter the basis.

> When using LINDO, a positive reduced cost represents the necessary *decrease* in the objective function coefficient for *minimization* problems and the necessary *increase* for *maximization* problems.

The Dual Prices column provides shadow price information. For LINDO the dual price is defined as a *marginal rate of improvement*. For the inactive constraints in our solution (those having slack), the dual prices are zero. The active constraints (those satisfied as equations) are constraints 2, 5, and 6. For constraint 2, the positive dual price indicates that the objective function would *improve* (decrease) in value by 1.4125 if the RHS constant were increased from 500 to 501. The negative dual price for constraint 5 indicates that there would be *negative improvement* (or an increase) of 3.0 in the value of the objective function if the RHS constant increased from 500 to 501. And the dual price for constraint 6 indicates negative improvement (an increase) of 6.13 in the value of the objective function if the RHS constant increases from 700 to 701.

> When using LINDO, a positive dual price represents a marginal improvement (i.e., a *marginal increase* in the objective function for *maximization* problems and a *marginal decrease* for *minimization* problems).

[6]Remember from Example 4.6 that LINDO labels the objective function as row 1, labels constraint 1 as row 2, and so on.

FIGURE 5–9 LINDO Output for Example 5.4

```
LP OPTIMUM FOUND AT STEP 3

        OBJECTIVE FUNCTION VALUE

1            5084.75000

VARIABLE          VALUE          REDUCED COST
   X1          500.000000          .000000
   X2             .000000         1.706250
   X3           75.000010          .000000
   X4          625.000000          .000000

   ROW        SLACK OR SURPLUS     DUAL PRICES
   2)           39.999990          .000000
   3)             .000000         1.412500
   4)         1000.000000          .000000
   5)         3950.000000          .000000
   6)             .000000        -3.000000
   7)             .000000        -6.130000

RANGES IN WHICH THE BASIS IS UNCHANGED

                          OBJ COEFFICIENT RANGES
               CURRENT          ALLOWABLE         ALLOWABLE
VARIABLE        COEF            INCREASE          DECREASE
   X1         3.000000          1.706250          INFINITY
   X2         4.000000          INFINITY          1.706250
   X3         6.130000          INFINITY          1.130000
   X4         5.000000          1.130000          INFINITY

                          RIGHT-HAND-SIDE RANGES
               CURRENT          ALLOWABLE         ALLOWABLE
   ROW           RHS            INCREASE          DECREASE
   2          350.000000        INFINITY          39.999990
   3          500.000000        60.000010         39.999990
   4         6000.000000        INFINITY        1000.000000
   5        10000.000000        INFINITY        3950.000000
   6          500.000000        79.999980        500.000000
   7          700.000000        49.999990         75.000010
```

Regarding sensitivity analysis, LINDO provides objective function coefficient analysis (Obj. Coefficient Ranges) and RHS constant analysis (Right-Hand–Side Ranges). For both types of analysis, the original parameter value and allowable increases and decreases are shown. Although the interpretations are straight forward, let us examine a couple of parameters. For x_2 the original objective function coefficient was 4.00. The output indicates that this coefficient can increase by an infinite amount or decrease by 1.70625 before the current basis is no longer optimal. This is consistent with the reduced cost interpretation examined earlier. Although there is a certain subjectivity in the interpretation of the results of sensitivity analysis (there are no definitive rules for stating when a solution is sensitive or insensitive to parameter changes), we can make the statement that the optimal basis is "insensitive" to any increases in the parameter c_2 and that it is "somewhat sensitive" to decreases in c_2. That is, if c_2 increases (all other parameters held constant), the current basis will not change. However, if it decreased by more than 1.70625, a new optimal basis exists.

Regarding RHS constants, the output indicates that b_2 (which currently equals 500) can increase by as much as 60 or decrease by as much as 40 before the current basis will no longer be feasible. Stated differently, the current basis will remain feasible as long as $460 \leq b_2 \leq 560$. Remember that the b_i sensitivity analysis is used to qualify the interpretations of shadow prices. Thus the shadow, or dual, price of 1.4125 associated with constraint 2 is valid over the range $460 \leq b_2 \leq 560$.

FOLLOW-UP EXERCISES

As mentioned in Exercise 23 (Chapter 4), the LP model discussed in Example 5.4 is the same as that formulated for the multiperiod, product mix model in Example 3.3. The only difference is the absence of the 60 in the objective function. Review Example 3.3, and then attempt the following exercises.

15. Provide a verbal *interpretation* of the meaning of each shadow (dual) price (interpret within the context of the multiperiod, product mix model). Discuss the range of validity for each.
16. What is the minimum price we should accept for delivering an extra unit of product B? If the buyer is willing to pay $8 per unit for delivery of an additional 50 units of product B, should we accept? Explain.
17. What can you conclude if the current cost coefficient on x_4 ($c_4 = 5$) increases to *exactly* $6.13?
18. *a.* Provide a verbal interpretation of the sensitivity analysis for objective function coefficients (again, within the context of Example 3.3).
    b. LINDO shows in Figure 5–9 that the optimal solution is insensitive to decreases in the x_1 objective function coefficient. A second computer package indicates that the solution is sensitive to decreases that put the coefficient at less than zero. Which package is right?
19. Our analysis indicates that it's desirable to increase available labor hours in the second quarter from the current 500 if doing so doesn't cost more than $1.41 per hour. An astute observer, you point out that we have 40 hours of slack in the first quarter. So maybe we can shift these 40 hours to the second quarter by reducing b_1 to 310 and increasing b_2 to 540, since both changes are within the limits given in the b_i-sensitivity output. Do you care to comment on this?

5.6 OTHER FORMS OF POSTOPTIMALITY ANALYSIS

Postoptimality analyses are not restricted to those types we have illustrated. In this section we briefly discuss other forms.

Parametric Programming

Parametric LP is a form of systematic postoptimality (sensitivity) analysis that automatically allows selected parameters (b_i's and c_j's) to be varied continuously over specified ranges. The output from this analysis shows the optimal solution as a function of these changes.

To be more specific, consider the usual objective function for LP,

$$z = c_1x_1 + c_2x_2 + \ldots + c_nx_n,$$

and its parametric LP equivalent for varying objective function contributions (c_j's):

$$z(\Delta) = (c_1 + k_1\Delta)x_1 + (c_2 + k_2\Delta)x_2 + \ldots + (c_n + k_n\Delta)x_n.$$

In this case, $z(\Delta)$ indicates that the criterion is a function of Δ, the **ranging parameter.** Note that the case $\Delta = 0$ yields the original objective function. The k_j's represent *relative rates of change* when the (c_j) parameters are to be varied *simultaneously*. If a selected k_j is set equal to unity, and the remaining k_j's are set equal to zero, then the analysis only varies the selected objective function contribution. This is equivalent to varying a selected c_j *independently* of the other c_j's.

Parametric programming software typically require specific input values for each k_j and a range of values for Δ. A simplex-based procedure is then utilized to provide optimal values of z as a function of Δ, $z^*(\Delta)$, and optimal values of decision variables as a function of $\Delta, x_j^*(\Delta)$. The function $z^*(\Delta)$ is called the **optimal value function.**

▶ Example 5.5 Air Cargo Problem Re-Revisited

In this chapter we have performed extensive sensitivity analyses on the following problem:

Maximize

$$z = 20x_1 + 10x_2$$

subject to

$$5x_1 + 4x_2 \leq 24 \quad \text{(Volume)}$$

$$2x_1 + 5x_2 \leq 13 \quad \text{(Weight)}$$

$$x_1, x_2 \geq 0$$

where x_1 and x_2 represent, respectively, the number of containers of beef and pork to be shipped by air cargo; z states profit in \$100s; the first constraint represents 24 cubic yards of volume capacity for the aircraft; and the last constraint represents 13,000 pounds of weight capacity.

The parametric LP equivalent for varying profit contributions simply involves a rewrite of z:

$$z(\Delta) = (20 + k_1\Delta)x_1 + (10 + k_2\Delta)x_2.$$

If we assume independence between variations in the two profit contributions, then to vary c_1 between 20 and 30 requires the specification of $k_1 = 1$, $k_2 = 0$, and $0 \leq \Delta \leq 10$. To vary c_2 between 10 and 25, we specify $k_1 = 0$, $k_2 = 1$, and $0 \leq \Delta \leq 15$. If increases in marginal pork profit are only possible at the expense of corresponding decreases in marginal beef profits, then $k_1 = -1$, $k_2 = 1$, and Δ may be varied as desired.

Parametric LP formulations for right-hand–side constants are stated analogously:

$$a_{i1}x_1 + a_{i2}x_2 + \ldots + a_{in}x_n \quad (\leq, =, \geq) \quad b_i$$

becomes

$$a_{i1}x_1 + a_{i2}x_2 + \ldots + a_{in}x_n \quad (\leq, =, \geq) \quad b_i + k_i\Delta .$$

FOLLOW-UP EXERCISES

20. In the air cargo problem, state the parametric equivalent of z if marginal profit gains in beef are double the corresponding declines in marginal pork profit.
21. State the parametric LP model of the air cargo problem for each of the following cases:
    a. Independence between volume and weight and sensitivity based on increases in volume capacity of up to 16 cubic yards.
    b. Same Δ as in part *a*, but where 1 cubic yard of additional volume yields 500 pounds of additional weight capacity.

**22. Either by the methods of Chapter 4 or by a parametric LP computer program available to you, fill in the following table for sensitivity of the air cargo solution to changes in
    a. Profit contributions where $k_1 = 0$, $k_2 = 1$, and $-10 \leq \Delta \leq 50$.
    b. Capacities where $k_1 = 1$, $k_2 = 0.5$, and $0 \leq \Delta \leq 50$.

Optimal z	Optimal x_1	Optimal x_2	Δ
.	.	.	.
.	.	.	.
.	.	.	.

**23. *Diminishing Margin Returns and the Optimal Value Function.* The plot of optimal z against a specific RHS constant gives the optimal value function $z^*(b_i)$. This function has interesting economic interpretations. For example, given a max type problem and a $\leq$ constraint, the general slope of the optimal value function is shown in Figure 5–10.

FIGURE 5–10 Optimal Value Function for $\leq$ Constraint in a Max Problem (holding b_j constant for $j \neq i$)

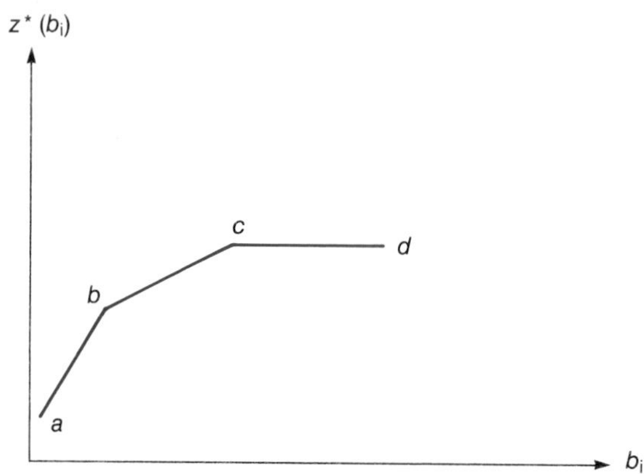

a. What do the slopes represent for the line segments $\overline{ab}$, $\overline{bc}$, and $\overline{cd}$?

b. Assuming b_i represents available resource and z is a return on that resource, explain why the optimal value function illustrates the economic phenomenon of "diminishing marginal returns."

c. Sketch $z^*(b_1)$ for the air cargo problem. Plot specific coordinates. Use Figure 5–8 to help you.

Other Forms of Sensitivity Analysis

Other forms of sensitivity analysis include analysis of changes in the structural coefficients (a_{ij}'s) for the system of constraints. Graphically, a change in an a_{ij} coefficient results in a change in the slope of the related constraint. The analysis by the simplex method varies both in form and degree of difficulty depending on whether the a_{ij} value is associated with a basic or nonbasic variable.

In addition, postoptimality analysis can be used to examine simultaneous variations in the parameters and structural variations in the LP model. For instance, it's possible to determine the impact on the optimal solution if a constraint that was originally omitted needs to be included in the model. Similarly, it's possible to determine the effects of adding a new variable to the problem.

If it's revealed that an optimal solution is extremely sensitive to variations in a particular parameter, then the decision maker should weigh the costs and benefits asociated with acquiring a better estimate of the parameter. For example, if the optimal decision in a media mix problem is particularly sensitive to the estimated television exposures per dollar of advertising budget, the decision maker might weigh the costs and associated benefits of having an additional marketing research survey conducted to determine a better estimate of this parameter. The benefits would take the form of the opportunity costs associated with making a nonoptimal decision, and the costs would be any direct and indirect costs associated with acquiring the improved estimate.

FOLLOW-UP EXERCISES

24. Graphically examine the effects of independent changes in the a_{ij} coefficients in the air cargo problem in Section 5.2. Allow each parameter to change by ± 50 percent of its original value.
25. Assess simultaneous changes in c_j's for the air cargo problem by determining the ranges of $-c_1/c_2$ that give optimal solutions at each of the corner points a, b, and c.

5.7 THE DUAL PROBLEM

Duality is the state of having two distinct but related parts. The concept represents the possibility of an intriguing universal state that has been proposed and debated in diverse disciplines. For example, philosophers speak of mind and matter as underlying all known phenomena; theologians propose the underlying principles of good and bad, and the doctrine that people have both a physical and a spiritual nature; and chemists have proved that every definite compound consists of two parts having opposite electrical activity.[7]

It turns out that every LP problem has a related problem called the **dual problem** or **dual**. The dual is formulated from information contained in the original problem called the **primal problem** or **primal** and when solved, the dual provides all essential information about the solution to the primal.

This section illustrates the formulation of the dual and discusses why it has considerable theoretical, economic, and computational importance.

Dual Problem Formulation

The parameters of an original (primal) LP problem provide all of the information needed to formulate the corresponding dual problem. Example 5.6 illustrates the formulation of the dual for a simple primal.

▶ Example 5.6 Primal/Dual Relationships

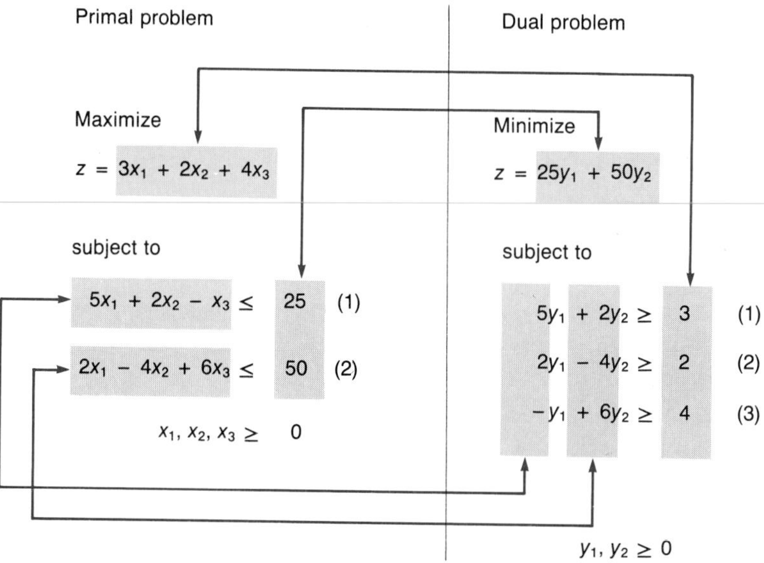

Let us make some observations about the primal and dual problems in Example 5.6.

a. The primal is a maximization problem, and the dual is a minimization problem. The sense of optimization is always opposite for corresponding primal and dual problems.

b. The primal has three variables and two constraints; the dual has two variables and three constraints. The number of variables in the primal (n) always equals the number of constraints in the dual and vice versa.

---

[7]Modern physicists have postulated a dual universe with the matter in one the energy of the other and vice versa. For business purposes, one can imagine that maximizing return subject to a resource constraint is somewhat analogous to minimizing the opportunity cost of the resource subject to a return constraint.

c. The coefficients in constraint 1 of the primal are the column coefficients for the first dual variable (y_1) in the three dual constraints. The same relationship is true for constraint 2 of the primal and the column for y_2 in the dual. The technological coefficients (a_{ij}) in the primal are transposed to a_{ji} in the dual; that is, row coefficients in primal constraints become column coefficients in dual constraints and vice versa, or the matrix A in the primal becomes the transposed matrix A^T in the dual.

d. The objective function coefficients for variables x_1, x_2, and x_3 in the primal become the RHS constants for constraints 1–3 of the dual. The objective function coefficient for the *j*th primal variable (c_j) equals the RHS constant for the *j*th dual constraint.

e. The RHS constants in constraints 1 and 2 of the primal equal the objective function coefficients for y_1 and y_2 in the dual. The RHS constant for the *i*th primal constraint (b_i) equals the objective function coefficient for the *i*th dual variable.

Example 5.6 illustrates the formulation of the dual problem from a so-called **canonical primal problem,** that is, a maximization problem having all ≤ constraints and all variables nonnegative. Given a canonical primal, the resulting dual is a **canonical dual problem,** that is, a minimization problem with all ≥ constraints and all variables nonnegative. The **symmetry** between a canonical primal and its canonical dual is illustrated by the following generalizations.

Canonical Primal	Canonical Dual
Maximize $$z = \sum_{j=1}^{n} c_j x_j$$ subject to $$\sum_{j=1}^{n} a_{ij} x_j \le b_i, \quad i = 1, \ldots, m$$ $$x_j \ge 0, \quad j = 1, \ldots, n$$	Minimize $$z = \sum_{i=1}^{m} b_i y_i$$ subject to $$\sum_{i=1}^{m} a_{ji} y_i \ge c_j \quad j = 1, \ldots, n$$ $$y_i \ge 0, \quad i = 1, \ldots, m$$

Thus the transformation from primal to dual is perfectly symmetric: In the objective function, max becomes min, c_j becomes b_i, and x_j becomes y_i; in the constraints, a_{ij} becomes a_{ji}, x_j becomes y_i, b_i becomes c_j, and ≤ becomes ≥. Interesting phenomenon, isn't it?

Obviously, original problems are not usually canonical primals. In such cases the rules for formulating the dual are more comprehensive. Table 5–2 presents primal/dual transformation rules for formulating the dual of any primal.

Our earlier example and the relationships in Table 5–2 clearly show that duality is a symmetric relationship between the primal and dual problems: One problem is like a mirror image of the other. Moreover, by convention we call the original problem the primal, although in reality either problem is the dual of the other. For these rea-

TABLE 5–2 Primal/Dual Transformation Rules

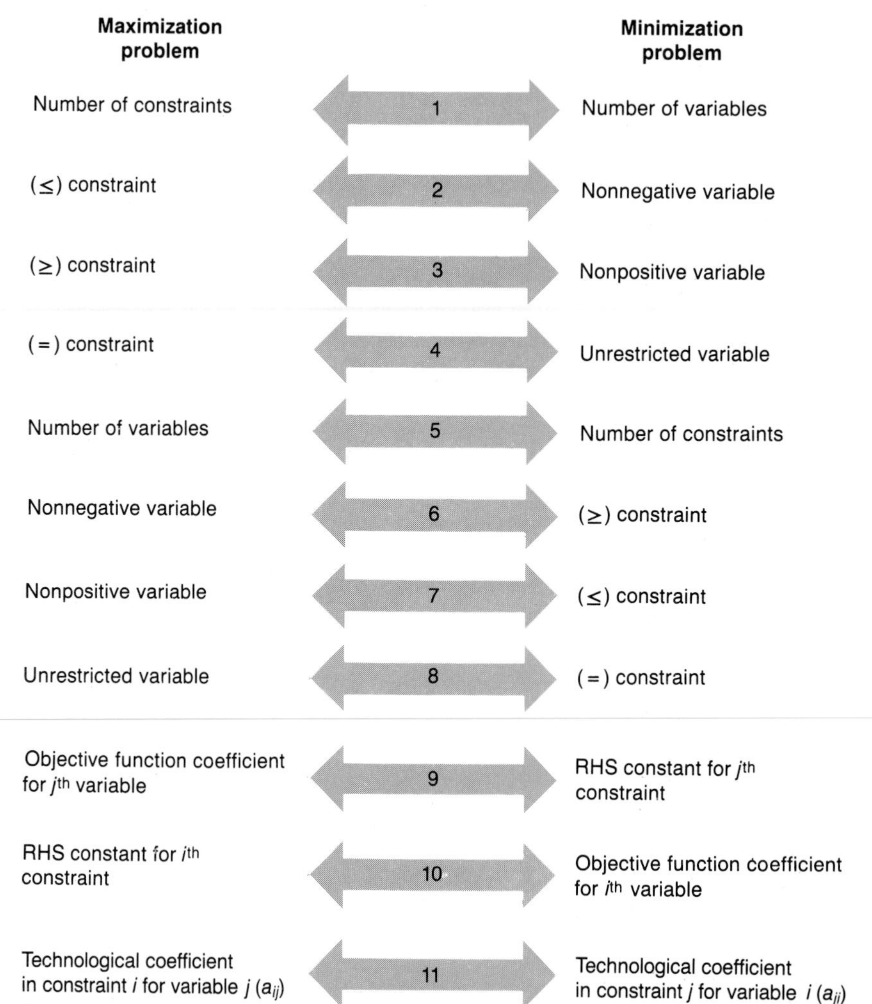

Maximization problem		Minimization problem
Number of constraints	1	Number of variables
(≤) constraint	2	Nonnegative variable
(≥) constraint	3	Nonpositive variable
(=) constraint	4	Unrestricted variable
Number of variables	5	Number of constraints
Nonnegative variable	6	(≥) constraint
Nonpositive variable	7	(≤) constraint
Unrestricted variable	8	(=) constraint
Objective function coefficient for j^{th} variable	9	RHS constant for j^{th} constraint
RHS constant for i^{th} constraint	10	Objective function coefficient for i^{th} variable
Technological coefficient in constraint i for variable j (a_{ij})	11	Technological coefficient in constraint j for variable i (a_{ji})

sons, Table 5–2 does not distinguish between primal and dual problems. If the primal is of the **max** type, then the left column in Table 5–2 is the primal, and the right column is the dual. Conversely, a min type primal is given by the right column and its dual by the left column.

Relationships 4 and 8 in Table 5–2 indicate that an unrestricted variable in one problem corresponds to an = constraint in the other problem. As you might recall from Section 3.4, an *unrestricted variable* can take on either positive, zero, or negative values. In practice, unrestricted variables are rare in primal problems, but common in dual problems. As you know, our usual (generalized) LP formulation specifies nonnegative variables, since this is a requirement of the simplex method of solution. Thus, if the dual itself is to be solved (rather than the primal), any unrestricted variable would be converted to the difference between two nonnegative variables. Note that this increases the number of dual variables.

Relationships 3 and 7 in Table 5–2 state that a *nonpositive variable* in one problem corresponds to a $\geq$ constraint in the max problem or a $\leq$ constraint in the min problem. Nonpositive variables are quite rare in primal problems but common in dual problems. If the dual is the problem chosen to be solved, then each nonpositive variable y_i would be replaced by the negative of a nonnegative variable; that is, replace nonpositive y_i with $-y_i'$ where y_i' is a *nonnegative variable*.

Example 5.7

Given the primal:

Minimize

$$z = 5x_1 + 4x_2 + 8x_3 + 7x_4$$

subject to

$$2x_1 + 3x_2 + x_3 + 2x_4 \leq 250 \quad (1)$$

$$4x_1 - 2x_2 + 2x_3 + x_4 \geq 125 \quad (2)$$

$$x_1 + x_3 - x_4 = 30 \quad (3)$$

$$x_1, x_2, x_3 \geq 0$$

$$x_4 \quad \text{unrestricted.}$$

We now call these sign conventions, since they are more comprehensive than nonnegativity conditions.

The corresponding dual is:

Maximize

$$z = 250y_1 + 125y_2 + 30y_3$$

subject to

Dual		Transformation Rules in Table 5.2
$z = 250y_1 + 125y_2 + 30y_3$		5, 9
$2y_1 + 4y_2 + y_3 \leq 5$	(1)	2, 10, 11
$3y_1 - 2y_2 \leq 4$	(2)	2, 10, 11
$y_1 + 2y_2 + y_3 \leq 8$	(3)	2, 10, 11 1
$2y_1 + y_2 - y_3 = 7$	(4)	4, 10, 11
$y_1 \leq 0$		7
$y_2 \geq 0$		6
y_3 unrestricted.		8

Don't forget the sign conventions for the dual.

Note that in this case the primal is the right column, and the dual is the left column in Table 5–2. In effect, we "mapped" from right to left in transforming a min primal to a max dual. Because they provide a failsafe way to formulate duals for computer solution, we encourage you to study exercises 32 and 33.

FOLLOW-UP EXERCISES

26. Is it true that the "dual of the dual is the primal?" Illustrate this for Example 5.7 using Table 5–2.
27. Modify the dual in Example 5.7 so that all variables are nonnegative.
28. Formulate the dual of the primal:

   a. Maximize

$$z = 6x_1 + 10x_2 + 8x_3$$

   subject to

$$\begin{aligned} x_1 + x_2 + x_3 &= 80 && (1)\\ 2x_1 + 3x_2 + 4x_3 &\le 650 && (2)\\ x_1 - 2x_2 + x_3 &\ge 45 && (3)\\ 8x_2 - 5x_3 &\le 30 && (4)\\ x_1 &\text{ unrestricted}\\ x_2, x_3 &\ge 0. \end{aligned}$$

   b. Minimize

$$z = 15x_1 + 20x_2$$

   subject to

$$\begin{aligned} x_1 + x_2 &\ge 90 && (1)\\ 3x_1 + 2x_2 &\ge 150 && (2)\\ x_1 - 3x_2 &\le 25 && (3)\\ -2x_1 + 5x_2 &= 65 && (4)\\ x_1 &\ge 0\\ x_2 &\text{ nonpositive.} \end{aligned}$$

29. Given the canonical primal

   Maximize

$$z = \{\mathbf{cx} \mid \mathbf{Ax} \le \mathbf{b}, \quad \mathbf{x} \ge \mathbf{0}\}$$

   where **c** is $(1 \times n)$, **x** and **b** are $(n \times 1)$, and **A** is $(m \times n)$, formulate the equivalent canonical dual.
30. ***Multiperiod, Product Mix Model.*** Formulate the dual for the primal in Example 3.3.
31. ***Solid Waste Management Model.*** Describe the dual of the primal in Example 3.9 by indicating: max or min; the number of variables and which are nonnegative, nonpositive, and unrestricted; the number of constraints and which are $\le$, $\ge$, and $=$.
32. ***The Nonpositive Variable and Unrestricted Variable Connections.*** Given the primal:

   Maximize

$$z = 3x_1 + 5x_2$$

subject to

$$x_1 + x_2 \geq 10 \quad (1)$$

$$2x_1 - 5x_2 = 6 \quad (2)$$

$$x_1, x_2 \geq 0,$$

show that y_1 is nonpositive and y_2 is unrestricted. *Hint*: First convert constraint 1 in the primal to the equivalent constraint

$$-x_1 - x_2 \leq -10. \quad (1)$$

Next convert constraint 2 into the two equivalent constraints given by

$$2x_1 - 5x_2 \leq 6 \quad (2)$$

$$2x_1 - 5x_2 \geq 6, \quad (3)$$

and then convert constraint 3 into the equivalent constraint

$$-2x_1 + 5x_2 \leq -6. \quad (3)$$

This gives a canonical primal that is ready for transformation to the canonical dual.

33. ***Primal to Canonical Primal to Canonical Dual to Dual Transformations.*** An alternative to using the relationships in Table 5–2 is to first convert a given primal to a canonical primal and then to use the symmetry illustrated on page 211 to convert to a canonical dual. We can convert any primal to a canonical primal by using the following transformations:
    a. Any nonpositive variable is converted to the negative of a nonnegative variable; any unrestricted variable is converted to the difference between two nonnegative variables. (See Section 3.4.)
    b. Min z is equivalent to max $-z$. (Can you demonstrate this using two-space geometry?)
    c. A $\geq$ constraint is converted to a $\leq$ constraint by multiplying both sides of the constraint by negative one, as done in the preceding exercise.
    d. An $=$ constraint is converted to two inequality constraints as shown in the preceding exercise.

    Once the canonical dual is written, we can then state a dual by applying any necessary transformations from the above four. Use this approach to write the dual of the primal in Example 5.7. Do you now have a better appreciation for Table 5–2?

Primal-Dual Properties

Certain properties regarding the primal and dual have considerable theoretical and practical significance. Before describing some of these properties, let us recall that a feasible solution to either the primal or dual is one wherein the solution values satisfy both the set of constraints and the specified *sign conditions* for nonnegative, nonpositive, and unrestricted variables. Moreover, any LP problem (primal or dual) falls into *one* of the following three classes:

1. The problem has a finite optimal solution.
2. The problem has an unbounded solution, implying that z approaches infinity for a max problem and negative infinity for a min problem.
3. The problem is infeasible (has no feasible solution).

Property 1: Symmetry The dual of the dual problem is the primal problem.

Because of this property, it doesn't matter which problem is the dual and which problem is the primal. We can simply say that one problem is the maximization problem and the other is the minimization problem (as done in Table 5–2). The two problems taken together are called **dual linear programs.** If each problem is in canonical form, then we have **canonical dual linear programs.** (Did you solve Exercise 29?)

Property 2: Fundamental Inequality of Duality Theory If $x_1, x_2, \ldots, x_n$ is any feasible solution to the maximization problem and $y_1, y_2, \ldots, y_m$ is any feasible solution to the minimization problem, then $c_1x_1 + c_2x_2 + \ldots + c_nx_n \leq b_1y_1 + b_2y_2 + \ldots + b_my_m$.

In other words, the value of the objective function for *any* feasible solution in the maximization problem is *always* less than or equal to the value of the objective function for *any* feasible solution in the minimization problem.

Property 3: Dual Theorem Any pair of dual linear programs falls into one of the following three categories:

a. Both (primal and dual) problems have finite optimal solutions for which the values of the objective functions are equal. In other words, if $(x_1^*, \ldots, x_n^*)$ and $(y_1^*, \ldots, y_m^*)$ are optimal solutions for the primal and dual problems, respectively, then

$$\sum_j c_j x_j^* = \sum_i b_i y_i^*$$

b. One problem has an unbounded solution, and the other problem is infeasible.

c. Both problems are infeasible.

These categories are exhaustive. For example, we can't have unbounded solutions for both the primal and the dual.

Properties 2 and 3*a* taken together suggest the relationship shown in Figure 5–11, where we assume a simplex algorithm independently operating on each of the primal and dual problems.

FIGURE 5–11 Evolution of Simplex-Based Solutions for Primal and Dual Problems with Finite Optimal Solutions.

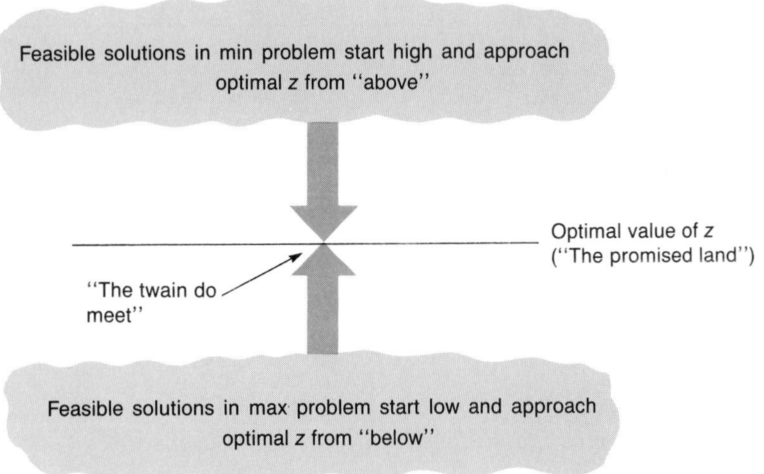

Property 4*a*: Weak Theorem of Complementary Slackness If a constraint is inactive (satisfied as a strict inequality) in an optimal solution of the primal problem, then the corresponding optimal dual variable equals zero. Conversely, an inactive constraint in an optimal solution of the dual problem is consistent with a zero-value for the corresponding optimal primal variable.

Property 4*b*: Strong Theorem of Complementary Slackness In addition to the weak theorem in Property 4*a*, if a constraint is active (satisfied as an equality) in an optimal solution of the primal problem, then the corresponding optimal dual variable is unequal to zero. Conversely, an active constraint in an optimal solution of the dual problem corresponds to an optimal primal variable with value unequal to zero.

To better understand the complementary slackness properties, consider the variable relationships in Table 5–3. Thus, as suggested by the symmetric relations in dual linear programs, the jth decision variable in the primal is related to the jth constraint in the dual. More precisely, x_j in the primal is related to slack (S_j) or surplus (E_j) in the dual. Conversely, S_i or E_i in the primal is related to the dual variable y_i.

Now we can restate the complementary slackness theorems according to Table 5–4. The next example illustrates these relationships, and other parts of the book make use of them.

TABLE 5–3 Primal-Dual Correspondence of Variables

Corresponding variable in		
Primal		Dual
x_j	⟷	S_j or E_j
S_i or E_i	⟷	y_i

TABLE 5–4 Complementary Slackness Theorems*

	Weak (Property 4*a*)	Strong (Property 4*b*)†
Primal	If $S_i^* > 0$ or $E_i^* > 0$, then $y_i^* = 0$	If $S_i^* > 0$ or $E_i^* > 0$, then $y_i^* = 0$
Dual	If $S_j^* > 0$ or $E_j^* > 0$, then $x_j^* = 0$	If $S_j^* > 0$ or $E_j^* > 0$, then $x_j^* = 0$
		If $S_i^* = 0$ or $E_i^* = 0$, then $y_i^* > 0$
		If $S_j^* = 0$ or $E_j^* = 0$, then $x_j^* > 0$

*In problems having either degenerate optimal solutions (one or more basic variables with zero value) or alternative optimal solutions, the strong theorem doesn't guarantee the result. The * represents "optimal value of."
†For problems not in canonical form, it's possible to have negative y_i^* and x_j^*; in this case we replace $y_i^* > 0$ and $x_j^* > 0$ with $y_i^* \neq 0$ and $x_j^* \neq 0$.

Example 5.8 Air Cargo Again

Let us illustrate these properties with our air cargo example. The primal problem is:

Maximize

$$z_p = 20x_1 + 10x_2$$

subject to

$$5x_1 + 4x_2 \leq 24 \quad (1)$$

$$2x_1 + 5x_2 \leq 13 \quad (2)$$

$$x_1, x_2 \geq 0$$

and the corresponding dual problem is:

Minimize

$$z_d = 24y_1 + 13y_2$$

subject to

$$5y_1 + 2y_2 \geq 20 \quad (1)$$

$$4y_1 + 5y_2 \geq 10 \quad (2)$$

$$y_1, y_2 \geq 0$$

where for purposes of our discussion we distinguish between the primal objective function (z_p) and the dual objective function (z_d).

Let us consider Property 2. A *feasible* solution to the primal is $x_1 = 2$ and $x_2 = 1$, with a resultant z-value of 50. Would you agree that a *feasible* solution to the dual is $y_1 = 5$, $y_2 = 3$, and $z_d = 159$? Both solutions are feasible, and $z_p < z_d$. In fact (according to Property 2) if we identify *any* feasible solution to the dual (minimization problem), we would find that $z_p \le z_d$.

Given that each problem has *a* feasible solution, Property 3 suggests that both problems have finite optimal solutions with equal values for the optimal objective functions. This is indeed the case, as shown in Table 5–5.

TABLE 5–5 Optimal Solutions for Air Cargo Model

Primal (Max)		Dual (Min)
$z_p^* = 96$	← Property 3a →	$z_d^* = 96$
$x_1^* = 4.8$	← Property 4b →	$E_1^* = 0$
$x_2^* = 0$	← Property 4a →	$E_2^* = 6$
$S_1^* = 0$	← Property 4b →	$y_1^* = 4$
$S_2^* = 3.4$	← Property 4a →	$y_2^* = 0$

This table also gives insight into Property 4, the complementary slackness property. In the optimal primal solution the second constraint is inactive ($S_2^* = 3.4$). According to Property 4*a*, we should expect that the second dual variable (y_2^*) will equal zero in the optimal dual solution. Similarly, the fact that constraint 2 of the dual is inactive ($E_2^* = 6$) suggests that x_2^* will equal zero in the optimal primal solution. Both of these conditions are confirmed by the results.

Moreover, property 4*b* in Table 5–4 is confirmed: $S_1^* = 0$ in the primal and $y_1^* > 0$ in the dual; $E_1^* = 0$ in the dual and $x_1^* > 0$ in the primal. It's beautiful, isn't it?

Consider one last property that ties together some of the earlier properties. From Section 4.5 we know that basic solutions are enumerated by setting selected nonbasic variables to zero and solving the system of simultaneous equations for basic variables. Table 5–6 enumerates all basic solutions for the air cargo model.

TABLE 5–6

Basis Solution Number	Basis	Values of Basic Variables	Feasible?	z
1	(S_1, S_2)	(24.0, 13.0)	yes	0.0
2	(S_1, x_1)	(−8.5, 6.5)	no	—
3	(S_1, x_2)	(13.6, 2.6)	yes	26.0
4	(S_2, x_1)	(3.4, 4.8)	yes	96.0
5	(S_2, x_2)	(−17.0, 6.0)	no	—
6	(x_1, x_2)	(4.0, 1.0)	yes	90.0

Note from Table 5–6 that basic solutions are either feasible or infeasible. Solutions 1, 3, 4, and 6 are feasible, whereas solutions 2 and 5 are infeasible. Violation of the sign condition on a variable renders the solution infeasible.

Also from Table 5–6, each basic solution is: (1) **optimal** with value z^*; (2) **suboptimal**, where z is less than z^* in a max problem and greater than z^* in a min problem ; or (3) **superoptimal**, where z is greater than z^* in a max problem and less than z^* in a min problem. In Table 5–6 solution 6 is optimal; solutions 1, 3, and 4 are suboptimal; and solutions 2 and 5 are superoptimal. Note that *superoptimal solutions are necessarily infeasible*.

Now, suppose we were to enumerate all basic solutions in *both* the primal and dual problems. It turns out that *each* basic solution in one problem has a corresponding solution in the other problem called the **complementary basic solution.** For example, the two solutions in Table 5–5 are complementary basic solutions. Property 5 summarizes the characteristics of complementary basic solutions.

Property 5: Complementary Basic Solutions The following conditions hold for complementary basic solutions:

a. The value of z in the max problem equals the value of z in the min problem.

b. Complementary slackness applies in the sense that basic variables in one problem have corresponding nonbasic variables in the other problem.

c. If the solution is suboptimal and feasible in one problem, it is superoptimal and infeasible in the other.

d. If the solution is optimal in one problem, it is optimal in the other problem.

Example 5.9 Complementary Basic Solutions

Table 5–7 gives the set of complementary basic solutions to the air cargo dual linear programs in Example 5.8. You should note from this table that complementary basic solutions necessarily have equal values for z according to Property 5*a*. Moreover, from Property 5*b*, complementary slackness suggests that basic variables unequal to zero in one problem have corresponding nonbasic variables (that is, equal to zero) in the other problem. For example, in solution number 3 we have $S_1 \neq 0$ in the primal and $y_1 = 0$; $E_1 \neq 0$ in the dual and $x_1 = 0$; $S_2 = 0$ in the primal and $y_2 \neq 0$; $E_2 = 0$ in the dual and $x_2 \neq 0$.

Property 5*c* should be apparent from Figure 5–11. For example, solution number 3 in Table 5–7 is a suboptimal feasible solution in the max problem with $z = 26$; it follows that its complementary basic solution in the min problem with $z = 26$ must be superoptimal (and therefore infeasible), since $z = 26 < z^* = 96$. In other words, looking at Figure 5–11, the domain of feasible solutions for the min problem is above the optimal-z line. Since $z = 26$ is below the line given by $z^* = 96$, it follows that $z = 26$ corresponds to a superoptimal and infeasible solution in the min problem.

Finally, Property 5*d* reflects Property 3*a*, and is confirmed by solution number 4 in Table 5–7. If you really want to understand Property 5, try solving Exercise 35.

TABLE 5–7 Complementary Basic Solutions to Air Cargo Problem

	Primal (Max)					Dual (Min)			
Number	**Basis**	**Values**	**Feasible?**	**Optimality?**	**z**	**Basis**	**Values**	**Feasible?**	**Optimality?**
1	(S_1, S_2)	(24.0, 13.0)	Yes	Suboptimal	0	(E_1, E_2)	(−20.0, −10.0)	No	Superoptimal
2	(S_1, x_1)	(−8.5, 6.5)	No	Superoptimal	130	(E_2, y_2)	(40.0, 10.0)	Yes	Suboptimal
3	(S_1, x_2)	(13.6, 2.6)	Yes	Suboptimal	26	(E_1, y_2)	(−16.0, 2.0)	No	Superoptimal
4*	(S_2, x_1)	(3.4, 4.8)	Yes	Optimal	96	(E_2, y_1)	(6.0, 4.0)	Yes	Optimal
5	(S_2, x_2)	(−17.0, 6.0)	No	Suboptimal	60	(E_1, y_1)	(−7.5, 2.5)	No	Superoptimal
6	(x_1, x_2)	(4.0, 1.0)	Yes	Suboptimal	90	(y_1, y_2)	(80/17, 30/17)	No	Superoptimal

FOLLOW-UP EXERCISES

34. State the dual for each primal, and classify the dual linear programs into one of the categories in Property 3 by sketching solutions to the dual linear programs.
   a. Maximize

$$z = 3x_1 + 5x_2$$

   subject to

$$x_1 + x_2 \geq 2 \quad (1)$$

$$-1.5x_1 + x_2 \geq 0 \quad (2)$$

$$x_1, x_2 \geq 0$$

   b. Same as part *a* except change max to min.

35. ***Complementary Basic Solutions for Example 3.1.* State dual linear programs for the model in Example 3.1, and enumerate complementary basic solutions as in Table 5–7. Confirm each part in Property 5. If a solution is infeasible in one problem, is its complementary basic solution necessarily feasible? If a solution is superoptimal, is it necessarily infeasible? If a solution is infeasible, is it necessarily superoptimal?

**36. One of the mathematical conditions below is a formal statement of weak complementary slackness, and the other is a formal statement of strong complementary slackness. Reason out which is which, based on the statements in Table 5–4.
   a. $y_i^* \times S_i^*$ (or E_i^*) $= 0, \quad i = 1, \ldots, m$
   and
   S_j^* (or E_j^*) $\times x_j^* = 0, \quad j = 1, \ldots, n.$
   b. S_i^* (or E_i^*) $+ y_i^* > 0, \quad i = 1, \ldots, m$
   and
   S_j^* (or E_j^*) $+ x_j^* > 0, \quad j = 1, \ldots, n.$

Dual Variables, Primal Shadow Prices, and Their Relationship

We suggested earlier in this section that an original LP problem can be solved using either the primal or dual. Example 5.8 confirmed that the primal and dual do achieve the same optimal value for the objective function when both problems have finite optimal solutions. In fact the optimal solution to one problem contains all the information needed to specify the optimal solution to the other problem.[8] In this section we relate the shadow prices discussed in Section 5.4 to the optimal values of dual variables.

> The optimal values of the dual variables, sometimes referred to as dual prices, are the shadow prices for the corresponding primal constraints.

Table 5–8 presents shadow prices for the air cargo primal and dual problems given in Table 5–5. Compare the data in Table 5–8 with that in Table 5–5. The shadow price of 4.0 for constraint 1 of the primal is the optimal value for y_1 in the dual. The shadow price of zero for constraint 2 in the primal is the optimal value for y_2 in the dual. Similarly, the shadow prices given for the dual problem equal the optimal values for the primal variables. The shadow price of 4.8 for constraint 1 of the dual is the optimal value for x_1 in the primal and the shadow price of zero for constraint 2 in the dual is the optimal value for x_2 in the primal.

TABLE 5–8 Shadow Prices for Air Cargo Primal and Dual

Constraint	Primal Shadow Price	Dual Shadow Price
1	4.0	4.8
2	0.0	0.0

Do you see why this makes sense? The right-hand–side constant in a constraint of the primal is the coefficient of the corresponding dual variable in the objective function of the dual. Hence a one-unit change in that right-hand–side constant (if feasible) corresponds to an *optimal* change in the objective function given by the value of the corresponding *optimal* dual variable.

This is precisely the definition of a shadow price: The change in optimal z for a one unit increase in b_i. If the RHS constant of constraint 1 in the air cargo primal on page 218 is increased from $b_1 = 24$ to $b_1 = 25$, z^* will increase by 4 as follows:

$$z_d = b_1 y_1 + b_2 y_2$$

$$\text{Old } z_d^* = 24y_1^* + 13y_2^*$$

$$\text{New } z_d^* = (24 + 1)y_1^* + 13y_2^*$$

If $y_1^* = 4$, then new z_d^* minus old z_d^* is precisely y_1^*, or 4.

FOLLOW-UP EXERCISES

37. Explain the relationship between complementary slackness and item 3 in Section 5.4 (on page 201).

38. ***Multiperiod, Product Mix Model.*** In Exercise 30 we asked you to formulate the dual for the primal given on page 99. In Example 4.6 and in Figure 5–9, we show

[8]Those going on to Chapter 6 will confirm this statement by computational examples.

computer output for the primal. Based on the output and on your understanding of primal-dual properties and dual/shadow prices, specify as much as possible about the optimal solution to the dual.

Economic Interpretations: The Pricing Problem

The shadow price/dual price equivalency states that the optimal value of the ith dual variable is the amount by which the optimal value of the primal objective function will change per allowable unit increase in b_i, all other parameters held constant. For a maximization primal where the $\leq$ constraints represent limited resources, *the corresponding dual price is a measure of the marginal value of additional units of a resource*. Let us pursue this interpretation a little further.

The air cargo model in Example 5.8 expresses for a Boston meat wholesaler the maximization of profit contribution from airfreighting two meat types, subject to volume and weight constraints. The corresponding dual problem is concerned with placing a monetary value (price) on the two resources, volume and weight capacity of the plane. The optimal solution indicates dual/shadow prices of $y_1^* = 4$ and $y_2^* = 0$ for the volume and weight constraints, respectively. This means that the Boston company should be willing to lease additional volume capacity from the airfreight company if the charge is less than \$400 per cubic yard, since each additional unit of the resource (volume) would increase profit contribution by \$400. Additional units of the weight resource have no economic value ($y_2^* = 0$), which makes sense given that the optimal solution shows excess weight capacity.

Now let us take a look at this problem from another perspective. Suppose the Boston meat wholesaler has already signed the airfreight lease agreement, but the airfreight company suddenly has an unusual (and profitable) opportunity to lease the Boston company's capacities to another customer. In effect the airfreight company wishes to rent back the resources (volume and weight capacities) from the Boston company by buying back the lease agreement. Let us construct an LP model for the airfreight company, where

y_1 = Rental cost (\$100) per cubic yard of space.
y_2 = Rental cost (\$100) per 1,000 pounds of weight.

The total rental from leasing the full capacity of the airplane is

$$z = 24y_1 + 13y_2$$

where the 24 and 13 are the volume and weight capacities, respectively. This total cost is to be minimized, since it represents the cost to the airfreight company of buying back the lease agreement.

The airfreight company realizes that the Boston company will not be interested in giving up the airplane capacity unless it can earn as much as it would by taking delivery of the two meats. The utilized capacities of volume and weight to airfreight a container of beef are 5 cubic yards and 2 (1,000) pounds. If these capacities are rented back to the airfreight company, the rental income received by the Boston company is $5y_1 + 2y_2$. The Boston company would require that this income be at least as much as the \$20 (100s) it would earn by airfreighting the container of beef, or

$$5y_1 + 2y_2 \geq 20\,.$$

Similarly, a container of pork uses 4 cubic yards and 5 (1,000s) pounds of the plane's capacity. The rental income from leasing these capacities would equal $4y_1 + 5y_2$. Since the Boston company would require that this income be at least as much as the $10 (100s) earned by airfreighting a container of pork, we have

$$4y_1 + 5y_2 \geq 10\,.$$

This leads us to the formulation

Minimize

$$z = 24y_1 + 13y_2$$

subject to

$$5y_1 + 2y_2 \geq 20 \qquad (1)$$

$$4y_1 + 5y_2 \geq 10 \qquad (2)$$

$$y_1, y_2 \geq 0\,,$$

which is the dual of the air cargo model.

The optimal dual solution indicates that the rental income is minimized at 96 ($100s) when $y_1^* = 4$ ($100s) and $y_2^* = 0$. The optimal rentals are $400 per cubic yard and $0 per 1,000 pounds. In effect the dual prices y_1^* and y_2^* are the minimum prices the Boston company should be willing to accept from the airfreight company for renting back the volume and weight capacities of the airplane. The airfreight company would have to pay at least $9,600 to buy back the lease agreement, which may or may not be worthwhile, depending on their alternative uses for the airplane.

Based on these economic interpretations, the canonical dual problem is often called a **pricing problem.** Its optimal solution yields the minimum prices that management should accept for selling or liquidating resources; the optimal value of the objective function is the minimum acceptable payment for all of these resources.

In the economic theory of the firm, the dual prices are also called **imputed prices,** since to the firm they are equivalent to the ascribed or attributed marginal values of resources. A perfectly competitive economic system would suggest that market prices and imputed prices are equal, which establishes an optimizing equilibrium; resources would be used optimally, since there is no incentive to either acquire or liquidate resources when the marginal cost (market price) of the resource is identical to the marginal revenue (dual price) generated by that resource. As you might recall from a course in microeconomics, the equality between marginal revenue and marginal cost is a necessary condition for profit maximization.

Computational Advantages

As we have seen, duality is useful both from a theoretical perspective (based on primal-dual properties) and an interpretive or economic perspective (based on shadow prices and the pricing problem). Additionally, certain computational advantages further underscore the usefulness of duality: (1) The dual is often easier to solve than the primal; (2) the dual can be extremely useful in performing the types of postoptimality analyses previously discussed; and (3) the dual can be applied more efficiently to the solution of certain types of models (e.g., the transportation algorithm in Chapter 7).

The amount of computer processing time required to solve an LP problem usually depends more on the number of constraints (m) than the number of variables (n), since the solution involves an $m \times m$ system of equations. Consequently, if the primal has a significantly larger number of constraints (say, $m = 5{,}000$) than variables (say, $n = 500$), then the solution of the dual may be much more efficient. That is, generally it takes much less time to solve a 500×500 than a $5{,}000 \times 5{,}000$ system of equations.[9]

In addition to computational efficiency, the theory of the dual is particularly well-suited to performing certain types of sensitivity analyses. If you recall for a moment the transpose nature of the primal-dual relationships, you should convince yourself of the equivalence between performing sensitivity analysis on the objective function coefficients of one problem and the right-hand–side value of the other. Furthermore, the advantages that accrue from using the dual go beyond the types of sensitivity analyses we demonstrated. The dual is useful in studying the effects of changes in the technological coefficients, the addition of new variables, and the addition of new or supplemental constraints. Moreover, as mentioned at the beginning of this chapter, the decision maker may be concerned about the simultaneous variation in the structure and/or parameters of an LP problem. The analyses presented in this chapter focused only on *independent* variation of parameters. Although the analysis of simultaneous variation is much more involved than that of independent variation, the dual greatly facilitates the process.

In an effort to try to tie together our discussions of the dual, the next example presents a comparative analysis of the solutions to the air cargo model and its dual as generated using LINDO.

▶ Example 5.10

Figure 5–12 presents the computer output from LINDO for the air cargo model and its dual. Also shown are the formulations of the two models. You should note the following linkages between the two problems:

1. Both objective functions are optimized at the same value of 96.
2. The optimal values for x_1 and x_2 are the same as the dual (or shadow) prices for constraints 1 and 2 of the dual problem. (Remember LINDO's sign convention for dual prices: a negative dual price for a minimization problem implies a corresponding *increase* in the value of the objective function.)
3. The optimal values for y_1 and y_2 are the same as the dual prices for constraints 1 and 2 of the air cargo model.
4. The results of the objective function coefficient sensitivity analysis for the air cargo model are the same as the results for the RHS constant ranges for the dual.

[9]We can't guarantee that an $n \times n$ LP system takes less time to solve than an $m \times m$ LP system where $n < m$, since it not only depends on the values of n and m but also on the *structure* of the data and the *closeness* of the initial simplex solution to the eventual optimal solution. Empirical evidence, however, clearly favors the smaller system of equations.

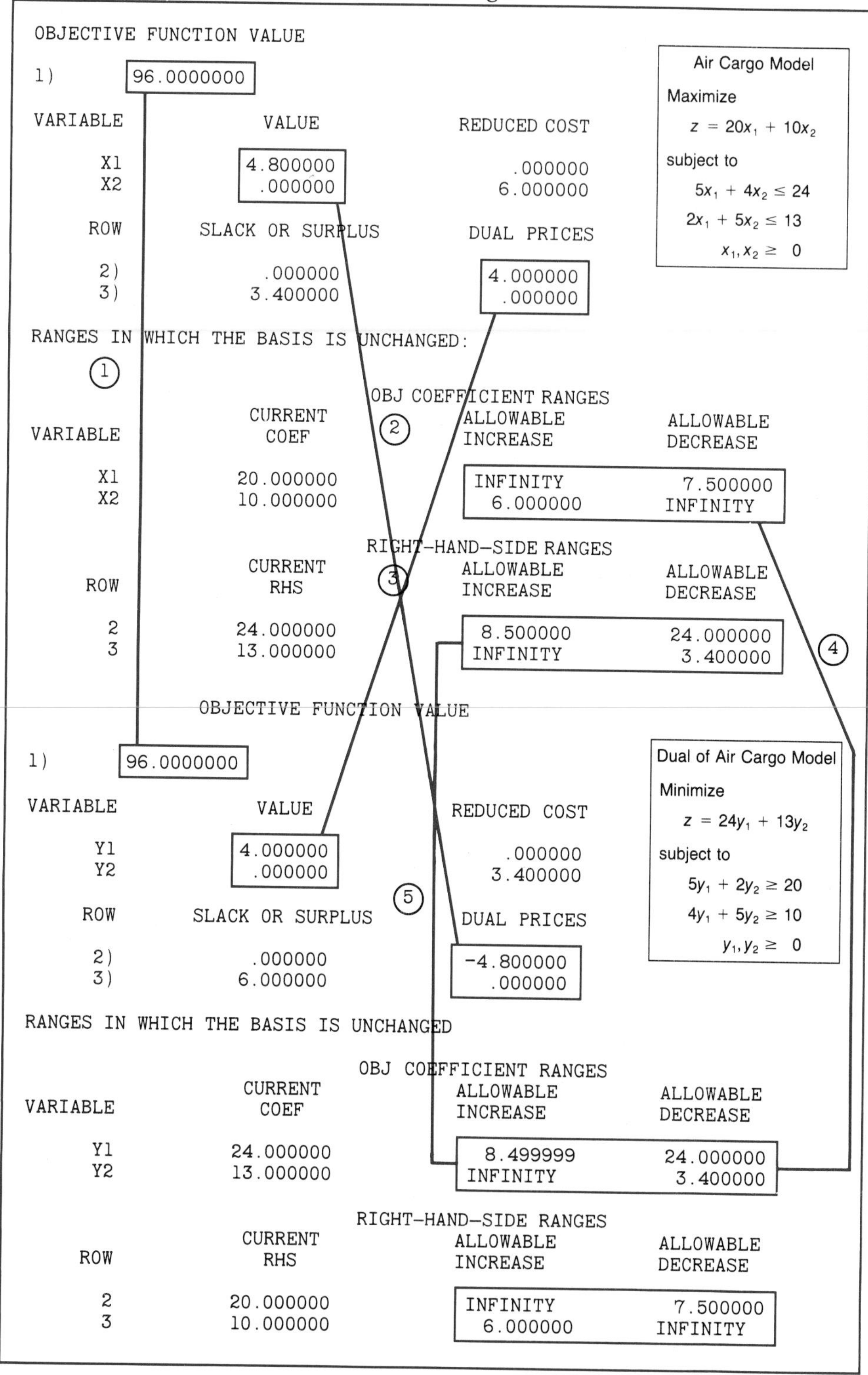

```
OBJECTIVE FUNCTION VALUE

1)        96.0000000

VARIABLE          VALUE          REDUCED COST
      X1        4.800000             .000000
      X2         .000000            6.000000

     ROW     SLACK OR SURPLUS     DUAL PRICES
      2)         .000000            4.000000
      3)        3.400000             .000000

RANGES IN WHICH THE BASIS IS UNCHANGED:

                          OBJ COEFFICIENT RANGES
VARIABLE        CURRENT        ALLOWABLE        ALLOWABLE
                 COEF          INCREASE         DECREASE
      X1       20.000000       INFINITY          7.500000
      X2       10.000000        6.000000        INFINITY

                          RIGHT-HAND-SIDE RANGES
     ROW        CURRENT        ALLOWABLE        ALLOWABLE
                  RHS          INCREASE         DECREASE
       2       24.000000        8.500000        24.000000
       3       13.000000       INFINITY          3.400000

              OBJECTIVE FUNCTION VALUE

1)        96.0000000

VARIABLE          VALUE          REDUCED COST
      Y1        4.000000             .000000
      Y2         .000000            3.400000

     ROW     SLACK OR SURPLUS     DUAL PRICES
      2)         .000000           -4.800000
      3)        6.000000             .000000

RANGES IN WHICH THE BASIS IS UNCHANGED

                          OBJ COEFFICIENT RANGES
VARIABLE        CURRENT        ALLOWABLE        ALLOWABLE
                 COEF          INCREASE         DECREASE
      Y1       24.000000        8.499999        24.000000
      Y2       13.000000       INFINITY          3.400000

                          RIGHT-HAND-SIDE RANGES
     ROW        CURRENT        ALLOWABLE        ALLOWABLE
                  RHS          INCREASE         DECREASE
       2       20.000000       INFINITY          7.500000
       3       10.000000        6.000000        INFINITY
```

Air Cargo Model
Maximize
$z = 20x_1 + 10x_2$
subject to
$5x_1 + 4x_2 \leq 24$
$2x_1 + 5x_2 \leq 13$
$x_1, x_2 \geq 0$
Dual of Air Cargo Model
Minimize
$z = 24y_1 + 13y_2$
subject to
$5y_1 + 2y_2 \geq 20$
$4y_1 + 5y_2 \geq 10$
$y_1, y_2 \geq 0$
1
2
3
4
5

FIGURE 5–12 LINDO Solutions for Air Cargo Model and the Dual

5. The results of the RHS constant sensitivity analysis for the air cargo model are the same as the results for the objective function coefficient ranges in the dual problem.

Study these results until you are comfortable with the relationships that exist between the primal and dual.

Duality and the Kuhn-Tucker Conditions

An understanding of the rudiments of the Kuhn-Tucker conditions should help consolidate your thinking on duality. These conditions arise partly from the rather innocuous-looking sign conditions on the primal variables. If x is constrained to be greater than or equal to zero, then we should examine the cases where x equals zero and where it is greater than zero. Consider a continuous function $f(x)$ defined for x greater than or equal to zero. Convince yourself that the optimal solution cannot be at $x = 0$ if the derivative of $f(x)$ at 0 is positive and we are seeking a maximum. For a maximum at $x = 0$, the derivative at $x = 0$ must be zero or negative. For a maximum at $x > 0$, on the other hand, the derivative must be zero. These conditions can be conveniently summarized by requiring that x times the derivative of x must be zero and the derivative of $f(x)$ must be less than or equal to zero.

Applying this idea to the air cargo model, we begin with the Lagrangian formulation:

$$\max\ 20x_1 + 10x_2 - y_1(5x_1 + 4x_2 - 24) - y_2(2x_1 + 5x_2 - 13)$$

$$\text{all } x \text{ and } y \text{ nonnegative}$$

Notice that y_1 and y_2 are the Lagrange multipliers. Requiring that the derivative with respect to x_1 should be less than or equal to zero gives $20 - 5y_1 - 2y_2 \leq 0$. From the above discussion, we also require $(20 - 5y_1 - 2y_2)x_1 = 0$. Similarly, for x_2 we get $10 - 4y_1 - 5y_2 \leq 0$ and $(10 - 4y_1 - 5y_2)x_2 = 0$. Noting that the dual prices in Figure 5–12 are the Lagrange multipliers y_1 and y_2, check that the solution given in the figure satisfies the conditions stated here.

Continuing with the air cargo model, the derivative with respect to y_1 must be less than or equal to zero, and that derivative times y_1 must equal zero, giving $5x_1 + 4x_2 - 24 \leq 0$ and $(5x_1 + 4x_2 - 24)y_1 = 0$. Similarly, for y_2 the Kuhn-Tucker conditions require $2x_1 + 5x_2 - 13 \leq 0$. Complementary slackness can also be seen in $(2x_1 + 5x_2 - 13)y_2 = 0$. Check now that the results in Figure 5–12 satisfy all the conditions.

As an aside, note that the optimal solution to any LP problem must satisfy the Kuhn-Tucker conditions and that any solution satisfying the conditions is optimal. (In general nonlinear programming problems, the Kuhn-Tucker story is somewhat more complicated.) In a sense, we do not care what algorithm generates LP solutions for us because we can always verify optimality and perform sensitivity analysis. Should Robert J. Serling propose the world's fastest LP algorithm, we could check and analyze his solutions.[10]

[10]Robert J. Serling is a well-known author. He recently wrote an interesting article entitled "History's Famous Hoaxes," *USAIR*, April 1987, p. 29. He has also used such pseudonyms as Arthur Hailey, Herman Wouk, and Ernest Hemingway.

5.8 ASSESSMENT

In this chapter, we see the heart of linear programming in its pricing ability. Although we estimate and provide coefficient inputs on the objective function and the resource constraints, the linear program provides us with values on the resources as well as estimates of the objective function coefficient changes required to allow other decision variables to enter the solution.

Reduced costs on the decision variables allow a decision maker to understand the changes needed in the decision variable costs before he or she will purchase them as inputs. The dual price tells the decision maker the marginal rate of improvement in the objective function per unit increase in a resource. This allows one to know how much to pay for additional resources on a purchase or rental basis.

Sensitivity analysis with reduced costs and shadow prices provides even further estimates on what it would take to change the solution. The linear program output provides a range on both the objective function coefficients and the resource limits within which the decisions remain the same. One can thus rethink estimates to see how probable they are to stay within the specified ranges. This process can ferret out model parameters to which the optimal solution is sensitive and about which the decision maker has little confidence in his or her estimates.

The forms of postoptimality analysis discussed in this chapter truly help provide a more complete understanding of the implications of the outputs of an LP model. To the extent that these types of analyses are conducted, the user and the designer can have greater confidence in the relevance of LP-derived decision inputs.

Finally, the last section in this chapter discussed the dual LP problem. Aside from the fascinating implications of duality, you should also have an appreciation for the computational efficiency of using the dual in solving certain LP structures. Now, forge on to the next chapter and the simplex algorithm.

SELECTED REFERENCES

Gal, T. *Postoptimal Analyses, Parametric Programming and Related Topics,* New York: McGraw-Hill, 1979.

Gribik, P. R., and K. O. Kortanek, *Extremal Methods of Operations Research,* New York; Marcel Dekker, 1985.

Jeter, M. W. *Mathematical Programming: An Introduction,* New York: Marcel Dekker, 1986.

Lev, B., and H. J. Weiss, *Introduction to Mathematical Programming,* New York: Elsevier, North-Holland, 1982.

Luenberger, D. G. *Linear and Nonlinear Programming.* 2nd ed. Reading, Mass.: Addison-Wesley Publishing, 1984.

ADDITIONAL EXERCISES

39. For the following LP problem:

Maximize

$$z = 10x_1 + 6x_2$$

subject to

$$x_1 + x_2 \leq 40 \quad (1)$$
$$3x_1 + 2x_2 \geq 30 \quad (2)$$
$$2x_1 + 3x_2 \leq 90 \quad (3)$$
$$x_1, x_2 \geq 0.$$

a. Solve the problem graphically.
b. Intuitively analyze and suggest the anticipated effects of increases and decreases in the objective function coefficients for x_1 and x_2.
c. Graphically verify the sensitivity of the optimal basis to changes in the two objective function contributions.

40. Figure 5–13 contains excerpts from the LINDO output for Exercise 39.
a. Determine the range for each RHS constant within which the current optimal basis remains feasible.
b. Determine each shadow price.
c. Interpret the meaning of each shadow price, and note the range of the corresponding RHS constant over which this interpretation is valid.
d. Using the appropriate shadow price, predict optimal z if:
(1) b_1 changes from 40 to 43.
(2) b_1 changes from 40 to 35.
(3) b_1 changes from 40 to 50.
(4) b_2 changes from 30 to 40.
(5) b_3 changes from 90 to 60.
e. Graphically confirm your answers to part *d.*

FIGURE 5–13

```
                    OBJECTIVE FUNCTION VALUE

 (1)       400.000000

 VARIABLE            VALUE              REDUCED COST
       X1          40.000000              .000000
       X2            .000000             4.000000

      ROW     SLACK OR SURPLUS          DUAL PRICES
       2)            .000000            10.000000
       3)          90.000000              .000000
       4)          10.000000              .000000

                               RIGHT-HAND-SIDE RANGES
                 ____________________________________________________
                   CURRENT              ALLOWABLE        ALLOWABLE
      ROW            RHS                INCREASE         DECREASE
        2          40.000000             5.000000        30.000000
        3          30.000000            90.000000        INFINITY
        4          90.000000            INFINITY         10.000000
```

41. For the LP problem:

Minimize

$$z = 3x_1 + 6x_2$$

subject to

$$4x_1 + x_2 \geq 20 \quad (1)$$

$$x_1 + x_2 \leq 20 \quad (2)$$

$$x_1 + x_2 \geq 10 \quad (3)$$

$$x_1, x_2 \geq 0$$

a. Solve the problem graphically.
b. Intuitively analyze and suggest the anticipated effects of increases and decreases in the objective function coefficients for x_1 and x_2.
c. Graphically verify the sensitivity of the optimal basis to changes in the two objective function contributions.

42. Figure 5–14 contains excerpts from the LINDO output for Exercise 41.

FIGURE 5–14

```
            OBJECTIVE FUNCTION VALUE

 (1)        30.0000000

VARIABLE          VALUE              REDUCED COST
      X1        10.000000               .000000
      X2          .000000              3.000000

     ROW      SLACK OR SURPLUS       DUAL PRICES
       2        20.000000               .000000
       3        10.000000               .000000
       4          .000000             -3.000000

                             RIGHT-HAND-SIDE RANGES

                 CURRENT             ALLOWABLE          ALLOWABLE
     ROW           RHS                INCREASE           DECREASE
       2        20.000000            20.000000           INFINITY
       3        20.000000            INFINITY            10.000000
       4        10.000000            INFINITY             5.000000
```

a. Determine the range for each RHS constant within which the current optimal basis remains feasible.
b. Determine each shadow price.
c. Interpret the meaning of each shadow price and note the range of the corresponding RHS constant over which this interpretation is valid.
d. Using the appropriate shadow price, predict optimal z if:
(1) b_1 changes from 20 to 12.
(2) b_1 changes from 20 to 50.

(3) b_3 changes from 10 to 3.
(4) b_3 changes from 10 to 5.
(5) b_3 changes from 10 to 15.

e. Graphically confirm your answers to part *d*.

43. If you have access to an LP package that performs sensitivity analysis, verify your results in
    a. Exercises 39 and 40.
    b. Exercises 41 and 42.

44. ***Production-Vendor Model.*** The LP model for Sniffy Smoke Sensors, Inc. (Exercise 35, Chapter 3) is:

Maximize

$$z = 2.00\text{ACPR} + 3.75\text{BAPR} + 1.50\text{ACSB} + 3.25\text{BASB}$$

subject to

$$\begin{array}{llll}
.15\text{ACPR} + .10\text{BAPR} & & \leq 1{,}000 & \text{(Production dept.)} \\
.20\text{ACPR} + .20\text{BAPR} & & \leq 1{,}800 & \text{(Assembly dept.)} \\
.10\text{ACPR} + .15\text{BAPR} & & \leq 1{,}200 & \text{(Packaging dept.)} \\
 & \text{ACSB} + \text{BASB} & \leq 15{,}000 & \text{(Sub capacity)} \\
 & \text{ACSB} & \leq 6{,}000 & \text{(Sub AC capacity)} \\
 & \text{ACSB} + \text{BASB} & \geq 2{,}500 & \text{(Sub min order)} \\
\text{ACPR} + & \text{ACSB} & \geq 10{,}000 & \text{(Seers min AC)} \\
\quad\quad \text{BAPR} + & \text{BASB} & \geq 8{,}000 & \text{(Seers min battery)} \\
 & \text{ACPR, BAPR, ACSB, BASB} & \geq 0 &
\end{array}$$

Figure 5–15 presents the LINDO output for this problem.

a. Interpret the meaning of each dual (shadow) price. Specify its range of validity.
b. Interpret the results of the objective function coefficient sensitivity analysis.
c. Interpret the results of the RHS constant sensitivity analysis.

45. ***Transportation Model.*** The LP model for the transportation model (Exercise 41, Chapter 3) is:

Minimize

$$z = 30x_{11} + 4x_{12} + 8x_{13} + 5x_{21} + 10x_{22} + 20x_{23}$$

subject to

$$\begin{array}{lll}
x_{11} + x_{12} + x_{13} \leq 50 & & \text{(Plant 1 capacity)} \\
x_{21} + x_{22} + x_{23} \leq 70 & & \text{(Plant 2 capacity)} \\
x_{11} + x_{21} & = 40 & \text{(Depot 1 demand)} \\
x_{12} + x_{22} & = 60 & \text{(Depot 2 demand)} \\
x_{13} + x_{23} & = 20 & \text{(Depot 3 demand)} \\
 & x_{ij} \geq 0 &
\end{array}$$

where x_{ij} = Number of thousands of gallons shipped from plant i to depot j.

FIGURE 5–15 Production-Vendor Model

```
OBJECTIVE FUNCTION VALUE

(1)      61250.0000

VARIABLE          VALUE           REDUCED COST
  ACPR         4000.000000           .000000
  BAPR         4000.000000           .000000
  ACSB         6000.000000           .000000
  BASB         9000.000000           .000000

     ROW     SLACK OR SURPLUS      DUAL PRICES
      2)           .000000         37.500000
      3)        200.000100           .000000
      4)        200.000000           .000000
      5)           .000000          3.250000
      6)           .000000          1.875000
      7)      12500.000000           .000000
      8)           .000000         -3.625000
      9)       5000.000000           .000000

RANGES IN WHICH THE BASIS IS UNCHANGED:

                             OBJ. COEFFICIENT RANGES
                CURRENT            ALLOWABLE          ALLOWABLE
VARIABLE         COEF              INCREASE           DECREASE
  ACPR         2.000000            1.875000           INFINITY
  BAPR         3.750000            INFINITY           1.250000
  ACSB         1.500000            INFINITY           1.875000
  BASB         3.250000            1.875000           3.250000

                             RIGHT-HAND-SIDE RANGES
                CURRENT            ALLOWABLE          ALLOWABLE
     ROW          RHS              INCREASE           DECREASE
      2       1000.000000         100.000000         400.000000
      3       1800.000000          INFINITY          200.000100
      4       1200.000000          INFINITY          200.000000
      5      15000.000000          INFINITY         5000.000000
      6       6000.000000        1600.000000        2666.667000
      7       2500.000000       12500.000000          INFINITY
      8      10000.000000        2666.667000        1600.000000
      9       8000.000000        5000.000000          INFINITY
```

Figure 5–16 presents the LINDO output for this problem.

a. Interpret the meaning of each dual (shadow) price. Specify its range of validity.

b. Interpret the results of the objective function coefficient sensitivity analysis.

c. Interpret the results of the RHS constant sensitivity analysis.

46. ***Blending Model I.*** The LP model for the blending model (Exercise 43*b*, Chapter 3) is:

Maximize

$$z = 3.7375x_1 + 4.70x_2 + 4.10x_3$$

FIGURE 5–16 Transportation Model

```
OBJECTIVE FUNCTION VALUE

(1)      780.000000

VARIABLE           VALUE           REDUCED COST
   x11            .000000          31.000000
   x12          30.000000            .000000
   x13          20.000000            .000000
   x21          40.000000            .000000
   x22          30.000000            .000000
   x23            .000000           6.000000

      ROW     SLACK OR SURPLUS     DUAL PRICES
       2)         .000000            6.000000
       3)         .000000             .000000
       4)         .000000           -5.000000
       5)         .000000          -10.000000
       6)         .000000          -14.000000

RANGES IN WHICH THE BASIS IS UNCHANGED:

                         OBJ. COEFFICIENT RANGES
                 ------------------------------------------
                 CURRENT         ALLOWABLE        ALLOWABLE
VARIABLE          COEF           INCREASE         DECREASE
   x11          30.000000        INFINITY         31.000000
   x12           4.000000        6.000000          6.000000
   x13           8.000000        6.000000         INFINITY
   x21           5.000000       31.000000         INFINITY
   x22          10.000000        6.000000          6.000000
   x23          20.000000        INFINITY          6.000000

                           RIGHT-HAND-SIDE RANGES
                 ------------------------------------------
                 CURRENT         ALLOWABLE        ALLOWABLE
      ROW          RHS           INCREASE         DECREASE
       2        50.000000       30.000000          .000000
       3        70.000000        INFINITY          .000000
       4        40.000000         .000000        40.000000
       5        60.000000         .000000        30.000000
       6        20.000000         .000000        20.000000
```

subject to

$$.2x_1 + .1x_2 + .3x_3 \leq 50{,}000 \quad \text{(Availability comp. 1)}$$

$$.15x_1 + .4x_2 + .1x_3 \leq 40{,}000 \quad \text{(Availability comp. 2)}$$

$$.3x_1 + .2x_2 + .1x_3 \leq 30{,}000 \quad \text{(Availability comp. 3)}$$

$$.1x_1 + .1x_2 + .2x_3 \leq 10{,}000 \quad \text{(Availability comp. 4)}$$

$$.25x_1 + .2x_2 + .3x_3 \leq 20{,}000 \quad \text{(Availability comp. 5)}$$

$$x_1 + x_2 + x_3 \leq 125{,}000 \quad \text{(Plant capacity)}$$
$$x_1 \geq 20{,}000 \quad \text{(Min production blend 1)}$$
$$x_2 \geq 20{,}000 \quad \text{(Min production blend 2)}$$
$$x_3 \geq 10{,}000 \quad \text{(Min production blend 3)}$$
$$x_1, x_2, x_3 \geq 0$$

where x_j = Number of gallons produced of final blend j.

Figure 5–17 presents the LINDO output for this problem.

a. Interpret the meaning of each dual (shadow) price. Specify its range of validity.
b. Interpret the results of the objective function coefficient sensitivity analysis.
c. Interpret the results of the RHS constant sensitivity analysis.

47. ***Media Mix Model.*** The LP model formulated for the media mix problem in Example 3.7 is:

Maximize

$$z = 22x_1 + 12x_2 + 15x_3 + 10x_4 + 5x_5$$

subject to

$$x_1 + x_2 + x_3 + x_4 + x_5 \leq 10 \quad \text{(Total budget)}$$
$$x_1 + x_2 \leq 5 \quad \text{(Max for TV and radio)}$$
$$x_1 \leq 3 \quad \text{(Max TV)}$$
$$x_2 \leq 3 \quad \text{(Max radio)}$$
$$x_3 \leq 3 \quad \text{(Max magazines)}$$
$$x_4 \leq 3 \quad \text{(Max newspapers)}$$
$$x_5 \leq 3 \quad \text{(Max outdoor ads)}$$
$$10x_1 + 5x_2 + x_3 + x_5 \geq 25 \quad \text{(Min exposures—youth)}$$
$$10x_1 + 5x_2 + x_3 + x_5 \leq 35 \quad \text{(Max exposures—youth)}$$
$$6x_1 + 4x_2 + 7x_3 + 2x_4 + 2x_5 \geq 40 \quad \text{(Min exposures—women)}$$
$$3x_1 + x_2 + 4x_3 + 5x_4 + x_5 \geq 35 \quad \text{(Min exposures—col. ed.)}$$
$$x_j \geq 0, \quad j = 1, 2, \ldots, 5$$

where x_j = Thousands of dollars allocated for advertising in medium j.

Figure 5–18 presents the LINDO output for this problem.

a. Interpret the meaning of each dual (shadow) price. Specify its range of validity.
b. Interpret the results of the objective function coefficient sensitivity analysis.
c. Interpret the results of the RHS constant sensitivity analysis.

48. Use an LP package to solve the dual of the primal in
a. Exercise 39. Relate your results to the analyses in Exercises 39 and 40.
b. Exercise 41. Relate your results to the analyses in Exercises 41 and 42.

49. Formulate the dual given the primal:

Minimize

$$z = 10x_1 + 5x_2$$

FIGURE 5–17 Blending Model I

```
OBJECTIVE FUNCTION VALUE

(1)      397750.000000

VARIABLE            VALUE              REDUCED COST
   x1          20000.000000              .000000
   x2          60000.000000              .000000
   x3          10000.000000              .000000

     ROW      SLACK OR SURPLUS         DUAL PRICES
      2        37000.000000              .000000
      3        12000.000000              .000000
      4        11000.000000              .000000
      5             .000000            47.000000
      6             .000000              .000000
      7        35000.000000              .000000
      8             .000000             -.962500
      9        40000.000000              .000000
     10             .000000            -5.300000

RANGES IN WHICH THE BASIS IS UNCHANGED:

                           OBJ. COEFFICIENT RANGES

                    CURRENT          ALLOWABLE          ALLOWABLE
VARIABLE             COEF             INCREASE           DECREASE
   x1              3.737500            .962500           INFINITY
   x2              4.700000           INFINITY            .962500
   x3              4.100000           5.300000           INFINITY

                           RIGHT-HAND-SIDE RANGES

                    CURRENT          ALLOWABLE          ALLOWABLE
     ROW              RHS             INCREASE           DECREASE
      2          50000.000000         INFINITY       37000.000000
      3          40000.000000         INFINITY       12000.000000
      4          30000.000000         INFINITY       11000.000000
      5          10000.000000          .000000        4000.000000
      6          20000.000000         INFINITY            .000000
      7         125000.000000         INFINITY       35000.000000
      8          20000.000000          .000000       20000.000000
      9          20000.000000     40000.000000           INFINITY
     10          10000.000000     20000.000000            .000000
```

subject to

$$x_1 + x_2 \geq 20 \quad (1)$$

$$6x_1 - x_2 \leq 75 \quad (2)$$

$$x_2 \geq 10 \quad (3)$$

FIGURE 5–18 Media Mix Model

OBJECTIVE FUNCTION VALUE

(1) 147.750000

VARIABLE	VALUE	REDUCED COST
$x1$	3.000000	.000000
$x2$	.250000	.000000
$x3$	3.000000	.000000
$x4$	3.000000	.000000
$x5$	.750000	.000000

ROW	SLACK OR SURPLUS	DUAL PRICES
2	.000000	3.250000
3	1.750000	.000000
4	.000000	1.250000
5	2.750000	.000000
6	.000000	10.000000
7	.000000	6.750000
8	2.250000	.000000
9	10.000000	.000000
10	.000000	1.750000
11	7.500000	.000000
12	2.000000	.000000

RANGES IN WHICH THE BASIS IS UNCHANGED:

	OBJ. COEFFICIENT RANGES		
VARIABLE	CURRENT COEF	ALLOWABLE INCREASE	ALLOWABLE DECREASE
$x1$	22.000000	INFINITY	1.250000
$x2$	12.000000	.555556	7.000000
$x3$	15.000000	INFINITY	10.000000
$x4$	10.000000	INFINITY	6.750000
$x5$	5.000000	5.400000	1.000000

	RIGHT-HAND-SIDE RANGES		
ROW	CURRENT RHS	ALLOWABLE INCREASE	ALLOWABLE DECREASE
2	10.000000	1.000000	.600000
3	5.000000	INFINITY	1.750000
4	3.000000	.111111	.600000
5	3.000000	INFINITY	2.750000
6	3.000000	.750000	.666667
7	3.000000	.600000	.500000
8	3.000000	INFINITY	2.250000
9	25.000000	10.000000	INFINITY
10	35.000000	3.000000	1.000000
11	40.000000	7.500000	INFINITY
12	35.000000	2.000000	INFINITY

$$2x_1 + 4x_2 \leq 125 \quad (4)$$

$$2x_1 + 3x_2 = 80 \quad (5)$$

$$x_1 \geq 0$$

$$x_2 \text{ unrestricted.}$$

50. Formulate the dual given the primal:

Maximize

$$z = 3x_1 + 5x_2 - 6x_3 + 4x_4$$

subject to

$$x_1 + x_2 + x_3 + x_4 = 35 \quad (1)$$

$$2x_1 - 3x_3 \leq 45 \quad (2)$$

$$2x_1 - x_2 + 3x_3 + 4x_4 \leq 60 \quad (3)$$

$$x_1 + x_2 \geq 20 \quad (4)$$

$$x_3 - x_4 = 5 \quad (5)$$

$$x_1, x_2 \quad \text{nonnegative}$$

$$x_3 \quad \text{unrestricted}$$

$$x_4 \quad \text{nonpositive.}$$

51. Use an LP package to solve *both* the primal and dual in
   a. Exercise 49.
   b. Exercise 50.
   Are the primal/dual solutions consistent with respect to values of z, shadow/dual prices, and complementary variables? *Note:* You must change all unrestricted and nonpositive variables to equivalent nonnegative variables in the formulations before you submit the problem to the computer.

52. Interpret postoptimality results using an LP package for
   a. Hospital Administration Model (Example 3.5).
   b. Blending Model (Example 3.6).
   c. Financial Mix Model (Example 3.8).
53. Formulate the dual of
   a. Hospital Administration Model (Example 3.5).
   b. Blending Model (Example 3.6).
   c. Financial Mix Model (Example 3.8).

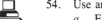

54. Use an LP package to solve *both* the primal and dual in
   a. Exercise 53*a*.
   b. Exercise 53*b*.
   c. Exercise 53*c*.
   Are the primal/dual solutions consistent with respect to values of z, shadow/dual prices, and complementary variables? List the results that illustrate primal/dual symmetry with respect to solution values and sensitivity analysis.

SELECTED READING

In the following reading look for sensitivity analysis. Also notice that all the data are provided so that you can run the linear programming problem yourself and carry out sensitivity analysis with the aid of a microcomputer package.

The Shanghai Urban Construction Bureau*

STEPHEN C. GRAVES

One of the more interesting projects was performed for the Shanghai Urban Construction Bureau (UCB), which is responsible for all residential construction. This bureau controls both the factories that produce building materials (for example, bricks) and the construction brigades that put up residential buildings, primarily apartment buildings. The bureau is under great pressure to expand and update the housing stock in Shanghai. It was considering adding two new factories that would use fly ash, the residue from coal combustion, to make wall materials. These factories would serve two purposes: they would make Shanghai more self-sufficient with regard to building material, and they would help to dispose of the large quantities of fly ash (an environmental hazard) produced by Shanghai's factories. The UCB needed to decide what mix of wall materials should be produced by these factories. Basically, three categories of wall materials could be made; bricks, blocks, and panels. The various bricks were generally the cheapest to manufacture and required the least investment, while panels were the most expensive to manufacture and required the most investment. At the prices set by the state for inputs and outputs, it was most profitable for the building materials factories to make a mix of bricks and blocks. However, for construction purposes, bricks were the most labor-intensive and resulted in the highest total construction costs. Both blocks and panels required less construction labor. Indeed, the panels required only 57 percent of the labor needed for comparable construction using bricks. Consequently, the construction brigade much preferred using blocks and panels.

In a market economy, market forces would probably solve such problems through price adjustment. However, this was not likely in Shanghai. Production mix decisions were made through negotiation between the interested parties, with the process overseen by the UCB. To support this, the research arm of the UCB proposed this problem as a project for one of the students. This student viewed the problem from a systems perspective and ignored the boundaries created by the building material organization and the construction brigade organization. He realized that much of the difference in opinion was due to the prices at which the bricks, blocks, and panels were transferred from the building material factories to the construction brigades, but that this was immaterial to deciding what was best for the UCB. He developed a linear programming model, analogous to the product mix LP found in any introductory operations research textbook, that took a systems perspective of minimizing the total cost of both manufacturing wall material and constructing residences. The model included constraints to ensure that all of the fly ash was used and that the expected needs for building materials were met. Other constraints limited the factory's usage of coal, electricity, and labor, and set a limit on the allowable capital investment level. Finally, there were constraints that limited the usage of cement, steel, and labor by the construction brigades and limited the total building weight. These usage constraints represented the resource levels expected to be available to the factory or to the construction brigades.

The general form of the LP is as follows:

$$\min Z = \sum_{j=1}^{m} C_j X_j$$

subject to

$$\sum_{j=1}^{m} X_j \geq D,$$

$$\sum_{j=1}^{m} B_{ij} X_j \leq (=) R_i, \qquad i = 1, 2, \ldots, n,$$

$$\text{ALL} \quad X_j \geq 0, \qquad j = 1, 2, \ldots, m,$$

where

Z is the total annual construction cost including material costs, labor costs, depreciation, overhead, and other indirect material costs used to build buildings.

C_j indicates the construction costs per unit for using wall material j. The construction costs include the

*Reprinted by permission of Stephen C. Graves, "Reflections on Operations Management in Shanghai, *Interfaces* 16, no. 2 (March–April 1986), Copyright 1986, The Institute of Management Sciences.

(continued)

X_j is the annual production quantity of wall material j.

D is the total annual demand for wall materials to satisfy the construction requirements, and equals 1.5 million cubic meters.

B_{ij} is the amount of resource i needed per cubic meter of wall material j.

R_i indicates the total annual supply of resource i.

m is the number of distinct wall materials (13).

n is the number of resources (nine).

The student collected data from both the building materials factories and the construction brigades to parameterize the model (Table 1). There are 13 distinct types of building materials: three types of bricks, six types of blocks, and four types of panels. Block 6 and panel 4 are light building materials with distinct technological processes; hence, we have not put all of the same types of building materials together.

The basic solution to this LP uses 262,000 cubic meters of bricks (17 percent), 706,000 cubic meters of blocks (47 percent), and 532,000 cubic meters of panels (36 percent) and has an objective value of 449 million yuan. Binding constraints are those for the usage of fly ash, coal, construction labor, and steel, and building weight.

This solution indicates that there is no dominant type of wall material for Shanghai. Since two new factories were being considered, the recommendation suggested by this solution is to devote the first factory to blocks and the second factory to a mix of bricks and panels. The student also explored the sensitivity of the solution to various parameter changes, for instance, how the mix of wall materials would change if more construction labor were available (Figure 1). As we would expect, with more construction labor, usage of bricks and blocks increases at the expense of panel usage. Furthermore, the savings in construction costs exceed the cost of the additional laborers, which suggests that the construction brigades should consider expanding.

While I do not know how this study affected the decisions facing the UCB, I do think the study is

TABLE 1 The Basic Data of Wall Building Materials

		Data from Building Material Factories					Data from Construction Brigades			
	Construction Cost (¥/m³)	Fly Ash (T/m³)	Coal (kg/m³)	Electricity (KWH/m³)	Labor (man-day/m³)	Capital Investment (¥/m³)	Labor (man-day/m³)	Weight (T/m³)	Steel usage (kg/m³)	Cement usage (T/m³)
Brick 1	282.2	0.36	27.5	16.1	2.52	35	8.7	1.22	50	0.45
Brick 2	282.2	1.11	56.9	19.3	1.21	70	8.7	1.43	50	0.45
Brick 3	282.2	0.55	34	26.9	1.97	55	8.7	1.25	50	0.45
Brick 1	282.2	0.51	34.08	9.4	0.6	50	8.17	1.37	50	0.417
Brick 2	280.2	0.54	38.24	9.64	0.6	53	8.17	1.3	50	0.415
Brick 3	296.7	1.21	34.08	9.4	0.6	75	8.17	1.18	50	0.415
Brick 4	296.7	1.31	34.08	9.4	0.6	115	8.17	1.15	50	0.415
Brick 5	282.2	0.79	52.8	12.6	0.6	60	8.17	0.98	50	0.415
Panel 1	335.3	0.97	48	12	1.53	165	5	1.07	69.5	0.35
Panel 2	330	0.54	48	12	1.53	103	5	12	69.5	0.35
Panel 3	348.2	0.25	48	12	1.53	165	5	1.05	69.5	0.35
Block 6	311	0.49	52.8	12.6	0.6	62.5	7.3	0.58	53.3	0.5
Panel 4	320	0.49	52.8	12.6	0.6	72	7	0.49	53.3	0.5
Supply = R_i		100	6,400	2,000	180	12500	1,100	164	8,300	63

The resource supplies R_i have been scaled by 10,000; that is, there are 100 · 10,000 = 1 million tons of fly ash that must be consumed by the building factories.

(continued)

indicative of the type of systems analysis that can be valuable to Chinese enterprises. The research arm of UCB, with whom the student worked closely, seemed to agree that a single model that encompassed both the manufacture of wall material and residential construction was the right approach; but clearly the model would be just one input, albeit a fairly objective input, into a complex decision-making process.

FIGURE 1 Sensitivity of Production Mix to Construction Labor Availability

With more construction labor, usage of blocks and bricks increases, while panel usage decreases.

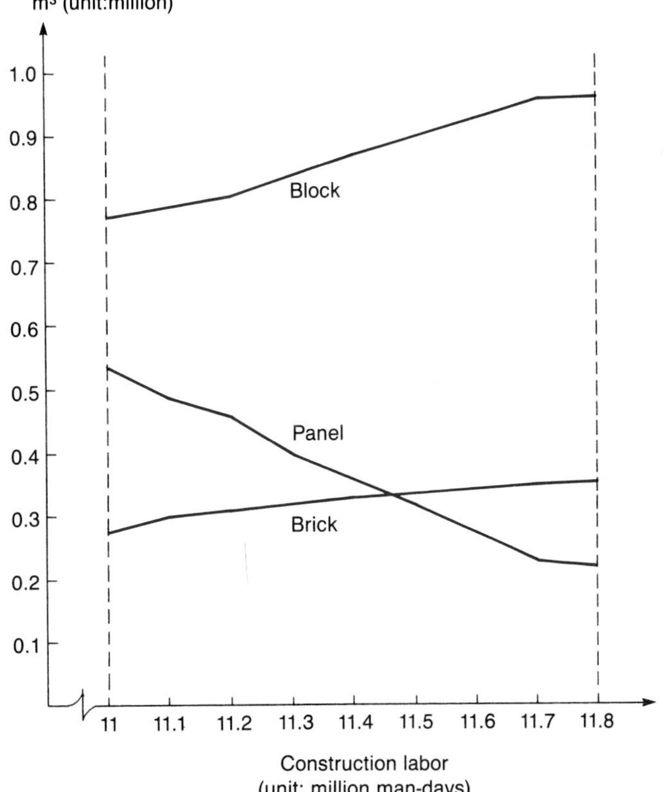

6

Linear Programming: The Simplex Method

Chapter Outline

In this chapter we take a "close-up" look at the simplex method of solving LP models. A **simplex** is a bounded convex polyhedron of n-dimensions determined by $n + 1$ points in a space of dimension equal to or greater than n. For example, a triangle together with its interior as determined by its three vertices forms a two-dimensional simplex in the plane or in *any* space of higher dimension. The simplex method is a procedure for finding the "point" within the simplex that optimizes the objective function. In addition to studying the mechanics of the simplex method, we illustrate the recognition of various solution aberrations (no feasible solution, alternative optimal solutions, etc.). We also present the treatment of sensitivity analysis and interpretation of primal/dual solution relationships. Finally, we summarize simplex-based alternative algorithms and briefly discuss recent developments challenging the superiority of simplex methods.

6.1 ON SYSTEMS OF LINEAR EQUATIONS

Before introducing the simplex method, we need to consider some characteristics and solution procedures for systems of linear equations.

Characteristics of Solutions

A linear system of m equations in n unknown variables may have *no* solution, a *unique* solution, or an *infinite* number of solutions. When solving linear programming problems using the simplex method, we will be solving systems of equations where $m < n$. Let us focus briefly on characteristics of these types of systems.

First consider the case where $m < n$ and the system has an infinite number of solutions. For this case any m variables can be expressed in terms of the *remaining* $(n - m)$ variables. Since an infinite number of arbitrary values can be assigned to the remaining variables, the system has an infinite number of possible solutions. For example, the following system has two equations ($m = 2$) and three variables ($n = 3$):

$$x_1 + x_2 + x_3 = 10 \quad (6.1)$$

$$2x_1 + x_2 + 5x_3 = 24\,. \quad (6.2)$$

Note that *any* two variables can be solved for in terms of the remaining variable. For example, verify that x_1 and x_2 can be expressed in terms of x_3 as

$$x_1 = 14 - 4x_3 \quad (6.3)$$

$$x_2 = 3x_3 - 4\,. \quad (6.4)$$

Choosing *any* value for x_3 provides unique values for x_1 and x_2. To illustrate, for $x_3 = 2$, $x_1 = 14 - 4(2) = 6$ and $x_2 = 3(2) - 4 = 2$. Hence this system has an infinite number of solutions.

Similarly, consider the following system of equations:

$$2x_1 + x_2 - 3x_3 = 20 \quad (6.5)$$

$$6x_1 + 3x_2 - 9x_3 = 80\,. \quad (6.6)$$

By observation, you should conclude that the left side of Equation 6.6 is three times the left side of 6.5. However, the right side of 6.6 does not equal three times the right side of 6.5. This system of equations is characterized by *no solution*. The two equations can be represented geometrically by two parallel planes in three-space (dimensions). Try to solve for two of the variables in terms of the third and observe what happens.

A Method of Solution

When an infinite number of solutions is possible (as is the case with most LP problems), we can arbitrarily choose a subset of variables and specify the remaining variables at zero. For example, with Equations 6.1 and 6.2, choose x_1 and x_3 as the subset and hence set x_2 equal to zero.

$$x_1 + 0 + x_3 = 10 \tag{6.1a}$$

$$2x_1 + 0 + 5x_3 = 24\,. \tag{6.2a}$$

Solving for x_1 in 6.1*a*, we have:

$$x_1 = 10 - x_3\,.$$

Substituting into 6.2*a*,

$$2(10 - x_3) + 5x_3 = 24$$

or

$$20 - 2x_3 + 5x_3 = 24$$

$$3x_3 = 4$$

$$x_3 = 4/3\,.$$

Substituting this result into Equation 6.1*a*,

$$x_1 = 10 - 4/3 = 30/3 - 4/3$$

$$= 26/3\,.$$

The **Gauss-Jordan elimination procedure** allows us to solve linear equations more easily. Two fundamental properties of systems of linear equations form the heart of this method.

1. The solution set for an equation remains the same if both sides of the equation are multiplied or divided by a nonzero constant.
2. The solution set for an equation remains the same if it is replaced by the sum of itself and a nonzero multiple of any other equation.

▶ Example 6.1

Given the system

$$x_1 + x_2 + x_3 = 10 \quad (1)$$

$$2x_1 + x_2 + 5x_3 = 24, \quad (2)$$

convince yourself that replacing Equation 1 by twice itself (property 1) gives the equivalent system

$$2x_1 + 2x_2 + 2x_3 = 20 \quad (1a)$$

$$2x_1 + x_2 + 5x_3 = 24. \quad (2)$$

To solve the resulting system, start by setting x_2 equal to zero:

$$2x_1 + 2x_3 = 20 \quad (1b)$$

$$2x_1 + 5x_3 = 24. \quad (2a)$$

We can eliminate x_1 by utilizing property 2. Multiplying 1*b* by −1 and adding to 2*a* results in

$$-1(2x_1 + 2x_3) = -1(20) \quad -1(1b)$$

$$2x_1 + 5x_3 = 24 \quad (2a)$$

$$0 + 3x_3 = 4 \quad (2b)$$

which when solved for x_3 gives $x_3 = 4/3$, the same result as before.

An approach which we refer to as the **identity matrix method** uses these two fundamental properties to transform one system of equations into an equivalent system whose solution set is easy to determine. For example, the identity matrix method would transform the following initial system of equations

$$\begin{aligned} 5x_1 + 4x_2 &= 24 \\ 2x_1 + 5x_2 &= 13 \end{aligned} \quad \text{(Initial)}$$

into an equivalent system having the form

$$\begin{aligned} 1x_1 + 0x_2 &= 4 \\ 0x_1 + 1x_2 &= 1\,. \end{aligned} \quad \text{(Final)}$$

The only set of values uniquely satisfying the final system (and consequently the initial system) is $x_1 = 4$ and $x_2 = 1$.

The transformations in proceeding from the initial system to the final system are often called **row operations.** If, as above, there is a unique solution to an $(m \times m)$ system of simultaneous equations, then the identity matrix method systematically utilizes row operations on the original system of equations to produce a new system of equations with a particular property. The desired end result is to transform the original system of equations into an equivalent system for which the resulting matrix of variable coefficients is in the form of an **identity matrix:**

$$I = \begin{pmatrix} 1 & 0 & \cdots & 0 \\ 0 & 1 & \cdots & 0 \\ \vdots & \vdots & \ddots & \vdots \\ 0 & 0 & \cdots & 1 \end{pmatrix}$$

Once this is achieved, the solution is read directly from the right-hand–side constants.

As we illustrate in Example 6.2, the most efficient process for performing this transformation of the original system is to create the identity matrix one column at a time. In each instance the column element that is equal to "one" should be created first, followed by the remaining "zero" elements in the column.

Example 6.2

Let us illustrate the identity matrix method using the (2 × 2) system just discussed. By way of explanation, we indicate algebraic operations along the right margin where Equation i is denoted as e_i. Repeated below is the original system of equations

$$5x_1 + 4x_2 = 24 \qquad e_1$$

$$2x_1 + 5x_2 = 13. \qquad e_2$$

Our first objective will be to transform the column of coefficients on x_1 from $\begin{pmatrix} 5 \\ 2 \end{pmatrix}$ to $\begin{pmatrix} 1 \\ 0 \end{pmatrix}$. Dividing ($e_1$) by 5 forces the coefficient of x_1 to 1:

$$1x_1 + 0.8x_2 = 4.8 \qquad e_3 = e_1/5$$

$$2x_1 + \quad 5x_2 = 13 \qquad e_2$$

Moving down the first column, a zero coefficient can be obtained for x_1 in the second equation by multiplying e_3 by −2 and adding the resulting equation to e_2:

$$1x_1 + 0.8x_2 = 4.8 \qquad e_3$$

$$0x_1 + 3.4x_2 = 3.4 \qquad e_4 = e_2 - 2e_3$$

Now we want to transform the coefficients on x_2 from $\begin{pmatrix} 0.8 \\ 3.4 \end{pmatrix}$ to $\begin{pmatrix} 0 \\ 1 \end{pmatrix}$. Dividing e_4 by 3.4 yields

$$1x_1 + 0.8x_2 = 4.8 \qquad e_3$$

$$0x_1 + \quad 1x_2 = 1.0 \qquad e_5 = e_4/3.4$$

Multiplying e_5 by −0.8 and adding this result to e_3 produces the desired coefficient of zero for x_2 in e_6:

$$1x_1 + 0x_2 = 4.0 \qquad e_6$$

$$0x_1 + 1x_2 = 1.0 \qquad e_5$$

Thus x_1 and x_2 equal the right-hand–side constants in e_6 and e_5, respectively.

In the next example, we illustrate the use of the identity matrix method in generating one solution for our previously examined (2×3) system.

▶ Example 6.3

As before, let us set $x_2 = 0$. Using the identity matrix method, we want to transform from the original system

$$1x_1 + 1x_2 + 1x_3 = 10 \qquad e_1$$

$$2x_1 + 1x_2 + 5x_3 = 24 \qquad e_2$$

to an equivalent system having coefficients of a (2×2) identity matrix associated with x_1 and x_3. Our first step is to transform the column for x_1 from $\begin{pmatrix}1\\2\end{pmatrix}$ to $\begin{pmatrix}1\\0\end{pmatrix}$. Since the coefficient is already equal to one in e_1, we transform the 2 in e_2 to zero by multiplying e_1 by -2 and adding to e_2. The result is:

$$1x_1 + 1x_2 + 1x_3 = 10 \qquad e_1$$

$$0x_1 - 1x_2 + 3x_2 = 4 \qquad e_3 = -2e_1 + e_2$$

The remaining transformations for x_3 follow with the appropriate row operations indicated to the right of the equations.

$$1x_1 + 1x_2 + 1x_3 = 10 \qquad e_1$$

$$0x_1 - \frac{1}{3}x_2 + 1x_3 = 4/3 \qquad e_4 = e_3/3$$

$$1x_1 + \frac{4}{3}x_2 + 0x_3 = 26/3 \qquad e_5 = e_1 - e_4$$

$$0x_1 - \frac{1}{3}x_2 + 1x_3 = 4/3 \qquad e_4$$

With x_2 assumed equal to zero, we can read the values for x_1 and x_3 from this last system as $x_1 = 26/3$ and $x_3 = 4/3$.

FOLLOW-UP EXERCISES Solve the following systems by the identity matrix method.

1. $2x_1 + 5x_2 = 0$
   $7x_1 + 5x_2 = 25.$
2. $x_1 + x_2 + x_3 = 8$
   $2x_1 - x_2 + 3x_3 = 17$
   $4x_1 + x_2 - 5x_3 = 7.$
3. In Example 6.3, set $x_1 = 0$, and solve for x_2 and x_3 using the identity matrix method.

4. Given the system of equations

$$\begin{aligned} 3x_1 + 2x_2 + x_3 + x_4 &= 5 \\ x_1 + x_2 + x_3 + x_4 &= 2 \\ x_1 - 2x_2 + x_3 - 2x_4 &= 5, \end{aligned}$$

set $x_4 = 0$ and solve for x_1, x_2, and x_3 using the identity matrix method.

6.2 STANDARD FORM OF THE LP MODEL

As we know from Section 4.3, a unique optimal solution to an LP problem, if it exists, lies at a corner point. Because the coordinates of a corner point are determined by solving a system of equations, the inequalities in an LP formulation *must be converted to equalities*.

A preliminary step required by the simplex method is the transformation of the problem to the so-called **standard form** such that the following three conditions are met:

1. The structural constraints are expressed as equalities.
2. The right-hand–side constants in the structural constraints are nonnegative.
3. All the variables are nonnegative.

Condition 1 is necessary for application of the identity matrix method of solution; the rationale for the other two conditions will be clear in Sections 6.3 and 6.4.

Given an LP problem having m structural constraints of the $\leq$ type,

Optimize

$$z = c_1x_1 + c_2x_2 + \cdots + c_nx_n,$$

or

$$z = \sum_{j=1}^{n} c_jx_j,$$

subject to

$$\begin{array}{ccccccccc} a_{11}x_1 & + & a_{12}x_2 & + & \cdots & + & a_{1n}x_n & \leq & b_1 \\ a_{21}x_1 & + & a_{22}x_2 & + & \cdots & + & a_{2n}x_n & \leq & b_2 \\ \vdots & & \vdots & & & & \vdots & & \vdots \\ a_{m1}x_1 & + & a_{m2}x_2 & + & \cdots & + & a_{mn}x_n & \leq & b_m, \end{array}$$

or

$$\sum_{j=1}^{n} a_{ij}x_j \leq b_i, \qquad i = 1, \ldots, m,$$

and

$$x_j \geq 0, \qquad j = 1, \ldots, n,$$

the **standard form** is expressed as

optimize

$$z = \sum_{j=1}^{n} c_j x_j + \sum_{j=n+1}^{n+m} c_j x_j$$

subject to

$$\sum_{j=1}^{n} a_{ij} x_j + x_{n+i} = b_i, \qquad i = 1, \ldots, m, \tag{6.7}$$

and

$$x_j \geq 0, \qquad j = 1, \ldots, n + m,$$

where x_{n+i} is the **slack variable** (what we used to call S_i) for the ith constraint. Remember from Section 4.4 that a $\leq$ inequality is converted to an equality by adding a slack variable to the left-hand side.

▶ Example 6.4

Let us return to the original formulation of the air cargo model (Example 4.1)

Maximize

$$z = 7x_1 + 10x_2$$

subject to

$$5x_1 + 4x_2 \leq 24 \tag{1}$$

$$2x_1 + 5x_2 \leq 13 \tag{2}$$

$$x_1, x_2 \geq 0.$$

The standard form for this problem is expressed as:

Maximize

$$z = 7x_1 + 10x_2 + 0S_1 + 0S_2$$

subject to

$$5x_1 + 4x_2 + S_1 \qquad = 24 \tag{1}$$

$$2x_1 + 5x_2 \qquad + S_2 = 13 \tag{2}$$

$$x_1, x_2, S_1, S_2 \geq 0.$$

Note our return to S_i notation for slack variables. This helps us distinguish decision variables from supplemental variables.

Condition 2 of the standard form requires nonnegative right-hand–side constants, b_i. Should there be a negative b_i, it is a simple matter to multiply both sides of the inequality by a minus one (−1). Note that doing so reverses the sense of the inequality.

Condition 3 requires nonnegative variables. In effect this condition was imposed in the generalized form of the LP model of Section 3.2 by specifying nonnegativity conditions. Unrestricted and nonpositive decision variables must be restated by methods described in Section 3.4.

FOLLOW-UP EXERCISES

5. Rewrite the following LP problem in standard form.

Maximize

$$z = 6x_1 + 7x_2 - 3x_3$$

subject to

$$x_1 + x_2 + x_3 \le 300 \quad (1)$$
$$2x_1 + x_2 + 8x_3 \le 450 \quad (2)$$
$$2x_1 - 3x_2 - 6x_3 \le 100 \quad (3)$$
$$x_1, x_2, x_3 \ge 0.$$

6. Rewrite the following LP problem in standard form:

Maximize

$$z = 2x_1 + 5x_2 + 3x_3$$

subject to

$$x_1 - 3x_2 + 2x_3 \le 60 \quad (1)$$
$$8x_1 - 3x_3 \ge -40 \quad (2)$$
$$x_1 \ge 0$$

x_2 unrestricted

x_3 nonpositive.

6.3 SIMPLEX METHOD: ≤ CONSTRAINTS

As discussed in Chapter 4, the simplex method of solution is an iterative procedure (algorithm) that avoids infeasible solutions and improves the objective function value at each iteration. The method of solution is similar to the identity matrix method presented in Section 6.1; it differs only in the criteria that guide row operations while searching for the optimal solution. This section illustrates the solution of problems with ≤ constraints; Section 6.5 generalizes the simplex algorithm to problems with mixed constraints.

Tableau Form

It is convenient to consolidate all equations in the LP model by adding the objective function to the constraints in the standard form, Equation 6.7, as follows:

$$\begin{aligned}
1z - c_1x_1 - c_2x_2 - \cdots - c_nx_n - 0S_1 - 0S_2 - \cdots - 0S_m &= 0 \\
0z + a_{11}x_1 + a_{12}x_2 + \cdots + a_{1n}x_n + 1S_1 + 0S_2 + \cdots + 0S_m &= b_1 \\
0z + a_{21}x_1 + a_{22}x_2 + \cdots + a_{2n}x_n + 0S_1 + 1S_2 + \cdots + 0S_m &= b_2 \\
\vdots \qquad\qquad & \quad \vdots \\
0z + a_{m1}x_1 + a_{m2}x_2 + \cdots + a_{mn}x_n + 0S_1 + 0S_2 + \cdots + 1S_m &= b_m.
\end{aligned} \qquad (6.8)$$

Note that z is now treated in the same manner as the other variables in the problem. Its role as a dependent variable becomes obscured by its inclusion as just another variable in a system of equations.

An equivalent representation to 6.8 is given by the following table of variable coefficients and RHS constants (see Table 6–1). This **tableau form** provides an efficient structure for writing and solving (both by hand and by computer) the standard LP model.

TABLE 6–1

	Criterion Value	Decision Variables				Slack Variables				Right-Hand-Side Constants
	z	x_1	x_2	$\cdots$	x_n	S_1	S_2	$\cdots$	S_m	b_i
z-equation	1	$-c_1$	$-c_2$	$\cdots$	$-c_n$	0	0	$\cdots$	0	0
Constraint equations	0	a_{11}	a_{12}	$\cdots$	a_{1n}	1	0	$\cdots$	0	b_1
	0	a_{21}	a_{22}	$\cdots$	a_{2n}	0	1	$\cdots$	0	b_2
	$\vdots$	$\vdots$	$\vdots$	$\ddots$	$\vdots$	$\vdots$	$\vdots$	$\ddots$	$\vdots$	$\vdots$
	0	a_{m1}	a_{m2}	$\cdots$	a_{mn}	0	0	$\cdots$	1	b_m

Example 6.5

The standard form of the air cargo model (from Example 6.4) is

Maximize

$$z = 7x_1 + 10x_2 + 0S_1 + 0S_2$$

subject to

$$5x_1 + 4x_2 + S_1 + 0S_2 = 24 \quad (1)$$

$$2x_1 + 5x_2 + 0S_1 + S_2 = 13 \quad (2)$$

$$x_1, x_2, S_1, S_2 \geq 0.$$

Incorporating the objective function in the manner given by system 6.8 gives the following:

$$1z - 7x_1 - 10x_2 - 0S_1 - 0S_2 = 0 \quad (0)$$

$$0z + 5x_1 + 4x_2 + 1S_1 + 0S_2 = 24 \quad (1)$$

$$0z + 2x_1 + 5x_2 + 0S_1 + 1S_2 = 13. \quad (2)$$

In tableau form this is expressed as:

Basis	z	x_1	x_2	S_1	S_2	b_i
m	1	−7	−10	0	0	0
S_1	0	5	4	1	0	24
S_2	0	2	5	0	1	13

For the sake of convenience, the basic variables are identified in the first column of the tableau. The selection of S_1 and S_2 for the basis is equivalent to setting x_1 and x_2 to zero; hence, the system of three equations is reduced to

$$1z + 0S_1 + 0S_2 = 0 \qquad (0)$$

$$0z + 1S_1 + 0S_2 = 24 \qquad (1)$$

$$0z + 0S_1 + 1S_2 = 13, \qquad (2)$$

which provides an immediate solution of $z = 0$, $S_1 = 24$, and $S_2 = 13$. Note that the first solution is at the origin (point A) in Figure 6–1.

FIGURE 6–1 Solution Space for Example 6.5

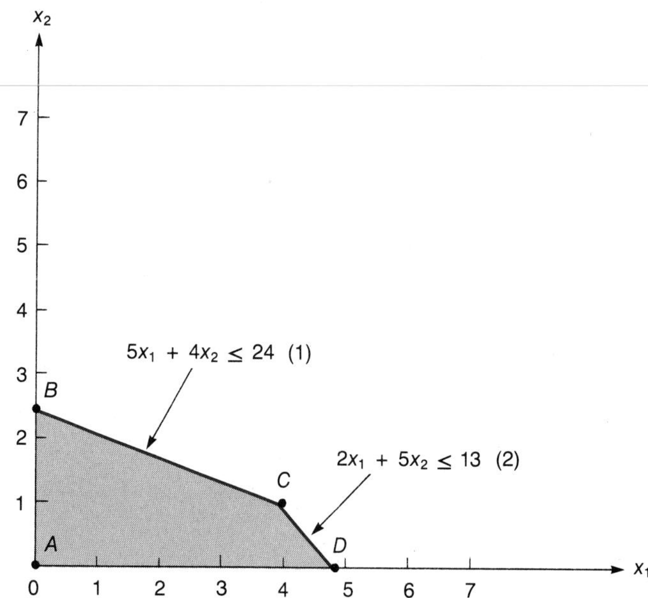

Suppose that an informant told us that the optimal extreme point involved x_1 and x_2 with S_1 and S_2 both equal to zero. Perhaps the informant read Chapter 4 carefully! *If* we knew what variables were in the final solution, we could easily solve this problem.

Again, assuming that we knew that x_1 and x_2 were basic variables in the optimal solution, we would want to transform the system of equations

$$1z - 7x_1 - 10x_2 - 0S_1 - 0S_2 = 0 \qquad e_1$$
$$0z + 5x_1 + 4x_2 + 1S_1 + 0S_2 = 24 \qquad e_2$$
$$0z + 2x_1 + 5x_2 + 0S_1 + 1S_2 = 13 \qquad e_3$$

into the form

$$1z + 0x_1 + 0x_2 + \cdots$$
$$0z + 1x_1 + 0x_2 + \cdots$$
$$0z + 0x_1 + 1x_2 + \cdots$$

using the identity matrix method. With this objective in mind, we can proceed on with the necessary row operations.

$$1z - 7x_1 - 10x_2 - 0S_1 - 0S_2 = 0 \qquad e_1$$
$$0z + 5x_1 + 4x_2 + 1S_1 + 0S_2 = 24 \qquad e_2$$
$$0z + 2x_1 + 5x_2 + 0S_1 + 1S_2 = 13 \qquad e_3$$

$$1z - 7x_1 - 10x_2 - 0S_1 - 0S_2 = 0 \qquad e_1$$
$$0z + 1x_1 + \frac{4}{5}x_2 + \frac{1}{5}S_1 + 0S_2 = \frac{24}{5} \qquad e'_2 = \frac{e_2}{5}$$
$$0z + 2x_1 + 5x_2 + 0S_1 + 1S_2 = 13 \qquad e_3$$

$$1z + 0x_1 - \frac{22}{5}x_2 + \frac{7}{5}S_1 + 0S_2 = \frac{168}{5} \qquad e'_1 = e_1 + 7e'_2$$
$$0z + 1x_1 + \frac{4}{5}x_2 + \frac{1}{5}S_1 + 0S_2 = \frac{24}{5} \qquad e'_2$$
$$0z + 0x_1 + \frac{17}{5}x_2 - \frac{2}{5}S_1 + 1S_2 = \frac{17}{5} \qquad e'_3 = e_3 - 2e'_2$$

$$1z + 0x_2 - \frac{22}{5}x_2 + \frac{7}{5}S_1 + 0S_2 = \frac{168}{5} \qquad e'_1$$
$$0z + 1x_1 + \frac{4}{5}x_2 + \frac{1}{5}S_1 + 0S_2 = \frac{24}{5} \qquad e'_2$$
$$0z + 0x_1 + 1x_2 - \frac{2}{17}S_1 + \frac{5}{17}S_2 = 1 \qquad e''_3 = \frac{5}{17}e_3$$

$$1z + 0x_1 + 0x_2 + \frac{15}{17}S_1 + \frac{22}{17}S_2 = 38 \qquad e''_1 = e'_1 + \frac{22}{5}e''_3$$
$$0z + 1x_1 + 0x_2 + \frac{5}{17}S_1 - \frac{4}{17}S_2 = 4 \qquad e''_2 = e'_2 - \frac{4}{5}e''_3$$
$$0z + 0x_1 + 1x_2 - \frac{2}{17}S_1 + \frac{5}{17}S_2 = 1 \qquad e''_3$$

Converting this solution into the tableau format, we have:

Basis	z	x_1	x_2	S_1	S_2	b_i
—	1	0	0	$\frac{15}{17}$	$\frac{22}{17}$	38
x_1	0	1	0	$\frac{5}{17}$	$-\frac{4}{17}$	4
x_2	0	0	1	$-\frac{2}{17}$	$\frac{5}{17}$	1

Without our informant, however, we do not know what variables will be "in solution" or in the basis of the optimal tableau. The simplex method provides an orderly way to proceed from one solution to another, solving for variables depending on how they contribute to the criterion function.

Again, we start with our initial formulation and move step by step but now without knowing which of the variables will be in the final solution.

Solution Procedure

The following steps generalize the simplex algorithm.

1. **Select a convenient starting basis of m variables.** Remember that variables *outside* the basis are set to zero and that the appearance of an *identity matrix* for the coefficients of variables in a system of linear equations is a convenient solution. From Table 6–1, we see that $S_1, S_2, \ldots, S_m$ represent a convenient starting basis with immediate solution values of $b_1, b_2, \ldots, b_m$, respectively.

   Please note the following important points: First, the appearance of an identity matrix in the tableau *underneath z and the variables in the basis* immediately provides the right-hand–side (RHS) constants as the solution; second, the RHS constants must be *nonnegative* in order to guarantee a feasible solution.[1]

   The next solution is generated by replacing a variable in the basis with a variable outside the basis such that the value of z is improved.

2. **Select the "entering variable" by applying the "optimality criterion":** Select the *non*basic variable that has the *best per unit contribution* to the objective function. For *maximization* problems, select the variable having the *most negative* coefficient in the z equation of the tableau; for minimization problems, select the variable that is *most positive*.[2] In case of a *tie*, arbitrarily select one of the tied variables.

[1] See condition 2 of the standard form in Section 6.2.

[2] If this seems the opposite from what you would expect, recall that the c_j coefficients in the tableau are opposite in sign from the original formulation of the problem.

3. **Select the "leaving variable" and the amount of the entering variable by applying the "feasibility criterion":** Determine the quantities of the entering variable required to force *each* basic variable to a value of zero. Select the leaving variable as the one corresponding to the smallest of these quantities. This value not only identifies the variable that departs from the basis but also represents the amount (value) of the entering variable.

▶ Example 6.6

Continuing Example 6.5, we select x_2 as the entering variable because it has the most negative coefficient (−10) of the nonbasic variables in the z equation of the tableau; this is equivalent to the best per-unit contribution in the original objective function. Each unit of x_2 *increases* z by 10.

Because there are two constraint equations, only two variables are allowed in the basis; hence either S_1 or S_2 must leave; the value of one or the other must be set to zero. The feasibility criterion determines the maximum value that can be assigned to x_2 while assuring that all remaining basic variables do not violate the nonnegativity condition. Consider the two constraints

$$5x_1 + 4x_2 + S_1 \qquad = 24 \qquad (1)$$

$$2x_1 + 5x_2 \qquad + S_2 = 13. \qquad (2)$$

Since x_1 is not in the basis, it may be ignored ($x_1 = 0$). Solving for the current basic variables S_1 and S_2, we get

$$S_1 = 24 - 4x_2 \qquad (1a)$$

$$S_2 = 13 - 5x_2. \qquad (2a)$$

If S_1 is selected as the leaving variable, its value must be set to zero. From Equation 1*a*, S_1 equals zero when the entering variable x_2 has a value of 24/4 or 6. If S_2 is selected to leave the basis, Equation 2*a* indicates that x_2 must be assigned a value of 13/5, or 2.6. Note, however, that a value of 6 for x_2 would cause S_1 to be negative based on 2*a*, which results in an infeasible solution. Hence, the largest value that can be assigned to x_2 such that one of the variables (S_2) leaves the basis and the remaining variable S_1 does not become negative is 2.6. The next solution is therefore:

$$\text{Basic} \quad \begin{cases} x_2 = 2.6 \\ S_1 = 24 - 4(2.6) \\ \quad\; = 13.6 \end{cases}$$

$$\text{Nonbasic} \quad \begin{cases} x_1 = 0 \\ S_2 = 0 \end{cases}$$

$$z = 7(0) + 10(2.6)$$

$$= 26.$$

The simplex method thus generates point *B* in Figure 6–1 as the next solution.

The feasibility criterion can be operationalized more effectively as:

a. Calculate the ratios $r_1, r_2, \ldots, r_m$ by dividing the RHS constants by the corresponding constraint coefficients of the entering variable; that is,

$$r_i = b_i / a^*_{ij} \tag{6.9}$$

where b_i is the ith RHS constant in the tableau, a^*_{ij} is the coefficient of the *corresponding* (ith) constraint for the *entering* variable, x_j, and r_i is the maximum amount allowed for the entering variable by the ith constraint.

b. Select the leaving variable as the one in the basis corresponding to the *minimum* r_i where $r_i \geq 0$; the quantity of the entering variable is given by this minimum r_i value.

In the preceding example,

$$r_1 = 24/4$$

$$r_2 = 13/5\,.$$

Since r_2 is minimum, the basic variable associated with the second constraint (S_2) is selected as the leaving variable. The variable x_2 will enter the basis with a value of 13/5 or 2.6.

Because *zero* or *negative* a^*_{ij} imply that an infinite amount of the entering value can be assigned (Can you show this?), their corresponding ratios are simply ignored whenever they appear.

4. **Modify the tableau to reflect the new solution.** The objective is to force an identity matrix immediately underneath z and the *new* set of basic variables by performing *row operations* as in Examples 6.2 and 6.3

Example 6.7

The original tableau of Example 6.5 is modified by including row numbers and an r_i column. The new tableau is shown below.

Basis	z	x_1	x_2	S_1	S_2	b_i	Row No.	r_i
I	1	−7	−10*	0	0	0	0	—
S_1	0	5	4	1	0	24	1	24/4 = 6.0
S_2	0	2	5	0	1	13	2	13/5 = 2.6*
II	1	−3*	0	0	2	26	0	—
S_1	0	17/5	0	1	−4/5	68/5	1	13.6/3.4 = 4.0*
x_2	0	2/5	1	0	1/5	13/5	2	2.6/0.4 = 6.5

Key column

Pivot element

Key row

In order to follow the movement of the identity matrix, each unity element is identified by the symbol □. Since the column corresponding to z always remains intact, we omit the symbol for its unity element. Note that the portion of the identity matrix in the constraint equation section is associated only with basic variables and that a one must be located at the intersection of the row and column corresponding to each basic variable, *with zeroes elsewhere in that column.* Thus the columns under S_1 and S_2 in Tableau I have all zero's except for the one's at the $S_1 - S_1$ and $S_2 - S_2$ intersections; likewise for the columns under x_2 and S_1 (the new basis) in Tableau II.

In Tableau I, the asterisk (*) above the -10 in the z equation identifies x_2 as the entering variable according to the optimality criterion; the asterisk following the 2.6 in the r_i column identifies S_2 as the leaving variable according to the feasibility criterion; hence, in the new basis, x_2 will replace S_2.

The row associated with the leaving variable (S_2 in this case) is termed the *pivot equation* or *key row.* The column associated with the entering variable (x_2) is called the *key column.* The constraint coefficient found at the intersection of the key row and key column is called the *pivot element.* We identify the pivot element by circling it ((5)).

Tableau II is generated using row operations by creating the new identity matrix for the new set of basic variables. The objective is to transform the coefficients in the key column into those formerly found in the column representing the departing variable. This is accomplished by creating a one in the pivot element position and zeros elsewhere in the key column.

a. In Tableau I, divide the pivot equation, Row 2, by the pivot element 5. This gives Row 2 in Tableau II. Note that a value of one has been forced in the $x_2 - x_2$ intersection.
b. To force the necessary zero in Row 1 of the key (x_2) column, multiply Row 2 of Tableau II by -4 and add it to Row 1 in Tableau I. This gives Row 1 in Tableau II.
c. To force the necessary zero in Row 0 of the key column, multiply Row 2 of Tableau II by 10 and add it to Row 0 of Tableau I. This gives the new Row 0 in Tableau II.

Now, note the following: First, the identity matrix plus the fact that the nonbasic variables (x_1 and S_2) equal zero make the RHS (right-hand–side) constants the solutions for the respective basic variables (S_1 and x_2); second, in Row 0, the zero values for x_1 and S_2 coupled with zero coefficients for S_1 and x_2 provide the RHS constant as the solution to z. In other words, essentially we have created the following system of equations:

Note how we shade columns in Tableau II to identify the system at right.

$$\begin{cases} 1z + 0S_1 + 0x_2 = 26 & (0) \\ 0z + 1S_1 + 0x_2 = 68/5 & (1) \\ 0z + 0S_1 + 1x_2 = 13/5. & (2) \end{cases}$$

Consequently, at the second iteration, the solution is

$$z = 26$$

$$\text{Basic} \begin{cases} S_i = 68/5 \\ \quad = 13.6 \\ x_2 = 13/5 \\ \quad = 2.6 \end{cases}$$

$$\text{Nonbasic} \begin{cases} x_1 = 0 \\ S_2 = 0 \end{cases}$$

5. **Repeat steps 2 through 4 until no further improvement is possible in the objective function.** Note that, for a maximization problem, no further improvement is possible when the coefficients in Row 0, the z equation, are all zero or positive.

▶ Example 6.8

Continuing the previous problem, we see from Tableau II that x_1 is the entering variable (optimality criterion) and S_1 is the leaving variable (feasibility criterion). The new pivot equation is 1 and the new pivot element is 17/5. The next tableau follows:

Basis	z	x_1	x_2	S_1	S_2	b_i	Row No.	r_i
III	1	0	0	15/17	22/17	38	0	
x_1	0	1	0	5/17	−4/17	4	1	
x_2	0	0	1	−2/17	5/17	1	2	

Since no coefficients in Row 0 are negative, improvement (increase) in the objective function is impossible. The optimal solution, at the third iteration, is

$$z = 38$$

$$\text{Basic} \begin{cases} x_1 = 4 \\ x_2 = 1 \end{cases}$$

$$\text{Nonbasic} \begin{cases} S_1 = 0 \\ S_2 = 0. \end{cases}$$

Note that the simplex algorithm iteratively generated solutions corresponding to points A, B, and C in Figure 6–1.

▶ Example 6.9

To further reinforce what we have discussed, the following problem is converted to standard form and solved by the simplex procedure.

Maximize

$$z = 3x_1 + 10x_2 + 4x_3 + 6x_4$$

subject to

$$2x_1 + 2x_2 + 5x_3 + x_4 \le 50 \quad (1)$$

$$x_1 - 2x_2 + x_3 + 5x_4 \le 40 \quad (2)$$

$$10x_1 + 5x_2 + 2x_3 + 4x_4 \le 150 \quad (3)$$

$$x_1, x_2, x_3, x_4 \ge 0.$$

Basis	z	x_1	x_2	x_3	x_4	S_1	S_2	S_3	b_i	Row No.	r_i
			*								
I	1	−3	−10	−4	−6	0	0	0	0	0	—
S_1	0	2	(2)	5	1	[1]	0	0	50	1	50/2 = 25*
S_2	0	1	−2	1	5	0	[1]	0	40	2	—
S_3	0	10	5	2	4	0	0	[1]	150	3	150/5 = 30
					*						
II	1	7	0	21	−1	5	0	0	250	0	—
x_2	0	1	[1]	5/2	1/2	1/2	0	0	25	1	25 ÷ 1/2 = 50
S_2	0	3	0	6	(6)	1	[1]	0	90	2	90/6 = 15*
S_3	0	5	0	−21/2	3/2	−5/2	0	[1]	25	3	25 ÷ 3/2 = 50/3
III	1	15/2	0	22	0	31/6	1/6	0	265	0	
x_2	0	3/4	[1]	2	0	5/12	−1/12	0	35/2	1	
x_4	0	1/2	0	1	[1]	1/6	1/6	0	15	2	
S_3	0	17/4	0	−12	0	−11/4	−1/4	[1]	5/2	3	

To aid you in following the row operations from Tableaus I to II and from Tableaus II to III, try following Table 6–2. For example, Row 0 of Tableau II was determined by multiplying Row 1 of Tableau II by 10 and adding the resulting equation to Row 0 of Tableau I.

TABLE 6–2 Row Operations for Example 6.4

New Row *i* in Tableau *k* (R_iT_k)	Was Determined by (=)	The Indicated Row Operations
R_1T_2	=	$R_1T_1/2$
R_0T_2	=	$10R_1T_2 + R_0T_1$
R_2T_2	=	$2R_1T_2 + R_2T_1$
R_3T_2	=	$-5R_1T_2 + R_3T_1$
R_2T_3	=	$R_2T_2/6$
R_0T_3	=	$R_2T_3 + R_0T_2$
R_1T_3	=	$(-1/2)R_2T_3 + R_1T_2$
R_3T_3	=	$(-3/2)R_2T_3 + R_3T_2$

To reiterate a previous point, the new tableau is determined from the previous tableau by forcing a one in the pivot element position and zeros elsewhere in the column of the entering variable.

In Tableau I, r_2 is not considered because the corresponding coefficient of the entering variable is negative ($a_{22} = -2$). Since all of the coefficients in Row 0 of Tableau III are greater than or equal to zero, the optimal solution is given by the RHS constants:

$$z = 265$$

$$\text{Basic} \begin{cases} x_2 = 35/2 \\ x_4 = 15 \\ S_3 = 5/2 \end{cases} \qquad \text{Nonbasic} \begin{cases} x_1 = 0 \\ x_3 = 0 \\ S_1 = 0 \\ S_2 = 0. \end{cases}$$

You should verify that with $S_1 = 0$ and $S_2 = 0$, the implication is that constraints 1 and 2 are active or binding; that is, constraints associated with these slack variables are satisfied as strict equalities; conversely, a positive value for a slack variable ($S_3 = 5/2$) indicates that the constraint associated with the slack variable is inactive or satisfied as an inequality; that is, the RHS constant of constraint 3 could be 5/2 less without affecting the optimal solution.

FOLLOW-UP EXERCISES

7. By both the simplex method and a graphical solution, verify that the optimal solution to the problem below is $x_1 = 50$, $x_2 = 20$, $S_2 = 30$, and $z = 19$. Note that the basis contains three variables.

   Maximize

$$z = 0.3x_1 + 0.2x_2$$

   subject to

$$6x_1 + 6x_2 \leq 420 \quad (1)$$

$$3x_1 + 6x_2 \leq 300 \quad (2)$$

$$4x_1 + 2x_2 \leq 240 \quad (3)$$

$$x_1, x_2 \geq 0.$$

8. Solve Exercise 5 by the simplex method.

6.4 INTERPRETATION OF COEFFICIENTS

Section 6.3 concentrated primarily on the mechanics and mathematical justification for the simplex method. This section provides a greater understanding of the interpretation and meaning of the data provided in a simplex tableau. This is reinforced by interpreting the solution to the air cargo model. Table 6–3 repeats the information needed to formulate the air cargo model. For convenience, Tableau II is also reproduced.

Algebraic Interpretation of Simplex Procedure

As demonstrated earlier in the chapter, the identity matrix procedure for solving simultaneous equations transforms an original system of equations into an equivalent

TABLE 6–3 Data for Air Cargo Problem

Meat Type	Profit Contribution ($100 per container)	Volume (cu. yd. per container)	Weight (1,000 lb. per container)
1(beef)	7	5	2
2(pork)	10	4	5
Availabilities		24	13

Basis	z	x_1	x_2	S_1	S_2	b_i	Row No.	r_i
II	1	* −3	0	0	2	26	0	—
S_1	0	$\frac{17}{5}$	0	1	$-\frac{4}{5}$	$\frac{68}{5}$	1	$\frac{13.6}{3.4} = 4.0$*
x_2	0	$\frac{2}{5}$	1	0	$\frac{1}{5}$	$\frac{13}{5}$	2	$\frac{2.6}{0.4} = 6.5$

*Denotes entering and leaving variables.

system. Examining Tableau II we see that the information contained within can be written alternatively in equation form as

$$1z \quad - 3x_1 + 0x_2 + 0S_1 + \quad 2S_2 = 26 \tag{0}$$

$$0z + \left(\frac{17}{5}\right)x_1 + 0x_2 + 1S_1 - \left(\frac{4}{5}\right)S_2 = \frac{68}{5} \tag{1}$$

$$0z + \left(\frac{2}{5}\right)x_1 + 1x_2 + 0S_1 + \left(\frac{1}{5}\right)S_2 = \frac{13}{5}. \tag{2}$$

Recall that the nonbasic variables x_1 and S_2 were set equal to zero in this second solution. After substituting these values of zero into the equation, we find that the values $z = 26$, $S_1 = 68/5$, and $x_2 = 13/5$ can be read directly from the right-hand–side constants. Notice once again that the coefficients on these variables form the columns of a (3×3) identity matrix.

The simplex procedure uses a "marginal analysis" approach to determine if a better solution exists. The essential question being asked is "What are the marginal effects of introducing one unit of a nonbasic variable into the solution?" The effects can be categorized as *those that influence the value of the objective function* and *those that influence values of the current basic variables*. The marginal effects can be seen readily by rewriting the previous system of equations as follows:

$$z = 26 + \quad 3x_1 - \quad 2S_2 \tag{0}$$

$$S_1 = \frac{68}{5} - \left(\frac{17}{5}\right)x_1 + \left(\frac{4}{5}\right)S_2 \tag{1}$$

$$x_2 = \frac{13}{5} - \left(\frac{2}{5}\right)x_1 - \left(\frac{1}{5}\right)S_2 . \tag{2}$$

This revised system of equations expresses the value of z and the values of the current basic variables in terms of the nonbasic variables (x_1 and S_2). This first equation suggests that the current value of z is 26, but if x_1 is increased from zero to one, z will increase by 3; if one unit of S_2 is introduced, z will decrease by 2. Thus the coefficients for x_1 and S_2 can be thought of as representing **marginal rates of change** in the objective function. The effects on the basic variables are read from the next two equations. Equation 1 implies that S_1 has a value of 68/5, that increasing x_1 by one unit will reduce S_1 by 17/5, and that increasing S_2 by one unit will increase S_1 by 4/5. A similar interpretation can be given for Equation 2 in terms of the basic variable x_2. The coefficients for x_1 and S_2 in these equations represent **marginal rates of substitution** between the basic variables and the nonbasic variables that are *candidates* for entrance into the solution (basis).

In summary, the marginal effects of introducing any nonbasic variable into the basis can be found by observing the column of coefficients for that variable in Equations 0, 1, and 2.

Generalized Interpretation of Tableau Elements

We now consider a generalized interpretation of the basis column, RHS constants (b_i column), r_i column, Row 0, and Row 1 through Row (m)—but first, a note of warning. The algebraic interpretation in the previous section can be helpful in understanding the elements in a simplex tableau; however, to avoid confusion in interpreting marginal effects, keep in mind that the coefficients of the variables in the algebraic formulation are opposite in sign from the coefficients in the tableau. Thus a positive coefficient in a tableau suggests a marginal *decrease* in either the objective function or the corresponding basic variable. A negative coefficient suggests a marginal increase.

Basis Column This column contains the m basic variables whose values have been determined by setting all other variables to zero and by solving the set of m constraint equations. Note that the basic variables are those corresponding to the columns of an identity matrix in the constraint equation section of the tableau. For this reason, the row in which a basic variable is indicated contains a one (1) in the column representing that basic variable.

b_i Column The right-hand–side constant for Row 0 always represents the current value of the objective function. The right-hand–side constants for the remaining m rows—Row 1–Row (m)—represent the values of the m basic variables. The values, of course, correspond to the variables listed in the Basis column.

r_i Column r_i values indicate the maximum amount of the entering variable permitted by the ith constraint. Another way of viewing these values is that they represent the number of units of the entering variable required to drive the corresponding basic variable to a value of zero.

Row 0. The coefficients in this row represent the marginal effects on the value of the objective function of entering a unit of the variable represented by each column. The coefficients are the negative of the actual marginal effect. Consequently, a given coefficient can be interpreted as the decrease (positive value) or increase (negative value) of introducing one unit of the column variable. Interpreted from an alternative perspective, these coefficients reflect the *opportunity gain* (positive value) or *opportunity loss* (negative value) of excluding one unit of the column variable. Note that Row 0 values for basic variables always equal zero. We demonstrate in Section 6.8 that Row 0 values for slack variables in the *final* tableau represent **shadow prices.**

Row 1 through Row *m*. The coefficient values for the last m rows represent the previously mentioned marginal rates of substitution. For any given column, the coefficients represent the marginal changes expected in the existing basic variables by introducing a unit of the column variable. As with the coefficients of Row 0, the coefficients are opposite in sign to their actual effect on the basic variable. That is, a negative coefficient implies an *increase* in the value of the corresponding basic variable; a positive coefficient implies a *decrease*.

Interpretation of Air Cargo Problem

Let us now turn to an interpretation of Tableau II within the context of the application.

Present Solution. Since columns z, x_2, and S_1 have the form of a (3×3) identity matrix (the z column will always appear the same) x_2 and S_1 are identified as the basic variables in this solution. Since a one (1) appears in Row 1 of column S_1, the variable S_1 is placed in this row of the Basis column. Similarly, the appearance of a one (1) in Row 2 of the x_2 column requires the presence of x_2 in this row of the Basis column.

The corresponding values in the b_i column indicate that $z = 26$, $S_1 = 68/5$, and $x_2 = 13/5$. This solution suggests that 2.6 containers of pork should be shipped at a profit of $2,600.

A value of 68/5 for S_1 indicates slack of 68/5 in the first constraint; that is, 13.6 cubic yards of unused volume remain in the cargo hold when 2.6 containers of pork are shipped. (Can you verify this directly from the first constraint?)

Since x_1 and S_2 are not in the basis, their values are zero in this solution. This means that no shipments are recommended for beef and that there is no slack in constraint 2. The shipment of 2.6 containers of pork exhausts fully the 13-ton capacity of the cargo hold.

Implications for Improvement. If a better solution exists, it can be determined by looking at Row 0. The -3 under x_1 indicates that shipping one unit (container) of beef will *increase* profits by three units ($300). Similarly, the 2 under S_2 implies that bringing in a unit (1,000 pounds) of slack weight (that is, displacing 1,000 pounds of cargo) will result in a two-unit ($200) reduction in profit. Consequently, a better solution exists, and it can be found by introducing x_1 (shipping containers of beef).

Examination of Rows 1 and 2 for the x_1 column indicates the marginal effects on the current basic variables of introducing one unit of x_1. The first row value, $17/5 = 3.4$, means that the introduction (shipment) of one unit (container) of beef would displace 3.4 cubic yards of unused volume. From the original data in Table 6–2, each unit of beef requires 5 cubic yards, so why the inconsistency? Bear with us. According to the coefficient immediately below 17/5, each unit of beef additionally will displace 2/5 unit of pork. Since the removal of 2/5 unit of pork will free 1.6 cubic yards of space (2/5 unit times 4 cubic yards per unit), the *effective* space requirement for each *additional* unit of beef is only 3.4 cubic yards $(5 - 1.6)$. Why will the inclusion of one unit of beef in the shipment displace 2/5 unit of pork? Because the weight constraint is *binding* in the current solution; thus the inclusion of beef must be accompanied by the removal of pork. Since beef and pork weigh 2,000 pounds and 5,000 pounds per container, respectively, 2/5 container of pork must be removed for each container of beef included.

Why is the *marginal* increase in profits only three ($100s) when a profit contribution of seven (100s) is indicated in the original objective function? The inclusion of one container of beef results in the displacements of 2/5 container of pork (x_2) and 17/5 units of volume capacity (S_1), which gives a marginal change in the original objective function of 3, that is, $7 - (2/5)(10) - (17/5)(0) = 3$.

Finally, the r_i values indicate the number of units of x_1 required to drive the existing basis values to zero. In Row 1, $r_1 = 4.0$ indicates that, with the addition of the fourth unit of beef, S_1 or excess volume in the cargo hold will be eliminated. Similarly, the 6.5 in Row 2 indicates that 6.5 units of beef could be introduced before eliminating shipments of pork. Can you verify that the introduction of 6.5 units of beef would be impossible? Why?

Interestingly, an examination of Row 0 in the final tableau of Example 6.8 indicates that 15/17 and 22/17 represent, respectively, the shadow prices associated with constraints 1 and 2. Thus, if it were possible to increase the volume constraint from 24 to 25 cubic yards, the optimal profit would increase by 15/17; similarly, a relaxation of the weight limitation to 14,000 pounds would increase optimal profit by 22/17. If it were equally costly to create either an additional cubic yard of volume or an additional 1,000 pounds of weight capacity, which would you create?

6.5 SIMPLEX METHOD: MIXED CONSTRAINTS

To handle a variety of formulations, we need to generalize the simplex method to problems with $\leq$, $\geq$, and $=$ constraints. We will use the notation that m_1, m_2 and m_3 represent the number of $\leq$, $\geq$, and $=$ constraints respectively.

Converting LP Model to Standard Form

In the standard form of LP problems with $\leq$ constraints, the inequalities were converted to equalities by adding slack variables to the left sides. Furthermore, the slack variables provided a convenient starting basis in the simplex method.

For problems including $\geq$ constraints, the left-hand side of the inequation must be at least equal to the RHS constant; hence the inequality can be forced into the form of an equation by subtracting a **surplus variable** from the left side. Doing so, however, precludes the use of a surplus variable in the starting basis, for the coefficient of -1 yields an infeasible (negative) solution; hence, it's necessary to *add* to the left-hand side yet another variable, termed an **artificial variable,** which can be used in the starting basis. Finally, in order to guarantee the elimination of the artificial variable from the final solution, a very heavy penalty is assigned to the artificial variable in the objective function. This takes the form of a very large *negative* coefficient in the objective function of *maximization* problems and a very large *positive* coefficient for *minimization* problems. Although other methods are available, this so-called **method of penalties** remains the most popular.

Problems containing *equality constraints* can be treated in several ways. The most convenient method is to simply add an artificial variable to the left-hand side of every equality restriction. The method of penalties will guarantee, should a solution exist, that the artificial variable will not appear in the final solution.[3] This technique is utilized in our development of the simplex method.

Based on this discussion, the generalized objective function is expressed as

$$z = \sum_{j=1}^{n} c_j x_j \pm \sum_{i=m_1+1}^{m} MA_i \tag{6.10}$$

where A_i is the artificial variable for the ith constraint, M is the penalty (a very large number) assigned to artificial variables in the objective function,[4] m_1 is the number of $\leq$ constraints and m is the total number of constraints. If z is to be maximized, the coefficient for any artificial variable must be $-M$; for minimization problems $+M$ is used. (Do you see the logic?) Constraints of the $\leq$ type are treated as before,

$$\sum_{j=1}^{n} a_{ij} x_j + S_i = b_i, \qquad i = 1, \ldots, m_1 \tag{6.11}$$

Constraints of the $\geq$ type are written in the standard form as

$$\sum_{j=1}^{n} a_{ij} x_j - E_i + A_i = b_i, \qquad i = m_1 + 1, \ldots, m_1 + m_2 \tag{6.12}$$

where E_i is the surplus (excess) variable for the ith constraint, and m_2 is the number of $\geq$ constraints. Finally, equality constraints are expressed as

$$\sum_{j=1}^{n} a_{ij} x_j + A_i = b_i, \qquad i = m_1 + m_2 + 1, \ldots, m. \tag{6.13}$$

Note that for the purpose of notational convenience we have ordered the $\leq$ constraints first, the $\geq$ constraints next, and the $=$ constraints last.

---

[3]Should the problem not have a solution, at least one artificial variable will appear in the final basis with a positive value. See Example 6.13.

[4]Because of this choice of letter, the method of penalties is also known as the **M-technique.**

Table 6–4 summarizes the nomenclature for the standard form of the LP problem.

TABLE 6–4 Nomenclature for Standard Form of LP Problems

Constraint Type	Number of Constraints	Type of Supplemental Variable	Number of Supplemental Variables
$\leq$	m_1	Slack (S_i)	m_1
$\geq$	m_2	Surplus (E_i) and Artificial (A_i)	$2m_2$
$=$	m_3	Artificial (A_i)	m_3
Total	m		$m_1 + 2m_2 + m_3$

Note that the **supplemental variables** now include three types: slack, surplus, and artificial. Furthermore, the total number of variables (n') is given by the sum of **real variables** (x_j's) and supplemental variables, or

$$\begin{aligned} n' &= n + (m_1 + 2m_2 + m_3) \\ &= n + m + m_2 . \end{aligned} \tag{6.14}$$

Generating Tableaus

As before, the first step in applying the simplex method is the conversion of the LP model to the standard form. Thereafter, the generation of tableaus follows readily, with some minor modifications. Figure 6–2 summarizes the simplex algorithm.

▶ Example 6.10

Given the problem:

Minimize

$$z = 2x_1 + 4x_2$$

subject to

$$x_1 + 5x_2 \leq 80 \qquad (1)$$

$$4x_1 + 2x_2 \geq 20 \qquad (2)$$

$$x_1 + x_2 = 10 \qquad (3)$$

$$x_1, x_2 \geq 0,$$

the standard form is expressed as:

Minimize

$$z = 2x_1 + 4x_2 + 0S_1 + 0E_2 + MA_2 + MA_3$$

FIGURE 6–2 Simplex Algorithm for Problems with Unique Optimal Solutions

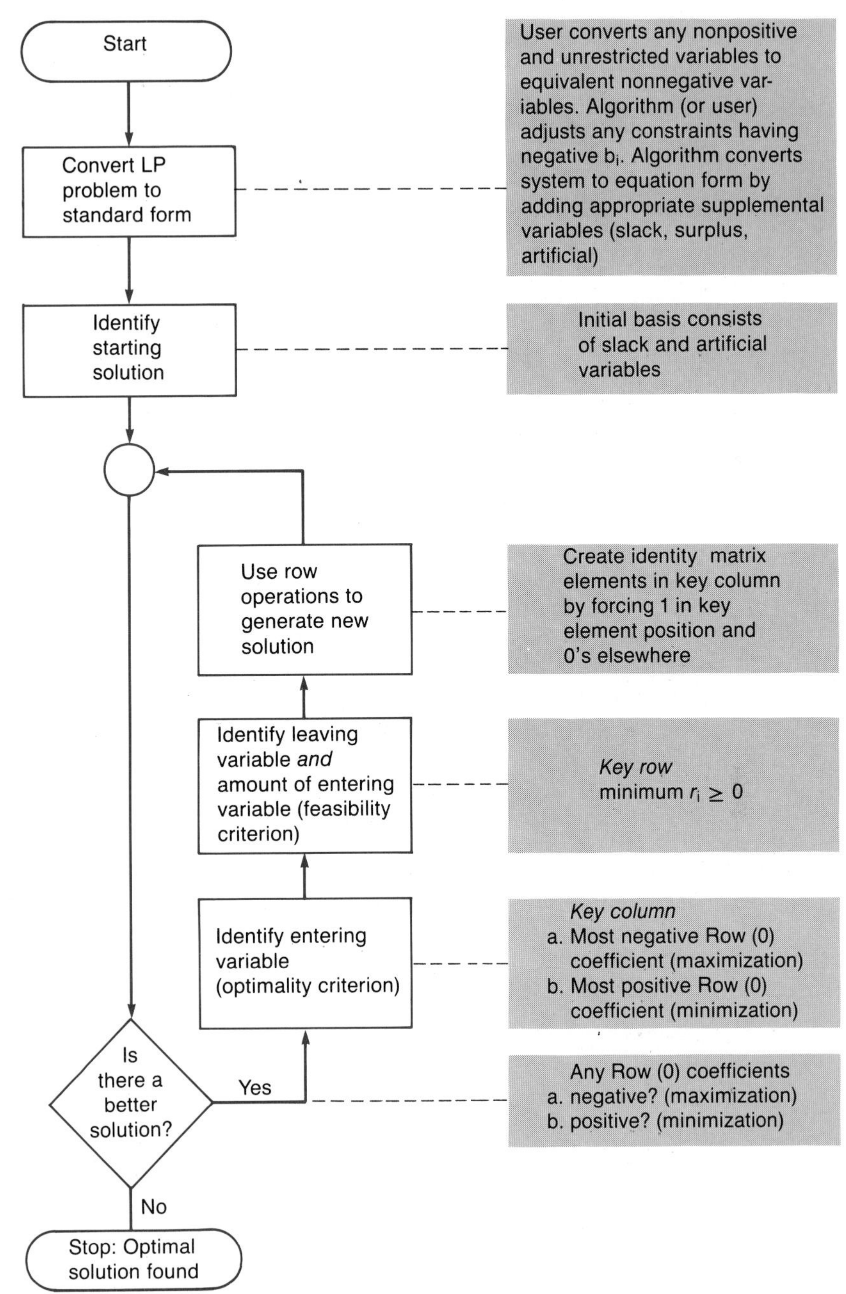

subject to

$$\begin{aligned} x_1 + 5x_2 + S_1 &= 80 &\quad (1)\\ 4x_1 + 2x_2 - E_2 + A_2 &= 20 &\quad (2)\\ x_1 + x_2 + A_3 &= 10 &\quad (3) \end{aligned}$$

$$x_1, x_2, S_1, E_2, A_2, A_3 \geq 0\,.$$

Note that the *minimization* of z requires *positive* Ms in the objective function. Expressing the system of equations in tableau form gives:

These must be forced to zeros. (→ the $-M$ entries under A_2 and A_3)

Basis	z	x_1	x_2	E_2	S_1	A_2	A_3	b_i	Row No.	r_i
I	1	−2	−4	0	0	$-M$	$-M$	0	0	—
S_1	0	1	5	0	1	0	0	80	1	
A_2	0	4	2	−1	0	1	0	20	2	
A_3	0	1	1	0	0	0	1	10	3	

Note that surplus variables E_i cannot appear in the starting basis, since infeasible solutions would result; for example, including E_2 in the starting basis would yield $E_2 = -20$. This was the purpose for introducing artificial variables. *The starting basis will therefore always consist of slack and artificial variables*—S_1, A_2, and A_3 in the present example.

Further note that Row 0 of Tableau 1 is inconsistent because basic variables A_2 and A_3 have *nonzero* coefficients. Because of this the RHS constant does not give the correct value of z; that is, the starting basis dictates that $A_2 = 20$ and $A_3 = 10$, which should give $z = 30M$. It is worth repeating that Row 0 provides the value of z as the RHS constant if and only if the coefficients of the basic variables in Row 0 are zero, as dictated by the identity matrix; the coefficients of the *nonbasic* variables in Row 0 need not be zero because those variables, themselves, have values of zero. The upshot of this observation is that *Row 0 must be modified, by row operations, to yield coefficients of zero for the artificial variables.*

Tableau II is generated by replacing Row 0 of Tableau I by the sum of itself plus M times Row 2 plus M times Row 3, or

$$R_0T_2 = R_0T_1 + M \cdot R_2T_1 + M \cdot R_3T_1\,.$$

Basis	z	x_1	x_2	E_2	S_1	A_2	A_3	b_i	Row No.	r_i
II	1	* $-2 + 5M$	$-4 + 3M$	$-M$	0	0	0	$30M$	0	—
S_1	0	1	5	0	1	0	0	80	1	$80/1 = 80$
A_2	0	(4)	2	−1	0	1	0	20	2	$20/4 = 5$*
A_3	0	1	1	0	0	0	1	10	3	$10/1 = 10$

Recall that the optimality criterion for *minimization* problems identifies the entering variable as the one having the *largest positive coefficient* in Row 0 of the tableau, which is equivalent to the greatest *marginal reduction* in the objective function. Consequently, x_1 is the first variable to enter the basis, since the coefficient $(-2 + 5M)$ is larger than any other coefficient (remember that M is a very large positive number).

From Tableau II on, the procedure is the same as before except for one item: *For minimization problems, the optimal solution has been found when all coefficients in Row 0 are either zero or negative.*

Basis	z	x_1	x_2	E_2	S_1	A_2	A_3	b_i	Row No.	r_i
			*							
III	1	0	$-3 + M/2$	$-1/2 + M/4$	0	$1/2 - 5M/4$	0	$10 + 5M$	0	—
S_1	0	0	9/2	1/4	[1]	−1/4	0	75	1	$75 \div 9/2 = 16\ 2/3$
x_1	0	[1]	1/2	−1/4	0	1/4	0	5	2	$5 \div 1/2 = 10$
A_3	0	0	(1/2)	1/4	0	−1/4	[1]	5	3	$5 \div 1/2 = 10^*$
				*						
IV	1	0	0	1	0	$-1 - M$	$6 - M$	40	0	—
S_1	0	0	0	−2	[1]	2	−9	30	0	—
x_1	0	[1]	0	−1/2	0	1/2	−1	0	2	—
x_2	0	0	[1]	(1/2)	0	−1/2	2	10	3	$10 \div 1/2 = 20^*$
V	1	0	−2	0	0	$-M$	$2 - M$	20	0	—
S_1	0	0	4	0	[1]	0	−1	70	1	
x_1	0	[1]	1	0	0	0	1	10	2	
E_2	0	0	2	[1]	0	−1	4	20	3	

In Tableau III r_2 and r_3 were tied; arbitrarily, A_3 was chosen to leave, although x_1 could have left instead. In Tableau IV, r_1 and r_2 were ignored because they were negative. (Why?) The final solution, from Tableau V, is

$$z = 20$$

$$\text{Basic} \begin{cases} S_1 = 70 \\ x_1 = 10 \\ E_2 = 20 \end{cases} \qquad \text{Nonbasic} \begin{cases} x_2 = 0 \\ A_2 = 0 \\ A_3 = 0. \end{cases}$$

Finally, you should note that in reality the solutions corresponding to Tableaus II and III are infeasible for the original problem though feasible for the problem as reformulated with artificial variables. For example, the solution in Tableau III indicates that $x_1 = 5$, $x_2 = 0$, and $A_3 = 5$. In the original formulation, this violates the third constraint $x_1 + x_2 = 10$. Of course, as far as the simplex algorithm is concerned, the constraint $x_1 + x_2 + A_3 = 10$ is satisfied. Thus, *the appearance of $A_i > 0$ in a solution indicates that the original constraint i is violated (an infeasible solution).*

FOLLOW-UP EXERCISES

9. In Example 6.10 break the tie in Tableau III by selecting x_1 as the leaving variable and continue the problem.
10. Draw a geometric figure for the model in Example 6.10, and relate each tableau in the example to a specific point in the figure.
11. Solve the following LP problem by the simplex method.

Minimize

$$z = 4x_1 + 5x_2 - 2x_3$$

subject to

$$2x_1 + x_2 - x_3 = 10 \quad (1)$$

$$x_1 + x_2 = 5 \quad (2)$$

$$x_1 \text{ unrestricted}$$

$$x_2, x_3 \text{ nonnegative.}$$

6.6 ABERRATIONS IN SOLUTIONS

Four typical contingencies may arise in the solution of an LP problem: alternative optimal solutions, unbounded solutions, nonexisting feasible solutions, and degeneracy.

Alternative Optimal Solutions

Chapter 4 indicated (see Figure 4–10) that an *infinite* number of alternative optima exist if the *objective function is parallel to a binding constraint.*[5] Example 6.11 illustrates the detection of this condition in the simplex tableau.

▶ Example 6.11 Alternative Optimal Solutions

Consider this problem:

Maximize

$$z = x_1 + 2x_2$$

subject to

$$2x_1 + 4x_2 \le 9 \quad (1)$$

$$3x_1 + x_2 \le 12 \quad (2)$$

$$x_1, x_2 \ge 0.$$

A comparison of variable coefficients indicates that the objective function is parallel to constraint 1. You should easily verify by a sketch that 1 is also a binding constraint. The simplex solution follows.

[5] By definition, a binding or active constraint has no slack or surplus; it is satisfied as an equality.

Alternative optima indicated

Basis	z	x_1	x_2	S_1	S_2	b_i	Row No.	r_i
I	1	−1	−2*	0	0	0	0	—
S_1	0	2	(4)	[1]	0	9	1	9/4*
S_2	0	3	1	0	[1]	12	2	12
II	1	0	0	1/2	0	9/2	0	—
x_2	0	1/2	[1]	1/4	0	9/4	1	9/2
S_2	0	(5/2)	0	−1/4	[1]	39/4	2	39/10*
III	1	0	0	1/2	0	9/2	0	—
x_2	0	0	[1]	3/10	−1/5	3/10	1	
x_1	0	[1]	0	−1/10	2/5	39/10	2	

Tableau II gives the optimal solution as $S_2 = 9.75$, $x_2 = 2.25$, and $z = 4.5$. Note, however, that *nonbasic* variable x_1 has a *coefficient of zero in Row 0* of the optimal tableau (Tableau II). This means that the inclusion of x_1 in the basis will have no effect on z, *implying that an alternative optimal solution exists.* In other words, a new solution having $x_1 > 0$ will yield the same optimal value of z. Tableau III enters x_1 at the expense of S_2 to give an alternative optimal solution of $x_1 = 3.9$, $x_2 = 0.3$, and $z = 4.5$. (Note that the nonbasic variable S_2 now has a zero coefficient in the z row). Thus any one of the infinite number of feasible points along constraint 1 will yield an optimal solution.

A coefficient of zero for a nonbasic variable in Row 0 of the optimal tableau indicates alternative optimal solutions.

Computationally, the family of alternative optima is determined as *weighted averages* of the **basic** (that is, corner point) **alternative optima:**

$$x_{aj} = \sum_{i=1}^{k} w_i x_{ij}, \qquad j = 1, \ldots, n \tag{6.15}$$

where

x_{aj} = Alternative optimum value for variable j.

x_{ij} = ith basic alternative optimum value for variable j.

w_i = Weight for ith basic alternative optimum.

k = Number of basic alternative optima.

Recall from your basic course in statistics that two conditions must hold with respect to weights in a weighted average:

$$0 \le w_i \le 1$$

$$\sum_{i=1}^{k} w_i = 1 .$$

In the present example, $k = 2$, $x_{11} = 0$, $x_{21} = 3.9$, $x_{12} = 2.25$, and $x_{22} = 0.3$; hence

$$x_{a1} = 0w_1 + 3.9w_2$$

$$x_{a2} = 2.25w_1 + 0.3w_2 .$$

The following family of alternative optima is generated for arbitrarily selected values of w_1 and w_2:

w_1	w_2	x_{a1}	x_{a2}
0.0	1.0	3.900	0.300
0.2	0.8	3.120	0.690
0.5	0.5	1.950	1.275
0.8	0.2	0.780	1.860
1.0	0.0	0.000	2.250

Thus the coordinates x_{a1}, x_{a2} are alternative optimal solutions along the binding edge defined by constraint 1 with the *basic* alternative optimum 0, 2.25 at one end of the edge and the basic alternative optimum 3.9, 0.3 at the other end of the edge.

FOLLOW-UP EXERCISES

12. Verify that the above family of alternative optima yields the same maximum value for z.
13. Determine the basic alternative optima for the problem

    Maximize

    $$z = 3x_1 + 2x_2$$

    subject to

    $$3x_1 + 5x_2 \le 60 \quad (1)$$

    $$6x_1 + 4x_2 \le 48 \quad (2)$$

    $$x_1, x_2 \ge 0 .$$

    Generate a family of optimal solutions.
14. How many basic alternative optima (extreme points) are possible with two decision variables (i.e., what values are possible for k when $n = 2$)? What values are possible for k when $n = 3$? (*Hint:* Conceptualize the problem geometrically.)

Unbounded Solutions

The relationship between an *unbounded solution space* and a *bounded* or *unbounded solution* was treated in Chapter 4. To refresh your memory we repeat a salient point:

An unbounded solution space yields an unbounded solution if and only if the optimization of the objective function is in the direction of the unbounded portion of the solution space. Otherwise, the solution is bounded. Example 6.12 illustrates the nature of the simplex calculations for both cases.

▶ Example 6.12 Unbounded Solution Space and Bounded/Unbounded Solutions

Optimize

$$z = -2x_1 + x_2$$

subject to

$$5x_1 - x_2 \leq 20 \qquad (1)$$

$$x_1 \leq 5 \qquad (2)$$

$$x_1, x_2 \geq 0.$$

As previously indicated, a negative or zero coefficient ($a_{ij} \leq 0$) in *a less than or equal to* structural constraint for a particular variable (x_j) implies that an infinite amount of that variable can be introduced into the solution without violating that constraint. In our present problem, assigning infinity to x_2 does not violate constraints 1 and 2. Figure 6–3 illustrates the unbounded solution *space* for this problem. The starting tableau is given below.

FIGURE 6–3 Unbounded Solution Space with Bounded and Unbounded Solutions

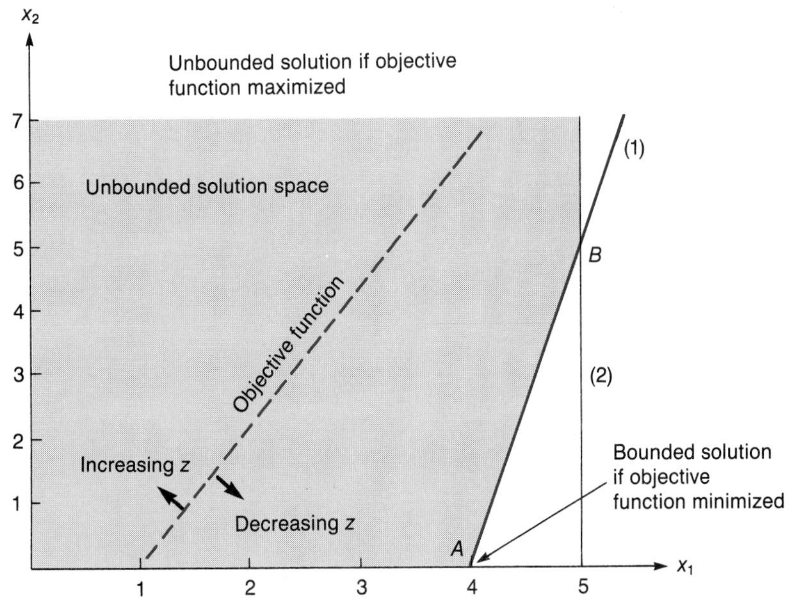

Basis	z	x_1	x_2	S_1	S_2	b_i	Row No.	r_i
—	1	2	−1	0	0	0	0	—
S_1	0	5	−1	1	0	20	1	
S_2	0	1	0	0	1	5	2	

Suppose the problem is to *maximize z.* The (−1) value associated with x_2 in Row 0 of the tableau indicates that the introduction of one unit of x_2 would increase the current value of z by one. Since all of the marginal rates of substitution are less than or equal to zero for column x_2, an infinite number of units can be introduced without driving any of the current basic variables to zero (Remember the interpretation given in Section 6.4?); consequently, the value of z has no bound ($z \to \infty$). If the problem were to *minimize z,* no longer would it be desirable to enter x_2. The problem then has a *bounded solution* (point *A* in Figure 6–3) because x_1, the variable to be entered, is bounded.

In general, having *all* negative or zero marginal rates of substitution in a column represents a *necessary* condition for an unbounded optimal solution. The *sufficient* condition is established by determining the desirability of entering the unbounded variable. This leads to the conclusion that *an LP problem has an unbounded optimal solution if at any iteration (tableau) the variable chosen to enter the basis has all zero or negative marginal rates of substitution.*

FOLLOW-UP EXERCISES

15. In Example 6.12 change the objective function to $z = -10x_1 + x_2$, and use the original constraints. Analyze the problem both graphically and by the simplex method for the case that minimizes z.
16. In Example 6.12 change the objective function to $z = 2x_1 - x_2$, and use the original constraints. Analyze the problem both graphically and by the simplex method for the two cases of minimizing and maximizing z. Note that, graphically, minimization implies shifting the z function upward. Why?
17. By graph and simplex tableaus analyze each of the following variations of Example 6.12:

    a. Maximize

    $$z = -2x_1 + x_2$$

    subject to

    $$5x_1 - x_2 \geq 20 \quad (1)$$

    $$x_1 \leq 5 \quad (2)$$

    $$x_1, x_2 \geq 0.$$

    b. Reverse the inequality in constraint (2) of part *a*.

    c. Maximize

    $$z = -2x_1 + x_2$$

    subject to

    $$5x_1 + x_2 \geq 20 \quad (1)$$

$$x_1 \qquad \leq 5 \qquad (2)$$

$$x_1, x_2 \geq 0.$$

d. Minimize z in part *c*.

No Feasible Solution

A problem has no feasible solution if its solution space is empty. Example 6.13 illustrates the detection of this condition by the simplex method.

▶ Example 6.13 No Feasible Solution

Maximize

$$z = 2x_1 + 3x_2$$

subject to

$$x_1 + x_2 \leq 10 \qquad (1)$$

$$x_1 + x_2 \geq 20 \qquad (2)$$

$$x_1, x_2 \geq 0.$$

Constraints 1 and 2 are clearly inconsistent (show this by graph). The simplex method provides the following.

Basis	z	x_1	x_2	E_2	S_1	A_2	b_i	Row No.	r_i
I	1	$-2-M$	* $-3-M$	M	0	0	$-20M$	0	—
S_1	0	1	(1)	0	[1]	0	10	1	10*
A_2	0	1	1	-1	0	[1]	20	2	20
II	1	1	0	M	$3+M$	0	$30-10M$	0	—
x_2	0	1	[1]	–	–	0	10		
A_2	0	0	0	-1	-1	[1]	10	2	

Since all Row 0 coefficients are nonnegative, Tableau II suggests that the optimal solution has been reached. A positive value for the artificial variable $A_2 = 10$, however, indicates that constraint 2 has not been satisfied; hence the solution is not feasible.

When an artificial variable appears in the final solution (basis) at a positive level, the problem has no feasible solution. Should the artificial variable appear at a *zero level*, the solution would be optimal and feasible, although the problem may have either a redundant constraint or basic feasible solutions that are degenerate (see the following section).

FOLLOW-UP EXERCISES

Solve the following problems and draw conclusions based on your results.

18. Maximize

$$z = x_1 + 2x_2 + 3x_3$$

subject to

$$2x_1 + x_2 + x_3 \leq 1 \quad (1)$$

$$5x_1 + 7x_2 + 4x_3 \geq 15 \quad (2)$$

$$5x_1 + 7x_2 + 4x_3 \geq 2 \quad (3)$$

$$x_1, x_2, x_3 \geq 0.$$

19. Change the RHS constant of constraint 2 to a value of 4.

Degeneracy

A **degenerate basic solution** is one where one or more basic variables has a value of zero. This can happen when a tie occurs for the leaving variable in the previous iteration. The leaving variable is forced to zero by the amount chosen for the entering variable according to the feasibility criterion. The tied variable that remains in the basis, however, also drops to a zero level. At this point, one of three things can happen: (1) the solution is temporarily degenerate; (2) the solution is a degenerate optimal solution; or (3) the optimal solution, if it exists, is not reached due to cycling.

The first case was demonstrated in Example 6.10. In Tableau III, x_1 and A_3 were tied for the "honor" of leaving variable, and the latter was selected arbitrarily. Accordingly, x_1 dropped to a zero level in the degenerate solution of Tableau IV. Degeneracy proved to be temporary, however, as indicated by the optimal solution of Tableau V. A degenerate optimal solution is not a problem in itself, although *it does affect shadow price and sensitivity analysis interpretations,* as mentioned in Chapter 5 and in the next section. To better understand this issue, try solving Exercise 48 at the end of this chapter.

Geometrically, a degenerate optimal solution is indicated when more than n constraints and x_j-axes pass through the optimal extreme point. For example, in the two-space case, an extreme point is degenerate if three (or more) lines pass through the point. These three lines can be either three constraints or two constraints plus, say, the x_1-axis.

The danger of degeneracy is the potential for cycling or returning to a previously generated intermediate (nonoptimal) solution. If this were to happen, the simplex algorithm would "stall" in its attempt to reach the optimal solution. The algorithm loops repetitively through a subset of nonoptimal (basic) solutions without changing the value of the objective function. Improved solutions are indicated by Row 0 values, but the minimum r_i value always equals zero. Advanced procedures, not to be treated here, have been developed to overcome this rare problem—although simply returning to the point where the r_i values were originally tied and selecting another of the tied variables for removal often resolves the cycling problem.

FOLLOW-UP EXERCISES

20. Solve the following both graphically and by the simplex method:

Maximize

$$z = 2x_1 + 6x_2$$

subject to

$$x_1 + 2x_2 \leq 20 \qquad (1)$$

$$2x_1 + 3x_2 \leq 30 \qquad (2)$$

$$x_2 \leq 10 \qquad (3)$$

$$x_1, x_2 \geq 0.$$

6.7 SENSITIVITY ANALYSIS

In Chapter 5 we focused on sensitivity analysis using intuitive, geometric, and computerized methods of analysis. In this section we complete our treatment by illustrating the simplex method of analysis actually used by most computer programs.

Let us continue with the air cargo model from Chapter 5.

Maximize

$$z = 20x_1 + 10x_2$$

subject to

$$5x_1 + 4x_2 \leq 24 \qquad (1)$$

$$2x_1 + 5x_2 \leq 13 \qquad (2)$$

$$x_1, x_2 \geq 0.$$

The original and final tableaus for this problem follow.

Basis	z	x_1	x_2	S_1	S_2	b_i	Row No.	r_i
I Initial	1	* −20	−10	0	0	0	0	
S_1	0	5	4	1	0	24	1	24/5*
S_2	0	2	5	0	1	13	2	13/2
II Final	1	0	6	4	0	96	0	
x_1	0	1	4/5	1/5	0	24/5	1	
S_2	0	0	17/5	−2/5	1	17/5	2	

*Denotes entering or leaving variable.

Objective Function Coefficients (Nonbasic Variables)

The analysis of objective function coefficients for nonbasic variables is relatively easy using the simplex method. Note from the final tableau that x_2 is a nonbasic variable. Essentially, we want to determine the range of variation in c_2 that keeps the current basis optimal. Let us define the contribution on c_2 as $c_2 = 10 + \Delta_2$, where 10 equals the original contribution plus some change in c_2, "delta 2" (Δ_2). If this newly defined value for c_2 is used, Row 0 in the *initial* simplex tableau appears as follows.

Basis	z	x_1	x_2	S_1	S_2	b_i	Row No.	r_i
I (Initial)	1	−20	$-(10 + \Delta_2)$	0	0	0	0	

↖Note that $-\Delta_2$ is the only difference.

Fortunately, there is no need to completely rework the problem with new parameters. In this instance we are interested in knowing how the addition of Δ_2 influences the *final* tableau. The key is remembering how Row 0 values are updated from tableau to tableau. If you think about this for a moment (or longer) you should realize that Row 0 values are determined solely by the row operation of adding multiples of other rows to Row (0). Look at the original and final tableaus presented earlier for this problem. The Row 0 coefficient for x_2 has changed from −10 to +6 in going from the initial to the final tableau (or +16 has been added). If the original Row 0 coefficient had been $-(10 + \Delta_2)$, then the simplex algorithm would result in the coefficient $-(10 + \Delta_2) + 16$, or $(6 - \Delta_2)$, in the final tableau.

$-\Delta_2$ carries through to final tableau.

Basis	z	x_1	x_2	S_1	S_2	b_i	Row No.	r_i
II Final	1	0	$6 - \Delta_2$	4	0	96	0	
x_1	0	1	4/5	1/5	0	24/5	1	
S_2	0	0	17/5	−2/5	1	17/5	2	

Without redoing the entire problem, we have shown that *the only effect of changing the objective function contribution on a nonbasic variable is to change the Row 0 coefficient for that variable in the final tableau*. The question still remains, though, by how much can c_2 change while maintaining the same optimal basis? Recall, that in a *maximization* problem, the solution is optimal as long as all Row 0 coefficients are greater than zero. In this problem, the existing basis will remain optimal as long as

$$6 - \Delta_2 > 0$$

or

$$\Delta_2 < 6.$$

Since $c_2 = 10 + \Delta_2$ and $\Delta_2 < 6$, this solution remains optimal as long as $c_2 < 16$. If $\Delta_2 > 6$ or $c_2 > 16$, then the Row 0 coefficient for x_2 becomes negative, and x_2 would enter the solution. Note that the inequality would be reversed for minimization type problems. (Why?)

Sometimes, the interpretation of Δ-values can be confusing in sensitivity analysis. For this example, it might take you a few minutes to conclude that $\Delta_2 < 6$ implies that $c_2 < 16$. We suggest the use of number lines like that shown in Figure 6–4. We have superimposed a Δ_2-axis on top of a c_2-axis to assist in drawing conclusions about possible values for c_2. Notice that $\Delta_2 = 0$ corresponds to the original value of c_2, which is 10. This type of approach may be useful to you later on in this chapter.

FIGURE 6–4 $\Delta_2 < 6 \rightarrow c_2 < 16$

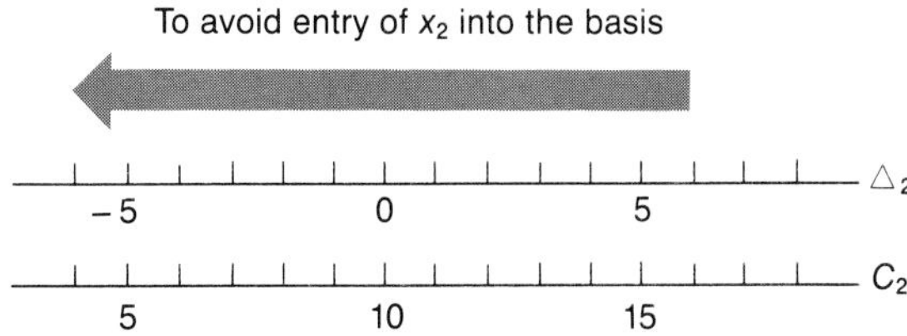

FOLLOW-UP EXERCISES

21. If the change in c_j is within the allowable range given by sensitivity analysis, then what does change and what does not change in the optimal solution? To be specific, describe the optimal solution (x_1^*, x_2^*, z^*) in our example if the real value of c_2 is 12 instead of 10. What happens if $\Delta_2 = 6$ or $c_2 = 16$?
22. For Example 6.9, determine the ranges over which the contributions on x_1 and x_3 can independently fluctuate and have the existing basis remain optimal.

Objective Function Coefficients (Basic Variables)

Sensitivity analysis on objective function coefficients is slightly more involved for basic variables. In the final tableau on page 277, x_1 is a basic variable. To conduct sensitivity analysis on c_1, we begin as with nonbasic variables. If we define $c_1 = 20 + \Delta_1$, Row 0 of the initial tableau changes accordingly.

Basis	z	x_1	x_2	S_1	S_2	b_i	Row No.	r_i
I (Initial)	1	$-(20 + \Delta_1)$	-10	0	0	0	0	

Note that $-\Delta_1$ is the only difference.

You should verify that in going from the initial to the final tableau of the original problem, +20 was added to the original Row 0 coefficient of x_1 to force the final value of zero. Thus, if the initial Row 0 coefficient had been $-(20 + \Delta_1)$, then the final tableau would appear as below.

$-\Delta_1$ would carry through to final tableau.

Basis	z	x_1	x_2	S_1	S_2	b_i	Row No.	r_i
II (Final)	1	$-\Delta_1$	6	4	0	96	0	
x_1	0	1	4/5	1/5	0	24/5	1	
S_2	0	0	17/5	−2/5	1	17/5	2	

If we examine this tableau carefully, we see that it is not in the format required for reading off the optimal solution. The Row 0 elements for basic variables should always equal zero. Because this is not true for x_1, row operations must be performed to create the desired condition. Multiplying Row 1 by Δ_1 and adding to Row 0, produces the following tableau.

$-\Delta_1$ has been eliminated.

Basis	z	x_1	x_2	S_1	S_2	b_i	Row No.	r_i
II (Final)	1	0	$6 + (4/5)\Delta_1$	$4 + (1/5)\Delta_1$	0	$96 + (24/5)\Delta_1$	0	
x_1	0	1	4/5	1/5	0	24/5	1	
S_2	0	0	17/5	−2/5	1	17/5	2	

This tableau indicates how the change in the objective function contribution for x_1 affects the optimal tableau. Notice that Δ_1 appears in Row 0 for the nonbasic variables x_2 and S_1. In addition, the appearance of the Δ_1 term in the b_i column shows the effect of a change in c_1 on the current optimal value of the objective function.

Again, the question is over what range of values for Δ_1 is the current solution still optimal? The variable x_2 would not become a candidate for entrance into the basis as long as

$$6 + \left(\frac{4}{5}\right)\Delta_1 > 0$$

or

$$\Delta_1 > -7.5\,.$$

If Δ_1 were less than -7.5 (if the contribution from beef were to drop from 20 to less than 12.5), then the Row 0 coefficient for x_2 would be less than zero, and x_2 would be identified as the new entering variable.

S_1 would not be a candidate for entrance as long as

$$4 + \left(\frac{1}{5}\right)\Delta_1 > 0$$

or

$$\Delta_1 > -20\,.$$

If Δ_1 were less than -20 (if the contribution from shipping beef were to drop from 20 to less than zero), then S_1 would be a new entering variable. Right? If $\Delta_1 = 20$, we have alternative optima.

Since we are concerned with the range of variation over which the present all-beef solution remains optimal, it is necessary to compare the Δ_1 values leading to the entrance of the nonbasic variables.

Figure 6–5 is a sketch of the two allowable ranges that were determined by separately considering the nonentry of variables x_2 and S_1. Entry into the basis of variable S_1 can be avoided by values of $\Delta_1 > -20$, but in order to avoid the entry of x_2, Δ_1 must be greater than -7.5; hence, the present solution remains optimal as long as $\Delta_1 > -7.5$, or $c_1 > 12.5$, or $12.5 < c_1 < \infty$. This result is consistent with our geometric analysis on page 193.

FIGURE 6–5 Allowable Changes in c_j

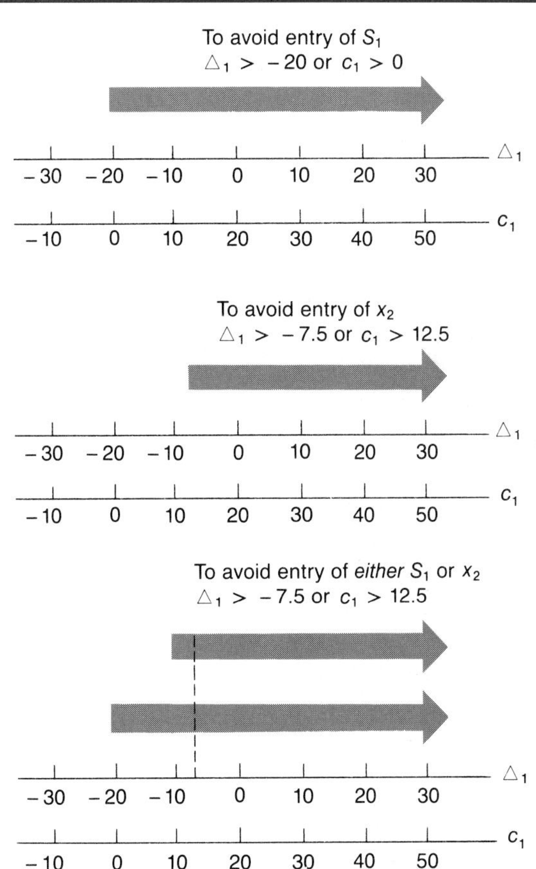

In this example, the optimal solution is insensitive to increases in c_1. As mentioned in Chapter 5, however, often the optimal solution is sensitive to variations in both directions (see the follow-up exercises). Thus care must be taken in examining Δ-values for basic variables.

In summary, sensitivity analysis for the coefficients of basic variables requires a translation of the change (Δ_j) from the initial to the final tableau. This leads ultimately to a nonzero Row 0 coefficient for a basic variable that subsequently must be removed by a row operation. The latter operation always creates a Δ_j term in Row 0 for some or all of the nonbasic variables. It is at this stage that the allowable ranges of variation are determined. Again, the beauty is that these ranges of allowable values are determined without reworking the entire problem using trial-and-error values for the parameters.

FOLLOW-UP EXERCISES

23. Suppose c_1 actually changes from 20 to 15 ($\Delta_1 = -5$).
    a. Without reworking the problem (just based on the final tableau), indicate the new optimal solution (x_1^*, x_2^*, z^*).
    b. What happens if c_1 exactly equals 12.5?
    c. In general, if Δ_j is within the allowable range, by what amount does z^* change if x_j is a basic variable? If x_j is a nonbasic variable?
24. Conduct a sensitivity analysis on the objective function contributions for the basic variables in Example 6.8.
25. Within what ranges can the coefficients of x_2 and x_4 in the objective function vary such that the solution of Example 6.9 remains optimal?

Right-Hand–Side Constants

Section 5.4 stated that this type of sensitivity analysis is concerned with the range over which the right-hand–side constant can fluctuate such that the optimal solution remains feasible. As with the objective function coefficients, we redefine the right-hand side of constraint 1 as:

$$b_1 = 24 + \Delta_1$$

where Δ_1 represents the change in value of the original b_1. The initial tableau follows.

Add Δ_1 here

Basis	z	x_1	x_2	S_1	S_2	b_i	Row No.	r_i
I (Initial)	1	−20	−10	0	0	0	0	
S_1	0	5	4	1	0	$24 + \Delta_1$	1	
S_2	0	2	5	0	1	13	2	

Now, pay very close attention! We would like to know what the final tableau would look like had we started with Δ_1 added to the right-hand side of constraint 1. Again it is unnecessary to rework the entire problem. If we think of the b_i-column in the manner below, Δ can be thought of as having a column of coefficients exactly like those for S_1, but on the opposite side of the equal sign.

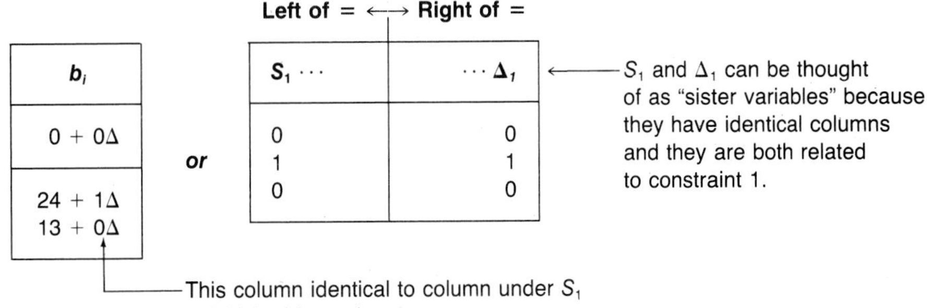

Since the same row operations are performed on both the left-hand and right-hand sides of the equations, Δ_1 will have the same column of coefficients in the final tableau as S_1. Or, the final tableau would appear as below (refer to the final tableau on page 277).

Basis	z	x_1	x_2	S_1	S_2	b_i	Row No.	r_i
II (Final)	1	0	6	4	0	$96 + 4\Delta$	0	
x_1	0	1	4/5	1/5	0	$24/5 + (1/5)\Delta$	1	
S_2	0	0	17/5	−2/5	1	$17/5 - (2/5)\Delta$	2	

Identical columns in final tableau for sister variables.

What values can Δ_1 assume for this solution to remain feasible? These values are determined by solving for the Δ_1's that allow x_1 and S_2 to remain nonnegative, or

$$x_1 = \frac{24}{5} + \left(\frac{1}{5}\right)\Delta_1 \geqslant 0 \quad \text{as long as } \Delta_1 \geqslant -24$$

and

$$S_2 = \frac{17}{5} - \left(\frac{2}{5}\right)\Delta_1 \geqslant 0 \quad \text{as long as } \Delta_1 \leqslant 8.5\,.$$

We can say, then, that this solution remains feasible as long as

$$-24 \leqslant \Delta_1 \leqslant 8.5$$

or

$$0 \leqslant b_1 \leqslant 32.5\,.$$

The current solution remains feasible (and optimal) as long as the right-hand–side of constraint 1 is greater than or equal to zero but no greater than 32.5. This result is consistent with our geometric analysis on page 196.

The key to this analysis is identifying a "sister variable" ("sibling variable"?) to the Δ_i that has been added to the right-hand side of the constraint under study (that is, a variable that has the same column of coefficients as Δ_i). *This sister variable is always the slack or artificial variable that was originally added to the constraint.*

Finally, suppose that $\Delta_1 = 6$ for b_1 (that is, the new value of b_1 is 30). Since this value is within the permissible range, the above basis remains feasible and optimal; however, the optimal *values* of the basic variables change according to the derived relationships under b_i in the final tableau. Thus $x_1 = (24/5) + (1/5)(6) = 6$ and $S_2 = (17/5) - (2/5)(6) = 1$.

In summary, permissible values for Δ_i related to *right-hand–side constants* result in the *same* set of optimal basic variables but with *different* values for one or more basic variables. For permissible Δ_i's associated with *objective function coefficients,* neither the mix nor the optimal values of basic variables changed—only optimal z changed whenever x_j was basic.

Section 5.4 defined the shadow price associated with the ith constraint as the amount by which the optimal value of the objective function would change if b_i were increased by one unit. Now note the Row 0 coefficient on Δ_1 (the 4) for the b_i-column in the preceding tableau. Over the range of variability permissible for Δ_1, the 4 is precisely the marginal change in the optimal z per unit increase in b_1. It is therefore the shadow price for constraint 1.

If we remember that the Row 0 coefficient on Δ_i in the b_i column of the final tableau is identical to the Row 0 coefficient on the sister variable, and that y_i is the shadow price, then we can state that:

The change in z^* is evident from the b_i column in the final tableau: $y_i\Delta_i$ where $y_i \neq 0$ whenever constraint i is active and $y_i = 0$ whenever constraint i is inactive.

The shadow price y_i associated with the ith constraint appears in Row 0 of the final tableau underneath the slack or artificial variable associated with that constraint.

FOLLOW-UP EXERCISES

26. Perform sensitivity analysis on the right-hand side of constraint 2. Also, what is the marginal effect (shadow price) on the value of optimal z over the permissible range of values for Δ_2? What would be the new values of z^*, x_1^*, x_2^*, S_1^*, and S_2^* if $\Delta_2 = -2$?

27. Perform sensitivity analysis for all right-hand–side constants in Example 6.9. Also specify the shadow prices.

A Minimization Problem with Mixed Constraints

To further reinforce the simplex approach for performing sensitivity analysis, we now solve a problem characterized by both a *minimization* objective and *mixed* constraints. We continue Example 6.10 by reproducing below the initial and final tableaus. Carefully note that the initial tableau is given by Tableau II, not Tableau I. (Do you remember why?)

Example 6.14

Basis	z	x_1	x_2	E_2	S_1	A_2	A_3	b_i	Row No.	r_i
II (Initial)	1	* $-2 + 5M$	$-4 + 3M$	$-M$	0	0	0	$30M$	0	—
S_1	0	1	5	0	1	0	0	80	1	80
A_2	0	4	2	−1	0	1	0	20	2	5*
A_3	0	1	1	1	0	0	1	10	3	10
V (Final)	1	0	−2	0	0	$-M$	$2 - M$	20	0	—
S_1	0	0	4	0	1	0	−1	70	1	
x_1	0	1	1	0	0	0	1	10	2	
E_2	0	0	2	1	0	−1	4	20	3	

*Denotes entering and leaving variables.

$-\Delta_2$ would be added here for sensitivity on c_2 (points to the −2 entry under x_2 in Row 0 of Tableau V)

Objective Function Coefficients (Nonbasic Variables). Inspection of the final tableau indicates that x_2 is the relevant nonbasic variable. Since the original objective function (ignoring the artificial variables) was

$$z = 2x_1 + 4x_2,$$

the revised objective function becomes

$$z = 2x_1 + (4 + \Delta_2)x_2.$$

The entry under x_2 in Row 0 of Tableau II would now appear as $(-4 - \Delta_2 + 3M)$. In the row operations that carried us from Tableau II to Tableau V, the entry under x_2 in Row 0 changed from $(-4 + 3M)$ to -2; hence $(-2) - (-4 + 3M)$ or $(2 - 3M)$ must have been added to the initial entry. To our new initial tableau entry of $(-4 - \Delta_2 + 3M)$ we add, therefore, $(2 - 3M)$ to arrive at our new final tableau entry of $(-2 - \Delta_2)$.

For our current basis to remain optimal, the Row 0 entry in the final tableau for x_2 must remain *negative* (remember that this is a *minimization* problem); that is,

$$-2 - \Delta_2 < 0$$

or

$$\Delta_2 > -2 .$$

Having specified that $c_2 = 4 + \Delta_2$, we see that $c_2 > 2$ for our current basis to remain optimal.

Objective Function Coefficients (Basic Variables). Letting $c_1 = 2 + \Delta_1$, or

$$z = (2 + \Delta_1)x_1 + 4x_2 ,$$

we see that the entry under x_1 in Row 0 of Tableau II becomes $(-2 - \Delta_1 + 5M)$. Since $(2 - 5M)$ must be added to arrive at the final tableau value (can you show this?), the following tableau results.

$-\Delta_1$ remains in final tableau.

Basis	z	x_1	x_2	E_2	S_1	A_2	A_3	b_i	Row No.	r_i
V (Final)	1	$-\Delta_1$	-2	0	0	$-M$	$2 - M$	20	0	—
S_1	0	0	4	0	1	0	-1	70	1	
x_1	0	1	1	0	0	0	1	10	2	
E_2	0	0	2	1	0	-1	4	20	3	

The entry $(-\Delta_1)$ under x_1 (a basic variable) in Row 0 is an inconsistency that must be removed (look at the column under x_1 and state why). Multiplying Row 2 by Δ_1 and adding to Row 0 gives the following.

$-\Delta_1$ has been eliminated.

Basis	z	x_1	x_2	E_2	S_1	A_2	A_3	b_i	Row No.	r_i
V	1	0	$-2 + \Delta_1$	0	0	$-M$	$2 - M + \Delta_1$	$20 + 10\Delta_1$	0	

For the current solution to remain optimal, the allowable range of Δ_1 must ensure that neither x_2 nor A_3 is allowed to enter the basis; that is,

$$-2 + \Delta_1 < 0$$

$$\Delta_1 < 2$$

and

$$2 - M + \Delta_1 < 0$$

$$\Delta_1 < M - 2 .$$

Recalling that M is a very large penalty, we see that only the $\Delta_1 < 2$ ensures that neither variable enters the basis. Consequently, c_1 must be less than 4 for the current solution to remain optimal.

Right-Hand–Side Constants. For constraint 3 we let $b_3 = 10 + \Delta_3$. The relevant parts of the new initial and final tableaus follow.

Basis	$\ldots A_3$	b_i
(Initial)	0	$30M + 0\Delta_3$
S_1	0	$80 + 0\Delta_3$
A_2	0	$20 + 0\Delta_3$
A_3	1	$10 + 1\Delta_3$

↑ identical ↑

Basis	$\ldots A_3$	b_i
(Final)	$2 - M$	$20 + (2 - M)\Delta_3$
S_1	-1	$70 - 1\Delta_3$
x_1	1	$10 + 1\Delta_3$
E_2	4	$20 + 4\Delta_3$

↑ identical ↑

Notice in the initial tableau that the column of coefficients for Δ_3 in the b_i column has identical coefficients to the A_3 column; hence, whatever operations are performed on the A_3 column must necessarily be performed on the Δ_3 column. Consequently, the corresponding coefficients are the same in the final tableau.

For the optimal basis to remain feasible, the allowable range for Δ_3 must ensure that no basic variable is allowed to assume a negative value; that is,

$$S_1 = 70 - \Delta_3 \geqslant 0 \quad \text{as long as } \Delta_3 \leqslant 70;$$

$$x_1 = 10 + \Delta_3 \geqslant 0 \quad \text{as long as } \Delta_3 \geqslant -10;$$

$$E_2 = 20 + 4\Delta_3 \geqslant 0 \quad \text{as long as } \Delta_3 \geqslant -5.$$

Figure 6–6 indicates the three regions corresponding to these allowable Δ_3 ranges; hence, the above optimal solution remains feasible as long as

$$5 \leqslant b_3 \leqslant 80 \quad (\text{that is, } -5 \leqslant \Delta_3 \leqslant 70).$$

Now carefully note the following. If b_3 was really 50 and not 10 (that is, $\Delta_3 = 40$), what would be the optimal solution? From the above final tableau (realizing that Δ_3 is within the allowable range), we have

$$S_1 = 70 - \Delta_3 = 70 - 40 = 30;$$

$$x_1 = 10 + \Delta_3 = 10 + 40 = 50;$$

and

$$E_2 = 20 + 4\Delta_3 = 20 + 4(40) = 180.$$

Since

$$z = 2x_1 + 4x_2,$$

the optimal value of the objective function is

$$z = 2(50) + 4(0) = 100.$$

FIGURE 6–6 Allowable Changes in b_3

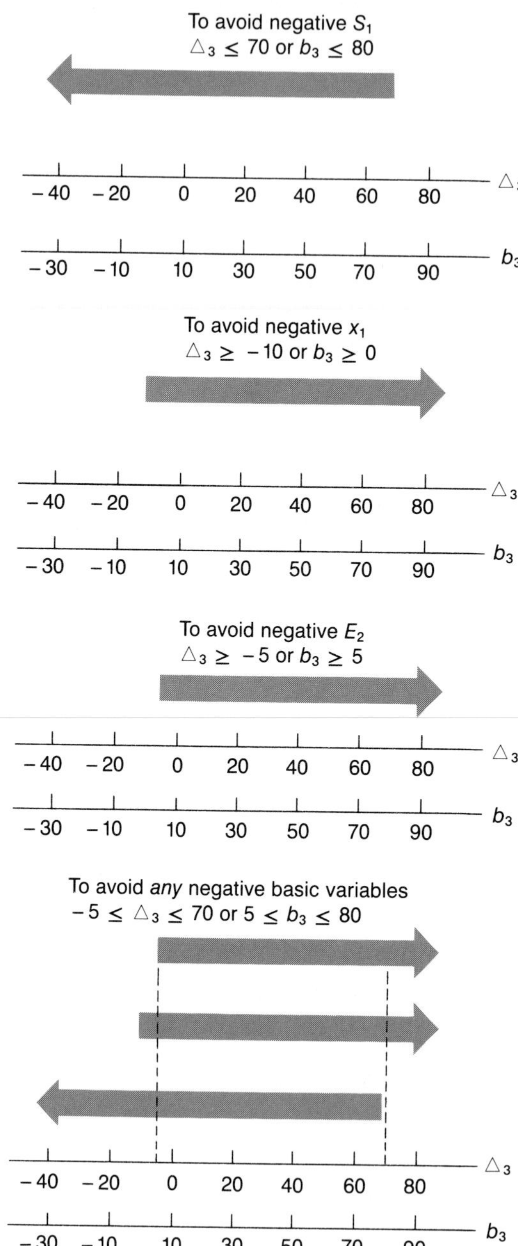

If you're an accountant, you might have realized that the immediately preceding final tableau in its present form is inconsistent with our result of 100 for z; that is,

$$z = 20 + (2 - M)\Delta_3 .$$

It is apparent, therefore, that *the original coefficient in the objective function for* A_3 (*that is,* +M) *must be added to the coefficient* on Δ_3. This gives the correct value

$$z = 20 + 2\Delta_3$$
$$= 20 + 2(40)$$
$$= 100\,.$$

It follows that the shadow price for the third constraint is the coefficient 2 on Δ_3, or the pure number in Row 0 under A_3 in the final tableau.

> The shadow/dual price corresponding to a ≥ or = constraint equals the pure number in Row 0 immediately under the corresponding artificial variable in the final tableau.

FOLLOW-UP EXERCISES

28. Use the simplex procedure to show that the allowable range for b_1 is 10 or above and for b_2 is 40 or below. What would be the new values for z^*, x_1^*, x_2^*, S_1^* and E_2^* if $b_2 = 30$? In general, can you conclude that z^* and all x_j^* are unaffected by a permissible change in Δ_i whenever constraint i is inactive? Explain.
29. What happens if the value for Δ_i or b_i exactly equals one of its boundary values on the allowable range? To be specific, what happens in Example 6.14 if $b_3 = 80$? Do you think this could affect the interpretation of a shadow price? Explain.
30. Would you agree that the shadow price corresponding to a ≥ constraint is the negative of the coefficient in Row 0 immediately under the corresponding surplus variable in the final tableau? Explain.

6.8 THE DUAL

Section 5.7 illustrated that the solutions to both the primal and dual problems can be found by solving either problem. Before illustrating this using the simplex method, let us state an additional primal-dual property.

> **Optimal Primal-Dual Solution Property** The optimal values in one problem are read from the optimal tableau of the other problem as Row 0 coefficients immediately under the corresponding variable.

Remember:

1. Either the dual or the primal can be the max problem.
2. Variable correspondences are x_j in the primal to S_j or E_j in the dual; S_i or E_i in the primal to y_i in the dual. (See Table 5–2.)

3. Table 5–1 indicates the proper sign conditions on the x_j and y_i variables. For example, if the primal is the max problem, and it has a $\geq$ constraint, then the primal E_i corresponds to a nonpositive y_i. Thus we would read the optimal value of y_i as the *negative* of the coefficient in Row 0 under E_i in the optimal primal tableau. Alternatively, from our results in Section 6.7 (the shadow price property on page 289 and Exercise 30), we can look at the coefficient in Row 0 under A_i instead of E_i, or under A_j instead of E_j. In this case, the sign on y_i is consistent with the sign on the pure number in Row 0 under a corresponding A_i. Similarly, the sign on x_j is consistent with the sign on the pure number in Row 0 under a corresponding A_j.

The following example illustrates this property.

Example 6.15

In Example 5.8 we formulated the dual of the air cargo problem. The simplex solution to this dual follows.

Min Problem

Basis	z_d	y_1	y_2	E_1	A_1	E_2	A_2	c_i	Row No.	r_i
I	1	* $9M - 24$	$7M - 13$	$-M$	0	$-M$	0	$30M$	0	
A_1	0	5	2	-1	1	0	0	20	1	$20/5 = 4$
A_2	0	4	5	0	0	-1	1	10	2	$10/4 = 2.5^*$
II	1	0	$-17M/4 + 17$	$-M$	0	* $5M/4 - 6$	$-9M/4 + 6$	$30M/4 + 60$	0	
A_1	0	0	$-17/4$	-1	1	5/4	$-5/4$	30/4	1	$\frac{30/4}{5/4} = 6^*$
y_1	0	1	5/4	0	0	$-1/4$	1/4	10/4	2	—
III (Final Dual)	1	0	$-17/5$	$-24/5$	$24/5 - M$	0	$-M$	96	0	
E_2	0	0	$-17/5$	$-4/5$	4/5	1	-1	6	1	
y_1	0	1	8/20	$-1/5$	1/5	0	0	4	2	

Max Problem

Basis	z_p	x_1	x_2	S_1	S_2	b_i	Row No.	r_i
II (Final Primal)	1	0	6	4	0	96	0	
x_1	0	1	4/5	1/5	0	24/5	1	
S_2	0	0	17/5	$-2/5$	1	17/5	2	

*Denotes entering or leaving variable.

The final tableau for the primal is repeated for purposes of comparison. Variable correspondences are as follows:

Max (primal) Variable	Corresponding Min (dual) Variable
x_1	E_1 (or A_1)
x_2	E_2 (or A_2)
S_1	y_1
S_2	y_2

The relationships indicated in the final tableaus confirm the optimal primal-dual solution property. In particular, note that the optimal value of $x_1 = 24/5$ is the negative of the Row 0 value under E_1 in the optimal dual tableau (or alternatively, it is the pure number under A_1). Also note that the optimal value for S_2 in the primal is 17/5 and not $-17/5$, since all slack (and surplus) variables are nonnegative.

FOLLOW-UP EXERCISES

31. Confirm that the solutions in Example 6.15 satisfy complementary slackness (property 4 on page 217).
32. Under what conditions in the primal is it possible to have negative values for optimal dual variables if:
    a. The primal is a max problem.
    b. The primal is a min problem.
33. How can you tell that nonoptimal simplex iterations in the dual represent infeasible complementary solutions in the primal?
34. Specify the optimal solution to the dual given the optimal primal tableau in Example 6.10 on page 266. Confirm your answer by solving the dual directly.
35. Given the following primal, formulate and solve the dual. Write down the optimal solution to the primal and verify that it is correct.

    Minimize

    $$z = 32x_1 + 34x_2$$

    subject to

    $$3x_1 + x_2 \geq 5 \quad (1)$$

    $$2x_1 + 4x_2 \geq 6 \quad (2)$$

    $$x_1, x_2 \geq 0.$$

6.9 ELLIPSOID AND OTHER LP ALGORITHMS

This section overviews some common extensions to the simplex algorithm and briefly discusses an alternative to simplex-based procedures.

Extensions of the Simplex Algorithm

The widespread use of linear programming has promoted the development of simplex-based procedures, which more efficiently solve either large-scale problems or problems with special structure. The transportation method in Chapter 7 is a good illustration of the latter. This section describes three popular extensions (from many available) of the simplex method.

The **revised simplex method** is geared to computer implementation by carrying tableau information more efficiently and by performing calculations using matrix algebra. In a tableau we need only carry the coefficients for nonbasic variables, since the coefficients for basic variables are always known (the identity matrix). Thus the matrix that represents the tableau in computer memory need not include the columns for the basic variables. These two extensions allow the efficient solution of problems having in the neighborhood of 6,000 constraints and several times that number of variables.

The **dual simplex method** essentially applies the simplex method to the equivalent dual problem without directly specifying the dual. The method generates complementary basic solutions to the primal. Thus from the "point of view" of the primal, dual simplex nonoptimal iterations are infeasible and superoptimal.[6] This method is computationally efficient when the initial dual simplex basis is "closer" to the optimal solution than the initial simplex basis. For example, when the primal has a large number of artificial variables (say, k), then it takes k simplex iterations in the primal just to "flush out" the artificial variables from the basis. Additionally, the dual simplex method considerably simplifies the process of sensitivity analysis.

The **decomposition method** applies the revised simplex method to large-scale multidivisional problems. Multidivisional problems are those that can be decomposed into separate divisions or subproblems for individual optimization. Thereafter, the separate optimal solutions are synthesized into an overall optimal solution. A large corporation with many autonomous divisions represents a typical arena for this approach.

Ellipsoid Algorithm (Khachian's)

In November 1979 a *New York Times* front-page headline proclaimed "A Soviet Discovery Rocks World of Mathematics." The accompanying story reported the discovery of a new mathematical algorithm by a Soviet mathematician, L. G. Khachian. The article startled mathematicians, OR/MS professionals, and computer scientists by suggesting a remarkably simple algorithm for solving LP problems with the potential to far outperform the computational efficiency of the simplex method. The suggestion that inroads might be made in solving the elusive "traveling salesman" class of problems (Chapter 8) generated particular interest.

The Khachian procedure can be described in terms of the geometry of **ellipsoids** (multidimensional ellipses). At a given point during the computational process it can be proved that an optimal solution, if it exists, lies within a given ellipsoid. The center of the ellipsoid is tested to see if it is optimal; if it is not, the ellipsoid is sectioned in two by a plane defined by one of the constraints in the original problem. An optimal solution is known to exist within one of the resulting semiellipsoids. The semiellipsoid containing the optimal solution is identified and then cleverly surrounded by

[6]If you're "fuzzy" here, see Section 5.7, page 209.

a new ellipsoid. The process is repeated with successively smaller ellipsoids, the center of one ultimately yielding an optimal solution.

One commonly accepted practice for evaluating computational efficiency is to test a procedure against the most complex problem of a given size, called the "worst case" problem. The original excitement over the ellipsoid algorithm was based on the fact that the ellipsoid method is "polynomially bounded"; that is, the amount of computation required by the algorithm to reach an optimal solution for worst case problems is a polynomial function of the size of the problem. In contrast, the simplex method is "exponentially bounded," meaning that the amount of computation is an exponential function of the size of the problem. For a sufficiently large problem, a solution in exponential time takes much longer than a solution in polynomial time. Because the simplex method has had poor performance experiences with some *very* large LP problems (e.g., large traveling salesman problems), the Khachian algorithm potentially offers relatively efficient computer-based solutions to such problems.

Computational benchmarks for the Khachian algorithm have been disappointing. Although the algorithm has demonstrated some efficiency for worst case problems, computational experiences for average or typical problems have been much poorer compared with the simplex method. Even with the disappointing practical results, the ellipsoid algorithm has been of great theoretical interest. It is still possible that the algorithm may realize its promise with future modifications and enhancements.

Enter Karmarkar

In November 1984 the newest simplex competitor was announced by an American Telephone & Telegraph Company Bell Laboratories researcher Narendra Karmarkar. With claims that his algorithm had solved LP problems 50 to 100 times faster than the simplex, the announcement was greeted with as much excitement and fanfare as the Khachian algorithm. Corporations that are heavy users of linear programming (such as the airlines and petroleum companies) are particularly eager to learn more about the new algorithm.

Karmarkar's algorithm is, as Khachian's was purported to be, a polynomial time algorithm. Converting a linear programming problem into an equivalent nonlinear problem, Karmarkar's algorithm is similar to the simplex in that it moves from a feasible point to a better feasible point. The algorithm is different in that the feasible points examined are located in the interior of the feasible polyhedron (solution space), ultimately converging to the optimal boundary (corner) point.

At the time of this writing, the jury is still out regarding the validity of the claims and applicability of the algorithm. Earliest reported results by individuals who have attempted to implement the algorithm using their own computer code suggest great potential, although inconsistent performance. Efforts seem to suggest that, compared with the simplex, Karmarkar's algorithm requires (sometimes, significantly) fewer iterations in moving from the starting solution to the optimal solution. However, the results also suggest that the computational burden at each iteration can be extremely great as compared with the simplex. Therein, seemingly, lies the challenge.

So, as the LP sweepstakes continue, a new challenger has stepped forward and seems to have the potential to succeed the champion simplex. However, until more is known about the algorithm and it is subjected to thorough and independent computational testing, no verdict can be reached. Stay tuned![7]

ADDITIONAL EXERCISES

36. For each of the following phenomena, summarize the way in which you become aware of it when solving graphically and when solving by the simplex method.
    a. Alternative optimal solutions.
    b. No feasible solution.
    c. Unbounded solution.
    d. Redundant constraints.
    e. Degenerate solution.
37. *a.* Solve the following problem using the simplex method:

    Maximize

    $$z = 7x_1 + 5x_2$$

    subject to

    $$5x_1 + 3x_2 \le 50 \qquad (1)$$

    $$4x_1 - 2x_2 \le 30 \qquad (2)$$

    $$x_1, x_2 \ge 0 .$$

    b. Verify your solution by solving graphically and relate tableaus to specific corner points.
    c. Determine the shadow prices and interpret their meaning.
    d. Change the RHS constant in the first constraint to 51 and determine optimal z. Is the change in optimal z consistent with the shadow price?
    e. Perform sensitivity analyses on the c_j's and b_i's.
38. *a.* Solve the following problem by the simplex method:

    Minimize

    $$z = 4x_1 + 2x_2 + x_3$$

    subject to

    $$x_1 + x_2 + x_3 \le 40 \qquad (1)$$

    $$2x_1 + x_2 + .5x_3 \ge 10 \qquad (2)$$

    $$x_1, x_2, x_3 \ge 0 .$$

    b. What is your conclusion?
    c. Perform sensitivity analysis on the c_j's and b_i's.
    d. Determine and interpret shadow prices.

[7]A reasonably intuitive explanation of Karmarkar's algorithm can be found in J. N. Hooker, "Karmarkar's Linear Programming Algorithm," *Interfaces*, July–August, 1986, pp. 75–90. See also G. Strang, *Introduction to Applied Mathematics* (Wellesley, Mass.: Wellesley-Cambridge Press, 1986).

39. *a.* Solve the following problem by the simplex method:

Maximize

$$z = 3x_1 + 5x_2$$

subject to

$$6x_1 - 4x_2 \geq 24 \qquad (1)$$

$$-4x_1 + 2x_2 \leq 12 \qquad (2)$$

$$x_1, x_2 \geq 0 .$$

b. Verify your solution by solving graphically.
c. What is your conclusion?
d. By the simplex method, solve the problem if z is to be minimized. Confirm graphically.

40. *a.* Solve the following problem by the simplex algorithm.

Maximize

$$z = x_1 + 3x_2 + 4x_3 - 2x_4$$

subject to

$$x_1 + x_2 + x_3 - x_4 \leq 100 \qquad (1)$$

$$2x_1 + x_2 \geq 20 \qquad (2)$$

$$-x_2 - 2x_3 + x_4 \geq -80 \qquad (3)$$

$$x_1, x_2, x_3 \geq 0$$

x_4 nonpositive

b. Determine and interpret shadow prices.
c. Perform sensitivity analyses on c_j's and b_i's.

41. *a.* Solve the following problem by the simplex algorithm.

Minimize

$$z = 4x_1 + 3x_2 + x_3$$

subject to

$$2x_1 + 5x_2 + x_3 \geq 30 \qquad (1)$$

$$4x_1 + x_2 + 2x_3 = 25 \qquad (2)$$

$$x_1, x_2 \geq 0$$

x_3 unrestricted.

b. Determine and interpret shadow prices.
c. Perform sensitivity analyses on c_j's and b_i's.

42. For the following LP problem:

Maximize

$$z = 4x_1 + 2x_2 + x_3 + 3x_4$$

subject to

$$
\begin{aligned}
2x_1 + x_2 \quad\quad + x_4 &\le 4 \\
2x_1 - x_2 + 2x_3 \quad\quad &\le 3/2 \\
3x_1 + 2x_2 + x_3 + 2x_4 &\le 8 \\
x_1, x_2, x_3, x_4 &\ge 0,
\end{aligned}
$$

the final simplex tableau is given below.

Basis	z	x_1	x_2	x_3	x_4	S_1	S_2	S_3	b_i
(Final)	1	1/2	1	1/2	0	0	0	3/2	12
x_4	0	3/2	1	1/2	1	0	0	1/2	4
S_1	0	1/2	0	−1/2	0	1	0	−1/2	0
S_2	0	2	−1	2	0	0	1	0	3/2

a. Determine the permissible ranges over which the objective function coefficients for x_1, x_2, and x_3 can vary such that the basis above continues to be optimal.
b. Do the same for x_4.
c. Is the value of optimal z altered as the objective function coefficients vary? Do the values change for the decision variables?

43. In the previous problem:
a. Conduct a sensitivity analysis for each of the right-hand–side constants.
b. What are the shadow prices associated with each constraint?
c. Over what ranges in the right-hand–side constants are the shadow prices valid?
d. Without reworking the problem, predict optimal z, x_4, S_1, and S_2 if:
(1) b_3 changes from 8 to 9.5.
(2) b_3 changes from 8 to 40.
(3) b_3 changes from 8 to 6.

44. For the primal problem in Exercise 42:
a. State the dual problem.
b. Read the optimal solution to the dual problem from the optimal tableau in Exercise 42.

45. For the following LP problem:

Minimize

$$z = 5x_1 + 6x_2 + 7x_3$$

subject to

$$
\begin{aligned}
x_1 + x_2 + x_3 &= 1{,}000 \\
x_1 \quad\quad &\le 300 \\
x_2 \quad &\ge 150 \\
x_3 &\ge 200 \\
x_1, x_2, x_3 &\ge 0,
\end{aligned}
$$

the final simplex tableau is given below.

Basis	z	x_1	x_2	x_3	A_1	S_2	E_3	A_3	E_4	A_4	b_i
(Final)	1	0	0	0	$(6 - M)$	-1	0	$-M$	-1	$(1 - M)$	5,900
E_3	0	0	0	0	1	-1	1	-1	1	-1	350
x_1	0	1	0	0	0	1	0	0	0	0	300
x_2	0	0	1	0	1	-1	0	0	1	-1	500
x_3	0	0	0	1	0	0	0	0	-1	1	200

a. Conduct a sensitivity analysis on the objective function coefficients for x_1, x_2, and x_3.

b. To which of these three parameters is the optimal basis most sensitive?

46. In the previous problem:

a. Conduct a sensitivity analysis for each of the right-hand–side constants.

b. To which of these parameters is the optimal basis most sensitive?

c. What are the shadow prices associated with each constraint, and over what ranges in RHS constants are their interpretations valid?

d. Without reworking the problem, predict optimal z, x_1, x_2, and x_3 if

(1) b_1 changes from 1,000 to 900.

(2) b_1 changes from 1,000 to 1,200.

(3) b_1 changes from 1,000 to 350.

47. For the primal problem in Exercise 45:

a. State the dual problem.

b. Read the optimal solution to the dual problem from the optimal tableau in Exercise 45.

48. ***Degeneracy: A Caveat.*** As mentioned earlier, degeneracy occurs when one or more variables in the basis have values of zero. This means that more than n constraints pass through the extreme point, when in reality we only need n constraints to define the extreme point. One result of this is the existence of one or more slack (or surplus) variables in the basis at a zero level. Thus we can "trade" zero-valued basic variables for zero-valued nonbasic variables without affecting the extreme point itself. In effect, we have a situation where multiple bases can define the same extreme point, instead of the usual one-for-one correspondence between a basis and an extreme point. To illustrate, consider the problem below taken from Evans and Baker.[8]

Maximize

$$z = 2x_1 + x_2$$

subject to

$$x_1 + x_2 \leq 10 \qquad (1)$$

$$x_1 \leq 5 \qquad (2)$$

[8] J. R. Evans and N. R. Baker, "Degeneracy and the (Mis)Interpretation of Sensitivity Analysis in Linear Programming," *Decision Sciences,* April 1982, pp. 348–54.

$$x_2 \leq 5 \tag{3}$$

$$x_1, x_2 \geq 0$$

a. Graph the geometry of this solution, and generate the three optimal tableaus corresponding to the following bases: (x_1, x_2, S_3), (x_1, x_2, S_2), (x_1, x_2, S_1).

b. Determine the sensitivity range for c_1 corresponding to each tableau. What are your conclusions?

**49. The optimality criterion relies on the marginal change in z for a one-unit increase in the nonbasic variable under consideration. Define a new optimality criterion that selects the entering variable as the one yielding the best *total* improvement in z. (*Hint*: The maximum amount for the entering variable is still determined according to the feasibility criterion.) Apply this new optimality-feasibility criterion to the solution of the problem in Example 6.4. Graph the area of feasible solutions, and relate the tableaus to specific corner points. What advantages and disadvantages do you foresee for this new criterion?

7

Transportation and Assignment Models

Chapter Outline

All linear programming problems can be solved by the simplex method. However, due to their specialized structure, certain classes of LP problems lend themselves to solution by other techniques that are computationally more efficient than the simplex method. These types of linear problems can be represented by so-called **network models** because they can be drawn pictorially as **nets**. The **transportation model** and the **assignment model** are two important subclasses of network models treated in this chapter. We defer network representations and a more generalized treatment of such models until Chapter 10.

This chapter overviews the characteristics and assumptions of transportation and assignment models, examines applications of each model, and discusses solution algorithms that may be employed to solve them. Also, computer-based implementations of these algorithms are discussed and illustrated in the last section of the chapter.

7.1 THE TRANSPORTATION MODEL

Structure of the Model

The typical transportation problem involves the shipment of some homogeneous commodity from various **origins** or sources of supply to a set of **destinations**, each demanding specified levels of the commodity. Each origin can theoretically ship all, part, or none of its supply to any of the destinations. The assumption of a homogeneous commodity implies no difference in commodity characteristics among origins. The goal is to allocate the supply available at each origin so as to optimize a criterion while satisfying the demand at each destination. The usual objective function is to minimize the total transportation cost or total weighted distance or to maximize the total profit contribution from the allocation. Example 7.1 illustrates a transportation model.

▶ Example 7.1 Yew Haw Trucking Company

A national truck rental firm, Yew Haw Trucking Company, is planning for a heavy demand of rental trucks during the month of June. An inventory of its trucks (all 16-foot vans) combined with projections for demand indicate that three western metropolitan areas will be short of the number of trucks required to satisfy expected demand. Three other metropolitan areas have surplus trucks during this period. These projections reflect anticipated movements of trucks between now and the first day of June.

To prepare for the period of heavy demand, company officials wish to relocate trucks from those metropolitan areas expected to have a surplus to those having shortages. Drivers can be hired to drive the trucks between cities, and the company would like to redistribute its trucks at a minimum cost. The costs (in dollars) of driving a truck between two cities are provided in Table 7–1, as well as the surplus and shortage figures for each metropolitan area. Conveniently, the total surplus (supply) and total shortage (demand) are equal at 420 trucks.

TABLE 7–1 Transportation Table for Yew Haw Trucking Company

Origin (surplus area)	Destination (shortage area) 1	2	3	Supply (surplus of trucks)
1	$ 50	100	100	110
2	200	300	200	160
3	100	200	300	150
Demand (shortage of trucks)	140	200	80	420 / 420

If x_{ij} represents the number of trucks reallocated from surplus area i to shortage area j, the LP statement of this problem is:

Minimize

$$z = 50x_{11} + 100x_{12} + 100x_{13} + 200x_{21} + 300x_{22} + 200x_{23} + 100x_{31} + 200x_{32} + 300x_{33}$$

subject to

Supply constraints

$$\begin{cases} x_{11} + x_{12} + x_{13} = 110 & \text{(Surplus area 1)} \\ x_{21} + x_{22} + x_{23} = 160 & \text{(Surplus area 2)} \\ x_{31} + x_{32} + x_{33} = 150 & \text{(Surplus area 3)} \end{cases}$$

Demand constraints

$$\begin{cases} x_{11} + x_{21} + x_{31} = 140 & \text{(Shortage area 1)} \\ x_{12} + x_{22} + x_{32} = 200 & \text{(Shortage area 2)} \\ x_{13} + x_{23} + x_{33} = 80 & \text{(Shortage area 3)} \end{cases}$$

$$x_{ij} \geq 0 \quad \text{for all } i \text{ and } j$$

The optimal solution to this LP model is z = \$67,000, $x_{12} = 110$, $x_{21} = 80$, $x_{23} = 80$, $x_{31} = 60$, and $x_{32} = 90$. This optimal solution is incorporated in the transportation table as shown in Table 7–2. For example, the optimal solution shows that 110 trucks are to be driven along the route from origin 1 to destination 2. The optimal cost is computed by multiplying entries in occupied cells by corresponding costs and summing. Thus we see that

TABLE 7–2 Transportation Table with Optimal Solution

Origin	Destination 1	Destination 2	Destination 3	Supply
1	50	100 110	100	110
2	200 80	300	200 80	160
3	100 60	200 90	300	150
Demand	140	200	80	420 / 420

x_{12} x_{23} x_{21} x_{32} x_{31}

$$z = 110 \times 100 + 80 \times 200 + 80 \times 200 + 60 \times 100 + 90 \times 200$$
$$= \$67{,}000 .$$

Given a **classical transportation model** with m origins, n destinations, and a minimization objective, the LP formulation can be generalized as

Minimize

$$z = \sum_{i=1}^{m} \sum_{j=1}^{n} c_{ij} x_{ij}$$

subject to

$$\text{Supply constraints:} \quad \sum_{j=1}^{n} x_{ij} = s_i \qquad i = 1, \ldots, m$$

$$\text{Demand constraints:} \quad \sum_{i=1}^{m} x_{ij} = d_j \qquad j = 1, \ldots, n \qquad (7.1)$$

$$x_{ij} \geq 0 \qquad \text{for all } i \text{ and } j,$$

where x_{ij} = Number of units shipped from origin i to destination j; c_{ij} = cost of shipping one unit from origin i to destination j; s_i = Number of units available at the ith origin; and d_j = Number of units demanded at the jth destination.

This formulation assumes that total supply and total demand are equal to one another, or

$$\sum_{i=1}^{m} s_i = \sum_{j=1}^{n} d_j \qquad (7.2)$$

This "balance" between total demand and total supply ensures a feasible solution. Shortly we will show a procedure for handling imbalance between total demand and total supply, which is the more common situation.

The generalized LP model for the transportation problem is best represented by the **generalized transportation table** shown in Table 7–3.

TABLE 7–3 Generalized Transportation Table

Origin	Destination 1	2	. . .	n	Supply
1	x_{11} [c_{11}]	x_{12} [c_{12}]	. . .	x_{1n} [c_{1n}]	s_1
2	x_{21} [c_{21}]	x_{22} [c_{22}]	. . .	x_{2n} [c_{2n}]	s_2
⋮	⋮	⋮	⋱	⋮	⋮
m	x_{m1} [c_{m1}]	x_{m2} [c_{m2}]	. . .	x_{mn} [c_{mn}]	s_m
Demand	d_1	d_2	. . .	d_n	$\sum_{j=1}^{n} d_j$ \ $\sum_{i=1}^{m} s_i$

Although any transportation problem can be solved by the simplex method, specialized **transportation algorithms** that work directly with transportation tables are preferred from the standpoint of formulation ease and solution efficiency. We discuss specific transportation algorithms later in the chapter.

Applicability and Special Structure

Transportation models are an important class of models for two reasons: applicability to many real world problems and special mathematical structure that promotes the design of computationally efficient algorithms.

Distribution systems in organizations are typically concerned with the storage and transportation of goods. Their analysis can be divided into three areas: (1) *location* of such facilities as factories, warehouses, and outlets; (2) *allocation* of routes between origins and destinations; and (3) *transportation* of goods from origins to destinations. Our concern in this chapter is with the last area, from which this class of models gets the name "transportation." Models that analyze facility location and route allocation are left to the chapters on integer programming and network models.[1]

Classical applications of the transportation model include those in the private sector and those in the military. In a commercial environment, transportation models are widely applied to distribution channels that include the movement of goods from plants to regional warehouses to wholesale outlets to retail outlets. In the military, distribution systems are usually called *logistics systems*. In this case the emphasis is on the distribution of personnel and material to vessels, installations, or troop locations.

In recent years transportation models have been applied to the "distribution" of people, services, money, information, and other resources. Moreover, the transportation structure often applies to problems that have nothing to do with distribution systems. For example, variations of the model have been used for production scheduling and inventory control; the scheduling of meals, freighters, and airplanes; the assignment of machines to jobs and personnel to tasks; and many other applications. We present some of these applications in Section 7.2.

Transportation models are important not only for their widespread applicability, but also for their specialized mathematical structure. To see what we mean, look at Figure 7–1, which shows the constraint coefficients (a_{ij}'s) and right-hand–side constants (b_i's) for the LP formulation in Example 7.1. *Special structure* in this case means that *each* column of coefficients has exactly two ones and the rest zeros, and each right-hand–side constant is a nonnegative integer.

Transportation algorithms have been designed to exploit this special structure, with two important payoffs: significant computational efficiencies over simplex-based procedures and the guarantee that any basic feasible solution consists of variables having nonnegative integer values. These payoffs are especially significant in large-scale integer programming problems (Chapter 8).

Overview of Solution Algorithms

The transportation model, once formulated, can be solved in a variety of ways.

1. *Simplex algorithm.* Given that the transportation model is a special class of LP models, it follows that the simplex method can be used as a solution algorithm. This has the advantage of availability on computer systems, but

[1]See Example 8.7 in Chapter 8 and Example 10.2 in Chapter 10.

FIGURE 7–1 Special Structure for Yew Haw LP Model

Constraint Coefficients for Variable

x_{11}	x_{12}	x_{13}	x_{21}	x_{22}	x_{23}	x_{31}	x_{32}	x_{33}	b_i	
1	1	1							= 110	Supply constraints
			1	1	1				= 160	
						1	1	1	= 150	
1			1			1			= 140	Demand constraints
	1			1			1		= 200	
		1			1			1	= 80	

disadvantages with respect to tedious input and increased processing time over transportation algorithms.

2. *Transportation algorithms.* These algorithms have several advantages over LP algorithms.
   a. They exploit special structure both to reduce computer processing time and to increase precision.
   b. They simplify model formulation and computer input. The transportation model is formulated according to a transportation table; the data in the table (m, n, s_i's, d_j's, and c_{ij}'s) then serve as input data to a computerized transportation algorithm. We discuss these algorithms in Sections 7.5 through 7.8.
3. *Network algorithms.* Transportation models can be viewed as networks and solved by specialized network procedures. We discuss these in Chapter 10.
4. *Heuristic algorithms.* "Rule of thumb" approaches can be used to solve transportation models based on transportation tables. These methods usually give nonoptimal solutions and are primarily used to generate initial solutions to transportation algorithms (as you will see in Section 7.5). We also use heuristic algorithms as "quick and dirty" solutions, primarily to get a "feel" for solution characteristics. The following examples illustrate two popular heuristic algorithms

▶ Example 7.2 Northwest Corner Algorithm

The **northwest corner algorithm** is a popular (but arbitrary) technique for arriving at an initial solution. The scheme is to start in the upper left-hand cell (northwest corner) of a transportation table and assign units from origin 1 to destination 1. Assignments are continued in such a way that the supply at origin 1 is completely allocated before moving on to origin 2. The supply at origin 2 is completely allocated before moving to origin 3, and so on. The same type of sequential allocation applies to assignments made to destinations. The demand at destination 1 is satisfied before making allocations to destination 2, and so forth. This pattern of assignments leads to a sort of staircase arrangement of assignments in the transportation table.

To illustrate the northwest corner algorithm, we develop an initial solution for Example 7.1.

1. Beginning in cell 1,1, the capacity of 110 trucks at origin 1 is less than the 140 units demanded at destination 1. Consequently, all of the capacity at origin 1 is allocated to cell 1,1. (See Table 7–4.)
2. With the supply at origin 1 exhausted, we move to origin 2. The 160 units available at origin 2 are compared with the 30 remaining trucks required at destination 1. This leads to the assignment of 30 trucks to cell 2, 1.
3. The preceding assignment leaves 130 trucks available at origin 2 and the requirements of destination 1 satisfied. Moving to the needs of destination 2, a comparison of the 200 trucks required with the 130 remaining at origin 2 results in the assignment of 130 units to cell 2, 2.
4. Having exhausted the capacity of origin 2, the 150 units available at origin 3 are compared with the 70 units still required at destination 2. This leads to an assignment of 70 units to cell 3, 2.
5. The remaining 80 units at origin 3 exactly equals the demand at destination 3. Thus 80 units are assigned to cell 3, 3.

Since our solution method requires that total supply and demand be equal, you should always find that your final allocation (in the southeast corner) exhausts the remaining supply and satisfies the remaining demand.

The decision rule for making allocations to each relevant cell is based on selecting the minimum of the unused supply for the row and the unsatisfied demand for the column, or in considering an assignment to cell i, j:

$$x_{ij} = \min(s_i - s'_i,\ d_j - d'_j) \tag{7.3}$$

where s'_i = the sum of previous allocations from origin i and d'_j = the sum of previous allocations to destination j.

The complete solution appears in Table 7–4. It indicates that 110 trucks should be delivered from the city representing origin 1 to the city representing destination 1, 30 from origin 2 to destination 1, 130 from origin 2 to destination 2, 70 from origin 3 to destination 2, and 80 from origin 3 to destination 3. Total cost for this redistribution is summarized in Table 7–5. Note that this solution is $21,500 more expensive than the optimal solution shown earlier.

▶ Example 7.3 Greedy Algorithm

Consider the following heuristic procedure for solving the transportation model: Select the lowest cost cell (route) within the transportation table and assign the most you can to this cell (hence the term *greedy*) such that you do not violate or exceed the supply and demand constraints associated with that cell. Repeat this procedure for the next lowest cost cell, and so on, until all supply and demand constraints are satisfied.

TABLE 7–4 Northwest Corner Algorithm Solution

Origin	Destination 1	Destination 2	Destination 3	Supply
1	[50] 110	[100]	[100]	110
2	[200] 30	[300] 130	[200]	160
3	[100]	[200] 70	[300] 80	150
Demand	140	200	80	420 / 420

TABLE 7–5 Cost Summary for Northwest Corner Solution

Variable	Value		Unit Delivery Cost		Contribution to Total Cost
x_{11}	110	×	50	=	$ 5,500
x_{21}	30	×	200	=	6,000
x_{22}	130	×	300	=	39,000
x_{32}	70	×	200	=	14,000
x_{33}	80	×	300	=	24,000
					$88,500

Table 7–6 illustrates the solution for the trucking example by the greedy algorithm. To start, the least cost element in the table is identified ($c_{11} = 50$) and the maximum feasible amount is allocated to the corresponding cell ($x_{11} = 110$). Since row 1 is satisfied, it is crossed out.

The next lowest cost element *among feasible cells* is located ($c_{31} = 100$), and the maximum feasible amount is entered ($x_{31} = 30$). This eliminates column 1. The next lowest cost element of 200 is given by either c_{23} or c_{32}. Arbitrarily selecting the former gives $x_{23} = 80$ and the elimination of column 3. The value 120 is next placed in cell 3, 2, which eliminates row 3. The solution is completed by entering 80 in cell 2, 2 to satisfy the requirements of destination 2. The total cost for this solution is $72,500, which is lower than the solution given by the northwest corner algorithm but higher than the optimal solution given in Table 7–2.

In practice, transportation models are usually solved by computerized transportation and network algorithms. For a good general understanding of transportation models and their solutions, you need only study Sections 7.1 through 7.4, coupled with some formulations and computer implementations on your local system. For greater solution detail, study Sections 7.5 through 7.10.

TABLE 7–6 Greedy Algorithm

Origin	Destination 1 (cost)	1 (ship)	2 (cost)	2 (ship)	3 (cost)	3 (ship)	Supply
1	50	110	100		100		110
2	200		300	80	200	80	160
3	100	30	200	120	300		150
Demand		140		200		80	420 / 420

FOLLOW-UP EXERCISES

1. ***Chemical Distribution.*** A chemical company manufactures liquid hydrogen at two different locations. The two plants supply three storage depots in the same geographical region. Given the limited capacity at each plant and the demand at each depot, management wants to determine the strategy that minimizes total distribution costs. Plants 1 and 2 can supply 50,000 gallons and 70,000 gallons, respectively. Depots 1, 2, and 3 have demands of 40,000, 60,000, and 20,000 gallons, respectively. Shipping costs per thousand gallons to the three depots are $30, $4, and $8 from plant 1 and $5, $10, and $20 from plant 2.
   a. Carefully define variables and formulate the LP model for this problem.
   b. Construct the transportation table (as in Table 7–1) for this problem.
2. ***Simplex Algorithm Computer Implementation.*** Use an LP package to solve the LP model in
   a. Example 7.1.
   b. Exercise 1*a*.
   Does the LP solution indicate a degenerate solution? Can you explain why it should?
3. ***Transportation Algorithm Computer Implementation.*** Use a transportation package (if available) to solve the transportation model in
   a. Table 7–1.
   b. Exercise 1*b*.
   If you worked Exercise 2, compare the transportation versus LP approaches with respect to (1) ease of input, (2) readability of output, and (3) processing time.
4. ***Heuristic Solutions.*** Solve the model in Exercise 1 by the
   a. Northwest corner algorithm.
   b. Greedy algorithm.
   Compare the solutions to one another and to the optimal solution (if you solved either Exercise 2*b* or 3*b*).

7.2 VARIATIONS ON THE CLASSICAL TRANSPORTATION MODEL

The *classical transportation model* is a minimization problem subject to supply and demand equality constraints with total demand equaling total supply. Variations on this structure are certain to occur in most real applications. This section presents a few of these formulation issues. After discussing these, we will challenge you to try your hand at formulations in the next section.

Maximization Objective

In some applications we may wish to *maximize* an objective function such as profit contribution. In an LP context, we simply change the objective function from "minimization" to "maximization." If a computerized transportation package does not provide a maximization option, then we simply input negative c_{ij}'s, since maximization of an objective function (z) is equivalent to minimization of its negative ($-z$). As in the simplex method, the difference between solving maximization and minimization problems is merely a matter of interpretation.

FOLLOW-UP EXERCISE

5. Consider a maximization objective for Example 7.1.
   a. Find the optimal solution using a computerized LP or transportation package.
   b. Find a solution using the Northwest corner algorithm.
   c. Find a solution using the greedy algorithm.

Unbalanced Conditions

Another common variation arises from **unbalanced conditions.** Imbalance between total supply and total demand is the rule rather than the exception. Since the primary solution method for these problems requires equality between total supply and total demand, a procedure equivalent to adding slack variables in the simplex method is used to ensure balance for problems having unbalanced conditions.

Example 7.4 Total Supply Exceeds Total Demand

If total supply exceeds total demand, than a **dummy destination** is added with an artificial demand exactly equal to the surplus supply. If origin (surplus area) 1 in Example 7.1 had 150 surplus trucks (rather than 110), total supply would exceed total demand by 40 trucks (460 > 420). Table 7–7 illustrates how a dummy destination is added to artificially bring total supply and demand into balance. Note that we assigned costs of zero to the cells. This makes sense because no trucks would actually be relocated to the dummy destination. Even though dummy costs are typically assigned values of zero, to assign that value automatically could cause problems (as illustrated later in Example 7.9).

If total supply is less than total demand, then a **dummy origin** is introduced, which has a capacity exactly equal to the excess demand. As in the previous case, objective function contributions of zero are often assigned to all allocations from the dummy origin. In so doing, however, the implication is that there is no preference (and associated penalty) for which destination will have unfulfilled demand.

TABLE 7–7 Transportation Table for Yew Haw Trucking with Dummy Destination

Origin (surplus area)	Destination (shortage area)				Supply (surplus of trucks)
	1	2	3	Dummy	
1	$50	100	100	0	150
2	200	300	200	0	160
3	100	200	300	0	150
Demand (shortage of trucks)	140	200	80	40	460 / 460

Many computerized transportation algorithms generate their own dummy row or column whenever the user inputs a transportation table with unbalanced conditions. Check this feature if you have a computerized algorithm available.

FOLLOW-UP EXERCISES

6. Formulate the LP model for Example 7.4. What structural changes have occurred when compared with the original formulation in Example 7.1?
7. What assumptions might result in the assignment of positive costs for the dummy destination in Example 7.4?
8. ***Total Demand Exceeds Total Supply***
   a. Modify Table 7–1 if the shortage of trucks at destination 1 is 175 rather than 140. Does the assignment of zero costs to the dummy origin make sense? Under what assumptions might positive costs be warranted?
   b. Formulate the LP model for this problem.
   c. Use a computerized package to solve the model in part *a* or part *b*.

Excluded Routes and Bounds

One assumption in the classic model is that each origin is capable of supplying each destination. For many problems, restrictions are imposed on routes (x_{ij}'s). These can take the form of exclusions or constraints of the ($\leq, =, \geq$) type. The following examples illustrate some possibilities.

▶ Example 7.5 Excluded Routes

Routes can be excluded for reasons of managerial discretion or infeasibility of assignment. For example, the commodity supplied by different origins may not be entirely homogeneous. As a result, management might decide that certain origins should not supply specified destinations. In certain problems, infeasible routes are necessary to avoid logical inconsistencies, as illustrated in Examples 7.7 and 7.9. In other cases, physical or natural barriers may make certain routes infeasible. For instance, suppose in the Yew Haw example that winter conditions routinely close a mountain route between origin 3 and destination 2. We can account for this in two ways:

1. In Table 7–1 we simply cross out cell 3, 2, effectively eliminating x_{32}, or
2. We can assign a unit contribution to cell 3, 2 that makes that route undesirable. In a minimization problem, we assign a *very* large positive contribution (much larger than any other in the problem) and in a maximization problem a very large negative contribution.[2]

Example 7.6 Lower Bounds on x_{ij} Values

Minimum values may be specified for selected variables in transportation problems. Assume in the Yew Haw example that management has declared a minimim of 75 vans must be supplied to shortage area 1 by surplus area 1. We can incorporate this policy in the following manner:

1. *Make a preliminary assignment of 75 units to* x_{11}. We account for this by reducing the available supply at shortage area 1 and the demand at surplus area 1 by 75 units. Table 7–1 would be modified as shown in Table 7–8. This assignment results in a cost of (75 vans × \$50/van =) \$3,750.

TABLE 7–8 Yew Haw Problem: Lower Bound of 75 for Cell 1, 1

Origin (surplus area)	Destination (shortage area)			Supply (surplus of trucks)	
	1	2	3		
1	\$50	100	100	35	Origin 1 supply reduced by 75
2	200	300	200	160	
3	100	200	300	150	
Demand (shortage of trucks)	65	200	80	345 \ 345	

Destination 1 demand reduced by 75.

Total supply and demand reduced by 75.

2. *Solve the new problem based on the changes made in step 1.* In this modified form, total supply and demand are reduced (and equal), and the variable x_{11} represents the number of vans (in excess of 75) relocated from origin 1 to destination 1.

[2] Those who studied the simplex method might recognize this approach as the M-technique for handling artificial variables.

3. *Modify and interpret the solution.* Once the solution has been found, we must correct for the preliminary assignment of 75 vans. To do so we add 75 to the optimal value for x_{11} (if $x_{11} = 20$, the optimal solution actually will recommend relocation of 95 vans from origin 1 to destination 1) and we add \$3,750 to the optimal value of the objective function.

We have thus far described procedures for handling **excluded routes** ($x_{ij} = 0$) and **lower bounds** on routes (that is, $x_{ij} \geq b_{ij}$). The procedure for **precise assignments** or **exact assignments** (that is, $x_{ij} = b_{ij}$) is a combination of the procedures for excluded routes and lower bounds, which we leave to Exercise 15. **Upper bounds** restrictions (that is, $x_{ij} \leq b_{ij}$) require considerations that go beyond the scope of this chapter.[3]

FOLLOW-UP EXERCISES

9. How would you handle excluded routes for a transportation model that is to be solved by the simplex method? How are lower bounds accounted for in an LP formulation? Upper bounds? Exact assignments?
10. Solve the problem in Example 7.5 using:
    a. A computer package.
    b. The greedy algorithm.
11. Solve the problem in Example 7.6 using:
    a. A computer package.
    b. The greedy algorithm.
12. For the chemical company discussed in Exercise 1 construct a transportation table to reflect all of the following changes:
    a. At least 30,000 gallons should be shipped from origin 1 to destination 2.
    b. No shipments should be made from origin 1 to destination 1.
    c. The supply at origin 1 has increased to 75,000 gallons, and the demand at destination 3 has increased to 40,000 gallons.
13. Formulate the LP model for the problem in the preceding exercise.
14. For the model in Exercise 12 or 13:
    a. Find the optimal solution using a computer package.
    b. Find a solution using the greedy algorithm.
15. *Precise (Exact) Allocations.*
    a. Formulate a procedure (using a transportation algorithm) for modifying and solving problems that make precise assignments to one or more routes.
    b. Modify Table 7–1 if Yew Haw management specifies that *exactly* 100 vans should be relocated from origin 1 to destination 1 and *exactly* 40 from origin 2 to destination 1.
    c. Solve this problem using a computer package.
    d. Solve this problem using the greedy algorithm.

Other Variations

Other variations and extensions to the transportation model include the following:

1. The use of **nonhomogeneous goods** (e.g., qualitative differences in goods means that not all suppliers are acceptable sources). This case can be treated

[3] If you dare, see G. B. Dantzig, *Linear Programming and Extensions* (Princeton, N.J.: Princeton University Press, 1963); or M. Simonnard, *Linear Programming*, trans. W. S. Jewell (Englewood Cliffs, N.J.: Prentice-Hall, 1966).

by various ad hoc procedures, including the exclusion of routes and weights on c_{ij} coefficients.

2. The location of facilities or selection of supply points (origins) from a set of alternatives, each characterized by route setup costs (e.g., selecting from among four landfill sites, two which can be used for garbage processing). These cases are modeled by the **conditional transportation model** described in the next chapter (Example 8.7). It is solved by integer programming algorithms (Chapter 8).
3. **Variable c_{ij}** as a function of the value for x_{ij}. This case applies, for example, when there are quantity discounts or economies or diseconomies of scale. These situations can be modeled and solved by mathematical programming methods, such as separable programming and dynamic programming (Chapter 12).
4. Structural coefficients (a_{ij}'s) in the supply constraints, that is,

$$\sum_{j=1}^{n} a_{ij}x_{ij} = s_i \qquad i = 1, \ldots, m.$$

This is called the **generalized transportation model** and can be solved by either the simplex method or by a special procedure that exploits its structure.[4]

5. The existence of transshipment points that receive goods from supply points (origins) and distribute goods to demand points (destinations). This important model is called the **transshipment model,** which we describe as a *network* in Section 10.1.

7.3 SELECTED APPLICATIONS OF THE TRANSPORTATION MODEL

In this section, we present and formulate three sample problems to illustrate a variety of formulation issues.

The first example illustrates a modification of the classical transportation model. Involving the distribution of a "relatively" homogeneous commodity, the example uses the flow-distance criterion, and it illustrates the natural and logical restriction of routes.

▶ Example 7.7 Public Works

Chicago has five locations around the city in which sand and salt stockpiles are maintained for winter icing and snow storms. For most major storms, all salt and sand is distributed from these five shelters to five different city zones. In fact, there is usually a need for additional sand and salt; however, it is currently impractical to gain access to additional stores that are maintained at a central depot in time to be of benefit (officials keep their fingers crossed that the city will not be hit by back-to-back storms).

---

[4]For example, see Hamdy A. Taha, *Operations Research: An Introduction*, 3rd ed. (New York: Macmillan, 1982); or G. Hadley, *Linear Programming* (Reading, Mass.: Addison-Wesley Publishing, 1962).

The Director of Public Works, an M.B.A. graduate with a public service inclination, wishes to determine the best way to allocate the salt and sand supplies during a storm. Her criterion is to minimize the time required to meet the needs of the five zones. In the absence of reliable time estimates (especially during storms) she has decided to use the *flow-distance criterion.* This criterion is a weighted measure that assigns a relative cost in proportion to the volume (units, weight, etc.) distributed and the distance traveled. In this example the criterion is computed by multiplying volume (truckloads) transported times distance (miles) yielding the surrogate criterion of "truckload-miles." Table 7–9 summarizes the distances (miles) between the sand and salt shelters and the center of each zone. Note that because of either department policy or geographical restrictions (natural barriers), shelters 1, 3, and 5 do not supply all five zones.

TABLE 7–9 Public Works Data

	Zone					
Shelter	**1**	**2**	**3**	**4**	**5**	**Truckloads Available**
1	1.2	—	2.2	—	—	200
2	3.8	4.5	5.2	2.3	3.2	250
3	—	6.4	—	4.2	1.8	150
4	2.9	3.1	5.2	4.1	3.8	300
5	1.5	—	4.0	6.1	2.2	100
Truckloads demanded	150	200	300	175	175	1,000

FOLLOW-UP EXERCISES

16. In Example 7.7:
    a. Define x_{ij}.
    b. Do you agree with the chosen criterion? What other surrogates might be chosen?
    c. How would you handle the infeasible routes for input to a computerized routine?
17. Solve this problem using
    a. Either a computerized LP algorithm or a computerized transportation algorithm.
    b. The greedy algorithm. Compare to the solution in part *a*.

    State the decision (solution) in words (plain English).

Our second example illustrates a nonclassical application involving the allocation of investment dollars over a multiperiod time horizon. In addition to being a maximization problem, the model provides some interesting considerations (addressed in the follow-up exercises) regarding imbalance. Transportation models involving allocations over time are known as **multistage transportation models.** Such models can also be solved (less efficiently) by dynamic programming (Chapter 12).

▶ Example 7.8 Multiperiod Investment Model

A company wishes to determine an investment strategy for each of the next four years. Five investment types have been selected, investment capital has been allocated for each of the coming four years, and maximum investment levels have been established for each investment type. An assumption is that amounts invested in any year will remain invested until the end of the four-year planning horizon. For example, an investment at the beginning of year 2 remains for a term of three full years. Table 7–10 summarizes the data for this problem. The values in the body of the table represent *net return on investment factors* (before taxes). These factors account for effects of compounding and reflect the *cumulative* return over the life of the investment. For example, a dollar invested in investment type 2 at the beginning of year 1 will grow to $1.90 by the end of the fourth year, yielding a net return of $0.90.

TABLE 7–10 Investment Model Data

		Investment Type					Dollars Available
		1	2	3	4	5	
Year Investment Made	1	0.80	0.90	0.60	0.75	1.00	500,000
	2	0.55	0.65	0.40	0.60	0.50	600,000
	3	0.30	0.25	0.30	0.50	0.20	750,000
	4	0.15	0.12	0.25	0.35	0.10	800,000
Maximum Dollar Investment		750,000	600,000	500,000	800,000	1,000,000	2,650,000 / 3,650,000

The objective in this problem is to determine the number of dollars to invest at the beginning of each year in each investment so as to *maximize* the net dollar return for the four-year period.

FOLLOW-UP EXERCISES

18. For the problem in Example 7.8:
    a. Construct the transportation table. Note that there is imbalance.
    b. State the meaning of the dummy in plain English. What would be the meaning of the dummy if total dollars available were to exceed total maximum allowable investments?
    c. State the meaning of x_{ij}.
    d. State the LP objective function and explain its meaning. How is this related to the criterion "total worth at the end of four years"?
19. Solve the problem in Exercise 18*a* using:
    a. Either a computerized LP algorithm or a computerized transportation algorithm.
    b. The greedy algorithm. Compare to the solution in part *a*.
    State the decision (solution) in words (plain English).
20. In example 7.8, suppose that the maximum capital available in each year is the same, but investment types 4 and 5 are excluded from consideration. For the remaining three investments, assume that the $750,000, $600,000, and $500,000

represent minimum recommended dollar investments in each type, respectively. To bring supply and demand into balance, can we simply add a "dummy investment type"? If not, how might we handle this special situation?

The final application in this section is a multiperiod production scheduling and inventory control model. Note carefully the definition of origins, the restriction of routes, and the costing of dummy destinations. Stick with this example—it is not as bad as it looks, and it helps you to see that "transportation" models apply to problems unrelated to transportation.

Example 7.9 Production Scheduling and Inventory Control

The transportation model can be applied to the problem of scheduling production and controlling inventory over several periods. The typical case is the manufacturer with a seasonal sales pattern; production can remain completely stable (thereby absorbing seasonal fluctuations with inventory buildups and depletions), production can vary to meet the sales pattern (no inventories), or production can follow some midground approach between these two extremes.

The most straightforward formulation involves a trade-off between overtime costs and inventory holding costs. In this formulation, for each period, such as a month, we define regular and overtime capacity in units, such as production hours. We also estimate the unit costs of regular and overtime production and the cost per period of holding a unit in inventory.

The transportation formulation identifies regular and overtime production capacities in each period as "origins" and demands for each period as "destinations." The decision variables are defined in terms of production quantities in a given period manufactured by a given method (regular or overtime) for delivery in the present or some future period. The cost associated with each cell is determined as the sum of production cost per unit and the cost of holding a unit in inventory (if any).

For example, consider a four-period model with projected (or contracted) demands of 40, 60, 75, and 60 units in periods 1, 2, 3, and 4, respectively. The costs are $4 per unit for regular time, $6 per unit for overtime, and $1.50 for holding a unit in inventory for one period. For simplicity, we assume that these costs are identical in each period. Furthermore, in each period, regular production capacity is 50 units and overtime production capacity is 20 units. Table 7–11 illustrates the transportation table for this example.

To illustrate the calculation of costs, consider origin 3. The first cell is infeasible because it is impossible to produce in period 2 for delivery in period 1 (assuming backordering is not allowed). The cost in the second cell is simply the cost per unit of regular production ($4). The cost of $5.50 in the third cell represents the cost of producing a unit on regular time in period 2 for delivery in period 3, or $4 plus the cost of holding the unit for one period ($1.50)—and so forth.

Since total supply is greater than total demand, a dummy destination is created to pick up the slack. Each dummy in this case represents unused production capacity. An interesting question concerns the cost values to assign to the dummy column. Although it may be tempting to uniformly assign zero, that would infer an ability to hold regular production costs completely variable. That would be equivalent to assuming that workers can be sent home when not needed at no cost to the company. The zero

TABLE 7–11 Transportation Table for Example 7.9

Origin (source of production)	Destination (demand in period)					Supply (production capacity
	1	2	3	4	Dummy	
1 Regular period 1	$4.00	$5.50	$7.00	$ 8.50	?	50
2 Overtime period 1	6.00	7.50	9.00	10.50	?	20
3 Regular period 2		4.00	5.50	7.00	?	50
4 Overtime period 2		6.00	7.50	9.00	?	20
5 Regular period 3			4.00	5.50	?	50
6 Overtime period 3			6.00	7.50	?	20
7 Regular period 4				4.00	?	50
8 Overtime period 4				6.00	?	20
Demand	40	60	75	60	45	280 / 280

assumption may be valid for overtime, but if workers remain on the job for 40 hours pe week with or without something to do, the dummy cost for an origin associated with regular production may better be estimated as the cost per unit of regular production ($4). Alternatively, if product costing is based on direct labor plus raw materials plus overhead, then dummy regulars should be costed as a proportion of $4.

FOLLOW-UP EXERCISES

21. Solve Example 7.9 using a computerized simplex or transportation algorithm. Assume that the raw material cost is 25 percent of the cost of producing a unit on regular time. Excess regular time production capacity is to be costed at 75 percent of unit regular time costs. Excess overtime production capacity is costed at zero.
    a. State the optimal production schedule as follows:

	Period				
	1	2	3	4	Totals
Units produced, regular					
Units produced, overtime					
Ending inventory					

    b. State the optimal cost breakdown as follows:

	Period				
Costs ($)	1	2	3	4	Totals
Regular time					
Overtime					
Raw material					
Inventory					
Excess capacity					
Totals					

22. In Example 7.9 consider an inflation rate of 10 % per period for regular time, overtime, and holding costs.
    a. Modify Table 7–11 accordingly. Assume that dummy regulars are costed at 75 % of regular time costs; dummy overtimes are costed at zero.

    b. Use a computerized package to solve this problem. State the solution as described in the preceding exercise. Is the solution sensitive to inflation?
23. Suppose back ordering is allowed in Example 7.9. An administrative cost and customer dissatisfaction charge of $1 per unit per period is to be levied.
    a. Modify Table 7–11 accordingly. Assume that dummy regulars are costed at 75 % of regular time costs; dummy overtimes are costed at zero.

    b. Use a computerized package to solve this problem. State the solution as described in Exercise 21. Is the solution sensitive to back ordering?

7.4 THE LINEAR ASSIGNMENT MODEL

A special case of the transportation model is the **linear assignment model.** Just as the special structure of the transportation model allows more efficient solution procedures than the simplex method, the characteristics of the linear assignment model allow its solution by more efficient procedures than the transportation method.

Assumptions and General Structure

In an assignment problem, the objective is to optimally allocate n origins or activities to n destinations or needs. Unlike the transportation model, a resource must be allocated *totally* or uniquely to a given task. The typical example includes assigning n persons or machines to n different jobs so as to minimize (or maximize) some objective function. Other examples include assigning sales personnel to sales districts in order to maximize sales effectiveness, assigning airline crews to flights in order to minimize costs, assigning rescue units to rescue tasks in order to minimize total combined time to complete all rescue tasks, assigning boats or planes to charter trips in order to maximize total profit, assigning social workers to welfare cases in order to maximize the number of cases closed within a specified period, and assigning snowplow crews to areas of a city so as to optimize transportation mobility. Consider the following example.

▶ Example 7.10 Court Scheduling

In recent years, OR/MS specialists have become increasingly involved in applications relating to the criminal justice system. One factor that interferes with the administration of justice is court congestion. A simplified version of the problem is a district court attempting to assign four judges to four court dockets. The objective is to minimize the total time required to complete all of the cases on the four dockets. Based on the composition of the cases scheduled on each docket and given district court records to indicate the ability of judges to process different types of cases, it is possible to estimate the number of days each judge would take to clear each docket. These data are displayed in Table 7–12.

TABLE 7–12 Estimated Days to Clear Docket

	Docket			
Judge	**1**	**2**	**3**	**4**
1	14	13	17	14
2	16	15	16	15
3	18	14	20	17
4	20	13	15	18

This problem can be formulated as a linear assignment model with decision variables

$$x_{ij} = \begin{cases} 1 \text{ if judge } i \text{ assigned to docket } j \\ 0 \text{ if judge } i \text{ not assigned to docket } j. \end{cases}$$

Using this *zero-one* (don't assign-assign) decision variable, days to process a court docket are incurred only if a judge is assigned to a docket. Thus the total days necessary to clear all four court dockets is expressed by the objective function

Minimize

$$z = 14x_{11} + 13x_{12} + 17x_{13} + 14x_{14} + 16x_{21} + \ldots + 18x_{44}$$

Two *types* of constraints are required for this problem. First, a set of constraints must be formulated which assure that each judge is assigned to *exactly* one docket. For judge 1 the appropriate constraint is

$$x_{11} + x_{12} + x_{13} + x_{14} = 1 .$$

Similar constraints are required for the other three judges.

In addition, a set of constraints is needed to assure that each docket is assigned exactly one judge. For example, the constraint for docket 3 is

$$x_{13} + x_{23} + x_{33} + x_{43} = 1 .$$

The complete LP formulation for this problem is

Minimize

$$z = 14x_{11} + 13x_{12} + 17x_{13} + 14x_{14} + 16x_{21} + 15x_{22} + 16x_{23} + 15x_{24} + 18x_{31} + 14x_{32} + 20x_{33} + 17x_{34} + 20x_{41} + 13x_{42} + 15x_{43} + 18x_{44}$$

subject to

$$\begin{aligned}
x_{11} + x_{12} + x_{13} + x_{14} &= 1 \\
x_{21} + x_{22} + x_{23} + x_{24} &= 1 \\
x_{31} + x_{32} + x_{33} + x_{34} &= 1 \\
x_{41} + x_{42} + x_{43} + x_{44} &= 1 \\
x_{11} + x_{21} + x_{31} + x_{41} &= 1 \\
x_{12} + x_{22} + x_{32} + x_{42} &= 1 \\
x_{13} + x_{23} + x_{33} + x_{43} &= 1 \\
x_{14} + x_{24} + x_{34} + x_{44} &= 1 \\
x_{ij} = 0 \text{ or } 1 \quad &\text{for all } i,j
\end{aligned}$$

The generalized mathematical statement of the linear assignment model is

Minimize (maximize)

$$z = \sum_{i=1}^{n} \sum_{j=1}^{n} c_{ij}x_{ij} \tag{7.4}$$

subject to

$$\sum_{j=1}^{n} x_{ij} = 1, \qquad i = 1, \ldots, n, \tag{7.5}$$

$$\sum_{i=1}^{n} x_{ij} = 1, \qquad j = 1, \ldots, n, \tag{7.6}$$

$$x_{ij} = 0 \text{ or } 1 . \tag{7.7}$$

Notice from Equation 7.7 that the decision variables are assigned values of either zero or one. Zero is assigned to x_{ij} if resource i is *not* allocated to task j; x_{ij} is assigned a value of one if resource i is assigned to task j. Constraint set 7.5 assures that each resource can be assigned to one task only. Constraint set 7.6 ensures that each task is assigned one and only one of the resources. Other characteristics worth noting are that the number of resources is equal to the number of tasks and the right-hand–side constants are all equal to one. In the context of the transportation model given by Equation 7.1, it follows that $m = n$ and $s_i = d_j = 1$ for the assignment model.

Overview of Solution Algorithms

We can identify six general categories of solution algorithms for linear assignment models, from least to most efficient:

1. **Total Enumeration.** The brute force approach to finding the optimal solution would enumerate (list) all possible solutions and then select the best. For example, if we had to assign three airline crews to three flights based on some criterion, we could proceed by listing the six possible assignments (any of three crews to the first flight × any of two crews to the second flight × the remaining crew to the third flight, or $3 \times 2 \times 1 = 6$) and selecting the best. In general, total enumeration requires the examination of $n!$ solutions. For problems of meaningful size, this approach is far too costly; if $n = 25$, then 25! or about 1.55×10^{25} solutions must be examined. To put this in perspective, this would take 4.92×10^{15} years of continuous computer processing time at 0.01 second per solution!
2. **Zero-one (Binary) Linear Programming.** LP problems with decision variables restricted to values of zero or one, as in the model given by Equations 7.4–7.7, are called 0–1 or binary LP problems (we discuss these in the next chapter).[5] Algorithms for binary LP are costly to implement because they often require exorbitant computer processing time to reach an optimal solution. An assignment problem with only $n = 25$ (that is, 625 variables and 50 constraints) could require many hours of expensive processing time.
3. **Simplex Algorithm.** The simplex method is a reasonable computational alternative for the model given by Equations 7.4–7.7, although severe degeneracy is guaranteed, since half (n) of the variables in the basis will be zero. If we formulate 16 variables for a 4×4 matrix, we have eight constraints. Only four variables will be in the final solution at nonzero values. This implies redundancy in half of the constraints. Still, the accessibility of simplex-based computer packages capable of solving large problems and the certainty of an integer (0–1) solution are persuasive factors for using the simplex method if more efficient computerized procedures are not available.
4. **Transportation Algorithms.** Since the linear assignment model is a special case of the transportation model, a transportation algorithm can be used as a method of solution. This alternative is more efficient than the simplex method, although severe degeneracy makes for an "unclean" solution. We discuss the problems associated with degeneracy in Section 7.7.

[5] We can guarantee that each x_{ij} will have a solution value of zero or one because of the special structure in Figure 7–1, where each $b_i = 1$.

5. **Assignment Algorithms.** Assignment algorithms have been designed to exploit the special structure of the assignment model. Among the most popular of these algorithms is the **Hungarian method,** an iterative technique that utilizes opportunity costs. We discuss this algorithm in Section 7.9.
6. **Network Models.** As with transportation models, assignment models can be viewed as networks. On a commercial basis, network methods form the current best approach to assignment problems. Using network formulations, enormous problems can be solved with relative ease. We will discuss the network formulation of assignment models in Chapter 10.

FOLLOW-UP EXERCISES

24. For example 7.10, explain why the first four constraints alone are insufficient.
25. ***Referee Assignments.*** The National Collegiate Athletic Association (NCAA) Division I basketball tournament is under way. In preparing for the four regional tournaments the tournament committee has selected four teams of referees judged to be the most qualified for this year's tourney. Each team of officials consists of three regular referees and one alternate, who also travels to the regional tournament in the event that illness, injury, or other circumstances preclude the participation of one of the regular officials. The committee has selected the teams in such a way that each official is from a different athletic conference. (This is to give the appearance of unbiased officiating.)

    Officials are paid a standard tournament fee plus travel expenses. The travel expenses vary depending on the location of the regional tournament assigned. Table 7–13 summarizes the estimated travel expenses for each team according to regional tournament assigned. The committee wants to assign the four teams of officials so as to minimize total travel expenses.

    a. Formulate the LP model for this problem.

TABLE 7–13

	Regional Tournament Assignment			
Team of Officials	**(1) Eastern**	**(2) Midwest**	**(3) Far West**	**(4) Southwest**
1	\$2,600	\$3,200	\$2,750	\$3,050
2	2,400	2,800	3,250	3,400
3	2,950	3,000	3,400	2,950
4	3,600	2,900	3,300	3,000

    b. Use your own approach to identify what you think is the optimal solution.

26. ***Charter Airplane Assignment.*** An airline company has five airplanes available for charter flights this weekend. Seven organizations have requested the use of a plane. Based on an analysis of the expected revenues from each requested charter and of estimated operating expenses, the company has arrived at expected profit figures resulting from the assignment of each of the five planes to each proposed charter. These figures are displayed in Table 7–14.

    If the objective is to assign the five airplanes to five of the charters,

    a. Formulate the objective function and constraints.

    b. Use your own approach to identify what you think is the optimal solution.

TABLE 7–14

	Charter Request						
Airplane	1	2	3	4	5	6	7
1	$2,500	$3,000	$1,000	$2,800	$3,200	$3,500	$2,400
2	1,800	3,500	2,800	4,300	2,700	3,400	3,000
3	2,300	4,000	1,800	4,000	2,800	3,600	3,600
4	3,000	3,600	2,100	2,000	2,500	3,000	3,200
5	2,800	3,800	2,500	2,700	3,000	2,500	3,700

7.5 A TRANSPORTATION ALGORITHM

Up to now our focus has been on the structure, formulation, and computerized solution of transportation models. If you want computational detail for transportation algorithms, then the remainder of this chapter is just what you're looking for.

Transportation Table and the Initial Solution

The transportation algorithms use the general transportation table shown earlier as Table 7–3. Note that there is one row for each origin and one column for each destination. The objective function coefficients are contained in the subcells at the intersection of each row and column. In addition the last column and the last row contain, respectively, the capacities of each origin and the requirements for each destination. These are the right-hand sides for the constraints and are often referred to collectively as **rim requirements.** Finally, values for the decision variables are indicated as entries in the main cells. (For keglers, this tabular format has a "striking" similarity to a bowling scoresheet.)

Remember that if total supply exceeds total demand, we add a column for a *dummy destination,* with a rim requirement equal to the excess supply; if total demand exceeds total supply, then we add a row for a *dummy origin,* with a rim requirement equal to the unfulfilled demand.

Also remember that infeasible or excluded routes require us either to "cross out" the corresponding cells or to assign undesirable objective function coefficients. In cases requiring either lower bounds on decision variables or exact values for decision variables, the table data must be suitably modified, as discussed in Section 7.2. A **feasible solution** contains solution variables called **basic variables** whose values satisfy the structural constraints and nonnegativity conditions. Basic variables are those selected for solution; variables not selected for solution are set to zero and called **nonbasic variables.** The set of basic variables is called a **basis**.

> Given a transportation problem with m origins and n destinations (including any dummy origin or destination) a basic feasible solution has $m + n - 1$ basic variables.

As an example, only seven variables form the basis when $m = n = 4$. Although eight variables would be in the final solution if we solved by the simplex (because we have eight constraints), the eighth is uniquely determined by the first seven. Hence the basis has seven variables.

The **stepping-stone algorithm** first requires an initial solution (obtained by any heuristic method) consisting of $m + n - 1$ basic variables.[6] Then the method employs marginal analysis to evaluate the desirability of a pairwise exchange. If an improved solution is possible, a new variable enters the basis, replacing one of the original basic variables, and the new solution is developed. This procedure is continued until no further improvement is possible.

▶ Example 7.11 Stepping-Stone Algorithm for Yew Haw Trucking Company

Before we begin, we ask that you now develop a commonsense solution to the problem shown in Table 7–15. Engaging your mind in the trade-offs will help you understand the next section. We also remind you that common sense is important in its own right, even though it doesn't always give the "best" answer.

Starting with the initial solution for the trucking example given by the northwest corner algorithm (Example 7.2), the steps of the solution algorithm are as follows:

TABLE 7–15 Closed Path for Cell 1,2

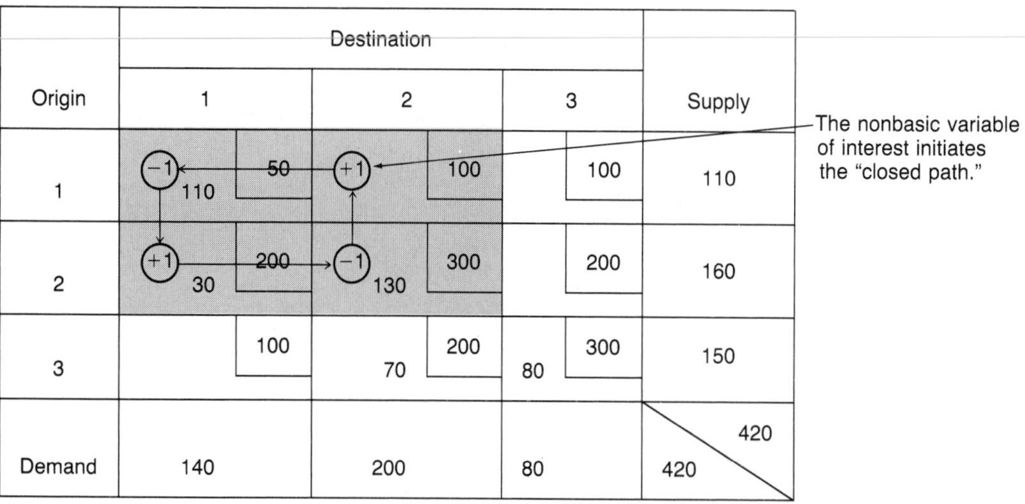

	Destination			
Origin	1	2	3	Supply
1	(−1) 50 / 110	(+1) 100	100	110
2	(+1) 200 / 30	(−1) 300 / 130	200	160
3	100	200 / 70	300 / 80	150
Demand	140	200	80	420 / 420

The nonbasic variable of interest initiates the "closed path."

Step 1: Determine the Improvement Index for Each Nonbasic Variable (Cell). As mentioned previously, the idea is to determine the effects on the existing solution of introducing one unit of a nonbasic variable (i.e., a variable not currently in the basis). As we examine a nonbasic variable, we will focus on two marginal effects associated with the entry of one unit of the variable: (1) What adjustments must be made to the

[6]Degeneracy (basic variables at zero level) presents some special problems, which we examine in Section 7.7.

values of the current basic variables (in order to continue satisfying all supply and demand constraints)? (2) What is the resulting change in the value of the objective function?

To illustrate (see Table 7–15) we focus on cell 1, 2, which by virtue of being empty indicates that no trucks are being shipped from origin 1 to destination 2. The question we want to ask is what trade-offs (or adjustments) with the existing basic variables (i.e., those "in solution") would be required if one truck is delivered from origin 1 to destination 2? If one truck is allocated to cell 1, 2, then 111 trucks would be designated for delivery from origin 1 (and 201 trucks would be designated for delivery to destination 2). Since this exceeds its capacity, an adjustment is necessary *with existing basic variables.* A reduction by one in deliveries from origin 1 to destination 1 to 109 trucks reestablishes balance in the supply constraint for origin 1. The reduction by one truck in cell 1, 1, however, results in an undershipment to destination 1. This can be compensated for by increasing the deliveries in cell 2, 1 to 31. As expected (Will this ever end?), this allocation results in an overshipment from origin 2. Finally, if deliveries in cell 2, 2 are reduced to 129, overall balance is restored (including 200 trucks designated for delivery to destination 2). That is, the *rim requirements* (row and column constraints) are satisfied. The series of required exchanges are indicated in Table 7–15 by the closed path of directed arrows.

Now that the required trade-offs or adjustments have been identified to compensate for the entry of x_{12}, the important question is the resulting effect on the current value of the objective function. For each cell i, j receiving an increased allocation of one unit, costs increase by the corresponding cost coefficient (c_{ij}). Similarly, costs decrease by the value of the cost coefficient wherever allocations have been reduced by one unit. These effects are summarized in Table 7–16. The net effect is that the relocation of one truck from origin 1 to destination 2 would lead to a \$50 reduction in total costs. This marginal change in the objective function (−\$50) is called the *improvement index* for cell 1, 2.

The following statement summarizes the required exchanges from introducing a nonbasic variable.

Calculation of Improvement Index. Trace a "closed path" that begins at the unoccupied cell of interest, moves alternately in horizontal and vertical directions pivoting only on occupied cells, and terminates on the unoccupied cell. A ⊕1 (circled +1) is assigned to the unoccupied cell (indicating an increase of one unit), and succeeding corner points on the path are alternately assigned (circled −1) and (circled +1) values. The pluses and minuses indicate the necessary adjustments for satisfying the row and column (rim) requirements.

Defining c^{+}_{kl} and c^{-}_{kl} as objective function coefficients corresponding to (circled +1) and (circled −1) cells, respectively, the improvement index for cell i, j is calculated as

$$I_{ij} = \sum_{k,l} c^{+}_{kl} - \sum_{k,l} c^{-}_{kl} \qquad (7.8)$$

where k, l are subscript values along the closed path.

TABLE 7–16 Marginal Effects on Value of Objective Function from Introducing One unit in Cell 1, 2

Cell (i, j)	Change in x_{ij} (Δx_{ij})	Change in Total Cost $(c_{ij} \cdot \Delta x_{ij})$
(1, 2)	+1	+100
(1, 1)	−1	− 50
(2, 1)	+1	+200
(2, 2)	−1	−300
Net change		− 50 (Improvement Index, I_{12})

For example, given Table 7–15 we have from Equation 7.8

$$I_{12} = (100 + 200) - (50 + 300)$$
$$= -50$$

which is what we got in Table 7–16.

It is important to understand that if the basis contains $(m + n - 1)$ variables (occupied cells), there is *one* unique path that can be traced that satisfies the rim requirements. The direction taken in tracing the closed path (clockwise or counter-clockwise) makes no difference. The procedure is a bit more tricky than merely jumping from the cell of interest to any occupied cell in the same row or column. It's necessary to go to *the* occupied cell which allows us to trace a closed path and not lead to a dead end. For example, if in starting with cell 1, 2 we next decided to jump to cell 3, 2 and thereafter to cell 3, 3, we would be "stuck." If you find yourself in this predicament and don't see any easy way out, then return to the nonbasic cell of interest and go another way.

As a demonstration of one more path, Table 7–17 indicates the closed path and corresponding adjustments to basic variables for cell 1, 3. You should verify that the improvement index for cell 1, 3 is −150.

The paths for each unoccupied cell in this initial solution and their associated improvement indices are summarized in Table 7–18 (check these out to test your understanding).

Step 2: If a Better Solution Exists, Determine Which Variable (Cell) Should Enter the Basis. An examination of the improvement indices in Table 7–18 indicates that the introduction of three of the four nonbasic variables would lead to a reduction in total delivery costs.

> For minimization problems, a better solution exists if there are any negative improvement indices. An optimal solution has been found when *all* improvement indices are nonnegative. Once the optimal solution has been found, the existence of one or more improvement indices at zero level indicates alternative optimal solutions.

As in the simplex method, we select the variable (cell) that leads to the greatest marginal improvement in the objective function.[7] In our example, cell 2, 3, or x_{23}, is selected as the *entering variable.*

TABLE 7–17 Closed Path for Cell 1, 3

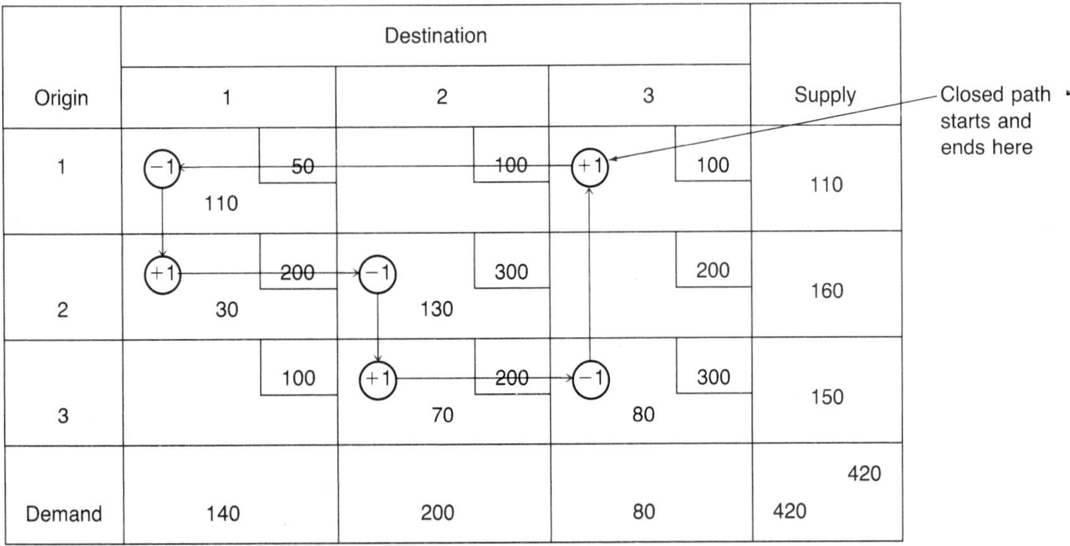

TABLE 7–18 Improvement Indices for Initial Solution to Yew Haw

Nonbasic Cell i,j	Closed Path	Improvement Index I_{ij}
1, 2	1, 2 → 1, 1 → 2, 1 → 2, 2 → 1, 2	− 50
1, 3	1, 3 → 1, 1 → 2, 1 → 2, 2 → 3, 2 → 3, 3 → 1, 3	−150
2, 3	2, 3 → 2, 2 → 3, 2 → 3, 3 → 2, 3	−200*
3, 1	3, 1 → 3, 2 → 2, 2 → 2, 1 → 3, 1	0

Step 3: Determine the Departing Variable and the Number of Units to Assign the Entering Variable. This step is performed by returning to the closed path associated with the incoming cell. Figure 7–2 is a section of the starting table showing the closed path for cell 2, 3. Since each unit assigned to x_{23} decreases total cost by \$200 (according to the improvement index), we would like to allocate as many deliveries as possible from origin 2 to destination 3. For every unit introduced in cell 2, 3, the quantities contained in cells 2, 2 and 3, 3 decrease by one unit. We simply introduce exactly enough units to drive *one* of the existing cells (basic variables) to zero. This preserves the $m + n - 1$ allocations without allowing other cells to become negative (which preserves feasibility). The only candidate cells that can be driven to zero are those cells in a *minus* position along the path. They are the cells that must be reduced to compensate for allocations to the new basic variable. The variable that leaves the basis is always the one having the smallest quantity among those in minus positions. Since the trade-off is one for one, its value also indicates the maximum amount assigned to the entering variable. In our example that value of 80 associated with cell 3, 3 is the

[7]As in the simplex method, *any* nonbasic variable that offers an improvement in z can be selected for entry.

smallest in a minus position on the path; hence, x_{23} is assigned 80 units and x_{33} (the *departing variable*) is assigned a value of zero. (What would happen to the values of the basic variables if 81 units were introduced?)

FIGURE 7–2 Closed Path for Cell 2, 3

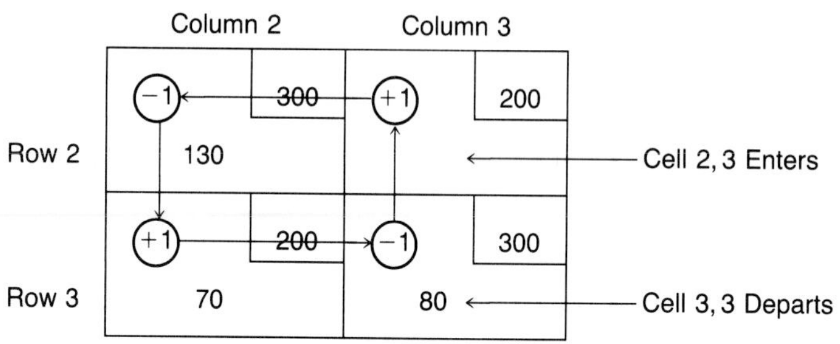

To summarize:

The departing variable is identified by the smallest cell in a minus position on the closed path for the entering variable.[8] The entering variable is assigned the number of units previously given the departing variable. Thus

$$x_d = \min_{k,l} x_{kl}^{-} \tag{7.9}$$

$$x_e = x_d \tag{7.10}$$

where x_d is the previous value of the departing variable, x_{kl}^{-} is the value of a variable along the closed path in a negative position, and x_e is the value of the entering variable.

For example, given Figure 7–2, we have from Equations 7.9 and 7.10

$$x_d = \text{Min}(x_{22}^{-}, x_{33}^{-})$$

$$= \text{Min}(130, 80)$$

$$x_d = 80$$

$$x_e = 80 \quad (\text{or entering } x_{23} = 80).$$

Step 4: Develop the New Solution, and Return to Step 1. Again referring to the closed path for the incoming variable, add the quantity determined in step 3 to all cells in a plus position and subtract it from those in a minus position. Thus, given the entering variable $x_{23} = 80$ from step 3, we have according to Figure 7–2:

$$x_{23} = 80 \quad (\text{enters})$$

$$x_{22} = 130 - 80$$

[8]It is possible to have more than one variable leave the basis. If so, degeneracy results—a condition we treat later in the chapter.

$$= 50$$

$$x_{32} = 70 + 80$$

$$= 150$$

$$x_{33} = 80 - 80$$

$$= 0 \quad \text{(departs)}.$$

Since variables off the closed path are unaffected, we need only update the previous table according to the changes along the closed path corresponding to the entering variable. Table 7–19 presents the new solution. Rather than multiplying the new values of all basic variables times their corresponding unit costs to compute the new value of the objective function, we can subtract from the previous value of the objective function the total reduction in costs from entering the new variable. Since each unit introduced to cell 2, 3 reduces total cost by $200 according to $I_{23} = -200$, and we have assigned 80 units to entering cell 2, 3, the new value of z is

$$z = \$88{,}500 + (\$-200)(80)$$

$$= \$88{,}500 - \$16{,}000$$

$$= \$72{,}500.$$

To summarize once again:

x_{ij} values off the closed path are unaffected.
x_{kl} values along the closed path are updated as follows:

$$\text{New } x_{kl}^{+} = \text{Old } x_{kl}^{+} + x_e \tag{7.11}$$

$$\text{New } x_{kl}^{-} = \text{Old } x_{kl}^{-} - x_e. \tag{7.12}$$

The value of the objective function is updated as follows:

$$\text{New } z = \text{Old } z + I_{ij} \cdot x_e \tag{7.13}$$

where I_{ij} is the improvement index associated with the entered variable.

The solution to this problem is completed in Tables 7–19 through 7–21. Closed paths and improvement indices for unoccupied cells are summarized for your convenience.

Since all of the improvement indices are greater than or equal to zero, the solution presented in Table 7–21 is optimal. It indicates that the redistribution of trucks can be achieved at a minimum total cost if 110 trucks are delivered from the city represented by origin 1 to the city represented by destination 2, 80 each from origin 2 to destinations 1 and 3, 60 from origin 3 to destination 1, and 90 from origin 3 to destination 2. The total (optimal) cost for the redistribution is $67,000. Note that we have an alternative optimal solution, which we ask you to generate in Exercise 27.

By the way, you can't strictly rely on intuition where the situation calls for analytic procedures. Looking at Table 7–21, one would think that the best solution would surely utilize the lowest cost cell (1, 1). Right?

Figure 7–3 summarizes the steps of the transportation algorithm.

TABLE 7–19 Second Iteration for Trucking Example

Origin	Destination 1	Destination 2	Destination 3	Supply
1	110 [50]	[100]	[100]	110
2	30 [200]	50 [300]	80 [200]	160
3	[100]	150 [200]	[300]	150
Demand	140	200	80	420 / 420

$z = \$72{,}500$

Cell	Closed Path	I_{ij}
1, 2	1, 2 → 1, 1 → 2, 1 → 2, 2 → 1, 2	−50*
1, 3	1, 3 → 1, 1 → 2, 1 → 2, 3 → 1, 3	+50
3, 1	3, 1 → 3, 2 → 2, 2 → 2, 1 → 3, 1	0
3, 3	3, 3 → 2, 3 → 2, 2 → 3, 2 → 3, 3	+200

At the next iteration:
Cell 1, 2 Enters the basis.
Cell 2, 2 Departs the basis.

FOLLOW-UP EXERCISES

27. Find the alternative optimal solution for Yew Haw. To do so, treat cell 2, 2 as an entering variable and repeat steps 3, 4, and 1. How many all-integer alternative optimal solutions are there? On what basis might management select *the* one solution to implement?
28. Solve Example 7.4 by the stepping-stone algorithm using the data in Table 7–7. Does the surplus of trucks result in any improvement over the solution found in Example 7.11?
29. Solve the chemical distribution problem in Exercise 1 using the stepping-stone algorithm.
30. ***Excluded Routes.*** Solve Example 7.5 using the stepping-stone algorithm. Assign a cost of M dollars to the excluded route (3, 2) where $M \gg c_{ij}$, for any i and j.
31. ***Lower Bounds.*** Solve Example 7.6 using the stepping-stone algorithm. Is there any cost attached to management's policy that at least 75 trucks must be relocated from origin 1 to destination 1? (*Hint:* Compare this solution with that of Example 7.11.)

TABLE 7–20 Third Iteration for Trucking Example

Origin	Destination 1	Destination 2	Destination 3	Supply
1	[50] 60	[100] 50	[100]	110
2	[200] 80	[300]	[200] 80	160
3	[100]	[200] 150	[300]	150
Demand	140	200	80	420 / 420

$z = \$70{,}000$

Cell	Closed Path	I_{ij}
1, 3	1, 3 → 1, 1 → 2, 1 → 2, 3 → 1, 3	+50
2, 2	2, 2 → 1, 2 → 1, 1 → 2, 1 → 2, 2	+50
3, 1	3, 1 → 3, 2 → 1, 2 → 1, 1 → 3, 1	−50*
3, 3	3, 3 → 2, 3 → 2, 1 → 1, 1 → 1, 2 → 3, 2 → 3, 3	+150

At the next iteration:
Cell 3, 1 Enters the basis.
Cell 1, 1 Departs the basis.

32. ***Public Works.*** Solve the problem discussed in Example 7.7 using the stepping-stone algorithm.
33. ***Production Scheduling and Inventory Control.*** Solve Exercise 21 using the stepping-stone algorithm.
34. ***Vogel's Approximation Method.*** Another algorithm for developing an initial solution is Vogel's Approximation Method (VAM). Using an opportunity cost criterion, the procedure begins by finding the two lowest cost cells for each row and column. Subtracting the smaller of these costs from the other produces a Vogel number for each row and column. We select the *largest* Vogel number and make the first assignment to the corresponding *lowest* cost cell; as before, we assign the maximum amount for the corresponding decision variable, as limited by row and column constraints. Ties can be broken arbitrarily. After each assignment, the Vogel numbers are recomputed based on the remaining rows and columns. The procedure is repeated until all assignments have been made. Apply VAM to the Yew Haw problem, and compare your result with those obtained in Example 7.11. (Remember that a sample of one is not statistically significant!)

TABLE 7–21 Fourth (and Final) Iteration for Trucking Example

Origin	Destination 1	Destination 2	Destination 3	Supply
1	[50]	[100] 110	[100]	110
2	[200] 80	[300]	[200] 80	160
3	[100] 60	[200] 90	[300]	150
Demand	140	200	80	420 / 420

z = $67,000 (optimum)

Cell	Closed Path	I_{ij}
1, 1	1, 1 → 3, 1 → 3, 2 → 1, 2 → 1, 1	+50
1, 3	1, 3 → 1, 2 → 3, 2 → 3, 1 → 2, 1 → 2, 3 → 1, 3	+100
2, 2	2, 2 → 2, 1 → 3, 1 → 3, 2 → 2, 2	0
3, 3	3, 3 → 2, 3 → 2, 1 → 3, 1 → 3, 3	+200

Since all $I_{ij} \geq 0$, this solution is optimal. $I_{22} = 0$ indicates an alternative optimal solution.

**Relations to Simplex Algorithm

By now the similarities between the stepping-stone method and the simplex method must be apparent. There is indeed a one-for-one correspondence between the steps of these solution procedures. In addition, you should recognize the relative efficiencies offered by the transportation method. In the simplex method successive solutions are generated by computationally burdensome row (matrix) operations, which include addition, subtraction, multiplication, and division. Additionally, the simplex procedure further taxes us (and computers) by augmenting the variable set with slack, surplus, and artificial variables. By contrast, the transportation method strictly utilizes the more efficient operations of addition and subtraction (except for the trivial multiplication in evaluating z) and works exclusively with the original set of decision variables (except, perhaps, for the addition of a dummy variable).

Furthermore, given integer s_i and d_j, the resulting x_{ij} *must necessarily be integers,* since only additions and subtractions are required. This feature, coupled with the

FIGURE 7–3 Flow Diagram for Transportation Algorithm *(Minimization case)*

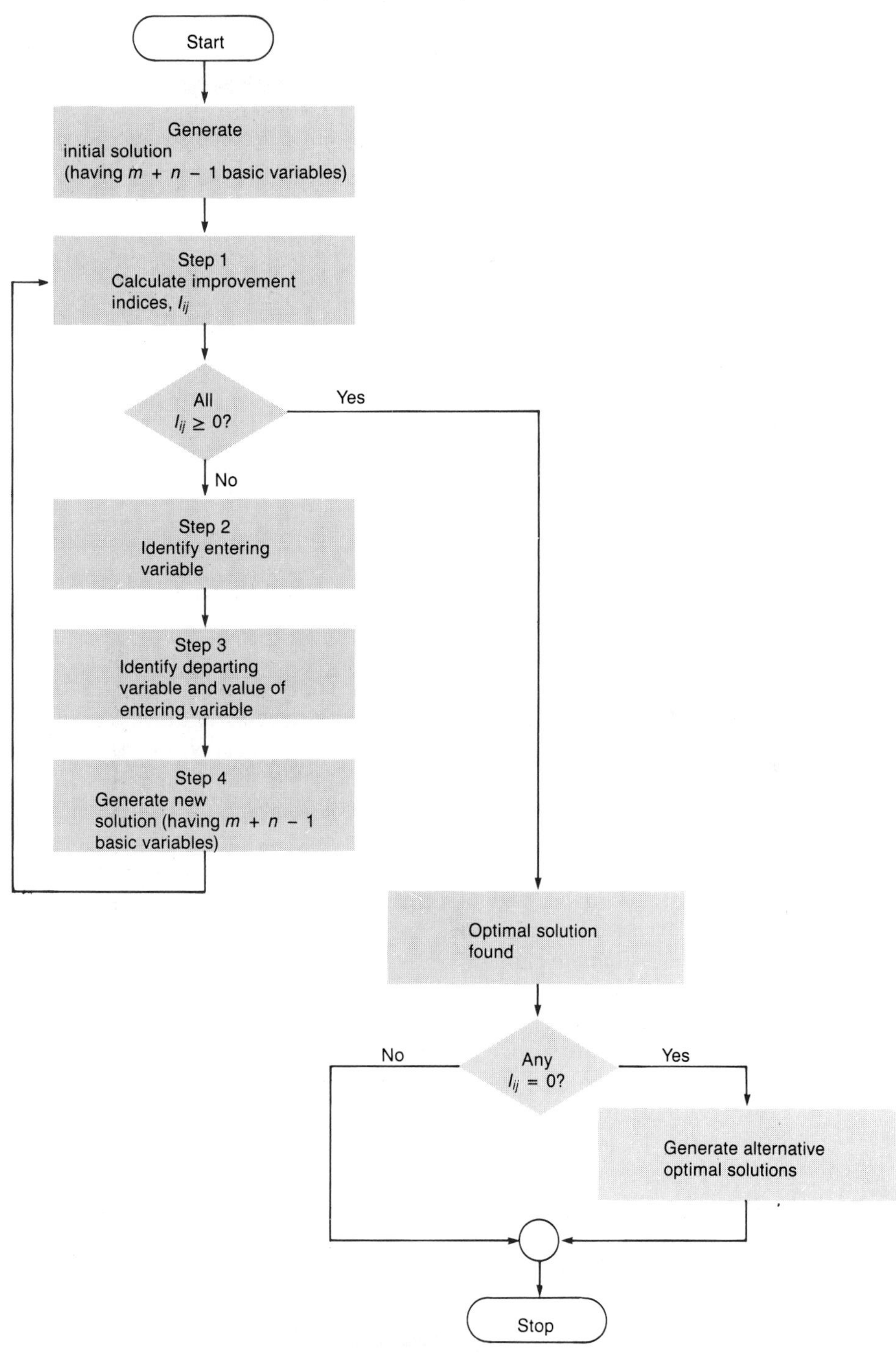

speed of the transportation method, allows the solution of some large-scale integer programming (Chapter 8) problems in the real world which otherwise would be computationally infeasible.

7.6 ALTERNATIVE TRANSPORTATION ALGORITHM

In this section we illustrate how the simplex-based stepping-stone algorithm is made more efficient by utilizing concepts from the dual of the transportation model.

The Dual Transportation Model[9]

The dual problem of the primal transportation model possesses properties that improve the efficiency of solving these types of problems. We can show easily from Table 5–1 that the dual problem for the transportation model given by Equation 7.1 is

Maximize

$$z_d = \sum_{i=1}^{m} s_i u_i + \sum_{j=1}^{n} d_j v_j \tag{7.14}$$

subject to

$$u_i + v_j \leq c_{ij} \quad \text{for all } i, j \tag{7.15}$$

$$u_i, v_j \quad \text{unrestricted.}$$

The variable u_i is the dual variable corresponding to the ith supply constraint in the primal, and v_j is the dual variable corresponding to the jth demand constraint.

Section 5.7 demonstrated that for each equality constraint in a primal problem there exists a corresponding dual variable that is unrestricted. Consequently, the m supply constraints and n demand constraints in the transportation model lead to the unrestricted variables u_i and v_j, respectively, in the dual problem. (Note that we have defined the two classes of dual variables to conveniently distinguish between the supply constraints and the demand constraints of the primal problem.)

Given the definitions of these dual variables, the function in Equation 7.14 should be clear from properties 5 and 9 in Table 5–1; the inequality in Equation 7.15 follows from properties 1, 2, 10, and 11 in Table 5–1. The left-hand–side of Equation 7.15 should be clear if you take a brief look at the special structure in Figure 7–1. The primal has two ones and the rest zeros in each column of structural coefficients; therefore, the dual has only two ones and the rest zeros in each row of structural coefficients. Moreover, the two ones in the primal column for variable x_{ij} are precisely located in supply constraint (i) and demand constraint (j); thus only $u_i + v_j$ appear in the corresponding dual row, with c_{ij} as the right-hand side!

Now here's the interesting part. According to Table 5–2, primal x_{ij} corresponds to the dual slack variable implicit in constraint 7.15. If an allocation is made between origin i and destination j (i.e., primal x_{ij} is a basic variable and $x_{ij} > 0$), then the

[9] You might find it useful to review Section 5.7 before proceeding.

slack in dual constraint (i, j) must be a nonbasic variable equal to zero, according to property $5b$ on page 220. If the slack is zero in constraint 7.15, then 7.15 can be restated as 7.16 whenever the corresponding $x_{ij} > 0$ giving

$$u_i + v_j = c_{ij} . \tag{7.16}$$

In words, when any allocation is made between origin i and destination j ($x_{ij} > 0$), the sum of the dual variables associated with the constraints for the particular origin and destination (u_i and v_j) will equal the objective function contribution c_{ij}. If an allocation is not made ($x_{ij} = 0$), then the sum of the dual variables is less than c_{ij}. This relationship is valid for basic variables in any nondegenerate, complementary basic solution, whether optimal or not.[10]

▶ Example 7.12 Dual Complementary Basic Solution

Given the primal, intermediate solution in Table 7–22, we would like to determine the corresponding values of the dual variables. The following equations reflect the property given by Equation 7.16 for the four basic variables:

TABLE 7–22 Sample Nonoptimal Primal Solution

Origin	Destination 1	Destination 2	Destination 3	Supply
1	cost 5; 60	cost 10; 30	cost 15	90
2	cost 1	cost 20; 70	cost 30; 80	150
Demand	60	100	80	240 / 240

Basic Variable	Corresponding Dual Constraint
x_{11}	$u_1 + v_1 = 5$
x_{12}	$u_1 + v_2 = 10$
x_{22}	$u_2 \quad v_2 = 20$
x_{23}	$u_2 + v_3 = 30$

[10] We treat degeneracy in the next section.

Note that this system involves four equations and five unknown variables. The reason for fewer equations than dual variables is the one redundant constraint that is characteristic of transportation problems.

To solve for values of the dual variables, we *arbitrarily* assign a value of zero to one of them. Indirectly this declares one of the primal constraints as redundant and allows us to solve for the dual variables associated with the remaining $m + n - 1$ constraints. Letting $u_1 = 0$, verify that the dual variables have the following values: $v_1 = 5$; $v_2 = 10$; $u_2 = 10$; and $v_3 = 20$.

FOLLOW-UP EXERCISES

35. In Example 7.12,
    a. Show that the dual objective function gives the same value as the primal objective function. Is there a primal-dual property from Chapter 5 that verifies this?
    b. Recompute the dual solution by setting $v_1 = 0$. Show that the value of the dual objective function is unchanged from that in part *a*. Pretty amazing?
    c. The dual problem has six constraints. Why? Write down the remaining two dual constraints. Are these satisfied by the dual solution in the example? Can you explain this result by citing a primal-dual property from Chapter 5?
36. Write the dual of the Yew Haw primal in Example 7.1, and verify that it has the form of Equations 7.14 and 7.15.

MODI Algorithm

Primal-dual properties provide the foundation for a much more efficient method of computing improvement indices. The method, referred to as the **Modified Distribution (MODI) algorithm,** eliminates the need to trace closed paths for *each* nonbasic variable as in the stepping-stone method.

The MODI algorithm is nothing more than the stepping-stone algorithm with a "souped-up" technique for computing improvement indices. This method provides a tabular approach to determining the values of the dual variables associated with any solution to a transportation problem. Once the values of the dual variables have been identified, the improvement index for any nonbasic variable can be computed using the equation

$$I_{ij} = c_{ij} - u_i - v_j. \tag{7.17}$$

How do we get 7.17? If x_{ij} is a *nonbasic* variable ($x_{ij} = 0$), its corresponding dual slack variable is a basic variable and (unequal to zero) in the dual complementary basic solution according to Property 5*b* on page 000. Thus the dual slack variable implicit in constraint 7.15 has a value other than zero whenever $x_{ij} = 0$. If we use the symbol I_{ij} for this dual slack variable, add it to the left-hand side of 7.15, and solve for I_{ij}, then we get 7.17.

It turns out that in the magical world of duality *the value of the dual slack variable is the marginal effect on the value of the primal objective function from introducing an additional unit of nonbasic* x_{ij}. This is precisely the definition of the improvement index, I_{ij}. Thus *the values of the dual slack variable and the improvement index are one and the same!*[11]

The bottom line of all this theorizing is that at any iteration of the primal problem, we can avoid the messy procedure of finding closed paths for all nonbasic variables. We simply calculate each I_{ij} from 7.17 after solving for the dual variables u_i and v_j. The next example illustrates a simple procedure for calculating the values of dual variables and improvement indices.

▶ Example 7.13 MODI Iteration

To illustrate, we modify Table 7–22 by including a column for u_i values and a row for v_j values as in Table 7–23. Rather than writing and solving the system of equations as was done in Example 7.12, we assign an arbitrary value to any u_i or v_j and place it in the appropriate row or column. As we did in Example 7.12, let $u_1 = 0$ and place this value in the first row of the u_i column. Now for each *basic cell* (i,j) $u_i + v_j$ must equal c_{ij}, according to Equation 7.16. Using the arbitrary value for u_1, we can proceed sequentially through each *basic* cell by identifying at each step the value for another dual variable (u_i or v_j). For instance, from Equation 7.16

$$c_{12} = u_1 + v_2$$

or

$$v_2 = 10 - 0.$$

TABLE 7–23 MODI Transportation Table

	Destination				
Origin	1	2	3	Supply	u_i
1	[5] 60	[10] 30	[15]	90	0
2	[1]	[20] 70	[30] 80	150	10
Demand	60	100	80	240 \ 240	
v_j	5	10	20		

[11] Example 6.14 illustrates this result.

This gives an entry of 10 in the second column of the v_j row. Can you verify the remaining assignments in Table 7–23?

Having found the values for all u_i and v_j, we use Equation 7.17 to determine the improvement index for each nonbasic cell.

Cell	I_{ij}
1, 3	$15 - 0 - 20 = -5$
2, 1	$1 - 10 - 5 = -14$*

For this solution, improvement (assuming a minimization objective) is possible and x_{21} would enter the solution.

Once a cell is designated for entrance, its closed path must be identified to determine the necessary exchanges with the current basic variables and the amount ot enter of the incoming variable, just as in the stepping-stone method.

To summarize, the steps of the MODI method for *computing improvement indices* are:

1. Arbitrarily assign a value to any u_i or v_j and place it in the appropriate row or column.
2. Using this initial value, complete the assignment of u_i and v_j values using Equation 7.16.
3. Compute the improvement index for each nonbasic cell using Equation 7.17.

Note that these steps must be repeated at *each iteration* of the solution algorithm.

FOLLOW-UP EXERCISES

37. Using the MODI method, recompute the improvement indices associated with the initial solution in Yew Haw given in Table 7–15. Did you get the same results as Table 7–18?
38. Verify that the initial u_i/v_j assignment is truly aribitrary. For example, be daring and assign a negative value to any one of the u_i or v_j values in Example 7.13. Compute the remaining values and then recompute the improvement indices. Are they the same?
39. Starting with a northwest corner initial solution and using the MODI algorithm, solve the following problem. What happens if you start with a greedy initial solution?

Minimize

$$z = 20x_{11} + 15x_{12} + 5x_{21} + 10x_{22} + 20x_{31} + 5x_{32}$$

subject to

$$\begin{aligned}
x_{11} + x_{12} \qquad\qquad\qquad\qquad\qquad\qquad &= 75\\
x_{21} + x_{22} \qquad\qquad\qquad &= 125\\
+ \; x_{31} + x_{32} &= 100\\
x_{11} \quad + x_{21} \quad + x_{31} \qquad &= 150\\
x_{12} \quad + x_{22} \quad + x_{32} &= 150\\
x_{ij} &\geq 0.
\end{aligned}$$

7.7 SPECIAL CONSIDERATIONS IN SOLVING TRANSPORTATION PROBLEMS

In this section we consider some special cases in solving transportation problems.

Maximization

As with the simplex method, the only difference between solving minimization and maximization problems is in the interpretation of the improvement indices. Improvement in a maximization problem is indicated by the existence of any positive indices in the stepping-stone of MODI algorithms. For initial solutions, the greedy algorithm favors high coefficients, the northwest corner algorithm is unaffected, and VAM (Exercise 34) is based on the highest and next highest values, again using highest resultant Vogle numbers. Otherwise the procedures are exactly the same.

FOLLOW-UP EXERCISES

40. Find the optimal allocation of trucks for Yew Haw if the contributions in Table 7–1 represent profits.
41. ***Multiperiod Investment Model.*** Solve the investment problem discussed in Example 7.8. State the optimal solution in words that would be understood by a nontechnical person.

Degeneracy

With the simplex method, the unlikely possibility of cycling was the main concern of degeneragy. In the transportation model, degeneracy is of much greater importance because a degenerate solution produces an inability to compute improvement indices for all nonbasic variables (cells).

Degeneracy occurs when the basis contains less than $(m + n - 1)$ basic variables. This condition can arise either in developing the initial solution or at some intermediate solution. *If in the initial solution an allocation results in the simultaneous exhaustion of the capacity for an origin and the fulfillment of the remaining demand at a destination, we end up with fewer than* m + n − 1 *basic variables*. Table 7–24 portrays a situation where the initial assignment exhausts the capacity of origin 1 and satisfies the demand at destination 1. The resulting solution has only three basic variables.

TABLE 7–24 Degeneracy in Initial Solution

Origin	Destination 1	Destination 2	Destination 3	Supply
1	(5) 75	(10) ϵ	(8)	75
2	(4)	(15) 60	(12) 65	125
Demand	75	60	65	200 / 200

Add epsilon to any unoccupied cell in the exhausted row or column.

Allocation in cell 1, 1 simultaneously exhausts s_1 and d_1.

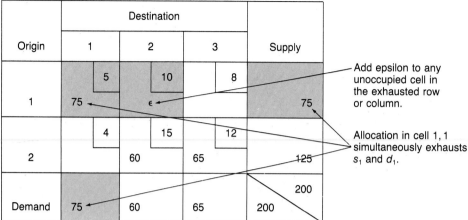

To resolve this problem we can adjust the degenerate solution by adding an artificial allocation, ϵ, to one of the unoccupied cells. ϵ is assumed to be an infinitesimally small quantity that would never actually be allocated. Its presence, though, allows for $(m + n - 1)$ basic variables and the ability to continue with the solution process. The *placement* of ϵ cannot be in just *any* unoccupied cell; it has to be placed in either the column or the row associated with the cell which simultaneously fulfilled the supply and demand constraint. The cell with epsilon is considered an occupied cell and is modified in the same manner as other occupied cells. In some instances ϵ may drop out in later solutions; in others it may be a part of the final basis.

Degeneracy occurs in an intermediate solution when the values of more than one basic variable go to zero with the entrance of a new variable. This occurs, as in the simplex method, whenever there is a tie for the departing variable (Step 3 of the stepping-stone algorithm). For example, assume that in the partial table below the unoccupied cell has been selected for entrance. Introducing 80 units will result in two of the three basic variables going to zero. If degeneracy occurs at any intermediate solution, then introduce ϵ to one of the two cells that dropped out of the basis and continue as before.[12]

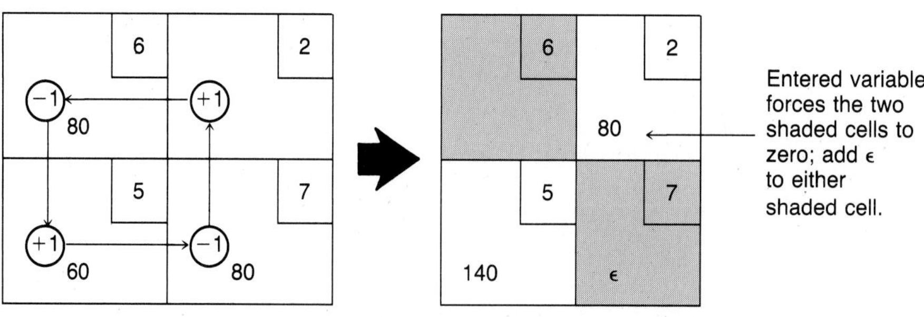

[12]If more than two cells drop out of the basis (say, k), then occupy $k - 1$ cells with epsilons.

FOLLOW-UP EXERCISES

42. Solve the transportation problem given below starting with the northwest corner algorithm.

Origin	Destination 1	Destination 2	Supply
1	[5]	[4]	25
2	[2]	[7]	45
3	[3]	[6]	30
Demand	75	25	100 \ 100

43. Given the following initial solution, continue on to determine the optimal solution.

Origin	Destination 1	Destination 2	Destination 3	Supply
1	[20] 150	[10] 50	[25]	200
2	[20]	[30] 150	[5] 175	325
3	[10]	[30]	[10] 300	300
Demand	150	200	475	825 \ 825

44. In the preceding exercise, confirm that the placement of ϵ-cells cannot be arbitrary. When introducing cell 3, 1 into the basis, place an ϵ in cell 2, 1, rather than in cell 1, 1 or 2, 2. What is the result?

45. Solve the problem in Exercise 43 if the demand at destination 3 is 325 rather than 475 and the supply at origin 3 is 150 rather than 300. Use the northwest corner algorithm to develop your initial solution.

7.8 SENSITIVITY ANALYSIS

The motivation for sensitivity analysis was well-established in Chapter 5. This section illustrates sensitivity analysis (in the framework of the transportation algorithm) on objective function coefficients for nonbasic and basic variables, supplies, and demands.

Objective Function Coefficients (Nonbasic Variables)

As you know, the optimal solution (for a minimization problem) has been found when $I_{ij} \geq 0$ for all nonbasic variables (cells). In this case we are interested in determining the amount by which the coefficient c_{ij} for a nonbasic variable can change and the current solution remain optimal. We accomplish this easily by using Equation 7.17 on the *final* tableau, as illustrated next.

▶ Example 7.14

The final computational tableau (MODI method) for the Yew Haw problem is given by Table 7–25. Can you verify the u_i and v_j using Equation 7.16? To conduct a sensitivity analysis for nonbasic cell 1, 1, let us define $c_{11} = 50 + \Delta_{11}$. The current solution remains optimal as long as all I_{ij} are greater than zero. As we conduct sensitivity analysis for a nonbasic variable, we would first like to know which I_{ij} values will be affected if a nonbasic c_{ij} is changed. In our example, which I_{ij} values will be affected by defining $c_{11} = 50 + \Delta_{11}$? To answer this question you may (*a*) think back to the method of tracing closed paths or (*b*) recall the MODI procedure. Both of these procedures ultimately yield I_{ij} values. See if you can verify the following:

> For sensitivity analysis on a nonbasic variable objective function coefficient c_{ij}, the only improvement index affected by changes in c_{ij} is that for the nonbasic variable being examined.

Test this by defining $c_{11} = 50 + \Delta_{11}$ in Table 7–25, and recompute all improvement indices either by tracing closed paths or by using the MODI method. If you trace closed paths, you should discover that the *only* path passing through cell 1, 1 (and thus incorporating c_{11} in the computation of an improvement index) is the path used to compute I_{11}. If you use the MODI method, you will find that the only I_{ij}

TABLE 7–25 Final MODI Tableau for Yew Haw

Origin	Destination 1	Destination 2	Destination 3	Supply	u_i
1	50	100 110	100	110	0
2	200 80	300	200 80	160	200
3	100 60	200 90	300	150	100
Demand	140	200	80	420 \ 420	
v_j	0	100	0		

stated as a function of Δ_{11} is I_{11}. Thus the current solution remains optimal as long as $I_{1i} > 0$, or by using Equation 7.17 as long as

$$c_{11} - u_1 - v_1 > 0$$

or

$$50 + \Delta_{11} - 0 - 0 > 0$$

or

$$\Delta_{11} > -50 .$$

Conversion from permissible Δ ranges to permissible ranges for the corresponding parameter is sometimes slippery, as illustrated in Section 6.7. Figure 7–4 illustrates an aid in interpreting these results. Parallel axes portray permissible values for Δ_{11} and corresponding values of c_{11}. The current solution remains optimal as long as $c_{11} > 0$. We might say that the current solution is *relatively* insensitive to changes in c_{11}.

For cell 2, 2 we define $c_{22} = 300 + \Delta_{22}$. The current solution will remain optimal, given changes in c_{22}, as long as

$$I_{22} > 0$$

or

$$300 + \Delta_{22} - 200 - 100 > 0$$

FIGURE 7–4 Allowable Changes in c_{11} Such that Current Solution Remains Optimal

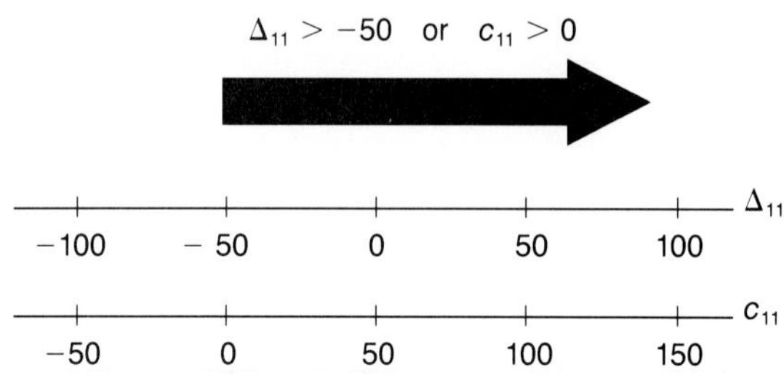

or

$$\Delta_{22} > 0 .$$

Referring to Figure 7–5, we conclude that the current solution remains optimal as long as $c_{22} > 300$. Since $c_{22} = 300$ for this problem, it follows that alternative optimal solutions exists. Thus the current solution is insensitive to increases in c_{22} but extremely sensitive to any decreases.

FOLLOW-UP EXERCISES

46. Verify that $c_{13} > 0$ and $c_{33} > 100$ for the current solution in this example to remain optimal. What happens if $c_{33} = 100$?

47. Given the following optimal solution to a minimization problem, perform a sensitivity analysis on the objective function coefficients of nonbasic variables.

	Destination				
Origin	1	2	3	4	Supply
1	35 (1.0)	5 (7.5)	(8.5)	(11.0)	40
2	(7.5)	15 (4.5)	(3.0)	35 (7.5)	50
3	(10.0)	(6.5)	25 (1.0)	10 (6.0)	35
Demand	35	20	25	45	125 / 125

FIGURE 7–5 Allowable Changes in c_{22}

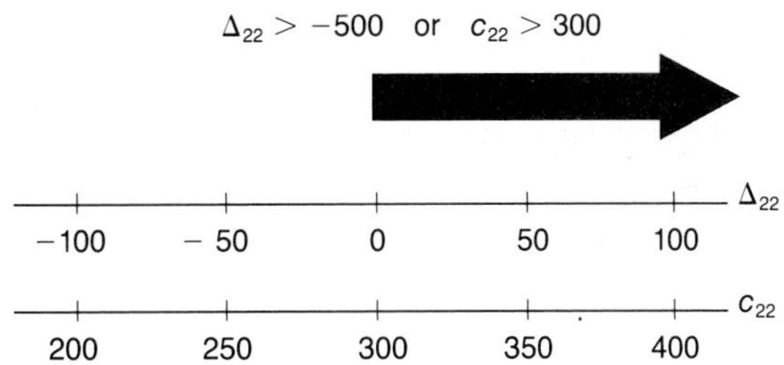

48. Given the following optimal solution to a *maximization* problem, perform a sensitivity analysis on the objective function coefficients of nonbasic variables, excluding the nonbasic dummy cells (be careful!).

Origin	Destination 1	Destination 2	Destination 3	Dummy	Supply
1	[12] 30	[13]	[11] 70	[0]	100
2	[13] 30	[17] 120	[8]	[0]	150
3	[5]	[6]	[4]	[0] 40	40
4	[8] 20	[12]	[3]	[0] 10	30
Demand	80	120	70	50	320 / 320

Objective Function Coefficients (Basic Variables)

When we conduct sensitivity analysis for basic variables, we want to know (as with nonbasic variable analysis) which I_{ij} values will be affected if c_{ij} changes.

For sensitivity analysis on a basic variable objective function coefficient, the number of improvement indices affected by changes in c_{ij} varies. As few as one and as many as all improvement indices may be affected.

This generalization suggests that the basic variable being considered may have to be adjusted in value when considering the effects of entry of anywhere from one to all of the nonbasic variables. In a path tracing context, the basic variable cell being examined may appear on as few as one or as many as all of the closed paths for the set of nonbasic variables.

Again utilizing Equation 7.17, we can easily conduct sensitivity analysis on the objective function coefficients for basic variables. Let us illustrate in the following example.

▶ Example 7.15

Given the final tableau (Table 7–25) for Yew Haw, examine the range over which the \$200 delivery cost for basic route 2, 1 can vary and still allow the existing basis to remain optimal. Defining $c_{21} = 200 + \Delta_{21}$, we substitute the new coefficient into the final tableau, as illustrated in Table 7–26. This new value for c_{21} causes some adjustments in certain u_i and v_j values. Since $I_{ij} = c_{ij} - u_i - v_j = 0$ for all basic variables, either u_2 or v_1 must be *increased* by Δ_{21} in order for I_{21} to remain equal to zero. Increasing v_1 to $0 + \Delta_{21}$, or Δ_{21} requires a readjustment of other u_i and v_j values.[13] Applying Equation 7.17 to the remaining basic variables results in the changes that appear in Table 7–26. To determine the impact of the change in c_{21} on the nonbasic variables, their improvement indices are recomputed using the new u_i, v_j values. The new indices are computed below. The fact that three of the four improvement indices are stated as a function of Δ_{21} implies that the closed paths traced for the corresponding nonbasic cells pass through cell 2, 1. The path for cell 1, 1 does not pass through cell 2, 1, implying that entry of x_{11} requires no adjustment in the value of x_{21}. Verify that the current basis will remain optimal as long as $-100 < \Delta_{21} < 0$, or $100 < c_{21} < 200$.

FOLLOW-UP EXERCISES

49. Complete the sensitivity analysis on the objective function coefficients for the other basic variables in Yew Haw.
50. Perform a sensitivity analysis on the objective function coefficients of basic variables in Exercise 47.
51. Perform a sensitivity analysis on the objective function coefficients of basic variables in Exercise 48.

Supplies and Demands (RHS Constants)

As demonstrated in Chapter 5, the dual variable associated with the ith constraint is a shadow price; that is, u_i is the relative implicit contribution of one additional unit

[13] We could just as well have selected to increase u_2 to $200 + \Delta_{21}$. It doesn't matter. Try it.

TABLE 7–26 Modified Final MODI Tableau for Yew Haw

Origin	Destination 1	Destination 2	Destination 3	Supply	u_i
1	[50]	110 [100]	[100]	110	$0 - (\Delta_{21})$
2	80 [$200 + \Delta_{21}$]	[300]	80 [200]	160	200
3	60 [100]	90 [200]	[300]	150	$100 - (\Delta_{21})$
Demand	140	200	80	420 / 420	
v_j	$0 + (\Delta_{21})$	$100 + (\Delta_{21})$	0		

Δ_{21} causes changes in u_i's and v_j's according to equation 7.17.

Cell	I_{ij}
1, 1	$50 - (-\Delta_{21}) - (\Delta_{21}) = 50$
1, 3	$100 - (-\Delta_{21}) - (0) = 100 + \Delta_{21}$
2, 2	$300 - (200) - (100 + \Delta_{21}) = -\Delta_{21}$
3, 3	$300 - (100 - \Delta_{21}) - 0 = 200 + \Delta_{21}$

from origin i, and v_j is the relative implicit contribution of one additional unit to destination j. Note that this economic interpretation is entirely consistent with the dual objective function given by Equation 7.14. For example, an increase of one unit in the supply of origin 2 from s_2 to $(s_2 + 1)$ and a simultaneous decrease of one unit in the supply of origin 1 from s_1 to $(s_1 - 1)$ imply a change in the optimal value of the objective function (Δz) given by $(u_2 - u_1)$.

Based on the above, the changes in the optimal value of the objective function for various cases are given by the relationships below.

Case 1. Simultaneous *increase* of one unit in the supply of origin p and *decrease* of one unit in the supply of origin q. *Change in z:*

$$\Delta z = u_p - u_q . \tag{7.18}$$

Change in basic x_{ij}: Trace "dead-end" path for unit (±) adjustments in basic x_{ij} to reflect new s_p and s_q.

Case 2. Simultaneous *increase* of one unit in the demand by destination p and *decrease* of one unit in the demand by destination q. *Change in* z:

$$\Delta z = v_p - v_q. \tag{7.19}$$

Change in basic x_{ij}: Trace "dead-end" path for unit ($\pm$) adjustments in basic x_{ij} to reflect new d_p and d_q.

Case 3. Simultaneous *increases* of one unit in the supply of origin p and the demand by destination q. *Change in* z:

$$\Delta z = u_p + v_q. \tag{7.20}$$

Change in basic x_{ij}: Trace "closed" path for unit ($\pm$) adjustments in basic x_{ij} as if one unit were *removed* from cell p, q.

Case 4. Simultaneous *decreases* of one unit in the supply of origin p and the demand by destination q. *Change in* z:

$$\Delta z = -u_p - v_q. \tag{7.21}$$

Change in basic x_{ij}: Trace "closed" path for unit ($\pm$) adjustments in basic x_{ij} as if one unit were *added* to cell p, q.

Case 5. *Increase* of one unit in the supply of origin p. *Change in* z:

$$\Delta z = u_p - \max_i u_i. \tag{7.22}$$

Change in basic x_{ij}: Trace "dead-end" path for unit ($\pm$) adjustments in basic x_{ij} by creating *oversupply* at the origin associated with max u_i.

Case 6. *Increase* of one unit in the demand by destination p. *Change in* z:

$$\Delta z = v_p - \max_j v_j. \tag{7.23}$$

Change in basic x_{ij}: Trace "dead-end" path for unit ($\pm$) adjustments in basic x_{ij} after allocating *unsatisfied demand* to the destination associated with max v_j.

Case 7. *Decrease* of one unit in the supply of origin p. *Change in* z:

$$\Delta z = -u_p - \max_j v_j. \tag{7.24}$$

Change in basic x_{ij}: Trace "dead-end" path for unit ($\pm$) adjustments after allocating *unsatisfied demand* to the destination associated with max v_j.

Case 8. *Decrease* of one unit in the demand by destination p. *Change in* z:

$$\Delta z = -v_p - \max_i u_i. \tag{7.25}$$

Change in basic x_{ij}: Trace "dead-end" path for unit ($\pm$) adjustments in basic x_{ij} after allocating *oversupply* to the origin associated with max u_i.

For each case above, values for the dual variables must be obtained from a *non-degenerate optimal* tableau. We now illustrate some of these by example.

▶ Example 7.16

Case 1: In Table 7–25, suppose $s_1 = 111$ and $s_2 = 159$. From Equation 7.18, $\Delta z = 0 - 200 = -200$. The "dead-end" path begins with a +1 adjustment in basic cell 1, 2 to reflect the new supply (increase of 1 in s_1) and continues with ± unit adjustments in basic variables such that all s_i and d_j are satisfied (*if feasible*). We term this type of path "dead-end" because it never returns to the originating cell. The path (shown in Table 7–27) is given by $(1, 2) \rightarrow (3, 2) \rightarrow (3, 1) \rightarrow (2, 1)$, resulting in the following *adjusted* basic variables: $x_{12} = 111$, $x_{32} = 89$, $x_{31} = 61$, and $x_{21} = 79$.[14] Verify that the net change in the optimal value of z is −200 by netting out the increases and decreases along the dead-end path in Table 7–27.

TABLE 7–27 Dead-End Path for Case 1 of Yew Haw

Origin	Destination 1	Destination 2	Destination 3	Supply	u_i
1	50	100; (+1); ~~110~~ 111	100	~~110~~ 111	0
2	200; (−1); ~~80~~ 79	300	200; 80	~~180~~ 159	200
3	100; (+1); ~~60~~ 61	200; (−1); ~~90~~ 89	300	150	100
Demand	140	200	80	420 / 420	
v_j	0	100	0		

Case 4: Supply $s_2 = 159$ and $d_2 = 199$. Then, according to Equation 7.21, $\Delta z = -200 - 100 = -300$. The "closed" path begins and ends with the addition of one fictitious unit of flow to cell 2, 2: $(2, 2) \rightarrow (3, 2) \rightarrow (3, 1) \rightarrow (2, 1) \rightarrow (2, 2)$. The adjusted basic variables are $x_{32} = 89$, $x_{31} = 61$, and $x_{21} = 79$. Note that $x_{12} = 110$ and $x_{23} = 80$ remain unchanged. The new solution is optimal and satisfies the new set of supplies and demands.

Case 5: Suppose $s_3 = 151$. From Equation 7.22, $\Delta z = 100 - 200 = -100$ where $u_2 = \max u_i$. Oversupply, therefore, will be created at origin 2; that is, only 159 trucks

[14] This path could also begin with a −1 adjustment in basic cell 2, 1 in order to satisfy $s_2 = 159$. The same path, in reverse, would result. Try it. Note that a −1 adjustment in basic cell 2, 3 would not work. Why? Because all s_i and d_j would not be satisfied by a path originating in this cell. Try it.

will be sent from origin 2. Do you see the logic? If a truck is not to be sent (which is to say that a truck is to be sent to a dummy destination with an assumed cost of zero), then utilize the extra unit at origin 3 with a relative cost of $100 ($u_3 = 100$) and reduce by one truck the shipment from the origin that gives us the maximum possible relative cost reduction (that is, $200 for origin 2 since $u_2 = 200$); hence, the optimal z will decrease by $100. The adjusted basic variables are $x_{31} = 61$ and $x_{21} = 79$; that is, the dead-end path runs between cells 3, 1 and 2, 1.

FOLLOW-UP EXERCISES

52. Using Table 7–25, evaluate Cases 2, 3, 6, 7, and 8 for $p = 1$ and $q = 2$.
53. Evaluate all eight cases for the optimal solution to Exercise 47, given that $p = 2$ and $q = 1$.

7.9 AN ASSIGNMENT MODEL ALGORITHM

The Hungarian Method

Section 7.4 indicated six different categories of solution methods for linear assignment models, including conventional LP methods (e.g., simplex) and transportation algorithms (because the assignment model can be thought of as a special case of the transportation model). As indicated in that section, special algorithms have been developed that capitalize on the special structure of the assignment model. This section presents the *Hungarian method,* one such algorithm. Although we will not take time to develop the underlying theory, we do illustrate its use.

The Hungarian method is based on the concept of opportunity costs. There are three steps in implementing the method. First, an opportunity cost table is constructed from the table of assignment costs. Second, it is determined whether an optimal assignment can be made. If an optimal assignment cannot be made, the third step involves a revision of the opportunity cost table. Let us illustrate the algorithm by solving the court scheduling example (Example 7.10).

Step 1: Determine Opportunity Cost Table. Table 7–28 repeats the data for Example 7.10. To determine the opportunity cost table, two steps are required. First, the least cost element in each row is identified and subtracted from all elements in the row. The resulting cost table is sometimes called the *row-reduced cost table.* Having accomplished this, the least cost element in each column is identified and subtracted from all other elements in the column resulting in the *opportunity cost table.* Table 7–29 is the row-reduced cost table for our example. Table 7–30 is the opportunity cost table.

TABLE 7–28 Estimated Days to Clear Docket

	Docket			
Judge	**1**	**2**	**3**	**4**
1	14	13	17	14
2	16	15	16	15
3	18	14	20	17
4	20	13	15	18

TABLE 7–29 Row-Reduced Cost Table

	Docket			
Judge	1	2	3	4
1	1	0	4	1
2	1	0	1	0
3	4	0	6	3
4	7	0	2	5

TABLE 7–30 Opportunity Cost Table

	Docket			
Judge	1	2	3	4
1	0	0	3	1
2	0	0	0	0
3	3	0	5	3
4	6	0	1	5

Step 2: Determine whether an Optimal Assignment Can Be Made. The technique for determining whether an optimal assignment is possible at this stage consists of drawing straight lines (vertically and horizontally) through the opportunity cost table in such a way as to minimize the number of lines necessary to cover all zero entries. If the number of lines equals either the number of rows or columns in the table, an optimal assignment can be made. If the number of lines is less than the number of rows or columns, an optimal assignment cannot be determined, and the opportunity cost table must be revised. Table 7–31 illustrates this step as applied to Table 7–30. As shown, three lines are required to cover all zeros in the table, and an optimal assignment cannot be determined.

TABLE 7–31

	Docket			
Judge	1	2	3	4
1	0	0	3	1
2	0	0	0	0
3	3	0	5	3
4	6	0	1	5

Step 3: Revise the Opportunity Cost Table. If it is not possible to determine an optimal assignment in Step 2, the opportunity cost table must be modified. This is accomplished by identifying the smallest number in the table not covered by a straight line and subtracting this number from all numbers not covered by a straight line. Also, this same number is *added* to all numbers lying at the *intersection* of any two lines. Looking at Table 7–31, the smallest element not covered by a straight line

is the 1 at the intersection of row 4 and column 3. If this number is subtracted from all elements not covered by straight lines and if it is added to the numbers found at the intersection of any two straight lines, the revised opportunity cost table is shown in Table 7–32. Step 2 is repeated at this point.

TABLE 7–32 Revised Opportunity Cost Table

	Docket			
Judge	1	2	3	4
1	0	1	3	1
2	0	1	0	0
3	2	0	4	2
4	5	0	0	4

Step 2: Determine whether an Optimal Assignment Can Be Made. Repeating Step 2, Table 7–32 shows that four lines are required to cover all of the zero elements. Thus an optimal assignment can be made. The optimal assignments may not be apparent from the table. One procedure for identifying the assignments is *to select a row or column in which there is only one zero, and make an assignment to that cell.* There is only one zero in column four. Thus the first assignment is Judge 2 to Docket 4. Since no other assignments can be made in row 2 or column 4, we cross them off. With row 2 and column 4 crossed off, look for a row or column in which there is only one zero. As can be seen in Table 7–33, the remaining assignments are apparent, since there are three zero elements that are the only such elements in a row or column. Thus optimal assignment of the four judges results in 58 judge-days to clear the four dockets.

TABLE 7–33 Optimal Assignments

	Docket				Final Assignments	Days
Judge	1	2	3	4		
1	(0)	1	3	1	Judge 1—Docket 1	14
2	0	1	0	(0)	Judge 2—Docket 4	15
3	2	(0)	4	2	Judge 3—Docket 2	14
4	5	0	(0)	4	Judge 4—Docket 3	15
					Total days	58

Summary of the Hungarian Method

Step 1: Determine the opportunity cost table.

a. Determine the row-reduced cost table by subtracting the least cost element in each row from all elements in the same row.

b. Using the row-reduced cost table, identify the least cost element in each column, and subtract from all elements in that column.

Step 2: Determine whether or not an optimal assignment can be made. Draw the minimum number of straight lines necessary to cover all zero elements in the opportunity cost table. If the number of straight lines is less than the number of rows (or columns) in the table, the optimal assignment cannot be made. Go to Step 3. If the number of straight lines equals the number of rows (columns), the optimal assignments can be identified.

Step 3: Revise the opportunity cost table. Identify the smallest element in the opportunity cost table not covered by a straight line.

a. Subtract this element from every element not covered by a straight line.

b. Add this element to any element(s) found at the intersection of two straight lines.

c. Go to Step 2.

The Hungarian method can be used when the objective function is to be maximized. Two alternative approaches can be used in this situation. The signs on the objective function coefficients can be changed, and the objective function can be minimized; or opportunity costs can be determined by subtracting the largest element (e.g., profit) in a row or column rather than the smallest element.

FOLLOW-UP EXERCISES

54. Use the Hungarian method to determine the optimal assignment of referees in Exercise 25.

55. Five jobs are to be assigned to five people; each person will do one job only. The expected times (in hours) required for each person to complete each job have been estimated and are shown in the following table. Use the Hungarian method to determine the optimal assignments.

	Person				
Job	**1**	**2**	**3**	**4**	**5**
1	12	15	13	14	15
2	16	18	15	14	16
3	18	16	15	18	20
4	15	20	18	17	19
5	16	15	18	14	15

7.10 COMPUTER-BASED ANALYSIS

The next three examples illustrate computer-based analysis of transportation and assignment models. The packages shown implement special-purpose transportation and assignment algorithms, respectively. If you have used an LP package to solve such models, note how the special structure of transportation and assignment models allows for efficient input of the problem. Compare this effort with that required to solve the same problems using a generalized LP package.

▶ Example 7.17 Computer-Based Solution to Yew Haw

Figure 7–6 illustrates the use of a software package designed to solve transportation problems. Shown is the solution to the Yew Haw example. Notice the interactive nature of the package; user responses are shown in color to distinguish them from responses given by the package. Compare these results with those shown in Table 7–21. The interpretation of results is straightforward.

▶ Example 7.18 Computerized Sensitivity Analysis for Yew Haw

The computer package illustrated in Example 7.17 also provides sensitivity analysis for objective function coefficients and the RHS constant sensitivity analysis options discussed in Section 7.8. Figure 7–7 presents the sensitivity analysis output for Yew Haw.

The sensitivity analysis for objective function coefficients is divided into that for basic variables and that for nonbasic variables. For basic variables LOWER DELTA and UPPER DELTA represent the permissible decreases and increases in the coefficient such that the current basis remains optimal. The LOWER LIMIT and UPPER LIMIT are the corresponding range of values permitted for the coefficient. For example, the objective function coefficient for cell 1, 2 is *not* permitted to decrease but is allowed to increase by 50 (rounding), or $100 \leq c_{12} \leq 150$.

Nonbasic variables were not included in the basis because their objective function coefficients were too large. The only way in which they might become candidates for entrance to the basis would be if they decreased in value. Thus for cell 1, 1 the current basis remains optimal as long as c_{11} *does not decrease* more than 50, or as long as $c_{11} \geq 0$.

For RHS constants, this package examines eight different types of ranging possibilities. The options include the effect of allowing one RHS constant to change as well as the simultaneous ranging of supply and demand parameters. We show the results from three of the options, the same three discussed in Example 7.16. The first option analyzes the marginal effect of increasing the supply at one origin while decreasing the supply at another origin. For example, if the supply at origin 1 is increased by 1 and the supply at origin 2 is decreased by 1, the optimal distribution cost will be *decreased* by 200.

Option 4 examines the marginal effect of simultaneously decreasing the supply at one origin and the demand at one destination. For example, decreasing the supply at origin 2 and the demand at destination 2 results in a *decrease* in the optimal distribution cost by 300. Lastly, option 5 examines the effect of increasing the supply at one of the origins. For example, increasing the supply at origin 3 by one unit will result in a decrease in the optimal value of the objective function by 100.

The next example illustrates the solution to the Court Scheduling problem discussed in Example 7.10 and solved in Table 7–33 (see Figure 7–8). The objective in this problem was to assign each of four judges to four individual court dockets in such a way as to minimize the total number of days required to clear all of the dockets. The problem is solved using the program ASGT1, one of several OR/MS pro-

FIGURE 7–6 Computer-Based Solution for Yew Haw

```
TRANSPORTATION MODEL  (maximum size 20 rows by 20 columns)
IF YOU WANT TO USE A FILE FOR INPUT ENTER FILE NAME:
ENTER THE NUMBER OF SUPPLY POINTS:3
ENTER THE NUMBER OF DEMAND POINTS:3
  NOW ENTER THE SUPPLY QUANTITY FOR EACH POINT
SUPPLY QUANTITY FOR POINT  1? 110
SUPPLY QUANTITY FOR POINT  2? 160
SUPPLY QUANTITY FOR POINT  3? 150
  NOW ENTER THE DEMAND QUANTITY FOR EACH POINT
DEMAND QUANTITY FOR POINT  1  140
DEMAND QUANTITY FOR POINT  2  200
DEMAND QUANTITY FOR POINT  3  80
NOW ENTER TRANSPORTATION COEFFICIENTS ROW BY ROW

  SUPPLY      DEMAND
     ROW      COLUMN
       1           1 :50
       1           2 :100
       1           3 :100
       2           1 :200
       2           2 :300
       2           3 :200
       3           1 :100
       3           2 :200
       3           3 :300

ENTER MAXIMUM OR MINIMUM:min
DO YOU WANT A TABLEAU OF YOUR DATA PRINTED?  YES OR NO:yes
-------------------------------------------------------------
                    1            2             3       SUPPLY
   1            50.00       100.00        100.00       110.00
   2           200.00       300.00        200.00       160.00
   3           100.00       200.00        300.00       150.00
DEMAND         140.00       200.00         80.00
-------------------------------------------------------------
! ! ! ! ! ! !  FINAL SOLUTION REACHED  ! ! ! ! ! ! !
-------------------------------------------------------------
ORIGIN          DESTINATION          QUANTITY            COST
     1                2                110.00       $11000.00
     2                1                 80.00       $16000.00
     2                3                 80.00       $16000.00
     3                1                 60.00        $6000.00
     3                2                 90.00       $18000.00
   YOUR TOTAL ALLOCATION COST WILL BE ======>>> $67000.00
```

grams included in the software package *Computer Models for Management Science*.[15]

[15]See Warren J. Erikson and Owen P. Hall, Jr. (Reading, Mass.: Addison-Wesley Publishing, 1986).

FIGURE 7–7 Computerized Sensitivity Analysis for Yew Haw

```
DO YOU WANT SENSITIVITY ANALYSIS?  YES OR NO:yes

NOTE:  A LOWER LIMIT OF -9999999 OR AN UPPER LIMIT
       OF 9999999 SHOULD BE INTERPRETED AS INFINITY
OBJECTIVE FUNCTION COEFFICIENTS BASIC VARIABLES
CELL   LOWER DELTA    UPPER DELTA    LOWER LIMIT    UPPER LIMIT
1 2           0.00          49.99         100.00         149.99
2 1        -100.05           0.00          99.95         200.00
2 3    -9999999.00         100.05    -9999799.00         300.05
3 1           0.00          49.99         100.00         149.99
3 2         -50.03           0.00         149.97         200.00
OBJECTIVE FUNCTION COEFFICENTS NONBASIC VARIABLES
CELL        LOWER DELTA           LOWER LIMIT
1 1              -50.00                  0.00
1 3             -100.00                  0.00
2 2                0.00                300.00
3 3             -200.00                100.00

    RHS SENSITIVITY OPTIONS
1  INCREASE IN ONE SUPPLY AND DECREASE IN ANOTHER SUPPLY
2  INCREASE IN ONE DEMAND AND INCREASE IN ANOTHER DEMAND
3  INCREASE IN BOTH A DEMAND AND SUPPLY
4  DECREASE IN BOTH A DEMAND AND SUPPLY
5  INCREASE IN ONE SUPPLY
6  INCREASE IN ONE DEMAND
7  DECREASE IN ONE SUPPLY
8  DECREASE IN ONE DEMAND
9  NONE OF THE ABOVE
   WHAT TYPE OF RHS SENSITIVITY DO YOU WANT? 1
       SUPPLY POINT        SUPPLY POINT          CHANGE IN
        INCREASED           DECREASED          OPTIMAL COST
            1                   2               -$200.0
            1                   3               -$100.0
            2                   1                $200.0
            2                   3                $100.0
            3                   1                $100.0
            3                   2               -$100.0

   WHAT TYPE OF RHS SENSITIVITY DO YOU WANT? 4
       SUPPLY POINT        DEMAND POINT          CHANGE IN
        DECREASED           DECREASED          OPTIMAL COST
            1                   1                  $0.0
            1                   2               -$100.0
            1                   3                  $0.0
            2                   1               -$200.0
            2                   2               -$300.0
            2                   3               -$200.0
            3                   1               -$100.0
            3                   2               -$200.0
            3                   3               -$100.0

   WHAT TYPE OF RHS SENSITIVITY DO YOU WANT? 5
       SUPPLY POINT         CHANGE IN
        INCREASED          OPTIMAL COST
            1                -$200.0
            2                   $0.0
            3                -$100.0
```

FIGURE 7–8 Computer-Based Solution for Court Scheduling Example

```
      *********************
      *                   *
      *  ASSIGNMENT MODEL *
      *     ANALYSIS      *
      *                   *
      *********************

 MODEL SIZE.
   NUMBER OF ROWS (1 TO 25) ? 4

   PROBLEM TYPE (1=MAX, -1=MIN) ? -1

 MODEL INPUT BY ROW.
   ROW 1
COLUMN 1 PAYOFF (ANY NUMBER) ? 14
COLUMN 2 PAYOFF (ANY NUMBER) ? 13
COLUMN 3 PAYOFF (ANY NUMBER) ? 17
COLUMN 4 PAYOFF (ANY NUMBER) ? 14

   ROW 2
COLUMN 1 PAYOFF (ANY NUMBER) ? 16
COLUMN 2 PAYOFF (ANY NUMBER) ? 15
COLUMN 3 PAYOFF (ANY NUMBER) ? 16
COLUMN 4 PAYOFF (ANY NUMBER) ? 15

   ROW 3
COLUMN 1 PAYOFF (ANY NUMBER) ? 18
COLUMN 2 PAYOFF (ANY NUMBER) ? 14
COLUMN 3 PAYOFF (ANY NUMBER) ? 20
COLUMN 4 PAYOFF (ANY NUMBER) ? 17

   ROW 4
COLUMN 1 PAYOFF (ANY NUMBER) ? 20
COLUMN 2 PAYOFF (ANY NUMBER) ? 13
COLUMN 3 PAYOFF (ANY NUMBER) ? 15
COLUMN 4 PAYOFF (ANY NUMBER) ? 18

      *********************
      *                   *
      *  ASSIGNMENT MODEL *
      *     ANALYSIS      *
      *                   *
      *********************

      ** INFORMATION ENTERED **

   NUMBER OF ROWS:  4
   NUMBER OF COLS:  4

             PAYOFFS

ROW 1     14      13      17      14

ROW 2     16      15      16      15

ROW 3     18      14      20      17

ROW 4     20      13      15      18
```

```
      ** RESULTS **

ROW ASSIGNMENTS

 1    A    ___  ___  ___

 2   ___   ___  ___   A

 3   ___    A   ___  ___

 4   ___   ___   A   ___

MINIMUM TOTAL PAYOFF = 58

      ** END OF ANALYSIS **
```

▶ Example 7.19 Court Scheduling

Notice the interactive nature of this package. User responses are shown in color. The results are displayed in a tabular format and they indicate that judge 1 should be assigned to docket 1, judge 2 should be assigned to docket 4, judge 3 should be assigned to docket 2, and judge 4 should be assigned to docket 3. The total number of days required to clear all four dockets is minimized at 58.

SELECTED APPLICATION REVIEW

EARTHMOVING APPLICATION

The redevelopment of the Brisbane International Airport provided a classical application of the transportation model. During the construction project, sand was brought to various sites to compress the swampy land in that area. A surplus of sand ended up at the sites and had to be redistributed to other areas around the airport. Two LP models were formulated, one of which was a simple, classic four-source, five-destination transportation model for planning how to best redistribute the excess sand. The analysis led to a plan that resulted in a demonstrable savings of $400,000 when compared with the engineering plan that would have been used prior to the LP analysis. This application illustrates the potential application of linear programming in the field of civil engineering as well as the potential benefit from applying rather straightforward, "textbook type" models.

SOURCE: Chad Perry and Mike Iliff, "From the Shadows: Earthmoving on Construction Projects," *Interfaces*, February 1983, pp. 79–84.

E. I. du Pont de Nemours & Co. uses a state-of-the-art computerized vehicle-routing methodology for scheduling delivery of a group of its products to more than 3,000 customers located in more than 1,000 cities throughout the continental United States and Canada. A three-tier distribution network, consisting of plants, regional distribution centers, and truck terminals is utilized. Du Pont uses a flexible, computerized vehicle routing package called ROVER (Real-Time Optimizer for Vehicle Routing) to address various tactical and strategic decisions related to serving its customers. ROVER assigns customers to vehicles by solving a linear generalized assignment model (a variation on the model presented in this chapter) and then determines a delivery sequence for the customers assigned to each vehicle using a

(continued)

traveling salesrep problem (Chapter 8) heuristic. The result has been a reduction in delivery costs by more than 15 percent as well as a management tool that continues to assist in planning future distribution strategies.

Logo reproduced courtesy of E. I. Du Pont de Nemours and Company.

SOURCE: Marshall L. Fisher, Arnold J. Greenfield, R Jaikumar, and Joseph T. Lester III, "A Computerized Vehicle Routing Application," *Interfaces*, August 1982, pp. 42–52.

SELECTED REFERENCES

Bradley, Stephen P.; Arnoldo C. Hax; and Thomas L. Magnanti. *Applied Mathematical Programming*. Reading, Mass.: Addison-Wesley Publishing, 1977.

Chvatal, Vasek. *Linear Programming*. New York: W. H. Freeman, 1983.

Gass, S. I. *Linear Programming: Methods and Applications*. 4th ed. New York: McGraw-Hill, 1975.

Hillier, Frederick S., and Gerald J. Lieberman. *Introduction to Operations Research*. 3rd ed. San Francisco: Holden-Day, 1980.

Ignizio, James P. *Linear Programming in Single- & Multiple-Objective Systems*. Englewood Cliffs, N.J.: Prentice-Hall, 1982.

Lee, Sang M. *Linear Optimization for Management*. New York: Petrocelli Books, 1976.

Lev, Benjamin, and Howard J. Weiss. *Introduction to Mathematical Programming*. New York; Elsevier North-Holland, 1982.

McMillan, Claude, Jr. *Mathematical Programming: An Introduction to the Design and Application of Optimal Decision Machines*. New York: John Wiley & Sons, 1970.

Wagner, Harvey M. *Principles of Operations Research*. 2nd ed. Englewood Cliffs, N.J.: Prentice-Hall, 1975.

ADDITIONAL EXERCISES

56. If the values in the body of the table reflect unit transportation costs, find the minimum cost solution.

		Destination			
		1	2	3	Supply
Origin	1	$10	$15	$40	400
	2	5	20	35	600
	3	15	10	30	500
	Demand	800	600	400	

57. If the data in the preceding exercise represent unit profits, determine the profit maximization solution.
58. ***Contract Award Problem.*** The Department of the Army wishes to award supply contracts to companies who supply hairnets. The "Modern" Army is experiencing (hair) growing pains, and it has reached a compromise in which recruits may retain their lengthy locks provided they wear hairnets while on duty. The Army has agreed to supply the nets. Four suppliers have submitted sealed bids that quote the price per case of nets (delivered) to four regional locations. The bids are summarized in the following table. Also shown are estimates of the maximum number of cases each supplier can provide and the regional requirements. Notice that supplier 4 has submitted a bid for region 1 only.

	Region				
Supplier	**1**	**2**	**3**	**4**	**Max. Supply (cases)**
1	$30	$25	$40	$35	800
2	35	32	38	40	1000
3	28	30	35	38	1500
4	25	—	—	—	600
Required number of cases	1,000	800	1,200	750	

Suppliers may receive contracts to provide all or part of the needs of any region. Given the objective of minimizing the cost of providing the hairnets:

a. Formulate this as a linear programming problem.
b.. Is this in the mathematical form of a transportation model?
c. Cite two different ways in which you might handle the unquoted bids by vendor 4 in the LP formulation.
d. Solve for the optimal solution (using a computer package if one is available).

59. For the previous problem:
a. Find an initial basic feasible solution using the northwest corner algorithm.
b. Continue from this initial solution to determine the contract awards that will result in minimum total cost.

60. ***Gasoline Reallocation.*** A major oil company is planning for the summer boost in vacation driving. In an effort to better accommodate the needs of motorists, the company has surveyed its 10 operating regions to determine summer needs and normal gasoline supplies. The analysis reveals that three regions will have surplus supplies, six regions will fall short of their needs, and supply and demand will be in balance for the remaining region. Company officials want to develop a plan that reallocates supplies from surplus areas to shortages areas. The accompanying table indicates the surplus and shortage quantities by region and the cost (stated in thousands of dollars) per million gallons of diverting gasoline from one region to another. If the objective is to minimize the total cost of reallocating the gasoline:

Surplus Region	Shortage Region						Surplus (millions of gallons)
	1	2	3	4	5	6	
1	$10.0	$ 5.0	$15.0	$7.5	$12.0	$8.0	900
2	8.0	7.0	12.0	9.0	10.0	6.0	850
3	11.5	10.0	10.0	8.5	15.0	9.0	1,000
Shortage (millions of gallons)	200	150	600	300	750	500	

a. Carefully define your variables and formulate the LP model for this problem.
b. Determine the optimal solution, and state your decision in plain English.

61. ***Media Mix.*** A manufacturer of designer jeans is interested in developing an advertising campaign that will reach four different age groups. Advertising campaigns can be conducted within TV, radio, and magazines. The following table indicates the estimated cost per exposure in each age group according to the medium employed. In addition, maximum exposure levels desired within each medium as well as minimum desired exposures within each age group are identified. If the objective is to minimize the cost of attaining the minimum exposure level in each age group:

Media	**Age Groups**				**Max. Exposure (millions)**
	13–18	**18–22**	**22–35**	**35 and older**	
TV	$0.12	$0.07	$0.10	$0 .10	40
Radio	0.10	0.09	0.12	0.10	30
Magazines	0.14	0.12	0.09	0.12	20
Minimum number of exposures (millions)	30	25	15	10	

a. Formulate this problem as a transportation model, and find the optimal solution.
b. Solve this problem if the policy is to provide at least 4 million exposures through TV in the 13–18 age group and at least 8 million exposures through TV in the 18–22 age group.

62. ***Plant Distribution.*** A company is engaged in a plant distribution study. The plant has four main work centers at which end items are assembled. Each center uses, among others, a common part. The part is stored in bins at three locations within the plant. Although alternative locations are being considered for the bins, the production manager wishes to determine the best way in which to allocate parts from the existing bins to the four work centers. The criterion selected to evaluate the current layout is a measure of volume of parts multiplied times the distance over which the parts are moved.

The table summarizes the distances (in meters) between each bin and each work center, the number of parts available in each bin, and the number required at each work center.

	Work Center				
Bin	**1**	**2**	**3**	**4**	**Parts Available**
1	25	40	75	20	2,000
2	50	40	65	25	1,500
3	25	50	70	40	1,500
Parts required	800	1,200	1,500	1,000	

If the objective is to minimize the weighted measure of volume times distance, then:

a. Formulate this problem as a transportation model and find the optimal solution.

b. Solve this problem if exactly 500 parts must be delivered to work center 3 from bin 2 and at least 400 from bin 1 to work center 4.

63. ***Processing Welfare Applications.*** A state welfare agency hires some social workers on a part-time basis in order to get through particularly busy periods. One activity for which these persons are hired is the review and evaluation of welfare applications. During the coming month the agency projects a need to hire part-timers. Workers are paid on a piecework basis according to the type of application reviewed and the experience of the social worker. Five social workers have been contacted to determine their interest in employment for the coming month. All have provided an estimate of the maximum number of welfare applications they would be willing to evaluate this month (the agency makes certain that the number of applications is within the capability of the social worker).

The table summarizes the cost per application per social worker, the maximum number of applications per social worker, and the number of applications that must be evaluated of each type. Social workers 2 and 4 have insufficient experience to evaluate certain application types. This is denoted in the table by the absence of a cost estimate. Because of the extensive experience of social worker 5 in evaluating the elderly, the agency director wants her to be assigned at least 75 applications of this type.

	Social Worker					
Type of Application	**1**	**2**	**3**	**4**	**5**	**Number of Applications**
Aid to individuals	$10	$12	$11	$12	$10	200
Aid to families with dependent children	8	9	8	—	8	100
Benefits for the elderly	7	—	6	8	8	150
Maximum number of applications per social worker	80	100	120	60	130	

a. Define x_{ij} and formulate an appropriate LP model. Is this model in the general form of an LP/transportation structure? Explain.

b. Set this problem up as a transportation model and find the optimal solution. State this solution in plain English.

64. ***Computer Programmer Assignment.*** A data processing department wishes to assign five programmers to five programming jobs. Management has estimated the total number of days each programmer would take if assigned to the different jobs. These are summarized in the following table.

	Programming Job				
Programmer	**1**	**2**	**3**	**4**	**5**
1	50	25	78	64	60
2	43	30	70	56	72
3	60	28	80	66	68
4	54	29	75	60	70
5	45	32	70	62	75

a. Determine the assignment that minimizes total time to complete the five jobs.

b. How would your solution change if programmer 3 could not be assigned to either job 2 or job 4?

65. ***Police Patrol Assignment.*** Sin City's police chief wishes to allocate five tactical patrol units to five precincts that have recently experienced large increases in crime. The five teams are different with respect to number of officers, years of experience, and mode of operation. Crime analysts have estimated the number of "Index" (serious) offenses expected in each precinct during the coming month. Based on the demographic and crime incidence characteristics of each precinct, analysts have also determined a *crime deterrence factor,* which represents the portion of anticipated crimes expected to be deterred as a result of the tactical unit's efforts. The table summarizes these factors.

Crime Deterrence Factors

	Precinct				
Team	**1**	**2**	**3**	**4**	**5**
A	0.25	0.28	0.40	0.22	0.30
B	0.35	0.18	0.32	0.26	0.34
C	0.22	0.26	0.29	0.24	0.32
D	0.36	0.40	0.44	0.38	0.42
E	0.18	0.24	0.15	0.22	0.20

The estimated number of Index offenses for the next month (assuming no assignment of tactical units) are summarized for each precinct as follows: 500 for precinct 1; 600 for precinct 2; 250 for precinct 3; 400 for precinct 4; and 550 for precinct 5. The chief wishes to allocate the five teams in such a way as to minimize the *expected* number of Index offenses for the five precincts during the coming month.

a. Formulate the objective function and constraints for this model.

b. Find a computerized LP, transportation, or assignment package, and solve this problem.

c. Solve this problem by the Hungarian Method.

66. ***Solid Waste Disposal.*** A major Canadian city has three incinerator sites for processing solid waste. There are six garbage collection areas within the city. The city wants to determine the least-cost method of disposing of their trash. Costs are broken into two components. Each incinerator is characterized by an operating cost, c_j, which is the cost of processing each ton of waste. There is also the cost t_{ij}, which expresses the cost of transporting each ton of waste from collection area i to incinerator j. Each collection area generates w_i tons of waste per month, and each incinerator has a processing capacity of p_j tons per month.

a. The accompanying table summarizes the transportation costs per ton of waste. Values for w_i and p_j are also indicated. Incinerator sites 1, 2, and 3 have variable operating costs of \$95, \$80, and \$100 per ton, respectively. Provide the transportation table for these data. (Note: We have purposely reversed rows and columns in the table; we don't want you to get lazy.)

	Collection Area						
Incinerator Site	**1**	**2**	**3**	**4**	**5**	**6**	**Capacity per Month (tons)**
1	\$60	\$50	\$70	\$40	\$45	\$55	3,000
2	75	30	45	55	80	70	4,000
3	40	50	25	60	50	35	5,000
Tons generated per month	1,000	800	1,200	1,500	2,000	1,600	

b. Define decision variables and formulate a *generalized* LP model for this problem. Next formulate the LP model *specific* to the data in part *a*.

c. Find the optimal solution to this problem.

***d.* Perform sensitivity analyses for the costs associated with the first incinerator site.

***e.* Suppose that the six collection areas represent potential collection areas being considered for purchase by the city. At least four must be purchased. The monthly interest charges to finance the purchases for collection areas 1 through 6 would be, respectively, \$50, \$75, \$60, \$85, \$100, \$70. Appropriately modify the formulation in part *b*. (Hint: Define a new set of decision variables, $y_i = 0$ if area i is not selected; 1 otherwise, $i = 1, \ldots, 6$.) Is this formulation still a transportation model? Explain.

67. An optimal solution to a transportation problem with a minimization objective is presented in the accompanying table.

a. Verify that the optimal solution has been found.

b. Conduct sensitivity analysis on the objective function coefficients for all real nonbasic variables.

c. Conduct sensitivity analysis for the objective function contributions for all real basic variables.

***d.* Conduct sensitivity analysis for Cases 1 through 8 for $p = 3$ and $q = 2$.

Origin	Destination 1		Destination 2		Destination 3		Supply
		60		88		64	
1	180				150		330
		100		70		66	
2			200		200		400
		0		0		0	
3			180				180
Demand	180		380		350		

68. ***Committee Assignments I.* Suppose that m members of a college faculty are to be assigned to n standing committees according to their preferences for the coming academic year. Let x_{ij} = one if the ith person is assigned to the jth committee; zero otherwise; c_{ij} = Preference score (low score implies high preference) of the ith person for the jth committee. In this problem each faculty member becomes an "origin" that can "supply" either zero or one "unit" to satisfy committee ("destination") demands. The objective is to maximize the cumulative preference of the faculty or to *minimize* the cumulative preference score.

If any one faculty member is to serve on one and only one committee and if assignments are to be made uniformly such that each committee has the same number of members:

a. Formulate the *generalized* LP model (you may wish to use summation notation).

b. If m/n is not integer, what is the implication? How can this be handled if solved as a transportation model?

69. ***Committee Assignments II.* Given the data in the following table, determine the committee assignments that minimize cumulative preference. (Remember, the lower the score the greater the preference.)

Individual	Preferences for Committee 1	2	3	Committees to Be Served
1	0.5	0.7	0.1	1
2	0.8	0.2	0.4	1
3	0.0	0.8	0.9	1
4	0.6	0.5	0.5	1
5	0.9	0.0	0.5	1
6	0.2	0.1	0.7	1
7	0.1	0.6	0.0	1
8	0.5	0.3	0.8	1
9	0.0	0.7	1.0	1
10	1.0	0.5	0.0	1
Committee membership	3	3	4	10

70. ***Committee Assignments III.* Let x_{ijk} represent the assignment variable for individual i from department k on committee j. Suppose there are six college departments and that committee 1 requires representation from each department. If c_{ijk}, s_i, and d_j are defined as before, state the mathematical formulation of this model. Is this a transportation model? Can you think of a scheme for avoiding the subscript "k" given that m_1 members are in department 1, m_2 members are in department 2, and so forth?

71. ***Caterer Model.* Cap and Gown Enterprises (C&G) has contracted to provide caps and gowns for graduation ceremonies for four local colleges. College A will have ceremonies Friday night, graduating 700 students; college B will hold ceremonies Saturday morning, graduating 600 students; college C will hold ceremonies Saturday night, graduating 700 students; and college D will hold ceremonies Sunday afternoon graduating 500 students. C&G currently has 400 sets of caps and gowns. It wishes to minimize the cost of providing graduation dress for the four schools. C&G can have Friday night's caps and gowns cleaned and ready for Saturday night's ceremonies at a cost of $2.50 per set. Saturday morning's sets can be cleaned at the same price for Sunday morning. New cap and gown sets cost $50.

a. Formulate this problem as a transportation model by setting up a table identifying all origins and destinations and appropriate costs.

b. How should C&G provide (cater) the caps and gowns?

CASE Bartholomew Electric Company

Bartholomew Electric Company (BEC) is a distributor of major household appliances. Management at BEC is somewhat concerned about distribution costs of its product line. BEC has two plants supplying five distribution warehouses, which serve as intermediate holding locations. The five distribution warehouses supply the needs of 20 major demand points (markets) across the country. In preparing the budget for the coming year, management wishes to examine the possibility of adding new distribution warehouses. Three locations have been proposed and relevant costs identified. Management is open to considering the addition of any or all of the three proposed locations as long as it is cost justified.

Table 7–34 reflects distribution costs per unit from plant to distribution warehouse to final demand point. Management has predetermined which plant should supply units to each distribution warehouse. The values in Table 7–34 incorporate those transportation costs. Aside from monthly capacities at each distribution warehouse and monthly demand for appliances at each demand point, the table also reflects handling costs per unit at each distribution warehouse. Not shown in the table are monthly amortization costs for the five existing and three proposed warehouses. These values are $4,500, $5,000, $4,000, $3,800, $4,200, $6,000, $7,000, and $5,500, respectively.

Required:

a. Determine which (if any) of the proposed distribution warehouses should be added and the quantities of new appliances that should be shipped from each (existing and new) distribution warehouse to each demand point on a monthly basis in order to minimize the sum of monthly distribution, handling, and amortization costs for BEC.

b. Write a report summarizing your analysis and results. In preparing your report, assume that it is to be submitted to top management personnel who are not technically or quantitatively (in an operations research sense) oriented.

TABLE 7–34 Distribution Costs/Unit: Plant → Distribution Warehouse → Demand Point

Distribution Warehouse	Demand Point 1	2	3	4	5	6	7	8	9	10	11	12	13	14	15	16	17	18	19	20	Monthly Capacity	Handling Costs Per Unit
1	$20	$18		$15	$22	$25			$10	$15		$24	$22	$26				$18	$14	$23	1,200	$ 8
2		20	24		20		40	22	18				20		42	26	35		13		1,800	7
3	30			18	24	22		26			23	30			38		32	21		21	800	10
4	25		32	22	18		45	25	15				26		35	25	36		16	20	1,500	8
5		22	30	16	30	$28	38			18	25				40	22		23		24	1,000	9
6*			22	20		20	40	20		13	20			18	30		25	16		18	1,200	$ 7
7*		16	24		20	24		18	13	10			18			18		16	10		1,000	6
8*	24	18		14	16		38		12	12		15		28			28			15	1,500	8
Monthly demand	250	350	100	200	325	175	400	250	150	300	375	125	425	300	250	180	420	500	340	160		

*Possible distribution warehouses

8

Integer and Zero–One Programming

Chapter Outline

In our formulations of certain LP models, some of you may have been concerned about the validity of using *continuous variables* in certain applications. That is, you may have challenged the assumption of divisibility. The implication of this assumption was "that fractional levels for decision variables are permissible". The consequences of this assumption are that final solutions to certain LP problems may recommend the production of fractional units of products, the investment in a portion of a project, or the assignment of a fractional number of workers to jobs.

If fractional or continuous values for decision variables are inappropriate or undesirable, then we need to work with **integer variables.** In some applications, integer variables are restricted to values of zero or one and are termed **zero-one** or **binary variables.** In practice, binary variables are quite common because they represent frequent two-choice decisions (to build or not to build?). As we will see in Sections 8.2 and 8.3, they also uniquely model a wide-ranging assortment of real-world circumstances. (Have we or have we not incurred a fixed charge?) Integer programming is the branch of mathematical programming that explicitly takes integer variables into consideration.

This chapter examines integer programming in general and the more specialized area of binary or zero-one programming in particular. We keep the theory of integer programming to a minimum; instead, we present specific issues in problem formulation, extensive examples where integer programming has been applied, and an overview of solution approaches. With emphasis on computer-based solutions, computational experience, and an overall assessment of the real-world potential of integer programming models, we maintain an applications focus.

8.1 THE NATURE OF INTEGER PROGRAMMING PROBLEMS

This section elaborates on some characteristics of integer programming, revisits the air cargo problem first presented in Example 4.1, and presents a geometric perspective of the integer programming model.

Characteristics of Integer Programming

The important body of knowledge called **integer programming (IP)** addresses the problem of optimizing an objective function subject to constraints, *where all (or some) variables are integer.* If *all* variables are integer, then we have **pure integer programming.** If only selected variables are integer and the remaining variables are continuous, then we have **mixed integer programming.** If all variables are binary, then the term **binary** or **zero-one programming** applies. If the objective function and structural constraints in an IP problem are *all* linear, it is customary to talk about **linear integer programming;** otherwise we have **nonlinear integer programming.** Our focus in this chapter is on *linear* integer programming, including mixed IP, pure IP, and binary programming.

If you think back to Chapter 7, you should recognize that the transportation and assignment models are both examples of IP models. As long as the s_i and d_j values in a transportation problem are integer, an all-integer optimal solution is guaranteed. The transportation problem is an example of a pure IP problem. Similarly, the typical assignment problem is an example of a 0–1 programming problem. If a linear IP problem has the special structural characteristics of these models, the specialized solution procedures presented in Chapter 7 are appropriate.

Realizing that linear IP problems are special cases of LP problems, you should agree that the **optimal continuous (LP) solution** to an IP maximization (minimization) problem will always be greater (less) than or equal to the **optimal integer solution.** In fact, if an IP problem is solved by the simplex method and an all-integer basis results, then we have found the optimal integer solution. Both LP and IP problems start with the same area of feasible solutions. However, the integer requirement is *more restrictive* and usually reduces the feasible solution space. The integer requirement never results in an increased set of feasible solution points. **Thus the optimal solution to an IP problem can never be better than the solution to its continuous counterpart.**

Section 3.2 briefly addressed the issue of noninteger solutions. For the most part, you were probably left with the impression that the issue was not too serious and that simply rounding a continuous solution would provide a close approximation to the optimal integer solution. This approach may produce the desired results for some problems, as when x_j values are large. In general, however, we have one of two potentially serious consequences when we force an integer solution by rounding an optimal LP solution: The solution either becomes infeasible (the solution "falls" outside the solution space) or is nonoptimal (one or more other integer solutions give better results).[1]

Over the years many IP solution algorithms have been developed, and these guarantee optimal integer solutions. Although they do not have the shortcomings associated with heuristic procedures, such as rounding LP solutions, these algorithms do exact a price: *General IP algorithms are computationally costly.* For example, an IP model with several hundred variables is likely to cause a syndrome in analysts that we might call computational anxiety. By way of contrast, LP models with several thousand variables and constraints hardly cause a murmur. Computational anxiety comes from the combinatorial nature of the integer problem. With 20 zero-one variables there are 2^{20}, or more than 1 million possible solutions to examine. Fortunately, special IP algorithms have been developed to exploit the special structure found in many IP problems, thereby significantly reducing computational times.

As you study the formulations in Sections 8.2 and 8.3, keep in mind the twin issues of computational difficulty and search for special structure. A relatively nontechnical overview of solution algorithms and their performance is left to Sections 8.4 and 8.6.

Example 8.1 Air Cargo, Again

We can illustrate some solution issues by referring to the air cargo problem presented in Chapters 4 through 6. The modified problem, as rewritten using an IP format, has this form:

---

[1]In special cases rounding always gives infeasible results. See Fred Glover and David C. Sommer, "Pitfalls of Rounding in Discrete Management Decision Problems," *Decision Sciences*, April 1975, pp. 211–20.

Maximize

$$z = 20x_1 + 10x_2$$

subject to

$$5x_1 + 4x_2 \leq 24 \qquad \text{(volume)}$$

$$2x_1 + 5x_2 \leq 13 \qquad \text{(weight)}$$

$$x_j = \text{Nonnegative integers}, \qquad \text{for } j = 1, 2$$

or

$$x_j = 0, 1, 2, \ldots \qquad \text{for all } j$$

where x_1 and x_2 represent, respectively, the number of containers of beef and pork to be shipped in a cargo plane subject to volume and weight constraints. Note that the only difference between LP formulations and pure IP formulations is the replacement of the nonnegativity condition ($x_j \geq 0$) by the condition of nonnegative integers.

The optimal continuous (LP) solution recommended the shipment of 4.8 containers of beef (x_1) and no containers of pork (x_2). The maximum profit was \$96(100s). This solution assumes that 0.8 of a container can be shipped, which in reality is not possible. The problem is in fact a pure IP model, since we are restricted to shipping whole containers of meat. We might therefore suggest that simple *rounding* of the continuous solution will provide the optimal integer solution. However, by rounding x_1 up to 5, verify that the volume constraint is violated and the solution ($x_1 = 5, x_2 = 0$) is infeasible. Rounding down to $x_1 = 4$, the solution ($x_1 = 4, x_2 = 0$) is feasible and integer but, unfortunately, nonoptimal ($z = 80$). As we will show graphically, the optimal integer solution occurs at $x_1 = 4$ and $x_2 = 1$ with a resulting profit of \$90(100s).

This example shows that, although simple rounding of optimal continuous solutions is appealing, optimal or feasible results are not necessarily achieved. In the optimal integer solution, another variable entered the basis, and the results were \$10(100s) better than in the rounded down version. Moreover, the complexity exhibited in rounding continuous solutions in small problems can become overwhelming in large-scale problems. It is also important to note that without exhaustive enumeration of all combinations of integer-valued solutions or some other way to assure optimality, rounding offers no signal that we are even close to the optimal IP solution.

Geometric Perspective

For problems with two decision variables, a graphical approach lends itself very well to explaining the nature of integer solutions. Figure 8–1 portrays the solution to the air cargo problem. The optimal continuous solution occurs at point c. Notice that **lattice marks** (+) have been used to identify the feasible set of integer solution points. Since the optimal continuous solution found at point c is noninteger, the objective function, z, must be moved parallel to itself toward the origin until it intersects a feasible integer solution point. The first such point is point b, which occurs at $x_1 = 4$, $x_2 = 1$. Thus point b is the optimal integer solution. Again, notice what happens when we round the optimal continuous solution. The difference in values for z between the optimal continuous and optimal integer solutions is often called the **cost of indivisibility.** The difference—in this example 96 − 90 = \$6(100's)—represents the opportunity cost of being forced to assign integer rather than continuous values to basic variables in the optimal solution.

FIGURE 8–1 Graphical Solution to Air Cargo Problem

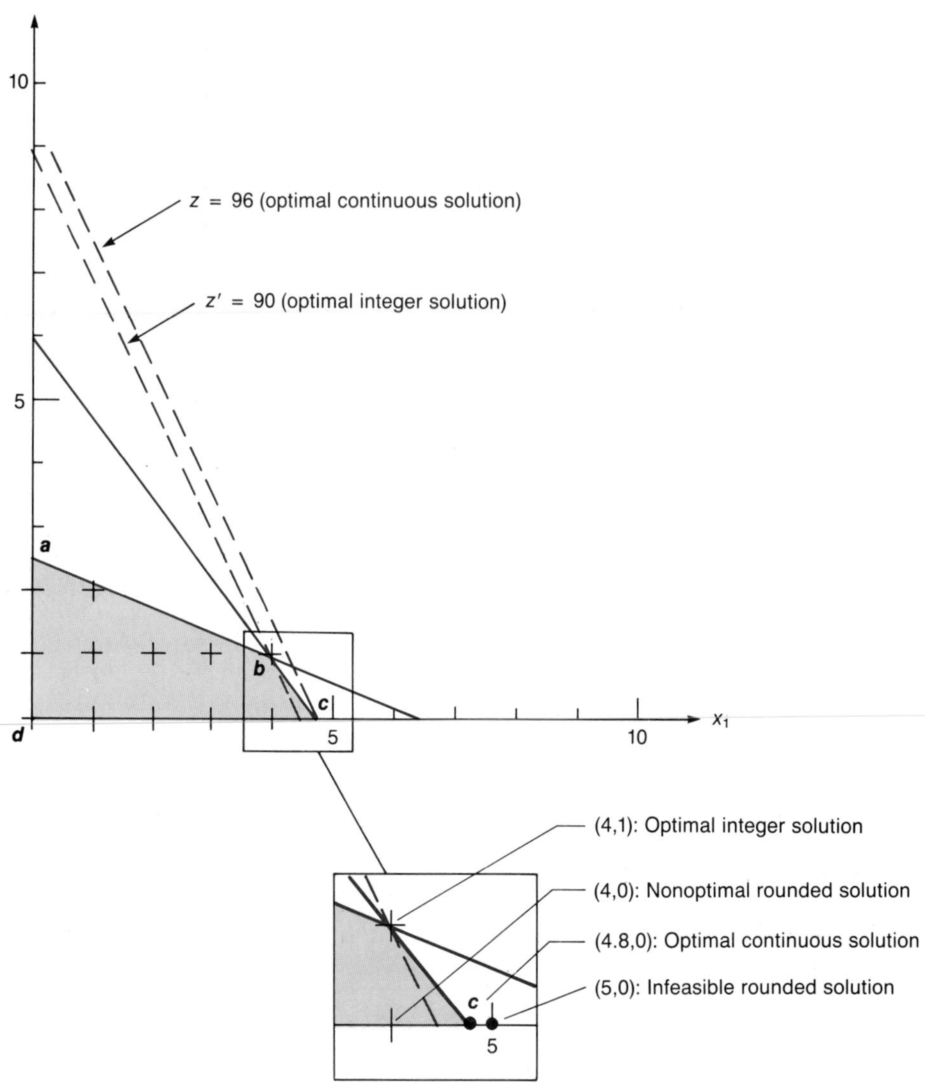

8.2 ISSUES IN PROBLEM FORMULATION

IP models make up an important class because of their widespread applicability. Many managerial problems are inherently integer programming problems. Other problems are not necessarily integer but possess *special characteristics that can be modeled accurately only through the use of binary variables*. This section presents some of these special conditions and the manner in which they can be modeled.

Mutually Exclusive Constraints

Consider a situation whereby a research and development program might be approved if available scientific personnel were used from one of two laboratory facilities but not from both laboratories. This is an example of the simplest case of mutually exclusive constraints—either-or constraints.

▶ Example 8.2 Either-Or Constraints

A company produces three different products. All products must be processed through a department that has 50 labor hours available per day. The hours required per unit of each product depend on the type of machine purchased for the department. In this instance there are two different machines available, one more highly automated than the other. If x_j = Number of units produced of product j, constraints 1 and 2 reflect the limited labor available in the department assuming the use of machines 1 and 2, respectively. Coefficients in the constraints represent hourly labor usage for production of one unit of products 1, 2, and 3, respectively. The coefficients in constraint 2 suggest that it represents the situation with the more automated machine. Why?

$$2.5x_1 + 1.8x_2 + 3.2x_3 \leq 50 \qquad (1)$$

$$2.2x_1 + 1.4x_2 + 2.5x_3 \leq 50\,. \qquad (2)$$

Only one of these constraints can be relevant, depending on the machine purchased. We use the term *relevant* to describe those constraints that have the potential to affect the solution space in a problem.

To model this situation, a new 0-1 variable, y, is introduced in the following manner to modify the original constraints:

$$2.5x_1 + 1.8x_2 + 3.2x_3 \leq 50 + My \qquad (1')$$

$$2.2x_1 + 1.4x_2 + 2.5x_3 \leq 50 + M(1-y)\,. \qquad (2')$$

M is our way of defining an arbitrarily large constant, such as 100,000. With y restricted to a value of either zero or one, the effect is as follows:

a. If $y = 1$, then the second constraint 2′ reverts to its original form (2) and becomes a relevant constraint. With M chosen sufficiently large, the right-hand side of constraint 1′ becomes so large that any values of x_1, x_2, and x_3 satisfying constraint 2 will easily satisfy 1′, making 1′ redundant.

b. If $y = 0$, then the first constraint (1′) reverts to its original form (1) and becomes relevant; constraint 2′ becomes redundant.

Note that the inclusion of y makes this a four-variable mixed-integer problem: x_1, x_2, and x_3 are the original continuous decision variables, and y is a zero-one variable that mathematically satisfies the either-or constraint. (See Exercise 1 for another interpretation of y.)

Also note that the usual formulation for computer input would place y on the left-hand sides of constraints 1′ and 2′. Thus

$$2.5x_1 + 1.8x_2 + 3.2x_3 - My \leq 50 \qquad (1')$$

$$2.2x_1 + 1.4x_2 + 2.5x_3 + My \leq 50 + M\,. \qquad (2')$$

Our choice of the variable name y is arbitrary; we could just as well have used x_4 or any other symbol. We have chosen y so as to clearly distinguish this 0-1 variable from continuous or other integer variables, x_j. Finally, the purpose of this example has been to illustrate the modeling of either-or $\leq$ constraints. We assume that these two constraints are part of a larger model. Ultimately we will deal with such issues as "How is y treated in the objective function?"

If there are m_1 mutually exclusive less-than-or-equal-to constraints, then the term My_j is added to the right-hand side of each. Each y_j is a 0-1 variable. To assure that only one of the m_1 constraints is relevant, we add an additional constraint of the form

$$\sum_{j=1}^{m_1} y_j = m_1 - 1 .$$

▶ Example 8.3 m_1 Mutually Exclusive Constraints

Given the four mutually exclusive constraints

$$x_1 + x_2 + x_3 \leq 5 \quad (1)$$

$$2x_1 - x_2 + x_3 \leq 10 \quad (2)$$

$$4x_1 - x_2 - x_3 \leq 12 \quad (3)$$

$$5x_1 - x_2 \leq 6, \quad (4)$$

four 0-1 variables must be added in the manner below in order to assure that only one of the constraints applies.

$$x_1 + x_2 + x_3 \leq 5 + My_1 \quad (1')$$

$$2x_1 - x_2 + x_3 \leq 10 + My_2 \quad (2')$$

$$4x_1 - x_2 - x_3 \leq 12 + My_3 \quad (3')$$

$$5x_1 - x_2 \leq 6 + My_4 \quad (4')$$

$$y_1 + y_2 + y_3 + y_4 = 3 \quad (5)$$

$$y_j = 0 \text{ or } 1, \quad \text{for } j = 1, 2, 3, 4 .$$

m_1 Constraints, k of Which Must Be Relevant

Some problems may require that a subset of constraints must apply in defining the solution space to the problem. Assume that of m_1 less-than-or-equal-to constraints, k of these must be relevant. As with the treatment of mutually exclusive constraints, a 0-1 variable is multiplied by an arbitrarily large constant, M, and added to the right-hand side of each constraint. To assure that only k of the m_1 constraints are relevant, the constraint below should be added to the set.

$$\sum_{j=1}^{m_1} y_j = m_1 - k$$

Number of ($\leq$) constraints in subset [m_1]

Number of constraints that apply in defining the solution space [k]

If in Example 8.3 we want three of the four constraints to be relevant, the first four constraints are treated as before, but the last constraint is replaced by

$$\begin{aligned} y_1 + y_2 + y_3 + y_4 &= 4 - 3 \\ &= 1 \end{aligned}$$

Remember, *a constraint is relevant if its associated* y_j *equals zero.*

This type of situation might arise in a problem having multiple criteria. Chapter 1 discussed the problems of multiple criteria and the concept of satisficing. A firm may establish satisfactory or minimum expected levels for a group of criteria (say, m_2), such as net profit, gross sales, market share, and a rate of return on investment. In determining whether or not to make a capital investment, management may specify that the minimum satisfactory levels for a given subset (say, k) of these criteria must be attained. (We leave the treatment of $\geq$ and $=$ constraints to Exercises 4 and 8.)

Fixed Charge Problems. In our discussions of linear programming, any cost minimization problems assumed that fixed costs are constant and need not be explicitly accounted for in the formulation of the LP model. Such was the case in Example 3.3 (Multiperiod, Product Mix Model). Many problems involve a fixed charge element that cannot be realistically modeled by linear programming. The conversion of the original problem to a mixed integer programming problem allows variations in fixed charges and related effects on variable costs.

Example 8.4 Economies of Scale

Economies of scale are well-recognized within production systems. A product mix problem may contain the alternatives of using different types of machinery to produce an item (as in Example 8.2). A more expensive machine or a more automated production process may result in lower variable production costs per unit at higher levels of output than a less expensive machine designed to operate at lower levels of output. The typical rule is that higher fixed cost configurations lead to the trade-off of lower per-unit variable cost.

Suppose a company is considering the alternative of using three different production processes in order to satisfy production requirements for a given item. Let x_j be the number of units produced using process j; k_j be the setup or fixed cost associated with operating process j; and c_j be the variable production cost per unit for process j. Although we will assume that other constraints exist in the problem, our concern here is to demonstrate how to represent the *fixed cost element.* Based on our definitions, the total cost for each process is represented by the equations

$$C_j = \begin{cases} k_j + c_j x_j & \text{if } x_j > 0 \\ 0 & \text{if } x_j = 0, \end{cases} \qquad \text{for } j = 1, 2, 3.$$

To represent this situation, we introduce the 0-1 variable y_j, which assumes a value of one if process j is used ($x_j > 0$) and a value of zero if process j is not used ($x_j = 0$). The objective function for minimizing overall total cost becomes

Minimize

$$\begin{aligned} z &= \quad C_1 \quad + \quad C_2 \quad + \quad C_3 \\ &= (k_1 y_1 + c_1 x_1) + (k_2 y_2 + c_2 x_2) + (k_3 y_3 + c_3 x_3). \end{aligned}$$

Our other concern is that each y_j takes on the appropriate value. That is, y_j must equal zero or one, only, and must equal one whenever $x_j > 0$. Depending on the computer code used, we specify zero-one variables in one of two equivalent ways:

(a) $$y_j = 0 \quad \text{or} \quad 1 \qquad \text{for } j = 1, 2, 3$$

or

(b) $$y_j \leq 1 \qquad \text{for } j = 1, 2, 3$$

and

$$y_j = \text{Nonnegative integer} \qquad \text{for } j = 1, 2, 3.$$

We would use alternative (a) for solution algorithms that explicitly identify binary variables and alternative (b) for solution algorithms that identify only continuous and integer variables. In the latter case, the $y_j \leq 1$ conditions would be input either as explicit constraints or as "upper bounds" on integer variables, depending on the algorithm. If y_j must be integer and less than or equal to one, y_j must be either zero or one.

To make sure that fixed costs are added in when process j is used, we must ensure that $y_j = 1$ whenever $x_j > 0$. Moreover, when $x_j = 0$ we want $y_j = 0$. This relationship between a continuous or integer x_j variable and a corresponding binary y_j variable is a common characteristic of fixed-charge problems. We can satisfy the (x_j, y_j) relationship by specifying the constraints

$$x_j \leq My_j$$

or

$$x_j - My_j \leq 0 \qquad \text{for } j = 1, 2, 3.$$

M, as before, is a constant having a value much larger than any value possibly assumed by x_j. The only way for x_j to assume a value greater than zero is for y_j to equal one. Verify that if x_j is greater than zero and $y_j = 0$, then there is a contradiction. Also notice that when $x_j > 0$ and $y_j = 1$ the above constraint is satisfied but is redundant (presuming M has been assigned a large enough value). Moreover, the constraint together with the nonnegativity condition guarantees the case $x_j = 0$ and $y_j = 0$.

Interdependent Variables

In some problems, a mutual dependence may exist between variables. An example might be such a project as building a second floor that requires the first floor project to precede it.

▶ Example 8.5 Dependent Projects

Let us define x_j as a 0-1 variable representing the acceptance ($x_j = 1$) or rejection ($x_j = 0$) of project j. If project 3 cannot be accepted unless project 2 has been accepted, then this restriction can be accounted for by including the constraint

$$x_3 \leq x_2$$

or

$$-x_2 + x_3 \leq 0.$$

If projects 2 and 3 must be undertaken together or not at all, then the condition can be represented by the constraint

$$x_2 - x_3 = 0.$$

FOLLOW-UP EXERCISES

This section has shown the manner in which certain special conditions that arise in problem formulation can be handled by integer programming. The conditions treated are by no means exhaustive of all that you might encounter. Try your luck on the following problems, not all of which have been discussed in the previous section.

1. Consider Example 8.2.
   a. Interpret the meaning of $y = 0$ and $y = 1$ with respect to machine purchases.
   b. Would we have an equivalent model by using $50 + My_1$ and $50 + My_2$ as the right-hand sides of constraints 1′ and 2′, where $y_j = 0$ or 1? Explain. Would any other changes be required? Interpret the meaning of $y_j = 0$ and $y_j = 1$.
2. Suppose in Example 8.2 that three machines can be used in the department. The third alternative is represented by the constraint

$$2.3x_1 + 1.6x_2 + 2.8x_3 \leq 50. \qquad (3)$$

   a. Any conclusions about machine 3 as compared with machines 1 and 2?
   b. Model the condition that results in one of the three being used.
3. Consider Example 8.4.
   a. Do any of the constraints prevent the contradiction $x_j = 0$ and $y_j = 1$? Explain. Would you expect that an optimal solution would ever give us this contradiction? Explain.
   b. Explain how the formulation guarantees the results in the table below.

	$y_j = 0$	$y_j = 1$
$x_j = 0$	Consistent	Contradictory
$x_j > 0$	Contradictory	Consistent

4. **≥ *Constraints.*** If there are two either-or (≥) constraints, does the formulation change from the way in which ≤ constraints were treated in this section? If so, demonstrate by example.
5. Given the following mutually exclusive constraints, reformulate them so as to assure the condition of mutual exclusiveness (i.e., that one and only one constraint applies).

$$x_1 + x_2 + x_3 \leq 40 \qquad (1)$$

$$2x_1 - x_2 + x_3 \geq 20 \qquad (2)$$

$$x_1 - x_3 \geq 15. \qquad (3)$$

6. Of a set of projects being considered for investment purposes, three projects are interrelated. If x_j is a 0-1 variable representing the rejection or acceptance of project j:
   a. Formulate the condition that assures at least two of the three projects must be accepted.
   b. Formulate the conditions that assure either all three projects are accepted or all three are rejected.

7. ***Lot Sizes.*** Suppose product j can be purchased or manufactured only in minimum lot sizes L_j such that either $x_j = 0$ or $x_j \geq L_j$, where x_j = Units of product j. Formulate the two constraints that guarantee minimum lot-sizing for product j.

8. ***Equality Constraints.* The treatment of mutually exclusive equality constraints is considerably different than for $\leq$ or $\geq$ constraints. How would the following either-or constraints be treated? (Hint: Equality constraints can be rewritten in an equivalent inequality form.)

$$x_1 + x_2 + x_3 = 25 \quad (1)$$

or

$$x_1 + x_2 + x_3 = 40. \quad (2)$$

**9. Given the following constraint set, reformulate such that two of the three constraints are relevant.

$$2x_1 + 4x_2 + x_3 \leq 200 \quad (1)$$

$$x_1 + x_2 + x_3 \geq 50 \quad (2)$$

$$3x_1 - x_2 + 5x_3 = 35. \quad (3)$$

8.3 SELECTED APPLICATIONS

This section illustrates problems that lend themselves to formulation as integer programming models. A number of the formulation issues discussed earlier are illustrated by these applications. In all cases we defer solutions until Section 8.4.

▶ Example 8.6 Fire Unit Model (Set Covering/Zero-One)

Emergency response systems have received considerable attention by operations researchers. One concern is positioning of emergency response units within a city. Units in this instance may refer to fire-fighting units, ambulance units, or police patrol units. Questions that have been addressed include the *prepositioning* of units prior to the beginning of a tour of duty and the *repositioning* of remaining units when certain units become unavailable.

Assume that a city has eight fire stations, which service 22 fire districts within the city. Figure 8–2 indicates relative locations of the fire stations and fire districts. Analysis of historical response time data has led to the identification of fire stations that can respond to fires in each fire district within a predetermined maximum allowable average response time. The branches of Figure 8–2 indicate the districts that each fire station can service within the average allowable response time. The absence of a branch between any station and fire district implies that the station cannot respond within the allowable time.

The Board of Fire Commissioners is interested in considering if some of the existing fire stations can be closed. Can the city get by with fewer than the existing eight stations and, if so, which can be eliminated? One way to look at this question is to find the smallest set of fire stations required to *cover* all fire districts. *Cover* in this instance means that at least one fire station would be able to respond to all fire districts within the maximum allowable average response time. Problems of this type are called **set-covering problems,** and have been applied to such diverse problems as airline crew scheduling and political districting.

FIGURE 8–2 Fire Station and Fire District Locations

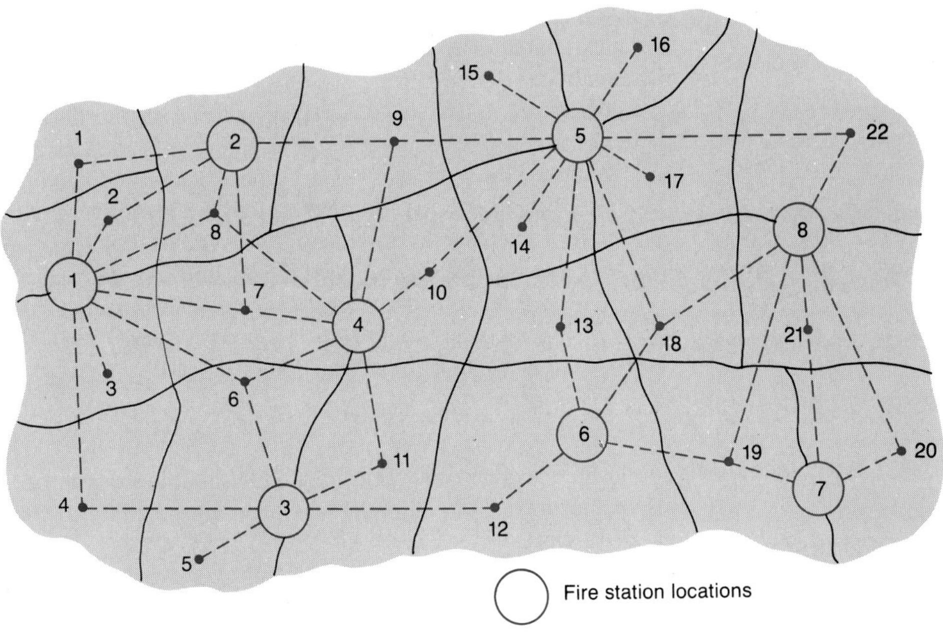

This problem can be formulated as a 0-1 programming model. Since we are going to focus on a set of applications in this section, let us utilize the problem-solving framework for this example. You may find it useful as you attempt problem formulations and solutions in this chapter.

1. **Verbal Statement of Problem**
   Determine the fire station locations at which fire equipment should be positioned so as to minimize the number of locations used.

2. **Decisions**
   a. **Verbal Statement**
   Locations where equipment should be positioned.
   b. **Mathematical Definition**

$$x_j = \begin{cases} 0 & \text{if equipment not positioned in location } j \\ 1 & \text{if equipment positioned in location } j. \end{cases}$$

3. **Criteria**
   a. **Verbal Statement**
   Minimize the number of fire station locations used.
   b. **Mathematical Statement**

   Minimize

$$z = x_1 + x_2 + x_3 + \ldots + x_8$$

$$= \sum_{j=1}^{8} x_j$$

4. **Constraining Conditions**

   a. **Verbal Statement**

   Assure that at least one fire station can respond to each fire district within the maximum allowable response time.

   b. **Mathematical Statement**

   The constraint set includes one constraint for each fire district. To develop these constraints, we must refer to Figure 8–2. For each fire district we identify those fire stations that can respond within the maximum allowable response time. In Figure 8–2 these stations are identified by the dashed line connecting the station and fire district. For fire district 1, dashed lines from locations 1 and 2 indicate that these are the only two that can respond to district 1. Therefore, as we go about making decisions about the location of equipment, equipment should be positioned in at least one of these two locations. The mathematical representation of this is

$$x_1 + x_2 \geq 1 .$$

   To illustrate another constraint, Figure 8–2 indicates that three locations can respond to district 18 within the maximum allowable time. The corresponding constraint is

$$x_5 + x_6 + x_8 \geq 1 .$$

   The remaining 20 constraints are developed in a similar manner.

5. **Mathematical Model**

   Although we leave the detailed formulation to you in Exercise 10, the complete model has the following structure:

   Minimize

$$z = x_1 + x_2 + x_3 + \ldots + x_8$$

   subject to

$$\begin{aligned} x_1 + x_2 &\geq 1 \quad \text{(district 1)} \\ x_1 + x_2 &\geq 1 \quad \text{(district 2)} \\ &\vdots \\ x_5 + x_8 &\geq 1 \quad \text{(district 22)} \\ x_j = 0 \quad &\text{or} \quad 1, \qquad \text{for all } j \end{aligned}$$

A general formulation for the set-covering problem is given by:

Minimize

$$z = \sum_{j=1}^{n} c_j x_j$$

subject to

$$\sum_{j=1}^{n} a_{ij}x_j \geq 1, \qquad i = 1, \ldots, m$$

$$x_j = 0 \quad \text{or} \quad 1 \qquad \text{for } j = 1, \ldots, n$$

where a_{ij} is a 0-1 coefficient. If all constraints were equalities, then we would have a **set-partitioning problem.** What assumptions in the fire unit scenario would result in a set-partitioning model?

FOLLOW-UP EXERCISES

10. Complete the formulation of the fire station problem.
11. Examination of Figure 8–2 should reveal that units *must* be located at certain fire stations, such as station 5. Show how this observation as well as other related redundancies allow the original formulation to be simplified considerably. By trial and error, solve for the optimal solution.
12. High fire incidence districts may require the services of more than one fire unit. Specify appropriate constraints if districts 1 and 6 require coverage from at least two and three fire units, respectively.
13. Discuss other issues of fire unit response that this simplified scenario fails to address. Also, discuss other criteria that might be considered in this problem.

▶ Example 8.7 Facility Location: Solid Waste Location/Distribution Model (Fixed Charge/*m* Constraints, *k* of *m* Relevant)

A major city is currently using three incinerator sites for processing solid waste. Garbage is collected from six collection areas and transported to the different incineration sites.

Overcome by smoke and public outcry, the city council has proposed the development of two new landfill areas. Four sites are being considered for purchase by the city; only two will be purchased. Based on a projected 10-year period of use for each landfill area selected, monthly tonnage capacities have been estimated.

The city comptroller also has estimated relevant costs for the system. Variable costs include both transportation and operating costs at each site. In addition, a monthly amortization cost (based on the anticipated purchase price) has been estimated for each proposed site. The estimated transportation costs per ton and other data are summarized in Table 8–1.

The objective is to determine the two sites to purchase and the number of tons to be transported from each collection area to each site so as to minimize the sum of monthly amortization, transportation, and operating costs.

This problem is an extension of the transportation problem and can be formulated as a *mixed integer programming model.* Let x_{ij} equal the number of tons of garbage transported from collection area i to landfill j. Also let us define the binary variable:

$$y_j = \begin{cases} 1 & \text{if site } j \text{ is purchased;} \\ 0 & \text{otherwise,} \qquad \text{for } j = 1, \ldots, 4. \end{cases}$$

TABLE 8–1 Solid Waste Transportation Data

Collection Area	Landfill Site 1	2	3	4	Forecasted Collections (tons/month)
1	$70	$80	$50	$40	1,500
2	60	55	60	70	1,750
3	65	40	45	55	2,500
4	50	75	70	60	2,000
5	40	60	50	55	2,800
6	55	50	40	30	2,200
Capacities (tons/month)	7,000	6,000	5,500	6,000	
Operating costs ($/ton)	40	50	55	45	
Amoritization costs ($/month)	5,000	4,000	3,500	4,500	

Starting with the objective function, let us focus on the variable costs per ton. If a ton of garbage is transported from area 1 to landfill 1, the transportation cost is $70 and the processing cost at the landfill is $40. Thus variable cost per ton is $110, and total variable cost for tonnage distributed between this collection area–landfill combination is $110x_{11}$. Monthly amortization cost for landfill 1 is computed as $5{,}000y_1$. If landfill 1 is not purchased, $y_1 = 0$, and this expression equals zero. By applying similar logic to the remaining routes, we state the objective function as:

Minimize

$$z = \text{Monthly transportation and operating costs} + \text{monthly amortization cost.}$$

$$= 110x_{11} + 130x_{12} + 105x_{13} + 85x_{14} + \dots + 75x_{64} + 5{,}000y_1 + 4{,}000y_2 + 3{,}500y_3 + 4{,}500y_4.$$

Can you verify the coefficients on x_{ij}? Note that monthly amortization costs are examples of fixed charges.

Two sets of structural constraints exist for this problem: monthly supply of garbage from each collection area and monthly capacity at each landfill site. The six supply constraints have the form

$$x_{11} + x_{12} + x_{13} + x_{14} = 1{,}500 \quad (1)$$

$$\vdots \qquad\qquad \vdots \qquad\qquad \vdots$$

$$x_{61} + x_{62} + x_{63} + x_{64} = 2{,}200. \quad (6)$$

The capacity constraints at each landfill must reflect the fact that capacity is available only if the site is purchased. The four capacity constraints are thus stated in the form

$$x_{11} + x_{21} + x_{31} + x_{41} + x_{51} + x_{61} \leq 7{,}000y_1 \quad (7)$$

$$x_{12} + x_{22} + x_{32} + x_{42} + x_{52} + x_{62} \leq 6{,}000y_2 \quad (8)$$

$$x_{13} + x_{23} + x_{33} + x_{43} + x_{53} + x_{63} \leq 5{,}500y_3 \quad (9)$$

$$x_{14} + x_{24} + x_{34} + x_{44} + x_{54} + x_{64} \leq 6{,}000y_4 \quad (10)$$

Note that the capacity for the jth landfill becomes zero if the landfill is not purchased ($y_j = 0$). Also, in the standard form for computer input, these four constraints would be rewritten with the right-hand side equaling zero. For example, constraint 7 would have the form

$$x_{11} + x_{21} + x_{31} + x_{41} + x_{51} + x_{61} - 7{,}000y_1 \leq 0\,.$$

Since only two of the four landfills will be purchased, we need the constraint

$$y_1 + y_2 + y_3 + y_4 = 2\,. \tag{11}$$

Finally, the nonnegativity constraints have these forms:

$$x_{ij} \geq 0 \qquad \text{for all } i, j$$

and

$$y_j = 0 \quad \text{or} \quad 1 \qquad \text{for all } j\,.$$

This particular problem is a variation of a class of transportation problems variously called **facility** or **plant** or **warehouse location problems.** (Try Exercise 16 for the generalized model.) If all demands can be satisfied, then the plant location problem is said to be **uncapacitated**; otherwise, it's termed **capacitated**.

FOLLOW-UP EXERCISES

14. With respect to Example 8.7:
    a. Modify the formulation such that the number of sites purchased is not fixed (at two) but is allowed to vary between one and four.
    b. The typical fixed-charge problem (see Example 8.4) would ensure the proper relationship between x_{ij} and y_j (that is, $x_{ij} > 0$ only if $y_j = 1$) by specifying the constraints

    $$x_{ij} - M_j y_j \leq 0 \quad \text{for all } i \text{ and } j$$

    where M_j in this case would be the landfill capacities. This approach would require 24 distinct constraints for our example. Explain why we don't need these constraints here.
15. ***Fixed-Charge Transportation Model.*** Modify the general transportation model LP formulation in Chapter 7 (page xxx) to include fixed charges f_{ij} for each route. If $x_{ij} > 0$, then the lump-sum charge f_{ij} is incurred for using that route; if $x_{ij} = 0$, then the fixed charge is not incurred.
16. ***Plant Location I.*** In a plant location problem assume that m sites are being considered as possible supply points to meet the demand at n destinations. Each potential site i has an available supply, s_i, each destination j has a demand, d_j. The objective is to select the sites and the amounts to be shipped from each site to each demand point so as to minimize total costs. Costs can include transportation cost per unit shipped from site i to demand point j (t_{ij}), manufacturing cost per unit at site i (c_i), and fixed overhead costs (f_i) that depend on the supply sites selected.

    Let x_{ij} equal the number of units shipped from origin i to destination j, and let y_i be a 0-1 variable that equals 1 if site i is selected as a plant location. Formulate the generalized IP model for this situation.

17. ***Plant Location II.* Refer to the preceding exercise.
    a. Suppose each destination is allowed to receive shipments from no more than r origins. How would this affect the formulation?
    b. Suppose each origin could ship to no more than p destinations. How would the formulation be affected?

18. ***Plant Location III.*** Formulate the plant location problem (as described in Exercise 16) for the case where two sites and four demand points are under consideration. The fixed costs associated with sites 1 and 2 are $80,000 and $50,000, respectively. Other pertinent data are provided in Table 8–2 (all costs have been discounted to the present).

TABLE 8–2 Data for Plant Location Problem

Supply Point	Demand Point 1	2	3	4	Capacity per Planning Period
1	1.00 3.00	1.20 2.00	1.10 3.00	0.50 1.00	40,000
2	0.75 5.00	0.60 3.00	2.00 2.00	1.05 4.00	35,000
Demand per Planning Period	20,000	15,000	17,000	22,000	74,000 / 75,000

Note: The first entry in each cell represents unit transportation cost (dollars per unit) for the given route; the second entry represents unit manufacturing cost (dollars per unit) at each plant.

▶ Example 8.8 Quantity Discount/Lot Size Model (Piecewise Linear Functions)

Opple Inc., a microcomputer manufacturer located in the Sunbelt, plans to award contracts for the supply of 50,000 random access memory (RAM) units. Three subcontractors have submitted bids. Subcontractor 1 bid $30 per unit for orders up to 10,000 units and $15 per unit for any units in excess of 10,000. This contractor placed no restrictions on the size of the order. Subcontractor 2 will supply no more than 20,000 units at a price of $20 per unit. Subcontractor 3 will supply no less than 30,000 units at a price of $17 per unit.

RAM units are standardized and essentially equally reliable, so all units need not be supplied by the same subcontractor. Moreover, Opple need not give an award to the low bidder (unlike certain agencies we know). Opple's objective, of course, is to determine how many units to order from each subcontractor so as to fulfill its requirement of 50,000 units at the lowest possible overall cost.

If we define the integer variable x_j as the number of units to award contractor j, then the objective function is given by

Minimize

$$z = 30d_1 + 15d_2 + 20x_2 + 17x_3.$$

The terms $20x_2 + 17x_3$ follow readily from the statement of the problem. The expression $30d_1 + 15d_2$ reflects the **quantity discount** structure offered by subcontractor 1. To understand this, consider Figure 8–3, which shows the **piecewise linear function** that describes the prices offered by subcontractor 1. For example, if Opple were to

FIGURE 8–3 Quantity Discount Function

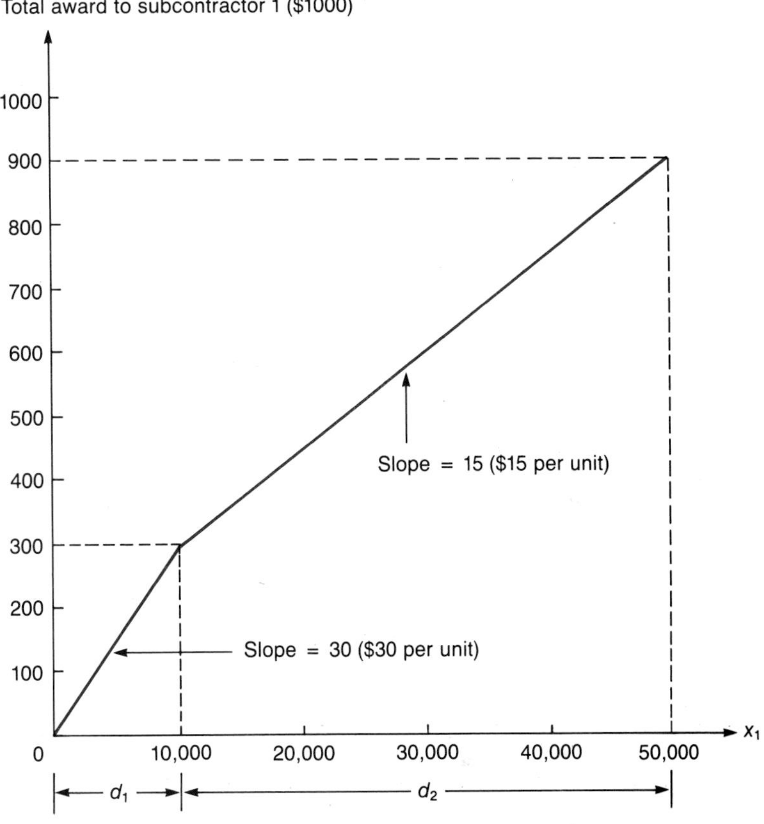

order all 50,00 units from subcontractor 1, it would cost \$30 per unit for the first 10,000 units and \$15 per unit for the next 40,000 units, for a total of \$90,000.

To model this piecewise linear function, we introduce new nonnegative integer variables d_1 and d_2 for each piecewise segment. In this case, d_1 is the amount by which x_1 exceeds 0, but is less than or equal to 10,000; d_2 is the amount by which x_1 exceeds 10,000, but is less than or equal to 50,000. Thus $0 \leq d_1 \leq 10{,}000$ and $0 \leq d_2 \leq 40{,}000$. For example, if Opple orders 40,000 units from subcontractor 1, then $d_1 = 10{,}000$ and $d_2 = 30{,}000$. For an order of 5,000 units, $d_1 = 5{,}000$ and $d_2 = 0$. In effect, we have defined the relationship

$$x_1 = d_1 + d_2,$$

which translates into the first constraint

$$x_1 - d_1 - d_2 = 0. \tag{1}$$

We must further ensure that $d_1 \leq 10{,}000$, that $d_1 = 10{,}000$ whenever $d_2 > 0$, and that $d_2 \leq 40{,}000$. We can do this by specifying the conditions

$$10{,}000y \leq d_1 \leq 10{,}000$$
$$0 \leq d_2 \leq 40{,}000y$$

where y is a binary variable. These conditions translate into the constraints

$$d_1 \leq 10{,}000 \tag{2}$$

$$d_1 - 10{,}000y \geq 0 \tag{3}$$

$$d_2 - 40{,}000y \leq 0. \tag{4}$$

Note that

$$y = \begin{cases} 1 & \text{if } d_1 \text{ is at its upper bound of } 10{,}000; \\ 0 & \text{otherwise}. \end{cases}$$

For example, if the algorithm assigns optimal values of $d_1 = 10{,}000$ and $d_2 = 30{,}000$, then the algorithm sets $x_1 = 40{,}000$ to satisfy constraint 1 and sets $y = 1$ to satisfy constraints 3 and 4.[2]

The restriction on the size of the order from subcontractor 2 is given by

$$x_2 \leq 20{,}000. \tag{5}$$

To handle the restriction of an order for no less than 30,000 units from subcontractor 3, we might be tempted to write $x_3 \geq 30{,}000$. Before reading on, do you see a problem with this? This constraint would force us to use subcontractor 3. What we really want to model is either $x_3 = 0$ or $x_3 \geq 30{,}000$. The following **lot-size constraints** handle this condition:

$$x_3 \leq Mw$$

or equivalently

$$x_3 - Mw \leq 0 \tag{6}$$

and

$$x_3 \geq 30{,}000w$$

or equivalently

$$x_3 - 30{,}000w \geq 0 \tag{7}$$

where, as before, M is any large constant (in this case we should use at least 50,000 for M because x_3 should not exceed the total requirement of 50,000 units) and w is a binary variable. Thus, if $w = 0$, we have $x_3 = 0$ from constraints 6 and 7. However, if $w = 1$, then 6 becomes redundant and 7 ensures $x_3 \geq 30{,}000$.

The requirement for 50,000 RAM units is given by

$$x_1 + x_2 + x_3 = 50{,}000. \tag{8}$$

Finally, we specify the sign/variable type conditions:

x_j = Nonnegative integer for $j = 1, 2, 3$.
d_k = Nonnegative integer for $k = 1, 2$.
y = 0 or 1.
w = 0 or 1.

[2]Piecewise linear functions are also used to approximate nonlinear continuous functions in nonlinear programming.

This problem illustrates two frequent modeling conditions. **Quantity discount structures** are common in pricing environments and in production processes that exhibit *economies of scale.* **Lot sizes** are common to production and ordering environments, as when products are produced or received in minimum-size batches. Lot sizes also apply to certain portfolio models where the number of shares purchased of security j (x_j) is subject to some lower bound.

FOLLOW-UP EXERCISES

19. Based on constraints 1 through 4 in Example 8.8:
    a. What values would be assigned to y, d_1, and d_2 if $x_1 = 5{,}000$? If $x_1 = 0$?
    b. According to the objective function, a minimization algorithm will try to assign values to d_2 before d_1. Show how these constraints would prevent the incorrect result $x_2 = 25{,}000$, $d_1 = 0$, $d_2 = 25{,}000$.
20. Modify the formulation in Example 8.8 as follows:
    a. Award contracts to no more than two subcontractors.
    b. Make sure we place an order with at least one domestic firm. (Subcontractors 2 and 3 are domestic firms.)

21. ***Multiple-Quantity Discounts.* If a piecewise linear function has p segments, then we need to ensure the conditions

$$x_j - \sum_{k=1}^{p} d_k = 0$$

$$L_k y_k \le d_k \le L_k y_{k-1} \qquad k = 1, \ldots, p$$

where d_k and y_k follow from the example, L_k is the length of the kth piecewise segment projected on the x_j axis, and $y_0 = 1$.

a. Show that constraints 1 through 4 and the nonnegativity condition on d_p reflect these general conditions.
b. Reformulate Example 8.8 if subcontractor 1 offers the following discount structure:

Quantity Break (units)	Price ($/unit)
10,000	30
20,000	25
30,000	20
40,000	15
50,000	10

▶ Example 8.9 Political Campaign Tour (Zero-One/Interdependent Variables)

The campaign manager for a presidential candidate is planning a campaign tour to the capitals of four states believed to be critical to winning. Leaving from Washington, D.C., the candidate wants to visit each capital and then return to Washington. Because of rapidly diminishing balances in campaign coffers, as well as investigative reporters interested in efficient use of public campaign funds, the campaign manager wishes to minimize transportation costs of the trip for the candidate and his traveling staff.

Finding the minimum cost tour is a classic **traveling salesman** problem that can be formulated as a 0-1 integer programming problem. The decision variable x_{ij} equals one if the tour includes a leg in which there is travel *from* city i *to* city j and x_{ij} equals zero if there is no trip from city i to city j. The usual objective is to minimize either travel cost or travel distance, where c_{ij} is defined as the cost (or distance) associated with traveling from city i to city j. This leads to the general form of the objective function:

Minimize

$$z = \sum_{i=1}^{n} \sum_{j=1}^{n} c_{ij}x_{ij} \tag{1}$$

where n equals the *total number* of cities (including the starting point). For example, $n = 5$ for the campaign tour above. A value of $x_{ij} = 1$ when $i = j$ makes no sense. (Do you see why?) In order to prevent the assignment of a value of one to these variables, they may be excluded in the formulation or assigned extremely large cost coefficients in the objective function.

The constraint set typically consists of three types of constraints. The first assures that each city is visited exactly one time:

$$\sum_{\substack{i=1 \\ i \neq j}}^{n} x_{ij} = 1 \quad \text{for } j = 1, 2, \ldots, n. \tag{2}$$

For example, the constraint for city 3 in a five-city problem would read

$$x_{13} + x_{23} + x_{43} + x_{53} = 1 .$$

The second subset of constraints assures that there is exactly one departure from each of the n cities:

$$\sum_{\substack{j=1 \\ j \neq i}}^{n} x_{ij} = 1 \quad \text{for } i = 1, 2, \ldots, n. \tag{3}$$

The constraint

$$x_{21} + x_{23} + x_{24} + x_{25} = 1 ,$$

for example, ensures this condition for city 2.

If no other constraints were to be specified, this problem would have the exact form of the *assignment model* discussed in Chapter 7. However, there can be values for the decision variables that satisfy constraint sets 2 and 3 but that do not fulfill the travel, objectives. The formulation, as it now stands, allows **subtours** (a return to the same city). Figure 8–4 illustrates one subtour solution to a five-city problem that is to originate and terminate at city 1. Note that this solution represents a valid mathematical solution to the problem specified by constraint sets 2 and 3. Since a complete tour is not accomplished, however, it represents a meaningless (real-world) solution. Consequently, it's necessary to include a third constraint set that prohibits such subtours as those illustrated in Figure 8–4.

To prevent two-city subtours, we simply specify that if there is travel from city i to city j, then there cannot be travel from j to i. For example, to prevent a subtour between cities 1 and 3, we formulate this constraint.

$$x_{13} + x_{31} \leq 1 .$$

FIGURE 8–4 Two City and Three-City Subtours for Five-City Problems

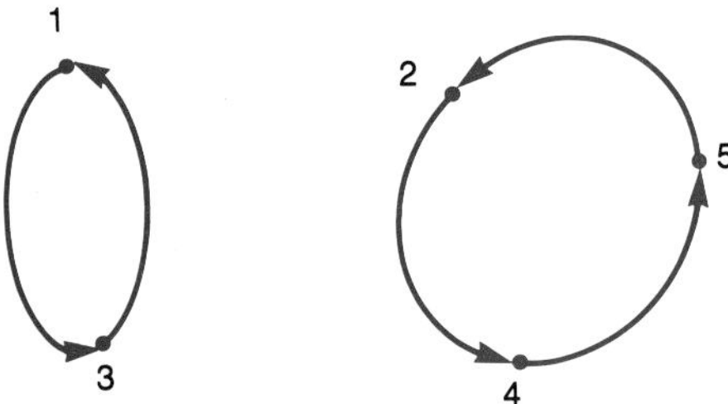

To prevent three-city subtours, two constraints must be constructed for *each combination* of three cities. For example all three-city subtours among cities 2, 4, and 5 can be prevented by specifying the following two constraints:

$$x_{24} + x_{45} + x_{52} \leq 2$$

$$x_{25} + x_{54} + x_{42} \leq 2 .$$

Note that the first of these two constraints eliminates the subtour indicated in Figure 8–4. Further note that the first constraint implies travel from city 2 to city 4 to city 5 and back to city 2. Algebraically, you should confirm that it does not matter where one begins in a circular subtour. For example, write down the constraint preventing travel from city 4 to city 5 to city 2 and back to city 4, and mathematically compare this to the first constraint above.

Now carefully consider the following: For a tour involving five cities, only two-city subtours need to be prevented to eliminate the possibility of all subtours. If all two-city subtours are eliminated, then all three-city subtours are automatically eliminated in a five-city problem, as guaranteed by constraint sets 2 and 3. In Figure 8–4, for example, if the subtour between city 1 and city 3 is eliminated by the appropriate constraint, then the indicated three-city subtour is not possible if at the same time we are to satisfy constraint sets 2 and 3. Furthermore, for a five-city problem, four-city subtours are impossible because one-city subtours ($x_{ij} = 1$ for $i = j$) are disallowed by simply eliminating all x_{ij} variables. The number of two-city subtours in a five-city problem is given by combinations of 5 taken two at a time, or 10. Since a single constraint eliminates a given two-city subtour, it follows that 10 constraints are required to eliminate all subtours in a five-city problem. Finally, we specify the nonnegativity/variable type conditions:

$$x_{ij} = 0 \quad \text{or} \quad 1 \qquad \text{for all } i \text{ and } j .$$

The traveling salesrep model is an example of a general class of models called **sequencing**, **scheduling**, and **routing problems.** Important applications include truck routings, pipeline distribution systems, and production scheduling. For example, a series of products may need to be scheduled on a common production facility so as to minimize setup costs. Consider soap making at a company such as Procter & Gamble, where Tide, Oxydol, Dreft, Cheer, and other brands are made. The cost of switching from Tide to white Oxydol is low, higher from Tide to blue Cheer, and still higher from Cheer to Tide. By conceptualizing each soap as a "city" and the facility as the "salesrepresentative," it follows that the above model is applicable.

Sequencing, scheduling, and routing problems are all examples of so-called **combinatorial problems.** As the size of the problem (measured by n) increases, the number of feasible solutions "explodes," as shown in Table 8–3. Combinatorial problems are usually straightforward to conceptualize and formulate but difficult to solve because of formulation size and computer processing time limitations. As a result, much effort has gone into developing special-purpose and heuristic algorithms for solving these problems.

TABLE 8–3 Combinatorial Explosion for Traveling Salesman Problem

n	Number of Feasible Solutions*
5	0.24×10^{2}
10	0.36×10^{6}
15	0.87×10^{11}
20	0.12×10^{18}
50	0.61×10^{63}

FOLLOW-UP EXERCISES

22. Answer the following:
   a. In a six-city tour, why need we only eliminate two-city and three-city subtours?
   b. In a seven-city tour, why need we only eliminate two-city and three-city subtours?
   c. In an eight-city tour, all two-city, three-city, and four-city subtours must be eliminated. Write down the necessary constraints to eliminate all subtours among cities 2, 5, 6, and 8. (*Hint:* Six constraints are needed to eliminate all subtours among four specific cities.)
   d. How many two-city, three-city, and four-city subtours are possible in an eight-city tour? How many constraints are needed to eliminate all of these two-city, three-city, and four-city subtours? How many total constraints in an eight-city problem? How many variables?
   e. How many variables and constraints must be specified in a seven-city problem? A six-city problem?
23. Let k represent the number of cities in a subtour. Write general algebraic expressions for the following.
   a. For an n-city problem, what values of k must be considered?
   b. How many constraints are needed to eliminate all subtours among k specific cities?
   c. How many constraints are needed to eliminate all k-city subtours given n total cities?
   d. How many constraints are needed to eliminate all subtours given n total cities?
   e. For the number of cities below indicate the number of variables and the total number of constraints in the model. How might you describe the rate of increase in the size of the model relative to the rate of increase in the number of cities?
      (1) $n = 5$
      (2) $n = 10$
      (3) $n = 20$
      (4) $n = 40$

*Given n cities, $(n - 1)!$ is the number of tours or feasible solutions. Convince yourself by listing the number of possible tours for three-city, four-city, and five-city problems.

24. Given the estimated transportation costs for each pair of cities in Table 8–4, completely formulate the five-city campaign tour problem. Does it matter what number you label Washington, D.C.? How many five-city tours are possible?

TABLE 8–4 Transportation Costs ($1,000s)

	To City				
From City	**1**	**2**	**3**	**4**	**5**
1	—	22	34	10	25
2	22	—	15	56	48
3	34	15	—	45	24
4	10	56	45	—	9
5	25	48	24	9	—

Note: City 1 is Washington, D.C.

25. Consider the following situations:
   a. Suppose the presidential candidate wishes to visit city 5 directly after city 3. How is this represented in the model? Does this result in any simplification of the model?
   b. Because of the good press coverage and the support expected in cities 4 and 2, the presidential candidate wants to visit city 5 directly after a visit to either 4 or 2. (City 5 is believed to be the city of weakest support.) How would you represent this constraint in the model?
26. ***Complete Enumeration.*** Given the data in Table 8–4, list each of the 24 possible tours together with their associated cost. State the optimal tour and its cost.
27. ***Greedy Algorithm.*** Solve the five-city problem in Table 8–4 by applying the following heuristic algorithm: Select the least-cost city from the remaining cities as the next city to be visited. Start and end in Washington, D.C. (Compare this solution to that in the preceding exercise.)

Example 8.10 Knapsack Problem (Zero-One)

The *knapsack problem* is a classical OR allocation problem that has a wide range of applications. In the classical problem a knapsack is to be filled with a selection from n possible items. If $x_j = 1$, then item j is selected for inclusion in the knapsack; otherwise, $x_j = 0$. The available quantity of each item is limited to one unit, and each item has attributes of weight (w_j) and relative benefit (c_j). The problem is to select which of the n items should be packed in the knapsack in order to maximize the total benefit contributed by the items without violating a specified maximum weight (W).

The formulation readily follows from these definitions:

Maximize

$$z = \sum_{j=1}^{n} c_j x_j$$

subject to

$$\sum_{j=1}^{n} w_j x_j \leq W$$

$$x_j = 0 \text{ or } 1, \quad j = 1, \ldots, n.$$

This is another combinatoric problem with a large number of potential solutions. The number of different combinations of items that may be selected for inclusion in the knapsack is 2^n. For a problem with 10 items, there are 1,024 different combinations of items; for 15 items there are more than 30,000 different combinations; and for 30 items we get more than 1 billion combinations (of course, these are not all feasible).

Solutions to knapsack problems are important, not only because many real-world problems have a knapsack structure, but also because the knapsack problem is often a subset problem within some larger problems. Indeed, in theory, any IP problem can be reduced to a knapsack problem.[3] Efficient special-purpose algorithms can solve *binary* knapsack problems with 1,000 variables in less than 2 seconds.

Variations on the classical problem allow additional constraints and the inclusion of more units of item j. **Cargo-loading problems,** of which the air cargo problem at the beginning of this chapter is a specific example, are knapsack-type problems. Efficient solution can become difficult with multiconstrained knapsack problems.

FOLLOW-UP EXERCISES

28. ***Space Shuttle Loading.*** Space Express, Inc. specializes in filling orders for weekly shuttle flights that deliver heavy equipment to scientific laboratories in orbit around Earth. The shuttle vehicle has an overall payload limitation of 30,000 kilograms. Delivery prices are negotiable, depending on such factors as weight, insurance, and specialized handling needs. Table 8–5 indicates prices and weights for five items under consideration for the coming flight. Space Express wants to determine the set of items to deliver on its next flight in order to maximize total revenue. Only one unit of each item is offered for delivery.

TABLE 8–5 Shuttle Payload Data

Item	Price per Item ($1,000)	Weight per Item (kg)
1	$ 50	3,750
2	450	15,000
3	600	13,500
4	650	18,000
5	300	7,200

a. Formulate the appropriate model.

b. Suppose there are volume limitations in addition to weight limitations. Modify the formulation in part *a* if the overall volume limitation is 250 cubic meters and each item respectively takes up 17, 150, 125, 130, and 70 cubic meters.

29. ***Cargo-Loading Model.*** Besides the definitions in Example 8.10 for c_j, w_j, and W, suppose: v_j is the volume taken up by item j, V is the maximum allowable volume, and x_j is the number of units selected of item j.

a. Formulate this generalized model.

b. How does this model differ from the model in part *b* of the preceding exercise?

▶ Example 8.11 Capital Budgeting Model

Capital budgeting models are common to financial environments where capital rationing requires the selection of a subset of projects from among a list of n capital investment

[3]For example, see Hamdy A. Taha, *Integer Programming* (New York: Academic Press, 1975).

projects. Each project requires lump sum capital outlays over one or more of m periods, where each period is subject to a budgetary (capital) constraint. The objective is to select the set of projects that maximizes a measure of total return on investment (usually net present value) without violating the capital constraints in each period.

The basic general model is given by

Maximize

$$z = \sum_{j=1}^{n} c_j x_j$$

subject to

$$\sum_{j=1}^{n} a_{ij} x_j \leq b_i \qquad i = 1, \ldots, m$$

$$x_j = 0 \quad \text{or} \quad 1 \qquad j = 1, \ldots, n$$

where

$$x_j = \begin{cases} 1 \text{ if project } j \text{ is selected;} \\ 0 \text{ otherwise.} \end{cases}$$

c_j = Return on investment for project j.
b_i = Available capital in period i.
a_{ij} = Needed capital in period i for project j.

Unlike our earlier formulation in Example 3.4, this formulation requires binary decison variables—either the jth project is selected or it is not—which is typical in capital budgeting environments. The use of binary variables also allows the modeling of relationships among projects (see Exercise 31).

Note that the basic capital budgeting model is an extension of the knapsack model to m constraints. In Example 12.2 we present a dynamic programming variation of the capital budgeting model.

FOLLOW-UP EXERCISES

30. Formulate the capital budgeting model for the data given in Table 8–6.

TABLE 8–6 Capital Budgeting Data

	Capital Outlay ($100,000) in Period				
Project	**1**	**2**	**3**	**4**	**Net Present Value of Benefits ($100,000)**
1	3	0	0	0	2
2	0	5	1	0	3
3	1	2	1	2	1
4	10	4	2	0	5
5	2	0	5	1	4
Available capital ($100,000).	12	8	8	4	

31. Reformulate the preceding exercise with the following additional considerations.
    a. Projects 1 and 3 must be undertaken together, if at all.
    b. At most, four projects may be undertaken.

c. Projects 4 and 5 are mutually exclusive (i.e., if one is undertaken, the other cannot be undertaken).
d. Projects 2 and 4 are dependent (that is, project 4 cannot be undertaken unless project 2 is undertaken).

8.4 SOLUTION ALGORITHMS

A variety of solution methods are available for solving integer programming problems. Some of these are generalized for all types of integer programming structures; others are tailored to the special structure of certain integer programming problems (such as pure 0-1 problems). This section overviews categories of solution methods and describes three of the more widely used algorithms.

Taxonomy

A taxonomy of solution methods might include the following categories.

Graphical Method. The geometric approach described in Figure 8–1 gives an optimal solution (if it exists) to two-variable problems. Since 99.999 . . . percent of IP problems have more than two variables, the geometric approach is primarily used as a descriptive learning tool.

Brute Force Approach. One intuitive approach for solving pure IP problems would suggest **total enumeration** of all feasible integer combinations of the pertinent decision variables. With small-scale problems having relatively few decision variables, this approach is effective. However, for most realistic problems, the number of feasible combinations is overwhelming. For example, in a traveling salesrep problem involving travel to $n - 1$ different cities (not including the originating city) and return to the originating city, the number of different tours (not all necessarily feasible, of course) is $(n - 1)!$. For $n = 11$, the number of tours exceeds 3.6 million, and for $n = 21$, the number exceeds 2 quintillion! A pure binary problem with 50 variables has 2^{50}, or about 1.12×10^{15} possible solutions. For problems of this magnitude, many years of fast computer time would be required. It is easy to see why complete enumeration of combinatorial problems can be sheer folly.

Heuristic Algorithms. These methods typically apply custom-tailored logic with the objective of obtaining computationally efficient, satisfying solutions. Algorithms might be classified as those that (*a*) generate good *initial* solutions to feed another optimizing algorithm or (*b*) generate *final* solutions that may be optimal (but difficult to prove so). Algorithmic logic runs the gamut from simple common sense to mathematically sophisticated.

If you studied the transportation model, then you are aware that a heuristic method such as the **greedy algorithm** can yield a fast, often good solution. Another heuristic approach is rounding the optimal LP solution, as described in Section 8.1. The literature on heuristic algorithms is extensive and routinely includes applications to set covering, fixed-charge and plant location, traveling salesrep, and knapsack problems. Heuristic methods are best applied when "quick and dirty" solutions are needed, when obtaining an optimal solution to a large-scale IP problem would use up this year's computer budget (or give a solution in the next century), and when used in conjunction with an optimization algorithm (as in generating an initial solution). You might try Exercises 33–36 to get a better feel for heuristic algorithms.

Search Algorithms. By viewing the feasible region as a finite set of lattices (in the pure IP case) or as partitionable into distinct subregions (in the mixed IP case), search algorithms apply a divide and conquer strategy to find the optimal integer solution, if it exists. They search for the optimal solution by exploring promising regions and ignoring clearly nonoptimal or nonpromising regions. In effect, these methods *partially enumerate* the solution space. **Implicit enumeration** for pure binary problems and **branch-and-bound** methods for pure and mixed IP problems are examples of search algorithms. We discuss these in some detail later in this section.

Cutting Algorithms. These methods find the optimal integer solution, if it exists, by successive iterations that reduce the feasible region in such a way that feasible integer points are not excluded. These cuts are affected by adding one or more special constraints to the formulation in the preceding iteration. Then at each iteration the IP problem is treated like an LP problem and solved by one of the simplex-based procedures. This iterative process continues until a given solution satisfies the integer requirements. We discuss this approach in greater detail later in this section.

Specialized and Hybrid Algorithms. Specialized IP algorithms have been developed to optimally solve IP problems that exhibit special structure, including knapsacks, fixed-charge transportation, plant location, traveling salesrep, and set covering problems. In principle, these specialized problems can be solved by general search or cutting algorithms. However, in practice the relative computational efficiency of the specialized algorithms makes a significant difference. **Network algorithms** are another class of specialized IP algorithms, which we discuss in Chapter 10. These algorithms have become extremely efficient (relative to other algorithms) in solving certain classes of large-scale problems.

Lagrangian relaxation is a tool that has been increasingly applied in large-scale IP problems. This approach exploits problem structure by observing that certain complex IP models can be viewed as relatively easy problems complicated by a set of side constraints. The original problem is transformed into a Lagrangian problem (Chapter 2) in which the side constraints are incorporated in the objective function. When successfully implemented, the Lagrangian problem is relatively easy to solve and helps to identify a bound on the optimal value for the original problem.[5]

In recent years, much developmental research has gone into **hybrid IP algorithms** that combine heuristic, search, cutting, dynamic programming (Chapter 12), and other methods to optimally solve both generalized and specialized IP models. In almost every case, the hybrid algorithms have the primary objective of improved computational efficiency for large-scale IP problems.

Branch-and-Bound Algorithm

The branch-and-bound algorithm is suited for pure integer, mixed integer, and 0-1 problems. It uses as its starting point the optimal simplex solution to the original

[4]Marshall L. Fisher, "An Applications-Oriented Guide to Lagrangian Relaxation," *Interfaces*, March–April 1985, pp. 10–21.

problem. If this continuous solution does not satisfy the integer requirements, then the following ideas are implemented:

Branching. This operation partitions the solution space into subspaces, where each subspace is a unique LP problem identical to the original except for added constraints that define the subspace. This procedure eliminates portions of the solution space that fail to satisfy the integer requirements, *without omitting any feasible integer solutions*. The partitioning process is called branching because a diagram of the process gives the semblance of a tree with branches (see Figure 8–7).

Bounding. The optimal simplex solution for the maximization (minimization) problem in a given subspace provides an upper (lower) bound on the z-value for any optimal integer solution within that subspace. The use of bounds promotes the elimination of clearly nonoptimal subspaces and eventually guarantees the location of the optimal integer solution (if it exists).

Example 8.12 Branch-and-Bound Solution

Perhaps the easiest way to understand the nature of the branch-and-bound method is to illustrate by example. The geometric representation of an integer programming problem is shown in Figure 8–5. Note that the optimal continuous (LP) solution occurs at point b with neither variable assuming an integer value ($x_1 = 4.809$, $x_2 = 1.817$, and $z = 355.890$).

The branch-and-bound algorithm next considers an integer variable with a noninteger value.[5] For instance we might select $x_1 = 4.809$. It stands to reason that the optimal integer solution will have an integer value assigned to x_1 such that $x_1 \leq 4$ or $x_1 \geq 5$. The noninteger region between $x_1 = 4$ and $x_1 = 5$ is not feasible in the integer version of the problem. Consequently, the branch-and-bound algorithm **branches** from the original problem, or partitions it into two further constrained problems, which eliminate this noninteger area. Figure 8–6 illustrates the graphic representation of these two problems. For the sake of reference, we will number the original problem as problem 1 and **descendant problems** as problems 2, 3, and so forth.

Solving each of the newly formed problems by the simplex method as if they were continuous problems yields the following solutions:

Problem 2	Problem 3
$z = 349.000$	$z = 341.390$
$x_1 = 4.000$	$x_1 = 5.000$
$x_2 = 2.100$	$x_2 = 1.571$

Again, neither solution is all-integer, although both indicate integer values for x_1. Since we excluded no feasible integer solution points in creating these two problems, the values of 349.000 and 341.390 act as upper **bounds** for any feasible integer solutions. That is, 349.000 is an upper bound for solution descendants from problem 2 since any

[5]Packages like IBM's MPSX/MIP give the user choices regarding the order of selection for integer variables. For example, we can specify order according to input ($x_1, x_2, \ldots$), or according to c_j-magnitude (x_2 then x_1 in our example), or according to a priority specified by the user.

FIGURE 8–5 Continuous Solution for Problem 1

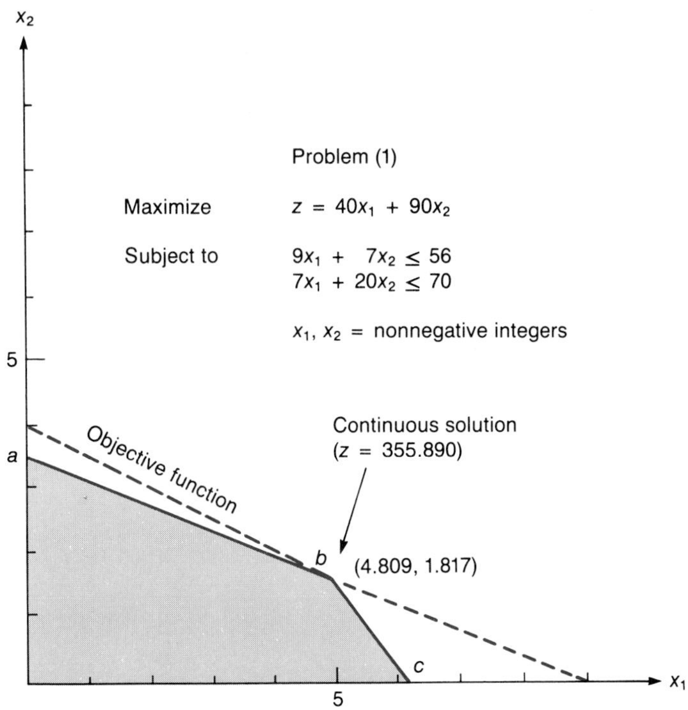

FIGURE 8–6 Partitioned Descendants from Problem 1

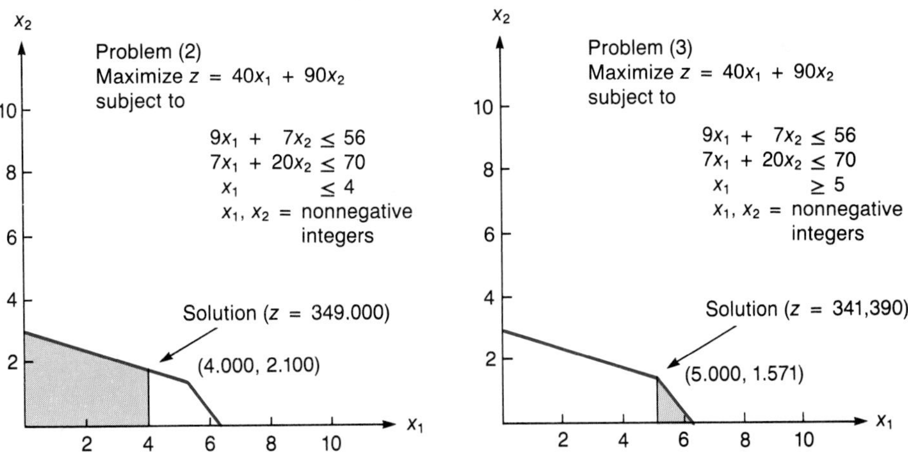

descendant problems will have additional constraints. Similarly, 341.390 is an upper bound for descendants from problem 3.

The branch-and-bound algorithm works on the principle of searching problem subsets to find feasible solutions, but discarding (not searching) subsets that cannot produce results superior to those already attained. Continuing the analysis, we could branch or partition from either problem 2 or problem 3 in an effort to integerize x_2. However, the "potential" associated with partitioning from problem 2 is more promising. This is because the upper bound on any descendant problem that further constrains problem 2 is $z = 349.000$, whereas the best that can be expected from descendants of problem 3 is $z = 341.390$. Thus the next step begins with problem 2 by adding branching constraints $x_2 \leq 2$ (problem 4) and $x_2 \geq 3$ (problem 5). In this subset of problems, the noninteger area between $x_2 = 2$ and $x_2 = 3$ is excluded, since $x_2 = 2.1$ in the solution to problem 2.[6]

Figure 8–7 summarizes in the form of a **tree** the remaining steps leading to the identification of the optimal integer solution. In problem 4 an all-integer solution is identified with an objective function valued at 340. In problem 5, the other descendant problem from problem 2, the optimal solution is not integer. However, since any descendant problems cannot produce z values greater than 327.120, we can discard problem 5 and prune its descendants from further consideration.

FIGURE 8–7 Summary of Branch-and-Bound Solution

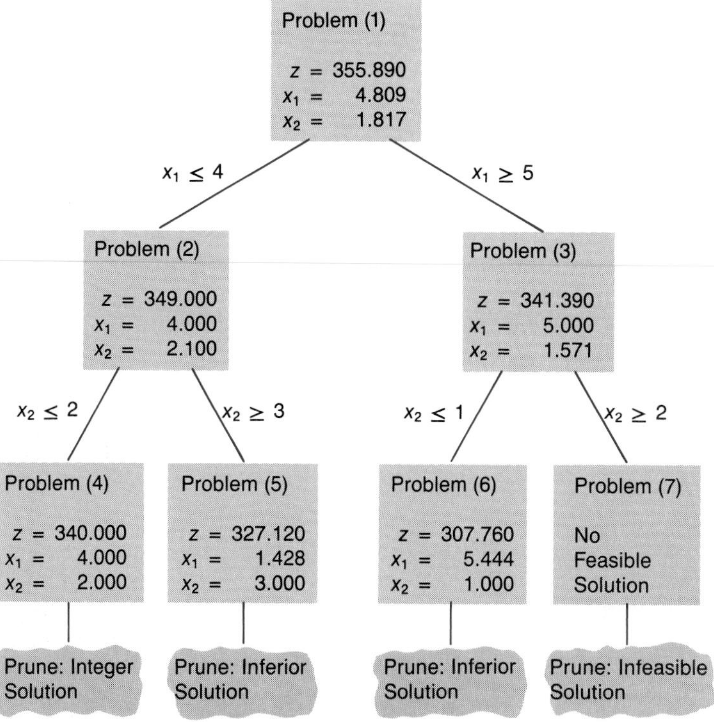

We might be inclined to conclude that the optimal integer solution has been found. However, there is potentially a better solution from one of the descendants of problem

[6]Our choice for branching according to the best bound is based on a popular rule often called the best bound rule. Another popular branching rule is the last-in-first-out (LIFO) rule. In this case our next branch is based on the latest problem available for branching, or problem 3 in our example. This rule is appealing when problems are stored on sequential files, such as magnetic tape (since retrieval times are reduced), or when it is desirable to increase the likelihood of a current feasible integer solution (since we are likely to continue along a path with many previous branching constraints).

3. The value of $z = 341.390$ is greater than the 340 found in problem 4. Therefore, it is necessary to partition problem 3 into problems 6 and 7 by adding the constraints $x_2 \leq 1$ and $x_2 \geq 2$, respectively. As we see in Figure 8–7 the results for these two problems are inferior to the solution found in problem 4. Any descendants from problem 6 would have optimal values for z no greater than 307.76, and any descendants of problem 7 would be infeasible. Thus the optimal integer solution is $x_1 = 4$, $x_2 = 2$, and $z = 340$.[7]

The problem boxes in the tree of Figure 8–7 are often called **nodes**. A branch is terminated or pruned whenever a node represents (1) an integer solution, (2) an infeasible solution, or (3) a solution with a z-value inferior to any current integer solution.

Finally, as mentioned earlier, the branch-and-bound algorithm is suited for both pure and mixed integer problems. Referring to Figure 8–7 we see that had x_1 been the only required integer variable, the optimal solution would have been that found in problem 2 with $z = 349.000$, $x_1 = 4$, and $x_2 = 2.100$.

The flow diagram in Figure 8–8 summarizes the branch-and-bound algorithm used in Example 8–12. Study it carefully and trace through the problems in Figure 8–7 to verify that this is indeed the procedure we used.

The branch-and-bound algorithm in our example is not the only one available. Other branch-and-bound algorithms differ with respect to the branching and bounding rules, tree representation, and other esoterica. The literature is lively with the search for branch-and-bound algorithms that are kind to computer storage and processing requirements.[8]

In summary, the branch-and-bound algorithm provides an intelligent search of the feasible solution space. As opposed to the brute force approach of complete enumeration, the search is restricted to partial enumeration of promising integer solution points. However, you should not conclude that branch-and-bound algorithms always produce optimal solutions with computational ease. *Relative ease,* yes, but not absolute ease; a 99.9 percent reduction of 2 quintillion potential solutions is still a big number. We reconsider this issue in Section 8.6.

FOLLOW-UP EXERCISES

32. State the objective function and constraints, and graph the solutions to problems 4 and 6 in Example 8.12 (Figure 8–7).
33. Solve Example 8.12 by the branch-and-bound procedure if x_2 is required to be integer and x_1 is not.
34. Solve Example 8.12 by selecting x_2 in problem 1 as the variable that causes descendants. Draw a tree as in Figure 8–7.
35. Solve the problem below by:
    a. Rounding the simplex solution (note that this is not obvious).
    b. Graphical means.
    c. Branch-and-bound method. Draw a tree as in Figure 8–7.

    Maximize

$$z = 8x_1 + 20x_2$$

[7]If we were to prune the branch at problem 3 and accept problem 4 as our solution, then we would be assured of having a "good" solution that is within (341.390 − 340.00 =) 1.39 of the optimal integer solution. Of course, problem 4 turned out to be our optimal solution in this case, but this idea is used by some heuristic algorithms to truncate all remaining tree branches once an integer solution is found with a z-value within a user-specified tolerance from the z-value(s) of all remaining tree branches.

[8]For the original branch-and-bound algorithm, see A. H. Land and A. Doig, "An Automatic Method for Solving Discrete Programming Problems, *Econometrica,* 28 (1960), pp. 497–520.

FIGURE 8–8 The Branch-and-Bound Algorithm

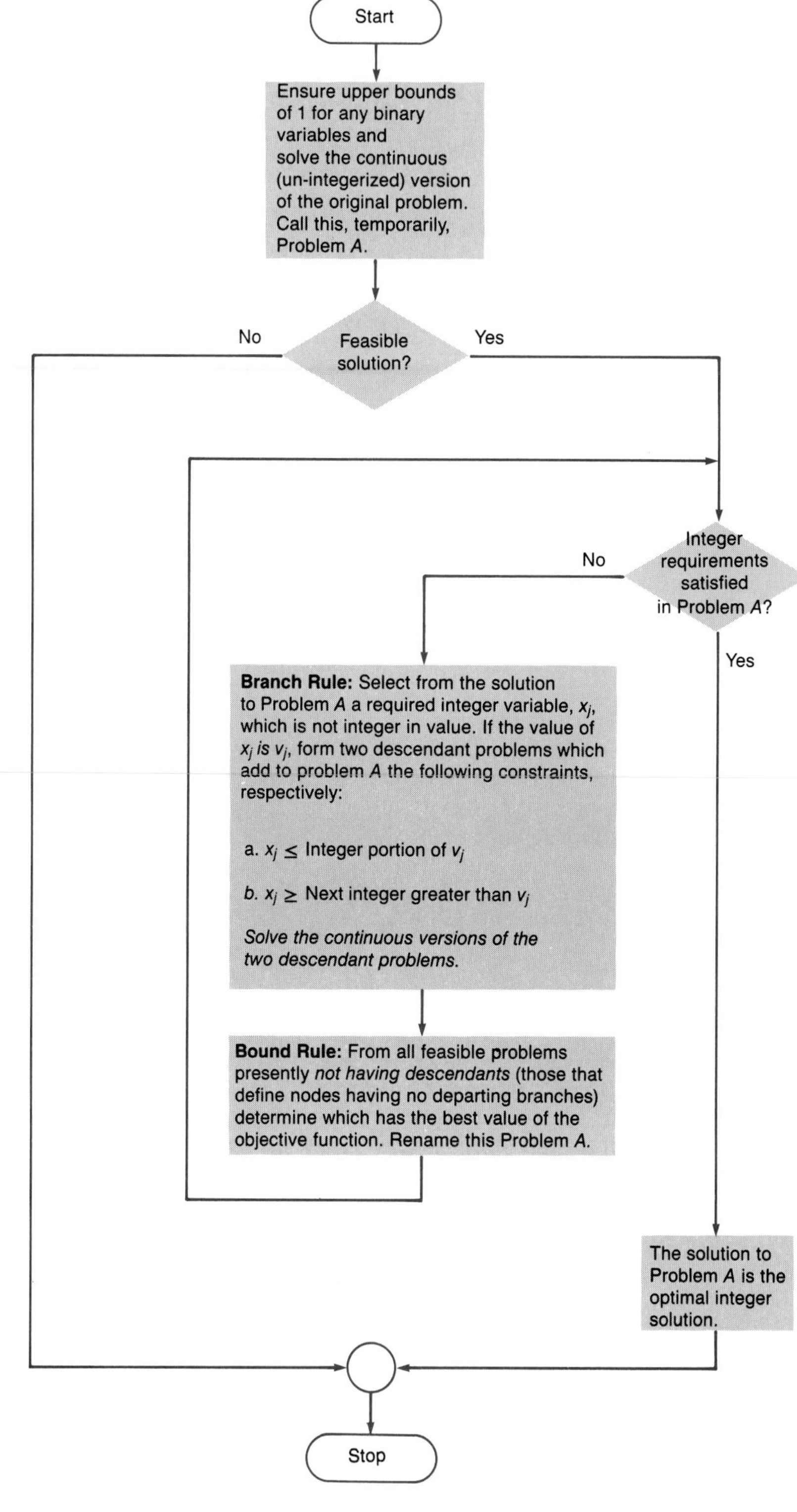

subject to

$$x_1 + 3x_2 \le 9$$
$$9x_1 + 7x_2 \le 56$$
$$x_1, x_2 = \text{Nonnegative integers.}$$

**36. Use an LP computer package to simulate the branch-and-bound procedure by solving the following pure IP problem. Construct a tree similar to Figure 8–7.

Maximize

$$z = 5x_1 - 3x_2 + 8x_3$$

subject to

$$x_1 + 6x_3 \le 12 \quad (1)$$
$$x_1 + x_2 - x_3 \le 1 \quad (2)$$
$$7x_1 - 6x_2 \le 0 \quad (3)$$
$$x_1, x_2 = \text{Nonnegative integers.}$$
$$x_3 = 0 \text{ or } 1 .$$

**37. Use an LP computer package to simulate the branch-and-bound algorithm by solving the following problem. Construct a tree similar to that in Figure 8–7.

Maximize

$$z = 7x_1 + 2x_2 + 5x_3$$

subject to

$$x_1 + 3x_2 + x_3 = 35$$
$$2x_1 + x_2 + x_3 \le 50$$
$$x_1 + x_2 + 2x_3 \le 40$$
$$x_1, x_2, x_3 = \text{Nonnegative integers.}$$

38. ***Branch-and-Bound Heuristic Algorithm.* There are many branch-and-bound heuristic algorithms that implement an array of rules and procedures to zero in on a good integer solution early in the process. Here we suggest one simple procedure to promote additional pruning.

a. Modify Figure 8–8 according to note 6.

b. Apply this heuristic to the tree in Exercise 34, 35, 36, or 37. Work with a tolerance equal to 1 percent of the *z*-value corresponding to the optimal continuous solution.

Gomory's Cutting Plane Algorithm

An early and popular technique for solving either pure or mixed integer programming problems is Gomory's cutting plane algorithm. This technique begins, as with the branch-and-bound algorithm, with the optimal solution to the continuous version of the problem. If the optimal solution does not satisfy the integer requirements of the problem, new constraints are formulated and added to the problem. These constraints represent planes (in two-space) or hyperplanes (in n-space) that effectively "cut away" portions of the feasible solution space while assuring that no feasible integer solution points are eliminated.

The principle behind the use of these cutting planes can be tied back to our discussions of linear programming. In Chapter 3 we concluded that at least one of the optimal solutions to an LP problem occurs at a corner point of the feasible solution space. The simplex algorithm provides a systematic search of corner points until it identifies the one that is optimal. Since all corner points are not necessarily integer, the cutting plane method attempts to pare down the feasible solution space such that it contains integer corner points. If this is accomplished, then application of the simplex method results in the identification of the optimal integer solution.

Figure 8–9 illustrates an area of feasible solutions (*abcd*) for a pure IP maximization problem in two-space. Aside from the origin, none of the other corner points are all-integer. The cutting plane method reduces the area of feasible solutions to "force" integer corner points. Figure 8–10 illustrates the extreme case in which all corner points are forced to integer coordinates. Three cutting planes (1, 2, and 3) have been added, which slice into the solution space, thereby eliminating the hatched portions of the original area of feasible solutions. Note that no feasible integer-valued points have been eliminated. The boundaries of the reduced area of feasible solutions make up a **convex hull.** This is the smallest convex set necessary to include all of the feasible integer solution points.[9] Application of the simplex method would now lead directly to the optimal integer solution.

We will not present the mechanics of how cutting plane constraints are developed; rather, we will offer some feeling for how the procedure works.[10] First, cutting planes are developed in order to force the noninteger-valued variables to integer values. If a starting solution includes a number of integer variables with noninteger values, then generally one variable is selected to provide the basis for developing a new constraint (cutting plane). Once this constraint has been identified, it can be added to the original constraint set, and the entire problem can be re-solved by the simplex method. Or, an advanced simplex procedure, called the **dual simplex method,** can be used to incorporate the constraint in the final tableau of the previous solution and allow the optimal solution of the larger problem to be found without starting from scratch.

We should mention that it is usually not necessary to add enough cutting planes to reduce the solution space all the way down to its convex hull. Depending on the objective function for the problem in Figure 8–10, it might take as little as one cutting plane to reach the optimal integer solution.

Compared with the branch-and-bound algorithm, several significant differences are evident. Thinking in terms of two-space, both methods add new constraints or cutting planes to the original problem. The cutting planes in the branch-and-bound method

---

[9]See Section 4.3 for the definition of a convex set.

[10]For detailed treatments see Harvey M. Wagner, *Principles of Operations Research,* 2nd ed. (Englewood Cliffs, N.J.: Prentice-Hall, 1975); Narendra Paul Loomba and Efraim Turban, *Applied Programming for Management* (New York: Holt, Rinehart & Winston, 1974); Hamdy A. Taha, *Integer Programming* (New York: Academic Press, 1975); or Stephen P. Bradley, Arnoldo C. Hax, and Thomas L. Magnanti, *Applied Mathematical Programming* (Reading, Mass.: Addison-Wesley Publishing, 1977).

FIGURE 8–9 Area of Feasible Solutions for Pure IP Maximization Problem

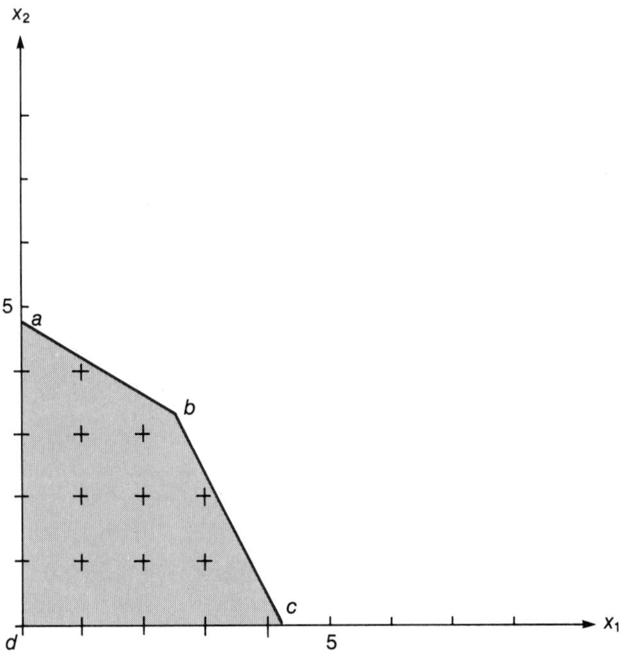

FIGURE 8–10 Convex Hull (*All extreme points are integer*)

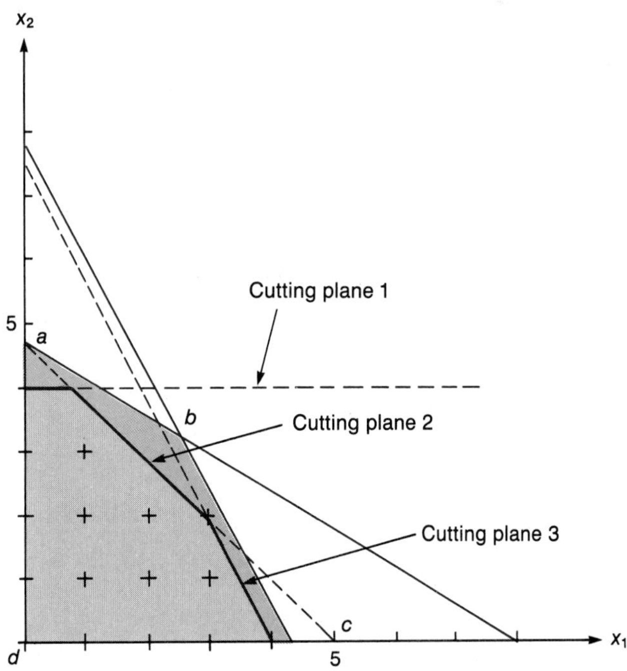

are always perpendicular to one of the coordinate axes, whereas this is not necessarily the case with Gomory's cutting planes. Also, Gomory's planes always result in a reduction of the original area of feasible solutions without any exclusion of feasible integer-valued points. Conversely, the branch-and-bound algorithm often defines solution spaces which exclude feasible but clearly nonoptimal integer-valued points.

Implicit Enumeration

Implicit enumeration is a technique for solving 0-1 programming problems. Since procedures exist for converting any integer programming problem into a 0-1 problem, implicit enumeration is more generally applicable than we might first believe. For realistic problems, we dismissed complete enumeration of all integer solution values as a procedure having appeal only to the dedicated masochist. Implicit enumeration, like branch-and-bound, only enumerates a subset of all possible combinations of variables.

Implicit enumeration builds from *partial solutions*. The building is in the fashion of a tree where whole branches can be dismissed from further consideration. The partial solution simply means the assignment of zero or one to a subset of the decision variables. Given a partial assignment, an analysis of the constraint set, objective function, and unassigned decision variables can lead to the elimination of certain subsets of solutions. As in the branch-and-bound algorithm, these subsets might be infeasible, or a lower (upper) bound on the objective function might indicate they are not promising. Thus certain sets of solution points associated with completion of a partial solution can be ignored and are said to be *implicitly enumerated* or *fathomed*. These terms, by the way, are also applied to branch-and-bound algorithms.

A number of implicit enumeration algorithms have been proposed for solving 0-1 problems. Most are variations of the Balas algorithm.[11] To get a feeling for the general approach let us illustrate with an example. Without loss of generality, we assume a canonical form of the 0-1 problem, which consists of (1) a minimization objective with all $c_j \geq 0$ subject to (2) all $\geq$ structural constraints.[12]

▶ Example 8.13 Solution by Implicit Enumeration

Consider the following 0-1 problem in canonical form.

Minimize

$$z = 2x_1 + 5x_2 + 3x_3 + 4x_4$$

subject to

$$-4x_1 + x_2 + x_3 + x_4 \geq 0 \quad (1)$$

$$-2x_1 + 4x_2 + 2x_3 + 4x_4 \geq 4 \quad (2)$$

[11] Egon Balas, "An Additive Algorithm for Solving Linear Programs with Zero-One Variables," *Operations Research*, July–August, 1965, pp. 517–46.

[12] Problems not in canonical form are easily converted to canonical form by the methods in Exercises 32 and 33 in Chapter 5.

$$x_1 + x_2 - x_3 + x_4 \geq 1 \quad (3)$$

$$x_j = 0 \quad \text{or} \quad 1 \qquad \text{for all } j.$$

The best possible solution would be an assignment of zero to all decision variables resulting in $z = 0$. However, such an assignment is infeasible in this problem because constraints 2 and 3 are violated. Given an infeasible solution, we now use a procedure similar to the branch-and-bound method. We subdivide (partition) a subset of variables by assigning them values of zero or one to yield a partial solution. The remaining variables in the problem are *unassigned* (free), yet to be given values.

Let us begin with an assignment to x_1. We are interested in minimizing z; therefore, making an assignment of $x_1 = 1$ is a reasonable place to begin, since it has the smallest c_j value.[13] This partial assignment violates constraints 1 and 2. Although the violation of constraint 2 can be rectified by certain choices for the remaining decision variables, constraint 1 can never be satisfied with $x_1 = 1$. (Do you see why?) Thus in Figure 8–11, any complete solutions descending from the partial solution at node ① can be discarded. They have been **implicitly enumerated** or **fathomed** because of their infeasibility. Evaluation of this one partial assignment reduces the number of solutions that must be explicitly enumerated by 50 percent (from 2^4 to 2^3 solutions).

FIGURE 8–11 Partial Solution (x_1)

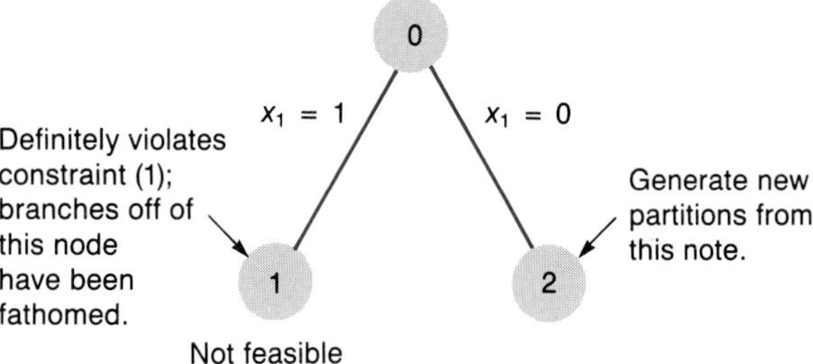

The partial solution at node ② in Figure 8–11 must be further subdivided. We know that we must consider an assignment of one to at least one other variable, since our starting solution of $(x_1 = x_2 = x_3 = x_4 = 0)$ or $(0, 0, 0, 0)$ was infeasible. Thus we arbitrarily select x_2 and subdivide into two new partial solutions. The new partial solutions are $(x_1 = 0, x_2 = 1)$ and $(x_1 = 0, x_2 = 0)$, shown as nodes ③ and ④ in Figure 8–12.

The partial solution at node 3 is feasible, since all constraints are satisfied. Because this is a minimization problem, the only reasonable completion of this partial solution is an assignment of the values $x_3 = x_4 = 0$, leading to a value of $z = 5$. Assigning a value of one to either or both of these variables would lead to values of z that are greater than five. Thus the complete solution $(0, 1, 0, 0)$ at node 3 implicitly enumerates three more solutions: those that would complete the partial solution with $x_3 = x_4 = 1$ or $x_3 = 0$, $x_4 = 1$ or $x_3 = 1$, $x_4 = 0$.

The partial solution at node 4 must now be subdivided. Noting that c_j-values for x_3 and x_4 are less than 5, there is potential for a better solution than the "incumbent" best solution of $z = 5$ at node 3. (If both c_3 and c_4 were greater than 5, then the solution at node 3 would be optimal. Right?)

[13]In fact, at least one algorithm adds the requirement that variables be ordered such that $c_1 \leq c_2 \leq c_3 \leq \ldots \leq c_n$. This suggests a logical order for adding new variables to partial solution sets.

FIGURE 8–12 Partial Solution (x_1, x_2)

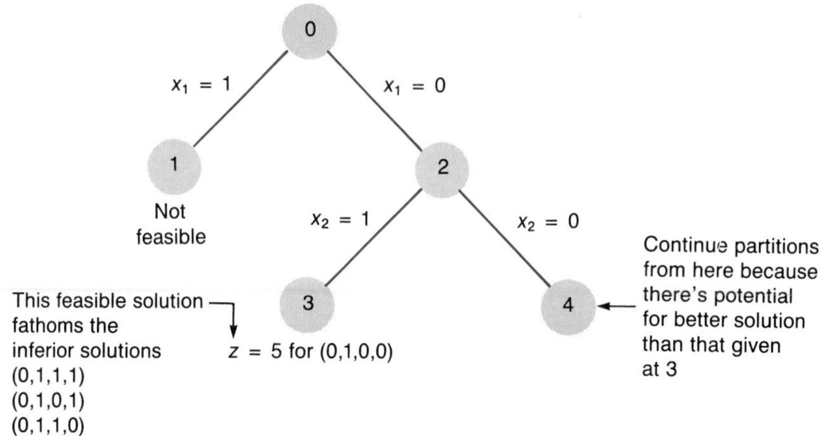
0
$x_1 = 1$
$x_1 = 0$
1
2
Not feasible
$x_2 = 1$
$x_2 = 0$
Continue partitions from here because there's potential for better solution than that given at 3
This feasible solution fathoms the inferior solutions (0,1,1,1) (0,1,0,1) (0,1,1,0)
3
4
$z = 5$ for (0,1,0,0)

Subdividing on x_3, we generate two new partial solutions $(x_1 = 0, x_2 = 0, x_3 = 1)$ and $(x_1 = 0, x_2 = 0, x_3 = 0)$. The partial solution $(0, 0, 1)$ at node 5 in Figure 8–13 is infeasible because constraint 3 can never be satisfied (regardless of the assignment to x_4). Thus we must subdivide on x_4 to generate two new solutions for consideration, which are in fact complete solutions. The solution $(0, 0, 0, 1)$ shown at node 7 in Figure 8–13 is feasible with $z = 4$, and the solution $(0, 0, 0, 0)$ at node 8 was determined infeasible at the very beginning. Since the solution at node 7 is an improvement over the incumbent at node 3, it is the optimal solution.

Our example illustrates the essentials of implicit enumeration algorithms. As you might expect, algorithms have been proposed to more efficiently solve large-scale problems, all of which have two common characteristics for success:

1. The algorithm must ensure that *all* solutions are enumerated, either explicitly or implicitly, and that the optimal solution is never implicitly enumerated. This guarantees optimality.
2. The enumeration scheme must specify a precise set of rules that attempts to minimize the number of explicit enumerations (or maximize the number of implicit enumerations). This promotes computational efficiency.

FOLLOW-UP EXERCISES

39. For Example 8.13, fully enumerate all possible solutions. How many of these were implicitly enumerated in the example?
40. Re-order the variables in Example 8.13 such that $c_1 \leq c_2 \leq c_3 \leq c_4$, and solve by implicit enumeration. Draw an enumeration tree similar to that in Figure 8–13 for this newly formulated problem. Is there any improvement in efficiency resulting from this re-ordering? (*Hint:* Instead of reordering variables, you could simply change the order of variable selection in the tree. Right?)
41. Solve one of the following by implicit enumeration:
    a. Space shuttle loading I (Exercise 28*a*).
    b. Space shuttle loading II (Exercise 28*b*).
    c. Capital budgeting (Exercise 30).

FIGURE 8–13 Enumeration Tree for Example 8.13

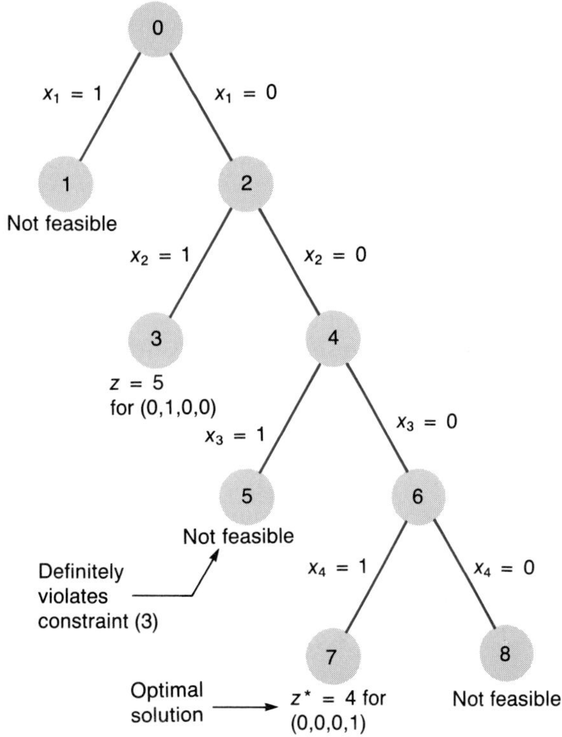

8.5 COMPUTER-BASED SOLUTIONS

Meaningful IP problems are invariably solved on the computer, as is the case with LP, transportation, assignment, and other mathematical programming models. A variety of commercially available software exists. Some packages are generalized to solve different integer programming structures. Others are more specific in focus, emphasizing efficiency in solving selected problem structures such as mixed integer or zero-one models.

▶ Example 8.14

For purposes of illustration, consider the following MIP model:

Minimize

$$z = 4x_1 + 15x_2 + 5x_3 - 60y_1 + y_2 + 6y_3$$

subject to

$$\begin{aligned} 10x_1 + 6x_2 + 4x_3 &\leq 75.2 \quad \text{(First)} \\ 5x_1 + 15x_2 \qquad\qquad + 20y_3 &\geq 100.8 \quad \text{(Second)} \\ x_3 - 7y_1 &\geq 5.5 \quad \text{(Third)} \\ y_1 + y_2 + y_3 &= 1 \quad \text{(Fourth)} \\ x_j &\geq 0 \quad \text{for } j = 1, 2. \\ x_3 &= \text{Nonnegative integer.} \\ y_j &= 0 \text{ or } 1 \quad \text{for } j = 1, 2, 3. \end{aligned}$$

Note that this problem includes continuous variables (x_1, x_2), an integer variable (x_3), and binary variables (y_1, y_2, y_3).

Figure 8–14 presents the solution to this problem as solved using the software module *Mixed Integer Programming Optimizer.*[14] This software utilizes a spreadsheet format for data input. Notice that three constraints of the form $y_j \leq 1$ were added to the original formulation. These were necessary because the program does not allow for explicit specification of zero-one variables. In this situation, such variables are declared integer with the provision that the maximum value equals one. Also note in the spreadsheet the specification of integer variables as compared with real variables. These were identified by typing an I in the S.T. row of the spreadsheet.

The objective function is minimized at a value of 114.440 when $x_1 = 2.36$, $x_2 = 4.60$, $x_3 = 6$, $y_1 = y_2 = 0$, and $y_3 = 1$. Substitute these values into the constraints to confirm the slack and surplus variable values shown in the output.

Figure 8–15 presents the solution to Example 8.7 (Facility Location: Solid Waste Location/Distribution Model). You will be asked in a follow-up exercise to provide a verbal interpretation of these results.

FOLLOW-UP EXERCISES

42. Provide a verbal interpretation of the results to Example 8.7 shown in Figure 8–15. Include in the summary a description of the extent to which all constraints are satisfied. What is the significance of the artificial variable in the list of basic slack and surplus variables?

43. Use an integer programming software package to solve the small IP model used to illustrate the branch-and-bound approach in Example 8.12.

44. Use an available MIP package to solve the following problems:
    a. Air cargo model (Example 8.1).
    b. Fire unit set covering model (Example 8.6).
    c. Plant location model (Exercise 18).
    d. Quantity discount/lot size model (Example 8.8).
    e. Political campaign tour (Exercise 24).
    f. Space shuttle loading (Exercise 28*b*).
    g. Capital budgeting model (Exercise 30).

8.6 CONCLUSION

Efficient solution of integer programming problems is a major concern. Solving such problems can become very time-consuming and costly. Researchers classify problems

[14]Gordon H. Dash, *Operations Research Software,* vol. I (Homewood, Ill.: R. D. Irwin, Inc., 1988).

FIGURE 8–14 Computer-Based Solution for Example 8.14

Cons	Var 1	Var 2	Var 3	Var 4	Var 5	Var 6	Sense	Rhs
Name	x1	x2	x3	y1	y2	y3		
Obj	4.000	15.000	5	-60	1	6		
S.T. (I)ntgr->			I	I	I	I		
1	10.000	6.000	4				≤	75.200
2	5.000	15.000				20	≥	100.800
3			1	-7			≥	5.500
4				1	1	1	=	1.000
5				1			≤	1.000
6					1		≤	1.000
7						1	≤	1.000

OPTIMAL SOLUTION

Solution Time 00h 00m 35s

OBJECTIVE FUNCTION VALUE IS: 114.440

VARIABLE	VALUE
1 x1	2.360
2 x2	4.600
3 x3	6
4 y1	0
6 y3	1

BASIC SLACK AND SURPLUS VARIABLES

Variable	Constraint	Type	Value
10 Surplus	3	>=	0.500
13 Slack	5	<=	1.000
14 Slack	6	<=	1.000
15 Slack	7	<=	0.000

according to the degree of difficulty required to solve them. Those classified as **P-time** are the relatively easy problems. For these, algorithms exist having solution times that are a polynomial function of the size of the problem. Those classified as **NP-complete** are the difficult problems; it is unlikely that there are algorithms that can solve these problems in a time stated as a polynomial function of the size of the problem. Included in this latter class are many combinatorial problems (e.g., traveling salesrep, sequencing, scheduling, and routing problems). For these problems, there is exponential growth in solution difficulty as the size of the problem increases. Although knowledge that a problem fits one of these two categories does not change the difficulty of the problem, it can assist in devising a strategy for solution. If we know our problem is in the NP-complete category, our effort might be focused on finding efficient algorithms that will generate good feasible solutions rather than those that are less efficient and less likely to reach an optimal solution.

Experiences in using various solution procedures are best described as inconsistent and disappointing. Each method has its advantages and disadvantages. What works well for one problem may fail miserably with a very similar problem. The main problem with integer programming is that there are no optimality conditions to check. The

FIGURE 8–15 Computer-Based Solution for Example 8.7

```
                         OPTIMAL SOLUTION

Solution Time        OBJECTIVE FUNCTION VALUE IS:      1131999.999
 00h 02m 10s
                       VARIABLE                          VALUE
                        4  x14                         1500.000
                        5  x21                         1750.000
                        9  x31                          200.000
                       10  x32                            0.000
                       11  x33                            0.000
                       12  x34                         2300.000
                       13  x41                         2000.000
                       17  x51                         2800.000
                       24  x64                         2200.000
                       25  y1                                 1
                       26  y2                                 0
                       27  y3                                 0
                       28  y4                                 1

                   BASIC SLACK AND SURPLUS VARIABLES

       Variable             Constraint          Type          Value

   35  Slack                 7                   <=         250.000
   41  Slack                13                   <=           1.000
   42  Slack                14                   <=           1.000
   46  Artificial           17 Structural        >=           0.000
```

solution procedure might find the optimal solution very quickly but continue working for a long time to verify that it is optimal. A number of authors have stated that the selection of the best solution algorithm is an art, but it is an art form which few have mastered in real-world applications. Some experiences associated with these solution procedures are shared below.

Cutting Algorithms

Cutting algorithms were the first to guarantee convergence on the optimal integer solution in a finite number of iterations. Unfortunately, their sensitivity to round-off errors and the often large number of cutting planes that must be added tend to promote a very large number of iterations. Cutting algorithms also sometimes "stall," whereby many cutting planes are added with relatively small changes in z-values. Moreover, they can be extremely sensitive to the structure of the IP model. For example, simply rearranging the order of constraints can dramatically change the required number of cutting planes in achieving an optimal solution. Finally, cutting methods rely on dual-simplex procedures, which give infeasible intermediate iterations until the final (optimal) interation. This means that the user is left with no "near optimal" or "good" feasible solution should there be a need to halt execution due to excessive computer processing times.

In practice, cutting algorithms are rarely used today, since they perform poorly relative to search algorithms. They have proved useful, however, in the evolution of IP algorithms. In particular, they have provided insight and technique in the development of certain hybrid algorithms.

Search Algorithms

Branch-and-bound procedures are effective in optimally solving general IP problems with a small number of integer variables. However, if problems have more than, say, 100 integer variables and if the continuous solution is distant from the optimal integer solution, then the required solution time may be prohibitively long. To further complicate matters, solution times are also a function of the number of continuous variables, the number of constraints, and the structure of the constraints. Certain problems permit the pruning of large branches, whereas others require the examination of many branch tips.

Pure binary models are better solved by implicit enumeration algorithms than by branch-and-bound algorithms. In particular, implicit enumeration computer codes that use integer arithmetic eliminate rounding problems and increase computational efficiency (operations are much faster in integer arithmetic than in real arithmetic). As mentioned earlier, any pure IP problem can be converted to an equivalent pure binary problem. However, the resulting increase in the number of variables renders this approach impractical.

Although search algorithms can severely tax computer time and memory resources, they do have a significant advantage over cutting algorithms: Failure to converge on the optimal solution within a specified time still leaves the user with a feasible solution that may be of some value.

Formulation/Solution Interface

The structure or specific formulation of an IP model very much affects solution times. The following brief guidelines should give you a feel for this interactive effect.

1. **Special structure.** If possible, formulate a problem with special structure for solution by special-purpose algorithms. For example, reasonably efficient optimization (exact) algorithms have been developed for fixed-charge transportation problems with about 200 binary variables,[15] for uncapacitated and capacitated plant location problems with 10,000 variables [16] and 1,000 variables,[17] respectively, and for knapsack problems with more than 1,000 variables.[18]

[15] J. Kennington and E. Unger, "A New Branch-and-Bound Algorithm for the Fixed-Charge Transportation Problem," *Management Science* 22 (1976), pp. 1116–26.

[16] D. Erlenkotter, "A Dual-Based Procedure for Uncapacitated Facility Location," *Operations Research* 26 (1978), pp. 992–1009.

[17] U. Akine and B. Khumawala, "An Efficient Branch-and-Bound Algorithm for the Capacitated Warehouse Location Problem" *Management Science* 23 (1977), pp. 585–94.

[18] G. P. Ingargiola and J. F. Korsh, "A General Algorithm for One-Dimensional Knapsack Problems," *Operations Research* 25 (1977), pp. 752–59.

2. **Non-IP formulations.** Instead of formulating a model as an IP model, one might best formulate it as another type of model. The transportation model is an obvious example. As another example, a mixed IP problem with 511 continuous variables, 126 binary variables, and 173 constraints was terminated on an IBM 370/168 machine using MPSX/MIP after seven hours of processing, without achieving an optimal solution! The same problem was formulated as a network model (Chapter 10), and after 30 minutes gave a feasible solution with a z-value that was 8 percent better than the MPSX z-value.[19]
3. **Number of integer variables.** Processing time is very much dependent on the number of integer variables. If possible, reduce the number of binary variables and approximate integer variables by continuous variables where large solution values are expected. For example, if we specify continuous x_j instead of integer x_j and the optimal solution indicates $x_j = 1983.2$, then rounding to 1983 or 1984 should not introduce much error.
4. **Solution space restrictions.** Restricted solution spaces facilitate the search for an optimal solution. Thus specify upper and lower bounds for integer variables when possible and interrelate integer variables through new constraints if appropriate.
5. **Hybrid and heuristic algorithms.** Exact hybrid algorithms, if available, tend to be more efficient than pure cutting or search algorithms. In particular, *interactive algorithms* that allow decisions by the user during execution can promote faster processing times. For example, a switch from a cutting routine to either a search routine or a heuristic routine at a crucial point during the computations might prove advantageous. Of course, this approach requires a very knowledgeable user. Finally, if optimization proves too costly for a large-scale problem, a heuristic algorithm might prove the best bet. For example, plant location problems with as many as 360,000 candidate plant locations and 52,000 constraints have been solved by heuristic algorithms.[20]

A Caveat

Consider the following quote from one of the prototype articles of R. E. D. Woolsey. This sage of real-world pragmatism entitled his article "A Candle to Saint Jude, or Four Real-World Applications of Integer Programming"[21]

> *In most of the standard texts of MS/OR, integer programming is treated just as any other mathematical programming technique. The fact that most of the algorithms proposed are extremely difficult to use in practice is simply ignored. To be blunt, the difference between theory and practice in integer programming can only be marked by the thousands of dollars spent getting these algorithms to converge in an eco-*

---

[19] F. Glover, J. Hultz, and D. Klingman, "Improved Computer-Based Planning Techniques, Part II," *Interfaces* 9 (1979), pp. 12–20.

[20] Jame P. Ignizio, "Solving Large-Scale Problems; A Venture into a New Dimension," *Journal of Operational Research Society* 31 (1980), pp. 217–25.

[21] Reprinted by permission of R. E. D. Woolsey, "A Candle to Saint Jude or Four Real-World Applications of Integer Programming," *Interfaces* 2, no. 2 (Feb. 1972). Copyright 1972 The Institute of Management Sciences.

nomic amount of time; because the Management Scientist says that the algorithm will "converge in a finite number of steps" is no guarantee that the company might not be bankrupted by the expense first. Thus, many of those who actually solve problems turn to heuristic methods to get good starting solutions, followed by some kind of branch-and-bound scheme to take every possible advantage of problem structure. But these methods are often given short shrift in OR/MS texts and journals due to their "inelegance." One recalls the remark of Marshall Joffre upon seeing one of the world's last cavalry charges in WWI: "It is magnificent, but is it war?"

This quote still applies today, although state-of-the-art improvement in solving large-scale IP problems coupled with today's faster computers have somewhat eased the computational problem. Still, the solution of realistic combinatorial problems all-too-often involves a trade-off between solution quality and solution cost.

SELECTED APPLICATION REVIEW

DECISION SUPPORT SYSTEMS: PURCHASING AT IBM

The purchasing function within many corporations is responsible for a significant proportion of corporate costs. The problem faced by the corporate buyer is complicated by a variety of factors. The number of vendors is often large, contract terms may be difficult to compare because of the variety of structures offered by vendors, and the evaluation of foreign vendors (increasingly relevant in high-tech industries) is complicated by such issues as exchange rates with foreign currencies, differing inflation rates, and the risks of supply disruption.

In order to improve the productivity of the purchasing function, a computerized vendor selection system was implemented for the purchasing department at IBM's Poughkeepsie manufacturing facility. The Vendor Selection System (VSS) is an interactive decision support system that utilizes imbedded mixed integer programming optimization methods to improve the quality of purchasing decisions. The system has capabilities far exceeding the standard features of commercially available purchasing software systems. Buyers can examine a variety of different purchasing strategies using assumptions they have defined. The "what if" capabilities of the system are implemented using a menu-driven dialog. The use of mixed integer programming in the system is completely transparent to the user.

Implementation of the system has resulted in typical savings of between 5 and 10 percent on purchases. Estimated annual savings are expected to exceed $1 million.

SOURCE: Paul S. Bender, Richard W. Brown, Michael H. Isaac, and Jeremy F. Shapiro, "Improving Purchasing Productivity at IBM with a Normative Decision Support System," *Interfaces*, May–June 1985, pp. 106–15.

Energy Conservation. Energy conservation has become an issue of great concern to the public. It has been estimated that the petroleum refining business *consumes* more than 10 percent of all energy consumed by the industrial sector. Exxon Corporation developed a multiperiod mixed integer

(continued)

programming model to assist in selecting energy improvement projects at its processing units within the refinery and chemical plant at Baton Rouge. The Site Energy Optimization model is expected to result in incremental benefits of approximately $100 million at the Baton Rouge site between 1985 and the year 2000. Because of the success of the effort in Baton Rouge, Exxon plans on applying the methods at other major sites in the United States, Europe, Asia, and Latin America.

Logo reproduced courtesy of EXXON Corporation.

SOURCE: W. L. McMahan and P. A. Roach, "Site Energy Optimization, A Math Programming Approach," *Interfaces,* December 1982, pp. 66–82. This article was a prize-winning paper in the TIMS College on the Practice of Management Science (CPMS) competition in 1982.

AIR PRODUCTS

Air Products and Chemicals, Inc. is a leading supplier of industrial gases. A sophisticated decision support system has been developed to model their customer response in the distribution of industrial gases. Among other components of the system is a mathematical optimization module used to produce daily delivery schedules. The optimization module solves extremely large mixed integer programming models having as many as 800,000 variables and 200,000 constraints. Major tangible and intangible benefits have been realized from the system, not the least of which are annual savings in operating expenses of between 6 and 10 percent.

Logo reproduced courtesy of Air Products and Chemicals, Inc.

SOURCE: Walter J. Bell, Louis M. Dalberto, Marshall L. Fisher, Arnold J. Greenfield, Ri Jaikumar, Pradeep Keedia, Robert G. Mack, Paul J. Prutzman, "Improving the Distribution of Industrial Gases with an On-Line Computerized Routing and Scheduling Optimizer," *Interfaces,* December 1983, pp. 4–23. This article was a prize-winning paper in the CPMS/TIMS competition in 1983.

A mixed integer programming model was used to assist in planning the construction schedule for seven office buildings that are part of a 90-acre mixed use development near Dallas called Texas Plaza. The model aided in

(continued)

decisions related to scheduling the opening of each building, the amount of space to be leased in each building each year, the sale value of each building, and annual cash flows expected to the owner. Even though it was a low-cost application, the model resulted in an increase in the net present value of profits of more than $6 million.

SOURCE: Richard B. Peiser and Scot G. Andrus, "Phasing of Income-Producing Real Estate," *Interfaces*, October 1983, pp. 1–9.

RADIOISOTOPE PRODUCTION

Production scheduling for various grades of a radioisotope in a nuclear reactor has been assisted by the use of a multiperiod mixed integer programming model.

SOURCE: Spyros C. Economides and Wayne T. Crawford, "Radioisotope Production Scheduling in a Nuclear Reactor," *Decision Sciences*, July 1982, pp. 501–12.

SELECTED REFERENCES

Bradley, Stephen P.; Arnoldo C. Hax; and Thomas L. Magnanti. *Applied Mathematical Programming*. Reading, Mass.: Addison-Wesley Publishing, 1977.

Hillier, Frederick S., and Gerald J. Lieberman. *Introduction to Operations Research*. 3rd ed. San Francisco: Holden-Day, 1980.

Lev, Benjamin, and Howard J. Weiss. *Introduction to Mathematical Programming*. New York: Elsevier North-Holland Publishing, 1982.

Loomba, Narendra Paul, and Efraim Turban. *Applied Programming for Management*. New York: Holt, Rinehart & Winston, 1974.

McMillan, Claude, Jr. *Mathematical Programming: An Introduction to the Design and Application of Optimal Decision Machines*. New York: John Wiley & Sons, 1970.

Plane, Donald R., and Claude McMillan, Jr. *Discrete Optimization*. Englewood Cliffs, N.J.: Prentice-Hall, 1971.

Salkin, H. *Integer Programming*, Reading, Mass.: Addison-Wesley Publishing, 1975.

Taha, Hamdy A. *Integer Programming: Theory, Applications and Computations*. New York: Academic Press, 1975.

Wagner, Harvey M. *Principles of Operations Research*. 2nd ed. Englewood Cliffs, N.J.: Prentice-Hall, 1975.

ADDITIONAL EXERCISES

45. To what extent are the four underlying LP assumptions (see page 000) relevant in IP?
46. Suppose x_j is a nonnegative integer variable in the primal. How does this affect the dual?
47. ***Court scheduling.*** A court clerk wants to schedule the three district courts within a city. Depending on the hours of operation and number of judges available, each court is characterized by an estimated number of judge-hours. Four categories of hearings may be scheduled into each court. The clerk has estimates of the number of judge-hours required to process a hearing, which varies depending on the court.

    During the coming month there will be 1,400, 800, and 600 judge-hours available in courts 1, 2, and 3, respectively. The clerk wishes to determine the number of hearings of each type to schedule for each court. In doing so, at least 20 type-1, 10 type-2, 25 type-3, and 30 type-4 hearings are to be scheduled. Because of the usual backlog of type-1 hearings, the number of hours allocated to these hearings should be at least 20 percent of the total hours available in *each* court. In addition, the number of type-2 hearings scheduled should be no more than 60 percent of the total hearings scheduled. Table 8–7 gives the estimated judge-hours to process each type hearing through each court.

TABLE 8–7 Estimated Judge-Hours

Hearing Type	Court 1	Court 2	Court 3
1	20	18	22
2	2	3	2
3	12	13	10
4	5	6	7

a. If x_{ij} is defined as the number of hearings of type i scheduled in court j, formulate the IP model for scheduling the greatest number of hearings during the coming month.

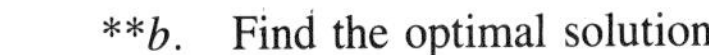

***b.* Find the optimal solution.

c. If the number of hours allocated to type-1 hearings is to be at least 20 percent of the total hours *scheduled* in each court, how would the formulation change?

48. ***Capital Expansion.*** Mac, Don, and Al's, a well-established hamburger chain, is planning an expansion. They wish to open a chain of health food restaurants over the next five years. Twelve potential cities have been explored; construction costs as well as annual (before-tax) profit figures have been estimated for each site. (See Table 8–8.)

    Mac, Don, and Al have appropriated $20 million for construction in this first phase of expansion. They have also specified some restrictions in allocating the funds. At least one restaurant *must* be built in each region. No more than two can be built in any one region. If a restaurant is built in Toronto, one must be built in Montreal. Similarly, one may be built in Los Angeles only if one is built in San Francisco. Mac, Don, and Al have agreed that restaurants should not be built in both Atlanta and Miami. Finally, Chicago and Detroit should receive equal treatment regarding the construction decision; that is, either build in both or don't build in either. (Note: If a city is selected, then only one restaurant is to be built.)

a. Formulate a model to maximize total annual profit.

***b.* Find the optimal solution.

TABLE 8–8 Capital Expansion Data

Cities	Construction Cost	Estimated Annual Profit
Northeast		
Boston	$2,500,000	$750,000
New York	3,000,000	900,000
South		
Atlanta	2,000,000	550,000
New Orleans	2,750,000	800,000
Miami	3,100,000	650,000
West		
Los Angeles	2,500,000	850,000
San Francisco	2,600,000	500,000
Midwest		
Detroit	1,750,000	450,000
Chicago	2,000,000	550,000
Cincinnati	1,800,000	400,000
Canada		
Toronto	2,900,000	800,000
Montreal	3,200,000	900,000

49. ***Bank Location.*** The law in one state allows banks to establish branch locations in a town provided that an adjacent (bordering) town has a main office. Figure 8–16 is a map showing 20 specific towns. Bank executives want to determine the towns in which main offices should be located if bank service is to be provided to all 20 towns.

Let $x_j = 1$ if a main office is located in town j and 0 if not. If the objective is to minimize the number of main offices needed,

a. Formulate the 0-1 programming problem that would allow the bank to determine the locations of main offices. (Hint: Remember that some form of bank service is desired in each town.)

b. Modify the formulation if main offices already exist in towns 1 and 3.

c. Solve the problems formulated in parts *a* and *b*.

50. ***Aircraft Purchase.*** Trans Oriental Pacific (TOP) Airlines is considering a capital expansion. The objective is to purchase new aircraft for Pacific runs. TOP is looking at the purchase of Boeing 767s, Airbus A310s, and Lockheed L-1011s. The budget for new purchases is $750 million. Boeing 767s cost $42 million, Airbus A310s cost $30 million, and Lockheed L-1011s cost $27.5 million. On the average, each type of plane is expected to generate annual after-tax profits of $3.5 million, $2.8 million, and $3.0 million. In an effort to have some uniformity with respect to spare parts and maintenance procedures, airline executives have specified that they would like to purchase at least 10 airplanes of the same type. They also wish to purchase at least two of each plane.

TOP has allocated up to $10 million per year for additional personnel hirings to support the operation of the new aircraft. Each 767 requires $200,000 in new hirings; each A310 requires $180,000; and each L-1011 requires $190,000.

Currently, available maintenance facilities allow 800 days of maintenance per year for new purchases. Each 767 requires 45 days of annual maintenance; each A310 requires 38 days; and each L-1011 requires 42 days. It is possible, however, to increase the available annual maintenance to 1,250 days. To accomplish this, the maintenance facilities

FIGURE 8–16 Town Locations

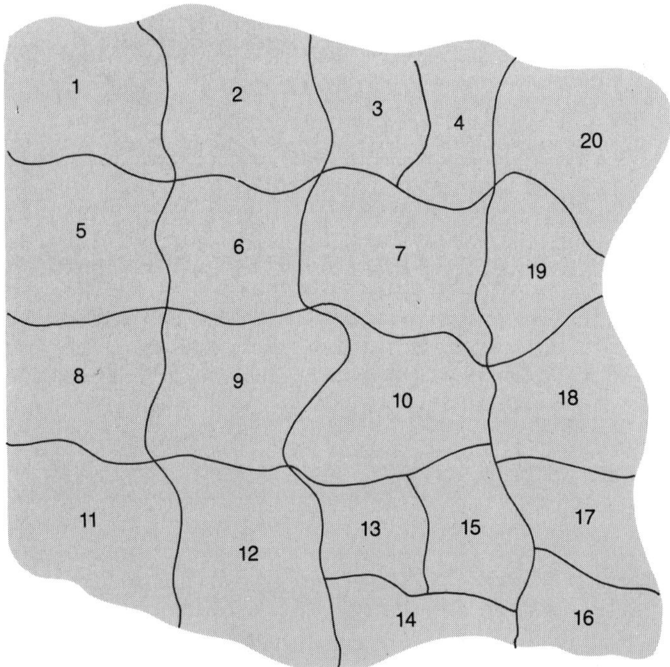

would have to be expanded at a capital cost of $10 million, which would come out of the budget for new purchases. If the objective is to maximize annual after-tax profit,

a. Explicitly define your decision variables and formulate this model.

***b.* Find the optimal solution.

51. ***Aircraft Purchase Continued.*** In the last exercise, suppose maintenance days can be expanded in increments of 50 days up to a maximum of 450 additional days. Accountants estimate that capital costs of $1 million would be required for each additional 50 days, again at the expense of the purchasing budget. How would you alter the formulation?

52. ***Management Training Program.*** One Big Eight accounting firm has a retraining program directed toward members of the staff who have been with the firm more than 10 years. The program lasts for one year and trains the staff in four new areas. A trainee spends three months in each module and then returns to a field office.

    Their experience during each three-month program consists of job training followed by actual field experience. When a person moves from one module to another, a certain number of hours are required for job training. In general, the training time in one module is a function of the immediately preceding module. Table 8–9 indicates estimated training times (in hours) in moving from one module to another. The training coordinators want to determine the module sequence that minimizes total training time for the four modules. Let

    x_{ij} = 1 if a trainee moves from module i to module j and
    0 if not.

    a. Formulate a 0-1 programming model. The model should account for entry into the program from a "field module" and reentry to the field at the conclusion of the program. What general class of problems does this model fall under?

TABLE 8–9 Job Training Times (Hours)

From/To	Field	A	B	C	D
Field	—	80	70	90	60
A	0	—	130	100	75
B	0	100	—	80	80
C	0	120	90	—	70
D	0	90	80	110	—

b. Find the optimal solution by enumeration.
c. Use the greedy algorithm as in Exercise 27. How good is your result?
***d*. Find the optimal solution using an IP algorithm.

53. ***Energy Conservation.*** In an effort to conserve gasoline, the mayor of a large Canadian city has proposed establishing commuter bus service from park-and-lock locations on the periphery of the city. Five such sites are being considered by the mayor's staff. These would service commuters from eight outlying suburban areas. Commuters could drive to one of the sites and obtain roundtrip bus transportation to the city. The mayor's objective is to minimize the total amount of fuel needed to transport people between their homes and the city. Table 8–10 indicates the average monthly fuel consumption (in liters) required to transport a commuter between home and the different park-and-lock sites. The empty cells indicate impractical suburb/park-and-lock combinations. The average monthly fuel consumption per commuter transported between a park-and-lock site and the city, estimates of the number of people interested in participating in this type of program, and capacities for handling commuters from each site are also indicated.

TABLE 8–10 Energy Conservation Data

	Monthly Fuel Consumption per Commuter (in liters) (home to park and lock) — Suburb 1	2	3	4	5	6	7	8	Bus: Monthly Fuel Consumption per Commuter (in liters)	Capacity (Number of Commuters)
Park-and-Lock Site 1	100.0	92.8		120.3			76.6		5.6	3,000
Park-and-Lock Site 2	84.8		91.2	98.8	81.6	79.4	98.2		6.4	4,000
Park-and-Lock Site 3	66.0		105.6		93.2	88.3		79.7	8.4	3,500
Park-and-Lock Site 4				107.5	108.9	83.9		93.8	7.2	2,800
Park-and-Lock Site 5	82.0	78.0	79.8		100.0		82.6	88.6	4.8	3,750
Number of Interested Commuters	600	750	1,500	800	700	550	1,000	400		

Given that no more than three of the sites will be selected, the problem is to determine which sites to select and how many commuters from each suburb to assign to each site. If the objective is to minimize total monthly fuel consumption,

a. Formulate the IP model.

***b*. Determine the optimal solution.

54. ***Air Traffic Control I.*** Officials of a major metropolitan airport are reviewing their staffing needs for air traffic controllers. The most recent labor agreement has specified hiring for eight different shifts consisting of eight hours per shift. FAA regulations specify that air controllers work two-hour intervals with an hour break between. Airport officials specify that each controller work the first two hours of a shift. Thus a controller is active for six of the eight hours.

Table 8–11 illustrates the hours of each shift and the periods during which a controller is on duty. Based on an analysis of daily traffic volume and FAA guidelines, airport officials have determined the minimum number of controllers on duty for each hour of the day. These are also indicated in Table 8–11.

TABLE 8–11 Air Traffic Controller Shifts and Requirements

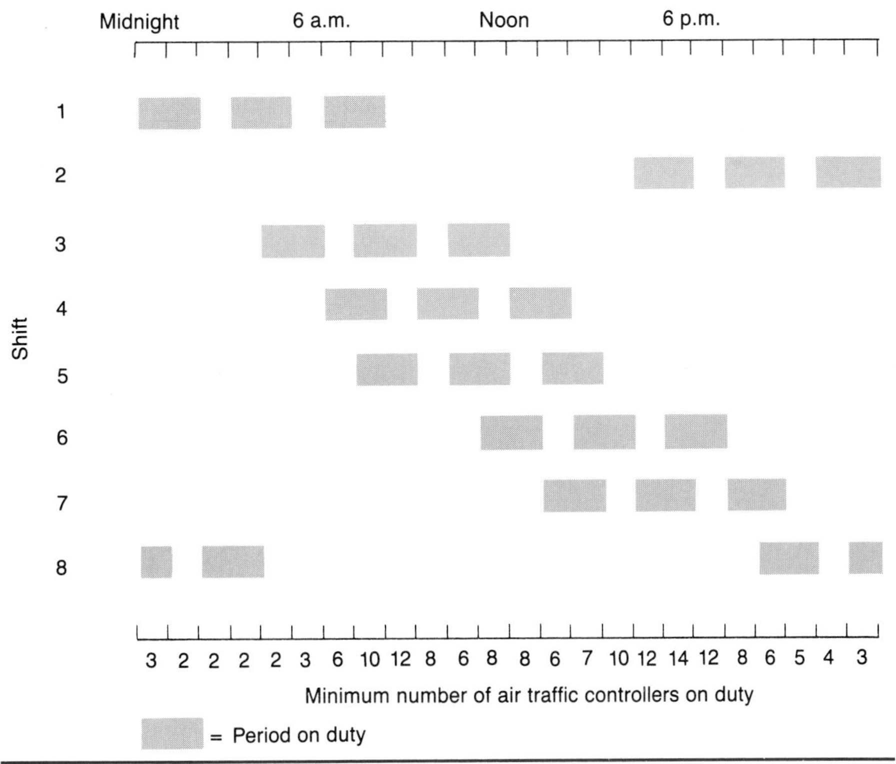

The base pay per controller is $80 per shift with differentials for certain shifts. Any shifts *beginning* between 4 P.M. and 11 P.M. (inclusive) are paid at a 10 percent premium for the entire shift; any *beginning* between midnight and 6 A.M. (inclusive) receive a 20 percent premium.

Airport officials want to determine the number of controllers to hire for each shift so as to meet the hourly requirements at a minimum cost per day.

a. Formulate an appropriate model.

b. Reduce the size of the model by eliminating unnecessary constraints or those automatically satisfied.

c. Find a solution to the formulation in part *b* using the greedy algorithm.

***d.* Solve using a computer package.

e. Reformulate the model if the objective is to minimize the surplus controller-hours above the required minimum for each hour of the day.

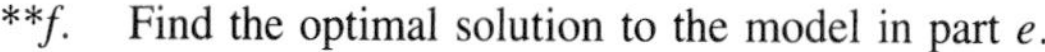

***f*. Find the optimal solution to the model in part *e*.

55. ***Air Traffic Control II.*** Suppose that in the previous exercise the FAA will allow overtime shifts of three hours provided the first hour of the three hours is off duty. Those working overtime receive credit for an additional half day of work and are paid time and a half (based on the pay/shift determined in the previous exercise) for the overtime period. The decisions under these assumptions are how many controllers should begin a regular shift and how many an overtime shift (of 11 hours) for each of the eight shifts.

a. Formulate this problem.

***b*. Find the optimal solution.

56. ***"Super Sunday."*** Super Sunday, the once-a-year TV extravaganza focused on the activities of the NFL Super Bowl, has almost become a tradition. CBS has received the TV contract for this year's family festivities. Producers have identified 12 potential camera locations within the stadium. They have also identified 25 stadium areas that may require camera coverage during the pregame, game, and postgame activities. Table 8–12 indicates each camera location and the stadium areas the camera can cover.

TABLE 8–12

Camera Location	Stadium Areas
1	1, 3, 4, 6, 7
2	8, 4, 7, 12
3	2, 5, 9, 11, 13
4	1, 2, 18, 19, 21
5	3, 6, 10, 12, 14
6	8, 14, 15, 16, 17
7	18, 21, 24, 25
8	2, 10, 16, 23
9	1, 6, 11
10	20, 22, 24, 25
11	2, 4, 6, 8
12	1, 6, 12, 17

CBS executives are concerned about costs for the production. Consequently, they have set an objective of minimizing the number of camera locations used. In seeking this objective they want at least one camera to be available to cover each stadium area. Camera location 9 is the "blimp," and executives have decided that the blimp *will* be used because of viewer expectation and fascination with the shots from this location. Stadium areas 1 and 2 are locker room locations. The viewer interest in football personalities has led the executives to request that at least two camera locations be available to cover each of these areas.

a. Formulate the 0-1 programming problem to allow for determining the minimum number of cameras needed for coverage.

b. In which locations are cameras required? Why? Which constraints does this eliminate in the formulation?

c. Find the optimal solution.

57. ***Diet Model.*** The diet problem is an LP/IP "classic." Basically, the objective is to ascertain the quantities of food to eat such that certain nutritional requirements are met at a minimum cost. In recent years, this type of model has been successfully extended and

generalized to applications in *food management,* whereby a given population (e.g., hospital, university, mental and penal institutions, navy base) is to be fed by converting raw food into menu items such that cost is minimized and nutritional, preference, and other constraints are satisfied.[22]

Consider the nutritional data in Table 8–13 where data have been gleaned from Adelle Davis' work.[23]

Define x_j as the daily measure or number of units (quarts, cups, etc.) to be consumed of food j.

a. Formulate an LP model that minimizes total cost and satisfies the following conditions:
 (1) Minimum and maximum daily allowances.
 (2) Daily potassium intake should be within ± 10 percent of daily sodium intake.
 (3) Daily calcium intake should be at least two thirds of daily phosphorous intake. (Note: x_j need not be integer.)

b. Find the optimal solution to the model in part *a*.

c. Modify the model in part *a* such that:
 (1) The meal must include at least 100 grams of one of the meat items.
 (2) One and only one item must come from each of the food groups diary, meat, and vegetable.

***d.* Find the optimal solution to the mixed IP model in part *c*.

e. Discuss shortcomings of the diet model with respect to its applicability in a food management environment.

58. ***Bartholomew Electric Company Revisited.* Review the case at the end of Chapter 7.

a. Formulate the problem as an integer programming problem.

b. Solve for the optimal solution.

c. Assume that Bartholomew is not necessarily committed to retaining the five existing distribution warehouses. Modify the formulation in part *a* such that you are determining which of the eight distribution warehouses should be utilized along with the quantities of new appliances to be shipped from each warehouse to each demand point.

d. Solve for the optimal solution using the assumptions in part *c*.

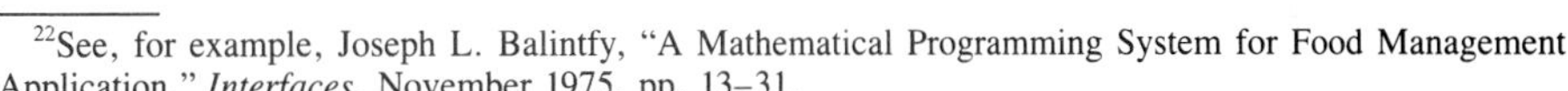

[22]See, for example, Joseph L. Balintfy, "A Mathematical Programming System for Food Management Application," *Interfaces,* November 1975, pp. 13–31.

[23]*Let's Eat Right to Keep Fit* (New York: Harcourt Brace Jovanovich, 1970).

TABLE 8–13 Nutritional Data

Food	Measure	Weight (g)	Cost ($/Measure)	Calories	Protein (g)	Fat (g)	Minerals (mg)					Vitamins			
							Iron	Calcium	Phosphorus	Potassium	Sodium	A (units)	B_1 (mg)	B_2 (mg)	C (mg)
Dairy															
Whole milk	1 qt.	976	0.60	660	32	40	0.4	1140	930	210	75	1,560	0.32	1.7	6
Ice cream	1 cup	188	0.55	300	6	18	0.1	175	150	170	140	740	0	0.3	0
Eggs (scrambled or fried)	2	128	0.25	220	13	16	2.2	60	222	140	338	1,200	0	0.4	0
Cheese (cheddar, American)	1 in. cube	17	0.10	70	4	6	0.1	133	128	30	180	230	0	0.1	0
Meat															
Lean ground beef	3 oz.	85	0.45	185	24	10	3.0	10	158	340	110	20	0	0	0
Broiled chicken	3 oz.	85	0.25	185	23	9	1.4	10	250	350	50	260	0	0.1	0
Baked flounder	3.5 oz.	100	0.40	200	30	8	1.4	22	344	585	235	0	0	0	0
Vegetable															
French fried potatoes	10 pieces	60	0.13	155	1	7	0.7	9	6	510	6	0	0	0	8
Green beans	1 cup	125	0.42	25	1	0	0.9	45	20	204	2	830	0	0.1	15
Fruit															
Frozen orange juice	6 oz. can	210	0.45	330	2	0	0.8	69	115	1,315	4	1,490	0.60	0.1	330
Grain															
Converted rice	1 cup uncooked	187	0.40	677	14	0	1.6	53	244	300	6	0	0.30	0	0
Min. daily allowance*				2,400	70	—	10	800	—	—	—	5,000	1.00	1.6	70
Max. daily allowance*				2,800	—	—	—	—	—	—	—	40,000	—	—	—

*For healthy men, 35–55 years old, 5′ 9″ height, and 154 lb. weight..

CASE Purr-Dew Chicken Corporation

John Purr and Dorothy Dew have pooled their collective resources and formed a corporation to sell processed chickens to major grocery chains. Purr-Dew has identified three large chicken suppliers who have agreed to supply fryer chickens to yet-to-be-determined processing plants. Purr-Dew has also reached tentative agreements with 20 major grocery chains around the country for supplying processed fryers. The problem now is to set up the processing plants. Twelve potential sites have been identified for the processing plants. Sites 1 and 2 are in the East; sites 3, 4, and 5 are in the Midwest; sites 6, 7, 8, and 9 are in the West; and sites 10, 11, and 12 are in the South. In making final decisions about the sites to choose, management has indicated that there should be at least one site in each region except for the West. In the West, at least two sites should be chosen. They have also indicated that because of the proximity of sites 6 and 7, both of these sites should not be selected—at most, one of the two.

Table 8–14 summarizes the transportation costs (per 100 pounds of fryers) from each supplier to each proposed processing plant. Where no entry appears in the table, costs have been judged too high for shipping to the plant location. Also shown in Table 8–14 are estimates of the maximum monthly quantities that can be provided by each supplier as well as the monthly processing capacities at each proposed processing plant (both stated in hundreds of pounds). Table 8–15 summarizes estimates of monthly amortization costs for each site as well as monthly overhead expenses.

TABLE 8–14 Transportation Costs per Hundred Pounds

		Processing Plant												
		1	2	3	4	5	6	7	8	9	10	11	12	Monthly Capacity (100s of lbs.)
Supplier	1	5.3	4.6	4.0	4.2		4.5		5.0		4.5	5.2	3.8	30,000
	2	4.8	4.4	4.2	3.8	5.1	4.8	5.2	4.8	3.8			3.5	25,000
	3			4.4	4.0	4.9	4.7	5.5		4.0	4.7	4.9	3.6	40,000
Monthly Capacity (100s of lbs.)		10,000	12,000	18,000	15,000	20,000	10,000	22,500	18,000	24,000	15,000	22,000	16,000	

John and Dorothy have determined the grocery chains that each proposed plant could reasonably supply. These combinations are shown in Table 8–16 along with estimates of the transportation costs (per 100 pounds) from each plant to each grocery chain. Table 8–16 also shown the monthly demands for fryers by each chain.

TABLE 8–15

Proposed Plant	Monthly Amortization	Monthly Overhead
1	$15,000	$22,000
2	18,000	36,000
3	24,000	48,000
4	16,000	30,000
5	30,000	55,000
6	16,000	24,000
7	36,000	52,000
8	20,000	28,000
9	32,000	50,000
10	18,000	40,000
11	28,000	52,000
12	21,000	36,000

John and Dorothy want to make the following decisions: (*a*) Which locations should be selected for processing plants? (*b*) How many pounds of fryers should be provided by each supplier to each processing plant? (*c*) How many pounds of processed fryers should each plant supply to each grocery chain? In making these decisions, John and Dorothy want to minimize the sum of monthly distribution, amortization, and overhead costs.

Required:

1. Formulate the integer programming model for this problem.

2. Solve the model for the optimal solution.
3. Verbally summarize your recommendations. An analysis of the extent to which constraints are satisfied and a breakout of expected weekly expenses by type should be included in the summary.

TABLE 8–16 Transportation Costs per Hundred Pounds

	Grocery Chain																			
	1	2	3	4	5	6	7	8	9	10	11	12	13	14	15	16	17	18	19	20
1	2.8	2.2	3.1	2.6			2.5	3.0		1.8										
2	2.0	2.3	4.0	2.8	3.5		2.3	2.6												
3				2.9	4.0	3.8	2.6	2.5	4.1											
4				3.0	3.8	4.0	3.0	2.4	4.3	2.0										
5			3.6		3.4	3.9	2.8	2.8	4.0	2.5										
6							2.5		3.9	2.6	3.5	4.2	5.0		4.3					
7									4.2	3.0	3.1	4.4	4.6	3.8	4.0					
8								2.9	4.0	2.8	3.3	4.1	4.5	4.0						
9						4.1			3.8	2.9	3.6	4.3	4.8	3.7	4.1		5.4			
10														4.1		5.2	5.6	4.2	3.6	2.9
11															4.0	5.0	5.3	4.5	3.8	3.2
12															4.2	4.8	5.5	4.1	4.0	3.4
Monthly Demand (100s of lbs.)	2,000	4,500	3,000	3,200	4,500	1,800	3,600	4,200	5,000	2,400	3,750	4,600	1,400	2,300	3,500	5,200	6,000	4,450	2,700	3,100

9

Multicriteria Mathematical Programming

The mathematical programming models and techniques presented thus far in the text have proved to be of significant value to decision makers. These techniques, under specified assumptions, determine values for decision variables that optimize a single quantifiable objective function (which may be a surrogate for the true objective in the problem). As indicated in Chapter 1, the assumption of a unidimensional criterion of choice is usually an oversimplification of reality. Frequently there are multiple goals (criteria or objectives) of interest to decision makers. These may be of different dimensions (maximize profit versus maximize market share); they may be difficult to quantify (maximize customer satisfaction); and they may conflict with one another (minimize cost of health care delivery versus maximize quality of health care services). These types of multicriteria issues are the primary concern of many managers on a daily basis.

Relatively new developments within the field of OR/MS have successfully dealt with the reality of multicriteria decision environments. Some of these are extensions of the mathematical programming techniques we have already examined. This chapter provides an overview of the methods of **multicriteria mathematical programming.** The largest part of the chapter will focus on the nature, applications, and solution methods of **goal programming (GP).** The last section of the chapter discusses extensions of goal programming and presents a brief description of other multicriteria methods.

9.1 GOAL PROGRAMMING

Goal programming is a powerful technique that has found wide application within organizations. Aside from addressing the multicriteria dilemma faced by so many decision makers, the solution method has the advantage of drawing heavily upon the simplex method.

Introduction

Goal programming is largely a variation of linear programming. Recent extensions, however, have branched into the area of nonlinear goal programming. First identified by Charnes and Cooper, the technique of goal programming was extended and refined by Ijiri.[1] Lee provided one of the first comprehensive presentations of the topic and was a pioneer in identifying areas of application.[2]

Goal programming is a form of linear programming that allows for consideration of a single goal or multiple goals. The goals may or may not be of the same dimension or unit of measurement. In addition, goal programming allows for consideration of conflicting goals. If multiple goals exist, the decision maker must specify an ordinal ranking of goals. The goal programming solution method operates in a way that addresses lower-priority goals only after higher-priority goals have been satisfied as well as possible. This forces decision makers into giving careful consideration to the relative importance of their goals. For example, in postoptimality analysis the decision maker is provided the opportunity to assess the effects of changing the priorities of multiple goals or of increasing or decreasing the number of goals.

[1]Y. Ijiri, *Management Goals and Accounting for Control* (Chicago: Rand McNally, 1965).

[2]Sang Lee, *Goal Programming for Decision Analysis* (Philadelphia: Auerbach Publishers, 1972).

Whereas linear programming identifies from the set of feasible solutions the point that *optimizes* a single objective, goal programming identifies the point that *best* satisfies either the single goal or set of goals in the problem. Given the number of goals, the priority structure specified by the decision maker, and the inevitable competition among goals, the best solution is often one that satisfices. (Remember this concept from Chapter 1.) With multiple goals, all goals usually cannot be realized exactly. Goal programming attempts to minimize the deviations from these goals with consideration given to the hierarchy of stated priorities.

In linear programming, goals can be stated individually as constraints. Suppose a hospital has a goal of adding 50 new rooms over the next two years and another goal of keeping capital expenditures during the same period below $1 million. These two goals could be specified as constraints in an LP model. If other capital commitments made it impossible to realize the goal of 50 new rooms, then the LP result would simply indicate no feasible solution. The goal programming treatment of this same situation, however, would provide a solution that, depending on the order of priorities, gives the hospital administrator information concerning possible trade-offs between rooms and budget. The infeasibility of meeting both goals has not changed, but a solution would be identified that minimizes the deviations from specified goals.

Let us illustrate the differences between an LP formulation and GP formulation of a simple, single-goal problem.

Example 9.1 Media Mix, Single Goal

Example 3.7 presented an LP formulation of a media mix problem. Here we examine a simplified version of this problem: how much money to allocate for television and radio advertisements. Rated exposures per $1,000 of advertising expenditure are 10,000 and 7,500, respectively, for television and radio. If the advertising budget for the next campaign is $100,000 and no more than 70 percent of the budget can be expended on television, then the **LP formulation** for maximizing total advertising exposures is

Maximize

$$z = 10{,}000x_1 + 7{,}500x_2$$

subject to

$$\begin{aligned} x_1 + x_2 &\leq 100 \\ x_1 \qquad &\leq 70 \\ x_1, x_2 &\geq 0 \end{aligned}$$

where x_1 = Thousands of dollars spent on TV advertising and x_2 = Thousands of dollars spent on radio advertising.

Now presume that management has set a target goal of 1 million exposures for the advertising campaign; that is, they would be satisfied if their campaign reached 1 million exposures. The LP approach would be to include this goal as a constraint having the form

$$10{,}000x_1 + 7{,}500x_2 \geq 1{,}000{,}000 .$$

You should be able to verify that there is no feasible solution to this revised problem.

The GP formulation of the same problem is

Minimize

$$z = 0x_1 + 0x_2 + d^- + d^+$$

or, more simply,

$$z = d^- + d^+$$

subject to

(Goal constraint)	$10{,}000x_1 + 7{,}500x_2 + d^- - d^+ = 1{,}000{,}000$	(1)
(System constraint)	$x_1 + x_2 \leq 100$	(2)
(System constraint)	$x_1 \leq 70$	(3)
	$x_1, x_2, d^-, d^+ \geq 0.$	

Let us examine the characteristics of this model:

> **Variables:** Two types of variables will be part of any goal programming formulation; they are **decision variables** and **deviational variables.**

The decision variables in the GP formulation are x_1 and x_2. Deviational variables represent the extent to which target goals are not achieved. The deviational variables are the nonnegative variables d^- and d^+ in the GP formulation. They represent the amount by which the exposure goal is *underachieved* (d^-) or *overachieved* (d^+). These variables appear in the first constraint, which sets total exposures equal to 1 million. *They behave in a manner similar to slack and surplus variables contained within the same constraint.* If x_1 and x_2 are chosen in such a way that total exposures are less than 1 million, d^- assumes a value that represents the amount by which total exposures fall short of 1 million. If x_1 and x_2 are assigned values such that total exposures are greater than 1 million, d^+ assumes a value equal to the amount by which the exposure goal is exceeded.

Linear dependency between the deviational variables assures that only one of the two can assume a positive value for any solution (i.e., it is impossible to have both underachievement and overachievement of a goal). If the goal is achieved *exactly,* then both deviational variables will equal zero.

> **Constraints:** Two classes of constraints may be formulated for a goal programming problem: (1) **system constraints,** which may influence but are not directly related to goals, and (2) **goal constraints,** which are directly related to goals.

In the media mix formulation, the first constraint would be considered a goal constraint, and the two budget constraints represent system constraints. With goal constraints, it is conceivable that the ultimate solution may result in either the underachievement or overachievement of the particular goal. For this reason *both* types of deviational variables should be included as a part of each goal constraint. Furthermore, *in all cases* goal constraints are of the equality (=) type.

In a goal programming formulation, system constraints have the same impact as in a linear programming model. Whereas goal constraints may involve over or underachieved, system constraints must be satisfied or there is no feasible solution.

> **Objective Function:** The objective function in a GP problem is always minimized and must be composed of deviational variables only (decision variables are implicitly assigned coefficients of zero).

We always minimize in GP problems in an effort to make deviations from stated goals as small as possible. As the problem was originally stated, the decision maker is interested in achieving the exposure goal exactly. Thus both deviational variables are included in the objective function. If overachievement of the exposure goal were acceptable, then only d^- would be included in the objective function (but both d^+ and d^- would be included in the goal constraint). The concern would be the minimization of the degree of underachievement of the exposure goal. Conversely, if only underachievement were acceptable for a given goal, then only d^+ would be included in the objective function. In this formulation, no preference or priority has been assigned to either underachievement or overachievement of the single goal in the problem. In the next section we will present examples of multiple goals; these problems require the decision maker to rank order the goals according to priorities.

FOLLOW-UP EXERCISES

1. Explain why it would be logically incorrect to
   a. Maximize $z = d^- + d^+$.
   b. Maximize $z = d^- - d^+$.
   c. Minimize $z = d^- - d^+$.
2. Modify z in the example if the decision maker finds overachievement of the goal to be desirable. Need you modify constraint 1? Explain.
3. Reformulate Example 9.1 if management wishes to spend as close as possible to the \$100,000 budget subject to (*a*) expenditures of less than \$70,000 on television and (*b*) achievement of a total exposure above 1.2 million. (*Hint:* Define the deviational variables in terms of overachievement and underachievement of the budget.)

Multiple Goals

When more than one goal exists:

a. Multiple goals must be assigned ordinal **priority factors** (that is, they must be rank ordered).

b. More than one set of deviational variables *may be* associated with any goal (or priority level).

c. When more than one deviational variable exists at a given priority level, **differential weights** may be assigned to the variables in the objective function to express decision-maker preferences within that priority level.

The following examples illustrate these issues for multiple-goal problems.

Example 9.2 Media Mix, Multiple Goals

In the previous example, assume that management has agreed that the campaign cannot be judged successful if total exposures are under 750,000. The campaign would be viewed as superbly successful if 1 million exposures occurred. In this example, management has rank ordered four goals it wishes to achieve, arranged from highest to lowest priority:

1. Minimize the underachievement of the exposure goal of 750,000 exposures.
2. Avoid expenditures of more than $100,000.
3. Avoid expenditures of more than $70,000 for television advertisements.
4. Minimize the underachievement of the goal of 1 million exposures.

Goals 1 and 4 are tiered in the sense that management's top priority is not to fall short of the exposure goal of 750,000. At a lower level of priority, management is effectively stating that they would not like to fall short of 1 million exposures. The GP formulation of the revised problem is

Minimize

$$z = P_1 d_1^- + P_2 d_2^+ + P_3 d_3^+ + P_4 d_4^-$$

subject to

(Total exposure goal)	$10{,}000x_1 + 7{,}500x_2 + d_1^- - d_1^+ = 750{,}000$	(1)
(Total budget goal)	$x_1 + x_2 + d_2^- - d_2^+ = 100$	(2)
(TV budget goal)	$x_1 + d_3^- - d_3^+ = 70$	(3)
(Total exposure goal)	$10{,}000x_1 + 7{,}500x_2 + d_4^- - d_4^+ = 1{,}000{,}000$	(4)

$$x_1, x_2, d_1^-, d_1^+, d_2^-, d_2^+, d_3^-, d_3^+, d_4^-, d_4^+ \geq 0,$$

where

d_1^- = Amount by which total exposures fall short of 750,000.
d_1^+ = Amount by which total exposures exceed 750,000.
d_2^- = Amount by which total expenditures fall short of $100,000.
d_2^+ = Amount by which total expenditures exceed $100,000.
d_3^- = Amount by which television expenditures fall short of $70,000.
d_3^+ = Amount by which television expenditures exceed $70,000.
d_4^- = Amount by which total exposures fall short of 1 million.
d_4^+ = Amount by which total exposures exceed 1 million.
P_k = Priority factor with rank k.
x_j = Thousands of dollars expended on jth medium (j = 1 for TV and j = 2 for radio).

Notice that deviational variables have been added to the two budgetary constraints; they have become goal constraints. Stating these original system constraints as goal constraints "loosens" their impact. System constraints must be satisfied or there is no feasible solution. As goal constraints, the incorporation of deviational variables acknowledges that under- or overachievement of these budgets may be required.

Within a given problem, either a condition must be satisfied in an absolute sense (and is modeled as a system constraint) or it is stated as a target or goal (and is modeled as a goal constraint). This frequently causes confusion for students who want to model a condition as both a system constraint and goal constraint.

Priority Factors: When a GP problem contains multiple goals that have been rank ordered, deviational variables are implicitly weighted in the objective function by ordinal priority factors, P_k, where P_1 represents the highest priority, P_2 the second highest priority, and so forth.

The priority factor P_k simply serves to identify the priority level (rank) for the goal it "weighs." These factors may be thought of as being preemptive in the sense that the goal associated with P_k must be satisfied as best as possible before considering the goal associated with P_{k+1}. Mathematically the relationship between these factors can be stated as $P_k >>> P_{k+1}$ where $>>>$ implies that P_k is much greater than P_{k+1}. Note, however, that the ordinal nature of P_k does not require the assignment of a numeric value.

Intuitively you might think of the priority factors as penalties or costs for having deviations from the stated goals. The greatest penalty (P_1) is assigned for any deviation from the highest priority goal. A large, but significantly smaller, penalty (P_2) is assigned for any deviation from the second highest priority goal. In general, a large penalty P_k is assigned for any deviations from the *k*th priority goal, where P_k is significantly larger than P_{k-1}.

In the objective function the highest priority (P_1) is associated with d_1^-, which represents the underachievement of the 750,000 exposure goal. Also, there is concern for exceeding both the total budget and the television budget, with the former having a higher priority (P_2) than the latter (P_3); consequently, d_2^+ and d_3^+ are included in the objective function with respective priority factors of P_2 and P_3. The variables d_2^- and d_3^- are not included in the objective function because of management's apparent lack of concern for spending less than budgeted amounts. The lowest priority goal is to minimize the underachievement of the exposure goal of 1 million; thus the inclusion of d_4^- and its priority factor P_4.

As a final reminder, objective functions in GP models consist of certain deviational variables weighted by priority factors (and sometimes, differential weights). All other variables in the model are asigned zero coefficients, implicitly.

FOLLOW-UP EXERCISES

4. Modify z in Example 9.2 if goals 3 and 4 have the same priority.
5. Suppose the priorities of the four goals in Example 9.2 were reversed. Reformulate the problem by
   a. Redefining the deviational variables.
   b. Changing the subscripts of the P_k's in z.

   Which approach requires less effort to reformulate?
6. Modify Example 9.2 if the condition in goal 3 is stated as a system constraint rather than as a goal constraint. In other words, eliminate goal 3 as a goal.

▶ Example 9.3 Media Mix, Differential Weights

Continuing the previous example, assume that the two most important audiences for the company are persons 18 to 21 years of age and persons 25 to 30 years of age. Table 9–1 presents estimates of the numbers of individuals in the two age groups expected to be exposed to advertisements per $1,000 of expenditure.

Management has established a goal of reaching at least 250,000 persons in each of the two age groups and ranks the achievement of these targets as the fifth most important goal. In addition, management realizes and wishes to account for the fact that the purchasing power of the 25-to-30 age group is twice the purchasing power of the 18-to-21 age group. The modified problem is formulated below.

TABLE 9–1 Exposures per $1,000

Age	Television	Radio
18–21 years	2,500	3,000
25–30 years	3,000	1,500

Minimize

$$z = P_1 d_1^- + P_2 d_2^+ + P_3 d_3^+ + P_4 d_4^- + P_5 d_5^- + 2P_5 d_6^-$$

subject to

(Total exposure goal)	$10{,}000x_1 + 7{,}500x_2 + d_1^- - d_1^+ =$	750,000	(1)
(Total budget goal)	$x_1 + x_2 + d_2^- - d_2^+ =$	100	(2)
(TV budget goal)	$x_1 + d_3^- - d_3^+ =$	70	(3)
(Total exposure goal)	$10{,}000x_1 + 7{,}500x_2 + d_4^- - d_4^+ =$	1,000,000	(4)
(18–21 year goal)	$2{,}500x_1 + 3{,}000x_2 + d_5^- - d_5^+ =$	250,000	(5)
(25–30 year goal)	$3{,}000x_1 + 1{,}500x_2 + d_6^- - d_6^+ =$	250,000	(6)

$$x_1, x_2, d_1^-, d_1^+, d_2^-, d_2^+, d_3^-, d_3^+, d_4^-, d_4^+, d_5^-, d_5^+, d_6^-, d_6^+ \geq 0,$$

where (in addition to the previous definitions)

d_5^- = Amount by which total exposures in the 18-to-21 age category fall short of 250,000.

d_5^+ = Amount by which total exposures in the 18-to-21 age category exceed 250,000.

d_6^- = Amount by which total exposures in the 25-to-30 age category fall short of 250,000.

d_6^+ = Amount by which total exposures in the 25-to-30 age category exceed 250,000.

P_5 = Priority factor with rank 5.

In the objective function both d_5^- and d_6^- (underachievement of exposure targets for the two markets) have the same priority factor (P_5), however, d_5^- and d_6^- have been assigned *differential weights* of 1 and 2, respectively, to account for the relative purchasing power of persons in the two age groups. These differentials imply that management perceives underachievement of the exposure goal in the 25-to-30 group to be twice as "costly" as underachievement in the other group. Also note that two sets of deviational variables (d_5^-, d_5^+ and d_6^-, d_6^+) are associated with the fifth most important goal.

When solving this problem, the goal programming algorithm will account for the fact that d_5^- and d_6^- are at the same level of priority. However, *at that level,* the differential weights will steer the algorithm toward minimizing d_6^- before d_5^- if possible.

FOLLOW-UP EXERCISES

7. What modification is necessary in Example 9.3 if the purchasing power differential is to be ignored?
8. Why would it be wrong to assign a priority factor of P_6 to d_6^- in the objective function of Example 9.3?
9. Does the number of goal constraints always equal the number of goals? Explain.
10. Reformulate Example 9.3 by accounting for relative purchasing power between the two age groups as follows: Eliminate the use of differential weights; make goal 5 the exposure target for the 25-to-30 age group; make goal 6 the exposure target for the 18-to-21 age group; and identify goal 6 as having lower priority than goal 5.
11. Suppose that management specifies a goal of keeping budget overruns for the campaign below \$5,000. Assume this goal to have the second highest priority, with goals 2 through 5 in the original formulation becoming goals 3 through 6. Define: d_7^- = Amount of budget overrun short of \$5,000 and d_7^+ = Amount of budget overrun in excess of \$5,000. With respect to Example 9.3:
    a. Appropriately modify z.
    b. Add a goal constraint exclusively in terms of deviational variables.
    c. Rewrite the constraint in part *b* using the decision variables x_1 and x_2.

9.2 ADDITIONAL APPLICATIONS OF GOAL PROGRAMMING

The diversity of applications of goal programming is as great as for linear programming. In this section we present some additional applications to illustrate the diversity.

Example 9.4 Contract Awards Model

An automobile manufacturer wants to award contracts for the supply of four different fuel injection system components. Four contractors have submitted bids on the components. Table 9–2 summarizes the prices bid per unit. Where no entry is made, the contractor submitted no bid.

TABLE 9–2 Bid Prices per Unit

	Contractor				
Component	**1**	**2**	**3**	**4**	**Demand (units)**
1	\$25	\$28	—	\$30	15,000
2	—	\$80	\$75	\$82	30,000
3	\$30	\$28	\$33	—	10,000
4	\$40	—	—	\$42	20,000

The demand for a component does not have to be supplied completely by one contractor. In fact certain contractors have indicated maximum quantities that can be supplied at the bid price. Contractor 1 can supply no more than 18,000 of item 4; contractor 2, no more than 3,000 of item 1; contractor 4, no more than 15,000 units of item 2 and no more than 5,000 units of item 4. There is no provision that awards must go to the low bidder. Contractor 4 has specified that it requires a minimum award of $500,000 if it is to supply any items at all.

In deciding how many units of each item to award to each contractor, management has stated the following goals in order of importance:

1. Minimize the extent to which total dollar awards to all contractors exceed $3.5 million.
2. Minimize the extent to which total dollar awards to contractor 4 fall short of $500,000.
3. Minimize the extent to which total dollar awards to each contractor exceed $1.2 million.
4. Because of a good relationship with contractor 1, minimize the extent to which his total awards fall short of $1 million.

As we go about formulating the model for this problem, let us return to the problem-solving framework.

1. **Verbal Statement of Problem**
   Determine the number of units of each item to award to each contractor so as to minimize the deviations from the stated set of goals.
2. **Decisions**
   a. **Verbal Statement**
      Number of units of each item to award to each contractor.
   b. **Mathematical Definition**
      x_{ij} = Number of units of component i awarded to contractor j.
3. **Criteria**
   a. **Verbal Statement**
      The multiple criteria in the problem are listed earlier as the four rank-ordered goals.
   b. **Mathematical Statement**
      For goal programming problems, formulation of the objective function is usually easier once the constraint set has been formulated. Thus we delay the mathematical statement.
4. **Constraining Conditions**
   a. **Verbal Statement (System Constraints)**
      The system constraints for this problem are of two types: demand constraints for each component and contractor restrictions on the number of units supplied of certain components. Demands for the four components are respectively 15,000, 30,000, 10,000, and 20,000 units. Contractor restrictions are 18,000 units(contractor 1/item 4), 3,000 units(contractor 2/item 1), 15,000 units(contractor 4/item 2), and 5,000 units(contractor 4/item 4).
   b. **Mathematical Statement (System Constraints)**
      Illustrating a few of these constraints, the demand constraint for component 1 is

$$x_{11} + x_{12} + x_{14} = 15,000 .$$

Similarly, the demand constraint for component 4 is

$$x_{41} + x_{44} = 20{,}000\,.$$

The restriction that contractor 1 can supply no more than 18,000 units of item 4 is stated as

$$x_{41} \leq 18{,}000\,.$$

c. **Verbal Statement (Goal Constraints)**
The following goal constraints are required: Total dollar awards to all contractors equal \$3.5 million. Total dollar awards to contractor 4 equal \$500,000. Total dollar awards to *each* contractor equal \$1.2 million. Total dollar awards to contractor 1 equal \$1 million.

d. **Mathematical Statement (Goal Constraints)**
The first goal constraint has the form:

$$25x_{11} + 28x_{12} + 30x_{14} + 80x_{22} + 75x_{23} + 82x_{24} + 30x_{31} + 28x_{32} + 33x_{33} + 40x_{41} + 42x_{44} + d_1^- - d_1^+ = 3{,}500{,}000\,.$$

In this constraint, d_1^- equals the amount by which total dollar awards fall short of \$3.5 million and d_1^+ the amount by which total dollar awards exceed \$3.5 million. The second goal constraint has the form

$$30x_{14} + 82x_{24} + 42x_{44} + d_2^- - d_2^+ = 500{,}000$$

where d_2^- = Amount by which contractor 4 is awarded less than \$500,000 and d_2^+ = Amount by which awards are greater than \$500,000. The third goal actually requires four goal constraints, one for each contractor. The four constraints correspond to four *subgoals* at this level of priority. Let us simply illustrate the constraint corresponding to contractor 1.

$$25x_{11} + 30x_{31} + 40x_{41} + d_3^- - d_3^+ = 1{,}200{,}000\,.$$

The last goal constraint has the form

$$25x_{11} + 30x_{31} + 40x_{41} + d_7^- - d_7^+ = 1{,}000{,}000\,.$$

5. **Mathematical Model**
The complete goal programming model for this problem follows:

Minimize

$$z = P_1 d_1^+ + P_2 d_2^- + P_3(d_3^+ + d_4^+ + d_5^+ + d_6^+) + P_4 d_7^-$$

subject to

System Constraints

$$\begin{aligned}
x_{11} + x_{12} + x_{14} &= 15{,}000 && (1)\\
x_{22} + x_{23} + x_{24} &= 30{,}000 && (2)\\
x_{31} + x_{32} + x_{33} &= 10{,}000 && (3)\\
x_{41} + x_{44} &= 20{,}000 && (4)\\
x_{41} &\leq 18{,}000 && (5)\\
x_{12} &\leq 3{,}000 && (6)
\end{aligned}$$

$$\begin{array}{llr}
x_{24} & \leq 15{,}000 & (7) \\
x_{44} & \leq 5{,}000 & (8)
\end{array}$$

$$\begin{aligned}
&25x_{11} + 28x_{12} + 30x_{14} + 80x_{22} + 75x_{23} + 82x_{24} \\
&\quad + 30x_{31} + 28x_{32} + 33x_{33} + 40x_{41} + 42x_{44} \\
&\quad + d_1^- - d_1^+ = 3{,}500{,}000 \quad (9)
\end{aligned}$$

Goal Constraints

$$\begin{array}{lr}
30x_{14} + 82x_{24} + 42x_{44} + d_2^- - d_2^+ = 500{,}000 & (10) \\
25x_{11} + 30x_{31} + 40x_{41} + d_3^- - d_3^+ = 1{,}200{,}000 & (11) \\
28x_{12} + 80x_{22} + 28x_{32} + d_4^- - d_4^+ = 1{,}200{,}000 & (12) \\
75x_{23} + 33x_{33} + d_5^- - d_5^+ = 1{,}200{,}000 & (13) \\
30x_{14} + 82x_{24} + 42x_{44} + d_6^- - d_6^+ = 1{,}200{,}000 & (14) \\
25x_{11} + 30x_{31} + 40x_{41} + d_7^- - d_7^+ = 1{,}000{,}000 & (15)
\end{array}$$

$$x_{ij} \geq 0 \quad \text{for all } i, j$$

$$d_k^-, d_k^+ \geq 0 \quad \text{for all } k$$

As you examine this model, note the construction of the objective function. As indicated in Step 3*b* of the problem-solving framework, it is usually easier to formulate the objective function *after* the constraint set has been formulated. For this goal structure, there are four levels of priority. At the third highest level, there is concern about four different deviational variables (those representing dollar awards exceeding \$1.2 million for each contractor). As the problem is stated, there is no preference expressed regarding excessive awards to any one contractor. Had a preference been stated, differential weights might have been assigned to the deviational variables d_3^+, d_4^+, d_5^+, and d_6^+. Finally, the GP model includes eight system constraints and seven goal constraints.

One modification to this model pertains to the last constraint. This goal constraint *can* be stated in the form

$$d_3^- + d_7^- - d_7^+ = 200{,}000$$

which involves deviational variables only. Remember that d_3^- represents the amount by which total dollar awards to contractor 1 fall short of \$1.2 million. An equivalent way of viewing the fourth-ranked goal is to minimize the extent to which d_3^- exceeds \$200,000. For this model, the original constraint (15) *or* the above modification can be used. The latter constraint is obviously simpler to write as long as you are comfortable with the logic. If the shorter version of the constraint is used, the fourth priority goal is represented in the objective function by the term $P_4d_7^+$. Do you see why?

FOLLOW-UP EXERCISES

12. Provide a verbal interpretation of the meaning of the deviational variables in constraints 11–14.
13. Provide a verbal interpretation of the meaning of d_7^- and d_7^+ as they appear in the modification to constraint 15.
14. Reformulate the model in this example if management has decided not to honor the request of contractor 4 for a minimum award of \$500,000. With the exception of the original goal 2, assume that the original set of goals is the same.

15. In the original problem, assume that management has stated a fifth goal: Minimize the extent to which total dollar awards to each contractor exceed \$1.5 million. Modify the original formulation in two *different but equivalent* ways to account for this new goal. Do you think the result will be any different than that obtained in the original formulation?

▶ Example 9.5 University Admissions

As noted in other chapters, educational planning has received increasingly more attention from OR/MS analysts. Let us illustrate how a much simplified university admissions planning problem can be examined with goal programming.

A small midwestern university is attempting to reach admission decisions for next year. It wants to determine the numbers of in-state and out-of-state students to admit to each of its three colleges—Arts and Sciences (A&S), Business Administration (BA), and Engineering (E). Each of the three colleges has quotas for the coming year of 1,500, 400, and 200 new students, respectively, and the university has an enrollment goal of 2,000 new students. The university also has benchmark goals that 75 percent of new students come from in-state and 25 percent from out-of-state. Furthermore, the university hopes that 40 percent of the new students will be women and that 1,300 new students will be added to the dormitories. Flexible living arrangements have allowed the elimination of dorm quotas for men and women. Table 9–3 indicates historical dorm percentages that have been fairly stable over time. The admissions office has estimated the maximum number of applicants it expects to meet the minimum requirements for admission to the various programs. These are listed in Table 9–4.

TABLE 9–3 Dorm Percentages by Residency and Sex

Residence	Men	Women
In-state	0.50	0.60
Out-of-state	0.80	0.95

TABLE 9–4 Maximum Number of Students Meeting Minimum Admission Requirements

Students	A&S	BA	E
In-state men	800	400	200
In-state women	400	100	10
Out-of-state men	300	100	50
Out-of-state women	150	50	5

University administrators have rank ordered the following goals, which are to be considered in making the admission decisions.

1. Exactly achieve the university admissions goal of 2,000 new students.
2. Achieve the college quotas (with preference given to achieving the goal for Business first, Engineering second, and A&S last).
3. Minimize the underachievement of the goal of 75 percent in-state admissions.

4. Minimize the overachievement of the goal of 25 percent out-of-state admissions.
5. Minimize the underachievement of the housing goal of 1,300 students.
6. Minimize the underachievement of the 40 percent goal for women.
7. Restrict the overachievement of the housing goal to 50 students.

If we let

x_1 = Number of in-state men admitted to A&S.
x_2 = Number of in-state men admitted to Business.
x_3 = Number of in-state men admitted to Engineering.
x_4 = Number of in-state women admitted to A&S.
x_5 = Number of in-state women admitted to Business.
x_6 = Number of in-state women admitted to Engineering.
x_7 = Number of out-of-state men admitted to A&S.
x_8 = Number of out-of-state men admitted to Business.
x_9 = Number of out-of-state men admitted to Engineering.
x_{10} = Number of out-of-state women admitted to A&S.
x_{11} = Number of out-of-state women admitted to Business.
x_{12} = Number of out-of-state women admitted to Engineering.

then the formulation of the problem is given by

Minimize

$$z = P_1(d_1^- + d_1^+) + 3P_2(d_3^- + d_3^+) + 2P_2(d_4^- + d_4^+) + P_2(d_2^- + d_2^+) + P_3 d_5^- + P_4 d_6^+ + P_5 d_7^- + P_6 d_8^- + P_7 d_9^+$$

subject to

System Constraints

$$
\begin{array}{lrr}
x_1 & \le 800 & (1) \\
x_2 & \le 400 & (2) \\
x_3 & \le 200 & (3) \\
x_4 & \le 400 & (4) \\
x_5 & \le 100 & (5) \\
x_6 & \le 10 & (6) \\
x_7 & \le 300 & (7) \\
x_8 & \le 100 & (8) \\
x_9 & \le 50 & (9) \\
x_{10} & \le 150 & (10) \\
x_{11} & \le 50 & (11) \\
x_{12} & \le 5 & (12)
\end{array}
$$

$$
\begin{array}{lrr}
x_1 + x_2 + x_3 + x_4 + x_5 + x_6 + x_7 + x_8 + x_9 + x_{10} + x_{11} + x_{12} + d_1^- - d_1^+ & = 2{,}000 & (13) \\
x_1 + x_4 + x_7 + x_{10} + d_2^- - d_2^+ & = 1{,}500 & (14) \\
x_2 + x_5 + x_8 + x_{11} + d_3^- - d_3^+ & = 400 & (15)
\end{array}
$$

Goal Constraints

$$x_3 + x_6 + x_9 + x_{12} + d_4^- - d_4^+ = 200 \quad (16)$$

$$x_1 + x_2 + x_3 + x_4 + x_5 + x_6 + d_5^- - d_5^+ = 0.75(x_1 + x_2 + \cdots + x_{12})$$

or

$$0.25x_1 + 0.25x_2 + 0.25x_3 + 0.25x_4 + 0.25x_5 + 0.25x_6 - 0.75x_7 - 0.75x_8 - 0.75x_9 - 0.75x_{10} - 0.75x_{11} - 0.75x_{12} + d_5^- - d_5^+ = 0 \quad (17)$$

$$x_7 + x_8 + x_9 + x_{10} + x_{11} + x_{12} + d_6^- - d_6^+ = 0.25(x_1 + x_2 + \cdots + x_{12})$$

or

$$-0.25x_1 - 0.25x_2 - 0.25x_3 - 0.25x_4 - 0.25x_5 - 0.25x_6 + 0.75x_7 + 0.75x_8 + 0.75x_9 + 0.75x_{10} + 0.75x_{11} + 0.75x_{12} + d_6^- - d_6^+ = 0 \quad (18)$$

$$0.5x_1 + 0.5x_2 + 0.5x_3 + 0.6x_4 + 0.6x_5 + 0.6x_6 + 0.8x_7 + 0.8x_8 + 0.8x_9 + 0.95x_{10} + 0.95x_{11} + 0.95x_{12} + d_7^- - d_7^+ = 1{,}300 \quad (19)$$

$$x_4 + x_5 + x_6 + x_{10} + x_{11} + x_{12} + d_8^- - d_8^+ = 0.40(x_1 + x_2 + \cdots + x_{12})$$

or

$$-0.40x_1 - 0.40x_2 - 0.40x_3 + 0.60x_4 + 0.60x_5 + 0.60x_6 - 0.40x_7 - 0.40x_8 - 0.40x_9 + 0.60x_{10} + 0.60x_{11} + 0.60x_{12} + d_8^- - d_8^+ = 0 \quad (20)$$

$$d_7^+ + d_9^- - d_9^+ = 50 \quad (21)$$

$$\text{all } x_j \text{ and } d_i \geq 0.$$

A few aspects of this formulation should be noted. First, constraints 1 through 12 are system constraints and 13 through 21 are goal constraints. Also, the second highest priority goal involves three subgoals. In the objective function, the deviational variables associated with these subgoals have been assigned the same priority factor, but they have been weighted differently by arbitrarily chosen differential weights (the highest of which is assigned to the most important subgoal). These subgoals might have been handled by simply assigning each a different priority factor. Either approach is acceptable. A final observation relates to the last constraint, which consists of deviational variables only. The deviational variable d_7^+ represents the degree of overachievement of the housing goal of 1,300 students. This constraint is specifically established in order to restrict this overachievement to no more than 50 students.

FOLLOW-UP EXERCISES

16. With respect to Example 9.5:
    a. Verify the system constraints using Table 9–4.
    b. Provide a verbal interpretation of the deviational variables, $d_i^{-,+}$.
    c. Verify the objective function.
17. Indicate changes in the formulation if the three subgoals of goal 2 were to be made goals 2, 3, and 4 (with the other goals appropriately renumbered).
18. What other method might have been used to represent the goal restricting overachievement of the housing goal to 50 students?
19. Is there interdependence between goals 3 and 4 that would allow for simplification of the formulation? If so, what are the simplifications in the model?
20. Describe how you would incorporate considerations relating to minority students classified by ethnic or racial characteristics.

21. What other goals might a university or college consider in making admissions decisions?

▶ Example 9.6 Diet Mix Model (Integer, Goal Programming Model)

Exercise 57 in Chapter 8 presented a diet mix problem where the purpose was to determine the quantities of different foods to provide so as to minimize total cost while satisfying certain nutritional requirements. The diet problem is an LP/IP classic successfully extended and applied in a variety of food management settings. Let us examine a goal programming version of the diet mix model.

The dietician for a local school system is planning the lunch menu for tomorrow. Table 9–5 lists the foods she is considering for lunch along with cost information and various nutritional data. The dietician wishes to include at least one serving from each of the five food groups, including exactly one from the meat group and exactly one beverage. The only foods for which there can be more than one serving (and foods are to be included in units of whole servings) are cheese and bread. Other requirements in planning the meal are that at least 30 percent of the minimum daily allowances (MDA) be provided for calcium and each of the four vitamins listed.

In deciding how many servings (measures) of each food type to include in the meal, the dietician has stated the following goals in order of importance:

1. Minimize the extent to which total cost per meal exceeds \$0.80.
2. Minimize the extent to which the protein content of the meal falls short of 50 percent of the MDA.
3. Minimize the extent to which the fat content of the meal exceeds 25 grams.
4. Minimize the extent to which the potassium content falls short of 400 mg.
5. Minimize the extent to which the sodium content exceeds 350 mg.

In formulating the integer goal programming model for this problem, let us define x_j as the number of servings (measures) of food j included in the meal, where $j = 1, \ldots, 15$ corresponds to the order of foods listed in Table 9–5. The requirement that foods be included in the meal in units of whole servings results in all x_j being integer. The further stipulation that only cheese and bread can be served in multiple servings restricts all x_j except x_3 and x_{13} to 0-1 values. The complete model formulation follows:

Minimize

$$z = P_1 d_1^+ + P_2 d_2^- + P_3 d_3^+ + P_4 d_4^- + P_5 d_5^+$$

subject to

System Constraints

$$x_1 + x_2 + x_3 \geq 1 \quad (1)$$

$$x_4 + x_5 + x_6 = 1 \quad (2)$$

$$x_7 + x_8 + x_9 \geq 1 \quad (3)$$

$$x_{10} + x_{11} + x_{12} \geq 1 \quad (4)$$

$$x_{13} + x_{14} + x_{15} \geq 1 \quad (5)$$

$$x_1 + x_{10} + x_{12} = 1 \quad (6)$$

$$385x_1 + 175x_2 + 133x_3 + 10x_4 + 10x_5 + 22x_6 + 9x_7 + 45x_8 + 38x_9$$
$$+ 15x_{10} + 8x_{11} + 27x_{12} + 23x_{13} + 16x_{14} + 157x_{15} \geq 240 \quad (7)$$

TABLE 9–5 Nutritional Information for Selected Luncheon Foods

Food	Measure	Cost/ Measure	Calories	Protein (gm)	Fat (gm)	Minerals			Vitamins (mg)			
						Calcium	Potassium	Sodium	B_1	B_2	Niacin	C
Dairy:												
1. Whole milk	1 cup	$0.15	165	8	10	385	52.5	19	0.08	.425	.2	1.5
2. Ice cream	1 cup	0.25	300	6	18	175	170	140	0.18	.30	.3	0
3. Cheese (cheddar)	1-in. cube	0.05	70	4	6	133	30	180	0	.10	0	0
Meat:												
4. Lean ground beef	3 oz.	0.45	185	24	10	10	340	110	0	0	5.3	0
5. Broiled chicken	3 oz.	0.22	185	23	9	10	350	50	0	0.1	7	0
6. Baked flounder	3.5 oz.	0.60	200	30	8	22	585	235	0	0	2.5	0
Vegetables:												
7. French fried potatoes	10 pieces	0.10	155	1	7	9	510	6	0	0	1.8	8
8. Green beans	1 cup	0.35	25	1	0	45	204	2	0	.1	.6	16
9. Carrots, cooked	1 cup	0.20	45	1	0	38	600	75	0	0	.7	6
Fruit:												
10. Apple juice	1 cup	0.18	125	0	0	15	200	5	0	0	0	2
11. Banana	1 medium	0.12	85	1	0	8	390	1	0.1	0	0.7	10
12. Orange juice, fresh	8 oz.	0.40	112	2	0	27	500	2	0.2	0	1	129
Grain:												
13. Bread, whole wheat	1 slice	0.05	55	2	1	23	40	144	0.05	0	0.7	0
14. Noodles	1 cup	0.04	200	7	2	16	0	0	0	0	0.7	0
15. Pizza, cheese	1 slice	0.20	180	8	6	157	96	525	0	0.1	0.8	8
Minimum daily allowance (MDA)*			2400	70	—	800	—	—	1.0	1.6	17	70

*For healthy men, 35–55 years old, 5′9″ tall, and weighing 154 pounds.

$$0.08x_1 + 0.18x_2 + 0.1x_{11} + 0.2x_{12} + 0.05x_{13} \geq 0.3 \quad (8)$$

$$0.425x_1 + 0.3x_2 + 0.1x_3 + 0.1x_5 + 0.1x_8 + 0.1x_{15} \geq 0.48 \quad (9)$$

$$0.2x_1 + 0.3x_2 + 5.3x_4 + 7x_5 + 2.5x_6 + 1.8x_7 + 0.6x_8 + 0.7x_9 + 0.7x_{11} + x_{12} + 0.7x_{13} + 0.7x_{14} + 0.8x_{15} \geq 5.1 \quad (10)$$

$$1.5x_1 + 8x_7 + 16x_8 + 6x_9 + 2x_{10} + 10x_{11} + 129x_{12} + 8x_{15} \geq 21 \quad (11)$$

Goal Constraints

$$0.15x_1 + 0.25x_2 + 0.05x_3 + 0.45x_4 + 0.22x_5 + 0.60x_6 + 0.10x_7 + 0.35x_8 + 0.20x_9 + 0.18x_{10} + 0.12x_{11} + 0.40x_{12} + 0.05x_{13} + 0.04x_{14} + 0.20x_{15} + d_1^- - d_1^+ = 0.80 \quad (12)$$

$$8x_1 + 6x_2 + 4x_3 + 24x_4 + 23x_5 + 30x_6 + x_7 + x_8 + x_9 + x_{11} + 2x_{12} + 2x_{13} + 7x_{14} + 8x_{15} + d_2^- - d_2^+ = 35 \quad (13)$$

$$10x_1 + 18x_2 + 6x_3 + 10x_4 + 9x_5 + 8x_6 + 7x_7 + x_{13} + 2x_{14} + 6x_{15} + d_3^- - d_3^+ = 25 \quad (14)$$

$$52.5x_1 + 170x_2 + 30x_3 + 340x_4 + 350x_5 + 585x_6 + 510x_7 + 204x_8 + 600x_9 + 200x_{10} + 390x_{11} + 500x_{12} + 40x_{13} + 96x_{15} + d_4^- - d_4^+ = 400 \quad (15)$$

$$19x_1 + 140x_2 + 180x_3 + 110x_4 + 50x_5 + 235x_6 + 6x_7 + 2x_8 + 75x_9 + 5x_{10} + x_{11} + 2x_{12} + 144x_{13} + 525x_{15} + d_5^- - d_5^+ = 350 \quad (16)$$

$$x_3, x_{13} = \text{Nonnegative integers.}$$

$$x_j = 0 \text{ or } 1, \quad j \neq 3, \quad j \neq 13$$

$$d_k^-, d_k^+ \geq 0, \quad k = 1, \ldots, 5.$$

Let us examine this model. First, the constraint set consists of 11 system constraints and 5 goal constraints. Constraints 1–5 assure at least one serving from each food group with constraint 2 assuring exactly one from the meat group. Constraint 6 satisfies the requirement of exactly one serving of a beverage. Constraints 7–11 require satisfaction of at least 30 percent of the MDA for calcium and each of the four listed vitamins. Constraints 12–16 are goal constraints associated with each of the five stated goals. Once the constraint set is formulated, the objective function follows readily. Examine the objective function to make sure you understand it.

FOLLOW-UP EXERCISES

22. How must the model be altered if whole servings of included foods are not required?
23. Suppose a sixth goal is to minimize the extent to which the vitamin content of the meal falls short of 30 percent of the MDA for each of the four listed vitamins. How would the formulation change?
24. Suppose the dietician has decided that a serving of milk will be included in the meal along with two pieces of whole wheat bread. How would the model be modified?
25. Suppose in the original model that the second goal specifies that the meal should provide *exactly* 50 percent of the MDA for protein. How would the model be modified?
26. How would the model be modified if the following requirements existed:
    a. Noodles must be served if ground beef is included in the meal.

b. French fries are included only if ground beef is served.
c. No more than three servings may be included from the meat and vegetables groups combined.
d. The 30 percent requirement stated in constraints 7–11 must be satisfied for *at least* three of the five nutritional items rather than for all five.

27. Discuss shortcomings of the model in terms of factors neglected in menu planning.

9.3 GOAL PROGRAMMING SOLUTION METHODS

A complete exposition of GP solution methods is inconsistent with the overview nature of this chapter. To give you an intuitive feeling for these procedures, however, we will illustrate graphical solutions, describe simplex-based solutions, and illustrate computer-based solutions.

Graphical Solutions

If you remember the graphical approach to solving LP problems, then you will find that procedure very similar to the one used in goal programming. As with LP, graphical solutions are restricted to situations in which there are two real decision variables. For these problems we must make certain that all constraints include real (decision) variables.[3]

Goal Programming Graphical Procedure:

1. Graph all system constraints (those not involving deviational variables) and identify the corresponding area of feasible solutions. If no system constraints exist, then the area of feasible solutions is the entire northeast quadrant. If no area of feasible solutions exists, there is no solution to the problem.
2. Graph the straight lines corresponding to the goal constraints, labeling the deviational variables.
3. Within the area of feasible solutions identified in step 1, determine the point or points that best satisfy the highest priority goal.
4. Sequentially consider the remaining goals and the points that satisfy them to the greatest extent possible. Make certain that a lower priority goal is not achieved by reducing the degree of achievement of higher priority goals.

▶ Example 9.7 Product Mix Problem

Consider a simple product mix problem in which a firm produces two products. Each product must be processed through two departments. Department 1 has available

[3]Goal constraints may sometimes be stated in terms of deviational variables only (as illustrated in Examples 9.4 and 9.5). In these situations, they must be restated in terms of the real variables prior to proceeding with the graphical analysis.

30 hours of capacity per day, and department 2 has 60 hours. Each unit of product 1 requires 2 hours in department 1 and 6 hours in department 2. Each unit of product 2 requires 3 hours in department 1 and 4 hours in department 2. Management has rank ordered (from highest to lowest priority) the following goals it would like achieved in determining the daily product mix:

1. Minimize the underachievement of management's goal of joint total production of 10 units.
2. Minimize the underachievement of management's goal of producing 7 units of product 2.
3. Minimize the underachievement of management's goal of producing 8 units of Product 1.

If we define x_j = Units produced of product j and $d_i^{-,+}$ = Underachievement (−) or overachievement (+) associated with goal i, then the formulation of this problem is:

Minimize

$$z = P_1 d_1^- + P_2 d_2^- + P_3 d_3^-$$

subject to

(Dept. 1 capacity)	$2x_1 + 3x_2 \leq 30$	(1)
(Dept. 2 capacity)	$6x_1 + 4x_2 \leq 60$	(2)
(Combined production goal)	$x_1 + x_2 + d_1^- - d_1^+ = 10$	(3)
(Product 2 production goal)	$x_2 + d_2^- - d_2^+ = 7$	(4)
(Product 1 production goal)	$x_1 + d_3^- - d_3^+ = 8$	(5)

$$x_1, x_2, d_1^-, d_1^+, d_2^-, d_2^+, d_3^-, d_3^+ \geq 0.$$

In this problem, constraints 1 and 2 are system constraints. Constraints 3 through 5 are goal constraints. Figure 9–1*a* illustrates the area of feasible solutions associated with the two system constraints. In Figure 9–1*b* the lines associated with the goal constraints have been added, and the deviational variables have been labeled. The farther a point is from a goal constraint line, the larger the value of the corresponding deviational variable. The closer a point is to a goal constraint line, the smaller the deviation from the associated goal.

In Figure 9–1*c*, the highest priority goal has been addressed. The highest priority was to minimize d_1^-, which represents underachievement of the total production goal of 10 units. In Figure 9–1*c* we have eliminated all feasible points that have positive values for d_1^-. The darkened area in this figure represents all combinations of products 1 and 2 that can be produced and that satisfy or exceed the production goal of 10 units.

In Figure 9–1*d* we have moved to the second highest priority goal and eliminated all points having positive values for d_2^-. The points eliminated are those that lie below the second goal constraint line. These represent combinations of products 1 and 2 that fall short of the production goal of seven units for product 2. What remains as we move on to the final goal is the shaded area *ABC*.

The final goal is to minimize the underachievement of the goal of producing 8 units of product 1. Of the points remaining (area *ABC*), each involves underachievement of this goal. The optimal solution occurs at *C* where d_3^- is made as small as possible. We might be tempted to move to points *D* or *E* in Figure 9–1*e* where d_3^- would equal zero. However, this movement would result in positive values for d_2^-, sacrificing what had been achieved for a higher priority goal. Goal programming does not allow this.

FIGURE 9–1 Graphical Solution to Product Mix Goal Programming Problem

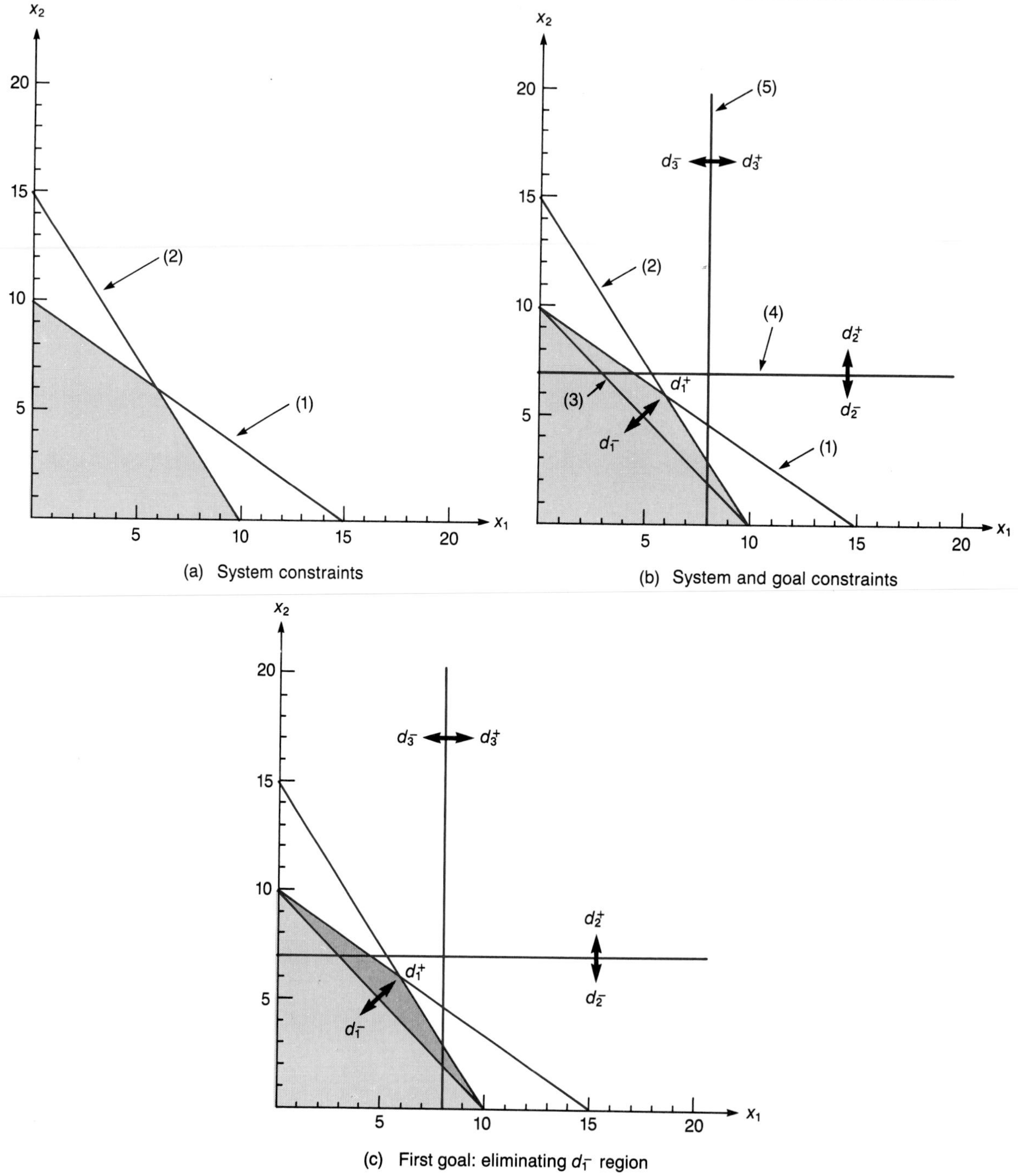

(a) System constraints

(b) System and goal constraints

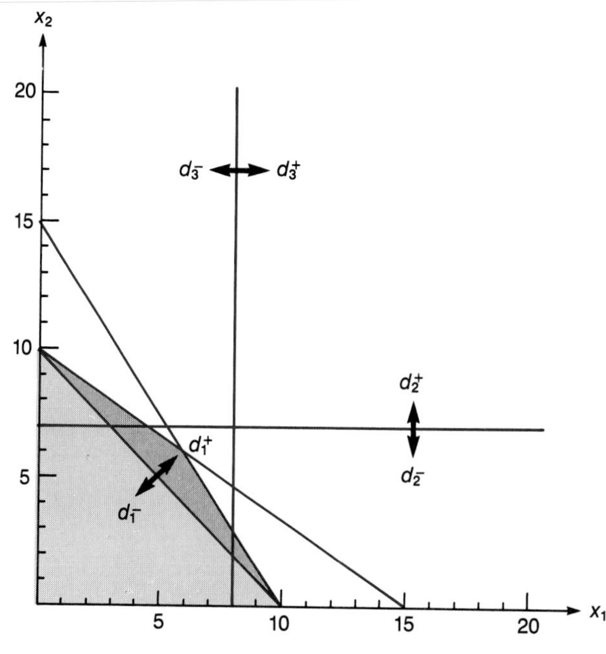

(c) First goal: eliminating d_1^- region

FIGURE 9–1 (*concluded*)

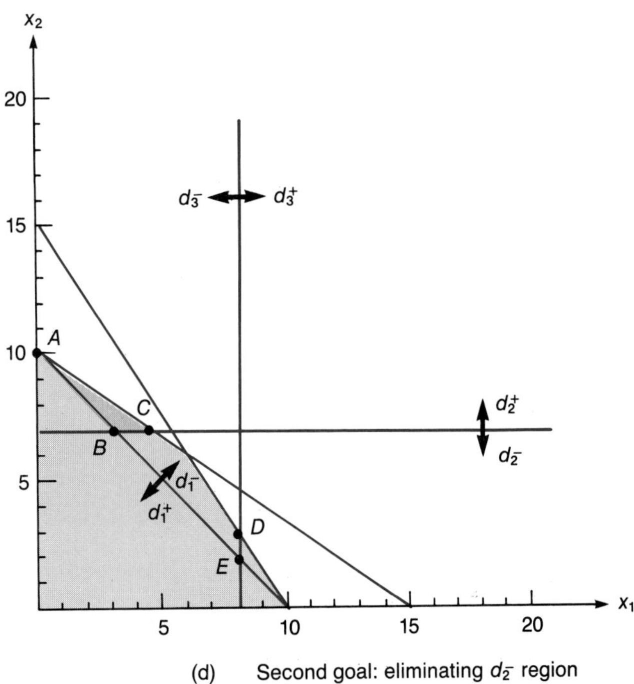

(d) Second goal: eliminating d_2^- region

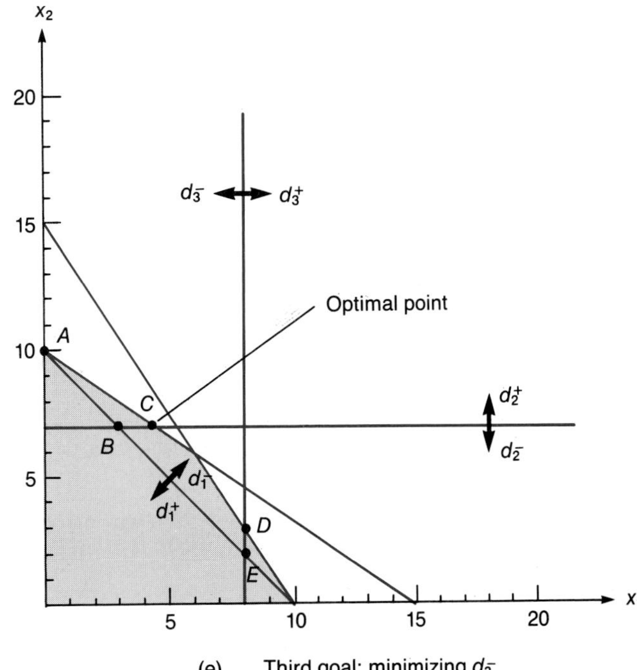

(e) Third goal: minimizing d_3^-

Let us summarize the solution we have generated. Point *C* occurs at the intersection of constraints 1 and 4. If we solve these two equations, we find that the optimal solution occurs at (4.5, 7) recommending production of 4.5 units of product 1 and 7 units of product 2. Verify that when these values are substituted into all constraints:

Department 1 operates at its maximum capacity of 30 hours.

Department 2 has 5 hours of slack or unused time.

There is overachievement of the joint production goal equal to (11.5 − 10) 1.5 units.

There is exact achievement of the production goal of 7 units for product 2.

There is underachievement of the production goal for product 1 of (8 − 4.5) 3.5 units.

FOLLOW-UP EXERCISES

28. Where would the optimal solution occur if goals 2 and 3 were reversed in their priority?
29. In the above problem, assume that the marginal profits associated with each unit of products 1 and 2 are, respectively, \$2 and \$5. Determine the optimal solution if the first two goals remain the same as in the original statement but the third is replaced by a goal that is to achieve a daily profit of \$60.
30. Perform sensitivity analysis that examines the effect on the production recommendation if the ranking of the three goals changes in different ways.

▶ Example 9.8 Graphical Solution to Example 9.2

The media mix problem in Example 9.2 is restated below. All four constraints are goal constraints, and they are shown in Figure 9–2. Notice that the absence of system constraints results in an *initial* area of feasible solutions that is the entire quadrant.

Minimize

$$z = P_1d_1^- + P_2d_2^+ + P_3d_3^+ + P_4d_4^-$$

subject to

$$10{,}000x_1 + 7{,}500x_2 + d_1^- - d_1^+ = 750{,}000 \quad (1)$$

$$x_1 + x_2 + d_2^- - d_2^+ = 100 \quad (2)$$

$$x_1 + d_3^- - d_3^+ = 70 \quad (3)$$

$$10{,}000x_1 + 7{,}500x_2 + d_4^- - d_4^+ = 1{,}000{,}000 \quad (4)$$

$$x_1, x_2, d_1^-, d_1^+, d_2^-, d_2^+, d_3^-, d_3^+, d_4^-, d_4^+ \geq 0.$$

Figure 9–3 illustrates the progression of steps leading to the identification of the optimal solution at (70, 30). In Exercise 31 you will be asked to interpret the result.

FOLLOW-UP EXERCISES

31. In Example 9.8 interpret fully the optimal solution. How could management realize its goal of 1 million exposures? Point B in Figure 9–3*d* requires less expenditure, but why is it nonoptimal?
32. Solve Example 9.1 graphically.
33. Solve graphically and compare:
    a. Example 9.3.
    b. Exercise 10.

FIGURE 9–2 Goal Constraints

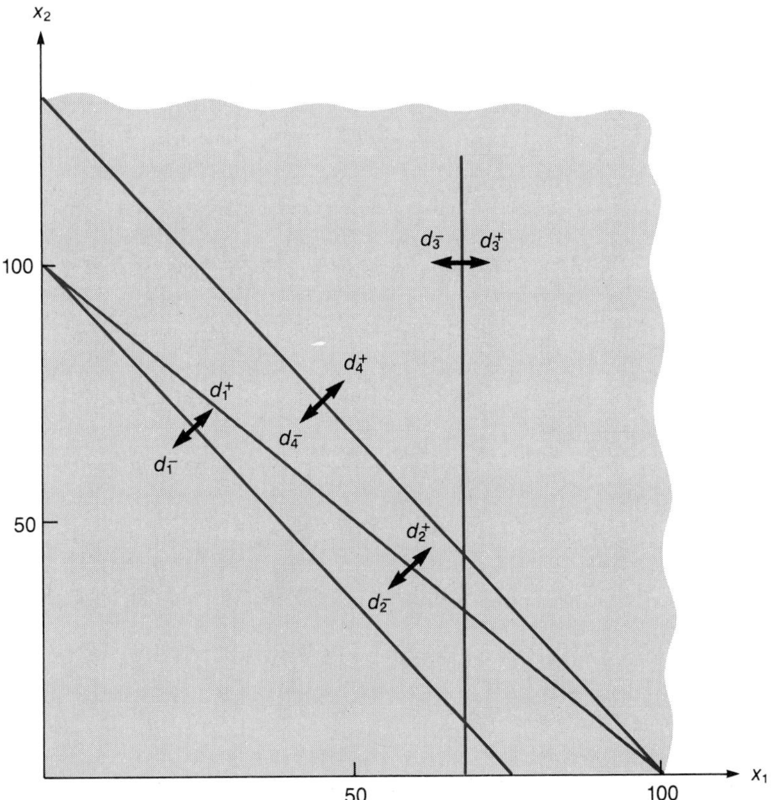

34. Solve Exercise 11 graphically. Note that the last constraint, which is constructed of deviational variables only, must be rewritten in terms of the real variables x_1 and x_2.

Simplex-Based Solutions

When a GP problem consists of more than two decision variables, nongraphical procedures must be utilized. Some procedures modify the initial GP formulation in a manner that allows the use of existing simplex computer programs.[4] Another procedure modifies the simplex algorithm itself.[5] In either case, the procedures are simplex-based.

In the former case, GP problems can be formulated and solved as LP problems. This is accomplished by including the deviational variables just as if they are decision variables in the goal constraints and modifying the objective function so as to express the priority structure reflected by the priority factors. To illustrate, let's reexamine the

[4]See J. P. Ignizio, *Linear Programming in Single- and Multiple-Objective Systems* (Englewood Cliffs, N.J.: Prentice-Hall, 1982).

[5]For specifics, see Sang M. Lee, *Management by Multiple Objectives* (Princeton, N.J.: Petrocelli Books, 1981).

FIGURE 9–3

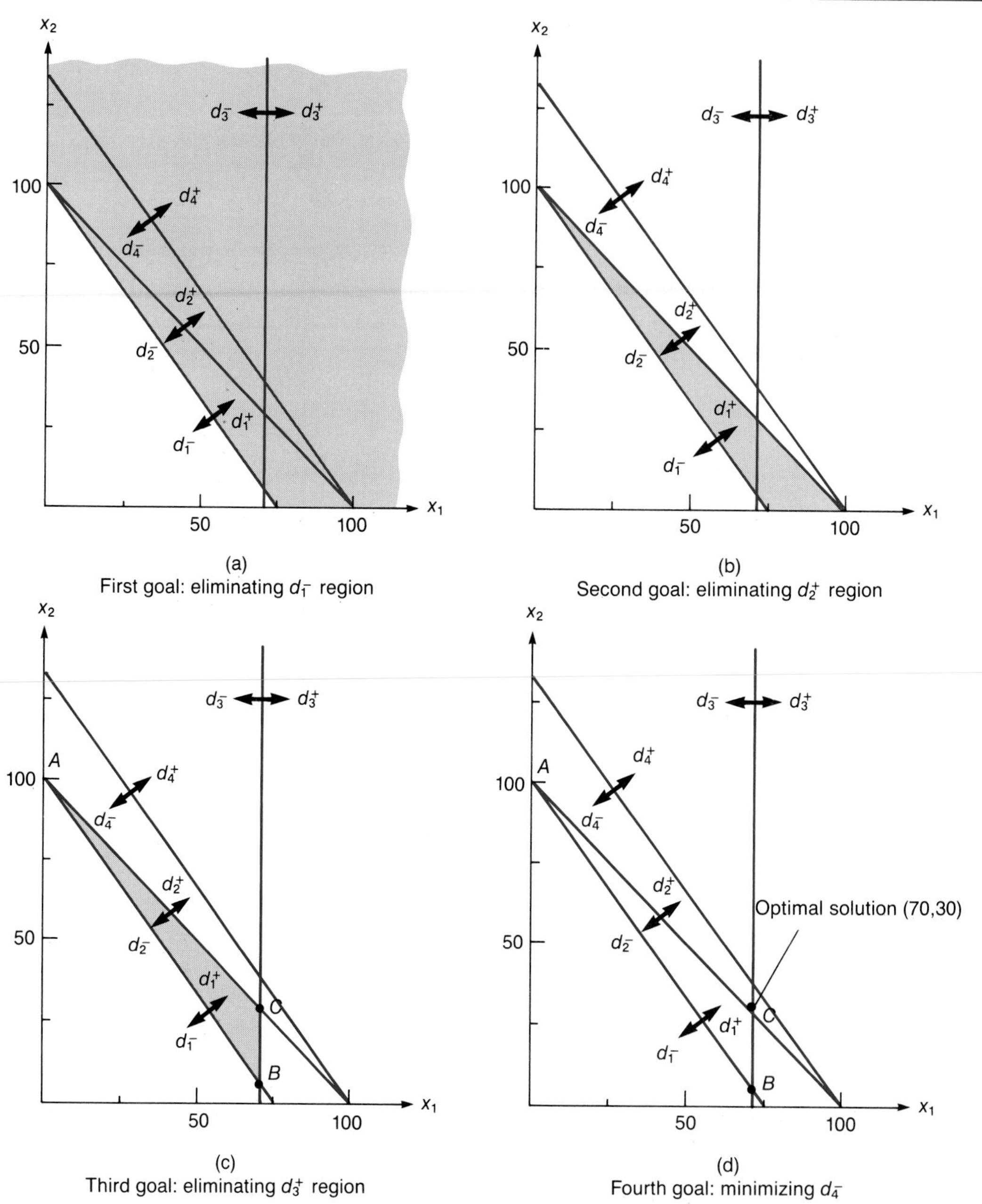

product mix problem solved graphically in Example 9.7. The original problem formulation was

Minimize

$$z = P_1 d_1^- + P_2 d_2^- + P_3 d_3^-$$

subject to

$$\begin{aligned} 2x_1 + 3x_2 \qquad\qquad\qquad &\leq 30 \\ 6x_1 + 4x_2 \qquad\qquad\qquad &\leq 60 \\ x_1 + x_2 + d_1^- - d_1^+ &= 10 \\ x_2 + d_2^- - d_2^+ &= 7 \\ x_1 \qquad + d_3^- - d_3^+ &= 8 \\ x_1, x_2, d_1^-, d_1^+, d_2^-, d_2^+, d_3^-, d_3^+ &\geq 0\,. \end{aligned}$$

This problem can be solved by the simplex method if the deviational variables are treated just like x_1 and x_2 and if appropriate numeric values are assigned to P_1, P_2, and P_3. For example, we might reflect the priority structure by writing the objective function

Minimize

$$z = 1{,}000{,}000d_1^- + 1{,}000d_2^- + 1d_3^-\,.$$

The assignment of values for priority factors can become tricky (and possibly infeasible) as the number of priority levels increases. Whatever values are assigned in place of the priority factors must adhere to the relationship $P_k >>> P_{k+1}$.

In the approach that uses a simplex-based GP algorithm, a modified simplex tableau is formulated much in the same manner as with LP. A row is established for each system constraint and each goal constraint, and a column is established for all variables including decision variables, deviational variables, and slack, surplus, or artificial variables where they are required. Slack, surplus, and artificial variables would be introduced for system constraints (nongoal constraints). Slack and surplus variables would be assigned objective function contributions of zero as in the simplex method. Artificial variables would be assigned contributions of $+M$ where $M >>> P_1$. This simply implies that artificial variables are introduced only for the purpose of generating the initial basic feasible solution, and they must be costed in the objective function as significantly less desirable than the deviational variables associated with the goal of highest priority.

In the simplex method the single objective function is embodied in Row (0). The simplex criterion for determining whether there is a better solution requires examination of this row. In the GP solution method, multiple criterion rows are established: one for each preemptive priority level in the problem. *These rows are usually arranged in order of priority.* In moving from one solution to the next, one seeks to satisfy as best as possible the criterion for the achievement of the highest priority goal, followed by the next highest, and so on. Since *goal programming problems are always stated as minimization problems,* the criterion row associated with the highest priority goal is examined for any *positive* coefficients. The entering variable is selected as the column having the largest positive coefficient. If all coefficients are eventually driven to nonpositive values, then that goal has been achieved and attention is then directed to the criterion row associated with the next highest priority goal. Precautions must be taken while moving from iteration to iteration to assure that the levels of achievement for higher priority goals are not sacrificed in an effort to better achieve lower priority goals. In effect, the solution at the highest priority level becomes a constraint for the remaining problem. Using this approach, P_k values are not needed. The priorities are established in the way the criterion rows are ordered.

Computer-Based Solutions

Computer packages can be used to generate solutions to goal programming problems. As indicated in the last section, GP problems can be solved by linear programming packages if modified appropriately. Figure 9–4 illustrates the computer output for the product mix example discussed in the last section. This output is from an LP package where the objective function was modified as suggested in the last section. You should confirm that this is the same result as obtained in Example 9.7.

FIGURE 9–4 Solution to Product Mix Problem (Example 9.7) Using LP Software Package

```
                OPTIMAL SOLUTION

OBJECTIVE FUNCTION VALUE IS:            3.500

VARIABLE                                VALUE
   x1                                   4.500
   x2                                   7.000
   d1+                                  1.500
   d3-                                  3.500
```

Figure 9–5 illustrates the solution to the same problem as solved using a goal programming software package. In the output section related to slack analysis, the column headings POS-SLK and NEG-SLK represent positive slack and negative slack. Since this section of the output is summarizing the extent to which all constraints are satisfied, we need to know how to interpret the columns. For a goal constraint, positive slack refers to the level of overachievement, and negative slack refers to the level of underachievement. For system constraints, positive slack is the same as "surplus" as in a $\geq$ constraint, and negative slack represents "slack" as in a $\leq$ constraint.

Figure 9–6 illustrates the solution to the Contract Awards Model (Example 9.4) as solved using an LP package. The objective function was rewritten as

Minimize

$$z = 1{,}000{,}000d_1^+ + 1{,}000d_2^- + 1d_3^+ + 1d_4^+ + 1d_5^+ + 1d_6^+ + .001d_7^-$$

Recall that we are implicitly looking at

$$z = 0x_1 + 0x_2 + 1{,}000{,}000d_1^+ + \ldots$$

Verbally summarize and interpret the results to this problem. Notice the minimum value for the objective function. Do you have an interpretation for this? When using LP packages to solve GP problems, care must be taken when interpreting the value of the objective function.

FIGURE 9–5 Solution to Product Mix Problem (Example 9.7) Using GP Software Package

OBJECTIVE FUNCTION ANALYSIS

PRIORITY	NONACHIEVEMENT
1	0
2	0
3	3.5

OPTIMAL SOLUTION

VARIABLE	VALUE
1	4.5
2	7.0

SLACK ANALYSIS

ROW	AVAILABLE	POS-SLK	NEG-SLK
1	30.0	0	0
2	60.0	0	5
3	10.0	1.5	0
4	7.0	0	0
5	8.0	0	3.5

9.4 EXTENSIONS

This final section briefly overviews extensions of the goal programming material discussed thus far and a system of classification for the ever-expanding set of modeling techniques for multicriteria decision making.

Goal Programming Extensions

As with linear programming, there are enhancements to the standard GP model that make it more robust and better able to represent the realities of a problem. A few such enhancements follow.

Sensitivity Analysis. As we discussed in earlier chapters, sensitivity analysis can be an effective tool for accounting for the uncertainty in a problem setting. As with the other mathematical programming topics discussed, sensitivity analysis can be used to examine model parameters in goal programming. As well as on the technological coefficients (a_{ij} values), sensitivity analysis can be conducted on the right-hand–side constants for system constraints and goal constraints. In the latter case, we are examining the impact of changes in goal levels ("What if we raise or lower our expectations?").

Sensitivity analysis can be conducted on parameters to a limited extent, but the effort required is considerably greater than with linear programming. A key to improvement in this process would be a better understanding of duality theory as

FIGURE 9–6 Solution to Example 9.4 Using LP Package

```
                    OPTIMAL SOLUTION

     OBJECTIVE FUNCTION VALUE IS: 20941703980.000

          VARIABLE                    VALUE
            x11                     15000.000
            x23                     30000.000
            x32                     10000.000
            x41                     18000.000
            x44                      2000.000
            d1+                    208999.989
            d2-                    416000.000
            d3-                    105000.011
            d4-                    920000.011
            d5+                   1050000.000
            d6-                   1116000.000
            d7+                     94999.989

                    BASIC SLACK AND SURPLUS VARIABLES

     Variable         Constraint        Type           Value

   31  Slack          Const  6           <=          3000.000
   32  Slack          Const  7           <=         15000.000
   33  Slack          Const  8           <=          3000.000
   34  Surplus        Const  9           =              0.000
   36  Surplus        Const 11           =              0.000
   37  Surplus        Const 12           =              0.000
   38  Surplus        Const 13           =              0.000
   40  Surplus        Const 15           =              0.000
```

it relates to goal programming. If it were possible to explicitly specify the dual of a GP problem, then it might be possible to achieve the degree of power and flexibility associated with postoptimality analysis of the LP model.

A different type of sensitivity analysis allows decision makers to examine the impact of changing priority factors. When asked to rank order their goals, decision makers may have difficulty stating preferences. Some or all of their rankings may be arbitrary. Examining different preferences can result in rather dramatic changes in recommended decisions. Thus this type of sensitivity analysis can be of particular value.

Integer and Nonlinear Goal Programming. As discussed in Chapter 8, many problems involve decision variables that must be integer valued or zero-one variables. This is also true for goal programming. We illustrated an integer, goal programming model in Example 9.6. As we indicated in Chapter 8, a major concern in integer programming (and this applies to integer, goal programming) is the development of algorithms that provide improved computational efficiency.

Another class of GP problems in need of additional research is that of nonlinear goal programming models. Nonlinear programming models are characterized by *at least* one nonlinear relationship, either an objective function or structural constraint. For a nonlinear goal programming model, there is at least one nonlinear system or goal constraint. Nonlinear programming problems suffer from the absence of a generalized solution algorithm that efficiently solves such problems. Approximation methods can be used to transform nonlinear relationships into linear relationships. When this is done, simplex-based approaches can be utilized to generate solutions that are near-optimal. As with integer GP models, there is considerable ground yet to be gained in addressing nonlinear GP models.

Interactive Goal Programming. Goal programming assumes a priori articulation of preferences. That is, we assume that complete information about a decision maker's preferences can be extracted prior to formulating the GP model and generating a solution. We ask that multiple criteria be identified and that the decision maker rank them in order of importance. *Interactive goal programming* methods recognize that preferences are neither always clearly defined nor fixed. They acknowledge that preferences depend on specific situations and the knowledge one has about the situation. As such, these methods allow for a progressive definition of preferences as a problem is analyzed and solved. They account for the learning that can take place when studying a problem.

An effective method for executing this approach is by using an interactive goal programming software package. Such a package should be capable of sensitivity analysis and should have the flexibility to easily modify the structure of the model. This type of decision support tool allows the decision maker to sit at a terminal and systematically analyze different model structures. Based on the results derived at various stages, the decision maker can come to understand better the interrelationships in the problem setting. Criteria structures may be experimented with, along with preferences. What may evolve is a model considerably different from the original model, but one more accurately representing the interests and aspirations of the decision maker.

For this type of human-machine interaction, *process* is critical in the evolution of a model. A real-time interactive environment can lead to random and exhaustive exploration of alternative model structures. The key to avoiding this is to allow and account for learning during the process. Such guidance can be provided either by an experienced analyst or by the software package itself.

One final point relates to computer graphics. To the extent that these capabilities exist within the software package, the interactive process can be facilitated. The use of graphs and tables for input or output purposes can expedite the process and enhance the communication and interpretation of model output.

Other Multicriteria Methods

The literature of multicriteria decision making is large and expanding. This chapter has focused on just one of many modeling techniques proposed to assist decision makers grapple with the priorities and interactions of multiple criteria. An interesting system classifies these techniques into four categories of preference articulation: (*a*) *a priori,* (*b*) *progressive,* (*c*) *a posteriori,* and (*d*) *no articulation* of preference information.[6]

With a priori methods, the analyst is given preference information prior to solving the problem. The preference information may be *cardinal* in nature, with target preference levels of specific trade-offs provided to the analyst. Alternatively, the preferences can be expressed as a combination of *ordinal* and cardinal information. Goal programming is an a priori modeling technique based on a mix of cardinal and ordinal information. When a priori preferences are cardinal in nature, utility function methods provide one approach to modeling the problem in a manner similar to that used by economists to model consumer theory.[7] A utility function is constructed that combines preference information regarding the multiple objectives. These functions are typically additive with respect to the utility associated with different objectives. One approach *weights* the utility components according to the relative importance of each objective.

Progressive articulation methods assume that the decision maker is unable to specify a priori preferences because of the complexity of the problem under study. However, it is assumed that the decision maker can specify preference information when provided with the outcomes of a particular solution. Using an interactive approach, these methods allow for learning about the behavior of the system and modification of aspirations. Typically, decision makers are presented with a current solution(s) and queried about trade-offs or preferences. Responses to these queries result in the generation of new solution sets, which in turn are examined in an effort to refine the articulation of preferences.

A posteriori articulation of preference information does not require any information regarding a decision maker's preferences. Decision makers are presented with a group of solution alternatives, selected because of their apparent superiority over other solutions. The decision maker compares these solutions using implicit trade-off relationships, eventually selecting the one judged most satisfactory. One disadvantage is that, in the absence of preference information, these methods often supply decision makers with a large number of solution alternatives to consider. Because comparison can become difficult, interactive methods similar to those used for progressive articulation of preferences have been recommended to help decision makers identify the most satisfactory solution.

Methods for no articulation of preference information essentially delegate the specification or assumption of preferences to the analyst. Once the problem structure has been defined, including identification of objectives, the analyst is left to make assumptions about the preferences of the decision maker and to generate a recommended solution. These methods are probably the least applicable and acceptable in a real-world context.

---

[6]See C. L. Hwang, S. R. Paidy, K. Yoon, and A. S. M. Masud, "Mathematical Programming with Multiple Objectives," *Computers and Operations Research* 7 (1980), pp. 5–31.

[7]See R. L. Keeney and H. Raiffa, *Decisions with Multiple Objectives: Preferences and Value Trade-offs*. (New York: John Wiley & Sons, 1976).

SELECTED APPLICATION REVIEW

MILITARY PLANNING

The Congressional Budget Office and the Office of the Assistant Secretary of Defense have made extensive use of a goal programming model for planning and evaluation of the All Volunteer Armed Forces. The Accession Supply Costing and Requirements model (ASCAR) determines the level of new recruits necessary to attain the personnel levels and quality requirements of each of the four military services. The model has facilitated the timely and efficient evaluation of a wide variety of alternative personnel policies and programs.

SOURCE: Roger W. Collins, Saul I. Gass, and Edward E. Rosendahl, "The ASCAR Model for Evaluating Manpower Policy," *Interfaces*, June 1983, pp. 44–53.

EDUCATION APPLICATION

A goal programming model was used in allocating teachers to 22 private schools in St. Louis. The Blue Hills Home Corporation contracted to provide remedial education services to children in the 22 schools, and the problem was to determine the way in which to assign teachers to the different schools. The criteria in making these decisions included balancing costs while considering the preference goals of the teachers, administrators, and schools. The model resulted in tremendous savings of time compared with the tedious trial-and-error approach used in the past, and it allowed all affected parties to provide inputs regarding their preferences.

SOURCE: Sang M. Lee and Mark J. Schniederjans, "A Multicriteria Assignment Problem: A Goal Programming Approach," *Interfaces*, August 1983, pp. 75–81.

SITE LOCATION

A goal programming model was used to help determine the new location for a trucking terminal for a firm based in East St. Louis, Illinois. In developing the model, goals were set to satisfy customer demands, driver requests for number of trips per period, driver preferences for terminal assignments, customer preferences for supplying terminals, cost of transportation between drivers' homes and terminals, and cost of servicing customers.

SOURCE: Mark J. Schniederjans, N. K. Kwak, and Mark C. Helmer, "An Application of Goal Programming to Resolve a Site Location Problem," *Interfaces*, June 1982, pp. 65–72.

ECONOMIC POLICY ANALYSIS

An interactive goal programming methodology was combined with an input-output model to simulate the effects of different economic policies in the Netherlands. Three contrasting economic strategies were identified as the possible options to consider for developing the Netherlands during the 1980s. The main options were balanced growth, export-led growth, and voluntary austerity. In examining the effects of these strategies, aspiration levels were set for a variety of economic measures related to consumption, employment, balance of trade, energy, and pollution. The significance of this research is that the methodology provided an important learning tool for both decision makers and analysts.

SOURCE: Jaap Spronk and Frank Veeneklaas, "A Feasibility Study of Economic and Environmental Scenarios by Means of Interactive Multiple Goal Programming," *Regional Science and Urban Economics*, February 1983, pp. 141–60.

SELECTED REFERENCES

Gass, Saul I. "A Process for Determining Priorities and Weights for Large-Scale Linear Goal Programs." *Journal of the Operational Research Society*, August 1986, pp. 779–85.

Ignizio, J. P. *Goal Programming and Extensions*. Lexington, Mass: D. C. Heath, 1976.

________ . *Linear Programming in Single- & Multiple-Objective Systems*. Englewood Cliffs, N.J.: Prentice-Hall, 1982.

Kornbluth, J. S. H. "A Survey of Goal Programming," *Omega* 1 (1973), pp. 115–17.

Lee, Sang M. *Goal Programming for Decision Analysis*. Philadelphia: Auerbach Publishers, 1972.

________ . *Management by Multiple Objectives*. Princeton, N.J.: Petrocelli Books, 1981.

Markland, R. E., and S. K. Vickery. "The Efficient Computer Implementation of a Large-Scale Integer Goal Programming Model." *European Journal of Operations Research*, September 1986, pp. 341–54.

Starr, M. K., and M. Zeleny, eds. *Multiple Criteria Decision Making*. TIMS Studies in the Management Sciences, Vol. 6. Amsterdam: North-Holland Publishing, 1977.

Zeleny, Milan. *Multiple Criteria Decision Making*. New York: McGraw-Hill, 1982.

ADDITIONAL EXERCISES

35. Given the following goal programming problem:

Minimize

$$z = P_1 d_1^- + P_2 d_2^- + P_3 d_3^- + P_4 d_3^+$$

subject to

$$4x_1 + 2x_2 \leq 64 \quad (1)$$

$$2x_1 + 3x_2 \leq 48 \quad (2)$$

$$5x_1 + 6x_2 + d_1^- - d_1^+ = 60 \quad (3)$$

$$x_1 + d_2^- - d_2^+ = 8 \quad (4)$$

$$x_2 + d_3^- - d_3^+ = 6 \quad (5)$$

$$x_1, x_2, d_1^-, d_1^+, d_2^-, d_2^+, d_3^-, d_3^+ \geq 0.$$

a. Solve graphically.
b. Solve graphically if the right-hand side of constraint 4 equals 20.
c. Solve the original problem if the objective function is

$$z = P_1(d_1^- + d_1^+) + P_2 d_2^- + P_3 d_3^- + P_4 d_3^+ .$$

36. Given the following goal programming problem:

Minimize

$$z = P_1(d_1^- + d_1^+) + P_2 d_2^- + P_3 d_3^+$$

subject to

$$2x_1 + 4x_2 \geq 20 \quad (1)$$

$$5x_1 + 3x_2 \geq 30 \quad (2)$$

$$x_1 \geq 3 \quad (3)$$

$$x_1 + x_2 + d_1^- - d_1^+ = 12 \quad (4)$$

$$x_2 + d_2^- - d_2^+ = 4 \quad (5)$$

$$x_1 + d_3^- - d_3^+ = 6 \quad (6)$$

$$x_1, x_2, d_1^-, d_1^+, d_2^-, d_2^+, d_3^-, d_3^+ \geq 0.$$

a. Solve graphically.
b. Solve the original problem graphically if there is an added constraint ($x_2 + d_4^- - d_4^+ = 12$) and an added term in the objective function ($P_4 d_4^-$).

37. Solve Exercise 35 if x_1 and x_2 are restricted to nonnegative integer values. What does this restriction imply about the values of the deviational variables?
38. Solve Exercise 36 if x_1 and x_2 are restricted to nonnegative integer values. What does this restriction imply about the values of the deviational variables?
39. Given the following goal programming problem:

Minimize

$$z = P_1 d_1^+ + P_2 d_3^+ + P_3 d_2^-$$

subject to

$$\begin{aligned} 4x_1 + 2x_2 & \geq 8 \\ 3x_1 + 4x_2 & \leq 36 \\ 2x_1 + 3x_2 + d_1^- - d_1^+ &= 18 \\ x_1 + d_2^- - d_2^+ &= 10 \\ x_2 + d_3^- - d_3^+ &= 6 \\ x_1, x_2, d_1^-, d_1^+, d_2^-, d_2^+, d_3^-, d_3^+ &\geq 0. \end{aligned}$$

a. Solve graphically and identify the values of all variables.
b. Solve if the objective function is

Minimize

$$z = P_1 d_3^- + P_2 d_1^- + P_3 d_2^-.$$

40. A company manufactures two products. Each unit of product *A* requires two hours of labor in department 1 and five hours in department 2. Product *B* requires four hours in department 1 and two hours in department 2. Departments 1 and 2 have 104 hours and 132 hours, respectively, available each week. The profit margins on products *A* and *B* are \$20 and \$25.

As management plans the production schedule for the coming week, the following goals have been stated in order of priority.

(1) Minimize the extent to which total weekly profit falls short of \$700.
(2) Minimize the extent to which weekly production of product *B* exceeds 15 units.
(3) Minimize the extent to which the total hours used in both departments falls short of the 236 available.

a. Formulate the goal programming model for determining the number of units to produce of each product.
b. Solve graphically, summarizing the resulting values of *all* variables including slack, surplus, and deviational variables. Interpret the meaning of all variables and their values.

41. ***Product Mix Problem.*** Example 3.3 on page 97 involved a product mix decision. In addition to the information given in that problem regarding constraints, assume that management has specified the following goals (in order of preference):

(1) The total number of units produced of product *A* during the two periods must be exactly 500 units.

(2) The total number of units produced of product B during the two periods must be exactly 700 units.
(3) The amount by which total costs exceed \$5,000 is to be minimized.

a. Formulate this as a goal programming problem.
b. Solve using an LP or goal programming computer package.

42. ***Cargo Loading.*** Good old Hugh Moore is retired on Nantucket and spends his summers driving an ice cream truck he purchased two years ago. Recently, Hugh completed a college-by-mail course entitled "Management Science for the Elderly." This gave him the idea to ask his progressive supplier, the O. R. Ice Cream Company, to advise all of its 10,000 drivers as to the best mix of ice cream products to put on their trucks each week. Table 9–6 indicates (for Hugh's operation) the possible products, their volume, profit margin, minimum weekly demand (based on past experience), and maximum weekly demand.

TABLE 9–6

Item	Volume (ft.^{3})	Profit Margin	Minimum Demand	Maximum Demand
Popsicles (doz.)	0.25	\$0.36	40	80
Cones (doz.)	0.30	0.24	24	64
Sandwiches (doz.)	0.20	0.30	32	56
Cups (doz.)	0.25	0.30	36	76
Sundaes (doz.)	0.30	0.60	16	48
Pints	0.05	0.10	96	240
Quarts	0.10	0.22	96	200
Half gallons	0.20	0.50	120	280

Hugh's truck has a volume capacity of 128 ft.^{3} In deciding on the mix of products to carry, Hugh has specified the following goals (in order of importance):

(1) Minimize the underachievement of making \$300 in profit each week.
(2) Minimize the underachievement of meeting the expected minimum demand for each item (differentially weighted according to relative profit margin).
(3) Fill the truck exactly to capacity.
(4) Minimize the overachievement of carrying no more than the maximum expected weekly demand for each item (differentially weighted according to relative volume of the items).

a. Formulate the goal programming model for this problem.
b. Solve using an LP or goal programming computer package.

43. ***Forest Management.*** Consider the following simplified forest management problem for a small national forest. In the next fiscal year 20,000 acres are to be allocated in a manner that comes as close as possible to meeting a set of four specified goals. Goals relate to the four uses this particular forest can be put to: backpacking, hunting, special habitats for timber wolf, and timber cutting. Each acre of forest can accommodate 1,000 visitor-days for backpacking, 100 visitor-days for hunting, two wolves, and 12,000 cubic feet of timber. The operating cost per year associated with each type of land use differs because of the nature of supervision, types of personnel, and so on. Per acre annual operating costs are estimated as \$15 for backpacking, \$20 for hunting, \$5 for wolves, and \$4 for timber cutting. Operating expenses for these activities, however, *must* be paid out of revenue from leasing timber land to the lumber companies. Each acre designated

for timber cutting is leased for \$240 per year. Goals, in order of importance, have been dictated by "top brass" in the Department of Interior:

(1) Minimize the overachievement of cutting 6 million cubic feet of timber (because of pressure from environmentalists).

(2) Minimize the underachievement of 700,000 visitor-days for hunting (the hunting lobby is strong in Washington).

(3) Exactly achieve the goal of sustaining 20,000 wolves (the head administrator owns a pet wolf).

(4) Minimize the overachievement of 5 million visitor-days for backpacking (a backpacking lobby does not exist).

a. Formulate the goal programming model for this problem.

b. Solve using a computer package.

44. ***Salvage Operations (Assignment Model).*** Davey Jones Salvage, Inc. specializes in recovering and salvaging sunken ships. Davey has identified three sunken ships he would like to recover. He has three salvage rigs and crews he would like to assign to the three salvage operations. Only one rig/crew can be assigned to any salvage operation. Table 9–7 summarizes Davey's estimates of (*a*) the probability of a successful salvage operation, (*b*) the expected cost of a salvage operation, (*c*) the expected time to complete the operation, and (*d*) the expected profit from the salvage operation if each of the three rig/crew teams is assigned to any of the salvage operations.

TABLE 9–7

	P (success) Salvage Operation			Expected Cost (\$100,000s) Salvage Operation			Expected Salvage Time (months) Salvage Operation			Expected Profit (\$100,000s) Salvage Operation		
	1	2	3	1	2	3	1	2	3	1	2	3
Rig/Crew 1	0.10	0.20	0.25	20	40	25	24	36	30	40	80	60
Rig/Crew 2	0.20	0.15	0.40	15	30	45	30	45	36	64	72	45
Rig/Crew 3	0.30	0.50	0.10	30	35	35	20	40	28	50	60	52

In making assignments, Davey has set the following goals (in order of preference).

(1) Minimize the extent to which the *combined* probability of success from the three salvage operations falls short of 0.80

(2) Minimize the extent to which expected profit from the three operations falls short of \$15 million.

(3) Minimize the extent to which *combined* expected cost of the three operations exceeds \$7.5 million.

(4) Minimize the extent to which the expected time of completing *each* salvage operation exceeds 30 months.

a. Formulate the goal programming model that will assist Davey in making assignments.

b. Solve using a computer package.

45. Modify the formulation in the previous exercise to account for the option that the rig/crew teams do not have to be assigned to any operations.

46. ***Transportation Model.*** A distributor of asphalt has three processing plants that have contracted to supply asphalt for five major road construction projects. Asphalt is delivered to the construction sites in trucks with a volume capacity of 20 cubic yards. Table 9–8 summarizes the weekly capacity of each plant, the weekly demand at each construction site, the distribution cost per truckload, the distance from each plant to each site, and the estimated round-trip travel time between each plant and site.

TABLE 9–8 Cost, Distance, and Round-Trip Travel Time

		Construction Site					Weekly Supply (truckloads)
		1	2	3	4	5	
Plant	1	$25 15 mi. 0.8 hr.	$28 12 mi. .6 hr.	$22 20 mi. 1.0 hr.	$40 10 mi. .5 hr.	$20 25 mi. 1.6 hr.	750
	2	$24 18 mi. 1.2 hr.	$26 15 mi. 1.4 hr.	$28 24 mi. 1.6 hr.	$38 15 mi. 1.1 hr.	$24 30 mi. 1.8 hr.	900
	3	$28 20 mi. 1.1 hr.	$30 16 mi. .9 hr.	$26 16 mi. 1.2 hr.	$34 12 mi. .9 hr.	$18 20 mi. 1.2 hr.	600
Weekly demand (truckloads)		200	150	300	250	500	

Management wants to determine the number of truckloads to distribute each week from each plant to each construction site. In making these decisions, the following goals have been stated in order of priority.

(1) Minimize the extent to which total weekly distribution costs exceed $35,000.
(2) Minimize the extent to which the total *round-trip* distance traveled per week exceeds 50,000 miles.
(3) Minimize the extent to which total weekly travel time exceeds 1,500 hours.
(4) Minimize the extent to which total shipments from *each* plant falls short of its weekly capacity.

a. Formulate the goal programming model for this problem.

b. Solve using a computer package.

47. ***Personnel Model.*** Exercise 39 in Chapter 3 (on page 129) involved recruiting for a new federal agency.

a. Formulate this as a goal programming model if management has specified the following goals (in order of preference):

(1) Minimize the amount of overexpenditure for recruiting purposes if the budget is $2.5 million.
(2) Minimize the underachievement of the goal that women constitute at least 50 percent of new hirings.
(3) Minimize the underachievement of the goal that minorities constitute at least 40 percent of new hirings.
(4) Restrict the overexpenditure for recruiting costs to $250,000.

b. Solve using a GP computer package.

48. ***Portfolio Model.*** Exercise 45 in Chapter 3 (on page 131) involved determining the best investment portfolio for an endowment fund.

a. Formulate this as a goal programming model if the fund manager has specified the following goals (in order of preference):

(1) Minimize the underachievement of the goal of a 7 percent return on investment.
(2) Minimize the overachievement of the goal that the weighted risk of the portfolio equal 10 percent.
(3) Minimize the underachievement of the goal of $10,000 in annual dividends.
(4) Minimize the underachievement of the goal that 10 percent of the total investment be in alternatives 1 and 2 (combined).
(5) Restrict the overachievement of the weighted risk goal to 1 percent

b. Solve using a computer package.

49. Figure 9–7 presents the computer-based solution to the University Admissions problem formulated in Example 9.5. Provide a complete interpretation of the results to this problem summarizing admission decisions, the extent to which system constraints are satisfied, and the extent to which goals have been realized.

FIGURE 9–7 Solution to University Admissions Problem (Example 9.5)

OBJECTIVE FUNCTION ANALYSIS

PRIORITY	NONACHIEVEMENT
1	0.0
2	100.0
3	0.0
4	0.0
5	68.25
6	85.0
7	0.0

OPTIMAL SOLUTION

VARIABLE	VALUE
1	555.0
2	250.0
3	185.0
4	400.0
5	100.0
6	10.0
7	295.0
8	0.0
9	0.0
10	150.0
11	50.0
12	5.0

SLACK ANALYSIS

ROW	AVAILABLE	POS-SLK	NEG-SLK
1	800.0	0.0	245.0
2	400.0	0.0	150.0
3	200.0	0.0	15.0
4	400.0	0.0	0.0
5	100.0	0.0	0.0
6	10.0	0.0	0.0
7	300.0	0.0	5.0
8	100.0	0.0	100.0
9	50.0	0.0	50.0
10	150.0	0.0	0.0
11	50.0	0.0	0.0
12	5.0	0.0	0.0
13	2000.0	0.0	0.0
14	1500.0	0.0	100.0
15	400.0	0.0	0.0
16	200.0	0.0	0.0
17	0.0	0.0	0.0
18	0.0	0.0	0.0
19	1300.0	0.0	68.25
20	0.0	0.0	85.0
21	1350.0	0.0	118.25

CASE

Example 9.4 discussed a contract award model involving four contractors submitting bids on four different fuel injection systems. The formulation of the model appears on page 440. The solution, generated using an LP package, appears on page 458. You should first review the formulation and interpret the solution. Regarding the solution, the automobile manufacturer's top priority goal was overachieved by \$209,000. That is, total awards of \$3,709,000 exceeded the \$3,500,000 target by \$209,000. At the second priority level, awards of \$84,000 to contractor 4 were \$416,000 under the minimum request of \$500,000. At the third priority level, total dollar awards to contractor 3 were \$2,250,000, exceeding the maximum target of \$1,200,000 by \$1,050,000.

There are several variations in assumptions that can be examined in this application in order to define an award strategy for the automobile manufacturer. This case explores some of these variations.

Required:

a. Because the recommended award to contractor 4 is only \$84,000, there is a good chance contractor 4 will not do any business with the manufacturer. In anticipation of this, eliminate contractor 4 completely in the formulation, and solve the revised model.

b. Another approach is to try to work with contractor 4. Solve the original model making the contractor 4 goal the top priority and making the total dollar awards goal the second goal.

c. Solve the original model with the contactor 4 goal expressed as a system constraint (resulting in three rather than four goals). Is the result any different from part *b*?

d. The \$2,250,000 award to contractor 3 may be viewed as excessive given the targeted ceiling of \$1,200,000 for each contractor. Given the original formulation, test the impact of tightening this requirement. Do this by reversing priorities 2 and 3. Is contractor 4 included at an acceptable level of award?

e. With regard to part *d*, test the impact by changing constraints 11–14 from goal constraints to system constraints.

f. Select another realistic modification in assumptions or policies, and examine the impact of the modification on the recommendations and satisfaction of goals.

10

Network Models

Chapter Outline

Network modeling is one of the more widely applied modeling techniques within the area of mathematical programming. The diversity of applications includes distribution, transportation, financial management, inventory control, production planning, project planning, facility location, and many others. There are several reasons for the wide range of applications. First, many problems that can be formulated as LP or IP models, can also be visualized within the context of **networks**. Second, network models of problems are often easier to formulate than alternative LP models of the same problem. Third, the pictorial representation of network models makes them relatively easy to understand, particularly by the nontechnical decision maker (user). Finally, the advances in network optimization procedures have resulted in some astonishing results in solving network models. Models involving thousands of constraints and millions of variables have been solved with *relative* ease. Also, when pitted against more conventional mathematical programming algorithms, specialized network algorithms have often proved to be more than 100 times faster.[1]

This chapter will introduce the terminology and notation of networks, illustrate the flexibility of modeling using networks, and show the relationship between certain LP models and their network representations. Having established a solid foundation in network modeling, we will present several specialized network algorithms for solving selected network problems and will illustrate computer implementation of these algorithms.

10.1 INTRODUCTION TO NETWORK MODELS

Terminology and Representation

A network can be represented visually by a graph or **network diagram** consisting of nodes and arcs. **Nodes** usually indicate locations or junction points and are represented by numbered or labeled circles in the diagram. Nodes might represent warehouses, cities, computer terminals, satellites, project milestones, and so on. Typically, nodes represent points at which a flow (e.g., products, travelers, electricity, or effort in achieving a project) originates, terminates, or is relayed. **Arcs** (or branches) are used to connect pairs of nodes, and they imply a relationship between the connected nodes. An arc connecting two nodes may suggest that movement or flow is possible between the two nodes. In such networks, arcs can represent roads, airline routes, telephone wires, pipelines, and so on. In other cases, arcs may represent logical sequences of activities or precedence relationships. The arc connecting nodes i and j in Figure 10–1 is called an **undirected arc.** An undirected arc assumes that flow or movement between the arcs may occur in either direction.

FIGURE 10–1 Undirected Arc

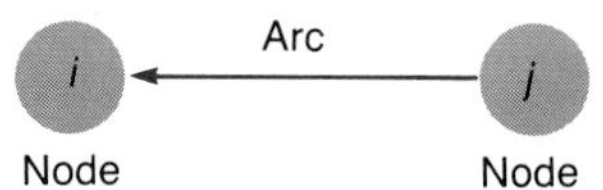

[1]See Fred Glover, John Hulty, and Darwin Klingman, "Improved Computer-Based Planning Techniques, Part I," *Interfaces,* August, 1978, pp. 16–25.

Directed arcs have a specified direction of flow. The directed arc in Figure 10–2 indicates possible movement *from* node j *to* node i. We would refer to this as the directed arc j–i.

FIGURE 10–2 Directed Arc

The sequence of arcs and nodes connecting any two nodes is called a **chain**. In Figure 10–3 *one* chain between nodes 1 and 4 consists of arcs 1–2 and 2–4 or 1–2–4. Other chains connecting nodes 1 and 4 include those consisting of arcs 1–3 and 3–4 or 1–3–4; arcs 1–3, 3–2, and 2–4 or 1–3–2–4; and 1–2–3–4. When the direction of travel along a chain is specified, the chain is called a **path.** In Figure 10–4, 1–2–3–4–5 is *one* path from node 1 to node 5. A **cycle** is a chain that connects a node to itself. The path consisting of arcs 1–2, 2–3, 3–4, and 4–1 is an example of a cycle. A **loop** is a cycle consisting of one node and arc. In Figure 10–4 arc 2–2 is a loop.

FIGURE 10–3

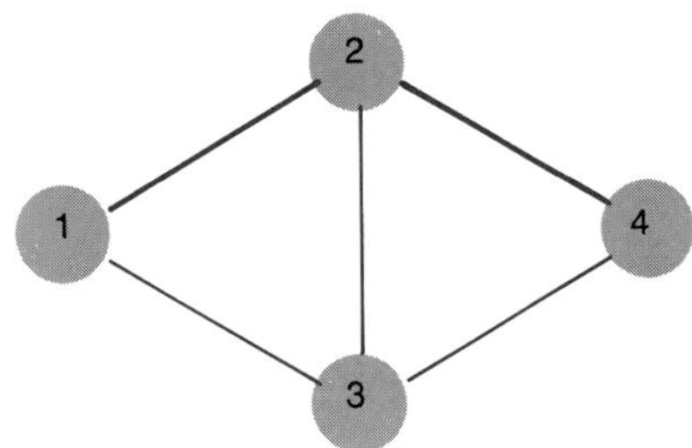

FIGURE 10–4

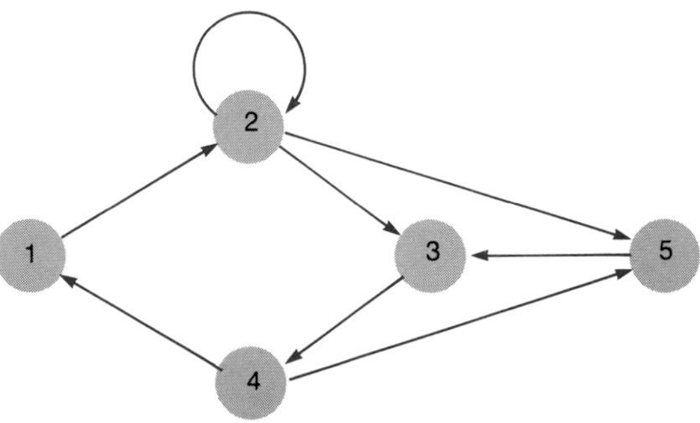

A network is *connected* if there is at least one chain or path joining *any* pair of nodes in the network. The network in Figure 10–5*a* is connected, since a path can be identified from any node to any other. A **tree** is a connected set of nodes containing no cycles. Figure 10–5*b* illustrates a tree for the network in Figure 10–5*a*. If in Figure 10–5*b* an arc connected nodes 6 and 7, the resulting graph would not be a tree because of the cycle connecting nodes 3, 4, 6, and 7. A **spanning tree** contains every node in the network. Figure 10–5*c* illustrates one spanning tree for the same network.

FIGURE 10–5

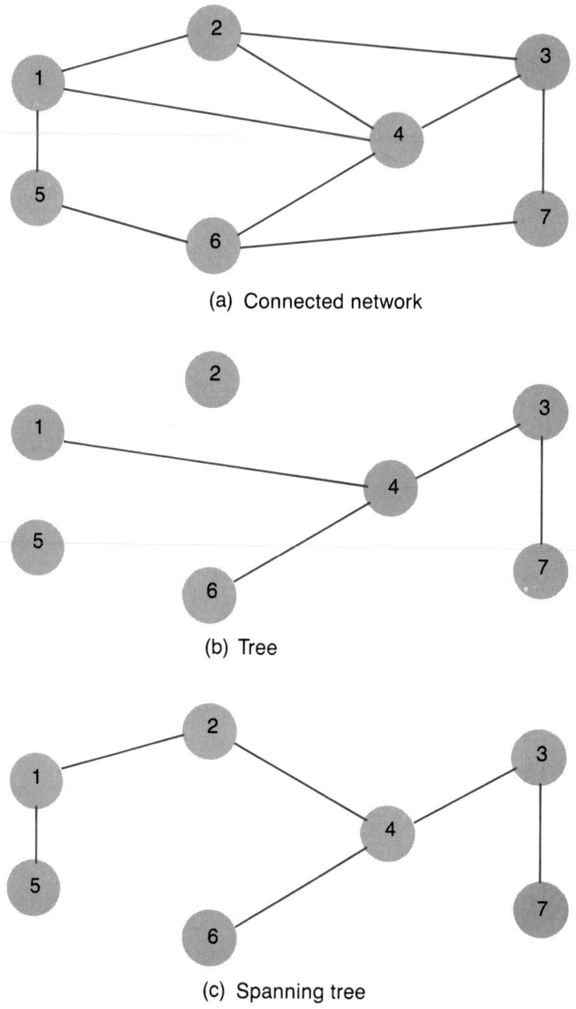

(a) Connected network

(b) Tree

(c) Spanning tree

Suppose the network diagram in Figure 10–6 represents a network where a commodity flows from node 1 to node 4. When all arcs associated with a node are oriented (directed) away from the node, it is referred to as a **source** (or origin). Node 1 is a source node having a supply of 100 units of the commodity. When all arcs associated with a node are directed toward (into) it, the node is called a **sink** (or destination). In Figure 10–6 node 4 is a sink having a demand of 90 units. Nodes that are neither supply points nor demand points are called **transshipment nodes.** Such nodes

FIGURE 10–6

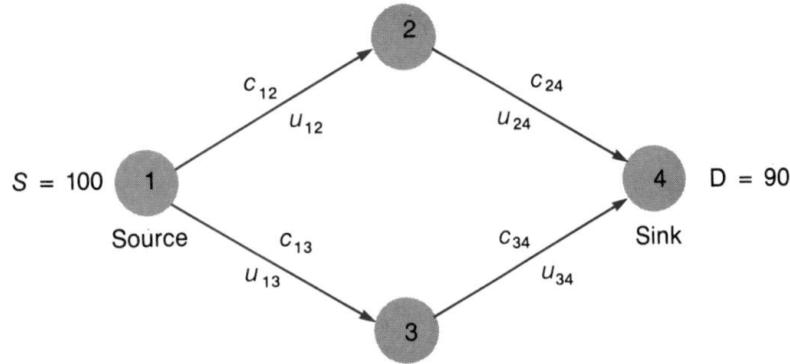

appear in a network diagram with arcs directed both toward and away from the node. Nodes 2 and 3 are examples of transshipment nodes.

Depending on the network application, flow along arcs may have a measurable cost (e.g., dollars/unit, time/unit) or return (e.g., revenue/unit, profit/unit). In Figure 10–6 the c_{ij} represents the cost (or return) per unit of flow along arc i–j. Finally, arcs may be characterized by a **flow capacity.** Flow capacity indicates any limit on the quantity of flow along an arc. In Figure 10–6, u_{ij} represents the maximum flow capacity along arc i–j.

▶ Example 10.1 The Transportation Model

The transportation model discussed in Chapter 7 can be viewed as a network model. Figure 10–7 is a network representation of the classic model having m origins (sources) and n destinations (sinks). Each source node is characterized by a supply capacity, and each sink node is characterized by a known demand. Remember that the classic model assumes total supply and demand to be equal. The directed arcs connecting each source node and sink node represent possible distribution routes. Each arc (route) is characterized by a unit distribution cost c_{ij}. In addition, it is implicit in the classic transportation model that the maximum flow capacity across any given arc i–j equals infinity, or $u_{ij} = \infty$ (i.e., *uncapacitated network*). In a practical sense, u_{ij} = The smaller of s_i and d_j. The LP formulation for this network model is:

Minimize

$$z = \sum_{i=1}^{m} \sum_{j=m+1}^{m+n} c_{ij}x_{ij}$$

subject to

$$\sum_{j=m+1}^{m+n} x_{ij} = s_i \qquad i = 1, \ldots, m$$

$$\sum_{i=1}^{m} x_{ij} = d_j \qquad j = m + 1, \ldots, m + n$$

$$x_{ij} \geq 0 \qquad i = 1, \ldots, m$$

$$j = m + 1, \ldots, m + n$$

FIGURE 10–7 Network Model for Transportation Model

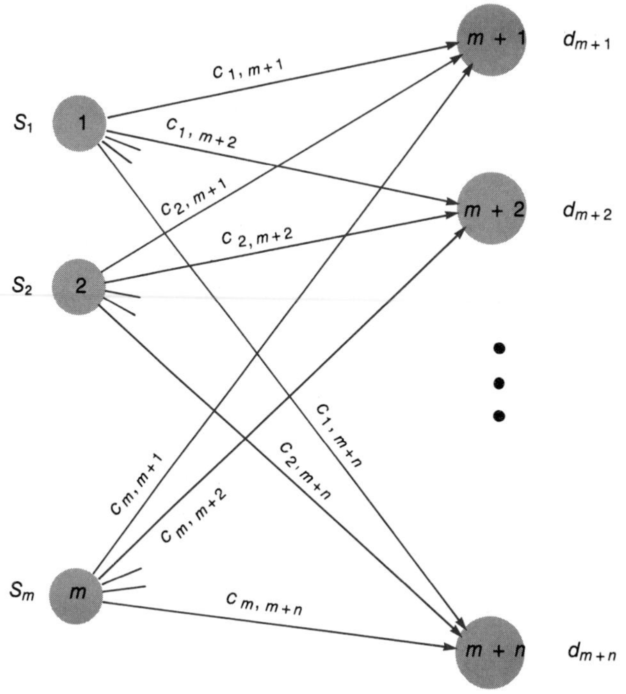

The Transshipment Model

The **transshipment model** is an extension of the classic transportation model. This widely applied model allows for intermediate transshipment nodes that lie between source nodes and sink nodes. A transshipment node acts as *both* a receiver and supplier of flow. Examples of transshipment nodes might include intermediate warehouses between plants and customers, connecting airports between the starting point of a trip and the final destination, and satellites that act as relay stations between a source of a transmitted TV signal and the point of final reception of that signal.

Figure 10–8 is the network diagram for a transshipment problem involving one plant, two distribution (transshipment) warehouses, and five final destinations. Notice that directed arcs between the distribution warehouses indicate possible flow from one to the other. Also note that the quantities demanded at final destinations are shown as negative quantities. Our convention will be that if a node is a net supplier (source) of flow, this will be reflected by a *positive* supply for the node. If a node is a net receiver (sink) of flow, this will be denoted as a *negative* supply. Intermediate (transshipment) nodes will be indicated (implicitly) by zero supply values.

The problem is to determine the number of units to distribute from the plant to each warehouse and the number to distribute from each warehouse to each final destination so as to minimize total costs of distribution. We will assume in this problem that there are no limits on the flow capacity along the various arcs (routes). Because

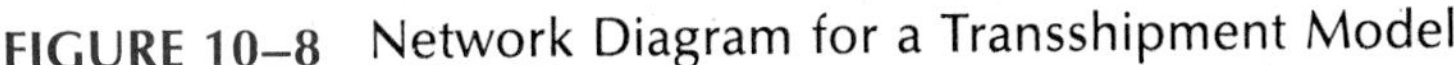

FIGURE 10–8 Network Diagram for a Transshipment Model

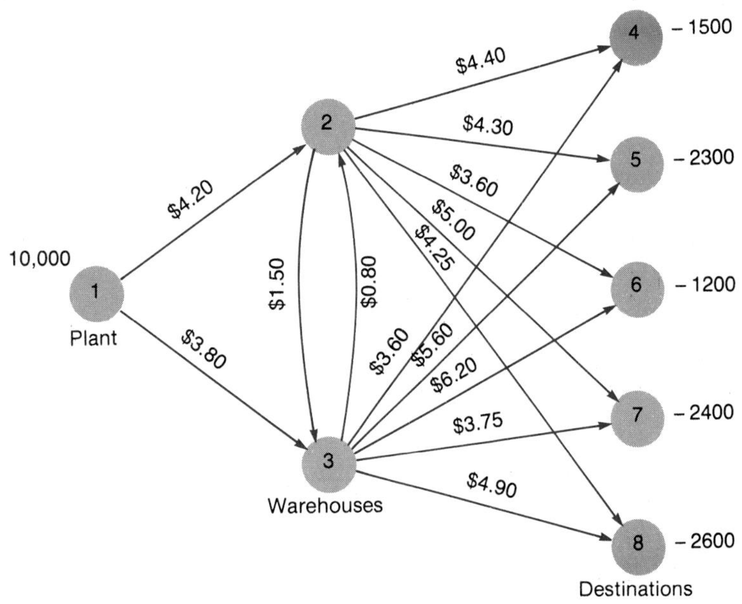

of this assumption, the model is referred to as an **uncapacitated transshipment model.**

If x_{ij} = Number of units distributed from node i to node j, the equivalent LP formulation of this model is:

Minimize

$$\begin{aligned} z = {} & 4.20x_{12} + 3.80x_{13} + 1.50x_{23} + 0.80x_{32} + 4.40x_{24} \\ & + 4.30x_{25} + 3.60x_{26} + 5.00x_{27} + 4.25x_{28} + 3.60x_{34} \\ & + 5.60x_{35} + 6.20x_{36} + 3.75x_{37} + 4.90x_{38} \end{aligned}$$

subject to

$$\begin{array}{lr} x_{12} + x_{13} & = 10{,}000 \quad \text{(Node 1)} \\ -x_{12} + x_{23} - x_{32} + x_{24} + x_{25} + x_{26} + x_{27} + x_{28} & = 0 \quad \text{(Node 2)} \\ -x_{13} - x_{23} + x_{32} + x_{34} + x_{35} + x_{36} + x_{37} + x_{38} & = 0 \quad \text{(Node 3)} \\ -x_{24} - x_{34} & = -1{,}500 \quad \text{(Node 4)} \\ -x_{25} - x_{35} & = -2{,}300 \quad \text{(Node 5)} \\ -x_{26} - x_{36} & = -1{,}200 \quad \text{(Node 6)} \\ -x_{27} - x_{37} & = -2{,}400 \quad \text{(Node 7)} \\ -x_{28} - x_{38} & = -2{,}600 \quad \text{(Node 8)} \\ & x_{ij} \geq 0 \quad \text{for all } i,j \end{array}$$

Let us make a few observations about this model. First, the constraint set consists of one constraint for each node in the network. Second, each constraint states the net flow requirements for the particular node. Each constraint has the form

$$\begin{matrix}\text{Total flow away} \\ \text{from node } j\end{matrix} - \begin{matrix}\text{Total flow} \\ \text{into node } j\end{matrix} = \begin{matrix}\text{Net flow} \\ \text{for node } j.\end{matrix}$$

These constraints are referred to as *flow balance* constraints because flow into and flow from each node offset each other to equal the net flow for each node. (Flow in must equal flow out for transshipment nodes.) To illustrate this second observation, source node 1 has two directed arcs away from the node. The corresponding LP constraint has the form

$$\begin{matrix}\text{Flow from node 1} \\ \text{to node 2}\end{matrix} + \begin{matrix}\text{Flow from node 1} \\ \text{to node 3}\end{matrix} = 10{,}000\,.$$

Similarly, transshipment node 2 has two arcs directed toward the node and six arcs directed away from the node. The corresponding LP constraint has the form

$$(\text{Flow } 2 \rightarrow 3 + \text{Flow } 2 \rightarrow 4 + \text{Flow } 2 \rightarrow 5 + \text{Flow } 2 \rightarrow 6 + \text{Flow } 2 \rightarrow 7$$
$$+ \text{Flow } 2 \rightarrow 8) - (\text{Flow } 1 \rightarrow 2 + \text{Flow } 3 \rightarrow 2) = 0$$

Third, for simplicity we assume total supply at the source node equals total demand at the sink nodes. Finally, there is a special structure to this network model. This structure can be seen by constructing a **node-arc incidence matrix,** which is a tabular representation of network constraints. Figure 10–9 is the node-arc incidence matrix for the network in Figure 10–8. One row exists for each node (constraint) in the network and one column exists for each arc (decision variable). If you examine the column of constraint coefficients for each variable (arc) in the formulation, you will see one coefficient equal to +1, one equal to −1, and the remaining equal to zero. The +1 coefficient occurs in the row corresponding to the node from which the arc originates. The −1 coefficient occurs in the row corresponding to the node at which the arc terminates.

FIGURE 10–9 Node-Arc Incidence Matrix for Network in Figure 10–8

Node	1–2	1–3	2–3	3–2	2–4	2–5	2–6	2–7	2–8	3–4	3–5	3–6	3–7	3–8	RHS
1	1	1	0	0	0	0	0	0	0	0	0	0	0	0	10,000
2	−1	0	1	−1	1	1	1	1	1	0	0	0	0	0	0
3	0	−1	−1	1	0	0	0	0	0	1	1	1	1	1	0
4	0	0	0	0	−1	0	0	0	0	−1	0	0	0	0	−1,500
5	0	0	0	0	0	−1	0	0	0	0	−1	0	0	0	−2,300
6	0	0	0	0	0	0	−1	0	0	0	0	−1	0	0	−1,200
7	0	0	0	0	0	0	0	−1	0	0	0	0	−1	0	−2,400
8	0	0	0	0	0	0	0	0	−1	0	0	0	0	−1	−2,600

This example has shown three different ways of portraying the transshipment model. We can represent the problem using (*a*) the network diagram in Figure 10–8, (*b*) the standard LP formulation, and (*c*) the node-arc incidence matrix. In fact the node-arc incidence matrix can be formulated directly from the network diagram and vice versa. In terms of solving this problem, we can use the simplex method to solve the LP formulation. However, more efficient network algorithms can be used to exploit the special structure of this type of model, as was done in Chapter 7.

FOLLOW-UP EXERCISES

1. For the network diagram in Figure 10–10, the numbers labeled on each arc represent costs per unit of traveling between nodes. The supply at each plant and demand at each warehouse are indicated next to each node.

FIGURE 10–10

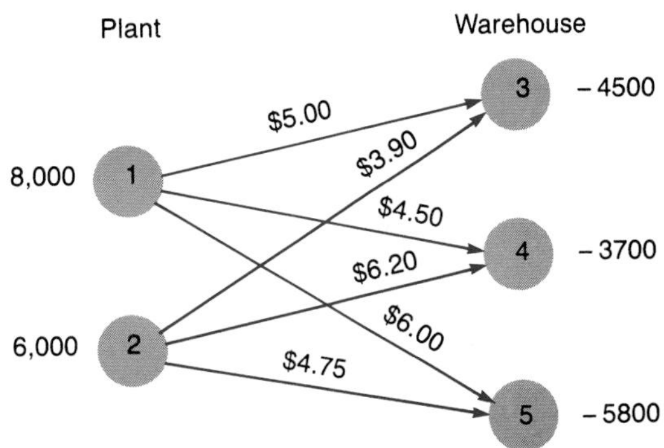

   a. Formulate the equivalent LP model for minimizing total travel cost.
   b. Formulate the node-arc incidence matrix for the network.

2. For the network diagram in Figure 10–11, the numbers labeled on each arc represent the distance between the two nodes. Supplies available at each source and demand at each destination are also shown.

FIGURE 10–11

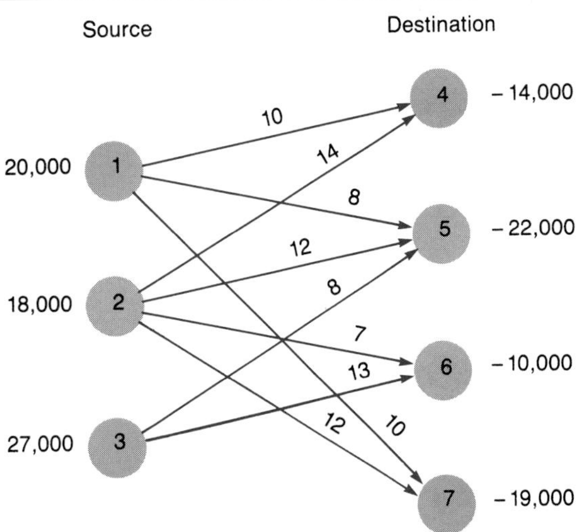

a. Formulate the equivalent LP model for minimizing the total flow-distance (units times distance shipped).
b. Formulate the node-arc incidence matrix for the network.

3. Given the transshipment problem represented in Figure 10–12,

FIGURE 10–12

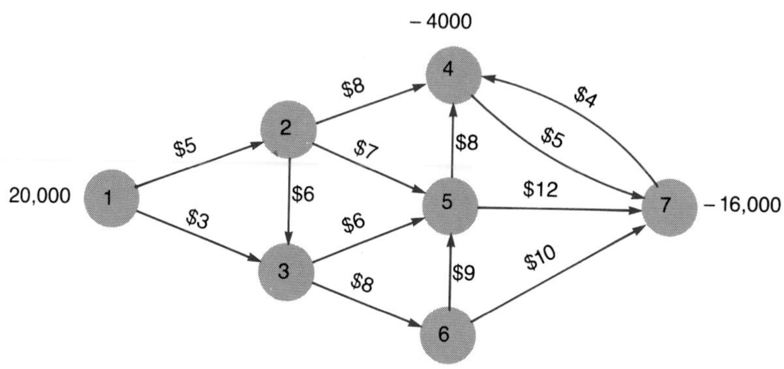

a. Formulate the equivalent LP model.
b. Formulate the node-arc incidence matrix for the network.
Assume that the arc labels represent unit flow costs and the objective is to minimize total cost.

4. Given the transshipment problem represented in Figure 10–13,

FIGURE 10–13

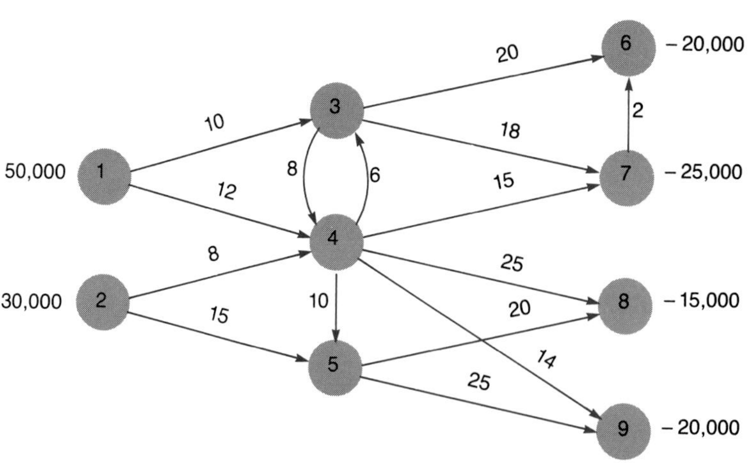

a. Formulate the equivalent LP model.
b Formulate the node-arc incidence matrix for the network.
Assume that the arc labels represent unit flow revenues and the objective is to maximize total revenue.

5. ***Excess Supply.*** Suppose in Exercise 1 that the supply at node 2 equals 10,000. The result is that total supply exceeds total demand. One way of accounting for this is to create a new sink node connected to nodes 1 and 2. This "dummy" node will have a "demand" equal to the surplus supply and appropriate costs assigned to flows across the arcs.
   a. Draw the new network diagram.
   b. How would the LP formulation be modified?
   c. How would the node-arc incidence matrix change?
   d. What conditions would lead to assuming zero arc costs for the dummy sink node? What conditions might result in positive costs?
6. Construct the network diagram corresponding to the following node-arc incidence matrix.

Node	1–3	1–4	1–5	2–3	2–5	RHS
1	1	1	1	0	0	5,000
2	0	0	0	1	1	10,000
3	−1	0	0	−1	0	−6,000
4	0	−1	0	0	0	−4,000
5	0	0	−1	0	−1	−5,000

7. Construct the network diagram corresponding to the following node-arc incidence matrix.

Node	1–0	1–3	1–4	2–0	2–4	2–5	3–6	4–3	4–5	4–6	5–6	RHS
0	−1	0	0	−1	0	0	0	0	0	0	0	−10,000
1	1	1	1	0	0	0	0	0	0	0	0	20,000
2	0	0	0	1	1	1	0	0	0	0	0	30,000
3	0	−1	0	0	0	0	1	−1	0	0	0	0
4	0	0	−1	0	−1	0	0	1	1	1	0	0
5	0	0	0	0	0	−1	0	0	−1	0	1	0
6	0	0	0	0	0	0	−1	0	0	−1	−1	−40,000

8. Construct the network diagram corresponding to the following node-arc incidence matrix.

Node	1–4	1–2	2–4	2–5	2–3	3–5	4–6	4–7	4–5	5–4	5–7	5–8	RHS
1	1	1	0	0	0	0	0	0	0	0	0	0	500
2	0	−1	1	1	1	0	0	0	0	0	0	0	800
3	0	0	0	0	−1	1	0	0	0	0	0	0	1,200
4	−1	0	−1	0	0	0	1	1	1	−1	0	0	0
5	0	0	0	−1	0	−1	0	0	−1	1	1	1	0
6	0	0	0	0	0	0	−1	0	0	0	0	0	−750
7	0	0	0	0	0	0	0	−1	0	0	−1	0	−450
8	0	0	0	0	0	0	0	0	0	0	0	−1	−1,300

10.2 MODELING WITH NETWORKS

In order to demonstrate the flexibility of network representation, this section will illustrate how to formulate network models for a variety of managerial applications.

Minimal Spanning Tree Model

A classic network problem requires selecting arcs for a network which provide a route between all pairs of nodes and minimize the total distance (cost or time) to do so. Another way of viewing this problem is that it involves selecting the network that forms a *tree* that *spans* (connects) the nodes of interest.

This type of problem has wide applicability, especially to transportation and telecommunication networks. Consider a planned community in the process of drawing up blueprints for sewer service. The planner knows the locations of the users (nodes) and wishes to provide sewer service to all users at a minimum cost of construction. The minimum spanning tree problem requires identifying the network of sewers that reaches all users and minimizes the total amount of sewer pipe. Other applications include transportation networks wherein nodes represent locations and arcs represent such transportation links as roads, railways, and airline routes.

▶ Example 10.2 Agricultural Irrigation

A corporate food producer has many farms under its "umbrella." One major farm for producing corn is in the planning stage. The farm has 10 fields in which corn will be planted. A primary concern is providing an adequate water supply to the fields. Supply of water itself is not the problem. The firm wishes, though, to minimize the cost of installing a water-pipe network that reaches all fields. A well will be drilled at one of the fields from which all others will be supplied. Figure 10–14 is a network diagram where each node represents a field and each arc represents a potential water-pipe link between respective fields. The numbers attached to each arc represent costs (in $1,000s) associated with installing the link. Costs primarily reflect the cost of pipe, labor, and equipment. Although cost is typically a linear function of pipe length, some differentials exist according to difficulty in laying the pipe (e.g., blasting rock formations or installing overhead pipes).

The problem is to determine the water-pipe network that connects all fields at a minimum total cost of installation. Section 10.3 will revisit this problem, using it to demonstrate a specialized minimal spanning tree algorithm.

Shortest Route Models

One popular class of network models is the **shortest-route model.** This type of model can be represented by a network diagram where the arc i–j has an associated value c_{ij}, which might represent the distance separating nodes i and j. In some problems c_{ij} could represent the time to travel arc i–j or the cost of moving one unit of flow across i–j. In the classic model, the problem is to determine the shortest distance path from a specified node to another node. You will see this problem approached from a different vantage point in Chapter 12 (Dynamic Programming

FIGURE 10–14 Network for Farm Irrigation Example

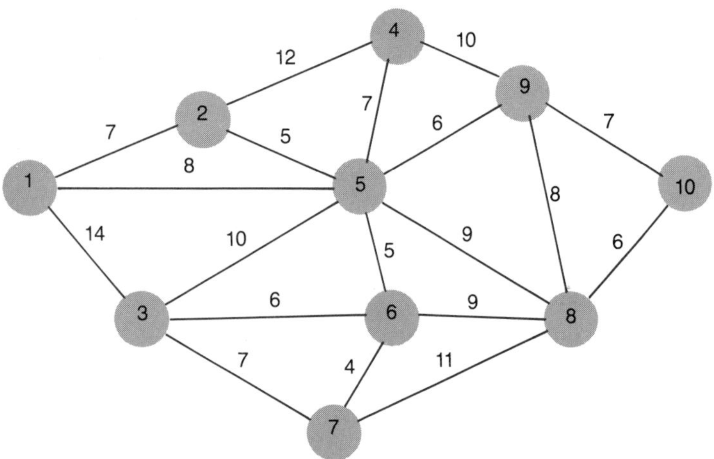

and Sequential Decisions). There are many variations on the problem, including modeling the equipment replacement decision. Example 10.3 illustrates such a model.

Example 10.3 Equipment Replacement

A company has a contract that will require the use of a particular type of equipment over the next five years. The equipment must be available for the five years of the contract and will be disposed of at the end of the five-year period. The demands on the equipment over the life of the contract are such that the equipment *might* have to be replaced one or more times. Table 10–1 reflects estimated costs as a function of the year of purchase and the period of ownership. These costs reflect capital costs (based on assumed purchase costs and estimated salvage value) as well as operating and maintenance expenses.

TABLE 10–1 Total Cost of Ownership

		Years of Ownership				
		1	2	3	4	5
Year Purchased	1	$15,000	$28,000	$48,000	$65,000	$85,000
	2	16,500	30,000	50,000	67,500	
	3	18,500	34,000	58,000		
	4	19,500	41,000			
	5	20,000				

This problem can be represented by the network diagram shown in Figure 10–15. In this diagram node *j* represents the beginning of year *j*. We have six nodes because the contract takes us from the beginning of year 1 to the beginning of year 6. Each arc (*i–j*) has been labeled with the cost (c_{ij}) of owning and operating the equipment from the beginning of year *i* to the beginning of year *j*. For example, the cost of buying new equipment at the beginning of year 2 and keeping it until the end of the contract (beginning of year 6) is $67,500. The fact that all paths terminate at node 6 accounts for the fact that whatever equipment is in use at the beginning of year 6 will be sold or disposed.

FIGURE 10–15 Equipment Replacement Network Diagram

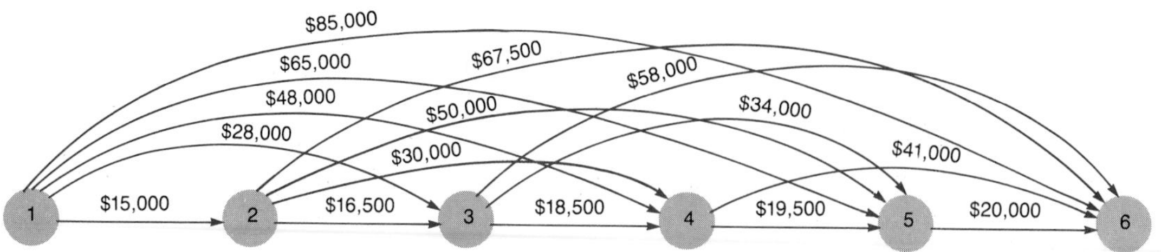

This problem is analogous to trying to find the least cost route from node 1 to node 6. You can see from this network diagram that many options are possible for providing equipment over the life of the contract. One option is represented by the path consisting of arcs 1–2, 2–3, 3–4, 4–5, and 5–6, or 1–2–3–4–5–6. This option represents the decision to purchase new equipment at the beginning of each year. Another option is to travel arc 1–6, which represents buying the equipment at the beginning of year 1 and keeping it over the life of the contract. The solution to this problem can be attained in several ways, using mathematical programming and special purpose algorithms. One shortest-route algorithm will be illustrated in Section 10.3.

Maximal Flow Model

The maximal flow model is concerned with determining the maximum flow that can pass from one input node or *source* through a network and out one output node or *sink* during a specified period. Examples include maximizing the flow of oil through pipelines, cars through highway systems, and passengers through airports. Flow capacities associated with arcs of the network set restrictions on the amount of flow between nodes. Pipe size, number of traffic lanes, and number of check-in counters and gates all affect flow capacities in the examples above.

The following example illustrates the nature of the maximal flow problem and presents a simple solution algorithm.

▶ Example 10.4 Postal Routing

The post office at city 1 is preparing for the Christmas rush, during which a heavy volume of mail always moves from city 1 to city 3. Mail moves by either air, truck, or rail from city 1 through city 2 to city 3. Mail may move via the same mode of transportation for the complete trip, or it may switch modes at city 2. Figure 10–16 is a network diagram of the delivery network. Arcs labeled *A*, *T*, and *R* represent air, truck, and rail links, respectively. Nodes 2′, 2″, and 2‴ all represent city 2 in the network. The flow capacities (in 10,000s of pieces per day) along an arc are indicated next to each node. Notice that these capacities may vary according to direction of flow and that each node indicates the flow capacities in a direction *away from* the node.

FIGURE 10–16 Network for Example 10.4

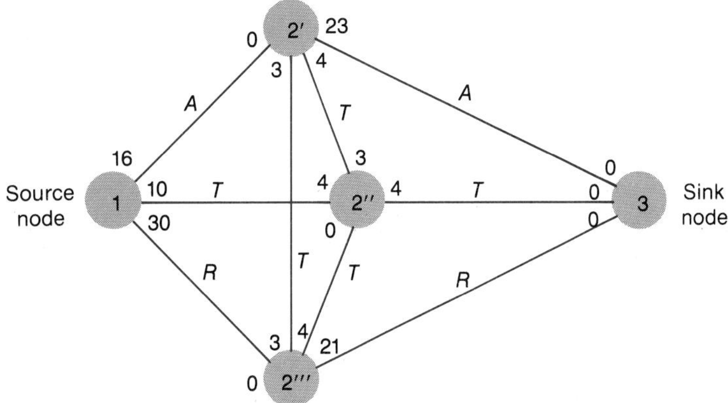

For example, the flow capacity from node 1 to node 2′ is 16(10,000) or 160,000 pieces of mail per day. The flow capacity from node 2′ to node 1 is zero. Similarly, the daily flow capacity from node 2′ to node 2″ is 4(10,000) or 40,000 pieces of mail and from node 2″ to node 2′ is 3(10,000) or 30,000 pieces per day.

The post office wants to determine the maximum number of pieces of mail that can be moved each day from city 1 to city 3 using the existing capacitated transshipment network. The unique network structure of the maximal flow problem lends itself to specialized solution algorithms. We will revisit this example in Section 10.3 where we discuss such an algorithm.

Generalized Capacitated Flow Network

The transshipment model discussed in Section 10.1 is an example of an **uncapacitated flow network model.** It is uncapacitated because there are no limits on the amount of flow across any arc. This is a special case of the generalized capacitated flow network model, which follows. The capacitated model assumes upper, and possibly lower, limits on the flow across a given arc.

Suppose we let:

f_{ij} = Amount of flow across arc i–j.
c_{ij} = Unit cost for flow across arc i–j.
u_{ij} = Maximum flow capacity for arc i–j.
l_{ij} = Minimum flow capacity for arc i–j.
b_i = Net flow for node i, where $b_i > 0$ for source nodes; $b_i < 0$ for sink nodes; and $b_i = 0$ for transshipment nodes.
n = Number of nodes.

The generalized minimum cost flow model is:

Minimize

$$z = \sum_i \sum_j c_{ij} f_{ij}$$

subject to

$$\sum_j f_{ij} - \sum_j f_{ji} = b_i \qquad i = 1, \ldots, n$$

$$l_{ij} \le f_{ij} \le u_{ij} \qquad \text{for all } i, j$$

Many applications can be modeled as capacitated flow networks. The following example illustrates a production planning application.

Example 10.5 Production Planning Model

Consider the XYZ Corporation, which has signed a contract to provide certain quantities of a product for each of four quarters. XYZ can produce units and/or subcontract with another company to supply units. Units can be produced or purchased from the subcontractor during the period in which they are demanded, or they can be produced or purchased during one period and held in inventory to satisfy demand in a future period. An inventory carrying cost of $2 per unit per quarter is incurred when units are held in inventory. Table 10–2 summarizes XYZ's production capacity for each quarter, production cost per unit, subcontractor capacity for each quarter, and associated unit purchase costs, as well as quarterly demand for the product.

TABLE 10–2

Quarter	Production Capacity (units)	Production Cost	Subcontractor Capacity	Purchase Cost	Demand
1	125	$8.00	50	$9.00	150
2	140	9.60	60	10.40	180
3	150	11.00	70	12.50	250
4	200	13.50	120	14.25	300
	615		300		880

The problem is to determine the production/purchase schedule that satisfies the quarterly demands of the contract at a minimum total cost. This problem can be represented by the network diagram in Figure 10–17. The nodes represent the eight sources of supply (produce or subcontract) in each of the four quarters, (P_j and S_j), the four quarterly demands (D_j), and an additional sink node that has a demand equal to the combined *excess* capacity of XYZ and its subcontractor. Notice that source nodes P_j and S_j may supply (connect) with any demand nodes D_k where $k \ge j$; that is, units produced or purchased in one period cannot be used to satisfy demand for a previous period (no *back ordering*).

For this capacitated flow network, the arcs are labeled in the following manner,

$$\text{(}i\text{)} \xrightarrow{(l_{ij},\ u_{ij},\ c_{ij})} \text{(}j\text{)}$$

where

l_{ij} = Minimum flow capacity for arc i–j.
u_{ij} = Maximum flow capacity for arc i–j.
c_{ij} = Unit cost for flow across arc i–j.

FIGURE 10–17 Network Flow Diagram for Production-Planning Example

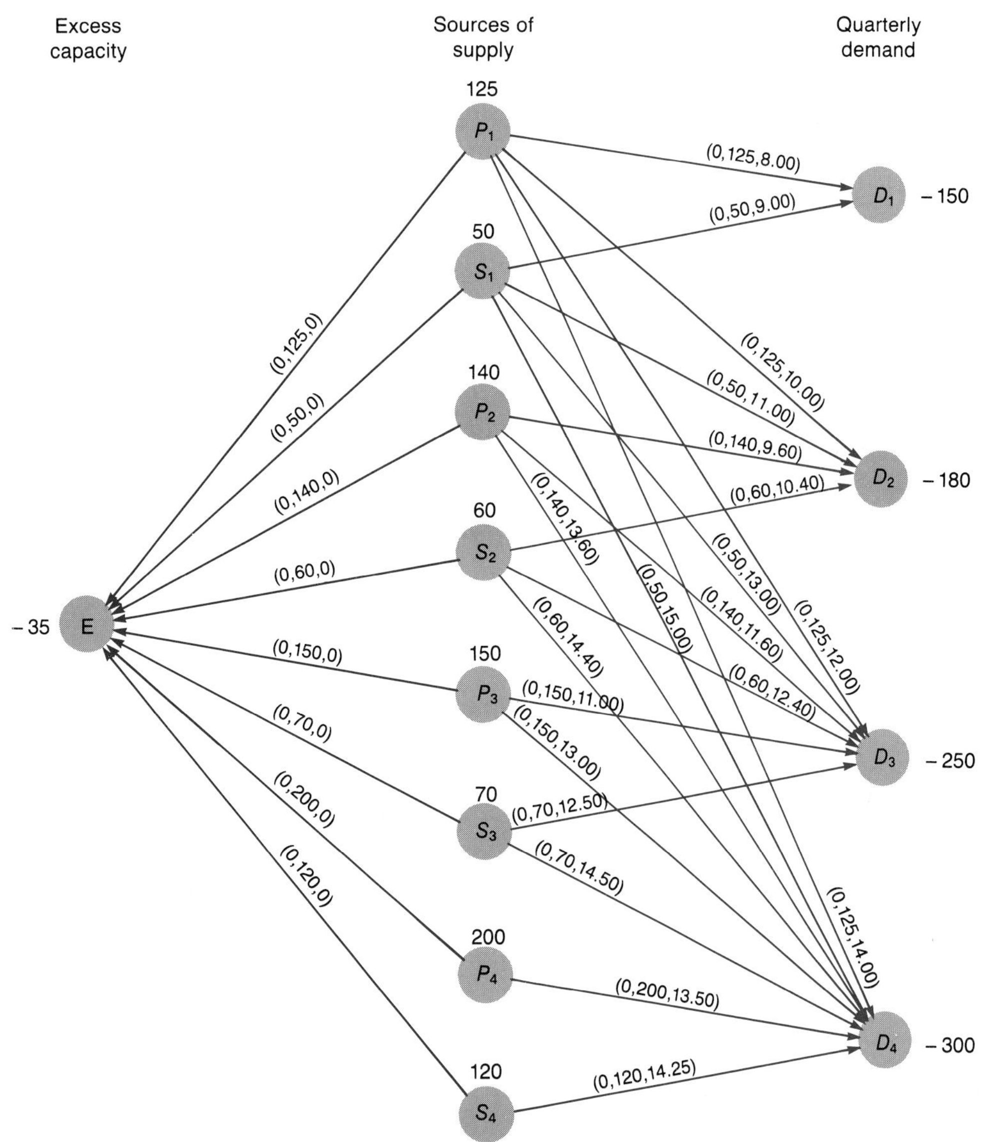

Minimum capacities are zero for all arcs in our example. The maximum capacities reflect the production capacity or subcontractor capacities in the respective quarters. The c_{ij} values include production (or purchase) cost *plus* inventory carrying cost. Note the labels for arcs P_1–D_1 and P_1–D_2. The unit cost on arc P_1–D_2 is $2 greater than the cost for P_1–D_1. This is because units produced in quarter 1 to satisfy demand in quarter 2 must be held in inventory for one quarter. The cost for arcs P_j–E and S_j–E assumes that excess (unused) capacity has no explicit cost. What circumstances might justify an assumption of zero cost for unused capacity?

This problem could be solved as a minimum-cost flow problem using either the transportation algorithm of Chapter 7 or the **out-of-kilter algorithm.** The out-of-kilter algorithm is considered one of the more generalized and widely applied algorithms for solving deterministic, capacitated network flow problems. However, the procedural detail of the method is too involved to be discussed in this chapter.[2]

FOLLOW-UP EXERCISES

9. A local natural gas company is planning service for eight new residential areas. A variety of routes are possible for interconnecting the areas. The company is interested in installing natural gas pipelines that will interconnect the eight areas at a minimum cost. Table 10–3 indicates the possible interconnections and the cost of laying the pipe (in $10,000s). Construct the network diagram for this system, labeling each arc with the corresponding cost. What type of network problem is this?

TABLE 10–3

Area	1	2	3	4	5	6	7	8
1	—	45	75	30	—	—	—	—
2		—	60	—	—	90	35	—
3			—	80	50	70	—	—
4				—	85	—	—	—
5					—	40	—	65
6						—	55	70
7							—	30
8								—

10. ***Automobile Purchase/Replacement.*** A company is planning its strategy for ownership of a fleet of company cars over the next five years. Cars will be purchased at the beginning of the first year and can be held for varying lengths of time. It is assumed that the fleet will be disposed of at the end of the five–year period. Table 10–4 reflects estimated costs of car ownership stated as a function of the year of purchase and the number of years the car is owned. These cost estimates reflect expected capital cost (purchase price less salvage value) plus maintenance cost.

TABLE 10–4 Capital Cost Plus Maintenance Cost

	Years of Ownership				
	1	2	3	4	5
1	$3,200	$6,000	$ 8,400	$11,800	$15,800
2	3,500	6,450	9,200	12,500	
3	4,000	7,200	10,300		
4	4,200	7,900			
5	4,750				

[2]For a detailed discussion of the out-of-kilter algorithm, see Don T. Phillips and Alberto Garcia-Diaz, *Fundamentals of Network Analysis* (Englewood Cliffs, N.J.: Prentice–Hall, 1981).

The problem is to develop a purchase/replacement strategy that results in minimum cost of ownership over the five-year time horizon. Construct the network diagram for this problem. What type of network problem does this represent?

11. A network contains seven nodes. The desire is to maximize the total flow from node 1 to node 7. The directed arcs and their respective flow capacities are listed in Table 10–5.

TABLE 10–5

Arc	**(1–2)**	**(1–3)**	**(1–4)**	**(2–3)**	**(2–5)**	**(3–5)**	**(3–6)**	**(3–7)**	**(4–3)**	**(4–6)**	**(5–7)**	**(6–7)**
Flow Capacity	300	200	400	100	250	150	100	100	100	225	400	300

Construct the network flow diagram for this maximal flow problem.

12. Suppose in the Production Planning Model (Example 10.5) that XYZ has an initial inventory of 75 units that had been produced at a cost of $6.50 per unit in the previous period. How would this alter the network diagram in Figure 10–17?

13. A company has signed a contract to provide specified quantities of a product for each of four periods. The company can produce units and/or subcontract with another company to supply units. Units can be produced or purchased from the subcontractor during the period in which they are demanded, or they can be produced or purchased during one period and held in inventory to satisfy demand in a future period. An inventory carrying cost of $3 per unit per period is incurred when units are held in inventory. Table 10–6 summarizes the production capacity for each period, production cost per unit, subcontractor capacity for each period, and associated unit purchase costs as well as the demand for each period.

TABLE 10–6

Period	**Production Capacity (units)**	**Production Cost**	**Sub-capacity**	**Purchase Cost**	**Demand**
1	250	$10.00	100	$12.00	275
2	200	11.00	100	13.50	325
3	250	12.50	50	15.00	300
4	300	14.50	100	16.00	350

Construct the network diagram for this production planning problem.

10.3 SPECIALIZED NETWORK ALGORITHMS

Having looked at various formulations of network models, this section presents specialized solution algorithms for the *minimal spanning tree model*, the *shortest-route model*, and the *maximal flow model*. Computer implementation of these algorithms will also be illustrated by solving representative problems.

Minimal Spanning Tree Algorithm

The previous section defined the minimal spanning tree problem as one requiring selection of the set of arcs for a network that provides a route between all pairs of nodes and minimizes the total distance (cost or time) to do so. A very simple algorithm exists for solving this type of problem.

Minimal Spanning Tree Algorithm

Step 1: Select *any* node and identify the least distant (cost or time) node. Connect the two. (Break any ties arbitrarily.)

Step 2: Identify the *unconnected* node that is least distant from any *connected* node, and connect the two. (Break any ties arbitrarily.)

Step 3: Repeat step 2 until all nodes have been connected.

This algorithm is in the class of **greedy algorithms** so-named because at each step they choose the largest improvement possible. In the minimal spanning tree algorithm, the least distant unconnected node is sought at each step. This is one of the few types of problems in which the greedy approach guarantees an optimal solution.

Example 10.6 Agricultural Irrigation — Revisited

Let us return to the agricultural irrigation problem (Example 10.2) in which the object was to determine the water-pipe network that connects all fields at a minimum total cost of installation. The network diagram is repeated in Figure 10–18. To illustrate the algorithm, begin arbitrarily with node 1. The shortest arc (costwise) emanating from node 1 is that leading to node 2. Thus these two nodes are connected as shown in Figure 10–19. Applying step 2, the next shortest arc from a connected node to an unconnected node leads from node 2 to node 5. Thus these nodes are connected as shown in Figure 10–20. Repeating step 2, the next least costly arc results in node 5 being connected to node 6 (Figure 10–21).

FIGURE 10–18 Original Network

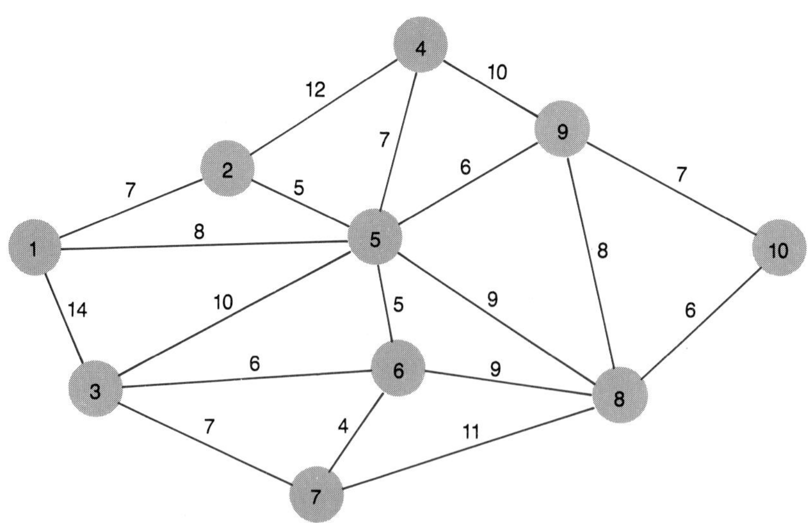

FIGURE 10–19 Iteration 1

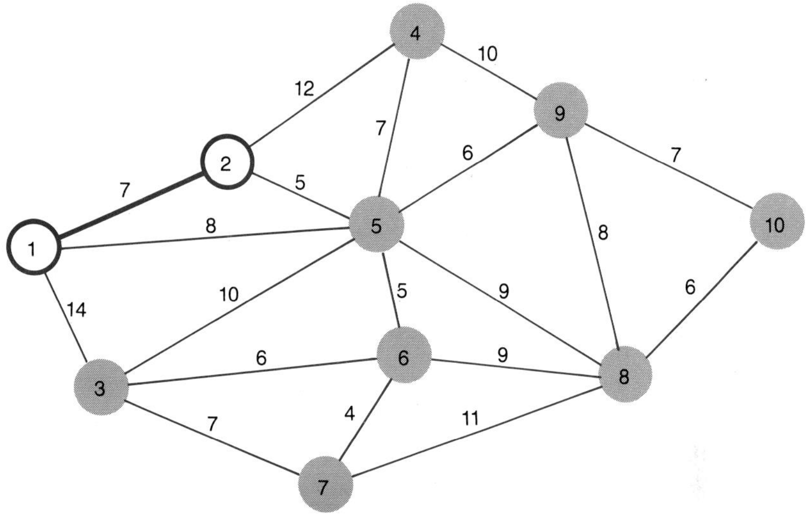

FIGURE 10–20 Iteration 2

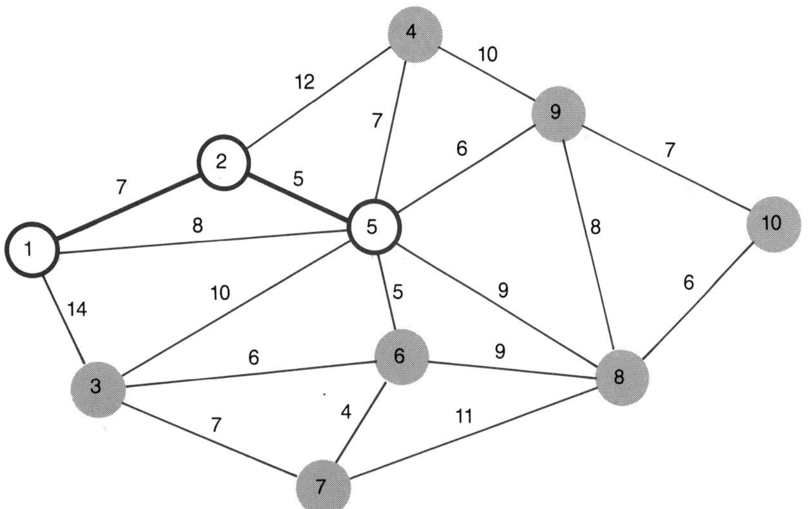

Table 10–7 summarizes the ($n - 1 = 9$) steps leading to the minimum cost spanning tree for this problem. Figure 10–22 illustrates the final network with total installation costs minimized at $53,000.

Tabular Approach for Minimal Spanning Tree Algorithm

As opposed to the graphical version of the algorithm, a tabular approach can be used which lends itself nicely to computer implementation. This version begins by constructing a matrix of arc distances (costs or times). Table 10–8 is the matrix for the agricultural irrigation example.

FIGURE 10–21 Iteration 3

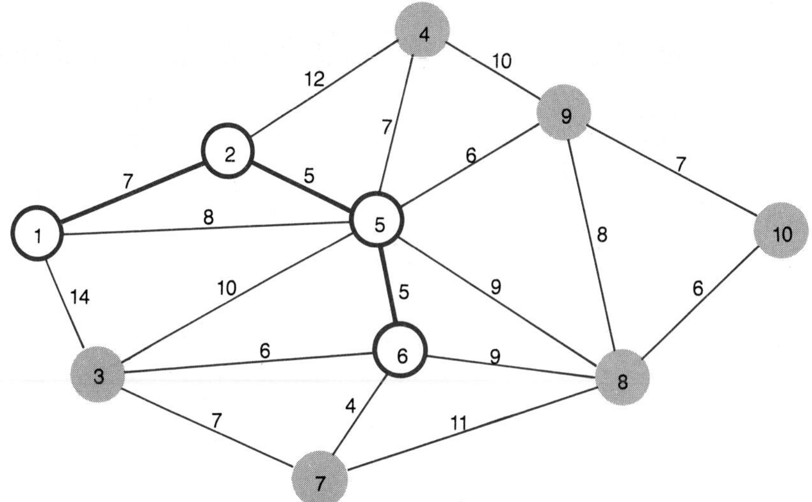

TABLE 10–7 Solution Summary for Example 10.6

Solution Step	Nodes Connected	Cost of Connection ($1,000s)	Cumulative Cost ($1,000s)
1	1–2	7	7
2	2–5	5	12
3	5–6	5	17
4	6–7	4	21
5	6–3	6	27
6	5–9	6	33
7	5–4	7	40
8	9–10	7	47
9	10–8	6	53

FIGURE 10–22 Minimal Spanning Tree for Farm Irrigation Problem

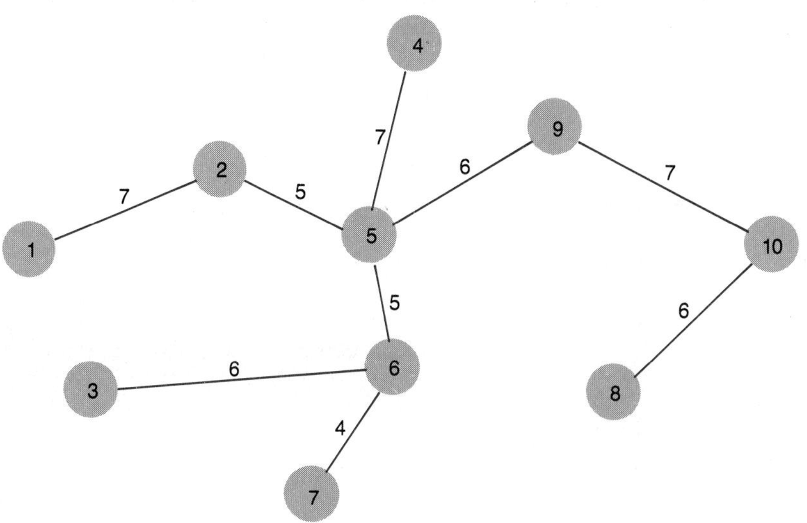

TABLE 10–8 Matrix of Installation Costs

From Field	To Field 1	2	3	4	5	6	7	8	9	10
1	—	7	14	—	8	—	—	—	—	—
2	7	—	—	12	5	—	—	—	—	—
3	14	—	—	—	10	6	7	—	—	—
4	—	12	—	—	7	—	—	—	10	—
5	8	5	10	7	—	5	—	9	6	—
6	—	—	6	—	5	—	4	9	—	—
7	—	—	7	—	—	4	—	11	—	—
8	—	—	—	—	9	9	11	—	8	6
9	—	—	—	10	6	—	—	8	—	7
10	—	—	—	—	—	—	—	6	7	—

Tabular Approach: Minimal Spanning Tree Algorithm

Step 1: Select *any* node and declare it *connected*. Label the row corresponding to the connected node with an asterisk (check mark, etc.) and cross off the *column* corresponding to this node.

Step 2: Examine the rows labeled as connected, and circle the smallest remaining element in these rows (ties broken arbitrarily). The column in which the element lies represents the new connected node. Label the row corresponding to this node as connected, and cross off the corresponding column.

Step 3: Repeat step 2 until all nodes are connected. The minimal spanning tree is represented by the circled elements.

Tables 10–9 and 10–10 illustrate the application of the tabular approach to the irrigation example. Table 10–9 illustrates the first connection of nodes 1 and 2, and Table 10–10 illustrates the second connection of nodes 2 and 5.

TABLE 10–9 Connection of Nodes 1 and 2

From Field	To Field 1	2	3	4	5	6	7	8	9	10
*1	—	(7)	14	—	8	—	—	—	—	—
*2	7	—	—	12	5	—	—	—	—	—
3	14	—	—	—	10	6	7	—	—	—
4	—	12	—	—	7	—	—	—	10	—
5	8	5	10	7	—	5	—	9	6	—
6	—	—	6	—	5	—	4	9	—	—
7	—	—	7	—	—	4	—	11	—	—
8	—	—	—	—	9	9	11	—	8	6
9	—	—	—	10	6	—	—	8	—	7
10	—	—	—	—	—	—	—	6	7	—

TABLE 10–10 Connection of Nodes 2 and 5

From Field	To Field 1	2	3	4	5	6	7	8	9	10
*1	—	(7)	14	—	8	—	—	—	—	—
*2	7	—	—	12	(5)	—	—	—	—	—
3	14	—	—	—	10	6	7	—	—	—
4	—	12	—	—	7	—	—	—	10	—
*5	8	5	10	7	—	5	—	9	6	—
6	—	—	6	—	5	—	4	9	—	—
7	—	—	7	—	—	4	—	11	—	—
8	—	—	—	—	9	9	11	—	8	6
9	—	—	—	10	6	—	—	8	—	7
10	—	—	—	—	—	—	—	6	7	—

Computer-Based Analysis

Figure 10–23 presents the computer output from solving the irrigation problem using the special minimal spanning tree algorithm software module **SPNT1**. This module is one of several included in the software package *Computer Models for Management Science*.[3] The output is split into two parts. The first part summarizes the information entered regarding the network. The second part summarizes the results. The results section indicates the included arcs in the minimal spanning tree along with their lengths and the total length (53) of the tree.

FOLLOW-UP EXERCISES

14. Verify that the algorithm presented in this section is valid regardless of the initial node selected by beginning the irrigation problem (*a*) at node 10 and (*b*) at node 7. (*Hint:* To ease your effort, start with a network diagram having only nodes and no arcs. Thereafter, connect the appropriate nodes at each step of the algorithm.)
15. Use the tabular approach beginning with Table 10–10, and continue to the optimal solution. Your steps should follow those in Table 10–7.
16. Given the network diagram in Figure 10–24, use the graphical version of the minimal spanning tree algorithm to determine the minimal spanning tree.
17. Determine the minimal spanning tree for Figure 10–24 using the tabular approach.
18. Determine the minimal spanning tree for the network in Exercise 9.

Shortest-Route Algorithm

The shortest-route problem is to determine the shortest distance path from a specified node to another node. Remember in the previous section the equipment replacement model (Example 10.3), which could be visualized as a shortest-route model. Let us discuss one specialized algorithm that capitalizes on the network structure of this problem.

[3]See Warren J. Erikson and Owen P. Hall, Jr. (Reading, Mass.: Addison-Wesley Publishing, 1986).

FIGURE 10–23 SPNT1 Output

```
* * * * * * * * * * * * * * * * * * * * *
*                                       *
*           SPANNING TREE               *
*              ANALYSIS                 *
*                                       *
* * * * * * * * * * * * * * * * * * * * *

**   INFORMATION ENTERED  **

NUMBER OF NODES:  10
NUMBER OF LINKS:  19
```

LINK NUMBER	START NODE	END NODE	LINK LENGTH
1	1	2	7
2	2	4	12
3	4	9	10
4	9	10	7
5	10	8	6
6	7	8	11
7	3	7	7
8	1	3	14
9	1	5	8
10	3	5	10
11	3	6	6
12	6	7	4
13	5	6	5
14	6	8	9
15	5	8	9
16	8	9	8
17	5	9	6
18	5	4	7
19	2	5	5

** RESULTS **

MINIMUM SPANNING TREE

START NODE	END NODE	LINK LENGTH
1	2	7
2	5	5
5	6	5
6	7	4
5	9	6
6	3	6
5	4	7
9	10	7
10	8	6

TOTAL LENGTH = 53

** END OF ANALYSIS **

FIGURE 10–24

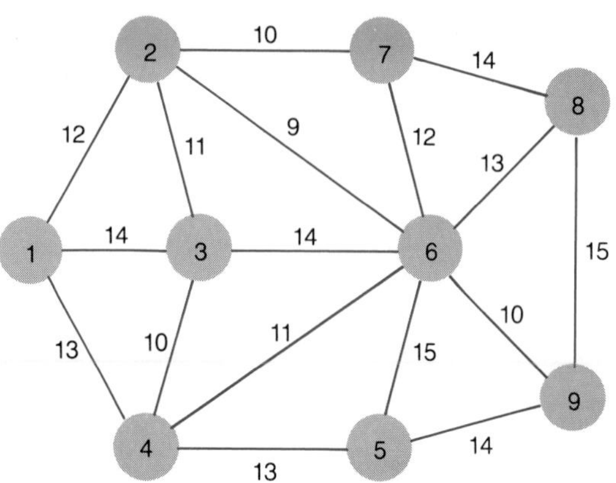

The shortest-route algorithm that we discuss determines the shortest path from one specified node to all other nodes. The algorithm assumes that the distance c_{ij} separating nodes i and j is nonnegative. The algorithm is also iterative in nature. If a network consists of n nodes, $n - 1$ iterations will be required to reach the optimal solution. The algorithm consists of two parts. A **labeling procedure** is used to determine the shortest distance from one specified node to *each* of the other nodes. The second part of the algorithm is a **backtracking procedure** used to define the actual shortest-distance route to each node.

Consider the simple network shown in Figure 10–25. Let us illustrate the algorithm in finding the shortest distance from node 1 to the remaining six nodes.

FIGURE 10–25 Original Network

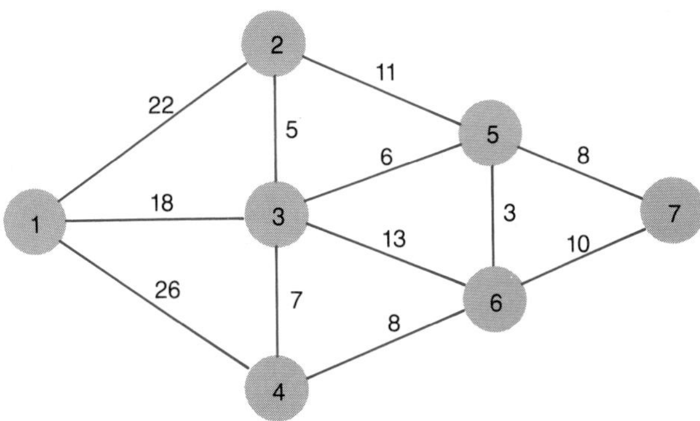

If we consider node 1 as the *origin*, the labeling procedure results in all remaining nodes being assigned a label. The label assigned to node n has the form (d_n, p), where

d_n = Distance from the origin to node n using a specified route.
p = The node preceding node n on the route.

As the algorithm progresses, the labels will be classified as either *temporary labels* or *permanent labels*. Nodes are initially assigned temporary labels. The temporary labels may change as the algorithm progresses. When the shortest route to a given node is identified, the node is assigned a permanent label. A summary of the labeling procedure follows.

Labeling Procedure

Step 1: Consider all nodes connected directly to the origin. Assign temporary labels to each where the distance component equals the distance from the origin. The predecessor part of the label is the origin.

Step 2: Permanently label the node whose distance from the origin is the minimum. (Break any ties arbitrarily.) Refer to this as node L, implying the "latest" node to be permanently labeled. If all nodes are permanently labeled, perform the backtracking procedure.

Step 3: Identify all unlabeled or temporarily labeled nodes that can be connected directly with node L. Compute for each of these unlabeled or temporarily labeled nodes the *sum* of the distance from the origin to node L *and* the distance from node L to the node of interest. If the node of interest is unlabeled, assign a temporary label. If the node already has a temporary label, update the label only if the newly calculated distance is less than that for the previous label. *Updating must also include the predecessor part of the label*. Go to step 2.

Example 10.7

Let us apply the labeling procedure to the network in Figure 10–25. In Figure 10–26 all nodes connected directly to the origin have been identified and labeled. The least distant node from the origin is node 3. This node is permanently labeled (indicated by the darkened arc 1–3, node, and node label).

FIGURE 10–26 First Iteration

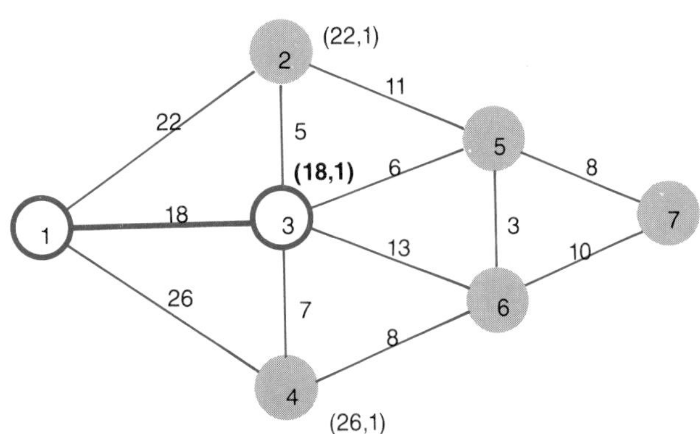

Applying step 3, we identify all unlabeled or temporarily labeled nodes that can be directly connected to node 3. This set includes nodes 2, 4, 5, and 6. Distances are calculated for each of these nodes by adding the distance label for node 3 to the distance from node 3 to the respective nodes. These are shown in Table 10–11. The new distance to node 2 equals 23, which is greater than that for the temporary label. Thus the label for node 2 remains unchanged in Figure 10–27.

TABLE 10–11 Second Iteration

Temporarily Labeled Node (j)	Node 3 Distance Label	Distance From Node 3 to Node j	Calculated Total	Previous Distance Label	New Distance Label
2	18	+ 5 =	23	22	22*
4	18	+ 7 =	25	26	25
5	18	+ 6 =	24	no label	24
6	18	+ 13 =	31	no label	31

FIGURE 10–27 Second Iteration

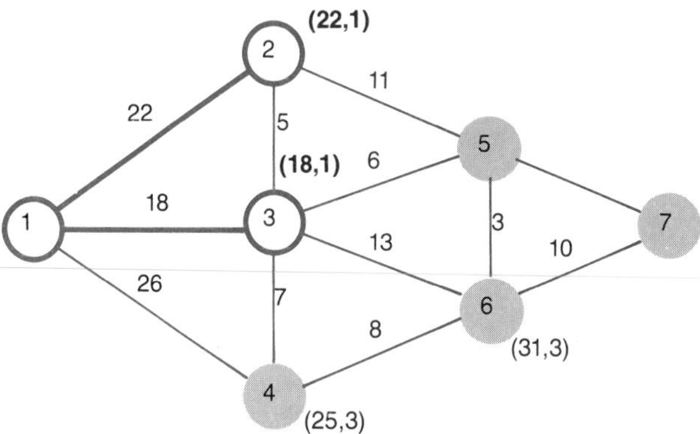

The newly calculated distance for node 4 equals 25, compared with the labeled distance of 26. Since the new distance is less, node 4 is relabeled as (25, 3). Note the relabeling of the predecessor node. Nodes 5 and 6 were previously unlabeled. In Figure 10–26 these nodes are assigned temporary labels. Given the nodes having temporary labels (2, 4, 5, and 6), node 2 has the smallest distance label. Applying step 3, node 2 becomes permanently labeled in Figure 10–27.

Repeating step 3, the only node that can be connected directly with node 2 is node 5. As can be seen in Table 10–12, the newly calculated distance to node 5 equals 33, which exceeds the temporary distance label for that node. Thus, the temporary label for node 5 is unchanged. Applying step 2, node 5 has the minimum distance label for all temporarily labeled nodes. Thus, it becomes permanently labeled in Figure 10–28.

TABLE 10–12 Third Iteration

Temporarily Labeled Node (j)	Node 2 Distance Label	Distance From Node 2 to Node j	Calculated Total	Previous Distance Label	New Distance Label
4	22	No connection	–	25	25
5	22	+ 11 =	33	24	24*
6	22	No connection	–	31	31

FIGURE 10–28 Third Iteration

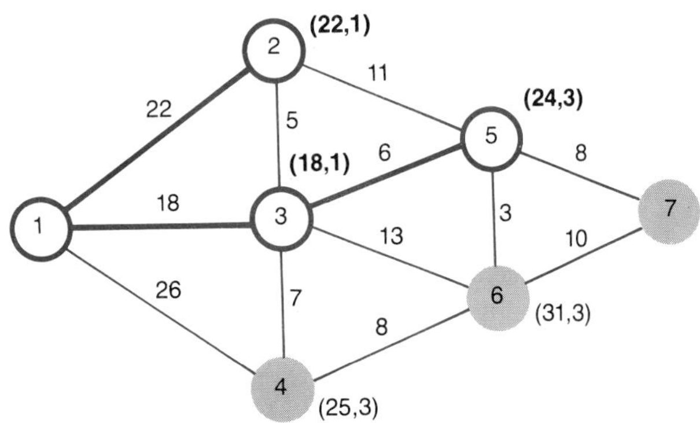

Tables 10–13 through 10–15 and Figures 10–29 through 10–31 summarize the remaining iterations of the labeling procedure for this problem. The permanent labels in Figure 10–31 represent the shortest distances from the origin to each node. Notice that all nodes except the origin have labels. In order to state the specific route that results in the shortest distance to any node, we must use the *backtracking procedure.*

TABLE 10–13 Fourth Iteration

Temporarily Labeled Node (*j*)	Node 5 Distance Label	Distance From Node 5 to Node *j*	Calculated Total	Previous Distance Label	New Distance Label
4	24	No connection	–	25	25*
6	24	+ 3 =	27	31	27
7	24	+ 8 =	32	no label	32

FIGURE 10–29 Fourth Iteration

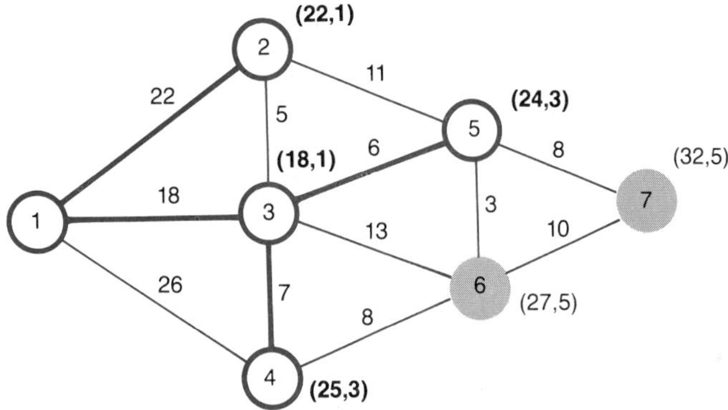

TABLE 10–14 Fifth Iteration

Temporarily Labeled Node (*j*)	Node 4 Distance Label	Distance From Node 4 to Node *j*	Calculated Total	Previous Distance Label	New Distance Label
6	25	+ 8 =	33	27	27*
7	25	No connection	–	32	32

FIGURE 10–30 Fifth Iteration

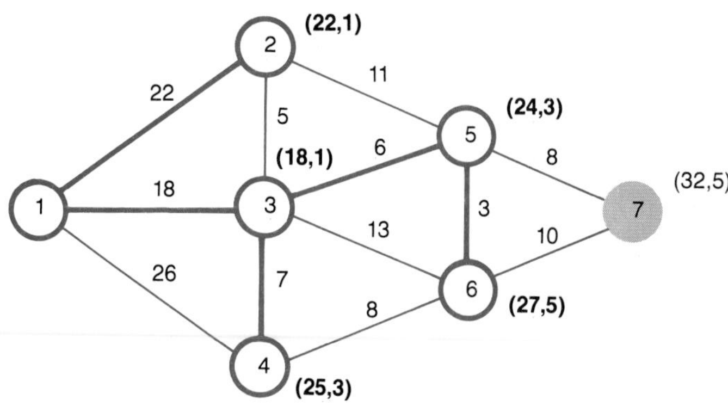

TABLE 10–15 Sixth Iteration

Temporarily Labeled Node (*j*)	Node 6 Distance Label	Distance From Node 6 to Node *j*	Calculated Total	Previous Distance Label	New Distance Label
7	27	+ 10 =	37	32	32*

FIGURE 10–31 Sixth Iteration

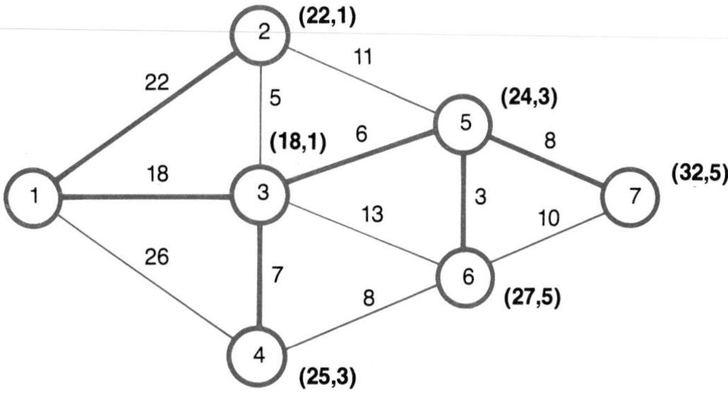

Backtracking Procedure. To find the shortest route from the origin to any node, identify the predecessor part of its permanent label, and move backward to that node. Identify the predecessor part of the permanent label for this node, and move backward to that node. Continue in this manner until arriving at the origin. The sequence of nodes traced forms the shortest route from the origin to the node in question.

Figure 10–32 indicates the shortest route between the origin and node 7. This route was identified by moving from node 7 to node 5. The predecessor label at node 5 indicates movement from node 5 to node 3. The predecessor label at node 3 indicates a final movement backward to the origin.

FIGURE 10–32 Shortest Route to Node 7

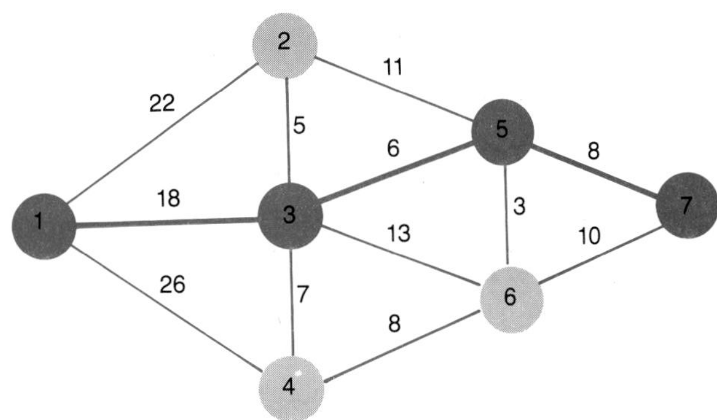

Computer-Based Analysis

Figure 10–33 illustrates the output for our example from a computer package that uses the shortest-route algorithm. The software module **SHOR1** is included in the Erikson and Hall software package. As with the minimal spanning tree module SPNT1, the output is divided into two parts. The first part summarizes the data input to the computer package. The second part summarizes the results of the analysis—the shortest route from node 1 to node 7. Included arcs, their lengths, and the shortest distance are shown.

When solving network problems manually using the shortest-route algorithm, the labeling procedure enables you to determine the shortest route from the origin (node 1) to any other node in the network. The software module SHOR1 determines the shortest route from the origin (node 1) to the highest-numbered node in the network.

FOLLOW-UP EXERCISES

19. Referring to Figure 10–31, specify the shortest routes and their distances from node 1 to nodes 4, 5, and 6.
20. ***Equipment replacement.*** Determine the solution to the equipment replacement problem formulated in Example 10.3. Verbalize the recommended optimal policy.
21. ***Agricultural Irrigation.*** Refer to the network diagram in Figure 10–18. Determine the shortest routes from node 1 to nodes 4 through 10. Specify the routes and their distances.
22. Given the network diagram in Figure 10–34, determine the shortest routes from node 1 to all other nodes in the network.
23. ***Automobile Purchase/Replacement.*** Solve the automobile problem stated in Exercise 10.

Maximal Flow Algorithm

The last network algorithm we will discuss is the maximal flow algorithm. Recall that the maximal flow problem is concerned with determining the maximal flow that can pass from one input node, or source, through a network to one output node, or sink, in a specified period.

FIGURE 10–33 SHOR1 Output

```
* * * * * * * * * * * * * * * * * * * * *
*                                       *
*          SHORTEST ROUTE               *
*             ANALYSIS                  *
*                                       *
* * * * * * * * * * * * * * * * * * * * *

**   INFORMATION ENTERED  **

NUMBER OF NODES  7
NUMBER OF LINKS  12
TYPE:  SYMMETRIC
```

LINK	START NODE	END NODE	DISTANCE	REVERSE DISTANCE
1	1	2	22	22
2	1	3	18	18
3	1	4	26	26
4	2	3	5	5
5	3	4	7	7
6	2	5	11	11
7	3	5	6	6
8	3	6	13	13
9	4	6	8	8
10	5	6	3	3
11	5	7	8	8
12	6	7	10	10

** RESULTS **

START NODE	END NODE	DISTANCE
1	3	18
3	5	6
5	7	8

TOTAL DISTANCE 32

** END OF ANALYSIS **

Before we present a special algorithm for solving this type of problem, we will state three assumptions: First, except for source and sink nodes, whatever flows into a node must flow out of the node. Second, when allocating flow across a path from the source to the sink, the maximum amount that can flow equals the minimum capacity of any arc lying on the path. Finally, as we search for the optimal allocations of flow along various paths in a network, we must provide a mechanism for making

FIGURE 10–34

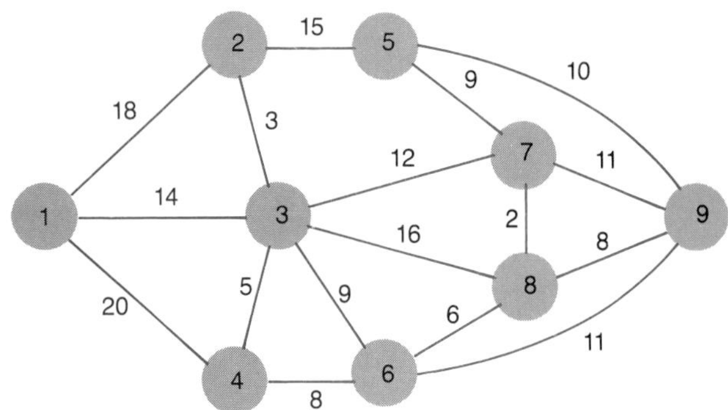

allocations and adjusting or changing those allocations at a later stage in the search if they are not optimal. The mechanism we will employ involves a two-step process. When making an allocation f along a path, (1) we reduce the flow capacities in the direction of flow for all arcs on the path by an amount equal to f, and (2) we increase the flow capacity in the opposite direction for all arcs on the path by f. To illustrate, suppose in Figure 10–35 that five units of flow are allocated along arc 6–8. The flow capacity is reduced by five units along the arc and increased in the reverse direction by five units.

FIGURE 10–35

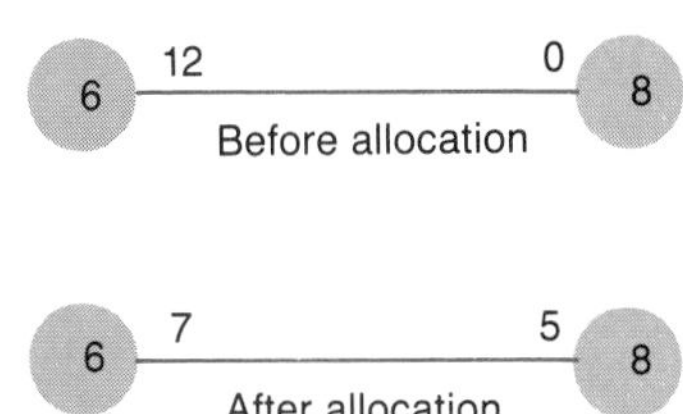

The following algorithm finds the solution to the maximal flow problem, where f_{ij} is the flow capacity from node i to node j.

Maximal Flow Algorithm

Step 1: Identify *any* path from the origin to the sink having *positive* flow capacities, f_{ij}, (in the direction of the path) along each arc of the path. If no such path exists, then the optimal solution has been found.

Step 2: Determine the *minimum* positive flow capacity between any two nodes on the path, f^*_{ij}. Increase the flow along the path by f^*_{ij}.

Step 3: Compensate for the flow assignment in Step 2 by *reducing* the flow capacities in the direction of the flow assignment by f^*_{ij} for all nodes on the path. *Increase* the respective capacities in the reverse direction along the path by the same quantity.

Step 4: Repeat steps 1 through 3 until an optimal solution has been identified.

▶ Example 10.8 Postal Routing—Revisited

Let us illustrate the algorithm by returning to the Postal Routing problem (Example 10.4). Figure 10–36 repeats the network diagram for this problem. Referring to Figure 10–36, we first identify path 1–2′–3 (shipment by air from city 1 to city 3) as allowing positive flows through each arc on the path. The flow capacity for arc 1–2′ ($f_{12'} = 16$) is compared with that for arc 2′–3 ($f_{2'3} = 23$), which gives $f^*_{12'} = 16$. Thus 16 (10,000s) pieces of mail are allocated along this path. Flow capacities for all nodes on the path are adjusted according to step 3, as indicated in Figure 10–37*a*.

FIGURE 10–36 Network for Postal Routing Problem

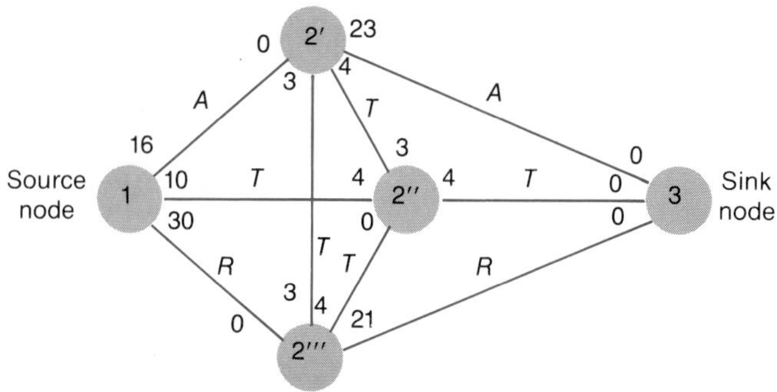

Arbitrarily, we next identify flow potential along the path 1–2‴–3. Comparing $f_{12'''} = 30$ to $f_{2'''3} = 21$, we see that 21 (10,000s) pieces of mail can be allocated to move by rail from city 1 to city 3. Flow capacities for all nodes on this path are adjusted as indicated in Figure 10–37*b*.

From Figure 10–37*b*, flow potential is identified for the path 1–2″–3. You should verify that 4 (10,000s) pieces of mail may be delivered by truck from city 1 to city 3. The resulting network is shown in Figure 10–37*c*.

At this stage, single mode delivery alternatives have been exhausted. There are, however, other possibilities for shipping mail from city 1 to city 3. For example, mail can go by rail to city 2, then by truck to the air terminal in city 2, then by air to city 3. How many paths are possible in this network?

You should verify that the maximal flow between cities 1 and 3 is 470,000 pieces of mail per day. Table 10–16 summarizes the allocations.

TABLE 10–16

Allocation	Path	Quantity
1	1–2′–3	16
2	1–2‴–3	21
3	1–2″–3	4
4	1–2″–2′–3	3
5	1–2‴–2′–3	3
		47

FIGURE 10–37 Intermediate Networks for Example 10.8

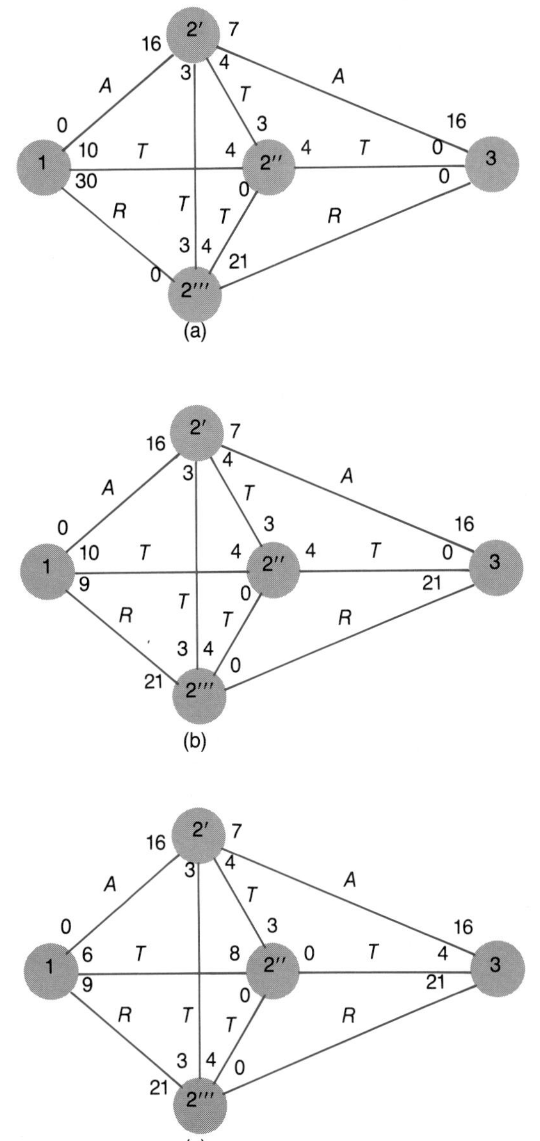

Computer-Based Analysis

Figure 10–38 presents the computer output from solving the postal routing example using the special maximal flow algorithm software module **MAXF1**. This is also from the Erickson and Hall management science software package. As with the SPNT1 and SHOR1 modules, the output is divided into sections that summarize the information entered about the network and the results of the maximal flow analysis.

FIGURE 10–38 **MAXF1** Output

```
* * * * * * * * * * * * * * * * * * *
*                                   *
*         MAXIMUM FLOW              *
*           ANALYSIS                *
*                                   *
* * * * * * * * * * * * * * * * * * *

**  INFORMATION ENTERED **

NUMBER OF NODES:  5
NUMBER OF LINKS:  12
```

LINK	START NODE	END NODE	FLOW
1	1	2	16
2	1	3	10
3	3	1	4
4	1	4	30
5	2	4	3
6	4	2	3
7	4	3	4
8	2	3	4
9	3	2	3
10	2	5	23
11	3	5	4
12	4	5	21

** RESULTS **

OPTIMAL FLOW OVER ALL PATHS FROM
NODE 1 TO NODE 5:

FLOW	NODES THAT DEFINE EACH PATH			
16	1	2	5	
3	1	3	2	5
3	1	4	2	5
4	1	3	5	
21	1	4	5	

OPTIMAL FLOW OVER EACH LINK:

START NODE	END NODE	FLOW
1	2	16
1	3	7
1	4	24
2	5	22
3	2	3
3	5	4
4	2	3
4	5	21

MAXIMUM TOTAL NETWORK FLOW: 47

** END OF ANALYSIS **

Legend: Node 2 = Node 2′; Node 3 = Node 2″; Node 4 = Node 2‴; Node 5 = Node 3.

The results show the optimal allocations along different paths and the optimal flow over each arc of the network. It is important to note that the resulting optimal flows shown in Figure 10–38 are not necessarily unique.

FOLLOW-UP EXERCISES

24. Draw the intermediate networks associated with allocations 4 and 5 in Table 10–16. What in the delivery network specifically restricts the shipment of more mail? What alternatives are available to increase the flow? Are there other criteria the postal authorities should be considering in this problem?
25. Resolve Example 10.8 by making the initial allocation of four units along the path 1–2′–2″–3. Do you get the same solution? Draw the final network diagram for both this solution and the solution in Example 10.8. Compare the final flow capacities for the two diagrams. Are they the same?
26. In Exercise 25 there is an initial flow of four units along arc 2′–2″. At a later step in the solution process a flow of seven units occurs in the reverse direction from 2″–2′. When a reverse flow occurs along an arc, one can think of this as canceling the previous equivalent flow along the arc. The net effects of the seven-unit allocation are:
    (1) The original flow of four units along path 1–2′–2″–3 is negated, and these four units are "reallocated" to path 1–2′–3.
    (2) Four of the seven units of flow from 1–2″ are allocated along the path 1–2″–3.
    (3) The remaining three of the seven units are allocated along the path 1–2″–2′–3.

    Verify a similar reversal of flow along arc 2‴–2′ if the *initial* allocation in Exercise 25 is a three-unit flow along the path 1–2′–2‴–3. Verify that the solution in this instance is the same as that for Exercise 25.
27. Find the maximal flow for the network in Exercise 11. What are the allocations across each arc?

10.4 ASSESSMENT

Network modeling is one of the more widely applied modeling techniques within the area of mathematical programming. Reasons for this include the flexibility of network modeling techniques and advances in the theory and implementation of network solution methods. This chapter has presented several classic network models and some selected network algorithms. These network algorithms exploit the special structure of the models.

Aside from the classic network problems, great potential exists for solving a wide diversity of problems that can be formulated (in part, or entirely) as network models. The **netform**[4] (*network formulation*) modeling technique has been successfully applied in a variety of areas. "Successfully applied" means that problems have been modeled as networks and that network solution methods have generated results efficiently. These experiences have occurred for problems too large or too complex to be solved by more traditional methods.

One area in which the netform approach has realized significant returns is discrete optimization problems, such as scheduling, production, distribution, and inventory.

[4]See Randy Glover and Paul Talmey, "Modeling and Solution of Practical Management Problems through Netforms," *Omega,* 6, no. 4 (1978), pp. 305–11.

Problems have been solved much more efficiently than by other mathematical programming methods. In many instances, the network approach has yielded solutions where other methods have failed. Inventory problems have also benefited from network approaches. Whereas traditional approaches tend to provide different models for different situations (often compromising reality by overly restrictive assumptions), network formulations of these problems tend to be more generalized, allowing for incorporation of a variety of assumptions within the same model. Single models embracing a diversity of assumptions are intuitively more satisfying than a collection of models and formulas used by classic approaches.

Finally, an appealing attribute of network modeling techniques is the graphical or pictorial representation. This attribute enhances the understanding of both the user and designer. The graphical representation conveys much more meaning to the user than an algebraic model. It also assists the designer in uncovering and understanding interrelationships that might otherwise be difficult to grasp.

In conclusion, network modeling is a powerful addition to the arsenal of tools possessed by OR/MS practitioners. Over time it should prove to be one of the more adaptable and efficient OR/MS methods as we know them today.

SELECTED APPLICATION REVIEW

DECISION SUPPORT SYSTEMS: PRODUCT PLANNING AT CITGO

Citgo Petroleum Corporation is one of the largest industrial companies in the United States, having more than $4 billion in sales during 1986. Jointly owned by The Southland Corporation and Petroleos De Venezuela, Citgo is the largest independent refiner and marketer of petroleum products in the United States. Citgo has a distribution network of pipelines, tankers, and barges covering the eastern two thirds of the United States. With Southland owning 7-Eleven stores, Citgo markets to all of the 48 contiguous states. The distribution network includes five distribution centers, 36 owned or leased product storage terminals, and more than 350 exchange terminal agreements that have been negotiated with other petroleum marketers.

The Problem

During the 1970s and early 1980s the price of crude oil increased dramatically, as did short-term interest rates. The cost of crude increased to more than $31 per barrel, and short-term interest rates went over 20 percent, causing some state usury laws to be reexamined. The result was that the cost of financing working capital (e.g., crude and product inventories, trade and credit card receivables) increased thirtyfold. It became very clear that Citgo's working capital had to be tightly controlled if Citgo was to remain profitable.

The Response

To respond to this need, a Supply, Distribution, and Marketing Modeling System was developed for Citgo. This network optimization-based decision support system is believed to be the first of its type for major downstream petroleum refiners. Based on an 11-week planning horizon, the system is used to assist management in making weekly decisions concerning refinery run levels, where to buy products and what prices to pay, where to sell products and what prices to charge, how much product inventory to hold at each location, how much product to distribute by each mode of transportation, and how to schedule the receipt and delivery of products exchanged in some manner with other refiners. The system is used not only by top management, but also by operations personnel.

(continued)

The primary users fall into four groups. *Product managers* use the system's what-if capabilities to identify strategy alternatives to planned and forecasted operations. *Pricing managers* use the system to set ranges for terminal prices of each product. In addition, they set prices and recommended quantities to be sold in bulk for the purpose of reducing excess inventory levels.

Product traders are responsible for product purchases and sales on the spot markets, as well as exchanges occurring with other refiners. These individuals use the system to determine which side of the trading board Citgo should be on for each product. They also utilize the system's what-if capabilities to determine the sensitivity of spot prices to the required purchase or sales volumes as prices fluctuate during a week. The *budget manager* represents the last category of major user of the system. This person uses the system to generate the selected components of the monthly and quarterly budgets.

The Model

At the core of the system is a collection of network optimization models, one for each product. Each model is a minimum cost flow (or maximum profit flow) transshipment model. The constraints are product flow balance conditions for each terminal, distribution center, transportation mode, exchange contract, and purchase, sale, or trade agreement. For each product, the model consists of approximately 3,000 nodes and 15,000 arcs. Solution times using specialized network algorithms are modest.

Benefits

The major tangible benefit from using the system was a significant reduction in product inventories with no drop in service levels. Given the dramatic increase in the sales of automotive gasoline since Citgo was purchased by Southland, and compared with former inventory management policies, the new system is estimated to have reduced gasoline inventories by 2.9 million barrels, or $91.3 million during the first six months of 1985. Combining this with the reductions for distillates (number 2 fuel oil and diesel fuel), total reductions in inventory were valued at $116.5 million. This equates to an approximate $14 million reduction in interest expenses, even at the new and lower interest rates.

A second tangible benefit related to improved operational decision making. This was evidenced by lower purchase prices for both spot and traded products, higher profits on terminal sales, and improved planning and profitability on bulk sales of excess inventories. Analysts estimated conservatively that these improvements resulted in savings of $2.5 million per year.

(continued)

Among many indirect benefits cited, a major intangible benefit was the establishment of a corporate database that provides current, online information for decision support.

Logo reproduced courtesy of CITGO Petroleum Corporation.

SOURCE: Darwin Klingman, Nancy Phillips, David Steiger, Ross Wirth, and Warren Young, "The Challenges and Success Factors in Implementing an Integrated Products Planning System for Citgo," *Interfaces*, May–June 1986, pp. 1–19.

PERSONNEL SCHEDULING

United Airlines has developed a highly successful personnel scheduling system for planning shift schedules at its reservations offices and airports. United's Station Manpower Planning System (SMPS) was implemented in 1983 and used to determine work schedules for approximately 4,000 reservation sales representatives and support personnel. This computer-based system utilizes linear programming, integer programming, and network optimization methods to determine schedules. Preliminary direct labor cost savings amounted to more than $6 million per year. Management at United believes that intangible benefits may even outweigh these significant tangible benefits. One of the most notable intangibles has been the improvement in customer service. United hopes to expand the use of the system to schedule as many as 10,000 of its employees, or approximately 20 percent of the total labor force.

SOURCE: Thomas J. Holloran and Judson E. Byrn, "United Airlines Station Manpower Planning System," *Interfaces*, January–February 1986, pp. 39–50. This was an award-winning article in reporting on the application of OR/MS.

OFFICE LOCATION

Significant tax revenues are generated for the state of Texas by out-of-state taxpayers (primarily corporations). In order to improve the tax collection process, a warehouse location-allocation network model was adapted to de-

(continued)

termine the best locations for out-of-state audit offices. Out-of-state audits were previously conducted by auditors based in Austin who traveled to out-of-state locations. This system was characterized by large travel expenses and high turnover of auditors. The network model recommended cities in which offices were to be located, the states to be serviced by the offices, and the number of auditors to assign to each office. The objective was to minimize the cost of operating the offices plus travel expenses of auditors. Implementation resulted in creation of six out-of-state offices.

SOURCE: James A. Fitzsimmons and Lou Austin Allen, "A Warehouse Location Model Helps Texas Comptroller Select Out-of-State Audit Offices," *Interfaces*, October 1983, pp. 40–46.

PRODUCTION, DISTRIBUTION, AND INVENTORY (PDI) PLANNING

Agrico Chemical Company is one of the nation's largest chemical fertilizer companies. Because of Agrico's inability to respond adequately to certain market behaviors in the mid 1970s, distribution costs escalated, and profit margins eroded. To counter this trend, Agrico developed a sophisticated network-based production, distribution, and inventory (PDI) planning system. The model had capabilities for both long-run and short-run planning. The long-run planning model addressed issues related to the sizing and configuration of the distribution system. The short-run model focused on production and distribution decisions for an existing distribution system configuration. Typical short-run models involved 6,000 equations and 35,000 variables. Long-run models involved 6,250 equations and 23,000 variables. The models proved highly effective and resulted in approximately $18 million savings during the first three years of operation and projected savings of $25 million for the next two years.

SOURCE: F. Glover, G. Jones, D. Karney, D. Klingman, and J. Mote, "An Integrated Production, Distribution, and Inventory Planning System," *Interfaces*, November 1979, pp. 21–35.

SELECTED REFERENCES

Ford, L. R., Jr., and D. R. Fulkerson. *Flows in Networks*. Princeton, N.J.: Princeton University Press, 1962.

Frank, H., and I. T. Frisch. *Communication, Transmission, and Transportation Networks.* Reading, Mass.: Addison-Wesley Publishing, 1971.

Glover, F.; J. Hultz; and D. Klingman. "Improved Computer-Based Planning Techniques, Part I." *Interfaces* 8 (1978), pp. 16–25.

________. "Improved Computer-Based Planning Techniques, Part II." *Interfaces* 9 (1978), pp. 12–20.

Gould, F. J., and G. D. Eppen. *Introductory Management Science.* Englewood Cliffs, N.J.: Prentice-Hall, 1984.

Kennington, Jeff L., and Richard V. Helgason. *Algorithms for Network Programming.* New York: John Wiley & Sons, 1980.

Phillips, Don T., and Alberto Garcia-Diaz. *Fundamentals of Network Analysis.* Englewood Cliffs, N.J.: Prentice-Hall, 1981.

Srinivasan, Venkat, and Yong H. Kim. "Payments in International Cash Management: A Network Optimization Approach." *Journal of International Business Studies,* Summer 1986, pp. 1–20.

ADDITIONAL EXERCISES

28. In the following LP formulation x_{ij} equals the number of units shipped from node i to node j.

Minimize

$$z = 12x_{14} + 15x_{16} + 11x_{17} + 14x_{25} + 12x_{27} + 10x_{34} + 13x_{35} + 9x_{36} + 10x_{37}$$

subject to

$$\begin{aligned} x_{14} + x_{16} + x_{17} \qquad &= 10{,}000 \\ x_{25} + x_{27} &= 20{,}000 \\ x_{34} + x_{35} + x_{36} + x_{37} &= 15{,}000 \\ -x_{14} - x_{34} &= -8{,}000 \\ -x_{25} - x_{35} &= -16{,}000 \\ -x_{16} - x_{36} &= -10{,}000 \\ -x_{17} - x_{27} - x_{37} &= -11{,}000 \\ x_{ij} &\geq 0 \qquad \text{for all } i, j \end{aligned}$$

a. Draw the network diagram that corresponds to this LP formulation.
b. What type of network problem is represented by this formulation?

29. In the following LP formulation, x_{ij} equals the number of units shipped from node i to node j.

Minimize

$$\begin{aligned} z = {} & 10x_{13} + 15x_{14} + 18x_{24} + 20x_{25} + 8x_{34} + 12x_{36} + 14x_{46} + 16x_{54} \\ & + 18x_{57} + 3x_{76} \end{aligned}$$

subject to

$$
\begin{aligned}
x_{13} + x_{14} &= 25{,}000 \\
x_{24} + x_{25} &= 25{,}000 \\
-x_{13} + x_{36} + x_{34} &= 0 \\
-x_{14} - x_{34} - x_{24} - x_{54} + x_{46} &= 0 \\
-x_{25} + x_{54} + x_{57} &= 0 \\
-x_{57} + x_{76} &= -10{,}000 \\
-x_{36} - x_{46} - x_{76} &= -40{,}000 \\
x_{ij} &\geq 0 \quad \text{for all } i, j
\end{aligned}
$$

a. Draw the network diagram that corresponds to the LP formulation.
b. What type of network problem is represented by this model?

30. ***Production Planning/Back Ordering.*** A company has assigned a contract to provide certain quantities of a product for each of the next three months. The company can produce units using regular production capacity or using overtime capacity. Units can be produced during the period in which they are demanded. Units can also be produced during one period and used to satisfy demand for a previous period. These *back-ordered* units have a penalty cost of $5 per unit per period since the original demand. For example, a unit produced in period 3 to satisfy demand for period 1 incurs a penalty of (2 × $5 =) $10 because of the two-period delay in satisfying the demand. Units may be produced in one period and held in inventory to satisfy demand in a future period. An inventory carrying cost of $2.50 per unit per period is incurred when units are held in inventory.

Table 10–17 summarizes the regular time and overtime production capacities and production costs per unit for each period as well as the demand for each period.

TABLE 10–17

Period	Regular Production Capacity	Unit Cost	Overtime Production Capacity	Unit Cost	Demand
1	10,000	$20.00	2,000	$30.00	10,000
2	7,500	15.00	1,000	23.00	12,000
3	12,500	25.00	2,000	36.00	13,000

a. Draw the network diagram that corresponds to this problem.
b. How would the diagram be modified if back ordering were not permitted?

31. ***Materials Handling.*** A company is planning an automated two-way conveyor system to move materials between areas within its production facility. Table 10–18 indicates the feasible connections between the 15 areas and the cost of installing a conveyor linkage between two areas (in $10,000s).

a. Draw the network diagram corresponding to this problem.
b. If the objective is to minimize total installation costs, determine the set of interconnections that will allow parts to be carried from any area to any other area in the production facility.

TABLE 10–18 Installation Cost ($10,000s)

From Area	To Area 1	2	3	4	5	6	7	8	9	10	11	12	13	14	15
1	—	5	4	—	10	—	8	—	—	—	—	—	—	—	—
2		—	—	7.5	6	—	—	—	—	—	—	—	—	—	—
3			—	—	6	8	—	—	—	—	—	—	—	—	—
4				—	8	—	—	7	4.5	—	—	—	—	—	—
5					—	7.5	8.5	6.5	—	—	—	—	—	—	—
6						—	6	—	—	—	—	—	—	—	—
7							—	7.5	—	—	5	10	—	—	—
8								—	6	7	5	—	—	—	—
9									—	8	—	—	5	—	—
10										—	7	—	8	6	—
11											—	6	—	9	7
12												—	—	—	12
13													—	10	—
14														—	8
15															—

32. In the previous exercise, assume that Table 10–18 shows *existing* conveyor linkages between areas. Also assume that the values in the table represent the time (in minutes) required to move an item from one area to another. If area 1 is the central receiving department, determine the route from area 1 *to each* of the other 14 areas that minimizes distribution time.

33. ***Physical Plant Management.*** A new community college is being established, and the director of physical plant is planning the sewer system that will be used to service the 10 buildings to be constructed on the campus. The director wants to minimize the amount of sewer pipe necessary to link all of the buildings.

    In Figure 10–39 the nodes represent the building locations and the arcs represent the pairs of buildings that can be feasibly linked. The distances (in yards) between buildings are denoted on the arcs. Determine the minimum amount of sewer pipe needed to connect all buildings.

FIGURE 10–39

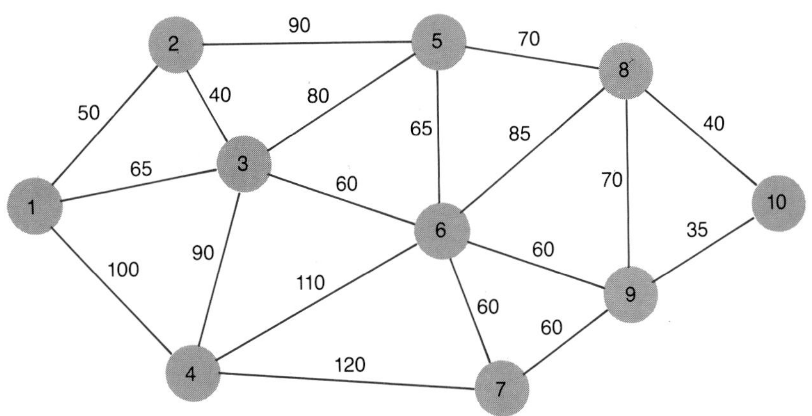

34. ***Sprinkler System.*** Figure 10–40 is a network diagram that illustrates the relative locations of 24 desired sprinkler outlets in a four-story warehouse. The arcs connecting the nodes represent the possible sprinkler connections, and the labels on each arc represent the distance separating each sprinkler (in feet). Determine the connections that will provide water to each sprinkler while minimizing the total number of feet of pipe required. What is the minimum amount of pipe?

FIGURE 10–40

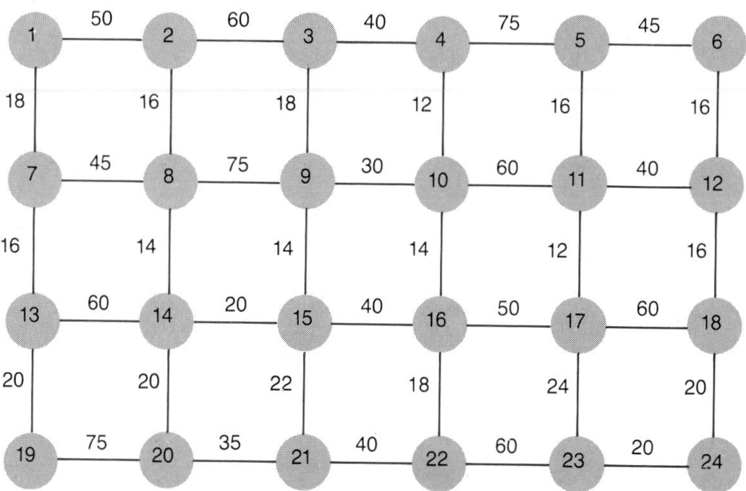

35. Given the network diagram in Figure 10–41, determine the shortest route from node 1 to all other nodes in the network.

FIGURE 10–41

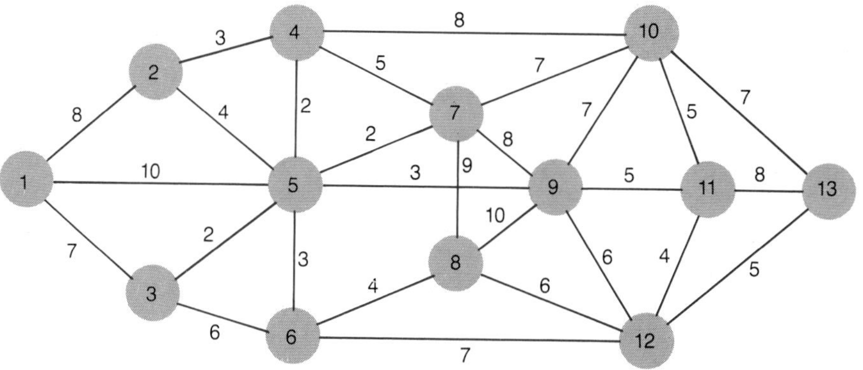

36. ***Air Freight.*** Figure 10–42 is a network diagram showing the relative locations of a major metropolitan airport and 13 distribution warehouses used by an air freight company. The arcs in the network represent possible linkages between the various distribution warehouses and the airport. The arc labels are distances stated in miles. Determine the shortest route from the airport to *each* of the distribution warehouses.

FIGURE 10–42

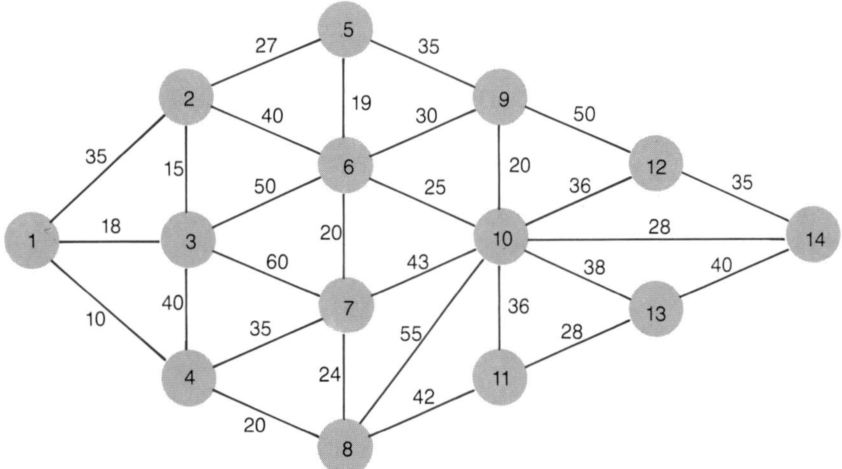

37. Determine the maximal flow from node 1 to node 11 for the network in Figure 10–43. Indicate the flow for each arc in the network.

FIGURE 10–43

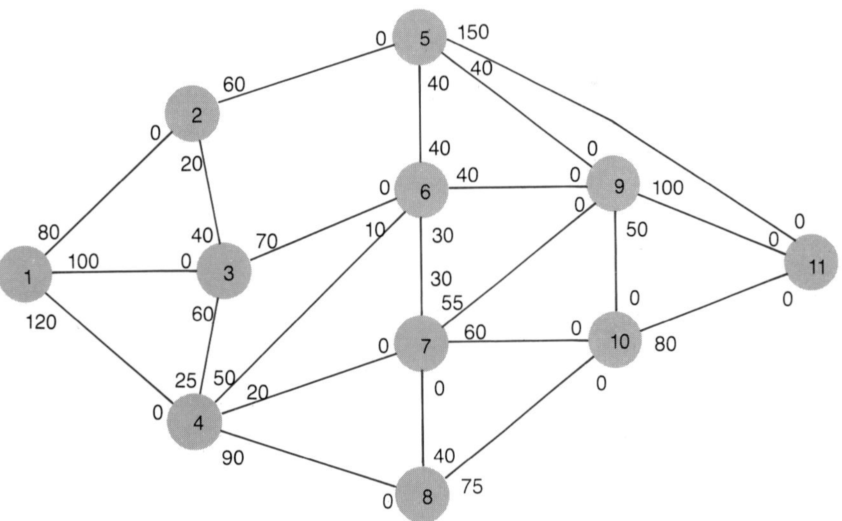

38. ***Ski Resort Management.*** A Colorado ski resort is planning for the coming season. Management wishes to determine the maximum number of skiers who can be transported to the top of the mountain with existing lift facilities. Figure 10–44 indicates the network of lifts and flow capacities (in 100s of skiers per hour).
    a. Determine the maximal flow per hour to the top of the mountain.
    b. What are the constraining arcs for this network?
    c. How much flow should go through each lift facility?

FIGURE 10–44

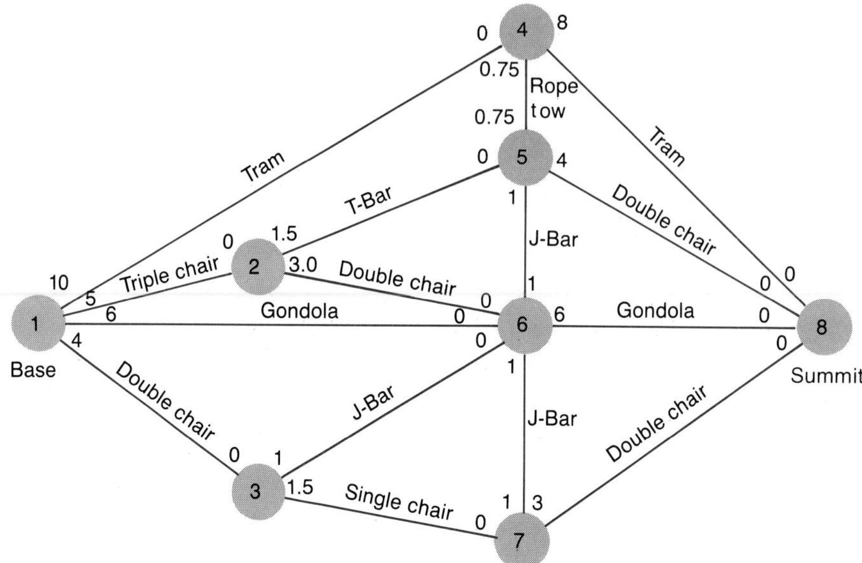

39. ***Highway System Capacity.*** A European city has been named host for the upcoming summer Olympics. Municipal officials are concerned about the ability of the existing highway network to handle the volume of vehicles converging on Olympic Village. All vehicular traffic must cross a river via one bridge and then choose different routes (as illustrated in Figure 10–45) to the village.

FIGURE 10–45

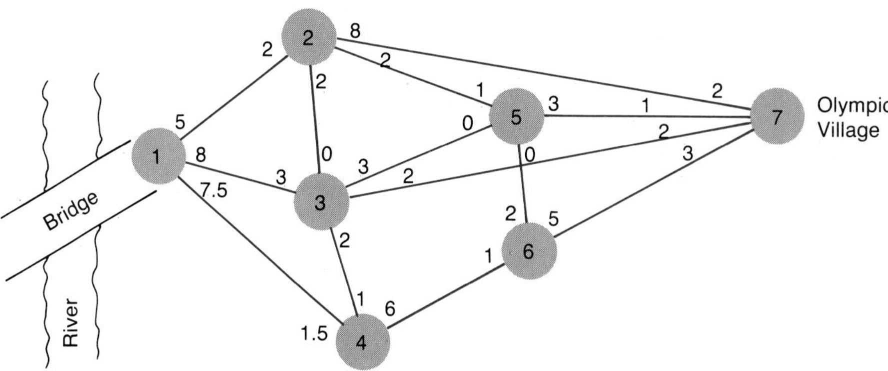

The network indicates flow capacities along each arc (in 1,000s of vehicles per hour). What would a capacity of zero indicate?

a. Determine the maximum number of vehicles per hour that can reach the Olympic Village via the current network of highways.

b. How much flow should go over each road to achieve this maximum?

c. What highways are most restrictive to the flow of traffic?

40. ***Highway Planning.*** Suppose the network in the preceding exercise represents the layout for a proposed Olympic Village. Assume that no roads have been constructed and that each node represents a spectator interest area (e.g., stadium, or swimming complex). The Board of Olympic Governors wants to establish a road network that links each area. However, budget overruns on other construction activities require that the total length of roads be minimized. Given that d_{ij} equals the distance in miles between nodes i and j, the accompanying table enumerates distances for road links under consideration (links may not be included because of such natural barriers as rivers or because of distances that are obviously too long).
   a. Draw the network, labeling each node and the length of each arc.
   b. Determine the plan that minimizes the total length of roads necessary to span all spectator areas. If road construction costs $10,000 per mile, then how much funds should be allocated for the highway plan?

i–j	$d_{i,j}$	i–j	$d_{i,j}$
1–2	2.5	3–5	2.2
1–3	2.2	3–6	2.4
1–4	2.7	4–5	2.8
2–3	1.9	4–6	2.5
2–5	2.4	5–6	1.0
2–7	4.2	5–7	2.6
2–6	3.1	6–7	2.4
3–4	1.8		

41. Determine the maximal flow from node 1 to node 13 for the network in Figure 10–46. Indicate the flow for each arc in the network.

FIGURE 10–46

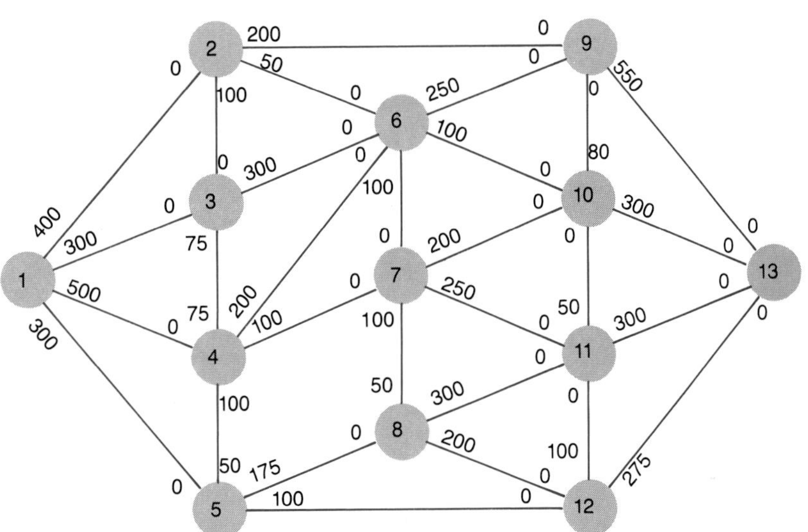

11

Project Scheduling

Chapter Outline

A project consists of the planning, design, and implementation of a set of tasks leading to the accomplishment of a goal, such as a completed house or a person on the moon. Projects often involve special teams and perhaps a matrix form of organization. In a matrix, the team members are responsible to their own department leader as well as to their project leader, who manages across departments. Scheduling the team members' time can be tricky, since each member may be dedicated to other projects as well. The coordination and scheduling of projects has our attention in this chapter.

An aid to implementing change in many organizations is to clearly delineate projects; to determine the detailed activities necessary to complete a particular project; to estimate the resources and times required for each activity; to plan start and completion times for each activity; to prepare a schedule of resource needs (especially labor) over the life of the proposed project; to commit the resources (from within the organization and outside it) to specified periods; and to monitor and control time and cost performance for the project.

This chapter presents some models well-suited to the design and implementation of major projects. Variations of these models have been successfully applied in the construction of large buildings or public works, in military research and development programs, and in the development and introduction of new products. We also deal with some important organizational issues for users of project management models, and we include an appendix on the use of mathematical programming for solving these models.

11.1 PLANNING WITH THE BASIC MODEL

Prior to the 1950s, organizations used *Gantt charts* for scheduling projects. A Gantt chart is a bar chart that simply lists the activities of the project down the left-hand side of the calendar with coded bars across the days or weeks to show when the activity will be (has been or is being) worked on. Most of us use Gantt charts to schedule our own class times and meeting times in our weekly calendars.

Not able to manage the Polaris submarine project with Gantt charts, the Navy and the Booz Allen consulting firm jointly developed a network approach called **Program Evaluation and Review Technique (PERT).** At the same time in the 1950s, Du Pont developed a very similar approach called **Critical Path Method (CPM).** These methods became very popular even though they were also criticized. One story is that the Navy Department had a visual display with colored lights for their Polaris PERT network, that the network was used for public relations purposes, and that the actual application was somewhat superficial. Whether the story is true or not, we find that the applications are numerous and that PERT/CPM software is readily available today for microcomputers. We will discuss both of these points at the end of this chapter.

Although PERT and CPM were developed concurrently and independently, they were surprisingly similar. Aside from minor differences in terminology, notation, and structure, only two major differences usefully distinguished the two methods. First, PERT acknowledged uncertainty in the times to complete activities, and CPM did not. Second, PERT restricted its attention to the time variable, whereas CPM included time-cost trade-offs. For our purposes we will not differentiate between the two methods, as subsequent developments have blurred the distinctions between them. The most straightforward way to understand project management models is by example.

▶ Example 11.1 Choo-Chew Restaurants, Inc., or CCRI

A franchised restaurant operation, Choo-Chew Restaurants, Inc. (CCRI) grew from a highly successful first restaurant made from two turn-of-the-century railroad cars. Similar restaurants followed, and the decor, menus, and operating procedures were standardized.

One critical aspect of the franchise arrangement is design and construction of the restaurant itself. CCRI has broken this job into the set of tasks or activities presented as Table 11–1.

TABLE 11–1 Restaurant Design and Construction Activities

	Activity	Preceding Activities	Estimated Duration (days)
A	Purchase and renovate coaches	—	10
B	Purchase restaurant equipment	—	3
C	Hire personnel	—	1
D	Select and purchase site	—	2
E	Obtain necessary permits and licenses	*D*	7
F	Site preparation	*E*	3
G	Move coaches onto site	*A, F*	5
H	Install utilities	*G*	4
I	Install equipment	*B, H*	4
J	Decorate	*B, H*	3
K	Stock bar and kitchen	*I, J*	6
L	Advertise and promote	*G*	3
M	Train personnel	*C, I*	4
N	Undertake Pilot Operation	*K, L*	7

Precedence Requirements

As noted in Table 11–1, the project can begin with purchases of the coaches, the restaurant equipment, and the site. The purchases are divided into three activities because they involve different procedures and vendors. At the same time, we can undertake the hiring process for the required personnel. The other activities should be self-explanatory.

In the second column of the table, **precedence requirements** are presented. That is, it is necessary to accomplish activity D (select and purchase site) before starting activity E (obtain necessary permits and licenses). Similarly, we need to obtain the permits associated with activity E before activity F (site preparation) can be started. Activity G (move coaches onto site) requires the completion of both site preparation (F) and purchase-renovation of coaches (A). Note, however, that activities I (install equipment) and J (decorate) have the same sequential requirements; this means that these two activities can proceed simultaneously. Do the other precedence relationships make sense?

The third column of Table 11–1 contains an estimate for the time required to accomplish each activity. Methods for estimating durations include those discussed in Appendix A (Sections A.5 through A.7).

We might mention that the construction of a table such as Table 11–1 represents a rather formidable task for complex projects. First, the nature and number of activities must be specified, which relates to the *level of aggregation* problem discussed in Chapter 1; that is, what level of detail should define activities? For example, should we separate the renovation of coaches from the purchase of coaches? Is renovation itself complex enough to warrant separate activities? Ultimately, these and other answers must be based on experience, "art," and the usefulness of results. Second, great care must be exercised in establishing meaningful precedence relationships, as their nature can very much affect differences between predicted and actual results.

Network Representation

Before illustrating the so-called network representation of Table 11–1, we formalize the previous discussion with some key definitions.

Events are specific accomplishments that occur at recognizable points in time. For example, the *completion* of activity *J* (decorate) in Table 11–1 represents an event. Similarly, the *initiation* of activity *N* represents an event.

An **activity** is the work required to complete a specific event. Activities, unlike events, require time and utilize resources.

The **project** is the complete set of interrelated activities. By convention, the "start" of the project is indicated by an **originating event;** the "end" of the project is denoted by a **terminal event.**

The **network** for the project is a display of its activities and events and their interrelationships. Figure 11–1 represents a network for the restaurant project defined in Table 11–1. Activities are represented by **directed arcs.** Events are represented by **nodes**. Note that nodes 1 and 11 represent, respectively, the originating event **(source)** and terminal event **(sink).**

Two rules must be observed in the construction of such a network:

Rule 1:	Each activity must be represented by one and only one directed arc.
Rule 2:	No two activities may begin *and* end on the same two nodes.
Convention:	The numbering of the nodes designates direction so that the head of the arrow should have the higher number.

To gain some feeling for how to draw a network, look at activities *A* through *H* in Table 11–1. Notice that *H* must be preceded only by *G* and *G* only by *A* and *F*. Also *E* must precede *F* and *D* must precede *E*. Thus activities *A*, *D* , *E*, and *F* all culminate in *G*. Also notice that *B* precedes *I* and *J*, *C* precedes *M*, and these do not culminate in *G*. With these observations in mind, try sketching activities *A*, *D*, *E*, *F*, and *G*. Check your sketch against Figure 11–1. Use of the three rules should help you develop a figure similar to Figure 11–1.

FIGURE 11–1 Network for Restaurant Project in Table 11–1

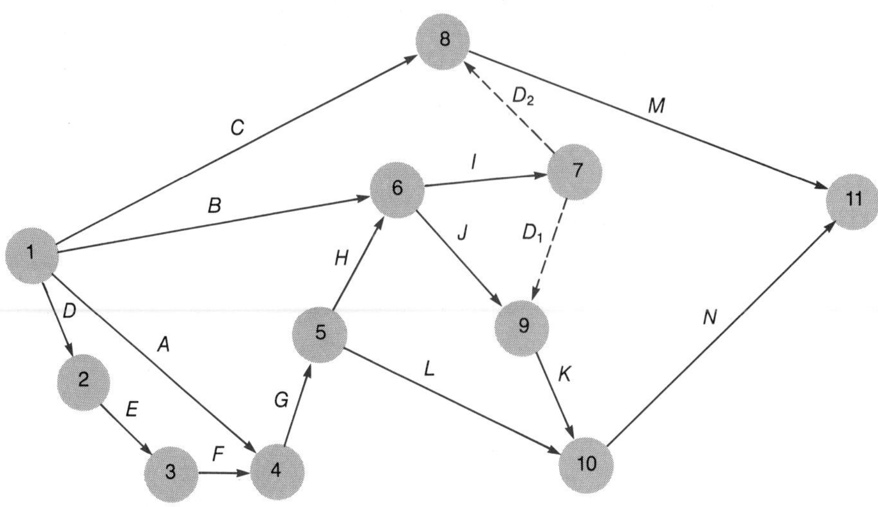

Rule 1 is needed to represent activities uniquely. Rule 2 is necessary to avoid notational problems when using solution methods. For example, activities I and J are concurrent activities that must precede activity K. Figure 11–2*a* shows an incorrect representation because I and J cannot be uniquely identified when using the "coordinate" convention of coding an activity by its beginning and ending event; that is, the coordinate 6–9 would fail to distinguish between activities I and J. Part *b* of the figure (as does Figure 11–1) correctly identifies activity I as 6–7 and activity J as 6–9.

FIGURE 11–2 Use of Dummy Activity to Avoid Notational Problems

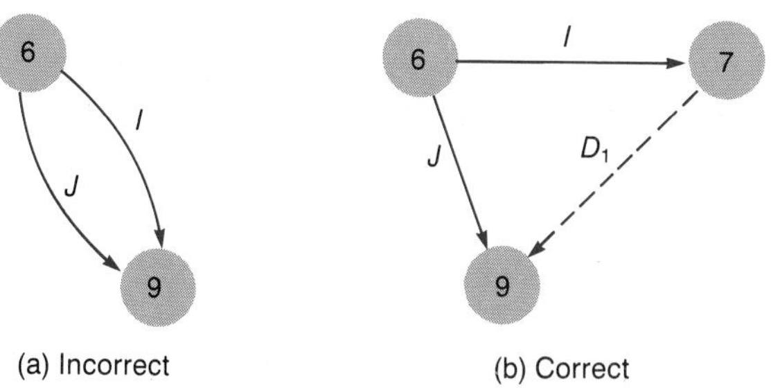

The implementation of Rule 2 in Figure 11–2*b* required the use of a **dummy activity** (D_1). Such activities do not require time or utilize resources, but they are necessary either (1) to preserve Rule 2 or (2) to properly represent certain logical relationships. To illustrate the latter, consider Figure 11–3. Part *a* shows an incorrect precedence relationship for activity K. According to Table 11–1, I and J are to precede K; and C and I are to precede M. The dummy (D_2) is therefore inserted to allow

I to precede *K*. Doing so, however, implies that *C also* must precede *K*, which is incorrect. Part *b* of Figure 11–3 (as does Figure 11–1) shows the correct relationships. Note that dummies are represented by "broken" directed arcs.

FIGURE 11–3 Use of Dummy Activities to Avoid Precedence Problems

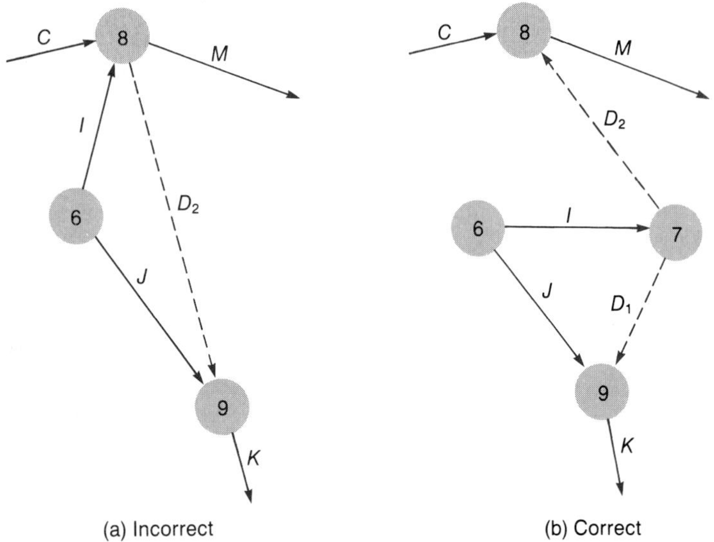

FOLLOW-UP EXERCISES

1. Confirm that Figure 11–1 is correctly based on Table 11–1. Do so by answering the following questions for each activity in the network: (*a*) What activity or activities must be completed immediately before this activity can start? (*b*) What activity or activities must immediately follow this activity? (*c*) What activity or activities must occur concurrently with this activity?
2. Construct a new network for the restaurant project if activity *J* need not precede
   activity *K* but must precede activity *N*.
3. Construct a new network for the restaurant project if activities *C* and *K* (rather than *C* and *I*) must precede activity *M*.
4. Construct a new network which combines the conditions in Exercises 2 and 3.

Time Concepts

A primary objective in project management is the determination of a schedule that shows starting and finishing dates for each activity. Concepts helpful in the construction of such a schedule are discussed next.

Figure 11–4 shows the network for the restaurant project (Table 11–1) with estimated durations for each activity (d_{ij}) labeled on the arcs. Note that activities are now referenced using *i–j* notation. For example, activity *C* in Figure 11–1 is now activity 1–8 in Figure 11–4, with duration $d_{18} = 1$.

We begin with two important definitions associated with each activity (all times reflect the end of the period—the end of the day in this example):

Two important definitions associated with each activity are:

1. The **earliest starting time** E_{ij} for activity i–j is the earliest time at which the activity can start such that all precedence relationships for that activity are completed.
2. The **latest starting time** L_{ij} for activity i–j is the latest time at which the activity can start without delaying the completion of the project.

FIGURE 11–4 Restaurant Network with Estimated Durations

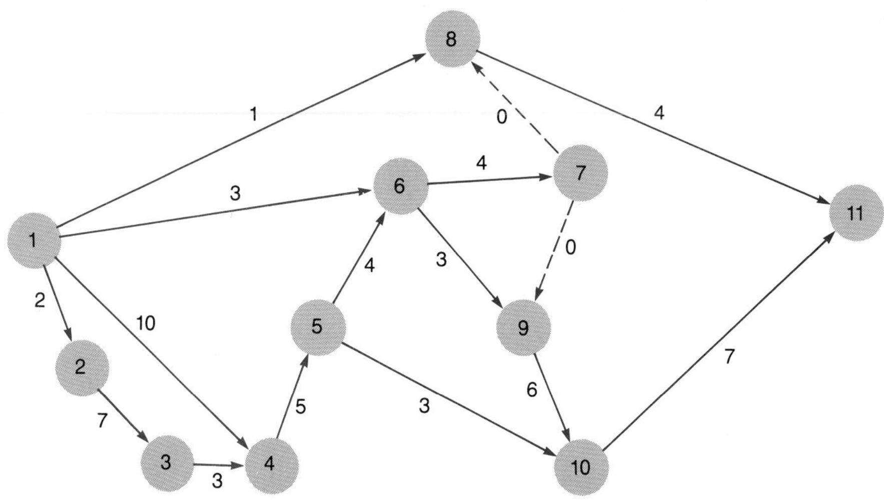

E_{ij} for each activity is calculated during a *forward pass* on the network. Any activity branching directly from node 1 can begin at time 0 giving $E_{18} = E_{16} = E_{14} = E_{12} = 0$. Subsequently, activity 2–3 can begin only after 1–2 has been completed, yielding $E_{23} = 2$. By formula

$$E_{jk} = 0 \qquad \text{for } j = 1$$

$$E_{jk} = \max_{i}\{E_{ij} + d_{ij}\} \qquad \text{for } j > 1\,. \tag{11.1}$$

Consider activity 4–5. The two preceding activities are 1–4 and 3–4, so we have

$$E_{34} = E_{23} + d_{23} = 2 + 7 = 9$$

$$\begin{aligned} E_{45} &= \max\{E_{14} + d_{14}, E_{34} + d_{34}\} \\ &= \max\{0 + 10, 9 + 3\} = 12\,. \end{aligned}$$

In words, the earliest starting time for activity 4–5 is the end of the 12th day, since all activities along the path 1–2–3–4 must be completed first. Table 11–2 shows each E_{ij}. Try confirming these by tracing through Figure 11–4. Note that *the earliest starting time for an activity is the path of maximum length that precedes that activity.* L_{ij} for each activity can be calculated once $E_{j,12}$ has been determined where there are 11 nodes in the network and "activity 12," the artificial activity of finishing the project, has a 0 duration. In this example, $E_{j,12} = 38$.

By specifying $L_{j,12} = E_{j,12}$, we can determine the L_{jk} through a *backward pass* on the network to assure that the project can be completed on time. *On time* is defined as the earliest project completion time. By formula, we have

$$L_{ij} = \min_k \{L_{jk} - d_{ij}\} \tag{11.2}$$

For example, noting that $L_{11,12} = E_{11,12} = 38$, we have

$$L_{10,11} = L_{11,12} - d_{10,11} = 38 - 7 = 31$$

$$L_{45} = \min\{L_{5,10} - d_{45}, L_{56} - d_{45}\} = \min\{28 - 5, 17 - 5\} = 12.$$

In words, activity 10–11 must start no later than the end of the 31st day if the project is to be completed on time (by the end of the 38th day); activity 4–5 must start by the end of the 12th day so as not to delay the completion of the project beyond 38 days.

Table 11–2 also shows the latest starting times for each activity.

TABLE 11–2 E_{ij}, and L_{ij} for Restaurant Project

Activity		
i–j	E_{ij}	L_{ij}
1–8	0	33
1–6	0	18
1–4	0	2
1–2	0	0
2–3	2	2
3–4	9	9
4–5	12	12
5–6	17	17
5–10	17	28
6–7	21	21
6–9	21	22
7–8	25	34
7–9	25	25
8–11	25	34
9–10	25	25
10–11	31	31
11–12	38	38*

*Setting latest starting time equal to earliest starting time.

Slacks

The **slack** for activity *i–j*, or S_{ij}, is the difference between its earliest starting date and its latest starting date. By formula, we have

$$S_{ij} = L_{ij} - E_{ij} \tag{11.3}$$

For example, the slacks for activities 1–6 and 3–4 are, respectively,

$$\begin{aligned} S_{16} &= L_{16} - E_{16} \\ &= 18 - 0 \\ &= 18 \text{ days} \end{aligned}$$

and

$$\begin{aligned} S_{34} &= L_{34} - E_{34} \\ &= 9 - 9 \\ &= 0 \text{ day}. \end{aligned}$$

This means that we have 18 days of "play" or "float" within which we can choose to delay the *start* of activity 1–6 *without delaying the 38-day completion time for the project.* No delay, however, is allowed in the start of activity 3–4 if we wish to complete the project in 38 days. Table 11–3 summarizes relevant time calculations for each activity.

Table 11–3 summarizes relevant time concepts for each activity. We also include two new time definitions that are commonly used in describing activity schedules. These are simply computed as follows:

Earliest finishing time = Earliest starting time + duration

$$E'_{ij} = E_{ij} + d_{ij} \tag{11.4}$$

Latest finishing time = Latest starting time + duration

$$L'_{ij} = L_{ij} + d_{ij} \tag{11.5}$$

For example, activity M can't start any earlier than the end of the 25th day ($E_{8,11} = 25$) and can't finish earlier than the 29th day given that its duration is 4 days ($E'_{8,11} = 25 + 4 = 29$). Similarly, to avoid a project delay, activity M can start no later than the 34th day ($L_{8,11} = 34$) and can finish no later than the 38th day ($L'_{8,11} = 34 + 4$).

TABLE 11–3 Time Summaries for Restaurant Project

Activity	Code i–j	Duration d_{ij}	Earliest Starting Time E_{ij}	Latest Starting Time L_{ij}	Slack S_{ij}	Earliest Finishing Time E'_{ij}	Latest Finishing Time L'_{ij}
A	1–4	10	0	2	2	10	12
B	1–6	3	0	18	18	3	21
C	1–8	1	0	33	33	1	34
D	1–2	2	0	0	**0**	2	2
E	2–3	7	2	2	**0**	9	9
F	3–4	3	9	9	**0**	12	12
G	4–5	5	12	12	**0**	17	17
H	5–6	4	17	17	**0**	21	21
I	6–7	4	21	21	**0**	25	25
J	6–9	3	21	22	1	24	25
D1	7–9	0	25	25	**0**	25	25
D2	7–8	0	25	34	9	25	34
K	9–10	6	25	25	**0**	31	31
L	5–11	3	17	28	11	20	31
M	8–11	4	25	34	9	29	38
N	10–11	7	31	31	**0**	38	38

The Critical Path

The **critical path** for a project is a path that spans the network such that activities along the path (termed **critical activities**) have zero slack. Thus a delay in the start of any activity along the critical path delays the entire project. In effect, the critical path is the *longest path* in the network. Put another way, the sum of durations for critical activities represents the *shortest* possible time to complete the project.

The critical activities in Table 11–3 are those having zero slack. Since they represent activities on the critical path, they must form a chain that spans the network, as indicated in Figure 11–5.

FIGURE 11–5 Restaurant Network and Critical Path (→)

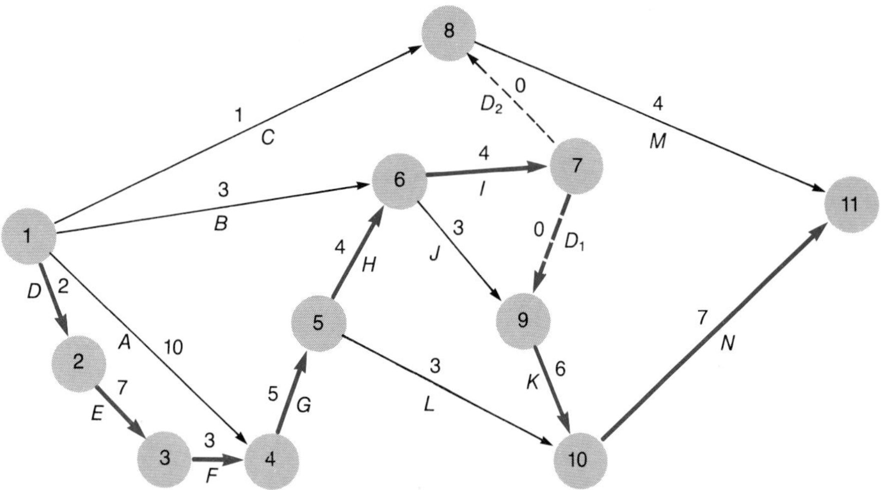

In the appendix of this chapter, we present mathematical programming procedures for finding the critical path directly.

Computerized Analysis[1]

Many software packages available on mainframes, minis, and micros perform critical path network analysis. Figure 11–6 illustrates one such package and its output for the restaurant project.[2] Note the echo of the data input to the package. This is useful in checking entry errors or problems in model formulation. Compare these results with those in Table 11–3.

Arc-Node Conventions

PERT originally followed an activity on arrow convention, and CPM often followed an activity on node convention. Today the terms *PERT* and *CPM* are used interchangeably, and often the technique is simply called PERT/CPM. Nevertheless, you will occasionally encounter the activity on node convention. In that convention, the 14 activities in Example 11.1 would be represented by 14 nodes. Arrows would indicate precedence relationships.

---

[1]For a listing of PERT/CPM software and vendors, see Joseph J. Moder, Cecil R. Phillips, and Edward W. Davis, *Project Management with CPM, PERT, and Precedence Diagramming*, 3rd ed. (New York: Van Nostrand Reinhold, 1983), pp. 363–70.

[2]Terry L. Dennis and Laurie B. Dennis, *Microcomputer Models for Management Decision Making: Software and Text* (St. Paul, Minn.: West Publishing, 1986).

FIGURE 11–6 Computer-Based Analysis for Restaurant Example

```
* * * * * * * * * * * * * * * * * * *
*                                   *
*          PERT ANALYSIS            *
*                                   *
* * * * * * * * * * * * * * * * * * *
```

HERE IS WHAT YOU ENTERED:

ACTIVITY	IMMEDIATE PREDECESSOR	EXPECTED TIME
A	–	10
B	–	3
C	–	1
D	–	2
E	D	7
F	E	3
G	A,F	5
H	G	4
I	B,H	4
J	B,H	3
K	I,J	6
L	G	3
M	C,I	4
N	K,L	7

OUTPUT: DETERMINISTIC, LETTERED ACTIVITIES & PREDECESSORS

ACT	EARLY START	LATE START	EARLY FINISH	LATE FINISH	SLACK (LS–ES)	CRITICAL PATH
A	0.0	2.0	10.0	12.0	2.0	
B	0.0	18.0	3.0	21.0	18.0	
C	0.0	33.0	1.0	34.0	33.0	
D	0.0	0.0	2.0	2.0	0.0	YES
E	2.0	2.0	9.0	9.0	0.0	YES
F	9.0	9.0	12.0	12.0	0.0	YES
G	12.0	12.0	17.0	17.0	0.0	YES
H	17.0	17.0	21.0	21.0	0.0	YES
I	21.0	21.0	25.0	25.0	0.0	YES
J	21.0	22.0	24.0	25.0	1.0	
K	25.0	25.0	31.0	31.0	0.0	YES
L	17.0	28.0	20.0	31.0	11.0	
M	25.0	34.0	29.0	38.0	9.0	
N	31.0	31.0	38.0	38.0	0.0	YES

CRITICAL PATH: D–E–F–G–H–I–K–N

NETWORK COMPLETION TIME = 38

FOLLOW-UP EXERCISES

5. Confirm the calculations in Table 11–2 using the formulas given by Equations 11.1 through 11.3
6. Confirm the calculations in Table 11–3.
7. Convince yourself that a critical path need not be unique by changing the duration of activity 5–10 in Figure 11–4 from 3 days to 14 days.
8. Complete a table such as Table 11–3 for the network in Exercise 4. Identify the critical path for this network.

11.2 SCHEDULING

The network calculations provided by the basic PERT model serve as the planning tool for actually scheduling the activities. In this section we illustrate the construction of a time chart for scheduling activities, and then touch on the important topic of allocating resources.

Time Chart

The **time chart** for the restaurant project is given in Figure 11–7. The first step is the scheduling of critical activities. From Table 11–3, critical activities are located as those having zero total slack. Then they are plotted sequentially, the length of each line corresponding to the duration of the corresponding activity. Note that dummy activities need not be plotted, as they take up zero time. Next, each noncritical activity is plotted separately. The beginning and end of each line correspond, respectively, to the *earliest starting time* (E_{ij}) and the *latest finishing time* (L'_{ij}) for the given activity. For example, activity J can begin as early as (the end of) day 21 and must be completed by (the end of) day 25. Since its duration is 3 days, its *latest starting time* is (the end of) day 22, which necessarily corresponds to a total slack of 1 day (i.e., 22 minus 21). Latest starting times for noncritical activities are located by dots (●) on the solid lines.

The time chart readily identifies scheduling flexibilities because of the visual ease in identifying the total slack associated with each noncritical activity (as given by the distance between the beginning of each line and the dot, which is the difference between earliest and latest starting times). For example, the purchase of restaurant equipment (B) and the hiring of personnel (C) represent activities with very flexible starting dates. Scheduling the start of purchase-renovation of coaches (A) or decoration (J), however, is not very flexible.

Resource Leveling

Up to now we have assumed unlimited resources in scheduling activities. In actual practice, it is probable that the initial schedule will call for more labor, equipment, funds, or other resources than is available for a particular period.

To illustrate our point, consider the labor requirements in Table 11–4. Figure 11–8 provides a schedule of labor requirements over time based on the scheduling of all noncritical activities according to the earliest starting time (part *a*) or the latest starting time (part *b*). For example, in part *b*, the number of personnel required for days 10, 11, and 12 (i.e., for the end of day 9 to the end of day 12) is 7. If the maximum

FIGURE 11–7 Time Chart for Restaurant Project

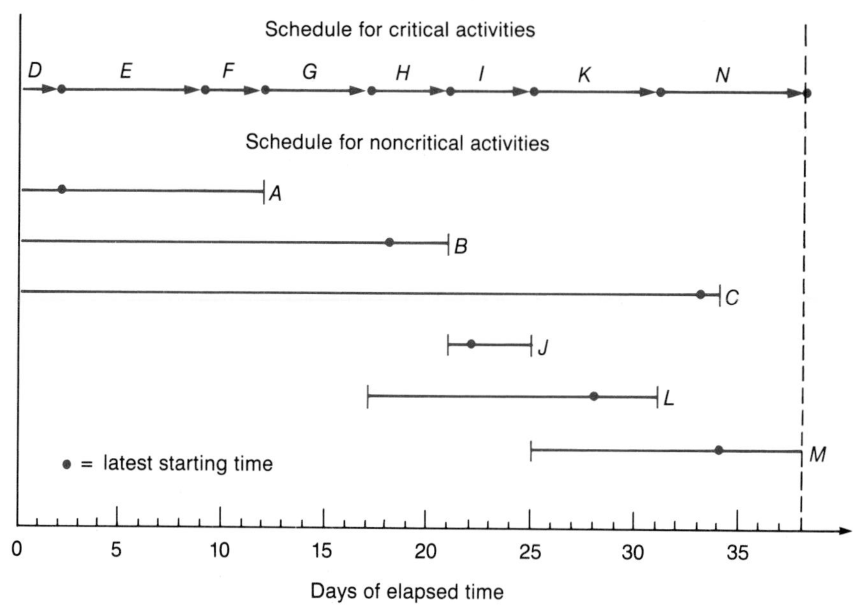

number of available personnel is 7, then it would not be desirable to schedule activities *A*, *B*, and *C* as early as possible (as in part a of Figure 11–8), since 9 and 8 personnel would be required in days 1 and 2, respectively.

TABLE 11–4 Labor Requirements for Restaurant Project

Activity	A	B	C	D	E	F	G	H	I	J	K	L	M	N
Number of Personnel	4	2	1	2	1	3	2	4	5	2	3	1	2	2

It should be evident that by shifting noncritical activities between earliest and latest *starting* times, either reduction in the maximum number of personnel or **resource (or load) leveling** can be achieved (assuming that units of the resource are perfect substitutes for one another). By load leveling we mean the smoothing of fluctuations in the requirements for a particular resource. At this time, computationally feasible models for optimizing the allocation of resources do not exist. Good heuristic (rule-of-thumb) approaches do exist, however.

PERT/MRP

As we shall see in a subsequent chapter on inventory control, Material Requirements Planning (MRP) has become a dominant inventory scheduling system. MRP shows the time-phased quantities of components, subassemblies, and end products produced at every stage of the production process. PERT has been successfully integrated with MRP.[3]

FIGURE 11–8 Labor Schedules for Restaurant Project

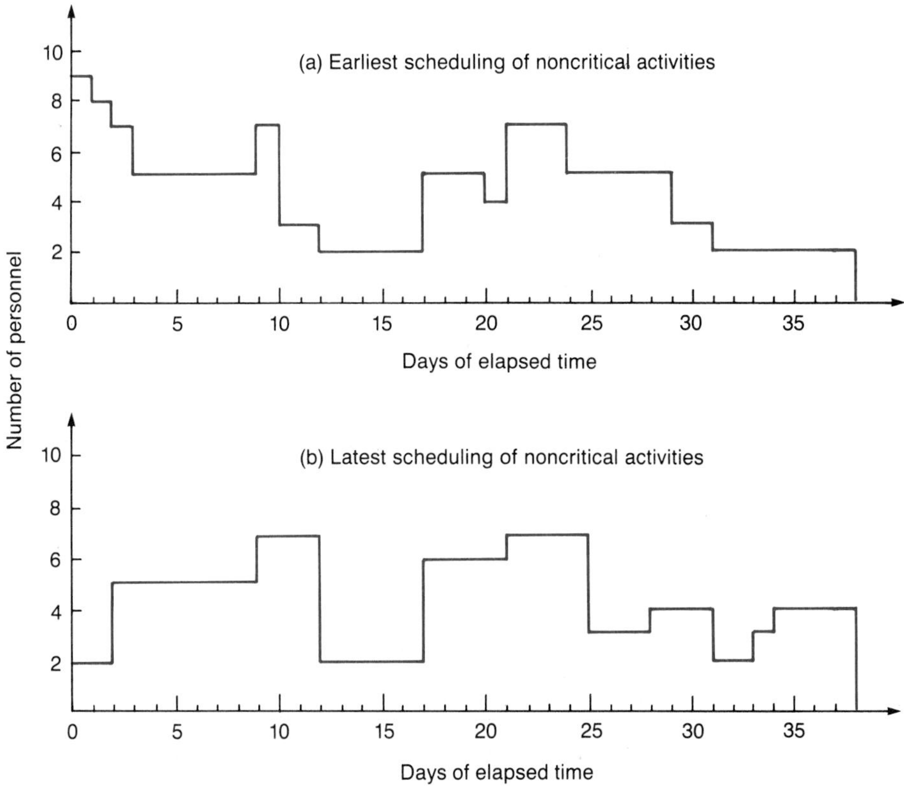

FOLLOW-UP EXERCISES

9. Construct a time chart for the project in Exercise 8. Identify what appear to be scheduling flexibilities.
10. With respect to Figure 11–8:
    a. Confirm the personnel needs in part *a*.
    b. Confirm the personnel needs in part *b*.
    c. Construct a labor schedule for the restaurant project by scheduling noncritical activities midway between earliest and latest starting dates. Compare to parts *a* and *b*. (*Hint*: First label Figure 11–7 to include labor needs and duration of each activity; then use this revised figure to aid you in answering parts *a*, *b*, and *c*.)
    d. For the 38 daily observations of the variable "number of personnel," calculate the mean and variance for part *a* and for part *b*. Based on these measures, which schedule best levels the load?
    e. By shifting the starting times of noncritical activities, is it possible to reduce maximum requirements below seven personnel? Illustrate your answer.
11. Construct labor schedules as in Figure 11–8 for the project of Exercise 9. Compare results to the needs in Figure 11–8.

[3]For an excellent presentation of this aspect of resource planning, see N. J. Aquilano and D. E. Smith, "A Formal Set of Algorithms for Project Scheduling with Critical Path Scheduling/Material Requirements Planning," *Journal of Operations Management*, November 1980, pp. 57–67.

12. Why must there be perfect substitutability across activities among resource units when leveling? Given the nature of the labor resource (people) and the variety of activities in the restaurant project, does this assumption appear tenable? (Assume some people can work on certain activities and not others.) Can you think of ways to overcome this problem? Can you think of resources that are more homogeneous than labor?

11.3 INCORPORATING PROBABILITIES

Up to now the duration of each activity has been treated as a deterministic variable. For example, the time required to purchase and renovate coaches in the restaurant project had been fixed at 10 days, with no possibility of variation. In this section a model is presented that defines the time to complete each activity as a random variable.

Activity Durations as Random Variables

The original version of PERT requires three time estimates of the duration of activity i–j from people who are most intimately involved with accomplishing the activity, as follows:

1. An *optimistic* time (a_{ij}), such that the probability is "small" that the activity can be completed in less time.
2. A *most likely* (*modal*) time (m_{ij}), which should occur under "normal" operating conditions.
3. A *pessimistic* time (b_{ij}), such that the prabability is "small" that the activity will take longer.

The time (d_{ij}) to complete activity i–j is assumed to be a random variate from a probability distribution with a specified mean and variance. The *mean* ($\bar{d}_{ij}$) is estimated as a weighted average of the three time estimates, with the mode receiving four times the weight of either extreme:

$$\bar{d}_{ij} = \frac{a_{ij} + 4m_{ij} + b_{ij}}{6}. \tag{11.6}$$

The *variance* (v_{ij}) for the time to complete activity i–j is estimated by assuming that the range given by ($b_{ij} - a_{ij}$) encompasses six standard deviations of the distribution.[4] Thus

$$6\sqrt{v_{ij}} = b_{ij} - a_{ij}$$

or

$$v_{ij} = \left(\frac{b_{ij} - a_{ij}}{6}\right)^2. \tag{11.7}$$

[4]According to the Chebyschev Inequality, we can guarantee that *at least* 89 percent of the durations will fall within the range given by ($b_{ij} - a_{ij}$) regardless of the specific form of the probability distribution. If the probability distribution is normal, for example, then the probability is 0.9973 that d_{ij} falls within this range. For an interesting commentary on PERT times, see M. W. Sasieni, "A Note on PERT Times," *Management Science*, vol. 32, no. 12 (December 1986), pp. 1652–1653.

Under certain restrictive assumptions, it can be proved that $\bar{d}_{ij}$ and v_{ij} are the mean and variance of a Beta distribution (Section A.3). As illustrated in Figure 11–9, this continuous distribution has finite limits, is unimodal, and can assume flexible shapes. The main concern in our calculations, however, is not the exact form of the probability distribution, but rather the "goodness" of $\bar{d}_{ij}$ and v_{ij} as estimates.

FIGURE 11–9 Beta Distributions for Durations of Actitivy *i–j*

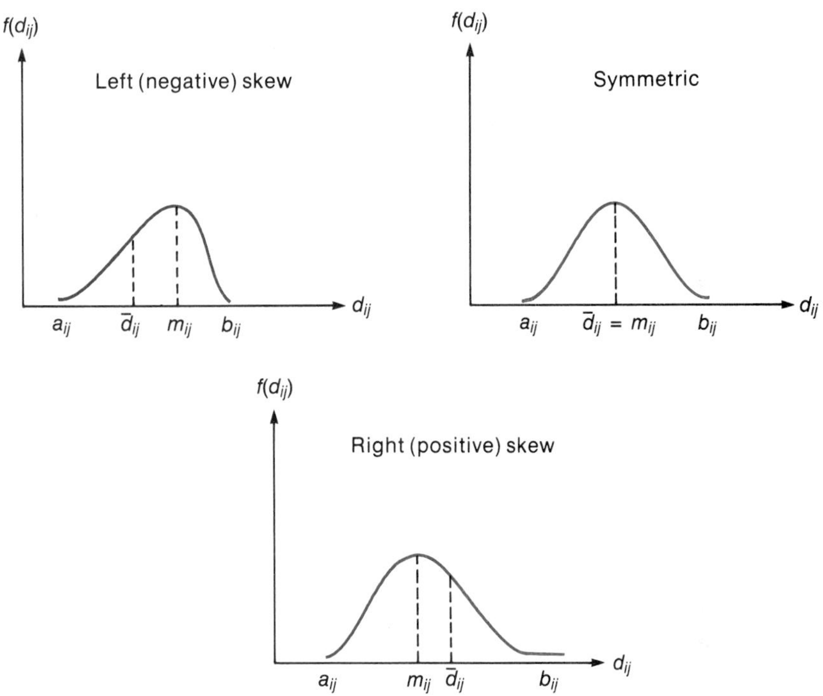

Table 11–5 provides time estimates and calculations of mean and variance for each activity of the restaurant project. Note that we have cleverly "fixed" the time estimates (a_{ij}, m_{ij}, and b_{ij}) to give us the same durations as before (i.e., $\bar{d}_{ij}$ equals the previously used d_{ij} for all *i* and *j*).

Probabilistic Events

Given probabilistic durations of activities along specific paths in the network, it follows that elapsed times for achieving events along those paths are also probabilistic. We now present a procedure for assessing the probability that an event will be attained within its allotted time according to a given schedule.

Let e_i represent a random variate from the distribution of "*earliest times for achieving event* i." If durations along the *longest* path into event *i* are statistically independent, then the mean, $E(e_i)$, and the variance, $V(e_i)$, of the distribution of earliest times for achieving event *i* can be estimated as the sums of the means ($\bar{d}_{ij}$'s) and vari-

TABLE 11–5 Time Estimates, Means, and Variances for Restaurant Project*

Activity	Code for Activity i–j	a_{ij}	m_{ij}	b_{ij}	$\bar{d}_{ij}$	v_{ij}
A	1–4	5	7	27	10	13
B	1–6	0	3	6	3	1
C	1–8	1	1	1	1	0
D	1–2	0	1	8	2	2
E	2–3	3	6	15	7	4
F	3–4	1	3	5	3	0
G	4–5	0	6	6	5	1
H	5–6	1	2	15	4	5
I	6–7	2	4	6	4	0
J	6–9	2	3	4	3	0
K	9–10	3	5	13	6	3
L	5–10	3	3	3	3	0
M	8–11	2	3	10	4	2
N	10–11	1	8	9	7	2

*All estimates and calculations to the nearest day.

ances (v_{ij}'s), respectively, of the durations for activities along the longest path.[5] (See Figure 11–10.) To illustrate, turn to Figure 11–4. For event 4,

$$\begin{aligned} E(e_4) &= \bar{d}_{12} + \bar{d}_{23} + \bar{d}_{34} \\ &= 2 + 7 + 3 \\ &= 12 \end{aligned}$$

and (from Table 11–5)

$$\begin{aligned} V(e_4) &= v_{12} + v_{23} + v_{34} \\ &= 2 + 4 + 0 \\ &= 6\,. \end{aligned}$$

FIGURE 11–10 $E(e_i)$ and $V(e_i)$ Estimates

Longest Path into Event i

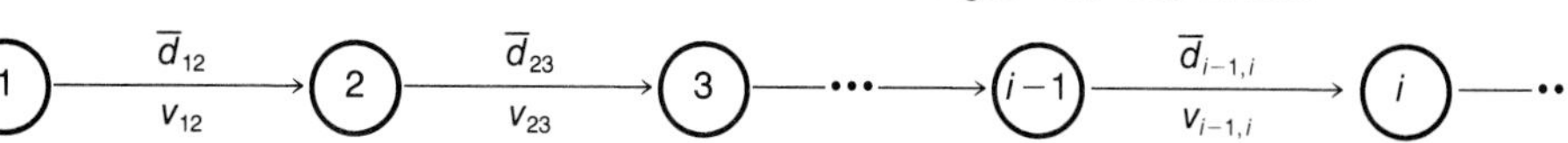

Mean of "earliest times for achieving event i":

$$E(e_i) = \bar{d}_{12} + \bar{d}_{23} + \cdots + \bar{d}_{i-1,i}\,.$$

Variance of "earliest times for achieving event i":

$$V(e_i) = v_{12} + v_{23} + \cdots + v_{i-1,i}\,.$$

{Where, for each activity, $\bar{d}_{ij}$ represents mean duration and v_{ij} represents variance in durations.}

[5] The justification for this statement is based on theorems in statistics which state that : (1) The expected value of a sum of n variables equals the sum of the n expected values; (2) the variance of a sum of n variables equals the sum of the n variances, provided the n variables are statistically independent (uncorrelated).

Note that 1–2–3–4 and not 1–4 is the *longest* path into event 4. Also note that $E(e_i)$ is equivalent to the earliest starting time (E_{ij}), since the latter was determined by summing expected durations along the longest path into event i. In other words, $E(e_i) \equiv E_{ij}$ for all i, as calculated in Table 11–2. Finally, if two or more paths into event i are of equal length, then $V(e_i)$ is conservatively estimated from the path yielding the highest sum of variances.

Given that k independent activities precede event i (on the longest path into i) and that e_i is the sum of the k independent and identically distributed observations (i.e., the k durations represent a random sample), then according the the **Central Limit Theorem** (Section A.5) e_i is approximately normally distributed with mean $E(e_i)$ and variance $V(e_i)$ for "large" k. This allows us to estimate the probability that the "earliest time for achieving event i" (e_i) is less than or equal to some "scheduled time for event i" (kT_i). In other words, $P(e_i \leq T_i)$ is given by the shaded area of the normal curve shown in Figure 11–11, where the "standardized random variate" (z_i) is defined by

$$z_i = \frac{T_i - E(e_i)}{\sqrt{V(e_i)}}. \tag{11.8}$$

FIGURE 11–11 Normal Curve for e_i

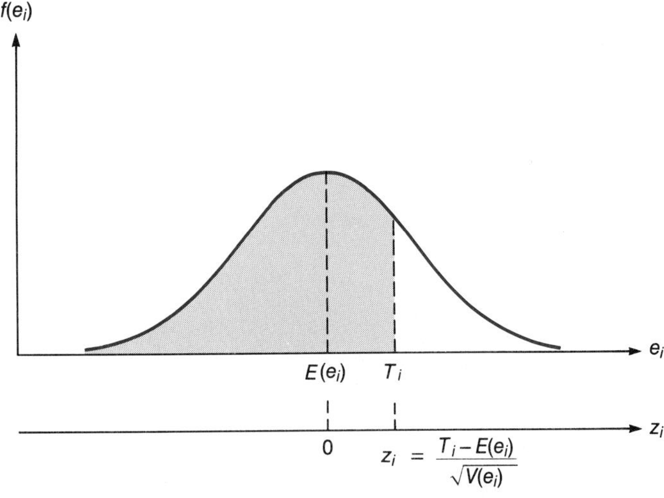

To illustrate the calculation of event probabilities, consider the probability that event 4 in the restaurant project occurs prior to the end of day 14. Previously we found that $E(e_4) = 12$ and $V(e_4) = 6$. Thus

$$P(e_4 \leq T_4) = P\left(Z_4 \leq \frac{T_4 - E(e_4)}{\sqrt{V(e_4)}}\right)$$

$$P(e_4 \leq 14) = P\left(Z_4 \leq \frac{14 - 12}{\sqrt{6}}\right)$$

$$= P(Z_4 \le 0.82)$$

$$= 0.79 \,.$$

If $T_4 = 9$, then

$$P(e_4 \le 9) = P\left(Z_4 \le \frac{9 - 12}{\sqrt{6}}\right)$$

$$= P(Z_4 \le -1.22)$$

$$= 0.11 \,.$$

Thus the probability is 79 percent that event 4 is achieved in 14 days or less and 11 percent that it is achieved in 9 days or less.

Table 11–6 presents the calculations for determining the probability that each event in the restaurant project finishes by a time (T_i) according to some schedule. Note that determinations of $E(e_i)$ are based on E_{ij} from Table 11–2; $V(e_i)$ calculations are based on the sum of v_{ij}'s from Table 11–5 for the longest path into event i.

TABLE 11–6 Event Probabilities for Restaurant Project

Event (i)	Longest Path into Event i	$E(e_i)$	$V(e_i)$	T_i	z_i	$P(e_i \le T_i)$, or $P(Z_i \le z_i)$
2	1–2	2	2	2	0.00	0.50
3	1–2–3	9	6	10	0.41	0.66
4	1–2–3–4	12	6	11	−0.41	0.34
5	1–2–3–4–5	17	7	20	1.13	0.87
6	1–2–3–4–5–6	21	12	24	0.87	0.81
7	1–2–3–4–5–6–7	25	12	27	0.58	0.72
8	1–2–3–4–5–6–7–8	25	12	34	2.60	1.00
9	1–2–3–4–5–6–7–9	25	12	28	0.87	0.81
10	1–2–3–4–5–6–7–9–10	31	15	32	0.26	0.60
11	1–2–3–4–5–6–7–9–10–11	38	17	40	0.49	0.69

Probability tables of this type aid project planners in assessing whether or not schedules and resource commitments are reasonable. For example, the probability that the project is completed in 40 days or less is estimated as 0.69. If this is considered too low, then additional resources must be committed along the critical path to reduce estimated durations and/or variances (or, perhaps, the scheduled completion date needs to be increased).

The procedure provided by PERT for assessing uncertainties, although not rigorous in a probabilistic sense, has been workable in actual practice. We must caution, however, that a number of assumptions have been made in this section. To recap, we have assumed that:

1. Expected activity durations and variances are accurately estimated by Equations 11.6 and 11.7.
2. Activities are statistically independent for computing event variances.
3. Time observations for activity durations represent "large enough" random samples for the Central Limit Theorem to be operable.

4. The distribution of times for the longest path into an event represents a reasonable estimate of earliest times for that event, which means that it is not possible for alternative paths into i to have greater cumulative times. (This assumption considerably simplifies statistical manipulations.)

PERT: What Ifs and Sensitivity

In actual networks, the PERT time estimates for completion of the project may be quite inaccurate. These estimates are biased by the fact that we ignore all paths except the critical path. With the activity time variability, however, long durations on noncritical activities can change the critical path. Several attempts have been made to improve the estimates, and work still continues in this area.[6]

In PERT networks, we are likely to ask questions about sensitivity. What if it takes longer than expected to carry out a particular activity? With computer programs, a sensitivity analysis feature would allow us to determine what would happen on the network. Indeed, we will find in Chapter 17 that the technique of simulation will allow us to generate thousands of networks with activity times obeying the probabilities assigned to them. For example, a 0.20 probability that an activity will take two days would mean that close to 200 of our 1,000 networks would show that activity at two days. How will these activity times be generated? Basically, we will use a table of random numbers and specify that any number 00 through 19 will be associated with two days. Since the 100 random numbers 00 through 99 are equally likely, there is a 0.20 probability of finding a random number 00 to 19.

Once we have "simulated" our 1,000 networks, we can create a table showing the percentage of time each activity was critical. Activities can then be ranked according to an index of criticality: What percentage of time is the activity on a critical path?

Related to these "what if" questions are "yeah, but" questions. "Yeah, but I would have handed in my term paper on time but for a delay due to illness." The military often requires contractors to use PERT networks to manage large procurement projects. When blame for the lateness becomes an issue, each party will attempt to show that the contract would have been completed on time "but for" a delay caused by the other party. To prove the "but for" statement, a PERT network with and without the delay in question can help.

FOLLOW-UP EXERCISES

13. Verify the calculations in Table 11–5.
14. For each activity in Table 11–5 identify whether its durations are symmetric, negatively skewed, or positively skewed (be careful with B). What can you say about activities C and L? Is it reasonable to state that activities having low variance are fairly standardized or routine?
15. Confirm the calculations in Table 11–6.
16. Determine the probability that the project is completed by its earliest expected completion date of 38 days.
17. In general, what can you say about the probability that an event along the critical path is completed by its latest date? In other words, $P(e_j \leq L'_{ij}) = ?$ when event j is critical.

[6] K. P. Anklesaria and Z. Drezner, "A Multivariate Approach to Estimating the Completion Time for PERT Networks," *Journal of the Operational Research Society*, 37, no. 8 (1986), pp. 811–15.

18. Find the following probabilities for the restaurant project:
    a. That the project is completed in 45 or less days.
    b. That the project is completed in 35 or less days.
    c. That the project is completed between 35 and 45 days, inclusive.
    d. That event 8 has not been completed by the end of day 30.
19. Compute a probability table for the project of Exercises 4 and 8. Assume all scheduled times are 20 percent higher than latest finishing dates; that is, $T_j = 1.2\, L_{ij}'$ for all i. Also, assume the time estimates in Table 11–5.
20. With respect to the four assumptions outlined at the end of the section:
    a. Do Equations 11.6 and 11.7 appear to be reasonable or logical? Why or why not? On what basis do they appear to be statistically justified?
    b. Activities are assumed to be statistically independent in order to avoid statistical problems associated with estimating covariances or correlations. Can you think of factors or circumstances in a real project that would cause dependence?
    c. For purposes of the Central Limit Theorem (CLT), a "large enough" sample is usually assumed to be 30 or more. Under what conditions is normality approximated for small samples? (*Hint:* It has to do with the shapes of the distributions of activity durations.) Would you say that size restrictions imposed on k (number of activities preceding event i along the longest path) by the CLT are a problem for real-world projects? (*Hint:* Real-world projects using PERT/CPM consist of hundreds and even thousands of activities.) Why do you feel more confident in probability estimates for events in the late part of the network than for events in the early part? (*Hint:* It has to do with the size of k and the CLT.) Since (1) variances associated with durations are estimated rather than known and (2) sample sizes (k) may be small, what probability distribution for event times is more appropriate than the normal curve?
    d. Would you say that the longest elapsed time into, say, event 4 of the restaurant project is *always* given by path 1–2–3–4? (See Figure 11–4.) The answer is no because, given probabilistic durations, it is quite possible that it will take longer to complete activity 1–4 than to complete the sequence of activities given by 1–2, 2–3, and 3–4. To convince yourself, assume that the elapsed time along path 1–4 is normal with mean 10 and variance 13 (from Table 11–5), and that elapsed time along path 1–2–3–4 is normal with mean 12 and variance 6 (from Table 11–6). Determine (1) the probability that elapsed time along 1–4 is *greater* than 12 days, (2) the probability that elapsed time along 1–2–3–4 is *less* than 12 days, and (3) the probability that the events in 1 and 2 occur simultaneously. Note that when elapsed time along 1–4 is greater than along 1–2–3–4, activity 1–4 becomes critical, and activities 1–2, 2–3, and 3–4 becomes noncritical. Can you think of alternative definitions for the critical path?
21. Criticisms of Equations 11.6 and 11.7 for estimating the means and variances of activities have led to the development of alternative formulas:

$$\bar{d}_{ij} = \frac{a_{ij} + 0.95m_{ij} + b_{ij}}{2.95} \qquad (11.9)$$

and

$$v_{ij} = \left(\frac{b_{ij} - a_{ij}}{3.25}\right)^2, \qquad (11.10)$$

where a_{ij} and b_{ij} are estimates for the 5 and 95 percentiles of the probability distribution and m_{ij} is the mode.[7] The authors claim that these formulas are more accurate than Equations 11.6 and 11.7 and are relatively distribution free (e.g., their use is not predicated on the assumption of a specific distribution such as the Beta). Based on 11.9 and 11.10, generate alternative tables to Tables 11–5 and 11–6. Comment on the differences.

11.4 INCORPORATING COSTS

Our presentation up to now has strictly focused on the time element of project management. In this section, we introduce the idea of time-cost trade-offs in rescheduling activities and follow with a brief description of PERT/Cost.

Crashing

Three categories of cost can be identified for any given project: (1) *direct* costs associated with the commitment of resources (labor, materials, equipment, etc.) to activities; (2) *indirect* or *overhead* costs, such as expenses associated with utilities, administration, and supervision; and (3) *opportunity* costs, such as penalties for completing a project beyond a certain date or bonuses (benefits or negative costs) for completing a project prior to a specified date.

In general, the time to complete an activity can be shortened by committing additional resources to that activity; necessarily, the direct costs for that activity will increase. By decreasing the durations of critical activities, it follows that the project can be completed at an earlier data than previously scheduled, but at higher direct costs and lower indirect and opportunity costs. Figure 11–12 illustrates the identification of a schedule that resolves this trade-off by minimizing the total cost (sum of direct, indirect, and opportunity costs) of a hypothetical project.

The original version of CPM approached this problem by first requiring the identification of normal and crash points for each activity. The **normal point** for activity i–j is identified as a coordinate on its **direct cost-time function,** which indicates the duration (DN_{ij}) and associated direct cost (CN_{ij}) for this activity under "normal" conditions. DN_{ij}, for example, can be represented by the most likely duration (m_{ij}) or the expected duration ($\bar{d}_{ij}$) defined in Section 11.3. The **crash point** for activity i–j is the coordinate on its direct cost-time function which indicates the duration (DC_{ij}) and associated direct cost (CC_{ij}) if direct cost were of no concern in expediting this activity. In other words, DC_{ij} is the limiting duration for activity i–j such that an additional commitment of resources cannot futher expedite this activity. Figure 11–13 illustrates these concepts under the usual *linear* assumption for the direct cost-time function. Note that the crash point is necessarily "northwest" of the normal point, but the function passing through the two points is not necessarily linear. Further note that the slope (or first derivative) of this function gives the *cost of expediting this activity per unit of time*.

Given the determination of a critical path based on normal times, the act of **crashing** involves the sequential time compression of critical activities from normal dura-

[7]C. Perry and I. D. Greig, "Estimating the Mean and Variance of Subjective Distributions in PERT and Decision Analysis," *Management Science* 21, no. 12 (1975), pp. 1477–80.

FIGURE 11–12 Costs of Hypothetical Project

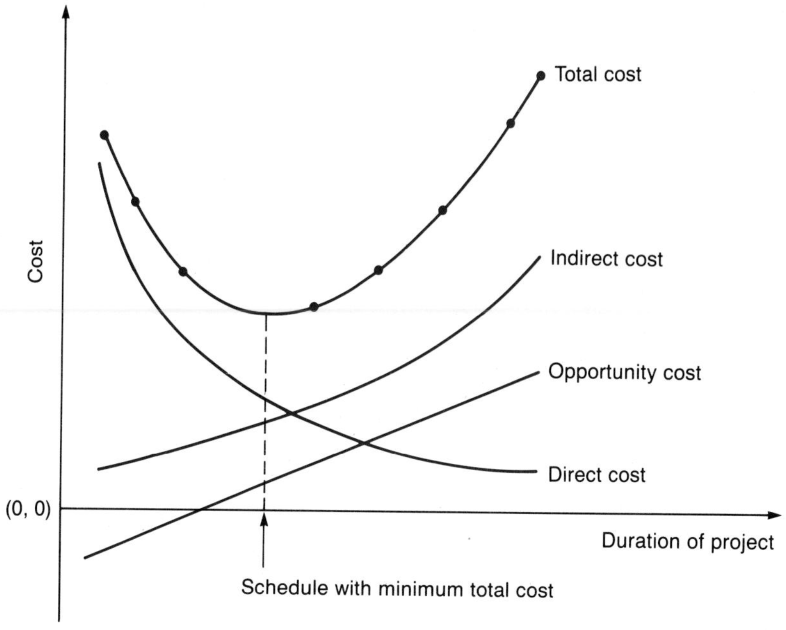

FIGURE 11–13 Direct Cost-Time Function for Activity *i–j*

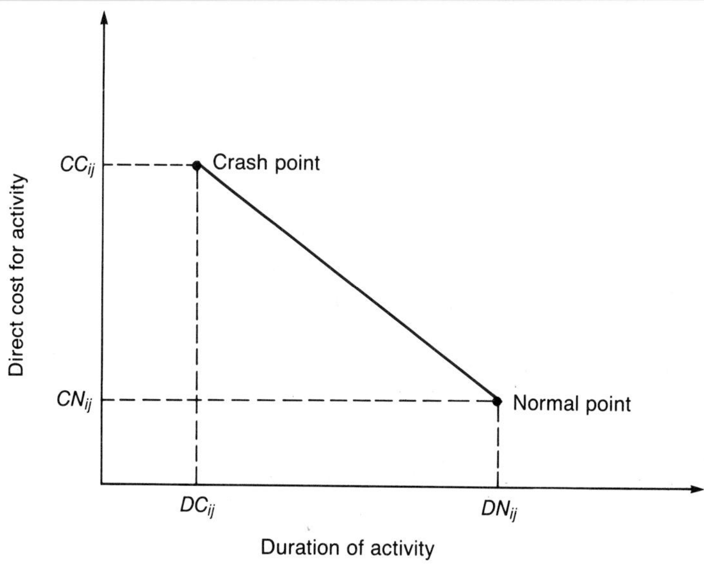

tions to crash durations. The end result of this effort is a set of schedules yielding direct cost as a discrete function of project duration. When its function is combined with the indirect and opportunity cost functions, a discrete version of the total cost function in Figure 11–13 can be constructed. We now illustrate one of many approaches to crashing. In the appendix to this chapter, a more rigorous linear programming version is presented.

In general, at each step of the crashing procedure, our heuristic (rule-of-thumb) calls for crashing the *uncrashed critical activity,* which yields the least linear direct cost per unit of time to expedite, or the minimum ratio

$$R_{ij} = \frac{CC_{ij} - CN_{ij}}{DN_{ij} - DC_{ij}} \qquad (11.11)$$

for all i–j along the *current* critical path.

Example 11.2 "Crashing in One Easy Lesson"

Table 11–7 provides cost and time estimates for a seven-activity project. As indicated in part *a* of Figure 11–14 the earliest time to complete the project under "normal" conditions is 16 weeks, for a total direct cost of \$82,000. Part *b* illustrates the extreme (but unnecessary) act of crashing *all* activities. It serves the useful purpose of providing the least possible duration for the project (9 weeks). As you will see, however, this same duration can be achieved at a cost lower than \$134,000.

TABLE 11–7 Cost-Time Estimates

	Duration Time Estimates (weeks)		Direct Cost Estimates (\$1,000)		Linear Slope (cost to expedite) ← This column is calculated from the others.
Activity i–j	**Normal** DN_{ij}	**Crash** DC_{ij}	**Normal** CN_{ij}	**Crash** CC_{ij}	R_{ij}
1–2	2	1	10	15	5
1–3	8	5	15	21	2
2–4	4	3	20	24	4
3–4	1	1	7	7	—
3–5	2	1	8	15	7
4–6	5	3	10	16	3
5–6	6	2	12	36	6
			82	134	

The first step is to expedite an activity along the critical path of the normal network. Noncritical activities are ignored because further reductions in their durations do not lower the earliest completion date for the project. Of the three critical activities given by 1–3, 3–5, and 5–6, activity 1–3 is crashed because it has the *least* cost per unit time to expedite; that is, according to the last column of Table 11–7, it costs \$2,000 per week to expedite activity 1–3, whereas it costs \$7,000 per week and \$6,000 per week to expedite activities 3–5 and 5–6, respectively. Crashing activity 1–3 from 8 weeks to 5 weeks reduces the time of project completion from 16 weeks to 13 weeks and increases direct cost from \$82,000 to \$88,000. For convenience, a **crashed activity** (i.e., an activity at its crash point) is identified by an asterisk (*) above its duration along the appropriate arc in the network. Note that activity 3–4 is already at its crash point.

FIGURE 11–14 Crashing a Project

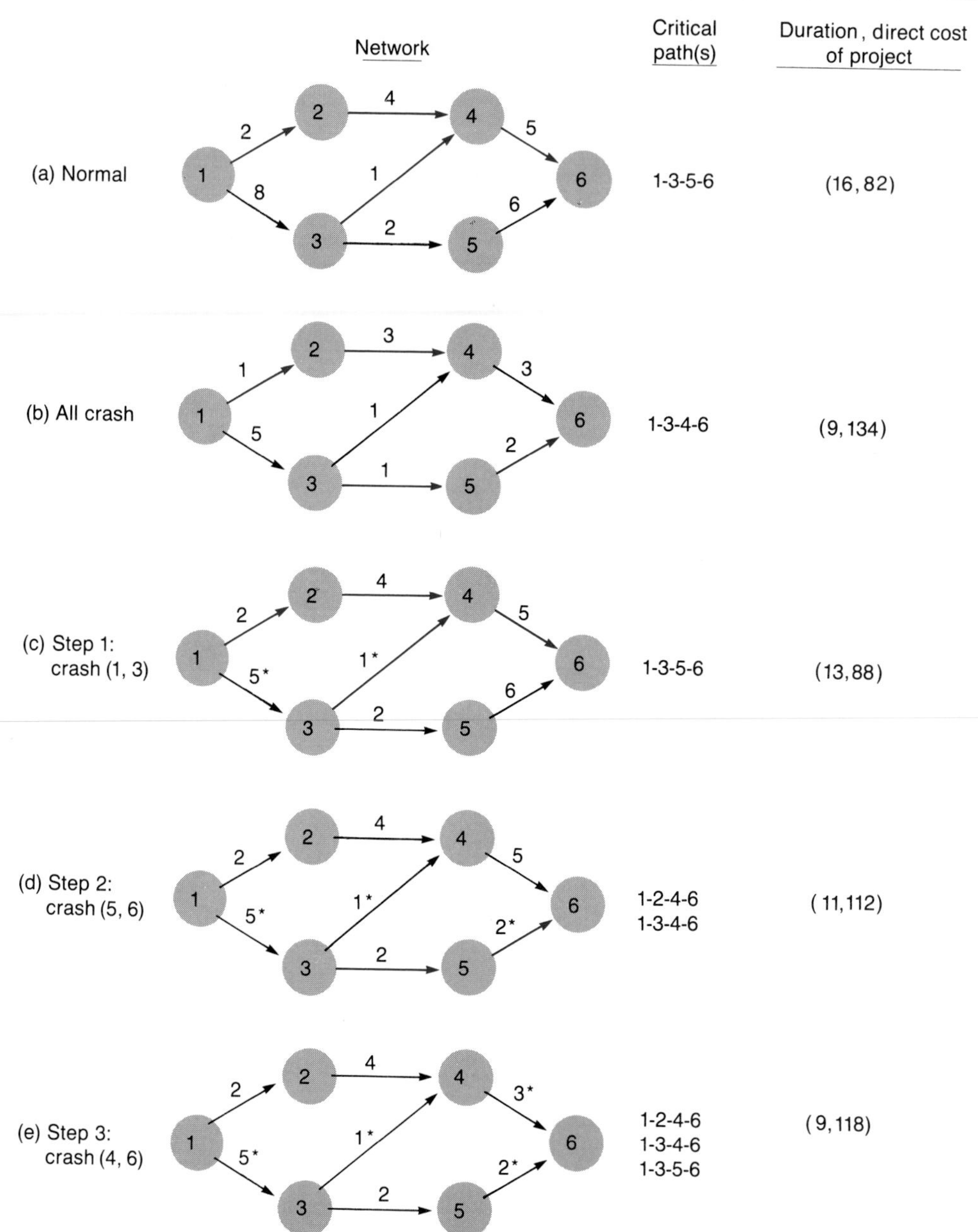

Given the current critical path 1–3–5–6 in part *c*, it is evident that activities 3–5 and 5–6 are critical and uncrashed. Because $R_{56} = 6$ is less than $R_{35} = 7$, we crash activity 5–6 in Step 2. Now the estimated duration of the project is 11 weeks at a direct cost of $112,000. Note that two paths are now critical. Activity 4–6 is chosen next for crashing

TABLE 11–8 Total Cost Calculations for Project of Example 11.2

Elapsed Time (weeks)	Direct Cost ($1,000)	Indirect Cost ($1,000)	Opportunity Cost (1,000)	Total Cost ($1,000)
16	82	35	12	129
15	84	33	9	126
14	86	31	6	123
13	88	29	3	120
12	94	27	0	121
11	100	25	−3	122
10	109	23	−6	126
9	118	21	−9	130

because it has the minimum R_{ij} (that is, $R_{46} = 3$) of all uncrashed activities along the two critical paths.

Step 3 yields a project duration of 9 weeks, a direct cost of $118,000, and three critical paths. According to the all-crash network in part *b*, we cannot lower the project's completion below 9 weeks. Furthermore, all activities that were previously crashed are currently critical; hence our procedure terminates at this point.

In general, crashing terminates when the "all-crash" time is reached *and* when current *noncritical* activities that have been crashed (or compressed), and have the *highest* R_{ij}, are *uncrashed* (or uncompressed) up to the point where they become critical.[8] To illustrate the second part of this stopping rule, suppose the network in part *d* satisfies the first part (i.e., 11 represents the all-crash time). Activity 5–6 is currently noncritical and has been crashed previously. By increasing its duration from 2 to 4 weeks, it follows that 1–3–5–6 also becomes critical, that the project's duration remains at 11 weeks, and that direct cost declines from $112,000 to $100,000.

Note, therefore, that the *least* direct cost is achieved *for each step* by uncrashing previously crashed (or uncompressing previously compressed) activities with *highest* R_{ij} along *uncritical* paths up to the point where they become critical. This gives a minimum direct cost of $100,000 for step 2 after activity 5–6 is uncrashed from 2 to 4 weeks.[9]

Now suppose that indirect cost ($1,000s) is given by the function $3 + 2t$ and opportunity cost ($1,000s) is given by the function $-36 + 3t$, where t represents elapsed time in weeks. According to the calculations in Table 11–8, total cost for the project is minimized at $120,000 for the 13-week schedule suggested by the network in part *c* of Figure 11–14.

FOLLOW-UP EXERCISES

22. Confirm the R_{ij} calculations in the last column of Table 11–7.
23. What difficulties do you foresee in crashing if the function passing through the normal and crash points is nonlinear?
24. Confirm the calculations in Table 11–8. Determine direct costs by compressing critical activities with lowest R_{ij} *one week at a time.* That is, for direct costs, generate a figure such as Figure 11–14 but having seven steps. Note that when two or more paths are currently critical, as in part *d* of Figure 11–14, a reduction of one period in the completion of the project requires the compression of the activity

[8]Take care with our terminology. If an activity is at its crash point, then we say it is crashed; moving it off its crash point is called uncrashing. If an activity is between its crash and normal points, then we say it is compressed; increasing its time further is called uncompressing.

[9]That is, $112,000 − (4 weeks − 2 weeks) · R_{56}, or $112,000 − (2 weeks) · ($6,000 per week).

with lowest R_{ij} (and no asterisk) along each critical path. This method, compared with the method in the example, requires more calculations but provides more comprehensive schedules.

**25. Given Table 11–9 for the restaurant project (Example 11.1), determine the minimum total cost schedule using the crashing procedure described in (*a*) Example 11.2 and (*b*) Exercise 24. Assume that indirect cost ($1,000) is given by $2 + t$, and opportunity cost is given by $-15 + 0.5t$, where t is elapsed time in days.

TABLE 11–9

Activity	Time Estimates (days)		Direct Cost Estimates ($1,000)	
i–j	Normal	Crash	Normal	Crash
1–4	10	6	50	60
1–6	3	1	35	36
1–8	1	1	1	1
1–2	2	1	25	27
2–3	7	5	1	1
3–4	3	2	8	11
4–5	5	4	12	20
5–6	4	2	3	8
6–7	4	3	8	12
6–9	3	2	5	8
9–10	6	4	12	15
5–10	3	3	2	2
8–11	4	2	3	8
10–11	7	4	5	6

PERT/Cost

PERT/Cost is a cost accounting technique for achieving realistic estimates of costs associated with activities and for providing an information system that allows excellent control of interim project costs. The federal government, which originally published the technique, uses it regularly for controlling cost overruns in governmental contracts.

The need for an accounting system that is conceptually consistent with project management becomes evident when one considers that traditional cost accounting systems group costs not by activities but by organizational areas, flows of materials, and time periods. PERT/Cost provides a means for structuring costs consistent with project management models.

With respect to planning and scheduling, PERT/Cost generates cumulative and average expenditures on a period-by-period basis for alternative schedules. This feature is useful in deciding when activities should be started between their earliest and latest starting dates.

Additionally, the information system for PERT/Cost provides reports that allow project managers to control costs and evaluate performance with respect to the schedule. For example, suppose *actual* cost for an activity is 80 percent of *budgeted* cost at some time. One might think that cost is under control; however, the activity may be only 50 percent complete. PERT/Cost provides this information routinely each period, for each activity, and for the project as a whole.

11.5 ASSESSMENT

After more than a quarter of a century of experience with PERT/CPM, this project-scheduling technique must be considered well established. The network approach to picturing a project is so natural that networks are to projects what spreadsheets are to accounting. Beyond the basic network diagram, however, users vary in what they gain from PERT/CPM. The diagram itself and the process of defining activity interrelationships and definitions may provide 95 percent of the payoff from PERT/CPM.

In an article describing new uses of CPM in the construction industry, Gary Glenn provides interesting insights about the actual use of the technique.[10] He points out that early uses stressed planning in the belief that the technique was not as reliable for control. Early uses also led to the technique taking the blame for project schedule failures as well as the technique being used ineffectively and only grudgingly to satisfy contractual requirements.

Glenn discusses the natural evolution of CPM into the area of resource analysis made possible by the model of the time or cash flow aspects of the project. Related to this is the cost-on-schedule payments approach applied by some owners and construction managers. In this approach, payments to the contractor are made on the dollars associated with each activity as it is completed.

Finally, Glenn mentions new developments in the use of PERT/CPM. The use of CPM as a database of historical scheduling information for projects has been useful for litigation on cost overruns and for maintenance of cost schedules. Also, the emergence of new interactive computer packages has allowed the scheduler to perform "what if" analysis.

In another key area for PERT/CPM, Dougherty, Stephens, and Ezell provide an excellent survey of the use of PERT for managing research and development in Fortune 500 companies.[11] They found that PERT was still very popular with project managers who have complex and expensive undertakings. Those managers who oppose the use of PERT find it too sophisticated, inflexible, and expensive. Nevertheless, it is used on approximately 40 percent of today's development projects, 27 percent of today's applied research projects, but only 16 percent of today's basic research projects. In most R&D projects, the authors found that the PERT system expense was less than 5 percent of the budgetary outlay of the project.

Finally, we must mention the popularity of PERT/CPM software packages on the computer. Gido provides a list of 127 project management systems, some allowing up to 10,000 activities or more.[12] Assad and Wasil review microcomputer packages

---

[10]G. O. Glenn, "CPM-Established and Then Some," *American Association of Cost Engineers Transactions*, (1985) pp. E7.1–E7.4.

[11]D. M. Dougherty, D. B. Stephens, and D. E. Ezell, "The Lasting Qualities of PERT: Preferences and Perceptions of R&D Project Managers," *R&D Management* 14, no. 1 (1984) pp. 47–56.

[12]J. Gido, *Project Management Software Directory* (New York: Industrial Press, 1985)

and mention that some claim a larger potential market for project management software than for spreadsheets.[13] Others believe the software will find much wider use as one component of large integrated packages. Hundreds of applications in American industry could be cited. Instead, we characterize most applications as having fewer than 200 activities with the majority of these under 75.[14] With many microcomputer PERT/CPM packages selling for under $1,000, there is increased interest in PERT/CPM software, as shown in the microcomputer magazines listed in the Selected References section of this chapter.

---

[13] A. A. Assad and E. A. Wasil, "Project Management Using a Microcomputer," *Computers & Operations Research* 13, no. 2/3 (1986), pp. 231–60.

[14] E. Davis and R. Martin, *"Project Management Software for the Personal Computer: An Evaluation,"* *Industrial Management* 27, No. 1 (1985), pp.1–21.

SELECTED APPLICATION REVIEW

THE AMERICAN THREAD CORPORATION

The American Thread Corporation produces textiles and is now owned by Tootell, a British company. One of the hundreds of unheralded applications of PERT took place at the American Thread Corporation as it developed a centralized order processing computer system. Raymond Proctor managed this project with the aid of a hand-drawn PERT network that covered an entire wall of his office

SOURCE: Personal observation from one of the authors' consultation visits.

AMERICAN PETROLEUM INSTITUTE

The American Petroleum Institute (API) represents oil companies and lobbied to have some provisions changed in the Outer Continental Shelf Lands Act of 1977. The API was concerned that uncertainties created by the legislation would lengthen the time between the sale of an offshore lease and commercial production of oil in the lease area. A consulting team developed a PERT network to determine the time to commercial production with and without the amendments. The challenge in that application was to separate those activities that could be done in parallel from those that would be sequential. Many participants in the legislative process viewed any delays as extending the time to production; but our knowledge of PERT/CPM has shown us that only delays on the critical path will extend the time. For example, one critical delay occurred because oil companies would no longer order platform rigs in advance of final development approval. The legislation rightly created uncertainties about approval. Previously, these site-specific rigs were ordered in the Gulf of Mexico on the expectation of development approval.

SOURCE: More details on this application can be found in D. W. McLeavey, "Projected Time to Commerical Production in Outer Continental Shelf Frontier Areas," *Outer Continental Shelf Lands Act Amendments of 1977, Part 2* (Washington, D.C.: U.S. Government Printing Office, 1977), pp. 1357–78.

THE POLARIS PROJECT

Nuclear-powered submarines were developed in the 1950s. The Polaris project was the first major undertaking, and included the solution of many technical and engineering problems. As construction planning got serious, however, the extremely difficult management problem of planning, scheduling, coordinating, and controlling such a vast project became evident. Each prime contractor and subcontractor alone represent at least one activity on the network, and there were more than 9,000 contractors! The potential for delays just from "bottlenecks" (precedence problems) alone was staggering.

The solution to this management problem was the joint development of PERT by the Navy Special Projects Office and the management consulting firm of Booz, Allen, & Hamilton. The Navy Department has since claimed that the Polaris Missile Submarine was combat-ready at least two years ahead of the originally scheduled (pre-PERT) date.

SOURCE: Richard I. Levin, and Charles A. Kirkpatrick, *Planning and Control with PERT/CPM* (New York: McGraw-Hill, 1966.

ETHAN ALLEN FURNITURE COMPANY

One of the authors served as a consultant to the Ethan Allen furniture company for several years. At that time, a critical need for additional capacity led to major plant expansion projects in seven furniture factories (in addition to minor increases in the other factories). The typical expansion project consisted of a 100 percent or greater increase in volume, design and construction of large buildings, layout and purchase of new equipment, rearrangement of existing facilities, and the hiring and training of new employees.

Large capital expenditures were committed to these expansion projects, and there were substantial pressures to get the additional capacities on line as quickly as possible. The vice president of manufacturing was very concerned about cost and time performance. This was the largest set of expansion projects ever taken on by the company; if past time-cost experiences were to be repeated, the company would need to go back into the money markets and customer complaints would reach an all-time high.

At the outset most of the plant managers responsible for the major projects did not understand the PERT/CPM models. They had all participated in expansion projects before, felt they knew how to do them, and that the PERT/CPM approach was largely a "pain in the neck."

(continued)

Initial responsibility for preparing the PERT/CPM plan was often delegated to someone who did not understand the complexities of the project. As a result, original plans had great variability in quality. Eventually, the requirement of PERT/CPM planning and reporting forced managers to understand the technique as well as to explain early deviations in plans. The result was better control and attention to meeting detailed objectives. Furthermore, extensive replanning resulted in better matches of time and cost schedules to reality than would otherwise have been achieved.

At one point, it was necessary to plan an education program for people actively engaged in major expansion projects. Included were the basics of project management models, the reporting and control procedures, and a case study. This session was intensive, lasted three days, and took place after the projects had been in the design stages for several months. At that point, each person had made major mistakes which could be shared, and the validity of project management models became obvious.

A critical reason for previous poor time-cost performance at Ethan Allen was a tendency to focus attention on the physical or "hard" aspects of a plant expansion. For example, the construction of buildings, placement of utilities, and ordering of equipment received a great deal of attention; but the design of a production scheduling system for the expanded volume or the training of 150 new employees did not receive the same degree of concerted effort.

This tendency to focus on hard activities to the detriment of "soft" activities was clearly shown in the planning models for Ethan Allen. Almost all of the projects included no provision for activities such as project scheduling, quality control procedures, plant maintenance and protection, shop floor control, production scheduling, personnel planning, capital budgeting, start up budgets and pro forma statements, standard cost calculations, product engineering, safety, hiring, training, or incentive wage determination.

When attention was clearly focused on the importance of considering soft activities as well as the hard activities, a very interesting learning experience took place. When each of these activities is included, it is necessary to identify the resources that will be used. That is, for example, *who* will design the new production scheduling system? The resources required for soft activities are almost always managerial people, and the analysis of the work loads placed on these individuals can be frightening. It is not hard to see why past failures were so prevalent.

SOURCE: Author's consultation.

SELECTED REFERENCES

Ang, A. H. S.; J. Abdeknour; and A. A. Chaker. "Analysis of Activity Networks under Uncertainty." *Journal of the American Society of Civil Engineering (Mechanical Division)* 101 (1975), pp. 373–87.

Assad, A. A., and B. Golden. "PERT." In *Encyclopedia of Statistical Sciences* Vol. 6. Ed. S. Kotz and N. Johnson, New York: John Wiley & Sons, 1985, pp. 691–97.

Clelland, D. and W. King. *Systems Analysis and Project Management.* 3rd ed. New York: McGraw-Hill, 1983.

Charnes, A.; W. W. Cooper, and G. L. Thompson. "Critical Path Analysis via Chance Constrained and Stochastic Programming." *Operations Research* 12, no. 3 (1964), pp. 460–70.

Devroye, L. P. "Inequalities for the Completion Time of Stochastic PERT Networks." *Mathematical Operations Research* no. 4 (1979), p. 441–47.

Edwards, K., et al. "Project Management with the PC: Part I." *PC Magazine* 3, no. 21 (1984), pp. 109–56.

________. "Project Management with the PC: Part III." *PC Magazine*. 3, no. 24 (1984), pp. 193–277.

Hart, Gary, et al. "Project Management with the PC: Part II." *PC Magazine* 3, no. 22 (1984), pp. 211–68.

Kerzner, H. *Project Management*. 2nd ed. New York: Van Nostrand Reinhold, 1984.

Krakow, I. *Project Management with the IBM PC Using Microsoft Project, Harvard Project Manager, Visischedule, and Project Scheduler.* Bowie, Md.: Brady Communications Company, 1985.

Kress, M. "The Chance Constrained Critical Path with Location-Scale Distributions." European Journal of Operational Research 18, no. 3 (1984), pp. 359–63.

Lindsey, J. H. "An Estimate of Expected Critical-Path Length in PERT Networks." Operations Research 20, no. 4 (1972), pp. 800–812.

Miller, R. "How to Plan and Control with PERT." *Harvard Business Review,* 40 no. 2 (1969), pp. 93–104.

Moder, J.; C. Phillips; and E. Davis. *Project Management with CPM, PERT and Precedence Diagramming*. 3rd ed. New York; Van Nostrand Reinhold, 1983.

Needle, D. Managing Time and Resources. *Personal Computing* 9, no. 5 (1985), pp. 85–93.

Pantumsinchai, P.; M. Hassan; and I. Gupta. *Basic Programs for Production and Operations Management*. Englewood Cliffs, N.J.: Prentice-Hall 1983.

Robillard, P., and M. Trahan. The Completion Time of PERT Networks. *Operations Research* 25, no. 1 (1977), pp. 15–29.

Smith, L., and S. Gupta. "Evaluation of Project Management for Microcomputers for Production and Inventory Management Projects." *Production Inventory Management Review* 5, no. 6 (1985), pp. 66–70.

Webster, F. *Survey of Project Management Software Packages*. Drexel Hill, Penn.: Project Management Institute, 1985.

Wiest, J. D., and F. K. Levy. *A Management Guide to PERT/CPM*. Englewood Cliffs, N.J.: Prentice-Hall 1977.

ADDITIONAL EXERCISES

26. ***Product Development.*** Consider the simplified scenario for the development of a consumer product through the market test phase shown in Table 11–10.

TABLE 11–10

Activity	Symbol	Preceding Activities	Time Estimate (weeks)
Design promotion campaign	*A*	—	3
Initial pricing analysis	*B*	—	1
Product design	*C*	—	5
Promotional costs analysis	*D*	*A*	1
Manufacture prototype models	*E*	*C*	6
Product cost analysis	*F*	*E*	1
Final pricing analysis	*G*	*B, D, F*	2
Market test	*H*	*G*	8

a. Draw the network for this project.
b. Calculate slacks and interpret their meaning.
c. Determine the critical path and interpret its meaning.
d. Construct a time chart and identify scheduling flexibilities.

27. For the product development project in the preceding exercise consider the detailed time estimates given in Table 11–11. Note that time estimates in the preceding exercise are equivalent to modal time estimates in this exercise.

TABLE 11–11

	Time Estimates (weeks)		
Activity	Optimistic	Most Likely	Pessimistic
A	1	3	4
B	1	1	2
C	4	5	9
D	1	1	1
E	4	6	12
F	1	1	2
G	1	2	3
H	6	8	10

a. Relabel your network in the preceding exercise to include $\bar{d}_{ij}$ (in place of d_{ij}) and v_{ij}. Use Equations 11.6 and 11.7.
b. Compare slacks to the preceding exercise.
c. Has the critical path changed?
d. Determine the following probabilities:
(1) That the project will be completed in 22 weeks or less.
(2) That the project will be completed by its earliest expected completion date.
(3) That the project takes more than 30 weeks to complete.

28. Use Equations 11.9 and 11.10 to calculate $\bar{d}_{ij}$ and v_{ij} and answer the same questions as in the preceding exercise. Compare results to the preceding exercise.
29. Consider the cost-time estimates for the product development project of Exercise 26 as given in Table 11–12.

TABLE 11–12

	Time Estimates (weeks)		Direct Cost Estimates ($1,000s)	
Activity	**Normal**	**Crash**	**Normal**	**Crash**
A	3	1.0	3.5	10.0
B	1	0.5	1.2	2.0
C	5	3.0	9.0	18.0
D	1	0.7	1.0	2.0
E	6	3.0	20.0	50.0
F	1	0.5	2.2	3.0
G	2	1.0	4.0	9.0
H	8	6.0	100.0	150.0

Indirect cost is made up of two components: a fixed cost of $5,000 and a variable cost of $1,000 per week of elapsed time. Also, for each week the project exceeds 17 weeks, an opportunity cost of $2,000 per week is assessed.

a. Construct a time chart for the minimum total cost schedule.

b. Construct a two-part schedule of direct costs (of the type illustrated in Figure 11–6) based on the time schedule in part *a*. Of the two, which schedule yields the lowest peak cost? Of the two, which schedule levels cost the most based on variance?

30. ***Space Module Assembly.*** An aerospace company has received a contract from NASA for the final assembly of a space module for an upcoming mission. A team of engineers has determined the activities, precedence constraints, and time estimates given in Table 11–13.

TABLE 11–13

Activity	Symbol	Preceding Activities	Time Estimate (days)
Construct shell of module	*A*	—	30
Order life support system and scientific experimentation package from same supplier	*B*	—	15
Order components of control and navigational system	*C*	—	25
Wire module	*D*	*A*	3
Assemble control and navigational system	*E*	*C*	7
Preliminary test of life support system	*F*	*B*	1
Install life support system in module	*G*	*D, F*	5
Install scientific experimentation package in module	*H*	*D, F*	2
Preliminary test of control and navigational system	*I*	*E, F*	4
Install control and navigational system in module	*J*	*H, I*	10
Final testing and debugging	*K*	*G, J*	8

a. Draw the network for this project. (*Hint:* You should have 10 events and two dummy activities.)
b. Calculate slacks, and interpret their meaning.
c. Determine the critical path and interpret its meaning.
d. Construct a time chart and identify scheduling flexibilities.

31. A more careful analysis of time estimates for the space module assembly of the preceding exercise is given in Table 11–14. Note that the "most likely estimates" are identical to the "time estimates" in the preceding exercise.

TABLE 11–14

Activity	Time Estimates (days)		
	Optimistic	Most Likely	Pessimistic
A	25	30	45
B	10	15	20
C	20	25	35
D	3	3	5
E	5	7	12
F	1	1	1
G	4	5	7
H	2	2	3
I	4	4	6
J	8	10	14
K	6	8	15

a. Relabel your network in the preceding exercise to include $\bar{d}_{ij}$ (in place of d_{ij}) and v_{ij}. Use Equations 11.6 and 11.7.
b. Compare slacks to the preceding exercise.
c. Has the critical path changed?
d. Determine the following probabilities.
(1) That the project will be completed in 54 days or less.
(2) That the project will be completed by its earliest expected completion date.
(3) That the project takes more than 70 days to complete.

32. Use Equations 11.9 and 11.10 to calculate $\bar{d}_{ij}$ and v_{ij}, and answer the same questions as in the preceding exercise. Compare results to the preceding exercise.

33. A project has 11 activities that can be accomplished either by one person working alone or by several people working together. The activities precedence constraints, and time estimates are shown in Table 11–15.
Suppose you have up to five people who can be assigned on any given day. A person must work full days on each activity, but the number of people working on an activity can vary from day to day.
a. Prepare a network diagram, and calculate the critical path and slacks assuming that one person (independently) is working on each task.
b. Prepare a time chart.
c. Prepare a daily assignment sheet for personnel so as to finish the project in minimum time.
d. Prepare a daily assignment sheet to "best" balance the work force assigned to this project.
e. How many days could the project be compressed if unlimited personnel resources were available?

TABLE 11–15

Activities	Preceding Activities	Person-Days Required
A	—	10
B	*A*	8
C	*A*	5
D	*B*	6
E	*D*	8
F	*C*	7
G	*E, F*	4
H	*F*	2
I	*F*	3
J	*H, I*	3
K	*J, G*	2

34. The Sour Grapes Winery has the following project defined for refurbishing one of their vats (see Table 11–16):

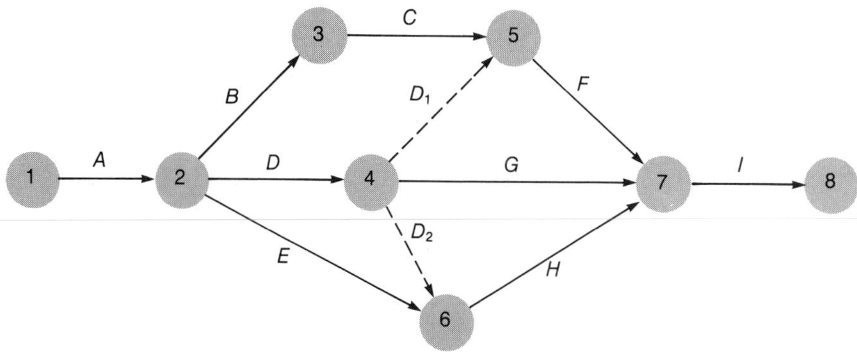

TABLE 11–16

			Crash Data	
Task	$\bar{d}_{ij}$ (days)	$\sqrt{v_{ij}}$ (days)	Maximum Possible Compression (days)	Expediting Cost per Day ($)
A	6	2	0	—
B	2	0	1	50
C	12	3	2	80
D	8	1	2	175
E	7	2	1	100
F	16	4	0	—
G	23	2	1	100
H	25	5	3	300
I	4	1	1	1,000

a. Find the critical path and slacks.
b. Find the probability of completion within 45 days.

c. Find the minimum cost increase to reduce the expected project duration by one day.
d. Find the minimum cost increase to reduce the expected project duration by two days.
e. Find the minimum project duration and the expected cost increase.

APPENDIX
Mathematical Programming Applied to Project Management Models

In this appendix we illustrate the use of mathematical programming in determining (1) the earliest completion time for the project, (2) the critical path, and (3) the schedule that minimizes direct cost for the project. Although there are fast network methods to solve this problem, the formulation here can help you understand the problem more precisely.

Earliest Event Times and Critical Path

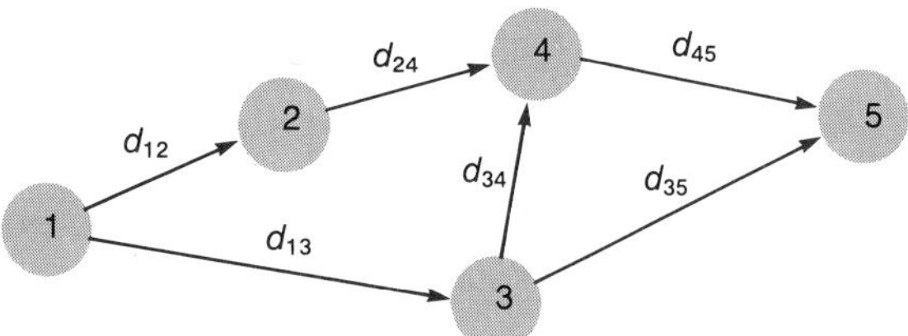

For the illustrative network given by the accompanying figure, we define E_j as the earliest time for event j and d_{ij} as the duration of activity i–j. Our objective is to *minimize* the earliest time of completing the project (as given by E_5) such that constraints imposed by the definition of E_j are not violated. That is, our constraints must guarantee that E_j is at least equal to or greater than the sum of durations along *all* paths leading into event j. For example, with respect to event 4, the following two constraints guarantee that E_4 is no less than the *longest* path into event 4, as suggested by Equation 11.1:

$$E_4 \geq E_2 + d_{24}$$

and

$$E_4 \geq E_3 + d_{34}.$$

For the entire network, you should easily confirm the following LP formulation for determining earliest event times:

Minimize

$$z = E_5$$

subject to

$$E_2 \qquad\qquad \geq d_{12} \qquad (1)$$

$$
\begin{aligned}
E_3 \qquad\qquad\qquad & \geq d_{13} \qquad (2)\\
-E_2 \qquad + E_4 \qquad & \geq d_{24} \qquad (3)\\
- E_3 + E_4 \qquad & \geq d_{34} \qquad (4)\\
- E_3 \qquad + E_5 & \geq d_{35} \qquad (5)\\
- E_4 + E_5 & \geq d_{45} \qquad (6)\\
E_j & \geq 0 \quad \text{for all } j.
\end{aligned}
$$

Inspection of the right-hand–side constants in 1 through 6 should convince you that the number of constraints always equals the number of activities. Furthermore, it can be shown that the dual of this primal problem (after certain modifications) is equivalent to a formulation for finding the *longest* path in the network. The optimal values of dual variables (*shadow prices*) indicate whether an activity is critical (value of unity) or noncritical (value of zero). Hence the critical path can be determined by examining shadow prices in the optimal solution to the primal problem. Since for each constraint in the primal there is a corresponding dual variable, it follows that (in our example) the shadow price corresponding to constraint 1 indicates whether or not activity 1–2 is critical; the shadow price corresponding to constraint 2 determines the nature of activity 1–3 and so forth.

FOLLOW-UP EXERCISES

35. Formulate the LP model for the restaurant project.
36. Confirm our solution to the restaurant project by solving the LP model. Inspect shadow prices to determine the critical path. Interpret the meaning of surplus variables.
37. Formulate and solve (by linear programming) the network given in part *a* of Figure 11–14. Confirm the critical path from shadow prices and interpret the meaning of surplus variables.
38. What recourse do you have if all E_j are restricted to integer values?

Minimum Cost Schedules

In Section 11.4 we presented a cumbersome "hand" technique for generating direct cost curves based on the concept of crashing. Assuming a linear function between crash and normal points (see Figure 11–13) and an intercept on the cost axis given by A_{ij}, the direct cost contribution of activity *i–j* is given by

$$A_{ij} - R_{ij} \cdot x_{ij}\,, \qquad (1)$$

where R_{ij} is the ratio defined by Equation 11.11, and x_{ij} is the *scheduled duration* for activity *i–j*. The objective function is determined by summing (1) over all defined *i–j* activities:

Minimize

$$z = \sum_{(i,j)} (A_{ij} - R_{ij} \cdot x_{ij})\,. \qquad (2)$$

The first set of constraints ensure that all x_{ij} are assigned values between crash (DC_{ij}) and normal (DN_{ij}) durations:

$$x_{ij} \leq DN_{ij}, \quad \text{all defined } i\text{–}j$$
$$x_{ij} \geq DC_{ij}, \quad \text{all defined } i\text{–}j\,. \tag{3}$$

The next set of constraints avoids a scheduling inconsistency:

$$E_j - E_i - x_{ij} \geq 0, \quad \text{all defined } i\text{–}j\,, \tag{4}$$

where E_j is the earliest time for event j. Note that (4) avoids the inconsistency of a duration being longer than its allotted time, as given by $(E_j - E_i)$. Also, in addition to all x_{ij}, all E_j are treated as decision variables. Finally, the duration of the project, as specified by t, must conform to the earliest time for the terminal event (n):

$$E_n = t\,. \tag{5}$$

The solution to this LP problem yields the schedule (E_j's and x_{ij}'s) that minimizes direct cost for a project of length t, which represents a point on the "Direct Cost" function of Figure 11–12. The entire function can be be constructed by varying t in steps between its appropriate limits and solving 2 through 5 for each step. A far more efficient (and elegant) approach is the use of parametric linear programming for generating optimal z as a function of t.

FOLLOW-UP EXERCISES

39. Explain why it would be valid to

    Maximize

    $$z' = \sum_{(i,j)} R_{ij} \cdot x_{ij}$$

    in finding optimal values for x_{ij} and E_j. Is z' equivalent to direct cost?
40. In general, within what limits can t be varied?
41. How can you be sure that E_j represents the *earliest* time for event j?
42. Formulate the LP version for the project in Example 11.2.
43. Solve the preceding exercise (and compare to Table 11.8) for
    a. $t = 9$.
    b. $t = 10, \ldots, 16$.
44. Formulate the LP version for the restaurant project as given in Exercise 25.

**45. Solve the preceding exercise for $t = 25, \ldots, 38$.

CASE Rocky Road University

Rocky Road University has decided to field an Executive MBA program (EMBA program). Such a program brings together business executives with five years or more of managerial experience in a class of 25 students per year for a two-year MBA program. Classes are taught on Friday afternoons and all day Saturday at the university's Cushy Plush Conference facility.

In developing this program, the MBA director has hired you as a graduate assistant to develop a PERT chart of the project—developing and delivering this new program. She provides you with her list of activities needed for the project, but she is uncertain of the times involved and thinks she may have overlooked some vital activities. Sketch out your plan of attack, and sketch a rough PERT chart. What can be done in parallel, and what must be done sequentially?

Design program.	3 months.
Obtain faculty approval.	3 months.
Obtain university approval.	6 months.
Obtain board of governors approval.	6 months.
Schedule courses (20 courses × 48 hours per course).	6 months.
Choose microcomputer for program.	3 months.
Recruit students for program.	12 months.
Advertise and promote program.	8 months.
Recruit faculty for program.	3 months.
Arrange meals and accommodations for weekends scheduled	3 months.

The program is projected to begin in July, one and a half years from now, and it is currently January. Twenty-five students per year will pursue the program. Prices have not yet been set, but it is expected that half of the participants will be sponsored by their companies. Can the program start in one and a half years?

12

Dynamic Programming and Sequential Decisions

Chapter Outline

Dynamic programming is a recursive optimization approach to solving sequential decision problems. By **recursive optimization procedure,** we mean one that *optimizes on a step-by-step basis using information from the preceding steps*. In short, we "optimize as we go." Recall that in the previous mathematical programming algorithms, optimization was also achieved on a step-by-step basis, but it was iterative rather than recursive; that is, each step represented a unique solution that was nonoptimal. In dynamic programming, a single step is sequentially related to preceding steps and is not itself a solution to the problem. A single step contains information that identifies a segment of the optimal solution.

Because of these features, dynamic programming is most often applied to problems requiring a sequence of interrelated decisions. Many time-dependent (dynamic) processes are characterized by sequential decision problems that need to be solved; hence the term **dynamic programming (DP)**. Other applications particularly well-suited to dynamic programming involve interrelationships rather than time dependencies per se, although time dependencies are a common basis for expressing interrelationships among variables. A more apt term for dynamic programming, therefore, might be **recursive optimization.**

In everyday life, we continually face sequential decision problems. If a graduating student has a good job offer in hand, should he or she decline it in anticipation of a better offer from another company? In sports, the athlete continually makes decisions about the best shot to take by evaluating where he or she will be left for the next one. Chess players make optimal opening moves depending on what type of middle game they want to be left facing. House buyers decide whether to buy now or wait for interest rates or house prices to decline.

As you proceed in this chapter, we believe you will be struck by the elegance and simplicity of the dynamic programming approach. We begin by orienting you to some basic concepts and terminology with a simple example. We follow with computational procedures applied to the simple example and other realistic problems. Additional applications are presented, followed by an assessment of the contributions, potential, and shortcomings of recursive optimization.

12.1 FUNDAMENTALS

Terminology and Principles

The fundamental approach of dynamic programming involves (1) the breaking down of a multistage problem into its subparts, steps, or **single stages,** a process called **decomposition**; (2) making decisions one at a time, or recursively, at **each stage,** according to a specific optimization objective; and (3) combining the results at each stage to solve the entire problem, a process called **composition**. The act of composition results in a set of sequential decision rules called a **policy**. For example, dynamic programming would optimize an n-decision variable problem by decomposing it into a series of n stages (each decision variable a stage), assigning an optimal value to each variable, and combining the results from each stage to generate the overall solution to the problem.

At each stage, the decision rule is determined by evaluating a criterion or objective function, called the **recursive equation** or **functional equation** (functional because it is a function yielding a single real number). This evaluation utilizes Bellman's famous **principle of optimality:**

> An optimal set of decision rules has the property that, regardless of the *i*th decision, the remaining decisions must be optimal with respect to the outcome that results from the *i*th decision.

Note that if this were not so, the entire policy could not possibly be optimal. The movement from one stage to another, or the decision made in any one stage, affects the **state** (a specific measurable condition of the system), which most often is determined by mathematical equations called **transformation functions.**

For example, the problem of maximizing the return from several different investment projects subject to an investment budget constraint might be decomposed into stages with each project as a stage. The criterion would be the investment return, and the recursive or functional equation might specify the cumulative return through the *i*th stage. Once decisions have been made for the first i stages, the state would be the amount of budget remaining. The transformation function simply specifies that the amount of resource left after the next stage is the amount of resource entering the stage minus that used up in the stage.

Two basic computational approaches have been developed. The **backward computational procedure,** or **backward recursion,** is illustrated first using the classical shortest route problem. After reinforcing backward recursions with a capital budgeting example, we will develop the **forward recursion** approach in the shortest route problem before proceeding to some time-dependent problems. We will use forward recursions to mimic the passage of time in these time-dependent problems.

Backward Recursion Method

Figure 12–1*a* is a schematic representation of a problem involving a sequence of n decisions. Dynamic programming decomposes the problem into a set of n stages of analysis, each stage corresponding to one of the decisions. Each stage of analysis is described by a set of elements—*decision(s), input state(s), output state(s),* and *return(s)* (measures of performance)—which can be represented schematically as in Figure 12–1*b*. Figure 12–1*c* shows the notational representation of these elements when a backward recursion analysis is used.

Figure 12–1*d* is a schematic representation of the decomposed problem and the n stages of analysis. We can formalize the notation with the following definition of symbols:

i = Stage number (or stage of analysis).
x_i = Decision variable associated with stage i.

FIGURE 12–1

(a) Sequence of n decisions

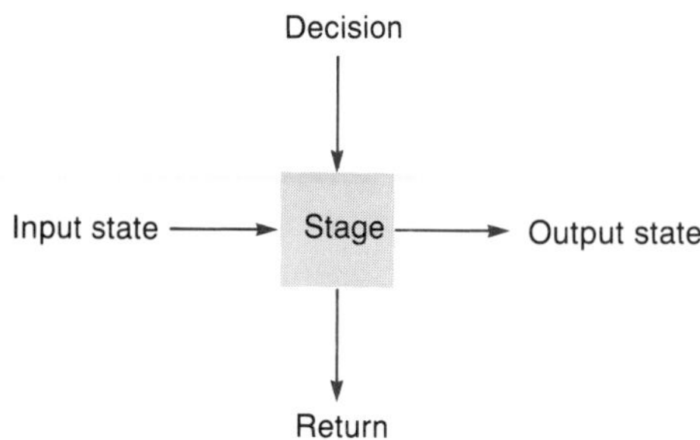

(b) Model elements for a stage of analysis

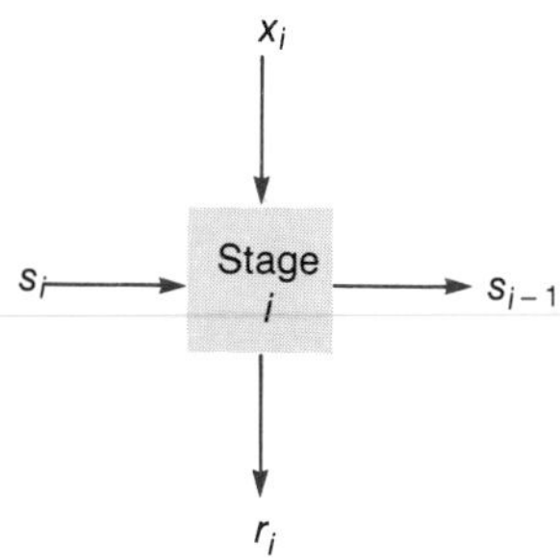

(c) Notational representation for a stage of analysis

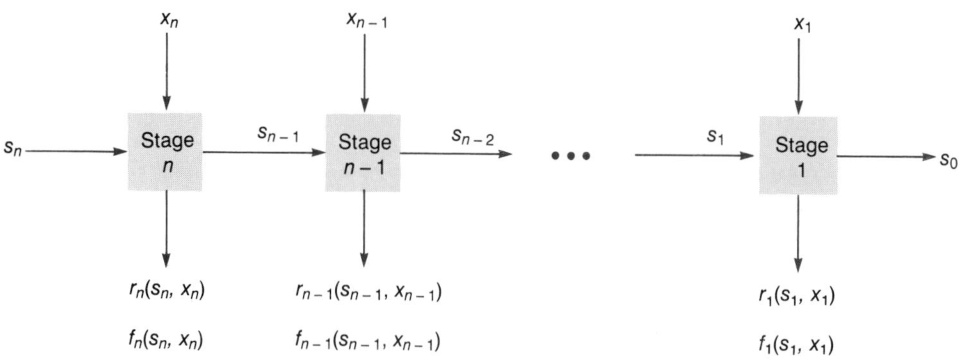

(d) Symbolic representation of n stages of analysis using backward recursion

s_i = State of the system *prior to* stage i.
$r_i(s_i, x_i)$ = Direct criterion return at stage i.
$f_i(s_i, x_i)$ = Cumulative criterion return from stages 1 through i.

Two observations should be made. To begin with, the backward recursion approach results in the last decision in the sequence corresponding to the first stage of analysis. Similarly, the first decision in the sequence corresponds to the last stage of analysis—thus the reverse-order labeling of stages. A second observation concerns the measure of performance, or returns from each stage. There are two types of returns—the direct return from stage i and the cumulative return (which is of greatest interest) from stages 1 through i. Notice that both of these depend on the input state *and* the decision(s) made at a given stage.

The general form of the recursion equation used to compute cumulative return is

$$\begin{matrix}\text{Cumulative return} \\ \text{through stage } i\end{matrix} = \begin{matrix}\text{Direct return} \\ \text{from stage } i\end{matrix} + \begin{matrix}\text{Cumulative return} \\ \text{through stage } i-1\end{matrix}$$

or,

$$f_i(s_i, x_i) = r_i(s_i, x_i) + f_{i-1}(s_{i-1}, x_{i-1}).$$

The following example illustrates the backward recursion approach of dynamic programming.

Example 12.1 Shortest Route Problem

Figure 12–2 illustrates a **network** that represents the "stagecoach" version of the shortest-route problem. The objective is to determine the path from the origin (I) to the destination (VIII) that minimizes the sum of the numbers along the **directed arcs** of the path. A directed arc is a line segment with an arrow to show the direction of travel between two **nodes**. The nodes are identified by roman numerals and are used to represent the beginning and end of directed arcs. Typically, the number associated with each arc represents the distance, cost, or time of "traveling" along that particular segment of the "journey." The terms *traveling* and *journey* are used loosely because many important applications of the shortest route model are unrelated to travel. In a follow-up exercise to this section, we will see an application of this model to an equipment replacement problem (as was illustrated in Chapter 10).

Simple observation and counting indicate the existence of five distinct paths through the network and reveal the optimal path given by I–II–VI–VIII, with a total distance of 8. In typical applications, the number of paths is too great to solve by enumeration; hence there is a real need for procedures that efficiently solve this type of problem. Although other more efficient procedures exist for the shortest route problem, the model allows the simplest dynamic programming formulation to be presented, and so it is a good place to start.

As mentioned earlier, the backward recursion approach solves a dynamic programming problem by analyzing the last stage first. The result of the analysis is the definition of optimal policies (decisions), which are contingent on the state of the system when entering the final stage. In the shortest route problem, backward recursion will focus on the third leg of the trip and determine the best destination node (this must be node VIII), given one's location at the beginning of the final leg.

The backward recursion approach then *reaches back* to incorporate information from the previous stage. *The result of stage 2 analysis is a set of policies that are optimal for the last two stages of the problem, contingent on the state of the system when entering stage 2.* In the shortest route problem, the backward recursion method reaches

FIGURE 12–2 Shortest Route Problem

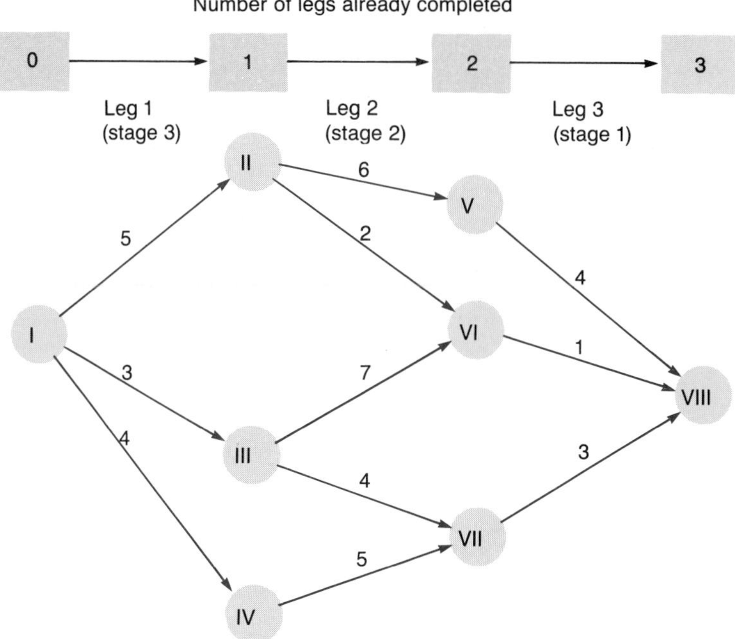

back to leg 2 of the trip and determines the best possible sequence of paths to follow for the rest of the trip, given one's location prior to leg 2. The final phase of the analysis incorporates information regarding leg 1 of the trip, resulting in an optimal sequence of paths for the entire journey. Let us now illustrate this approach.

As we have seen, dynamic programming decomposes this problem into three stages, one for each leg of the journey. Note that nodes are useful in identifying where one is located prior to or following the completion of a leg of the journey. For example, if path III–VI is followed, the location prior to leg 2 is node III, and the location at the completion of this leg is node VI. Node VI in this instance would be the location prior to the starting point for the next leg of the journey.

Given where one is located following any leg of the trip, it is simple to illustrate how a decision is made using a recursive equation in the context of Bellman's principle of optimality. Consider the third leg of the trip and the only end point for this portion of the trip (node VIII). If we found ourselves at node V, the optimal (and only) path to node VIII would be V–VIII. Similarly, VI–VIII and VII–VIII are the optimal paths from nodes VI and VII, respectively. But what if we found ourselves at node II? Where do we go from there? To answer this question, we must solve a subproblem.

The optimal path from node II must minimize the sum of the distance to the next node plus the optimal distance from the next node to the end point. In this case there are two alternatives to consider:

From Node II

Alternative paths:	II–V and V–VIII	or	II–VI and VI–VIII
Distance traveled:	6 and 4 = 10		2 + 1 = 3

Path II–VI–VIII is the best with a distance of 3. Further, we store this information for future reference. If we ever find ourselves at node II, we automatically know that the optimal path from node II is II–VI–VIII with a distance of 3.

Similarly, the optimal path from node III is III–VII–VIII with a distance of 7. This is identified by comparing the following alternatives:

From Node III

Alternative paths:	III–VI and VI–VIII	or	III–VII and VII–VIII
Distance traveled:	7 + 1 = 8		4 + 3 = 7

From Node IV

Alternative paths:	IV–VII and VII–VIII
Distance traveled:	5 + 3 = 8

From node IV, the optimal path is the only path, IV–VII–VIII, with a distance of 8. We have now determined the optimal (minimum distance) paths for the last two legs of the trip given any location prior to leg 2.

We now reach back and incorporate information pertaining to leg 1 of the trip. Starting at node I, we have three paths to consider for leg 1. If we take path I–II, we will travel a distance of 5. In our second stage of analysis, we decided that we would take II–VI–VIII with a distance of 3 if we ever found ourselves at node II. Thus a decision to move from node I to node II should be followed by movements II–VI and VI–VIII for a total distance of 8. The three paths from node I can best be considered in a table.

Decision	Distance to Next Node	Optimal Path from Next Node	Optimal Distance from Next Node	Total Distance from Node I to Node VIII
I–II	5	II–VI–VIII	3	8*
I–III	3	III–VII–VIII	7	10
I–IV	4	IV–VII–VIII	8	12

The best decision in this table is I–II, with a total distance of 8. The other alternatives involve distances of 10 and 12.

This example can also be formulated using our problem-solving framework. As we go through the formulation steps, we will begin to develop a generalized notation common to dynamic programming models.

1. **Verbal Statement of the Problem.**
   Minimize the distance traveled from node I to node VIII.
2. **Decisions.**
   a. **Verbal Statement**
      Paths to follow between node I and node VIII.
   b. **Mathematical Definition**

$$x_{ij} = \begin{cases} 1 & \text{if arc chosen from node } i \text{ to node } j, \\ 0 & \text{otherwise.} \end{cases}$$

3. **Criterion.**
   a. **Verbal Statement**
      Total distance
   b. **Mathematical Statement**

   Let t_{ij} be the distance between nodes i and j.

   Minimize

$$z = g(x_{ij}) = t_{\mathrm{I,II}}x_{\mathrm{I,II}} + t_{\mathrm{I,III}}x_{\mathrm{I,III}} + t_{\mathrm{I,IV}}x_{\mathrm{I,IV}} + \dots + t_{\mathrm{VII,VIII}}x_{\mathrm{VII,VIII}}$$

   Using the notation of backward recursions and Arabic numerals,

   Minimize

$$z = f_3(1)$$

   where

$$f_3(1) = \min\{t_{12}x_{12} + f_2(2), t_{13}x_{13} + f_2(3), t_{14}x_{14} + f_2(4)\}.$$

4. **Constraints.**
   None except the obvious—that we plan to make the trip (i.e., start at node I and end at node VIII).
5. **Mathematical Model.**

   Minimize

$$f_3(1)$$

   where

$$f_i(j) = \min_k \{t_{jk}x_{jk} + f_{i-1}(k)\}$$

   and

$$f_0(j) = 0.$$

Tabular Approach

For many dynamic programming problems, the analysis can be organized and displayed within tables, one for each stage of the analysis. Table 12–1 displays the tabular solution to the shortest route problem. For any given table (stage), the following elements exist:

One row corresponding to each possible entering state for that stage.

One column corresponding to each decision alternative for that stage. The values in these columns reflect the cumulative return through that stage of analysis, or $f_i = r_i + f^*_{i-1}$, where f^*_{i-1} represents the *optimal* cumulative return through stage $i - 1$.

Two columns that define the optimal policy *given* the entering state for the stage. One column defines the optimal decision, and the other column, the cumulative return associated with making the optimal decision.

TABLE 12–1 Tabular Solution to Shortest Route Problem

Stage 1 (Leg 3): Cumulative distance through stage 1 = Distance for stage 1 + Optimal cumulative distance through stage 0 ($f_1 = r_1 + f_0^*$)

Entering State, s_1 (travel from node) \ Decision, x_1	Travel to Node	Optimal Policy	
	VIII	x_1^* Decision	f_1^* Cumulative Distance
V	4 + 0 = 4	VIII	4
VI	1 + 0 = 1	VIII*	1
VII	3 + 0 = 3	VIII	3

Stage 2 (Leg 2): Cumulative distance through stage 2 = Distance for stage 2 + Optimal cumulative distance through stage 1 ($f_2 = r_2 + f_1^*$)

Entering State, s_2 (travel from node) \ Decision, x_2	Travel to Node			Optimal Policy	
	V	VI	VII	x_2^* Decision	f_2^* Cumulative Distance
II	6 + 4 = 10	2 + 1 = 3		VI*	3
III		7 + 1 = 8	4 + 3 = 7	VII	7
IV			5 + 3 = 8	VII	8

Stage 3 (Leg 1): Cumulative distance through stage 3 = Distance for stage 3 + Optimal cumulative distance through stage 2 ($f_3 = r_3 + f_2^*$)

Entering State, s_3 (travel from node) \ Decision, x_3	Travel to Node			Optimal Policy	
	II	III	IV	x_3^* Decision	f_3^* Cumulative Distance
I	5 + 3 = 8	3 + 7 = 10	4 + 8 = 12	II*	8

The tables generated are *contingency tables,* which define optimal policies *contingent on* the entering state. For example, the table for stage 2 has three rows, reflecting the possible locations prior to the second leg of the trip, and three columns, representing the three possible decision alternatives (locations at the end of the second leg). The cells of the table found at the intersection of these rows and columns contain the cumulative return *through* stage 2, contingent on the entering state and the decision alternative chosen. These returns are the sum of the direct return from the decision at stage 2 and the *best* return from stage 1, *given* the decision at stage 2. Notice that all cells do not contain return values. Why is this?

In the table for stage 2, the optimal policy is defined contingent on the entering state. Given a possible entering state, the optimal policy is identified by comparing the feasible returns from the different decision alternatives. For example, given that we are at node II prior to leg 2, the minimum distance traveled from that point on would equal 3 if we choose to travel from node II to node VI.

Table 12–2 illustrates the composition of the optimal policy for this problem. Working forward from stage 3, the best decision for leg 1 of the journey is to travel to node II. This decision defines the entering state for stage 2. The table for stage 2 indicates that given an entering state of node II, the best decision is to travel to node VI. Finally, the last step of composition indicates that given an entering state of node VI for stage 1, the best decision (of course) is to travel to node VIII.

FOLLOW-UP EXERCISES

1. Verify the entries in each cell of Table 12–1. Verbalize their meanings.
2. Change the distance of arc II–VI to 5 and completely solve for the shortest route using backward recursion.
3. Using dynamic programming, determine the longest route in Figure 12–1.
4. Add arc I–VIII in Figure 12–1 with a distance of 9. How can this be handled?
5. ***Equipment Replacement.*** A piece of equipment must be in service for five years. At the beginning of year 6 it will be replaced regardless of what we do in the meantime. Each year the equipment loses 25 percent of its remaining value. Worth $10,000 on original purchase, the equipment is worth only $7,500 at the end of the first year and loses another $1,875 during the second year of its life.

   Operating and maintenance expenses are $500 for the first year and increase by $100 each year. Each year, we face a decision to keep or replace the equipment. (*a*) Formulate as a shortest route problem, and solve by dynamic programming with the objective of minimizing costs. (*b*) List the assumptions made in this problem. (*c*) What modifications in assumptions would make the model more realistic?

12.2 THE KNAPSACK PROBLEM AND DYNAMIC PROGRAMMING

The attractive feature of dynamic programming is its ability to handle a wide variety of optimization problems. One common problem is the knapsack problem. A scout plans to climb Mount Washington and needs to decide what to pack in the knapsack. The constraint of space available prevents the scout from taking everything needed, and yes/no decisions must be made on the basis of the value or utility of each item. Most scouts pack a pup tent and a sleeping bag, but not all pack granola. These yes/no or zero/one decisions make the problem nonlinear. Here we formulate the knapsack problem as a zero/one integer programming problem, where n items are being considered for inclusion in the knapsack.

TABLE 12–2 Composition of Optimal Policy

Stage 1 (Leg 3): Cumulative distance through stage 1 = Distance for stage 1 + Optimal cumulative distance through stage 0 ($f_1 = r_1 + f_0^*$)

Leaving State, s_1 (travel from node) \ Decision, x_1	Travel to Node	Optimal Policy	
	VIII	x_1^* Decision	f_1^* Cumulative Distance
V	4 + 0 = 4	VIII	(4)
[VI]	1 + 0 = 1	[VIII*]	(1)
VII	3 + 0 = 3	VIII	(3)

Stage 2 (Leg 2): Cumulative distance through stage 2 = Distance for stage 2 + Optimal cumulative distance through stage 1 ($f_2 = r_2 + f_1^*$)

Leaving State, s_2 (travel from node) \ Decision, x_2	Travel to Node			Optimal Policy	
	V	VI	VII	x_2^* Decision	f_2^* Cumulative Distance
[II]	6 + (4) = 10	2 + (1) = 3		[VI*]	(3)
III		7 + (1) = 8	4 + (3) = 7	VII	(7)
IV			5 + (3) = 8	VII	(8)

Stage 3 (Leg 1): Cumulative distance through stage 3 = Distance for stage 3 + Optimal cumulative distance through stage 2 ($f_3 = r_3 + f_2^*$)

Entering State, s_3 (travel from node) \ Decision, x_3	Travel to Node			Optimal Policy	
	II	III	IV	x_3^* Decision	f_3^* Cumulative Distance
[I]	5 + (3) = 8	3 + (7) = 10	4 + (8) = 12	[II*]	8

Maximize

$$z = f(x_j) = u_1x_1 + u_2x_2 + \ldots + u_nx_n$$

subject to

$$a_1x_1 + a_2x_2 + \ldots + a_nx_n \leq b$$

$$x_j = 0 \quad \text{or} \quad 1, \qquad j = 1, 2, \ldots, n$$

where u_j is the utility of the jth item, a_j is the volume required for the jth item, and b is the volume of the knapsack.

The following example shows how a knapsack-type problem can be solved by dynamic programming.

Example 12.2 Capital Budgeting Model

The comptroller of a company has a \$5 million budget for capital investment to allocate among three divisions. Each division was asked to submit new project proposals together with relevant cost and revenue data. Based on the proposals, the comptroller constructed Table 12–3 by discounting all future cash flows (costs and revenues) and expressing them in terms of net present values. For example, project A3 requires a present outlay of \$2 million and yields a net (after subtracting the initial capital outlay and the discounted future costs) present value of \$2 million. As can be seen, not every division proposed the same number of projects. Note that the first project of each division represents a decision not to select a project from that division. Furthermore, projects across divisions are independent. To avoid morale problems in the divisions, however, *no more than one project can be selected from any one division.* Alternatively, the projects for any one division can be treated as being mutually exclusive.

TABLE 12–3 Capital Investment Data (*Millions of dollars*)

	Capital Outlay	NPV of Future Cash Flow	NPV of Benefits (r) (after subtracting capital outlay)
Division A:			
Project A1	0	0	0
Project A2	1	3	2
Project A3	2	4	2
Project A4	3	5	2
Division B:			
Project B1	0	0	0
Project B2	3	6	3
Division C:			
Project C1	0	0	0
Project C2	1	2	1
Project C3	2	5	3

The dynamic programming approach decomposes this problem into three stages ($n = 3$), one for each division. This approach is illustrated by Figure 12–3.

FIGURE 12–3 DP Representation of Capital Budgeting Example: Backward Recursion

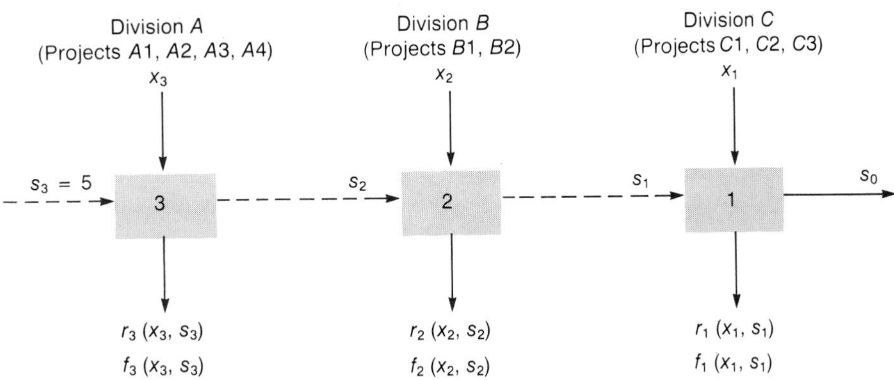

The decision variable in the ith stage (x_i) represents adoption of one of the available projects under consideration in the corresponding division (including the decision of no investment). The return associated with each stage (r_i) is defined in terms of the net present value for the project selected. Working with backward recursion, the state of the system and recursive function (criterion) are defined as follows:

s_i = Remaining capital available prior to stage i.
f_i = Cumulative net present value of benefits generated from stages 1 thru i.

Assuming independence of projects across divisions, the optimal return for stages 1 through i is additive and given by

$$f_i = r_i + f_{i-1}.$$

The selection of a particular project (a decision) in stage i uniquely transforms the state of the system according to

$$s_i = s_{i+1} - c_{i+1}$$

where c_i represents the outlay required by the selected project in stage i. In words, total capital available for allocation at stage i equals total capital available at stage $i + 1$ minus the capital outlay specified in stage $i + 1$.

Stage 1 Analysis

Beginning with stage 1, there are six possible entering states. Refer to Figure 12–3 and convince yourself that the amount of capital that might be available following allocations in stages 3 and 2 equals 0, 1, 2, 3, 4, or 5. Ask yourself how much money could be available for Division C after making allocations to Divisions A and B. Once you are convinced that these are the possible entering states for stage 1, our objective is to determine the optimal policy for this stage, contingent on each possible state.

Table 12–4 presents the tabular analysis for this stage. Note that $f_0 = 0$ means there is no return from projects prior to the first stage of analysis. Also notice in the table that, for convenience, we have indicated (parenthetically) below each project the required capital outlay and the net present value of benefits.

TABLE 12–4 Stage 1 Analysis, Capital Budgeting Model

Stage 1 (Division C) $f_1 = r_1 + f_0$ (capital outlay/NPV of benefits)

Possible Remaining Budget s_1	Possible Decisions (x_1)			Optimal Policy	
	C1 (0/0)	C2 (1/1)	C3 (2/3)	x_1^*	f_1^*
0	0 + 0 = 0	—	—	C1	0
1	0 + 0 = 0	1 + 0 = 1	—	C2	1
2	0 + 0 = 0	1 + 0 = 1	3 + 0 = 3	C3	3
3	0 + 0 = 0	1 + 0 = 1	3 + 0 = 3	C3	3
4	0 + 0 = 0	1 + 0 = 1	3 + 0 = 3	C3	3
5	0 + 0 = 0	1 + 0 = 1	3 + 0 = 3	C3	3

Let us examine the various possible entering states and the recommended decisions for each. If there is no available budget in stage 1, we must select project C1, which represents no project for division C and zero return to the company. If there is \$1 million available, the best we could do would be project C2, which requires a capital outlay of \$1 million and a net return of \$1 million. If the available budget coming into stage 1 is between \$2 million and \$5 million, we choose project C3, which has a capital outlay of \$2 million and a return of \$3 million.

Stage 2 Analysis

Using the backward recursion approach, we now reach back to the second stage and consider the investment decision associated with division B. Our goal at this stage is to define a set of decision policies that would maximize the combined net benefit from projects selected for divisions B and C. These decision policies will be stated contingent on the state of the system (remaining capital budget) prior to making a decision about division B.

For stage 2, the possible decisions are B1 and B2. We might be tempted to define the possible states of the system (s_2) as the same six values as in stage #1. However, the values of s_2 depend on the decision made for division A. Starting with a budget of \$5 million, the decision made for division A could involve investment of 0, 1, 2, or 3 million. Therefore, the remaining budget prior to stage 2 could be 5, 4, 3, or 2 million. Think about that for a moment. Do you agree? Table 12–5 reflects these values. The contingency table for stage 2 indicates that we have no choice but project B1 unless there is \$3 million or more to allocate. With \$3 million available, we could invest everything at stage 1 or else everything at stage 2 with the same return from both policies. If more than \$3 million were available, we should invest in project B2 at this stage. Make sure that you understand how the return values ($r_2 + f_1^*$) are computed in each cell and the linkage between this contingency table and that for stage 1.

TABLE 12–5 Stage 2 Analysis, Capital Budgeting Model

Stage 2 (Division B) ($f_2 = r_2 + f_1^*$)

Possible Remaining Budget s_2	Possible Decisions (x_2)		Optimal Policy	
	*B*1 (0/0)	*B*2 (3/3)	x_2^*	f_2^*
2	0 + 3 = 3	—	B1	3
3	0 + 3 = 3	3 + 0 = 3	B1 or B2	3
4	0 + 3 = 3	3 + 1 = 4	B2	4
5	0 + 3 = 3	3 + 3 = 6	B2	6

Stage 3 Analysis

Our final stage of analysis reaches back to incorporate the decision for division A. The goal at this stage is to define the set of decisions for all three divisions that will maximize combined net benefit. The possible decisions at this stage are A1, A2, A3, and A4. The single possible state of the system (s_3) prior to making an allocation to division A is \$5 million. From Table 12–6, we see that choosing either A1 or A2 in this stage will result in a policy maximizing total net benefit at \$6 million. This indicates alternative optimal decision policies. Again, make sure that you understand how the return values ($r_3 + f_2^*$) have been computed.

TABLE 12–6 Stage 3 Analysis, Capital Budgeting Model

Stage 3 (Division A) ($f_3 = r_3 + f_2^*$)

Possible Remaining Budget s_3	Possible Decisions (x_3)				Optimal Policy	
	*A*1 (0/0)	*A*2 (1/2)	*A*3 (2/2)	*A*4 (3/2)	x_3^*	f_3^*
5	0 + 6 = 6	2 + 4 = 6	2 + 3 = 5	2 + 3 = 5	A1 or A2	6

Composition of Optimal Policies

To compose the alternative optimal decision policies, we begin with the contingency table for stage 3 and link successively with the tables for stages 2 and 1. For example, choosing A1 in stage 3 results in no expenditure of money, and \$5 million is available in stage 2. From the contingency table for stage 2, if $s_2 = 5$, the optimal decision for division B is to select E2. Since B2 requires an investment of \$3 million, \$2 million remains for stage 1. Given \$2 million remaining at stage 1, the contingency table indicates an optimal decision for division C is to select C3. Figure 12–4 defines this optimal policy schematically. Verify for yourself that the alternative optimal policy involves selection of projects A2, B2, and C2.

FIGURE 12–4 One Optimal Policy for Capital Budgeting Example

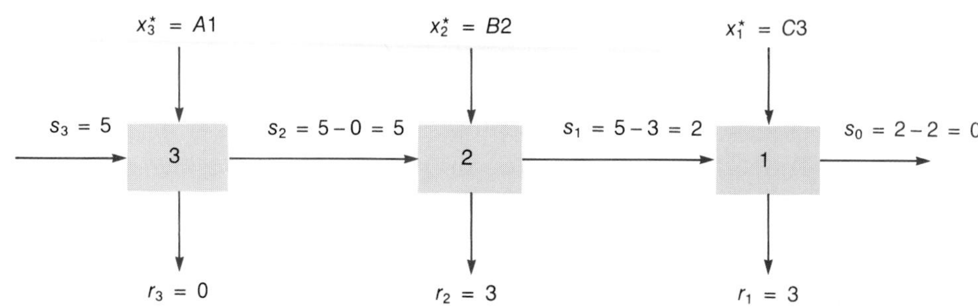

Note: In this example, there is no explicit or required sequence for the set of three decisions. Thus the correspondence between stages and divisions of the company is arbitrary. That is, stage 1 of the analysis could have corresponded to division A, stage 2 to division B, and stage 3 to division C. In other decision problems, the sequence of decisions is rigidly defined, such as decisions made over time. For these problems, backward recursion methods require that the first stage of analysis corresponds to the last decision in the sequence.

FOLLOW-UP EXERCISES

6. For the stage 1 analysis, all six values for s_1 are unlikely. Which values can be eliminated and why?
7. What is the optimal policy and net present value if only \$3 million is available for capital outlays? Based on this and the results when \$4 million is available, can you make a recommendation?
8. Formulate this problem as an integer (0–1) programming model.
9. Solve the problem with the model formulated in the preceding exercise using an integer programming package. Which approach for formulating and solving (dynamic programming or integer programming) do you prefer and why?
10. Solve Example 12.2 if a fourth division has submitted the following projects for consideration:

Project	Capital Outlay	Net Present Value Cash Flow	Net Present Value of Benefits
D1	0	0	0
D2	1	3	2
D3	2	4	2
D4	2	5	3

You do not have to re-solve from scratch. Use part of the analysis in Example 12.2.

12.3 FORWARD RECURSIONS AND DYNAMIC PROGRAMMING

We have illustrated the backward recursion approach to solving dynamic programming problems in the previous sections. The forward recursion approach takes a problem decomposed into a sequence of n stages (as shown if Figure 12–5) and analyzes the problem starting with the first stage in the sequence, working forward to the last stage.

FIGURE 12.5 Generalized Notation for Forward Recursion

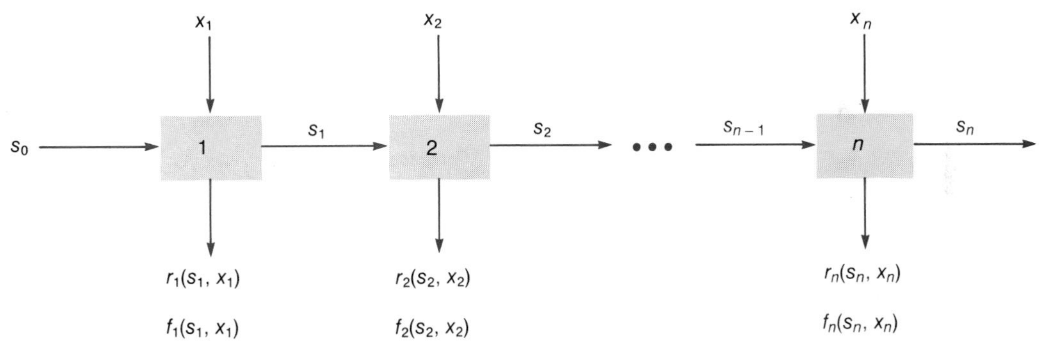

In Figure 12–5, the symbols are defined as follows:

n = Number of stages.
x_i = Decision variable for stage i.
s_i = State of the system *following* stage i.
$r_i(s_i, x_i)$ = Return or result associated with a particular state-decision combination (s_i, x_i) in stage i.
$f_i(s_i, x_i)$ = Value of criterion for the first i stages of analysis, given a particular state-decision combination (s_i, x_i) in stage i.

Let us illustrate the forward recursion approach by solving the shortest route problem. Figure 12–2 is repeated for convenience in Figure 12–6.

FIGURE 12–6 Shortest Route Problem: Forward Recursion (*Repeat of Figure 12–2*)

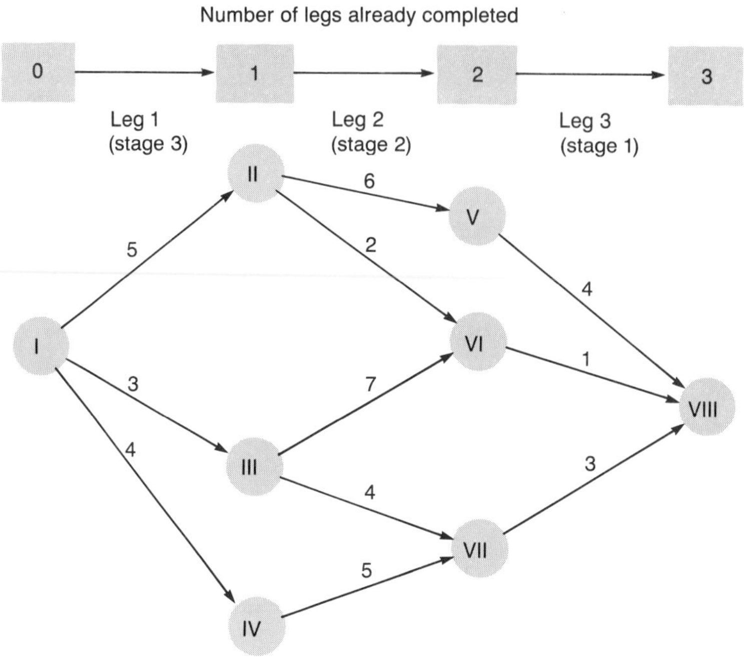

▶ Example 12.3 Shortest Route Problem: Forward Recursions

Stage (leg) 1 Analysis. For the shortest route problem, the state of the system in a forward recursive approach is the location of the traveler at the end of each leg. Thus for stage (leg) 1, the possible states of the system are nodes II, III, and IV. The decision in each stage is what node we should depart from so as to minimize the distance to each state (node). For leg 1 of the journey, we have no choice. The only way to arrive at nodes II, III, or IV is by departing from node I. The contingency table (Table 12–7) summarizes the stage 1 analysis. Note that the return values are $(r_1 + f_0^*)$, where f_0^* represents the minimum distance traveled to node I (which of course equals zero). The table answers the following question: "Given that I wish to be at state (node) s_1 at the end of leg 1 of the journey, which node should I depart from so as to minimize total distance traveled?

Let us examine the table. One possible ending state for leg 2 is node V. We can only arrive at node V by traveling from node II. The distance associated with that leg is 6, combined with the distance of 5 required to get to node II, for a minimum total distance of 11 to arrive at node V.

Given that we wish to arrive at node VI at the conclusion of leg 2, we may leave from either nodes II or III. Going from node II to VI has a direct distance of 2 plus a distance of 5 required to get to node II. Similarly, travel from III to VI has a direct distance of

7 plus a distance of 3 required to get to node III. Thus if we wish to minimize the total distance required to get to node VI, we should travel from I to II to VI, for a total distance of 7. Similar thinking reveals the best way to get to node VII.

Note in the contingency table that our criterion values are computed using the relationship $f_2 = r_2 + f_1^*$.

TABLE 12–7 Shortest Route Problem, Stage 1 Analysis (*Forward recursions*)

$f_1 = r_1 + f_0^*$

Possible Ending Nodes	Possible Decisions (x_1) (originating nodes)	Optimal Policy	
s_1	I	x_1^*	f_1^*
II	5 + 0 = 5	I	5
III	3 + 0 = 3	I	3
IV	4 + 0 = 4	I	4

Stage (Leg) 2 Analysis. For stage 2 the heart of the forward recursion approach becomes apparent. On the second leg, we may end up at node V, VI, or VII. What is the best way to get to each of those nodes? The contingency table for this stage (Table 12–8) follows.

TABLE 12–8 Shortest Route Problem, Stage 2 Analysis (*Forward recursions*)

$f_2 = r_2 + f_1^*$

Possible Ending Nodes	Possible Decisions (x_2) (originating nodes)			Optimal Policy	
s_2	II	III	IV	x_2^*	f_2^*
V	6 + 5 = 11	—	—	II	11
VI	2 + 5 = 7	7 + 3 = 10	—	II	7
VII	—	4 + 3 = 7	5 + 4 = 9	III	7

Stage (Leg) 3 Analysis. In stage 3 we are interested only in getting to node VIII. We will be trying to get there from node V, VI, or VII. What is the best way to get to node VIII? That is the original question—so solving stage 3 will solve the problem. Table 12–9 shows us that the only ending state is node VIII and that we may arrive at this node from V, VI, or VII. Verify the computations in this table, and compare the results of the analysis to show that the optimal policy is I–II–VI–VIII, with a total distance of 8.

FOLLOW-UP EXERCISES

11. Solve Exercise 3 using forward recursions.
12. Solve Example 12.2 using forward recursions.

TABLE 12–9 Shortest Route Problem, Stage 3 Analysis (*Forward recursions*)

$f_3 = r_3 + f_2^*$

Possible Ending Nodes	Possible Decisions (x_3) (originating nodes)			Optimal Policy	
s_3	V	VI	VII	x_2^*	f_3^*
VIII	4 + 11 = 15	1 + 7 = 8	3 + 7 = 10	VI	8

12.4 FORWARD RECURSIONS AND TIME-SEQUENTIAL DECISIONS

Elton and Gruber claimed in 1971 that most of the analytical work in the field of finance has been based on static analysis.[1] Although this situation has been somewhat corrected since, the difference between static analysis and dynamic programming analysis can be studied in the context of the bond refunding problem presented in the Elton and Gruber article. This section extends the forward recursion approach to dynamic programming but also shows that dynamic programming is much more than a programming technique; it is an approach to decision making.

▶ Example 12.4 The Bond Refunding Problem

A company wishes to maintain a constant level of debt in its capital structure for the next five years, after which it will have no debt (i.e., a five-year horizon). All debt is in the form of callable bonds issued in $100 denominations with maturities of three years. Because of possible fluctuations in interest rates, management would like to be in a position to reduce the cost of its debt should interest rates drop.

Bond refunding is done for a variety of reasons. One is that it is a method of capitalizing on lower interest rates by exchanging lower cost debt for higher cost debt. The process involves repaying (calling) of the existing debt and issuing new bonds at the lower interest rate. The callable bond provides a mechanism whereby existing debt can be repaid prior to maturity. Early repayment usually involves a penalty called the call premium. Similarly, issuing new bonds involves floatation costs. In bond refunding, management seeks to more than offset the expenses of calling existing bonds and floating new bonds with the savings of reduced interest expenses.

Suppose in our example that the call premiums are $2 on a one-year bond and $1 on a two-year bond. Also, assume that floatation expenses on new debt are $2 per bond. For our company, management is willing to base its decisions on the point estimates of future rates shown in Table 12–10.[2] Assume that the existing debt consists of two-year-old bonds with a five percent coupon rate. Management faces the decision of

[1]E. J. Elton, and M. J. Gruber, "Dynamic Programming Applications in Finance," *Journal of Finance*, May 1971, pp. 473–505.

[2]Although these rates may be low in today's world, we use the Elton and Gruber figures so that you can work your way more easily through this article should you want to go further. We also present a variation of the Elton-Gruber formulation.

TABLE 12–10 Projected Interest Rates on Three-Year Callable Bonds

Period	Interest Rate
Past	5%
Year 1	4
Year 2	5
Year 3	5
Year 4	7
Year 5	7

whether or not to refund the bonds. This decision can be based on a marginal analysis of refunding a single bond.

Static Analysis

One procedure for making the refunding decision is to minimize cost over the life of the original bond. Since our two-year-old bond has only one period until maturity, the decision would be based only on the costs for period 1. Not refunding gives a cost of $5, the interest cost for period 1. Refunding would cost $7 ($1 to refund a two-year-old bond plus $2 floatation expense plus $4 interest). Clearly, the optimal decision would be to *not* refund. Do you agree?

Dynamic Programming Analysis

Based on the decision problem we face, dynamic programming provides a superior approach to this problem. We will use forward recursion to find the optimal solution. Figure 12–7 portrays the problem in a DP context. The decision at each stage is whether or not to refund the bond we have. The state of the system, s_t, is the age of the bond at the end of stage (year) t. Notice that $s_0 = 2$ (at the beginning of year 1 we have a two-year-old bond).

FIGURE 12–7 Bond Refunding Problem: Five-year Time Horizon

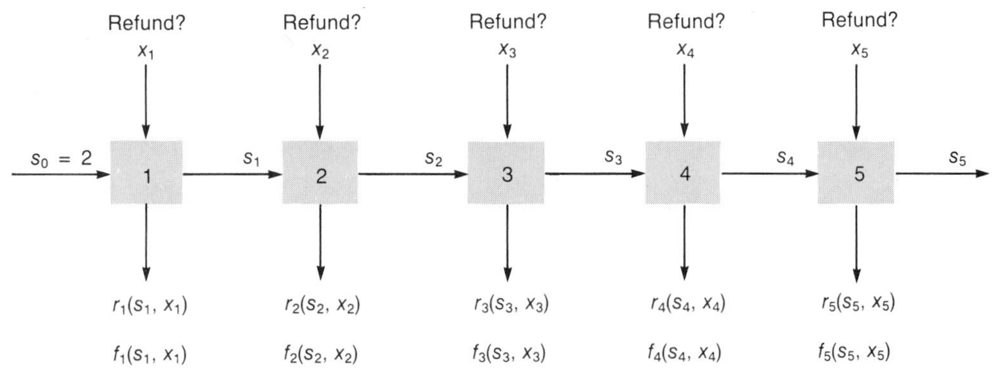

Stage 1 (Year 1)

At the end of stage (year) 1, we could have either a one-year-old bond if we refund at the beginning of the year, or a three-year-old bond if we do not refund. If the bond is refunded, the cost will be \$7 as in the static analysis (i.e., \$1 to refund plus \$2 to float plus \$4 interest). If the bond is not refunded, interest expense for the year will be \$5. (See Table 12–11.)

TABLE 12–11 Stage 1 (Year 1) Analysis

Age of Bond after Stage 1 s_1	Possible Decisions (x_1)		Optimal Policy	
	Refund	Do Not Refund	x_1^*	$f_1^*(s_1, x_1)$
1	(1 + 2 + 4) = 7	—	Refund	7
3	—	5	Do not refund	5

Stage 2 (Year 2)

At the end of period 2 we could have either a one-year-old or a two-year-old bond. To have a one-year-old, we could refund a one-year-old *or* a three-year-old bond depending on our period 1 decisions. The cost of refunding a one-year-old bond would be \$9 (the \$2 call premium plus \$2 floatation plus \$5 interest) plus \$7 (the cost of having a one-year-old bond at the end of period 1. But we could also refund a three-year-old bond. The cost of refunding a three-year-old bond would be \$7 (\$0 call premium plus \$2 floatation plus \$5 interest) plus \$5 (the cost of having a three-year-old bond at the end of period 1). (See Table 12–12.)

TABLE 12–12 Stage 2 (Year 2) Analysis

s_1	Age of Bond after Stage 2 s_2	Possible Decisions (x_2)		Optimal Policy	
		Refund	Do Not Refund	x_2^*	$f_2^*(s_2, x_2)$
1	1	(2 + 2 + 5) + 7 = 16	—		
3	1	(0 + 2 + 5) + 5 = 12		Refund	12
1	2	—	(4) + 7 = 11	Do not refund	11

Having a two-year-old bond at the end of stage 2 implies not refunding a one-year-old bond. The cost of this decision is the interest of \$4 plus the cost of \$7 associated with refunding the bond in stage 1.

The contingency tables (12–13 through 12–15) for stages 3 through 5 follow. Verify the computations in these tables to test your understanding. Notice that we have included one extra column, which indicates the state of the system at the end of the previous stage. This is intended to help you keep track of the linkages between stages (which can become a bit confusing in this example).

Stage 3 (Year 3)

TABLE 12–13 Stage 3 (Year 3) Analysis

s_2	Age of Bond after Stage 3 s_3	Possible Decisions (x_3)		Optimal Policy	
		Refund	Do Not Refund	x_3^*	$f_3^*(s_3, x_3)$
1 2	1 1	(2 + 2 + 5) + 12 = 21 (1 + 2 + 5) + 11 = 19	— —	Refund	19
1	2	—	(5) + 12 = 17	Do not refund	17
2	3	—	(4) + 11 = 15	Do not refund	15

Stage 4 (Year 4)

TABLE 12–14 Stage 4 (Year 4) Analysis

s_3	Age of Bond after Stage 4 s_4	Possible Decisions (x_4)		Optimal Policy	
		Refund	Do Not Refund	x_4^*	$f_4^*(s_4, x_4)$
1 2 3	1 1 1	(2 + 2 + 7) + 19 = 30 (1 + 2 + 7) + 17 = 27 (0 + 2 + 7) + 15 = 24	— — —	Refund	24
1	2	—	(5) + 19 = 24	Do not refund	24
2	3	—	(5) + 17 = 22	Do not refund	22

Stage 5 (Year 5)

TABLE 12–15 Stage 5 (Year 5) Analysis

s_4	Age of Bond after Stage 5 s_5	Possible Decisions (x_5)		Optimal Policy	
		Refund	Do Not Refund	x_5^*	$f_5^*(s_5, x_5)$
1 2 3	1	(2 + 2 + 7) + 24 = 35 (1 + 2 + 7) + 24 = 34 (0 + 2 + 7) + 22 = 31	— — —	Refund	31
1	2	—	(7) + 24 = 31	Do not refund	31
2	3	—	(5) + 24 = 29	Do not refund	29*

Notice from Table 12–15 that the cost of $100 in debt for the five-year period will be minimized at $29. The optimal policy can be traced back from stage 5. In year 5, do not refund a two-year-old bond. Year 4 sees the bond age from a one-year-old to a two-year-old bond. In year 3, we refund a two-year-old bond. Year 2 sees a one-year-old bond age to two. For this to happen, we must replace our original two-year-old bond at the beginning of year 1. Remember that our static analysis told us *not* to refund our original two-year-old bond! This illustrates the power of dynamic programming in analyzing time-dependent sequences of decisions.

FOLLOW-UP EXERCISES

13. What lies behind the different result obtained by static versus dynamic analysis in the bond refunding problem? Put your finger on exactly what static analysis misses in this problem.
14. Solve the bond refunding problem with backward recursions.

12.5 ADDITIONAL APPLICATIONS

This section presents three additional examples that illustrate not only the diversity of applications of DP, but also the flexibility of modeling capabilities.

▶ Example 12.5 Production-Inventory Model

A manufacturing firm wishes to prepare a production-inventory schedule over n periods (quarters) for an expensive low-volume product that has been contracted. Due to time and labor constraints, the number of items produced during the tth period (x_t) cannot exceed a maximum capacity for that period (K_t). The demand in the tth period (d_t) can be met both by production in that period and by the *ending* inventory (s_{t-1}) from the previous period, although the latter cannot exceed the storage capacity (S). In other words, items can be produced in one period and carried over in inventory (at a cost) for consumption in a subsequent period. For simplicity we assume that the beginning inventory for the horizon, s_0, is zero and no ending inventory is desired ($s_n = 0$). Furthermore, we assume that negative inventories (i.e., back orders or lost sales) are not allowed. The cost per period of holding an item in inventory is given by h_t and the total cost of producing x_t items in period t is given by some production function $C_t(x_t)$.

An integer programming formulation for this problem is given by

Minimize

$$z = \sum_{t=1}^{n} [C_t(x_t) + h_t \cdot s_t]$$

subject to

$$\left.\begin{aligned} s_1 &= x_1 - d_1 \\ s_t &= s_{t-1} + x_t - d_t \qquad t = 2, 3, \ldots, n - 1 \\ s_n &= 0 \end{aligned}\right\} \qquad (1)$$

$$x_t \leq K_t \qquad t = 1, \ldots, n \qquad (2)$$

$$s_t \leq S \qquad t = 1, \ldots, n \qquad (3)$$

x_t, s_t nonnegative integers.

Ideally, the cost criterion is expressed in terms of present value. Constraint set 1 ensures the appropriate accounting identity among beginning inventory, ending inventory, production, and demand. (Can you verbalize these?)
Constraint sets 2 and 3 account for production and storage constraints. For notational convenience, s_t is treated as a decision variable along with x_t, although in reality it represents the surplus associated with constraints that meet demand. (Could you express this problem without the use of s_t?)

If the production and inventory costs were stationary (constant over time) and if $C_t(x_t)$ were linear, an integer programming algorithm (Chapter 8) could be used to solve this type of model. Suppose, however, that the total cost function for production (in \$1,000's) is estimated as

$$C_t(x_t) = \begin{cases} (12 + t) - 6x_t + x_t^2, & 0 < x_t \leq 5 \\ 0, & x_t = 0 \end{cases} \quad t = 1, \ldots, n. \qquad (12.1)$$

Clearly, a linear formulation is inappropriate. Note that a setup cost is incurred, which is a function of the period, and that the function is U-shaped with a minimum total cost at three units. Dynamic programming, however, is uniquely suited to solve this type of *nonlinear optimization problem.*

Letting each time period represent a stage (that is, quarter 1 is stage 1, quarter 2 is stage 2, and so forth), we define the following symbols:

x_i = Number of units produced in quarter i.
s_i = *Ending inventory* in quarter i, or *leaving state* for stage i.
r_i = Production cost plus inventory holding cost in quarter i.
f_i^* = Optimal cumulative cost through the first i quarters.

Since the ending inventory for a period must equal the beginning inventory for that period plus the amount produced in that period less the demand in that period (that is, $s_i = s_{i-1} + x_i + d_i$), it follows that the *transformation function* is given by

$$s_{i-1} = s_i - x_i + d_i. \tag{12.2}$$

The "return" for stage i is given by

$$r_i = \text{Production Cost} + \text{Inventory holding cost}$$
$$= C_i(x_i) + h_i \cdot s_i$$

where $C_i(x_i)$ is defined by Equation 12.1. Thus for $x_i = 0$,

$$r_i = h_i \cdot s_i \tag{12.3}$$

and, for $0 < x_i \leq 5$,

$$r_i = 12 + i - 6x_i + x_i^2 + h_i \cdot s_i. \tag{12.4}$$

Note that the holding cost of inventory for any period is based on the ending inventory for that period. Furthermore, note that states and stage returns are influenced by the *exogeneous variable* d_i; that is, demand represents an influence from outside the production-inventory system.

As in the preceding examples, the *optimal recursive equation* is additive:

$$f_i^* = \min[r_i + f_{i-1}^*]. \qquad x_i = 0, \ldots, K_i \tag{12.5}$$

Note that x_i is restricted to integer values between 0 and K_i inclusive.

Consider the data presented in Table 12–16 for a four-quarter model ($n = 4$) in which maximum production and inventory capacities are five and three, respectively (that is, $K_t = 5$ for all t and $S = 3$). For convenience, production costs have been tabulated in Table 12–16 according to Equation 12.1

TABLE 12–16 Data for Example 12.5*

Period (t)	Stage (i)	Production Costs, $C_i(x_i)$ When x_i Equals: 0	1	2	3	4	5	Holding Cost per Unit (h_i)	Demand (d_i)
1	1	0	8	5	4	5	8	1	2
2	2	0	9	6	5	6	9	1	2
3	3	0	10	7	6	7	10	2	3
4	4	0	11	8	7	8	11	2	3

*All costs in $1,000; all demands in units.

Utilizing Equation 12.3 or 12.4 to determine r_i (with the aid of Table 12–16) and Equation 12.2 to calculate the relevant s_{i-1} for determining f_{i-1}^* in the table for the preceding stage, you should be able to verify (after some tedium) the results in Tables 12–17 through 12–20. (Can you verbalize the computations for any given cell in the context of this application?)

As usual, each column for a particular table represents a specific decision alternative for that stage, and each row represents a possible leaving state for that stage. In this example, each row represents a possible ending inventory for that period.

Note that infeasible cells are a direct result of the avoidance either of negative inventories ($s_{i-1} < 0$) or of excessive storage ($s_{i-1} > 3$). For example, the cell given by $s_2 = 1$ and $x_2 = 5$ in stage 2 is infeasible because according to the transformation function, the ending inventory in quarter 1 would be negative; that is, $s_1 = s_2 - x_2 +$

TABLE 12–17 Stage 1: $f_1 = r_1 + f_0^* = C_1(x_1) + 1 \cdot s_1 + 0$

Ending Inventory Quarter 1 s_1	Possible Decisions (x_1) (number of units produced during quarter 1)						Optimal Policy	
	0	1	2	3	4	5	x_1^*	f_1^*
0			5 + 0 + 0 = 5				2	5
1				4 + 1 + 0 = 5			3	5
2					5 + 2 + 0 = 7		4*	7
3						8 + 3 + 0 = 11	5	11

TABLE 12–18 Stage 2: $f_2 = r_2 + f_1^* = C_2(x_2) + 1 \cdot s_2 + f_1^*$

Ending Inventory Quarter 2 s_2	Possible Decisions (x_2) (number of units produced during quarter 2)						Optimal Policy	
	0	1	2	3	4	5	x_2^*	f_2^*
0	0 + 0 + 7 = 7	9 + 0 + 5 = 14	6 + 0 + 5 = 11				0*	7
1	0 + 1 + 11 = 12	9 + 1 + 7 = 17	6 + 1 + 5 = 12	5 + 1 + 5 = 11			3	11
2		9 + 2 + 11 = 22	6 + 2 + 7 = 15	5 + 2 + 5 = 12	6 + 2 + 5 = 13		3	12
3			6 + 3 + 11 = 20	5 + 3 + 7 = 15	6 + 3 + 5 = 14	9 + 3 + 5 = 17	4	14

TABLE 12–19 Stage 3: $f_3 = r_3 + f_2^* = C_3(x_3) + 2 \cdot s_3 + f_2^*$

Ending Inventory Quarter 3 s_3	Possible Decisions (x_3) (number of units produced during quarter 3)						Optimal Policy	
	0	1	2	3	4	5	x_3^*	f_3^*
0	0 + 0 + 14 = 14	10 + 0 + 12 = 22	7 + 0 + 11 = 18	6 + 0 + 7 = 13			3*	13
1		10 + 2 + 14 = 26	7 + 2 + 12 = 21	6 + 2 + 11 = 19	7 + 2 + 7 = 16		4	16
2			7 + 4 + 14 = 25	6 + 4 + 12 = 22	7 + 4 + 11 = 22	10 + 4 + 7 = 21	5	21
3				6 + 6 + 14 = 26	7 + 6 + 12 = 25	10 + 6 + 11 = 27	4	25

TABLE 12–20 Stage 4: $f_4 = r_4 + f_3^* = C_4(x_4) + 2 \cdot s_4 + f_3^*$

Ending Inventory Quarter 4 s_4	Possible Decisions (x_4) (number of units produced during quarter 4)						Optimal Policy	
	0	1	2	3	4	5	x_4^*	f_4^*
0	0 + 0 + 25 = 25	11 + 0 + 21 = 32	8 + 0 + 16 = 24	7 + 0 + 13 = 20			3*	20
1		11 + 2 + 25 = 38	8 + 2 + 21 = 31	7 + 2 + 16 = 25	8 + 2 + 13 = 23		4	23
2			8 + 4 + 25 = 37	7 + 4 + 21 = 32	8 + 4 + 16 = 28	11 + 4 + 13 = 28	4, 5	28
3				7 + 6 + 25 = 38	8 + 6 + 21 = 35	11 + 6 + 16 = 33	5	33

$d_2 = 1 - 5 + 2 = -2$. Furthermore, you should confirm that the stipulation of a beginning inventory of zero for period 1 (that is, $s_0 = 0$) results in only four feasible cells for stage 1.

Since the ending inventory for the planning horizon is to be zero, then $s_4 = 0$ and the overall minimum cost (from the table for stage 4) is $20,000 for the year (that is, $f_4^* = 20$ is the cumulative cost for periods 1 through 4). The optimal policy in stage 4 (period 4) indicates a production of three units. This means that, given the delivery of three units in this period ($d_4 = 3$) and no ending inventory ($s_4 = 0$), zero units must be left in inventory at the end of the third period. In other words, according to Equation 12.2, $s_3 = 0 - 3 + 3 = 0$. Entering the table for stage 3 at $s_3 = 0$, the optimal policy dictates the production of three units ($x_3^* = 3$) in period 3. Continuing in this manner, the entire optimal production schedule of 3, 3, 0, and 4 units for periods 4, 3, 2, and 1, respectively, can be determined. Can you verify directly from the tables that ending inventories for periods 1, 2, 3, and 4 are 2, 0, 0, and 0, respectively? (Look at the s_i's for the optimal rows.)

Since s_4 represents the ending inventory for the planning horizon, a sensitivity analysis based on ending inventory can be carried out easily. For instance, an ending inventory of three units for period 4 would call for a production schedule of four, zero, four, and five units in periods 1, 2, 3, and 4, respectively, with an optimal cost of $33,000.

Finally, the treatment of periods as stages gives dynamic programming the powerful capability of both performing sensitivity analysis on the planning horizon (value of n) and treating *infinite time horizons.* The latter is possible (in a forward recursion) if the system achieves an "effective" steady state (i.e., the process essentially becomes time independent) beyond some finite horizon or if the objective function is bounded. For example, steady state for our inventory model essentially occurs at some finite horizon if all costs are discounted to time zero. The treatment of unbounded horizons is also possible either in the case of stationary cycles in the processes (e.g., periodic quarterly demands such as 2, 2, 3, 3, 2, 2, 3, 3, . . .) or by the use of more advanced mathematical procedures.[3]

FOLLOW-UP EXERCISES

15. With respect to the computational tables:
    a. Why must $0 \le s_i \le 3$ and $0 \le x_i \le 5$ for each table? Do these *bounds* on s_i and x_i reflect constraints in the integer programming formulation?
    b. Confirm that an ending inventory of three units for the planning horizon results in an optimal production schedule of four units in period 1; zero units in period 2; four units in period 3; and five units in period 4.
    c. Confirm that ending inventories for the schedule in part *b* are two, zero, and one units for periods 1, 2, and 3, respectively, according to the following two methods. *Method 1:* Fill in the table below using simple algebra.

t	Beginning Inventory	Production	Demand	Ending Inventory
1				
2				
3				
4				

[3]As discussed in R. E. Bellman, *Dynamic Programming* (Princeton, N.J.: Princeton University Press, 1957); and G. L. Nemhauser, *Introduction to Dynamic Programming* (New York: John Wiley & Sons, 1966).

Method 2: Look up s_i's in the computational tables for rows giving the optimal production schedule.

d. From the table for stage 4, $f_4^* = \$33{,}000$ when $s_4 = 3$. Confirm this figure by summing up production and inventory costs for the four periods.

16. From Table 12–19, $f_3^* = \$13{,}000$ for the optimal production policy. Confirm that this represents the sum of production and inventory costs for the first three periods.
17. Extend the forward recursion to five periods, given that demand is five units in period 5 and holding cost is two. Assess the change in the optimal production-inventory schedule.
18. Solve the production-inventory problem if the beginning inventory for period 1 is two units.

**19. Formulate and solve a production-inventory dynamic programming model that allows shortages (i.e., negative inventories). Use a shortage cost of 1 ($1,000) per item per period. Assume that items must be back ordered; that is, the total order of 10 items must be filled by the end of the four periods. Explicitly state the new recursive equation.

▶ Example 12.6 Reliability Model

Since the inceptions of large-scale military and space programs and the concurrent growth of the electronics industry, reliability models have enjoyed a great deal of attention from mathematicians, engineers, and operations researchers. To capture the essence of these models, consider the problem of designing an electronic device with four components aligned in series. "In series" means that the components are arranged one after the other, as in the first column of Figure 12–8. Failure of any of the components means failure of the entire electronic device. The problem is to determine the number of parallel units for each component (i.e., the number of units of a given type of component, which includes the working unit plus backup units of the same type) such that reliability is maximized subject to a cost constraint and a limit of 3 units per component. (See Figure 12–8). *Reliability* is defined as the probability that the device does not fail over a particular planning horizon.

If, in our example, two units represent a particular component (i.e., the original component plus a backup), then the failure of the first unit results in the second unit switching in automatically (we assume the switching process is completely reliable). It follows that by increasing the reliability of each component, the reliability of the device itself increases.

Suppose that the probabilities of *failure* for *each unit* of components 1, 2, 3, and 4 are 0.2, 0.5, 0.4, and 0.3, respectively. Now consider a design that specifies two parallel units for the first component. In order for component 1 to fail, each of its two parallel units must fail (we assume independence among parallel units). The probability of this occurrence, according to the elementary multiplication rule of probability, given by Equation A.7 in Appendix A, is $(0.2) \cdot (0.2)$ or 0.04. Hence the reliability of the first component (r_1) when two parallel units are used is $(1.0 - 0.04)$ or 0.96. Table 12–21 provides cost (c_i) and reliability (r_i) calculations for each of the possible alternatives for each component (x_i).

FIGURE 12–8 Design for Electronic Device

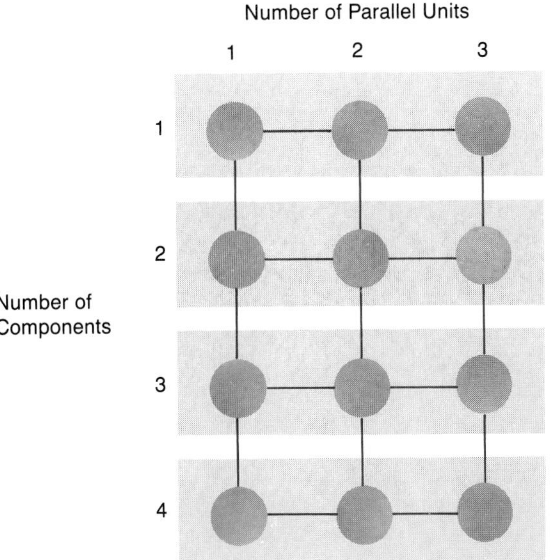

TABLE 12–21 Reliability (r_i) and Cost (c_i) Data*

Component Number (i)		Number of Parallel Units (x_i) 1	2	3
1				
	c_1	3	4	5
	r_1	0.80	0.96	0.99
2				
	c_2	1	2	3
	r_2	0.50	0.75	0.88
3				
	c_3	2	4	5
	r_3	0.60	0.84	0.94
4				
	c_4	1	2	2
	r_4	0.70	0.91	0.97

*Costs expressed in units of $1,000; reliabilities expressed to two significant digits.

To illustrate the calculation of reliability for the entire device, consider the decision of two units for component 1 ($x_1 = 2$), one unit for component 2 ($x_2 = 1$), and three units each for components 3 and 4 ($x_3 = 3$ and $x_4 = 3$). The entire device fails if any one of its components fails. In other words, the device continues to operate so long as *all* of the components continue operation. The reliability of the system, therefore, is given by $(0.96) \cdot (0.50) \cdot (0.94) \cdot (0.97)$, or approximately 0.44.

The objective then is to maximize the product of component reliabilities ($r_1 \cdot r_2 \cdot r_3 \cdot r_4$) subject to a cost constraint of, say, \$10,000.[4] In general, this problem is formulated as

Maximize

$$z = \prod_{i=1}^{n} r_i(x_i)$$

subject to

$$\sum_{i=1}^{n} c_i(x_i) \leq b$$

$$x_i \leq u_i, \qquad i = 1, \ldots, n,$$

$$x_i \geq 1, \qquad i = 1, \ldots, n,$$

$$x_i \text{ positive integer},$$

where n represents the number of components, b denotes the budget, u_i stipulates the upper limit on parallel units for the ith component, and where it is understood that component reliabilities (r_i's) and costs (c_i's) are functions of the number of parallel units per component (x_i's). Note that both the objective function and budget constraint are nonlinear.

Letting the components correspond to stages in a forward recursion, you should have no difficulty (by now) in understanding the following transformation function and **multiplicative recursive equation.**[5]

$$s_i = \text{Available funds for Components } 1, 2, \ldots, i$$
$$= s_{i-1} + c_i$$

or

$$s_{i-1} = s_i - c_i$$

and

$$f_i^* = \text{Optimal reliability for Components } 1, 2, \ldots, i$$
$$= \max\,(r_i \cdot f_{i-1}^*)\,. \tag{12.6}$$
$$x_i = 1, 2, 3$$

FOLLOW-UP EXERCISES

20. Get out your electronic calculator and determine the optimal design for the device in the preceding example by partially (intelligently) enumerating all of the feasible designs.
21. Determine the optimal design by dynamic programming.
22. Draw conclusions based on a sensitivity analysis of the budget.

---

[4]A shorthand notation for product forms (comparable to Σ for summation) is the use of the symbol Π. In general, $\prod_{i=1}^{n} f_i(x) = f_1(x) \cdot f_2(x) \cdot \ldots \cdot f_n(x)$.

[5]A necessary condition for the decomposition of multiplicative recursive equations is that the r_i be non-negative real numbers; otherwise, optimization will not be achieved.

▶ **Example 12.7 Work Force Planning Model

Up to this point, optimization at each stage (for each subproblem) has been accomplished by the process of *enumeration* with the aid of tables. This procedure is feasible when the decision variable (x_i) and state variable (s_i) for each stage are finite and discrete. If these variables are discrete but can take on an infinite number of values, *integer programming* (Chapter 8) techniques *may* be appropriate for finding the optimal policies at each stage. If x_i and s_i are *continuous*, however, the appropriate procedures include (1) *classical calculus* (Chapter 2) for unconstrained subproblems, (2) *Lagrangian functions* for subproblems with equality constraints, (3) *Kuhn-Tucker conditions* for subproblems with inequality constraints, (4) *linear programming* (Chapter 3 through 6) for subproblems with linear criteria and linear constraints, and (5) other *mathematical programming* and *search procedures,* depending on the characteristics of the problem. If optimization for any given stage is not possible, then *heuristic procedures* represent the only recourse.

To illustrate a procedure that utilizes classical calculus, consider the problem of scheduling a work force over four quarters ($n = 4$) for an organization. Each quarter has a projected demand for labor in hours. Assuming that the labor requirements must be met and that overtime is not allowed, management is faced with the cost trade-off of hiring-firing on the one hand and idle labor on the other. The objective is to propose a work force schedule that (1) meets requirements for labor of 30,000, 40,000, 35,000, and 50,000 hours in quarters 1, 2, 3, and 4, respectively, and (2) minimizes the sum of costs associated with changes in the work force and idle labor over the planning horizon of four quarters.

Suppose that the work force level prior to quarter 1 stands at 32,000 hours and that an analysis indicates a cost of $6 per hour for idle labor and a cost associated with work force changes (hours) equal to 1 percent of the square of the change.

Working with a backward recursion to facilitate the stage transformations we define the following:

d_i = Demand in Stage i.[6]
x_i = Hours of work force hired ($x_i > 0$) or fired ($x_i < 0$) in Stage i.
s_i = Work force level (hours) with i more quarters to go.
r_i = Costs (dollars) of idle time and hiring-firing in Stage i.

The transformation function and recursive equation follow easily from the definitions

$$s_{i-1} = s_i + x_i \tag{12.7}$$

and

$$f_i = \min_{x_i \geq d_i - s_i}[r_i + f^*_{i-1}]$$

or

$$f_i = \min_{x_i \geq d_i - s_i}[6(s_{i-1} - d_i) + 0.01x_i^2 + f^*_{i-1}]. \tag{12.8}$$

[6]Note that $d_1 = 50{,}000$, $d_2 = 35{,}000$, $d_3 = 40{,}000$, and $d_4 = 30{,}000$.

Substituting Equation (12.7) into (12.8) gives

$$f_i^* = \min[6(s_i - d_i) + 6x_i + 0.01x_i^2 + f_{i-1}^*]. \tag{12.9}$$
$$x_i \geq d_i - s_i$$

Note that the condition which requires meeting the demand for labor in each quarter is expressed as

$$s_{i-1} \geq d_i \tag{12.10}$$

or substituting Equation (12.7) into Equation (12.10) as

$$x_i \geq d_i - s_i . \tag{12.11}$$

Further note that the unit of measurement for the decision variable (hours) and the availability of part-time labor make x_i and s_i continuous variables.

Stage 1:

$$f_1 = 6(s_1 - 50{,}000) + 6x_1 + 0.01x_1^2 + 0. \tag{12.12}$$

The requirement of 50,000 hours in stage 1 (period 4) and the nonoptimality of having idle labor in the last period dictate that

$$x_1^* = 50{,}000 - s_1; \tag{12.13}$$

that is, hire as much as you need to reach the requirement. Note that an optimal policy necessarily specifies that s_1 never exceed the maximum requirement of 50,000. Plugging Equation (12.13) into (12.12) gives the optimal recursion in stage 1 as

$$f_1^* = 0.01(50{,}000 - s_1)^2. \tag{12.14}$$

Stage 2:

$$f_2 = 6(s_2 - 35{,}000) + 6x_2 + 0.01x_2^2 + 0.01(50{,}000 - s_1)^2 \tag{12.15}$$

Substituting Equation (12.7) into (12.15) we can express f_2 strictly in terms of s_2 and x_2, or

$$f_2 = 6(s_2 - 35{,}000) + 6x_2 + 0.01x_2^2 + 0.01(50{,}000 - s_2 - x_2)^2. \tag{12.16}$$

To find the optimal policy in stage 2, we take the partial derivative of f_2 with respect to x_2, set it to zero, and solve for x_2, giving

$$x_2^* = 24{,}850 - 0.5s_2. \tag{12.17}$$

The second-order condition identifies x_2^* as a global minimum. The crucial question now is "Does x_2^* satisfy the constraints imposed by Equation (12.11)?" The answer is yes, as found by plugging Equation (12.17) in (12.11) and given that $s_2 \geq 40{,}000$ according to Equation (12.10); hence, (12.17) represents the optimal policy in stage 2 and the optimal recursion is given by

$$f_2^* = 12{,}439{,}550 - 497s_2 + 0.005s_2^2 \tag{12.18}$$

after substituting Equation (12.17) into (12.15) and simplifying.

Stages 3 and 4 proceed in the same manner to arrive at

$$x_3^* = 40{,}000 - s_3 \tag{12.19}$$

$$f_3^* = 16{,}560{,}000 - 800s_3 + 0.01s_3^2 \tag{12.20}$$

$$x_4^* = 19{,}850 - 0.5s_4 \tag{12.21}$$

and

$$f_4^* = 16{,}380{,}000 - 794(s_4 + x_4) + 0.02s_4x_4 + 0.01s_4^2 + 0.02x_4^2. \qquad (12.22)$$

Note that Equation (12.19) satisfies (12.11) strictly, which should indicate to you that the stationary point in stage 3 did not satisfy (12.11).

Given that $s_4 = 32{,}000$, we successively evaluate Equations (12.21), (12.19), (12.17), and (12.13), making use of (12.7), to get $x_4^* = 3{,}850$, $x_3^* = 4{,}150$, $x_2^* = 4{,}850$, and $x_1^* = 5{,}150$; that is, hire 5,150; 4,850; 4,150; and 3,850 hours of labor in quarters 1, 2, 3, and 4 respectively. Given an optimal hiring-firing policy in each stage, the work force levels for quarters 1, 2, 3, and 4 are 35,850; 40,000; 44,850; and 50,000, respectively. The optimal cost, as given by Equation (12.22), is \$915,550 over four quarters.

FOLLOW-UP EXERCISES

23. What is the optimal policy and associated cost if the initial labor force is 40,000? 50,000?
24. Formulate and solve the work force problem by defining x_i as *work force level* with i more quarters to go. Which approach is easier?

On Selecting A Procedure: Forward or Backward Recursion?

The analyst's decision regarding the use of forward or backward recursions will be determined by personal preference, by the difficulty of effecting stage transformations for the particular application, by the type of sensitivity analysis desired, or by the specification of initial or final states. Transformations of state that occurred in the stage decisions for the shortest route problem were straightforward in either the forward direction or the backward direction; however, for many other applications, especially time-dependent processes, the backward procedure facilitates the conceptualization and computation of transformations. For this reason, there is a decided preference in the literature for backward recursions.

12.6 ASSESSMENT

We conclude our treatment of dynamic programming by assessing its strengths, weaknesses, and future prospects.

Advantages

1. The process of breaking down a complex problem into a series of interrelated subproblems often provides insight into the nature of the problem. This advantage of dynamic programming is especially evident for sequential types of processes (e.g., production smoothing and scheduling on an ongoing basis or control of a chemical process), some of which can be solved only by dynamic programming.
2. Because dynamic programming is an approach to optimization rather than a technique, it has a flexibility that allows application to other types of mathematical programming problems. Essentially, each term or variable in the objective function is assigned a stage, the decision at each stage is based on the level or value for that variable, and the amount of unused or used

resource (right-hand–side constant) for a constraint is represented by a state variable. Integer programming problems and linear programming problems can be solved in this manner, the former using tabular form (Example 12.2) and the latter using a nontabular (continuous) form. The approach can be used to solve nonlinear integer programs (Example 12.6), nonlinear continuous programs (Example 12.7), and other optimization problems characterized by nonconvex or discontinuous functions. Additionally, dynamic programming is applicable to either deterministic or stochastic processes and to adaptive processes (e.g., feedback-control systems in the making of steel).

3. The computational procedure in dynamic programming allows for a built-in form of sensitivity analysis based on state variables and on the variable represented by the stages. For example, the final tableaus for the capital budgeting model (Example 12.2) and the reliability model (Example 12.6) allow for examination of the sensitivity of the solution to the budget; the final tableau of the production-inventory model (Example 12.5) related sensitivity of the solution to the level of ending inventory; the final optimization equation for x_4^* in the work force planning model (Example 12.7) readily allows for an examination of solution sensitivity to the beginning level of work force; and the extension of the number of stages in the forward versions of the production-inventory model and the work force planning model allows the treatment of varying planning horizons. This latter capability also opens the way to the treatment of unbounded planning horizons, especially under the circumstances of a present value criterion or stationary cycles.

4. Finally, dynamic programming achieves computational savings over complete enumeration. For example, complete enumeration of a problem with two variables ($n = 2$) and 10 alternatives per variable requires the examination of 10^2 or 100 solutions; an increase to four variables ($n = 4$) generates 10^4 or 10,000 solutions; for six variables ($n = 6$) the number of possible solutions is 10^6 or 1,000,000. In short, difficulty in enumeration increases exponentially as the number of variables increases linearly. In contrast, the number of stages in dynamic programming would increase from two to four to six, which essentially represents a linear increase in computational difficulty. As the size of the problem increases, the disparity in calculations between the two approaches becomes pronounced.

Disadvantages

1. Although dynamic programming is conceptually more powerful than its sister techniques in mathematical programming, the high degree of expertise, insight, and "art" required in the efficient formulation of complex problems (especially with regard to the specification of transformations) has to be considered a disadvantage.

2. A further disadvantage is the lack of a general algorithm akin to, say, the simplex method. This is not an inconsequential problem as it restricts the availability of generalized computer codes necessary for widespread

and inexpensive implementation of dynamic programming. Some progress has been made, however, in classifying applications by type and developing computational procedures that, although not identical, have similar structures.[7]

3. The most formidable shortcoming of dynamic programming is the so-called curse of **dimensionality**. This problem is encountered when a particular application is characterized by multiple states (termed a multidimensional state vector). For such formulations, the storage capacity and computational capabilities of computers can be taxed severely. To illustrate, consider a discrete three-stage problem ($n = 3$) that has 10 decision alternatives per stage (10 columns in a tableau excluding the optimal policy columns), and one state variable with 100 alternatives (rows). The number of storage cells required per matrix (tableau) would be $(10) \cdot (100)$ or 1,000. The addition of second and third state variables, each with 100 alternatives, would increase the required number of cells to 100,000 and 100 million, respectively.[8] Thus storage requirements increase geometrically as the dimensions of the state variable increase linearly. Computation time will increase roughly by the same magnitude. Although more efficient computation procedures and increased computer capabilities will tend to compensate for these effects, "breakthroughs" will be required to relegate them to the status of minor problems.

Potentialities

Dynamic programming procedures and concepts have had a significant impact both in the development of other academic areas (e.g., Markov processes, game theory, and numerical analysis) and in the successful solution of certain applied problems (e.g., inventory replenishment, production scheduling, equipment replacement and maintenance, and chemical control processes). Its scope is broad and its areas of application are being extended continually.

---

[7]Allocation processes (Examples 12.2 and 12.6), dynamic processes (Examples 12.5 and 12.7), multistage production processes, feedback-control processes, network processes, and Markov processes (Chapter 14). For details see R. E. Bellman and S. E. Dreyfus, *Applied Dynamic Programming* (Princeton, N.J.: Princeton University Press, 1962); and N. P. Loomba and E. Turban, *Applied Programming for Management* (New York; Holt, Rinehart & Winston, 1974).

[8]An efficiently written computer program would carry only one full matrix for calculations in the current stage and one additional matrix to store the optimal decision for each stage. The number of cells in the computational matrix can be reduced even further with an additional dosage of ingenuity. Any ideas?

SELECTED APPLICATION REVIEW

EQUIPMENT REPLACEMENT

The Phillips Petroleum Company utilizes a dynamic programming algorithm to provide guidance in equipment replacement decisions for its fleet of large highway tractors. The overall fleet includes approximately 1,500 passenger cars and 3,800 trucks, among which are the tractors. The criterion used in making replacement decisions is discounted outgoing cash flow (DOCF). Compared with its former replacement model, this model allows for consideration of such issues as the relative fuel economies of existing versus new models, timing replacements to take maximum advantage of tax depreciation laws, and scheduling upcoming replacements prior to license renewals to avoid these costs. Aside from substantial savings being realized for the highway tractor fleet, the model is being used to establish policies for company passenger cars and light trucks. Anticipated annual savings are expected to be more than $90,000 annually.

Logo reproduced courtesy of Phillips Petroleum Company.

SOURCE: Richard Waddell, "A Model for Equipment Replacement Decisions and Policies," *Interfaces*, August 1983, pp. 1–7.

TIMBER MANAGEMENT

The Edelman Award for Management Science Achievement honors excellence in the practice of management science. The first prize winner in the 1985 competition was an application at the Weyerhaeuser Company, one of the the largest forest products companies in the world. Weyerhaeuser harvests approximately 15 million trees per year. The value of a tree varies depending on its length, curvature, diameter, knots, and the decisions about

(continued)

how to cut the tree into logs. A decision simulator has been developed for Weyerhaeuser that incorporates a dynamic programming optimization procedure for determining the most profitable cutting pattern for individual trees. The decision simulator looks like a video game and helps "wood buckers" (workers responsible for selecting trees to cut and determining the way in which they should be cut) and mill personnel to improve their cutting decisions. When using the decision simulator, trees are shown on a video screen with all of their knots, curves, and flaws. The user makes decisions about how to cut the tree. The resulting values of the lumber and sawdust produced by the cuts are immediately tallied. The optimal cutting pattern and its values are then displayed for comparison. In the first seven years since implementation, it is estimated that improved decisions have resulted in increased profits exceeding $100 million.

Logo reproduced courtesy of Wezerhaeuser Company.

SOURCE: Mark R. Lembersky and Uli H. Chi, "Weyerhaeuser Decision Simulator Improves Timer Profits," *Interfaces*, January–February, pp. 6–15.

HYDROTHERMAL ELECTRICAL GENERATION

The second place prize winner in the 1985 Edelman Awards was an application of dynamic programming in helping to manage the Brazilian hydrothermal generating system. Consisting of 18 member utilities, which share the costs of operating the thermoelectric system, a stochastic (probabilistic) dynamic programming model determines the optimal allocation of hydro and thermal resources within the system. The system consists of several hundred generating units interconnected by thousands of miles of transmission lines. The model deals with the uncertainty of water supply, trade-offs that exist between hydro and thermal generation, conflicting demands for water use, and other factors influencing the efficiency of operating the system. Implemented in 1979, the actual savings (compared with the formerly used management system) from 1979 to 1984 were approximately $260 million.

SOURCE: L. A. Terry, M. V. F. Pereira, T. A. Araripe Neto, L. F. C. A. Silva, and P. R. H. Sales, "Coordinating the Energy Generation of the Brazilian National Hydrothermal Electrical Generating System," *Interfaces*, January–February 1986, pp. 16–38.

MANAGEMENT OF MUNICIPAL WATER SUPPLY

For municipal water companies, water distribution systems consume significant amounts of electricity. In the town of Lancaster, Ohio, dynamic programming was used to develop water pumping policies to minimize the consumption (cost) of electricity. Both a deterministic DP model and a probabilistic DP model were used to determine the combination of water pumps, the amounts of water to be pumped to the different demand points within Lancaster, and the pumping schedule (dividing a week into 42 four-hour intervals).

SOURCE: Subhash C. Sarin and Wahib Ei Benni, "Determination of Optimal Pumping Policy of a Municipal Water Plant," *Interfaces*, April 1982, pp. 43–49.

SELECTED REFERENCES

Bellman, R. E. *Dynamic Programming*. Princeton, N.J.: Princeton University Press, 1957.

Bellman, R. E. and S. E. Dreyfus. *Applied Dynamic Programming*. Princeton, N.J.: Princeton University Press, 1962.

Denardo, E. V. *Dynamic Programming: Theory and Application*. Englewood Cliffs, N.J.: Prentice-Hall, 1975.

Dykstra, Dennis P. *Mathematical Programming for Natural Resource Management*. New York: McGraw-Hill, 1984.

Hadley, G. F. *Nonlinear and Dynamic Programming*. Reading, Mass.: Addison-Wesley Publishing. 1964.

Loomba, N. P., and E. Turban. *Applied Programming for Management*. New York: Holt, Rinehart & Winston, 1974.

Nemhauser, G. L. *Introduction to Dynamic Programming*. New York: John Wiley & Sons, 1966.

Oren, Shmuel S., and Shao Hong Wan. "Optimal Strategies Petroleum Reserve Policies: A Steady-State Analysis." *Management Science*, January 1986, pp. 14–29.

Rosenblatt, Meir J. "The Dynamics of Plant Layout." *Management Science*, January 1986, pp. 76–86.

Wagner, H. M. *Principles of Operations Research*. Englewood Cliffs, N.J.: Prentice-Hall, 1975.

ADDITIONAL EXERCISES

The **structure** of a dynamic programming (DP) problem is identified by the following:

1. Definition of stage and number of stages.
2. Identification of decision variables.

3. Definition of state variable and statement of transformation function.
4. Statement of return function (algebraic or tabular).
5. Statement of optimal recursive equation.

25. ***Fire Station Allocation.*** Planners for a city are to recommend the "best" allocation of fire stations to three districts. Anywhere from zero to three stations can be located in a district. Not suprisingly, the number of stations located in a district has a bearing on the annual property damage caused by fires for that district. Table 12–22 reflects this relationship. Differences among districts are due to such factors as population, residential-commercial mix, socioeconomic makeup, and quality of construction. A budget constraint restricts the total number of allocations to five stations.

TABLE 12–22 Annual Property Damage (*Millions of Dollars*)

	Number of Stations per District			
District	**0**	**1**	**2**	**3**
1	2.0	0.9	0.3	0.2
2	0.5	0.3	0.2	0.1
3	1.5	1.0	0.7	0.3

a. Identify the *DP* structure for this problem. Do you have "quarrel" with the criterion? Explain.

b. Determine the optimal allocation by *DP*.

26. ***Police Patrol Allocation.*** Assume that a police administrator wishes to allocate *all* 12 patrol teams of two officers to four precincts. A departmental policy prescribes that at least one two-officer team must be assigned to each precinct, but no more than four teams to any one precinct. The primary objective in allocating the 12 teams is to minimize the expected number of serious crimes among the four precincts during an eight-hour tour of duty. Statisticians within the department have estimated expected numbers of serious crimes for these four precincts as a function of the number of partol teams assigned. These are presented in Table 12–23.

TABLE 12–23 Estimated Serious Crimes per Tour of Duty

	Precinct			
Number of Two-Officer Teams	**1**	**2**	**3**	**4**
1	20	40	8	36
2	18	38	4	34
3	16	36	2	32
4	12	30	1	25

The optimal allocation of police officers can be determined by dynamic programming. The problem can be solved as a four-stage model in which each stage represents a precinct; the state variable represents the total number of two-officer teams available for allocation to i precincts; the decision variable is the number of teams allocated at each stage (precinct); and the return function represents the total expected number of serious crimes.

Determine the optimal solution to this problem using the backward recursion method.

27. In the previous exercise,
    a. Determine the optimal solution if the departmental policy requires at least two teams but no more than four per precinct.
    b. Solve the original exercise if there are 14 teams available.
28. Figure 12–9 is a network diagram showing alternative routes for a four-day trip from Boston to Denver. Using backward recursions, determine the shortest route for the trip.

FIGURE 12–9

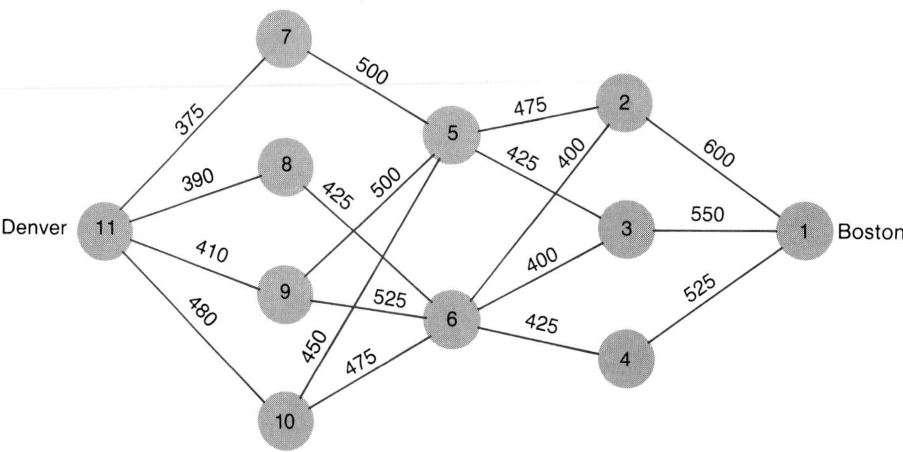

29. ***Advertising Budget.*** A company has $12 million it wishes to allocate for advertising five products. Company officials wish to allocate the budget in such a way as to maximize expected profit from the five products. Table 12–24 indicates the expected profit from each product as a function of the amount allocated from the advertising budget. Assuming that no one product will be allocated more than $4 million, use dynamic programming to determine the optimal allocations.

TABLE 12–24 Expected Profit (*Stated in $millions*)

	Product				
	1	**2**	**3**	**4**	**5**
0	5.1	2.4	1.8	3.2	5.4
1	7.3	4.8	4.2	5.9	4.6
2	9.3	7.2	5.8	6.8	6.2
3	10.4	9.8	7.9	9.1	8.8
4	11.6	10.6	9.8	10.6	11.2

30. In the preceding exercise, assume that each product is to receive at least $1 million of the advertising budget. Determine the optimal solution, and compare the results with the original problem.
31. ***Research Funds Allocations.*** An agency in the Department of Health, and Human Services (HHS) has $6 million for allocation to three cancer research clinics. In general, the

greater the size of a grant for a particular clinic, the greater will be the subsequent savings of lives over a specified planning horizon. By consensus, experts have provided the data in Table 12–25.

TABLE 12–25 Savings in Lives over the Next Decade (*$millions*)

	Funds Allocation (millions of dollars)						
Clinic	**0**	**1**	**2**	**3**	**4**	**5**	**6**
1	5	7	10	15	25	40	60
2	10	15	20	24	27	30	32
3	1	10	15	20	30	35	45

Note that funds are allocated in increments of $1 million.

a. Identify the *DP* structure for this problem.

b. Determine the optimal allocation by *DP*.

c. What would be the effects on the criterion and on the allocation if only $5 million were available?

d. What would be the effects if each clinic must receive a minimum of $1 million?

32. ***Cargo-Loading Model.*** A lunar space vehicle is to be loaded with three types of geological kits for purposes of experimentation. At least one kit, but no more than four kits, of each type must be loaded. In general, the more kits of a certain type the better, since a greater quantity of experimental information can be gathered. Unfortunately, the payload of the vehicle limits the total weight of the experimental kits to 250 pounds (volume is not restrictive). Relevant data are given in Table 12–26.

TABLE 12–26 Measure of Experimental Value

		Number of Kits Loaded			
Type of Kit	**Weight per Kit (lb.)**	**1**	**2**	**3**	**4**
1	20	4	7	9	10
2	50	6	7	8	9
3	30	3	6	8	9

a. Identify the *DP* structure for this problem.

b. Determine the optimal loading by *DP*. (*Hint:* You should be efficient in specifying leaving states for each stage, lest you have 251 rows in a tableau. For example, you need only consider four leaving states in stage 2).

c. What is the value of s_0 and what does it represent?

33. ***Feedlot Optimization.*** A simplified feedlot optimization problem is concerned with the amounts of a certain type of ration (x_t) a feedlot operation is to feed an animal over a planning horizon ($t = 1, 2, \ldots, T$) such that the profit contribution per animal is maximized.[9]

A feedlot purchases animals from livestock growers when the animals reach a certain age or weight. While in the feedlot, animals are fed a special diet for T periods, after

[9]For a more realistic (and more complex) formulation, see C. F. Meyer and R. J. Newett, "Dynamic Programming for Feedlot Optimization," *Management Science* 16, no. 6 (1970), pp. B410–26.

which they are sold to a slaughter-house. The variable cost of the ration per period is a function of the amount in the ration, as indicated by $c_t(x_t)$ in Table 12–27.

TABLE 12–27

x_t (lb.)	$c_t(x_t)$ ($)
150	20
200	30
250	35

The weight of an animal at the end of period t is given by its weight at the end of the preceding period plus the weight gain during period t. The weight gain during period t is a function of the amount of feed in period t, as indicated by $g_t(x_t)$, shown in Table 12–28.

TABLE 12–28

$g_t(x_t)$ (lb.)	x_t (lb.)
50	150
70	200
80	250

Higher weight gains during a period tend to be associated with higher operating costs (e.g., maintenance costs, veterinary costs). Moreover, these costs increase over time, as given by the function

$$m_t(x_t, t) = 0.01t \cdot g_t(x_t),$$

where $m_t(x_t, t)$ represents these operating costs. Any other costs are considered fixed.

The feedlot purchases animals initially weighing 500 pounds and sells them after three periods at a weight of 700 pounds. The operator wishes to determine a feeding schedule such that total feeding cost is minimized.

a. Identify the *DP* structure for this problem.

b. Determine the optimal decision and value of the criterion by *DP*. (*Hint:* In a forward recursion, the three leaving states for stage 1 are 550, 570, and 580; the three leaving states for stage 2 are 620, 630, and 650; and the leaving state for stage 3 is 700.)

34. Suppose the feedlot operator in the preceding exercise is willing to consider all possible ending weights (i.e., weight at the end of three periods).

a. Generate *DP* tableaus. (*Hint:* The number of leaving states for stages 1, 2, and 3 are, respectively, 3, 6, and 9.)

b. Determine optimal contribution to profit and overhead for each ending state if the feedlot pays $0.40 per pound for an animal and receives $0.50 per pound after three periods. What optimal ending weight and feeding schedule do you recommend?

35. ***Replacement Model.* An expensive capital asset (e.g., printing press, freighter, airplane) is characterized by a purchase price at the *beginning* of period i (P_i) that increases over time, a salvage value at the *beginning* of period j (S_j) that decreases over time, and an operating cost *during* period t (C_t) that increase over time. Based on past experience, the followng functions have been determined.

$$P_i = 2 + 0.1i \qquad \text{(millions of dollars).}$$

$$S_j = P_i \cdot (0.8)^{j-i}, \quad j > i \qquad \text{(millions of dollars).}$$

$$C_t = 0.05 + 0.01t, \quad i \le t < j \qquad \text{(millions of dollars).}$$

Thus, the total cost for an asset purchased at the beginning of period i and replaced at the beginning of period j is given by

$$TC_{ij} = P_i - S_j + \sum_{t=i}^{j-1} C_t, \qquad j > i.$$

For example, if the asset is purchased at the beginning of period 3 ($i = 3$) and replaced at the beginning of period 5 ($j = 5$), then

$$\begin{aligned} TC_{35} &= P_3 - S_5 + \sum_{t=3}^{4} C_t \\ &= P_3 - P_3 \cdot (0.8)^{5-3} + (C_3 + C_4) \\ &= P_3[1 - (0.8)^2] + C_3 + C_4 \\ &= [2 + 0.1(3)](1 - 0.64) + [0.05 + 0.01(3)] + [0.05 + 0.01(4)] \\ &= 0.998\,. \end{aligned}$$

a. For a planning horizon of four years, compute a table for TC_{ij}. Note that the table has four rows ($i = 1, 2, 3, 4$) and four columns ($j = 2, 3, 4, 5$).

b. Identify the DP structure for this problem. (*Hint:* Let each stage represent a point in time at the beginning of a year. A backward recursion may be easier to conceptualize.)

c. Solve this problem by *DP*.

36. ***Solar Energy Installation.* An experimental solar energy system for residential heating consists of three major components; a solar collector made up of plate glass that is oriented toward the sun; a water tank for storing thermal energy; and a piping-control system for regulating flows, pressure, and temperature.

Suppose that three surface areas for the collector are under consideration: 500, 600, and 700 square feet. Engineering tests show that the area of the collector directly affects its ability to increase average ambient (outdoor) temperatures. The 500-square-foot collector increases ambient temperature by a factor of 6; the 600-square-foot collector, by a factor of 7; and the 700-square-foot collector, by a factor of 8. For example, given an average ambient temperature of 30°F, the 600-square-foot collector has the capability of sending water into the storage tank, which is heated to 210°F (30 × 7). Over the life of a typical home (estimated at 40 years), the amortized cost of the collector is $.50 per square foot per year.

Two choices are available for the size of the storage tank: 800 gallons and 1,000 gallons. Generally, the larger tanks have a greater ability to store thermal energy for use during the nighttime or during cloudy weather. The effective heat retention of the smaller tank is 0.7, and that of the larger tank is 0.8. For example, the larger tank is capable of effectively maintaining the water at 168°F, when the collector delivers water at 210°F (210 × 0.8). The amortized cost of the storage facility is $0.15 per gallon per year.

Two choices also are available for the piping and control system. These are amortized at $50 per year and $100 per year. The efficiency factor for the cheaper alternative is 0.4 and that for the more expensive alternative is 0.5. For example, if the effective temperature of water in a tank is 168°F, then an efficiency factor of 0.5 means that the effective temperature that can be delivered to the residence is 84°F (168 × 0.5).

The effective delivery temperature is important because it determines the average cost of supplying conventional heat to supplement the solar system. For a 2,000-square-foot residence heated to 70°F, the average annual cost of the conventional heating system has been estimated by the following relationship:

$$h = 150 + 10(70 - \text{Effective delivery temperature}).$$

Note that effective delivery temperatures above 70°F reduce h below \$150 per year. Moreover, if a calculation yields $h < 0$, then h should be set to zero.

a. Identify the *DP* structure for this problem.

b. Determine the optimal design by *DP*. (To simplify the problem, round off the effective delivery temperature to the nearest 10°F).

13

Decision Analysis

Chapter Outline

This chapter introduces a formal analytic framework for analyzing decisions in the face of uncertainty. Uncertainty about where interest rates or exchange rates will go or about the market potential of a product are examples of uncertainty about a future state of nature. If we can somehow assign probabilities to the possible outcomes, then we can make decisions based on the calculated risks involved.

To begin, we will calculate expected returns for decisions using our initial or prior probability estimates. Then we will consider how these probability estimates could be improved, perhaps as a result of a forecast or a market survey. These new and improved "posterior" probabilities will allow us to calculate new expected returns, this time with decisions based on better information. We will then question whether or not the forecast or survey is worth its cost. After answering this question with preposterior analysis, we will show how all of our decision analysis could also be carried out using a decision tree. Finally, we explore the decision maker's attitude toward risk and incorporate risk preferences into our models.

13.1 FUNDAMENTALS

Decision analysis, which is often called **decision theory,** is a popular field of study that provides an insightful framework for statistically analyzing decisions characterized by uncertain environments. Before illustrating the basic structure of decision models, we present a motivating example.

▶ Example 13.1 Portfolio Model

In financial analysis *portfolio* refers to the number and types of investments undertaken by an individual or institution. The usual investment alternatives are represented by stocks and bonds, which allows for wide latitude in the number and types of investments in the portfolio.

Consider a decision whereby an institutional investor plans to invest \$10 million in one of two or both investment alternatives. Such a situation might arise in deciding how much to invest in each of two alternatives for a retirement fund.[1] To simplify matters, only three decisions are under consideration:

D_1 ≡ All \$10 million invested in alternative A.
D_2 ≡ \$5 million invested in alternative A and \$5 million invested in alternative B.
D_3 ≡ All \$10 million invested in alternative B.

To further simplify (or complicate, depending on your point of view) the illustration, suppose that the annual rate of return for alternative A will be either −0.05 or 0.10 and that for alternative B will be either −0.10 or 0.20; however, which return will be associated with each investment alternative is not known with certainty.[2] Furthermore, the rates of

[1]College professors might recognize this as being similar to the TIAA-CREF portfolio decision.

[2]Annual rate of return = (Value at end of year + Dividends or interest − Value at beginning of year) ÷ (Value at beginning of year). For example, if a share of stock is bought for \$10, provides \$0.20 dividend, and sells for \$11 one year later, then the rate of return is (11 + 0.2 − 10)/10, or 0.12.

TABLE 13–1 Rates of Return Relationships

	θ_1	θ_2	θ_3	θ_4
Alternative A	−0.05	−0.05	0.10	0.10
Alternative B	−0.10	0.20	−0.10	0.20

return between the two investment alternatives are statistically dependent. The interactions are shown in Table 13–1. Thus θ_1 represents a year in which alternative A had a −0.05 rate of return and alternative B had a −0.10 rate of return; θ_2 represents the outcome −0.05 for A and 0.20 for B; and so forth.

Basic Structure of Decision Tables

Table 13–2 illustrates a type of decision table called a **payoff table.** Rows represent the **decision alternatives** to be considered, and columns represent the possible **states of nature.** In a decision theory context, states of nature represent conditions outside the control of the decision maker that influence the outcomes associated with decisions. States of nature may be indicated by values for continuous random variables, such as the rate of inflation during a particular period, or they may be reflected by discrete or categorical random variables, such as weather conditions (rain, snow, sunny, and so forth).

TABLE 13–2 Payoff Table for Example 13.1 (*Millions of dollars*)

	θ_1	θ_2	θ_3	θ_4
D_1	9.50	9.50	11.00	11.00
D_2	9.25	10.75	10.00	11.50
D_3	9.00	12.00	9.00	12.00

The interaction of a decision D_i and a state of nature θ_j results in a **consequence.** In this case, consequences are represented by monetary "payoffs," as indicated by the cell values in Table 13–2. For example, if all $10 million are invested in alternative A (that is, decision D_1) and both investments have positive rates of return over the following year as indicated in Table 13–1 (that is, state of nature θ_4), then the investor will end up with $11 million at the end of the year.[3] This payoff, then, is entered in cell D_1, θ_4 of the payoff table.

If consequences are represented by a measure that reflects "cost," then the decision table is called a **loss table** rather than a payoff table; otherwise its structure is identical to that of a payoff table.

[3]$10 million original investment plus $1 million increase in value due to the 0.10 rate of return for investment alternative *A*. Can you confirm the other entries in Table 13.2?

Measures of subjective preferences, called **utilities**, are still another way of reflecting consequences. Utilities represent individualized desirability measures for risky consequences. In essence, these measures reflect the extent of need satisfaction as perceived by the decision maker. A simple way of relating to utility is to think of the satisfaction that \$50 would bring to a pauper versus the satisfaction that \$50 would bring to a millionaire. Most likely the utility measure of that identical payoff would be quite different between these two individuals. When utilities replace payoffs, the payoff table is labeled a **utility table.** When utilities replace losses, however, the loss table is called a **disutility table** as the consequences reflect measures of dispreferences. Section 13.6 will discuss procedures for "quantifying" utilities.

As an alternative to payoff, loss, and utility tables, for some applications it is desirable to specify an **opportunity loss** or **regret table** as given by Table 13–3. The **opportunity loss** for a given decision-state of nature combination is the numerical difference between the realized consequence (payoff, loss, or utility) and the consequence associated with the optimal decision for the given state of nature. For example, suppose decision D_3 is made and θ_3 occurs, resulting in a \$9 million payoff according to Table 13–2. In retrospect, if we had known that θ_3 would occur, then the best decision would have been D_1 with a payoff of \$11 million. The difference of \$2 million between the optimal decision and the nonoptimal decision for state of nature θ_3 represents a loss we would not have incurred (or a "missed opportunity") if we had made the best decision. Hence it is termed an opportunity loss or regret for cell D_3, θ_3. Can you confirm the other entries in Table 13–3?

TABLE 13–3 Regret or Opportunity Loss Table for Example 13.1 (*Millions of dollars*)

	θ_1	θ_2	θ_3	θ_4
D_1	0.00	2.50	0.00	1.00
D_2	0.25	1.25	1.00	0.50
D_3	0.50	0.00	2.00	0.00

Components of Decision Problems

In general four components must be specified for the analysis of all decision problems:

1. $\{D\}$, the *set* of decision or action variables (alternatives).
2. $\{\theta\}$, the *set* of uncontrollable variables or states of nature.
3. $f(\theta)$, the probability distribution for the states of nature.
4. The payoff function, $R(D, \theta)$, the loss function $L(D, \theta)$, or the utility function, $U(D, \theta)$.

Decision variables can be *discrete* or *continuous*. As described, the portfolio problem identified three discrete alternatives: $\{D\} = \{D_1 D_2 D_3\}$. If the decision, however, had been stated in terms of the proportion of funds to be invested in each alternative, then the decision variable would have been continuous.

Another issue relating to decision variables is the number and timing of decisions. **Single stage decision problems** are those that require a single decision followed by some chance event. The portfolio example is this type. **Multistage or sequential decision problems** are characterized by a sequence of decisions. Following each decision a chance event occurs, which in turn influences the next decision. This topic is discussed more fully in Section 13.7.

States of nature can also be discrete or continuous. In the portfolio problem, each investment alternative was characterized by only two possible rates of return, which gave four permutations when the investments were considered jointly. The permutations represent four discrete states of nature, $\{\theta\} = \{\theta_1\theta_2\theta_3\theta_4\}$, as depicted in Table 13–1. Note that the use of payoff, loss, or utility tables is restricted to discrete $\{D\}$ and $\{\theta\}$. Why?

The solution of a decision problem also requires the specification of a probability distribution $f(\theta)$ for states of nature. If states of nature are discrete, then a probability mass function must be specified; continuous states of nature require the identification of a probability density function. As discussed in Appendix A, these probability distributions can be empirical, subjective, or theoretical. In the theoretical case, empirical evidence should substantiate the use of a specific theoretical distribution. In this chapter, we will focus on the solution of decision problems having discrete decisions and discrete states of nature.

Finally, a payoff function, a loss function, or a utility function must be specified. Each of these functions provides a measure for the specific consequences resulting from the interaction of decisions and states of nature. For this reason we attach the argument D, θ to the symbols that represent payoffs, losses, and utilities, or, $R(D, \theta)$, $L(D, \theta)$, and $U(D, \theta)$. In effect, these functions embody the criterion set with which the decision maker evaluates actions. **Payoffs** are generally represented by gains, profits, revenues, net worth, or any other measure that reflects something desirable. **Losses** are usually taken to mean opportunity losses or some other measure that reflects something to be avoided (e.g., costs, error). The literature on decision theory exhibits a distinct preference for reflecting consequences in terms of losses, primarily because losses are easier to determine and can give useful theoretical insights, as demonstrated in Section 13.3. **Utilities** represent preference measures for consequences. Conceptually, they are superior to payoffs or losses in that they take into account a decision maker's subjective attitude toward risk. Section 13.6 develops this concept in more detail.

Once the four elements of a decision problem have been specified, it is necessary to solve the problem. This is accomplished by determining the optimal act or decision with respect to some criterion. Methods of solution are presented in Sections 13.2 through 13.5

FOLLOW-UP EXERCISES

1. Construct a payoff table for the portfolio problem that also includes the following decisions:

$D_4 \equiv$ \$2.5 million in A and \$7.5 million in B.

$D_5 \equiv$ \$7.5 million in A and \$2.5 million in B.

2. Construct the regret table for Exercise 1.
3. Construct a payoff table for the portfolio problem that includes a 0.0 rate of return for investment alternative *A* and the same rates of return for alternative *B*.
4. Construct the regret table for Exercise 3.

13.2 PRIOR ANALYSIS

Prior analysis refers to methods of solving decision problems which utilize the originally specified probability distribution $f(\theta)$ for states of nature. This probability distribution is termed the **prior probability distribution** because it is specified *prior* to the act of seeking additional information about states of nature. Procedures that revise prior probabilities based on additional experimentation or sampling will be discussed in Section 13.3.

Assessment of Prior Probabilities

If past data are available, then the *relative frequency* or *empirical* definition of probability (Section A.1) may be used to define the probability distribution for states of nature. This procedure is quite acceptable if the future environment is not expected to differ appreciably from the historical environment that provided the data; however, if the decision maker believes that historical data will not be representative of future data, then empirical probabilities can be altered subjectively to accommodate this belief.

Subjective probabilities represent the likelihood of occurrences for the specific states of nature based on the personal feelings and experiences of the decision maker. They are not wild guesses, but rather represent degrees of belief based on informed judgment. In some cases these subjective probabilities may reflect or utilize available empirical data, as mentioned previously. In other cases, however, historical data may be unavailable, in which case subjective likelihoods represent the only alternative for specifying prior probabilities. Interestingly, the willingness of decision theorists to use subjective probabilities is a clear break with the classical school of statistics.

Alternatively, $f(\theta)$ can be based on a theoretical distribution, such as the binomial, Poisson, or normal. The use of theoretical distributions, however, should be justified by logic or by empirical evaluation.

▶ Example 13.2 New Product Model

A product manager must make a decision regarding whether or not a new product is to be developed and introduced to the market. Based on judgment and past experience with similar products, the payoff table for this venture is represented by Table 13–4. In this case, states of nature are defined by degrees of market penetration. For example, θ_1 indicates that the product will capture 5 percent ($p = 0.05$) of the market. Payoffs represent the present value of estimated profits in millions of dollars. Note that all pay-

TABLE 13–4 Payoffs ($1 million) for New Product Model

	$\theta_1: p = 0.05$	$\theta_2: p = 0.10$	$\theta_3: p = 0.15$
D_1: Introduce	−2	1	5
D_2: Do not introduce	0	0	0

offs for act D_2 are zero, as revenues are not generated and costs relating to development, manufacturing, and distribution are not incurred.

In actual practice, penetration would be a continuous random variable; however, the manager believes that the three specified penetrations adequately represent the states of nature. Table 13–5 suggests the reasoning behind this assertion. The product is expected to achieve no less than 2.5 percent and no more than 17.5 percent of the market. Penetrations within each of the first two class intervals are judged to occur with twice the likelihood of penetrations within the last class; hence, classes are represented by class midpoints, and prior probabilities for states of nature are defined by the given $f(\theta)$.

TABLE 13–5 Potential Market Penetrations

State of Nature θ	Range of Potential Penetration	Midpoint (p)	Probability $f(\theta)$
θ_1	0.025 but less than 0.075	0.05	0.4
θ_2	0.075 but less than 0.125	0.10	0.4
θ_3	0.125 but less than 0.175	0.15	0.2

The Expected Value Decision Rule

The **expected value rule** specifies the selection of the decision D* which maximizes expected return given by

$$E(R) = \sum_{\theta} R(D, \theta) f(\theta) \tag{13.1}$$

or minimizes the expected loss given by

$$E(L) = \sum_{\theta} L(D, \theta) f(\theta) , \tag{13.2}$$

where the decision set $\{D\}$ and the states of nature $\{\theta\}$ are both discrete. D^* is termed the *optimal prior decision,* where optimality is based on the expected value rule. We hasten to point out that this optimality also presumes that the decision maker is risk neutral. Risk neutrality will be discussed in Section 13.6. Here we simply point out that a risk-neutral individual would take the alternative with the higher expected return (or smallest expected loss), even though that alternative had considerably more risk or variability.

Table 13–6 indicates that decision D_1 (introduce) is the optimal prior decision for the new product model with an expected optimal return of $0.6 million.

TABLE 13–6 Expected Returns for New Product Model

Decision	Return $R(D, \theta)$	Prior Probability $f(\theta)$	Expected Return ($ millions) $R(D, \theta) \cdot f(\theta)$
D_1	−2	0.4	−0.8
	1	0.4	0.4
	5	0.2	1.0
Total		1.0	0.6
D_2	0	0.4	0
	0	0.4	0
	0	0.2	0
Total		0	0

Decision Rules under Uncertainty

In the case above, wherein prior probabilities can be determined, the decision-making situation is termed **decision making under risk. Decision making under uncertainty** occurs when no prior probabilities can be estimated. For this case, decision rules can accommodate varying degrees of optimism and pessimism on the part of the decision maker. We will see that the use of these decision rules implies subjective probability estimates, and so the uncertainty case can be brought back to the risk case through somewhat indirect subjective probability assessments. To see this, we need to look at some decision rules.

Min-max and **max-min** rules reflect a pessimistic decision maker who assumes that, given any decision made, the worst possible outcome will occur. Psychologists would call this person a horribilizer. Consequently, the decision maker identifies the worst outcome associated with each decision alternative and selects the decision giving the best of the worst outcomes. Table 13–7 indicates that the worst possible outcome is a $2 million loss for the decision to introduce the product and $0 for the decision not to introduce. These figures represent the minimum values for each row in the table. The max-min rule states that one should select the decision that maximizes the minimum profit. Thus a pessimistic marketing manager (if one existed) would decide not to introduce the product.

TABLE 13–7 Payoff Table for New Product Model with Values of Best and Worst Outcomes

	θ_1	θ_2	θ_3	Worst	Best	
D_1	−2	1	5	−2	[5]	← "Best of Best"
D_2	0	0	0	[0] ↑ "Best of Worst"	0	

Min-min and **max-max** rules accommodate the eternal optimist. This decision-maker expects that "fate" will deal the best possible outcome for whatever decision is selected. From Table 13–7, introducing the product could yield a maximum return of

\$5 million, and not introducing the product would yield a maximum return of \$0. The best of the best outcomes would be the \$5 million, and so the optimist would introduce the product.

A moderately optimistic person might weight the best outcome by 0.75 and the worst outcome by 0.25. Such a procedure would yield an "expected" outcome of $0.75(5) + 0.25(-2) = 3.25$ for introducing the product and 0 for not introducing. A moderately pessimistic decision maker might weight the outcomes in the reverse to yield $0.25(5) + 0.75(-2) = -0.25$ for introducing and 0 for not introducing (to be completely indifferent between introducing and not introducing, the decision maker would need to be fairly pessimistic with a weight of 2/7 to the best outcome and 5/7 to the worst outcome). Known as the **Hurwicz procedure,** the weighting approach highlights the subjectivity involved in the max-max and max-min rules. One simply weights the best outcome by a fraction representing the degree of confidence one has in the outcome occurring and the worst outcome by one minus that fraction. Of course, the Hurwicz procedure ignores all other outcomes and so in effect assigns zero probabilities to them. To use the Hurwicz procedure, simply specify a fraction as your "optimism coefficient" (α) and proceed as above.

Another decision rule takes a more detached view. The **Laplace** or **Bayes procedure** simply assigns equal probabilities to all possible outcomes. If you react by saying that all outcomes are not equally likely, then it sounds as though you are ready to assign prior probabilities. Remember, we are discussing decision rules under uncertainty. By definition, this is the case where we are unable to assign probabilities. For the Laplace method, we assign 1/3 probabilities to the three states of nature in the product introduction example to get: $\frac{1}{3}(-2) + \frac{1}{3}(1) + \frac{1}{3}(5) = \frac{4}{3}$ and $\frac{1}{3}(0) + \frac{1}{3}(0) + \frac{1}{3}(0) = 0$. With this method, we would decide to introduce the product. Sometimes this method is called the **equal likelihood method** or simply the **likelihood method.**

Finally, the **min-max regret** strategy selects the decision that minimizes the maximum regret for each decision. First a regret table is developed as in Table 13–8. Then, for each decision alternative, the maximum regret is identified. The min-max regret strategy calls for choosing the alternative that minimizes these maximum regret values, which would be the introduction alternative in this case.

TABLE 13–8 Regret Table for New Product Model

	θ_1	θ_2	θ_3	Maximum	
*D*1 (introduce)	2	0	0	[2]	← "Minimum of maxima"
*D*2 (don't)	0	1	5	5	

In some circumstances, one of the first five decision rules may be desirable. For example, max-min may be appropriate for the portfolio problem if the investor must have at least \$9.5 million by the end of the year. In general, however, the first five decision rules suffer because they ignore prior probabilities (if such information exists), even though they implicitly assign some subjective probabilities themselves. One cannot support the proposition that the first five rules are relevant when prior probabilities are unknown because subjective prior probabilities can always be assigned for use by the expected value rule. We remain interested in the rules for what they say about the decision maker and suggest that the rules can be used to elicit subjective probability estimates implied by the decision maker's choice of rule.

We now present output from the Erikson-Hall microcomputer package.[4] Again, we stress the idea that each computer package has its own idiosyncracies, but general familiarity with the techniques and definitions will allow us to use any of a variety of packages. The first quarter of Table 13–9, down to "information entered," is an echo check of the new product model data entered as input. The remainder of the table shows the payoffs and the analysis.

TABLE 13–9 Erikson-Hall Output for New Product Model

```
            COMPUTER MODELS FOR MANAGEMENT SCIENCE

DECISION MODELS

              -=*=-  INFORMATION ENTERED  -=*=-

NUMBER OF STATES          :  3

NUMBER OF ALTERNATIVES    :  2

HURWICZ COEFFICIENT       :  .3

                          PAYOFF TABLE

STATES        PAYOFF FROM EACH ALTERNATIVE
                 1        2

  1            -2.00      0
  2             1.00      0
  3             5.00      0

              DECISION MAKING UNDER UNCERTAINTY

                     -=*=-  RESULTS  -=*=-

      CRITERION                    ALTERNATIVE           PAYOFF

      1. MAXIMAX                       A1                  5.00

      2. MAXIMIN                       A2                  0.00

      3. LIKELIHOOD                    A1                  1.33

      4. MINIMAX REGRET                A1                  2.00

      5. HURWICZ RULE                  A1                  0.10

        ------------  END OF ANALYSIS  ------------
```

[4]Warren J. Erikson and Owen P. Hall, *Computer Models for Management Science*, 2nd ed. (Reading, Mass.: Addison-Wesley Publishing, 1986).

FOLLOW-UP EXERCISES In what follows, we will use the payoff table and prior probabilities from the portfolio problem.

	θ_1	θ_2	θ_3	θ_4
D1	9.50	9.50	11.00	11.00
D2	9.25	10.75	10.00	11.50
D3	9.00	12.00	9.00	12.00
Prior Probabilities	0.1	0.5	0.3	0.1

5. Determine the best decision according to the expected value rule.
6. Determine the best decision using the maximax, maximin, equal likelihood and Hurwicz ($\alpha = .3$) decision rules.
7. Determine the best decision by the minimax regret rule.
8. Determine the best decision for Table 13–2 using the maximax, maximin, equal likelihood, Hurwicz ($\alpha = .6$), and minimax regret rules. Would you conclude that diversification (investing in more than one investment alternative) is undesirable when expected monetary value is the only criterion? In general, why is diversification desirable?
9. Show that the maximin rule for Table 13–7 is nothing more than an expected value rule where $f(\theta_1) = 1.0$, $f(\theta_2) = 0$, and $f(\theta_3) = 0$ for both D_1 and D_2. Do these probability assignments make sense for the pessimist?
10. Show that the maximin rule for Table 13–2 is in reality an expected value rule where $f(\theta_1 \text{ or } \theta_2) = 1.0$, $f(\theta_3) = 0$, and $f(\theta_4) = 0$ for D_1; $f(\theta_1) = 1.0$, $f(\theta_2) = 0$, $f(\theta_3) = 0$, and $f(\theta_4) = 0$ for D_2; and $f(\theta_1 \text{ or } \theta_3) = 1.0$, $f(\theta_2) = 0$, and $f(\theta_4) = 0$ for D_3. Do these probability assignments make sense for the pessimist?
11. For Table 13–2, assign implicit subjective probabilities $f(\theta)$ according to the maximax rule. Find the decision which maximizes the expected value. Is this identical to the maximax rule?

13.3 POSTERIOR ANALYSIS

Up to now we have not considered the possibility of seeking additional information about the states of nature. For example, an investor might achieve a better return on a portfolio by subscribing to a service that forecasts stock prices. In this section we present methods which incorporate the availability of additional information.

Value of Perfect Information

In general, applications of decision theory include the option of seeking additional information about the states of nature. An interesting hypothetical question is the expected upper limit for the value of this information. In other words what would be the value of information so perfect that the true state of nature can be predicted with certainty?

Consider the new product example. If θ_1 were predicted with certainty, then D_2 should be chosen with payoff \$0; if θ_2 were predicted with certainty, then D_1 would be the best with payoff \$1 million; finally, if θ_3 were predicted with certainty, then D_1

would yield \$5 million. The expected value of this combination of best decisions and certain states of nature is determined by weighting these payoffs by their respective probabilities of occurrence, as defined by $f(\theta)$. Thus the **expected value under certainty (EVUC)** is $(0) \cdot (0.4) + (1) \cdot (0.4) + (5) \cdot (0.2)$, or \$1.4 (million). Given that \$600,000 is the expected value of the optimal act *prior* to any additional information about states of nature (we derived that result earlier using the expected value rule) and \$1.4 million would be the expected value if perfect information were available, it follows that \$800,000 is the most that the product manager should be willing to pay for perfect information.

In general,

$$\text{EVUC} = \sum_{\theta} R(D^*, \theta) \cdot f(\theta) \tag{13.3}$$

when consequences are expressed as payoffs and

$$\text{EVUC} = \sum_{\theta} L(D^*, \theta) \cdot f(\theta) \tag{13.4}$$

when consequences are in terms of losses, where D^* identifies the best act for a certain θ. Note that the calculation of EVUC requires that $f(\theta)$ *not be affected by decisions.*

The upper bound of \$800,000 is called the **expected value of perfect information (EVPI);** that is, it is the difference between the expected return or loss under certainty (\$1,400,000) and the expected return or loss of the optimal act given by prior analysis (\$600,000). In general,

$$\text{EVPI} = \text{EVUC} - E(R^*) \tag{13.5}$$

for payoffs and

$$\text{EVPI} = E(L^*) - \text{EVUC} \tag{13.6}$$

for losses, where $E(R^*)$ and $E(L^*)$ represent the appropriate expected values of the optimal act for prior analysis.

Revision of Prior Probabilities[5]

Posterior analysis provides a means for revising prior probabilities based on new information that has become available. The vehicle for revising probabilities is **Bayes' Rule,** which is given by

$$f(\theta \mid x) = \frac{f(\theta) \cdot f(x \mid \theta)}{f(x)} \tag{13.7}$$

for *discrete* θ and X where

θ = State of nature.
X = Random variable representing additional information based on a sample survey or an experiment.

[5]This section assumes knowledge of the concepts in Section A.1.

x = Specific value of X.
$f(\theta | x)$ = Revised or conditional probability of θ given x (termed the **posterior probability**).
$f(\theta)$ = Prior probability.
$f(x | \theta)$ = Conditional probability of x given θ.
$f(x)$ = Marginal probability of x.[6]

To continue the new product model, suppose that a market survey based on a consumer panel of 100 customers yields the additional information that only 3 customers would buy this product. In this case we assume that the binomial distribution is an adequate representation of the experimental process where $n = 100$, $X = 3$, and p is given by the appropriate θ in Table 13–6. The calculation of posterior probabilities is summarized in Table 13–10.

TABLE 13–10 Calculation of Posterior Probabilities

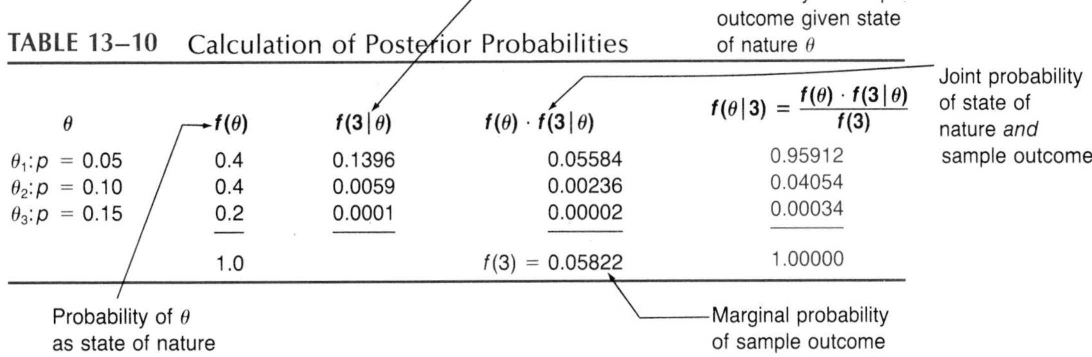

θ	$f(\theta)$	$f(3 \mid \theta)$	$f(\theta) \cdot f(3 \mid \theta)$	$f(\theta \mid 3) = \frac{f(\theta) \cdot f(3 \mid \theta)}{f(3)}$
$\theta_1: p = 0.05$	0.4	0.1396	0.05584	0.95912
$\theta_2: p = 0.10$	0.4	0.0059	0.00236	0.04054
$\theta_3: p = 0.15$	0.2	0.0001	0.00002	0.00034
	1.0		$f(3) = 0.05822$	1.00000

Note that $f(x | \theta)$ is in fact the binomial probability mass function. For example, 0.1396 is the probability of 3 "successes" ($X = 3$) in 100 trials ($n = 100$) of a binomial experiment when the probability of success in any one trial is $p = 0.05$.

The joint probability of θ and x is given by

$$f(\theta \text{ and } x) = f(\theta) \cdot f(x | \theta) \tag{13.8}$$

according to Equation A.6. For example, from Table 13–10, the joint probability of $X = 3$ *and* θ_1 is 0.05584. Since x can be achieved any number of mutually exclusive ways depending on the value of θ, it follows that Equation A.3 can be applied to the joint event (θ and x) across all possible values of θ:

$$f(x) = \sum_{\theta} f(\theta) \cdot f(x | \theta) . \tag{13.9}$$

Having determined that $f(3) = 0.05822$ according to Equation 13.9, we now apply 13.7 to revise the prior probabilities for the states of nature. This provides the last

[6]For posterior analyses based on continuous θ and/or X see G. Hadley, *Introduction to Probability and Statistical Decision Theory* (San Francisco: Holden-Day, 1967; L. Weiss, *Statistical Decision Theory* (New York: McGraw-Hill, 1961); Charles Holloway, *Decision Making under Uncertainty Models*, (Englewood Cliffs, N.J.: Prentice-Hall, 1979); and R. L. Winkler, *Introduction to Bayesian Inference and Decisions* (New York: Holt, Rinehart & Winston, 1972).

column in Table 13–10. Thus, based on the experimental result, we revise the probability of θ_1 (i.e., that the market penetration will be 0.05) from 0.4 to 0.95912, of θ_2 from 0.4 to 0.04054, and of θ_3 from 0.2 to 0.00034. This means that our current best likelihoods for achieving 0.05, 0.10, and 0.15 market penetrations are approximately 96, 4, and 0 percent, respectively. Note that the application of 13.7 ensures that these revised probabilities sum to unity. Further note that the experimental result (3 customers out of 100) is much more consistent with θ_1 than with θ_2 or θ_3. Hence the revised probabilities reflect the changes in likelihoods that one would logically expect.

To determine the optimal posterior decision $\mathbf{D}_B^*$, termed the **Bayes' decision,** the expected value rule given by Equation 13.1 or 13.2 is applied after replacing the prior probability distribution $f(\theta)$ by the posterior probability distribution $f(\theta \mid x)$:

$$E'(R) = \sum_{\theta} R(D, \theta) \cdot f(\theta \mid x) \tag{13.10}$$

or

$$E'(L) = \sum_{\theta} L(D, \theta) \cdot f(\theta \mid x) \tag{13.11}$$

where E' denotes the posterior expected value.

Table 13–11 illustrates calculations for the new product example. Since the expected return associated with introducing the new product (D_1) is now a loss of \$1,876,000, it follows that the Bayes' decision subsequent to the consumer panel results is not to introduce this product (that is, $D_B^* = D_2$) with an optimal expected return of $E'(R^*) = 0$.

TABLE 13–11 Expected Posterior Payoffs for New Product Model

Decision	Payoff $R(D, \theta)$	Posterior Probability $f(\theta \mid x)$	Expected Payoff $R(D, \theta) \cdot f(\theta \mid x)$
D_1	−2	0.95912	−1.91824
	1	0.04054	0.04054
	5	0.00034	0.00170
		1.00000	$E'(R) = -1.87600$
D_2	0	0.95912	0.0
	0	0.04054	0.0
	0	0.00034	0.0
		1.00000	$E'(R) = 0.0$

FOLLOW-UP EXERCISES

12. With respect to the portfolio problem:
    a. Up to how much should you be willing to pay for an investment service that guarantees you perfect forecasts for Table 13–2 (assume prior probabilities shown in Exercise 5)?
    b. It can be proved that EVPI *is equivalent to the minimum expected regret.* Show this for the portfolio problem of Tables 13–2 and 13–3. Is the decision associated with minimum expected regret the same as the decision associated with maximum expected payoff?

13. Determine D_B^* if 3 consumers out of a panel of 20 indicate their preference for the new product instead of the 3 in 100 demonstrated in Table 13–11.

14. Suppose that an investment service for the portfolio model of Table 13–2 accurately forecasts the correct θ with twice the likelihood of the other θ's. This means, for example, that $f(x_1 | \theta_2) = 0.2$, $f(x_2 | \theta_2) = 0.4$, $f(x_3 | \theta_2) = 0.2$, and $f(x_4 | \theta_2) = 0.2$, where x_j is the forecast for θ_j. Thus, if the actual state of nature turns out to be θ_2, then $f(x_1 | \theta_2) = 0.2$ indicates that 20 percent of the time θ_1 was forecasted erroneously, $f(x_2 | \theta_2) = 0.4$ says that θ_2 was forecasted accurately 40 percent of the time, and so on. Note that these conditional probabilities must sum to one. Further note that the above conditional probabilities are only 4 of the 16 that must be specified for this problem. Can you verbalize the following complete set of conditional probabilities?

Conditional Probabilities, $f(x | \theta)$

	Forecast				
State of Nature	x_1	x_2	x_3	x_4	Total
θ_1	0.4	0.2	0.2	0.2	1.0
θ_2	0.2	0.4	0.2	0.2	1.0
θ_3	0.2	0.2	0.4	0.2	1.0
θ_4	0.2	0.2	0.2	0.4	1.0

In Exercise 5 you should have confirmed that D_3 is the optimal decision by prior analysis with $E(R^*) = \$10.8$ million. Using the prior probabilities given in Exercise 5, determine the posterior probabilities, the expected values, and the Bayes' decision by posterior analysis if the forecast for next year is (*a*) x_1 and (*b*) x_3.

When you compare the posterior probabilities in this exercise to the prior probabilities in Exercise 5, are the directions of change logical? Based on the magnitudes of these changes, would you conclude that the forecasting service is effective?

15. In Exercise 14, change the elements in the main diagonal of the $f(x | \theta)$ table from 0.4 to 0.7, and change all other elements to 0.1. Rework the problem and draw a conclusion with respect to the "information content" of main-diagonal elements.

Prelude to Preposterior Analysis

There is a certain flow to thinking about decision theory problems, and it is important to grasp that flow in order to put the numbers into perspective. Regardless of the decisions, we can trace the following steps in decision analysis.

1. Given the alternative decisions, what are the current probabilities on the states of nature, and what is the expected result from each decision?
2. If I knew the state of nature with certainty, what decision would I make, and what would be the resulting payoff?
3. How much would it be worth to be closer to the position of certainty than the current position? A sample or experimental outcome or peek at the situation will surely allow me to revise current probabilities on outcomes.

4. Given the alternative decisions, what are the revised probabilities on the states of nature, and what would be the resulting expected payoffs?
5. How much better off would I be to base my decisions on these revised probabilities rather than on the current probabilities?
6. Is the value of the additional information worth more than its cost?

13.4 PREPOSTERIOR ANALYSIS

As you already know, prior analysis does not consider the act of obtaining new information about the states of nature, whereas posterior analysis provides a means to incorporate new information *after* it becomes available. Up to now, however, we have not considered the issue of whether additional information *should* be acquired in the first place. In other words, since the acquisition of information incurs a cost, it is of interest to assess *beforehand* whether or not the potential benefit of this information is worth the cost. **Preposterior analysis** addresses itself to this issue at a time preceding the actual acquisition of new information. Preposterior analysis can evaluate not only whether new information should or should not be acquired, but also the manner (i.e., alternative sample designs) by which this information is to be acquired.

▶ Example 13.3 Nuclear Power Plant Model

Although you might not think that the future of nuclear power in the United States appears very bright at the moment, companies are still making plans for nuclear plants because of projections in the growth of demand for electricity. Regulatory uncertainty is driving up the time and costs of building such plants. In the future companies interested in building nuclear plants will be forming consortia to spread the costs and the risks.

Consider a $1 billion nuclear power plant that, after 12 years, is nearing completion. It is being built by Ocean Gas & Electric (OG&E) in a certain western state that will remain unnamed (to protect the innocent). OG&E has applied for an operating license to the Nuclear Regulatory Commission (NRC). Unfortunately, the power needs of this most progressive state required that the plant be located in an area near a most famous geological fault. Should a severe earthquake rupture the plant, radioactive particles would be released into the atmosphere in the form of a colorless, odorless cloud that not only would contaminate everything in its path but also would cause untold death and human misery primarily in the form of cancers and genetic defects.

The NRC is well aware of the potential catastrophe. As a result, it requires that all atomic power plants located in earthquake zones be constructed to withstand the most severe shaking ever recorded in that location. To comply with this ruling, OG&E engineers designed a plant with a 15-feet-thick reinforced concrete foundation and a 4-feet-thick reinforced concrete dome over each reactor. It is estimated that this design would withstand a jolt of 7.0 on the Richter scale.

An analysis by the OR staff of NRC yields the information provided by Table 13–12, where

$\theta_1 \equiv$ Reading of $R \leq 7$ on the Richter scale over the life of the plant.
$\theta_2 \equiv$ Reading of $7 < R \leq 8$.
$\theta_3 \equiv$ Reading of $R > 8$.
$D_1 \equiv$ Award operating license unconditionally.

$D_2 \equiv$ Award operating license conditional on additional concrete reinforcement which is to withstand 8.0 on the Richter scale.

$D_3 \equiv$ Do not award operating license.

TABLE 13–12 Loss Table for Nuclear Power Plant Model (*Billions of dollars*)

License	$R \leq 7$ θ_1	$7 < R \leq 8$ θ_2	$R > 8$ θ_3
D_1 (Unconditional)	70.0	8,000.0	8,000.0
D_2 (Conditional)	70.1	70.1	8,000.1
D_3 (No)	100.0	100.0	100.0

The loss function $L(D, \theta)$ represents the present value of expected cost to the consumer in billions of dollars over the life of the plant. D_2 represents higher costs than D_1 because expensive construction rework must be undertaken, the cost of which eventually gets passed on to the consumer in the form of higher rates. This amounts to \$0.1 billion (i.e., the difference between 70 and 70.1 when no rupture occurs for D_1 and D_2). D_3 implies that the power plant is to be abandoned as a nuclear generating facility, resulting in higher rates for alternative sources of power and/or for reduced levels of commercial activity due to a lack of generating power. It follows that costs for D_3 are independent of θ. The consequence of a ruptured nuclear plant is costed at \$7,930 billion, which is reflected by the difference between 8,000.0 and 70.0 in the D_1-row or between 8,000.1 and 70.1 in the D_2-row.[7]

Now suppose that the prior probabilities for states of nature are estimated as $f(\theta_1) = 0.999990$, $f(\theta_2) = 0.000009$, and $f(\theta_3) = 0.000001$. You should confirm that prior analysis yields $E(L) = 70.0793$ for D_1, $E(L) = 70.10793$ for D_2, and $E(L) = 100.0$ for D_3; hence, the license should be granted unconditionally, based on prior analysis.

Bayes' Decision Rules

Prior to making one of the decisions D_1, D_2, or D_3 the NRC has the option of seeking additional information about the states of nature θ. Past geological surveys in other regions often have discovered new faults, causing revisions in the projected magnitudes of tremors. A special geological survey over an area encompassing a 50-mile radius centered on the plant can provide forecasts for θ, but at a cost of \$1 million to the consumers (courtesy of the NRC). Should the NRC require the survey? If so, what decision is best for each possible forecast?

Before answering these questions, it is of interest to determine EVUC and EVPI (the expected value under certainty and the expected value of perfect information). Thus, based on Equations 13.4 and 13.6,

$$\begin{aligned}\text{EVUC} &= (70.0) \cdot (0.999990) + (70.1) \cdot (0.000009) + (100.0) \cdot (0.000001) \\ &= 70.0000309\end{aligned}$$

[7]Any attempt to cost human death or suffering in terms of dollars is impossible to justify, yet costing is always implicit. For example, the "cost" of waiting in the emergency room of a hospital effectively can be reduced to zero by providing extremely costly facilities. Since such facilities are never provided, it follows that death and suffering caused by waiting are implicitly costed by our institutions; that is, a cost trade-off is acknowledged. The expression of losses in terms of disutilities (Section 13.6) perhaps provides a more meaningful approach to this dilemma.

and

$$\text{EVPI} = 70.0793000 - 70.0000309$$
$$= 0.0792691$$

This indicates that \$79.2691 million (exclusive of fee) is the most that can be gained by a perfect survey. Since the cost of an imperfect survey is \$1 million, it follows that a wide margin exists for the realization of cost gains. We have yet to answer, however, whether or not the benefit from an imperfect survey outweighs its cost.

The geological survey under consideration is capable of providing a forecast on the maximum magnitude of tremors for a particular region. Let the random variable X represent forecasted maximum reading on the Richter scale so that

x_1 = Forecast of $R \leq 7$.
x_2 = Forecast of $7 < R \leq 8$.
x_3 = Forecast of $R > 8$.

Needless to say, forecasts are not perfectly reliable. Past experience combined with expert judgement provides the conditional probabilities in Table 13–13.

TABLE 13–13 Conditional Probabilities $f(x \mid \theta)$

	State of Nature	Experimental Result (forecast) x_1	x_2	x_3
θ_1	$R \leq 7$	0.7	0.2	0.1
θ_2	$7 < R \leq 8$	0.3	0.5	0.2
θ_3	$R > 8$	0.0	0.1	0.9
		$R \leq 7$	$7 < R \leq 8$	$R > 8$

For example, the first row of probabilities can be interpreted as follows:

$f(x_1 \mid \theta_1) = 0.7$ means that in regions with maximum $R \leq 7$, the correct forecast is 70 percent reliable.
$f(x_2 \mid \theta_1) = 0.2$ means that in regions with maximum $R \leq 7$, the erroneous forecast $7 < R \leq 8$ is given with 0.20 probability.
$f(x_3 \mid \theta_1) = 0.1$ means that in regions with maximum $R \leq 7$, the erroneous forecast $R > 8$ is given with 0.10 probability.

Can you interpret the other rows? Why do row probabilities sum to unity?

From Section 13.3 we know that a specific forecast is going to cause a revision in the prior probability for each state of nature according to Bayes' Rule. Table 13–14 provides results that facilitate the calculation of these posterior probabilities. The nine cell entries in the main body of the table represent joint probabilities according to Equation 13.8. For example, the joint probability of θ_3 and x_3 is

$$f(\theta_3 \text{ and } x_3) = f(\theta_3) \cdot f(x_3 \mid \theta_3)$$
$$= (0.000001) \cdot (0.9)$$
$$= 0.0000009,$$

where $f(\theta_3)$ is the prior probability given in Example 13.3 and $f(x_3 | \theta_3)$ is the conditional probability given in Table 13–13. Note that the sum of the joint probabilities in a given row gives the prior probability $f(\theta)$ for that row, as expressed in the column of marginal probabilities. Similarly, the sum of any column gives the marginal probability $f(x)$. For example, $f(x_3) = 0.1000017$ is the probability of x_3 or a forecast $R > 8$.

TABLE 13–14 Joint and Marginal Probabilities, $f(\theta_i \text{ and } x_j) = f(\theta_i) \cdot f(x_j | \theta_i)$

	x_1	x_2	x_3	Priors Marginal, $f(\theta)$
θ_1	0.6999930	0.1999980	0.0999990	0.999990
θ_2	0.0000027	0.0000045	0.0000018	0.000009
θ_3	0.0000000	0.0000001	0.0000009	0.000001
Marginal, $f(x)$	0.6999957	0.2000026	0.1000017	1.000000

$f(x_j) = f(\theta_1) \cdot f(x_j | \theta_1) + f(\theta_2) \cdot f(x_j | \theta_2) + f(\theta_3) \cdot f(x_j | \theta_3)$

The results in Table 13–14 are now used to generate the nine posterior probabilities in Table 13–15. For example, if the forecast is $X = x_3$, then the posterior probability of θ_3 is given by Equation 13.7:

$$f(\theta_3 | x_3) = \frac{f(\theta_3) \cdot f(x_3 | \theta_3)}{f(x_3)}$$

$$= \frac{f(\theta_3 \text{ and } x_3)}{f(x_3)}$$

$$= \frac{0.0000009}{0.1000017}$$

$$= 0.0000090$$

where the numerator and denominator are taken from Table 13–14. Note the meaning of this result. Prior to a geological survey, the probability that a jolt registers above 8 on the Richter scale is $f(\theta_3) = 0.0000010$; however, if a geological survey forecasts that the given area will receive a jolt above 8, this prior probability is revised upward by a factor of nine to 0.0000090.

TABLE 13–15 Posterior Probabilities, $f(\theta | x) = \dfrac{f(\theta) \cdot f(x | \theta)}{f(x)}$

	$f(\theta)$ priors	x_1	x_2	x_3	
θ_1	(0.999990)	0.9999961	0.9999770	0.9999730	
θ_2	(0.000009)	0.0000039	0.0000225	0.0000180	← Posteriors $f(\theta | x_3)$ given forecast $R > 8$
θ_3	(0.000001)	0.0000000	0.0000005	0.0000090	
	Total	1.0000000	1.0000000	1.0000000	

Posterior Analysis with Forecast $R > 8$

We are now in a position to calculate the Bayes' decision for each possible forecast. Consider the forecast $X = x_3$. From Table 13–15 the revised probabilities for each state of nature are $f(\theta_1|x_3) = 0.9999730$, $f(\theta_2|x_3) = 0.0000180$, and $f(\theta_3|x_3) = 0.0000090$. Substituting these posterior probabilities and the losses in Table 13–12 into Equation 13.11, we get

$$\begin{aligned} E'(L) &= (70.0) \cdot (0.9999730) + (8{,}000.0) \cdot (0.0000180) \\ &\quad + (8{,}000.0) \cdot (0.0000090) \\ &= 70.21411 \quad \text{for } D_1, \\ E'(L) &= (70.1) \cdot (0.9999730) + (70.1) \cdot (0.0000180) \\ &\quad + (8{,}000.1) \cdot (0.0000090) \\ &= 70.17137 \quad \text{for } D_2, \end{aligned}$$

and

$$\begin{aligned} E'(L) &= (100.0) \cdot (0.9999730) + (100.0) \cdot (0.0000180) \\ &\quad + (100.0) \cdot (0.0000090) \\ &= 100.0 \quad \text{for } D_3. \end{aligned}$$

This result indicates that D_2 (award license conditional on more reinforcement) is the Bayes' decision should the results of the survey yield $X = x_3$ (a forecast for a tremor above 8 on the Richter scale). The optimal posterior expected loss is $E'(L^*) = 70.17137$ for this decision.

Posterior Analysis with All Forecasts

Table 13–16 summarizes the Bayes' decision for each possible experimental result. The first two columns of this table define the **Bayes' strategy, Bayes' policy,** or **Bayes' decision rule** for this model. A Bayes' decision rule Q is a function that

TABLE 13–16 Summary of Preposterior Analysis

(1) Forecast X	(2) Bayes' Decision D_B^*	(3) Optimal Posterior Expected Loss $E'(L^*)$	(4) Marginal Probability (Probability of Forecast) $f(x)$	(3) · (4) Expected Loss $E'(L^*) \cdot f(x)$
x_1	D_1	70.030927	0.6999957	49.021348
x_2	D_2	70.103965	0.2000026	14.020975
x_3	D_2	70.171370	0.1000017	7.017256
Total			1.0000000	70.059579

specifies the Bayes' decision to be taken for each possible experimental result (value of X); that is

$$D_B^* = Q(x) . \tag{13.12}$$

Thus if the geological survey yields $X = x_1$, then the NRC should select D_1; if $X = x_2$, then D_2 is the best decision; and if $X = x_3$, then D_2 is prescribed.

Expected Value of Experimentation

Although we have prescribed an optimal (Bayes') decision for each possible experimental result, we have yet to consider the issue of whether or not the geological survey should be commissioned. The third column in Table 13–16 gives the optimal posterior expected loss for each Bayes' decision. Since the probability of each Bayes' decision is exactly equivalent to the probability of the experimental outcome (value of X) that corresponds to each Bayes' decision, it follows that the probability of each $E'(L^*)$ is defined by $f(x)$, as indicated in the fourth column of Table 13–16 (which is taken from the last row in Table 13–14). The **expected loss with experimentation (ELE)** is the expected value of $E'(L^*)$:

$$\text{ELE} = \sum_x E'(L^*) \cdot f(x) . \tag{13.13}$$

For the atomic power plant example,

$$\begin{aligned}\text{ELE} &= (70.030927) \cdot (0.6999957) + (70.103965) \cdot (0.2000026) \\ &\quad + (70.171370) \cdot (0.1000017) + 0.001 \\ &= 70.05957933 .\end{aligned}$$

This means that the expected loss is \$70,059,579,330 if the geological survey is to be undertaken. By the prior analysis in Example 13.3, the optimal decision with no experimentation was determined as D_1, yielding $E(L^*) = 70.0793$, or an **expected loss without experimentation** of \$70,079,300,000. The difference between the expected loss without experimentation and the expected loss with experimentation is termed the **expected value of sample information**

$$\text{EVSI} = E(L^*) - \text{ELE} . \tag{13.14}$$

For the example,

$$\begin{aligned}\text{EVSI} &= 70.07930000 - 70.05957933 \\ &= 0.019721\end{aligned}$$

The **expected net value of sample information** (ENVSI) is EVSI $- C$ where C is the cost of experimentation. This indicates that the decision to require a geological survey results in an expected net savings of approximately \$18.7 million over the decision not to direct the survey (i.e., $0.019721 - 0.001 = 0.018721$).

To summarize, the NRC first should require a geological survey. Based on the result of this survey, it should then make a decision according to the decision rule specified in Table 13–16.

If consequences are expressed as payoffs, then the **expected payoff with experimentation (EPE)** is given by

$$\text{EPE} = \sum_x E'(R^*) \cdot f(x) \tag{13.15}$$

and

$$\text{EVSI} = \text{EPE} - E(R^*) \tag{13.16}$$

$$\text{ENVSI} = \text{EVSI} - C. \tag{13.17}$$

When alternative experimental plans are available, let ENVSI_k represent the expected net value of experimentation for plan k. If $\text{ENVSI}_k < 0$ for all k, then experimentation should not be undertaken; otherwise, select the plan that yields maximum ENVSI_k.

FOLLOW-UP EXERCISES

16. For the portfolio problem, we provide the output from the Erikson-Hall package in Table 13–17. Check the information entered to assure that you understand the

TABLE 13–17

```
             COMPUTER MODELS FOR MANAGEMENT SCIENCE

   DECISION MODELS

              -=*=-  INFORMATION ENTERED  -=*=-

   NUMBER OF STATES          :  4

   NUMBER OF ALTERNATIVES    :  3

   NUMBER OF PREDICTIONS     :  4

   PROBLEM TYPE              :  MAXIMIZATION

                          PAYOFF TABLE

   STATES       PAYOFF FROM EACH ALTERNATIVE

                1           2           3

     1          9.50        9.25        9.00
     2          9.50       10.75       12.00
     3         11.00       10.00        9.00
     4         11.00       11.50       12.00

   STATES       PRIOR PROBABILITIES

     1          0.1000
     2          0.5000
     3          0.3000
     4          0.1000
```

TABLE 13–17 *(concluded)*

```
                                                CONDITIONAL TABLE
STATES                         CONDITIONAL PROBABILITIES

                  1              2              3              4

   1           0.7000         0.1000         0.1000         0.1000
   2           0.1000         0.7000         0.1000         0.1000
   3           0.1000         0.1000         0.7000         0.1000
   4           0.1000         0.1000         0.1000         0.7000

                     DECISION MAKING UNDER RISK

                        -=*=-  RESULTS  -=*=-

EXPECTED VALUE OF EACH ALTERNATIVE

   10.10          10.45            10.80

OPTIMAL ALTERNATIVE                        :       A3

EXPECTED PAYOFF WITH PERFECT INFO          :       11.45

EOL FOR OPTIMAL ALTERNATIVE                :        0.65

EXPECTED VALUE OF PERFECT INFO             :        0.65

PRED          MARGINAL PROBABILITIES

    1      0.1600
    2      0.4000
    3      0.2800
    4      0.1600

PRED          REVISED PROBABILITIES

    1      0.4375        0.3125        0.1875        0.0625
    2      0.0250        0.8750        0.0750        0.2050
    3      0.0357        0.1786        0.7500        0.0357
    4      0.0625        0.3125        0.1875        0.4375

           EXPECTED PAYOFF WITH ADDED INFO  :        11.09

           EXPECTED VALUE OF ADDED INFO     :         0.29
```

problem. Note that the states of nature are listed as rows and the columns as decisions—as contrasted to the arrangement in Table 13–2. All payoffs are in millions of dollars. The "number of predictions" refers to the number of forecasts or experimental outcomes. Thus the "conditional table" shows the columns as outcomes and the rows as states, just as we have done throughout the chapter. Unlike our analysis in Table 13–9, we specified decision making under risk rather than uncertainty in response to an input query. With this understanding of the input, explain the output with particular reference to the following:

a. What is the maximal number of dollars that should be paid for perfect information?

b. Given the four experimental outcomes, the computer output provides the marginal and the revised or posterior probabilities. The table of revised probabilities shows the states as columns and the rows as experimental outcomes. What is the maximal number of dollars that should be paid for sample information? What is the Bayes' decision rule for this problem? Recall that the Bayes' decision rule is a function specifying the decision to be taken for each possible outcome. Although not supplied as part of the output, enough information is given for you to figure it out. Verify the figure given for the expected payoff with added information. Note that the EOL (expected opportunity loss) for the optimal alternative is the difference between the expected payoff with perfect information and the expected value of the optimal alternative. In our terminology, this would be EVUC-E(R).

17. You can easily write your own software to perform the calculations involved in the analysis so far in this chapter. In doing this you will be able to consolidate your thinking on what we have done so far. Using 1–2–3 from Lotus or any other spreadsheet package available, set up the calculations needed to determine expected values for a payoff table and to revise probabilities.

18. Confirm the results for x_1 and x_2 in Table 13–16.

19. Suppose that the NRC has the option of a more elaborate and reliable geological survey costing $5 million. Determine

a. $D_B^* = Q(x)$ with $f(\theta) = 0.99$, $f(\theta_2) = 0.009$, $f(\theta_3) = 0.001$, and the conditional probabilities $f(x|\theta)$ given the the table below.

	x_1	x_2	x_3
θ_1	0.9	0.1	0.0
θ_2	0.1	0.8	0.1
θ_3	0.0	0.0	1.0

b. EVSI and ENVSI. Should the NRC select this survey over the other survey?

c. Judging from the conditional probabilities, why do we say this survey is more "reliable" than the other? Would you say that good estimates for prior probabilities become less important as more reliable experiments are used? Explain.

d. Based on joint probabilities, show that the probability of a correct forecast for this survey is greater than for the other survey. Is this a good measure of reliability?

20. For the portfolio problem in Exercise 15, modify the element on the main diagonal of the $f(x|\theta)$ table to 0.91, and change all other elements to 0.03.

a. Generate the table of joint and marginal probabilities.

b. Generate the table of posterior probabilities.

c. Determine $D_B^* = Q(x)$.

d. Calculate ENVSI if the investment service (providing the forecasts) costs $50,000. Do you recommend subscribing to the investment service? What is the maximum the investor should be willing to pay the investment service?

21. For the new product model described in Example 13.2, consider a consumer panel of 4 members (instead of 100 members). Also, assume that you are at a point in time prior to a market survey.
    a. Theoretically, what is the most the company should be willing to pay for a market survey?
    b. Generate the table of conditional probabilities.
    c. Generate the table of joint and marginal probabilities.
    d. Generate the table of posterior probabilities.
    e. Determine $D_B^* = Q(x)$.
    f. Calculate ENVSI if the market survey costs $100,000. Do you recommend a market survey? What maximum cost should the company tolerate for a market survey? Should a larger consumer panel be considered? Explain.

22. ***Optimal Sample Size.* An interesting issue for binomial sampling plans of the type in the preceding exercise is the determination of the optimal sample size. As the size of the sample n becomes larger, the expected value of the optimal posterior expected loss $E'(L^*)$ becomes smaller [or the expected value of the optimal posterior expected return $E'(R^*)$ gets larger]. Can you reason why? As n becomes larger, however, the cost of the experiment C increases. Right? This trade-off is reflected by ENVSI, so that the optimal sample size n^* is that which maximizes ENVSI. The solution for n^* is straightforward once C is specified as a function of n. In fact, ENVSI is well behaved (i.e., exhibits a single maximum, which is global) so that by incremental analysis the following must be true: $\text{ENVSI}_{n^*} > \text{ENVSI}_{n^*-1}$ and $\text{ENVSI}_{n^*} > \text{ENVSI}_{n^*+1}$. Right? Thus the computational procedure "only" needs to determine ENVSI_n for $n = 1, 2, \ldots, n^* + 1$.
    a. Determine n^* for Example 13.2 if $C = 400{,}000 + 50{,}000n$.
    b. In general, would you say that the computer is recommended for solving optimal binomial sampling plans? Explain by example.

13.5 DECISION TREES

Decision trees represent a useful means by which to structure decision problems. Figure 13–1 illustrates the complete decision tree for the nuclear power plant model of the previous section. (At this point we recommend that you close your eyes and breathe deeply if you're in a state of panic from an overabundance of visual stimuli.) It is not as bad as it looks. In fact, we would be willing to bet that decision trees will become your preferred tool for analyzing decision problems.

First, study the legend to reorient yourself to this model. Note that the decisions to not undertake or to undertake the geological survey are identified by the new decision variables D_4 and D_5, respectively. Next, take each of the following steps in sequence.

Basic Tree Structure

The first step is preliminary: Determine all relevant states of nature θ, decisions D, and experimental outcomes X. Next, structure the relationships among these variables in the form of a tree having "forks" and "branches." Branches identify specific values

FIGURE 13–1 Decision Tree for Nuclear Power Plant Model

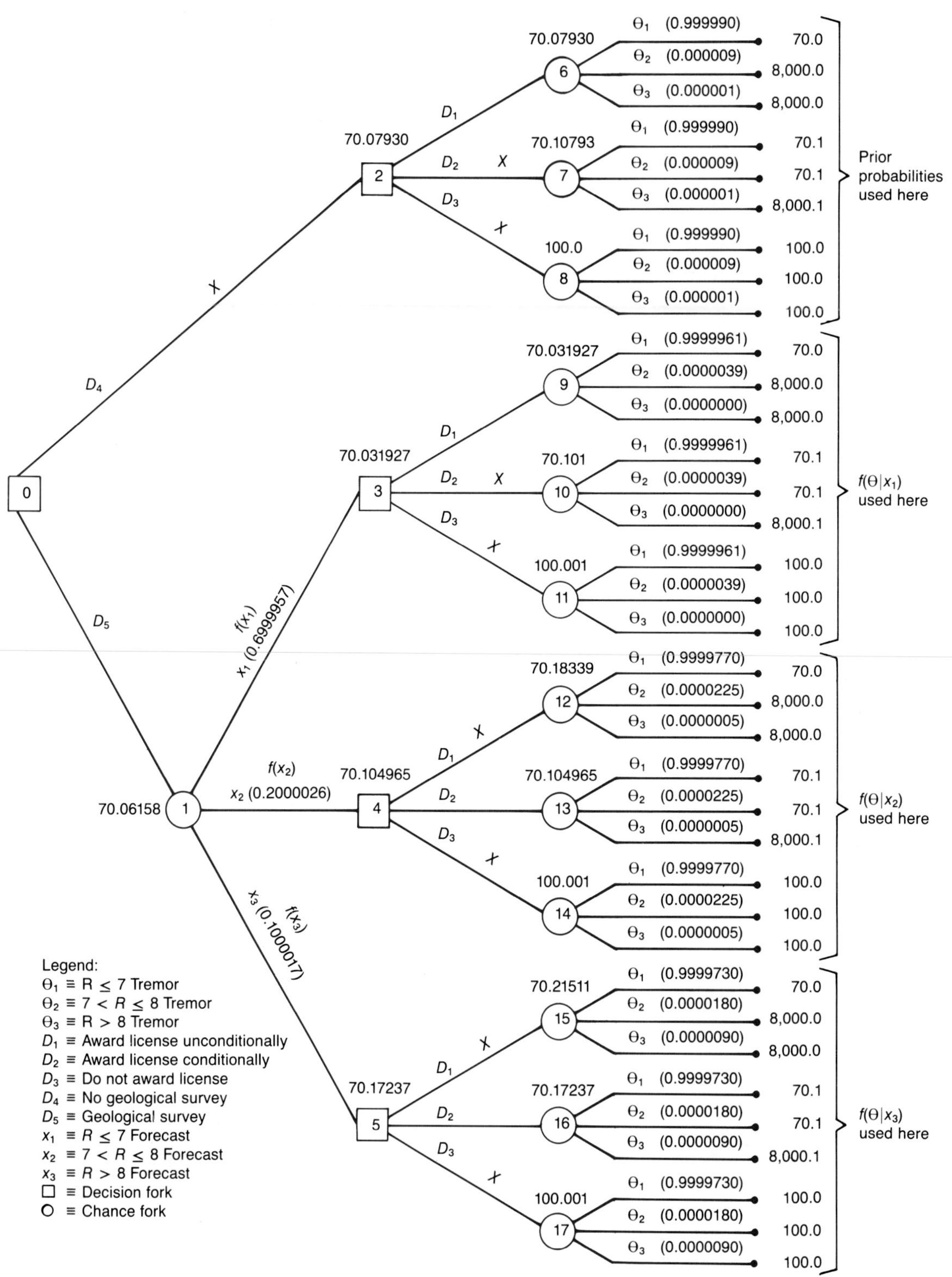

of θ, D, and X. A fork identifies the type of branches that emanate from the fork. The branches following **decision forks** identify specific decisions D. The branches following **chance forks** identify either specific states of nature θ or specific experimental outcomes X.

The tree "flows" from left to right in chronological order. For example, the Nuclear Regulatory Commission first must decide D_4 or D_5; hence, D_4 and D_5 are the first set of branches. Since these are decision branches, they must emanate from a decision fork (labeled [0]). If D_4 is selected, then the NRC must next decide on D_1, D_2, or D_3, which gives [2] and its three branches. For each of these three branches, any one of three possible states of nature will follow; thus θ_1, θ_2, and θ_3 depart from the chance forks given by (6), (7), and (8). If the NRC selects D_5, then the experimental results of the geological survey will follow. This gives the chance fork (1) and its three possible branches (x_1, x_2, and x_3). Following the experimental result, the NRC must decide D_1, D_2, or D_3. Since three experimental results are possible, this gives [3], [4], and [5], with their sets of decision branches. These decision branches, in turn, must lead into the chance forks (9) through (17), each of which provides a fork for the states of nature θ. Right? (Don't let the numbers bother you at this point; just focus on the relationships indicated by the flows.)

Incorporating Probabilities

Now we are ready to include probabilities in the decision tree. First of all, note that probabilities parenthetically follow chance outcomes only (that is, θ_1, θ_2, θ_3, x_1, x_2, and x_3). The probabilities for θ_1, θ_2, and θ_3 following (6), (7), and (8) are the *prior probabilities* specified in Example 13.3: $f(\theta_1) = 0.999990$, $f(\theta_2) = 0.000009$, and $f(\theta_3) = 0.000001$. This must be so because no experimental outcomes precede these chance forks.

Now consider the probabilities for θ_1, θ_2, and θ_3 following (9), (10), and (11). For each of these chance forks, the experimental outcome x_1 is a precedent; hence these probabilities must be the *posterior probabilities* $f(\theta|x_1)$. Similarly, the posterior probabilities $f(\theta|x_2)$ follow (12), (13), and (14); and $f(\theta|x_3)$ follow (15), (16), and (17). These posterior probabilities are given, respectively, by the columns in Table 13–15.

Finally, the probability for each experimental outcome must be the *marginal probability* $f(x)$. They cannot be the conditional probabilities $f(x|\theta)$ because θ does not precede X in the tree. Thus $f(x_1) = 0.6999957$, $f(x_2) = 0.2000026$, and $f(x_3) = 0.1000017$, according to Table 13–14.

Backward Induction

The optimal set of decisions is found by the method variously called **backward induction, roll-back principle,** or **averaging out and folding back.**

First, place the appropriate loss $L(D, \theta)$ or payoff $R(D, \theta)$ at each terminal point of the tree. For example, the losses in the first row of Table 13–12 are placed following the appropriate end points of branches not involving a survey and emanating from (6), (7), and (8). *All other end points have the cost of the survey added to give a terminal payoff* as shown for branches emanating from (9) through (17).

Second, move backward or "rollback" on the tree to the chance forks labeled (6) through (17). Immediately above each chance fork place the expected loss for the outcomes following this fork. You should recognize the entries above (6), (7), and (8) as the expected losses $E(L)$ for prior analysis. Thus for D_1, we place

$$E(L) = (70.0) \cdot (0.999990) + (8{,}000.0) \cdot (0.000009) + (8{,}000.0) \cdot (0.000001)$$
$$= 70.07930$$

above fork (6). The procedure is identical for forks (7) through (17).

Next, we roll back to the decision forks [2] through [5]. Above each of these decision forks we place the loss of the optimal decision following that fork. For example, above [3] we place 70.031927, since D_1 yields the lowest expected loss following [3]. At the same time we "prune" the nonoptimal branches by labelling them with the symbol ×. You should recognize that the branches *not* pruned following [3] through [5] represent the Bayes' decisions in Table 13–15.The decision D_1 following [2] represents the optimal prior decision.

Finally, we roll back to (1) and calculate the expected loss at this point in the tree:

$$(70.031927) \cdot (0.6999957) + (70.104965) \cdot (0.2000026)$$
$$+ (70.17237) \cdot (0.1000017) = 70.06058\,.$$

Since the expected loss for D_5 is less than the expected loss for D_4, the latter is pruned.

The optimal set of decisions can be summarized now: Select D_5; if x_1 is the experimental outcome, then select D_1; if x_2 or x_3, then D_2.

FOLLOW-UP EXERCISES

Our investor faces a slightly simpler version of the problem presented in Example 13.1. Alternative A returns minus 5 percent or else plus 10 percent with probabilities 0.6 and 0.4, respectively. Alternative B returns nothing or else 7½ percent with probabilities 0.6 and 0.4, respectively. Alternative C offers a return of 5 percent regardless of the two possible economic scenarios that carry the probabilities 0.6 and 0.4 as above. The investor has $10 million to invest and plans to invest all in one of the three alternatives. Additionally, the investor could pay for the predictions of an investment service costing $10,000. The service provides forecasts that are 80 percent reliable. The investor could buy the predictions and then choose one of the three investment alternatives.

23. What is the optimal set of decisions based on decision tree analysis? Draw a decision tree to model this problem.
24. Examine the Erikson-Hall decision tree output, and draw their tree (See Table 13–18).
25. Determine EVPI, EVSI, and ENVSI for this problem. Note that decision tree analysis incorporates the experimentation costs into the terminal payoffs.

TABLE 13–18

```
COMPUTER MODELS FOR MANAGEMENT SCIENCE

DECISION TREE MODEL

        -=*=-    INFORMATION ENTERED    -=*=-
```

TABLE 13–18 (*continued*)

MAXIMIZATION

-=-*=- DECISION NODES -=*=-

NODE	BRANCHES	ALTERNATIVE NUMBER	ENDING NODE
0	4	1	1
		2	2
		3	3
		4	4
11	3	1	13
		2	14
		3	15
12	3	1	16
		2	17
		3	18

-=*=- CHANCE NODES -=*=-

NODE	BRANCHES	PROBABILITY	ENDING NODE
1	2	0.6000	5
		0.4000	6
2	2	0.6000	7
		0.4000	8
3	2	0.6000	9
		0.4000	10
4	2	0.5600	11
		0.4400	12
13	2	0.8571	19
		0.1429	20
14	2	0.8571	21
		0.1429	22
15	2	0.8571	23
		0.1429	24
16	2	0.2727	25
		0.7273	26
17	2	0.2727	27
		0.7273	28
18	2	0.2727	29
		0.7273	30

TABLE 13–18 *(continued)*

-=*=- TERMINAL NODES -=*=-

NODE	PAYOFF
5	9.50
6	11.00
7	10.00
8	10.75
9	10.50
10	10.50
19	9.49
20	10.99
21	9.99
22	10.74
23	10.49
24	10.49
25	9.49
26	10.99
27	9.99
28	10.74
29	10.49
30	10.49

-=*=- RESULTS -=*=-

MAXIMIZATION PROBLEM

NODE	EXPECTED PAYOFF	SELECTED ALTERNATIVE
0	10.54	4
1	10.10	
2	10.30	
3	10.50	
4	10.54	
5	9.50	
6	11.00	
7	10.00	
8	10.75	
9	10.50	
10	10.50	
11	10.49	3
12	10.59	1
13	9.71	
14	10.10	
15	10.49	
16	10.59	
17	10.54	
18	10.49	
19	9.49	
20	10.99	
21	9.99	

TABLE 13–18 *(concluded)*

```
22          10.74
23          10.49
24          10.49
25           9.49
26          10.99
27           9.99
28          10.74
29          10.49
30          10.49

            EXPECTED PAYOFF = 10.53502

   ------------  END OF ANALYSIS  ------------
```

13.6 UTILITY THEORY

Section 13.1 noted that consequences can be expressed in terms of a preference measure $U(D, \theta)$ called a utility function. This section justifies and illustrates the use of utility functions.

Rationale

Consider the following hypothetical scenario. A benefactor offers you two alternative decisions:

$D_1 \equiv$ Flip a coin once, wherein either you win \$1 million if a head comes up or you win nothing if a tail comes up.
$D_1 \equiv$ Accept a gift of \$300,000.

What would *you* decide? Experience shows that most people would accept the *certain* payoff of \$300,000 for D_2 rather than the *expected* payoff of \$500,000 for D_1. Why? Because the consequences associated with D_1 are risky, and most decision makers are risk avoiders. In this case we would say that the expected preference for D_2 is greater than the expected preference for D_1.

The above scenario suggests that the selection of an act based on the decision rule of optimal expected value may not be appropriate when "great" risk is involved. Consider another scenario. A Las Vegas casino offers you a coin-flip game. If head comes up, then you win \$2; otherwise, you lose \$1. The expected monetary value of this game to you is $(2) \cdot (0.5) + (-1) \cdot (0.5)$, or \$0.50. Most likely you would play against this foolish casino. Suppose, however, that the payoffs were \$2,000 and −\$1,000 instead of \$2 and −\$1, respectively. Your expected payoff is now \$500. Would you still play? How about if the payoffs were \$200,000 and −\$100,000?

The lesson should be evident by now. A decision involving less expected payoff and less risk is often selected over a decision involving greater expected payoff and greater risk. Evidence of this type of risk-avoiding behavior is common, particularly in life and casualty insurance applications. For example, almost all homeowners carry homeowners' insurance; yet the expected values of such policies to homeowners must be negative, as the insurance companies presumably set rates to yield expected profits. What is needed, then, is a preference measure that incorporates the subjective risk associated with uncertain monetary payoffs.

In other situations, a preference measure is desirable when the use of monetary payoffs or losses may be inappropriate. For example, monetary cost is not the most desirable measure to use when reflecting human casualties due to the rupture of a nuclear power plant.

Besides the ability to incorporate subjective risk and nonmonetary payoffs, utility concepts can be used in *multiple criteria environments*. For example, utility functions have been applied to the solution of mathematical programming problems characterized by multiple concave objective functions.[8]

Construction of Utility Functions

We define a **utility index** $U = U(D, \theta)$ as a real number that represents the preference measure for some consequence. This section illustrates one procedure for constructing the utility function $U(D, \theta)$ when it is based on monetary payoffs. In other words, rather than expressing U functionally in terms of the consequences (D, θ), we express U functionally in terms of the monetary payoffs:[9]

$$\begin{aligned} U &= U[R(D, \theta)] \\ &= U(R). \end{aligned}$$

Consider once again the portfolio model of Example 13.1. The payoff table is reproduced here as Table 13–19. Our present purpose is to replace these monetary payoffs with utility indices, based on the following procedure.

TABLE 13–19 Monetary Payoffs *(Millions of dollars)*

	θ_1	θ_2	θ_3	θ_4
D_1	9.50	9.50	11.00	11.00
D_2	9.25	10.75	10.00	11.50
D_3	9.00	12.00	9.00	12.00

1. Determine the lowest ($R_{min} = 9$) and the highest ($R_{max} = 12$) monetary payoffs and assign corresponding utility indices of $U_{min} = 0$ and $U_{max} = 1$. The selection of end points on the utility scale is arbitrary (as long as $U_{max} > U_{min}$); however, the selection of 0 and 1 as end points makes for an attractive interpretation of utility indices as probabilities (see Exercise 31). We have now established coordinates 1 and 2 on the utility function, or **preference curve,** for the investor, as illustrated in Figure 13–2.

[8]S. Zionts and J. Wallenius, "An Interactive Programming Method for Solving the Multiple Criteria Problem," *Management Science*, 22, no. 6 (1976), pp. 652–63. For multicriteria applications, see also Holloway, *Decision Making under Uncertainty Models*, (Englewood Cliffs, N.J.: Prentice-Hall, Inc., 1979).

[9]For other procedures see the references at the end of the chapter.

FIGURE 13–2 Preference Curve for Portfolio Model

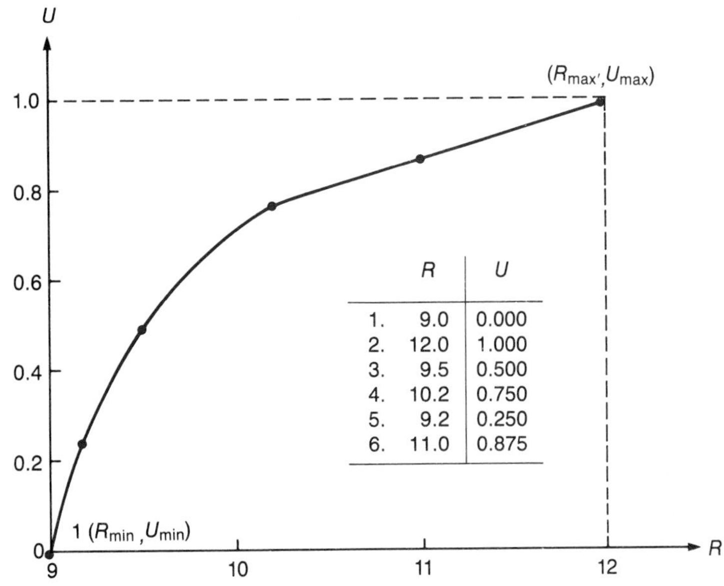

2. Next, the **certainty equivalent (CE)** is established. The *CE* represents a payoff for which the decision maker is indifferent between (*a*) the option of receiving the uncertain payoffs R_1 and R_2, each with probability 0.5, and (*b*) the option of receiving the *CE* with certainty. For example, suppose that it were possible to offer the investor the following options: (*a*) an asset position of \$9 million ($R_1 = 9$) with probability ½ or an asset position of \$12 million ($R_2 = 12$) with probability ½; (*b*) an asset position of \$9.2 million with certainty. If the investor selects option *a*, we then increase option *b* to, say, \$10 million. If now the investor prefers option *b*, we then revise the certain figure downward and ask the same question. Suppose that after a number of such questions the investor decides that a certain asset position of \$9.5 million is no more or less desirable than uncertain asset positions of \$9 million or \$12 million, each with probability ½. In this instance, we conclude that the $CE = 9.5$ when $R_1 = 9$ and $R_2 = 12$. Note that the expected value of option *a* is \$10.5 million, yet the investor is willing to accept option *b* if just over \$9.5 million can be guaranteed with certainty. This means that our investor is exhibiting risk-averse (avoidance) behavior; that is, the 50 percent probability of ending up with \$9 million is considered so risky that the investor is willing to accept a riskless \$9.5 million over a risky expected payoff of \$10.5 million. The difference of \$1 million between \$10.5 million and \$9.5 million is called a **risk premium;** that is, in effect the investor is willing to "sacrifice" an expected value of \$1 million to avoid this risk.

3. Given the *CE* from the preceding step, it is now possible to establish another coordinate on the preference curve. Since the investor is indifferent between

the riskless \$9.5 million of option b and the equally likely $R_1 = 9$ and $R_2 = 12$ of option a, it follows that the utility associated with the $CE = 9.5$ must be equal to the *expected* utility associated with $R_1 = 9$ and $R_2 = 12$; hence,

$$\begin{aligned} U(9.5) &= \frac{1}{2} \cdot U(9) + \frac{1}{2} \cdot U(12) \\ &= \left(\frac{1}{2}\right) \cdot (0) + \left(\frac{1}{2}\right) \cdot (1) \\ &= 0.5 . \end{aligned}$$

This gives 9.5, 0.5 as the third coordinate on the preference curve of Figure 13–2. In general,

$$U(CE) = \frac{1}{2} \cdot U(R_1) + \frac{1}{2} \cdot U(R_2) . \tag{13.18}$$

4. Steps 2 and 3 are repeated a number of times until a reasonably smooth preference curve is obtained. Note that you are free to select values of R_1 and R_2 so long as the values selected have known utility indices. Thus R_{min} and R_{max} must always be used for R_1 and R_2 to establish the third coordinate. Table 13–20 provides the R_1, R_2, CE triads and the corresponding utilities that were used to establish the preference curve of Figure 13–2. For example, given $R_1 = 10.2$, $R_2 = 12.0$, and $CE = 11.0$, it follows from Equation 13.18 that

$$\begin{aligned} U(11.0) &= \frac{1}{2} \cdot U(10.2) + \frac{1}{2} \cdot U(12.0) \\ &= \left(\frac{1}{2}\right) \cdot (0.750) + \left(\frac{1}{2}\right) \cdot (1.000) \\ &= 0.875 . \end{aligned}$$

Can you confirm $U(10.2) = 0.750$ and $U(9.2) = 0.250$? Note that the CE and $U(CE)$ columns in Table 13–20 represent, respectively, the R and U coordinates in Figure 13–2.

TABLE 13–20 Certainty Equivalents and Corresponding Utilities

R_1	R_2	CE	$U(R_1)$	$U(R_2)$	$U(CE)$
9.0	12.0	9.5	0.000	1.000	0.500
9.5	12.0	10.2	0.500	1.000	0.750
9.0	9.5	9.2	0.000	0.500	0.250
10.2	12.0	11.0	0.750	1.000	0.875

Based on the sketched preference curve, it is now possible to replace the payoffs in Table 13–19 by utility indices.[10] For example, consider $R(D_2, \theta_3) = 10$ for the portfolio model in Table 13–19. From Figure 13–2, $R = 10$ approximately corresponds to $U = 0.7$; hence, in Table 13–21 we let $U(D_2, \theta_3) = U(10) = 0.7$. Can you confirm the remaining entries in Table 13–21?

TABLE 13–21 Utility Table for Portfolio Model

	θ_1	θ_2	θ_3	θ_4
D_1	0.50	0.50	0.88	0.88
D_2	0.31	0.85	0.70	0.95
D_3	0.00	1.00	0.00	1.00

Incorporating Utility Functions

Once $U(D, \theta)$ is specified as in Table 13–21, prior, posterior, and preposterior analyses are undertaken as before. The primary differences are notational: $U(D, \theta)$ is used in place of $R(D, \theta)$ or $L(D, \theta)$; $E(U)$ in place of $E(R)$ or $E(L)$; and $E'(U)$ in place of $E'(R)$ or $E'(L)$.

We might note that $U(D, \theta)$ is interpreted as a **disutility function** when it replaces the loss function $L(D, \theta)$. In other words, rather than minimizing expected loss we minimize expected dispreference.[11]

Additionally, when undertaking preposterior analysis, the cost of experimentation (C) must be added to $L(D, \theta)$ or subtracted from $R(D, \theta)$ *before* $U(D, \theta)$ is determined because $U(10) \neq U(1) + U(9)$. For example, the losses at the end points of forks (9) through (17) in Figure 13–1 must be increased by 0.001 before losses are converted to disutilities. This is the same as saying that $R(D, \theta)$ and $L(D, \theta)$ must include the cost of experimentation as they did in our decision tree analysis.

To illustrate the use of $U(D, \theta)$, consider the prior analysis for the portfolio problem. Given $f(\theta_1) = 0.1, f(\theta_2) = 0.5, f(\theta_3) = 0.3$, and $f(\theta_4) = 0.1$ and the payoffs in Table 13–19, we get $E(R^*) = \$10.8$ million and $D^* = D_3$. This says that an investment of \$10 million in alternative B is optimal according to the $E(R)$ decision rule, yielding an expected worth of \$10.8 million one year hence.

According to the utilities in Table 13–21, however, we get $E(U) = 0.652$ for D_1, $E(U) = 0.761$ for D_2, and $E(U) = 0.600$ for D_3. Thus $E(U^*) = 0.761$ and $D^* = D_2$. This means that the investor should diversify (i.e, invest \$5 million in A and \$5 million in B) when risk is taken into consideration.

The selection of D_2 as optimal in the utility sense yields an $E(R)$ of \$10.45 million; hence the investor pays a "price" of \$350,000 (that is, \$10.80 − 10.45) by selecting the alternative with lower risk. In effect the investor is willing to trade-off a higher

[10] The estimation of an analytic utility function is an alternative to curve-fitting by hand. See Exercise 32.

[11] Based on a set of axioms, it can be proved that maximization of expected utility or minimization of expected disutility is consistent with the optimizing behavior of a "rational" decision maker. See R. L. Winkler, *Introduction to Bayesian* Inference and Decision (New York: Holt, Rinehart and Winston, 1972).

expected return for a lower expected risk. Those of you who are financial wizards recognize this as the key argument for diversification in portfolios.[12]

Behavioral Implications

As mentioned earlier, utility theory provides an attractive means by which to describe the subjective preferences of decision makers in environments characterized by risk. Figure 13–3 illustrates three prototype configurations to describe risk behavior. You are already familiar with the conservative individual who exhibits **risk-aversion.** This decision maker is willing to pay a risk premium for averting risk, resulting in a concave preference curve .

FIGURE 13–3 Behavioral Prototypes

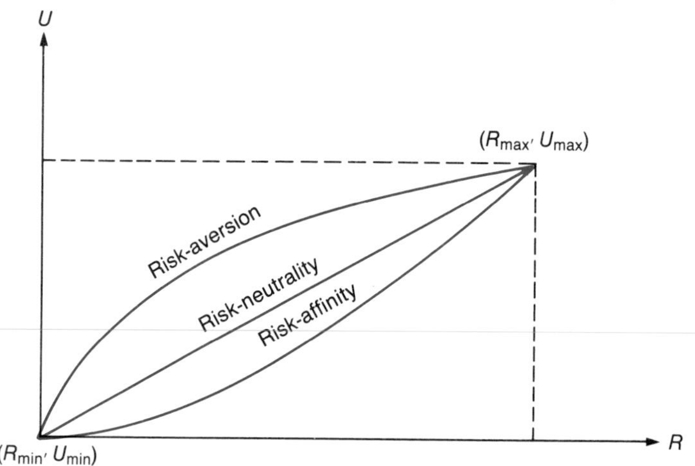

If the preference curve for a decision maker is linear, then the decision maker professes **risk-neutrality;** that is, this individual is indifferent toward risk. Note that a linear preference curve equates the *CE* to the expected value of R_1 and R_2. Thus the linear function always yields the expected value of R_1 and R_2.

More important, it can be proved that *maximization of* E(U) *and maximization of* E(R)—*or minimization of* E(U) *and minimization of* E(L)—*yield identical results for linear preference curves.* This result is significant in justifying the simpler approach of utilizing payoffs or losses for situations characterized by either low risk or small disparities in monetary values.

A decision maker with a convex utility function exhibits **risk-affinity**. This individual can be characterized as a gambler, as there is a willingness (up to a point) to favor risk situations having a lower expected payoff than no-risk situations. This is

[12] We know that the investor is risk-averse because of the concave utility function of Figure 13–2. By deduction, therefore, we might conclude that if D_2 yields a lower expected return, then it must also yield a lower expected variance (the traditional measure of risk). Using A.14 on Table 13–21 and $f(\theta)$ from above gives $V(R) = 0.54$ for D_1, $V(R) = 0.36$ for D_2, and $V(R) = 2.16$ for D_3, which is consistent with our reasoning. This result also is consistent with the thrust of mathematical programming applications of portfolio theory.

evident by the fact that the CE is greater than the expected value of the R_1, R_2 gamble for any given utility (i.e., for any U, the R-value for the curve with risk-affinity is greater than the R-value for the linear function).

FOLLOW-UP EXERCISES

26. Conduct a prior analysis for the portfolio model of Exercise 1 that includes a fourth decision of 25 percent invested in alternative A and 75 percent in alternative B as well as a fifth decision of 75 percent in A and 25 percent in B. Use the utilities $U(R)$ given in this section. The monetary payoff table would be:

Priors	0.1	0.5	0.3	0.1
	θ_1	θ_2	θ_3	θ_4
D_1	9.5	9.5	11	11
D_2	9.25	10.75	10	11.5
D_3	9	12	9	12
D_4	9.125	11.375	9.5	11.75
D_5	9.375	10.125	10.5	11.25

27. Construct $U(R)$ for the portfolio model in this section given the following triads:

R_1	R_2	CE
9.0	12.0	10.0
10.0	12.0	10.5
9.0	10.5	9.9
9.0	9.9	9.7
9.0	9.7	9.5

What type of behavior is exhibited by $U(R)$? Determine $U(D, \theta)$ and conduct a prior analysis using $f(\theta_1) = 0.1$, $f(\theta_2) = 0.5$, $f(\theta_3) = 0.3$, and $f(\theta_4) = 0.1$.

28. Modify the decision tree in Exercise 23 such that all consequences are expressed in terms of utility indices. Use Figure 13–2 as the utility function. (Don't forget the $10,000 cost of experimentation.) Determine $D_B^* = Q(x)$. Is the investment service desirable?

29. Construct $U(R)$ and $U(D, \theta)$ for the new product model of Example 13.2 if the triads below are relevant.

R_1	R_2	CE
−2.0	5.0	0.5
−2.0	0.5	−0.5
0.5	5.0	2.5
2.5	5.0	3.7
−2.0	−0.5	−1.0

Assess the behavioral implications of this preference curve. Modify the analysis in Exercise 21 accordingly. Don't forget the $100,000 cost of the market survey. Compare prior and preposterior results to what was obtained previously.

30. Construct $U(L)$ and $U(D, \theta)$ for the nuclear power plant model of Example 13.3 if the triads below are relevant. Note that L replaces R in the notation.

L_1	L_2	CE
70.0	8,000.1	2,000.0
70.0	2,000.0	700.0
70.0	700.0	200.0
2,000.0	8,000.1	3,000.0
3,000.0	8,000.1	4,000.0

Assess the behavioral implications of this dispreference curve. Modify the analysis in Exercise 20 accordingly. Compare prior and preposterior results to what was obtained in Section 13.4.

31. The choice of $U_{min} = 0$ and $U_{max} = 1$ for end points on the utility scale makes for the following interpretation of utility: The utility $U(R)$ for a certain payoff R is equivalent to an **indifference probability** (p) for the option of receiving R_{max} with probability p and R_{min} with probability $(1 - p)$. Show this algebraically.

**32. Determine an appropriate *analytic* utility function for the preference curve of Figure 13–2. Try regression analysis for
a. The quadratic, $U = b_0 + b_1R + b_2R^2$.
b. The third degree polynomial, $U = b_0 + b_1R + b_2R^2 + b_3R^3$.
c. The modified exponential, $U = 1 - e^{-bR}$.
Compare estimated values of U based on the analytic function to the values of U in Table 13–21. Which approach do you prefer, analytic utility functions or hand-sketched utility functions? Explain.

13.7 OTHER DECISION STRUCTURES

In this chapter we have focused strictly on discrete and finite decisions and states of nature. This allowed the construction of a payoff, loss, or utility table and the mathematically straightforward development of prior, posterior, and preposterior analyses. In the current section we overview other decision structures of interest.

Continuous States of Nature and Decisions

Textbooks that specialize in decision theory usually include a relatively extensive treatment of various cases where $\{\theta\}$ is continuous and $\{D\}$ is discrete. Various situations arise depending on the probability density function (pdf) specified for θ and the functional form of $R(D, \theta)$ or $L(D, \theta)$. A common case is a *normal* pdf for $f(\theta)$ combined with a *linear* payoff or loss function. In general, the mathematical requirements for these cases include integral calculus and concepts from mathematical statistics.

The treatment of D as a continuous decision variable introduces another level of mathematical complexity. In this case optimization requires the application of differential calculus or other mathematical programming procedures.

Sequential Decision Processes

In recent years a great deal of effort has been expended in defining and solving sequential (multistage) decision problems. For such processes a time variable is relevant; that is, decisions are made chronologically. The observed process is termed sequential because a decision is followed by a chance event, followed by another decision, followed by another chance event, and so on. Often the occurrences of chance events can be described as Markovian, in which case the decision framework of Section 13.5 can be adapted for what is called a **Markovian sequential decision process.**

Without realizing it, you have already dealt with a special case of sequential decision processes. The type of preposterior analysis exhibited in Figure 13–1 requires the consideration of two sequential decisions (D_5 and D_1, D_2, or D_3) separated in time by the occurrence of a chance event (x_1, x_2 or x_3). It follows that the roll-back procedure represents one approach for solving sequential problems.

A second, widely used approach for solving sequential decision problems is **probabilistic dynamic programming.** If you were assigned Chapter 12, then you might have realized (being the whiz that you are) that the backward induction procedure of Section 13.5 is conceptually the same as a backward recursion in dynamic programming. In this case, the stage is indexed on a time variable and the state is a random variable.

Many real problems are so large that enumerative decision tree procedures and semienumerative dynamic programming procedures are computationally infeasible. For this reason, research interest continues to be expressed in developing efficient algorithms for solving large-scale sequential decision processes.

Game Theory

Game theory represents an analytic approach to decision making involving conflict and cooperation among two or more decision makers.

> *It recognizes that conflict arises naturally when various participants have different preferences and that such problems can be studied quantitatively rather than as a mere illness or abnormality which should be cured or rectified. Game theory attempts to abstract those elements which are common and essential to many different competitive situations and to study them by means of the scientific method. It is concerned with finding optimal solutions or stable outcomes when various decision makers have conflicting objectives in mind. In brief, a game consists of players who must choose from a list of alternatives which will then bring about expected outcomes over which the participants may have different preferences. The game model describes in detail the potential payoffs which one expects to occur, and it points out how one should act in order to arrive at the best possible outcome in light of the options open to one's opponents. Game theory attempts to provide a normative guide to rational behavior for a group whose members aim for different goals.*[13]

[13]William F. Lucas, "An Overview of the Mathematical Theory of Games," *Management Science* 18, no. 5, pt. 2 (1972), p. 3.

The placement of game theory in this textbook implies that it is a special case of decision theory, whereby a decision maker "plays" against other decison makers rather than against an indifferent state of nature. A strong advocate of game theory, however, would counter that decision theory is a special case of game theory, whereby the set of opposing players is represented by Mother Nature. We suspect that the truth is somewhere in between. Without question, however, game theory is an important area of specialization in OR/MS which is quite distinct from decision theory.

Most introductory textbooks of OR/MS treat the topic of game theory in its simplest form: **two-person, zero-sum games** with no cooperation. Zero-sum refers to a strictly competitive situation whereby what one player loses, the other player gains. Real-world interest in game theory, however, is concerned with more than two players, nonzero sum games, cooperation as a way of life, and sequential (over time) games. Unfortunately, the mathematics for such games are esoteric for the nonspecialist. For these reasons, we have chosen to entirely omit detailed game theory models.

Game theory scenarios have been formulated in such diverse fields as economics, management theory, political science, military science, and psychology. For the most part, these models have been normative (what should be done) rather than descriptive (what is done). To date, unlike other OR/MS models, game theory models have had a negligible impact with respect to operating decisions; however, their usefulness as a conceptual and insightful framework for structuring certain types of real-world phenomena is generally acknowledged. For example, Hauser and Fader at MIT have been studying three-person pricing games with linear profit functions. Coalition building and degrees of "niceness" have a large impact on successful pricing in this marketing game environment, and insights from these games may have a bearing on successful marketing strategy.

Multicriteria Decision Problems

Choice problems with multiple attributes and uncertainty have been studied extensively. Dominance, satisficing, and lexicographic procedures can be used for multiattribute problems under certainty. An alternative that is at least as good as other alternatives on all attributes and better on one or more is said to dominate the other alternatives and should thus be preferred. Rather than comparing alternatives against each other, satisficing compares each alternative against acceptable levels for each attribute. Those alternatives falling short on any attribute are then excluded from further consideration. Those alternatives that pass the satisficing test might then be subjected to the lexicographic procedure—a fancy name for ranking the attributes in order of importance and choosing based on how the alternatives look on the ranked attributes. Of course these three procedures have not really faced up to the problem of trade-offs. Can an alternative make up for weakness in one attribute by strength in others?

For decision making under certainty and under risk, the concept of trade-offs provides the basis for multicriteria methods. Suppose that two alternatives are to be evaluated on two dimensions and that the first alternative has a lower payoff on the first dimension and higher on the second dimension as compared with the second alternative. How to resolve the situation? Create a third alternative in the vein of certainty equivalents. The third alternative has the same value as the second alternative on the second dimension; but on the fist dimension it has a value somewhere between the high value of the first alternative and the low value of the second alternative. The secret is to set the third alternative's value on the first dimension at the point that produces indifference between the first and third alternative. Then it is a simple matter to compare the third alternative with the second in a type of finesse procedure. To see what has happened, consider the two alternatives in Table 13–22 along with the third artificial alternative.

TABLE 13–22

	Payoff on Dimension 1	Payoff on Dimension 2
Alternative 1	10 apples	100 bananas
Alternative 2	100 apples	15 bananas
Alternative 3	75 apples	15 bananas

Clearly, alternative 2 dominates 3, and yet the decision maker is indifferent between 1 and 3 by construction of 3. By transitivity, then, the decision maker should prefer 2 over 1.

With this brief taste of multicriteria decision making, we hope that you have gained insight into the basic role played by trade-offs and indifference. The landmark book in this field is Keeney and Raiffa.[14]

13.8 ASSESSMENT

This chapter has explored methods to aid decision making in cases of both uncertainty and risk. We began the chapter by looking at decision making rules for the case of uncertainty. The definition of uncertainty versus risk predates decision theory and goes back to the work of the famous economist Frank Knight. With the advent of decision theory, the dichotomy between uncertainty and risk no longer really exists because probabilities can always be assigned if we allow subjective probabilities. Probabilities allow us to use the expected value decision rule as the underlying rule throughout the chapter. Nevertheless, our study of decision rules for the case of uncertainty introduced us to one of decision theory's major contributions, insights on how people's choices reflect their attitudes toward risk. Later in the chapter, concepts from utility theory helped formalize the description of risk attitudes.

Subjective probability estimates bother classical statisticians, and we ought to think about their concern rather than simply dismiss them as arcane purists. Here is the concern: Suppose you were placing a bet on the last game of the World Series in 1986 and you gave the Boston Red Sox a 50/50 chance of beating the New York Mets. Presumably you would have studied all the statistics of the players and tried to make an informed probability assessment. You are a little concerned because all your

[14]R. Keeney and H. Raiffa, *Decisions with Multiple Objectives: Preferences and Value Trade-offs* (New York: John Wiley & Sons, 1976).

statistics are based on regular season play, and the World Series seems to have little to do with the regular season. Classical probabilities call for repeated trials of the same experiment, and because the World Series seems to be unique you do not place much stock in the season's statistics. In your 0.5 probability assessment you thus found yourself forced away from simply running the numbers, and you actually made an educated subjective assessment. Now suppose that a hurricane cut off power to your neighborhood on the evening of the last game, and no one in your neighborhood had a working radio that night or the next morning. The next morning your neighbor suggests a bet on the game since neither of you yet know who won. You like the idea, but something bothers you about your 0.5 probability assessment. You do not know that the Mets won the night before, but that does not make the outcome random; so how can you think in terms of probability? If you could only find your transistor radio you could learn the outcome of the game and forget about your 0.5 probability assessment. A classical statistician would not consider assigning probabilities to an event that has already occurred.

The value of a transistor radio or the value of information becomes a matter of great importance to the decision theorist. As we have seen in this chapter, sample information allows the decision maker to update the probabilities of outcomes. Ivan F. Boesky was so attracted by perfect information that he raised a furor on Wall Street in late 1986 by getting caught at trading on inside information. Most decision makers deal with only imperfect tests. Financial statement analysis and capital asset pricing models help financial analysts to obtain better subjective probabilities on the future performance of stocks, but analysts' forecasts are imperfect to say the least.

With imperfect information, we see an underlying pattern in all decision theory situations. We begin with a payoff matrix and prior probabilities on the states of nature in the matrix. Experimental evidence, tests, forecasts, or predictions may be available, and these can be summarized by the conditional probability table showing the likelihood or probability of obtaining the test outcome or the forecast, given the underlying state of nature. These are the only inputs needed in a decision theory problem. Bayesian probability revision allows us to determine the posterior probabilities on the states of nature given the priors and the likelihoods. With the posteriors in hand, we can return to the payoff table to calculate expected payoffs.

The payoffs considered may be monetary payoffs or utilities. The insights gained from utility analysis help explain many real-world phenomena. For example, individuals insure themselves even though the expected monetary value is negative. The insurance company makes a profit by insuring hundreds of individuals in this gambling situation and thus faces repeated trials of the same experiment. Meanwhile the individual fears the somewhat unique case of needing to collect on the insurance. The individual exhibits risk-averse behavior or a high marginal utility for money when buying insurance.

In this chapter, we see the dual nature of decision theory. Not only is it a prescriptive theory of how to update probabilities and determine expected utilities in decision making situations; it is also a benchmark against which to compare individual information-processing and decision-making skills. Indeed, research opened up by decision theory has greatly enhanced our understanding of how people make decisions. Inconsistencies are rampant in utility and probability assessments, and so we see that people differ in their information-processing skills. Two equivalent gambles presented in a different fashion can evoke different responses.[15]

Also, people use various rules to aid their decision making when unaided by Bayesian analysis, and these rules have been unearthed by human information-processing studies. Case studies have been developed to help train auditors in judgment and decision making to overcome the biases of these rules.[16] Unaided by Bayesian training, people tend to use (1) *anchoring and adjustment,* (2) *representativeness,* and (3) *availability heuristics* when faced with uncertain situations. Anchoring and adjustment means that the individual establishes some starting or anchor value and then makes adjustments to that value, but the anchor value may be entirely ill-conceived. People use the representativeness heuristic when they tend to place a higher probability on an event occurring when a similar event has occurred. Finally, the availability heuristic leads people to place a higher probability on an event the more easily occurrences can be brought to mind. Because these three heuristics can lead to significant errors in judgment, the Bayesian-flavored case studies are designed to help the auditor assess and revise probabilities more precisely.

We can perhaps best summarize this chapter by mentioning the story of one of our colleagues whose son faced a blood transfusion. The father was upset and concerned when he read a newspaper report that a test to detect the AIDS virus in a blood sample was 95 percent reliable. Thinking that his son faced a 5 percent chance of contracting AIDS, our colleague was distraught until his Bayesian training allowed him to overcome his emotions and realize that he had misestimated the probabilities. Why? Because the test yields conditional probabilities, not posterior probabilities.

---

[15]See for example John C. Hershey and Paul J. H. Schoemaker, "Probability versus Certainty Equivalence Methods in Utility Measurement: Are They Equivalent?" *Management Science* (October 1985, pp. 1213–31.

[16]R. H. Ashton, "Integrating Research and Teaching in Auditing: Fifteen Cases on Judgement and Decision Making," *The Accounting Review,* January 1984, pp.78–96.

SELECTED APPLICATION REVIEW

EASTMAN KODAK

Eastman Kodak has an enormous foreign currency exposure with as much as 35 percent of its sales coming from abroad. The manager of $1.5 billion in foreign currencies has a sign on the trading room wall: "Minimize your maximum regret." That maxim drives Kodak's approach to the currency market.

SOURCE: M. R. Sesit, "Avoiding Losses," *The Wall Street Journal*, March 5, 1985.

TOMCO OIL CORPORATION

Tomco Oil Corporation is a small independent oil and gas producer drilling wildcat wells in Kansas. In choosing between sites for drilling exploratory wells, Tomco uses geologic and engineering information. However, the risks are high, the information is limited, and the capital expenditures are intensive. Key aspects of the decision tree model-building process at Tomco were the assessment of probabilities on geologic, engineering, economic, and political variables, as well as the assessment of a utility function. Basing their decision on decision theory methods, the company drilled and produced oil from the chosen location. Note that the decision was made on expected utilities rather than expected monetary values.

SOURCE: J. Hosseini, "Decision Analysis and Its Application in the Choice between Two Wildcat Oil Ventures," *Interfaces*, March–April 1986, pp. 75–85.

SELECTED REFERENCES

Arborist. Palo Alto, Calif.: The Scientific Press, 540 University Avenue, Palo Alto, CA 94301 (decision tree micro package).

Boffey, Philip M. "Booster Seals and Cold Emerge as Key Issues in Decision to Launch Shuttle." *New York Times*, February 20, 1986.

Bunn, Derek W. *Applied Decision Analysis*. New York: McGraw-Hill, 1984.

Curnow, H. J. "Artificial Intelligence—A Survey." *Information Age (UK)*, January 1985, pp. 10–14.

D'Agapayeff, A. "A Short Survey of Expert Systems in UK Business." *R&D Management (UK)*, April 1985, pp. 89–99.

De Groot, M. H. *Optimal Statistical Decisions*. New York: McGraw-Hill, 1970.

Hadley, G. *Introduction to Probability and Statistical Decision Theory*. San Francisco: Holden-Day, 1967.

Halter, A. N. and G. W. Dean. *Decisions under Uncertainty*. Cincinnati: South-Western Publishing, 1971.

Hershey, John C., and Paul J. H. Schoemaker. "Probability versus Certainty Equivalence Methods in Utility Measurement: Are They Equivalent?" *Management Science*, October 1985, pp. 1213–31.

Keeney, Ralph L., and Robert L. Winkler. "Evaluating Decision Strategies for Equity of Public Risks." *Operations Research*, September–October 1985, pp. 955–76.

Newman, J. W. *Management Applications of Decision Theory*. New York: Harper & Row, 1971.

Raiffa, H. *Decision Analysis*. Reading, Mass.: Addison-Wesley Publishing, 1968.

Rotenberg, Jonathan. "Decision-Making Software: Lightyear's Ahead." *Computer Update*, March–April 1985, pp. 18–21.

Saul, George K. "Business Ethics: Where Are We Going?" *Academy of Management Review*. 6, no. 2 (1981), pp. 269–76.

Schlaifer, R. *Analysis of Decisions under Uncertainty*. New York: McGraw-Hill, 1969.

"Science and Technology." *The Economist*. November 9, 1985, pp. 99–102.

Singer, Alan; John Davies; and Ming S. Huang. "Talking about Probabilities: A Logical Problem for OR/MS." *Decision Sciences*, Fall 1984, pp. 488–96.

Turner, Michael. "A Consultant's View of Expert Systems." *Data Processing (UK)*, May 1985, pp. 12–14.

Weiss, L. *Statistical Decision Theory*. New York: McGraw-Hill, 1961.

Winkler, R. L. *Introduction to Bayesian Inference and Decisions*. New York: Holt, Rinehart & Winston, 1972.

Winter, Frederick W. "An Application of Computerized Decision Tree Models in Management-Union Bargaining." *Interfaces*, March–April 1985, pp. 74–80.

ADDITIONAL EXERCISES

33. Table 13–23 is a payoff table for a particular venture.

TABLE 13–23

		State of Nature				
		θ_1	θ_2	θ_3	θ_4	θ_5
	D_1	150	225	180	210	250
Decision	D_2	180	140	200	160	225
Alternative	D_3	220	185	195	190	180
	D_4	190	210	230	200	160

Determine the optimal decision using:

a. Max-min criterion.

b. Max-max criterion.

c. Min-max regret criterion.

d. Maximum expected payoff (assuming equal likelihood of states of nature).

34. Assume that Table 13–23 is a loss table rather than a payoff table. Determine the optimal decision using (*a*) the min-max criterion, (*b*) the min-min criterion, (*c*) the min-max regret criterion, and (*d*) the minimum expected loss criterion (again assuming equal likelihood of states of nature).

35. Table 13–24 is a payoff table for a particular venture.

TABLE 13–24

		State of Nature					
		θ_1	θ_2	θ_3	θ_4	θ_5	θ_6
	D_1	280	300	260	360	400	450
Decision	D_2	320	420	540	300	280	380
Alternative	D_3	200	360	400	440	250	320
	D_4	350	260	390	500	380	260

The relative likelihoods of occurrence for the states of nature are $f(\theta_1) = 0.18$, $f(\theta_2) = 0.10$, $f(\theta_3) = 0.16$, $f(\theta_4) = 0.24$, $f(\theta_5) = 0.20$, and $f(\theta_6) = 0.12$.

a. Determine the decision alternative that maximizes expected payoff.

b. Determine the expected value under certainty.

c. What is the expected value of perfect information?

36. Rework Exercise 35 assuming that Table 13–24 is a loss table.

37. Rework Exercise 35 with experimental outcomes depending on the state of nature, as shown in Table 13–25.

TABLE 13–25

	Conditional Probabilities	
States	x_1	x_2
θ_1	0.95	0.05
θ_2	0.90	0.10
θ_3	0.85	0.15
θ_4	0.15	0.85
θ_5	0.10	0.90
θ_6	0.05	0.95

Use the payoffs as given in Exercise 35.

38. ***Investment Banking.*** A trust officer for a major banking institution is planning the investment of a $1 million family trust for the coming year. The trust officer has identified a portfolio of stocks and another group of bonds that might be selected for investment. The family trust can be invested in stocks or bonds exclusively, or a mix of the two. This trust officer prefers to divide the funds in increments of 10 percent; that is, the family trust may be split 100 percent stocks/0 percent bonds, 90 percent stocks/10 percent bonds, 80 percent stocks/20 percent bonds, and so on.

The trust officer has evaluated the relationship between the yields on the different investments and general economic conditions. Her judgment is as follows:

(1) If the next year is characterized by solid growth in the economy, bonds will yield 12 percent and stocks 20 percent.
(2) If the next year is characterized by inflation, bonds will yield 18 percent and stocks 10 percent.
(3) If the next year is characterized by stagnation, bonds will yield 12 percent and stocks 8 percent.

a. Formulate a payoff table where payoffs represent the annual yield, in dollars, associated with the different investment strategies and the occurrence of various economic conditions.

b. Determine the optimal investment strategy using the max-max, max-min, Hurwicz ($\alpha = 0.4$), equally likely, and regret criteria.

c. Suppose that a leading economic forecasting firm projects P (solid growth) = .4, P (inflation) = .25, and P (stagnation) = .35. Use the expected value criterion to select the appropriate strategy.

d. What is the expected value with perfect information?

39. ***Single-Period Inventory Model.*** Consider an inventory situation whereby an item is to be stocked at the *beginning* of some period for the purpose of meeting stochastic demand *during* that period. It is not possible to restock during the period; hence, if demand is greater than the amount stocked, then sales are lost. If more units are stocked than are demanded, however, then items are left over, which *must* be disposed of at some salvage value. We are dealing, then, with a perishable product that must be totally renewed at the beginning of the next period, which implies that decisions can be made in isolated periods without regard to other periods, providing that lost sales do not affect subsequent demand distributions. Note that this model is particularly suitable to perishable products. This classic scenario in inventory theory is often referred to as the "newsboy" problem.

Suppose a large supermarket chain is in the process of reassessing its inventory policy for ½-gallon containers of milk, which are dated and good for one week. The current policy of stocking 2,500 containers at the beginning of the week has been questioned. Each container sells for \$0.90 and costs the store \$0.60. Unsold containers left over at the end of the week can be sold to a food salvage company for \$0.20 per container. The penalty cost for shortages has been assessed at \$0.35 per container, which includes lost profit and ill will. A recent analysis of demands for a "pilot" store indicates the probability distribution shown in Table 13–26.

TABLE 13–26

Weekly Demand	Probability
1,000	0.1
1,500	0.3
2,000	0.4
2,500	0.2

a. Denote unit selling price by p, cost by c, salvage value by s (where $s < c$), and penalty cost by C_p (where $C_p > p\text{-}c$). Define D and θ, and state a general expression for $R(D, \theta)$ in terms of p, c, s, C_p, D, and θ, where R represents weekly "contribution to profit and overhead" in dollars. (*Hint:* $R(D, \theta)$ requires two expressions, depending on whether $\theta \leq D$ or $\theta > D$.)

b. Construct a payoff table for the stocking alternatives 1,000, 1,500, 2,000, and 2,500 containers. How many containers should be stocked at the beginning of the week? What is the expected savings in contribution to profit and overhead of this optimal policy versus the current policy?

40. Rework the preceding exercise if a carrying cost (C_h) of $0.05 per container per week is assessed on *average* inventory for the week.

41. A time-sharing company has offered its services to the supermarket chain described in Exercise 39. For an estimated $50 per week, each supermarket can access a forecasting program for predicting demand in the coming week. Past experience with this forecasting package shows that, given any realized demand, the probability of a correct forecast is 70 percent; the probabilities of erroneous forecasts, given any realized demand, are approximately evenly distributed among the remaining 30 percent. Does the time-sharing service appear worthwhile for the pilot supermarket? If so, how many containers of milk should be stocked for each possible forecast?

42. In actual practice, it is unnecessary to construct the payoff table for the single-period inventory model described in Exercise 39, as it can be proved that D^* is the *smallest* number of units stocked (d) for which the following expression holds:[17]

$$F(d) \geq \frac{p + C_p - c}{p + C_p - s}.$$

The symbols p, C_p, c, and s have been defined in Exercise 39; $F(d)$ represents the cumulative distribution function for demand, that is, the probability that demand is less than or equal to some specific value (d). Confirm that the described decision rule yields the same D^* as in Exercise 39.

43. The decision rule described in the preceding exercise is particularly useful for considering stocking alternatives in increments of one unit when demand is represented by some theoretical probability distribution. Consider a single-period inventory situation whereby a certain type of spare part for a highly technological aircraft is to be stocked for one year. The price is $500, the cost is $400, the salvage value is $1, and the penalty cost is $150.

a. Determine the optimal number of parts to stock if demand is Poisson with mean five parts per year.

b. Determine the range in penalty cost outside of which the optimal decision in part *a* changes. Would you say that the optimal decision is sensitive to this parameter?

44. ***Forest Management Model.*** A pulp and paper firm wishes to determine the percentage of timber for the next fiscal year which it will supply itself from company-owned timberlands. Three possible alternatives are under consideration: 25 percent internal supply and 75 percent external supply; 50 percent internal and 50 percent external; 75 percent internal and 25 percent external. Demand for timber (in thousands of cords) is estimated to be 600, 700, or 800 for the year, with respective probabilities 0.3, 0.5, and 0.2. The cost per cord for externally supplied wood has been guaranteed by the supplier at $30 per cord, regardless of the amount purchased. The internal cost to the firm of supplying its own wood is estimated as a convex function of the amount of harvested wood, as indicated in Table 13–27.

a. Construct a loss table for this problem in terms of annual cost of supplying wood in millions of dollars. How should the firm supply its wood and what is the expected annual cost?

[17] See Hadley, *Introduction to Probability*, p. 170.

TABLE 13–27

	Thousands of Cords Harvested Internally								
	150	**175**	**200**	**300**	**350**	**400**	**450**	**525**	**600**
Cost (dollars per cord)	36	34	32	30	29	29	29	35	40

b. Suppose that the external supplier guarantees prices of \$30 or \$34 with probabilities 0.6 and 0.4, respectively. What is the optimal decision and associated annual cost for the firm? (*Hint:* You must redefine θ.)

45. ***Environmental Protection Model.* The following scenario is based, in part, on a description in *Time,* June 28, 1976, p. 53. Among other duties, a regional office of the Environmental Protection Agency (EPA) is charged with investigating complaints regarding industrial pollution, when "warranted." A complaint is investigated by sending a panel of three experts, collectively called the "proboscis patrol," to the site of the alleged offender. By consensus, the proboscis patrol renders one of three opinions; low level, medium level, or high level of pollution. (We might note that the human nose has yet to find an electronic "equal" in detecting offending odors.) Following an opinion, the regional director of the EPA has the option of issuing or not issuing a citation to the offender. Alternatively, the EPA may choose not to investigate the complaint and then make a decision regarding issuance or nonissuance of a citation.

A joint team of economists, ecologists, and management scientists has determined the economic impact to the region of various consequences. If a citation is issued, the present values of "net pollution costs" are \$3 million, \$5 million, and \$10 million, respectively, should low, medium, or high levels of pollution come to be realized. The equivalent costs for not issuing a citation are 0, 8, and 25 (in millions of dollars). By "net pollution costs" we mean the direct costs associated with pollution (e.g., medical illness, purifying water, and cleaning buildings) plus the costs of altered economic activity as a result of enforcing pollution standards (e.g., potential reduction in tax revenues or higher prices for consumer goods). For present value purposes, a 20-year planning horizon and an 8 percent per year discount rate have been assumed. The cost of maintaining the proboscis patrol is estimated at \$50,000 per year, which in present value terms over a 20-year horizon at 8 percent translates into approximately \$490,000.

Past experience and judgment indicate that alleged offenders achieve low, medium, and high actual levels of pollution with probabilities 0.5, 0.4, and 0.1, respectively. Also, for any given actual level of pollution, the proboscis patrol has been accurate in predicting the correct level 80 percent of the time and equally wrong in predicting each of the other two levels the remaining 20 percent of the time.

Completely analyze this problem in order to advise the director of the EPA as to (1) whether or not to investigate complaints and (2) whether or not to issue citations depending on the circumstances.

46. Completely analyze the preceding exercise based on the following disutility function: $U(L) = 0.065L - 0.01L^2$.

47. ***Single-Stage Capital Investment Model.*** An industrial plant is faced with two capital investment alternatives for a planning horizon encompassing the next five years: Modernize the existing plant at a capital cost of \$10 million or do not modernize the existing plant. The effect of the capital investment decision is realized through the capacity of the company to operate efficiently and to meet sales demand over the next five years. For example, if market demand over the next five years is high, then a modernized plant can

meet projected demand and operate more efficiently. The projected present values of net cash flows (revenues less operating costs) in millions of dollars for the six possible consequences are given in Table 13–28. Probabilities for low, medium, and high demands are estimated as 0.2, 0.5, and 0.3, respectively. Construct an appropriate payoff table, and apply the four decision rules with which you are familiar. Relate these decision rules to behavioral prototypes.

TABLE 13–28

Demand	Modernize	Do Not Modernize
Low	8	10
Medium	38	30
High	75	50

48. ***Two-Stage Capital Investment Model.*** Suppose that the analysis of the capital investment model of the preceding exercise is extended to a second stage (the years 6 through 10). At the beginning of the sixth year, a decision on modernization or no modernization is to be made once again. If the plant was modernized at the beginning of the first year, then the alternative at the beginning of the sixth year is no modernization. However, if modernization was not carried out in the first year, then both options are open once again in the sixth year. Treating this problem as a sequential decision is attractive because one of the chance (experimental) events has occurred by the sixth year. In other words, the company is in a better position to assess subsequent demands. Table 13–29 reflects these relationships by indicating the conditional probabilities of demand in stage 2 given demand in stage 1.

TABLE 13–29

Demand During First-Stage	Demand during Second Stage		
	Low	Medium	High
Low	0.8	0.2	0
Medium	0.1	0.7	0.2
High	0.1	0.3	0.6

The present value of the capital investment for modernizing in the sixth year is estimated as $12 million. The present values of net cash flows in the second stage are projected as indicated in Table 13–30.

TABLE 13–30

Demand in Stage 2	Decision in Stage 2	
	Modernize	Do Not Modernize
Low	9	10
Medium	40	30
High	80	50

Using the expected value decision rule, determine the optimal decision for the first year. Specify the decision to be made in the sixth year for each possible demand level during the first five years. (*Hint:* Draw a decision tree.)

49. ***Pipeline Construction Model.* The following exercise is a variation of the classical "machine set-up" problem. The installation of an oil pipeline which runs from an oil field to a refinery requires the welding of 1,000 seams. Two alternatives have been specified for conducting the weldings: strictly use a team of ordinary and apprentice welders (B-Team) or use a team of master welders (A-Team) who check and rework (as necessary) the welds of the B-Team. If the B-Team is strictly used, it is estimated from past experience that 5 percent of the seams will be defective with probability 0.30, or 10 percent will be defective with probability 0.50, or 20 percent will be defective with probability 0.20. However, if the B-Team is followed by the A-Team, a defective rate of 1 percent is almost certain.

Material and labor costs are estimated at $400,000 when the B-Team is used strictly, whereas these costs rise to $530,000 when the A-Team is also brought in. Defective seams result in leaks, which must be reworked at a cost of $1,200 per seam, which includes the cost of labor and spilled oil but ignores the cost of environmental damage.

a. Determine the optimal decision and its expected cost. How might environmental damage be taken into account?

b. A worker on the pipeline with a Bayesian inclination (from long years of wagering on sporting events) has proposed that management consider X-ray inspections of five randomly selected seams *following* the work of the B-Team. Such an inspection would identify defective seams, which would provide management with more information for the decision on whether or not to bring in the A-Team. It costs $5,000 to inspect the five seams. Financially, is it worthwhile to carry out the inspection? If so, what decision should be made for each possible result of the inspection?

CASE To Be Vaccinated or Not to Be Vaccinated*

Every so many years a new strain of flu appears in the United States and individuals are faced with the decision of whether or not to be vaccinated when and if a vaccine becomes available. As an analyst for a health maintenance organization, you have been asked to come up with some guidelines to help individuals with the decision. A *pandemic* is a major epidemic due to a single virus type, often appearing around the world in a short period of time. In 1918, a pandemic killed 20 million people. The current strain of flu is related to the one causing the pandemic in 1918.

The probability of an adverse reaction to the newly developed vaccine is approximately 0.03. Experts estimate that the probability of an epidemic is 0.12, and the attack rate will be 30 percent for those not vaccinated. The vaccine is 75 percent effective, meaning that it will reduce by a factor of 0.75 an individual's probability of being attacked by this flu strain. If the individual does not get the flu shot and contracts the disease, the probability of dying is about 0.0010 according to experts. These experts also believe that the shot will reduce the probability of dying from the flu by a factor of 0.72 for those who receive the vaccine but get the flu anyway. You begin your analysis by drawing the decision tree. Once you have completed that task, you will need to develop a method to assign utility values to the outcome. You might want to demonstrate your method and show how it might work with a representative person assigning utility values.

---

*This case is based loosely on D. L. Zalkind and R. H. Shachtman, "A Decision Analysis Approach to the Swine Influenza Vaccination Decision for an Individual," *Medical Care,* January 1980, pp. 59–72.

14

Markov Processes

Chapter Outline

A stochastic process is a sequence of events with random outcomes. For example, two flips of a coin could be called a stochastic process. Normally, we use a slightly more restrictive definition of a stochastic process as one in which the events are indexed by time. If we flip a coin every hour on the hour, we have a stochastic process with hourly trials and equiprobable outcomes. Similarly, closing Wall Street prices are the outcomes of a stochastic process.

In this chapter, we begin by establishing the nature of stochastic processes, follow with the development of a specific type of stochastic process called a Markov process, and thereafter present analytical models of Markov processes that have been useful in actual applications.

14.1 NATURE OF STOCHASTIC PROCESSES[1]

As noted above, a stochastic process is a random experiment over time whereby some attribute of interest assumes numerical values according to chance factors (probability laws). This attribute, which may take on nominal (categorical) values, is termed a *random variable*.

A **stochastic process** is defined by the family or *set* of random variables $\{X_t\}$, where t is a time parameter (index) from a given *set* T. For example, if X_t is defined as the number of customers observed in a camera shop queuing system at the end of each hour (i.e., at time t), then $\{X_1, X_2, X_3, X_4, X_5, X_6, X_7, X_8\}$ represents a stochastic process for an eight-hour working day, and $\{2, 5, 3, 6, 10, 4, 3, 5\}$ represents the *realization* of this process (i.e., two customers were observed at the end of the first hour, five at the end of the second hour, . . .). In this case T represents the set of hours in an eight-hour working day, or $T = \{1, 2, 3, 4, 5, 6, 7, 8\}$.

A specific value for the random variables is termed a **state**. Hence in the terminology of stochastic processes, the random variable X_t is termed a **state variable.** The **state space** (S) is simply the sample space for all possible values of X_t. If S exclusively contains discrete values, then $\{X_t\}$ is termed a **discrete state stochastic process.** In other words, S contains the mutually exclusive and exhaustive states (outcomes) associated with the process (experiment). The camera shop queuing example represents such a process since $S = \{0, 1, 2, \ldots, N\}$ is the possible number of customers in the shop. In this case, N represents the capacity of the camera shop. The **index parameter** T can be discrete or continuous. If T is restricted to integer values, that is, $T = \{0, 1, 2, \ldots\}$, then $\{X_t\}$ is a **discrete parameter stochastic process.**

▶ Example 14.1 IRS Income Tax Audits

Consider a problem dear (not to mention frightening) to many of us: the possibility that the Internal Revenue Service (IRS) will audit our tax return. Suppose that records for a particular taxpayer are shown in the accompanying table.

[1] Knowledge of the concepts in Sections A.1 and A.2 in Appendix A at the end of the book is assumed throughout this chapter.

Year (t)	1	2	3	4	5	6	7	8	9	10
Audit?	No	No	No	Yes	No	No	Yes	Yes	Yes	No

In this case, the state variable is discrete and can take on one of two values. Let $X_t = 0$ if there is no audit in year t and $X_t = 1$ if there is an audit in year t. $\{X_t\}$ then is a discrete state and discrete parameter stochastic process where $S = \{0, 1\}$ and $T = \{1, 2, \ldots\}$. For a 10-year period, $\{X_t\} = \{X_1, X_2, \ldots, X_{10}\}$ is a general representation of this stochastic process, and $\{0, 0, 0, 1, 0, 0, 1, 1, 1, 0\}$ is its realization.

14.2 MARKOV PROCESSES

Markov processes represent one of the best-known and most useful classes of stochastic processes. In this section we present some of their fundamental properties.

Markovian Property

A stochastic process is a **Markov process** if it satisfies the following condition, which is called the **Markovian property:**

> Given that the present (or most recent) state is known, the *conditional* probability of the next state is independent of states prior to the present (or most recent) state.

More specifically, for a discrete state and discrete parameter stochastic process, the conditional probability of a specific *next* state (i.e., of $X_{t+1} = x_{t+1}$) given the *present* state (i.e., given $X_t = x_t$) and given all states prior to the present state (i.e., given $X_0 = x_0, X_1 = x_1 \ldots, X_{t-1} = x_{t-1}$) is identical to the conditional probability of a specific next state given the present state:

$$P(X_{t+1} = x_{t+1} | X_0 = x_0, X_1 = x_1, \ldots, X_t = x_t) = P(X_{t+1} = x_{t+1} | X_t = x_t) \qquad (14.1)$$

for $t = 0, 1 \ldots.$ and all possible sequences for state values. Note that an uppercase letter represents the *random variable*, and a lowercase letter represents a specific value of the random variable (termed a *random variate*).

Stated a little differently,

> A Markov process is a time-based process where the probability of a state on the next trial (time period) depends only on the state in the current trial (time period) and not on how we got to the present state.

Because of the Markovian property, these processes are often referred to as being "memoryless."

Markov processes describe the dynamics of a system. Specifically, they describe movement among the different states of a system as a function of time. Movements of people, inventories, and money have been described as Markov processes. Let us examine some examples of Markov and non-Markov processes.

Markov process. The probability that a hospital patient will have a given state of health (satisfactory, fair, critical, etc.) on a particular day depends only on the condition of the patient the previous day.

Non-Markov process. The probability that a hospital patient will have a given state of health on a particular day depends not only on the condition the previous day, but also on the patient's condition for each day in the hospital as well as the number of relapses the patient has had with the illness.

Markov process. The probability that a person's next automobile purchase will be a foreign car depends only on whether or not the person's last purchase was a foreign car.

Non-Markov process. The probability that a person's next automobile purchase will be a foreign car depends not only on whether the last purchase was a foreign car, but also on the past several purchases and the experiences the person has had with those automobiles.

Markov process. The probability of selling a house the next day remains constant regardless of how long the house has been on the market (i.e., depends only on the state "unsold").

Non-Markov process. The probability of selling a house the next day declines the longer the house has been on the market (i.e., depends on the state "unsold" and on how you arrived at the state . . . how many previous days the state "unsold" occurred).

▶ Example 14.2 IRS Again

If the discrete state and discrete parameter stochastic process in Example 14.1 is known to be Markovian, then the conditional probability of an audit in the 11th year can be stated according to the Markovian property given by Equation 14.1:

$$P(X_{11} = 1 \mid X_1 = 0, X_2 = 0, \ldots, X_{10} = 0) = P(X_{11} = 1 \mid X_{10} = 0).$$

This implies that *how* we got to the present state is not a factor in affecting the probability of the next state. In other words, the probability of an audit in year 11 is only conditional (dependent) on the fact that no audit occurred in year 10.

FOLLOW-UP EXERCISES

1. For the IRS example, state the Markovian property given by Equation 14.1 for the state "no audit in year 11."
2. Would you consider the process of coin flipping to be Markovian in nature? Why or why not? Hint: Let 1 be heads and 0 tails and use the formula given in Example 14.2.

Transition Probabilities

The conditional probability given by the right-hand side of Equations 14.1 represents a **transition probability.** Thus a transition probability is defined as the conditional probability that the process will be in a specific future state given its most recent state. These probabilities are also termed *one-step* transition probabilities, since they describe the system between t and $t + 1$. Similarly, we refer to an *m-step* transition probability as the conditional probability describing states in the system between t and $t + m$.

A convenient representation of one-step transition probabilities for the discrete state case is given by the following **transition matrix:**[2]

$$\mathbf{P} = \begin{array}{c} \\ 1 \\ 2 \\ \vdots \\ n \end{array} \overset{\displaystyle \begin{array}{cccc} 1 & 2 & \cdots & n \end{array}}{\begin{pmatrix} p_{11} & p_{12} & \cdots & p_{1n} \\ p_{21} & p_{22} & \cdots & p_{2n} \\ \vdots & & & \\ p_{n1} & p_{n2} & \cdots & p_{nn} \end{pmatrix}} \tag{14.2}$$

(Rows: *From State*; columns: *To State*)

where n is the number of exhaustive and mutually exclusive states and p_{ij} is the transition probability of going from the present (ith) state to the next (jth) state. Thus rows represent the possible present states, and columns represent the possible future states for the next outcome. Note that the specific values of i and j represent identification numbers for discrete states, not their values. For example, the identification numbers for the possible states in Example 14.1 are 1 and 2; however, the value of state 1 is $X_t = 0$ and for state 2 is $X_t = 1$.

By definition, the elements in **P** must satisfy the following two properties:

1. $0 \leq p_{ij} \leq 1 \quad \text{for all } i, j.$
2. $\sum_{j=1}^{n} p_{ij} = 1, \quad i = 1, 2, \ldots, n.$

The first property follows from the definition of a probability. The second property states that each row of the transition matrix must sum to one. This follows from the Rule of Addition for mutually exclusive events that are exhaustive; that is, given that the system is presently in the ith state, the probability of its being next in state 1 or state 2 or . . . or state n is one.

[2] The notion of a matrix is reviewed in Appendix B at the end of the book.

▶ Example 14.3 IRS Rides Again

Suppose the stochastic process in Example 14.1 is Markovian and the transition matrix between year 10 and year 11 is given by

$$\mathbf{P} = \begin{pmatrix} p_{11} & p_{12} \\ p_{21} & p_{22} \end{pmatrix} = \begin{pmatrix} 0.6 & 0.4 \\ 0.5 & 0.5 \end{pmatrix}.$$

As illustrated in Figure 14–1, row 1 ($i = 1$) represents a state of no audit in year 10 (that is, $X_{10} = 0$), and row 2 ($i = 2$) represents an audit in year 10 (that is, $X_{10} = 1$); column 1 ($j = 1$) represents no audit in year 11 (that is, $X_{11} = 0$), and column 2 ($j = 2$) represents an audit in year 11 (that is, $X_{11} = 1$).

The transition probability p_{11} states that the probability of not having an audit in the 11th year ($j = 1$) given that no audit was performed in the tenth year ($i = 1$) is 0.6. Mathematically,

FIGURE 14–1 Transition Matrix for IRS Audit

		Year II	
		No Audit ($X_{11} = 0$)	**Audit ($X_{11} = 1$)**
Year 10	No audit ($X_{10} = 0$)	0.6	0.4
	Audit ($X_{10} = 1$)	0.5	0.5

$$p_{11} = P(X_{11} = 0 \mid X_{10} = 0) = 0.6.$$

Similarly,

$$p_{12} = P(X_{11} = 1 \mid X_{10} = 0) = 0.4.$$

Note that both properties of **P** are satisfied by this matrix. In particular, all rows sum to one.

Markov Chains

A **Markov chain** is a stochastic process with the following properties:

1. Discrete state space.
2. Markovian property.
3. One-step transition probabilities that remain constant over time (termed *stationary* transition probabilities).

If additionally the discrete state space has a finite number of states, then a **finite-state Markov chain** has been defined.

Markov chains constitute a prominent class of Markov processes that have desirable computational properties for real-world implementation. As we show in Section 14.4, a Markov chain is completely determined once we specify the transition matrix and the set of unconditional probabilities for initial states. Knowledge of these two sets of probabilities allows the probabilistic prediction of specific states at future times. Prior to computational considerations, however, we take the time in the next section to present some actual applications.

▶ Example 14.4 IRS Contingency Table

Example 14.3 presented a transition matrix for the Markov process described in Example 14.1. If a finite-state Markov chain is to be assumed, then the property of stationary transition probabilities prescribes that

$$\mathbf{P} = \begin{pmatrix} 0.6 & 0.4 \\ 0.5 & 0.5 \end{pmatrix}$$

remains constant over time.

Typically, the theoretical or true transition matrix is unknown in actual practice. The usual procedure for specifying **P** first assumes that the observed (historical) stochastic process is a random sample from the true process. If this is the case, there is theoretical justification for basing point estimates of transition probabilities on the empirical probabilities obtained from a contingency table. To illustrate, the historical stochastic process in Example 14.1 given by

$$\{X_t\} = \{0, 0, 0, 1, 0, 0, 1, 1, 1, 0\}$$

can be described by this *contingency* table. For example, three times the state of the system went from "no audit" to "no audit" in successive years (i.e., from $X_1 = 0$ to $X_2 = 0$, from $X_2 = 0$ to $X_3 = 0$, and from $X_5 = 0$ to $X_6 = 0$); hence a 3 is placed in cell 1, 1 of the table. (Can you confirm the other entries?)

	To a Specific State in the Following Year		
From a Specific State in a Given Year	**No Audit**	**Audit**	**Row Sum**
No audit	3	2	5
Audit	2	2	4

By definition, p_{11} is the probability of "no audit" in a succeeding year given that there was "no audit" in the current year. From the contingency table, out of 5 "no audit" current years (the sum of row 1), 3 "no audit" succeeding years followed; hence $p_{11} = 3/5$. Similarly, $p_{12} = 2/5$, or 2 "audit" years followed "no audit" years out of a possible 5. For the entire matrix, we have

$$\mathbf{P} = \begin{pmatrix} p_{11} = 3/5 & p_{12} = 2/5 \\ p_{21} = 2/4 & p_{22} = 2/4 \end{pmatrix},$$

which is consistent with the matrix we used previously.

FOLLOW-UP EXERCISES

3. Verbalize the implication and plausibility of each of the three assumptions (properties) in treating Example 14.1 as a Markov chain.
4. In estimating **P** for the IRS problem, would you prefer more observations? Explain.
5. Suppose that a year has passed in the IRS problem. If an audit was performed in year 11, how would you update **P**? Would you say that the history of the stochastic process is relevant when **P** is not known with certainty? Explain. If so, does this necessarily violate the Markovian property? Explain.
6. Let f_{ij} represent the number of observations in cell i, j of a contingency table for **P**. Write down a general expression for calculating all p_{ij}.

14.3 APPLICATIONS OF MARKOV CHAINS

Early uses of Markov models are found in the physical sciences. For example, this type of analysis has been used to study the behavior of gas particles in a container, to model the development of biological populations, and to forecast weather patterns in meteorology. More recently, managerial applications include analyses of inventory and queuing systems; replacement and maintenance policies for machines; brand loyalty in marketing; time series of economic data, such as price movements of stocks; accounts receivable in accounting; hospital systems, such as the movements of coronary and geriatric patients; management of resources, such as water and wildlife; and expected payout of life insurance policies. This section describes scenarios for three of these applications. In every case, a Markov chain is assumed. In the exercises at the end of the chapter, other applications will be described for you to formulate and analyze.

Brand Switching Model

Markov chains of brand-switching behavior in the marketplace have been used as diagnostic tools for suggesting marketing strategies. To illustrate a specific formulation, consider the brand-switching behavior depicted in Table 14–1 for a panel of 500 consumers. According to the first row, of the 100 consumers enjoyed by brand 1 in

TABLE 14–1 Number of Consumers Switching from Brand i in Week 26 to Brand j in Week 27

Brand	(j) 1	2	3	Total
(i)				
1	90	7	3	100
2	5	205	40	250
3	30	18	102	150
Total	125	230	145	500

week 26, 90 repurchased brand 1 in week 27, 7 switched to brand 2, and 3 switched to brand 3. Note, however, that 5 customers switched from brand 2 to brand 1, and 30 customers switched from brand 3 to brand 1 (according to the first column). Hence for brand 1 the loss of 10 customers (7 + 3) was more than compensated by the gain of 35 customers (5 + 30), yielding a net gain of 25 customers from one week to the next (100 versus 125). The market share for brand 1 increased from 0.2 of the sample market (100/500) to 0.25 of the sample market (125/500).

Contingency tables of this type are useful because they not only show the net changes and market shares but also show the sources of change. For example, brand 1 showed a net loss of 2 customers (5 − 7) to brand 2 and a net gain of 27 customers (30 − 3) from brand 3.

Additionally, such tables directly yield the *current* one-step matrix of transition probabilities, as given in Table 14–2. Note that **P** in this case represents a sample estimate of the underlying or true transition matrix. (See Example 14.4.) Further note that p_{ii} is a reflection of the "holding power" of brand i since it represents the probability that a consumer purchases brand i, given that the preceding purchase was brand i. Similarly, p_{ij} reflects the "attraction power" of brand j, in that it is an estimate of the probability that brand j is purchased next given that brand i was the preceding purchase.

Figure 14–2 is a "lily pad" representation of the transition matrix for the brand-switching model. This provides a convenient way of visualizing the behavior of a finite state Markov process.

FIGURE 14–2 Lily Pad Model for Brand Switching Model

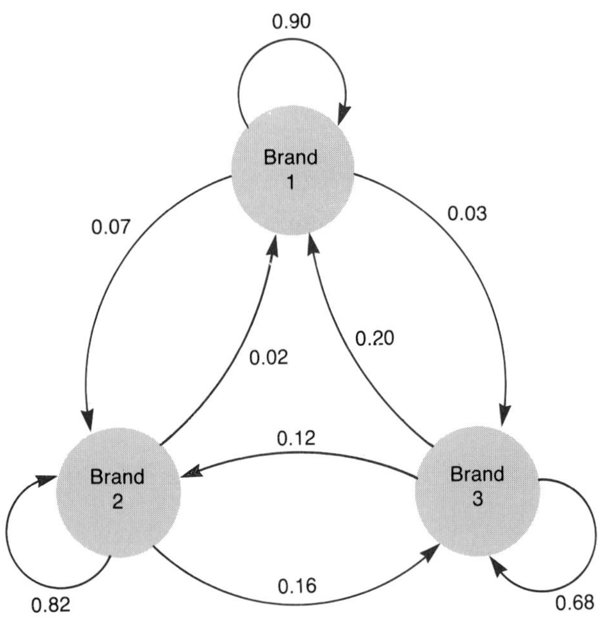

If we define the state variable X_t as the brand purchased in week t, then $\{X_t\}$ represents a discrete state and discrete parameter stochastic process where $S = \{1, 2, 3\}$ and $T = \{0, 1, 2, \ldots\}$. If we can establish that $\{X_t\}$ exhibits the Markovian property given by Equation 14.1 and that **P** is stationary, then a Markov chain should be a reasonable representation of *aggregate* consumer brand-switching behavior.

Uses of Markov analyses of brand-switching behavior include, but are not restricted to, the following:

1. Prediction of market shares at specific future times.
2. Assessment of rates of change in market shares over time.
3. Prediction of market share equilibriums (if they exist).
4. Assessment of the specific effects of marketing strategies in changing undesirable market shares.
5. Evaluation of the process for introducing new products.

FOLLOW-UP EXERCISES

7. With respect to Table 14–2:
   a. Interpret the meanings of $p_{11} = 0.90$, $p_{22} = 0.82$, and $p_{33} = 0.68$.
   b. To which brand is brand 2 most likely to lose customers?
   c. Which brand has the most "loyal" customers?
   d. Which brand has the least "loyal" customers?
8. Add a fourth state to the state space that represents "no purchase of brands 1, 2, or 3 in week *t*." Construct a new transition matrix given the contingency table below.

Brand (*i*)	(*j*) 1	2	3	4	**Total**
1	90	5	3	2	100
2	5	200	40	5	250
3	25	15	80	10	130
4	5	10	5	0	20
Total	125	230	128	17	500

   Is this table more comprehensive than the preceding table? Interpret the meaning of p_{44}. Identify two explanations for the occurrence of $X_t = 4$. (*Hint*: When $X_t = 4$, does it necessarily mean that the consumer did not purchase this product in week *t*?)
9. Consider the three-brand market presented in the example. Define a state space that includes the possibilities of zero, one, or two purchases of the product in a given week.
10. ***Homogeneity Assumption.*** You should realize that a contingency table such as Table 14–2 and the resulting matrix of transition probabilities represent the *aggregate* switching behavior in a *sample* of the defined *population*. They do not represent *individual* consumer behavior in the sense of predicting what a particular consumer will do. The purchasing pattern for a particular consumer represents a stochastic process, which could be modeled by a Markov chain. To illustrate, you should construct **P** for the following nine-week purchasing pattern of a specific

consumer: {2, 2, 2, 1, 1, 3, 1, 1, 1}. For practical reasons firms are interested in aggregate rather than individual behavior. The act of aggregating consumers, however, implicitly assumes that consumers are *homogeneous* with respect to their transition matrices. Put another way, the construction of empirical probabilities as point estimates for true probabilities requires that the experiments (i.e., consumer trials in the sample) be performed under "identical" conditions (i.e., homogeneous consumers). Can you think of procedures for designing the sample which more nearly guarantee homogeneity?

11. ***Marketing Strategies.*** To illustrate how marketing strategy can affect consumer switching behavior in a Markov model, consider the following. Suppose the relationship below is empirically valid:

$$p'_{ij} = p_{ij} + a(s_{it} - \bar{s}_{it})$$

where

p_{ij} = Current (stationary) transition probability.
p'_{ij} = New (stationary) *unadjusted* transition probability.
s_{it} = Selling price of brand i in week t.
$\bar{s}_{it}$ = Mean selling price of all brands other than brand i in week t.
a = Parameter ($a = 0.01$ when $i \neq j$ and $a = -0.05$ when $i = j$).

Thus when $i \neq j$, a price for brand i in week t that is above the market average of all other prices (that is, $s_{it} > \bar{s}_{it}$) will have the effect of increasing the attraction power of other brands (that is, p'_{ij} will be greater than p_{ij}). Given expected prices in week t, it follows that this prediction model can be used to construct a new transition matrix. Note, however, that row sums will not be unity; hence the unadjusted p'_{ij} for each row must be adjusted to yield a sum of unity. For example, if unadjusted $p'_{11} = 0.9$, $p'_{12} = 0.5$, and $p'_{13} = 0.6$, then the adjusted values for the first row would be determined as follows (noting that unadjusted $p'_{11} + p'_{12} + p'_{13} = 2.0$): $p'_{11} = 0.9/2.0 = 0.45$; $p'_{12} = 0.5/2.0 = 0.25$; $p'_{13} = 0.6/2.0 = 0.3$. *Note*: if unadjusted $p'_{ij} < 0$, then set to zero before adjusting.

a. Reason out changes in p_{ij} when $s_{it} > \bar{s}_{it}$ and $i = j$; $s_{it} < \bar{s}_{it}$ and $i \neq j$; $s_{it} < \bar{s}_{it}$ and $i = j$; $s_{it} = \bar{s}_{it}$. Does the logic of this model reflect the phenomenon of "price-snobbery?"

b. Construct the new transition matrix for the main example (Table 14–2) given that expected market prices in week 28 are \$1, \$3, and \$2 for brands 1, 2, and 3, respectively. Reflect on the changes.

Hospital Administration Model

Decision problems in the field of health administration have proved to be fertile territory for OR/MS models. Here we illustrate a Markov model for analyzing the flow of patients in the geriatric ward of a state hospital.[3]

For the hospital in question, a resocialization program (RP) has been initiated in the geriatric ward to reduce the number of patients who become "institutionalized," or totally dependent on the hospital for their needs. After five years of running RP, hospital administrators felt that it was a success but were unsure of means to measure its effectiveness in terms of both monetary cost to the state and the welfare of its

[3]This model is based on Jack Meredith, "A Markovian Analysis of a Geriatric Ward," *Management Science*, February 1973, pp. 604–12.

patients. Fortunately, one of the administrators (a young, aspiring M.B.A. graduate) had recently taken a course in Management Science and so suggested that the services of her professor (a young, aspiring Ph.D. graduate) be commissioned.

Following a fair amount of interaction with the administrators, much study, and tedious data collection, the consultant constructed Table 14–3. The problem has been conceptualized as a discrete state (four states) and discrete parameter (one-month time unit) stochastic process. Thus $S = \{1, 2, 3, 4\}$ and $T = \{0, 1, 2, \ldots\}$, where $T = 0$ represents an initial month.

TABLE 14–3 Transition Probabilities

State	1	2	3	4
1 RP	0.85	0.03	0.11	0.01
2 Ward	0.01	0.97	0.01	0.01
3 Home	0.02	0.02	0.95	0.01
4 Dead	0.00	0.00	0.00	1.00

Based on the information provided in the table, patients are classified in one of four states in any given month. Patients who are in RP live in a special ward of the hospital and participate in a four-step program that combines group activities and special training aimed at fostering independence. Patients who are not in RP but who live in the hospital are classified as "Ward" ($X_t = 2$). Patients classified in state 3 have been discharged to an approved boarding home outside the hospital grounds. Patients living in such homes are deemed resocialized because they are more active and independent than their peers living in the hospital. The other (very real) possibility for the geriatric patient is death. In the literature, this state is referred to as an "absorbing state" because there is no possibility of leaving the state.

Based on data analysis using statistical procedures, the consultant concluded (1) that patients were essentially homogeneous (see Exercise 10), (2) that future states were basically dependent only on the present state (Markovian property), and (3) that the transition matrix was independent of time (stationary). Hence a Markov chain is a satisfactory representation of this flow of patients. It was noted, however, that a patient's aging affects the probability of death. This means that the Markov chain may be unreliable for long-run predictions. Furthermore, the probability of moving from one state to another was a function of not only the current state but also how long a patient had been in the current state. This effect, however, was weak.

The transition matrix for this problem is a good indication of RP's effectiveness. For example, we might conclude that for patients beginning their stay in the regular ward of the hospital ($X_0 = 2$), the probability of being discharged to a home in the next month is no better than the probability of dying [that is, $P(X_1 = 3 | X_0 = 2) = P(X_1 = 4 | X_0 = 2) = 0.01$]. However, for a patient beginning in RP ($X_0 = 1$), the odds of being discharged in the next month rather than dying are 11 to 1, that is, 11 percent probability versus a 1 percent probability, or $P(X_1 = 3 | X_0 = 1) = 0.11$ versus $P(X_1 = 4 | X_0 = 1) = 0.01$.

FOLLOW-UP EXERCISES

12. Draw a lily pad diagram for the hospital example. Notice the representation for the absorbing state.

13. If the amount of time in a given state affects the probabilities of subsequent states very much, do we still have a Markov chain? A Markov process? A stochastic process? Explain.

Stock Market Model

The fluctuation of stock prices over time is an example of a stochastic process of an economic time series. The field of finance known as security analysis is concerned with predicting the future behavior of prices of securities (stocks, bonds, Treasury bills, and so forth) for the purpose of formulating investment strategy. A popular class of models for this type of decision making is mathematical programming applied to portfolio analysis. In the present example, we describe a simplified Markovian scenario based on an actual application.[4]

Let $\{C_t\}$ and $\{D_t\}$ represent, respectively, the stochastic process of *closing daily prices* over time and the stochastic process over time of *differences in closing prices* from one day to the next (that is, $D_t = C_t - C_{t-1}$). Based on these price movements, we can now define a discrete three-state and discrete parameter stochastic process $\{X_t\}$ with respect to actual changes in the price of a stock from one day to the next, as indicated in Table 14–4. For example, if the price of a stock at the end of a trading day (day t) has increased from the preceding day, then state 1 ($X_t = 1$) has occurred on this day. It follows that $\{X_t\}$ represents a discrete state and discrete parameter stochastic process with $S = \{1, 2, 3\}$ and $T = \{0, 1, 2, \ldots\}$, where T is indexed on days.

TABLE 14–4 States for Stock Market Model

X_t	Description	Realization if
1	Up	$c_t > c_{t-1}$ or $d_t > 0$
2	No change	$c_t = c_{t-1}$ or $d_t = 0$
3	Down	$c_t < c_{t-1}$ or $d_t < 0$

Note: c_t represents actual price at close of day t; d_t represents actual difference between two successive daily closing prices, or $d_t = c_t - c_{t-1}$.

Table 14–5 shows the realization of $\{C_t\}$, $\{D_t\}$, and $\{X_t\}$ over a 20-day period for a selected stock. The stochastic process given by $\{X_t\}$ is a Markov chain if the assumptions relating to dependence (Markovian property) and stationarity are satisfied. In the next two sections we develop computational procedures for you to further analyze this model.

FOLLOW-UP EXERCISES

14. In the context of this problem, what two conditions must be statistically validated if $\{X_t\}$ is to be considered a Markov chain? Comment on the logical reasonableness of these two conditions.
15. Based on $\{X_t\}$ in Table 14–5, construct a matrix of transition probabilities. In words, what is $P(X_t = 1 \mid X_{t-1} = 3)$?

[4] B. D. Fielitz and T. N. Bhargava, "The Behavior of Stock Price Relatives—A Markovian Analysis," *Operations Research*, November–December 1973, pp. 1183–99.

TABLE 14–5 Realization of Stochastic Processes for Stock Market Model

Day T	Closing Price (dollars per share)	Price Difference (dollars per share)	Classification of Price Difference
0	10¼	—	—
1	10⅞	⅝	1
2	11½	⅝	1
3	11	− ½	3
4	13½	2½	1
5	13½	0	2
6	12¼	−1¼	3
7	15⅛	2⅞	1
8	18¾	3⅝	1
9	16	−2¾	3
10	15⅞	− ⅛	3
11	14½	−1⅜	3
12	14	− ½	3
13	16⅛	2⅛	1
14	20¾	4⅝	1
15	20	− ¾	3
16	19¼	− ¾	3
17	19½	¼	1
18	21	1½	1
19	21½	½	1
20	19⅞	−1⅝	3

16. It can be argued that Up, No Change, and Down states should be based not only on the direction of change, but also on the magnitude of change. Consider the following scheme for assigning states where $\bar{d}$ is the mean of price differences and $\hat{\sigma}_d$ is the unbiased estimate of the standard deviation of price differences: If $d_t > \bar{d} + 0.5\hat{\sigma}_d$, then $X_t = 1$; if $d_t < \bar{d} - 0.5\hat{\sigma}_d$, then $X_t = 3$; otherwise, $X_t = 2$.
    a. State in words the meaning of these "state rules."
    b. State an advantage of this scheme with respect to small changes in price.
    c. Generate $\{X_t\}$ for $\{D_t\}$ given in Table 14–5. (*Note:* $\bar{d} = 0.5$ and $\hat{\sigma}_d = 1.9$.)
    d. Construct a transition matrix and compare to Exercise 15. Comments?

14.4 COMPUTATIONAL PROPERTIES OF MARKOV CHAINS

Up to now we have presented the nature, uses, and sample formulations of stochastic processes in general and Markov chains in particular. This section illustrates computational techniques for the probability analysis of future states in a Markov chain.

Transient Solutions: Classical Approach

Consider the IRS problem previously presented (Example 14.1). Assuming the validity of a Markov chain (Example 14.4), we can predict the probability of any future state given any present state.

Figure 14–3 illustrates a **probability tree,** which depicts the present state in year 10 ("no audit" or $X_{10} = 0$) and possible future states in years 11, 12, and 13. Each node in the tree represents a specific state in year t that is either "no audit" ($X_t = 0$) or "audit" ($X_t = 1$). The branch between any two states represents a possible path of travel between those two states. For convenience, the conditional or branch probabilities are included in the figure just above each branch. Note that these branch probabilities are, in fact, the transition probabilities between any two successive states. Now, what is the probability of "no audit" in year 13? First, the probability of "no audit" in year 11 ($X_{11} = 0$) given "no audit" in year 10 ($X_{10} = 0$) is simply

$$\begin{aligned} P(X_{11} = 0 \mid X_{10} = 0) &= p_{11} \\ &= 0.6\,. \end{aligned}$$

FIGURE 14–3 Probability Tree for IRS Problem

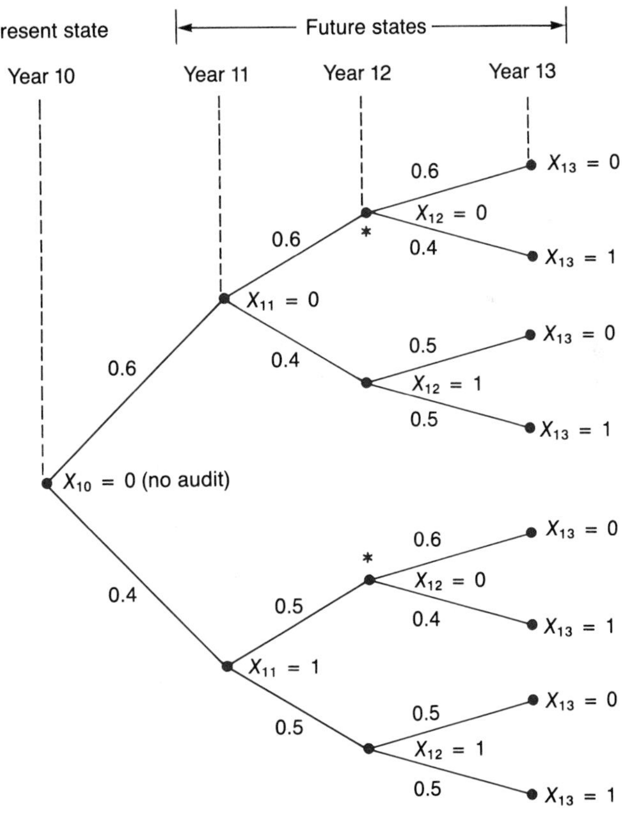

The probability of "no audit" in year 12 ($X_{12} = 0$) given "no audit" in year 10 ($X_{10} = 0$) depends on the paths to the * in Figure 14–3 and is given by

$$\begin{aligned} P(X_{12} = 0 | X_{10} = 0) &= P(X_{11} = 0 | X_{10} = 0) \cdot P(X_{12} = 0 | X_{11} = 0) \\ &\quad + P(X_{11} = 1 | X_{10} = 0) \cdot P(X_{12} = 0 | X_{11} = 1) \\ &= (0.6) \cdot (0.6) + (0.4) \cdot (0.5) \\ &= 0.36 + 0.20 \\ &= 0.56\,. \end{aligned}$$

Looking at the tree, we reason that it is possible to achieve $X_{12} = 0$ by one of two paths. The first takes us from $X_{10} = 0$ to $X_{11} = 0$ to $X_{12} = 0$ with probability $(0.6) \cdot (0.6)$ according to the Probability Rule of Multiplication for dependent events. The second path runs from $X_{10} = 0$ to $X_{11} = 1$ to $X_{12} = 0$ with probability $(0.4) \cdot (0.5)$. Since these paths are mutually exclusive, the probability of achieving $X_{12} = 0$ given that we started at $X_{10} = 0$ is given by the sum of the separate path probabilities $(0.36 + 0.20)$ according to the Probability Rule of Addition for mutually exclusive events. Finally, the probability of "no audit" in year 13 given "no audit" in year 10 is given by the sum of four path probabilities:

$$\begin{aligned} P(X_{13} = 0 | X_{10} = 0) &= (0.6) \cdot (0.6) \cdot (0.6) + (0.6) \cdot (0.4) \cdot (0.5) \\ &\quad + (0.4) \cdot (0.5) \cdot (0.6) + (0.4) \cdot (0.5) \cdot (0.5) \\ &= 0.216 + 0.120 + 0.120 + 0.100 \\ &= 0.556\,. \end{aligned}$$

To summarize, given "no audit" in year 10, the probabilities of "no audit" in years 11, 12, and 13 are 0.6, 0.56, and 0.556, respectively. These conditional probabilities for the "no audit" state are known as **transient probabilities** because they are changing over time.

FOLLOW-UP EXERCISES

17. Using Figure 14–2, determine the transient probabilities for audits in years 11, 12, and 13 given that "no audit" was performed in year 10.
18. Confirm that $P(X_{14} = 0 | X_{10} = 0) = 0.5556$. Do you notice anything interesting about the behavior of the transient probabilities over time given by $P(X_t = 0 | X_{10} = 0)$, $t = 11, \ldots, 14$?
19. Draw a probability tree and determine the following transient probabilities for a "typical" customer in the brand-switching model of Table 14–2: Given that the current purchase is brand 3 ($X_0 = 3$), determine the conditional probabilities that brand 1 will be purchased next week ($X_1 = 1$), two weeks hence ($X_2 = 1$), and three weeks hence ($X_3 = 1$).
20. For the hospital administration model depicted in Table 14–3, draw probability trees and determine the following:
    a. The probabilities that a customer currently in RP will be in a home next month, two months from now, and three months from now.
    b. The probabilities that a customer currently in a ward will be in a home next month, two months from now, and three months from now. Compare these to part *a*, and draw a conclusion as to the effectiveness of RP.
21. For the stock price model with transition matrix given in Exercise 15, find the probabilities that two days from now the price will increase, remain the same, and

decrease given that the current state is "down." Why should these probabilities sum to unity?

Transient Solutions: Matrix Approach

The method of probability trees for calculating transient probabilities is instructive but cumbersome. A more efficient (and elegant) procedure involves the application of matrix multiplication, as we now demonstrate.[5]

▶ Example 14.5 IRS with Matrices

For the IRS problem (Examples 14.1 through 14.4), with transition matrix given by

$$\mathbf{P} = \begin{pmatrix} 0.6 & 0.4 \\ 0.5 & 0.5 \end{pmatrix}$$

we know that the first row represents the conditional probabilities of possible states in the *next* period given that state 1 (no audit) is observed in the *current* period. Thus, given "no audit" in the current period, $p_{11} = 0.6$ and $p_{12} = 0.4$ are the probabilities of "no audit" and "audit," respectively, in the next period. Similarly, the second row represents all conditional probabilities in the next period given that state 2 (audit) is observed in the current period (that is, $p_{21} = 0.5$ and $p_{22} = 0.5$).

To determine all conditional probabilities two periods hence (that is, $p_{ij}^{(2)}$ for all i and j), we simply square **P** as follows:

$$\begin{aligned} \mathbf{P}^2 &= \mathbf{P} \cdot \mathbf{P} \\ &= \begin{pmatrix} 0.6 & 0.4 \\ 0.5 & 0.5 \end{pmatrix} \cdot \begin{pmatrix} 0.6 & 0.4 \\ 0.5 & 0.5 \end{pmatrix} \\ &= \begin{pmatrix} 0.56 & 0.44 \\ 0.55 & 0.45 \end{pmatrix} \end{aligned}$$

This indicates, for example, that $p_{11}^{(2)} = 0.56$ is the probability of "no audit" two years hence given that in the current year there was "no audit," and $p_{22}^{(2)} = 0.45$ is the probability of an audit two years from now given that there was an audit in the current year. Can you interpret $p_{12}^{(2)}$ and $p_{21}^{(2)}$?

Figure 14–4 illustrates the detail behind the computation of $\mathbf{P}^2$. The expanded multiplication should help you understand the computation of elements $p_{ij}^{(2)}$ as well as their meaning. For example, to compute $p_{11}^{(2)} = 0.56$, there are two paths: stay in state one through two transitions *or* leave state one and return again through two transitions.

Three years from now, the conditional probabilities are given by

$$\begin{aligned} \mathbf{P}^3 &= \mathbf{P}^2 \cdot \mathbf{P} \\ &= \begin{pmatrix} 0.56 & 0.44 \\ 0.55 & 0.45 \end{pmatrix} \cdot \begin{pmatrix} 0.6 & 0.4 \\ 0.5 & 0.5 \end{pmatrix} \\ &= \begin{pmatrix} 0.556 & 0.444 \\ 0.555 & 0.445 \end{pmatrix} \end{aligned}$$

[5]For a review of matrix multiplication, see Appendix C at the end of the book.

FIGURE 14–4 Computation of $\mathbf{P}^2$

$$\begin{pmatrix} p_{11} & p_{12} \\ p_{21} & p_{22} \end{pmatrix} \begin{pmatrix} p_{11} & p_{12} \\ p_{21} & p_{22} \end{pmatrix} = \begin{matrix} \text{From} \\ \text{current} \\ \text{state} \end{matrix} \begin{matrix} & \text{to state two periods hence} & \\ & 1 & 2 \\ 1 & \multicolumn{2}{l}{\left(p_{11}p_{11} + p_{12}p_{21}, \quad p_{11}p_{12} + p_{12}p_{22} \right.} \\ 2 & \multicolumn{2}{l}{\left. p_{21}p_{11} + p_{22}p_{21} \quad p_{21}p_{12} + p_{22}p_{22} \right)} \end{matrix}$$

$$= \begin{pmatrix} p_{11}^{(2)} & p_{12}^{(2)} \\ p_{21}^{(2)} & p_{22}^{(2)} \end{pmatrix}$$

$$\begin{pmatrix} 0.6 & 0.4 \\ 0.5 & 0.5 \end{pmatrix} \begin{pmatrix} 0.6 & 0.4 \\ 0.5 & 0.5 \end{pmatrix} = \begin{Bmatrix} [(0.6)(0.6) + (0.4)(0.5)] & [(0.6)(0.4) + (0.4)(0.5)] \\ [(0.5)(0.6) + (0.5)(0.5)] & [(0.5)(0.4) + (0.5)(0.5)] \end{Bmatrix}$$

$$= \begin{pmatrix} 0.56 & 0.44 \\ 0.55 & 0.45 \end{pmatrix}$$

Thus, $p_{12}^{(3)} = 0.444$ represents the probability that there is an audit three years from now given that there was no audit in the current year.

For the conditional probabilities four years into the future, we simply evaluate $\mathbf{P}^4$ by taking $\mathbf{P}^3 \cdot \mathbf{P}$ or $\mathbf{P}^2 \cdot \mathbf{P}^2$. In general, so-called *k-step transition probabilities* for k time periods into the future (which we label as $p_{ij}^{(k)}$) are determined by calculating $\mathbf{P}^k$.

Notice that the $p_{11}^{(2)} = 0.56$ and $p_{11}^{(3)} = 0.556$ transient probabilities which were determined in the previous section for years 12 and 13 (two and three years beyond the current year given by year 10) are readily located in cell 1, 1 of $\mathbf{P}^2$ and $\mathbf{P}^3$, respectively.

FOLLOW-UP EXERCISES

22. Why must *each row* of $\mathbf{P}^k$ sum to unity?
23. Confirm the probability for year 14 requested in Exercise 18 by calculating $\mathbf{P}^4$. Label this probability using $p_{ij}^{(k)}$ notation.
24. Use matrix multiplication to answer (*a*) Exercise 19, (*b*) Exercise 20, and (*c*) Exercise 21. Does the matrix approach readily provide more information than the classical approach? Illustrate for any one of the problems in parts *a*, *b*, or *c*.

Unconditional versus Conditional Probabilities

In the preceding section, $p_{ij}^{(k)}$ was defined as the k-step transition probability between states i and j. Just as in the case of the one-step transition probability (p_{ij}), this probability is a *conditional* probability because the probability of state j after the Markov chain goes through k transitions is statistically dependent on the initial state i. If the *unconditional* or *absolute* probability of state j after k transitions ($u_j^{(k)}$) is desired, then the following product must be determined:

$$\mathbf{u}^{(k)} = \mathbf{u}^{(o)} \cdot \mathbf{P}^k \tag{14.3}$$

where $\mathbf{u}^{(k)} = [u_1^{(k)} u_2^{(k)} \ldots u_n^{(k)}]$ is the row vector of unconditional probabilities for all n states after k transitions, $\mathbf{u}^{(o)}$ is the row vector of *initial* unconditional probabilities, and $\mathbf{P}$ is the one-step transition matrix.

▶ Example 14.6 Market Share Prediction

In the brand-switching model, the column totals in Table 14–1 represent market shares for the current week (week 27). Alternatively, we can say that the absolute probability is 125/500 (or 0.25) that a consumer selected at random (from among the 500 in the sample) has purchased brand 1 in the current week. Similarly, the unconditional probabilities that brands 2 and 3 were purchased in the current week are 0.46 and 0.29, respectively. These probabilities represent the initial unconditional probabilities, so

$$\mathbf{u}^{(o)} = (0.25 \quad 0.46 \quad 0.29)\,.$$

To predict market shares for, say, week 29 (i.e., two weeks into the future), we simply apply Equation (14.3) with $k = 2, \mathbf{u}^{(o)}$ as above, and $\mathbf{P}$ as given by Table 14–2:

$$\mathbf{u}^{(2)} = (0.25 \quad 0.46 \quad 0.29) \cdot \begin{pmatrix} 0.90 & 0.07 & 0.03 \\ 0.02 & 0.82 & 0.16 \\ 0.20 & 0.12 & 0.68 \end{pmatrix}^2$$

$$= (0.25 \quad 0.46 \quad 0.29) \cdot \begin{pmatrix} 0.8174 & 0.1240 & 0.0586 \\ 0.0664 & 0.6930 & 0.2406 \\ 0.3184 & 0.1940 & 0.4876 \end{pmatrix}$$

$$= (0.32723 \quad 0.40604 \quad 0.26673)\,.$$

Thus the expected market shares two weeks hence are 32.723 percent for brand 1, 40.604 percent for brand 2, and 26.673 percent for brand 3.

FOLLOW-UP EXERCISES

25. Interpret the elements in column 1 (0.8174, 0.0664, and 0.3184) of $\mathbf{P}^2$.
26. Calculate expected market shares three weeks into the future by
    a. Utilizing $\mathbf{u}^{(o)}$ and the fact that $\mathbf{P}^3 = \mathbf{P}^2 \cdot \mathbf{P}$, where $\mathbf{P}^2$ has already been determined.
    b. Taking the product of $\mathbf{u}^{(2)}$ and $\mathbf{P}$. Which approach is easier?
27. Show that, in general,

$$\mathbf{u}^{(k)} = \mathbf{u}^{(k-1)} \cdot \mathbf{P}\,. \tag{14.4}$$

28. Suppose that the transition matrix in the IRS problem was based on a sample of homogeneous taxpayers. Calculate the proportion of taxpayers that will be audited (*a*) next year, (*b*) two years from now, and (*c*) four years from now, if we have knowledge that the number of taxpayers audited in the current year was 10 percent.
29. For the hospital administration problem, determine $\mathbf{u}^{(2)}$ given that $\mathbf{u}^{(o)} =$ (0.3 0.4 0.2 0.1). Interpret $\mathbf{u}^{(2)}$ and compare to $\mathbf{u}^{(o)}$.

Steady-State Solutions

To illustrate the nature of steady-state (time-independent) probabilities in Markov chains, consider the calculations in Table 14–6 for the IRS problem. First of all, focus on any $p_{ij}^{(k)}$ as k increases. For example, the series given by $p_{11} = 0.6$, $p_{11}^{(2)} = 0.56$, $p_{11}^{(3)} = 0.556$, $p_{11}^{(4)} = 0.5556$, and $p_{11}^{(5)} = 0.55556$ indicates that these transient probabilities change by smaller and smaller increments for each step. This implies that $p_{ij}^{(k)}$ is asymptotically approaching a steady-state value as k increases.

TABLE 14–6 *K*-Step Transition Matrices for IRS Problem

k	$\mathbf{P}^k$
1	$\begin{pmatrix} 0.6 & 0.4 \\ 0.5 & 0.5 \end{pmatrix}$
2	$\begin{pmatrix} 0.56 & 0.44 \\ 0.55 & 0.45 \end{pmatrix}$
3	$\begin{pmatrix} 0.556 & 0.444 \\ 0.555 & 0.445 \end{pmatrix}$
4	$\begin{pmatrix} 0.5556 & 0.4444 \\ 0.5555 & 0.4445 \end{pmatrix}$
5	$\begin{pmatrix} 0.55556 & 0.44444 \\ 0.55555 & 0.44445 \end{pmatrix}$

Now, focus on the rows of $\mathbf{P}^k$ as k increases. As you can see, the rows are becoming identical. For example, the rows of $\mathbf{P}^5$ are identical to four significant digits. This illustrates the interesting phenomenon that *the probability of any future state is becoming independent from its initial state* as we go further and further into the future. In addition, from our previous observation, this probability is converging to its steady-state value (u_j^*) either from above (if $p_{ij} > u_j^*$) or from below (if $p_{ij} < u_j^*$), as indicated in Figure 14–5.

Carefully note that the steady-state probability for state j indicates that the probability of finding the stochastic process in state j after a "large" number of transitions tends toward the value given by u_j^*. Since this tendency manifests itself regardless of initial states or initial probability distributions, it follows that u_j^* is an *unconditional* probability for state j.

From the preceding observation, we can conclude that absolute probabilities do not change once steady state is reached; hence, based on Equation 14.4, the following must be true:

$$\mathbf{u}^* = \mathbf{u}^* \cdot \mathbf{P} \tag{14.5}$$

where $\mathbf{u}^*$ is the row vector of n steady-state probabilities. This condition, together with the fact that the elements in $\mathbf{u}^*$ must sum to one, that is,

$$\sum_{j=1}^{n} u_j^* = 1, \tag{14.6}$$

allows us to readily calculate steady-state probabilities, as we now illustrate.

FIGURE 14–5 Transient Probability Asymptotically Approaches Steady-State Probability

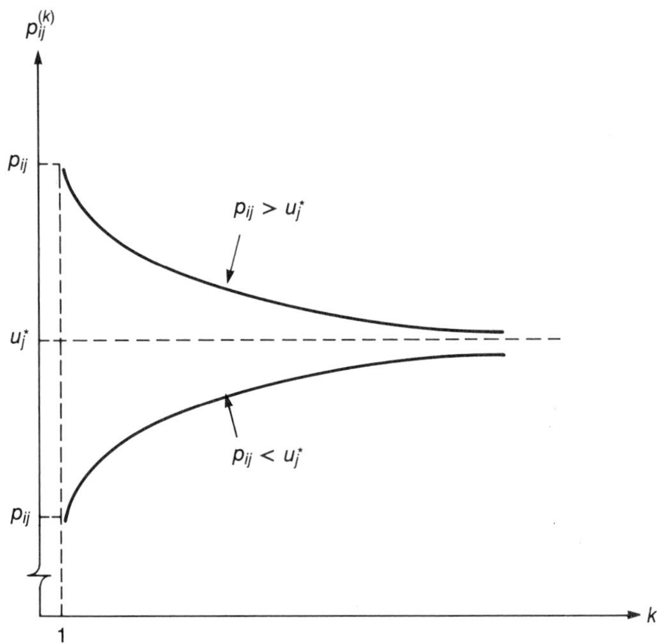

▶ Example 14.7 Steady-State Market Shares

Applying Equation 14.5 to the brand-switching model, we get

$$(u_1^* \quad u_2^* \quad u_3^*) = (u_1^* \quad u_2^* \quad u_3^*) \cdot \begin{pmatrix} 0.90 & 0.07 & 0.03 \\ 0.02 & 0.82 & 0.16 \\ 0.20 & 0.12 & 0.68 \end{pmatrix},$$

which translates into three equations in three unknowns after multiplication:[6]

$$u_1^* = 0.90u_1^* + 0.02u_2^* + 0.20u_3^* \quad (1)$$

$$u_2^* = 0.07u_1^* + 0.82u_2^* + 0.12u_3^* \quad (2)$$

$$u_3^* = 0.03u_1^* + 0.16u_2^* + 0.68u_3^* . \quad (3)$$

Furthermore, from Equation 14.6, the following must be true:

$$u_1^* + u_2^* + u_3^* = 1 . \quad (4)$$

This gives a total of four equations in three unknowns. Since $\mathbf{u}^* = (0 \quad 0 \quad 0)$ represents a trivial solution to Equations 1 through 3 which is invalidated by Equation 4, it

[6]Note that the product given by $\mathbf{u}^* \cdot \mathbf{P}$ results in a (1×3) matrix, which is then equated to $\mathbf{u}^*$ according to Equation 14.5. Equating term by term gives the first three simultaneous equations. In general, this procedure provides n simultaneous equations in n unknowns.

follows that there is one redundant equation among the first three. Arbitrarily discarding Equation 3 and solving Equations 1, 2, and 4 simultaneously, we get (to three significant digits) $u_1^* = 0.474$, $u_2^* = 0.321$, and $u_3^* = 0.205$.

These results indicate that, over time, the market share of brand 1 will increase from its present value of 0.25 (see Example 14.6) to its long-run stable value of 0.474. The market shares of brands 2 and 3 will erode, respectively, from 0.46 to 0.321 and from 0.29 to 0.205. Therefore, if present conditions continue, we can expect market share gains for brand 1 at the expense of losses for the other two brands. Note, however, that under steady-state conditions customers will continue to switch according to the stationary transition matrix. It is the absolute probabilities (market shares) that will change over time and finally stabilize.

Two points are in order at this time. First, steady-state predictions are never achieved in actual practice because of a combination of (1) error in estimating **P**, (2) changes in **P** over time, and (3) changes in the nature of dependence relationships among states; however, the use of steady-state values is an important diagnostic tool for the decision maker.

Second, not all transition matrices lend themselves to the analysis of steady-state properties as presented here. In fact, steady-state probabilities may not exist for certain types of Markov chains. If a Markov chain is **ergodic**, however, then u_j^* as the limit of $p_{ij}^{(k)}$ will exist; that is,

$$u_j^* = \lim_{k \to \infty} p_{ij}^{(k)}$$

is guaranteed. Basically, a Markov chain is ergodic if the process allows the achievement of any future state from any initial state after one or more transitions. For example, consider the following two matrices:

$$\mathbf{P}_1 = \begin{pmatrix} 0.4 & 0 & 0.6 \\ 0.3 & 0.3 & 0.4 \\ 0 & 0.5 & 0.5 \end{pmatrix}$$

and

$$\mathbf{P}_2 = \begin{pmatrix} 0.7 & 0 & 0 & 0.3 \\ 0.2 & 0.2 & 0.4 & 0.2 \\ 0.6 & 0.1 & 0.1 & 0.2 \\ 0.2 & 0 & 0 & 0.8 \end{pmatrix}$$

$\mathbf{P}_1$ is checked as follows. If state 1 is the initial state, then state 3 can be reached after one transition but not state 2; however, state 2 can be reached once state 3 is reached. Therefore any state can be achieved from an initial state given by state 1. If the initial state is state 2, then any state can be achieved after one transition. Finally, if state 3 is the initial state, then state 2 can be achieved after one transition, but not state 1. Once state 2 is achieved, however, state 1 can be achieved. Thus the chain described by $\mathbf{P}_1$ is ergodic, since it is possible for the process to go from any one state to any other state. Using the same reasoning along with Figure 14–6, determine why the chain described by $\mathbf{P}_2$ is *not* ergodic. What does this imply about steady state conditions?

FIGURE 14–6 Lily Pad Representation of Nonergodic Transition Matrix, $\mathbf{P}_2$

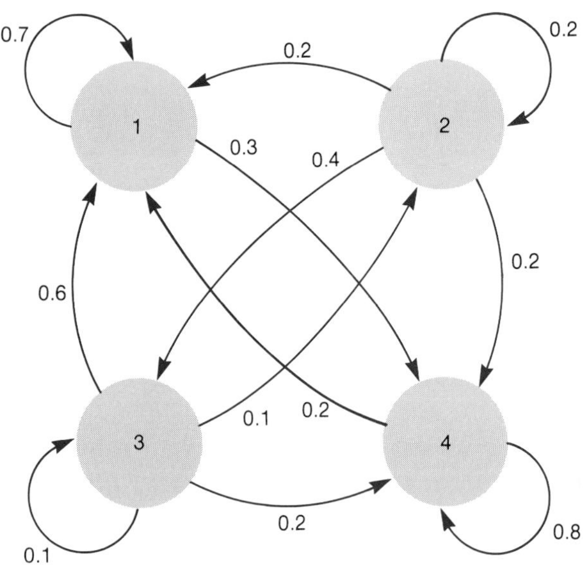

FOLLOW-UP EXERCISES

30. Confirm the calculations for $\boldsymbol{u}^*$ in Example 14.7.
31. Calculate steady-state probabilities for the IRS example. Interpret their meaning.
32. The nearly identical rows of $\mathbf{P}^5$ in Table 14–6 indicate the irrelevancy of initial states with respect to the probabilities of states far enough into the future. For the IRS example, demonstrate the long-run irrelevancy of initial absolute probability distributions by comparing $\mathbf{u}^5$ using $\mathbf{u}^{(o)} = (0.9\ 0.1)$ in Equation 14.3 against $\mathbf{u}^{(5)}$ using $\mathbf{u}^{(0)} = (0.1\ 0.9)$ in Equation 14.3. Compare $\mathbf{u}^{(5)}$ to $\mathbf{u}^*$. Conclusions?
33. The Markov chain described in the hospital administration model is not ergodic. Can you answer why? Certain long-run properties (e.g., expected number of time periods before absorption) for this type of chain can be analyzed by other procedures. Show that $\mathbf{u}^* = (0\quad 0\quad 0\quad 1)$ for this problem. Interpret this result.
34. Show what happens when you try to calculate $\mathbf{u}^*$ for the nonergodic chain described by the transition matrix $\mathbf{P}_2$ above.
35. If a transition matrix $\mathbf{P}$ has all nonzero entries, then does it necessarily describe an ergodic chain?

Computerized Analysis

Numerous software packages are available that perform Markov analysis. Figure 14–7 illustrates output from a Markov analysis module of a microcomputer-based management science software package.[7] Given the data from the brand-switching model (Examples 14.6 and 14.7), the output in Figure 14–7 illustrates the expected transient

[7] Laurie B. Dennis and Terry L. Dennis, *Microcomputer Models for Management Decision Making: Software and Text*, (St. Paul, Minn.: West Publishing, 1986).

FIGURE 14–7 Computerized Analysis for Brand-Switching Example

```
                    * * * * * * * * * * * * * * * * * * * * *
                    *                                       *
                    *          MARKOV ANALYSIS              *
                    *                                       *
                    * * * * * * * * * * * * * * * * * * * * *

HERE IS WHAT YOU ENTERED:

(0)  NUMBER OF STATES = 3

Transition Matrix:
       1       2       3
     ----------------
(1)  .9      .07     .03
(2)  .02     .82     .16
(3)  .2      .12     .68
     ----------------
(4)  TRANSITION (MARKET SHARE) ANALYSIS = Y
(5)  NUMBER OF TRIALS OR PERIODS = 2

Beginning Vector or Matrix:
       1       2       3
     ----------------
(6)  .25     .46     .29

OUTPUT SUMMARY:
TRANSITION MATRIX AFTER 1 TRIALS (PERIODS)

       1       2       3
     ----------------
1 :  .9      .07     .03
2 :  .02     .82     .16
3 :  .2      .12     .68
     ----------------

RESULTING VECTOR (MATRIX) - AFTER 1 PERIODS:

.292      .43      .278

TRANSITION MATRIX AFTER 2 TRIALS (PERIODS)

       1       2       3
     ----------------
1 :  .817    .124    .059
2 :  .066    .693    .241
3 :  .318    .194    .488
     ----------------

RESULTING VECTOR (MATRIX) - AFTER 2 PERIODS:

.327      .406      .267

STEADY STATE PROBABILITIES:

       1       2       3
     ----------------
     .474    .321    .205
     ----------------
```

behavior in the market. The expected market shares for each of the next two weeks (weeks 28 and 29), the matrix of k-step (two-week) transition probabilities, as well as the steady state probabilities are provided. Compare these results with those obtained in Examples 14.6 and 14.7.

14.5 MARKOVIAN DECISION MODELS

This section explicitly incorporates decision making in a Markovian framework. We begin by introducing concepts that relate criteria, decisions, and policies; thereafter, we illustrate solutions by enumeration and discuss more advanced optimization procedures.

Decision-Making Framework

Assume that a specific *discrete decision* (D_m) is made for period t which, when coupled with the *realized state* (X_t), results in a value for some *criterion*, $Z(D_m, X_t)$. In other words, a criterion of interest to the decision maker (e.g., cost, profit) is affected both by the state of a Markov process and by a decision that has been (or is to be) made. A **policy** (Q) is a statement or *decision rule* that specifies a *specific* decision for *each* possible state. For example, if $(D_1, D_2, \ldots, D_M)$ represents the set of decisions of interest, then a policy would assign a specific decision (D_1 or D_2 or $\cdots$ or D_M) to each possible value of the state variable.

Given a state that has just been observed (X_{t-1}) and a set of defined policies $(Q_1, Q_2, \ldots, Q_L)$, the problem is to determine the policy that optimizes the criterion.

In general, the Markov process given by $\{X_t\}$ now develops over time as a result of both probability laws (Markovian property) and decisions. Observed states, however, need not be affected by decisions. Furthermore, transition probabilities may or may not be affected by actions of the decision maker. Finally, the number of decision alternatives (M) may or may not be affected by the state of the system.

▶ Example 14.8 IRS Decision Problem

For our IRS problem, suppose you are considering two decisions: *Hire* (D_1) or *do not hire* (D_2) a "top flight" certified public accountant (CPA) to prepare your return for the current year. Suppose it costs \$250 to hire a CPA. It is widely held that the IRS usually collects "back taxes" whenever it audits a return. According to past records, if the return has been prepared by a CPA, the average collection of back taxes is \$50 when a return is audited. However, if the audited return has not been prepared by a CPA, then the taxpayer has had to pay average back taxes of \$500.

Our dilemma is to identify a policy (decision rule) regarding the hiring of a CPA so as to minimize expected annual costs. In order to provide some structure to this example, let us return to our problem-solving framework.

1. **Verbal Statement of Problem.**
   Determine the CPA hiring policy that minimizes expected annual costs.

2. **Decisions.**
   a. **Verbal Statement.**
   Given the Markovian nature of the audit process, we assume that our decisions to hire or not hire a CPA depend on the state of the system (whether or not there was an audit) in the preceding year. Thus our decision variable is the rule that decides whether or not to hire a CPA in year t given $X_{t-1} = 0$ (no audit in previous year) or $X_{t-1} = 1$ (audit in previous year).
   b. **Mathematical Definition.**
   Table 14–7 indicates the four possible policies for this problem. Each policy specifies a decision hire (D_1) or do not hire (D_2) depending on the audit outcome from the previous year. For example, Q_1 specifies that a CPA is not to be hired in year t if no audit was performed in year $t - 1$; a CPA is to be hired in year t if an audit was performed in year $t - 1$. The philosophy underlying the policy suggests that if they got you last year, there's an increased chance they will come after you again the next year. However, if they did not audit last year, chances increase that they will not the next. Can you verbalize Q_2, Q_3, and Q_4 and suggest an underlying philosophy for each?

TABLE 14–7 Policies for IRS Problem

	State from Preceding Year	
Policy	$X_{t-1} = 0$ **(no audit)**	$X_{t-1} = 1$ **(audit)**
Q_1	D_2 (don't hire)	D_1 (hire)
Q_2	D_1 (hire)	D_2 (don't hire)
Q_3	D_1 (hire)	D_1 (hire)
Q_4	D_2 (don't hire)	D_2 (don't hire)

3. **Criteria.**
   a. **Verbal Statement.**
   Expected annual costs that equal the sum of *back taxes* paid as a result of an audit and *costs of a CPA.*
   b. **Mathematical Statement.**
   For any policy, the expected annual costs in year t are a function of the decision to hire or not hire a CPA and the actual audit experience in year t. Table 14–8 illustrates possible values for the cost criterion (Z). For example, if a CPA is hired (D_1) and this year's return is audited ($X_t = 1$), then $Z(D_1, 1) = 300$, or it costs the taxpayer \$300 (\$250 for the CPA and \$50 to the IRS). See if you can account for the other values in Table 14–8.

TABLE 14–8 $Z(D_m, X_t)$ for IRS Problem

	State	
Decision	$X_t = 0$	$X_t = 1$
D_1	250	300
D_2	0	500

4. **Constraints.**
   None.

5. **Model.**

   With this particular type of analysis, we don't necessarily have a model statement of the form found in the mathematical programming chapters. We might, for this problem, state our model as

   Minimize

$$E[Z_L(D_m, X_t)], \qquad L = 1, 2, 3, 4$$

   where $E[Z_L(D_m, X_t)]$ is the expected annual cost associated with policy Q_L.

In this problem we assume that decisions in any one year affect neither states nor transient probabilities. In the next section, we illustrate the determination of an optimal policy for this problem.

Solution by Complete Enumeration

When the number of policies is small, a practical solution procedure involves the evaluation of expected values for the criterion for each possible policy. In this case, we find that the "optimal" policy is that policy (from among those enumerated) which yields the most favorable expected value for the criterion *per unit time, assuming the existence of steady-state probabilities*. If criteria are based on cash flows (e.g., costs, profits, revenues), a popular alternative is to optimize the discounted total flow.

▶ Example 14.9 Solution of IRS Decision Problem

In Exercise 31 you should have confirmed that $u_1^* = 5/9$ and $u_2^* = 4/9$. This means that in the long run 5/9 of the time there will *not* be an audit, and 4/9 of the time there will be an audit. Now consider policy Q_1 according to Table 14–7. Based on the long-run probabilities, it follows that 5/9 of the time decision D_2 (do not hire CPA) is made, and 4/9 of the time decision D_1 (hire CPA) is made. From the transition matrix,

$$\mathbf{P} = \begin{pmatrix} 0.6 & 0.4 \\ 0.5 & 0.5 \end{pmatrix}$$

TABLE 14–9 Expected Cost per Year for Policy Q_1

X_{t-1}	Verbal Joint Event	Symbolic Joint Event	Joint Probability	Cost	Expected Cost
0 (No audit year $t-1$)	Do not hire CPA and no audit in year t	D_2 and $X_t = 0$	$(5/9) \cdot (0.6) = 3/9$	0	$(3/9) \cdot (0)$
	Do not hire CPA and audit in year t	D_2 and $X_t = 1$	$(5/9) \cdot (0.4) = 2/9$	500	$(2/9) \cdot (500)$
1 (Audit year $t-1$)	Hire CPA and no audit in year t	D_1 and $X_t = 0$	$(4/9) \cdot (0.5) = 2/9$	250	$(2/9) \cdot (250)$
	Hire CPA and audit in year t	D_1 and $X_t = 1$	$(4/9) \cdot (0.5) = 2/9$	300	$(2/9) \cdot (300)$
	Total		9/9		2100/9 = \$233.33 per year

we know that given no audit in the preceding year (which for policy Q_1 is the same as saying "given decision D_2") the probability of no audit in year t is 0.6; hence, the long-run probability of no audit in the preceding year ($X_{t-1} = 0$) *and* no audit in the subsequent year ($X_t = 0$) is (5/9) · (0.6), or 3/9. Since under these circumstances decision D_2 will have been made and no audit will have occurred, it follows that a cost of zero dollars will have resulted according to $Z(D_2, 0) = 0$ in Table 14–8. A cost of \$500 will be incurred with probability (5/9) · (0.4), or 2/9, if D_2 is coupled with an audit in year t.

Table 14–9 summarizes for policy Q_1 the four possible joint events, their probabilities, and their costs. If policy Q_1 were to be adopted, then the expected (long-run) cost per year would be \$233.33. (Why must the sum of the joint probabilities always equal unity?)

Table 14–10 summarizes the calculations for the remaining policies Q_2, Q_3, and Q_4. (Can you verbalize the joint events and confirm their probabilities and costs by referencing Tables 14–7 and 14–8?) Based on this long-run criterion (expected cost per year), the best policy is Q_4 (never hire a CPA).

TABLE 14–10 Expected Costs per Year for Policies Q_2, Q_3, and Q_4

Policy	X_{t-1}	Joint Event	Joint Probability	Cost	Expected Cost
Q_2	0 (No audit year $t-1$)	D_1 and $X_t = 0$	$(5/9) \cdot (0.6) = 3/9$	250	750/9
		D_1 and $X_t = 1$	$(5/9) \cdot (0.4) = 2/9$	300	600/9
	1 (Audit year $t-1$)	D_2 and $X_t = 0$	$(4/9) \cdot (0.5) = 2/9$	0	0/9
		D_2 and $X_t = 1$	$(4/9) \cdot (0.5) = 2/9$	500	1000/9
Total			9/9		2350/9 = \$261.11 per year
Q_3	0 (No audit year $t-1$)	D_1 and $X_t = 0$	$(5/9) \cdot (0.6) = 3/9$	250	750/9
		D_1 and $X_t = 1$	$(5/9) \cdot (0.4) = 2/9$	300	600/9
	1 (Audit year $t-1$)	D_1 and $X_t = 0$	$(4/9) \cdot (0.5) = 2/9$	250	500/9
		D_1 and $X_t = 1$	$(4/9) \cdot (0.5) = 2/9$	300	600/9
Total			9/9		2450/9 = \$272.22 per year
Q_4	0 (No audit year $t-1$)	D_2 and $X_t = 0$	$(5/9) \cdot (0.6) = 3/9$	0	0
		D_2 and $X_t = 1$	$(5/9) \cdot (0.4) = 2/9$	500	1000/9
	1 (Audit year $t-1$)	D_2 and $X_t = 0$	$(4/9) \cdot (0.5) = 2/9$	0	0
		D_2 and $X_t = 1$	$(4/9) \cdot (0.5) = 2/9$	500	1000/9
Total			9/9		2000/9 = \$222.22 per year

FOLLOW-UP EXERCISES

36. Suppose that, in addition to the costs depicted in Table 14–8, a benefit of \$100 is realized when a CPA prepares a return. In other words, with the CPA's expert

knowledge you pay $100 less than what you would have paid if you had prepared the return yourself. Appropriately modify Table 14–8.

37. Determine the optimal policy for Exercise 36.

▶ Example 14.10 Brand Switching Problem

According to Table 14–1, brand 2 has a 50 percent market share in week 26; however, if present conditions were to continue, as represented by the transition matrix

$$\mathbf{P} = \begin{pmatrix} 0.90 & 0.07 & 0.03 \\ 0.02 & 0.82 & 0.16 \\ 0.20 & 0.12 & 0.68 \end{pmatrix},$$

then its long-run market share will slip to 32.1 percent according to the calculation for u_2^* in Example 14.7. Suppose that two promotion campaigns (A and B) are under consideration for reversing this trend:

Campaign A. Aims to achieve 90 percent retention of its customers (holding power) by reducing the attractive power that brand 3 has on brand 2 customers (i.e., aims to increase p_{22} from 0.82 to 0.90 and simultaneously decrease p_{23} from 0.16 to 0.08)

Campaign B. Aims to increase by half the attractive power of brand 2 for brand 3 customers at the expense of brand 1 (i.e., aims to increase p_{32} from 0.12 to 0.18 and decrease p_{31} from 0.20 to 0.14).

A marketing research study shows that **P** is representative of a potential market of 50 million customers. Exclusive of additional promotion, each customer represents a potential profit of $0.50 per week. What decision should be made by the company if the cost of A is $500,000 per week and the cost of B is $400,000 per week?

Since states (X_t) for this process are based on individual consumer behavior and **P** is based on aggregate behavior, it should be evident that X_{t-1} is not a factor for defining policies. In this case, therefore, policies and decisions are essentially synonymous. Let

$Q_1 \equiv D_1 \equiv$ No additional promotion campaign.
$Q_2 \equiv D_2 \equiv$ Undertake Campaign A.
$Q_3 \equiv D_3 \equiv$ Undertake Campaign B.
$Z(D_m) \equiv$ Long-run profit per week when decision D_m is made.

This problem, then, illustrates a situation wherein the most recent state (X_{t-1}) has no bearing on a policy, yet decisions affect transition probabilities and consequently affect the evolution of the stochastic process over time. We solve this problem next with the help of work that you will do in Exercises 38 and 39.

FOLLOW-UP EXERCISES

38. For the brand switching problem:
   a. State **P** and determine $\mathbf{u}^*$ for Q_2.
   b. State **P** and determine $\mathbf{u}^*$ for Q_3.
   Compare effects on long-run market shares relative to Q_1.

39. Let Q_4 represent a policy to undertake both promotion campaigns. If the effects of these campaigns are independent of each other, state **P** and determine $\mathbf{u}^*$. Compare to the preceding exercise.

▶ Example 14.11. Solution of Brand Switching Problem

In Example 14.10, three policies were enumerated. Table 14–11 shows the transition matrix and corresponding steady-state market shares for each policy. (Did you confirm **u*** for Q_2 and Q_3 in Exercise 38?) In Table 14–11, the transition probabilities affected by the two campaigns are circled. If we assume that (1) the effect of a promotion campaign on **P** is immediate, but weekly promotion expenditures must be continued to maintain the new **P**; and (2) prices, costs, size of potential market, and transition probabilities are all static and known with certainty, then the expected steady-state value of the criterion (profit per week) for policy Q_i is given by $Z(Q_i)$ = Expected market share for brand 2) × (Size of potential market) × (Marginal profit per week) − (Promotional expenditures per week).

TABLE 14–11 P and u* for Stated Policies

Policy	P	u*
Q_1	$\begin{pmatrix} 0.90 & 0.07 & 0.03 \\ 0.02 & 0.82 & 0.16 \\ 0.20 & 0.12 & 0.68 \end{pmatrix}$	(0.474 0.321 0.205)
Q_2	$\begin{pmatrix} 0.90 & 0.07 & 0.03 \\ 0.02 & \textcircled{0.90} & \textcircled{0.08} \\ 0.20 & 0.12 & 0.68 \end{pmatrix}$	(0.393 0.456 0.151)
Q_3	$\begin{pmatrix} 0.90 & 0.07 & 0.03 \\ 0.02 & 0.82 & 0.16 \\ \textcircled{0.14} & \textcircled{0.18} & 0.68 \end{pmatrix}$	(0.393 0.380 0.227)

Table 14–12 summarizes the calculations. Accordingly, policy Q_2 should be undertaken, which is to say that promotion campaign A yields the highest expected profit per week.

TABLE 14–12 Expected Values of Criterion for Stated Policies

Policy	Long-Run Profit per Week, $Z(Q_i)$
Q_1	(0.321) · (50,000,000) · (0.5) − 0 = \$ 8,025,000 per week
Q_2	(0.456) · (50,000,000) · (0.5) − 500,000 = \$10,900,000 per week
Q_3	(0.380) · (50,000,000) · (0.5) − 400,000 = \$ 9,100,000 per week

FOLLOW-UP EXERCISES

40. Determine $Z(Q_4)$ based on your results in exercise 39. Compare to the policies in Table 14–12. Conclusion?

41. For the stock market model, consider two decisions: Sell a share at the beginning of the trading day or buy a share at the beginning of the trading day. Now consider two policies: (1) Sell if the closing price from the preceding day increased or remained the same from its opening price on that day; buy if it declined; (2) buy if

the closing price from the preceding day increased or remained the same from its opening price on that day; sell if it declined.

a. Construct a Q_l v. X_{t-1} table.

b. From Table 14–6, determine the average price increase per day for the days when the stock closed up. Determine the average price decrease per day for the days when the stock closed down. Define your criterion in terms of gains or losses per share per day due to price changes. Construct a table for $Z(D_m, X_t)$.

c. Can you define additional policies? Can decisions affect **P** or X_t?

d. Determine the optimal policy based on **P** in (*a*) Exercise 15 and (*b*) Exercise 16.

14.6 ASSESSMENT

The simple fact that models of stochastic processes directly address an uncertain environment lends value and credibility to such approaches. For this reason alone, applications in economics and the social and physical sciences have been widespread.

As with all OR/MS modeling, however, problems arise in the divergence between the theoretical model and the real process itself. Since all models necessarily rely on assumptions for their derivations, it follows that analysts must assess the degree of this divergence by appropriate tests in inferential statistics. Specifically, for Markov chains, the goodness of the model should be assessed by appropriate tests for (1) stationarity, (2) the Markovian property, and (3) homogeneity (where applicable). All too often these assumptions are not tested.

Other problems that arise in implementation include the need for substantial data estimation and the cost of convergence for large-scale decision processes. Current research is alleviating the latter problem. Unfortunately, for many applications, the collection of adequate data is either too costly or impossible. In part, data collection is facilitated for consumer behavior applications (e.g., brand switching) by the existence of established consumer panels. In other cases, the existence of large data banks reduces the cost of data collection. In financial applications, for example, COMPUSTAT and CRSP tapes provide a wealth of time-series data for corporations and industries.

Another issue relates to the relevancy of long-run assumptions for decision problems. For example, stationarity and equilibrium are never really achieved for brand-switching models, because such markets are dynamic as a result of changing competitive strategies and changing consumer preferences. Even under these conditions, however, the use of equilibrium criteria is widespread. This leads us to conclude that equilibrium approaches appear to be valid diagnostic tools for making decisions.

Actual implementation of the results of Markov analysis has not been as widespread as with other modeling techniques, such as math programming. A recently published survey of reported Markov studies found that relatively few had directly implemented results.[8] Several of the studies, however, reported that although no

[8]Douglas J. White, "Real Applications of Markov Decision Processes," *Interfaces*, November–December 1985, pp. 73–83.

direct implementation of results had occurred, the process of analysis had proved beneficial. In some studies, the process resulted in better understanding of the problem and guidance in redirecting further analysis. The study also revealed an increase in the number of efforts to model phenomena as Markov decision processes, with a combined simulation-Markov approach holding the greatest promise.

SELECTED APPLICATION REVIEW

HIGHWAY MAINTENANCE

The Arizona Department of Transportation is responsible for the design, construction, preservation, and maintenance of a road network that consists of more than 7,400 miles of highways. The Arizona Pavement Management System was developed as a decision-making tool to help the state maintain its roads. At the core of the system is a mathematical model that recommends maintenance policies for achieving both short-term and long-term objectives at the lowest possible cost. At the core of this "hybrid" model is a Markov submodel having transition probabilities linking current road conditions and maintenance actions to future road conditions. The Markov model is linked to a linear programming model that determines optimal solutions.

The new system has changed the pavement decision-making process from a subjective nonquantitative method to one that is scientifically based. During the first year of implementation the system saved $14 million in maintenance funds. The forecasted savings over the next four years was estimated at $101 million.

Logo reproduced courtesy of the Arizona Department of Transportation.

SOURCE: Kamal Golabi, Ram B. Kulkarni, and George B. Way, "A Statewide Pavement Management System," *Interfaces*, December 1982, pp. 5–21.

VEHICLE REPLACEMENT

A vehicle replacement policy was developed for the British Army's nonarmored wheeled vehicles. At the time of the study, this group consisted of approximately 60,000 vehicles of 500 different types. The optimal policy specifies "repair limits" that consider a set of factors including the age of the vehicle and its cost. When a vehicle needs a repair that costs more than the

(continued)

predetermined repair limit, the vehicle is replaced rather than repaired. The repair limits may be adjusted to reflect exceptionally low or high mileage. A key part of the model is the assumption that the age of a vehicle follows a stochastic process. Specifically, the process is assumed Markovian between states. States, in this instance, refer to the age of the vehicle. When a vehicle is placed in service ($t = 0$), the process enters state 1. If a vehicle survives one year, the process enters state 2. If a vehicle is replaced by a new one, the process returns to state 1. Combining the Markovian assumption with dynamic programming to calculate optimal repair limits, significant savings were expected in the costs of owning and maintaining this group of vehicles.

SOURCE: B. H. Mahon and R. J. M. Bailey, "A Proposed Improved Replacement Policy for Army Vehicles," *Operational Research Quarterly* 26, no. 3, (1975) pp. 477–94.

MARKETING STRATEGIES

Hauser and Wisniewski provide an excellent analysis of consumer response to marketing strategies. Using a semi-Markov analysis, such responses as market penetration and expected sales to promotional campaigns are predicted. In a semi-Markov process, the time between a consumer's transitions is a random variable with density function dependent on the state the consumer is in prior to the transition. Aside from allowing the time between transitions to be random, all else remains the same as in a Markov process.

The authors examine the analgesics Bayer, Excedrin, and Tylenol. The brand-switching process among these creates some complex patterns. Because Tylenol contains no aspirin, switchers from the aspirin-based Bayer may be more likely to move to Excedrin, which also contains aspirin. Limited time offers and the relative strengths of the products may affect the time between purchases. A stronger product may last longer, and consumers might purchase earlier if they get a special offer. In fact a special offer can be considered a separate state so that we think of six states for the last purchase: Bayer-regular, Bayer-offer, Excedrin-regular, Excedrin-offer, and so on. The transition matrix of interest becomes a six by six.

At the time of publication, the authors' methodology had been applied twice—once to the launch of a new transportation service and once to the

(continued)

purchase of ground coffee. In the transportation application, a village in Illinois initiated a demand-actuated transportation service called DART. Using their methodology, the authors were able to predict ridership with a correlation of 0.83 between predicted and actual ridership.

SOURCE: John R. Hauser and Kenneth J. Wisniewski, "Dynamic Analysis of Consumer Response to Marketing Strategies," *Management Science*, May 1982, pp. 455–86.

SELECTED REFERENCES

Albright, S. C., and W. Winston. "Markov Models of Advertising and Pricing Decisions." *Operations Research*, July–August 1979, pp. 668–81.

Chapman, C. B., and D. F. Cooper. "Risk Engineering: Basic Controlled Internal and Memory Models." *Journal of the Operational Research Society*, January 1983, pp. 51–60.

Grassman, W. K. *Stochastic Systems for Management*. New York: Elsevier North-Holland, 1981.

Hillier, Frederick S., and Gerald J. Lieberman. *Introduction to Operations Research*. 3rd ed. San Francisco: Holden-Day, 1980.

Howard, R. *Dynamic Programming and Markov Processes*. Cambridge, Mass: MIT Press, 1960.

Kallberg, J. G., and A. Saunders. "Markov Chain Approaches to the Analysis of Payment Behavior of Retail Credit Customers." *Financial Management*, Summer 1983, pp. 5–14.

Kao, E. P. "Modeling the Movement of Coronary Patients within a Hospital by Semi-Markov Processes." *Operations Research*, July–August 1974, pp. 683–99.

Karlin, S. *A First Course in Stochastic Processes*. New York: Academic Press, 1966.

Parzen, E. *Stochastic Processes*. San Francisco: Holden-Day, 1962.

Ross, S. M. *Applied Probability Models with Optimization Applications*. San Francisco: Holden-Day, 1970.

Taha, H. A. *Operations Research: An Introduction*. 3rd ed. New York: Macmillan, 1982.

Urban, G. L. "SPRINTER Mod III: A Model for the Analysis of New Frequently Purchased Consumer Products." *Operations Research*. September–October 1970, pp. 805–53.

ADDITIONAL EXERCISES

42. Given the matrix of transition probabilities:

$$\mathbf{P} = \begin{pmatrix} 0.7 & 0.2 & 0.1 \\ 0.6 & 0.3 & 0.1 \\ 0.5 & 0.2 & 0.3 \end{pmatrix}$$

a. Specify whether or not this matrix could represent a Markov process.

b. Determine $\mathbf{P}^2$.
Explain the meaning of $\mathbf{P}^2$.

c. Determine the steady state probability vector.

43. ***Credit Ratings.*** A major bank evaluates the credit ratings of its credit card customers on a monthly basis. Customer credit ratings are evaluated as "poor," "good," and "excellent" depending on their payment histories. The following matrix of transition probabilities reflects the probabilities that a customer classified in one credit category during one month will be evaluated in a given category in the following month.

From \ To	Poor	Good	Excellent
Poor	0.80	0.18	0.02
Good	0.20	0.75	0.05
Excellent	0.00	0.16	0.84

a. Square the transition matrix and verbally interpret the elements.

b. Given an existing pool of 100,000 customers, is equilibrium possible in the distribution of credit ratings? If so, how many accounts would be classified in each category?

44. ***Brand Switching.*** Table 14–13 reflects the results of a recent survey of 750 consumers of a particular product.

TABLE 14–13

	Week 11 Brand			
Week 10 Brand	**1**	**2**	**3**	**Total**
1	216	12	12	240
2	36	306	18	360
3	6	18	126	150
Total	258	336	156	750

a. Construct the matrix of transition probabilities.

b. Using the data in Table 14–13, what were the market shares of the three products in week 11?

c. Predict the market shares for week 12. Week 14?

d. Determine the equilibrium market shares (if they exist).

45. ***Health Insurance.*** The personnel department for a large employer recently completed its annual reenrollment program for health insurance benefits. Three different health insurance options are offered: Blue Cross-Blue Shield, a health maintenance organization (HMO) plan, and a plan offered by the Wanderers Insurance Company. Table 14–14 summarizes the options selected this year versus options selected in the previous year.
If the data in Table 14–14 are representative of the general pattern of employee changes in preferences,

a. Construct the matrix of transition probabilities.

b. What are the current market shares for the three plans?

c. Predict the expected shares next year. The following year?

d. If the matrix of transition probabilities is raised to the fifth power, provide a general interpretation of the elements $p_{ij}^{(5)}$.

TABLE 14–14 Number of Employees Selecting Various Health Insurance Options

Option Selected Last Year	Option Selected This Year		
	BC/BS	HMO	Wanderers
BC/BS	6,400	800	800
HMO	200	4,750	50
Wanderers	300	300	1,400

e. Determine the equilibrium states (if they exist) for the percentage shares of the three health plans.

f. Critique the assumptions of equilibrium conditions.

46. ***Corrections System.*** The director of corrections for a state penitentiary has gathered data on the movements of people who have been convicted and admitted to the corrections system. The transition matrix in Table 14–15 summarizes the probabilities of various monthly movements. Notice that one possible movement is release from the system. Another possibility is reentry into the system.

TABLE 14–15

From \ To	High Security	Medium Security	Work Release	Halfway House	Release
High Security	0.70	0.30	0.00	0.00	0.00
Medium Security	0.10	0.60	0.15	0.05	0.10
Work Release	0.00	0.15	0.40	0.20	0.25
Halfway House	0.00	0.05	0.10	0.40	0.45
Released	0.02	0.08	0.00	0.10	0.80

Given a pool of 3,000 persons who have been admitted to the correction system, 600 are currently in the high-security section, 1,800 are in medium security, 200 participate in work release, 100 are in halfway houses, and 300 have been released.

a. For this pool, estimate the number expected to be in each program next month. The following month?

b. How many of these 3,000 persons will be in each program when the system is in equilibrium?

c. Estimate the number of months necessary to achieve equilibrium. (This can be achieved by using a computer package or writing a simple program to predict the distribution of convicts for future months.)

d. Construct a lily pad diagram for the transition matrix.

47. ***Dialysis Need-Projection.*** Markov models have been successfully applied to predict the need for kidney dialysis facilities.[9] The one-year transition matrix in Table 14–16 indicates five possible states for persons having potential need for dialysis therapy.

[9]See J. S. Pliskin and E. J. Tell, "Using a Dialysis Need-Projection Model for Health Planning in Massachusetts," *Interfaces*, December 1981, pp. 84–100.

TABLE 14–16

Year t \ Year $t+1$	Dialysis	T_2	LT	CT	Death
Dialysis	0.85	0	0	0	0.15
T_2	0.08	0.88	0	0	0.04
LT	0.20	0.75	0	0	0.05
CT	0.30	0.60	0	0	0.10
Death	0	0	0	0	1.00

The five possible states are those included in the dialysis pool, those who have lived more than one year with a transplanted kidney (T_2), those who are in their first year with a transplanted kidney from a living related donor (LT), those who are in their first year with a transplanted kidney from a cadaver, and those persons who have died.

a. Provide a verbal interpretation of the elements in the transition matrix.

b. Construct a lily pad type of diagram corresponding to the transition matrix.

c. Suppose of an original group of 1,000 persons, currently 600 are in dialysis, 100 have lived more than one year with a transplant, 80 are in their first year with a transplant from a living related donor, 120 are in their first year with a transplant from a cadaver, and 100 from the original group have died. Predict the number of persons expected to be in each state one year from now. Five years from now.

d. What are the equilibrium states expected to equal (if they exist)?

48. ***Air Pollution Control.*** A city classifies the air quality into eight categories. The probability of a given air quality on a particular day has been found to be conditional on the air quality for the previous day. Table 14–17 is a transition matrix for the eight categories. Determine whether or not equilibrium conditions exist and, if so, the expected number of days each year in which the air quality would be classified in each of the eight categories.

TABLE 14–17

Air Quality Day t \ Air Quality Day $t+1$	1	2	3	4	5	6	7	8
1	0.24	0.26	0.16	0.14	0.12	0.08	0	0
2	0.16	0.28	0.20	0.14	0.10	0.08	0.04	0
3	0.08	0.10	0.20	0.26	0.14	0.14	0.08	0
4	0	0.06	0.12	0.32	0.24	0.16	0.05	0.05
5	0	0.04	0.14	0.20	0.28	0.22	0.08	0.04
6	0	0	0.06	0.14	0.20	0.26	0.20	0.14
7	0	0	0.04	0.14	0.25	0.17	0.28	0.12
8	0	0	0	0.12	0.18	0.26	0.36	0.08

49. ***Accounts Receivable Control.*** Consider Table 14–18 based on the accounts (in millions) of Muster Charge, a nationally prominent credit card company. Of 10 million total

accounts, 5 million were 0–29 days past due on July 1. Of these 5 million, 3 million remained in the 0–29 status, and 2 million lapsed into the 30–59 category. Note that it is not possible in one month to go from 0–29 days past due to 60 or more days past due. Accounts remaining in the 0–29 category were paid on time (i.e., within 30 days). In actual practice, more past-due categories would exist.

TABLE 14–18

Days Past Due On July 1	Days Past Due on August 1			
	0–29	30–59	60+	Total
0–29	3.0	2.0	0.0	5.0
30–59	0.5	1.8	0.7	3.0
60+	0.6	0.8	0.6	2.0
Total	4.1	4.6	1.3	10.0

a. Predict the proportion of accounts in each category for September 1, October 1, and November 1. Show why this chain is ergodic. Predict the steady-state proportions, and interpret their meaning. (*Note*: Express the entries in **P** to two decimal places.)

b. What assumptions need to be realized for your predictions in part *a* to be valid?

c. A monthly total cost given by the sum of administrative cost, receivable carrying cost (including opportunity cost), and bad debt cost is associated with each account in each state. The estimated total costs (dollars per account per month) for the states 0–29, 30–59, and 60+ are, respectively, 2, 5, and 20. Predict monthly costs for the months ending on September 1, October 1, and November 1. Predict steady-state monthly costs. (Assume 10 million accounts throughout.)

****d.* Suppose that the company makes one of two decisions each month for customers in each state: "Do nothing other than the usual late notice" or "phone the customer." (Can you think of other alternatives in actual practice?) If the company selects the first decision, the *row* in the transition matrix *for that state* remains unaffected, and the expected cost per customer per month is the same as in part *d*. However, if the company phones the customer, the added expense of \$.50 per customer per month is incurred *and* that particular *row* of the transition matrix is altered as follows: Increase the 0–29 transition probability by 6 percentage points (i.e., by 0.06) and decrease all other nonzero entries uniformly. For example, row 2 of **P** would change from (0.17 0.60 0.23) to (0.23 0.57 0.20). Do you see the logic? Construct a Z-table and policy table for this problem and determine the policy that yields minimum expected (long-run) cost per month. (*Hint*: You must consider eight policies.)

50. ***Maintenance Model.* Markov processes have been applied to a wide variety of maintenance scenarios. To illustrate one approach, consider the following problem. Turbines in a power generating plant are inspected daily. At the end of each day, a turbine is classified into one of the following states: $X_{t-1} = 1$ if operating efficiently; $X_{t-1} = 2$ if operating inefficiently; and $X_{t-1} = 3$ if inoperable. The operating costs in day t for these states are estimated as \$100 per day, \$200 per day, and \$1,000 per day, respectively. The increased cost for state 3 reflects the higher operating cost of securing supplementary power from a regional combine of utility companies.

Current maintenance policy calls for "no repair" (D_1) in day t whenever state 1 or state 2 is observed the previous night (i.e., decision D_1 whenever $X_{t-1} = 1$ or $X_{t-1} = 2$) and "undertaking a major repair" (D_2) in day t whenever state 3 is observed the previous night (i.e., decision D_2 whenever $X_{t-1} = 3$). Assume that the major repair always takes one full day, is always successful in the sense of returning the turbine to state 1, and costs \$500. Note that when a turbine is being repaired, the daily cost for that turbine is \$1,500, or \$1,000 for auxiliary power and \$500 for the parts and labor associated with the repair.

The matrix for transitions between X_{t-1} and X_t is given by

$$\mathbf{P} = \begin{pmatrix} 0.8 & 0.2 & 0 \\ 0 & 0.9 & 0.1 \\ 1 & 0 & 0 \end{pmatrix}$$

Note that **P** is dependent on the policy. For example, row 3 indicates that if the machine is inoperable at the end of Day $t - 1$, then it is overhauled and will be operating efficiently by the end of day t; that is, if $X_{t-1} = 3$, then $X_t = 1$ with certainty.

a. What assumptions need to be realized for this problem to be modeled as a Markov chain? Is this chain ergodic? Explain.

b. In the long run, how many turbines will need repair per day on the average if the facility has 16 turbines?

c. Determine the expected cost per day for the current policy.

***d.* Determine the optimal policy by assessing all other possible policies. (*Hint*: For two decisions and three states there are eight possible policies; also note that **P** changes according to the policy.)

e. Can you think of other possible states and other possible decisions for this model?

51. Given the matrix of transition probabilities:

$$\mathbf{P} = \begin{pmatrix} 0.7 & 0.2 & 0.1 & 0 \\ 0.5 & 0.4 & 0 & 0.1 \\ 0 & 0 & 1 & 0 \\ 0 & 0 & 0 & 1 \end{pmatrix}$$

a. Determine whether or not **P** is ergodic.

b. State 3 (row 3) is termed an *absorbing* state. Why do you think this makes sense? What about state 4?

52. Given the matrix of transition probabilities:

$$\left(\begin{array}{cc|cc} 1 & 0 & 0 & 0 \\ 0 & 1 & 0 & 0 \\ \hline 0.1 & 0 & 0.7 & 0.2 \\ 0 & 0.1 & 0.5 & 0.4 \end{array}\right) = \left(\begin{array}{c|c} \mathbf{P}_1 & \mathbf{O} \\ \hline \mathbf{R} & \mathbf{Q} \end{array}\right)$$

where $\mathbf{P}_1$ is the matrix of recurrent states—those where eventual return to the original state is certain, **R** is the matrix of states with one-step transitions to the recurrent states, and **Q** is the matrix of transition states with probabilities of transition only among the transient states—transient states are those where the process *may* not eventually return to the original state.

a. Verify that the definitions hold for this example. Is an absorbing state a recurrent state? Construct an example of a recurrent state that is *not* absorbing.

b. The matrix in this problem is the canonical representation of the matrix in Exercise 51. Verify that the matrix in this problem is arranged so that the process can go from a given state to another in a preceding class, for example, class $\boldsymbol{R}$ to class $\boldsymbol{P}_1$, but *not* from a preceding class to a following class, for example, class $\boldsymbol{P}_1$ to class $\boldsymbol{Q}$.

**53. The *fundamental matrix* $\mathbf{M} = (\mathbf{I} - \mathbf{Q})^{-1}$ can be created from the matrices given in problem 50.

$$\mathbf{I} - \mathbf{Q} = \begin{bmatrix} 1 & 0 \\ 0 & 1 \end{bmatrix} - \begin{bmatrix} 0.7 & 0.2 \\ 0.5 & 0.4 \end{bmatrix}$$

$$\mathbf{M} = (\mathbf{I} - \mathbf{Q})^{-1} = \begin{bmatrix} 0.3 & -0.2 \\ -0.5 & 0.6 \end{bmatrix}^{-1}$$

Find the inverse or the fundamental matrix.

a. Review your mathematical background to establish that $1 + x + x^2 + \ldots = \dfrac{1}{1 - x}$. What kind of series is this (i.e., what is the name of this type of series)? For what values of x does this series converge?

b. Given that $\mathbf{Q}^0 = \mathbf{I}$, the matrix series $\mathbf{Q}^0 + \mathbf{Q}^1 + \mathbf{Q}^2 + \ldots$ behaves in the same manner as $1 + x + x^2 + \ldots$. What relation does this series have to the fundamental matrix **M**?

c. Interpret $\mathbf{Q}^n$. What happens to $\mathbf{Q}^n$ as n gets large? (*Hint*: Treat **Q** as a transition matrix in its own right.)

d. Interpret $\mathbf{Q}^0 + \mathbf{Q}^1 + \mathbf{Q}^2$.

$$\begin{pmatrix} 1 & 0 \\ 0 & 1 \end{pmatrix} + \begin{pmatrix} 0.7 & 0.2 \\ 0.5 & 0.4 \end{pmatrix} + \begin{pmatrix} 0.7 & 0.2 \\ 0.5 & 0.4 \end{pmatrix}^2$$

Given these two transitions, what is the mean number of times the system is in state 1? [*Hint*: Probability of being in state 1 to start (times one) + Probability of being in state 1 after 1 transition (times one) + Probability of being in state 1 after 2 transitions (times one).]

e. Interpret **M** element by element.

f. Sum the rows of **M**. What does each sum mean?

54. ***Scheduling Hospital Admissions.***[10] Consider the following definitons of variables for a model that schedules the admission of patients into a specific ward of a hospital:

X_t = Number of occupied beds at *end* (midnight) of day t.
N_t = Nonscheduled arrivals during day t.
A_t = Scheduled arrivals during day t.
D_t = Discharges, transfers, and deaths during day t.

For this stochastic process, X_t represents the state variable: N_t is a random variable over time that is independent and identically distributed; D_t is a random variable over time that is dependent (conditional) on the occupancy of the ward in day $t - 1$; and A_t represents the deterministic decision variable.

By policy of the hospital, all scheduled arrivals for day t are admitted, but nonscheduled arrivals are admitted into this ward only if beds are available. Hence N_t is not synonymous with admissions. Also, patients who are admitted on day t are never discharged on the same day. To keep the problem manageable for you, we limit the number of beds in this ward to three.

Empirical probability distributions have been determined for N_t and for D_t given X_{t-1}, as shown in Table 14–19. For example, the probability of three nonscheduled arrivals on any given day is 20 percent. Note that discharges, transfers, and deaths on any given day cannot exceed the number of occupied beds at the *beginning* of the day; that is,

[10]Based in part on Peter Kolesar, "A Markovian Model for Hospital Admission Scheduling," *Management Science*, February 1973, pp. 384–96.

$D_t \le X_{t-1}$. Also, the value of D_t is probabilistically dependent on the value of X_{t-1}. For example, if two beds are occupied at the beginning of any one day, then the probability that one patient is discharged, is transferred, or dies is 30 percent.

TABLE 14–19

N_t	$P(N_t)$	X_{t-1}	D_t	$P(D_t \mid X_{t-1})$
0	0.2	0	0	1.0
1	0.1	1	0	0.8
2	0.4		1	0.2
3	0.2	2	0	0.6
4	0.1		1	0.3
			2	0.1
		3	0	0.3
			1	0.4
			2	0.2
			3	0.1

a. Specify the state space and the index parameter for this stochastic process.

b. Finish constructing the following one-step transition matrix for this model if the hospital follows a policy of always scheduling one admission (that is, $A_t = 1$ for all t):

$$X_{t-1}\;\begin{matrix} \\ 0 \\ 1 \\ 2 \\ 3 \end{matrix}\overset{X_t}{\begin{matrix} 0 & 1 & 2 & 3 \end{matrix}}\begin{pmatrix} & & & \\ & & & \\ 0 & 0.02 & 0.07 & 0.91 \\ & & & \end{pmatrix}.$$

To help you along, we will describe the given calculations for the third row of the transition matrix. In general, the number of beds occupied at the end of day t will be either three (the capacity of the ward) or $(X_{t-1} + N_t + A_t - D_t)$, whichever is smaller. Can you verbalize the algebraic expression? Thus for $A_t = 1$, it follows that

$$X_t = \min[3, (X_{t-1} + N_t - D_t + 1)].$$

OK so far? Now, to determine the third row of **P**, it is necessary to evaluate the conditional probabilities $P(X_t \mid X_{t-1} = 2$ for all possible values of X_t. To help you conceptualize this, consider the probability tree given in Figure 14–8. A node (●) with a number on top represents a realized value for that random variable. The probability of achieving that node is labeled parenthetically on the branch leading into that node. To illustrate, consider the path with the starred (*) ending node. In this case, two beds were occupied at the beginning of the day ($X_{t-1} = 2$), two nonscheduled arrivals ($N_t = 2$) and one departure ($D_t = 1$) occurred, and one scheduled arrival was admitted (+1). Thus there was a demand for four beds ($2 + 2 - 1 + 1$). Since only three beds are available, it follows that the number of beds occupied at the end of the day must be three ($X_t = 3$). Since $N_t = 2$ *and* $D_t = 1$ must occur for this path, it should be evident that achieving $X_t = 3$ via this path is given by the *joint* probability

FIGURE 14–8 Probability Tree for Hospital Admission Model

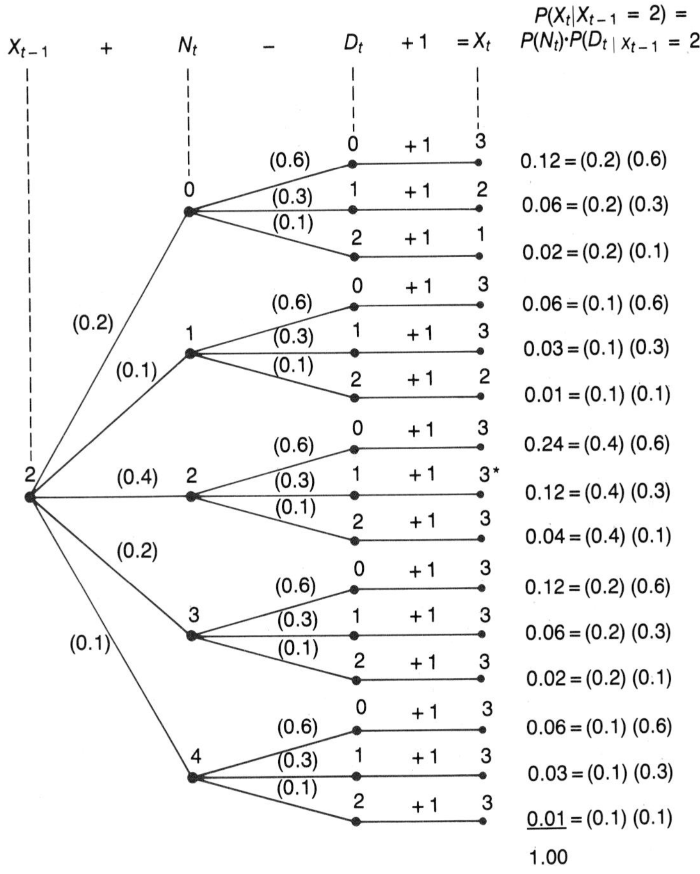

$$P(X_t = 3 | X_{t-1} = 2) = P(N_t = 2) \cdot P(D_t = 1 | X_{t-1} = 2)$$
$$= (0.4) \cdot (0.3) = 0.12 .$$

Noting that the paths through the tree are all mutually exclusive, you should readily confirm the entries in row 3 of **P** by the Rule of Addition in probability (Appendix A).

c. Explain why the described stochastic process is a finite state Markov chain. Do you have quarrel with any of the assumptions? Is this chain ergodic? Explain.

d. Calculate the steady-state probability distribution for number of occupied beds and the expected number of occupied beds.

e. In the preceding parts, the decision variable A_t was specified as 1 for all t. In actual practice, this analysis would be undertaken for the purpose of determining the policy that provides optimal control of the process. In this case, the possible number of policies $(Q_1, Q_2, \ldots, Q_L)$ is determined by the possible assignments of decisions to each possible value of the state variable X_{t-1}. In other words, given the number of occupied beds at the end of day $t - 1$, a decision is made for the number of admissions to schedule the next day (A_t). Criteria to be optimized include maximization of expected occupancy subject to a constraint for an upper limit on the probability that an arriving patient is rejected from the ward; or, conversely, minimizing this "overflow" probability subject to a constraint on average bed utilization. You might be surprised to learn that this model can be solved by linear programming. Determine the possible number of policies for the three-bed ward if more than three patients are never scheduled into the ward. How many policies are possible for a 20-bed ward if more than 20 patients are never scheduled for admission?

CASE Probabilistic Dynamic Programming

Chapter 12 treated the topic of dynamic programming in detail. In all cases, the models solved were deterministic. In this case we extend dynamic programming to include stochastic states. Since dynamic programming is a sequential approach to optimization, its use in a Markovian framework describes a **Markovian sequential decision process.**"[11]

To illustrate a Markovian sequential decision process, we return to the maintenance model of Exercise 50. The equivalent dynamic programming structure is as follows.

1. A **stage** is equivalent to a day. Therefore, the number of stages (n) will equal the number of days in the planning horizon.
2. The **decision variables** for stage i are defined as $x_i = 1$ for no repair in stage i and $x_i = 2$ for major repair in stage i.
3. The **state** *entering* stage i is labeled s_i. It will take on one of three values:

   $s_i = 1$ if the turbine is operating efficiently.
   $s_i = 2$ if the turbine is not operating efficiently.
   $s_i = 3$ if the turbine is inoperable.

4. The general **transformation function** can be depicted as in Chapter 12: $s_{i-1} = T(s_i, x_i)$. This means that, given s_i and x_i, it is possible to determine s_{i-1}. Note, however, that the state variable is now stochastic. Its next value is determined by a chance process based on the current state and decision. In other words, the current state and decision do not determine the next state (as in the deterministic case); they determine the *probability distribution* for the next state. In a Markovian framework, this probability distribution is based on a *row* of an enlarged transition matrix. The appropriate row is determined by both the current state s_i and the current decision x_i, as indicated by the transformation function. Since we have three states and two decisions, it is necessary to specify six distinct rows:

$$\begin{array}{cc} & \text{Next State } (s_{i-1}) \\ & \begin{array}{ccc} 1 & 2 & 3 \end{array} \\ \begin{array}{c}\text{Current} \\ \text{State-Decision} \\ (s_i, x_i)\end{array} \begin{array}{c} 1,1 \\ 1,2 \\ 2,1 \\ 2,2 \\ 3,1 \\ 3,2 \end{array} & \begin{pmatrix} 0.8 & 0.2 & 0 \\ 1 & 0 & 0 \\ 0 & 0.9 & 0.1 \\ 1 & 0 & 0 \\ 0 & 0 & 1 \\ 1 & 0 & 0 \end{pmatrix} \end{array}$$

[11]For applications in airline and hotel reservation systems, see M. Rothstein, "Hotel Overbooking as a Markovian Sequential Decision Process," *Decision Sciences* 5, no. 3 (1974), pp. 389–404.

For example, if the current state is "operating efficiently" ($s_i = 1$), then a decision "no repair" ($x_i = 1$) would yield transition probabilities of (0.8 0.2 0) for the next state (as in Exercise 50). However, again if $s_i = 1$, then a decision "major repair" ($x_i = 2$) would result in transition probabilities (1 0 0); that is, the next state is guaranteed to be "operating efficiently." Can you interpret the remaining four rows?

5. The **return** for stage i, r_i, depends on the state and decision associated with stage i. As in Exercise 50, it represents (Operating cost + Repair cost) for stage i.
6. The **optimal recursive equation** is given by

$$f_i^* = \min_{\text{all } x_i}[r_i + E(f_{i-1}^*)],$$

where f_i^* is the cumulative optimal cost per turbine over the first i stages and $E(f_{i-1}^*)$ is the *expected* cumulative optimal cost through stage i-1. The expected value for f_{i-1}^* is found by weighting each possible f_{i-1}^* by the probability of its associated state s_{i-1}. These probabilities are given by the appropriate row in the enlarged transition matrix.

Now, suppose that a turbine is currently in state 2 and we wish to determine an optimal policy (sequence of optimal decisions) for the next four days. Because of this given state, we formulate this as a **backward recursion** according to the diagram. Carefully note that

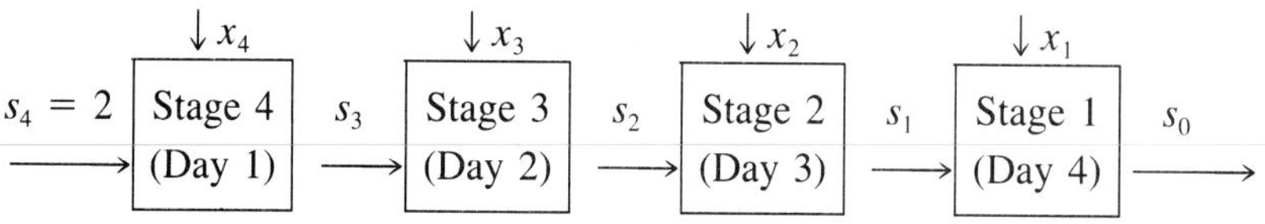

$$s_4 = 2 \longrightarrow \boxed{\begin{matrix}\downarrow x_4\\ \text{Stage 4}\\ \text{(Day 1)}\end{matrix}} \xrightarrow{s_3} \boxed{\begin{matrix}\downarrow x_3\\ \text{Stage 3}\\ \text{(Day 2)}\end{matrix}} \xrightarrow{s_2} \boxed{\begin{matrix}\downarrow x_2\\ \text{Stage 2}\\ \text{(Day 3)}\end{matrix}} \xrightarrow{s_1} \boxed{\begin{matrix}\downarrow x_1\\ \text{Stage 1}\\ \text{(Day 4)}\end{matrix}} \xrightarrow{s_0}$$

s_i is equivalent to the *beginning* state for the day associated with stage i. For example, $s_2 = 1$ would mean that the turbine is operating efficiently at the beginning of day 3. This of course also represents the ending state for day 2.

The tabular analysis for stages 1 and 2 follows. Carefully confirm the logic of all calculations based on the above explanations.

Stage 1 (Day 4): $f_1 = r_1 + E(f_0^*)$

	Possible Decisions (x_1)			
s_1	**$x_1 = 1$ (no repair)**	**$x_1 = 2$ (major repair)**	**x_1^***	**f_1^***
1	100 + 0 = 100	1,500 + 0 = 1,500	1	100
2	200 + 0 = 200	1,500 + 0 = 1,500	1	200
3	1,000 + 0 = 1,000	1,500 + 0 = 1,500	1	1,000

Note: $s_1 \equiv$ Beginning state for Day 4.

Stage 2 (Day 3): $f_2 = r_2 + E(f_1^*)$

s_2	Possible Decisions (x_2): $x_1 = 1$ (no repair)	$x_2 = 2$ (major repair)	x_2^*	f_2^*
1	100 + [(0.8)(100) + (0.2)(200) + (0)(1,000)] = 220	1.500 + [(1)(100) + (0)(200) + (0)(1,000)] = 1,600	1	220
2	200 + [(0)(100) + (0.9)(200) + (0.1)(1,000)] = 480	1,500 + [(1)(100) + (0)(200) + (0)(1,000)] = 1,600	1	480
3	1,000 + [(0)(100) + (0)(200) + (1)(1,000)] = 2,000	1,5000 + [(1)(100) + (0)(200) + (0)(1,000)] = 1,600	2	1,600

Note: $s_2 \equiv$ Beginning state for day 3.

Requirements:

a. Determine the optimal policy for days 1, 2, 3, and 4 and the associated optimal cost when the turbine is in state 2 at the beginning of day 1.

b. Same as part *a* for initial states of 1 and 3. Do the results make sense? Explain.

c. Answer part *a* for a five-day planning horizon. Assess differences in policy and optimal cost between the four-day and five-day problems. Why might a longer horizon be desirable?

d. Answer part *a* for the case where an additional decision is possible: $x_i = 3$ represents "minor repairs." A minor repair costs \$150 per day per turbine and guarantees the return of a previously efficient or inefficient turbine to an efficient state; however, a minor repair cannot restore an inoperable turbine to an operable state. Assume that auxiliary power for a minor repair is costed at \$300 per day. Compare optimal cost to part *a*.

15 Inventory Models

Chapter Outline

This chapter applies management science methods to the analysis and management of inventories. There are two kinds of aggregates in day-to-day affairs: *stocks* and *flows*. **Stocks** represent amounts on hand and can refer to widgets, cash, or whatever else is being held at a particular time. **Flows** are additions or subtractions to stock and thus have a time dimension. Saying that inventories are being increased by 30 units makes no sense unless we embellish the story by mentioning that we mean 30 units per hour. The inventory models in this chapter relate stocks and flows with a cost criterion.

Much inventory analysis takes place intuitively. For example, the geranium man of Kennebunk, Maine, annually grows 100,000 red geraniums, 30,000 pink geraniums, and 4,000 white geraniums from cuttings. "You can't sell a white! Pinks, they go along for the ride. If you want a geranium, you want red."[1]

Al Verrecchia and Carole Anderson of Hasbro have also described how stocks of toys must be sold through the retail level so that the retailers' shelves are empty after Christmas. This creates an aura of "hot" items that parents and children will want when they can find them. Some sales will be lost because of out-of-stock situations, but Hasbro is betting on the "hot aura" to create larger sales. The balance is struck intuitively by talking with retailers and by using experience to judge how lean to go.

This chapter will develop some inventory models that have helped companies to make inventory decisions. Successful inventory management calls for the skill to interpret the results of inventory models and to combine these with judgment and intuition where appropriate. The inventory model thus provides one input to the decision.

15.1 THE NATURE OF INVENTORY

An **inventory** may be thought of as a resource or as a list of some category of materials, machines, people, money, or information for some organizational unit at some time. Inventories are "added to" and "depleted from"; if the addition and depletion processes are stopped, what remains is inventory. Alternatively, an inventory can be conceived as a usable resource that is idle.

We all know that manufacturing firms typically "take inventory" once a year; included is the counting and valuation of all goods—raw materials, work-in-process, and finished goods. Similarly, retail firms count their stocks; and universities, hospitals, police departments, and other public or semipublic organizations take periodic inventories of equipment. Inventories of money tend to be verified more often through reconciliation of bank statements, petty cash funds, or cash registers. Formal analyses of personnel inventories are less frequent, but enlightened personnel departments in large organizations do indeed maintain accurate personnel inventory data. Personnel and money are being conceived and controlled as inventories. Information inventories are a bit more abstract; nonetheless, information is added and depleted from records (information inventories) ranging from lists to massive computer files.

Most inventory models are concerned with finding the best way to add and deplete inventories. Before turning our attention to these, however, a few basic questions need to be answered: (1) What is the function of an inventory? (2) What is the nature of the inventory environment? (3) What are inventory-related criteria?

---

[1]Franklin Emmons as quoted in Edie Clark, "The Geranium Man," *Yankee Magazine*, February 1986, p. 95.

Inventory Function

The basic function of an inventory is to allow demand and supply to be separated for physical and/or economic reasons. **Transaction stocks** support the transformation, movement, and sales operations of the firm. There are two kinds of transaction stocks. *Work-in-process stocks* are currently being worked on, waiting to be worked on, or moving between work centers. *Pipeline inventories* are inventories in transit to support sales at the retail center.

Beyond these transaction stocks, companies may invest in **organization stocks** if the benefits outweigh the costs. *Safety stocks* buffer the firm against uncertainty in demand. *Anticipation* or *leveling inventory* may be used as an alternative to changing production levels or capacity in the face of cyclical sales. *Lot size* or *cycle inventories* are held to avoid repeated setups to produce the same type of unit. *Scheduling stocks* are one type of work-in-process stock held between operations solely to achieve high resource utilization. *Speculative stocks* are held against anticipated price increases. All these organization stocks have the common characteristic that they can be reduced to zero if need be without shutting down normal sales transactions.

In most operations research textbooks, inventory control and scheduling are treated as separate topics. In this chapter, however, we insist on mentioning the scheduling aspects of inventory control. Indeed, many of the misapplications of inventory control can be traced to faulty problem definition and to an examination of inventory in isolation from scheduling, capacity, and quality control issues.

Inventory Environments

Before presenting some classical inventory models, we find it useful to overview possible inventory environments and to note the two predominant decisions addressed by inventory models: (1) In what quantity should the inventory be replenished? (2) When should the replenishment begin?

We distinguish in this chapter between **vendor** (purchasing) inventory models and **production** inventory models. Vendor models are those in which the inventoried item is purchased from suppliers outside the company. Production models are those in which the user of the item produces the replenishment supply.

Another distinction made in inventory analyses is the treatment of demand for an item as **deterministic** or **stochastic**. In a small number of cases, deterministic demand is reasonable, as when demand is contractual or otherwise relatively stable. In most cases, however, demand must be treated as a random variable. This requires the specification of an appropriate probability distribution for demand.

The time delay between the initiation of a replenishment order and the receipt of the items is called the **lead time.** Lead time, as with demand, can be either deterministic or stochastic. If both the demand during the lead time period and the lead time period are known with certainty, the development of an inventory model is straightforward; however, any uncertainty associated with lead time period or lead time demand makes for a more complex analytic model. As will be seen in Section 15.5, the use of buffer quantities of the inventoried item (referred to as **safety stocks**) is one approach to protecting against such uncertainties.

Order launching refers to the release of an order, either for production or purchase, and relates to the key question of when the order should be initiated. Classical ordering policies are of two types. **Fixed-order quantity systems,** to which we devote most of our attention, are those in which a perpetual inventory record is maintained. The records are reviewed on a continuous basis until the inventory level reaches a predetermined level referred to as the **reorder point.** At this time, an order is launched for a fixed replenishment quantity. The second type of ordering policy is the **periodic review system.** Rather than maintaining a continuous review of the inventory level, periodic checks are made, usually at fixed intervals. The quantity on hand is compared with the desired inventory level, and the difference between the two is ordered. Whereas the order quantity is always the same in fixed-order quantity systems, the order quantity is variable with this system. Many variations on these two basic alternatives exist. For example, it is possible to periodically review, estimate the probability of a stockout if an order is not placed until the next review, and then order in fixed (or varying) quantities.

The echelon structure of the inventory system also must be specified. A **single-echelon system** is one in which inventories directly service ultimate demand. Examples include the clothing inventories of a small independent retailer who services consumers, the hospital that inventories blood, and the manufacturer who ships to customers directly from the factory. Alternatively **multiechelon systems** move the inventoried item through various "levels" or "stocking points." This occurs whenever a stocking point serves as a warehouse for one or more other stocking points. For example, inventories for a major department store might be characterized as two echelon if inventories at regional warehouses service inventories at retail stores. Note that each of these could be treated independently as single-echelon systems. Doing so, however, generally results in suboptimization.

Another issue that must be considered includes the treatment of **single** versus **multiple items.** Generally, it is desirable to view an inventory in terms of multiple items; that is, most organizations carry not one but many different items in inventory. An approach that seeks to optimize the inventory policy for each separate item generally fails to optimize the overall inventory policy for the organization, as issues relating to storage, capital, dependencies among items, and other constraints have been ignored. The general modeling approach for multiple items employs mathematical programming, heuristic methods, or simulation.

The treatment of shortages must also be explicit. Shortages are either allowed or not allowed. If allowed, then it must be specified whether or not **back ordering** (fulfilling the shortage at a later date) is allowed. If back ordering is not possible, then a **lost sales environment** is assumed. In some cases, a mixture of back ordering and lost sales may be appropriate.

Also, the planning horizon of interest must be specified for modeling purposes. This means that the model must consider either a **finite discrete time horizon** or an **infinite continuous-time horizon.** The classic models in this chapter treat an infinite time horizon.

Finally, production systems create either a push or a pull environment. Pull systems are those in which the flow of material is triggered by stocking points closer to the customer. If one of these stocking points stops requesting inventory items, the stocking points further away from the customer will shut down the flow of inventory in a domino effect. By contrast, push systems work to a plan that dictates when an item should be produced or supplied. Classic order-launching systems are basically push systems. Many Japanese companies use pull systems associated with a **Kanban** or card technique, whereby requests for stock are conveyed by a card from a point closer to the customer. You may have heard the terms **MRP** and **JIT.** You will learn more about these later in this chapter where we show that material requirements planning (MRP) is a push system and just-in-time (JIT) can be either pull or push.

In a manufacturing environment, one can think of a pull system as one in which operations happen only in response to signals from an immediate downstream operation even though daily schedules do exist. The purpose is to have no excess inventory or unneeded inventory left over. In a push system, operations begin in response to a preplanned schedule without consideration of the real-time status of other operations and work centers. The intent is to operate to schedule.

Cost Criteria

The need for proper management of inventory resources is obvious merely from the pervasiveness of these inventories. One must always keep in mind that firms are investing in the inventory asset. Inventories are classified as a current asset in most cases. Because they are usually classified as current, inventories are part of working capital. They often compose 15 to 30 percent of the firm's total assets. For example, IBM's 1986 year-end balance sheet displays about $8.039 billion in inventory classified as a current asset against total assets of about $57.8 billion. Another $0.975 billion are shown as noncurrent, classified as work in process and field service parts. IBM valued inventory in 1986 at the lower of average cost or market, a procedure used with FIFO or first in, first-out. Recall that in periods of rising prices FIFO yields higher inventory values on the balance sheet because older lower-cost inventory layers have been removed. In Figure 15–1, IBM's 1986 current assets are shown. In Figure 15–2, we show a breakdown of inventories for the year ending 1986. Noting that IBM had gross income of approximately $51.25 billion in 1986, one gains some appreciation of the importance of inventory management at IBM.

One straightforward inventory criterion is minimization of cost; however, an understanding of inventory functions highlights inventory benefits as well as costs. A more appropriate criterion, therefore, might be overall return on investment to the firm. Unfortunately, this criterion is difficult to assess as it relates to the inventory decision; hence we must specify surrogate criteria. A discussion of all inventory surrogate criteria is beyond our scope. Included are such issues as speculative buying, product life cycles, and asset management.

In determining an optimal inventory policy, the criterion function is most often one of cost. Classical inventory analysis identifies four major cost components. Depending on the structure of the inventory environment, some or all of these cost components may be included in the objective function.

The first cost component is the **purchase cost** for vendor supply environments or **direct production costs** in case of items produced by the user. In either situation the unit cost may be constant for all replenishment quantities, or it may vary with the quantity purchased or produced. Vendors frequently offer discounts or price breaks if

FIGURE 15–1 Current Assets for 1986 Balance Sheet: International Business Machines Corporation and Subsidiary Companies (*Dollars in millions*). *Source: IBM 1986 Annual Report*

		1986
Assets		
Current assets		
Cash	$ 755	
Marketable securities, at cost, which approximates market	6,502	
Notes and accounts receivable-trade, net of allowances	9,971	
Other accounts receivable	854	
Inventories	8,039	
Prepaid expenses and other current assets	1,628	
		$27,749
Plant, rental machines and other property	38,121	
Less: Accumulated depreciation	16,853	
		21,268
Investment and other assets		8,797
		$57,814

FIGURE 15–2 Breakdown of IBM's 1986 (Year End) Inventory (*Dollars in millions*). *Source: IBM 1986 Annual Report*

Inventories	December 31, 1986
Current inventories	
Finished goods	$2,166
Work in process	5,645
Raw materials and operating supplies	228
Total current inventories	8,039
Work in process and field service parts included in Plant, rental machines and other property	975
Total inventories	$9,014

the user purchases quantities that exceed some specified quantity. Similarly, unit costs may decrease as larger production runs are made due to economies of scale.

The second cost component is **setup** or **ordering cost.** This cost is incurred whenever an inventory is replenished. Generally, it is independent of the quantity replenished. *Ordering cost* is the term used for purchasing or vendor models. In this context it is primarily clerical and administrative in nature; that is, it is the cost incurred for activities from the time the replenishment supply is requested to the time the order is received, paid for, and placed in inventory. Typical elements are the costs associated with processing and expediting the purchase order, follow-up, transportation, receipt, inspection, location of the items and payment for the order. In production models, the term "setup cost" is frequently used to include the same types of clerical and administrative costs; in addition, they include the costs of labor and materials used in setting up machinery for the production run.

The third cost component is **carrying (holding) cost.** This cost is proportional to the amount of inventory and the time over which it is held. It essentially represents the explicit and implicit costs of maintaining and owning the inventory. A significant component of carrying cost is the *opportunity cost* associated with owning the inventory. Although estimating procedures vary from firm to firm, this cost often reflects the rate of return the company might expect to earn on the money invested in inventory. Out-of-pocket costs normally accounted for include the cost of storage space (rent or cost of ownership), handling costs (including warehouse personnel, forklift trucks, and other equipment), insurance and taxes, allowances for depreciation, quality deterioration, obsolescence, and costs of administering inventory and maintaining records.

The fourth inventory cost component accounts for the explicit and implicit costs of being out of stock when items are requested. These **shortage costs** are computed differently depending on whether or not back ordering is possible. When back ordering is permitted, explicit costs are incurred for overtime, special clerical and administrative efforts, expediting, and special transportation. When the unavailable item is a finished good, there is often an implicit cost reflecting loss of goodwill. This is a difficult cost to measure, since it supposedly accounts for lost future sales. In other cases, it may not make sense to cost the "lost sale." For example, how would you cost unavailable blood that results in loss of life? If the item is a raw material being used in a production process, the shortage cost would also reflect costs of expediting, idle machines, and extra labor. When back ordering is not permitted, the primary costs reflect lost immediate and future sales, or in the case of raw materials inventory, the cost of idle facilities, disrupted schedules, and lost sales.

The shortage cost may be computed in different ways, depending on the situation. In some instances the cost may be a fixed amount regardless of the number of units short or the period of time over which the shortage exists. An example would be that the cost consists only of the added administrative and clerical expenses associated with processing a back order. In other situations, shortage costs vary as a function of the number of units short and/or the length of time over which there is a shortage. In some cases, explicit penalty clauses may be written into supply agreements that link costs to these two variables. Our models in this chapter are of the latter type.

15.2 CLASSIC ECONOMIC ORDER QUANTITY (EOQ) VENDOR MODEL

This section develops the classic deterministic economic order quantity (EOQ) model for vendor supply of inventory items. It is the simplest of the inventory models and will be followed in later sections by other deterministic models that are of greater complexity and that relax the initial set of assumptions. In all cases, the objective is to find the optimum order quantity (Q^*) and the optimum reorder point (R^*).

Model Assumptions

The following assumptions are made in this model:

1. Demand per year (D) is known with certainty and is at a constant (linear) rate.

2. Lead time (t_L) is known with certainty and specified as a fraction of a year.
3. Stockouts are not permissible.
4. The entire order is received in one batch.
5. Unit cost for items is constant (no discounts).
6. Single-item, single-echelon inventories are assumed.
7. Infinite planning horizon is assumed.
8. Demand, lead time, and costs are stationary (i.e., remain fixed over time).
9. Costs are known and accurate.

These assumptions lead to the type of inventory behavior depicted in Figure 15–3. Note that deterministic demand and deterministic lead time allow for the placement of orders in such a way that the new supply arrives at the instant the old stock is used up. In other words, for t_L fixed and for constant D, the reorder point R is determined as $t_L D$, the fraction of yearly demand occurring during lead time t_L. Each sawtooth portion of Figure 15–3 represents the behavior of inventory during an **inventory cycle,** which requires time t_c.

FIGURE 15–3 Inventory Behavior: Classic EOQ Model

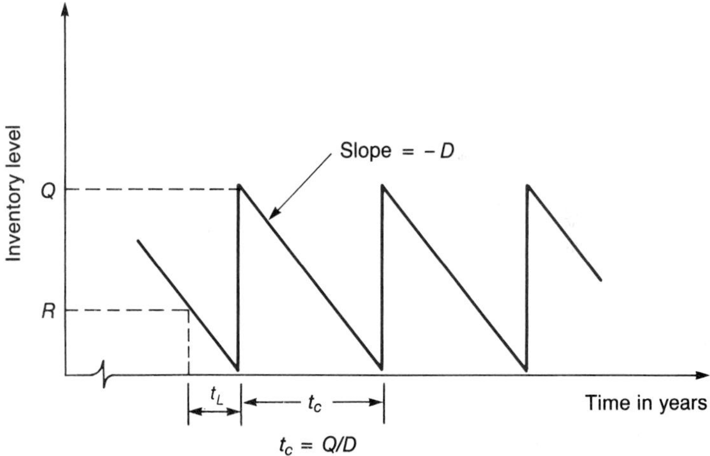

Although it is questionable whether or not the assumptions in this model closely approximate reality, this model provides a framework for the analysis of more complex models. In addition, situations do exist in which this model provides significant inputs for inventory policy.

Model Development

In addition to Q, R, D, t_c, and t_L, the following symbols are defined: C_h = Holding cost per unit of item per time period (exclusive of fixed costs), and C_o = Ordering cost per order. Holding (carrying) cost is often expressed as a percentage of the value of an item, e.g., $C_h = 0.10V$ where V is the value of the item.

As stated above, the criterion to be minimized (total cost) is the sum of the cost components discussed previously. Since no shortages are allowed under the assumptions of this model, no shortage cost will be incurred. And since unit purchase costs are assumed constant, this cost cannot be affected by inventory policy. Consequently, the pertinent variable costs per year are ordering cost plus carrying cost.

Since one order is placed per cycle, the *ordering cost per cycle* is C_o. Ordering cost per year is computed as

$$\begin{aligned}\text{Ordering cost per year} &= (\text{Number of orders per year}) \times (\text{Order cost per order}) \\ &= \text{NC}_0\end{aligned}$$

However, the *number of orders per year* can be defined as

$$\begin{aligned}N &= (\text{Number of units demanded per year}) \div (\text{Units of item per order}) \\ &= \frac{\text{D}}{\text{Q}}.\end{aligned}$$

In other words, if 500 units are demanded per year and 250 units are in each order, then two orders per year must be placed. Thus the *ordering cost per year* is given by

$$f_1(Q) = \left(\frac{D}{Q}\right)C_o. \tag{15.1a}$$

Carrying cost per inventory cycle is computed as Average number of units in inventory times holding cost per unit of item per year. Observation of Figure 15–3 should lead you to the conclusion that the average number of units in inventory during any inventory cycle equals $Q/2$. More rigorously, the average inventory over an inventory cycle is given by the area under the inventory curve divided by the length of the inventory cycle. The area of one triangle in Figure 15–3 is one half the base times the height, or $\frac{1}{2} t_c Q$. Dividing this result by t_c yields $Q/2$. Therefore, the *carrying cost per year* is:

$$f_2(Q) = \left(\frac{Q}{2}\right)C_h. \tag{15.1b}$$

Total cost per year now can be defined as

$$\begin{aligned}C(Q) &= f_1(Q) + f_2(Q) \\ &= \left(\frac{D}{Q}\right)C_o + \left(\frac{Q}{2}\right)C_h.\end{aligned} \tag{15.2}$$

Figure 15–4 indicates the behavior of ordering cost, carrying cost, and their sum as a function of Q. The order quantity Q^*, which minimizes total cost, is determined by differentiating $C(Q)$ with respect to Q and setting the derivative equal to zero. This procedure yields the classic EOQ formula:

$$Q^* = \sqrt{\frac{2DC_o}{C_h.}} = \sqrt{2D}\sqrt{\frac{C_o}{C_h}}. \tag{15.3}$$

FIGURE 15–4 Inventory Costs: Classic EOQ Model

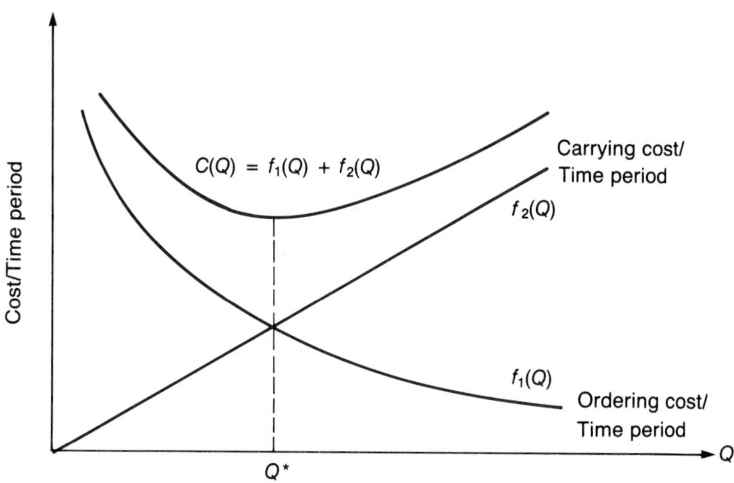

Based on the assumption of fixed lead time and the geometry of Figure 15–4, you should confirm that Q^* should be ordered whenever the inventory level drops to $t_L D$.

FOLLOW-UP EXERCISES

1. Critique the assumptions made in the classic EOQ model.
2. Verify that the stationary point defined by Equation 15.4 is a universal minimum by finding the first and second derivatives.
3. Articulate reasons for the trade-off (inverse) relationship that exists between ordering cost and carrying cost.
4. Mathematically verify
   a. That yearly ordering costs and carrying costs are equal when operating with an EOQ policy; that is, that $f_1(Q^*) = f_2(Q^*)$.
   b. That optimal cost is given by $C(Q^*) = \sqrt{2C_oC_hD}$.
5. The equation $N = D/Q$ implies a direct and obvious relationship between N (number of orders per time period) and Q. Thus the optimal EOQ policy can be stated alternatively by defining the optimal number of orders to place during each time period.
   a. Show that $N^* = \sqrt{DC_h/(2C_o)}$ *by substituting the expression for* Q^* into the equation above.
   b. Formulate total cost, Equation 15.3, in terms of N instead of Q. Having defined $C(N)$, determine N^* by (1) equating ordering cost $f_1(N)$ with carrying cost $f_2(N)$; (2) finding $C'(N)$ and setting it equal to zero.
   c. Graphically sketch $f_1(N)$, $f_2(N)$, and $C(N)$.

**6. Confirm that $Q/2$ is the average inventory as follows:
   a. Functionally state the level of inventory with respect to time for any given cycle. Use Figure 15.3 as a reference.
   b. Determine average inventory from

$$\bar{L} = \frac{\int_0^{t_c} L(t)\,dt}{t_c}.$$

▶ Example 15.1 Metrobus, Inc.

Metrobus, Inc. is a city-owned transit company that operates a fleet of 400 buses. The fleet includes buses used for public transit as well as school buses. Buses used in public transit average close to 400 miles per day, seven days a week. School buses also amass considerable mileage, though not nearly as much as public transit buses. Metrobus is interested in establishing an inventory policy for bus tires that minimizes the sum of annual ordering and carrying costs. All buses use the same type of tire, and the annual requirements are estimated at 5,000 tires. Ordering cost per order is $125, and the cost of carrying a tire in inventory for one year is estimated at $20. For practical purposes lead time is zero, as the supplier will deliver on the day an order is placed. Note that the basic unit of measurement for a period is one year in this case.

Applying Equation 15.3, we see that the order quantity that minimizes total inventory cost per year is

$$
\begin{aligned}
Q^* &= \sqrt{\frac{2DC_o}{C_h}} \\
&= \sqrt{\frac{2(5{,}000)(125)}{(20)}} \\
&= \sqrt{62{,}500} \\
&= 250\,.
\end{aligned}
$$

You should confirm that the annual carrying and ordering cost total $5,000 for this optimal policy or that $C(Q^*) = 5{,}000$.

The optimal number of orders each year is

$$
\begin{aligned}
N^* &= \frac{D}{Q^*} \\
&= \frac{5{,}000}{250} \\
&= 20\,.
\end{aligned}
$$

The length of the inventory cycle is 0.05 year; that is,

$$
\begin{aligned}
t_c^* &= \frac{Q^*}{D} \\
&= \frac{250}{5{,}000} \\
&= 0.05
\end{aligned}
$$

or

$$
\begin{aligned}
t_c^* &= \frac{1}{N^*} \\
&= \frac{1}{20}\,.
\end{aligned}
$$

This means that the time between any two successive order arrivals (or order placements) is approximately 2.5 weeks.

FOLLOW-UP EXERCISES

7. Determine Q^*, $C(Q^*)$, N^*, t_c^*, and R^* for Metrobus, Inc. for each of the three environments below.
   a. $D = 6{,}000$ and no other changes.
   b. $C_h = 10$ and no other changes.
   c. $C_o = 200$ and no other changes.

   Sketch inventory behavior. Are changes in optimal policy logical given the indicated changes in the parameters? In actual practice, what would you do about the fact that Q^* is noninteger?
8. If Metrobus must order tires by the dozen, compare the costs of purchasing in lots of 240 (20 dozen) versus 252 (21 dozen). Are the total costs "significantly" different from those of the EOQ model? What about lots of 264? Is it worse to order too much or too little?
9. Inventory costs for a particular item consist of a per-unit storage cost based on the maximum inventory level and a regular holding cost expressed as a percentage of the average dollar value of inventory. Develop an EOQ formula for these conditions.
10. A processor of raw sugar for health food stores processes 6.0 million tons of sugar cane per year. Ordering costs per order are estimated at \$4,000 (including shipping cost), and carrying costs per ton per year are estimated at \$2.25. The fixed lead time is zero days. What is the EOQ for this company? What is the total inventory cost per year? Sketch inventory behavior.
11. Assume that in Exercise 10 the supplier of sugar cane pays for shipping and gets the best price by shipping in tankers at full capacity. Cargo ships are available with capacities of 100,000 tons or 200,000 tons. The supplier has agreed to sell to the processor at the same price provided that the purchases are in quantities of 100,000 or 200,000 tons. The processor saves \$1,000 per order on shipping costs. What are the total costs under the two alternatives? Which size shipment should the processor accept? If the supplier gives the processor the option of unrestricted order quantities with payment of shipping charges (Exercise 10) versus the option of the above with no payment of shipping charges, what should the processor choose?

15.3 EXTENSIONS OF CLASSIC EOQ VENDOR MODEL

In this section we present EOQ models for vendors that relax the assumptions of instantaneous replacement and no shortages.

Usage during Production

Suppose replenishment is not instantaneous but rather takes place at the production rate p units per day where quantity demanded is d units per day. To produce the quantity Q would require Q/p days, but during those Q/p days $(Q/p)d$ units would be lost to demand. Hence the maximum inventory position would be $Q - (Q/p)d$ or $Q(1 - d/p)$. Noting that $(1 - d/p)$ is simply a constant and that this modification affects only the annual holding costs, we can write the cost function as

$$C(Q) = \left(\frac{Q}{2}\right)\left(1 - \frac{d}{p}\right)C_h + \left(\frac{D}{Q}\right)C_o. \tag{15.4}$$

This equation reflects the notion that the average inventory in this model is half the maximum inventory, but the maximum inventory is no longer Q as it was in the basic EOQ model. Figure 15–5 shows inventory behavior for this model.

Of course we could derive the economic production quantity (EPQ) in the same fashion as we did the EOQ formula. But notice that $(1 - d/p)$ is simply a constant, and we can think of that constant as attaching itself to the constant C_h. There then should be no surprise in the economic production quantity given by

$$\text{EPQ} = \sqrt{\frac{2DC_o}{[C_h(1 - d/p)]}} \tag{15.5}$$

FIGURE 15–5 Inventory Behavior with Usage during Production

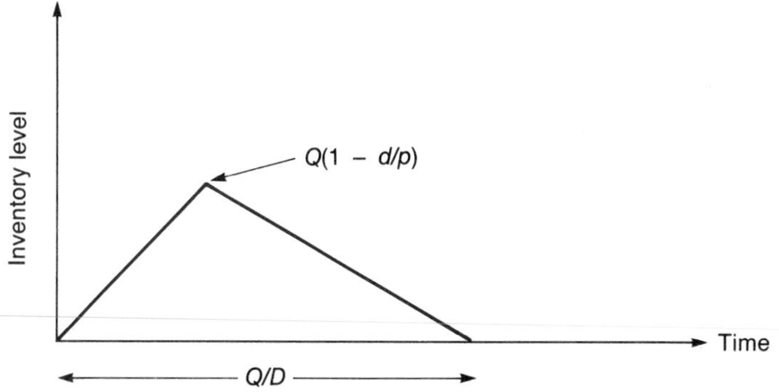

FOLLOW-UP EXERCISES

12. Annual quantity demanded is 3,000 units, setup costs are \$300, and annual per unit holding costs are 20 percent of the inventory value of \$15 per unit. The production rate is 100 units per day, and there are 250 working days in the year. Determine the economic production quantity. What would have been the EOQ if replenishment had been instantaneous? What is the maximum inventory level under the EOQ versus EPQ case ?
13. In the EPQ formula, how sensitive is the optimal Q to the ratio of setup to per unit holding cost? How sensitive to the ratio of the demand rate to the production rate? What happens when the demand rate is very small relative to the production rate?

EOQ with Planned Back Orders

We now present a more general case of the classic EOQ model discussed in Section 15.2. In this model we allow shortages of inventory that can be back ordered. As before, all demand must be met ultimately; hence, at the moment of replenishment, all back orders are satisfied prior to meeting new demands. These back orders, however, incur a shortage cost. Why might a vendor allow back orders? When back orders are allowed, the assumption of unaffected demand requires that all demand will be met. By delaying purchases, however, part of each incoming order is immediately allocated to back ordered demand. Consequently, fewer orders may be made resulting in lower ordering costs, and average inventory levels *may* be lower resulting in reduced carrying costs. This trade-off between ordering and carrying costs on the one hand and back ordering costs on the other hand is often exploited, particularly by the home furnishings industry.

Figure 15–6 portrays the inventory behavior for this model. We define the following variables in addition to those defined in Section 15.2: S = Maximum number of units short; C_s = Shortage cost per unit per time period; L = Maximum inventory level; t_1 = Time within a cycle during which inventory is held; and t_2 = Time within a cycle during which a shortage exists.

In this model, the decision variables are Q, the order quantity, and S, the maximum shortage. The order cost component is the same as earlier, or

$$f_1(Q, S) = \left(\frac{D}{Q}\right)C_o .$$

Carrying cost is determined as in the classic model. The carrying cost per cycle is based on the triangle in Figure 15–6 with t_1 as the base:

$$\left(\frac{L}{2}\right) \cdot t_1 \cdot C_h . \tag{15.6}$$

Using relationships of similar triangles, we see that

$$\frac{t_1}{t_1 + t_2} = \frac{L}{Q}$$

or

$$t_1 = \frac{(t_1 + t_2)(L)}{Q} .$$

FIGURE 15–6 Inventory Behavior: Classic EOQ with Back Orders

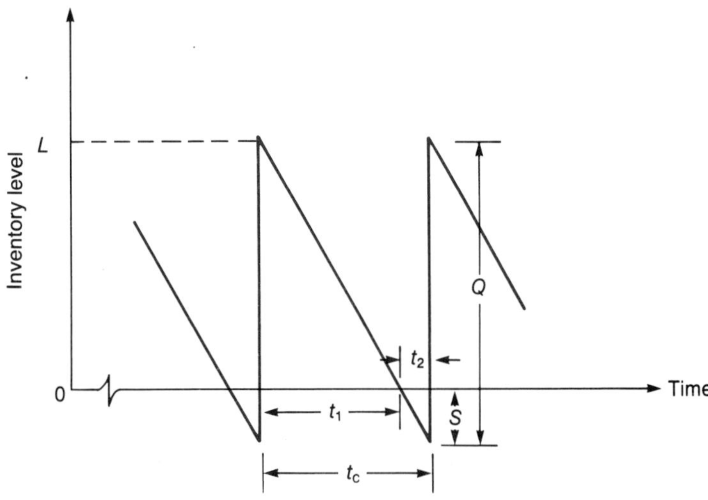

But the time of one complete cycle, $t_1 + t_2$, can be expressed equivalently as Q/D. Thus

$$t_1 = \frac{(Q/D)(L)}{Q} = \frac{L}{D}. \qquad (15.7)$$

Since the maximum inventory level L can be stated as $Q - S$, we can combine Equations 15.6 and 15.6 to compute the carrying cost per cycle as

$$\frac{(Q - S)^2}{2D} \cdot C_h.$$

Multiplying by the number of cycles per year, D/Q, we find total carrying cost per year is

$$f_2(Q, S) = \frac{(Q - S)^2}{2Q} \cdot C_h. \qquad (15.8)$$

The final cost component is the shortage cost. This is determined in a manner similar to that used for carrying cost. Shortage cost per cycle is given by (Average number of units short) × (Time short per cycle) × (Shortage cost per unit, per time period). Based on the triangle below the time axis in Figure 15–6, the shortage cost per cycle is

$$\left(\frac{S}{2}\right) \cdot t_2 \cdot C_s. \qquad (15.9)$$

Again by similar triangles,

$$\frac{t_2}{t_1 + t_2} = \frac{S}{Q}$$

or

$$t_2 = \frac{S}{Q}(t_1 + t_2).$$

Since $(t_1 + t_2) = Q/D$, as before, it follows that

$$t_2 = \frac{S}{Q} \cdot \frac{Q}{D} = \frac{S}{D}.$$

Combining this result with Equation 15.9 gives a shortage cost per cycle of

$$\frac{S^2 C_s}{2D}.$$

Multiplying the number of cycles, D/Q, we see that shortage cost per year is given by

$$f_3(Q, S) = \frac{S^2 C_s}{2Q}. \qquad (15.10)$$

Combining the three cost components, we see that the total variable cost function for this model can be expressed as

$$C(Q, S) = \frac{D}{Q}C_o + \frac{(Q - S)^2}{2Q}C_h + \frac{S^2 C_s}{2Q}. \tag{15.11}$$

Taking partial derivatives of Equation 15.11 with respect to Q and S and solving for the stationary point, we find that the optimal order quantity is

$$Q^* = \sqrt{\left(\frac{2DC_o}{C_h}\right) \cdot \left(\frac{C_h + C_s}{C_s}\right)} \tag{15.12}$$

and the maximum shortage quantity is

$$S^* = \sqrt{\frac{2C_o DC_h}{C_h C_s + C_s^2}}. \tag{15.13}$$

Note that C_h/C_s close to zero will leave us with the standard EOQ. Also, the definition of L gives:

$$L^* = Q^* - S^* \tag{15.14}$$

▶ Example 15.2 Cracked Block Associates

An Alaskan distributor of antifreeze is attempting to establish an optimal inventory policy. The clientele is relatively unchanging, and demand is approximately constant throughout the year. Because of limited competition, there is less concern with shortages than other businesses might experience. Any unsatisfied demand can be back ordered. Annual demand for antifreeze is 600,000 cases, ordering cost per order is \$100, carrying cost per case per year is \$0.25, and back order cost per case per year is \$2. Using Equation 15.12 we see that the optimal order quantity is approximately

$$Q^* = \sqrt{\left[\frac{2(600{,}000)(100)}{0.25}\right] \cdot \left[\frac{(0.25 + 2.00)}{2.00}\right]}$$

$$= 23{,}238 \text{ cases}.$$

Based on Equation 15.13 the maximum shortage is approximately

$$S^* = \sqrt{\frac{2(100)(600{,}000)(0.25)}{(0.25)(2.00) + (2.00)^2}}$$

$$= 2{,}582 \text{ cases}.$$

For this example, we illustrate output using the Erikson-Hall computer package in Figure 15–7. This and other packages allow options for usage during production as well as back orders and price discounts. Philosophically, however, we do not emphasize these computer packages for two reasons. First, the model should be formulated based on the facts of the inventory situation, and this may produce a total relevant cost function slightly different from the standard models given in the package. Second, the models are easy to implement with 1-2-3 from Lotus, so we encourage you to write your own inventory packages when needed.

FIGURE 15–7 Computer Models for Management Science* Inventory Models

```
                  -=*=-  INFORMATION ENTERED  -=*=-

PRODUCT DEMAND                         :           600,000.000
ORDERING COSTS                         :               100.000
HOLDING COSTS                          :                 0.250
DELIVERY LEAD TIME                     :                 0.000
SHORTAGE COSTS                         :                 2.000

                       -=*=-  RESULTS  -=*=-

OPTIMAL ORDER QUANTITY                 :            23,238.598
REORDER LEVEL                          :                 0.000
MAXIMUM INVENTORY                      :            20,655.291
ORDERING COSTS                         :             2,581.911
HOLDING COSTS                          :             2,295.033
SHORTAGE COSTS                         :               286.879
TOTAL INVENTORY COSTS                  :             5,163.823

              ----------  END OF ANALYSIS  ----------
```

*Warren Erickson and Owen Hall, Jr., *Computer Models for Management Science,* 2nd ed. (Reading, Mass.: Addison-Wesley Publishing, 1986).

FOLLOW-UP EXERCISES

14. For Example 15.2 specify
    - *a.* The annual ordering, carrying, and shortage costs under the optimal policy.
    - *b.* The time between orders (that is, the cycle time).
    - *c.* The proportion of demand that must be back ordered each year.
    - *d.* The time per cycle over which shortages exist.
    - *e.* The maximum inventory level.
    - *f.* The number of orders per year.
15. A distributor of 12-speed bicycles is enjoying its best year ever. Annual demand for this distributor is 200,000 bicycles. Ordering cost per order is estimated at \$1,000, carrying cost per bicycle per year at \$15, and shortage cost per bicycle per year at \$20. Determine the order quantity, Q^*, and maximum allowable shortage, S^*, which result in the minimization of variable costs. What are the component costs under this policy? What is the time between orders? What proportion of annual demand must be back ordered each year? What is the maximum inventory

level? What proportion of the time do back orders exist? How many orders per year are placed?

16. Suppose back orders are allowed for Metrobus, Inc. (Example 15.1) at a cost of \$80 per tire per year. Determine Q^*, S^*, and component costs for this policy. Compare to Q^* and component costs in Example 15.1.
17. Suppose the carrying cost curve reflects diseconomies of carrying larger amounts of inventory. Specifically, $f_2(Q) = (Q/2)^2 C_h$. Derive the EOQ under these conditions, and comment on the relation of annual holding and setup costs. Are they equal?
18. Show that Q^* in Equation 15.12 approaches Q^* in Equation 15.3 as the back order cost approaches infinity. What happens to S^* as back order cost approaches infinity? Do you conclude that the classic model in Section 15.2 is a special case of the EOQ model with back orders?

**19. Verify Equations 15.12 and 15.13 by finding partial derivatives of 15.11 and setting them equal to zero.

**20. Verify that the stationary point as expressed by Equations 15.12 and 15.13 is a global minimum for the cost function 15.11.

15.4 OTHER DETERMINISTIC MODELS

So far we have developed deterministic EOQ models that included back orders and usage during production. In this section we conclude the treatment of deterministic models by a brief overview of other models and the explicit development of a quantity discount model for vendors.

Overview

Other deterministic models that have been treated in the literature include, but are not restricted to, the following:

1. Vendor EOQ model with lost sales.
2. Periodic review models.
3. EOQ models with discrete demand and order quantities.
4. Multi-item EOQ models with resource constraints.
5. Production models with discrete time periods over finite time horizons.
6. Quantity discount models.

Interestingly, the EOQ model with lost sales yields the same optimal decision rule for Q^* and R^* as the classic EOQ model, as long as inventory is to be stocked in the first place. Similarly, deterministic periodic review models provide identical optimal decisions as deterministic reorder point (EOQ) models.

EOQ models with discrete D and Q require a marginal or difference equation type of analysis, as the calculus does not apply. Generally, the development of the model and the decision rules that result are more complex for the discrete case than for the continuous case. For this reason, "fudging" (rounding) the results of the continuous model is the typical approach to solving the discrete model, which works well if demand is high and unit costs are low.

Environments with multiple items subject to resource constraints are more typical of reality. Unfortunately, these models are difficult to solve. Typical constraints include limits on inventory levels, space, and capital. If the inventory costs of separate items are additive, then objective functions can be constructed easily based on single-item models; otherwise, complex interactions among items must be specified. Classical optimization with Lagrange multipliers and nonlinear mathematical programming techniques are the usual approaches to solving these types of models.

The production EOQ model is a classic model that can be approached in a different way. Mathematical programming approaches, particularly dynamic programming and integer programming, have proved successful in actual practice. For instance, the dynamic programming model of Example 12.5 takes into consideration a finite planning horizon, discrete time periods, discrete units for items, resource constraints, nonlinear and dynamic production costs, dynamic inventory costs, and fixed costs of production. The transportation model of Example 7.9 includes these same features except for nonlinearities and fixed costs.

Single Quantity Discount

All models presented thus far have assumed that the unit purchasing cost is constant. This allowed us to ignore purchasing costs in the objective functions, thereby simplifying the methods of solution. Frequently, however, suppliers offer discounts if buyers purchase in large quantities. The motivation for doing so is straightforward. In vendor models, the supplier moves more inventory forward in the distribution channel and lowers carrying costs if buyers purchase in larger quantities. Whoever pays for the transportation of the items can potentially benefit from lower unit shipping costs. Moreover, by purchasing a large lot size, the buyer is trading off lowered purchasing and ordering costs (fewer orders) with higher carrying costs.

Several different discount structures are possible. In this section we illustrate a total cost comparison for a single discount problem; in the next section we generalize this procedure.

If a company is offered a single quantity discount, one approach is to compare the total cost for the best inventory policy without the discount to the total cost if the discount is accepted. Total cost per period is defined as the sum of ordering cost per period, carrying cost per period, shortage cost per period, and purchasing cost per period, or

$$TC(Q,S,P) = C(Q,S) + D \cdot P \tag{15.15}$$

for the back order model and

$$TC(Q,P) = C(Q) + D \cdot P \tag{15.16}$$

for the no-shortage model, where $C(Q)$ is defined by Equation 15.2, $C(Q,S)$ is defined by Equation 15.11, D is demand per period, P is purchase cost per unit of item, and $D \cdot P$ represents the purchasing cost per period.

▶ Example 15.3 Metrobus, Inc.—Revisited

Suppose that the supplier of tires to Metrobus (Example 15.1) has made an offer in which a discount of 2 percent off the normal cost of $100 per tire will be applied if Metrobus purchases in quantities of 1,000 or more. Metrobus officials wish to analyze this proposal to see if it is worth their while. Analysts have decided to compare total costs under the current EOQ policy with those that would exist under the discount situation.

Recalling that $D = 5{,}000$ tires per year, $Q^* = 250$ tires, $C_o = \$125$ per order, and $C_h = \$20$ per tire per year, we see that

$$TC(Q^*, P) = \left(\frac{D}{Q^*}\right)C_o + \left(\frac{Q^*}{2}\right)C_h + D \cdot P$$

$$TC(250{,}100) = \left(\frac{5{,}000}{250}\right)(125) + \left(\frac{250}{2}\right)(20) + (5{,}000)(100)$$

$$= 505{,}000\,.$$

This means that an EOQ ordering policy with no discount incurs a cost of $505,000 per year.

Under the discount policy, $P = 98$ and Q is set to the minimum lot size that qualifies for a discount ($Q = 1{,}000$).[2] This reduces the ordering cost, increases the carrying cost, and reduces the purchasing cost:

$$TC(1{,}000, 98) = \left(\frac{5{,}000}{1{,}000}\right)(125) + \left(\frac{1{,}000}{2}\right)(20) + (5{,}000)(98)$$

$$= 500{,}625\,.$$

If total annual cost is the primary criterion, then there is an apparent savings of $4,375 per year. Comparing individual cost components between the two models, it can be seen that the increased carrying costs associated with buying the larger quantity, although not offset by the decrease in the ordering cost, is more than balanced by savings in the purchasing cost.

FOLLOW-UP EXERCISES

21. Using the formula for *TC*, prove to yourself that any order quantity greater than 1,000 will result in increased costs.
22. In Example 15.3 the discount offer was acceptable to Metrobus on a cost basis. In fact, Metrobus would have accepted the offer had there been less of a discount. The **indifference discount** is the discount per unit that equates total costs under the EOQ policy with those under the discount offer. Solve for the indifference discount, *d*, in the Metrobus example by redefining *TC* for the discount policy in terms of *d* and equating with the EOQ cost of $505,000.
23. Assume in Exercise 10 that the sugar processor has been offered a 2 percent discount on the purchasing cost of $100 per ton if purchases are in quantities of

[2]Assuming that carrying cost is unaffected, the lower P simply has the effect of shifting the total cost curve downward by a constant amount. Since $Q = 1{,}000$ is greater than $Q^* = 250$, it follows that further increases in Q result in higher total costs; that is, we would not wish to move further to the right when located to the right of the minimum point in a convex curve such as in Figure 15–4.

100,000 tons or more. Should the processor accept the offer on the basis of total cost comparisons?

24. What is the indifference discount for the preceding exercise?
25. ***Back Order Case.*** Compare annual ordering, carrying, shortage, purchasing, and total costs for the vendor in Example 15.2 if a discount of 0.2 percent is offered on the per-case purchase cost of $20 for purchases of 100,000 cases or more. What Q and S do you recommend? Sketch inventory behavior. *Note*: If Q is fixed at a particular discount level, then optimal S must be determined by differentiating Equation 15.11 with respect to S. This procedure yields $S = QC_h/(C_s + C_h)$. Can you show this?

Multiple Quantity Discounts

Often suppliers offer a progression of discrete discounts to buyers, each discount corresponding to a larger minimum purchase quantity. To simplify the presentation, assume a vendor model with no shortages and a constant carrying cost per unit per year.[3] This means that the purchasing price is not an element in the determination of Q^* according to Equation 15.3. Moreover, changes in the purchasing price have no effect on $C(Q)$. It follows, therefore, that decreases in the purchasing price of items do nothing but lower the vertical orientation of the total cost function. In other words, total inventory cost for any order quantity Q is less when the unit purchasing cost is lower. This is demonstrated in Figure 15–8 where, based on Equation 15.16, it follows that $TC(Q, P_1) > TC(Q, P_2) > TC(Q, P_3)$ for any Q when $P_1 > P_2 > P_3$.

FIGURE 15–8 Total Inventory Cost per Period; Multiple Quantity Discounts

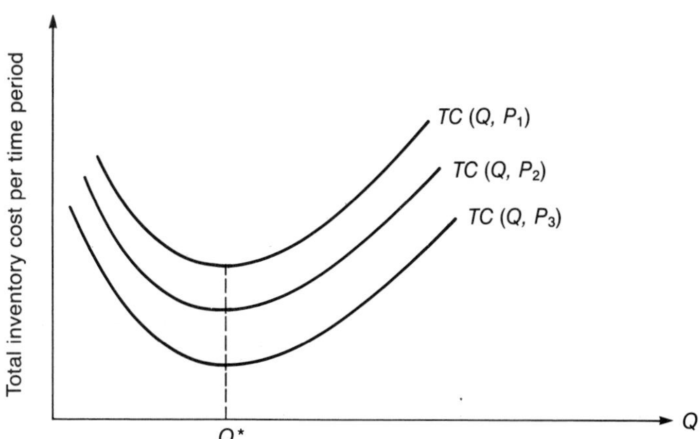

[3]In reality, carrying cost per unit per year may decrease as the unit cost decreases. The reason for this is that a major part of carrying cost reflects the opportunity cost associated with having an investment in inventory, where the value of the investment is directly related to the unit cost of the item. See Exercise 31 for the treatment of variable carrying cost.

Assume in Figure 15–8 that a supplier will sell at price P_1 unless the buyer agrees to purchase in quantities of Q_1 or more units, in which case P_2 is the selling price. Similarly, if the buyer agrees to buy in quantities of Q_2 or more units, the lower price P_3 applies. If the objective is to minimize the total inventory cost per period, then it is apparent that this is achieved when the order size is Q_2 units and the price is P_3. Note that Q^* is not permissible at price P_3 since $Q^* < Q_2$.

The result in this illustration cannot be generalized; that is, the lowest total inventory cost will not always be associated with the policy of purchasing the minimum allowable quantity at the lowest price offered. In general, the minimum cost solution is found by first computing Q^*. (Remember that Q^* is independent of purchasing price, provided that ordering cost and unit carrying cost remain the same.) Next, compute the total inventory cost for Q^* and the appropriate unit purchasing price for that order size, $TC(Q^*, P^*)$. The only way in which total cost might be lower is if the buyer purchases the minimum quantity corresponding to a unit purchasing price that is *lower* than P^*. Total costs under these lower price alternatives must be compared with $TC(Q^*, P^*)$ to determine the best policy (see Figure 15–9).

FIGURE 15–9 Total Inventory Costs: Two Price Discounts

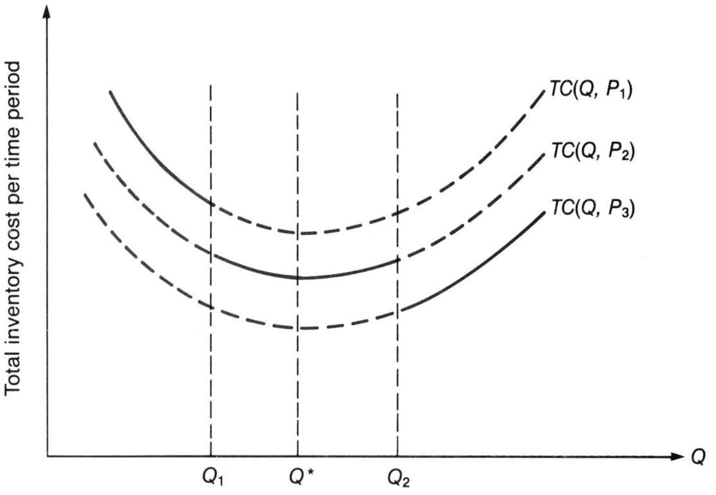

▶ Example 15.4 Term Papers, Inc.

A certain successful entrepreneur purchases high-quality term papers ("guaranteed A") from an even bigger entrepreneur for resale to unethical students. Annual demand is 25,000 papers, carrying cost is \$2.50 per paper per year, and ordering cost is \$100 per order. Students, being as desperate as they are, never back order. The purchase price is normally a stiff \$30 per paper; however, the supplier will sell at a 1 percent discount if the buyer purchases in lots of at least 5,000 papers and a 1.5 percent discount if the buyer purchases in lots of 10,000 papers or more.

Given the parameters, the economic order quantity at any price is

$$Q^* = \sqrt{\frac{2DC_0}{C_h}}$$
$$= \sqrt{\frac{2(25{,}000)(100)}{2.50}}$$
$$= \sqrt{2{,}000{,}000}$$
$$\doteq 1{,}414 \text{ papers.}$$

Since Q^* is not large enough to qualify for a quantity discount, the regular price of $30 applies (that is, $P_1 = 30$). Thus, according to Equations 15.16 and 15.2,

$$TC(1{,}414, 30) = \frac{25{,}000}{1{,}414}(100) + \frac{1{,}414}{2}(2.50) + (25{,}000)(30)$$
$$= 1{,}768 + 1{,}768 + 750{,}000$$
$$= 753{,}536.$$

The only possibilities for lower total cost would occur if the firm purchased the minimum quantity at each price beak. Total cost at the first discount level ($P_2 = 29.70$) is

$$TC(5{,}000, 29.70) = \frac{25{,}000}{5{,}000}(100) + \frac{5{,}000}{2}(2.50) + (25{,}000)(29.70)$$
$$= 500 + 6{,}250 + 742{,}500$$
$$= 749{,}250.$$

At the other discount level ($P_3 = 29.55$), we have

$$TC(10{,}000, 29.55) = \frac{25{,}000}{10{,}000}(100) + \frac{10{,}000}{2}(2.50) + (25{,}000)(29.55)$$
$$= 250 + 12{,}500 + 738{,}750$$
$$= 751{,}500.$$

From the standpoint of annual total cost, term papers should be bought in lots of 5,000 units at a price of $29.70 per paper.

FOLLOW-UP EXERCISES

26. Sketch the total cost curves for this example.
27. Determine the optimal decision if carrying cost is $6 per paper per year. Sketch the total cost curves and compare with the original example.
28. For Metrobus, Inc. (Example 15.3), suppose that demand remains the same ($D = 5{,}000$) but ordering cost increases to $200 per order, and holding cost decreases to $15 per tire per year. The normal price of a tire is still $100, but the following discounts apply: $P = 97$ if $250 \leq Q < 500$; $P = 96$ if $500 \leq Q < 1{,}000$; $P = 95$ if $1{,}000 \leq Q < 2{,}000$; and $P = 93$ if $Q \geq 2{,}000$. Determine the optimal policy. Sketch the total cost curves. Compare cost components (ordering, holding, and purchasing) for each Q you considered.
29. A regional automotive parts wholesaler purchases catalytic converters from the manufacturer for distribution to regional dealers and automotive repair shops. Annual demand is constant at 200,000 units, carrying cost is $30 per unit per

year, and ordering cost is \$250 per order. Without discounts, the purchase price is \$200 per converter. Assume that backorders are not allowed. The manufacturer offers a 2 percent discount for orders of at least 2,000 converters, a 3 percent discount for orders of at least 10,000, and a 3.5 percent discount for orders of at least 20,000. Determine the ordering policy that minimizes total cost per year. Sketch the total cost functions. Compare cost components (ordering, holding, and purchasing) for each Q you considered.

30. *Back Order Case.* Suppose back orders are allowed in the preceding exercise. For given Q, optimal S must be determined from $S = QC_h/(C_s + C_h)$, as discussed in Exercise 25. Determine the optimal policy. Sketch the total cost functions. Compare cost components (ordering, holding, shortage, and purchasing) for each Q you considered. Compare the optimal policy and total cost to that obtained in the preceding exercise.

31. ***Variable Carrying Cost.* Suppose carrying cost varies proportionally to the price paid for the item: $C_h = h \cdot P$ where h is the carrying cost proportion. For example, if $h = 0.20$ per period (i.e., carrying cost is 20 percent of the price), then $C_h = \$20$ per unit per period when $P = \$100$ per unit, and $C_h = \$10$ per unit per period when $P = \$50$ per unit. For this case, you should realize that the total cost curves of Figure 15–9 have their minima at different values of Q. Can you reason out why $Q_3^* > Q_2^* > Q_1^*$ for curves where $P_1 > P_2 > P_3$? Moreover, the shape of each curve is different because the $C(Q)$ component differs. It can be shown, however, that the curves never intersect. It follows that Q^* must be calculated for every price considered.

a. Outline a step-by-step methodology for determining the optimal policy where C_h is variable. *Hint:* Step 1 is the calculation of Q^* for the *lowest* price. If this Q^* is allowable, then the optimal policy has been found; otherwise, go on to the next lowest price. When the first allowable Q^* has been determined, then $TC(Q^*, P^*)$ must be compared with each TC corresponding to the minimum purchase quantity for prices lower than P^*.

b. Solve Example 15.4 if the carrying cost percentage is 8⅓ percent per year. Compare results.

c. Solve Exercise 28 if $h = 0.10$. Compare results.

d. Solve Exercise 29 if $h = 0.15$. Compare results.

15.5 STOCHASTIC INVENTORY MODELS[4]

Until this section all models have assumed that demand and lead times are deterministic. Although deterministic models often provide useful approximations to stochastic environments, models that directly incorporate uncertainties are more appropriate, particularly when variances are high. This section first overviews stochastic models and then presents in detail an EOQ model with probabilistic demands.

Overview

When we speak of stochastic inventory models, we refer to models that treat demand or lead times (or both) as random variables with specific probability distributions. As in the deterministic case, many models have been developed. A classic

[4]This section requires knowledge of the concepts in Sections A.1 and A.2 of Appendix A.

model is the single-period model with probabilistic demand, whereby a single stocking decision is made for one period for an item that is either perishable or salvable (i.e., has a salvage value at the end of the period). Examples include the stocking of newspapers, magazines, food items, and blood. Multiperiod periodic review models with stochastic demand represent another important class of models, with the usual variations relating to types of probability distributions, cost structures, the nature of shortages, and the treatment of lead times.

Needless to say, the incorporation of stochastic demand increases the level of modeling complexity. In many cases, particularly when both demand and lead times are probabilistic, closed-form solutions are not possible. This means that decision rules based on mathematical formulas are not available. This problem is particularly acute when dependencies exist both among items in a multi-item environment and among lead times (as when more than one order is outstanding).

Approaches to solving stochastic models include dynamic programming (Chapter 12), simulation (Chapter 17), Markov processes (Chapter 14), decision analysis (Chapter 13), and classical methods (e.g., mathematical statistics and calculus). In the remainder of this section we develop models with stochastic demand, fixed lead time, and an infinite continuous-time horizon. In Chapter 17 we incorporate stochastic lead time and solve by simulation.

Single-Period Model with Stochastic Demand: Model 1

In many situations, a retailer faces the decision of how much to order to cover a specified period. Newspapers and Christmas trees have been the classic examples of consumer goods having specified shelf lives, and the single-period model with stochastic demand has been called the newsboy or the Christmas tree model by the popular OR press. Whatever it is called, the single-period problem is probably the most common inventory problem faced. How many of each kind of toy should Toys-R-Us order for the Christmas season?

The expected profit on any unit will be the probability of selling the unit times the marginal profit (difference between the sales price and the unit cost). Similarly, the expected loss on any unit will be the probability of not selling the unit times the marginal loss (difference between the unit cost and any salvage value). Let p be the probability of selling the unit, MP the marginal profit, and ML the marginal loss.

Simply requiring that expected profit be at least as large as expected loss yields the relation $p(MP) > (1 - p)ML$. Rearranging slightly, we develop the requirement $p > ML/(MP + ML)$. Hence the retailer should stock one more unit of the item provided that the probability of selling that unit exceeds the ratio of the marginal loss to the difference between the sales price and the salvage value. Convince yourself of this by writing out $MP + ML$ and noticing that unit cost cancels out.

Now that we have a model, let us check it out. The higher the marginal loss, the higher the assurance we want of selling the unit (i.e., the higher the required probability on selling the unit). The higher the difference between the sales price and the salvage value, the lower the assurance we need that we will sell the unit. In the extreme, an exorbitant sales price might induce us to take more risk. Letting D be expected demand during the period and Q the order quantity, Q should be specified as large as possible subject to $P(D \geq Q) > ML(MP + ML)$.

FOLLOW-UP EXERCISES

32. Suppose the expected demand during a period is normally distributed with mean 100 and standard deviation 20. Sales price is $25, unit cost is $15, and salvage value is $5. How many units should the retailer stock?
33. Suppose the expected demand during a period is normally distributed with mean 100 and standard deviation 20. Sales price is $25 and unit cost is $15. Compare optimal order quantities with salvage values of $7 and $12. Explain.
34. Suppose the expected demand during a period is normally distributed with mean 100 and standard deviation 20. Sales price is $25 and salvage value is $5. Compare optimal order quantities with unit costs of $10 and $20.

EOQ with Stochastic Demand: Model 2

We now consider the same model as in Section 15.2, but allow both stochastic demand and back orders. One naïve approach to dealing with this situation is to determine the order quantity Q by Equation 15.3 and to set the reorder point R at a level equal to the expected (average) demand during the lead time. Unfortunately, lead time demand rarely equals its expected value and, as seen in Figure 15–10, the possibility exists of shortages.

FIGURE 15–10 Inventory Behavior: Constant Lead Time-Stochastic Demand

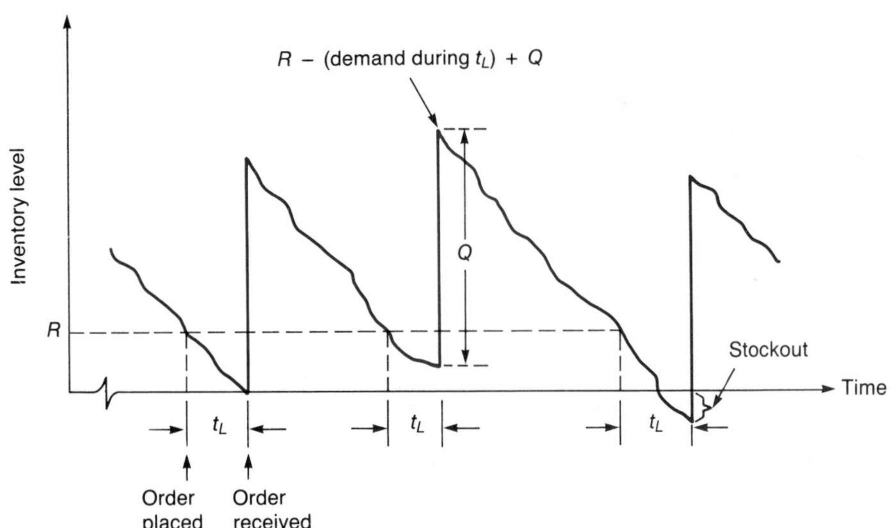

To protect against uncertainties, organizations often provide **safety (buffer) stocks** of inventory, which act as a buffer against variations in lead time demand or lead time period. The approach of the model in this section first determines the economic order quantity Q^* as given by Equation 15.3. Then the appropriate level of safety stock is determined by minimizing the sum of (1) the expected carrying cost per period associated with holding the safety stock and (2) the expected shortage cost per period.

(Can you reconcile the trade-off relationship between these two cost components?) The following symbols are defined:

d_L = Random variate for discrete demand during fixed lead time t_L.
$\overline{d}_L$ = Mean (average) demand during lead time.
$f(d_L)$ = Probability mass function for lead time demand.
R = Reorder point.
C_h = Holding cost per unit per time period.
$\overline{D}$ = Mean demand per time period (normally per year).
Q^* = Order quantity given by Equation 15.3.
C_p = Penalty cost per unit back ordered (independent of the length of the back order period).

All other assumptions in Section 15.2 are assumed to hold. Moreover, we assume a nonnegative expected safety stock (that is, $R \geq \overline{d}_L$) and no more than one order outstanding at any point in time.

Given the objective of minimizing the per period sum of expected safety stock carrying cost and expected shortage cost, the cost function can be established as a function of R:

$$\begin{aligned} C(R) &= \text{(Expected safety stock carrying cost per period)} \\ &\quad + \text{(Expected back ordering cost per period)} \\ &= C_h(R - \overline{d}_L) + C_p\left(\frac{\overline{D}}{Q^*}\right) \sum_{d_L > R} (d_L - R) f(d_L). \end{aligned} \tag{15.17}$$

Note that $(R - \overline{d}_L)$ represents the expected safety stock. Further note that whenever lead time demand exceeds the reorder point a stockout occurs. Thus the *summation* expression in Equation 15.17 represents the expected shortage in units per inventory cycle. $(\overline{D}/Q^*)$ indicates the expected number of orders (cycles) per period or, accordingly, the expected number of times during a period that a stockout is possible.

By finding the derivative of Equation 15.17 with respect to R, it can be shown that $C(R)$ will be minimized when

$$\sum_{d_L > R^*} f(d_L) = \frac{Q^* C_h}{C_p \overline{D}}$$

or

$$P(d_L > R^*) = \frac{Q^* C_h}{C_p \overline{D}}. \tag{15.18}$$

As in Section 15.2, this procedure assumes that the cost function is continuous. In this case it is not continuous, since d_L is assumed discrete.[5] For large demand, however, the approximation is reasonable. Additionally it is unlikely that Equation 15.18 will be satisfied as an equality because of discrete d_L. For this reason, the decision rule is to set the reorder point at the lowest value R^* that satisfies

[5]Continuous demand requires the use of integral calculus for expressing cumulative probabilities. See G. F. Hadley and T. M. Whitin, *Analysis of Inventory Systems*, (Englewood Cliffs, N.J.: Prentice-Hall, 1963), and M. Starr and D. Miller, *Inventory Control: Theory and Practice* (Englewood Cliffs, N.J.: Prentice-Hall, 1962).

$$P(d_L > R^*) \leq \frac{Q^* C_h}{C_p \overline{D}}. \tag{15.19}$$

Note that $P(d_L > R^*)$ represents the cumulative probability that d_L is greater than R^*, which is the same as $1 - P(d_L \leq R^*)$, the complement of the cumulative distribution function (CDF) at R^*, or $1 - F(R^*)$. Thus

$$1 - F(R^*) \leq \frac{Q^* C_h}{C_p \overline{D}}$$

or R^* is the smallest value for which

$$F(R^*) \geq 1 - \frac{Q^* C_h}{C_p \overline{D}}. \tag{15.20}$$

▶ Example 15.5 Gotham City Hospital Blood Bank

The management of blood is an important area within health care delivery systems. Blood banks have been developed to perform the functions of procurement, storage, processing, and distribution of blood. The uncertainties associated with both supply and demand usually result in the maintenance of relatively large buffer stocks. Blood bank inventory models are complex, for several reasons:

> *(1) both supply and demand are random; (2) approximately 50 percent of all bloods demanded, "crossmatched," and held for a particular patient are eventually found not to be required for that patient; (3) blood is perishable, the present legal lifetime being 21 days in most areas; and (4) each blood bank typically interacts with a number of other banks.*[6]

Assume that GCH is in the process of studying the inventory policies of its blood bank. It is interested in determining the optimal buffer stock to maintain. Needless to say, the assumptions of the model developed in the previous section need to be "stretched" to apply to the blood bank environment; however, assume that the analysts agree that the assumptions are close enough to use the model for a quick benchmark solution. The model is to be applied to the entire inventory of blood used by the hospital. Subsequently, further analyses can be conducted for each type of blood.

Mean annual demand is 160,600 units of blood (based on 365 days). Lead time for receiving replenishment supplies from the regional cooperative blood bank is deterministic and equal to two days. The carrying cost of blood is estimated at \$2.25 per unit per year. Ordering cost is estimated at \$63 per order. Based on Equation 15.3, Q^* is approximately 3,000 units of blood per order.

GCH has worked out a loan arrangement with a private blood bank in Gotham City whereby if GCH incurs a temporary shortage of blood, it can immediately borrow units at a cost of \$1.50 per unit. The agreement also specifies the replacement of the borrowed blood units when GCH receives its next replenishment supply.

[6]John B. Hennings, "Blood Bank Inventory Control," *Management Science*, February 1973, p. 637.

Lead time demand (i.e., demand for *any* two-day period) is stochastic. It is characterized reasonably well by the empirical distribution in Table 15–1. According to Equation A.12 in Appendix A, the mean of this distribution is 880.[7]

TABLE 15–1 Lead Time Demand: GCH

Class Intervals for Lead Time Demand	Lead Time Demand (d_L)	Probability $f(d_L)$	Cumulative Probability $F(d_L)$
790 but under 810	800	0.02	0.02
810 but under 830	820	0.05	0.07
830 but under 850	840	0.07	0.14
850 but under 870	860	0.18	0.32
870 but under 890	880	0.36	0.68
890 but under 910	900	0.18	0.86
910 but under 930	920	0.07	0.93
930 but under 950	940	0.05	0.98
950 but under 970	960	0.02	1.00

In order to determine the optimal reorder point R^* we first compute

$$1 - \frac{Q^*C_h}{C_p\overline{D}} = 1 - \frac{3{,}000(2.25)}{1.50(160{,}600)}$$

$$= 1 - 0.0280$$

$$= 0.9720 .$$

We conclude that the lowest value of R satisfying Equation 15.20 is $R^* = 940$. In other words, according to Table 15–1, R must be 940 for the cumulative probability to exceed 0.9720, or $F(940) \geq 0.9720$. Thus 3,000 units of blood should be ordered whenever inventory drops below 940 units. Since the expected lead time demand is 880, the recommended buffer stock is

$$R^* - \overline{d}_L = 940 - 880$$

$$= 60 \text{ units} .$$

FOLLOW-UP EXERCISES

35. Why is Equation 15.17 inappropriate for the case where a negative safety stock is allowed?
36. Show why it is necessary that demand during a lead time not exceed order quantity (that is, $d_L \leq Q^*$) in order to satisfy the assumption that no more than one order is to be outstanding at any time. Is it possible for d_L to exceed Q^* in Example 15.5? Why is the model given by Equation 15.17 not appropriate when more than one order is outstanding?
37. Estimate the probability of a blood shortage while an order is outstanding for Example 15.5. What reorder point should be established if this probability is to be approximately zero?

[7]Note that 880 is mean demand per two days. Per day the mean demand is 440, which when multiplied by 365 days gives $\overline{D} = 160{,}600$ units per year.

38. Fill in the table below for Example 15.5. Does the policy $Q^* = 3{,}000$ and $R^* = 940$ yield minimum $C(R)$?

R	Expected Safety Stock Carrying Cost per Year	Expected Number of Units Short per Cycle	Expected Shortage Cost per Year	$C(R)$
880				
900				
920				
940				
960				

39. Determine the recommended order quantity, reorder point, and buffer stock for Example 15.5 if
   a. $C_p = \$2.50$.
   b. $C_p = \$1.00$.
   c. $\overline{D} = 280{,}000$.
   d. $C_h = \$4.00$.

**40. Suppose that demand for blood is Poisson (see Section A.3) with $\lambda = 500$ units *per day*. Note that $\overline{D}$ now differs from before, but all other parameters remain unchanged. Take care that the lead time is still two days. What order quantity, reorder point, and buffer stock do you recommend? What is the probability of a stockout while an order is outstanding? *Hint:* Use the normal curve as an approximation to the Poisson cumulative probability $F(d_L)$, where the mean and variance are given by Equations A.25 and A.26 in Appendix A.

41. For Example 15.1 (Metrobus, Inc.) suppose that $C_o = \$125$ per order and $C_h = \$20$ per tire per year, as before, but demand is stochastic according to the following probability distribution for a five-day lead time:

d_L	60	64	68	72	76	80	84
$f(d_L)$	0.15	0.20	0.40	0.10	0.08	0.05	0.02

Determine Q^*, R^*, and expected buffer stock if the penalty cost is \$5 per tire back ordered. (Base the calculation of $\overline{D}$ on a 365-day year.)

**EOQ with Stochastic Demand: Model 3

The model developed in the preceding section is based on a *partial* cost trade-off: expected buffer stock carrying cost per period versus expected shortage cost per period. Moreover, Q^* is determined independently from the specified objective function $C(R)$. These two simplifications result in a model that is rather easy to solve; however, it suffers from the fact that it does not give an optimal policy in the sense of minimizing the expected *total* inventory cost.

The model developed in this section minimizes the following approximation to the expected total inventory cost per period:

$$\begin{aligned} C(Q,R) &= \text{(Expected ordering cost per period)} \\ &\quad + \text{(Expected carrying cost per period)} \\ &\quad + \text{(Expected back ordering cost per period)} \\ &= C_o(\overline{D}/Q) + C_h\left(\frac{Q}{2} + R - \overline{d}_L\right) \\ &\quad + C_p(\overline{D}/Q) \cdot \sum_{d_L > R} (d_L - R)f(d_L), \end{aligned} \tag{15.21}$$

where all symbols have been defined in the preceding sections. The logic behind the expected ordering cost per period is identical to that of the classic EOQ model. The expected back ordering cost per time period is identical to that of the preceding model. The expected carrying cost per period, however, is only an approximation to the exact carrying cost per period.

If we assume that the number of units back ordered is negligible, then the expected physical inventory when an order arrives is the safety stock $(R - \overline{d}_L)$. At this time, the expected physical inventory immediately rises by the amount Q to $(R - \overline{d}_L + Q)$, as indicated in Figure 15–11. We label this the beginning of a cycle. The ideal cycle ends when the physical inventory drops to the safety stock, at which time the next order of Q units arrives. It follows that average inventory is simply the expected safety stock $(R - \overline{d}_L)$ plus $Q/2$, as expressed in Equation 15.21. An exact (but complex) solution for carrying cost would take into consideration the likelihood that physical inventory reaches a level of zero *prior* to the arrival of an order, as illustrated at the end of the third cycle in Figure 15–10.

FIGURE 15–11 Behavior of Idealized Inventory with No Back Orders

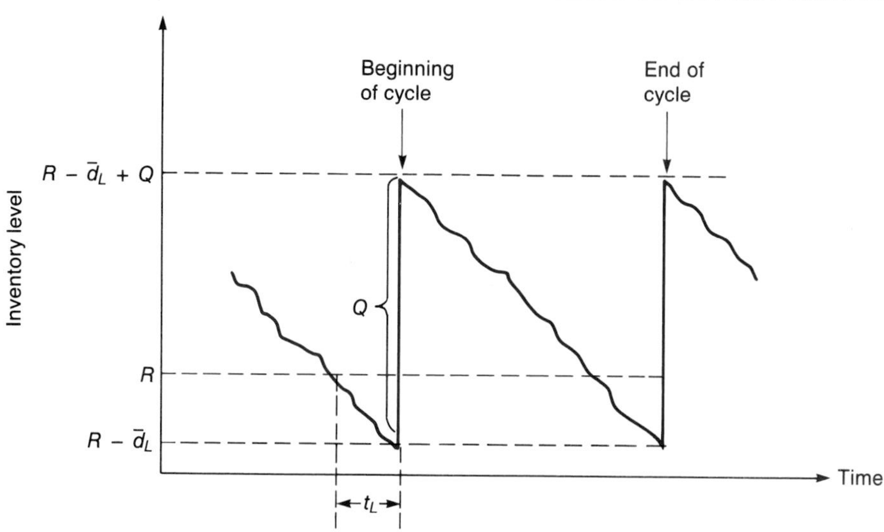

Finding partial derivatives with respect to both Q and R and setting these to zero leads to

$$Q^* = \sqrt{\frac{2D\left[C_o + C_p \sum_{d_L > R} (d_L - R^*) \cdot f(d_L)\right]}{C_h}} \tag{15.22}$$

and

$$F(R^*) \geq 1 - \frac{Q^* C_h}{C_p \overline{D}}, \tag{15.23}$$

which when solved simultaneously yield Q^* and R^*. Note that Equations 15.20 and 15.23 are the same. The algorithmic procedure outlined below can be used to solve for Q^* and R^*.

1. A trial value is established for Q by using the classic EOQ formula,

$$\sqrt{\frac{2DC_o}{C_h}}.$$

2. The value for Q found in step (1) is substituted into Equation 15.23 to find a corresponding value of R.
3. A new value for Q is computed by substituting the value of R into Equation 15.22.
4. R is recomputed from Equation 15.23 using the most recent value of Q.
5. Steps 3 and 4 are repeated until the values of Q and R have converged (sometimes to within some predetermined tolerance).

The algorithm usually converges within a few steps with trial values of Q getting larger at each iteration.

▶ Example 15.6 Simultaneous Determination of Q and R

Assume an inventoried item having the following characteristics: $C_o = 100$, $C_h = 50$, $C_p = 2.50$, $\overline{D} = 36{,}500$, and average lead time demand equals 500 with a distribution as indicated in Table 15–2.

TABLE 15–2 Lead Time Demand Distribution

d_L	$f(d_L)$	$F(d_L)$
460	0.020	0.020
470	0.060	0.080
480	0.130	0.210
490	0.165	0.375
500	0.250	0.625
510	0.165	0.790
520	0.130	0.920
530	0.060	0.980
540	0.020	1.000

1. Computing a trial value of Q, we get

$$Q = \sqrt{\frac{2(36{,}500)(100)}{50}}$$

$$= 382.10\,.$$

2. Substituting $Q = 382.1$ into Equation 15.23, we get

$$F(R) \geq 1 - \frac{(382.1)(50)}{(2.50)(36{,}500)}$$

$$\geq 1 - 0.209$$

$$\geq 0.791\,.$$

The smallest R for which $F(R) \geq 0.791$ is $R = 520$.

3. Substituting $R = 520$ into Equation 15.22, we get

$$Q = \sqrt{\frac{2(36{,}500)\{100 + 2.5[(530 - 520)(0.060) + (540 - 520)(0.020)]\}}{50}}$$

$$= 386.85\,.$$

4. Substituting $Q = 386.85$ into Equation 15.23 results in $F(R) \geq 0.7880$, implying $R = 510$.
5. Recomputing Q using Equation 15.22 yields $Q = 396.63$.

You should verify that beyond this step, computed R values will not change and neither, then, will computed Q values. Thus the algorithm has converged to optimal values of $R^* = 510$ and $Q^* = 396.63$. The safety stock implied by this solution is $R - \overline{d}_L = 510 - 500 = 10$ units. After the follow-up exercises, a spreadsheet program is included to solve this example.

FOLLOW-UP EXERCISES

42. Determine the optimal policy for the GCH blood bank (Example 15.5) using Model 3. Compare total inventory cost per year for both models based on Equation 15.21.

**43. Solve Example 15.6 with $C_o = 200$, $C_h = 25$, $C_p = 10$ and all else the same.

44. Solve Exercise 41 using Model 3. Compare $C(Q, R)$ for each model.

Spreadsheet Program for Example 15.6

```
A1: '   CO
B1: '   CH
C1: '   CP
D1: '   DBAR
E1: '  LTDAVE
F1: '     QR
H1: 'EOQ
A2: 100
B2: 50
C2: 2.5
D2: 36500
E2: 500
```

```
F2: @SQRT(2*D2*(A2+G8)/B2)
H2: @SQRT(2*D2*A2/B2)
A4: 'Trial EOQ
B4: '   F(R*)
F4: '    R
A5: 386.8492
B5: 1-(A5/D2)*(B2/C2)
F5: 510
A7: '      dl
C7: '     f(dl)
D7: '      F(dl)
E7: '
F7: '
G7: '  CP*SUM
A8: 460
C8: 0.02
D8: +C8
E8: (A8-$F$5)*C8
F8: @IF(E8>=0,E8,0)
G8: +C2*F18
A9: 470
C9: 0.06
D9: @SUM(C8..C9)
E9: (A9-$F$5)*C9
F9: @IF(E9>=0,E9,0)
A10: 480
C10: 0.13
D10: @SUM(C8..C10)
E10: (A10-$F$5)*C10
F10: @IF(E10>=0,E10,0)
A11: 490
C11: 0.165
D11: @SUM(C8..C11)
E11: (A11-$F$5)*C11
F11: @IF(E11>=0,E11,0)
A12: 500
C12: 0.25
D12: @SUM(C8..C12)
E12: (A12-$F$5)*C12
F12: @IF(E12>=0,E12,0)
A13: 510
C13: 0.165
D13: @SUM(C8..C13)
E13: (A13-$F$5)*C13
F13: @IF(E13>=0,E13,0)
A14: 520
C14: 0.13
D14: @SUM(C8..C14)
E14: (A14-$F$5)*C14
F14: @IF(E14>=0,E14,0)
A15: 530
C15: 0.06
D15: @SUM(C8..C15)
E15: (A15-$F$5)*C15
F15: @IF(E15>=0,E15,0)
A16: 540
```

```
C16: 0.02
D16: @SUM(C8..C16)
E16: (A16-$F$5)*C16
F16: @IF(E16>=0,E16,0)
E18: '   SUM =
F18: @SUM(F8..F16)
```

```
Instructions
1. Enter R value of 0 in F5.
2. Enter EOQ value from H2 into Trial EOQ cell A5.
3. Enter an R value such that F(dl)>F(R*).
4. Take the QR value and enter it as Trial EOQ.
5. Repeat steps 2 and 3 until no change in QR value.
```

CO	CH	CP	DBAR	LTDAVE	QR	EOQ
100	50	2.5	36500	500	396.6295	382.0994

Trial EOQ	F(R*)	R
386.8492	0.788027	510

dl	f(dl)	F(dl)			CP*SUM
460	0.02	0.02	−1	0	7.75
470	0.06	0.08	−2.4	0	
480	0.13	0.21	−3.9	0	
490	0.165	0.375	−3.3	0	
500	0.25	0.625	−2.5	0	
510	0.165	0.79	0	0	
520	0.13	0.92	1.3	1.3	
530	0.06	0.98	1.2	1.2	
540	0.02	1	0.6	0.6	
			SUM =	3.1	

LTDAVE is average lead time demand
$f(dl)$ is probability of demand shown
$F(dl)$ is cumulative probability of demand shown
$CP*SUM$ is $C_p \sum_{d_L > R} (d_L - R) f(d_L)$

15.6 AGGREGATE INVENTORY MANAGEMENT

Seldom does an inventory manager have only one inventory item to cause sleepless nights. Usually he or she is responsible for a large dollar volume of inventory made up of several hundred items. In this section, we examine two approaches to managing several items in inventory. The first approach focuses our attention on which items are worth the worry, and the second approach allows us to pay attention to the budget.

The ABC System of Aggregate Inventory Management

Whether or not you subscribe to the creationist, evolutionary, or big bang theory of the universe, you will probably already have encountered the fundamental law of nature that 20 percent of the whatevers create 80 percent of the action or problems. This law has been proved over and over whether in application to courses, professors, customers, in-baskets, or inventory.

To use the ABC system of inventory control, simply rank the inventory items by dollar volume — annual quantity demanded times cost or value per unit. Then classify as *A* items the 15–20 percent of items making up 80 percent of the total dollar volume of inventory. The next 30–40 percent become *B* items; and the remainder, *C* items.

To avoid sleepless nights, inventory managers pay close attention to *A* items and worry little about C items that account for only 5 percent of dollar volume. The best discussion of different inventory control systems for different classes is found in a classic work by Peterson and Silver.[8]

FOLLOW-UP EXERCISES

45. What percentage of items are classified as *C*, and what dollar volume do they constitute? How upset would you be if the percentages did not work out exactly?
46. Suppose you have five inventory items (known as stock-keeping units) as your responsibility. The first item has a dollar volume of $80,000, the next two have a dollar volume of $15,000; and the last two, $5,000. Listing these items as items 1 through 5, specify which are *A*, *B*, and *C*. Make up numbers for annual demand and unit value consistent with the dollar volumes given above and with annual demand in units declining from a high of 10,000 for item 1 to a low of 500 for item 5. Now do the same with annual demand in units increasing from a low of 500 for item 1 through a high of 10,000 for item 5. Any conclusions? (Note that dollar volumes always refer to annual dollar volumes in this section.)

Aggregate Inventory Analysis with Constraints

When there are many items in the inventory system, we must be concerned about total dollars tied up in inventory and also about the total number of orders or possibly setups in a factory. In this section, we examine the situation of an inventory volume constraint. Consider a simplified inventory situation whereby inventory is to be carried for each of two liquid items. Assume that conditions for the classic EOQ model are approximated, except that the maximum storage volume of both items combined must not exceed 400,000 gallons. Relevant weekly data are given in Table 15–3.

TABLE 15–3

	Item 1	Item 2
D	= 1 million gallons per week	2 million gallons per week
C_h	= $0.02 per gallon per week	$0.01 per gallon per week
C_o	= $200 per order	$300 per order
t_L	= 1 week	2 weeks

With this data, you ought to be able to calculate the unconstrained EOQ solutions as 141,421 and 346,410 gallons, respectively, for items 1 and 2. The total of the two exceeds the capacity constraint by 87,831 gallons.

What does it mean to exceed a capacity constraint? Holding costs have been underestimated! Suppose we multiply the per unit holding cost on both items by the same

[8]Rein Peterson and Edward A. Silver, *Decision Systems for Inventory Management and Production Planning* (New York: John Wiley & Sons, 1979).

factor and thereby increase the holding cost and decrease the EOQs by enough to satisfy the constraint. Try doubling the per-unit holding costs to \$0.04 and \$0.02, respectively, for items 1 and 2. The corresponding EOQs would be 100,000 and 244,949 gallons. This puts us below the capacity constraint, so we ought to look for a factor of less than 2 which will bring us right up against the constraint. Convince yourself that a factor of 1.49 does the job pretty well.

In Exercise 65 at the end of this chapter, we ask you to formulate this problem with an objective function and constraints. Once formulated in this fashion, you can form the Lagrangean function and solve to find that the Lagrange multiplier is the factor we are using above.

FOLLOW-UP EXERCISES

47. Suggest a simple procedure to solve for the factor needed to bring the EOQs in the example back to storage capacity. Use this simple procedure to find the factor 1.49.
48. Suppose the maximum storage capacity were 200,000 gallons per week. Find the optimal constrained EOQs.

15.7 MULTIECHELON INVENTORY MANAGEMENT AND SCHEDULING

As mentioned in Section 15.1, multiechelon inventory systems are those wherein inventory moves from one level or stocking point to another. A factory and a warehouse form a multiechelon system, just as do two workstations. In such systems, the classical EOQ approach does not hold water because ordering in EOQ amounts automatically negates the assumption of a constant demand rate at the level receiving the EOQ order. More importantly, however, multiechelon inventory systems also cause the scheduling issue to surface. Even in the discussion of aggregate inventory management earlier, you may have been bothered by an inventory-related scheduling issue. We do not have the capacity to hold both EOQ amounts together, but why not just schedule the lots so that the second item does not get put into inventory until the first one is depleted just enough to allow sufficient room? Once we introduce capacity constraints, we can no longer completely divorce inventory and scheduling considerations. Because different echelons have different capacities, we are beginning to look at a pretty interesting problem.

Several approaches have been taken to solving the multiechelon inventory problem. Material requirements planning (MRP) became the crusade of the 70s to help vanquish the straw man of order point or EOQ-based systems. In the 80s we are hearing about the Japanese zero inventory systems. Let us look at these not only to understand what is happening in the inventory world but also to study the process of modeling inventory systems as it has evolved. As we move into the era of computer-integrated manufacturing (CIM), we will see dramatic advances in inventory control as design for manufacturing becomes a reality.

Material Requirements Planning

The most important underpinning of MRP is the distinction between *independent* and *dependent (derived) demand*. Independent demand, where demand must be estimated or forecasted, is assumed by order point systems. Dependent demand, on the other hand, depends on other echelons, can be calculated exactly, and is not well-approximated by forecasting models. Once a production plan for the assembly of end items has been established, the exact demand for the component parts that are necessary to support the assembly plan can be calculated. For example, if a furniture plant were to assemble 600 chairs of a particular kind every six weeks, then the weekly demand for the chair seats would be 0, 0, 0, 0, 0, 600. The average weekly demand is 100; it can be shown, however, that the resultant 95 percent safety stock level would equal 343 units. These 343 units would be unneeded for five weeks out of six and *insufficient* for the sixth week!

The simple fact is that demand for component parts is usually not a random process. The furniture firm sells chairs not chair seats; the demand for seats is completely determined by (dependent on) assembly needs. We do not need a safety stock of chair seats when we are not assembling chairs. Moreover, the weakness of the order point approach is evident when one considers how the order point approach would operate in this example. If there were an inventory of chair seats that was being depleted by chair assembly, then 600 units would be withdrawn in week 6. This draw might reduce the inventory substantially below the reorder point, and interpretation of that low inventory might lead to a rush replenishment order. But, we will not *need* any more seats until week 12.

The superiority of an MRP system over an order point system can be nicely illustrated by the approach of a restaurant to meal planning. In an order point system, the chef would review the pantry inventory levels daily before deciding on replenishments. Any item that fell below the reorder point would be added to the shopping list in the amount given by the economic order quantity. A sample rule might be: Buy ten 50-pound sacks of Uncle Ben's rice whenever the inventory gets below 100 pounds.

The MRP approach would plan the meals to be offered during the week, which is equivalent to what is called the *master production schedule*. The set of meals (finished products) would then be *exploded* into the necessary ingredients (components or raw materials) by looking in the chef's cookbook (in manufacturing, the "cookbook" is called a *bill of materials*). The result would be a list of required ingredients and their necessary amounts. These *gross requirements* would then be compared with pantry inventories to determine the *net requirements* for the shopping list (economic order quantities could still be purchased). Additionally, the MRP system tells the chef when and in what amounts each ingredient is needed, which is called *time phasing*.

There should be no doubt in your mind that the MRP system would result in fewer stockouts and lower inventories. For example, consider an item such as poultry spice. If the inventory level fell below the reorder point immediately following the Christmas holidays, then the reorder point system would order more poultry spice even though the next large requirement for turkey in the "master production schedule" were not until Thanksgiving. A less severe case of the same phenomenon occurs when rice is replenished even though no meal with rice is planned during the next week. For planned meals using either a much larger than usual quantity of an ingredient or an ingredient not normally stocked, the order point system again will be inferior to the MRP system.

In conclusion, note that the benefits of MRP are not without costs. Forecasts, master production schedules, and bills of materials need to be precise. Large databases require extensive data maintenance, and concomitant procedural changes occur frequently. MRP can lead to substantial returns. This is particularly true if the final product is made up of complex assemblies, if lead times for components and/or raw materials are long, and if the manufacturing cycle for the finished product is long.

Example 15.7 Widget Production

The MRP approach can be completely understood by examining only one level in detail to see how it might possibly interact with every other level. Suppose a company has a demand for widgets. *Letting GR represent gross requirements, OH on hand inventory at the end of a period,* and *POR a planned order release* at the beginning of a period, we get the type of table shown in Table 15–4.

TABLE 15–4 MRP Table

Week	0	1	2	3	4	5	6	7	8
GR		0	0	0	0	0	600	0	0
OH	50	50	50	50	50	50	0	0	0
POR					550				

The table tells us that no units are required until the sixth week, at which time we need 600 units. Since we already hold 50 units in inventory, we need an additional 550 units. With a two-week production lead time, we should release an order to production at the beginning of week 4 in order to have the inventory available at the beginning of week 6.

The main points to consider in MRP are these:

1. The planned order release from an item becomes the gross requirement for any items making it up. If our widget is made up of two subassemblies, each subassembly must be ready by week 4.
2. The master production schedule specifies the production times and quantities for the end item, whether the end item be a finished widget or a high-level subassembly ready to be customized.
3. For each level in the system, we must know into what the item goes so that we can determine its gross requirements. If an item goes into three different subassemblies, it must be ready on time to meet the planned order release dates of these subassemblies. It is also important to know how many units of the item go into one unit of subasssembly.
4. The bill of materials gives the product structure outlining how the product is assembled.

Example 15.8 Widget Production—Revisited

Some of these principles of MRP can be seen in the following MRP tables. In these tables, the master production schedule (MPS) calls for the production of 600 widgets during week 6. This schedule has been arrived at with consideration of the load this would put on each workstation. Each widget has a gadget subassembly as well as a gozinto subassembly with two-week and three-week lead times, respectively. Assembly of the gadget and gozinto subassemblies to make a widget takes two weeks. Each widget uses two gozinto subassemblies. These relationships are shown in Figure 15–12 and Table 15–5.

FIGURE 15–12 Widget Product Structure

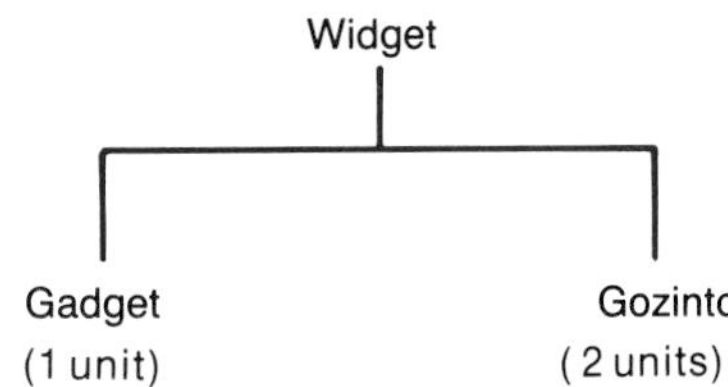

TABLE 15–5 MRP Tables for Widgets

				Widgets					
Week	**0**	**1**	**2**	**3**	**4**	**5**	**6**	**7**	**8**
MPS							600		

				Widgets					
Week	**0**	**1**	**2**	**3**	**4**	**5**	**6**	**7**	**8**
GR							600		
OH	50	50	50	50	50	50	0	0	0
POR					550				

				Gadget subassembly					
Week	**0**	**1**	**2**	**3**	**4**	**5**	**6**	**7**	**8**
GR					550				
OH	3	3	3	3	0	0	0	0	0
POR			547						

				Gozinto subassembly					
Week	**0**	**1**	**2**	**3**	**4**	**5**	**6**	**7**	**8**
GR					1,100				
OH	2	2	2	2	1,098	0	0	0	0
POR		1,098							

FOLLOW-UP EXERCISES

49. Suppose the MPS called for the production of 600 widgets in week 5 rather than week 6. Could this be done?
50. The MPS is revised and now calls for the production of 580 widgets in week 7 rather than 600 in week 6. Revise all tables appropriately.
51. The MPS is revised again and now calls for the production of 300 widgets in week 6 and 300 in week 8 rather than 580 in week 7. Revise all tables appropriately.

Just-in-Time Inventory Systems

The Japanese have generally been credited with developing just-in-time inventory systems, even though Lee Iacocca claims that American automobile companies had such systems with their suppliers in the 1920s (turning iron ore into steel and then engine blocks within 24 hours at River Rouge).[9] **Just-in-time (JIT)** should not be thought of as a technique for inventory control but as a general approach to production and quality control. The main ingredients of this approach are reduced set-up times, zero inventory, production and delivery just-in-time for need, a "pull" orientation, and a repetitive manufacturing environment. We will discuss each of these major JIT elements in turn.

Perhaps the most significant contribution of the Japanese approach is their total disregard of assumptions about setup times. Steadfastly refusing to accept long setup times, the Japanese devoted engineering efforts to minimizing set-up times while American companies were basing MRP implementations on setup and lead times as given. In this challenge to setup, the Japanese were taking a much more fundamental operations research approach than were the many researchers who spent time in the 1970s and 1980s still studying variations of EOQ in an MRP setting. What we must recognize is the intimate link between setup and lead time. Lead time is made up of setup plus run time plus some planned queue or waiting time. As well as making small lot sizes economical, reducing setup times cuts down on lead times. The importance of high quality standards also becomes apparent because buffer inventory is removed.

JIT is sometimes called stockless production, and the idea of zero inventories is that the Japanese try to operate without buffer stocks or inventories held in anticipation of need. For example, buffer stocks between work centers are not seen as important to decouple the work centers because the JIT response would be to have the worker at the faster work center help the worker at the slower center. Also a worker at a faster work center would not build up inventory because he or she would perform other activities, such as machine maintenance, or would be idle rather than build an inventory that is not being used up.

Consistent with the zero inventory philosophy, the main idea of JIT is to produce and deliver each item just in time for its intended use. In purchasing, the supplier delivers the inventory just in time for its use in the company and this requires considerable cooperation throughout the vendor-supplier chain.

JIT is often associated with **Kanban**, the Japanese implementation of a *pull system*. In English we think of Kanban as a card system. For our purposes, it is sufficient to note that containers of small lots are passed between work centers as authorized by a conveyance card. The conveyance signal comes from the using work center, establishing a pull mode. Further, production at the work center is triggered by a production card when the container is empty. Rather than producing to plan, Kanban calls for production to need established by downstream work centers.

Finally, JIT is associated with repetitive manufacturing just as MRP is associated with a job shop environment. In a job shop environment, production or final assembly awaits a specific customer order. Final level assemblies may be ready in anticipa-

[9] L. Iacocca, *Lee Iacocca: An Autobiography*, New York: Bantam Books Paperback, 1986, p. 197.

tion of the customer order, but in a real sense the final product is customized. Repetitive manufacturing systems are closer to assembly lines except that products are produced in batches with changeovers between runs. Inventory management with the JIT approach calls for designing common parts for different products so that manufacturing can be repetitive rather than job lot.

15.8 ASSESSMENT

Because of the enormous amount of money tied up in inventory, this application of the operations research approach has received widespread praise, criticism, and blame. Inventories can be quantified, and demand patterns can be examined statistically. The cost trade-offs can be modeled with approaches similar to EOQ or to MRP. Yet the popular press currently heralds the Japanese just-in-time and zero inventory systems as what American companies should have been doing all along. What benefit were the classic order quantity systems of the 1960s and the MRP crusade of the 1970s if the real solution was to keep zero inventories?

After reading this chapter, you ought to be able to discern the grain of truth in the latest consultant's fad, the computer vendor's sales pitch and the practitioner's skepticism. EOQ models do not apply in a multiechelon manufacturing situation, although they may apply at the retail and end item level. To sell MRP systems, the MRP crusade of the 1970s set up EOQ as the straw man. Yet both approaches have their place, as does the zero inventory approach.

First, we should emphasize that the simple EOQ may be the most widely misapplied tool of management science. The assumptions are so severe that the model can seldom yield insights about real-world inventory situations. The approach, however, remains valid, and variations of the model can indeed yield important insights. In approaching an inventory problem, the EOQ approach does not begin with a computer program. Rather, the first step is to provide a verbal statement of the problem. Then verbal and mathematical statements of both the decisions and the system criteria need to be developed. After specifying constraints, the management scientist develops a model to relate the decisions to the criteria.

Throughout this chapter, you have seen several inventory models developed. In the first third of the chapter, the models arose from relaxing one or another of the EOQ assumptions. As a manager, you should understand that these models are only suggestive of which model should actually be employed. You should value the approach more than any specific model, and you should recognize that the cost trade-offs cannot be avoided by any new system regardless of its acronym. In relaxing the EOQ assumptions, we moved into the cases of usage during production, planned back orders, and then quantity discounts. These models can, of course, be mixed together and also modified according to the actual nature of the cost criteria.

In the middle of the chapter, we presented several models for the more realistic case where demand is not certain but can be modeled statistically. In carrying finished goods, what probability of stockout are we willing to permit? Even though we may not be able to estimate a stockout cost, such a cost can be imputed from our behavior. The central portion of this chapter then deals with cost trade-offs in the face of stockouts.

The final portion of the chapter begins the study of much more complex systems. Aggregate inventory analysis considers the very realistic situation that inventories of many unique items are held at once within a given storage facility. Multiechelon inventory analysis considers the case of dependent demand where the demand at one level in the firm depends on demand at another level. In the manufacturing context, such systems as manufacturing resource planning (MRPII) and just-in-time (JIT) will be summarized in the following selected reading. The article provides an excellent summary of the state of the art of inventory control at several major manufacturing plants. Based on what you have learned in this chapter, you should be able to read the article and round out your knowledge of inventory control.

Just-In-Time in the MRP II Environment

SERGIO LOTENSCHTEIN

*On September 10 and 11 of last year, I had the pleasure of attending a Just-in-Time conference whose attendees were there to discuss the success of their JIT efforts. Perhaps this is not so unusual given that each month someone is sponsoring similar JIT conferences. What is uncommon is that the men and women who gathered for this conference work for companies that have attained the distinction of "Class A" in their Manufacturing Resource Planning (MRP II) environment; and that they, themselves, honor that distinction.**

Sponsored by the Oliver Wight Companies, these representatives gathered not to laud, defend, or denounce MRP II; rather, they were there to illustrate, with their contemporaries, the progress and benefits of using JIT in their MRP II environments.

The benefits of JIT are becoming well known. You may already be all too aware of what JIT has done for many American companies. Yet, there is still much talk of displacing the existing methods of manufacturing for the new ones. Is MRP an adjunct to JIT? Are CIM and MRPII complementary? Is Kanban-JIT and which is implemented first? Perhaps we've all been too consumptive about the amount of literature on the subject and the fact that much of it varies in statement of definition and purpose. One example is the subject of Kanban as it relates to JIT and the "push" versus "pull" maxims (as defined by the APICS Dictionary).

Kanban is not JIT, it is one way to apply JIT, but is Kanban a "pull" system if JIT is considered as such? In one interpretation by Walter E. Goddard, president of the Oliver Wight Educational Associates, this may not appear to be the case; "Those companies wherein components are being 'pulled from the stockroom and pulled from one operation to the next on demand' are generally calling this a pull system, and yet if it is replenishing inventory in anticipation of that component being needed again, I believe we would all consider that a push system."

Although many will argue with that and be logically correct, it is far more important to negotiate these definitions where they are operationally pertinent to the user. By defining JIT, MRP, Kanban, CIM, etc. in terms of interdependent functionality, we can adapt some or all of these methods to our present day manufacturing conditions, simply because in our present industrial flux, there is no room for "versus."

THE PLAYERS

Gathering MRPII Class "A" companies to discuss their JIT implementation is a formidable task. Companies like Hewlett-Packard, Black & Decker, Tektronix, Steelcase, Xerox, Bently Nevada, and The Tennant Company share in a mutual admiration, in that their venture into JIT has been successful, or as Dave Garwood, Executive VP of Oliver Wight Educational Services puts it, "Here we have a group of .300 hitters, people that are extremely knowledgeable, that have defined their existing problems before using JIT." The following are just a few examples of how these "players" have used the Just-in-Time philosophy to enhance the productive output of their organizations.

JIT 1: BENTLY NEVADA

As a $60 million company producing Machinery Protection Instrumentation, Bently Nevada often has to function in the capacity of a job shop as well as a batch manufacturing facility. They have been using MRP for eight years, MRPII for four, and have improved 100 percent in their control of the business, customer service, productivity and inventory to name a few. Their JIT concentration came in the form of vendor relations.

The initial and most important step in JIT implementation was the ability to communicate their needs to their vendors. Be they 5 or 50, if the vendor cannot provide the material you need just-in-time, then the whole concept is not worth implementing.

Reprinted with permission from *Production & Inventory Management Review with APICS News*, February 1986 pp. 26–29.

*MRPII systems are MRP systems operating in a closed loop fashion, checking the capacity requirements implied by the master production schedule and allowing revisions to the schedule. When extended to include business and financial planning, MRP becomes MRPII. A class A MRPII user can be thought of as having the inventory situation well in hand with top management support, realistic master production schedules, and little need for expediting. The closed loop concept is used for both priority and capacity planning.

(continued)

As well, it is important that the vendor understand the manufacturers drive toward JIT, the concepts of quality and the importance of timely execution of products delivered. But vendor relationsis not as easy as one might consider. Vendors look upon JIT implementation as a change device that makes them responsible for holding inventory. Ray Bacon, manufacturing manager at Bently Nevada, recommends that one should understand the vendors process of what's reasonable and what isn't. "If you are not willing to make some changes why should the vendor?"

The question is also of one between scheduled and the nonscheduled vendor. In some cases if you are the vendor you must be willing to be a scheduled one as much as you want your vendors to be one. Many benefits can be realized from this involvement:

Working with Bently some vendors had cause to implement MRP systems for scheduling.

Quality Control. Bacon says "As you get closer to JIT relationships with vendors, traditional roles have to change, for example your internal method has got to change, by actually reducing some factor like internal quality (meaning less inspection of received shipments)."

With JIT you can actually delete some people out of the loop. For example, vendors can bypass purchasing because committed orders are set, now the vendor can ask product questions right to the line supervisors.

Bently is not alone in their success with vendor relations. Xerox's Reprographic Divisions JIT/vendor relations have decreased the number of vendors from 5,000 to 300, "Fewer suppliers allow for quality control, since you can directly deal with 300," says Pierre C. Landry, materials manager at Xerox. "Trust does not come easy, you have to work at it, you're better at building trust with fewer suppliers than with many. For Xerox, these relations have reduced costs by 50 percent and decreased lead times."

Albeit, complete JIT vendor relations on all commodities are not always practical. At Bently some vendors are not near, and the uncertainty of winter road conditions over the Sierra mountains make JIT/Vendor execution a major obstacle.

JIT 2: THE TENNANT COMPANY

The Tennant Company is a manufacturer of industrial cleaning equipment. They have been using MRP for the past 18 years, and MRPII for the last 12. With their MRPII system Tennant has seen an improvement of inventory by 30 percent; a 50 percent control of their business and a productivity improvement of 20 percent. In 1981 Tennant decided to be a JIT user.

Duane S. Davis, Tennant's plant manager, says that "JIT is something that you have to have a fairly even demand picture of." With their 10 product families and their forecasts fairly stable, Tennant uses JIT methods to enhance the leveling of their master schedule. According to Mr. Davis, master scheduling for JIT requires several disciplines.

Stabilizing Production for a Fixed Time Period. This implies more than "don't change the schedule or leadtime." It implies providing a level schedule that is fixed in the first month, firm in the second and flexible beyond, but the key is the level schedule, not the fixed periods.

Knowing the Production Environment. Management by eyes and ears is very important. As Davis states, "You have to know what the people are doing, and how fast you can make changes."

Obtaining Commitments to Change. It is one thing to present a proposed change to people. It is entirely different for those people to make that change happen. JIT is a big change, training is a big component to obtaining commitments.

Sticking to the Plan. No matter what the size of the job, if it is worth starting, it is worth finishing.

The key to having a level schedule is short cycle scheduling. Because traditional production management emphasizes economical lots and product stocking, JIT rules say that one should produce only what the customer is buying. On short cycle, for example, a JIT schedule strives to build daily; by releasing weekly lots instead of economical lots it forces them to reduce setup costs, material handling, and order processing.

The production line itself follows the Kanban system to pull carts through the line. Tennant has achieved good results by reducing lots in a single product model with multiple configurations. Another

(*continued*)

goal is to build mixed models (different products of variable configurations) on the same assembly line.

The results, they've eliminated finished goods inventory; inventory decreased from $23 million to $16, a reduction of 20 percent and inventory turns went from four to nine.

The flexibility in JIT schedules requires that people be flexible, that they can be moved effectively from one production area to another. Most important though, Davis feels that when "one levels the schedule it should be done on a project by project basis instead of doing it all at one time."

Level scheduling is not the cure-all for all companies. For example at Steelcase, due to the diversity of the product lines, they need stable schedules rather than level schedules—since they are making all products at all times.

But what of MRP? "MRP will let you do whatever you want to level the schedule," says Davis. JIT is the execution.

JIT 3: STEELCASE CORP.

Steelcase is a Class A MRPII user, and they seem to feel the need to use JIT concepts to ensure the industrial advantage they possess. Steelcase had identified 11 elements of their JIT implementation project. Setup time reduction; leadtime reduction; card scheduling system; preventive maintenance; supplier program; focus processing/group technology/ cellular manufacturing; employee involvement; statistical process control; reduction in need of stockrooms; stable schedules; and containerization.

Setup time reduction was an important target to be accomplished. Gary Vredenburg, plant manager of Steelcase comments, "We spent more time deciding what kind of EOQ system to use instead of setup.... We realized that JIT is a real philosophy...we're not trying to avoid setups, we're going to do the same thing today, but we're going to do it better and one way to do it is by reducing lot sizes." Other reduction goals included decreasing down times and scrap as well as generating quality improvements.

Steelcase's emphasis on setups began two years ago. They created a steering committee that comprised many disciplines in the plant including foremen, production and inventory control, engineering, and quality control to name a few. This committee concentrated on employee involvement, education and enthusiasm. The committee selected which operations were to be targeted for JIT.

In order to reduce setups they observed and videotaped a specific operation including line shutdowns. By reviewing their recordings and concentrating on JIT education to the floor level, Steelcase created an ongoing improvement program. This included a continuing recommendation process from the tool operators and a preventive maintenance program that now puts a lot of pressure on the maintenance people. Employee enthusiasm? Vredenburg notes, "Once you turn it on, you can't turn it off... these resources were never hidden, we just never tapped them."

Steelcase has had success with this part of the program. Floor space has been reduced due to lower lot sizes, as well as reduction of scrap since quality now becomes part of the JIT process. As their JIT line perfects itself the next step is to develop a no work-order situation.

Steelcase is a large multiplant operation. In another application, a cell operation in their plants was able to decrease material handling and storage dramatically.

Pre-JIT and post-JIT results on components at Steelcase's File Cabinet production lines are worthy of notice. Prior to JIT, a weld operation performed on a product amounted to the use of 82 warehouse openings, 13 days inventory on hand, 55,000 pieces in process, 115 containers, and 11 forktruck moves.

Implementation of JIT processes via a card system included eliminating subassembly schedules from the MRP explosion—via linking to the final assembly number. Three- and two-day schedules changed to daily with prededuction from MRP, and a week's forecast would be given to the weld division for all end supports.

Repairs have been reduced from 15 percent to 1 percent, pieces in process went to 16,000, now there's 5 days of inventory on hand instead of 13, warehouse openings are zero, containers used went down to 31, forktruck moves are now two, and the number of warehouse moves went from four to one.

Robert Birch, P&IC manager at Steelcase, documents additional improvements which include:

1. Quicker reaction to quality problems because less inventory is in process.

(continued)

2. Problems are found quicker, and due to a decrease in repairs a 10 percent reduction in direct labor has resulted.
3. Improved operator safety by reducing wrist and back discomfort.
4. Operator input from design through implementation made the system work.
5. Less administration required to execute the schedule. Operators determine what needs to be run rather than shop floor control. Reduction in indirect labor relating to material handling and dispatching has also taken place.
6. Improved housekeeping, due to organization of queuing areas (inbound and outbound stock points).
7. Overall capacity has increased by 25 percent, and floor space has been reduced by 25 percent.

JIT 4: TEKTRONIX

JIT use in the MRPII environment has wielded results, and only begins to prove what many already believe. That both JIT and MRPII can be adjunct; more so, MRP II disciplines can be used directly to assist in the JIT implementation.

Tektronix has more than 30 plants under their corporate logo, and each one is committed in some degree to JIT.

In applying the JIT techniques, Tektronix has seen much progress. They've encountered manufacturing process improvements, operational improvements, and lead-time reductions: vendor lead-time reduction (internal vendors such as those from component plants as well as external vendors); level scheduling; use of MRP planning with JIT execution; warehousing and manufacturing floor space reduction . . . to name just a few.

In the preface of "A Guide To Manufacturing Excellence" Ralph Todd, MRP/JIT operations consultant at Tektronix, writes, "Manufacturing excellence is a journey, not a project. The intent of this booklet is to provide a method of measuring your progress toward manufacturing excellence and to highlight some of the practices and techniques. The solutions are in the participation and creativity of the people, where encouraged by management."

The "booklet" Todd refers to is a checklist, developed by Tektronix. This guide does not direct itself to one specific manufacturing philosophy and method. The checklist actually defines the "journey" as the effective use of

People Involvement.

Total Quality control.

Just-in-time.

Manufacturing resource planning.

The merits of the guide rest in the emphatic explanations of the different areas of the checklist. For instance; number 19 states that "Accounting Systems are redesigned to operate in a JIT environment . . . . Because work orders are eliminated, they are not available to report to. The industries that accomplish this will convert from job order costing to process costing."

And accounting has been quite the bone of contention where the application of JIT is concerned. For JIT implementation the accounting system needs to change. There appears to be too much resistance in the accounting world to the JIT philosophy. Accounting needs to be re-evaluated. In a recent interview done by *Corporate Accounting Magazine*, Robert Kaplan, former dean of Business School at Carnegie Mellon University, stated that "it is important to remember that accountants do not set strategy. Strategy is set by the senior operating executive committee of the company. What accountants can do is to understand the strategy, and then devise a consistent accounting and measurement system. This new role arises from the fact that the old reliable, generic accounting model used for the past 70 years is no longer applicable for the global competition of the 1980s." Since the push system uses the release of a work order to build a predetermined batch or lot size, the "lot size of one" approach in JIT clearly eliminates that specific function of the work order. "The work order is kept to appease accounting," commented Charlene Adair, specialist manufacturing and quality systems at Hewlett-Packard, "Traditional MRP is based on work order—things we do not need."

THE JIT PHILOSOPHY

How can JIT best be defined? Although definitions are not easy, one of the most accomplished tasks at this conference was the development of the JIT definition seen in Figure 1. The most ironic part of a

(continued)

Just-in-Time conscience is that it is not as difficult as one may perceive. Charlene Adair recommends that:

1. "One should make only what is required as it is required, eliminating waste."
2. Top management commitment is essential. It takes quite a turnaround for it to happen. "The real idea is to charge, to really get going."
3. Start small and build on your successes.
4. Small means manageable, visible with a high likelihood of success, no major yield problems.

VOTE FOR ONE OR THE OTHER?

If one looks further into the successes of the companies just described as well as others such as Black & Decker and Hewlett-Packard, one would find that there is much to be gained in implementing the Just-in-Time philosophy, and that these companies are very proud of their successes. Amidst the bottle throwing that can be presently found on the value of our inherent manufacturing practices, it is refreshing to see these numerous companies willing to share their thoughts on the many subjects faced by manufacturing every day.

Recently someone said that manufacturing managers tend to be people who have grown up on the factory floor. They think in terms of incremental improvements on "what is" instead of "what might be." Perhaps that is one perception, but apparently not the case where the individuals at this conference were concerned. In their eyes, JIT is appropriate to any kind of manufacturing, be it make-to-order, batch, repetitive, continuous, etc. They are also firmly committed to the MRP II facility that they have worked hard to make successful. To them it is not a choice of having to choose one or the other; it is one and the other, conjunctively and at best asymmetrically.

The disciplines required to learn any manufacturing methodology lies in the ability of its managements to communicate intelligently, first and foremost. Whether the discussions be CIM, MRP, JIT, SFC, and the cacophony of buzzwords, it is essential to note that each serves a purpose and there really is no room for "versus."

FIGURE 1

Just-in-Time is a philosophy of manufacturing excellence based on pursuit of the planned elimination of all waste and consistent improvement of productivity. Just-in-Time encompasses the successful execution of all activities required to satisfy customer requirements from product design to delivery. It includes all states from acquisition and conversion of raw material to delivery of the product.

The primary elements of Just-in-Time may include . . .

- Reduction of
  - Work-in-process (WIP)
  - Queue
  - Setup
  - Manufacturing and purchase lead times
  - Lot sizes
  - Transit time
  - Factory floor space
- Preventing maintenance
- Supplier program
- Frequent vendor deliveries
- Focus processing
- Group technology
- Cellular manufacturing
- People involvement
- Point-of-view storage
- Level schedules
- Mixed model scheduling
- Standard containers
- Zero defects
- Quality at source
- Flexible manufacturing
- Minimum bill of material levels
- Housekeeping
- Line balancing
- 100% ± zero schedule attainment

In the broad sense, JIT applies to all forms of manufacturing: job shop, and process, as well as repetitive.

SELECTED REFERENCES

Aggarwal, Sumer C. "MRP, JIT, OPT, FMS?" *Harvard Business Review*, September–October 1985, pp. 4–8.

Aquilano, N. J., and D. E. Smith. "A Formal Set of Algorithms for Project Scheduling with Critical Path Scheduling/Material Requirements Planning." *Journal of Operations Management,* November 1980, pp. 57–67.

Brown, R. G. *Materials Management Systems*. New York: John Wiley & Sons, 1977.

________. "The New Push for DRP." *Inventories and Production*, July–August 1981, pp. 25–27. Reprinted by permission.

________. *Advanced Service Parts Inventory Control*. 2nd ed. Norwich, Vt.: Materials Management Systems, 1982.

Clark, A. J., and H. Scarf. "Optimal Policies for a Multiechelon Inventory Problem." *Management Science,* July 1980, pp. 475–90.

Dicasali, Ray L. "MIS in the Computer Integrated Factory." *P & IM Review with APICS News,* April 1986, pp. 24–30.

Gardner, Everette S., and David G. Dannenbring. "Using Optimal Policy Surfaces to Analyze Aggregate Inventory Trade-Offs." *Management Science*, August 1979, pp. 709–20.

Graves, S. C., and L. B. Schwarz. "Single Cycle Continuous Review Policies for Arborescent Production/Inventory Systems." *Management Science*, January 1977, pp. 529–40.

Heskett, J. L.; N. A. Glaskowsky; and R. M. Ivie. *Business Logistics*. 2nd ed. New York: Ronald Press, 1973.

Hirsch, Albert A., and Michael C. Lovell, *Sales Anticipations and Inventory Behavior*. New York: John Wiley & Sons, 1969.

Kinnucan, Paul. "Flexible Systems Invade the Factory." *High Technology*, July 1983, pp. 32–42.

McLeavey, Dennis W., and Seetharama L. Narasimhan. *Production Planning and Inventory Control*. Boston: Allyn & Bacon, 1985.

Martin, Andre. "DRP—A Profitable New Corporate Planning Tool." *Canadian Transportation & Distribution Management,* November 1980, pp. 51–66.

Schonberger, Richard J. *Japanese Manufacturing Techniques*. New York: Free Press, 1982.

ADDITIONAL EXERCISES

52. ***Energy Inventories.*** A southern power company has recently made the publicly unpopular decision to resume burning coal. Although environmentalists have been lobbying to block this action, the Southern Regional Power Consortium approved the proposal that 20 percent of the energy requirements be generated using coal. The remaining 80 percent will originate from a combination of petroleum, nuclear, and hydroelectric sources.

    Energy demand tends to be relatively constant year-round because of the stability of the climate. Consequently, company analysts have projected a requirement of 10,000 tons of coal per day, or 3,650,000 tons per year. They are attempting to determine an optimal ordering policy that would lead to the minimization of total inventory costs. The supplier of their coal, Smokiest Mountain Coal Company, has quoted a delivered price of $60 per ton. Carrying costs are estimated at \$5 per ton per year and ordering costs at \$500 per order. Assuming that lead time is deterministic and constant at two days, determine:

a. The economic order quantity.
b. The optimal reorder point.
c. The optimal number of orders to place each year.
d. The minimum annual inventory costs.
e. What happens if lead time doubles to four days?

53. For Exercise 52 assume that the coal is shipped by train and that it must be purchased by the carload. Thus coal must be purchased in units of 60 tons (the capacity per jumbo hopper car).

a. Determine the minimum cost order quantity and reorder point given this constraint.
b. What is the optimal number of orders to place each year?
c. What are the total annual inventory costs under this policy?
d. What is the cost to the power company of the added restriction when compared with part *d* in Exercise 52.

54. By now we are all comfortable with sensitivity analysis. Company analysts admit that carrying costs can actually fluctuate between \$3 and \$6. Similarly, ordering cost per order can fluctuate between \$300 and \$650 per order. If the parameters assume their extreme values, analyze the effects of these fluctuations *independently* by determining the effects on the

a. EOQ.
b. Optimal reorder point.
c. Number of orders.
d. Total annual cost.

To which of these parameters do Q^*, N^*, and total cost seem to be most sensitive?

**55. Again referring to the initial data in Exercise 52, estimate the effect on Q^* and total cost of instantaneous changes in C_o and C_h by:

(1) Independently finding the derivatives of the expressions for Q^* and $C(Q^*)$ with respect to C_o and C_h.
(2) Evaluating these derivatives when all parameters assume the values given in Exercise 52.

Interpret the meaning of these derivatives. Would you say that Q^* and $C(Q^*)$ are very sensitive to changes in C_o and C_h? Explain.

56. Smokiest Mountain Coal Company has offered the power company a 1 percent discount if they will order in quantities of 100,000 tons or more.

a. What are total annual costs under the discount?
b. Should the power company accept the offer?
c. What is the indifference discount (see Exercise 22)?

57. Smokiest Mountain Coal Company has offered the power company a progression of discount possibilities. The offer is summarized here.

Purchase Price	**Minimum Purchase Quantity**
\$60.00	No minimum
59.00	100,000 tons
58.00	150,000 tons
57.50	200,000 tons

a. Determine the optimal order quantity and reorder point for the power company.
b. What is the minimum total annual inventory cost?

58. Assume that lead time is deterministic and equal to two days in Exercise 52. However, assume that lead time demand is stochastic with a mean of 20,000 tons and a distribution as given.

Class Intervals for Lead Time Demand (tons)	Lead Time Demand (d_L)	$f(d_L)$
16,500 but less than 17,500	17,000	0.02
17,500 but less than 18,500	18,000	0.08
18,500 but less than 19,500	19,000	0.20
19,500 but less than 20,500	20,000	0.40
20,500 but less than 21,500	21,000	0.20
21,500 but less than 22,500	22,000	0.08
22,500 but less than 23,500	23,000	0.02

The power company recognizes the penalty associated with incurring shortages. When a shortage of coal occurs, oil must be substituted at an effective additional cost of $1 per ton short. This $1 reflects additional costs associated with arranging and operating at higher levels of capacity at the oil-burning facilities. A company policy specifies that when replenished supplies of coal arrive following a shortage, the coal-burning facilities will reciprocate by operating at higher capacity so as to replace the energy units provided during the shortage (assume this is done at a negligible additional cost).

a. Determine the optimal order quantity and optimal reorder point.

b. What is the suggested buffer stock?

c. Rework parts *a* and *b* above if the penalty cost is $0.25 per ton short.

**59. *a.* *Simultaneously* compute Q^* and R^* for the data given in Exercise 58.

b. What should the safety stock be for this policy?

c. Based on Equation 15.21, compare the expected cost per day for this model to the expected cost per day for the policy in Exercise 58. Conclusion?

d. Compare the expected annual cost of the policy in part *a* to what the expected annual cost would be for the policy given in Exercise 52. Comment on the meaning of this difference.

60. Suppose that for the scenario in Exercise 58, the shortage cost is based not only on the amount short but also on the length of time over which the shortage exists, that is, $1 per ton per day.

a. Explicitly state why the model used in Exercise 58 is inappropriate.

b. Determine the optimal policy and associated cost using the deterministic back order model as an approximation. In which direction does this model bias Q^* and R^*?

c. Modify the policy in part *b* to account for the discounts indicated in Exercise 57.

***d.* Modify the policy in part *c* if the carrying cost is 10 percent of the purchase price.

61. ***Financial Management.*** Inventory models have been applied in arenas not usually thought of as involving inventory concepts. One such area is that of financial management. Any of you who have taken a finance course should readily concede that cash on hand is an inventoried item. Financial managers regularly deal with the problem of determining the optimal level of cash to keep on hand.

A variation on this treatment involves a company that has regular cash needs during a time period. The problem is to determine the optimal amount of new funds to obtain from borrowing. The objective is to minimize the costs of going to the market for funds and the opportunity cost associated with "carrying" the funds. Let

Q = Amount of cash obtained from each bond issue (dollars per issue).

C_o = Fixed cost associated with floating a bond issue (dollars per issue).

C_h = Annual opportunity (carrying) cost associated with having cash on hand (dollars per dollar per year).
D = Annual cash needs (dollars per year).

It is important to note that C_h is expressed as a proportion or percentage of a dollar. For example, if $C_h = 0.08$, then the opportunity cost is \$0.08 on the dollar per year, or 8 percent annually.

Assume that cash needs are uniform during the year, that funds can be obtained in a deterministic period of time, and that interest rates on bonds are constant and unaffected by the size of the bond issue.

a. Write a general expression for the total annual cost associated with borrowing and holding cash.

b. If D = \$100 million, C_o = \$100,000, and C_h = \$0.08 per dollar per year, determine the optimal size of each bond issue. How many times a year should bond issues be floated?

c. What is the annual cost of floating bonds? The annual opportunity cost associated with holding cash?

d. At what level of cash should a bond issue be initiated if it takes five days to float the issue? Assume 255 "trading" days in a year (i.e., days when the bond market and the firm actively engage in their affairs).

62. In Exercise 61 the opportunity cost associated with holding cash was estimated at 8 percent per year. Because of the dynamics of the money market, analysts concede that this percentage may fluctuate between 6.5 and 9.75 percent. By conducting sensitivity analyses, determine the effects on your answers to parts *b*, *c*, and *d* in Exercise 61 if C_h assumes these extreme values.

63. Suppose that cash withdrawals for the firm in Exercise 61 are probabilistic according to the distribution indicated here. As before, assume a 5-day fixed lead time and 255 trading days in a year.

Cash Withdrawals over Five Successive Trading Days (\$1,000)	Probability
170	0.05
180	0.10
190	0.30
200	0.40
210	0.05
220	0.10

a. Confirm that the mean demand during the lead time translates into an expected annual demand approximately consistent with the annual demand used in Exercise 61.

b. Assume a shortage cost of \$0.05 per dollar, which is independent of time. Determine Q^*, R^*, and optimal buffer stock based on Model 2 in Section 15.5. Would you say that the shortage cost for this application should include a time factor? Explain.

***c.* Determine the optimal policy by using Model 3 of Section 15.5. Use $C_p = 0.05$. Based on Equation 15.21, compare the expected annual cost of this policy to the expected annual costs of the policies in Exercise 61 and part *b* of this exercise.

**64. Derive expressions for Q^* and $C(Q^*)$ for a reorder point inventory model having the same assumptions as the classical model except that

$$C_o = a + b \cdot Q,$$

where a and b are fixed cost and variable cost parameters, respectively. Comment on differences between this model and the classic EOQ model.

65. ***Multi-Item Constrained EOQ Model.* Mathematical programming represents one approach to solving inventory models characterized by more than one item subject to constraints on capital, storage area, storage volume, or any other resource. Consider a simplified inventory situation whereby inventory is to be carried for each of two liquid items. Assume that conditions for the classic EOQ model are approximated, except that the maximum storage volume of both items combined must not exceed 400,000 gallons. Relevant weekly data are given below.

	Item 1	Item 2
D	1 million gallons per week	2 million gallons per week
C_h	\$0.02 per gallon per week	\$0.01 per gallon per week
C_o	\$200 per order	\$300 per order
t_L	1 week	2 weeks

a. Determine the unconstrained EOQ solution for each item, and show that the volume constraint is violated.

b. Formulate this model in terms of a mathematical programming format; that is, minimize z = (?) subject to (?).

c. Solve the model in part *b* by the Lagrange multiplier method. (*Hint:* Develop an expression for Q_i^* in terms of λ^*, and systematically assume trial values for λ^* until the constraint is approximately satisfied.)

66. In the single-period model with stochastic demand, confirm that the decision rule could be expressed as:

$$p \geqslant (uc - sv)/(sp - sv)$$

where p is the probability of selling the marginal unit, uc is the per-unit cost, sp is the selling price, and sv is the salvage value. Provide an intuitive explanation of this rule.

**67. Assume that the quantity demanded during a period is Poisson distributed with mean 100 and variance 100. Sales price is \$25, unit cost is \$15, and salvage value is \$5. How many units should the retailer stock?

**68. A periodic system is one in which we order every T years where T is a fraction, and we order enough to bring us up to a target M. Letting EOQ be the standard EOQ and D the annual demand, we can determine the optimal T as EOQ/D. Why is this so? Derive an expression for T as a function of C_o, C_h, and D where C_o is the setup cost per setup, C_h is the annual per-unit holding cost, and D is the annual demand. Letting L be the lead time, each order must cover the planning interval $T + L$ because the inventory on hand plus the inventory ordered must cover the demand between now and the time the next order is received. M, the target inventory level, can then be determined as the sum of expected demand during the planning interval plus a buffer stock to cover demand variations during this interval. In fact, if we ignore the interaction of T and M, we should be able to show that the optimal stockout risk is C_hT/C_p, where T is the review interval and C_p is the per-unit back order cost. With C_o = \$500, C_h = \$5, D = 8,000, L = 0.04 years, and C_p = \$10 per unit—calculate T and M. Draw a picture of the way this system would operate. Would it likely carry more or less safety stock than a continuous review system?

69. Distribution requirements planning (DRP) is the application of MRP principles to a distribution environment. Suppose a plant in Detroit serves warehouses in Chicago and Boston. Forecasts at the Chicago warehouse are for 53 units per week for the next eight weeks. The lead time between placing and receiving an order in Chicago is two weeks. The on-hand balance in Chicago is 200 units, and the economic order quantity is 300 units. Boston has forecasted demand of 68 units per week for the next eight weeks and a lead time of two weeks for receiving orders. At Boston the on-hand balance is 150 units, and the EOQ is 250 units. The factory in Detroit produces on a lot-for-lot basis (i.e., it does not use EOQ), has 500 units on hand, and takes two weeks of production lead time. Formulate the MRP-type tables for this problem, and specify production and shipment dates.

16

Queuing Models

Chapter Outline

A *queue* is a waiting line of "customers" (units) requiring service from one or more "servers" (service facility). With slight exaggeration, the comment has been made that "life is one big queue." Reflect for a moment about the waiting lines in which you have been a "unit": registration for the school term, red light at a traffic signal, ticket booth at a movie theater, checkout counter at a supermarket, busy signal when making a phone call, teller window at a bank, line or table at a dining hall or restaurant, and so on.[1]

Both the concept of "unit" and the concept of "service facility" can be applied very broadly. Although one first thinks of such examples as automobiles at toll booths, queuing models also are applicable to the arrival of rainfall to dams via rivers, arrivals of fire calls to fire departments, and money into and out of bank accounts.

Essentially, a queue forms whenever existing demand exceeds the existing capacity of the service facility; that is, whenever arriving customers cannot receive immediate service due to busy servers. This state of affairs is almost guaranteed to occur in any system that has probabilistic arrival and servicing patterns. Trade-offs between the cost of increasing service capacity and the cost of waiting customers prevent an easy resolution of the problem. If the cost of the service facility were no object, then theoretically enough servers could be marshaled to immediately service all incoming customers. It follows that a reduction in the capacity of the service facility results in a concurrent increase in the costs associated with waiting units. Consider the annual cost of acquiring and operating 24 hours per day an additional fire tructk. Compare this with the hard-to-measure cost of having people (fires) wait for the arrival of fire-fighting equipment. The basic objective in most queuing models is to achieve a balance in this cost trade-off.

The application of formal waiting line models began with the study of telephone congestion problems some seven decades ago. As with many models in MS/OR, the potential for application is almost unlimited; the theoretical "state of the art" continues to advance; and problems associated with implementation, although difficult, are being overcome slowly.

This chapter begins by discussing the fundamentals of queuing systems, follows with an exposition of the most popular models (including models in an optimization framework), and ends with an assessment of the field in general. The presentation is geared to your achieving an understanding of the assumptions and limitations for each model as well as to your acquiring a working knowledge of applied relationships for each model. The minor emphasis on proofs is relegated to Appendix 16A.

16.1 QUEUING SYSTEMS: AN OVERVIEW

Rather than immediately leaping into techniques of solution, we believe it is useful to first provide a foundation of concepts and a framework to help you establish your bearings. We start with a brief discussion of criteria and the managerial decision

[1]In an article using standard concepts found in this chapter, Ward Whitt shows that you might be better off joining the longer queue when deciding between two queues and seeking to minimize expected waiting time. For the conditions and assumptions giving rise to this counter-intuitive result, see Ward Whitt, "Deciding Which Queue to Join: Some Counterexamples," *Operations Research*, January–February 1986, pp. 55–62.

alternatives related to queuing models and thereafter provide a general representation of a queuing process. With this background, we can then examine in some detail the five basic features or characteristics of queuing systems, see how a taxonomy of queuing models can be structured by these features, and describe the analytical approaches that have been developed. At that point, the presentation of particular solution procedures can be accomplished in a more meaningful context.

Criteria and Decisions

Maximization of profit and minimization of cost represents two relatively global criteria for many queuing models. The optimal value is achieved when the costs of waiting are properly traded off with costs of providing service. A supermarket, for example, might wish to determine the number and type of servers that maximize the expected contribution to overhead and profit determined by expected revenue less costs of goods less server operating costs less implicit costs associated with customer waiting (or refusing to wait). The managerial decisions are what levels of service to provide and what operating conditions allow for the achievement of these service levels. For the supermarket example, long-term decisions include the number and type of checkout counters (conveyor belts, computers, and so forth). Medium-term decisions include the size and composition of the labor force (number of checkers and baggers) as well as work schedules. Short-term decisions include when to operate express lines, when to open and close checkout counters, and when and how to shift personnel from stocking shelves to bagging groceries.

If the decisions appear to be difficult to pin down exactly, the cost criteria are even more slippery. What is the cost of waiting in supermarket lines? In having customers choose not to enter a queue? For students waiting to register for classes? For patients waiting in a hospital emergency room?

Appealing as the optimal waiting-service cost trade-off may be, empirical problems often have surrogate criteria related to **operating or behaviorial characteristics** of queuing systems. Examples of operating characteristics include the average or expected waiting time and the probability that the server will be idle. Note that these two operating characteristics are respectively proportional to waiting and facility (idle) costs.

Thus the decision maker will want to examine various service level policies (decision rules) in terms of various operating characteristics. Interest may be focused on both long-run expectations and specific levels for relevant operating characteristics. For example, although it may be of interest to know that the average waiting time at a checkout counter is four minutes, a decision maker might also be interested in the maximum waiting time, demand during periods preceding holidays, and the influences of starting with an empty store every morning.

Before we turn to the five basic features of queuing systems, it is useful for you to explicitly understand the role played by variability in queuing systems. In fact, waiting occurs primarily because of randomness or variability in the arrival pattern of units and because of variability in the times required to service those units. You will not be surprised to find that waiting times and other operating characteristics can be improved by reducing variability in either of these areas. Examples in reducing arrival time variability include appointments (e.g., doctor's offices, beauty parlors, and automobile service centers) and smoothing via promotional efforts (e.g., family discounts and double trading stamps on specific days). Reduction in service time variability can be equally advantageous, which suggests that alternative service facilities need to be evaluated in terms of both means and variances in their servicing times.

General Representation

Figure 16–1 is a general model of a **queuing process.** Units arrive from some defined **calling source** or **population** to require service from a **service facility,** which can consist of none (self-service), one, or multiple servers. If the service facility can be entered immediately, the unit is served and then departs; otherwise, the unit joins a **queue or waiting line** (if it can or wants) to await service. The term **queue configuration** refers to the number of available queues and their arrangement. Note that the **queuing system** itself only includes one or more queues (made up of units) and the service facility (which can include one or more servers). **Queue and service disciplines** refer to the behavior and processing of units in the system. These will be discussed shortly.

FIGURE 16–1 Schematic of Queuing Process

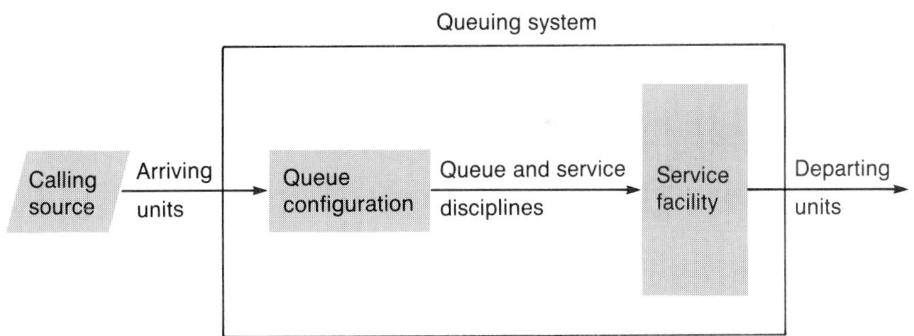

Table 16–1 identifies selected real-world queuing systems that have been analyzed. The examples clearly indicate the scope and flexibility of what we term a queuing system. Notice that (1) customers and servers can be animate or inanimate, (2) queues can exist conceptually or physically in one or many locations, and (3) customers can go to servers or vice versa. The last section of the table includes criteria that might be of interest in making decisions.

16.2 FEATURES OF QUEUING PROCESS

Variations in the treatment of queuing systems can be described in terms of five important features: arrival process, queue configuration, queue discipline, service discipline, and service facility.

TABLE 16–1 Queuing Examples

	Units	Servers	Queues	Possible Criteria
1.	Automobiles	Tollbooths	Automobiles waiting to pay	Driver waiting, tollbooth cost
2.	Machine breakdowns	Mechanics	Machines waiting to be fixed	Idleness of mechanics, cost of breakdown
3.	Patients	Surgeons	Patients waiting for surgery	Surgeon income, patient health
4.	Airplanes	Runways	Departing and arriving airplanes	Fuel costs, customer service
5.	Computer jobs	Computer	Jobs not yet begun	Machine utilization, turnaround time
6.	Boats	River locks	Waiting boats in both directions	River traffic, freight cost
7.	Vacationers	Rooms at resort hotel	Waiting list	Room utilization, "happy" travelers
8.	Callers	Reservations clerks	Calls on hold	Number of clerks, lost reservations
9.	Mechanics	Tool crib attendants	Waiting mechanics	Mechanic cost, attendant cost
10.	Freighters	Unloading docks	Freighters waiting to be unloaded	Stevedore cost; freighter leasing cost
11.	Documents	Typists	Documents to be typed	Size of typing pool, turnaround time
12.	Telephone calls	Switching equipment	Busy signals	Equipment needs, customer complaints
13.	River water	Dam locks	Quantity of water in reservoir	Flood control, irrigation benefits
14.	Orders	Sales personnel	Back orders	Lost back orders, payroll
15.	Criminal defendants	Trials	Defendants in jail or on bail	Justice, court cost, retention costs

Arrival Process

The arrival process characterizes the arrival of units into the queuing system. We will consider eight possible states or arrival conditions. These are not necessarily mutually exclusive.

1. The calling source can consist of *single or multiple populations*. For instance, a queuing system for operating rooms can be analyzed in terms of a specific type of surgery (e.g., brain or open heart) or in terms of several or all types of surgery combined.
2. The calling source can consist of a *finite or infinite number of units*. Water to replenish a reservoir originates from an infinite population, whereas malfunctioning machines in a particular machine shop are members of a finite population. For many applications, the populations, although not infinite, are large enough that models assuming infinite populations serve as adequate approximations.
3. *Single or bulk arrivals* can occur. At a restaurant, families may arrive singly to make reservations but in bulk to eat their meals.
4. Total, partial, or no *control of arrivals* can be exercised by the queuing system. The arrival of a component to be assembled in an automated assembly line is totally controlled; airplane arrivals at an airport are partially controlled; and automobiles arriving at tollbooths are not controlled at all. Appointment schedules exercise a degree of arrival control.
5. Units can emanate from a *deterministic or probabilistic generating process*. If total control is exercised, then the arrival process is deterministic; if the time between arrivals is a random variable, then the generating process is probabilistic. Needless to say, most queuing problems are represented by the latter process.
6. A probabilistic arrival process can be described by either an *empirical or a theoretical probability distribution*. The Poisson model, for example, is one of several theoretical distributions widely used to describe arrival processes.
7. The arrival process can be characterized by *independent or conditional (dependent) arrivals*. If the state of the system or the sequence of preceding arrivals does not affect subsequent arrivals, then arrivals are said to be independent; otherwise, arrivals are conditional. Arrivals can be conditional by virtue of *correlation* or *state-dependence*. For example, the number of succeeding arrivals per time interval can be correlated due to *seasonal factors,* as when traffic intensity increases or decreases along a highway according to the time of day and the day of the week. Arrivals also can be affected by the number of units in (state of) the system. For example, if a finite calling source consists of 10 operating machines, then the probability of four machine breakdowns in a one-hour period depends on how many machines are presently in the queue (broken down). *Behavioral factors* also account for state-dependence in the arrival rates. For instance, the rate at which customers queue for a particular amusement at Disney World may be affected by the length of the waiting line.

8. A *stationary arrival process* may or may not exist. If the process is stationary, then the parameters (e.g., mean and standard deviation) and form of the probability distribution that describes the arrival process remain constant over time. The usual assumption is a stationary process, as the mathematics become intractable otherwise. Nonstationary processes can be treated by monitoring changes in the process and/or by the use of forecasting models, in which cases stationary models can be reapplied.

Queue Configuration

Queue configuration refers to the number of queues in the queuing system, their relationship to the servers, and spatial considerations. A single queue can feed into a single server or multiple servers. Multiple queues typically align with an equal number of multiple servers (one queue in front of each server), although exceptions may exist as when several lanes of a highway converge into a smaller number of exit lanes. Queues may exist (1) physically in one place, (2) physically in disparate locations, as when telephone callers "hold the line" or machines wait to be repaired, (3) conceptually, as in a waiting list for hotel or airline reservations, or (4) not at all, as when calls to a busy number are rejected. Additionally, a queuing system may impose a restriction on the maximum number of units allowed in the queue (or system).

Queue Discipline

As used here, queue discipline refers to the behavior of arriving units both in the selection (or rejection) of a waiting line and in the act of waiting. We note six items which must be specified for any given queuing system.

1. If the system is filled to capacity, then the arriving unit is **rejected**. Examples include a busy signal when making a telephone call and a parking lot filled to capacity. Note that holding calls, such as is done by airlines, and waiting on the street for a parking space in the lot bring us back to queues. However, these queues also have a finite limit; at that point arriving units are rejected. In some instances a customer may be rejected by the primary system but accepted by a secondary system. A car that cannot enter a parking lot may "queue up" in an informal waiting line of cars driving around the block waiting for entrance into the parking lot.
2. If the arriving customer's estimate of the waiting time is intolerably large (as in a long queue moving slowly), then the customer might **balk**, or not join the queue. Note that this phenomenon is related to *state-dependence* in the arrival process.
3. If the customer does join the waiting line and subsequently decides that additional waiting is not worth it, then the customer **reneges**, or leaves the queue.
4. Customers exhibit **collusion** when the explicit processing of one unit represents the implicit processing of more than one unit, as when customers collude to buy movie tickets.

5. In multiple-queue systems, the possibility may or may not exist for customers to **jockey** between queues. (How many times have you had your grocery cart "revved up" as you continuously scan the cashier lines for the purpose of changing queues?)
6. *Selection of a queue from among multiple queues* may be done by a variety of decision rules, including random selection, and shortest expected waiting time selection.

Customers who do not balk, renege, collude, jockey, and nonrandomly select from among multiple queues are said to be **patient**.

Service Discipline

Service discipline refers to the policy established for the service facility in selecting customers for processing. We note five types of service disciplines, with the last accommodating many varieties. It is useful to note that the selection of a service discipline represents a decision that can affect cost criteria.

1. *First-come first-served* **(FCFS)** or *first-in first-out* **(FIFO)** is often dictated by "fairness," as in the ticket numbering system of bakeries, butcher shops, or delicatessens.
2. *Last-come first-served* **(LCFS)** or *last-in first-out* **(LIFO)** can be illustrated by an elevator queuing system whereby the last customers to enter are the first to exit on any given floor, or by coal to be removed from a coal pile.
3. *Service in Random Order* **(SIRO)** refers to some probabilistic process in selecting customers for service, as in a nail-packaging operation that packs nails randomly as they fall from a rotating drum, or in the selection of Bingo numbers. Service in random order does not require that anyone keep track of when units arrive at the queue.
4. **Round-robin service** is a sequential method of partially servicing units in the queuing system, as in the processing of jobs by a time-shared computer. Note that every unit in the queuing system is getting some service.
5. **Priority service** is a method of selection that biases the selection process according to predefined attributes. In general, units are serviced in order of decreasing priority. Examples include a time-sharing system that allocates CPU time on the basis of accumulated run time, favoring short-run jobs. Another is called "shortest operation next," which always processes that unit with smallest expected service time. The result is fewer units in the queue but longer expected waiting times for units with high service needs. A **preemptive** *priority discipline* specifies that a unit presently in service must be interrupted to service a newly arrived unit with higher priority; if the lower-priority unit presently in service is allowed to continue without interruption, then a **nonpreemptive** *priority discipline* has been specified. Emergency rooms in hospitals use priorities that are a function of the seriousness of the needs of the arriving customer and that of the customer being serviced.

Service Facility

In this section we describe characteristics associated with service facilities. These include both design attributes and operating characteristics.

1. The service facility can have *none, one, or multiple servers* **(channels)**. Queuing systems in supermarkets, for instance, include both self-service (no server) for grocery items and multiple servers for checkouts.
2. Multiple servers can be **parallel,** in **series (tandem),** or *both*. Figure 16–2 illustrates various queue-server configurations. Interestingly, assuming patient customers, the case in part *b* can be analyzed as *c* separate cases of the type in part *a*. The combined parallel-tandem case in part *e* is but one of many possible configurations. This case could be representative of a laundromat where the first type of service represents washing and the second represents drying. Channels in parallel can be **cooperative** (idle servers help busy servers) or **uncooperative**. By policy, parallel channels also can be **variable**, as when an additional teller's window is opened at a bank when the length of the queue exceeds a specified number. Job shop scheduling and network flow problems characterize the case of channels in tandem.

FIGURE 16–2 Queue-Server Configurations

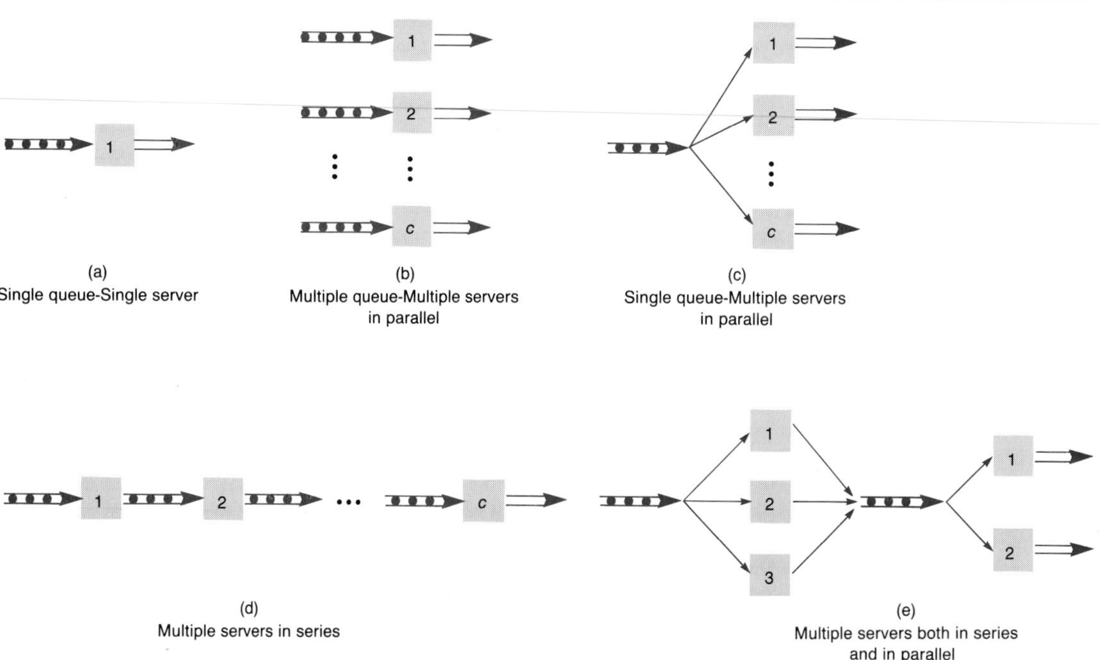

3. As in the arrival process, service times can be deterministic or probabilistic. The time to process a car in an automated car wash is essentially deterministic. Most service-time distributions, however, are represented by random variables according to some specified empirical or theoretical probability

distribution. For example, the exponential density function is commonly used to describe service times. As in the arrival process, *stationariness* is typically assumed.

4. *State-dependent service parameters* refer to cases where the mean, standard deviation, or other parameters of a service-time distribution are affected or changed by the **state** of (number of units in) the system. For example, cases wherein the service rate is affected by the length of a queue have been analyzed. Would you expect that the average service time increases or decreases as the length of the queue increases? Why? Can you think of examples?
5. *Breakdowns* among servers also can be considered. Such occurrences are possible not only among mechanical servers but also among human servers (as when someone takes ill).

Random Arrivals and Random Service Times

When the average arrival rate is less than the average service rate, a queue can build up during a specified interval. Suppose the arrival rate is three units per minute, and the service rate is four units per minute. On average, three units arrive per minute. On average, four units can be served per minute if there is always a unit present to be served. But suppose the range on arrivals is 0 to 10 per minute and the range on the number served per minute is also 0 to 10. There you have it. Arrivals can occur at a faster rate than can be served within a limited time interval.

The flip side of arrival and service rates is the interarrival and the service time. The ability to serve four units per minute translates into an average service time of 15 seconds per unit, and an arrival rate of three per minute means that arrivals are spaced 20 seconds apart on average. The interarrival time and the service time probability distributions are of great interest in queuing theory.

From the beginning of queuing theory, the exponential distribution has received a great deal of attention in modeling interarrival and service times. The exponential distribution possesses the *Markov* or *memory-less property*. If interarrival times are exponentially distributed, then the time to the next arrival is *independent* of the time of the last arrival. What about phone calls during the evening at your residence? During the hours of 7 to 9 P.M., phone calls might be random—you are as likely to receive a phone call at 8:05 P.M. whether or not you received one at 7:30 P.M. or at 8 P.M. If phone calls coming in are random in this sense, then they can be modeled by the exponential distribution where the variable is the interarrival time. If you protest that phone calls are not random—that the lack of a phone call from 7 to 8 P.M. means that this is going to be a quiet night—then you are explicitly ruling out the exponential distribution. Your next step would be to specify whether the likelihood of a call increases or decreases with the time since the last call. This would lead you to an alternative probability distribution.

We hope by now that you have developed some instinct for modeling and hypothesis testing and also for empiricism. If you believe that the great number of potential telephone callers leads to a random interarrival time distribution, your next step is to collect the data and use a chi-square test on the null hypothesis that the data are exponentially distributed. Suppose however, only one person is likely to call you, and that person is very likely to call between 8 and 9 P.M. If he or she had not called between

7 and 8 P.M., you would formulate a different model for hypothesis testing. In summary, an early step in queuing analysis will be the statistical analysis of arrival and service time data. If the exponential holds, you are facing *random* arrivals or service time.

Further, the exponential distribution for "time between arrivals" is the same as the Poisson distribution for number of arrivals per unit time. For intuition, you might allow each microsecond to be a trial with the constant conditional probability of an arrival equal to the arrival rate per hour times the fraction of an hour represented by a microsecond. Only the exponential probability distribution exhibits a constant conditional probability (same probability of an arrival no matter how long since the last arrival). Meanwhile the trials define a Poisson process.

This Poisson/exponential symmetry would also be the case for exponential service times and the number served per unit time if someone were always present to be served. Because sometimes the server will be ready to serve and no one will be there to be served, we do not talk about Poisson service, although we speak interchangeably about exponential and Poisson arrivals.[2]

16.3 CLASSIFICATIONS OF MODELS AND SOLUTIONS

In this section we first present an established scheme for classifying queuing models and then discuss general approaches for solving the models. The section ends with the very important consideration of time-dependency in the solutions.

Taxonomy of Queuing Models

Based on the various possibilities for each of the five queuing features, the number of distinct queuing models is almost endless. It goes without saying that the complete specification of any queuing model must include an explicit assumption with respect to each of the above variations. Still, it appears useful to broadly classify queuing models. D. G. Kendall has proposed a system of notation that has become popular for classifying parallel-server queuing models, as follows:

$$W/X/Y$$

where position W contains a descriptive symbol for the particular distribution of time between arrivals (interarrivals times), X contains a descriptive symbol for the specific distribution of service times, and Y contains the number of parallel servers. The descriptive symbols used for the arrival and service distributions include the following:

$M \equiv$ Exponential interarrival or service time distribution (equivalent, respectively, to Poisson arrivals or departures).[3]

---

[2]To predict traffic for new telephone switchboard installations at the turn of the century, M. C. Rorty of AT&T began to use probability theory. Edwin C. Molina then became involved and developed the Molina Formula as the basis for probability curves used at AT&T. Although years later it was discovered that the French mathematician Poisson had discovered the formula a century earlier, Molina made a significant contribution to practice at AT&T, and we consider him an exemplary operations researcher. See P. C. Mabon, *Mission Communications*, Bell Telephone Laboratories, Incorporated, Bell Laboratories, Technical Publications and Advertising, Murray Hill, 07974.

[3]See Section A.3 in Appendix A under the negative exponential distribution.

D ≡ Deterministic interarrival or service-time distribution.
E_k ≡ Erlangian distribution of order k. ($k = 1$ gives the exponential).
GI ≡ General (any) distribution of interarrival times (or arrivals) that are independent.
G ≡ General distribution of service times (or departures).

Thus $M/M/1$ represents a Poisson arrival–exponential service time–single-server model; $D/M/c$ is a model with deterministic arrivals, exponential service times, and c parallel servers (but only one queue); and $GI/G/1$ indicates a single-server model with any probabilistic arrival process (as long as it is independent) and any probabilistic distribution of service times. Extensions by Lee and Taha have augmented the system of notation to include the type of service discipline, the maximum number of units allowed in the system, and the type of calling source (whether finite or infinite). In this chapter, we will use Kendall's notation strictly and specify assumptions on the other characteristics in the description of the model.[4]

Methods of Solution

Two methods of solution are available for queuing models: analytic and simulation. The analytical approach seeks to derive mathematical expressions for operating characteristics and (perhaps) optimal values for decision variables using probability theory and mathematical manipulations (e.g., algebra and calculus), as illustrated in Appendix 16A and Section 16.7. The simulation approach seeks to artificially reproduce the queuing process itself. We demonstrate this approach in the simulation chapter.

Often the characteristics of certain real-world queuing problems can be "adequately" approximated by analytical models. The "adequacy" of the approximations can be judged by statistical tests on historical or experimental data, as illustrated in Example A.3 on page 000. If the assumptions of available analytical queuing models are invalid for a particular application, then two courses of action are open: Derive a unique analytical solution or simulate. Since the mathematics associated with queuing solutions are difficult to understand for *all* but a select few, the usual recourse is simulation. Simulation is appealing to most practitioners because it is conceptually uncomplicated. Great care (and expense), however, must be exercised in design, validation, and estimation.

Transient versus Steady-State Solutions

A final distinction is important at this time: the difference between transient-state and steady-state solutions. A solution in the **transient state** is one that is time-dependent (i.e., the values of the operating characteristics depend on time), whereas a solution in the **steady state** is in statistical equilibrium (i.e., time-independent). Typically, operating characteristics are transient during the early stages of operation because of

[4]A. M. Lee, *Applied Queuing Theory* (New York: St. Martin's Press, 1966); and H. A. Taha, *Operations Research; An Introduction*, 3rd ed., (New York: Macmillan, 1982). The simplest extension has $W/X/Y/Z$ with position Z containing a descriptive symbol for the maximum allowable number of customers in the queue plus the number of servers (i.e., a capacity position). Then an $M/M/c/K$ system means that at most $K \cdot c$ customers can wait in line.

their dependence on initial conditions, as illustrated by Figure 16–3. For example, the opening of a department store during a "normal" day or during a "big sale" day represent radically different initial conditions (small or nonexistent initial queue versus long initial queue, which will affect the operating characteristics during the early part of the operating period). However, as enough time goes on, the system will effectively settle down to its long-run or steady-state tendencies. Mathematically, this is equivalent to letting the time variable approach infinity, a device that considerably simplifies the necessary mathematical tools.

FIGURE 16–3 Transient versus Steady-State Behavior

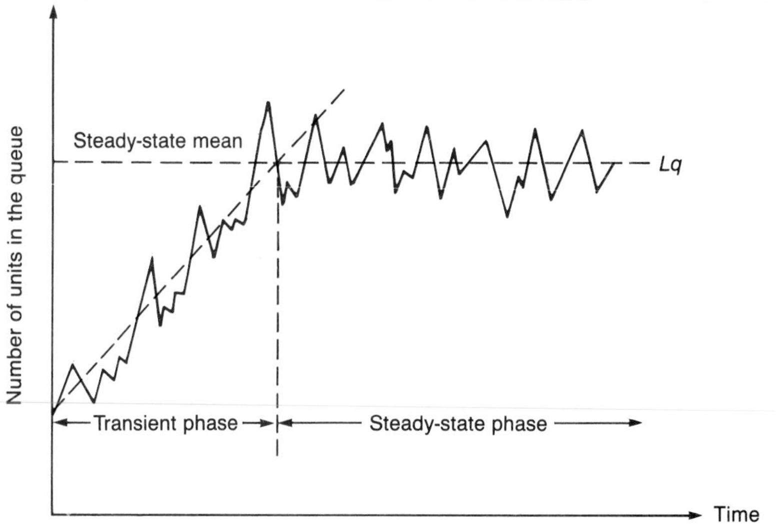

Unfortunately, many queuing systems may never achieve an effective steady state, as in the following two cases: (1) the average rate of arrivals exceeds the average servicing capacity of the system, and (2) the time span of operation for the system is too short (as in an eight-hour day). Bhat has illustrated the latter case for an $M/D/1$ system.[5] Given mean arrivals of six customers per hour and service requiring seven minutes per customer, it takes more than half of an eight-hour day to achieve equilibrium. For both of these cases either simulation or complex mathematical formulas that include time as a variable (when available) must be used to estimate operating characteristics, such as time spent in the queue or average number of units in the queue.

16.4 *M/M/1* MODELS

This section presents the best-known set of queuing models. For each case, we state the relevant assumptions and follow with analytically derived formulas for estimating operating characteristics.

[5] U. N. Bhat, "Sixty Years of Queuing Theory," *Management Science* 15 (1969), p. B–290.

Standard $M/M/1$ Model

Every queuing model requires specific assumptions with respect to the five features in Section 16.2. The application of any queuing model, therefore, should include validation with respect to these assumptions.

The derivation of the standard $M/M/1$ model requires the following set of assumptions about the queuing process:

1. Arrival process — Single population with infinite number of units; single arrivals with no control exercised by queuing system; arrivals are independent and behave according to Poisson probability mass function; and stationary arrival process exists.[6]
2. Queue configuration — Single waiting line with no restriction on maximum length.
3. Queue discipline — No rejections; patient customers, (i.e., no balking, reneging, or collusion). (Note that behavior associated with jockeying or queue selection need not be specified for a single queue.)
4. Service discipline — FCFS.
5. Service facility — One server (no parallel or series considerations); service times distributed according to exponential probability density function; service parameter and distribution are state-independent and stationary: no breakdowns.

There are several reasons for the popularity of this model, even though the above assumptions may seem unduly restrictive. First, transient and steady-state derivations of operating characteristics are possible and easily applied; second, the assumptions have proved reasonable (especially Poisson-distributed arrivals) in some (but not many) applied problems; and, finally, the model can be used for planning purposes and insight. For example, results based on this model may lead to suggestions for subsequent approaches.[7]

In Table 16–2 we provide formulas, without proof, for the *steady-state* operating characteristics of this model. For those of you who are interested, the derivations for this model are presented in Appendix 16A.

Given the assumptions, you should understand that λ and μ are the parameters of the Poisson and exponential probability distributions, respectively. The restriction on **traffic intensity** $[\rho \equiv (\lambda/\mu) < 1]$ should make sense to you. If it were not restricted to a value less than one, the steady state never would be achieved as an arrival rate greater than the service rate would result in an infinitely large queue as time approaches infinity. Also note that Equations 16.5, 16.7, 16.9, and 16.11 which are in Table 16–2, include customers who do not have to wait before moving into the service facility. Their inclusion results in lower expected values for these operating characteristics; Equations 16.8 and 16.12 provide operating characteristics that are

[6]The Poisson function given by A.24 implies independence between arrivals: Conversely, as already indicated, *interarrival times* are distributed according to the exponential density function given by A.31. (See pages and .)

[7]For an excellent example of what we mean by "insightful uses," see H. Deutsch and V. Mabert, "Queueing Theory and Teller Staffing: A Successful Application", *Interfaces*, October 1980, pp. 63–66.

TABLE 16–2 Steady-State Operating Characteristics for Standard *M/M/1* Model

Operating Characteristics	Formula	Formula Number
Probability of zero units in system (probability of idle system)	$P_o = 1 - \rho$	(16.1)
Probability of busy period or busy system (probability of waiting or of delaying a unit)	$P(n > 0) = \rho = 1 - P_o$	(16.2)
Probability of n units in system (geometric distribution)	$P_n = P_o\,\rho^n$	(16.3)
Probability density function for time in system (exponential distribution)	$f(w) = (\mu - \lambda)e^{-(\mu-\lambda)\omega}, w \geq 0$	(16.4)
Expected number of units in system	$L_s = \dfrac{\lambda}{\mu - \lambda}$	(16.5)
Variance of number of units in system	$V_{ls} = \dfrac{\lambda\mu}{(\mu - \lambda)^2}$	(16.6)
Expected number of units in queue	$L_q = \dfrac{\rho\lambda}{\mu - \lambda}$	(16.7)
Expected number of units in queue for busy system	$L_b = \dfrac{\lambda}{\mu - \lambda}$	(16.8)
Expected time in system	$W_s = \dfrac{1}{\mu - \lambda}$	(16.9)
Variance of time in system	$V_{\omega s} = \dfrac{1}{(\mu - \lambda)^2}$	(16.10)
Expected time in queue	$W_q = \dfrac{\rho}{\mu - \lambda}$	(16.11)
Expected time in queue for busy system	$W_b = \dfrac{1}{\mu - \lambda}$	(16.12)

λ ≡ Mean arrival rate (units per period).
μ ≡ Mean service rate (units per period).
ρ ≡ Traffic intensity (λ/μ).
w ≡ Random variate for time in system.
n ≡ Number of units in system.
Note: System refers to queue plus service facility; formulas are valid only if $\rho < 1$.

more representative for those customers who must wait. For example, Equation 16.8 represents the steady-state mean number of customers in the queue when the single server is busy. Alternatively, 16.7 is the steady-state mean number of customers in the queue, including the queues of zero length whenever the server is idle. The steady-state mean in Figure 16–3 is, in fact, L_q.

Finally, note that the number of customers in the system (n) is a random variable with an associated probability distribution given by Equation 16.3. In other words, the actual number of customers in the system (n) will fluctuate about the mean number of customers in the system (L_s) according to the specified probability distribution 16.3 with variance given by 16.6. (L_s and L_b happen to be equal for this model, but this is not true in general.)

FOLLOW-UP EXERCISES

Load the formulas from Table 16–2 into a spreadsheet, such as 1-2-3 from Lotus. For each of the problems below, check out your answers by plugging in numbers to confirm your intuitive answers. In plugging in numbers, assume Poisson arrivals averaging three per minute and exponential service times of 0.25 minute.

1. Show that Equation 16.2 is obtained easily from 16.1.
2. Interpret the meanings, with respect to **system utilization,** of low and high values for Equations 16.1 and 16.2.
3. Using Equations 16.1 and 16.2 show that the **expected number in service** is $(1 - P_o)$ or ρ. (Note that a unit is either in service or not in service.)
4. Show that the expected number of units in the system equals the expected number in service plus the expected number in the queue.
5. If $1/\mu$ is the expected time in service (right?), show that the expected time in the system equals the expected time in the queue plus the expected time in service.
6. Show that the expected time in the queue can be determined as the expected number of units in the queue divided by the arrival rate. Does this make sense? Is this equivalent to $L = \lambda W$ for the system, queue, and busy-system queue?
7. Show that L_b can be determined as L_q divided by the probability of delaying a unit. Can you show why this is valid? (*Hint:* See Equation 13 in Appendix 16.A.)
8. Show that W_b can be determined as W_q divided by the probability of waiting. Can you show why this is valid?
9. A measure of effectiveness for a queuing system is given by the **customer loss ratio,** (R), or the ratio of average time in waiting for service to the average time in service. Show that $R = \lambda/(\mu - \lambda)$ for the $M/M/1$ model. From the standpoint of the customer, are low or high values desired for R?

Example 16.1 Emergency Room Queuing System

In an emergency room queuing system, patients requiring treatment can be considered the units and the mechanism for treating them (e.g., beds and physicians) the servers. Suppose patients are treated by a single "server" on a FCFS basis, the arrival and service processes are as described in Examples A.1 and A.3 on pages 893 and 906, and other assumptions of the $M/M/1$ model are met.[8] (Note that the population is assumed infinite, which effectively means that it is of sufficient size to ensure that the assumption of infinity only minutely affects probabilities.)

Carefully note that the collection of data (step four in the paradigm) is a rather crucial step in the application of the correct queuing model. The chi-square test in Example A.3 indicates that the service distribution depicted in Table A–3 is exponential with mean 0.4 hour per patient. Thus $\mu = 2.5$ customers per hour (that is, $1/\mu = 0.4$). In actual practice, μ is best estimated by fixing the number of units served and dividing by the total elapsed busy (service) time.

If you carried out a chi-square test in Exercise 19 of Appendix A on page 908, then you should have verified that the arrival process is Poisson with $\lambda = 2.1$ patients per hour. In general, λ can be estimated by fixing the number of arrivals and dividing by the total elapsed time or vice versa.[9]

[8] In actual practice, as previously mentioned, emergency room queuing systems must be analyzed using a priority service discipline based on, say, two priorities (e.g., major and minor emergencies).

[9] These procedures for estimating λ and μ provide unbiased estimates of the population parameters; that is, the expected value of the sample statistic equals the population parameter. For Poisson and exponential distributions, respectively, they also provide maximum likelihood estimates; that is, they represent values for the parameters that maximize the probability of obtaining the observed sample outcome.

The traffic intensity for this example is $\rho = 0.84$ (that is, 2.1/2.5), which implies that the server is busy (the system is utilized) 84 percent of the time. In other words, according to Equation 16.2, the probability of a busy period, or a busy system, or of waiting, or of delaying a unit is 0.84. Conversely, according to Equation 16.1, the probability of an idle server is 0.16.

The expected (mean) number of patients in the system, queue, and busy-system queue are, respectively, 5.25, 4.41, and 5.25 according to Equations 16.5, 16.7, and 16.8. A customer loss ratio (see Exercise 9) of 5.25 indicates that, on the average, customers spend more time in the queue than in service by a factor of 5.25 (or 525 percent). We see that the variance and standard deviation for the number of patients in the system, using Equation 16.6, are 32.8 and 5.73, respectively. From Equation 16.9, the mean time to process a patient from arrival to departure is 2.5 hours; from 16.11, the mean time that customers spend in a queue is 2.1 hours; from 16.12, the average time of waiting *for those who wait* (84 percent of the cases) is 2.5 hours; and from 16.10, the variance and standard deviation for time through the system are 6.25 hours and 2.5 hours^2, respectively.

Now consider a sensitivity analysis based on the parameter μ. In Table 16–3 it can be seen that operating characteristics are highly sensitive to values of μ in the neighborhood of λ (i.e., when ρ is close to 1); hence, especially precise estimations are needed in this neighborhood of high traffic intensities. Further note that a high traffic intensity promotes a large expected value for number of units and waiting time, which in turn results in a longer period of time for the system to achieve steady state. Moreover, if the system got "out of whack" (e.g., a five-car accident), it would take a long time to get back into steady state.

The sensitivity table clearly is an important aid to decision making. If the hospital administrator finds that an average time above two hours for entirely processing a patient is intolerable, yet wishes to maintain a utilization (ρ) above 80 percent, then the service rate that must be achieved is 2.6 patients per hour, as indicated in Table 16–3. What controllable variables influence μ? In what ways can the hospital administrator increase the value of μ?

TABLE 16–3 Sensitivity Analysis Based on μ for Example 16.1

μ	P_o	ρ	L_s, L_b	L_q	W_s, W_b	W_q
2.2	0.05	0.95	21.00	20.05	10.00	9.50
2.3	0.09	0.91	10.50	9.55	5.00	4.55
2.4	0.12	0.88	7.00	6.16	3.33	2.64
2.5	0.16	0.84	5.25	4.41	2.50	2.10
2.6	0.19	0.81	4.20	3.40	2.00	1.62
2.7	0.22	0.78	3.50	2.73	1.67	1.30
2.8	0.25	0.75	3.00	2.25	1.43	1.07

FOLLOW-UP EXERCISES

10. What service rate must be achieved to attain an average waiting time in the system (queue and service) that is one hour or less? What values result for the other operating characteristics?
11. Find the probabilities of $0, 1, 2, \ldots, 7$ patients in the system using Equation 16.3; find the cumulative probabilities of $0, 1, 2, \ldots, 7$ and less patients in the system.
12. Find the probabilities of $0, 1, \ldots, 6$ patients in the queue using the results of the preceding exercise; determine the associated cumulative probabilities.

13. What values for μ yield a customer loss ratio below 4 and system utilization above 75 percent? Interpret the meaning of the 4 and the 75 percent.
14. What value of μ satisfies the requirement that the probability of exactly no patients in the queue is 0.50.?
15. What values of μ satisfy the condition that the probability of one or more patients waiting at any given time must be less than 0.05?
16. Noting that $(\mu - \lambda)$ represents the parameter for the exponential density function in Equation 16.4, use A.32 to determine the probability that a unit will take less than one hour to process. Between one and two hours? Between two and three hours?

▶ Example 16.2 Bank Queuing System

Suppose arrivals of customers to drive-in windows of a commercial bank are Poisson-distributed with rate $\lambda = 0.9$ car per minute. Goodness-of-fit tests indicate that the service time distribution for each of three tellers is exponential with rate $\mu = 0.4$ car per minute.

Notice that the example illustrates a multiple-server system; however, if we assume a queue in front of each teller, random selection of queues, and patient customers, then three separate single-server independent subsystems can be used to approximate the real system, as illustrated in Figure 16–4. If we adjust the arrival rate to 0.3 car per minute (that is, 0.9/3) for each subsystem, then $P_o = 0.25$, $P(n > 0) = 0.75$, $L_s = L_b = 3$ cars, $L_q = 2.25$ cars, $V_{ls} = 12$ cars^2. $W_s = W_b = 10$ minutes per car, $W_q = 7.5$ minutes per car, and $V_{\omega s} = 100$ minutes^2. For the system as a whole, tellers are idle 25 percent of the time, 75 percent of the customers must wait an average of 10 minutes, on the average the waiting time in the queue is 300 percent greater than the waiting time in service (that is, $R = 3$), the expected number of cars in the system is

FIGURE 16–4 Independent Subsystems for Bank

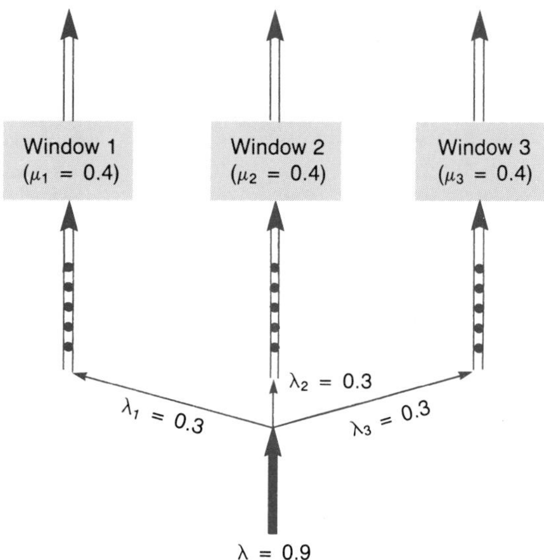

nine (that is, 3 tellers × 3 cars per teller), and the associated variance is 36 cars^2 for the system (that is, 12 + 12 + 12).

Figure 16–5 illustrates the output of selected operating characteristics for this example using the queuing module of the Erikson-Hall software package. We have appended the symbols for these characteristics in color.

FIGURE 16–5 Selected Operating Characteristics for Example 16.2 Using Erikson-Hall Package

```
            COMPUTER MODELS FOR MANAGEMENT SCIENCE
QUEUEING MODELS

              -=*=-  INFORMATION ENTERED  -=*=-

  ALTERNATIVE CHOSEN           :      SINGLE SERVER
  ARRIVAL RATE                 :              0.300   (λ)
  SERVICE RATE                 :              0.400   (μ)

  NUMBER OF SERVERS            :              1

                   -=*=-  RESULTS  -=*=-

  SERVER IDLE (PERCENT)        :             25.000   (Po · 100)

  EXPECTED NUMBER IN SYSTEM    :              3.000   (Ls)

  EXPECTED NUMBER IN QUEUE     :              2.250   (Lq)

  EXPECTED TIME IN SYSTEM      :             10.000   (Ws)

  EXPECTED TIME IN QUEUE       :              7.500   (Wq)

             ----------  END OF ANALYSIS  ----------
```

The use of $M/M/1$ formulas for approximating a multiple-queue $M/M/c$ system illustrates the flexibility of this simple model. In general, however, the realities of non-random queue selection, impatient customers, and utilization of indoor tellers due to rejection and balking suggest that the actual average time and average number of cars in the system will be less than 10 minutes and nine cars, respectively. At the very least, this model provides useful bounds for operating characteristics and serves as a benchmark for the application of more complex analytical or simulation models.

FOLLOW-UP EXERCISES

17. Draw a conclusion if only two drive-in windows are available.
18. Conduct a sensitivity analysis as in Table 16–3 for Example 16.2 based on $\mu = 0.3, 0.35, 0.5$. Conclusions?
19. What range of μ satisfies a customer loss ratio below two and system utilization above 60 percent? (Use data in Example 16.2.)
20. Determine operating characteristics if four drive-in windows are available, each with $\mu = 0.4$ car per minute, and compare to the results in the example.
21. How many drive-in windows, each with $\mu = 0.4$ car per minute, would be needed to reduce the average time for those who wait to less than five minutes? What

percentage of the time is each window busy? What is the probability a customer has to wait? What is the average number of customers in the system? In which direction are these figures biased and why?

22. Determine operating characteristics if four drive-in windows are available each with $\mu = 0.3$. Compare these results with the results in the example. (Note that the product $c \cdot \mu$, the average capacity of the entire system, equals 1.2 cars per minute for both cases.) Conclusions?

**23. Given three drive-in windows, each with $\mu = 0.4$ car per minute service and $\lambda = 0.3$ car per minute input, verify that the probability of exactly two cars in the *entire* system is given by $6(1 - \rho)^3\rho^2 = 0.053$. (*Hint:* Derive this expression by applying Equations A.6 and A.3 to 12.3 for the six possible combinations that give two cars in the system.)

Other Service Disciplines

Except for a priority service discipline, the derivation of P_n for the standard $M/M/1$ model (as illustrated in Appendix 16A) is independent of whether FCFS, LCFS, or SIRO is used; in fact, the only difference among these three service disciplines is in the form and shape (but not the mean) of the waiting time distribution for the system. Thus all equations in Table 16–2 are valid for these cases except for Equations 16.4 and 16.10. As noted before, however, service disciplines can affect operating characteristics in ways that are consistent with system design criteria.

Restriction on Maximum Number in System: $M/M/c/N$ Model

We now consider a modification to the standard $M/M/1$ model by introducing a restriction on the allowable number of customers in the system. Suppose N represents the maximum number of customers allowed in the system, or for a single-server model, $N - 1$ indicates the maximum number of units in the queue. Thus, if a customer arrives at a time when N units are in the system, then that customer is rejected (i.e., leaves the system without entering). Examples of this type of ***finite-queue*** (or **truncated-queue) model** include telephone reservations systems with a finite number of calls that can be "held," a drive-in window with a driveway coming in from a busy street where one cannot stop, and so forth.

Except for rejection, all assumptions of the standard $M/M/1$ model are identical for this case.

> Formulas for selected operating characteristics are given by 16.13 through 16.21 in Appendix 16B.

Since the waiting time distribution has not been considered explicitly, these formulas also hold for LCFS and SIRO service disciplines. *Note that a traffic intensity of unity ($\rho = 1$) or above is allowed for this model.* Can you explain why? Also, W_s and W_q relate to customers who join the system; otherwise, times of zero for those who are rejected would bias these characteristics downward. Furthermore, you should realize that P_N represents the **probability of rejection** and λP_N is the **expected number of customers rejected per unit time.** Finally, as you might have verified in Exercises 4 and 5, Equation 16.17 indicates that the expected number in the queue equals the expected number in the system less the expected number in service, and 16.20 suggests that the expected time in the queue equals the expected time in the system minus the expected time in service.

Example 16.3 Bank Queuing System

Suppose $N = 2$ for each teller in the bank queuing system of Example 16.2. Then, with $\rho = 0.75$, you should verify that for each teller $P_o = 0.43$, $P(n > 0) = 0.57$, $L_s = 0.81$ customer, $L_q = 0.24$ customer, $L_b = 0.43$ customer, $W_s = 3.6$ minutes, $W_q = 1.1$ minute, and $W_b = 1.9$ minutes. As expected, dramatic decreases over the previous case are experienced in system utilization, line lengths, and waiting times. Of course, these are achieved at the expense of a high rejection rate (see Exercise 24). Figure 16–6 illustrates the output of selected operating characteristics using the Erikson-Hall package. Remember that these operating characteristics are derived from the formulas in Appendix 16B.

FIGURE 16–6 Selected Operating Characteristics for Example 16.3 Using Erikson-Hall Package

```
          COMPUTER MODELS FOR MANAGEMENT SCIENCE
QUEUEING MODELS

              -=*=-  INFORMATION ENTERED  -=*=-

  ALTERNATIVE CHOSEN           :   SINGLE SERVER-FINITE QUEUE

  ARRIVAL RATE                 :          0.300  (λ)
  SERVICE RATE                 :          0.400  (μ)

  NUMBER OF SERVERS            :          1
  MAXIMUM QUEUE LENGTH         :          2      (N)

                  -=*=-  RESULTS  -=*=-

  BALKING RATE (PERCENT)       :         24.324  (Pn)

  SERVER IDLE (PERCENT)        :         43.243  (Po)

  EXPECTED NUMBER IN SYSTEM    :          0.811  (Ls)

  EXPECTED NUMBER IN QUEUE     :          0.243  (Lq)

  EXPECTED TIME IN SYSTEM      :          3.571  (Ws)

  EXPECTED TIME IN QUEUE       :          1.071  (Wq)

           ----------  END OF ANALYSIS  ----------
```

FOLLOW-UP EXERCISES

24. Use Equation 16.15 to verify that the probability of rejection, P_2, is approximately 0.24. On the average, how many customers will be rejected per minute? Per Hour? (Distinguish between each teller and the system.)
25. Calculate the customer loss ratio (R) for this example. Interpret its meaning.
26. Using data for this example, show that $P_0 + P_1 + \cdots + P_N = 1$.
27. What value for N would guarantee a rejection rate of less than 10 percent? What effect does this have on P_0, L_s, L_q, L_b, W_s, W_q, and W_b when compared to results in Example 16.3 above?

Finite Population

In many queuing systems, the calling source is finite. This means, in turn, that the number of units presently in the system alters the probabilities of future arrivals (note that infinite populations are not so affected). The most commonly analyzed problem of this type is that where m machines are to be repaired by one or more service representatives. In this case, machine breakdowns represent "arrivals," and the number of machines to be repaired represents the queue. Obviously, the number of machines presently in the queuing system (i.e., in the queue plus being serviced) affects the arrival rate and the probabilities of subsequent breakdowns. Conversely, any arrival or departure affects this probability. Other examples of finite populations as calling sources for queuing systems include those concerned with machine utilization by a limited number of personnel. Secretaries using a copying machine and analysts using computer terminals represent two common examples.

We might note that a subtle distinction exists between this model and other models with respect to the definition of the arrival rate. In the present case, λ is the arrival rate for *each* unit in a population of m units. This means that the *effective arrival rate* into the queuing system is given by the product of λ and the expected number of units outside the queuing system, that is, by $\lambda \cdot (m - L_s)$. Right? For example if each of 10 machines breaks down at the rate of 2 machines per day and the expected number of machines in the queuing system is 3, then the effective arrival rate is $2 \cdot (10 - 3)$, or 14 machines per day.

Except for the assumptions of a finite calling source and the manner in which λ is defined, all other assumptions of this model are identical to those in the standard $M/M/1$ model. As for the standard model, *LCFS* and *SIRO* also apply to this model. Finite populations that are "sufficiently" large can be treated as infinite populations with little or no error, as illustrated in the hospital emergency room and drive-in bank tellers problems. Rules-of-thumb for assessing the term *sufficiently* are not as clear-cut as in the case of sampling. Populations above 30 units may suffice if traffic intensity is low (say, below 75 percent). As ρ increases however, the number of units in the system must increase accordingly. Under these circumstances, the infinite population model will serve as a reasonable approximation to the finite population model if the size of the population is well above 30.

Formulas for selected operating characteristics are given by Equations 16.22 through 16.30 in Appendix 16B.

In formulas 16.22 through 16.30 m represents the number of units in the population, and other symbols are as previously defined. Since hand-solution of these formulas for a particular problem can be tedious, tables have been published to greatly simplify the effort.[10] Repeated applications of queuing formulas, however, may warrant the development of an appropriate computer program.

Example 16.4 Computer Terminal Service

The accounting office of a company is considering the installation of a single computer terminal for a staff of four members engaged in financial analysis. Trial runs have indicated that the time to complete a job is exponential with a mean of 48 minutes, and the demand on the terminal by *each analyst* is Poisson with a mean of 1/50 of a demand per minute. Thus $m = 4$, $\mu = 1/48$, and $\lambda = 1/50$, so that $\rho = 0.96$. For the probability of zero in the system, we get:

$$P_0 = \frac{1}{\frac{4!}{4!}(0.96)^0 + \frac{4!}{3!}(0.96)^1 + \frac{4!}{2!}(0.96)^2 + \frac{4!}{1!}(0.96)^3 + \frac{4!}{0!}(0.96)^4}$$

$$= \frac{1}{57.47} = 0.0174$$

The following operating characteristics are expected: Essentially, the terminal will be fully utilized (i.e., idle 1.73 percent of the time); on the average 2.98 analysts will be in the queuing system (L_s); both the overall average number of waiting analysts (L_q) and the average number of waiting analysts when the system is busy (L_b) will be approximately 2.0; the average time for waiting and using the terminal (W_s) will be 146 minutes; the average time lost in waiting (W_q) will be 97.6 minutes; and the average time of waiting for those analysts who wait (W_b) will be just over 99 minutes. Needless to say, a single terminal would appear overburdened (which increases the probability of a breakdown), and analysts would waste a great deal of time waiting (unless they have alternative uses for their time). Figure 16–7 illustrates the output of selected operating characteristics for this example using the Erikson-Hall package.

The expected cost per day for this queuing system can be estimated by summing the expected costs per day of the service facility and the analysts' lost time due to waiting. The cost of service is based on costs associated with subscription to a time-sharing service and costs relating to the terminal itself: cost per unit of connect time, cost per resource unit (ru), cost of magnetic disk storage, maintenance cost, and capital (depreciation) cost.[11] This being the accounting office, we can have great confidence in the following estimates: $10 per terminal per hour for connect time; $1 per resource unit; $5 per day for required disk space; $0.50 per terminal per day for a maintenance contract; and $3 per terminal per day for capital cost. For an eight-hour day, the expected connect time is $8(1 - P_0)$ or approximately 7.86 hours in this case. If each job averages 48 minutes, then the mean number of jobs per day will be given by the expected connect time per day (471.6 minutes) divided by the expected job time (48 minutes), or 9.825. If

[10] See, for instance, L. G. Peck and R. N. Hazelwood, *Finite Queuing Tables* (New York: John Wiley & Sons, 1958).

[11] A resource unit is based on the utilization of the Central Processing Unit (CPU), which primarily consists of CPU time and use of magnetic core.

FIGURE 16–7 Selected Operating Characteristics for Example 16.4 Using Erikson-Hall Package

```
                COMPUTER MODELS FOR MANAGEMENT SCIENCE
QUEUEING MODELS

                 -=*=-  INFORMATION ENTERED  -=*=-

ALTERNATIVE CHOSEN             :      SINGLE SERVER - FINITE POPULATION

ARRIVAL RATE                   :            0.020     (λ)
SERVICE RATE                   :            0.021     (μ)

NUMBER OF SERVERS              :            1
POPULATION SIZE                :            4         (m)

                     -=*=-  RESULTS  -=*=-

SERVER IDLE (PERCENT)          :             1.730    (P0)

EXPECTED NUMBER IN SYSTEM      :             2.978    (Ls)

EXPECTED NUMBER IN QUEUE       :             1.995    (Lq)

EXPECTED NUMBER IN SYSTEM      :           145.694    (Ws)

EXPECTED TIME IN QUEUE         :            97.617    (Wq)

          ----------  END OF ANALYSIS  ----------
```

on the average 5 resource units are used per job, then on the average 49.125 resource units will be used per day. Thus the total cost of service per day is illustrated in the accompanying table.

Connect[(hours/day) · $P(n > 0)$ · ($/hour) = (8) · (0.9826) · (10)]	$78.61
Resource[(jobs/day) · (ru's/job) · ($/ru) = (9.825) · (5) · (1)]	49.13
Disk space	5.00
Maintenance	0.50
Capital cost (depreciation)	3.00
Cost per day of service facility	$136.24

If the idle time of an analyst is costed at $15 per hour and the lost time per day is given as the product of L_q and the number of hours in a day, then the cost per day associated with waiting is ($15 per analyst-hour) · (2 analysts) · (8 hours per day), or $240 per day; hence, the expected total cost for this queuing configuration is $376.24 per day.[12] Needless to say (but we'll say it anyway), this cost per day should be compared with

[12] The cost of idle time is most easily estimated as the hourly rate of pay, although more precisely it should be the hourly "worth" of the employee, which includes the return to the company less some adjustment if the employee is not entirely idle while waiting.

the cost per day of alternative configurations, including the alternative of continuing under the present arrangement.

FOLLOW-UP EXERCISES

28. Calculate $P_1, P_2, \ldots, P_4$. What is the probability of two or less analysts in the system? More than three analysts? Does $P_0 + P_1 + \cdots + P_4 = 1$?
29. Besides the customer loss ratio (R = Mean time in queue divided by mean service time), other effectiveness measures for finite population models include E_1 = Average number in system (L_s) divided by number in population (m) and E_2 = Average number of facilities idle divided by number of facilities (c). Calculate R, E_1, and E_2 for this example.
30. Determine the operating characteristics and costs associated with two computer terminals. Treat this system in the manner of Example 16.2, that is, as two separate and independent single line-single server subsystems. (*Hint:* Maintenance and depreciation costs will double; however, connect and resource costs will *not* increase proportionally. Also, m must be adjusted but not λ. Can you reason why?)

16.5 $M/M/c$ MODELS

In this section we generalize single queue-single server models with Poisson arrivals and exponential service times to *single* queue–multiple server models.

Standard $M/M/c$ Model

The assumptions for this model are identical to the assumptions for the standard $M/M/1$ model except for the additional restrictions that servers are uncooperative and service rates across channels are independent and identical (that is, $\mu_1 = \mu_2 = \ldots = \mu_c$). Additionally, the given operating characteristics apply to FCFS, LCFS, and SIRO service disciplines.

> The standard $M/M/c$ model equations, Equations 16.31 through 16.39 appear in Appendix 16B.

The steady-state operating characteristics (given by Equations 16.31 through 16.39 in Appendix 16B) have the same interpretation as before, although the expressions are more complex. As before, $\rho = \lambda/\mu$. Note, however, that now $\rho < c$, or $(\lambda/\mu c) < 1$, is a necessary condition for steady state to be achieved. In other words, the mean overall service rate (μc) for the system must be greater than the mean arrival rate (λ). Further note that the probability of a busy period or of waiting is $P(n \geq c)$ and not $P(n > 0)$; that is, an arriving unit has to wait if the number of customers in the system is at least equal to the number of servers.

Interestingly, the distribution of *departures from the queuing system* for this model is Poisson. For a queuing system characterized by subsystems in tandem of the $M/M/c$ type, the above formulas can be used to analyze each subsystem separately.[13]

We now illustrate computations for this model. As you might imagine, the computations are *very* tedious. In actual practice, tables, graphs, or computer routines are used.

▶ Example 16.5 Bank Queuing System Continued

In the bank queuing system (Example 16.2), a queue formed in front of each of the three drive-in tellers. Suppose the system is redesigned such that one queue feeds into the service facility. In this case, we have an $M/M/c$ system with $c = 3$, $\lambda = 0.9$ car per minute, $\mu = 0.4$ car per minute, and $\rho = 2.25 < 3$. This gives

$$P_o = \frac{1}{\frac{(2.25)^0}{0!} + \frac{(2.25)^1}{1!} + \frac{(2.25)^2}{2!} + \frac{(2.25)^3}{3!(1 - 2.25/3)}}$$

$$= 0.0748\,.$$

You should verify that appropriate substitutions in Equations 16.33 through 16.39 give the results in column 1 of Table 16–4. The second column in this table allows a direct comparison to the results in Example 16.2. In comparing methods 1 and 2, it appears that substantial improvements in performance measures are realized in switching from three queues to a single queue.[14] Have you noticed in recent years how banks have forced single queues for the indoor system of tellers? Not only has performance improved, but also equity in the processing of customers and privacy of transactions have been gained. As is true for many real-world problems, however, perception can be a significant behavioral factor. For example, McDonald's tried a single queue, but gave it up because "balky" customers perceived long waits when confronted with one long line.

TABLE 16–4 *M/M/3 versus Three Subsystems of M/M/1*

Operating Characteristics	$M/M/3$ Model (1)	$M/M/1$ Model* (2)
P(wait)	0.57	0.75
L_s	3.95 cars	9.00 cars (overall system)
L_q	1.70 cars	2.25 cars (each of 3 queues)
L_b	2.98 cars	9.00 cars (overall system)
W_s	4.39 min. per car	10.00 min. per car
W_q	1.89 min. per car	7.50 min. per car
W_b	3.31 min. per car	10.00 min. per car

*Treated as three separate $M/M/1$ subsystems (as in Example 16.2)

[13] We treat such a system in Example 16.7 and Exercises 45 and 46.

[14] As pointed out previously, the results for the $M/M/1$ treatment are upward biased. Do you remember why? Still, the differences are so substantial that a single queue appears warranted.

Again, Figure 16–8 illustrates selected operating characteristics from Erikson-Hall.

FIGURE 16–8 Selected Operating Characteristics for Example 16.5 Using Erikson-Hall Package

```
             COMPUTER MODELS FOR MANAGEMENT SCIENCE
QUEUEING MODELS

              -=*=-  INFORMATION ENTERED  -=*=-

ALTERNATIVE CHOSEN                 :      MULTIPLE SERVER

ARRIVAL RATE                       :             0.900     (λ)
SERVICE RATE                       :             0.400     (μ)

NUMBER OF SERVERS                  :             3         (c)

                     -=*=-  RESULTS  -=*=-

SERVER IDLE (PERCENT)              :            25.005

EXPECTED NUMBER IN SYSTEM          :             3.948     (Ls)

EXPECTED NUMBER IN QUEUE           :             1.698     (Lq)

EXPECTED TIME IN SYSTEM            :             4.387     (Ws)

EXPECTED TIME IN QUEUE             :             1.887     (Wq)

          ----------  END OF ANALYSIS  ----------
```

FOLLOW-UP EXERCISES

31. Verify that the formulas for the $M/M/1$ model are special cases of the $M/M/c$ model for $c = 1$.
32. Confirm the calculations in column (1) of Table 16–4.
33. Repeatedly using Equation 16.32, find $P(n < 3)$ for Example 16.5. How is this result related to $P(n \geq 3)$, as given by (16.33)?
34. In general, the number of idle servers is a random variable given by $c - n$ when $n < c$ and by zero when $n \geq c$; hence, the **mean number of idle servers** is given by $cP_0 + (c - 1)P_1 + (c - 2)P_2 + \cdots + 1P_{c-1} + 0P_{n \geq c}$. Right? Find the mean number of idle servers for Example 16.5.
35. Perform a sensitivity analysis for $\lambda = 0.8$ and $\lambda = 1.0$ in Example 16.5. Conclusions?
36. To what degree does performance improve in the emergency room problem (Example 16.1) if $c = 2$? $c = 3$?

Restriction on Maximum Length of Queue

As in the $M/M/1$ model, if $N \geq c$ is the maximum number of customers allowed in the system, an arriving customer is rejected if $n = N$ or if the length of the queue is $N - c$. Other assumptions for this model are identical to the assumptions for the standard $M/M/c$ model.

Formulas for selected operating characteristics are given by Equations 16.40 through 16.48 in Appendix 16B.

As before, $(\rho/c) = (\lambda/\mu c)$ need not be less than one; W_s, W_q, W_b reflect customers who join the system; P_N represents the probability that a customer will be rejected; and λP_N yields the expected number of rejections per unit time.

FOLLOW-UP EXERCISES

37. Determine performance measures for the banking system of Example 16.5 if $N = 5$. Compare these to the results in the example. What is the probability of rejection? Expected number of rejections?
38. What value of N would guarantee a rejection rate of less than 10 percent for the banking example?

No Queue

In some cases the number of customers in the system is limited to the number of service facilities; that is, $n \leq c$. This situation, termed **absolute truncation,** is equivalent to stating that facilities are unavailable for the existence of a queue. Clearly, this represents a finite queue system with $N = c$; hence, the operating characteristics are given by Equations 16.40 through 16.48.

▶ Example 16.6 Parking Lot Queuing System

An underground parking lot with c parking spaces is a representative example of a queuing system that might not allow the formation of a queue. For instance, if the arrival of cars is Poisson with mean 20 cars per hour and the length of stay is exponential with mean 1 hour per car, then Equations 16.40 through 16.48 with $N = c$ can be used to evaluate the performance of a parking lot queuing system with c parking spaces (providing, of course, that other assumptions of the standard $M/M/c$ model are relevant). Note, however, that in reality this system has tandem service facilities if departing cars queue up at the exit to pay the parking fees.

FOLLOW-UP EXERCISES

39. Determine a set of formulas for the no-queue $M/M/c$ system by substituting $N = c$ in Equations 16.40 through 16.48.
40. Determine operating characteristics for the parking lot problem if $c = 5$.
41. Suppose implicit revenue is given by z = (Realized revenue) − (Lost revenue due to rejection), or $z = L_s \cdot T \cdot p - \lambda \cdot T \cdot P_N \cdot (1/\mu) \cdot p$, *where p* represents the price per car per unit time period for parking and T represents the number of time periods in the planning horizon. Note that $\lambda \cdot T \cdot P_N$ is the number of rejected cars and $\lambda \cdot T \cdot P_N(1/\mu)$ is the associated number of lost hours over T due to rejection. Agree? Determine z if $c = 5$, $T = 10$ hours, and $p = \$0.50$ per car per hour.
42. Use a software package to solve for the operating characteristics of a parking garage with $c = 15$.

Finite Population

If the calling source is limited to m units and m is small, then finite population models must be used.[15]

> Operating characteristics for an $M/M/c$ model with a finite population are given by Equations 16.49 through 16.57 in Appendix 16B.

As in the single-server model, $\rho/c \equiv \lambda/(\mu c)$ is not restricted to values less than unity for steady state to be achieved.[16]

FOLLOW-UP EXERCISES

43. Determine operating characteristics for the computer terminal problem (Example 16.4) if a single queue feeds into two terminals.
    a. Compare performance and costs to the results in Example 16.4.
    b. Compare L_s, L_q, W_s, and W_q to the results in Exercise 30. Comment?
44. For the preceding exercise, calculate R, E_1, and E_2 and compare to Exercise 29. In calculating E_2, the average number of idle facilities is given by $2P_0 + 1P_1$. Can you state a general experssion given c service facilities? (See Exercise 34 for the answer.)

Self-Service

Given the assumptions of the standard $M/M/c$ model and unlimited self-service facilities (for practical purposes), the self-service model is simply the standard $M/M/c$ model as c approaches infinity.

> Operating characteristics are given by Equations 16.58 through 16.60 in Appendix 16B.

In this case, $\rho \equiv \lambda/\mu$ can take on any value (less than infinity). Note that P_n is Poisson with mean ρ and that $L_q = W_q = 0$.

▶ Example 16.7 Supermarket Tandem System

The queuing systems at supermarkets are essentially tandem systems consisting of two subsystems or sets of servers. The first subsystem includes arrivals at the store of customers who self-serve groceries; the second subsystem entails arrivals at the checkout queues for servicing by clerks. Poisson arrivals at the store and exponential

[15]See the discussion under Finite Population in Section 16.4 for an interpretation of "small."

[16]L. G. Peck and R. N. Hazelwood, *Finite Queueing Tables* (New York: John Wiley & Sons, 1958), p. 210., also include computational tables for this model.

self-service result in Poisson departures from the first subsystem and, consequently, Poisson arrivals for the second subsystem. In fact, Saaty has proved that **Poisson systems in series** (where each system is either standard $M/M/1$ or standard $M/M/c$) can be analyzed independently, each having the same steady-state input rate given by λ.[17]

FOLLOW-UP EXERCISES

45. Suppose customer arrivals at a supermarket are Poisson with rate 30 customers per hour and times to complete the "shopping list" are exponential with mean one half hour per customer. What is the expected number of customers who are shopping? Find a cumulative Poisson table in some statistics text and determine the following: $P(n \leq 15)$, $P(n > 15)$, $P(n = 0)$, $P(n > 50)$, and $P(n > 75)$.
46. For the supermarket in the preceding exercise determine the expected number of customers and time spent in the checkout subsystem if management is experimenting with (*a*) a queue in front of each of four checkout counters and (*b*) one queue feeding into four checkout counters. Checkout times are exponential with a mean of four minutes. Conclusions?

16.6 OTHER QUEUING MODELS

Up to this point, the presentation has been limited to models of the Poisson type with varying assumptions regarding characteristics. Variations on the characteristics present an opportunity for an endless variety of models. As a result, the literature in this field is voluminous. For example, many models have been derived that treat Poisson-related distributions, non-Poisson distributions, priorities for service, bulk arrivals, impatient customers, facilities in series, and state-dependent arrival and service rates, to name a few. (See the references at the end of the chapter for some detailed treatments.)

In this section we begin by presenting some results that are rather general across models and end with the treatment of the $(M/G/1)$ model.

General Relationships

As you should have verified in Exercises 4 and 5, the following relationships hold generally by definition, where the symbol E denotes expected value or mean:

$$E[\text{number in system}] = E[\text{number in queue}] + E[\text{number in service}]$$

or

$$L_s = L_q + L_{se} \tag{16.61}$$ [18]

and

$$E[\text{time in system}] = E[\text{time in queue}] + E[\text{time in service}]$$

or

$$W_s = W_q + E[t]. \tag{16.62}$$

[17] T. L. Saaty, *Elements of Queuing Theory with Applications* (New York: McGraw-Hill, 1961).

[18] Note that Equations 16.13 through 16.60 are in Appendix 16B.

Additionally, Little has shown that the following relationships are relatively general providing the queuing process is stationary and steady state:[19]

$$L_s = \lambda W_s \tag{16.63}$$

and

$$L_q = \lambda W_q . \tag{16.64}$$

Did you verify these in Exercise 6 for the standard $M/M/1$ model? Can you give logical meaning to these?

If you were to check back over the various models we have presented, you would realize that Equations 16.61 through 16.64 either were directly used or can be proved in all cases. Their importance is evident if you realize that a knowledge of any three of the seven variables (either through sampling or analytical derivation) provides the solution to the remaining four variables. In some cases, however, care must be exercised in defining λ. For instance, in models with finite populations or finite queues, an *effective* λ must be used.[20]

Finally note that, although the relations hold for either single-server or multiple-server models with single queue, conditions for steady state must be met. This means that $\rho/c < 1$ must be satisfied where applicable and the period of sampling for statistical estimates must be sufficiently long to ensure an effective steady state.

FOLLOW-UP EXERCISES

47. Numerically confirm Equations 16.62 through 16.64 for the
    a. Standard $M/M/c$ model calculations in Table 16–4, column 1.
    b. Finite queue $M/M/1$ model of Example 16.3. [*Hint*: Effective λ is given by $\lambda \cdot (1 - P_N)$. Right?]
    c. Finite population $M/M/1$ model of Example 16.4. [*Hint*: Effective λ is given by $\lambda \cdot (m - L_s)$. Right?]
48. Consider a queuing system where $\lambda = 10$ units per day, $\mu = 5$ units per day, and $W_s = 0.5$ day per unit. Determine L_s, L_q, L_{se}, and W_q. Note that, for constant μ, $E[t] = 1/\mu$. Are your results valid for $c \leq 2$? What are the implications of λ, μ, and W_s were estimated by taking a "small" sample?

Pollaczek-Khintchine (P-K) Formula[21]

The P-K formula applies to an $M/G/1$ model having the same assumptions as the standard $M/M/1$ model except for the following: FCFS, LCFS, or SIRO service discipline; general (any) service time distribution with mean $E[t]$ and variance $V[t]$. Note that the condition $\rho < 1$ must still apply for the steady-state where $\rho = \lambda \cdot E[t]$.[22] Given these assumptions, we can prove that

---

[19] J. D. C. Little, "A Proof of the Queuing Formula: $L = \lambda W$, *Operations Research* 9 (1961), pp. 383–87. Also see W. S. Jewell, "A Simple Proof of $L = \lambda W$, "*Operations Research* 15 (1967), pp. 1109–16; and S. Stidham, Jr., "A Last Word on $L = \lambda W$," *Operations Research* 22 (1974), pp. 417–21.

[20] Effective λ was illustrated under Finite Population in Section 16.4. Remember?

[21] Correct pronunciation and spelling should be worth some sort of bonus for your course. Ask your instructor!

[22] If the average service rate (customers per unit time) is represented by μ, then $E[t] = 1/\mu$ so that $\rho = \lambda/\mu = \lambda \cdot E[t]$.

$$L_s = \rho + \frac{\rho^2 + \lambda^2 V[t].}{2(1 - \rho)} \tag{16.65}$$

Thus knowing λ, $E[t]$, and $V[t]$, L_s can be determined from Equation 16.65 and L_q, W_s, and W_q follow from 16.62 through 16.64.

This result is significant because of the generality of the service time distribution. In other words, given a specific distribution such as exponential, normal, or deterministic, Equations 16.62 through 16.65 can be used to determine relevant operating characteristics.

Also, note the following very important observation: The appearance of a variance term in 16.65 proves the fallacy of deriving expected values without the explicit consideration of probabilistic behavior (as exhibited through variance); only if $V[t] = 0$ does variance not affect E[number in system]. Thus we have shown explicitly what we said earlier in the chapter: Queues build up both because of traffic intensity (ρ) and because of variability in arrival and service times; improvements in operating characteristics can be effected from changes in either means or variances.

Example 16.8 Car Wash

Consider a planned car wash operation with four independent channels and a Poisson arrival pattern with rate 72 cars per hour for the entire system. Time-and-motion studies for similar service facilities indicate that $E[t] = 0.05$ hour per car and $V[t] = 0.01$ (hour per car)^2 for each server. For each channel it follows that $\lambda = 72/4 = 18$ and $\rho = \lambda \cdot E[t] = (18) \cdot (0.05) = 0.9$. According to 16.65,

$$\begin{aligned} L_s &= 0.9 + \frac{(0.9)^2 + (18)^2(0.01)}{2(1 - 0.9)} \\ &= 21.15 \text{ cars} \end{aligned}$$

for each channel, or approximately 85 cars for the entire system. From 16.63,

$$\begin{aligned} W_s &= \frac{L_s}{\lambda} \\ &= \frac{21.15}{18} \\ &= 1.175 \text{ hours} \end{aligned}$$

as the expected time in the system for each car. Rearranging 16.62 gives

$$\begin{aligned} W_q &= W_s - E[t] \\ &= 1.175 - 0.05 \\ &= 1.125 \text{ hours} \end{aligned}$$

as the expected time in the queues. Finally, from 16.64,

$$\begin{aligned} L_q &= (18)(1.125) \\ &= 20.25 \text{ cars} \end{aligned}$$

is the expected length of each queue.

Needless to say, the performance of this planned queuing system would be dismal. Costs aside, the number of servers definitely should be increased to avoid mass balking and reneging (if not rioting). Note also that these results differ from $M/M/3$ results (shown in Figure 16–9) because the variance of exponential service times would be 0.0025 (the square of the mean equals the variance for the exponential).

FOLLOW-UP EXERCISES

49. Noting that $\lambda = 24/c$ (cars per hour) for c independent single channel–single queue subsystems, determine operating characteristics for five car wash facilities. Is there much improvement?
50. At least how many car wash facilities would be needed to force the mean number of cars in each subsystem below three cars?
51. Suppose that total automation of each car wash facility effectively reduces variance to zero ($M/D/1$ model). Determine the resulting operating characteristics using the data in Example 16.8 and reflect on the results. Is the variance effect significant?
52. Using Equations 16.62 through 16.65, derive a set of formulas for the model $M/D/1$, noting that $E[t] = 1/\mu$ and $V[t] = 0$.
53. *a.* Do you remember the expression for the variance of an exponential distribution with parameter μ? (If not, see Appendix A) Prove that 16.62 through 16.65 provide the identical results for their equivalents in the standard $M/M/1$ model.

    b. Compare results from 16.65 (L_s) with $V(t) = 0.0025$ against the results for Example 16.8 in Figure 16–9.

FIGURE 16–9 Selected $M/M/3$ Operating Characteristics for Example 16.8 Using Erikson-Hall Package

```
          COMPUTER MODELS FOR MANAGEMENT SCIENCE
QUEUEING MODELS

              -=*=-  INFORMATION ENTERED  -=*=-

ALTERNATIVE CHOSEN                 :        MULTIPLE SERVER

ARRIVAL RATE                       :              72.000
SERVICE RATE                       :              20.000

NUMBER OF SERVERS                  :               4

                    -=*=-  RESULTS  -=*=-

SERVER IDLE (PERCENT)              :              10.480

EXPECTED NUMBER IN SYSTEM          :               9.283

EXPECTED NUMBER IN QUEUE           :               5.702

EXPECTED TIME IN SYSTEM            :               0.130

EXPECTED TIME IN QUEUE             :               0.080

         ----------  END OF ANALYSIS  ----------
```

16.7 QUEUING OPTIMIZATION MODELS

Up to this point, we have primarily stressed the behavior (operating characteristics) of a queuing system. This section explicitly considers queuing models that optimize some objective function, a topic that has received increasing emphasis in recent years.

General Considerations

Figure 16–10 illustrates the economic trade-off in a queuing system. Generally, increasing the degree of service results in lower waiting costs for customers at the expense of higher service costs for the facility. If the criterion to be optimized is stated in terms of minimizing these combined costs, then the decision is in terms of the best level of service to provide. An alternative objective relevant in retail establishments is the maximization of implicit contribution to overhead and profits, that is, revenue minus cost of service minus cost of waiting.

FIGURE 16–10 Economic Trade-off in Queuing System

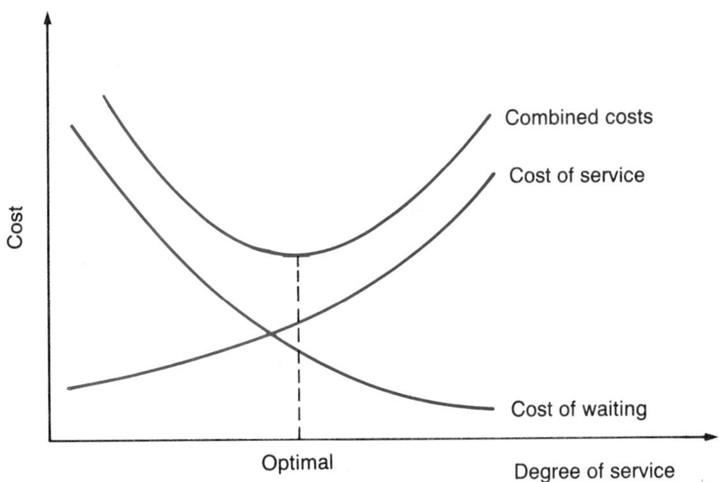

Typically, costs are stated on the basis of per unit time. The cost of service is based on *all* costs associated with the provision of that service. For instance, as in Example 16.4, the cost of a server (terminal) was composed of connect, resource, task, maintenance, and capital costs on a per-day basis. For the most part, service costs are readily attainable.

The estimated cost of waiting is another matter. If the waiting units are *internal* to the organization (e.g., office personnel waiting to use equipment or mechanics waiting for supplies from a tool crib), the cost of waiting usually can be estimated adequately. For units *external* to the organization, however, the cost of waiting is subtle. Examples include lost sales due to ill will, balking, or reneging; annoyances and "lost opportunities" due to waiting in long registration lines for the school term (usually costed at zero by universities); the "cost" (to the individual and society) associated with aggravated injuries or death in the queuing system of a hospital; and the "cost" of waiting for the response by fire or police departments. Because of the difficulty in estimating external waiting costs, many analyses focus on minimizing service costs subject to a constraint on a variable related to the cost of waiting (for example, W_q or L_q). Alternatively, **aspiration level models** seek to determine a level (or range) of service that satisfies two or more conflicting operating characteristics (e.g., number of servers that would simultaneously not exceed predetermined levels for percent idle time and expected waiting time).[23] In either case, costs are treated *implicitly*. In short, there is no way of avoiding cost considerations. As in the past, we can ease our anxiety for risky parameter estimates by sensitivity analysis.

The degree of service is loosely defined, as it can take many forms. To wit: service rate (μ) setting, as in machines that are adjustable or different configurations of servers (e.g., checkout clerk and bagger) or varying degrees of ability or experience; number of servers (c); traffic intensity (ρ); arrival rate (λ), as in scheduling patients for a clinic or setting the speed of conveyor belts in an automated assembly line; and allowable number of units in the system (N). More complicated cases include joint levels for decision variables (for example, μ and ρ, or μ and N, or λ and c) and the assignment of priority levels. (Can you think of examples for these?)

Methods of solution include marginal analysis for discrete variables, classical calculus for continuous variables, dynamic programming (Chaper 12), and Markov decision processes (Chapter 14). In this section, we illustrate the first two methods.

Optimal μ for $M/M/1$ Models

Assuming steady-state conditions and linear cost functions for service and waiting, we see that the expected *total cost per unit time* is given by

$$z = c_s \cdot \mu + c_w \cdot L_s \tag{16.66}$$

where c_s = Marginal cost of service (dollars per customer) and c_w = Cost of waiting (Dollars per customer − Unit time).

The expression for z in 16.66 is perfectly general for any single server model, excepting those that cost customers who renege or balk and those that truncate queues when N is a decision variable and rejected customers are costed. Substituting 16.5 for L_s gives the objective function for the standard $M/M/1$ model:

$$z = c_s\mu + c_w\left(\frac{\lambda}{\mu - \lambda}\right).$$

Setting the first derivative of z with respect to μ to zero and solving for optimal μ gives

$$\mu^* = \lambda + \left(\frac{c_w}{c_s} \cdot \lambda\right)^{1/2}. \tag{16.67}$$

Note that 16.67 ensures $\lambda < \mu$ or $\rho < 1$. Furthermore, the process of taking the derivative assumes that z (and hence μ) is continuous.

[23] This idea was illustrated using Table 16–3 in determining μ for an $M/M/1$ model. Exercises 13 and 19 also illustrate the aspiration-level approach.

FOLLOW-UP EXERCISES

54. Suppose a particular electronic component is assembled by a machine with an adjustable service rate. Parts for assembly exhibit random (Poisson) arrivals with a mean of 40 parts per hour. Processing times are exponential. Determine the optimal machine assembly rate given that delayed components are costed at $5 per hour each and that the marginal cost of assembling a component is $2. How sensitive is μ^* to variations in the cost ratio? To variations in λ?

**55. Verify Equation 16.67 and test the second-order condition for a minimum.

**56. Express z for a finite queue single-server model where both μ and N are decision variables. Let $C_c \equiv$ Cost per unit time of expanding the capacity of the facility to allow one more unit in the queue and $C_r \equiv$ Cost of a rejected unit. Why is it inappropriate to differentiate this expression? How might you solve for μ^* and N^*?

**57. If the cost of waiting is defined in terms of waiting in the queue, then L_q or L_b must be used in place of L_s in 16.66. Determine z using L_q for the standard $M/M/1$ model. Show that the expression for μ^* (that is, $dz/d\mu = 0$) is a polynomial of degree 4. Can you solve for μ^* given values for the parameters as in Exercise 54?

**58. For the finite population $M/M/1$ model, L_s is given by 16.25. Determine the expression that must be solved for μ^*.

Optimal c for M/M/c Models

Assuming steady-state conditions, linearity in the cost functions, and the number of servers as the only relevant decision variable, the expected total cost per unit time is given by

$$z = c_s' \cdot c + c_w \cdot L \tag{16.68}$$

where c_s' is the cost per server per unit time, L is the expected number of customers in the system (L_s), or the expected number in the queue (L_q), or the expected number of customers in a busy-system queue (L_b), and c and c_w are as previously defined.

Since z is discontinuous (that is, c is an integer), we use marginal analysis to determine optimal c. Defining $z(c^*)$ as the minimum value of z when c is optimal, then the necessary conditions for minimum costs are

$$z(c^*) \le z(c^* - 1)$$

and (16.69)

$$z(c^*) \le z(c^* + 1).$$

Try verbalizing these conditions. Substituting 16.68 into a combined inequality based on 16.69 gives

$$z(c^* - 1) \ge z(c^*) \le z(c^* + 1)$$

$$c_s' \cdot (c^* - 1) + c_w \cdot L(c^* - 1) \ge c_s' \cdot c^* + c_w \cdot L(c^*)$$

$$\le c_s' \cdot (c^* + 1) + c_w \cdot L(c^* + 1) \tag{16.70}$$

where $L(c^*)$ represents the value of L when using c^* servers. By algebraically manipulating 16.70, it can be shown that the necessary condition for an optimum number of servers is given by

$$L(c^*) - L(c^* + 1) \le \frac{c_s'}{c_w} \le L(c^* - 1) - L(c^*). \qquad (16.71)$$

▶ Example 16.9 Optimal Number of Tool-Crib Attendants

The tool crib in a production shop of a large industrial corporation services a large number of mechanics who are paid an average hourly wage of \$6 (excluding fringe benefits). Two attendants in the service facility dispense tools on an FCFS basis according to a numbering system. Recently, the vice president of production has been receiving complaints of excessively long waiting lines. Upon first hearing of this, the assistant to the vice president (a recent M.B.A. graduate) immediately diagnosed this as a queuing problem. A subsequent study indicated that $\lambda = 48$ mechanics per hour, $\mu = 25$ mechanics per hour, and that the conditions of Poisson arrivals and servicing were satisfied adequately. Assuming a very large population of mechanics, the standard $M/M/c$ model should serve as a reasonable approximation to this queuing system. If tool-crib attendants are paid wages of \$4 per hour (including fringe benefits), how many should be hired to service the facility?

In this case, $\rho = 1.92$, $c_s' = \$4$ per attendant-hour, and $c_w = \$6$ per mechanic-hour. If we assume that the time spent in the queue and in service is unproductive, then L_s, as given by 16.34, is appropriate for the criterion given by 16.68

Table 16–5 indicates that $c^* = 3$ and $z^* = \$27.87$ per hour. Note that the cost ratio ($c_s'/c_w = 0.667$) falls within the range (0.582 – 21.845) specified by Equation 16.71 for c^*. Figure 16–11 illustrates the results as generated using the Erikson-Hall package.

TABLE 16–5 Results for Optimum Number of Tool-Crib Attendants[24]

Number of Attendants c	Mean Number of Mechanics in System $L_s(c)$	Total Cost in Dollars per Hour* $z(c)$	l_1–l_2†
1	28.913	177.48	21.845–177.48
2	12.157	80.94	0.582– 21.845
3	2.645	27.87	0.111– 0.582
4	2.063	28.38	
5	1.952	31.71	

*From equation 16.68.
†l_1 and l_2 represent, respectively, the left-hand–side and right-hand–side inequalities in 16.71.

FOLLOW-UP EXERCISES

59. Verify the calculations in Table 16–5.
60. Suppose the plant is operating at full capacity so that any time lost by mechanics must be made up with overtime at time and a half. Determine the new cost ratio and find optimal c.
61. Should the cost of waiting be expressed in terms of forgone marginal revenues or profits? Discuss pros and cons.
62. Why is Equation 16.71 an inappropriate rule for determining the optimal number of computer terminals as presented in Example 16.4
**63. Verify Equation 16.71 starting with 16.70.

[24] W. K. Grassman claims to have a very simple approximation to solve this type of problem. See W. K. Grassmann, "Is the Fact that the Emperor Wears No Clothes a Subject Worthy of Publication?" *Interfaces*, March–April 1986, pp. 43–51.

FIGURE 16–11 Results for Example 16.9 Using Erikson-Hall Package

```
          COMPUTER MODELS FOR MANAGEMENT SCIENCE
QUEUING MODELS

              -=*=-  INFORMATION ENTERED  -=*=-

ALTERNATIVE CHOSEN          :          MULTIPLE SERVER

ARRIVAL RATE                :               48.000    (λ)
SERVICE RATE                :               25.000    (u)

NUMBER OF SERVERS           :                 1-12    (c)

SERVICE COST RATE           :                4.000    (c's)
WAITING COST RATE           :                6.000    (cw)

         MULTIPLE SERVER PARAMETRIC ANALYSIS

                 -=*=-  RESULTS  -=*=-
```

NUMBER OF SERVERS	SYSTEMS WAIT	SYSTEMS LENGTH	TOTAL COSTS
1	1.157	28.913	177.478
2	0.258	12.157	80.942
3	0.055	2.645	27.867
4	0.043	2.063	28.378
5	0.041	1.952	31.712
6	0.040	1.927	35.562
7	0.040	1.921	39.529
8	0.040	1.920	43.522
9	0.040	1.920	47.520
10	0.040	1.920	51.520
11	0.040	1.920	55.520
12	0.040	1.920	59.520

---------- END OF ANALYSIS ----------

16.8 ASSESSMENT OF QUEUING THEORY

In recent years, theoretical developments in queuing models have proliferated at a rapid rate. Not only are theoretical models based on more realistic assumptions (e.g., state-dependent parameters, dependent arrivals, general arrival and service distributions, and priority service disciplines), but also powerful and sophisticated mathematical procedures have been developed to treat complex problems and transient solutions.

As in most fields characterized by rapid technological or theoretical developments, the application or practice of queuing theory has lagged behind the theoretical state of the art. In part, this is due to a communications gap (or chasm) between mathematical theoreticians and applied researchers—a state of affairs for which both groups can share credit. For example, many of the theoretical results on, say, operating characteristics for complex models are in a form (called "transforms") that are either inconvenient or unusable for numerical calculations. Progress has been made, however, in developing results that are computationally manageable, including approximation techniques. The alternative of simulation is available also, as demonstrated in the next chapter.

Other criticisms regarding the practice of queuing theory include the absence of statistical procedures and the indiscriminate uses of $M/M/c$ models and steady-state results. All too often, a disconcerting absence of proper sampling, estimation, and hypothesis testing procedures is noted. All assumptions inherent in a model (e.g., types of distributions, parameters, state-independence, and independent arrivals) must be tested by such procedures, if possible, in order to select the correct model. While $M/M/c$ models are widely available and useful, their assumptions must be reasonably substantiated in any particular application. (Interestingly, Poisson input processes tend to be more common in real phenomena than exponential service times.) The limitations of and interpretations for steady-state solutions also must be assessed, as many queuing systems do not operate a sufficiently long period of time to achieve steady state. This is not to say that decisions based on steady-state solutions are unjustified, but rather that their interpretations are based on an idealized concept.

We conclude this assessment with a summary of the managerial implications of queuing theory.[25]

Queuing Models show us:

1. Why waiting lines form,
2. Why some waiting is necessary or very costly to eliminate,
3. The nonlinear effects resulting from:
   a. Increasing service capacity.
   b. Pooling service facilities.
   c. Decreasing variability in service times.

I. Congestion is a function of: (1) randomness in arrival patterns—50 percent; (2) variability in service times—50 percent.
   A. Understanding that the source of congestion is twofold requires managers to take a two-dimensional approach to managing waiting time situations:
      1. *Scheduling* to smooth demand fluctuations; for example, reservation/appointment systems.
      2. *Staffing multiple specialized service channels* to minimize service time variation.

[25] This summary of managerial implications are class notes developed by Dr. Richard Reid of the University of New Mexico.

B. Recognizing that if a service organization has *both* fluctuating arrival rates and service times, it will be difficult to achieve both:
   1. Good facility utilization.
   2. Good customer service levels.

C. Efficiencies and customer satisfaction increase through the utilization of the *self-service concept:*
   1. Requiring the customer to provide some of his/her own service yields a reduction in variability of organizationally provided service time.
   2. Requesting customer participation in service delivery process helps make idle time productive and reduces perceived wait time.

D. A *trade-off* exists between service facility idle time and rapid response to customer requests for service:
   1. If rapid service response is critical, significant amounts of service facility idle time will be required, for example, fire, ambulance, or other public safety services.
   2. If rapid service response is not critical, minimal total operational costs will necessitate some customer waiting.

II. Managerial intuition fails due to prevailing nonlinearities.

A. Adding *parallel* service channels causes a *disproportional reduction* in average line lengths and system times.

B. *Pooling service facilities* increases overall efficiencies:
   1. Total server idle time and customer waiting time at a single large facility are less than that recorded at a number of smaller facilities offering an equivalent processing service capacity.
   2. This reduced idle time is *not* the result of economies of scale, but results from the interplay of arrival rates and service times. That is, the single facility has shorter average lines and less server idle time because the randomness of arrivals and service times can be spread over more servers. At geographically dispersed facilities, customer waiting occurs at some facilities and server idleness occurs concurrently at others.

SELECTED APPLICATION REVIEW

OUTPATIENT DEPARTMENTS

An investigation was undertaken into the operation of outpatient departments in an attempt to arrive at a sensible and implementable appointment policy that would reduce patient waiting time. In 1983 the Management Science staff at the University of Kent (UK) conducted a survey of three outpatient departments at a hospital. Each department was observed for four sessions, and patients were asked to complete a questionnaire. The results revealed that: (1) physicians often started sessions late, (2) they were distracted by other matters, (3) a pool of patients was created at the start of the sessions, and (4) appointments were badly scheduled. Several courses of action were discussed. It was concluded that the determination of an implementable system, the education of participants into acceptance of that policy, and monitoring any policy once implemented are of great importance. This aproach is compared briefly with qualitative and soft approaches.

SOURCE: Robert M. O'Keefe, "Investigating Outpatient Departments: Implementable Policies and Qualitative Approaches," *Journal of the Operational Research Society (UK)*, August 1985, pp. 705–12.

COMMAND AND CONTROL

The fundamental question posed in this application is which of two alternative configurations (centralized or distributed) of a network of queues would, in general, move customers through the network faster? An application was developed for the Navy to evaluate alternative concepts for the Navy Command and Control System (NCCS). The NCCS was to consist of a network of command centers and possible support facilities. The network serves different levels of naval command authority, each of which makes decisions

(continued)

regarding the deployment of forces. The network was to support decision making, with particular attention given to those decisions needing to be made within a short period of time and requiring timely and accurate information feedback.

One particular activity supported by the NCCS is ocean surveillance. A ship can maintain continuous surveillance of an area on the order of 30 miles around its own location. Naval commanders must know the location and identity of all objects in this area. Ocean surveillance systems provide this information, but there is a trade-off between systems that provide good position accuracy versus those that provide good identification. The essential task of the NCCS is to provide for correlation of these reports from different systems and to provide good position *and* good identification. The analysis defined two alternatives: centralized and distributed processing networks. The advantage of the central network would be that all users would have the same picture but there was fear that the central processing network would become a bottleneck.

Queuing theory helped in two ways. First, the problem was not clearly defined in the beginning, and queuing theory helped elicit definitions and specifications of trade-offs. Second, taking the output rates of surveillance systems as arrivals to the NCCS and taking service time as the time to make that information available to naval commanders, the study found that central networks showed smaller time delays than distributed networks. This study became one input to the Navy in their decision making. Primarily, it removed an assumption or constraint on the decision by allaying fears about central bottlenecks.

SOURCE: Stan Siegel and Paul Torelli, "The Value of Queueing Theory: A Case Study," *Interfaces,* November 1979, pp. 148–51.

AUTOMATIC TELLERS

A study to determine customer service standards for the automatic teller machines (ATMs) of a large retail bank led to the formulation and calibration of a finite waiting room $M/M/c/K$ queuing model.* The model suggested that the percentage of lost customers be adopted as the service standard instead of line wait. The new standard was applied against existing transaction reports to identify those congested ATM facilities that could best

(continued)

profit from additional machines and lobby space. The magnitude of the increased business at the upgraded facilities partly confirmed the model's hypothesis that substantial numbers of customers had indeed been balking.

---

*An $M/M/c/K$ queuing model has a maximum capacity of K units in the system so that $K - c$ units is the maximum capacity of the queue. Recall that c is the number of servers and that M/M indicates Poisson arrivals and exponential service times.

SOURCE: Peter Kolesar, "Stalking the Endangered CAT: A Queueing Analysis of Congestion at Automatic Teller Machines," *Interfaces,* November–December 1984, pp. 16–26. An excerpt from this article is reprinted below.

Stalking the Endangered CAT: A Queueing Analysis of Congestion at Automatic Teller Machines*

PETER KOLESAR

Graduate School of Business
Uris Hall
Columbia University
New York, New York 10027

A study to determine customer service standards for the automatic teller machines (ATMs) of a large retail bank led to the formulation and calibration of a finite waiting room $M/M/c/K$ queueing model. The model suggested that the percentage of lost customers be adopted as the service standard instead of line wait. The new standard was applied against existing transaction reports to identify those congested ATM facilities that could best profit from additional machines and lobby space. The magnitude of the increased business at the upgraded facilities partly confirmed the model's hypothesis that substantial numbers of customers had indeed been balking.

Although studies on the impact of teller staffing and the like have appeared in the MS/OR literature [Deutch and Mabert, 1979, 1980; McClure and Miller, 1979; Momjian et al., 1976; Foote, 1976] actual applications of queueing models to control bank waiting lines are the exception rather than the rule.

The rapid and widespread introduction of automatic teller machines (ATMs) capable of carrying out many routine retail banking transactions makes the use of queueing or simulation modeling in retail banking more attractive, if not necessary. ATM facilities and the computer/telecommunications networks that link them have many of the characteristics that underly classical queueing models: Customer demands occur quite at random, customer service times are very unpredictable, and under most conditions customers form and maintain reasonably orderly queues. Although ATM systems do not obey the strictures of stationarity, the temporal patterns of customer arrivals are stable enough to be understood and modeled. Since managers are seldom present at ATM locations to observe operations and respond to problems on the spot, MS/OR modeling and the decision support tools it can produce are potentially more important for ATMs than for regular teller operations. Many managerial problems in the daily operation of ATMs, ATM engineering and system design, and the long-range strategic planning of ATM networks can all profit from queueing analysis — sometimes with the same simple models.

A model of ATMs has been developed and tested for the retail division of a large commercial bank that is heavily committed to expanding its ATM network. The key questions posed by bank management were how to set customer service standards at ATMs and how to determine which ATM locations were overloaded or congested. Management particularly wanted assistance in choosing ATM locations that would benefit most from additional terminals. It was also interested in a cost/ benefit analysis of two types of terminals: One an expensive general purpose terminal; the other a less expensive terminal limited to cash dispensing transactions.

The particular ATM studied was called a "Customer Activated Terminal" (CAT). An overloaded CAT was called "endangered," hence the title of this article.

THE PROBLEM AND THE MODEL

Most of the bank's nearly 500 ATMs are located in one large U.S. city. Each facility consists of one or more ATMs in a bank vestibule which is open throughout the regular banking day when the ATMs are an alternative to the human tellers inside the bank. After hours the banks are locked, but the vestibules can be entered by inserting into a slot in the locked door the same plastic card that accesses the ATM itself. The ATMs provide the most frequently used retail banking transactions: cash withdrawals, deposits, transfers of funds from one account to another, credit card payments, and so

Reprinted by permission of Peter Kolesar from *Interfaces*, 14, no. 6, November–December 1984, pp. 16–26.

(continued)

forth. As part of a corporation-wide program on improving customer service, bank management wanted to set "service standards" for customer delay at the ATMs. They chose line wait as the parameter of interest.

At the time most ATM locations had two machines in a vestibule of rather limited size configured as shown in Figure 1. Customers usually formed an orderly single queue on a first-come-first-served basis that fed both machines. This immediately suggests that a limited queue length two-server model might be appropriate. The simplest of these is, of course, the classic $M/M/c/K$ model [Gross and Harris, 1974] in which customers arrive one at a time according to a Poisson process at rate λ customers per hour, service times are independent identically distributed exponential random variables with mean service time $1/\mu$ hours, there are c identical and independent servers that never break down, and not more than $K - c$ customers can be in line. In real ATM facilities none of these assumptions are precisely true, yet it is my thesis that the simple $M/M/c/K$ model is still a very useful statistical descriptor of actual ATM facility performance.

When we began this project the bank had been using an $M/M/c/\infty$ type queueing model in their capacity and planning studies of the ATM network and its supporting computer system. That model had been calibrated with transaction counts and durations derived exclusively from the computer system that supported the ATM network. Using supplementary empirical data gathered by human observers and a finite queue-length model led bank management to important insights not obtainable from the extant $M/M/c/\infty$ models.

DATA COLLECTION

My interest in ATM operations had begun earlier with a series of student projects in an operations research course for Columbia Business School

FIGURE 1 A Typical Automatic Teller Facility Layout

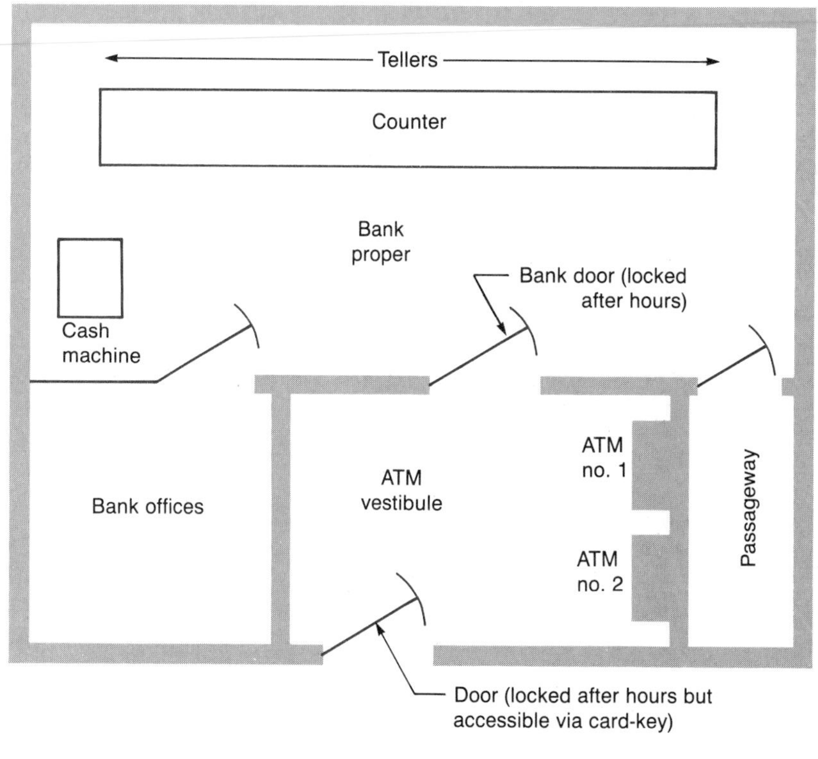

(*continued*)

M.B.A. students that at first had no connection with the client bank. Students collected data at several local retail branches of different commercial banks, built models for each bank, and then compared the different service systems from both the banks' and customers' viewpoints. At the end of the course we were retained by our client to study its own ATMs and tellers more intensively. (The teller study is ongoing and only the ATM study is reported on here.) The students measured service times by recording the entire period during which a customer "occupied" an ATM. Consequently their service times proved substantially longer than those derived by computer measured "card-in-card-out" intervals. Service times were recorded from continuous running digital stop watches. As long as there was a queue, the end of one service was taken as the beginning of the next service. Service end was defined as that moment when the customer stepped away or aside from the ATM so that another customer would have access. In those cases when there was not a queue, service starts were taken at the moment when the customer stepped up to the ATM and took "occupancy" of it. Since over 90 percent of the observed service starts began while a queue existed, there was little ambiguity in actual measurements. We also observed ATM "down times," customer balking, and reneging, and began to be impressed by the impact on customer behavior of the limited vestibule size.

Data were collected for one-hour intervals at ATM facilities at several branches during hours and days when we anticipated high traffic. This enabled us to collect a maximum amount of service time data, and observe the system at the congestion periods of most concern to management. However, because of the influence of the size of the vestibule on customer balking, peak-hour data provided only *censored* information on actual arrivals and limited measurements of fluctuations in the queue length.

In addition to manually collected data, we obtained computer generated transaction counts, an example of which is shown in Table 1.

TABLE 1 Successful ATM Transaction Counts for a Particular Site by Hour and by Day (*Third week of October 1982*)

Hour	Sunday	Monday	Tuesday	Wednesday	Thursday	Friday	Saturday	Total
0–1	0	5	18	11	12	18	17	81
1–2	1	0	9	3	10	4	16	43
2–3	0	4	2	8	8	6	7	35
3–4	0	0	7	4	5	2	8	26
4–5	0	0	3	14	2	6	1	26
5–6	0	4	2	3	11	6	3	29
6–7	1	7	22	12	26	42	2	112
7–8	0	70	55	53	80	86	11	355
8–9	6	112	120	138	137	162	4	679
9–10	5	72	93	91	68	115	14	458
10–11	4	78	58	69	85	106	8	408
11–12	9	98	78	99	147	122	14	567
12–13	5	161	98	183	166	168	18	799
13–14	3	154	98	170	172	181	21	799
14–15	7	149	91	151	148	141	12	699
15–16	4	126	67	82	105	119	17	520
16–17	8	88	72	96	98	124	13	499
17–18	6	133	82	90	84	148	15	558
18–19	3	57	70	59	64	89	7	349
19–20	0	36	33	50	53	40	8	220
20–21	7	25	24	8	49	24	5	142
21–22	3	11	25	20	21	29	3	112
22–23	3	4	9	8	9	11	0	44
23–24	1	17	7	5	21	1	1	53
Total	76	1411	1143	1427	1581	1750	225	7613

(continued)

CORRESPONDENCE OF THE MODEL TO REALITY

1. *Customer arrivals* do not actually occur according to a stationary Poisson process. Table 1, which counts experienced customer transactions, is indirect but telling evidence that actual arrivals occur in a rather marked temporal pattern that varies by hour of day and day of week. The data are incomplete since not all attempted arrivals actually join the system, and since many customers carry out several transactions in a single session. Data collected over several months and studied statistically show that these patterns are quite stable. The customer arrival process is further complicated in that persons frequently arrive in groups. At times each member of an arriving group actually became a customer, while at other times although each occupied a place in line only one became a customer.

The data obtained when there are strong surges in (attempted) arrivals, for example, at 5 P.M. on Friday afternoons, are greatly censored and nearly useless for studying whether arrivals follow a particular stochastic model. "Arrivals" cannot be measured with any accuracy at times of severe congestion, since although balking clearly occurs (and was sometimes explicitly observed) it cannot be directly recorded in a reliable manner. Indeed, one can conceive of three categories of balking: First, sometimes a customer could be observed to "balk," that is, begin to join the line and then turn away. Second, other customers, when interviewed, remarked that they often "balked" just by walking on past the bank when they observed a long line through the vestibule window. Third, still others "balked" by never even attempting a service at certain times. They learned not to try to arrive at times when they really desired service. (Reneging also occurs, although rather less frequently at ATMs than on the much longer teller lines inside the bank.) Data obtained when facilities were uncongested revealed that arrival in 10-minute intervals followed frequencies predicted by the Poisson distribution—with mean arrivals rates particular to hour and day of week. This all suggests that there is a time varying Poisson customer demand process driving the system. For a fuller statistical analysis supporting the use of the time varying Poisson process to model customer arrivals see Green and Kolesar [1983]. Were it not for the significant censoring, the methods reported there could be used with the bank transaction data which would follow a time varying compound Poisson process.

Recognizing -these characteristics we decided to base our model on stationary Poisson arrivals, but to create different models specific to each hour and day of week.

2. *Service times* are not identically exponentially distributed. Figure 2 is derived from 640 observations taken at a particular ATM location. Although this service time histogram peaks at small service times and is strongly skewed to the right, the mode is not zero as would be predicted by the exponential model, and there appears to be a minimum service time of almost half a minute. On the other hand, a plot of the tail of the distribution on semilog graph paper (Figure 3) does show the linear pattern consistent with the exponential model.

To test whether the exponential probability law is still a useful model of service times an $M/G/2/12$ model was simulated using the empirical service time distribution in Figure 2. In Table 2 simulation generated estimates of the probability of delay and mean delay are compared to predictions from the $M/M/2/12$ model over a broad range of traffic intensities, and there appeared to be no practical difference.

Mean service times that differed by site and by ATM are an additional complexity. (The statistical significance of these differences was confirmed by analysis of variance.) The former difference appears to reflect characteristics of the population of users at each site, while the latter reflects differences in hardware. (To increase the chance that at least one ATM would be working, the two devices at each site were supported by different host computers with rather different speeds. This substantial hardware difference was somewhat lost on customers for the differences observed were only about ± 3 percent. The site-to-site differences were in the range of ± 10 percent over the six locations studied.) Although statistically significant, these differences were neither large enough nor well enough understood to incorporate in a planning model. Therefore, an overall empirical average service time was used to estimate the expected service time ($1/\mu$) for all terminals. Service times were estimated from data

(*continued*)

FIGURE 2 A Histogram of ATM Service Times

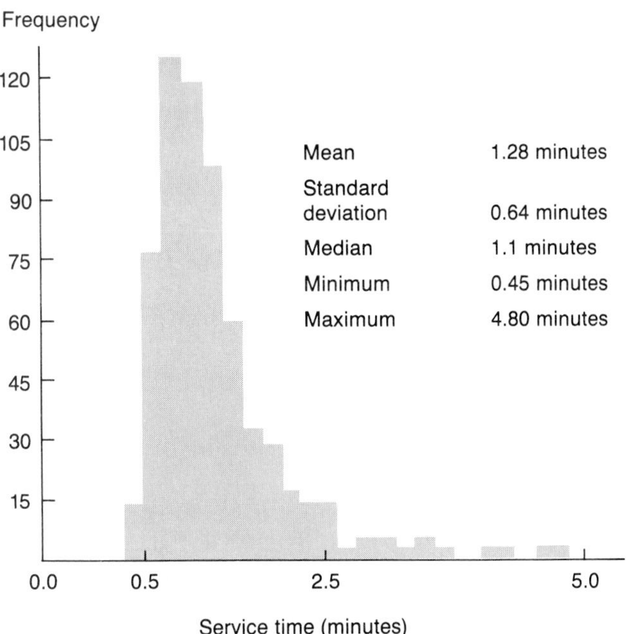

collected by human observers because, as indicated earlier, the detailed statistics gathered by the supporting computer system were for transaction times, and customer sessions often include several transactions and also include "setup" time not recorded by the computer.

The $M/M/c/K$ model presumes that ATMs are always available to serve customers. In practice, ATMs "go down" for several reasons: There may be a failure of the individual ATM, or the computer supporting the ATM may go down, or the ATM may simply run out of cash. These events happen with enough frequency to be of concern to management, but it was not necessary to model them for our purposes. (For a model with server breakdowns see Conway, Maxwell, and Miller [1967].)

3. ***Standard queue discipline*** **was usually followed by ATM customers.** In all situations observed, the customers formed a first-come-first-served single queue that fed both machines. Yet, customers were sometimes observed to renege (leave the queue after waiting in line for a while), and as mentioned earlier, a variety of balking behaviors were observed: Potential customers would arrive at the vestibule, observe the line length and turn away. Our questioning of some such persons confirmed that they had indeed balked.

The vestibules have a distinctly limited capacity. At the location we studied most intensively, even during peak hours there were rarely more than a dozen persons in line: More simply couldn't fit into the vestibule. Clearly the limited vestibule size had an effect, but it would be impossible to define precisely an upper limit on the queue. A model with a balking probability related to queue length would be more accurate—if its parameters could be estimated. Lacking the ability to gather such "metaphysical" data we proceeded with the fixed queue size model with the limit subjectively related to the physical size of the waiting room and the "typical maximum" queue length observed during congested periods.

APPLICATION OF THE MODEL

A simple BASIC program that could run in any personal computer calculates key performance measures of the $M/M/c/K$ system. Its inputs include λ,

(continued)

FIGURE 3 The Tails of the ATM Service Time Distribution

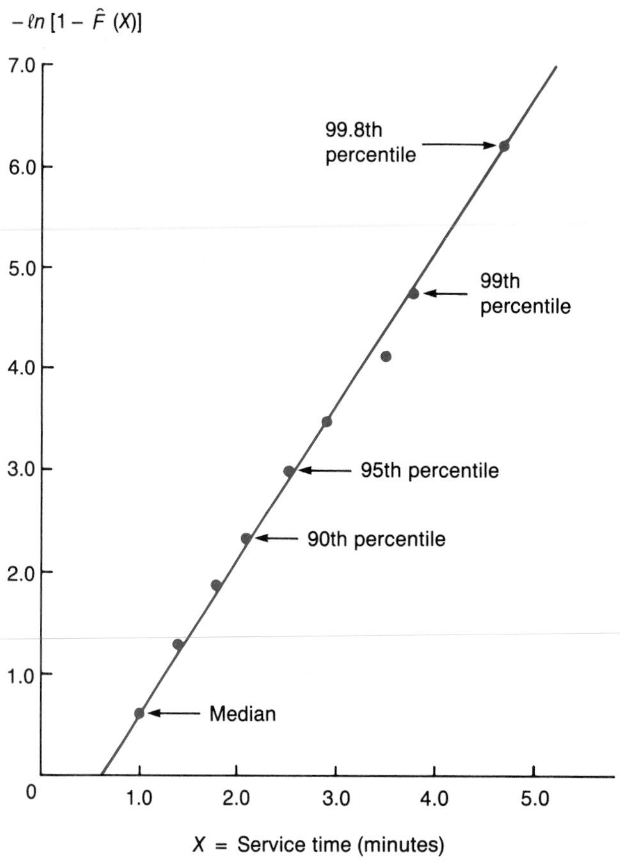

$1/\mu$, c, and $K - c$, as well as the expected number of transactions per customer session. The outputs include the load on the system ($\rho = \lambda/\mu$), the percent of arriving customers who are lost (balk), the percent of the served customers who are delayed (have to queue), the expected wait in queue of delayed customers, the expected length of the waiting line, and the utilization of the ATMs. The program runs for parameter values ranging over the conditions encountered in the field—different arrival rates, average service times, number of ATMs, and vestibule sizes showed the interrelations that determine the quality of customer service. Some insights such as how vestibule size and the number of ATMs jointly affected customer service are mostly relevant to system designers. Interesting as these were, it was what upper management learned that proved to have the most impact.

REFERENCES

Conway, R.; Maxwell, W.; and Miller, L. 1967, *Theory of Scheduling*, Addison-Wesley, Reading, Massachusetts.

Deutsch, H. and Mabert, V. 1980, "Queueing theory and teller staffing: A successful application," *Interfaces*, Vol. 10, No. 5 (October), pp. 63–66.

Deutsch, H. and Mabert, V. 1979, *Teller Staffing Guide: A Case Study*, The Bank Administration Institute, Park Ridge, Illinois.

(*continued*)

TABLE 2 A Comparison of Simulations and Model Predictions Using an Expected Service Time of 1.28 Minutes and Simulating 50,000 Customer Arrivals

(a) **Simulation vs. Model: *M/M/2/12* Systems**

	Proportion of Served Customers Who Are Delayed		Proportion of Arriving Customers Who Are Lost	
Utilization (ρ)	Model Prediction	Simulation with Empirical Distribution	Model Prediction	Simulation with Empirical Distribution
0.8	0.687	0.676	0.016	0.004
1.0	0.870	0.894	0.080	0.044
1.2	0.957	0.983	0.136	0.156
1.4	0.986	0.999	0.290	0.270
1.6	0.996	1.000	0.376	0.360
1.8	0.998	1.000	0.445	0.432
2.0	0.999	1.000	0.500	0.489

(b) **Simulation vs Model: *M/M/3/12* Systems**

	Proportion of Served Customers Who Are Delayed		Proportion of Arriving Customers Who Are Lost	
Utilization (ρ)	Model Prediction	Simulation with Empirical Distribution	Model Prediction	Simulation with Empirical Distribution
0.6	0.477	0.329	0.001	0.000
0.8	0.677	0.603	0.013	0.003
1.0	0.853	0.864	0.072	0.043
1.2	0.950	0.979	0.180	0.154
1.4	0.984	0.997	0.288	0.270
1.6	0.995	1.000	0.375	0.361
1.8	0.998	1.000	0.444	0.432
2.0	1.000	1.000	0.500	0.489

Feller, W. 1967, *An Introduction to Probability Theory and Its Applications,* Vol. 1, third edition, John Wiley, New York.

Foote, B. 1967, "A queueing case study of drive-in banking," *Interfaces,* Vol. 6, No. 4 (August), pp. 31–37.

Green, L. and Kolesar, P. 1983, "Testing the validity of a queueing police patrol," Columbia University School Working Paper No. 521.A, New York.

Gross, D. and Harris, C. 1974, *Fundamentals of Queueing Theory,* John Wiley, New York.

McClure, R. and Miller, R. 1979, "The applications of operations research in commercial banking companies," *Interfaces,* Vol. 9, No. 2 (February), Part 1, pp. 24–29.

Momjian, D.; Williams, S.; and Hoehenwarter, W. 1976, *Teller Staffing: A Guide to Improved Services at Lower Costs,* The Bank Administration Institute, Park Ridge, Illinois.

APPENDIX

The technical aspects of the $M/M/c/K$ model are described in most books on queueing theory (for example Gross and Harris [1974]), and some books on probability theory (for example Feller [1968]).

The model with arrival rate λ, service rate μ, c identical servers, and a waiting room of size $K - c$ is equivalent to a finite state birth and death process with rates

$$\lambda_n = \lambda, \qquad 0 \leq n \leq K,$$

$$\mu_n = \begin{cases} n\mu, & 0 \leq n \leq c, \\ c\mu, & c < n \leq K. \end{cases}$$

(continued)

The stationary probability of finding the system in state n (n customers present in total) are

$$P_n = \begin{cases} \dfrac{\rho^n P_o}{n!}, & 0 \leq n \leq c, \\ \dfrac{\rho^n P_o}{c^{n-c} c!}, & 0 < n \leq K, \end{cases}$$

where $\rho = \lambda/\mu$ is the presented load in the system, and P_o, the stationary probability that the system is empty, equals

$$P_o = \begin{cases} \left\{ \sum_{n=0}^{c-1} \dfrac{\rho^n}{n!} + \dfrac{\rho^c}{c!} \dfrac{1 - (\rho/c)^{K-c+1}}{(1 - \rho/c)} \right\}, & \rho \neq c \\ \left\{ \sum_{n=0}^{c-1} \dfrac{\rho^n}{n!} + \dfrac{\rho^c (K - c + 1)}{c!} \right\}^{-1}, & \rho = c. \end{cases}$$

The probability that the waiting room is full, P_K, is also the probability that a customer is lost, and $P_{delay} = \sum_{n=c}^{K-1} P_n$ is the probability that a customer is delayed. Thus, the probability that a served customer is delayed is $P_{delay}/(1 - P_K)$. The expected length of the queue is

$$EQ = \sum_{n=c}^{K} (n - C)P_n = \frac{P_o \rho^{c+1}}{(c - 1)!(c - \rho)^2} \cdot \left[1 - \left(\frac{\rho}{c}\right)^{K-c+1} - \left(1 - \frac{\rho}{c}\right)(K - c + 1)\left(\frac{\rho}{c}\right)^{K-c} \right].$$

Customers join the system at rate $\lambda(1 - P_K)$ and consequently from Little's equation the expected line wait, EW, is

$$EW = \frac{EQ}{\lambda(1 - P_N)}.$$

As the handled load is $\lambda(1 - P_N)/\mu$, the fraction of time a server is utilized is $\lambda(1 - P_N)/\mu c$.

SELECTED REFERENCES

Byrd, J. "The Value Of Queueing Theory." *Interfaces,* May 1978, pp. 22–26.

Fletcher, G. Y.; H. G. Perros; and W. J. Stewart. "A Queueing System Where Customers Require a Random Number of Servers Simultaneously." *European Journal of Operational Research (Netherlands)* March 1986, pp. 331–42.

Grassman, Winfried K. *Stochastic Systems for Management.* New York: Elsevier North-Holland Publishing, 1981.

Kleinrock, L. *Queueing Systems.* Vol. 1: Theory, 1975; Vol. 2: Computer Applications, 1976. New York: John Wiley & Sons.

Lee, T. I. "M/G/1/N Queue with Vacation Time and Exhaustive Service Discipline." *Operations Research,* July–August 1984, pp. 774–84.

Lemoine, A. J. "Networks of Queues—A Survey of Equilibrium Analysis." *Management Science,* December 1977, pp. 464–81.

Lindsay, C. M., and B. Feigenbaum. "Rationing by Waiting Lists." *American Economic Review,* June 1984, pp. 404–17.

Neuts, M. F. "Matrix Analytic Methods in Queuing Theory." *European Journal of Operational Research,* January 1984, pp. 2–12.

Stecke, Kathryn E. "A Hierarchical Approach to Solving Machine Grouping and Loading Problems of Flexible Manufacturing Systems." *European Journal of Operational Research (Netherlands),* March 1986, pp. 369–78.

Suri, Rajan, and Gregory W. Diehl. "A Variable Buffer-Size Model and Its Use in Analyzing Closed Queueing Networks with Blocking." *Management Science,* February 1986, pp. 206–24.

Vinod, B., and M. Sabbagh. "Optimal Performance Analysis of Manufacturing Systems Subject to Tool Availability." *European Journal of Operational Research (Netherlands),* March 1986, pp. 398–409.

Vinod, B., and T. Altiok. "Approximating Unreliable Queueing Networks under the Assumption of Exponentiality." *Journal of the Operational Reseach Society (UK),* March 1986, pp. 309–16.

Woodside, C. M., D. A. Stanford; and B. Pagurek. "Optimal Prediction of Queue Lengths and Delays in GI/M/m Multiserver Queues." *Operations Research,* July–August 1984, pp. 809–17.

ADDITIONAL EXERCISES

64. ***Gasoline Panic.*** Consider a one-pump gas station that satisfies the assumptions for the $M/M/1$ model. It is estimated that on the average, customers arrive to buy gas when the tank is one-eighth full. The mean time to service a customer is four minutes, and the arrival rate is six customers per hour.
    a. Determine the expected length of the queue and the expected number of minutes in the system.
    b. Suppose that customers perceive a gas shortage (when there is none) and respond by changing the fill-up criterion to more than one-eighth full on the average. Assuming that changes in λ are proportional to changes in the fill-up criterion, compare results to part *a* when the fill-up criterion is one-fourth full.
    c. Same as part *b* if the fill-up criterion is one-half full. Do we have the makings of a behaviorally induced gasoline panic?
    d. It is reasonable to assume that the time to service a customer will decrease as the fill-up criterion increases. Under "normal" conditions it takes an average of two minutes to pump gasoline and an average of two minutes to take the order, collect the money, and so forth. Rework parts *b* and *c* if the time to pump gasoline changes proportionally to changes in the amount of gasoline that must be pumped.
    e. Currently, we do not have a gasoline panic. Give two examples of inventory panic situations that seem plausible based on behavior in the face of shortage. Mortgage applications in the summer of 1986 required a two-month time in the system.
65. ***Dishwashing.*** You and your significant other are washing and drying dishes. As the washer, you can wash dishes at the Poisson rate of one per minute. Your helper can exponentially dry a dish in 45 seconds. You are cleaning up after a party and both face 1,000 dishes. What will be the "steady state" average queue between you?
66. ***Christmas Dolls.*** Toy manufacturers have discovered that a created shortage can make a toy desirable. Thinking back to various toy crazes, you might recall that Santa Claus had a rough time supplying enough dolls during Christmas 1984. In 1985 dolls became commonly available and somewhat less popular. If retail orders arrive at the rate of 10 truckloads per day (Poisson), how many truckloads should the plant supply to maintain a "desirable" shortage or waiting time of seven days?
67. ***Maintenance Service.*** Consider a company that holds maintenance contracts for repairing computer terminals whenever they break down. On the average each terminal breaks down every five days, where the time between breakdowns is exponential. The time to service a terminal, which includes travel time and repair time, is exponential with mean

one-quarter day. What is the maximum number of terminals that should be assigned to each service representative such that the probability of waiting to be serviced is less than 0.3?

68. ***Typing Pool Model.*** Suppose documents to be typed at an office arrive (Poisson) at the rate of 100 per day and secretaries can type (Poisson) at the rate 50 documents per secretary per day. Each secretary earns $40 per day, and the cost of holding documents in the system is estimated at $4 per document per day.
    a. Using the criterion total cost per day, find the optimal number of secretaries if each works with his/her own queue.
    b. Suppose that secretaries are to be combined into a typing pool with one queue. Determine the optimum number of secretaries and the associated cost by enumeration, that is, by evaluating 16.68 for 1, 2, 3, . . . secretaries. Is Equation 16.71 satisfied? Decision for pool or no pool? Any reservations about the validity of the analysis?
69. ***Quality Control.*** Consider the schematic below.

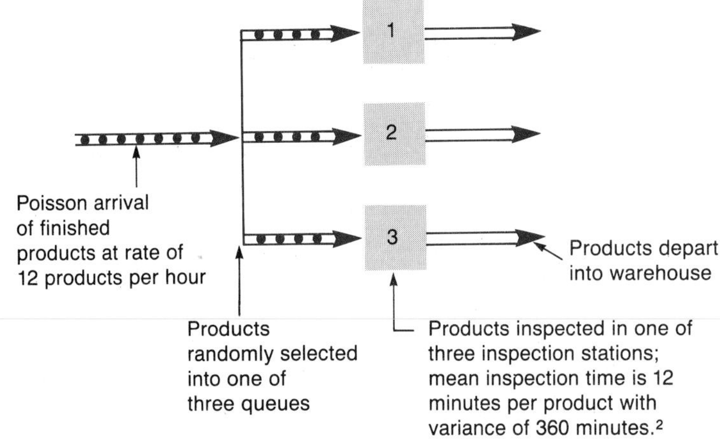

    a. Determine the expected waiting time for a product, the expected length of each queue, and the expected number of products in the *overall* system.
    b. Same as part *a* except for a variance of 36 min.^{2}
    c. Same as part *a* for $M/D/1$ model. Does the variance effect appear significant?
70. Given the schematic in the preceding exercise, determine the optimal number of inspection stations if each station costs $10 per hour to operate and the cost of holding each product in the system is $2 per hour.
71. ***Pollution Control Model.*** A manufacturing company continuously operates five independent treatment facilities for cleaning out the effluents discharged into a major river. The operation of each facility, however, is not completely reliable due to breakdowns. The time between breakdowns of each facility is exponential with mean 14 days. On the average, it takes a repair crew one day to repair a facility. As you might have guessed, repair times are exponential. Each repair crew costs the company $1,000 per day. The EPA does not allow the company to discharge untreated waste material; hence, whenever a facility is "down" the plant operates at less than planned capacity. This downtime is costed at $50,000 per day per facility. Determine the optimal number of repair crews to hire by enumerating total cost per day for 1, 2, 3, 4, and 5 repair crews. Is Equation 16.71 satisfied?
72. ***Airline Reservation System.*** An airline reservation system has four telephone lines. For a particular shift, incoming phone calls are Poisson with rate 10 calls per hour. The time to service a caller is exponential with a mean time of five minutes. If a call comes in

and all reservationists are busy, then the call is placed on hold, providing a line is available; otherwise, the call is lost; that is, a busy signal rejects the caller. Callers encountering a busy signal are assumed to place reservations elsewhere. It is further assumed that calls on hold never renege.

a. Determine the minimum number of reservationists needed to ensure a probability of rejection below 10 percent.

b. Assuming that one reservationist is to be used, determine the minimum number of phone lines needed to ensure a probability of rejection below 10 percent.

c. Discuss the trade-offs between the two types of decisions indicated in parts *a* and *b*. Specifically, determine the total cost per hour for each of the decisions above if \$5 per hour is the cost of a reservationist, \$0.25 per hour is the cost of a phone line, \$2 is the cost of a rejected call, and \$1 per hour per call in the system is the cost of waiting.

d. Describe how you would determine the optimal joint decision for c and N.

73. ***Production System.*** Consider the following tandem queuing system for a product that requires two steps to assemble.

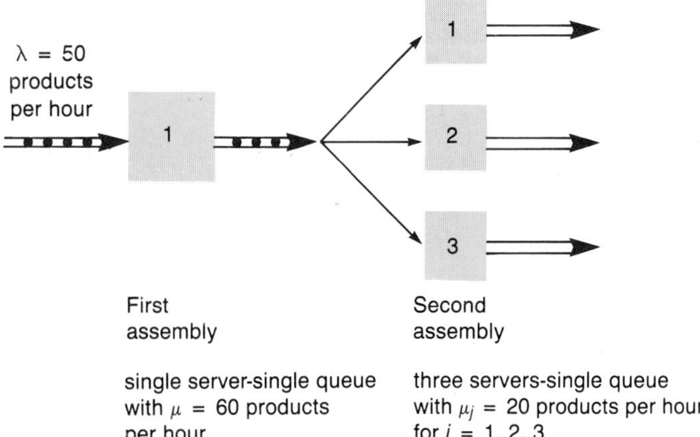

Given that the assumptions for the standard $M/M/c$ model are satisfied, determine the mean length of each queue and the expected time a product spends on the assembly line. (*Hint:* See Example 16.7.)

74. ***State Unemployment Compensation.*** The agency of a particular state that handles compensation for those who are unemployed is considering two options for processing applications of potential recipients.

Option 1: Four clerks process applications in parallel from a single queue. Each clerk fills out the form for the application in the presence of the applicant based on information verbally related to the clerk. Processing time is exponential with mean 45 minutes.

Option 2: Each applicant first fills out the application without the help of a clerk. The time to accomplish this is exponential with mean 65 minutes. When the applicant finishes filling out the form, he/she joins a single queue to await a review by one of the four clerks. The time to review a form is exponential (what else?) with mean 5 minutes.

Given that the arrival of applicants is Poisson with rate 4.8 applicants per hour, compare the two options with respect to expected number of applicants in the system and expected time in the system.

CASE

You are the bank manager who commissioned Dr. Kolesar to study the automatic teller machines (ATMs) discussed in the selected applications. Most of the bank's nearly 500 ATMs are located in one large U.S. city. As part of a corporation-wide program on improving customer service, you wanted to set "service standards" for customer delay at the ATMs. You chose line wait as the parameter of interest.

Dr. Kolesar presents you with an interim report summarized in Table 16–6 (reprinted from P. Kolesar as referenced in Selected Applications). As a manager, what would you conclude from the table? Would you continue to focus on line wait?

TABLE 16–6 ATM Model Results for a Two-Machine, Capacity 12-Vestibule Site

Arrival Rate (per hour)	Load	Customers Served Rate (per hour)	Handled Transactions Rate (per hour)	Percent Customers Lost	Percent Customers Delayed	Average Wait of Delayed (min.)	Average Queue Length (cust.)	ATM Utilization (percent)
10	0.2	10.0	18.0	0.0	2.0	0.01	0.00	10.4
20	0.4	20.0	36.0	0.0	7.2	0.06	0.02	20.8
30	0.6	30.0	54.0	0.0	14.9	0.14	0.07	31.3
40	0.8	40.0	72.0	0.0	24.5	0.26	0.17	41.7
50	1.0	50.0	90.0	0.0	35.6	0.46	0.38	52.1
60	1.3	59.9	107.8	0.2	47.8	0.77	0.77	62.4
70	1.5	69.5	125.1	0.7	60.5	1.23	1.42	72.4
80	1.7	78.2	140.7	2.3	72.4	1.84	2.40	81.4
90	1.9	85.2	153.3	5.4	82.3	2.56	3.63	88.7
100	2.1	90.0	162.0	10.0	89.5	3.26	4.90	93.7
110	2.3	92.9	167.2	15.6	94.1	3.87	6.00	96.7
120	2.5	94.4	170.0	21.3	96.7	4.36	6.85	98.4
130	2.7	95.2	171.4	26.8	98.2	4.72	7.48	99.2
140	2.9	95.6	172.1	31.7	99.0	4.98	7.94	99.6
150	3.1	95.8	172.4	36.1	99.4	5.18	8.27	99.8
160	3.3	95.9	172.6	40.1	99.7	5.33	8.52	99.9
170	3.5	95.9	172.7	43.6	99.8	5.45	8.71	99.9
180	3.8	96.0	172.7	46.7	99.9	5.54	8.86	100.0
190	4.0	96.0	172.8	49.5	99.9	5.61	8.98	100.0
200	4.2	96.0	172.8	52.0	100.0	5.67	9.08	100.0

Site Features: Number of automatic teller machines = 2,
Vestibule capacity = 10.*
Average session time = 1.25 minutes = 75 seconds,
Average number of transactions/session = 1.8

*Although Dr. Kolesar has presented the vestibule capacity as 10, it is clear from the average queue length of 9.08 for the 200 arrival rate that the system capacity is 12 (i.e., $K = 12$ and $K - c = 10$).

APPENDIX 16A
Derivation of Standard $M/M/1$ Model

In this appendix, we incompletely derive the operating characteristics given by Equations 16.1 through 16.10. Familiarity with the symbols and assumptions of the standard $M/M/1$ model are assumed.

Arrivals that are Poisson are said to occur randomly. This means that the probability of an arrival in some small interval of time (Δt) depends strictly on the length of Δt and not its starting point or the previous history of arrivals (*memoryless property*). Furthermore, it can be shown that Poisson arrivals with rate λ are equivalent to exponential interarrival times with parameter λ; hence, the probability of an interarrival time less than Δt, assuming *stationarity,* is given by A.32 on page 902, the CDF for the exponential distribution:

$$F(\Delta t) = 1 - e^{-\lambda \Delta t}. \tag{1}$$

This is equivalent to stating that $F(\Delta t)$ is the probability of an arrival in the interval Δt. Agree? It follows, then, that the probability of no arrival in the interval Δt is given by the complement of (1):

$$P(\text{no arrival in } \Delta t) = e^{-\lambda \Delta t}. \tag{2}$$

The expression in (2) can be estimated by its Taylor series expansion:[26]

$$e^{-\lambda \Delta t} = 1 - \lambda \Delta t + \frac{(-\lambda \Delta t)^2}{2!} + \frac{(-\lambda \Delta t)^3}{3!} + \cdots.$$

For sufficiently small Δt, this can be approximated by

$$P(\text{no arrival in } \Delta t) = 1 - \lambda \Delta t, \tag{3}$$

since higher order terms tend to vanish. Now, (1) can be reexpressed as

$$\begin{aligned} F(\Delta t) &= P(\text{arrival in } \Delta t) = \lambda \Delta t. \qquad (4) \\ &= 1 - P(\text{no arrival in } \Delta t) \end{aligned}$$

Similarly, assuming exponential service times with rate μ and that a customer is being serviced, we see that the corresponding probabilities are

$$P(\text{service not completed in } \Delta t) = 1 - \mu \Delta t \tag{5}$$

and

$$P(\text{service completed in } \Delta t) = \mu \Delta t. \tag{6}$$

Given (3) through (6), the basic derivation of operating characteristics hinges on the determination of $P_n(t)$, the probability that the *state* of the system is n at time t (i.e.,

---

[26] $f(x) = f(0) + \frac{f'(0)}{1!}x + \frac{f''(0)}{2!}x^2 + \cdots + \frac{f^n(0)x^n}{n!}$ + Remainder.

that n units are in the system at time t). If Δt is sufficiently small, then no more than one arrival or departure (or both) can occur during Δt. Three cases can be identified for the occurrence of n units in the system at time $t + \Delta t$: First, n units at t combined with no arrival and no departure during Δt; second, $n + 1$ units at t combined with no arrival and one departure during Δt; three, $n - 1$ units at t combined with one arrival and no departure during Δt. Assuming independence among an arrival, a departure, and the state of the system, we find that the probabilities for the preceding cases are determined by applying the multiplication rule given by A.6: First, $P_n(t) \cdot (1 - \lambda\Delta t) \cdot (1 - \mu\Delta t)$; second, $P_{n+1}(t) \cdot (1 - \lambda\Delta t) \cdot \mu\Delta t$; third, $P_{n-1}(t) \cdot \lambda\Delta t \cdot (1 - \mu\Delta t)$. Since the system can have n units at time t in any of these three mutually exclusive ways, it follows that $P_n(t + \Delta t)$ is given by the sum of the three separate probabilities:[27]

$$P_n(t + \Delta t) = P_n(t) \cdot (1 - \lambda\Delta t) \cdot (1 - \mu\Delta t) + P_{n+1}(t) \cdot (1 - \lambda\Delta t) \cdot \mu\Delta t + P_{n-1}(t) \cdot \lambda\Delta t \cdot (1 - \mu\Delta t). \tag{7}$$

Transposing $P_n(t)$ to the left-hand side of (7), dividing by Δt, and letting $\Delta t \to 0$, we get[28]

$$P'_n(t) = \begin{cases} \mu P_{n+1}(t) - \lambda P_n(t) & \text{for } n = 0 \\ \mu P_{n+1}(t) + \lambda P_{n-1}(t) - (\lambda + \mu)P_n(t) & \text{for } n > 0. \end{cases} \tag{8}$$

The solution to this system of *linear differential equations* provides the *transient probabilities*.

In the steady state, probabilities are independent of time; hence, rates of change in the probabilities with respect to time [that is, $P'_n(t)$ for $n = 0, 1, \ldots$] equal zero. This gives, from (8), the *steady-state difference equations for the system:*

$$\mu P_1 - \lambda P_o = 0 \tag{9}$$

$$\mu P_{n+1} + \lambda P_{n-1} - (\lambda + \mu)P_n = 0. \tag{10}$$

The solution for P_n is obtained recursively. Starting with (9) we have

$$P_1 = \left(\frac{\lambda}{\mu}\right)P_o = \rho P_o.$$

Proceeding to (10) with $n = 1$ gives

$$\mu P_2 + \lambda P_o - (\lambda + \mu)P_1 = 0.$$

Substituting ρP_o for P_1 and solving for P_2 gives

[27]Rule of Addition according to A.3.

[28]Note that the first derivative is defined in this case as

$$P'_n(t) = \lim_{\Delta t \to 0} \frac{P_n(t + \Delta t) - P_n(t)}{\Delta t}.$$

$$\begin{aligned} P_2 &= -\frac{\lambda}{\mu}P_o + \frac{(\lambda + \mu)}{\mu}(\rho P_o) \\ &= -\rho P_o + \rho^2 P_o + \rho P_o \\ &= \rho^2 P_o \,. \end{aligned}$$

Continuing in the same manner, we can verify easily that

$$P_n = \rho^n P_o \,, \tag{16.3}$$

which is a geometric probability mass function. By definition for a pmf,

$$\sum_{n=0}^{\infty} P_n = 1 \,.$$

Substituting Equation 16.3 provides

$$P_o \sum_{n=0}^{\infty} \rho^n = 1$$

or

$$P_o(1 + \rho + \rho^2 + \ldots) = 1 \,.$$

You should recognize the parenthetic expression as an infinite geometric progression with common ratio ρ. If $\rho \equiv (\lambda/\mu) < 1$, then the series converges to the well-known sum $1/(1 - \rho)$. Note that if $\rho \geq 1$, then the series does not converge; that is, it sums to infinity. We have then

$$P_o\left(\frac{1}{1 - \rho}\right) = 1$$

or

$$P_o = 1 - \rho \,. \tag{16.1}$$

By the definition of expected value, L_s is determined from

$$\begin{aligned} L_s &= \sum_{n=0}^{\infty} nP_n \\ &= P_o \sum_{n=0}^{\infty} n\rho^n \\ &= (1 - \rho) \cdot (0 + \rho + 2\rho^2 + 3\rho^3 + \cdots) \\ &= (\rho + 2\rho^2 + 3\rho^3 + \cdots) - (\rho^2 + 2\rho^3 + 3\rho^4 + \cdots) \\ &= \rho + \rho^2 + \rho^3 + \cdots \\ &= \rho(1 + \rho + \rho^2 + \cdots) \\ &= \frac{\rho}{1 - \rho} \end{aligned}$$

or, since $\rho \equiv \lambda/\mu$,

$$L_s = \frac{\lambda}{\mu - \lambda}. \tag{16.5}$$

The expression for the variance, as given by Equation 16.6, can be obtained in a similar manner, although the procedure is tedious (there are better ways).

By definition, the expected number in the queue, L_q, is the expected number in the system, L_s, minus the expected number in service, L_{se}, or

$$L_q = L_s - L_{se}. \tag{11}$$

With only one server, 0 and 1 are the only two possible values for the random variable "number in service." Since their respective probabilities are P_o and $1 - P_o$, then by the definition of expected value,

$$\begin{aligned} L_{se} &= 0 \cdot P_o + 1 \cdot (1 - P_o) \\ &= 1 - P_o. \\ &= \rho. \end{aligned} \tag{12}$$

By substituting Equation 16.15 and (12) into (11) and simplifying we have

$$L_q = \frac{\rho^2}{1 - \rho}$$

or

$$L_q = \frac{\rho\lambda}{\mu - \lambda}. \tag{16.7}$$

The expressions 16.9 and 16.11 for W_s and W_q can be obtained by respectively substituting 16.5 and 16.7 into 16.63 and 16.64. The expression for V_{ws}, Equation 16.10, is simply the variance of the exponential distribution for waiting times given by 16.4.

An alternative expression for L_q is

$$L_q = L_b \cdot (1 - P_o) + 0 \cdot P_o \tag{13}$$

where L_b is the expected number in the queue when the system is busy and $(1 - P_0)$ is the probability of a busy system. Solving for L_b gives

$$L_b = \frac{L_q}{1 - P_o}, \tag{14}$$

which can be verified easily as the equivalent of 16.8. Note that L_b simply removes the bias of an idle system; that is, it represents the mean queue length when the system is busy. Similarly,

$$W_b = \frac{W_q}{1 - P_o}, \tag{15}$$

which confirms 16.12.

With minor variations, the derivation of the standard $M/M/c$ model is identical (but messier).

APPENDIX 16B

Formulas for Selected $M/M/1$ and $M/M/c$ Models

Definition of Symbols

n = Number of units in system.
λ = Mean arrival rate (units per period).
μ = Mean service rate (units per period).
ρ = Traffic intensity (λ/μ).
N = Maximum number allowed in system.
m = Number of units in finite population.
c = Number of servers.
P_n = Probability of n units in system.
L_s = Steady-state mean number of units in system.
L_q = Steady-state mean number of units in queue.
L_b = Steady-state mean number of units in queue for busy system.
W_s = Steady-state mean time in system.
W_q = Steady-state mean time in queue.
W_b = Steady-state mean time in queue for busy system.

Finite Queue $M/M/1$ Model[29]

$$P_0 = \begin{cases} \dfrac{1-\rho}{1-\rho^{N+1}} & \text{for } \lambda \neq \mu \\ \dfrac{1}{N+1} & \text{for } \lambda = \mu \end{cases} \tag{16.13}$$

$$P(n > 0) = 1 - P_o \tag{16.14}$$

$$P_n = P_o\rho^n \quad \text{for } n \leq N \tag{16.15}$$

$$L_s = \begin{cases} \dfrac{\rho}{1-\rho} - \dfrac{(N+1)\rho^{N+1}}{1-\rho^{N+1}} & \text{for } \lambda \neq \mu \\ \dfrac{N}{2} & \text{for } \lambda = \mu \end{cases} \tag{16.16}$$

$$L_q = L_s - (1 - P_o) \tag{16.17}$$

$$L_b = \frac{L_q}{1 - P_o} \tag{16.18}$$

$$W_s = \frac{L_q}{\lambda(1 - P_N)} + \frac{1}{\mu} \tag{16.19}$$

[29]Note: $0 < \rho < \infty$.

$$W_q = W_s - \frac{1}{\mu} \tag{16.20}$$

$$W_b = \frac{W_q}{1 - P_0}. \tag{16.21}$$

Finite Population $M/M/1$ Model[30]

$$P_o = \frac{1}{\sum_{i=0}^{m}\left[\frac{m!}{(m-i)!}\cdot \rho^i\right]} \tag{16.22}$$

$$P(n > 0) = 1 - P_o \tag{16.23}$$

$$P_n = \frac{m!}{(m-n)!}\rho^n P_o, \qquad n \leq m \tag{16.24}$$

$$L_s = m - \frac{1}{\rho}(1 - P_o) \tag{16.25}$$

$$L_q = m - \frac{(\lambda + \mu)(1 - P_o)}{\lambda} \tag{16.26}$$

$$L_b = \frac{L_q}{1 - P_o} \tag{16.27}$$

$$W_s = \frac{m}{\mu(1 - P_o)} - \frac{1}{\lambda} \tag{16.28}$$

$$W_q = \frac{1}{\mu}\left(\frac{m}{1 - P_o} - \frac{\lambda + \mu}{\lambda}\right) \tag{16.29}$$

$$W_b = \frac{W_q}{1 - P_o}. \tag{16.30}$$

Standard $M/M/c$ Model[31]

$$P_o = \frac{1}{\left(\sum_{i=0}^{c-1}\frac{\rho^i}{i!}\right) + \frac{\rho^c}{c!\left(1 - \frac{\rho}{c}\right)}} \tag{16.31}$$

$$P_n = \begin{cases} \frac{\rho^n}{n!}\cdot P_o & \text{for } 0 \leq n \leq c \\ \left(\frac{\rho^n}{c!\,c^{n-c}}\right)\cdot P_o & \text{for } n \geq c \end{cases} \tag{16.32}$$

[30]Note: $0 < \rho < \infty$.

[31]Note: $0 < \rho < c$.

$$P(n \geq c) = \frac{\rho^c \mu c}{c!\,(\mu c - \lambda)} \cdot P_o \tag{16.33}$$

$$L_s = \frac{\rho^{c+1}}{(c-1)!\,(c-\rho)^2} \cdot P_o + \rho \tag{16.34}$$

$$L_q = L_s - \rho \tag{16.35}$$

$$L_b = \frac{L_q}{P(n \geq c)} \tag{16.36}$$

$$W_s = \frac{L_q}{\lambda} + \frac{1}{\mu} \tag{16.37}$$

$$W_q = \frac{L_q}{\lambda} \tag{16.38}$$

$$W_b = \frac{W_q}{P(n \geq c)}. \tag{16.39}$$

Finite Queue *M/M/c* Model[32]

$$P_o = \frac{1}{\left(\sum_{i=0}^{c} \frac{\rho^i}{i!}\right) + \left(\frac{1}{c!}\right) \cdot \left(\sum_{i=c+1}^{N} \frac{\rho^i}{c^{i-c}}\right)} \tag{16.40}$$

$$P_n = \begin{cases} \frac{\rho^n}{n!} \cdot P_o & \text{for } 0 \leq n \leq c \\ \frac{\rho^n}{c!\,c^{n-c}} \cdot P_o & \text{for } c \leq n \leq N \end{cases} \tag{16.41}$$

$$P(n \geq c) = 1 - P_o \sum_{i=0}^{c-1} \frac{\rho^i}{i!} \tag{16.42}$$

$$L_s = \frac{P_o \rho^{c+1}}{(c-1)!\,(c-\rho)^2}\left[1 - \left(\frac{\rho}{c}\right)^{N-c} - (N-c)\left(\frac{\rho}{c}\right)^{N-c} \cdot \left(1 - \frac{\rho}{c}\right)\right] + \rho(1 - P_N) \tag{16.43}$$

$$L_q = L_s - \rho(1 - P_N) \tag{16.44}$$

$$L_b = \frac{L_q}{P(n \geq c)} \tag{16.45}$$

$$W_s = \frac{L_q}{\lambda(1 - P_N)} + \frac{1}{\mu} \tag{16.46}$$

$$W_q = W_s - \frac{1}{\mu} \tag{16.47}$$

[32]Note: $0 < \rho < \infty$.

$$W_b = \frac{W_q}{P(n \geq c)}. \tag{16.48}$$

Finite Population $M/M/c$ Model[33]

$$P_o = \frac{1}{\left(\sum_{i=0}^{c} \frac{m!}{(m-i)!\,i!} \cdot \rho^i\right) + \left(\sum_{i=c+1}^{m} \frac{m!}{(m-i)!\,c!\,c^{i-c}} \cdot \rho^i\right)} \tag{16.49}$$

$$P_n = \begin{cases} \dfrac{m!\,P_o\rho^n}{(m-n)!\,n!} & \text{for } 0 \leq n \leq c \\[2ex] \dfrac{m!\,P_o\rho^n}{(m-n)!\,c!\,c^{n-c}} & \text{for } c \leq n \leq m \end{cases} \tag{16.50}$$

$$P(n \geq c) = 1 - P_o \sum_{i=0}^{c-1} \frac{m!}{(m-i)!\,i!} \cdot \rho^i \tag{16.51}$$

$$L_s = \frac{L_q + m\rho}{1 + \rho} \tag{16.52}$$

$$L_q = \sum_{n=c+1}^{m} (n - c)P_n \tag{16.53}$$

$$L_b = \frac{L_q}{P(n \geq c)} \tag{16.54}$$

$$W_s = \frac{L_s}{\lambda(m - L_s)} \tag{16.55}$$

$$W_q = \frac{L_q}{\lambda(m - L_s)} \tag{16.56}$$

$$W_b = \frac{W_q}{P(n \geq c)}. \tag{16.57}$$

Self-Service Model[34]

$$P_n = \frac{e^{-\rho}}{n!} \cdot \rho^n \qquad \text{for } n \geq 0 \tag{16.58}$$

$$L_s = \rho \tag{16.59}$$

$$W_s = \frac{1}{\mu}. \tag{16.60}$$

[33] Note: $0 < \rho < \infty$.

[34] Note: $0 < \rho < \infty$.

17

Simulation

Chapter Outline

Of all the tools in OR/MS, simulation leads the way in flexibility, comprehensiveness, and (most probably) frequency of use. Its flexibility is apparent when one begins to list areas of application. Table 17–1 presents a sampling of the many simulation applications. Simulation's ability to be comprehensive is evident with large-scale and complex systems. In its treatment of such systems, simulation permits less restrictive assumptions than do analytical approaches; thus simulation can handle a wider range of real-world problems. For example, operating characteristics for some complex queuing systems can be estimated by simulation methods but not by the analytic methods illustrated in the Chapter 16.

In this chapter we (1) define and classify simulation, (2) describe the motivation for using simulation, (3) focus on key aspects of the *process* of conducting a simula-

TABLE 17–1 Selected Applications of Simulation

Urban-social:	
Emergency-response vehicle location	Facilities scheduling
Mass transit system design	Air pollution control
Garbage collection patterns	Population planning
Traffic light sequencing	Air traffic control
Police beat design	Airport design
Political redistricting	Urban development
Educational planning	Schoolbus routing
Political campaign strategies	Urban dynamics
U.S. and world economic conditions	Courtroom scheduling
Health care:	
Health care planning	Hospital admissions
Emergency room design	Blood bank management
Organ transplant strategies	Diet management
Hospital staffing	Ambulance crew-scheduling
Disease control strategies	Patient flow
Drug interaction control policies	
Aerospace-military:	
Space system reliability	Search and rescue strategies
Equipment replacement policies	Equipment distribution
War games/strategies	Space defense systems
Armed forces recruiting strategies	Satellite positioning
Service Industry:	
Portfolio management	Fleet scheduling
Insurance and risk management	Bank teller scheduling
Professional sports draft strategies	Supermarket clerk scheduling
Auditing strategies	Telephone switching
Communication network design	Facility location
Feedlot management	
Industrial	
Food and chemical blending	Production scheduling
Inventory management	Product safety testing
Facility layout	Quality control
Repair crew scheduling	Tool crib personnel planning
Design of distribution channels	Labor negotiations

tion study, and (4) present examples of the use of simulation in several diverse and meaningful areas of application.

17.1 NATURE OF SIMULATION

Before presenting specific illustrations of simulation, we will take the time to provide a meaningful frame of reference on the nature of simulation.

Simulation Defined

In a broad sense, simulation is a methodology for conducting experiments using a model of the real system. OR/MS is primarily concerned with **digital** simulations, which involve the numerical manipulation of mathematical models. Other forms of simulation include **physical** simulations (e.g., wind-tunnel and water-tank models of space flight) and **analog** simulations (i.e., when one physical system is used to represent another, as when an electrical system is used to represent a mechanical system).

Given that the simulation (for our purposes) is based on a mathematical model, further distinctions can be cited: *deterministic* versus *stochastic,* and *static* versus *dynamic*. **Deterministic** simulations involve variables and parameters that are fixed and known with certainty, whereas **stochastic** simulations assign probability distributions to some or all variables and parameters. Both types are important, although many analysts are inclined to narrow their definition of simulation to those experiments based only on stochastic processes.

A **static** simulation is one in which experiments are performed on a model having variables and parameters that are not time-dependent. A **dynamic** simulation includes processes that change over time. Most simulations of economic and administrative interest are dynamic.

Digital simulation is the OR/MS analyst's experimental laboratory. Simulation is a means to derive sample data and statistical estimates from a computer model. As such it is distinguishable from the analytical procedures that seek to optimize some criterion (such as linear programming and inventory models) or seek to predict the behavior of a system by formulas that are analytically derived (as are queuing models).

Motivations for Simulation

Many reasons can be advanced in support of simulation. In this section we indicate the more obvious.

1. **Simulation can be useful when analytic models are unable to provide solutions.** For example, transient (time-dependent) solutions for complex queuing models are not possible by analytic methods but are readily obtained by simulation methods.
2. **Simulation can provide a simpler alternative when analytic techniques exist but are very complex to utilize.**
3. **With simulation, the configuration or structure of the model can be easily changed to answer "What happens if . . . ? questions.** This offers decided advantages compared to experimenting with the structure or policies

of the actual system. For example, various decision rules can be tested for increasing or decreasing the number of servers in a queuing system in response to different levels of customer demand.

4. **Simulation is often less costly than actual experimentation.** In other cases, it may be the only reasonable initial approach, as when the system does not yet exist, yet theoretical relationships are well known. For example, solar energy thermal collection systems for homes have been tested by simulation, prior to being built, in order to help solve particular applications problems or to indicate problems in design not known to exist.
5. **Simulation allows for time compression.** A simulation can accomplish in minutes what might require years of actual experimentation. These advantages are illustrated in Sections 17.5 and 17.6.
6. **Simulation can be used for pedagogical (teaching) purposes.** It may illustrate a model or allow one to better comprehend a process, as in management games. Management games allow decision makers to better understand the interrelationships within a decision-making setting, to test their understanding, and to develop their decision-making skills.
7. **Simulation tends to be relatively straightforward.** Simulation is often more easily understood by nontechnical managers, particularly when compared with sophisticated analytical methods. This is so partly because the simulation model imitates a setting in which the manager is familiar. He or she has an easier time understanding the results generated.

Limitations of Simulation

One might ask, "Why not approach all modeling through simulation?" There are several limitations with the use of simulation, including the following:

1. **Simulation can be time-consuming and costly.** Applying simulation involves a comprehensive process that parallels, in many respects, the decision-making paradigm. The person-days (months, years, etc.) expended can escalate rapidly if not managed carefully. Ad hoc model building, even using special computer languages, is very time-consuming (code, debug, validate, etc.).

   An added complication with simulation is the experimental nature of the study. Poor experimental design can result in the inexperienced going well over time and expense budgets as they approach total enumeration of possible alternative strategies.
2. **Optimal solutions are not guaranteed when using simulation approaches.** Simulations are not typically based on optimization algorithms, as was the case in the math programming part of this book.
3. **Certain key issues related to the design of models, the design of the simulation experiment, validation, and estimation are complex at best and unresolved at worst.** Some of these issues will be addressed later in the chapter.

4. **There can be an overreliance on simulation when other methods are more appropriate.** For example, a simulation to estimate optimal reorder levels and quantities for an inventory problem requires an extensive search for optimal values of controllable variables (as illustrated in Section 17.6), whereas an analytic solution would not. If complete analytic results exist for a model, these can be used rather than wasting large amounts of computer time to generate experimental results for specific parameter values.

17.2 MONTE CARLO SIMULATION

Perhaps the easiest way to begin to understand the nature of simulation is to see an illustration. This section presents a simple example involving the *manual* simulation of a stochastic process.

The Process Illustrated

When simulating a stochastic process, the objective is to imitate its behavior. A technique to accomplish this is **Monte Carlo simulation.** Given that the probability distribution for the real-life process is known (or can be approximated), the Monte Carlo method samples from the distribution to generate an experimental history of the behavior of the process. The Monte Carlo approach involves a five-step process.

Monte Carlo Process:

1. Determine the (actual or estimated) probability distribution for the stochastic process.
2. Construct the cumulative probability distribution.
3. Assign Monte Carlo numbers to the cumulative probability distribution.
4. Select a random sample from the Monte Carlo distribution.
5. Determine simulated values of the actual random variable.

We will illustrate this process in the following example.

Example 17.1 Production Planning

Navguide Corporation, a small electronics firm, manufactures a navigational instrument used on sailboats. Demand for the instrument is probabilistic, and a review of past records has yielded the weekly demand distribution shown in Table 17–2.

Navguide is considering the purchase of a sophisticated industrial robot to be used in the assembly of the instrument. Three different robots are being considered, each having different capacities, production efficiencies, and purchase costs. Table 17–3 summarizes the number of instruments that could be manufactured each week on a regular

TABLE 17–2 Weekly Demand

Demand	Probability
10	0.10
20	0.14
30	0.26
40	0.24
50	0.18
60	0.08
	1.00

TABLE 17–3

	Robot #1	Robot #2	Robot #3
Regular time capacity (units)/week	30	40	50
Overtime capacity (units)/week	30	40	50
Regular time cost/unit	$1,200	$1,100	$1,050
Overtime cost/unit	$1,600	$1,450	$1,350
Overhead cost/week	$10,000	$15,000	$20,000

time and overtime basis, the expected production cost per unit, and the weekly overhead costs—which include amortization costs for the robots. Given that Navguide sells the instruments for $1,800, management wants to determine which robot to purchase so as to maximize weekly profit.

The stochastic process in this example is weekly demand for the navigation instrument. Let us return to the five-step Monte Carlo process outlined earlier. *Step 1* requires identification of the probability distribution for weekly demand. This is given in Table 17–2. In *step 2* the cumulative probability distribution should be formed for weekly demand. This is shown in Table 17–4.

TABLE 17–4 Weekly Demand Distributions

Demand	Probability	Cumulative Probability
10	0.10	0.10
20	0.14	0.24
30	0.26	0.50
40	0.24	0.74
50	0.18	0.92
60	0.08	1.00

In *step 3* ranges of (Monte Carlo) numbers are assigned to each random outcome in proportion to the probability of occurrence of that outcome. Table 17–5 reflects the assignment of these numbers. Because the cumulative probability distribution is stated with two digits to the right of the decimal, two-digit Monte Carlo numbers 00–99 are assigned. *The assignment of the Monte Carlo numbers is in proportion to the probability of occurrence of each random outcome.* For example, of the 100 Monte Carlo numbers assigned, 10 (00–09) are assigned to the outcome "Demand = 10." That is, 10

TABLE 17–5 Assignment of Monte Carlo Numbers

Demand	Probability	Cumulative Probability	Monte Carlo Numbers (ranges)
10	0.10	0.10	00–09
20	0.14	0.24	10–23
30	0.26	0.50	24–49
40	0.24	0.74	50–73
50	0.18	0.92	74–91
60	0.08	1.00	92–99

percent of the Monte Carlo numbers are assigned to this outcome because there is a 10 percent chance of it occurring. Similarly, 14 (10–23) numbers are assigned to the outcome "Demand = 20," reflecting the 14 percent chance of this level of demand occurring.

For purposes of analyzing this problem, management has decided to simulate experiences for a 10-week time frame. The intent is to use Monte Carlo sampling to simulate demand experience for each of 10 weeks and compare the relative profit position assuming the purchase of each of the industrial robots. Data they wish to compile for the simulation period include:

Weekly demand.

Weekly production using regular time capacity.

Weekly production using overtime capacity.

Weekly revenue.

Weekly production cost.

Weekly overhead cost.

Total weekly cost.

Weekly profit.

Average weekly profit.

Step 4 of the Monte Carlo process requires selection of a random sample from the Monte Carlo numbers. Selection of a random number can be performed in several ways. A simple method for this example would be to place 100 balls (numbered 00–99) in an urn, stir well, and select one at a time, recording the number that appears on the ball. After recording the number on the ball, it should be returned to the urn, the urn stirred again, and another ball selected. Since we wish to simulate 10 weeks of experience, we would sample 10 times from the urn to generate 10 Monte Carlo numbers. These, in turn, would be mapped back into the cumulative probability distribution to produce the 10 weekly demand figures. An important aspect of the random sampling from the Monte Carlo numbers is that *each* Monte Carlo number have an equal chance of being selected (i.e., they are uniformly distributed).

Another way of selecting random numbers is using *tables of random numbers.* In addition, computer-based simulations employ numerical methods to generate *pseudo-random numbers.* We will return to this discussion later in the chapter.

Suppose that 10 random numbers have been generated by selecting 10 balls from an urn and that the numbers are (in order of their occurrence) 44, 46, 85, 99, 09, 95, 22, 87, 64, and 50. In *step 5,* the simulated values of weekly demand are determined.

This is accomplished by mapping the random sample of Monte Carlo numbers into the cumulative probability distribution. In essence, the range in which the Monte Carlo number falls is identified along with the corresponding outcome for the stochastic process. Figure 17–1 indicates this mapping for our example.

FIGURE 17–1 Mapping of Random Numbers for Example 17.1

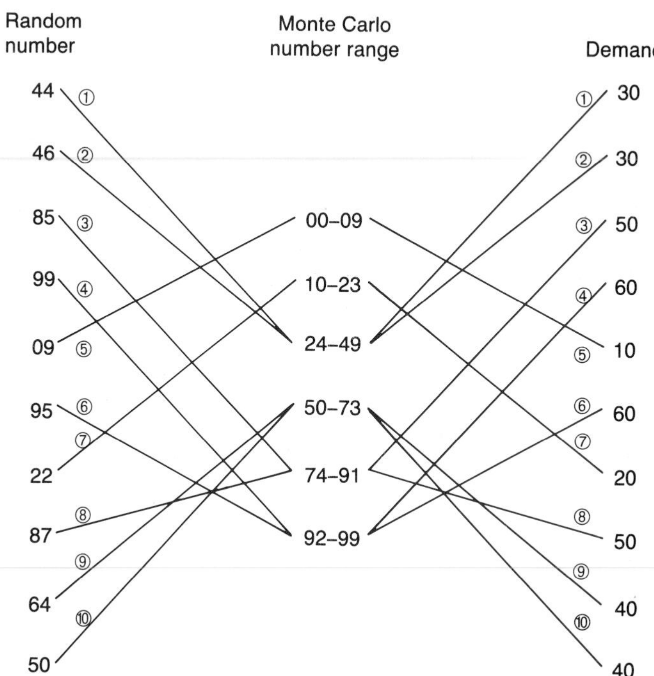

Once the weekly demand figures have been generated, the data from the simulation can be compiled. Table 17–6 is a tabular summary of the results of this 10-week simulation assuming the purchase and use of robot #1.

Let us make a few observations regarding the results. The stated regular time and overtime capacities represented upper limits of production for any given week. Thus when demand was less than regular time capacity, there was no requirement to produce to capacity. The simulation of a 10-week period resulted in total demand of 390 units, 270 of which were produced using regular time production capacity, and 120 of which required production on an overtime basis. Only one week resulted in a net loss, that occurring when demand was at its lowest possible level. Total profit for the simulated period was $86,000, averaging $8,600 per week. Average weekly profit fluctuated during the simulation from a low of $7,600 after week 5 to a high of $10,500 following week 4.

Do you think the average profit of $8,600 is close to what we might expect over the long run using this robot? If you are uncomfortable with this figure, how could you gain more confidence in it? What we are hinting at is the issue of whether or not we have an adequate sample to reach conclusions about this stochastic process. Is a simulation of 20 weeks sufficient? 100 weeks? We will address this issue later; however, our intention here was to provide a simple example to illustrate the nature of simulation. We leave for you (in an exercise) the question of which robot is best for Navguide.

TABLE 17–6 Ten-Week Simulation Summary for Robot #1

Week	Demand	Regular Time Production	Overtime Production	Revenue	Production Cost	Overhead Cost	Total Cost	Profit	Average Weekly Profit
1	30	30	0	$ 54,000	$ 36,000	$ 10,000	$ 46,000	$ 8,000	$8,000.00
2	30	30	0	54,000	36,000	10,000	46,000	8,000	8,000.00
3	50	30	20	90,000	68,000	10,000	78,000	12,000	9,333.33
4	60	30	30	108,000	84,000	10,000	94,000	14,000	10,500.00
5	10	10	0	18,000	12,000	10,000	22,000	−4,000	7,600.00
6	60	30	30	108,000	84,000	10,000	94,000	14,000	8,666.66
7	20	20	0	36,000	24,000	10,000	34,000	2,000	7,714.28
8	50	30	20	90,000	68,000	10,000	78,000	12,000	8,250.00
9	40	30	10	72,000	52,000	10,000	62,000	10,000	8,444.44
10	40	30	10	72,000	52,000	10,000	62,000	10,000	8,600.00
	390	270	120	$702,000	$516,000	$100,000	$616,000	$86,000	

FOLLOW-UP EXERCISES

1. Using the same 10 Monte Carlo numbers generated in Example 17.1, simulate the 10-day experience for the other two robots. Which robot results in maximum average weekly profit? What reason can you give for using the same 10 Monte Carlo numbers?
2. Determine the expected weekly demand in Example 17.1, and compute the expected weekly profit for each of the robots. How do these results compare with those from simulation?
3. Management would like to see the simulation extended to a 20-week experiment. A sample of 20 Monte Carlo numbers is selected, and the results are 47, 61, 58, 45, 81, 00, 09, 54, 48, 96, 27, 42, 77, 11, 52, 99, 97, 27, 83, 65. Manually simulate 20 weeks of experience with each of the three robots. Which one results in maximization of average weekly profit? How do the decision and the profit compare with the results of the 10-week simulation?
4. ***Epidemiology.*** The Center for Disease Control in Atlanta has been gathering data on a relatively rare type of viral infection. Table 17–7 summarizes data on the number of new cases reported to the center each day for the past 400 days.

TABLE 17–7 New Cases Reported/Day

New Cases Reported/Day	Frequency
0	35
1	68
2	74
3	55
4	48
5	36
6	32
7	25
8	17
9	8
10	2

a. Construct the probability distribution for the number of new cases reported per day.

b. Construct the cumulative distribution.

c. Assign Monte Carlo numbers to the cumulative distribution. Your numbers need to be four digits ranging from 0000–9999. Do you see why?

d. Given the following sample of 20 Monte Carlo numbers, record the simulated results of 20 days of reporting. 5921, 4303, 2716, 1224, 1890, 8497, 2426, 4398, 4405, 2036, 3275, 8414, 0546, 4283, 0389, 5884, 8307, 0861, 7443, 6056.

17.3 THE PROCESS OF SIMULATION

Simulation is primarily concerned with experimentally predicting the behavior of a real system for the purpose of designing the system or modifying behavior. In essence, it replaces the need for either direct experimentation on the real system or analytic solutions of system behavior. This section will focus on the *process* of simulation, which is critical to its successful application. In particular, we hope to highlight some of the critical issues that need particular attention in a simulation study.

The Process and the Paradigm

The process of simulation involves all eight steps of the decision-making paradigm discussed in Chapter 1. As discussed in that chapter, the words used to describe, or the steps used to characterize, a process may differ from author to author or from practitioner to practitioner. Even though the eight steps stated in Chapter 1 are appropriate, we believe the process as portrayed in Figure 17–2 is particularly good. This description of the process helps us to highlight some of its critical issues.

Perhaps the greatest difference between simulation and other forms of quantitative analysis is the focus on the simulation experiment. With the deterministic optimization methods discussed in the first part of the text, a model was developed, an optimization algorithm was applied to determine the recommended policy, and sensitivity analysis was conducted to account for possible effects of uncertainty. Without optimization algorithms or other analytical techniques, simulation could be viewed as a bit of a "fishing expedition," whereby knowledge about a system or recommended policies for that system are sought. As with a fishing expedition, the likely outcome depends on the extent to which the search is planned. Thus it is important that the experimental part of the simulation process be carefully planned and executed. Objectives for the experiment need to be defined, and an experimental design must be developed that provides the greatest likelihood of achieving the objectives.

The Systems Orientation

Because of the recurrent use of the word *system,* simulation is often cast in the context of **systems analysis.** A **system** is defined as a set of objects joined together for the purpose of accomplishing a common goal. For example, a production system can be thought of as a collection of machines, materials, and people organized in such a way as to manufacture a product.

The objects joined together to form a system are referred to as **entities**. The machines, materials, and people in a production system are examples of its entities. Entities can usually be described by their **attributes**. An attribute of a machine might be its output rate or capacity; an attribute of a raw material might be its cost per unit or some measure of its quality; attributes of people might be their skill levels and wage rates.

Entities of a system tend to interact with different types of behaviors within a system. These behaviors may be thought of as **activities**. Examples of activities within the production system might include assembly operations, fabrication operations, packing, and quality control. The **state** of a system is the set of variables necessary to provide an adequate description of the system at any given time. The definition of *adequate* depends on the objectives of the study. Examples of state variables for the production system might include the status of machines (busy or idle), the number of completed units in inventory, and the amounts of raw materials on hand. Finally, **events** are interactions or occurrences that can change the state of a system. A ma-

FIGURE 17–2 The Simulation Process*

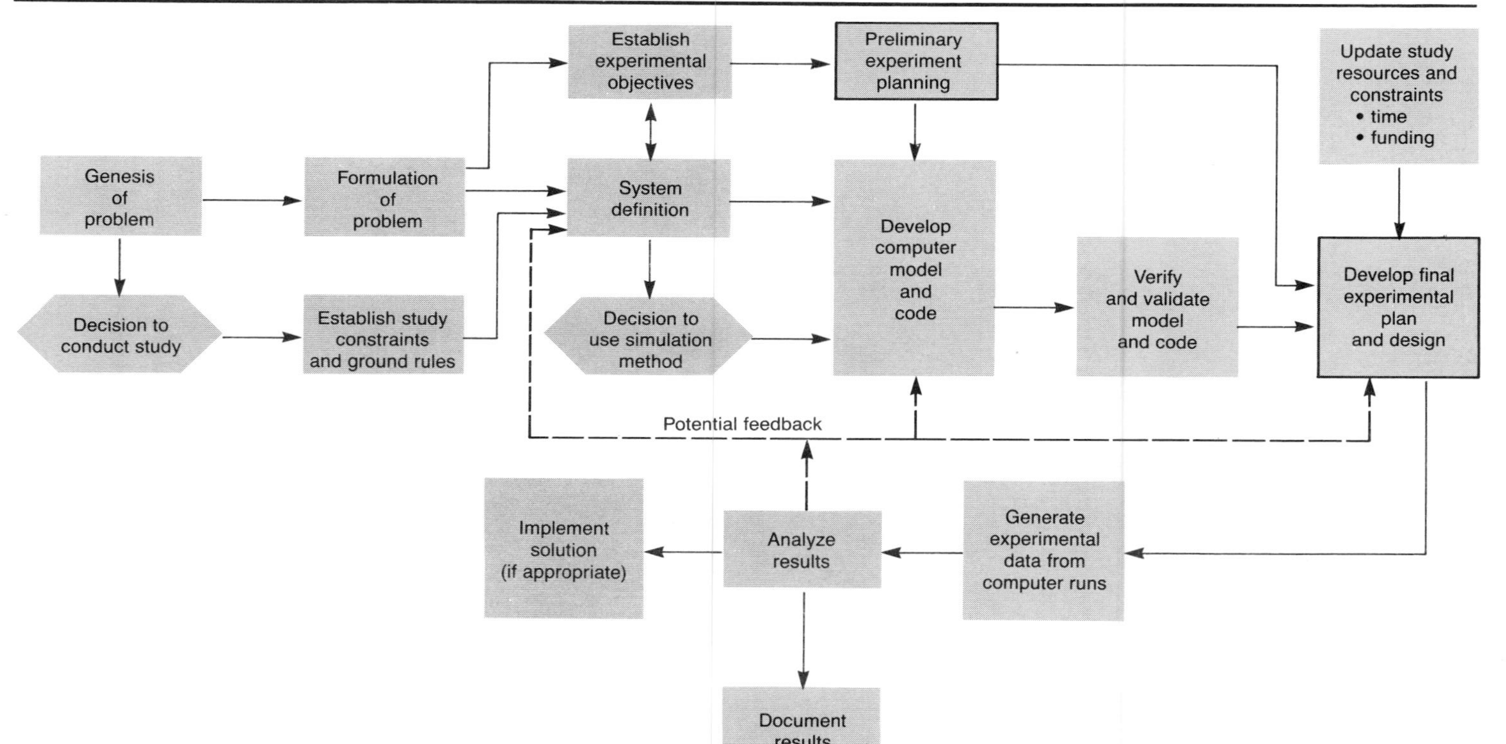

*From Pat R. Odom and Robert E. Shannon, "Nomographs for Computer Simulation," *Industrial Engineering,* November 1973, pp. 34–38.

chine breakdown or the submittal of a large order for finished goods are examples of events in the production system example.

Systems can be affected by changes from within (**endogenous**) and from outside (**exogenous**). For example, a production system will be affected by machine breakdown or by excessive absenteeism of workers. Similarly, a production system could be affected by general economic conditions or by the good or bad fortune of the firm's customers. Thus when developing a model of a system, it is necessary to include those elements (both within and outside the system) that can have a significant impact on the system. These elements are said to lie within the **system environment.** It is also important to define the **system boundaries** that delineate system entities from other entities within the system environment.

We have taken the time to briefly develop these systems concepts because they are important to the process. In addition, some of the terminology expressed in this section is likely to be common to the vocabulary of certain special-purpose simulation languages you may work with.

Some Key Issues in the Process

There is insufficient space in this text to provide all of the detailed knowledge necessary to be an effective user of simulation methods. However, this section highlights some important issues.

Model Design. In developing a model of the actual system of interest, our discussion from Chapter 1 still applies. In particular, the issue of *level of aggregation* (model detail) is significant. The goal is to strike an appropriate balance. In addition to these ideas about model design, a good simulation model includes the following characteristics:

1. **The model should be easy to understand, particularly for the user.** This has been one of the attractive features (from the perspective of the user) of simulation.
2. **The model should have an ability to evolve as the user and designer decide to add more detail and complexity.** There is a natural migration path from initial models that are relatively simple to those that incorporate more detail. To the extent that this can be anticipated in the initial design, the time and cost of later enhancements can be kept at lower levels.
3. **The model should adapt easily to changing conditions.** This characteristic speaks less to issues of changes in basic model structure but more to those dealing with changes in the experimental design. Such changes might include changes in model parameters, in the functional form of probability distributions, and in the number of runs or length of runs in the simulation experiment.

Experimental Design. The primary reason for simulation studies is to learn about the behavior of a system of interest. If simulation is to be used effectively, there must be careful planning of a design for the experiment so that the desired information will be generated in a timely manner and at reasonable expense. Some of the issues that must be considered when planning the experimental design include the **specification of experimental objectives.** This issue helps to clarify the reasons for conducting the simulation, and it provides a reference point for testing the relevance of each step of the process.

Related to this issue, both the attributes of interest and the measures of performance must be defined. For example, suppose a supermarket chain is interested in simulating the checkout system for its typical store. The experimental objective might be to determine the checkout system configuration (e.g., number of cashiers, physical layout of the system, use or nonuse of optical scanning devices, use or nonuse of baggers) that results in the best system performance. When simulating different alternative configurations, attributes of interest might include the number of customers waiting, customer waiting time, idle time of checkout personnel, and the time to service customers.

The attributes of interest may be measures of system performance, or they may be used to determine measures of system performance. In the supermarket example, customer waiting time may be one measure of performance. Another possible measure of performance is *cost* of customer waiting. This measure might be derived using customer waiting time. Similarly, the idle time of checkout personnel may be a measure of performance or may be used to determine the measure "cost of idle facilities." Another issue is whether steady-state conditions for measures of performance are necessary or averages will be sufficient for evaluation. In the supermarket example, will steady-state waiting times be required, or will average waiting time over the duration of the simulation be adequate?

Another aspect of the experimental design is establishing **initial conditions** for the experiment—the assumptions about the system at the time the simulation is "turned on." In the supermarket example, should we assume that the store is empty initially, or should we assume some normal level of activity. Are we simulating a particular time of day and day of the week? The choice of initial conditions can have a significant impact on how long the system will take to reach steady-state conditions.

Along with initial conditions, decisions need to be made regarding **parameter settings.** In the supermarket example, what parameters should be set for the interarrival time and service time distributions? How should those parameters be modified according to time of day and day of the week?

Another decision related to experimental design is the **length of each experimental run.** What criterion will be used to decide when a run should terminate? Often, the length of a run will be stated in terms of the *number of simulated observations (n)*. Prior to the experiment, sample sizes are determined that provide sample statistics for estimating population parameters within specified maximum errors and confidence levels according to the Central Limit Theorem. In the supermarket example, we might decide to simulate the processing of a specific number of customers. Another criterion might be a *simulated period.* We might decide to simulate the checkout system for 100 hours of supermarket operation. The *realization of steady-state conditions* might be another criterion for terminating a simulation run. Some simulation models that involve massive amounts of computation may (of necessity) require stopping rules based on *computer time and/or expense*. Any of the criteria mentioned above should be chosen scientifically. They should also reflect consideration of sample sizes that have a strong likelihood of generating statistically significant results. Finally, the length of run can be determined prior to the simulation run, or it can be developed during the course of the run as output data are being gathered.

Data Analysis. Because most simulations pertain to stochastic processes, the data generated as output from the simulation tend to be characterized by random variability. That is, the measures of performance for the system being studied tend to be stochastic. Thus simulation experiments of this type tend to be thought of as statistical experiments. Before any conclusions can be reached based on simulated output data, appropriate statistical analysis of the data is essential. Statistical analysis should be used to provide assurances of the accuracy of estimates derived from any single simulation experiment. Analysis can also be extremely useful in performing comparative evaluations of estimates derived from simulation experiments of alternative system designs.

If a steady-state estimate of criteria is desired, then care must be exercised so that **transient effects** do not bias the calculations. By definition, in steady state, succeeding observations of the criterion are time independent (observations are equally likely to be above or below the steady state criterion value). Hence the observations used to estimate the steady-state criterion should not exhibit correlation over time (termed **serial correlation**). One approach (of many) to this problem is to calculate a serial correlation coefficient for a block of the first k observations and test for significance. If significant, assume the first k observations are part of the transient phase, and repeat the procedure on the next k observations by continuing the simulation where it previously ended. This procedure is continued until the first block of k observations is found that accepts the null hypothesis of no correlation. At this point the k observations in that block can be used to estimate the steady-state criterion.

A more straightforward (but no less costly) approach is "reasonably" initializing values for the necessary parameters and variables and simulating until **stochastic convergence** is exhibited. The usual problem with this approach is that one may not know what "reasonable" (i.e., near steady-state) values to use. Because stochastic convergence is slow, its realization is costly in terms of computer time. For this reason, much research has centered on **variance reduction techniques,** which attempt to increase the precision of estimates for a fixed sample size or decrease the sample size necessary to obtain a desired level of precision. At present, however, there is no definitive answer to the problem of estimating steady-state criteria.

A multitude of different types of statistical analysis can assist in experimental data interpretation. This analysis is a routine and significant part of the simulation process and should be carefully planned as part of the experimental design.

Validation. The validation process seeks to answer the question, "Does the simulation experiment accurately represent the problem environment?" Two aspects of this process can be identified: (1) *internal validation* with respect to logical and programming errors and (2) *external validation* with respect to the degree to which the experiment replicates the phenomenon in question.

Various means can be used to internally validate what we assume to be a computer program of the simulation model. For example, hand calculations can be compared to generated output under various conditions. Another popular procedure is comparing simulated results to analytic results, which may be available.

External validation creates both philosophical and practical problems. The former relates to the issue of "What is truth?" which may well be irreconcilable. In contrast, the practical approach seeks to apply statistical tests to simulated data versus either historical data or future data (when they become available). For instance, a chi-square test (Section A.4) or other statistical tests can be performed to test the null hypothesis that simulated and actual data are from the same underlying distribution. Another approach for, say, time series data is to regress (Section A.6) generated data on actual data to test the null hypothesis that the population intercept equals 0 and the population slope equals 1.

Simulation Languages

Digital computers and programming languages have been important facilitators in increasing the frequency and ease of simulations. Without such technology the cost of implementing "meaningful" simulations would be prohibitive. Once the construction of a simulation model (in mathematical or flowchart form) is accomplished, the model must be programmed for simulated experiments on the computer. For this purpose, any of the available general-purpose languages can be used (FORTRAN, BASIC, PL/1, etc.). These languages have the advantage of providing flexibility in tailoring the program both to the model and to the needs of the user. However, they also require great amounts of programming effort, which translates into more time and expense, especially in the process of debugging errors.

An alternative to general purpose languages are **special-purpose simulation languages.** Examples of such languages are SIMSCRIPT, GPSS, SLAM, and DYNAMO. Different versions or revisions of these languages appear from time to time. In general, these languages simplify the process of transforming a model to a set of computer instructions and altering the model to answer "What if . . . ?" types of questions. Essentially, they accomplish this by providing a generalized and easily manipulated structure and a set of built-in capabilities common to most simulation experiments. For example, random number generation, time-sequencing and/or event-sequencing mechanisms, data tabulation and manipulation, and report-writing capabilities are fairly standard in most languages. The inclusion of such capabilities makes the programming of such model elements very easy compared with having to do so from scratch with general purpose languages. A thumbnail sketch of SIMSCRIPT, GPSS, SLAM, and DYNAMO follows.

SIMSCRIPT is a discrete event simulation language developed at the Rand Corporation in the early 1960s. The language is FORTRAN based, having all the capabilities of FORTRAN. However, it has additional features extremely useful in simulating discrete systems. These combined features result in a flexibility that allows the language to be used in simulating unusual and complex systems. SIMSCRIPT is relatively easy to learn and has excellent statistics-gathering capabilities, but tends to require large amounts of computer memory.

GPSS is also a discrete event language developed in the 1960s at IBM. This problem-oriented language has been used primarily in simulating queuing systems. GPSS is one of the easier simulation languages to learn, and it is excellent for conceptualizing a problem. On the negative side, computer run time tends to be very slow compared with other languages.

SLAM, developed in 1979, is similar to SIMSCRIPT in that it is FORTRAN based. However, SLAM is a more flexible modeling language than SIMSCRIPT.

SLAM has the capability of modeling discrete event systems and continuous systems. In addition, it has a capability of modeling network systems. SLAM is easy to learn, is excellent for conceptualizing problems, and has excellent statistics-gathering capabilities. It also is relatively efficient in terms of computer run times.

DYNAMO was developed at MIT in the late 1950s. Like GPSS, DYNAMO is a problem-based language. The systems modeled, however, must be continuous, unlike the discrete focus of GPSS. DYNAMO uses first-order difference equations to model the continuous relationships. It is also a language that executes very quickly on the computer. One drawback is that the language compiler for DYNAMO has not been written for all computer systems. Thus the availability of DYNAMO may not be as widespread as some other languages.

In closing out our discussion of computer languages, we should mention the increasing use and popularity of a group of languages referred to as financial planning languages. Leading examples of these include IFPS, PROFIT, and EXPRESS. These languages tend to be flexible modeling languages having capabilities ranging from optimization (as in mathematical programming) to the "What if . . . ?" capabilities of simulation. The last section in this chapter offers some evidence of the increasing use of these languages for purposes of simulation.

FOLLOW-UP EXERCISES

5. For each block in the flow diagram of Figure 17–2, identify the corresponding step in the paradigm stated in Chapter 1.
6. For each of the following systems of interest, identify examples of entities, attributes, activities, state variables, endogenous events, and exogenous events.
   a. Bank tellers.
   b. Horse racing.
   c. Hypothetical heavyweight fight between Rocky Marciano and Mohammed Ali.
   d. Distribution warehouse management.
   e. University dining services.

   In Exercises 7–11, a more narrow focus is given to the five systems mentioned in Exercise 6. For each of these, hypothesize a simulation experiment identifying (a) *experimental objectives,* (b) *design alternatives that might be considered,* (c) *examples of conditions that must be initialized and alternative values that might be assigned,* (d) *examples of parameters that would be assigned settings for any simulation run, and* (e) *examples of criteria that might determine the length of a simulation run.*
7. The bank is interested in evaluating system performance using the traditional parallel arrangement of tellers who handle all types of banking functions versus a parallel arrangement where one or more tellers is specified as express for single transactions (e.g., cash one check or make one deposit).
8. Gamblers at the track are interested in evaluating the wagering strategies of (*a*) selecting horses at random in any race versus (*b*) evaluating a horse's past three races to determine the choice.
9. Boxing enthusiasts have always wondered how these two great heavyweight boxers would have fared against one another when each was in his prime (in fact, there was indeed just such a simulated boxing match).
10. Given random demand for final goods from a distribution warehouse, managers want to evaluate different ordering policies from supplying manufacturers. The two options being considered are (*a*) to use a reorder point, EOQ system, or (*b*) to order 1⁄12 of the estimated annual demand at the beginning of each month.

11. Dining hall officials are thinking about closing one dining hall and expanding the capacity of another dining hall. The dining hall proposed to be abolished has two main serving lines in one dining room. The proposed expansion would add two new serving lines and one new dining room to an existing dining hall that already has five serving lines and two dining rooms.

17.4 FUNDAMENTALS OF MONTE CARLO SIMULATION

Section 17.2 gave a simple illustration of Monte Carlo simulation. We return to this topic briefly to provide a more in-depth treatment of selected issues. Before proceeding, review Sections A.1 through A.3 at the end of the book.

Inverse Transformation Method for Generating Random Variates

The inverse transformation method (ITM) is a popular technique for generating random variates for either discrete or continuous random variables.[1] To illustrate, consider the discrete random variable (X) "number of emergency room arrivals per hour" and the data in Table 17–8.[2]

TABLE 17–8 Distribution of Emergency Room Arrivals

Number of Arrivals per Hour (x)	Frequency of Occurrence	pmf f(x)	CDF F(x)	Range Along 0–1 Scale
0	10	0.10	0.10	0.00–0.10
1	28	0.28	0.38	0.10–0.38
2	29	0.29	0.67	0.38–0.67
3	16	0.16	0.83	0.67–0.83
4	10	0.10	0.93	0.83–0.93
5	6	0.06	0.99	0.93–0.99
6	1	0.01	1.00	0.99–1.00
	100	1.00		

According to the relative frequency definition of probability, the probability of zero arrivals, or $P(X = 0)$, is 0.10, $P(X = 1) = 0.28, \ldots,$ and $P(X = 6) = 0.01$. Now, if it were possible to generate another random variable (U) that is *uniformly distributed* in the range 0–1, then by definition $P(0.00 < U \leq 0.10) = 0.10$, $P(0.10 < U \leq 0.38) = 0.28, \ldots,$ and $P(0.99 < U \leq 1.00) = 0.01$.[3] Since the probabilities for the given ranges of U are respectively identical to the probabilities for the given values of X, it follows that occurrences of U can be used to simulate or "artificially reconstruct" occurrences of X. If you study Table 17–8 and Figure 17–3, you should realize that random variates of U within the specified intervals are equivalent to corresponding random variates of X. In other words, U can be used to artifi-

[1]Other methods exist. See T. H. Naylor et al., *Computer Simulation Techniques* (New York: John Wiley & Sons, 1966) for details.

[2]As in Appendix A, a random variate (specific value) of a random variable is represented by a lowercase letter and the random variable itself is denoted by an uppercase letter.

[3]See (1) under Continuous Probability Distribution in Section A.3.

FIGURE 17–3 *U-X* Equivalents Based on Table 17–8

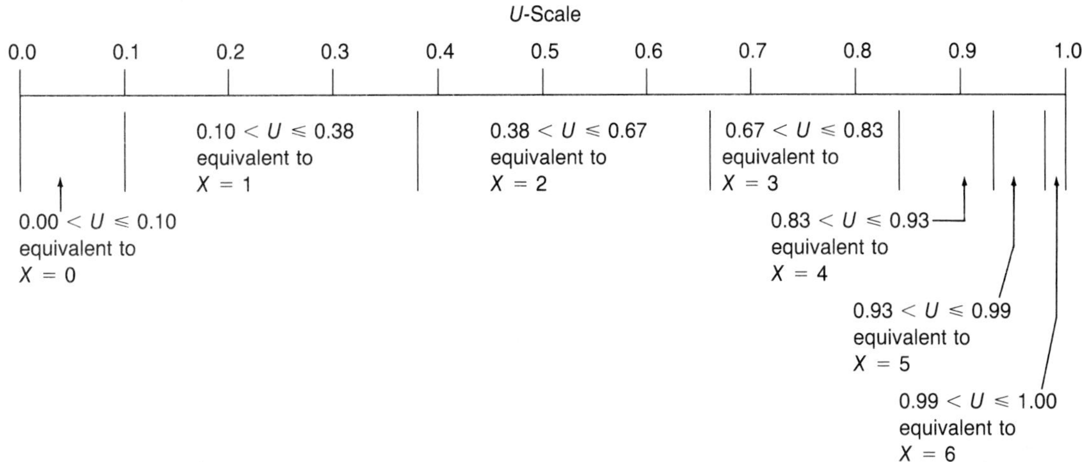

cially generate X precisely because the probabilities associated with the specified ranges of U are exactly equivalent to the probabilities associated with the corresponding values of X.

As you can see from Table 17–8, the Cumulative Distribution Function (CDF), $F(x)$, is equivalent to specified values of U. ITM gets its name from the fact that we are transforming from the U-scale to the X-scale. Note that this procedure is backward (inverse) from the usual procedure. Typically we map from specific X into specific U through $F(x)$, that is,

$$F(x) = u \tag{17.1}$$

where u represents a specific cumulative probability. By the approach of the ITM, this procedure is reversed since given u we need to specify x, that is,

$$x = F^{-1}(u)\,. \tag{17.2}$$

Table 17–9 illustrates a "hand" simulation for six one-hour periods based on the data in Table 17–8. The simulated number of arrivals for each period first requires the generation of a random variate (u) from the distribution of U. To accomplish this we provide Table 17–10, which illustrates 500 random variates (or values for u) in the interval 0–1. Arbitarily selecting column 5, we find the first number is 246, which represents U = 0.246. This corresponds to one simulated arrival ($X = 1$) between 10 A.M. and 11 A.M., since 0.246 falls between 0.10 and 0.38 on the scale given in Table 17–3. Continuing down column 5 of Table 17–10, we find that $U = 0.514$ falls in the interval 0.38–0.67, which corresponds to $X = 2$ (two arrivals between 11A.M. and noon). To check your understanding, you should confirm the remaining entries in Table 17–9. Approaches to generating values of U as in Table 17–10 are discussed in the next section.

The transformation of u to x for our present example is shown graphically in Figure 17–4. In general, the simulation of a *discrete* random variable can be represented by the graph of its CDF. Conceptually, the simulation of a *continuous* random variable is treated in the same manner, as indicated in Figure 17–5.

TABLE 17–9 Sample Simulation of Emergency Room Arrivals between 10 A.M. and 4 P.M.

Period (24-hour clock)	0–1 Random Variate (u)	Number of Arrivals during Specified Period (x)
10–11	0.246	1
11–12	0.514	2
12–13	0.898	4
13–14	0.030	0
14–15	0.152	1
15–16	0.573	2

FIGURE 17–4 Graphical Illustration of $2 = F^{-1}(0.514)$ for Discrete Random Variable

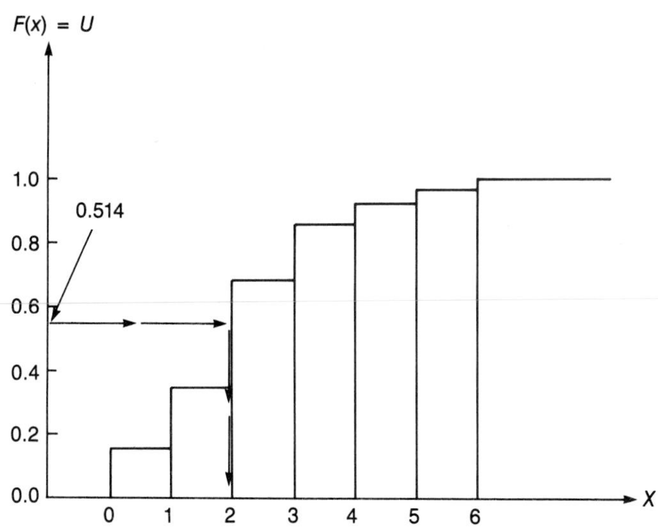

Actual simulations of *empirical* probability distributions can be effected in the manner of Tables 17–8 and 17–9. For *theoretical* distributions (e.g., Poisson and exponential), however, random variates of X are generated through the use of algorithms or formulas for $F^{-1}(u)$. The Appendix at the end of this chapter illustrates methods of generating exponential and Poisson variates. Given an empirical probability distribution, some analysts prefer to generate the simulation from a theoretical probability distribution for which the empirical distribution "fits" based on a goodness-of-fit test, as in Section A.4 on page 905.

Generation of 0–1 Uniformly Distributed Random Variates

As you now know, the simulation of a stochastic process (e.g., arrivals at the emergency room of a hospital) requires the generation of a sequence of random numbers (variates of U) uniformly distributed over the interval 0–1.

TABLE 17–10 Random Numbers

1	*2*	*3*	*4*	*5*	*6*	*7*	*8*	*9*	*10*
104	900	150	296	246	812	725	250	612	999
223	321	465	925	514	096	842	039	484	009
241	211	483	475	898	413	838	038	048	990
421	021	930	830	030	888	376	520	605	800
375	198	399	287	152	759	267	655	583	487
779	383	888	774	573	075	261	972	773	478
995	107	799	123	480	690	491	527	054	227
963	799	322	849	558	393	962	577	853	190
895	439	236	772	462	343	230	943	313	439
854	262	309	917	245	025	484	755	200	302
289	587	611	433	468	448	075	731	684	794
635	169	349	564	940	430	604	670	663	707
094	678	743	242	427	094	470	918	992	637
103	917	253	078	717	075	238	653	078	597
071	440	442	098	906	713	553	631	061	456
510	346	695	575	110	366	849	844	142	450
023	310	082	654	181	893	783	159	413	754
010	744	527	853	275	446	275	405	898	612
521	333	491	242	215	145	288	938	056	434
070	718	975	011	651	639	963	142	757	609
556	002	893	868	375	903	336	194	942	098
204	847	436	188	037	688	067	922	719	665
203	553	943	111	623	193	682	154	167	244
112	939	806	291	830	790	429	813	430	358
465	345	285	278	323	203	999	122	085	091
549	128	563	635	478	095	035	649	916	657
411	809	098	428	335	267	750	228	388	257
640	617	605	822	012	317	042	295	784	912
070	116	499	272	334	593	085	899	415	796
074	895	985	934	815	937	884	193	213	938
588	728	220	698	448	028	299	731	279	221
355	271	284	471	392	866	365	625	770	327
517	811	435	424	201	968	746	097	653	966
328	959	772	300	832	040	560	521	744	709
007	887	982	497	661	947	733	715	362	861
514	627	829	667	669	353	949	652	358	324
869	374	186	522	729	249	527	540	852	607
316	010	840	919	397	917	497	147	203	845
523	672	564	745	906	544	688	936	103	214
979	152	263	443	097	753	202	916	249	420
370	575	698	784	535	441	926	296	914	009
448	670	395	433	625	508	576	989	126	523
391	837	633	447	092	139	875	729	189	018
098	191	066	267	834	849	113	429	226	086
568	545	478	310	911	811	572	054	054	106
800	868	301	727	743	917	344	617	251	660
524	199	592	107	240	441	050	092	209	516
122	493	915	730	755	553	582	872	865	196
681	200	279	565	790	841	626	671	901	136
327	734	849	367	161	713	219	965	382	512

FIGURE 17–5 Graphical Illustration of $x = F^{-1}(u)$ for Continuous Random Variable

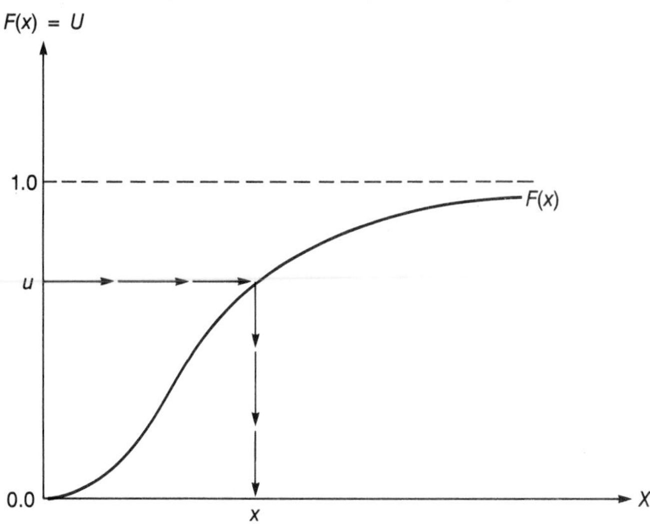

The process that generates U *must* satisfy the conditions of (1) a *uniform distribution* in the parent population and (2) *independence* (absence of correlation) in the sampled observations (variates) from that population. Additionally, it is desirable that the process be (3) *fast (or cheap)* and (4) have a *long period* should it repeat itself.

Processes for generating U include (*a*) the use of random number tables available either in published form or on computer tapes, (*b*) special machines or physical phenomena (e.g., fluctuations in some electronic process), and (*c*) application of a numerical process. Of these, numerical processes based on so-called *congruential methods* most nearly satisfy the four criteria outlined above. In fact, Table 17–10 was generated by a congruential method. Suffice it to say that all manufacturers of general-purpose digital computers make available computational procedures (usually in the form of subroutines) for generating random numbers. Therefore, a simulation model programmed for a digital computer need only incorporate the appropriate subroutine for generating U.

Random numbers for U based on numerical methods are called **pseudorandom numbers,** as opposed to *true* random numbers, which are generated by some physical process. Believe it or not, pseudorandom numbers are preferable because the exact same sequence of random numbers is capable of being repeated at will by the experimenter. This has control value when the experimenter wishes to alter a policy or decision variable in answering "What happens if . . . ?" questions. Without the capability of repeating the same sequence of random variates, experimental results would differ because of both conscious changes by the analyst and random changes due to a different random number sequence. The latter effect would represent a confounding factor that would have to be isolated by replications of the experiment. Pseudorandom numbers, therefore, uniquely isolate the effects of changes in controllable conditions. Furthermore, purely random effects can be estimated easily by rerunning experiments with changed **random number seeds.** (A random number seed is an arbitrary number provided by the experimenter that initializes the random number subroutine.) The value of using pseudorandom numbers will be illustrated in the next two sections.

FOLLOW-UP EXERCISES

12. Besides the methods indicated above for generating U, more pedestrian methods (e.g., manual) can be described. If you were given 100 poker chips and a felt-tip pen, describe how you could manually simulate the arrival process in Table 17–8. Comment on the degree to which the four criteria for generating U are satisfied.
13. Theoretically, why need we not worry about $U = 0.10$, $U = 0.38$, and so on in using the ITM for the process in Table 17–8? Need we be concerned from a practical standpoint?
14. Determine $f(u)$, $F(u)$, $E(U)$, $V(U)$, $P(U \leq 0.1)$, $P(0.10 \leq U \leq 0.38)$, and $P(0.38 \leq U \leq 0.67)$ when U is uniform over the interval $(0, 1)$. (*Hint:* Go back to Appendix A.) Are your probabilities consistent with corresponding values of $f(x)$ in Table 17–8?

17.5 SIMULATION OF QUEUING SYSTEMS

This section illustrates a manual simulation for a $GI/G/1$ system and presents the results of a simulation for an $M/M/c$ system with state-dependent service rates. The latter simulation is implemented using GPSS, the output of which we will illustrate. First, however, we motivate the use of simulation for queuing systems.

Motivation for Simulating Queuing Systems

As with inventory systems, the primary motivation for simulating queuing systems is the inability to generate meaningful analytic solutions for complex queuing structures. Typical system complexities include:

1. Arrival processes having empirical distributions with no theoretical counterparts, or characterized by certain theoretical distributions (e.g., normal), or exhibiting nonstationarity, seasonal patterns (e.g., rush hours) or serial correlation.
2. Service facilities with certain empirical or theoretical service time distributions, or specific forms of state dependence in the service rate (as illustrated later in this section), or tandem and parallel servers (as in job shop systems that process simultaneous orders and assembly line production systems), or breakdown and fatigue failures, or nonstationary service distributions.
3. Queuing processes for which transient solutions are required (i.e., the system never operates long enough to achieve steady state) but are unavailable (which is the case for most non-$M/M/c$ systems).

$GI/G/1$ System

To give you a better "feel" for the process of Monte Carlo simulation, we now illustrate a procedure for simulating any single-channel queuing system. For simplicity we adopt the assumptions of the standard $M/M/1$ model (page 773), except for the relaxation of interarrival times and service times to the general case.

Consider the interarrival-time (i.e., time between successive arrivals) distribution and service-time distribution given in Table 17–11. Two random variables are to be directly simulated: *interarrival time (B)* and *service time (T)*. Tables 17–12 and 17–13 provide the structure for simulating these random variables. Note that the random variates are determined as the midpoints of the ranges in Table 17–11. Further note the cumulative probabilities identify the upper point of each range for the random numbers on the U-scales.

TABLE 17–11 Empirical Probability Distributions for Queuing Simulation

Range of Interarrival Times (minutes)	Probability	Range of Service Times (minutes)	Probability
0 but under 4	0.4	0 but under 2	0.4
4 but under 8	0.3	2 but under 4	0.4
8 but under 12	0.2	4 but under 6	0.2
12 but under 16	0.1		

TABLE 17–12 Simulation Structure for B

Random Variates for Interarrival Times b	Probability $f(b)$	Cumulative Probability $F(b)$	Ranges of 0–1 Uniformly Distributed Random Number u_1
2	0.4	0.4	0.0–0.4
6	0.3	0.7	0.4–0.7
10	0.2	0.9	0.7–0.9
14	0.1	1.0	0.9–1.0

TABLE 17–13 Simulation Structure for T

Random Variates for Service Times t	Probability $f(t)$	Cumulative Probability $F(t)$	Ranges of 0–1 Uniformly Distributed Random Number u_2
1	0.4	0.4	0.0–0.4
3	0.4	0.8	0.4–0.8
5	0.2	1.0	0.8–1.0

Table 17–14 illustrates a simulation for a period encompassing 10 arrivals. The items below should help to clarify the logic.

1. The 0–1 random variates (u_1 and u_2) are taken from columns 2 and 9 in Table 17–10. The simulated random variates (b and t) are determined from Tables 17–12 and 17–13 once u_1 and u_2 are given.
2. CLOCK1 records the time of arrival of each unit into the system. CLOCK2 records the time each unit enters the service facility. The first arriving unit initializes CLOCK1. Because an empty initial system is assumed, unit 1 enters service immediately (CLOCK2 = 0) and departs at the end of 3 minutes. Other entries in this first row should be self-explanatory.

TABLE 17–14 *GI/G/1* Simulation

Arriving Unit	u_1	b	Enter System at Time (CLOCK1)	Length of Queue at Entry	Number in System at Unit Arrival	Time Spent in Queue	Enter Service at Time (CLOCK2)	u_2	t	Leave Service at Time (CLOCK3)	Server Idle Time
1	—	—	0	0	0	0	0	0.612	3	3	—
2	0.900	14	14	0	0	0	14	0.484	3	17	11
3	0.321	2	16	0	1	1	17	0.048	1	18	0
4	0.211	2	18	0	0	0	18	0.605	3	21	0
5	0.021	2	20	0	1	1	21	0.583	3	24	0
6	0.198	2	22	0	1	2	24	0.773	3	27	0
7	0.383	2	24	0	1	3	27	0.054	1	28	0
8	0.107	2	26	1	2	2	28	0.853	5	33	0
9	0.799	10	36	0	0	0	36	0.313	1	37	3
10	0.439	6	42	0	0	0	42	0.200	1	43	5

3. Unit 2 enters the system 14 minutes into the simulation (CLOCK1 = 14). Since unit 1 departed the system at time 3, it follows that unit 2 enters service immediately (CLOCK2 = 14). Given that it takes 3 minutes to service unit 2, this unit departs at time 17 (CLOCK3 = 17). Note that the server is idle for 11 minutes (i.e., the difference between CLOCK3 = 3 for unit 1 and CLOCK2 = 14 for unit 2).
4. Unit 3 enters at CLOCK1 = 16. Since unit 2 does not leave service until time 17, it follows unit 3 must wait 1 minute in the queue before entering service. Unit 3 enters at time 17 and departs at time 18. No idle time is experienced by the server between units 2 and 3.
5. The simulation continues in the same manner until the desired number of arriving units has been generated, after which relevant operating characteristics can be estimated.
6. Note that the length of the queue when a unit enters the system will be zero whenever CLOCK1 for the entering unit is *greater than* or *equal to* CLOCK2 for the immediately preceding unit; however, if CLOCK1 for the entering unit is *less than* CLOCK 2 for the immediately preceding unit, then a queue at least 1 unit long must exist (as "viewed" by the entering unit).

Time Flow Mechanisms

The simulation just described is classified as a **variable time increment** simulation because the clock that times the simulation is not changing by equal intervals of time. This simulation also can be labeled as a **next event** simulation because the simulation moves forward by the occurrence of "events." In this case events are based on the arrivals and departures of units, and the clock is updated by the amount of time necessary for the next event to occur. Alternatively, **fixed time increment** simulations proceed by equal increments of the clock. At each time interval the system is scanned in order to record the occurrence or nonoccurrence of events.

The choice of a **time flow mechanism** (fixed or variable) will affect the efficiency and cost of a particular simulation; hence, this represents a nontrivial design issue.[4]

FOLLOW-UP EXERCISES

15. Calculate the following operating characteristics for the queuing system of Table 17–14.
    a. Mean time in queue.
    b. Mean time in busy-system queue.
    c. Mean length of queue at entry.
    d. Mean length of queue weighted by the proportion of time the queue is at a given length. (*Note:* This is equivalent to L_q of Chapter 16 in the steady state.)
    e. Same as part *d* for busy-system queue.
    f. Mean time in system.
    g. Probability of an idle system (*Hint:* Total clock time for the simulation is given by CLOCK3 of the last unit.)
16. Extend the simulation of Table 17–4 to 25 units, and calculate the operating characteristics of the preceding exercise. (*Note:* Continue down columns 2 and 9 of Table 17–10). Explain why these are more reliable estimates than those in the preceding exercise.

Multiserver Queuing System with State-Dependent Service Rates and Implicit Profits

We now describe the development of a general single queue-multiserver queuing model with two distinguishing characteristics; *implicit* (as opposed to accounting) *profit* as a criterion and service rates that can be modified behaviorally as a function of queue length. The stated criterion provides a desirable economic framework for retail establishments that incorporate both facility costs and waiting time (*implicit* or *opportunity*) costs, the latter by formulating an opportunity cost function in terms of customer waiting time. Additionally, functionally relating service times to queue lengths may have its behavioral justifications, especially for retail establishments having human beings as servers. For instance, longer queues may decrease the mean time of service, perhaps because of an increased level of dissonance or anxiety in the server induced by irate customers, superiors, or the realization that long queues encourage lost sales (some empirical studies have borne out these allegations).

For known revenue and opportunity cost distributions, the implicit revenue contribution of the *i*th customer can be expressed as

$$r_i = q_i - w_i$$

where q is a variate of the random variable customer contribution to operating and overhead expenses (Q) or, alternatively, revenue from a sale less the cost of goods sold, and w is a variate of the random variable W, the opportunity cost ($W > 0$) or gain ($W < 0$).

A policy that creates ill will is said to represent an opportunity cost. Conversely, the creation of good will represents an opportunity profit (negative opportunity cost) to the firm. Ignoring such variables as courtesy, quality of service and merchandise, and price differentials, we can see that the reality of impatient or pleased customers

[4]See the references for greater detail on the cost implications of time flow mechanisms.

can be incorporated by expressing opportunity cost (W) as a function of the random variable waiting time in the queue.

For a specified time horizon, H, the total implicit revenue for K customers is

$$R_H = \sum_{i=1}^{K} r_i \tag{17.4}$$

and the implicit profit, exclusive of overhead, is

$$P_H = R_H - \sum_{j=1}^{c} O_j \tag{17.5}$$

where c is the number of servers in operation during H and O_j is the operating expense for the jth service station over H.

The objective is to determine a value for the decision variable c such that P_H is maximized. Since revenue contribution and marginal operating expenses are not treated as decision variables, the formulation implicitly assumes that product prices and factor costs are market-determined parameters.

The term **state-dependent service rate** refers to a service rate (customers per unit time) that is a function of the number of customers in the system (n). We incorporate this concept behaviorally as follows. Under "normal" operating conditions, a mean service time (time units per customer) for the jth service station, $E[t_j]$, is to be determined or assumed. Service time is to be a function of queue length (L) as defined by the following conditions:

1. The service time for the ith customer is to be modified by a *service time multiplier* (m) such that the resulting service time will be a variate from a distribution with mean

$$E[t_{ij}] = m_i E[t_j]. \tag{17.6}$$

2. The range of m will be specified by an upper limit (v) and a lower limit (k), which represent, respectively, the maximum increase and decrease in mean service time multiples, $k \leq m \leq v$.
3. The "normal" service time $E[t_j]$ has been observed when L_N customers have been in the queue; that is, $m = 1$ when $L = L_N$.

The last two assumptions suggest the curve in Figure 17–6 for the service-time multiplier function, which may be described as a modified exponential.[5]

We now illustrate the simulation of a queuing system having these types of characteristics.

Simulation Using GPSS

General Purpose System Simulation (GPSS) is a special purpose simulation language uniquely designed for implementing complex queuing simulations. Our intent is not to describe the simulation language itself, but rather to illustrate its convenient out-

[5]Its mathematical function is given by $m = k + ab^L$, where a and b can be determined given v, k, and $(L, m) = (L_N, 1)$.

FIGURE 17–6 Service-Time Multiplier Function

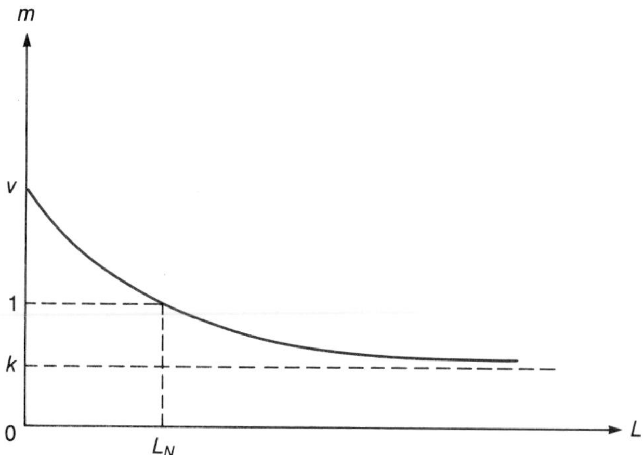

put.[6] The queuing system to be simulated is based on the model just described, according to the following conditions:

1. A multiserver retail establishment characterized by stationary exponential interarrival and service times ($M/M/c$), where mean interarrival time is 6 minutes and mean service time is 20 minutes.
2. Around-the-clock operation of the firm.
3. First-come, first-served service discipline from a single queue.
4. Service times independent from customer expenditures.
5. Absence of balking and reneging.
6. Normally distributed revenue contributions with mean of \$100 per customer and standard deviation of \$20 per customer.
7. Operating cost per hour per service station of \$100.
8. A positive opportunity cost that increases at a decreasing rate to a maximum of \$100 as waiting time increases above 10 minutes and a negative opportunity cost that decreases (becomes more negative) at a decreasing rate to a minimum of −\$50 as waiting time decreases below 10 minutes.[7]
9. Maximum changes of ±20 percent in mean service time (that is, $k = 0.8$ and $v = 1.2$) and normal service times at a queue length of five customers (that is, $L_N = 5$).

We might emphasize that the model described in the preceding section is in no way dependent on the specific conditions 1 through 6. Any specified service and arrival time distributions, empirical or theoretical, can be utilized. An $M/M/c$ queuing system was chosen for referencing (benchmarking). Should the assumption of 24-hour operation prove untenable, it would be an easy matter to reprogram the simulation.

[6]For details of the simulation language itself, see P. A. Bobillier, B. C. Kahan, and A. R. Probst, *Simulation with GPSS and GPSS V* (Englewood Cliffs, N.J.: Prentice-Hall 1976); and G. Gordon, *The Application of GPSS V to Discrete System Simulation* (Englewood Cliffs, N.J.: Prentice-Hall, 1975).

[7]To avoid unnecessary detail in the formulation, the specific functions for W have been omitted.

Such a procedure, while more realistic, necessitates replication runs and obviates a direct comparison with analytic steady-state solutions. Other conditions, such as multiple queues with specific selection heuristics, can also be programmed easily in GPSS. Should service times and customer expenditures exhibit covariation, a conditional probability distribution of service time given customer revenue contribution must be specified. Explicit balking and reneging can be programmed once the distributions are specified. If a space constraint is active, the likelihood of balking is certain (e.g., parking lot filled). Finally, should expected interarrival times exhibit seasonal variations across periods (i.e., hourly, daily, and so on), it might be of benefit to so vary the arrival distribution. One possible way of accommodating this condition is not unlike the multiplier used in changing the service-time distribution. Given each seasonal arrival time multiplier (index), it would be a simple matter to modify the mean and/or variance of the distribution.

Figure 17–7 illustrates the type of output provided by a GPSS simulation. This particular run generated 25,000 arrivals into a five-server queuing system as previously described. The first part of the exhibit summarizes statistics for each server (facility). For example, the third server was busy 78.4 percent of the time, served 5,115 customers, and averaged 21.262 minutes to service each customer.[8] The second part provides summary statistics for the queue. The third part is a frequency distribution for "waiting time in the queue." This distribution is one of many that can be specified by the programmer. For example, the same computer run also provided frequency distributions for revenue contribution (Q), opportunity cost (W), total implicit revenue (R_H), service-time multiplier (m), service times, and total implicit profit (P_H).

Table 17–15 provides simulated statistics for 1,500 arrivals. The results indicate that the "optimal" number of servers is six, with an associated maximum total implicit profit of \$126,000 over the time horizon.[9]

TABLE 17–15 Results of GPSS Simulation

Number of Servers (c)	Mean Waiting Time for Those Who Waited (minutes)	Mean Service Time Multiplier ($\bar{m}$)	Total Implicit Revenue in \$1,000 (R_H)	Total Implicit Profit in \$1,000 (P_H)
3	84.1	0.88	43	−1
4	26.6	1.06	156	99
5	14.0	1.14	195	124
6*	9.5	1.17	212	126*
7	7.4	1.18	219	119
8	5.2	1.19	222	108
9	3.6	1.19	224	96
10	3.0	1.19	224	82

* Optimal solution.

Table 17–16 summarizes some comparisons to theoretical steady-state predictions given by the analytic formulas of the standard $M/M/c$ model.

[8] In GPSS parlance, "entry" or "transaction" is synonymous with "'customer" or "unit."

[9] The resulting GPSS "clock count" was 8,620, which gives an elapsed time horizon of 8,620 minutes,

FIGURE 17–7 Partial GPSS Output

FACILITY	AVERAGE UTILIZATION	NUMBER ENTRIES	AVERAGE TIME/TRAN
1	.872	5589	21.631
2	.838	5379	21.613
3	.784	5115	21.262
4	.723	4673	21.476
5	.666	4244	21.774

QUEUE	MAXIMUM CONTENTS	AVERAGE CONTENTS	TOTAL ENTRIES	ZERO ENTRIES	PERCENT ZEROS	AVERAGE TIME/TRANS	$AVERAGE TIME/TRANS
1	17	1.444	25000	12190	48.7	8.011	5.636

$AVERAGE TIME/TRANS = AVERAGE TIME/TRANS EXCLUDING ZERO ENTRIES

TABLE 2

ENTRIES IN TABLE	MEAN ARGUMENT	STANDARD DEVIATION	SUM OF ARGUMENTS
25000	8.011	11.867	200299.000

UPPER LIMIT	OBSERVED FREQUENCY	PERCENT OF TOTAL	CUMULATIVE PERCENTAGE	CUMULATIVE REMAINDER	MULTIPLE OF MEAN	NON-WEIGHTED DEVIATION FROM MEAN
0	12190	48.75	48.7	51.2	-.000	-.675
5	3017	12.06	60.8	39.1	.624	-.253
10	2552	10.20	71.0	28.9	1.248	.167
15	1974	7.89	78.9	21.0	1.872	.588
20	1564	6.25	85.1	14.8	2.496	1.010
25	1235	4.93	90.1	9.8	3.120	1.431
30	814	3.25	93.3	6.6	3.744	1.852
35	569	2.27	95.6	4.3	4.368	2.274
40	429	1.71	97.3	2.6	4.992	2.695
45	286	1.14	98.5	1.4	5.616	3.116
50	147	.58	99.1	.8	6.240	3.538
55	123	.49	99.5	.4	6.864	3.959
60	51	.20	99.8	.1	7.488	4.380
65	26	.10	99.9	.0	8.112	4.802
70	19	.07	99.9	.0	8.736	5.233
75	2	.00	99.9	.0	9.361	5.644
80	1	.00	99.9	.0	9.985	6.644
85	1	.00	100.0	.0	10.609	6.487

REMAINING FREQUENCIES ARE ALL ZERO

When m is restricted to values of unity, the simulated model is identical to the standard $M/M/c$ model of Section 16.5. The "closeness" of the results is an indication of the validity of the simulation model (or of the analytic formulas, depending on your perspective). Note the predictable effect on mean waiting time and mean system utilization when average m is greater than one (i.e., from Table 17–15, $\overline{m} = 1.14$, 1.17,and 1.18, respectively, when $c = 5, 6, 7$)—increased service times increase both utilization and waiting times.

TABLE 17–16 Comparisons of Theoretical Steady State and Simulations*

	Waiting Time for Those Who Waited (minutes)			Average System Utilization		
Number of Servers (c)	Theoretical Steady State	Value of *m* Fixed at Unity	Variable *m*	Theoretical Steady State	Value of *m* Fixed at Unity	Variable *m*
5	12.0	11.9	14.0	0.67	0.70	0.78
6	7.5	8.4	9.5	0.56	0.58	0.67
7	5.5	5.4	7.4	0.48	0.50	0.57

*Based on 1,500 arrivals.

FOLLOW-UP EXERCISES

17. Sketch the service rate multiplier function for the data in conditon 9. Is the function conceptually reasonable? How might you go about designing a sampling plan for obtaining this function for, say, a state unemployment benefits agency with a numbering system for servicing potential recipients?
18. The literature on queuing theory defines two main approaches to handling the behavior of arrivals as a function of "number of customers presently in the system" (n): Modify the arrival rate as a function of n, or specify balking and reneging probability distributions.
    a. Discuss how each might be incorporated in a simulation.
    b. Discuss the pros and cons of these approaches versus our opportunity cost approach.
19. With respect to Figure 17–15:
    a. Determine overall average utilization for the queuing system. Compare to Table 17–16. (Note the difference in number of generated customers.)
    b. Identify consistencies in the generated statistics between the second and third parts of the output.
    c. Estimate the following probabilities: of more than 17 customers in the queue; of spending 10 minutes or less in the queue; of spending more than 30 minutes in the queue; of going into service without having to wait in the queue; of waiting in the queue.
20. With respect to Table 17–15:
    a. Describe the behavior of mean waiting time for those who waited as a function of number of servers. Is the function logical?
    b. Describe the behavior of $\overline{m}$ as a function of c. Is the function logical? What maximum value for $\overline{m}$ is approached as $c \to \infty$?
    c. Describe the behavior of R_H. Is the function logical?
    d. Describe the behavior of P_H. Is the function logical?
    e. Given an elapsed time horizon of 8,620 minutes and a cost of \$100 per server per hour, confirm P_H = \$126,000 given R_H = \$212,000.
21. With respect to Table 17–16, confirm (for $c = 5$) the mean steady-state waiting time for those who waited using Equation 16.39 on page 821.

17.6 SIMULATION OF INVENTORY SYSTEM

Our next illustration of a stochastic simulation is that of a reorder point inventory system with probabilistic demands and lead times. Although the model is conceptually simple, analytic solutions are restrictive and not generally available.

Motivation for Simulating Inventory Systems

Inventory systems are simulated when analytic solutions are not possible. System conditions under which it is necessary to simulate include:

1. Stochastic demands *and* lead times characterized by specific probability distributions that may be theoretical or empirical.
2. Nonstationarities as when demands exhibit pattern or trend over time.
3. Nonlinearities and/or discontinuities in the cost functions that negate analytic solutions.
4. Elaborate or comprehensive systems (e.g., constraints, multiproducts, multiechelons, and queuing considerations as in production inventory systems).

Extension of Reorder Point Inventory Model

As you may recall from Chapter 15, the reorder point model is concerned with estimating the reorder point (R) and reorder quantity (Q) that minimize the sum of average holding, ordering, and shortage costs per unit time. In this section we simulate a reorder point inventory model that incorporates both stochastic demands and stochastic lead times.

Tables 17–17 and 17–18 illustrate sample data for empirical probability distributions of demand per day (D) and days of lead time (T_L), respectively. As before, the assignments of random number ranges are based on the cumulative probabilities (CDF). Note that the random variates for D and T_L are approximated as class midpoints. Also, we assume that the given probability distributions typify the random behaviors of D and T_L, and are stationary.

TABLE 17–17 Assignment of Random Numbers to Daily Demand

Number of Units Demanded Daily	Number of Days in Which Specified Demand Occurred	Random Variate for Demand (d)	pmf $f(d)$	CDF $F(d)$	Ranges of 0–1 Uniformly Distributed Random Number (u_1)
0 but under 50	0	—	—	—	—
50 but under 70	24	60	0.07	0.07	0.00–0.07
70 but under 90	50	80	0.14	0.21	0.07–0.21
90 but under 110	65	100	0.18	0.39	0.21–0.39
110 but under 130	103	120	0.29	0.68	0.39–0.68
130 but under 150	59	140	0.16	0.84	0.68–0.84
150 but under 170	41	160	0.11	0.95	0.84–0.95
170 but under 190	18	180	0.05	1.00	0.95–1.00
190 but under ∞	0	—	—	—	—
	360		1.00		

Figure 17–8 and Table 17–19 describe the procedure for this type of inventory simulation. Carefully study these figures and relate them to one another. Note the following:

1. Holding cost for a given day (H) is based on the ending inventory (I) for that day as long as $I > 0$; that is, $H = C_h \cdot I$. If $I \leq 0$, then $H = 0$.

TABLE 17–18 Assignment of Random Numbers to Days of Lead Time

Number of Days between Placement and Receipt of Order	Number of Orders for Which Specified Lead Time Occurred	Random Variate for Lead Time (t_L)	pmf $f(t_L)$	CDF $F(t_L)$	Ranges of 0–1 Uniformly Distributed Random Number (u_2)
0	0	—	—	—	—
1	3	1	0.06	0.06	0.00–0.06
2	10	2	0.20	0.26	0.06–0.26
3	20	3	0.40	0.66	0.26–0.66
4	10	4	0.20	0.86	0.66–0.86
5	7	5	0.14	1.00	0.86–1.00
≥6	0	—	—	—	—
	50		1.00		

Depending on the application, C_h could also be based on the beginning inventory or average inventory for the day.

2. Shortage cost for a given day (S) is strictly based on the *lost sales* for that day; that is, $S = C_s \cdot |I|$, when $I < 0$. If ending inventory for a given day is negative ($I < 0$), then the beginning inventory for the next day is set to zero. (See days 8, 11, and 16.) Thus *back ordering* is not allowed. Other models could base this cost on the number of outstanding back orders per day, in which case the unit of measurement on C_s is dollars per unit per day. Still other models could use a mixture of lost sales and back orders, if appropriate.
3. If the ending inventory for a given day is less than the reorder point (that is, if $I < R$), then an order for Q units is placed and an ordering cost (C_o) is incurred. At this point a random number for the lead time variate is generated to determine when the order is to be received. (See days 3, 6, 9, 12, and 18.) For example, the order placed in day 3 can be used in day 5, since the lead time is two days. Note that only one order can be outstanding at any one time. Quantity discounts can be incorporated easily by making C_o a function of Q.
4. Beginning inventory is augmented by Q on the day an order is received. (See days 5, 9, 12, and 17.)
5. If a random number exactly equals a class boundary, then the event corresponding to the lower class limit is assigned. (See day 20.) This occurrence is rare in actual practice (when using, say, seven digits). For practical purposes, this slight bias may be ignored.

Note that Table 17–19 represents an illustration of a *20-day* simulation ($n = 20$) for *specific* values of the decision variables ($R = 300$, $Q = 400$). In an actual simulation, a greater number of days (sample size) would be needed to more accurately estimate the criterion mean total cost per day, $\overline{C} = \overline{H} + \overline{O} + \overline{S} = \$181 + \$5 + \$50 = \$236$. (Can you draw an analogy in assessing the balance of a coin in 10 flips versus 1,000 flips?) Also, you should realize that the beginning inventory for day 1 will affect cost calculations; however, this effect diminishes as n becomes larger.

FIGURE 17–8 Logic for Inventory Simulation

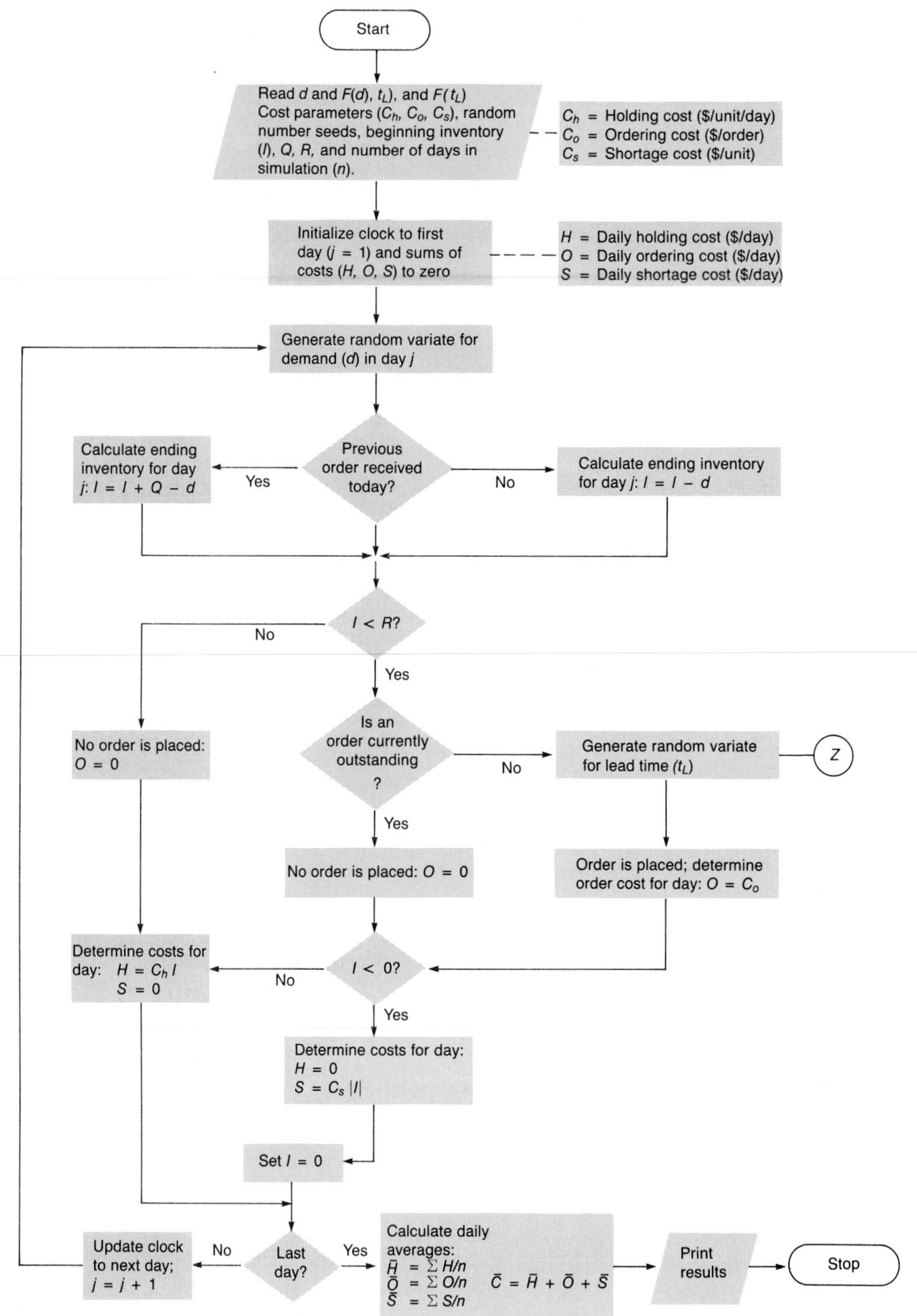

TABLE 17–19 Sample Inventory Simulation*

Day	Units of Beginning Inventory	Units Received (Q)	u for Demand (u_1)	Units of Demand (d)	Units of Ending Inventory	u for Lead Time (u_2)	Days of Lead Time (t_L)	Holding Cost in $ (H)	Order Cost in $ (O)	Shortage Cost in $ (S)	Total Cost in $ (C)
1	500	0	0.104	80	420	—	—	420	0	0	420
2	420	0	0.223	100	320	—	—	320	0	0	320
3	320	0	0.241	100	220	0.150	2	220	20	0	240
4	220	0	0.421	120	100	—	—	100	0	0	100
5	100	400	0.375	100	400	—	—	400	0	0	400
6	400	0	0.779	140	260	0.465	3	260	20	0	280
7	260	0	0.995	180	80	—	—	80	0	0	80
8	80	0	0.963	180	0	—	—	0	0	500	500
9	0	400	0.895	160	240	0.483	3	240	20	0	260
10	240	0	0.854	160	80	—	—	80	0	0	80
11	80	0	0.289	100	0	—	—	0	0	100	100
12	0	400	0.635	120	280	0.930	5	280	20	0	300
13	280	0	0.094	80	200	—	—	200	0	0	200
14	200	0	0.103	80	120	—	—	120	0	0	120
15	120	0	0.071	80	40	—	—	40	0	0	40
16	40	0	0.510	120	0	—	—	0	0	400	400
17	0	400	0.023	60	340	—	—	340	0	0	340
18	340	0	0.010	60	280	0.399	3	280	20	0	300
19	280	0	0.521	120	160	—	—	160	0	0	160
20	160	0	0.070	80	80	—	—	80	0	0	80
Totals	4,040	—	—	2220	3620	—	—	3,620	100	1,000	4,720
Average	202	—	—	111	181	—	—	181	5	50	236

*For R = 300 units, Q = 400 units, C_h = \$1 per unit per day, C_o = \$20 per order, C_s = \$5 per unit, and initial inventory of 500 units; u_1 and u_2 taken from columns 1 and 3 of Table 17–10.

Interactive Computer Model

An actual simulation of the inventory model would be characterized both by an adequately large sample size and by the search for an "optimal" $R - Q$ combination; hence, it would be desirable to implement the simulation using a computer package that automatically allows the systematic evaluation of mean total cost ($\overline{C}$) based on specified $R - Q$ ranges. Figure 17–9 illustrates the I/0 for a time-shared version of the inventory model presented in this section. A chronological explanation of the I/0 follows.

FIGURE 17–9 Computerized Inventory Simulation

```
Enter random number seed (any number)? 2001
How many simulations ?1000

What is the possible number of demands? 7

Enter the demand and associated cumulative probability, one pair
per line

?60,.07
?80,.21
?100,.39
?120,.68
?140,.84
?160,.95
?180,1.0

How many lead times are possible? 5

Enter the lead time and associated cumulative probability, one pair
per line

?1,.06
?2,.26
?3,.66
?4,.86
?5,1.0

What is the shortage cost, holding cost, order cost, beginning
inventory?5, 1, 20, 500

What is the first reorder point, last one, and the step? 0,700,100

What is the first order quantity, last one, and the step? 100,700,100


Do you want a printout for the first few days (ans. yes or no)? no


Reorder                              Quantities Ordered (Q)
Points (R)      100       200       300       400       500       600       700

   0          449.10    376.94    346.30    333.38    354.70    357.82    386.78
```

```
100          435.78   329.84   303.70   302.58   315.40   342.06   365.34
200          425.00   307.68   260.66   267.64   289.18   322.32   360.52
300          433.30   293.88   240.08   257.24   289.88   327.80   368.28
400          433.06   301.46   233.20   275.44   325.28   371.10   421.12
500          433.32   310.34   234.28   327.06   402.26   453.00   524.64
600          430.92   303.18   239.12   370.44   488.06   561.74   583.46
700          432.48   300.42   256.16   415.90   579.46   626.06   703.92

The lowest average total cost is $233.20 when R=400, Q=300

Do you want to make any input changes (ans. yes or no)? yes

How many changes? 3

Choose the change (one at a time) and type in the corresponding
number.

1=#simulation, 2=#demands, 3=demand vs. cum. prob., 4=#lead times
5=lead times vs. cum. prob., 6=costs and begin. inven., 7=reorder
points, 8=order quantities, 9=R.N. seed

?7

What is the first reorder point, last one, and the step? 250,550,50

?8

What is the first order quantity, last one, and the step? 250,350,50

?1

How many simulations? 5000

Any more changes (ans. yes or no)? no

Do you want a printout for the first few days (ans. yes or no)? no


Reorder       Quantities Ordered (Q)
Points (R)     250      300      350

250          262.60   240.29   246.95
300          261.59   235.99   240.91
350          258.60   236.48   240.80
400          257.52   235.35   249.64
450          258.16   239.96   255.04
500          258.85   238.35   266.05
550          258.79   240.89   279.38

The lowest average total cost is $235.35 when R = 400 and Q = 300.

Do you want to make any value changes (ans. yes or no)? no

Stop.
```

The purpose of the random number seed has been explained previously, and the issue of "how many days of simulation" will be taken up subsequently. Inputs for the demand and lead time distributions are consistent with Tables 17–17 and 17–18. The costs (C_s = \$5 per unit, C_h = \$1 per unit per day, and C_o = \$20 per order) and the beginning inventory (500 units) are identical to those used in the "hand" simulation of Table 17–19.

Next, the user must specify appropriate ranges for R and Q. In effect, this means that ranges for R and Q must be indicated *within* which (one hopes) the *universal optimal* $R - Q$ will be found. "Quick-and-dirty" starting points are provided by the basic EOQ formula for Q,

$$Q^* = \left[\frac{2C_o E(D)}{C_h}\right]^{1/2}, \tag{17.7}$$

and by the *expected* demand between placement and receipt of an order for R,

$$R = E(D) \cdot E(T_L) \tag{17.8}$$

where $E(D) \equiv$ Mean demand per unit time and $E(T_L) \equiv$ Mean time between placement and receipt of an order. Note that Equation 17.7 will tend to be too low, as shortage costs are ignored. The estimate given by 17.8 should make sense in that the computation provides the expected demand between the placement and receipt of an order; hence, on the average, inventory will be at zero level when an order arrives.

From Tables 17.17 and 17.18, using the formula given by A.12 on page 000, we get $E(D)$ = 117.2 units per day and $E(T_L)$ = 3.2 days. This gives Q^* = 68 units and $R \doteq 370$ units with Equations 17.7 and 17.8. Therefore, ranges of 0–700 for R and 100–700 for Q should be reasonable first approximations within which we might expect to find optimal $R - Q$, as shown in Figure 17–9.

Based on the first output matrix for $\overline{C}$, optimal R and Q are 400 and 300 units, respectively. This policy would cost a total of \$233.20 per day, on the average. At this point, we can be reasonably certain that the "universal" minimum $\overline{C}$ has been "bracketed," rather than some "local" optimum. This is because 233.20 is "well-embedded" in the matrix. That is, if you were to conceptualize the first cost matrix as a topographical map with "ridges" outlining a "valley," you can see that 233.20 is on the valley floor with high ridges all around the perimeter of the matrix. Right? Convince yourself that if we had specified ranges of 0–200 for R and 100–300 for Q, the minimum given by 260.66 would represent a local minimum, as suggested by its "hillside" location.

Now that we have located the approximate floor of the valley, we "zoom in" to get a better fix on optimal R and Q. The computer run continues by narrowing the ranges for R (250–550) and Q(250–350) and lowering the increments (steps) to 50 units instead of 100 units. Also note that the number of days in the simulation (n) has been increased from 1,000 to 5,000 in order to further reduce sampling error.

The results given by the second cost matrix indicate that the valley floor is fairly flat between 300 and 400 for R and 300 for Q. Thus an optimal policy is suggested by Q = 300 paired with R = 300 to 400.

FOLLOW-UP EXERCISES

22. Modify the logic of Figure 17–8 and the data in Table 17–19 if
    a. C_s is based strictly on back orders that are subsequently filled, where C_s = \$5 per unit per day.
    b. Forty percent of shortages represent lost sales and 60 percent back orders, where C_s for lost sales is \$5 per unit and C_s for backorders is \$2 per unit per day.
    c. The mix of lost sales and back orders when units are short is probabilistic as shown:

Percent of Shortages Going to		
Lost Sales	**Back Orders**	**Probability**
30%	70%	0.6
40	60	0.3
50	50	0.1

    Assume costs as in part *b.* (*Hint:* You need a third random number generator. Use column 10 of Table 17–10. *Note*: When back orders are outstanding, the receipt of a shipment first satisfies back orders; hence, track must be kept of outstanding back orders.)
23. Find $\overline{C}$ for the simulation in Table 17–19 if
    a. C_s = \$10 per unit (C_h and C_o as in the example).
    b. C_o = \$100 per order (C_s and C_h as in the example).
    c. C_h = \$1.50 per unit per day (C_s and C_o as in the example).
    d. Beginning inventory for Day 1 is 1,500 units.
    How sensitive is $\overline{C}$ to each of these changes?
24. Continue the use of columns 1 and 3 in Table 17–10 to extend the simulation of Table 17–19 to 40 days. Do you have more confidence in $\overline{C}$? (Check your result against the result in Figure 17–9.)
25. Appropriately modify Table 17–19 for
    a. R = 300 and Q = 700.
    b. R = 600 and Q = 400.
    Check each result against the corresponding cell in the matrix of Figure 17–9. Comment on the differences in $\overline{C}$ estimates.

17.7 SUMMARY/ASSESSMENT

This chapter has provided an overview of simulation. We have discussed the nature of simulation, the process of conducting a simulation study, the key issues when developing a simulation model and using it for experimentation, and several illustrations of simulation modeling. Our discussions should leave you with the impression that simulation is extremely useful as a modeling technique, particularly when examining stochastic systems that do not lend themselves easily to analytical modeling techniques. We discussed the advantages, as well as the limitations, of using this technique.

To provide additional insight about the status of simulation, we are going to end this chapter with some results from a study of nonacademic users of simulation.[10] Christy and Watson conducted their survey to determine the level of industrial interest and use of simulation. Some of their conclusions follow:

1. **There is a high level of simulation use in industry.** Of the firms responding, 89 percent currently use simulation.
2. **Simulation applications occur in almost all functional areas.** The most frequently mentioned areas were production (59 percent), corporate planning (53 percent), engineering (46 percent), finance (41 percent), and research and development (37 percent).
3. **The development of simulation models occurs both centrally and decentrally within organizations.** Of respondents 54 percent indicated that simulation activities occurred within functional area departments; 44 percent, in centralized MS/OR departments; and 30 percent, within corporate planning departments.
4. **Even though special-purpose simulation languages, and more recently financial planning languages, have become available, there is a reluctance to change from familiar general purpose languages.** Of those responding, 27 percent were unwilling to learn a new language and 52 percent said they would learn a new language only if the application clearly called for its use. FORTRAN was the leading language, used (but not necessarily exclusively) within 81 percent of respondent organizations. GPSS was the next most frequently used language, with 40 percent. Financial planning models seem to be gaining in popularity (35 percent).
5. **The climate for acceptance of simulation is generally favorable.** In terms of implementation problems, the largest percentage of respondents (40 percent) indicated that insufficient knowledge of quantitative methods on the part of top and middle management is a factor. The lack of good data and insufficient time to conduct a study were mentioned by 25 percent and 29 percent, respectively.

---

[10]For further details, see David P. Christy and Hugh J. Watson, "The Application of Simulation: A Survey of Industry Practice," *Interfaces*, October 1983, pp. 47–52.

SELECTED APPLICATION REVIEW

DECISION SUPPORT SYSTEMS: PRODUCTION PLANNING AT INTELSAT

INTELSAT provides satellite communication services to 112 countries that are members of this cooperative commercial venture. The INTELSAT communication satellite system handles virtually all of the world's live international television transmissions and approximately two thirds of all international telephone, telex, and other message services. Fifteen satellites and several hundred earth stations are part of the communications network. One of the major planning needs is the design and production of new and more sophisticated satellites to replace old satellites and to meet the growing and changing demand for communication services. With satellites costing between \$30 million and \$100 million, the objectives are to keep costs contained while providing high assurances that future communications requirements are satisfied.

A planning and decision support system (PDSS) was developed to provide assistance in deciding the number of satellites to purchase and the timing of these purchases. Significant factors needed to be considered include the length of time necessary to manufacture a satellite, the uncertainty of future costs, the uncertainty of communications demand, the likelihood of satellite failure, and the multiple, and sometimes conflicting, objectives that exist in this decision process.

The heart of the PDSS is the simulation of a large Markov decision process. The FORTRAN V, Monte Carlo simulation model allows for the evaluation of a variety of purchase strategies, some of which are generated by experts or heuristic methods, and those generated by the Markov model. At the time of the reporting of this application, INTELSAT was using the PDSS as an analytic adjunct to the overall decision-making process.

Logo reproduced courtesy of International Telecommunications Satellite Organization.

SOURCE: William T. Scherer and Chelsea C. White III, "A Planning and Decision-Aiding Procedure for Purchasing and Launching Spacecraft," *Interfaces*, May–June 1986, pp. 31–40

The Canadian National Railway is one of the most successful railways in the world. Owned by the Canadian government, CN Rail has a system consisting of approximately 33,000 miles of track that serves all provinces in Canada. In the late 1970's a major strategic planning effort was undertaken to make recommendations regarding capital expansion, given projections of a doubling of traffic volumes over the next decade. Simulation models were developed to analyze the effects of various factors on the capacity of the railway. These models resulted in proposals for a capital expansion program that would allow the railway to handle increased traffic volumes over the next decade. The proposed program resulted in the deferral of more than C$350 million in capital expenditures, compared with original cost estimates.

SOURCE: The Franz Edelman award-winning paper by Norma Welch and James Gussow, "Expansion of Canadian National Railways's Line Capacity," *Interfaces*, January–February 1986, pp. 51–64.

The Burger King Corporation has had considerable success due to operations research activities. One of the first applications (in the late 1970s) determined the type of meat to buy and the supplier to purchase from so as to provide the desired quality of hamburger at minimum cost. The recommendation resulted in a savings of $0.0075 per pound (which when multiplied times the 3 million pounds used per week *used at that time*, represented a weekly savings of approximately $22,000).

Burger King has also had great success with simulation models. A general-purpose restaurant simulation model has been used extensively to improve the productivity of company-owned as well as franchised restaurants. Able to model almost all aspects of the operation of a restaurant, the simulation studies have resulted in diagnostic and prescriptive tools that can be used by managers of existing restaurants. These tools assist managers in identifying potential problem areas in the operation of the restaurant, offer alternative ways of remedying the problems, and project the return on investment from implementing "productivity upgrades." The model can be applied to new restaurants by evaluating new location market potential and the sizing of restaurants (sales and service capacity) to match the needs of a particular location.

SOURCE: William Swart and Luca Donno, "Simulation Modeling Improves Operations, Planning, and Productivity of Fast Food Restaurants," *Interfaces*, December 1981, pp. 35–48.

Blue Bell, Inc. is one of the world's largest apparel manufacturers, with fiscal year 1983 yielding $1.2 billion. Its three major lines of apparel are Wrangler denim and corduroy lines, Red Kap durable garments for on-the-job, and Jantzen sports and casual apparel. In 1982 management became concerned about the high level of investment in working capital. Reduction in inventories seemed the most opportune way to reduce working capital. However, the planning of such a reduction would be complicated by the facts that lead times on orders from retailers were decreasing, and competition required that Blue Bell provide high levels of service for its customers.

Within 21 months Blue Bell reduced its inventory by more than 31 percent, from $371 million to $256 million. The reduction occurred with no decline in sales nor any deterioration in levels of service. Although the management science effort involved the use of several modeling techniques, a simulation model was key to diagnosing the problem, and it convinced senior management that a significant opportunity existed by way of reducing inventory levels. Top management's support for the management science effort is one of the unique aspects of this application.

Logo reproduced courtesy of Blue Bell.

SOURCE: Jerry R. Edwards, Harvey M. Wagner, and William P. Wood, "Blue Bell Trims Its Inventory," *Interfaces,* January–February 1985, pp. 34–52.

Simulation versus Analysis in Waiting Line Problems

MARVIN ROTHSTEIN

University of Connecticut

A recent paper by Paul and Stevens [4] in the Tutorial and Survey Section of *Decision Sciences* presents an application of waiting line concepts in staffing service activities. A retail department store is used as an illustration. The authors' well-planned approach to the problem, with its careful consideration of performance standards and scheduling, is commendable. So too is their methodology, involving the gathering of empirical data and the formulation of a model, *up to the point of solving the waiting line problem*. Here, however, the authors appear to have ignored a mathematical solution which is not only more general, instructive, and economical than the simulation approach they adopted, but would have kept them from presenting anomalous conclusions.

The department store problem was formulated as a first-in-line-first-served waiting line model with Poisson arrivals, multiple servers in parallel, exponential service times, and infinite system capacity. The objective was to determine the average customer waiting time and service personnel utilization for given numbers of servers. This was accomplished by running four simulations of the model, in which the average customer arrival rate (one every 3 minutes) and the average service time (9.18 minutes) were held fixed while the number of servers was varied from three to six. In each case 1,000 transactions were simulated, presumably to obtain estimates of system performance in the steady state. The simulation results were then used to demonstrate a method for optimal staffing.

In our opinion the article [4] lacks something essential for never mentioning that complete analytic results exist for this model, based upon queuing theory. It is instructive to review the relevant steady-state formulas. Let

λ = The customer arrival rate
μ = The reciprocal of the average service time
s = The number of servers

Then the average percent utilization of the servers is

$$\rho = \frac{\lambda}{s\mu} \tag{1}$$

The average waiting line length is

$$L_q = \frac{\rho(s\rho)^s}{s!\,(1-\rho)^2} P_0 \tag{2}$$

where P_0 is the probability that no customers at all are in the system and is given by the formula

$$P_0 = \left(\sum_{i=0}^{s-1} \frac{(s\rho)^i}{i!} + \frac{(s\rho)^s}{s!\,(1-\rho)} \right)^{-1} \tag{3}$$

The average waiting time in line exclusive of service is

$$W_q = \frac{L_q}{\lambda} \tag{4}$$

and the average waiting time for customers who are delayed in line is

$$W_q(>0) = \frac{W_q}{P(>0)} \tag{5}$$

where $P(>0)$ is the probability that a customer will wait at all for service to begin and is given by

$$P(>0) = \frac{(s\rho)^s}{s!\,(1-\rho)} P_0 \tag{6}$$

These formulas may be found in any standard reference work on queuing theory, for example [1, p. 307], [5, p. 865], [2, p. 231]. Computations are feasible with a desk calculator or a simple time-sharing program, and they certainly would not entail the "considerable degree of technical expertise" required, according to Paul and Stevens [4, p. 213] to program the simulation model. In fact Lee [2, p. 239] presents charts for Formulas 6 and 2 which

(*continued*)

virtually eliminate computation entirely. Other versions of such charts were published by Molina [3] as far back as 1927.

Table 1 compares the exact results we obtained from Formulas 1–6 with the approximations obtained by the Paul–Stevens computer simulations, for $s = 4, 5, 6$. The results apparently agree reasonably well except that the simulation estimates for the average waiting times and line lengths are always a little too low.* Observe that we have presented no theoretic results to match the case $s = 3$. The reason is that this case is *fundamentally different* from the other three cases, a circumstance not evident from the simulation results. When $s = 3$, it follows from Formula 1 that $\rho > 1$. Under this condition the system never reaches a steady state and the waiting line and waiting time durations tend to increase without limit over time [2, p. 27]. Even without delving too deeply into the theory the reader may appreciate this because of the factors in the denominators of Formulas 2, 3, and 6 which approach zero as ρ tends to unity.

Now there is something unexpected in the table of simulation results presented by Paul and Stevens [4, p. 217]. It appears that the system performance *deteriorates* as the number of servers increases from three to four, since the average waiting time for customers delayed in line *increases* from 6.77 minutes to 8.37 minutes as an additional server is added! The answer to this anomaly is that the simulation never arrived at a steady state for $s = 3$. Thus the outputs presented by Paul and Stevens for that case are not comparable with those obtained from their other runs and are, in fact, rather meaningless. An inkling of what was taking place might have been gleaned from the waiting *line* statistics they presented for $s = 3$. These show that during the simulation the waiting line averaged 22.57 customers and reached an unrealistic high point of 87. When the number of servers simulated was increased to four, their figures indicate that the average line length dropped dramatically to 1.60.

No inference should be drawn from these comments that our intention is to detract from the importance of simulation as a tool in the solution of waiting line problems. Examples of simulation applied in this way abound in the literature (e.g., a number of instructive case histories are to be found in [2, chap. 12 and 15]). Major points often made regarding these applications are that simulation can be used readily where attempts at analysis have been unsuccessful, that simulation is not tied to restrictive assumptions about the probability distributions of the model, and that simulation is more easily under-

* This may be the result of bias in the generation of the exponential interarrival times and service times by the simulation program. Our experience with the various versions of GPSS (the simulation compiler used by Paul and Stevens) indicates that the technique required in GPSS for representing the exponential distribution introduces bias.

TABLE 1 Comparison of Simulations with Theory

	4 Servers		5 Servers		6 Servers	
$\lambda = .3333$, $\mu = (9.18)^{-1}$	Sim.	Theory	Sim.	Theory	Sim.	Theory
Average percent utilization of service personnel	77.97	76.49	59.70	61.19	49.43	50.99
Average waiting line length	1.60	1.74	.37	.40	.09	.11
Average waiting time in line	4.65	5.22	1.10	1.19	.26	.33
Percent of customers not delayed in line	44.4	46.5	74.4	74.8	89.5	89.3
Average waiting time of customers delayed in line	8.37	9.76	4.31	4.73	2.49	3.12

(*continued*)

stood than queuing theory by individuals with a limited mathematical background. On the other hand theoretical analysis, if it can be applied, has the advantages of greater generality, economy, and insight. The formulas give results which are valid for *all* values of the parameters within some specified range, and it is unnecessary to consume a large amount of computer time to obtain answers applicable only to one set of numerical parameter values. Moreover, the general behavior of the system often may be deduced by considering limiting values of the parameters in the analytic expressions, as we have seen. These advantages make it highly desirable to search for a reasonable analytic solution before rushing off to simulate. Sometimes the two approaches can be combined. In any event, a tremendous wealth of theoretical queuing models and results have been developed over the years, and some patient research in the literature can often yield considerable practical benefits.

REFERENCES

1. Hillier, F. S., and G. I. Lieberman, *Introduction to Operations Research*. San Francisco: Holden-Day, 1967.
2. Lee, A. M. *Applied Queuing Theory*. London: Macmillan, 1966.
3. Molina, E. C. "Application of the Theory of Probability to Telephone Trunking Problems." *Bell System Technical Journal* 6 (July 1927).
4. Paul, R. J., and R. E. Stevens. "Staffing Service Activities with Waiting Line Models." *Decision Sciences* 2, no. 2 (April 1971).
5. Wagner, H. M. *Principles of Operations Research*. Englewood Cliffs, N.J.: Prentice-Hall, 1969.

M. Rothstein, "Simulation Versus Analysis in Waiting Line Problems." *Decision Sciences* 3, no. 2 (1972), p. 137–41. Reprinted with permission. *Decision Sciences* journal is published by the Decision Sciences Institute (formerly the Institute for Decision Sciences).

SELECTED REFERENCES

Banks, Jerry, and John S. Carson II. *Discrete-Event System Simulation*. Englewood Cliffs, N.J.: Prentice-Hall, 1984.

Bobillier, P. A.; B.C. Kahan; and A. R. Probst, *Simulation with GPSS and GPSS V*. Englewood Cliffs, N.J.: Prentice-Hall, 1976.

Carlson, J. G. H., and M. J. Misshauk. *Introduction to Gaming; Management Decision Simulations*. New York: John Wiley & Sons, 1972.

Dutton, J. M. and W. H. Starbuck. *Computer Simulation of Human Behavior*. New York: John Wiley & Sons, 1971.

Emshoff, J. R., and R. L. Sisson. *Design and Use of Computer Simulation Models*. London: Macmillan, 1970.

Forrester, J. W. *Industrial Dynamics*. Cambridge, Mass.: MIT Press, 1961.

________. *Urban Dynamics*. Cambridge, Mass. MIT Press, 1969.

________. *World Dynamics*. Cambridge, Mass.: MIT Press, 1971.

Gordon, G. *System Simulation*. Englewood Cliffs, N.J.: Prentice-Hall, 1969.

________. *The Application of GPSS V to Discrete System Simulation*. Englewood Cliffs, N.J.: Prentice-Hall, 1975.

Law, Averill M., and David W. Kelton. *Simulation Modeling and Analysis*. New York: McGraw-Hill, 1982.

McMillan, C., and R. F. Gonzalez. *Systems Analysis*. Homewood, Ill.: Richard D. Irwin, 1973.

Meier, R. C.; W. T. Newell; and H. L. Pazer. *Simulation in Business and Economics*. Englewood Cliffs, N.J.: Prentice-Hall, 1969.

Mize, J. H., and J. G. Cox. *Essentials of Simulation*. Englewood Cliffs, N.J.: Prentice-Hall, 1968.

Modianos, Doan, "Random Number Generation on Microcomputers," *Interfaces*, July–August 1984, pp. 81–87.

Naylor. T. H., J. L. Balintfy, D. S. Burdick, and K. Chu. *Computer Simulation Techniques*. New York: John Wiley & Sons, 1966.

Pritsker, A. Alan B., and Claude D. Pedgen. *Introduction to Simulation and SLAM*. New York: Halsted Press, 1979.

Schmidt, J. W., and R. E. Taylor. *Simulation and Analysis of Industrial Systems*. Homewood, Ill.: Richard D. Irwin, 1970.

Shannon, Robert E. *Systems Simulation: The Art and Science*. Englewood Cliffs, N.J.: Prentice-Hall, 1975.

ADDITIONAL EXERCISES

26. For Example 17.1, assume that regular and overtime costs for each of the robots are not known with certainty. Compared with the costs stated in Table 17–3, the costs per unit may fluctuate weekly according to the probability distribution in Table 17–20. Simulate 10 weeks of experience with each of the three robots. Assume the same weekly demand distribution and sample of 10 random variables as used in Example 17.1. Assign ranges of Monte Carlo numbers to the distribution in Table 17–20. Assume that 10 two-digit numbers have been selected to simulate the unit cost experience for the 10 weeks. The random numbers are (in order of appearance) 56, 42, 68, 81, 17, 49, 92, 87, 36, 05. Which robot should be selected?

TABLE 17–20 Percentage Change in Table 17–3 Unit Costs

Percent Change	Probability of Percent Change
−20%	0.05
−10	0.18
0	0.40
+ 10	0.28
+ 20	0.09

27. ***Simulation of Dependent Variables.*** For the inventory model of Section 17.6, consider the case where the random variable D, "number of units demanded per day," is determined by the random variable Y, "unit price in dollars," where Y fluctuates daily based on factors beyond the control of our firm. Thus we have a compound experiment with two statistically dependent events: First, a random variate of Y is generated for the day; next, based on the value of Y, a random variate from the appropriate distribution of D is generated.
    a. Run a 20-day simulation as in Table 17–19 given the probability distributions in Table 17–21.
    b. Can you think of an alternative procedure for generating D without first having to generate Y? (*Hint;* Determine the *marginal* distribution of D utilizing the Rules of Multiplication and Addition.) Is this approach theoretically equivalent to the approach in part *a*?

TABLE 17–21

		If Y = 5		If Y = 6		If Y = 7	
y	f(y)	d	f(d | Y = 5)	d	f(d | Y = 6)	d	f(d | Y = 7)
5	0.5	120	0.20	60	0.07	40	0.05
6	0.3	140	0.35	80	0.14	50	0.20
7	0.2	160	0.25	100	0.18	60	0.40
		180	0.10	120	0.29	70	0.25
		200	0.07	140	0.16	80	0.10
		220	0.03	160	0.11		
				180	0.05		

Note: In Table 17–10 use columns 7, 8, and 9 to generate Y, D, and T_L, respectively.

28. ***Patterned Behavior.*** As you might recall from Appendix A, the relative definition of probability requires that trials in the random experiment be as uniform as possible. This means, for example, that the probability distribution of demands exhibited in Table 17–17 must be free of identifiable irregularities and patterned behavior over time. By patterned behavior we mean the existence of trend, seasonal, and cyclical effects, or factors that can cause serial correlation.
    a. Suppose demand for the inventory problem exhibits stationary seasonal patterns by day of the week, with Monday through Friday seasonal indices of 0.8, 1.1, 0.9, 1.2, and 1.0 respectively (assuming a five-day week). Since the data in Table 17–17 have been deseasonalized, it is necessary to appropriately adjust (i.e., seasonalize) the random variate once it has been generated. For example, assuming day 1 in Table 17–19 represents Monday, we note that the demand of 80 is deseasonalized; hence, it must be seasonalized by its appropriate seasonal index to (0.8) · (80), or 64. Rework the simulation in Table 17–19 by seasonalizing each demand. Do you expect that steady-state $\overline{C}$ will be affected? Do you expect that the timing of orders will be affected?
    b. Suppose that, in addition to being seasonal, demand exhibits a simple linear trend of +5 units per day. In other words, the data in Table 17–17 have been detrended to the present by the time series model

    $$\hat{y}_t = 117.2 + 5t,$$

    where t represents the number of days from time zero. (Note that the intercept of 117.2 turns out to be the mean of the probability distribution for D. Right?) This means, for example, that Monday's ($t = 1$) generated demand of 80 must be adjusted for trend to 85 and then seasonalized to (0.8) · ((85), or 68; Tuesday's ($t = 2$) demand becomes (1.1) · [100 + (5) · (2)], or 121; Wednesday's ($t = 3$) demand becomes (0.9) · [100 + (5) · (3)], or 104; and so forth. Rerun the simulation in Table 17–19 by incorporating both trend and seasonal factors. What effect does trend have with respect to the interpretation of mean total cost ($\overline{C}$)? (*Hint:* Is steady state achievable?)
29. ***Port Facility Management.*** Consider a port with a single dock that can unload a specialized type of cargo off of a freighter. Frequency distributions based on 100 freighters are given in the Table 17–22 as determined empirically by a "hotshot" OR consultant. Freighters are unloaded on a first-come, first-served basis. Moreover, the port operates around the clock.
    a. Initialize the number of units in the system to zero, and simulate this port facility for 20 arrivals. Use columns 1 and 2 in Table 17–10, respectively, for the two probability distributions. Calculate the operating characteristics described in Exercise 14.

TABLE 17–22

Times between Arrivals of Successive Freighters (hours)	Frequency	Times to Unload Freighter (hours)	Frequency
5 but under 15	30	0 but under 12	40
15 but under 25	25	12 but under 24	25
25 but under 35	20	24 but under 36	16
35 but under 45	15	36 but under 48	9
45 but under 55	10	48 but under 60	6
		60 but under 72	4

b. Assuming that the assumptions for the standard $M/M/1$ queuing model are valid for this port facility, calculate the steady-state operating characteristics determined in part *a* by using appropriate analytic formulas from Chapter 16. Are the two sets of calculations consistent? Comment on reasons for any divergences. (*Hint:* First you must calculate mean interarrival and mean service times using Formula A.12. Then, you must determine λ and μ using Formula A.33.)

c. Initialize the simulation in part *a* to six freighters in the port facility (five waiting to be unloaded and one just starting to unload). Simulate 20 arrivals and calculate operating characteristics. Are these closer to the theoretical operating characteristics determined in part *b*? Comment. (*Note:* The first six service times must be assigned to the initial freighters in the port.)

***d*. Use appropriate statistical tests to test the null hypothesis that the probability distributions are exponential. (*Hint:* See Appendix A.) What other assumptions need to be realized for the $M/M/1$ model to hold? Of these, what assumptions are necessary for the simulation to be a valid representation of reality?

30. Construct a flowchart of the type given in Figure 17–8 for the $GI/G/1$ simulation in Section 17.5. Make sure that a variable name is assigned to each column of 17–14.

31. ***Coin Flip Game.*** Sharpie, a long-time resident of Las Vegas, has proposed a game to Orsa, the "budding" collegian who is the offspring of a prominent OR analyst (unknown to Sharpie, of course).

Sharpie: I have a game you can't refuse.

Orsa: O yeah?

Sharpie: Yeah. You flip a coin until the difference between the number of heads and the number of tails reaches three.

Orsa: What kind of bread are we talking about?

Sharpie: Well, you pay me $1 for each flip. When the games ends I pay you $8. OK?

Orsa: *(Skeptical)* Well, I'll tell you what. Give me a few minutes to interact with my computer terminal and then I'll get back to you.

Sharpie: *(Doubtful)* Well, OK.

How sharp is Sharpie? (*Hint:* Define a criterion in terms of an appropriate random variable that must be estimated and, using random numbers, simulate 10 games. You wouldn't be so crass as to use a real coin would you?) Identify some statistical issues in estimating the criterion.

32. ***Emergency Room.*** Design a simulation for the emergency room of Gotham City Hospital as described in Exercise 7 of Chapter 1 (page 15). Use five-minute *fixed time increments*. Assume one queue and the ability of the emergency room to treat 10 patients at one time. Use column 6 of Table 17–10 to simulate arrivals and column 7 to simulate

treatment times. Assume an empty emergency room at the beginning of the simulation, and simulate for one hour (12 periods). For simplicity, assume that treatment for any patient arriving during a time interval starts at the beginning of the time interval, which is the same as saying that patients arrive at the beginning of an interval. In your simulation table keep track of "number in system," "number in queue," and "number of idle servers," all defined at the *end* of a time interval.

Theoretically, what do you expect will happen in this system as time approaches infinity? How many "servers" would be needed to avert this theoretical happening? What factors in reality prevent this theoretical happening? In your simulation, indicate how you would handle 15 "servers." Will this increase in the number of servers improve operating characteristics? Explain.

33. ***Solar Energy Collection System.*** A solar energy collection system consists of four basic components: solar collection panels, thermal energy storage tank, thermal distribution system, and control system. The ability to provide the energy needs for a particular building or house is determined by the design configuration of the system (i.e., area and efficiency of collectors, quality of control system, size and efficiency of storage tank, design and efficiency of distribution system) and by uncontrollable variables, such as ambient temperatures and amount of sunlight. Meteorological data for the month of January in a particular geographical region are given in Table 17–23.

TABLE 17–23

Percent Amount of Sunlight per Day	Probability	Average Ambient Temperature per day (°F)	Probability
0	0.25	0	0.10
20	0.20	10	0.30
40	0.25	20	0.40
60	0.10	30	0.15
80	0.05	40	0.05
100	0.15		

A contractor for a large housing development is considering the installation of thermal collection systems in houses essentially similar with respect to construction and living area. Two designs are under consideration, each differing with respect to amortized cost per day of the system and cost per day of providing supplementary energy needs. This latter cost is a reality because solar energy systems may not be capable of providing 100 percent of the energy needs every day, in which case an auxiliary conventional heating system supplements the solar system. Relevant cost data are given in Table 17–24. Can you reason why weather factors in the preceding day have an effect on the current day's supplementary heating cost? How are the efficiencies of each design accounted for in the costs?

a. Estimate the average total cost per day in January for each design given that on December 31 the average temperature is 20°F and the average percent sunlight is 50 percent. (Use columns 1 and 2 of Table 17–10 for variates of S and T, respectively.) Recommendation?

***b.* Determine a 95 percent confidence interval for the average total cost of each design. (Ignore serial correlation in supplementary heating costs.) Conclusion?

34. ***Stock Market Investment Strategy.*** Adam Smith, Jr., is an up-and-coming investor. (It runs in the family.) For many trading days he has observed the closing price (per share) behavior of a particular stock that he has taken a fancy to, as depicted in Table 17–25.

TABLE 17–24

Design	Amortized Cost per Day ($)	Supplementary Heating Cost per Day* ($)
1	1.00	$\frac{30}{T_i + 0.5T_{i-1}} + \frac{20}{10 + S_i + 0.4S_{i-1}}$
2	1.50	$\frac{30}{T_i + 0.8T_{i-1}} + \frac{20}{20 + S_i + 0.7S_{i-1}}$

*$S_i \equiv$ Percent sunlight in day i; $T_i \equiv$ average °F in day i.

Adam's parents have just given him 100 shares of this very same stock, which currently closed up $1 at $20 a share. This gift, however, is not without a very specific condition: Adam must cash in his shares at the end of 30 days, as the cost realized from this sale will become his expense money for his first year in college. Needless to say, Adam is concerned with having a good (extracurricular) time his first year in college, so he has devised an investment strategy that "can't lose," as follows:

(1) Sell all shares owned at the end of a trading day whenever the price of the stock increases.

(2) Buy as many shares as cash allows whenever the price of the stock has declined at the end of a trading day.

(3) Do nothing if price remains the same.

TABLE 17–25

Price Change Any Given Day to Nearest $1	Price Change the Following Day			
	Down $1	Same	Up $1	Up $2
Down $1	0.4	0.3	0.2	0.1
Same	0.3	0.3	0.3	0.1
Up $1	0.2	0.4	0.2	0.2
Up $2	0.3	0.4	0.2	0.1

a. Simulate Adam's cash position at the end of 30 days given that 1 percent of the price of each share goes to the broker as commission whenever shares are bought or sold. Use column 6 of Table 17–10.

b. Would Adam have been better off at the end of 30 days if he had just let the shares "ride" while spending his time at the beach?

c. Can you think of other investment strategies.

35. ***Accounting Simulation.***[11] A firm wishes to predict the status of certain items in its financial structure one year from now. Specifically, it would like to know what its acid test ratio (the sum of cash plus accounts receivable divided by accounts payable), cash balance, accounts receivable, and accounts payable will be if current sales and credit patterns prevail and if current inventory and financial policies are maintained.

Merchandise is sold both for cash and on credit. Cash and credit sales vary from month to month, but these variations are not attributable to seasonal or cyclical factors. Rather, they reflect the influence of essentially chance or random forces. Analysts know that the basic factors underlying these chance variations have remained stable over the

[11]Adapted from the seminar "Monte Carlo Simulation for Financial Analysis," Executive Development Program, University of Cincinnati, 1970.

past several years and believe that they will not change significantly over the coming year. Table 17–26 shows these variations.

TABLE 17–26

Cash Sales (millions of dollars per month)	Probability	Credit Sales (millions of dollars per month)	Probability
3	0.5	6	0.1
4	0.3	7	0.2
5	0.1	8	0.4
6	0.1	9	0.2
		10	0.1

Each month, a certain percentage of the preceding month's accounts receivable (resulting entirely from credit sales) is collected. Table 17–27 shows the firm's credit payment experience over the past several years.

TABLE 17–27

Percentage of Preceding Month's Accounts Receivable Collected in Current Month	Probability
0.1	0.1
0.2	0.2
0.3	0.4
0.4	0.2
0.5	0.1

As part of its inventory policy, the firm finds it desirable to begin each month with an inventory level equal to a retail valuation of $16 million. Since inventory is obtained from outside vendors, and since the *markup* on each item is 20 percent of the selling price, the firm makes *purchases* at the end of each month that amount to 80 percent of that month's total dollar sales. These purchases are paid in full at the end of the next month. If the cash balance is not adequate for this purpose, the deficit is carried over to the next month under accounts payable and paid off then, if cash funds are sufficient. Carryovers to succeeding month's accounts payable continue as long as the cash balance remains inadequate. As a matter of policy, the firm pays cash dividends of $500,000 every third month.

At the beginning of the first month, the retail value of inventory is $16 million, the cash balance is $5 million, accounts receivable are $10 million, and accounts payable are $2 million.

a. Conduct a 12-month simulation by completing a table with the following headings: Month, Random Number for Cash Sales, Cash Sales, Random Number for Credit Sales, Credit Sales, Total Sales, Random Number for Percentage of Preceding Month's Accounts Receivable Collected, Percentage of Preceding Month's Accounts Receivable Collected, Preceding Month's Accounts Receivable Collected, Total Cash Inflow, Purchases, Dividends, Total Cash Outflow, Beginning Cash Balance, Ending Cash Balance, Accounts Receivable, Accounts Payable, Acid Test Ratio. (Use columns 8, 9, and 10 of Table 17–10, respectively, to generate the three random number sequences.)

b. What happens to the financial structure if the inventory policy is changed to beginning inventories of $12 million? (*Note:* If total sales for a month exceed beginning inventory, then assume that the difference is lost to credit sales.)

c. What happens to the financial structure if the markup is changed to 30 percent? (What else must you assume?)

d. Do you have statistical confidence in your estimates? Explain.

APPENDIX 17A
Process Generation of Exponential and Poisson Random Variates

In this appendix we illustrate methods of generating random variates from exponential and Poisson processes. The general approach typifies the treatment of process generation for many other theoretical probability distributions. We repeat that computer subroutines are widely available for process generation of standard probability distributions.

If X is an exponential random variable with parameter λ, then its pdf is given by

$$f(x) = \lambda e^{-\lambda x}, \qquad x \geq 0. \tag{1}$$

Its CDF, therefore, is given by

$$\begin{aligned} F(x) &= P(X \leq x) \\ &= \int_0^x f(x)\,dx \\ &= \int_0^x \lambda e^{-\lambda x}\,dx \\ &= -e^{-\lambda x}\Big|_0^x \\ &= 1 - e^{-\lambda x}. \end{aligned} \tag{2}$$

Letting $F(x) = u$, where u is a random variate in the interval 0–1, and noting that we wish to express x as a function of u when using the ITM, then from Equation 2:

$$\begin{aligned} u &= 1 - e^{-\lambda x} \\ e^{-\lambda x} &= 1 - u \\ -\lambda x \ell n e &= \ell n(1 - u) \\ x &= \frac{-\ell n(1 - u)}{\lambda}. \end{aligned} \tag{3}$$

Note that the right-hand–side expression in Equation 3 represents $F^{-1}(u)$. Thus given the ability to generate uniformly distributed random variates in the interval 0–1 as represented by u, exponential random variates of X are easily determined using 3.

If X is Poisson with parameter λ, it can be proved that the continuum (e.g., time) between any two Poisson occurrences is exponential with the same parameter λ. For example, if the number of arrivals per unit time (X) in a queuing process is Poisson with mean λ, the time between successive arrivals (S) is exponential with mean $1/\lambda$ (or parameter λ). Now, if x Poisson arrivals occur over some arbitrary number of unit time intervals (t), the sum of times between the x arrivals *must be* less than t. If s_i represents the time between arrivals $i - 1$ and i, the following must be true:

$$\sum_{i-1}^{x} s_i \leq t < \sum_{i=1}^{x+1} s_i \,. \tag{4}$$

Thus Poisson random variates (x) with parameter λ can be generated by summing exponential random variates (s_i) until (4) is satisfied. Note that s_i is based on 3; that is,

$$s_i = \frac{-\ell n(1 - u_i)}{\lambda}$$

where u_i is the ith 0–1 uniform random variate.

FOLLOW-UP EXERCISES

36. Is

$$F^{-1}(u) = \frac{-\ell nu}{\lambda}$$

as valid as Equation 3 for generating exponential random variates? Why or why not?

37. Using the u's in Table 17–9, determine x for the 10–11 period if X is Poisson with $\lambda = 2.1$ patients per hour (as in Table A–1 or Example 16.1) and $t = 1$. What if $t = 2$?

38. Suppose that the random variable X represents the time to service an emergency room patient, as in Examples A.3 and 16.1. Given that X is exponential with parameter $\lambda = 2.5$ patients per hour, simulate the times required to treat five patients using the first five random numbers in column 3 of Table 17–10.

39. Carry out the simulation in part *a* of Exercise 29 by assuming that interarrival times and service times are exponential with parameters $\lambda = 0.04$ and $\mu = 0.0468$, respectively. How is this procedure advantageous over the procedure in Exercise 29?

40. Determine $F^{-1}(u)$ if X is uniform in the interval a–b.

18

Management Science in Perspective

Chapter Outline

This chapter begins with a review of the basic nature of management science as an approach to solving problems, then reiterates our philosophy about the role of management science in the decision-making process. Throughout the text we have offered evidence of the applicability of the management science approach. Section 18.2 takes one last look at the implementation of this approach. Another theme woven into the book is that of decision support systems. Section 18.3 reexamines the relationship between decision support systems and management science. We also take a brief look at artificial intelligence and expert systems, which represent the next generation of resources aimed at assisting managers with problem solving and decision making.

18.1 MANAGEMENT SCIENCE, PROBLEM SOLVING, AND DECISION MAKING

Creative Problem Solving

In his delightful book on the art of problem solving, Russell Ackoff provides an excellent and nonquantitative description of the management science approach to a variety of societal problems.[1] One introductory puzzle mentioned by Ackoff illustrates the process of creative problem solving and highlights the importance of specifying assumptions. Recall that one of the merits of the management science approach is the explicit recognition of assumptions. In the puzzle suppose that you have a piece of paper containing nine dots as shown in Figure 18–1. Place a pen or pencil on one of the dots and then draw four straight lines without lifting the pen or pencil from the paper so that all nine dots are covered by the lines.

FIGURE 18–1

• • •
• • •
• • •

No, we are not going to supply the answer; however, we encourage you to challenge any unnecessary assumptions you may be making. Reread the problem and be sure that you are not putting any more constraints on yourself than specified by the problem.

The creative and systematic thinking that goes into solving the dot-covering problem is the same thinking that goes with the management science approach. Wall Street's financial institutions were challenged into creative problem solving when the Federal Reserve Board decided to concentrate on controlling the money supply rather than interest rates in late 1979. Interest rate gyrations in the early 1980s created enormous problems for financial institutions that had operated for years in a stable interest rate environment.

A particular dilemma was presented by the bond management problem. In order to cope with the new dynamic environment and associated complexity, financial institutions hired mathematicians, physicists, and management scientists.[2] Termed *rocket*

[1]Russell L. Ackoff, *The Art of Problem Solving*. (New York: John Wiley & Sons, 1978).

[2]"Rocket Scientists Are Revolutionizing Wall Street," *Business Week*, April 21, 1986, pp. 52–54.

scientists, these individuals possessed the technical skills as well as the creativity necessary to solve the problems. For example, knowing how to take a derivative is the only way to understand the meaning of the duration of a bond portfolio or to understand that duration is a measure of the sensitivity of the price of a bond to changes in interest rates.

As a result of the rocket scientist successes, many financial institutions are sending their top management to university seminars to understand what duration, convexity, and mathematical programming have to do with earning a profit and avoiding losses. In addition, significant career opportunities have opened up for Wall Street's new group of problem solvers. Aside from filling staff positions, bond houses have begun promoting these individuals, creating a new breed of financial managers.

In a less quantitative vein, we have observed a U.S. tire manufacturer using the management science approach in dealing with its marketing-distribution system. The problem for the company was how to hold on to the original equipment market (OEM). An automobile lasts an average of 120,000 miles in the United States. At the time the company faced the problem, tires were lasting an average of 20,000 miles. That meant one OE set of tires and five sets of replacement tires. For radials, averaging 30,000 miles per tire, one could expect one set of OE tires and three replacement sets.

For obvious reasons, the marketing people were lusting over the replacement market. However, their enthusiasm was dampened because of the company's lack of an adequate distribution system. To enter the replacement market, the company would need to set up a system of dealerships and inventories across the country. The investment needed for that was intimidating, and the company was financially constrained. With that problem definition, cover the next paragraph with a sheet of paper and develop a decision based on the decision-making paradigm of Chapter 1. If you are frustrated by a lack of information, rest assured that you have enough to come up with a solution.

The company initiated a project to design a tire to run the life of the car and subsequently achieved a tire life of between 60,000 and 75,000 miles. In doing so, they demonstrated that a simple arithmetic model and a management science approach can help with the solution of real-world business problems that are not as dissimilar from the point-covering problem as one would assume.

Management Science and Decision Making

As claimed in the beginning of this book, the elements of a decision environment frequently lend themselves to quantification. The appropriate analysis of these quantitative elements can yield significant inputs for the purpose of decision making. Although we are not so self-assured as to suggest that all problems lend themselves to such analysis, we believe that many problems are amenable to quantitative analysis and that such analysis holds the potential for more effective decision making.

When a problem is conducive to quantitative analysis, the results and recommendations of such analysis should be viewed as *one* of possibly many inputs to the ultimate decision maker(s). Along with the quantitatively based input(s), there may be subjective as well as experientially based inputs. In some cases the quantitative input may be significant; in other cases it may not be. From the perspective of the decision maker, the most important point is his or her ability to evaluate this input (as well as all others) and to utilize the inputs to make an effective decision.

Many readers of this text are managers or will become managers. You may be faced with evaluating quantitatively based decision inputs. Our hope is that having studied the material in this book, you will be in a better position to evaluate these inputs and to be a more effective decision maker.

18.2 IMPLEMENTATION OF MANAGEMENT SCIENCE

Throughout this book we have tried to convey the extent to which management science/operations research has been applied. Table 1–1 provided a partial listing of areas of application. Our chapter examples, as well as the annotated applications at the end of chapters, have also indicated the diversity of applications. Several studies have been conducted over the years to document the extent to which MS/OR has been implemented within organizations. One of the more recently reported studies of corporate utilization was conducted by Guisseppi A. Forgionne.[3] Surveys were sent to a random sample of firms selected from among the 1,500 largest (dollar sales) American-operated corporations listed in the *EIS* (Economic Information Systems) *Directory*. Among the issues addressed by the study, one related to the *areas* of application of MS/OR studies. Table 18–1 reflects the frequencies with which organizations have applied MS/OR to different problem areas.

TABLE 18–1 Areas of Application of MS/OR Techniques

	Frequency of Application (% of Respondents)		
Area	**Never**	**Moderate**	**Frequent**
Project planning	33.9	45.2	21.0
Capital budgeting	40.3	41.9	17.7
Production planning	43.5	27.4	29.0
Inventory analysis	48.4	30.6	21.0
Accounting	50.0	33.9	16.1
Marketing planning	53.2	35.5	11.3
Quality control	58.1	25.8	16.1
Plant location	59.7	35.5	4.8
Maintenance Policy	61.3	30.6	8.1
Personnel management	67.7	25.8	6.5

The Forgionne study concluded that MS/OR activities are being conducted by a large percentage of corporate organizations and are being applied to a wide range of problems. Other studies that have examined the implementation of MS/OR within organizations are referenced at the end of the chapter.

Utilization of Modeling Techniques

We have discussed a wide variety of modeling techniques and have tried to give a sense of their relevance in problem analysis. The Forgionne study examined this is-

[3]Guisseppi A. Forgionne, "Corporate Management Science Activities: An Update," *Interfaces*, June 1983, pp. 20–23.

sue by surveying the extent to which different techniques have been used. Table 18–2 presents the results. Shown is the relative use of the different modeling techniques within corresponding corporations. As can be seen, statistical analysis, simulation, PERT/CPM, and linear programming were the most frequently used methods.

TABLE 18–2 Use of MS/OR Modeling Techinques

	Frequency of Use (percent of respondents)		
Modeling Technique	**Never**	**Moderate**	**Frequent**
Statistical analysis	1.6	38.7	59.7
Computer simulation	12.9	53.2	33.9
PERT/CPM	25.8	53.2	21.0
Linear programming	25.8	59.7	14.5
Queuing theory	40.3	50.0	9.7
Nonlinear programming	53.2	38.7	8.1
Dynamic programming	61.3	33.9	4.8
Game theory	69.4	27.4	3.2

Although Table 18–2 shows separate techniques, many applications involve the use of multiple modeling techniques. A good example of this is the research that resulted in the development of a national water management policy for the Netherlands.[4] The paper reporting on this application won the 1984 CPMS/TIMS Management Science Achievement Award. The research project resulted in the development of an integrated set of 50 models designed to evaluate different policies including mixes of new facilities, operating rules for improving water supply, and price adjustment and regulatory strategies to reduce new demand for water. Included among the 50 models were 12 simulation models, 6 mathematical programming models, 2 heuristic optimization models, 11 fitted-function models (including multiple-regression and n-dimensional interpolation), 5 accounting models, and 7 miscellaneous models (including ones for data manipulation, statistical analyses, differential equations, input-output, and economic market models).

The integration of these models was a remarkable effort. The project required hundreds of person-years using state-of-the-art computer systems for implementation. The impact of the analysis included substantial changes in plans for future construction, changes in water-use regulations for industry, and recommendations aimed at international cooperation in water-use and pollution control. Tangible benefits of the project included savings of hundreds of millions of dollars in proposed investment expenditures and more than $15 million in estimated annual savings due to reduced salinity damage to agriculture.

On a smaller, yet extremely effective, scale, United Airlines developed a computerized personnel planning system that utilizes integer programming, linear programming, network optimization, forecasting, and queuing models.[5] A 1985

[4] Bruce F. Goeller and The PAWN Team. "Planning the Netherlands' Water Resources," *Interfaces*, January–February 1985, pp. 3–33.

[5] Thomas J. Holloran and Judson E. Byrn, "United Airlines Station Manpower Planning System," *Interfaces*, January–February, 1986 pp. 39–50.

award-winning application in the CPMS/TIMS competition, this system was implemented in 1983 and is used to develop work schedules for 4,000 employees working in United's reservations offices and airports. Ultimately, the system is expected to be used in scheduling 10,000 United employees (approximately 20 percent of the total work force). The scheduling system has resulted in annual savings of more than $6 million in labor costs and has received excellent reviews from the top management level as well as from affected employees.

Further Evidence of Successful Implementation

Since 1972 The Institute of Management Sciences College of the Practice of Management Science (TIMS/CPMS) has recognized excellence in the application of management science in the form of the Edelman Awards for Management Science Achievement. Kolesar has made some observations regarding the projects (more than 70) that have been recognized, offering some additional insight about the application of MS/OR.[6] First, he has observed a wide diversity in computer usage. Exemplary applications have ranged from the Netherlands' project, requiring hundreds of person-years and large, state-of-the-art computers, to a cargo loading project[7] that involved a portable microcomputer, to an inventory management application[8] that required the use of a hand-held calculator.

Another observation by Kolesar was the diversity of MS/OR models represented. Since 1974, more than 70 papers have been published in *Interfaces*. Although many linear programming applications have been included, almost every type of MS/OR model has been represented. One last observation relates to the diversity of applications represented by finalists' papers.

> *I was delighted to see the breadth represented. Among industries we can see automobile manufacturing, steel, telecommunications, electrical power generation, and distribution, fast food stores, emergency services, lumber processing, pharmaceuticals, air transportation, rail, trucking, banking, shipbuilding, and more. There are projects in long-range policy planning at the highest level of government and projects in minute-by-minute detailed operations management. It is not an exaggeration to say that there is something here for everyone.*[9]

Key Aspects of Successful Implementation

Chapter 1 discussed implementation and some of the keys to successful implementation. This is the phase where the behavioral sciences merge with MS/OR to provide greater assurances of success. We emphasized the *user-designer concept* as being fundamental to success because of participation by the ultimate decision maker. The

---

[6]Peter Kolesar, "Franz Edelman Award for Management Science Achievement," *Interfaces*, January–February 1986, pp. 1–5.

[7]Douglas D. Cochard and Kirk A. Yost, "Improving Utilization of Air Force Cargo Aircraft," *Interfaces*, January–February 1985, pp. 53–68.

[8]Donald B. Brout, "Scientific Management of Inventory on a Hand-Held Calculator," *Interfaces*, December 1981, pp. 57–69.

[9]Kolesar, p. 3.

hope is that his or her involvement will increase the likelihood of improved communication and understanding. We also discussed the essential need to prepare the organization for changes associated with implementing a solution. Inviting participation of ultimate users and/or planning a program of education are important considerations.

Several studies have examined applications to determine factors associated with successful and unsuccessful implementations. A survey by Watson and Marett was sent to 300 practitioners of MS/OR.[10] A response of 112 returned questionnaires resulted in classification of implementation problems into 10 categories, as shown in Table 18–3.

TABLE 18–3 Implementation Problems

	Implementation Problem	Percentage of Respondents
1.	Selling management science methods to management.	35
2.	Neither top nor middle management have the educational background to appreciate management science methods.	34
3.	Lack of good, clean data.	32
4.	There is never time to analyze a real problem using a sophisticated approach.	23
5.	Lack of understanding by those who need to use the results.	22
6.	Hard to define problems for applications.	19
7.	The payoff from using unsophisticated methods is insufficient.	16
8.	Shortage of personnel.	12
9.	Poor reputation of management scientists as problem solvers.	11
10.	Individuals feel threatened by management scientists and their methods.	10

Re-inforcing Table 18–3, which represents the perspective of MS/OR practitioners, a study by Green et al. surveyed vice presidents of production to determine their perceptions of the barriers to successful utilization of quantitative methods.[11] The highest rated barrier was a lack of understanding of the benefits of using quantitative techniques. The next highest factor was managers' lack of knowledge of quantitative techniques. These two studies come at the implementation issue from the perspectives of both the users and the designers. There seems to be general agreement from both groups that education of users needs attention.

18.3 THE PRESENT AND THE FUTURE

The decision support systems concept represents a new and increasingly important vehicle for assisting managers to make decisions and holds the potential for improving the quality of decision making.

[10]H. Watson and P. Marett, "A Survey of Management Science Implementation Problems," *Interfaces*, August, 1979, pp. 124–128.

[11]Thad B. Green, Walter B. Newsom, and S. Roland Jones, "A Survey of the Application of Quantitative Techniques to Production/Operations Management in Large Organizations," *Academy of Management Journal*, December 1977, pp. 669–76.

Decision Support Systems Revisited

In a world of buzzwords and acronyms, we feel obliged to delineate the bare essentials of **decision support systems (DSS),** which some feel is simply a new buzzword for management information systems. The next section tackles another popular buzzword—**expert systems.** The development of decision support and expert systems is a natural evolution of management science toward increasing intimacy with the decision maker.

A decision support system is an interactive computerized system capable of providing direct, personal support for the individual decision maker. The intent of such systems is not to replace managerial judgment, nor to automate the decision-making process. Rather, these systems are seen as best suited to assist decision makers in wrestling with unstructured problems that are less routine. Key attributes of decision support systems are their interactive features; their flexibility in allowing decision makers to modify assumptions, parameters, output requirements, and report formats; as well as their ease of use, employing English-like language commands to assist the decision maker in interacting with the computer.

A decision support system consists of *databases, model banks, software,* and *hardware*. Access to internal as well as external databases is essential. Many applications require integrating data from several databases. For a corporation, an application may require the use of several internal databases as well as external syndicated databases containing industry information. A model bank consists of a set of models that might be of use in analyzing a particular problem. Examples of the types of models included in a model bank are MS/OR models, statistical models, financial planning models, and long-range planning models. A model bank may also include *model building* capabilities to allow a decision maker to structure a model that cannot be represented by the other standard models in the model bank.

The software component of a decision support system brings the user, the databases, and the model banks together. There are different types of software in a decision support system. *Database management systems* are sets of computer programs that allow databases to be created, accessed, and updated. Other software includes the computer programs for the different models in the model bank. In addition, software is necessary to allow the user to communicate with the databases and model banks. These tend to be based more and more on natural languages that allow the user to "drive" the decision analyses and allow for appropriate interfacing with the other software in the decision support system. Operating in an online setting, the software should have good query capabilities, easy data entry facilities, flexible output formats, and (preferably) good graphics capabilities. The bottom line is that online queries of the needed databases and freedom of access to combinations of models and databases define the heart of a decision support system.

We have referred several times to **IFPS**, one type of decision support system software. IFPS consists of five subsystems: the executive subsystem, the modeling language subsystem, the report generator subsystem, the data file subsystem, and the command file subsystem. Marketed by Execucom System Corporation, IFPS was originally designed for financial and market research analysts. Evolution toward use by executives as opposed to staff researchers came as a natural consequence of the executive's desire to ask "What if . . . ?" questions and to develop more precise questions in response to feedback from the system. The focus switched to encouraging executives to analyze data themselves rather than waiting for results. IFPS, as well as other similar languages (e.g., **EXPRESS** and **NOMAD 2**) are increasingly finding their way into the executive suite.

The final component of a decision support system is hardware. Most decision support systems operate using mainframes, although more implementations will occur on minis and microcomputers as their capabilities grow. It is desirable to have hardware with graphical display capabilities, preferably in color.

Artificial Intelligence and Expert Systems

Artificial intelligence covers a very broad range of topics centering on the attempt to have a computer demonstrate intelligent behavior.[12] For example, we might want to present a computer with the dot-covering problem and have it draw the appropriate lines. Work in the artificial intelligence direction has moved in several different directions, including natural language processing. However, the current popularity of **expert systems** in business foretells potentially exciting new developments in the application of management science.

An expert system is a software package that attempts to emulate expert human performance. It is capable of limited reasoning and typically builds a knowledge base within a narrow area of application. The objective with an expert system is the achievement of high levels of performance in solving problems that require significant levels of human expertise. The intended man-machine dynamic is that a user interacts with the software in a manner similar to interacting with a human expert. An example of an area of applicability is that of medical diagnosis.

According to Assad and Golden the following characteristics are necessary for an expert system to consult like a human expert:[13]

Its performance should be comparable to the human expert in terms of reliability and accuracy of its solutions.

It should be able to justify and explain its results.

The knowledge it draws on should be easy to expand or update.

It should be able to generate multiple solutions and qualify its recommendations if necessary.

It should be able to accept the problem description in lay terms and translate it into its own representation of the problem space.

It must disregard irrelevant data.

It must be capable of checking the problem description and inputs for consistency and inaccuracies and provide the user with some measure or indication of the inconsistency.

Given a problem outside its domain of expertise, it should be able to identify it as such and decline offering a solution.

---

[12]Wendy B. Rauch-Hindin, *Artificial Intelligence in Business, Science, and Industry*, Vols. I and II (Englewood Cliffs, N.J.: Prentice-Hall, 1986).

[13]Arjang A. Assad and Bruce L. Golden, "Expert Systems, Microcomputers, and Operations Research," *Computers & Operations Research*, 13, no. 2–3 (1986), p. 303.

Even though efforts to integrate artificial intelligence and operations research have not been overly encouraging to date, many people think of expert systems as "applicable AI." These people see great promise for the applicability of expert systems in the areas of finance, accounting, and production. Although some question the ability of expert systems to interface effectively with the algorithmic discipline of operations research, others are optimistic that effective hybrids will be developed.

Are expert systems being oversold? Will they have the future impact that many believe? Only the future will tell. At this time, simple expert systems have been realized and are relatively straightforward to develop. More sophisticated "intelligent" expert systems, able to learn from their mistakes, capable of displaying simple, commonsense knowledge, and capable of dealing with conflicting information, require more powerful AI methods than currently exist.

SELECTED REFERENCES

Geoffrion, Arthur M., "An Introduction to Structured Modeling." *Management Science,* 33, no. 5 (May 1987), pp. 547–88.

Kitchener, Alan. "The Impact of Technology on the Information Systems and Operations Research Professions." *Interfaces,* May–June 1986, pp. 20–30.

Ledbetter, W., and J. F. Cox. "Are O.R. Techniques Being Used?" *Journal of Industrial Engineering,* February 1977, pp. 19–21.

Linstone, H. A. "Multiple Perspectives: Overcoming the Weaknesses of MS/OR." *Interfaces,* July–August 1985, pp. 77–85.

McDaniel, R. R., Jr., and D. P. Ashmos. "Marketing the Results of Analysis." *Interfaces,* July–August 1985, pp. 70–76.

Miller, James R., and Howard Feldman. "Management Science—Theory, Relevance, and Practice in the 1980s," *Interfaces,* October 1983, pp. 56–60.

Tilanus, C. B. "Failures and Successes of Quantitative Methods in Management." *European Journal of Operational Research* (Netherlands), February 1985, pp. 170–75.

Yadav, S. B., and A. Korukonda. "Management of Type III Error in Problem Identification." *Interfaces,* July–August 1985, pp. 55–61.

Zahedi, Fatemeh. "MS/OR Education: Meeting the New Demands on MS Education." *Interfaces,* March–April 1985, pp. 85–94.

Appendix A Review of Probability, Estimation, and Forecasting

Although probability and statistics are not usually considered fields of specialization in operations research, their concepts are utilized so extensively both by theoreticians and practitioners that it is worthwhile to review some highlights. We stress "review" and "highlights."

This appendix reviews basic probability, probability distributions, statistical inference, and forecasting. The review obviously cannot replace a two-semester statistics course; our objectives are to emphasize the use of these concepts in decision making through operations research and to lay a foundation for the chapters that directly utilize probability.

Essentially, OR's use for probability and statistics falls into two categories. First, the theory of probability plays a significant role in the derivation of all stochastic or probabilistic models. For example, probability distribution theory plays an integral part in the derivation of stochastic inventory models (Chapter 15), queuing models (Chapter 16), Markov processes (Chapter 14), and decision analysis (Chapter 13).

Second, the utilization of OR requires the estimation of parameters and uncontrollable variables—for both the deterministic models and the stochastic models. Procedures for effecting this step of data collection (step 4 of the paradigm in Chapter 1) include **sample survey methods, estimation** (including **regression analysis**) in inferential statistics, and statistical **forecasting**.

We cannot overemphasize the OR analyst's need for data collection tools. By and large the collection of viable data has not received proper emphasis from both practitioners and (especially) teachers of OR. We hope this appendix will rectify this deficiency. Why the importance? Because the most elegant OR model is only as useful as the data that drive it. (At this time, you might find it informative to reread Section 1.5.)

A.1 BASIC CONCEPTS IN PROBABILITY

Experiments and Events

A **random experiment** is a process of observation that can be repeated and that has two or more results (**outcomes** or **sample points**) affected by chance factors. A **sample space** (S) is the set of all possible outcomes in the experiment, an **event** (E_i) is a defined subset of S, and the **complement** of an event (E_i') consists of all outcomes not in E_i. Figure A–1 illustrates these concepts for an M.B.A. class of 100 students (sample points). In this case the experiment consists of selecting a student's file and observing (classifying) the attributes "entrance examination score" and "academic performance." The set E_1 consists of students whose scores on the GMAT examination were greater than 550 (60 out of 100 students). The set E_2 represents those students whose undergraduate academic grade point average is greater than 3.25 (65 out of 100 students). Note that E_1' has 40 outcomes and E_2' has 35 outcomes.

Another experiment might be defined as rolling a die and observing the face that comes up; the sample space has six outcomes, or $S = (1, 2, 3, 4, 5, 6)$. Two possible events are "the maximum value," $E_1 = (6)$, and "three or less," $E_2 = (1, 2, 3)$, as indicated in Figure A–2.

Two events are said to be **mutually exclusive** if they cannot occur simultaneously in the same experiment. E_1 and E_2 are mutually exclusive in the die experiment but

FIGURE A–1 Sample Space for M.B.A. Class

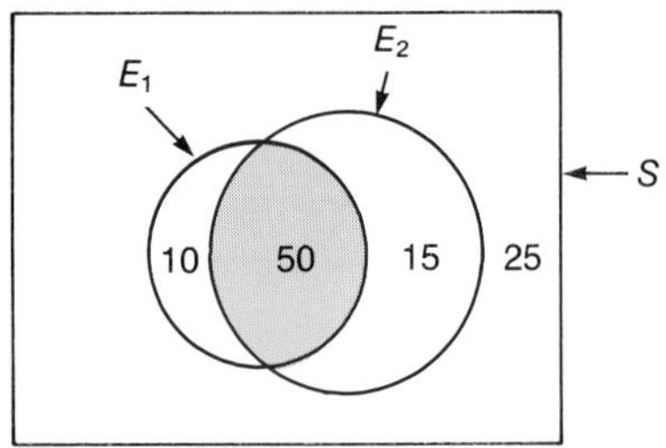

(a) Venn diagram

	E_1	E_1'
E_2	50	15
E_2'	10	25

(b) Contingency table

FIGURE A–2 Sample Spaces for Die Experiment

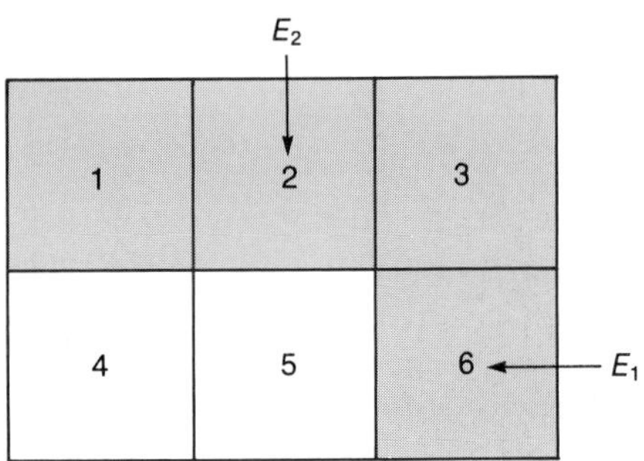

not in the M.B.A. experiment. A set of events is said to be **collectively exhaustive** if the outcomes represented by the set include all possible points in the sample space. E_1 and E_2 are not collectively exhaustive events in the die experiment because of their failure to account for the outcomes 4 and 5.

The **alternative event** (E_1 or E_2) is the event consisting of outcomes in either E_1 or E_2 or both. In set theory, the alternative event (E_1 or E_2) is represented by the *union* of E_1 and E_2. Thus (E_1 or E_2) can be represented by 75 outcomes in the M.B.A. experiment and by the outcomes $(1, 2, 3, 6)$ in the die experiment.

The **joint event** (E_1 and E_2), represented by the *intersection* between two events, consists of outcomes common to both events. Thus the joint event (E_1 and E_2) consists of 50 outcomes in the M.B.A. experiment (shaded region in Figure A–1*a*) and (E_1 and E_2) = $\varnothing$, the *null set,* in the die experiment.

A **compound random experiment** is two or more random experiments performed in succession, and its resulting event is termed a **compound event.** For example, three successive rolls of the die is a compound experiment which could result in the compound event E_1 and E_2 and E_2. Can you think of a compound experiment and event for the M.B.A. example?

Assignment of Probabilities to Single Events

The probability of an event is simply the likelihood of the occurrence of that event. When you conclude that the probability of flipping a balanced coin and obtaining the event "head" is 0.5, you really mean that on the average, over many flips of the coin, 50 percent of the flips will result in heads. Probabilities can assume values between 0 and 1, where a value of 0 implies certainty of nonoccurrence of an event and a value of 1 implies certainty of occurrence of the event.

Single events can be assigned probabilities in one of three ways: **a priori** (sometimes termed classical, predetermined, logical, or axiomatic), **empirical** (or relative frequency), and **subjective**. If the possible outcomes in E_i are known beforehand and if the outcomes in S are collectively exhaustive, mutually exclusive, and equally likely, then the probability that an event (E_i) occurs can be determined a priori as

$$P(E_i) = \frac{\text{Number of outcomes in } E_i}{\text{Number of outcomes in } S}. \tag{A.1}$$

For example, $P(E_2) = 3/6$ in the die experiment and $P(E_1) = 60/100$ if a file is selected at random from among the 100 files in the M.B.A. experiment.

If outcomes are not equally likely and/or if it is not practical or possible to draw up a collectively exhaustive list of outcomes, then an experiment can be performed n times *under identical conditions*. In this case the empirical probability of an event is defined as

$$P(E_i) = \lim_{n \to N} (f/n) \tag{A.2}$$

where f is the frequency of occurrence of E_i and where the sample size n approaches some maximum value N (which could be infinity). The probability of rolling a "1" with an unbalanced die, the probability that an American male of age 45 will live to be 55, the probability that an M.B.A. student taking the GMAT examination in 1986 scored above 600, and the probability that more than 50 units of a product will be demanded in one week are all examples of probabilities that could be estimated using the relative frequency definition. In actual practice, the critical issues are in satisfying conditions of "identical experiments" and of sufficient sample size. We will see that the sample size issue can be resolved by estimating the standard error of the sampling distribution.

The third approach to the assignment of probabilities is to use subjective opinion. Although this approach might not appear as elegant as a priori or relative frequency, for many kinds of problems it is very appropriate. This procedure allows for the translation of the experience and feelings of the decision maker into an estimate of the likelihood of occurrence of an event. This form of "educated guessing" can be effective in actual practice, for example, determining odds for sporting events and the estimation of success levels for new products by brand managers.

The probabilities for mutually exclusive alternative events can be determined by the **Rule of Addition:**

$$P(E_1 \text{ or } E_2 \text{ or } \ldots \text{ or } E_k) = \sum_{i=1}^{k} P(E_i) \tag{A.3}$$

If the events are not mutually exclusive, then the probability for two alternative events is

$$P(E_1 \text{ or } E_2) = P(E_1) + P(E_2) - P(E_1 \text{ and } E_2)\,. \tag{A.4}$$

For the M.B.A. experiment, $P(E_1 \text{ or } E_2) = 0.60 + 0.65 - 0.50 = 0.75$, and, for the die experiment, $P(E_1 \text{ or } E_2) = 1/6 + 3/6 = 2/3$ and $P(E_1' \text{ or } E_2) = 5/6 + 3/6 - 3/6 = 5/6$. Can you verify these results using a *Venn diagram* approach? (See Figure A–1*a*.)

The **marginal probability** of an event is simply the probability of the event. In the M.B.A. example, the probability of selecting a student having an undergraduate grade point average above 3.25, or $P(E_2)$, is 0.65. Note that this probability can be expressed opposite E_2 in the right-hand "margin" of the *contingency table* of Figure A–1*b*.

The **conditional probability** of E_i relative to E_j (i.e., the probability of E_i given the occurrence of E_j) is defined as

$$P(E_i \mid E_j) = \frac{P(E_j \text{ and } E_i)}{P(E_j)}\,. \tag{A.5}$$

For the M.B.A. example, given that a student has scored above 550 on the GMAT Examination, what is the probability that the student had an undergraduate grade point average above 3.25? In other words, given E_1 what is the probability of E_2? According to (A.5),

$$\begin{aligned} P(E_2 \mid E_1) &= \frac{P(E_1 \text{ and } E_2)}{P(E_1)} \\ &= \frac{0.50}{0.60} \\ &= \frac{5}{6} \\ &= 0.83\,. \end{aligned}$$

Carefully note that knowledge of E_1 has altered the probability of E_2; that is, the conditional probability is different from the marginal probability for this example.

The probability of a **joint event** for a single experiment is simply the probability that both E_1 and E_2 occur simultaneously in the same experiment; for example, $P(E_1 \text{ and } E_2) = 0.5$ in the M.B.A. example.

Assignment of Probabilities to Compound Events

Events can be classified as being either statistically **independent** or statistically **dependent**. When events are independent, the occurrence (or nonoccurrence) of any one event in no way affects the probabilities of the others. Examples of states of statistical independence include successive flips of a coin, rolls of dice, and sampling with replacement (such as drawing a card from a deck). Under statistical dependence, the probability of an event is related to or affected by the occurrence or nonoccurrence of other events. With certain types of illnesses, the probability of survival often depends on the number of days survived since contracting the disease. The likelihood of having your birthdate selected *next* in the former military draft lottery was dependent on the number of birthdates selected previously.

For a compound experiment, the probability of a joint or compound event is given by solving for the numerator in the right-hand side of A.5; that is,

$$P(E_j \text{ and } E_i) = P(E_j) \cdot P(E_i | E_j). \tag{A.6}$$

The presence of a conditional term in A.6 implies that the events E_i and E_j are dependent, or the occurrence of one event affects or alters the probability of the other event. The usual example of this dependence is sampling "without" replacement. Thus, in the M.B.A. example, removal of the file for a student having a GPA over 3.25 alters the probability that the random draw of the next file is for a student with a GPA over 3.25, unless the first file is returned before the second is drawn. If two files are removed without replacement and the first file indicates the occurrence of E_2, then the probability that the second file also yields E_2 is not $P(E_2)$ but $P(E_2$ in the second experiment $|$ E_2 in the first experiment), so according to A.6

$$P(E_2 \text{ and } E_2) = \left(\frac{65}{100}\right) \cdot \left(\frac{64}{99}\right).$$

If the events are not dependent, then (A.6) can be generalized by the **Multiplication Rule:**

$$P(E_1 \text{ and } E_2 \text{ and } \ldots \text{ and } E_k) = P(E_1) \cdot P(E_2) \cdot (\ldots) \cdot P(E_k)$$

$$= \prod_{i=1}^{k} P(E_i). \tag{A.7}$$

For example, the events in our compound die experiment of three rolls are independent so

$$P(E_1 \text{ and } E_2 \text{ and } E_2) = \left(\frac{1}{6}\right) \cdot \left(\frac{3}{6}\right) \cdot \left(\frac{3}{6}\right).$$

FOLLOW-UP EXERCISES

1. For the M.B.A. example, determine $P(E_1')$, $P(E_2)$, $P(E_2')$, $P(E_1'$ and $E_2')$, and $P(E_1'$ or $E_2')$ in a single experiment; for a compound experiment of drawing three files at random, determine the probability that all three are of students having scored below 550 in the GMAT.
2. For the die example, find the probability of (*a*) rolling four successive aces; (*b*) $P(E_1'$ or $E_2')$ in a single roll; and (*c*) $P(E_1 | E_2')$ in a single roll.

A.2 RANDOM VARIABLES AND PROBABILITY DISTRIBUTIONS

For most random experiments, interest is centered not on the individual sample points of the sample space but on some value associated with the attribute being measured. For instance, a market researcher might be interested in the probability that, out of n customers who purchase a particular type of product, p purchase brand Y; analysis of an inventory system would consider the demand per period (d) over the next n periods and the variability in that demand; and a study of emergency room operations in a hospital might center around the distribution of arrivals per unit time (a) and the distribution of times to serve patients (s). Attributes which assume numerical values based on the outcome of a random experiment, as in the examples above, are termed **random** or **stochastic variables.** In these instances, we need to be able to estimate probabilities that specific values will occur, such as the probability of selling 20 units next period. Also we are concerned with ranges such as the probability that sales next period will be between 15 and 25. We do this with probability distributions that, given some value for the random variable (x), permit the assignment of probabilities by the function $f(x)$.

Discrete Random Variables and Probability Mass Functions

If the sample space contains a countably infinite or finite number of sample points, then it is termed a **discrete sample space.** Variables defined on discrete sample spaces are identified as **discrete random variables;** that is, random variables that assume integer or discrete values. Conversely, a **continuous sample space** consists of elements that are uncountably infinite, and variables defined on them are termed **continuous random variables.** That is, for some kinds of experiments outcomes are restricted to certain values, such as 4 or 5 in rolling a die but not 4.3. For other experiments, the values, the time to run 100 yards or the diameter of a shaft, are only restricted by measurement equipment. In the illustrations above, p is discrete, d can be either discrete or continuous (e.g., units or pounds) a is discrete, and s is continuous.

▶ Example A.1 Emergency Room Arrivals

A study has been undertaken to improve the emergency room operation of a hospital. In Chapter 16 this project is treated as a waiting line or queuing model. For now, consider the collection of data pertaining to arrivals during "off-peak" hours. Assume that adjustments have been made for seasonal variations and other identifiable "noise," such as a natural disaster, a train derailment, and so forth.[1] (Can you guess why this must be done?)

[1]Raw data can be "deseasonalized" by dividing the value for each observation by its corresponding seasonal index. Methods for constructing seasonal indices are explained in textbooks on managerial, business, or economic statistics. Adjusting data for identifiable random movements can be accomplished by various ad hoc procedures; for example, if on a given day excessive arrivals at an emergency room can be traced to a local airplane disaster, then the number of victims involved in the disaster can be subtracted from the total number of arrivals on that day.

Let the discrete random variable X represent the number of arrivals per hour, x a particular value of X, $f(x)$ the probability of x arrivals per hour, and $F(x)$ the probability of x or less arrivals each hour. Table A–1 illustrates sample arrival data for 100 periods of one hour each. For the 100 periods under observation, seven or more arrivals per hour never occurred (although theoretically the sample space contains a finite number of points given by the population of the world). Carefully note that the process of data "deseasonalizing" and other "smoothing" is undertaken in order to ensure that trials in the experiment (periods) are as uniform as possible so that the relative frequency definition of probability is valid. The question of whether or not $n = 100$, is large enough will be taken up subsequently.

TABLE A–1 Distribution of Emergency Room Arrivals

x		Number of One-Hour Periods	f(x)	F(x)
0		10	0.10	0.10
1		28	0.28	0.38
2		29	0.29	0.67
3		16	0.16	0.83
4		10	0.10	0.93
5		6	0.06	0.99
6		1	0.01	1.00
	Total	100	1.00	—

The ordered pairs given by x, $f(x)$ in Table A–1 represent a **discrete probability distribution.** Thus, for example, the probability that the random variable X takes on a value of 3, that is, $P(X = 3)$, is given by $f(3) = 0.16$. For a discrete random variable, $f(x)$ is termed a **probability mass function (pmf),** a designation that becomes clear if the plotted points for the probability functions in Figure A–3 are perceived as "masses."

Notice that we use the convention of an uppercase symbol for the random variable itself (X) and a lowercase symbol for specific values that the random variable can take on (termed **random variates**).

In general, the pmf is defined as

$$f(x) = P(X = x) \tag{A.8}$$

such that the following two conditions are met:

$$0 \leq f(x_i) \leq 1, \qquad i = 1, \ldots, k \tag{A.9}$$

and

$$\sum_{i=1}^{k} f(x_i) = 1 \tag{A.10}$$

where k represents the possible number of values for the random variable. The condition given by Equation A.9 defines the acceptable probability range, and A.10 ensures that the defined events are collectively exhaustive and mutually exclusive. Note that A.10 is simply the application of (A.3).

FIGURE A–3 Plots for Example A.1

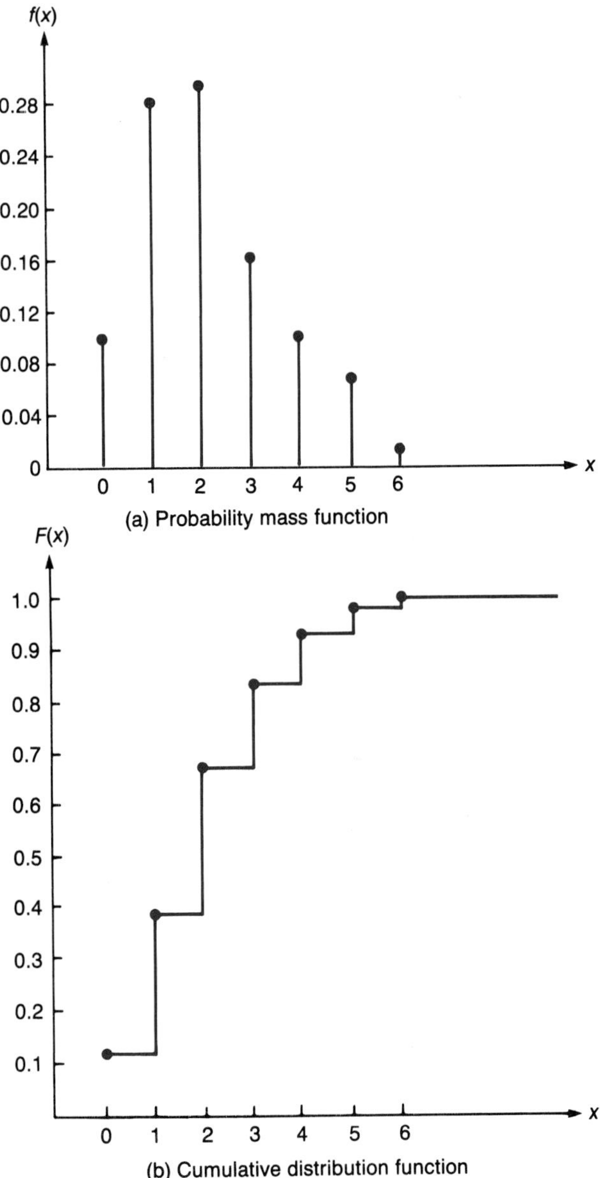

The **cumulative distribution function (CDF)** for a discrete random variable is defined as

$$F(x_i) = P(X \leq x_i)$$
$$= \sum_{j=1}^{i} f(x_j) . \qquad \text{(A.11)}$$

For Example A.1, the CDF is calculated in Table A–1 and plotted in Figure A–3*b*.

The **expected value** or **mean** for a discrete random variable is given by

$$E(X) = \sum_{i=1}^{k} x_i \cdot f(x_i), \tag{A.12}$$

and the extent of the dispersion about this mean, as measured by the **variance**, can be estimated from either

$$V(X) = \sum_{i=1}^{k} [x_i - E(X)]^2 \cdot f(x_i) \tag{A.13}$$

or

$$V(X) = \sum_{i=1}^{k} x_i^2 \cdot f(x_i) - [E(X)]^2. \tag{A.14}$$

The **standard deviation** (σ_X) is simply the square root of the variance. For example A.1, $E(X) = 2.1$, $V(X) = 1.93$, and $\sigma_X = 1.39$. The expected value indicates that during "off peak" hours there are an average of 2.1 arrivals per hour.

FOLLOW-UP EXERCISES

3. Does the pmf in Example A.1 satisfy Equations A.9 and A.10?
4. Verify the calculations for $E(X)$, $V(X)$, and σ_X in Example A.1.

Continuous Random Variables and Probability Density Functions

If X is a continuous random variable, then its probability function, $f(x)$, termed a **probability density function (pdf),** must satisfy the following two conditions:

$$f(x) \geq 0 \tag{A.15}$$

and

$$\text{Area under the function} = 1.0\,. \tag{A.16}$$

The first condition ensures nonnegative probabilities, and the second condition guarantees the property of a collectively exhaustive and mutually exclusive sample space. Note that A.15 and A.16 are analogs of A.9 and A.10.

The probability that the random variable assumes a real value in the interval a, b where $a < b$, is given by

$$P(a \leq X \leq b) = \text{Area (density) under } f(x) \text{ between } a \text{ and } b, \tag{A.17}$$

as depicted in Figure A–4a.[2] It follows that $P(X = x) = 0$ when X is a continuous random variable. (Can you reason this out logically if, say, X represents the weight of baby girls living in New York City on their second birthday?)

The CDF for a continuous random variable is given by

$$F(x) = P(X \leq x) \tag{A.18}$$

as illustrated in Figure A–4b. From A.18 it follows that A.17 can be expressed as

$$P(a \leq X \leq b) = F(b) - F(a)\,. \tag{A.19}$$

[2] As you probably know, such areas are typically determined by evaluating definite integrals.

FIGURE A–4 Probability Functions for Continuous Random Variables

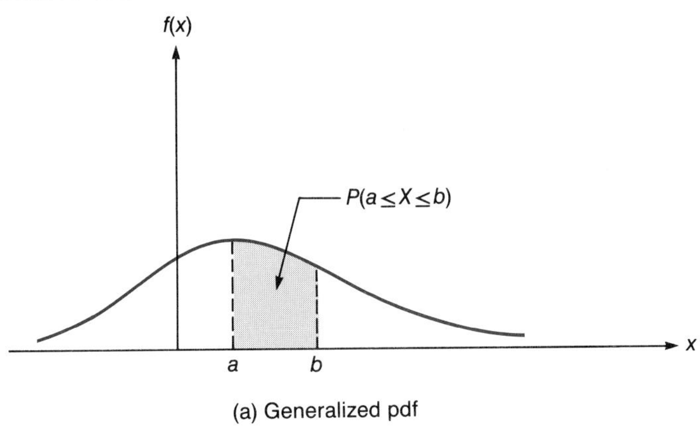

(a) Generalized pdf

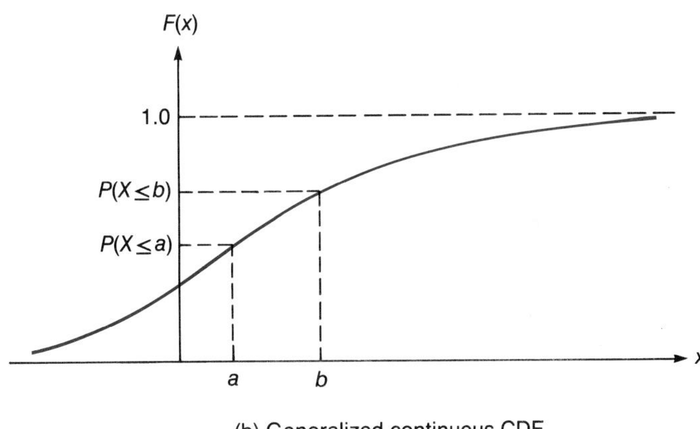

(b) Generalized continuous CDF

The expected value $E(X)$ and the variance $V(X)$ of a continuous random variable are defined in a manner similar to A.12 and A.13 by replacing the summation symbol by the integral symbol. Their values for a specific function can be determined by the methods of integral calculus.

▶ Example A.2

Suppose the random variable "air pollution index, x, in New York City" can be characterized by the following pdf:

$$f(x) = \begin{cases} \dfrac{-3}{80} + \dfrac{x}{800}, & 30 \leq x \leq 70 \\ 0, & \text{otherwise.} \end{cases}$$

The probability of an air pollution index between 40 and 50 units can be determined either by evaluating the area indicated in Figure A–5a or by integrating the definite integral of $f(x)$ using limits of 40 and 50. In either case, $P(40 \leq X \leq 50) = 3/16$. Alternatively, given the CDF in Figure A–5b and utilizing A.19, we see that $P(40 \leq X \leq 50) = F(50) - F(40) = 1/4 - 1/6 = 3/16$. The expected value and variance can be determined as 170/3 and 800/9, respectively,

FIGURE A–5 Probability Functions for Example A.2

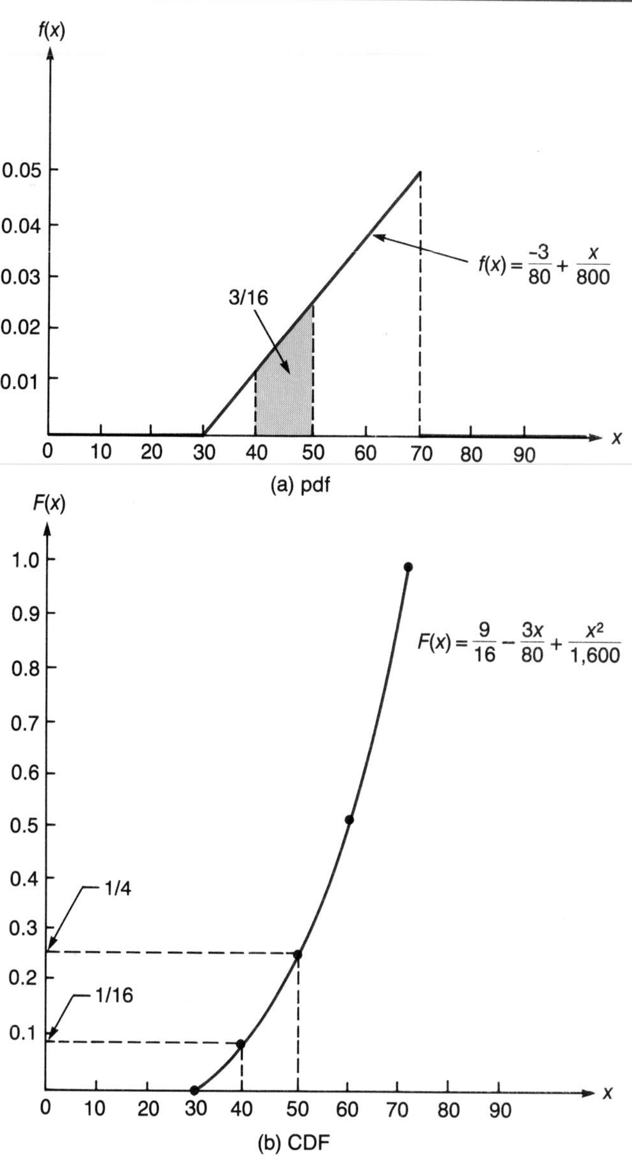

FOLLOW-UP EXERCISES[3]

5. Does the pdf in this example satisfy Equations A.15 and A.16? Can you state the distinctions between a pdf and a pmf?
6. Find $P(2 \leq X \leq 4)$ and $P(X \leq 3)$ by sketching $f(x)$ and $F(x)$ given that

$$f(x) = \begin{cases} 1/4, & 1 \leq x \leq 5 \\ 0, & \text{otherwise.} \end{cases}$$

Verify that this is a pdf.

**7. Integrate $f(x)$ for Example A.2 to verify that

$$F(x) = \frac{9}{16} - \frac{3x}{80} + \frac{x^2}{1600}.$$

**8. Verify that

$$f(x) = \begin{cases} \dfrac{1}{b-a}, & a \leq x \leq b \\ 0, & \text{otherwise} \end{cases}$$

is a pdf. Derive expressions for $F(x)$, $E(x)$, and $V(X)$. Let $a = 1$ and $b = 5$ and verify your results in this exercise using your results in Exercise 6.

**9. Determine $F(x)$, $P(X \leq 10)$, $P(4 \leq X \leq 8)$, $P(X > 12)$, $E(X)$, and $V(X)$ given that

$$f(x) = 0.1e^{-0.1x}, \qquad x \geq 0.$$

Sketch $f(x)$ and $F(x)$. (e is the base of natural logarithms.)

**10. Verify that

$$f(x) = \lambda e^{-\lambda x}, \qquad x \geq 0$$

is a pdf where e is the base of natural logarithms. Derive expressions for $F(x)$, $E(X)$, and $V(X)$. Do your results agree with Exercise 9?

A.3 SELECTED THEORETICAL PROBABILITY DISTRIBUTIONS

Both discrete and continuous probability distributions can be represented by theoretical functions of specific mathematical form. Theoretical pmfs and pdfs are useful for several reasons. First, they simplify the calculation of probabilities; second, they provide specific mathematical functions with which to "fit" empirical data; finally, they play a central role in the derivation of many stochastic models in operations research, for example, queuing, inventory, and decision theory models, among others. This section presents a review of distributions that have been especially useful.

Discrete Probability Distributions

First, a random variable X has a **binomial distribution** if its pmf is given by

$$f(x) = ({}_nC_x) \cdot (p^x) \cdot (1-p)^{n-x}, \qquad x = 0, 1, \ldots, n \tag{A.20}$$

where n is the number of *Bernoulli* trials (distinct random experiments with only two possible outcomes, "success" or "failure," per trial) performed under identical condi-

[3]Exercises preceded by two asterisks are for those who are "up" on integral calculus.

tions; p is the constant probability of success per trial; x is the total number of successes; and

$$_nC_x = \frac{n!}{(n - x)!\, x!} \tag{A.21}$$

is the number of combinations of n items taken x at a time. Note that only two parameters, n and p, completely describe this distribution.

The mean and variance for the binomial distribution are

$$E(X) = n \cdot p \tag{A.22}$$

and

$$V(X) = n \cdot p \cdot (1 - p)\,. \tag{A.23}$$

To illustrate, suppose 10 market survey questionnaires have been sent out to a "homogeneous" market segment, and past experience indicates that the probability of getting any one back is 0.2. The probability that four will be returned is

$$\begin{aligned} f(4) &= ({}_{10}C_4) \cdot (0.2)^4(0.8)^6 \\ &= 0.0881\,, \end{aligned}$$

the probability that four or more will be returned is 0.1209 (Can you verify this using a table in any statistics text?), the expected number that will be returned is 2, and the variance in the number returned is 1.6.

In OR, the binomial distribution has been useful in certain queuing models, in marketing research simulations, in the sample design related to survey data collection, and in some Bayesian decision theory models. We illustrate its usefulness in Chapter 13.

Second, a random variable X has a **Poisson distribution** if its pmf is given by

$$f(x) = \frac{(\lambda t)^x \cdot e^{-\lambda t}}{x!} \qquad x = 0, 1, 2, \ldots \tag{A.24}$$

where λ is the expected number of "successes" per unit of continuum (time, distance, area, and so forth); t is the number of continuum units; x is the number of successes over t continuum units; and e is the irrational number 2.71818 . . . (the base of natural logarithms).

Interestingly, the mean and variance are identical and given by

$$E(X) = \lambda \cdot t \tag{A.25}$$

and

$$V(X) = \lambda \cdot t\,. \tag{A.26}$$

Since both x and t must be specified in any given problem, λ is the only parameter in this distribution. This feature of the Poisson pmf makes it especially amenable to analytical use.

As an illustration, suppose that the hospital emergency room arrival data (Table A–1) are considered to be adequately represented by a Poisson distribution with mean (λ)

of two arrivals per hour. The probability of five arrivals in any three-hour off-peak period (noting that $\lambda = 2$ and $t = 3$) is

$$f(5) = \frac{(6)^5 \cdot e^{-6}}{5!}$$
$$= 0.1606\,.$$

Underlying assumptions for this model include a constant λ over the continuum and irrelevancy of the beginning point of the continuum (i.e., any three-hour off-peak period in the above example). As with the binomial distribution, tables for the Poisson distribution are readily available so that typically Equation A.24 does not have to be solved.

The Poisson distribution is extensively applied in waiting line systems (Chapter 16), has been used in estimating the demands for certain products, and can serve as an approximation to the binomial distribution if n is large (say, 100) and p is small (say, 0.1).

Continuous Probability Distributions

First, a random variable X has a **rectangular** or **uniform distribution** if

$$f(x) = \begin{cases} \dfrac{1}{b - a}, & a \leq x \leq b \\ 0, & \text{otherwise} \end{cases} \tag{A.27}$$

where a and b are specified parameters (Figure A–6a). Its CDF is given by

$$F(x) = \frac{x - a}{b - a}, \qquad a \leq x \leq b \tag{A.28}$$

and its mean and variance by

$$E(X) = \frac{b + a}{2} \tag{A.29}$$

and

$$V(X) = \frac{(b - a)^2}{12}. \tag{A.30}$$

(Is this what you got in Exercise 8?)

The primary use for the uniform distribution is the generation of uniformly distributed random numbers in the interval 0–1 for simulation, as you will see in Chapter 17.

Second, a random variable X has a **negative exponential distribution** if

$$f(x) = \lambda e^{-\lambda x}, \quad x \geq 0 \tag{A.31}$$

where λ is a specified parameter (Figure A–6b). Its CDF, mean, and variance are determined from

FIGURE A–6 Selected pdf's

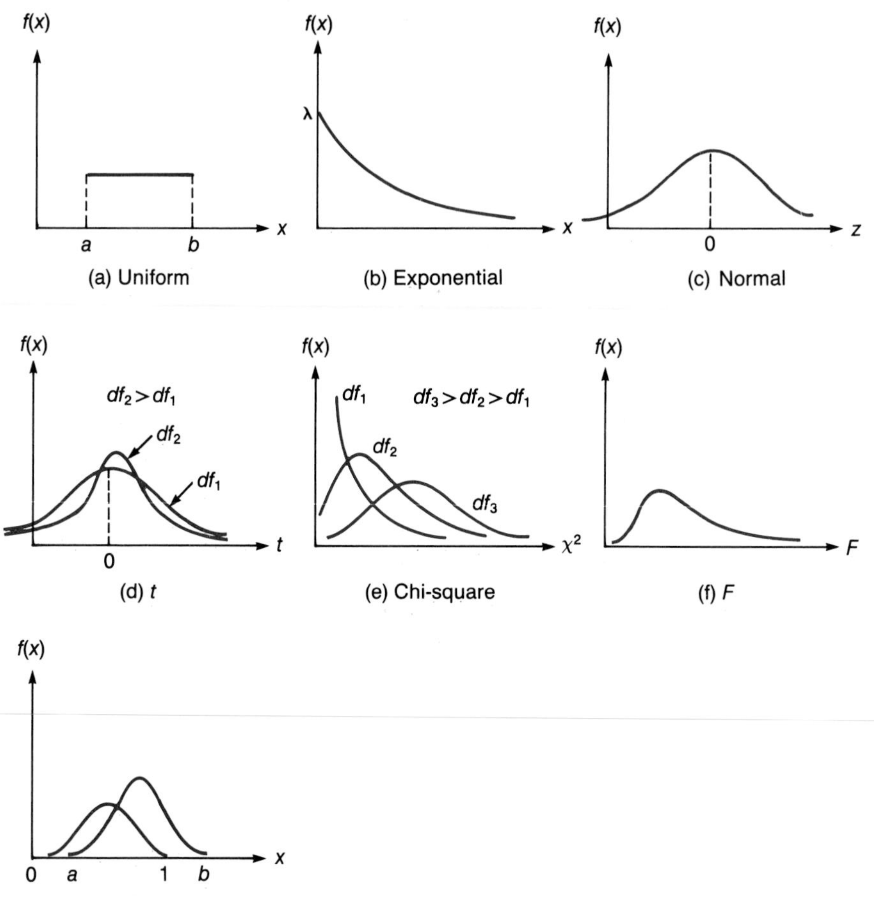

$$F(x) = 1 - e^{-\lambda x}, \qquad x \geq 0 \tag{A.32}$$

$$E(X) = 1/\lambda \tag{A.33}$$

and

$$V(X) = 1/\lambda^2. \tag{A.34}$$

(Do these agree with your results in Exercise 10?)

Interestingly, there is a unique relationship between the Poisson and exponential distributions. To illustrate, if X is the number of arrivals in a queuing system over a period of time t and it is Poisson-distributed with λ representing the average arrival rate per unit of time, then the random variable "time between successive arrivals" is distributed according to the exponential distribution with the same parameter λ. For example, if $\lambda = 2$ customers per hour, then according to A.32 the probability of an interarrival time of less than 0.5 hour is

$$F(0.5) = 1 - e^{-2(0.5)}$$
$$= 1 - \frac{1}{2.718\ldots}$$
$$= 0.6321 .$$

Further note that the mean of the exponential distribution is the inverse of the mean of the Poisson distribution, as it should be.

The exponential distribution has been exceedingly useful in queuing systems and in describing certain phenomena, such as the "life" of both telephone conversations and electronic components.

A **standardized** random variable

$$Z = \frac{X - E(X)}{\sigma_X} \tag{A.35}$$

has a **unit normal** or **Gaussian distribution** (Figure A–6c) if

$$f(z) = \frac{e^{-(1/2)z^2}}{\sqrt{2\pi}} \tag{A.36}$$

where e is as before and $\pi = 3.14\ldots$, the ratio of the circumference to the diameter of a circle. Recall that this distribution is perfectly symmetrical about its mean and that its tails approach the z-axis asymptotically.

Notice that X is also normally distributed with mean $E(X)$ and standard deviation σ_X. The standardized variable Z has a mean of zero and a standard deviation of unity. In effect, this scale change allows the application of a single normal CDF table to all normal curve problems.[4]

For those of you who are "rusty," turn to Table D.3 in Appendix D and confirm that if $x = 20$, $E(X) = 14$, and $\sigma_X = 4$, then $z = 1.5$ and

$$P(X \leq 20) = P(z \leq 1.5)$$
$$= 0.9332 .$$

The normal curve commands a central role in sampling, can be used to approximate either the binomial distribution for large n or p close to 0.5 or the Poisson distribution for large λ (say, greater than 15), has described a variety of real-world phenomena, and has been incorporated in queuing, inventory, and decision theory models.

For modeling and applications in OR, a familiarity with four other probability distributions would round out your repertoire. In the interest of avoiding "shell shock," we omit the pdf's. For greater detail, consult your statistics text. (You do have one, don't you?)

The **t distribution** is similar to the unit normal distribution in its symmetry about a mean of zero, its bell shape, and its asymptotic tails to the abscissa (Figure A–6d). Furthermore, the random variate t is calculated in the identical manner as z, that is, by Equation A.35. This distribution is central to inference based strictly on sample

[4]The CDF is tabulated because A.36 cannot be integrated.

data (see Section A.5). Its shape is a function of a parameter termed **degrees of freedom (df),** which is determined by the sample size less the number of parameters (including the parameter n or total frequency in a sample) used to calculate the statistic under investigation; that is, df is the number of independent random observations in the sample. As with the normal curve, its tabular CDF is commonplace. Find a t-table and verify that for $P(T \leq t) = 0.95$ and $df = 30$, the value of t is 1.697. Also note that for any probability in a t-table, as df approaches infinity, the t-value approaches the corresponding z-value in the normal curve table. Do you remember why?

The **chi-square** (χ^2) **distribution** (Figure A–6e) is useful primarily for testing statistical hypotheses relating to equality of variances, goodness-of-fit, frequencies, and statistical independence. As with the t distribution, its shape is strictly dependent on the degrees of freedom. In Section A.4, we illustrate its applied use for testing the fit of empirical data to theoretical probability distributions. Find a table for the chi-square distribution and verify that for $df = 3$, $P(\chi^2 \leq 7.81) = 0.95$.

The **F distribution** (Figure A–6f) as with chi-square and t, serves primarily to test statistical hypotheses. Its most common application is the analysis of variance (ANOVA). We will illustrate its use in testing the "goodness" of a regression model (Section A.6). Theoretically, the F distribution is the ratio of two chi-square distributions; hence, a degree of freedom is associated with the numerator (df_1) and another with the denominator (df_2). Interestingly, in the particular case of testing the fit of simple linear regression (i.e., the hypothesis that the population slope is zero), it turns out that $F = t^2$. Now that you are adept at finding tables, verify that $P(F \leq 4.17) = 0.95$ for $df_1 = 1$ and $df_2 = 30$.

The **Beta distribution** (Figure A–6g) is another two-parameter family of distributions that has been useful in project scheduling models (Chapter 11) and Bayesian decision theory (Chapter 13). By specific assignments of values to its parameters, it can be used to generate random numbers either uniformly or nonuniformly distributed between 0 and 1; by scale changes, other limits (a, b) can be chosen, as illustrated in the figure. Furthermore, wide latitude in the degree of symmetry or asymmetry is possible. Its cumulative distribution for $0 < x < 1$ is extensively tabulated in specialized texts as the **incomplete Beta distribution.**

FOLLOW-UP EXERCISES

11. If X is binomial with $n = 20$ and $p = 0.5$, find $P(X \leq 10)$, $P(X = 10)$, $E(X)$, and $V(X)$. Try it again for $n = 100$ and $p = 0.1$ and compare.
12. If X is Poisson with $\lambda = 5$ and $t = 2$, find $P(X \leq 10)$, $P(X = 10)$, $E(X)$, and $V(X)$. Compare your results to Exercise 11. Any conclusions? Recompute for $\lambda = 10$ and $t = 1$. Any conclusions?
13. What are the forms of $f(x)$, $F(X)$, $E(X)$, and $V(X)$ for the uniform distribution over the unit interval 0–1?
14. If X is exponential with $\lambda = 10$, find $P(X \leq 0)$, $P(X \leq 0.1)$, $P(X \leq 0.2)$, $P(X \leq 0.5)$, and $P(X \leq 1)$. Also find $E(X)$ and $V(X)$. What can you conclude about skewness?
15. If Z is normal, find z for $F(z) = 0.95$, $F(z) = 0.98$, $F(z) = 0.99$, $P(-z < Z < z) = 0.95$, $P(-z \leq Z \leq z) = 0.98$, and $P(-z \leq Z \leq z) = 0.99$. Distinguish between one-tail and two-tail probabilities.

16. If X is t-distributed, $E(X) = 14$, $\sigma_X = 4$, and $df = 10$, estimate $P(X \leq 20)$. Estimate again for $df = \infty$. Compare the latter to the sample normal calculation given in the third part of this section. Any conclusions? Compare the last row of the t-table ($df = \infty$) to its equivalent in a normal curve table. Would you conclude that $T \rightarrow$ normal Z as $df \rightarrow \infty$?

A.4 STATISTICAL INFERENCE: ESTIMATING PROBABILITY DISTRIBUTIONS

In this and the following two sections, we present some fundamental concepts regarding sampling, sample design, and statistical inference with respect to the nature of underlying probability distributions and the estimations of means. An understanding of these concepts is very important to the successful conduct of OR studies that require real data.

Sampling and Sample Design

For any study that requires data, there is a target set of objects about which information regarding some attribute is desired. This set of objects is termed the **universe** or **population**. Illustrative attributes and populations include the following; the probability distribution for "interarrival times" (attribute) for "all possible arrivals at the emergency room of a hospital" (population); the average "response velocity for a particular type of emergency vehicle" (attribute) among "all the possible responses in a given section of a city" (population); the expected "total cost of producing any given number of items over some planning horizon" (attribute) from among the "set of items of the same type that will be, could be, or would have been produced" (population).

If every item of the population is to be examined, a **census** is to be undertaken; if some subset of the population is to be examined, then a **sample** will be undertaken. **Inferential statistics** is the area of study concerned with making generalizations or inferences about some population characteristic based on the results of a sample.

The motivation for sampling is strong. In many cases, a census either is not feasible (e.g., an infinite population) or is insane (e.g., determination of the attribute requires the destruction of the object). In most cases, sampling is considerably less costly with little or no sacrifice in estimation error.

The method of selecting a sample is a field of study in itself (**sample survey methods**) requiring substantial expertise. Essentially, samples can be selected in one of two ways: **judgment samples** and **probability samples.**

In the first approach, an individual (or set of individuals) selects items "known" to be typical with respect to the desired attribute(s); in the latter approach, the selection of items is based on a plan requiring knowledge of the probability that any given item will be selected. Only for the latter can we estimate the degree of **sampling error,** which is a measure of the variability in estimating a statistic, such as the mean. Of the various methods for selecting probability samples (e.g., simple random, systematic, cluster, stratified random, and variants or combinations thereof), we will exclusively deal with **simple random sampling,** that is, where each element of the population has an equal probability of being selected.

Goodness-of-Fit Test

In this section, we illustrate the use of the chi-square distribution to test the hypothesis that an empirical distribution based on some random variable represents a sample from some theoretical distribution.

Given an empirical probability distribution with observed frequencies o_i and a theoretical probability distribution with expected frequencies e_i, both with k categories as illustrated in Table A–2, the statistic

$$s = \sum_{i=1}^{k} \frac{(o_i - e_i)^2}{e_i} \tag{A.37}$$

approaches a chi-square (χ^2) distribution with $df = k - m$ degrees of freedom as the sample size n approaches infinity (m stands for the number of parameters or restrictions that apply in the calculations). As a rule, $n \geq 50$ gives satisfactory results as long as all expected frequencies are greater than five; otherwise, additional refinements must be incorporated in the test. Note that small values for s imply "good" fits between the empirical and theoretical distributions; for example, if $o_i = e_i$ for all i, then the fit would be perfect (giving $s = 0$).

TABLE A–2 Setup for Chi-Square Test

Range of Random Variable $a_i \leq X \leq b_i$ (Category i)	Empirically Observed Frequency (o_i)	Theoretically Expected Frequency (e_i)
1	o_1	e_1
2	o_2	e_2
.	.	.
.	.	.
.	.	.
k	o_k	e_k

The idea then is to evaluate (A.37) utilizing the expected frequencies for some assumed theoretical distribution. The **null hypothesis** would state that the empirical distribution represents a sample of observations from the assumed theoretical distribution. If this were true, differences between observed and expected frequencies would be due only to sampling error and values for s would be small; on the other hand, a "surprisingly" high value for s would raise the suspicion that the empirical data are inconsistent with the assumed underlying distribution, which implies a rejection of the null hypothesis.

▶ Example A.3 Emergency Room Service

Consider the emergency room problem first introduced in Example A.1. A simple random sample of 100 cases has been selected from among a large number of case records and the attribute "time to treat a patient" was recorded as in Table A–3. As before, data have been smoothed to ensure the elimination of identifiable "noise." Furthermore, a previous statistical study showed no appreciable differences in the distribution of treatment times for various physicians.

TABLE A–3 Data and Computations for Exponential Service Distribution

Service Time per Patient in Hours ($a_i \le X < b_i$)		Observed Frequency (o_i)	For Exponential pdf with $\lambda = 2.5$: $P(X \le a_i)$ $F(a_i)$	$P(X \le b_i)$ $F(b_i)$	$P(a_i \le X \le b_i)$ $F(b_i) - F(a_i)$	Expected Frequency (e_i)	$\frac{(o_i - e_i)^2}{e_i}$
0.0	0.2	38	0.0000	0.3935	0.3935	39.35	0.05
0.2	0.4	25	0.3935	0.6321	0.2386	23.86	0.06
0.4	0.6	17	0.6321	0.7769	0.1448	14.48	0.44
0.6	0.8	9	0.7769	0.8647	0.0878	8.78	0.01
0.8	1.0	6	0.8647	0.9179	0.0532	5.32	0.09
1.0	1.2	5	0.9179	0.9507	0.0328	3.28	1.26
Over	1.2	0	0.9507	1.0000	0.0493	4.93	
Total		100					1.91

Using A.12, we calculate the sample mean as 0.4 hour. Suppose we formulate the null hypothesis that the observed distribution is a sample from an exponential distribution with $E(X) = 0.4$. Furthermore, suppose we specify a probability of no more than 0.01 for the wrong decision of rejecting a true hypothesis (this establishes a 0.01 **level of significance** or right-tail area and a corresponding value of the **critical value** of χ^2 as in Figure A–7).

According to A.33, $\lambda = 1/0.04 = 2.5$. Based on A.32, it follows that the assumed distribution has a CDF given by

$$F(x) = 1 - e^{-2.5x}.$$

We can now determine the probability of a theoretical observation within any specified category or class (a_i, b_i) in the table. For example, in the third class ($a_3 = 0.4, b_3 = 0.6$), we have

$$\begin{aligned} P(0.4 \le X \le 0.6) &= [1 - e^{-2.5(0.6)}] - [1 - e^{-2.5(0.4)}] \\ &= 0.7769 - 0.6321 \\ &= 0.1448. \end{aligned}$$

Expected frequencies for each class are now determined as the product of the total number of observations ($n = 100$) and the probability of an observation in that class. For the third class, $e_3 = 100(0.1448) = 14.48$. Calculations for each class are shown in Table A–3. Note that the last two classes in the table have been combined in order to avoid an expected frequency of less than five in any class. This changes the number of categories to $k = 6$.

The last column illustrates the calculation of $s = 1.91$ according to A.37. For $df = 6 - 2 = 4$ (two parameters, n and λ, were needed, or $m = 2$), the critical value of χ^2 that gives a 0.01 level of significance is 13.28. (See Figure A–7.) Since $s < 13.28$, we conclude that the exponential distribution with $\lambda = 2.5$ is a reasonable theoretical distribution to represent this process.

FOLLOW-UP EXERCISES

17. Plot the empirical and theoretical CDFs for this example and compare.
18. Test the null hypothesis that the empirical distribution in Table A–3 is a sample from an underlying normal distribution with $E(X) = 0.4$ and $V(X) = 0.16$. Use 1 percent and 5 percent levels of significance.

FIGURE A–7 Chi-Square Distribution for Hypothesis Test

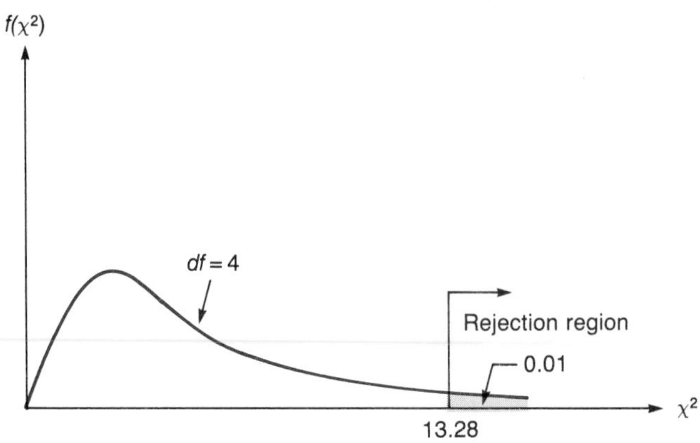

19. Test the null hypothesis that the empirical distribution in Table A–1 is a sample from an underlying Poisson distribution. Use a 5 percent level of significance. Calculate $E(X)$ according to A.12 to determine λ based on A.25.

A.5 STATISTICAL INFERENCE: ESTIMATING MEANS

In this section we review the concepts of a sampling distribution and point and interval estimations.

Sampling Distributions and Estimation of Population Parameters

Given the motivation to estimate the parameter of some population (e.g., mean or variance), the usual procedure is to design a probability sample that would provide a **sample statistic** for estimating the parameter of interest. For example, we might estimate the parameter true average cost (population mean, μ) with the statistic average cost (sample mean, $\bar{x}$) based on a sample; or we might estimate the proportion of taxpayers who cheated on their 1986 income tax returns (population proportion, π) by using the proportion based on a sample (sample proportion, p). When a single estimate based on a sample is used to estimate the population parameter ($\bar{x}$ for μ or p for π), it is termed a **point estimate.** Although such estimates are indispensible data for models (think back to all of our "estimates" in the LP examples), you can appreciate that they provide no judgement as to the extent of random sampling error. **Interval estimates** allow us to specify the maximum expected error and associated probability that a point estimate would diverge from the population parameter.

By realizing that the sample statistic calculated is only one of many possible that could be calculated, it is not difficult to conceptualize the existence of a distribution of possible sample statistics, termed the **sampling distribution of a statistic.**[5] Now for the crux of sampling theory. If the shape or form of the sampling distribution can

[5]If N is the size of the population and n is the size of the simple random sample, the number of possible samples (and therefore the number of $\bar{x}$'s if the population mean is being estimated) is given by combinations of N taken n at-a-time, as determined by A.21.

be specified, it is possible to base errors on probability judgements. For example, if p is used to estimate π, the sampling distribution of p turns out to be binomial (which can be approximated by the normal curve if n is sufficiently large), assuming the conditions underlying the binomial process are met; if $\bar{x}$ is used to estimate μ, the sampling distribution of $\bar{x}$ turns out to be approximately normally or t-distributed. Given a specified shape for the sampling distribution, interval estimates are made easily, as illustrated next.

Sampling Distribution of the Mean

If $x_1, x_2, \ldots, x_n$ represent independent and identically distributed random variates (i.e., variates from a random sample of size n), the sample mean (point estimate for the population mean, μ) can be calculated from:[6]

$$\bar{x} = \frac{\sum_{i=1}^{n} x_i}{n}. \tag{A.38}$$

If n is sufficiently large (say, above 30) and the population standard deviation is known, then we have the result guaranteed by the **central limit theorem (CLT):**

> *If* $x_1, x_2, \ldots, x_n$ *represents a random sample from a population with* $E(X) = \mu_x$ *and* $V(X) = \sigma_x^2$, *then the distribution of* $\bar{x}$ *approaches a* normal distribution *with*
>
> $$E(\bar{X}) = \mu_x \tag{A.39}$$
>
> *and*
>
> $$V(\bar{X}) = \sigma_{\bar{X}}^2 = \frac{\sigma_X^2}{n}. \tag{A.40}$$
>
> *as* n *approaches infinity.*

In short, this allows us to establish probability ranges of $\bar{x}$ about μ_X. Carefully note that the CLT is operative if and only if (1) the variates are independently and identically distributed, (2) n is sufficiently large, and (3) σ_X is known. Condition 1 and the derivation of A.40 require that sampling is from an infinite population or from a finite population with replacement; otherwise, a so-called **finite population correction** factor must be applied to A.40:

$$\sigma_{\bar{X}}^2 = \frac{\sigma_X^2}{n} \cdot \left(\frac{N - n}{N - 1}\right). \tag{A.41}$$

If n is small or σ_X is unknown, the sampling distribution of $\bar{X}$ will be distributed according to the t-distribution, providing the population for X is normally distributed. Note that the normality of $\bar{X}$ as specified by the CLT makes absolutely no assumptions about the form of the X distribution. The application of the t-distribution, how-

[6]Note that for a simple random sample, $P(X = x_i) = f(x_i) = 1/n$, so that A.38 is a special case of A.12. Also, we make no effort to explain methods of calculating point estimates (e.g., moments, maximum likelihood, Bayesian), although the Least Squares Method will be reviewed in the next section. Finally, a discussion on criteria for evaluating methods of point estimation (i.e., consistency, efficiency, sufficiency, and unbiasedness) is omitted.

ever, requires that X itself be normally distributed. If σ_X^2 is unknown (the usual case), it is estimated by the **unbiased sample variance:**

$$\hat{\sigma}_X^2 = \frac{\sum_{i=1}^{n} (x_i - \bar{x})^2}{n - 1}. \tag{A.42}$$

If n is large or small, σ_X is unknown, and X is *not* normally distributed, then the appropriate statistical procedure is "punt." For practical purposes, however, a large n (above 50) under these conditions will give satisfactory results.

Once $\bar{x}$ and the **standard error of the mean,** $\sigma_{\bar{x}}$, are determined, the maximum error and **confidence interval** in estimating μ_X are given by

$$\mu_X = \bar{x} \pm z \cdot \sigma_{\bar{x}} \tag{A.43}$$

or

$$\mu_X = \bar{x} \pm t \cdot \hat{\sigma}_{\bar{x}} \tag{A.44}$$

as the case may be, where $\hat{\sigma}_{\bar{x}}$ is the estimated standard error when A.42 is used in place of σ_X^2 in A.40 or A.41.

▶ Example A.4 Police Patrol Sector

In Example 3.1, 10 mph is used as the velocity of travel for a police patrol vehicle in an east-west (x_1) direction along a particular sector. Suppose this figure represents a point estimate (that is, $\bar{x} = 10$) for the mean of the population of all possible response velocities based on a simple random sample of 61 observations (that is, $n = 61$). The population variance (σ_X^2) is unknown, but has been estimated as $\hat{\sigma}_X^2 = 2$ using A.42. Seasonal factors based on shift, day of week, and month of year have been controlled to ensure as much as possible that random variates are independent and identically distributed.[7] The assumption of a random sample was further buttressed by a previous study which showed that response velocities do not vary significantly with individual drivers. Finally, a chi-square test on the null hypothesis that the random sample of 61 observed velocities came from a normal distribution was accepted. This cleared the way for using the t-distribution as representative of the $\bar{X}$ distribution.

Since the population is infinite, we substitute $\hat{\sigma}_X^2$ for σ_X^2 in A.40 which gives $\hat{\sigma}_{\bar{X}}^2 = 2/61$, or $\hat{\sigma}_{\bar{X}} = 0.18$ mph. For $df = n - 1 = 60$ and a 0.95 **level of confidence** (that is, 0.025 of the area lies in each tail), the value of t is 2.0; hence, according to (A.44),

$$\mu_X = 10 \pm (2.0)(0.18)$$
$$= 10 \pm 0.36.$$

This means that the probability is 95 percent that the estimate of 10 mph is *within* 0.36 mph of the population (true) average velocity. Alternatively, the 95-percent confidence interval for μ is 9.64 to 10.36 mph. These **confidence limits** can be used as extreme values of this parameter for performing sensitivity analysis.

---

[7] This can be accomplished by selecting the sample either from a particular shift-day-month combination or from a group of such combinations that appear to be statistically similar with respect to response velocities. A less likely alternative includes deseasonalizing velocities using seasonal indices.

FOLLOW-UP EXERCISES

20. Determine the confidence limits if $n = 21$, all other things equal. Conclusion?
21. Estimate maximum error for μ if $\bar{x} = 50$, $n = 30$, and $\sigma_X = 10$. Use 95 percent and 99 percent confidence intervals.
22. If σ_X is known, then the maximum error for a given level of confidence is given by $E = z \cdot \sigma_{\bar{x}}$ or $E = z \cdot \sigma_x/\sqrt{n}$ when A.40 applies. If follows that

$$n = \left(\frac{z \cdot \sigma_X}{E}\right)^2 \tag{A.45}$$

provides the required sample size that satisfies a given maximum error and confidence level. For the police sector problem, determine the required sample size if $\sigma_X = 1.41$ and an error of no more than 0.5 mph with 99-percent confidence is desired. What sample size must be taken if $E = 0.1$? Conclusion as to behavior of n as E changes?

A.6 STATISTICAL INFERENCE: REGRESSION ANALYSIS

The **least squares method** in regression analysis is an alternative method for point and interval estimates of population parameters. The gist of the technique is to discover linear association or covariation between the variable to be estimated (called the **dependent** or **criterion variable**) and some other set of variables (called the **independent** or **predictor variables**) having values accessible to or under the control of the decision maker.[8] If the set of predictor variables consists of a single variable, the form of the analysis is called **simple** or **bivariate regression;** otherwise, **multiple regression** applies. Throughout this section it should be understood that we are dealing only with **linear regression** (which *can* include nonlinear functions) and not **nonlinear regression.** The term *linear* refers to linearity in the parameters of the model and not to linearity in the variables themselves.

Estimating the Simple Regression Function

In bivariate regression, the objective is to find the function (mathematical) relationship between the criterion variable (y) and the predictor variable (x), that is, to explicitly determine

$$y = f(x)\,. \tag{A.46}$$

The simplest and most widely used form of A.46 is the linear function:

$$y_c = a + bx \tag{A.47}$$

where a is the y-intercept, b is the slope or **regression coefficient,** and y_c is the calculated or estimated value for y. Other forms of A.46 include nonlinear functions that by some transformation can be converted to linear form. For example, the popular *exponential*

$$y = a \cdot b^x \tag{A.48}$$

is converted easily to the form in A.47 by taking the logarithm of both sides.

[8]In some cases the purpose of regression analysis is not to predict or estimate some variable but rather to discover associations for explanatory purposes (e.g., as a means to structurally substantiate some theory such as "lip velocity in the combustion of a jet engine is related to the fuel/air ratio").

Given a set of n paired observations for the predictor and criterion variables, $[(x_1, y_1), (x_2, y_2), \ldots, (x_n, y_n)]$, based on a random sample, the method of least squares "fits" a linear function to these observations such that the sum of squared deviations from the line is minimized. (See Figure A–8.) In other words, we wish to find the values for a and b that minimize the **residual sum of squares** or **unexplained variation (UV):**

$$UV = \sum_{i=1}^{n} [y_i - (a + bx_i)]^2 . \tag{A.49}$$

The procedure involves taking the partial derivatives of UV with respect to a and b, setting the two simultaneous equations to zero, and solving for a and b. You can find computational equations for a and b in any textbook on statistics.

FIGURE A–8 Linear Function Fit to n Data Points

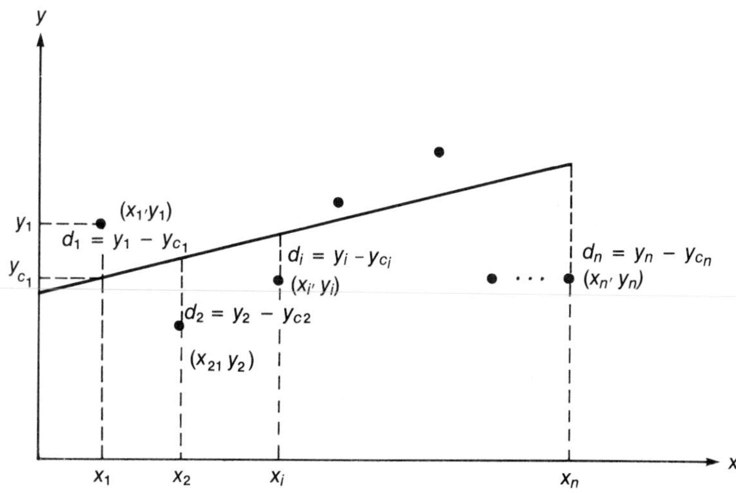

▶ Example A.5

Table A–4 illustrates regression information provided by a time-shared computer package (STATPACK) for the demand data in the MBTA example of Chapter 2. The results indicate a regression equation of the form

$$y_c = 22.5 - 0.5x .$$

Estimated y_i values (y_{c_i}) are determined by plugging corresponding x_i values in the regression equation. Note that the sum of the residuals will always equal zero (except for rounding errors).

FOLLOW-UP EXERCISES

23. Construct a **scatter diagram** for this example by plotting (x_i, y_i) and the regression line. Confirm the y_{c_i} and d_i columns in Table A–4.
24. Suppose a firm wishes to establish the relationship between the total cost of placing orders and the number of orders placed for an item it carries in inventory. A

TABLE A–4 Sample Statistics from Computer Output*

Volume y_i	Price x_i	Estimated Volume y_{c_i}	Residual $d_i = y_i - y_{c_i}$			
10.0	25	10.0	0.0	Intercept (a)	=	22.500
12.6	20	12.5	0.1	Regression coefficient (b)	=	−0.500
14.9	15	15.0	−0.1	Coefficient of determination (r^2)	=	1.000
17.4	10	17.5	−0.1	Coefficient of correlation (r)	=	−1.000
20.1	5	20.0	0.1	Estimated standard error of regression coefficient ($\hat{\sigma}_b$)	=	0.007
$\bar{y} = 15$	$\bar{x} = 15$		0.0	t-test on regression coefficient	=	−68.445
				Estimated standard error of estimate ($\hat{\sigma}_c$)	=	0.116

*Above results are standard output for most commercial computer packages. Computational formulas for these statistics are readily found in textbooks on managerial statistics.

"random" sample of eight observations (one observation for each of eight quarters) provides the following paired (cost, order) data where costs have been deflated by the consumer price index: ($560, 2), (640, 5), (780, 9), (620, 4), (700, 6), (580, 3), (640, 4), and (700, 7). Fit a least squares line to these data and construct a scatter diagram. Try to accomplish this by using an available computer program. On the average, what is the change in cost per unit change in orders?

Judging Goodness-of-Fit

The precision of a regression fit can be judged by the relationships exhibited in Table A–5.

TABLE A–5 Analysis of Variance (ANOVA) Table for Bivariate Regression

Source of Variation	Sum of Squares	Degrees of Freedom	Mean Square	F Statistic
Regression	EV	1	$MEV = \frac{EV}{1}$	
Residual	UV	$n - 2$	$MUV = \frac{UV}{(n-2)}$	$F = \frac{MEV}{MUV}$
Total	TV	$n - 1$	—	

Total variation *for the criterion variable* is given by the numerator of the variance term, or

$$TV = \sum_{i=1}^{n} (y_i - \bar{y})^2 . \quad \text{(A.50)}$$

The variation due to or explained by the regression fit (EV) represents the portion of TV we have been able to account for by the regression model. Ideally, we would like $EV = TV$, or a "perfect" fit. The variation that remains unexplained (UV) represents the extent to which the observations fall off the line. In fact, this was the objective of our minimization as given by A.49.

The mean squares are the sums of squares adjusted for (divided by) the degrees of freedom. The F-statistic allows the analyst to test the null hypothesis that the *population* regression coefficient (β) is zero (note that b represents the *sample* regression coefficient). If the null hypothesis were true, then there is no linear relationship between y and x. (Why?) If $\beta = 0$, then it can be proved that the expected value of F is unity. Note that if it were true that $\beta = 0$, it would still be possible for the sample statistics (F or b) to diverge from their expected values due to random sampling error. Note also that the greater the value of F, the better (or more significant) is the regression fit.

The **coefficient of determination (r^2)** also provides a measure of goodness in that it represents the proportion of variation explained by the model; that is,

$$r^2 = \frac{EV}{TV}. \tag{A.51}$$

The **coefficient of correlation (r)** is simply the square root of the coefficient of determiniation. If $r = 0$, the worst possible fit has occurred (a horizontal line); if $r = 1$, perfect positive correlation exists; if $r = -1$, perfect negative correlation exists. (Note that the sign on r is consistent with the sign on b.)

Because b is an observation from the **sampling distribution of b** with expected value β and the estimated **standard error of the regression coefficient** ($\hat{\sigma}_b$) is analogous to $\hat{\sigma}_{\bar{x}}$, the t-statistic given by

$$\begin{aligned} t &= \frac{b - \beta}{\hat{\sigma}_b} \\ &= \frac{b}{\hat{\sigma}_b} \end{aligned} \tag{A.52}$$

allows for the test of the null hypothesis that $\beta = 0$. As mentioned in Section A.3, $F = t^2$ for simple linear regression.[9]

▶ Example A.6

Continuing our previous example, we see that Table A–6 illustrates the computer output for the ANOVA table. As can be seen, out of a total variation of 62.54 in the criterion variable (volume), all but 0.04 remains unexplained. The F statistic of 4684.7 is extremely high, as the critical F value is only 34.1 for $df_1 = 1$ and $df_2 = 3$ at a significance level of 0.01.

---

[9]All inferences in regression analysis are predicated on the assumption that the residuals are independent, have zero mean, a constant variance, and are normally distributed. A rigorous analysis would test these assumptions.

TABLE A–6 ANOVA Table for Example A.5

Source	SS	df	MS	F
Regression	62.50	1	62.500	
Residual	0.04	3	0.013	4684.7
Total	62.54	4	—	—

To three significant digits, the coefficient of determination (from Table A–4) indicates that approximately 100 percent of the variance in volume was explained (actually it is 62.5/62.54). The coefficient of correlation correspondingly suggests a perfect negative correlation between price and volume. Finally, the *t* value of −68.445 concurs with a highly significant regression fit; that is, the null hypothesis of a zero population slope is soundly rejected. (Do you get the feeling we contrived the data?) In actual practice, regression fits never quite measure up to the standard we have just set. In fact, such a small number of observations rarely gives meaningful results in the sense of achieving reject signals from *F* and *t*.

FOLLOW-UP EXERCISES

25. Determine relevant goodness-of-fit statistics for the problem in Example 3.6. Compare these results with our results in Example A.6. Conclusions? Does $F = t^2$?
26. Determine goodness-of-fit statistics for the inventory problem in Exercise 24. Make a judgement as to the precision of the regression model.

Point and Interval Estimates

The calculated value, y_{c_i}, represents a point estimate for the mean (expected or average) value of y_i conditional on (or given) x_i.

The confidence interval for the *expected* value of y_i given x_i is determined from

$$\text{Expected } y_i = y_{c_i} \pm t \cdot \hat{\sigma}_m \tag{A.53}$$

where $\hat{\sigma}_m$ is the **estimated standard error of expected (mean) y_i**, a statistic also analogous to the standard error of the mean (i.e., it represents the estimate for the standard deviation of the sampling distribution of mean y_i). For bivariate regression analysis, $df = n - 2$ and

$$\hat{\sigma}_m = \hat{\sigma}_e \sqrt{\frac{1}{n} + \frac{(x_i - \bar{x})^2}{\Sigma (x - \bar{x})^2}} \tag{A.54}$$

where $\hat{\sigma}_e$ is the **estimated standard error of estimate** (as given in Table A–4). We might note that $\hat{\sigma}_e$ is an unbiased estimate of the standard deviation of residuals about the population regression line:

$$\hat{\sigma}_e = \sqrt{\frac{UV}{n - 2}}. \tag{A.55}$$

Similarly, the confidence interval for an *individual* y value given x_i is determined from

$$\text{Individual } y_i = y_{c_i} \pm t \cdot \hat{\sigma}_f . \tag{A.56}$$

where $\hat{\sigma}_f$ is the **estimated standard error of the forecast:**

$$\hat{\sigma}_f = \hat{\sigma}_e \sqrt{1 + \frac{1}{n} - \frac{(x_i - \bar{x})^2}{\Sigma(x - \bar{x})^2}}. \tag{A.57}$$

Again $df = n - 2$. Note that individual y_i values are distributed about the expected y_i value.

▶ Example A.7

Continuing our volume-price example, for $df = 3$ and 99 percent confidence, the critical value of t is 5.841, so that for, say, $x_i = 12$

$$\text{Expected } y_i = [22.5 - 0.5(12)] \pm (5.841)\left\{(0.116) \cdot \left[\frac{1}{5} + \frac{(12 - 15)^2}{250}\right]^{1/2}\right\}$$

$$= 16.50 \pm (5.841)(0.056)$$

$$= 16.50 \pm 0.33$$

and

$$\text{Individual } y_i = 16.50 \pm (5.841)\left\{(0.116) \cdot \left[1 + \frac{1}{5} + \frac{(12 - 15)^2}{250}\right]^{1/2}\right\}$$

$$= 16.50 \pm (5.841)(0.129)$$

$$= 16.50 \pm 0.75.$$

In other words, for a fare of $0.12, the expected number of passengers is 16.5 thousand. Alternatively, we can state that the probability is 99 percent that the mean number of passengers will fall between 16.17 thousand and 16.83 thousand when a fare of $0.12 is charged. Furthermore, the probability is 99 percent that a single observation falls in the interval 15.75 thousand to 17.25 thousand for a fare of $0.12. Note that the unexpected width of the intervals is due to the small *df* and its correspondingly high *t*.

FOLLOW-UP EXERCISES

27. For Exercise 25 establish a 95 percent confidence interval for the average price given a volume of 15; for the same volume establish a 95 percent confidence interval for an individual price. Interpret these intervals.
28. For the inventory problem in Exercise 26, construct a 99 percent confidence interval for average and individual cost given the placement of six orders. Interpret these intervals.

Multiple Regression

Functionally, conceptually, and computationally the multiple linear regression model given by

$$y_c = b_0 + b_1x_1 + b_2x_2 + \cdots + b_nx_n \tag{A.58}$$

is a straightforward extension of A.47.[10] Statistics of interest (as in Tables A–4 and A–5) and their interpretations remain almost the same.[11]

The model given by A.58 is useful from several perspectives: first, most real-world phenomena tend to be multivariate (e.g., incidence of coronaries is related to such factors as age, weight, blood pressure, and extent of cigarette smoking); second, if the analyst is having difficulty establishing what predictor variable(s) to use in the analysis, it saves time to overspecify the number of variables for the purpose of "cranking" through a multiple regression (preferably stepwise) analysis that effectively does some "fishing"; third, it is useful in assessing the results of sensitivity analysis; finally, A.58 can handle a nonlinear function, such as

$$y_c = b_0 + b_1 x_1 + b_2 x_1^2 + b_3 \cdot (\log x_1)\,, \tag{A.59}$$

by simply letting x_2 represent x_1^2 and x_3 represent $\log x_1$ in the data matrix.

A.7 FORECASTING

The term *forecasting,* as used here, refers to the estimation of some random variable *over time*. All of our previous estimating procedures implicitly assumed estimation for a given point in time (or that the estimate would not vary over time). Yet many models in OR require the specification of some variable or parameter that could vary over time (e.g., inventory models, production planning models). In this section we have the modest objective of simply making you aware of this particular specialization by very briefly describing a typology of forecasting procedures and illustrating one methodology in particular called exponential smoothing.

Typology of Forecasting Procedures

The first (and perhaps most often used) approach is **subjective forecasts,** primarily based on the intuition and expertise of the analyst regarding the variable or process being forecasted. If rapid responses are needed and/or if the cost of forecast error is small relative to the cost of implementing a more sophisticated forecasting system, then subjective forecasts can be justified; otherwise, mathematical and statistical procedures may be warranted.

Classical time series models express the criterion variable as a mathematical function of time (t) so as to provide forecasts ($\hat{y}_t$) by simple extrapolation:

$$\hat{y}_t = f(t)\,. \tag{A.60}$$

For instance, a polynomial model of degree 3 would appear as

$$\hat{y}_t = b_0 + b_1 t + b_2 t^2 + b_3 t^3 \tag{A.61}$$

[10] Using matrix algebra.

[11] A common oversight for this type of analysis is the problem of **multicollinearity** (correlation among the predictor variables), as its existence affects the precision and interpretation of individual regression coefficients. To some extent, **stepwise regression procedures** overcome this problem by sequentially including or excluding variables.

and an exponential model as

$$\hat{y}_t = a \cdot b^t \tag{A.62}$$

or

$$\hat{y}_t = a \cdot e^{bt} \tag{A.63}$$

where b is the growth rate and e is the natural number. Models of this type are most often fit by the use of linear regression procedures. More sophisticated versions first **decompose** the historical time series into trend, seasonal, cyclical, and noise components, analyze each component separately, and finally recompose for the forecast. Such models have fared well for long-term predictions of relatively stable processes (e.g., GNP and world population growth) but are far too unresponsive to short-term movements.

Hybrid time-series models express the criterion either as a function of both independent variables (x_i's) and time (t) or as a function of variables that lead-lag the criterion.

Naïve models include a plethora of models with ad hoc forecasting formulas; for example, the forecast in period $t + 1$ equals the value of the variable in the present period ($\hat{y}_{t+1} = y_t$); and include others founded on the important classes of **simple moving averages** and **exponentially weighted moving averages** based on past observations. For example, a moving average of n periods provides the following forecast one period ahead (period $t + 1$):

$$\hat{y}_{t+1} = \frac{1}{n}(y_t + y_{t-1} + \cdots + y_{t-n+1}) . \tag{A.64}$$

For the most part, naïve models have fared well, both from the standpoint of good forecast accuracy and ease of implementation. Among the most popular is the exponentially weighted moving average or **exponential smoothing.**

Econometric models specify structural relations among variables using mathematical and statistical methods. For instance, in a capital investment application the estimation of present value is dependent, among other things, on future prices, which in turn are dependent on supply-and-demand functions, which in turn. . . . If correctly specified, these models can be quite effective; however, the required expenditure of time and the need for personnel with specialized knowledge in econometrics discourage their widespread use other than in large organizations.

Stochastic time-series models include a host of mathematically sophisticated procedures that treat the time series (sequence of observations) as a set of jointly distributed random variables. From a theoretical perspective, these models are the most appealing and appear to be the most effective for certain **autoregressive** (future observations correlated to past observations) and nonstationary processes.

Often the distinction between a **forecast** and a **prediction** is useful. Any of the above procedures results in a forecast. There may be causal factors at work, however, that will not be exhibited in the data. For example, forecasted sales for some product can be strongly influenced by the introduction of a competitive product or by the onset of a recession. Inclusion of such anticipated events results in a prediction based on a subjective revision of the forecast. In such instances, the **Delphi method** of prediction has proved useful.[12]

Exponential Smoothing

The simplicity, low cost of implementation, and relative effectiveness of exponential smoothing models have been prominent factors in their widespread use. Here we illustrate the simplest of these, sometimes termed *single* exponential smoothing.

The smoothed value for the variable in the tth period ($\hat{y}_t$) is defined as a *weighted average* of the current and n past observations ($n \to \infty$);

$$\hat{y}_t = Ay_t + A(1 - A)y_{t-1} + A(1 - A)^2 y_{t-2} + \cdots + A(1 - A)^n y_{t-n} \tag{A.65}$$

where A is termed the **smoothing coefficient** ($0 < A < 1$). The smoothed value $\hat{y}_t$ approaches a true weighted average as n approaches infinity because the sum of the weights approaches unity (they form a geometric progression with a ratio less than unity). Factoring $(1 - A)$ beginning with the second term in A.65 gives the basic computational formula for single exponential smoothing as

$$\hat{y}_t = Ay_t + (1 - A)\hat{y}_{t-1}\,. \tag{A.66}$$

Thus the smoothed value in period t is simply a weighted average of the current observation and the smoothed value in the previous period.

Note that (1) past observations are progressively less important, an intuitively appealing feature;[13] (2) n should be large (say, above 30) to justify theoretically the concept of a weighted average and to ensure lower sampling error; (3) higher values for A place more emphasis on the current observation (y_t) than on the composite of all past observations ($\hat{y}_{t-1}$); and (4) we need only keep track of four calculations at one time and not the entire history (compare this feature to regression analysis).

The choice of a value for A poses an interesting dilemma for the analyst; High values for A (close to 1) make for a model that is highly responsive (but unstable) to changes in the time series; low values for the smoothing coefficient (close to 0) make for a model that is stable (but unresponsive) to changes in the time series. If the series is undergoing real changes, as when it is trending, then high values for A are called for. However, if much of the variability of the series is caused by random factors (noise), then low values for A are best. This trade-off in stability and responsiveness often can be resolved by an analysis that evaluates forecast errors over a range of values for A.

Assuming that the y_t's represent deseasonalized values and that no trend is present, we can forecast k periods into the future by

$$\hat{y}_{t+k} = \hat{y}_t \tag{A.67}$$

[12] Prediction by the Delphi method is based on a revised group consensus arrived at by a process that collates, summarizes, and "feeds" back to the group individual predictions of experts. For an overview, see J. Pill, "The Delphi Method: Substance, Context, a Critique and Annotated Bibliography," *Socio-Economic Planning Sciences* 5, no.1 (1969).

[13] By contrast, all past observations are equally important (weighted) in *classical* regression analysis. Alternatively, *Bayesian* regression analysis allows the revision of regression coefficients based on new observations.

and the forecast error by

$$d_{k,t} = y_{t+k} - \hat{y}_{t+k} \,. \tag{A.68}$$

Needless to say, more meaningful exponential smoothing models exist, including those that incorporate and smooth seasonal indices and trends.

▶ Example A.8

To illustrate the model given by A.66, consider the calculations in Table A–7 for the first five observations of a series using two values for A.

TABLE A–7 Calculations for Single Exponential Smoothing

		Smoothed Values A		One Period Forecast Error A	
		0.1	0.8	0.1	0.8
t	y_t	$\hat{y}_t$	$\hat{y}_t$	$d_{1,t}$	$d_{1,t}$
1	5	5.0	5.0	—	—
2	7	5.2	6.6	2.0	2.0
3	8	5.5	7.7	2.8	1.4
4	10	5.9	9.5	4.5	2.3
5	10	6.3	9.9	4.1	0.5
⋮					

In both cases, $\hat{y}_1$ was initialized by setting it to y_1.[14] Notice that a higher smoothing coefficient ($A = 0.8$) gives better results than a smaller coefficient ($A = 0.1$) for a series that exhibits trend as evidenced by closer fits of $\hat{y}_t$ to y_t and lower one-period forecast errors given by $d_{1,t} = y_t - \hat{y}_{t-1}$. (Can you explain why this is so?)

FOLLOW-UP EXERCISES

29. Given the time series (10, 15, 18, 22, 26, 32, 37, 44, 48, 55), construct a table such as Table A–7 and compare average $d_{1,t}$ and $d_{2,t}$ for $A = 0.1$ and 0.8. Conclusions?
30. Do as in Exercise 29 for the time series (50, 60, 42, 55, 47, 45, 55, 40). Conclusions?

[14] Better procedures exist. Can you think of any?

31. Use the first five observations of the series in Exercise 29 to fit the regression model $\hat{y}_t = a + bt$. Forecast the last five periods using this model and calculate average error. Compare this result to the one-period forecasts when $A = 0.8$ in Exercise 29 (for the last five periods).
32. Apply the model $\hat{y}_{t+1} = y_t$ to the series in Exercises 29 and 30. Compare errors.
33. What would be your forecast for the tenth observation of the series in Exercise 29 if you were to fit the regression model $\hat{y}_{t+1} = a + by_t$ to the first nine observations? Why is this model costly to implement?

APPENDIX B
Review of Differential Calculus

This appendix presents a *review* of differentiation and principles of classical optimization. Treatment is first given to functions of one independent variable, followed by functions of two independent variables. The appendix is intended to serve as a review for students who have had an exposure to calculus in the past. It may be adequate for students who have had little or no exposure to calculus, but who do have a firm grounding in algebra. The appendix is by no means a substitute for a separate course in calculus.

B.1 DIFFERENTIATION IN ONE EASY LESSON

For those of you who have not been introduced to the concepts of calculus, we will now spend a few pages helping you to "tool-up" for the calculus portions of the text. You need not fear what lies ahead. Newcomers to this topic should find the concepts rather palatable. Old-timers, who may have suffered from a case of mathematical indigestion when taking their first calculus course, will probably appreciate this direct and intuitive approach.

Think of the Derivative as a Slope

Differential calculus has a fundamental concern with the slope of continuous mathematical functions. Suppose in Figure B–1 you are interested in finding the slope of line $\overline{pq}$, which is tangent to the function $y = f(x)$ at point a. The slope of this line segment actually represents the *instantaneous slope* of the function for the specific value of x at point a. We refer to this as an instantaneous slope because the tangent slope continually changes for different values of the variable x. Only with linear functions would the tangent slope remain the same for all allowable values of x.

FIGURE B–1 Instantaneous Slope of $y = f(x)$

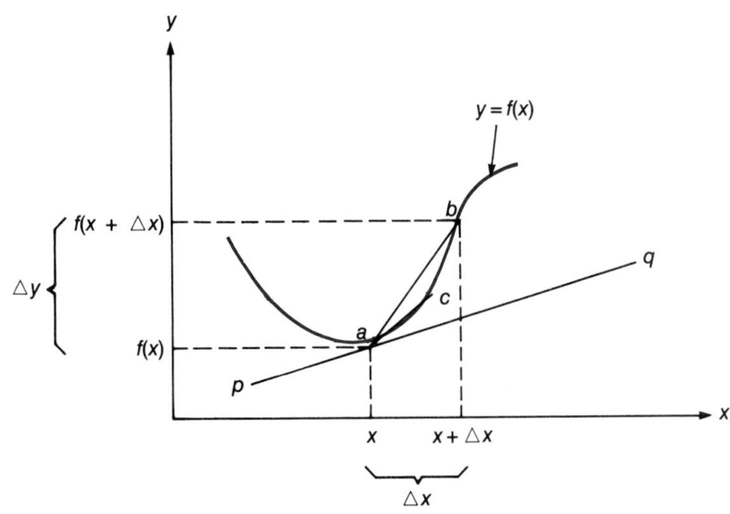

The slope of the tangent line could be determined by several different methods. A carefully constructed tangent line might be drawn using graph paper; the coordinates of any two points on the line could be determined and the slope calculated using the **two-point slope formula**

$$m = \frac{\Delta y}{\Delta x} = \frac{y_2 - y_1}{x_2 - x_1},$$

where Δy (delta y) represents the vertical displacement from point 1 to point 2, and Δx represents the horizontal distance between the two points. An alternative approach would be to identify another point on the curve, such as point b, connect it with the original point a by a straight line, and use the slope of the line segment $\overline{ab}$ as an "approximation" for the actual tangent slope. Obviously this is a poor approximation, but there is a method to our madness. Using the two-point slope formula, we compute the slope of $\overline{ab}$ as

$$m = \frac{\Delta y}{\Delta x} = \frac{(f(x + \Delta x) - f)x)}{\Delta x}. \tag{B.1}$$

This is a general formula providing the slope of the straight line connecting any two points on a function that are Δx units apart from each other along the x-axis.

Notice in Figure B–1 that if the adjacent point is selected closer to point a, as given by point c, the slope of the line segment $\overline{ac}$ becomes a better approximation than the slope of the line segment $\overline{ab}$ to the slope of the tangent line $\overline{pq}$. Recognizing that Δx is the distance along the x-axis separating points a and b, we might state that "in the limit," as Δx approaches zero, the slope of line segment $\overline{ab}$ will come closer and closer to the slope of $\overline{pq}$.

This type of reasoning enables us to generalize a definition for the **derivative** of a continuous mathematical function. The derivative can be thought of as a general equation from which the tangent slope can be determined exactly at any point x on the function. Mathematically, this slope relationship is derived as a "limit" of Equation B.1. Specifically, the derivative is defined as

$$\frac{dy}{dx} = \lim_{\Delta x \to 0} \left(\frac{f(x + \Delta x) - f(x)}{\Delta x} \right). \tag{B.2}$$

The dy/dx notation replaces $\Delta y/\Delta x$ to emphasize that the tangent slope at any point on a curve is a measure of the *instantaneous rate of change* in the variable y with respect to a change in x.

Equation B.2 can be read as saying "in the limit, as the distance along the x-axis separating the two points approaches zero, the slope of the line segment connecting the two points will equal the slope of the tangent at a specific value of x."

▶ Example B.1

For the function $y = x^2$,

a. Find the general slope equation, or derivative.

b. Find the slope of a tangent to this curve when $x = 1$.

According to Equation B.1 the derivative can be found by selecting any two points on the curve having coordinates $[x, f(x)]$ and $[x + \Delta x, f(x + \Delta x)]$. Thus, for the function $y = x^2$, the coordinates are, respectively, (x, x^2) and $[x + \Delta x, (x + \Delta x)^2]$. The slope of the line segment connecting these two points is

$$m = \frac{\Delta y}{\Delta x} = \frac{y_2 - y_1}{x_2 - x_1} = \frac{(x + \Delta x)^2 - x^2}{(x + \Delta x) - x}.$$

Simplifying, we get

$$\begin{aligned}\frac{\Delta y}{\Delta x} &= \frac{x^2 + 2x(\Delta x) + (\Delta x)^2 - x^2}{\Delta x}\\ &= \frac{2x(\Delta x) + (\Delta x)^2}{\Delta x}\\ &= 2x + \Delta x.\end{aligned}$$

Taking the limit as Δx goes to zero, we get

$$\begin{aligned}\frac{dy}{dx} &= \lim_{\Delta x \to 0}[2x + \Delta x]\\ &= 2x.\end{aligned}$$

Thus the derivative, or general slope equation, for the function $y = x^2$ is $dy/dx = 2x$. To determine the slope of the tangent to this function at any point, x, simply substitute the value for x into the derivative expression.

The slope of a tangent to the function when $x = 1$ is $dy/dx = 2(1) = 2$. If a tangent to the curve were constructed at $x = 1$, the *exact slope* of the tangent line would equal $+2$.

The notation $f'(x)$ is often used as an equivalent form for dy/dx. This notation is convenient for specifying the slope of a function when x assumes a particular value. To illustrate,

$$f'(0) = 2(0) = 0,$$

$$f'(-1) = 2(-1) = -2,$$

and

$$f'(5) = 2(5) = +10.$$

All specify the exact tangent slopes when $x = 0, -1$, and 5, respectively.

FOLLOW-UP EXERCISES

Determine the formula for the first derivative for each of the following and evaluate at $x = -2, 0, 2$.

1. $y = c$ (constant).
2. $y = x$.
3. $y = c \cdot x^2$.

Rules of Differentiation

The process of finding a derivative is called **differentiation.** Fortunately you do not have to go through the "limit" approach to find derivative expressions. The work has been done for you. A set of basic rules exists for finding derivative expressions in a manner similar to that of Example B.1. If you wish to find the slope expression for a mathematical function, it is simply a matter of applying the rule or rules appropriate for the particular functional form.

Table B–1 provides a list of the basic differentiation rules, and this is followed by examples of their application. You should keep in mind that every mathematical function of the form $y = f(x)$ can be expressed graphically. The derivative allows you to determine the instantaneous slope at any point on the curve.

TABLE B–1 Differentiation Rules*

Rule	Function $y = f(x)$	Derivative $\frac{dy}{dx} = f'(x) = y'$
1	$y = c$	0
2	$y = x$	1
3	$y = x^n$	nx^{n-1}
4	$y = u(x) + v(u)$	$u'(x) \pm v'(x)$
5	$y = c \cdot f(x)$	$c \cdot f'(x)$
6	$y = [u(x)]^n$	$n[u(x)]^{n-1} \cdot u'(x)$
7	$y = u(x)/v(x)$	$\frac{v(x) \cdot u'(x) - u(x) \cdot v'(x)}{[v(x)]^2}$
8	$y = u(x) \cdot v(x)$	$u'(x) \cdot v(x) + v'(x) \cdot u(x)$
9	$y = e^{u(x)}$	$e^{u(x)} \cdot u'(x)$
10	$y = c^{u(x)}$	$c^{u(x)} \cdot \ln(c) \cdot u'(x)$
11	$y = \ln[u(x)]$	$\frac{1}{u(x)} \cdot u'(x)$

*Functions such as $u(x)$ and $v(x)$ are used to distinguish between different functions having the form $y = f(x)$. c and n are constants. e = 2.718. . . , the base of natural or naperian logarithms (ln).

Example B.2

Using the rules in Table B–1, find the derivatives of the functions below (before looking at the answer, try to apply the rule yourself).

a. $y = 10$ $\quad \frac{dy}{dx} = 0$ [Rule 1]

b. $y = x^2$ $\quad \frac{dy}{dx} = 2x$ [Rule 3]

c. $y = x^{-1/2}$ $\quad \frac{dy}{dx} = -½x^{-3/2}$ [Rule 3]

d. $y = x^4 - 10$ $\quad \frac{dy}{dx} = 4x^3 - 0$

$= 4x^3$ [Rules 4, 3, 1]

e. $y = 5x^3 + 2x^2$ $\quad \frac{dy}{dx} = 5 \cdot (3x^2) + 2 \cdot (2x)$

$= 15x^2 + 4x$ [Rules 5, 4, 3]

f. $y = \frac{x^4}{7}$ $\quad \frac{dy}{dx} = \frac{1}{7} \cdot (4x^3)$

$= \frac{4x^3}{7}$ [Rules 5, 3]

g. $y = \frac{2x^2}{5x - 1}$ $\quad \frac{dy}{dx} = \frac{(5x - 1)[2(2x)] - (2x^2)(5)}{(5x - 1)^2}$

$= \frac{10x^2 - 4x}{(5x - 1)^2}$ [Rules 7, 1, 3, 5]

h. $y = (6x^3 + 1)(x^2 - 5)$ $\quad \frac{dy}{dx} = (18x^2)(x^2 - 5) + (2x)(6x^3 + 1)$

$= 30x^4 - 90x^2 + 2x$ [Rules 8, 1, 3, 5]

i. $y = (4x^2 - 1)^3$ $\quad \frac{dy}{dx} = 3(4x^2 - 1)^2 \cdot 8x$

$= 24x(4x^2 - 1)^2$ [Rules 6, 1, 3, 5]

j. $y = \left(\frac{3}{x + 1}\right)^5$ $\quad \frac{dy}{dx} = 5\left(\frac{3}{x + 1}\right)^4 \cdot \frac{(x + 1)(0) - (3)(1)}{(x + 1)^2}$

$= 5\left(\frac{3}{x + 1}\right)^4 \cdot \frac{(-3)}{(x + 1)^2}$

$= -\frac{1,215}{(x + 1)^6}$ [Rules 6, 7, 1, 2]

k. $y = e^x$ $\quad \frac{dy}{dx} = e^x \cdot (1)$

$= e^x$ [Rules 9, 2]

l. $y = e^{x2-3}$ $\quad \frac{dy}{dx} = e^{x2-3} \cdot 2x$

$= 2xe^{x2-3}$ [Rules 9, 1, 3]

m. $y = \ln x$ $\quad \frac{dy}{dx} = \frac{1}{x} \cdot (1)$

$= \frac{1}{x}$ [Rules 11, 2]

n. $y = \ln(x^2 - 1)$ $\quad \frac{dy}{dx} = \frac{1}{x^2 - 1} \cdot (2x)$

$= \frac{2x}{x^2 - 1}$ [Rules 11, 1, 3]

o. $y = 50(1 - 0.5^x)$ $\quad \frac{dy}{dx} = -50 \cdot (0.5)^x \cdot \ln(0.5) \cdot (1)$

$= -50 \cdot (0.5)^x \cdot (-0.69315)$

$= (34.6575) \cdot (0.5)^x$ [Rules 10, 1, 2, 5]

FOLLOW-UP EXERCISES

Verify the following:

4. The first derivative of $y = (7 + 4x + x^2)^{-2}$ is $y' = -4(2 + x)(7 + 4x + x^2)^{-3}$.
5. The instantaneous slope for $y = 2(3x^3 - 5x)^2$ at $x = 5$ is 308,000.
6. The instantaneous slope for $y = 1/(2x - 4)$ at $x = 3$ is $-½$.

7. The first derivative of $y = \ln(x^3 + 2)^4$ is $y' = 12x^2/(x^3 + 2)$.
8. For $y = e^{2x} \cdot (5 - \ln x^3)^4$, $y' = 2e^{2x} \cdot (5 - \ln x^3)^3 \cdot [5 - \ln x^3 - (6/x)]$.

Higher-Ordered Derivatives

Given a function of the form $y = f(x)$, one can define derivatives of an order higher than $f'(x)$, termed the **first derivative.** For example, the **second derivative** is simply the derivative of the first derivative. Denoted by $f''(x)$, the second derivative represents the instantaneous rate of change in the first derivative with respect to a change in the variable x. Another way of viewing the second derivative is that it represents the rate at which the slope of a function is changing with regard to a change in x. The rules used to find second derivatives are the same as those used in finding first derivatives except that the function differentiated is the first derivative. Third and higher-ordered derivatives can be found in the exact same manner. For instance, the **third derivative** is found by differentiating the second derivative of a function. Intuitive appreciation of the meaning of these derivatives becomes difficult beyond the second derivative.

▶ Example B.3

Find the first and all higher-ordered derivatives for the function $y = 12x^3 - 2x^2 - 2x + 1$:

$$f'(x) = 36x^2 - 4x - 2$$

$$f''(x) = 72x - 4$$

$$f'''(x) = 72$$

$$f''''(x) = 0.$$

All derivatives higher than the fourth derivative equal zero.

FOLLOW-UP EXERCISES

9. Find the second derivatives for the functions in Exercises 4, 5, and 7.
10. Find the second and third derivatives for the functions in parts *l* and *m* of Example B.2.

Later in this appendix we will return to higher-ordered derivatives to demonstrate their usefulness in classical optimization.

A word of caution is in order at this point. By no means have we done a thorough job of treating differentiation. Many important topics have been neglected, including *limits and continuity;* hence, even if you have mastered this section, your knowledge of differentiation is partial at best. We hope our limited objectives have been met; for the neophyte, an intuitive understanding of the essence of differentiation, a working knowledge of some basic rules of differentiation, and increased mathematical confidence (It's not so bad after all!); for the "pro," a clear and concise review and a reaffirmation of mathematical maturity (I told you it was easy!).

B.2 SINGLE-VARIABLE OPTIMIZATION

When an objective function can be formulated as a continuous function involving one independent variable, differential calculus easily can identify conditions for optimality, if they exist. This section discusses procedures for determining these conditions.

Stationary Points

In Chapter 2 the concepts of relative and global maximum and minimum points are introduced. These are also referred to, collectively, as **extreme points,** and they are particularly relevant in identifying conditions for optimality.

Figure B–2 represents a continuous function. Points a and c are both relative maxima, and points b and d are relative minima. Points c and d are respectively, the global maximum and minimum over the indicated range of values for x.

FIGURE B–2 Extreme Points

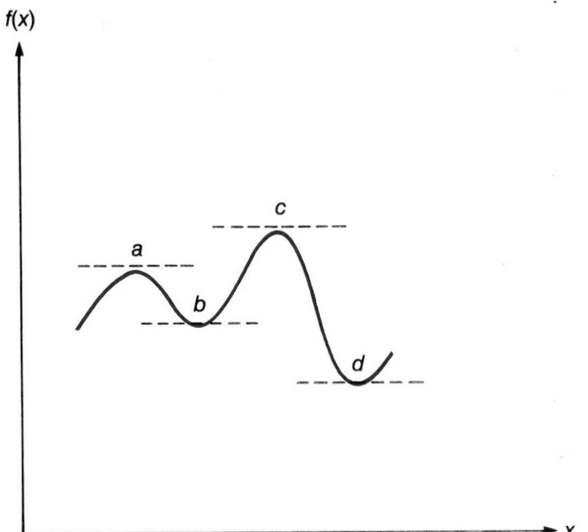

One characteristic common to these extreme points is that the slope of the line tangent to the curve at each point is equal to zero. This observation, in fact, leads to the **necessary condition** for identifying extreme points. That is, a necessary condition for an extreme point at $x = x^*$ is that the tangent to the function at $x = x^*$ has a slope equal to zero. Any point having a tangent slope equal to zero is called a **stationary point.** As will be shown later, stationary points do not have to be extreme points.

Recall that the first derivative of a function represents a general relationship for the slope of the function at any point on the function. Put another way, the first derivative of a function provides a mathematical expression in x that indicates the instantaneous rate of change for the function at any given point. Stationary points, if they exist, can be found by determining the values of x (roots) that satisfy the equation when the first derivative is set equal to zero. Stationary values of x will be distinguished from other values of x by the notation x^*.

▶ Example B.4

The first derivative of the function

$$y = f(x)$$
$$= 4x^2 + 4x + 2$$

is given by

$$f'(x) = 8x + 4$$

At $x = 0$, it follows that $f'(0) = +4$. This means that a line tangent to the original function at $x = 0$ has a slope equal to $+4$; alternatively, at $x = 0$, y is increasing at the instantaneous rate of four units for each unit increase in the value of x. Similarly, $f'(-2) = -12$; that is, the instantaneous rate of change (slope) at $x = -2$ is -12.

It can be shown easily, by setting the expression for $f'(x)$ to zero and solving for x, that a single stationary point exists at $x^* = -\frac{1}{2}$.

FOLLOW-UP EXERCISES

11. Find the stationary point(s) for the function in part (e) of Example B.2.
12. Find the stationary point(s) for $y = -x^2 + 5x$.

Determining the Nature of Stationary Points

A variety of situations can be characterized by an instantaneous slope of zero. Figure B–3 indicates some of the possibilities. Figures B–3a and B–3b represent maximum and minimum points, respectively. Over the indicated portion of Figure B–3a, the function is said to be **concave downward** (or **concave**). In Figure B–3b, the function is said to be **concave upward** (or **convex**).

FIGURE B–3 Instantaneous Slopes of Zero

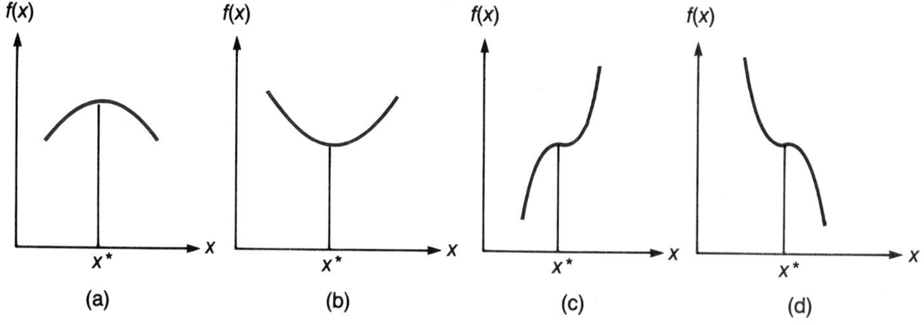

Figures B–3c and B–3d represent situations in which the slope equals zero, but the conditions for local extreme points are not satisfied. These are both cases wherein the functions are said to have stationary inflection points. **Inflection points** are points at which the concavity of a function changes from either concave upward to downward, or vice versa. **Stationary inflection points** are points at which the concavity of the function changes *and* the slope equals zero.

A number of tests can be used to test for the nature of a stationary point—that is, whether it is a relative maximum, a relative minimum, or a stationary inflection point. The tests range from rather intuitive tests that may be computationally cumbersome to tests less intuitive but more efficient computationally. We will examine the two most efficient tests.

Second Derivative Test. The second derivative test takes advantage of the fact that if the value of the second derivative is negative at some point, the function is *concave downward* at that point on the curve. This follows because the second derivative is the rate of change of the first derivative, just as the first derivative is the rate of change or slope of the original function; hence, if the rate of change of the slope is negative, the slope becomes less positive or more negative, and the curve must be concave downward. If the value of the second derivative is positive, the function is *concave upward* at that point on the curve. Consequently, if a stationary point has been identified and the function is concave upward, the stationary point is a relative minimum; if the concavity is downward, the stationary point must be a relative maximum.

To be more precise, *if the first derivative equals zero, and the second derivative,* $f'(x)$ *is defined, then*

1. $f(x^*)$ is a relative minimum if $f''(x^*)$ is greater than (>) 0.
2. $f(x^*)$ is a relative maximum if $f''(x^*)$ is less than (<) 0.
3. The test breaks down or is indeterminate if $f''(x) = 0$.

Verify for yourself that a *relative* minimum (maximum) is a *global* minimum (maximum) if the second derivative is positive (negative) throughout the relevant range of x.

▶ Example B.5

Testing the stationary point found at $x^* = -½$ in Example B.4, we get

$$f'(x) = 8x + 4$$

$$f''(x) = 8$$

$$f''(-½) = 8.$$

Therefore, the function $y = 4x^2 + 4x + 2$ has a relative minimum at $x = -½$. The minimum value for y can be verified as $f(-½) = 1$.

▶ Example B.6

The first derivative for the function $y = x^3 + 2x^2 + 5$ is given by

$$f'(x) = 3x^2 + 4x.$$

Setting $f'(x)$ equal to zero and solving for x yields

$$3x^2 + 4x = 0$$

$$x(3x + 4) = 0$$

and

$$x^* = 0, -4/3\,.$$

In this instance, two stationary points exist. Applying the second derivative test gives

$$f''(x) = 6x + 4$$

$$f''(0) = 6(0) + 4 = 4 > 0\,,$$

or a relative minimum occurs when $x^* = 0$, and

$$f''(-4/3) = 6(-4/3) + 4 = -4 < 0\,,$$

or a relative maximum occurs on the function when $x^* = -4/3$. This function is sketched in Figure B–4.

FIGURE B–4 Sketch of $y = x^3 + 2x^2 + 5$

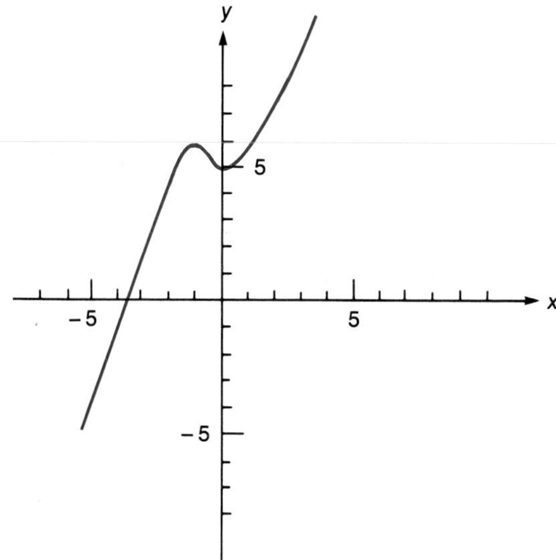

FOLLOW-UP EXERCISES

13. Identify the nature of the stationary point(s) in Exercise 11. Sketch the function.
14. Identify the nature of the stationary point(s) in Exercise 12. Sketch the function.
15. Find the stationary point(s) for and sketch the second-degree polynomial $y = -x^2 + 20x - 100$. Identify the nature of the stationary point(s) and indicate if a global extremum has been found.

Higher-Order Derivative Test. The second derivative test is actually a special case of tests based on higher-ordered derivatives. As opposed to the second derivative test, the higher-order derivative test will not fail in distinguishing the nature of stationary points. The test procedure is as follows:

1. Find the lowest-ordered derivative for which the value of the derivative is nonzero at the stationary point and denote this derivative as $f^n(x)$ where n is the order of the derivative.
2. If the order of this derivative is even, the stationary point is
   a. A relative maximum if $f^n(x^*) < 0$.
   b. A relative minimum if $f^n(x^*) > 0$.
3. If the order of this derivative is odd, the stationary point is a stationary inflection point.

▶ Example B.7

If $y = x^4$, then $f'(x) = 4x^3$. Setting the first derivative equal to zero and solving to x gives $x^* = 0$. Taking the second derivative, we get

$$f''(x) = 12x^2$$

and

$$f''(0) = 12(0)^2 = 0.$$

Since the value of the second derivative equals zero at the stationary point, higher-ordered derivatives must be examined.

$$f'''(x) = 24x$$

and

$$f'''(0) = 24(0) = 0.$$

Again, the value of the third derivative equals zero at the stationary point and the next highest derivative must be examined.

$$f''''(x) = 24$$

and

$$f''''(0) = 24.$$

Since the value of the fourth derivative is nonzero, the nature of the stationary point can be determined. In this case, the order of the first nonzero derivative is 4. Given that n is even, the stationary point is either a relative maximum or minimum. Because $f''''(x^*)$ is greater than zero, it is concluded that the function $y = x^4$ has a relative minimum at $x^* = 0$. This can be seen in Figure B–5.

▶ Example B.8

Given the function $f(x) = (x - 2)^3$, it follows that

$$f'(x) = 3(x - 2)^2(1)$$
$$= 3(x - 2)^2.$$

FIGURE B–5 Sketch of $y = x^4$

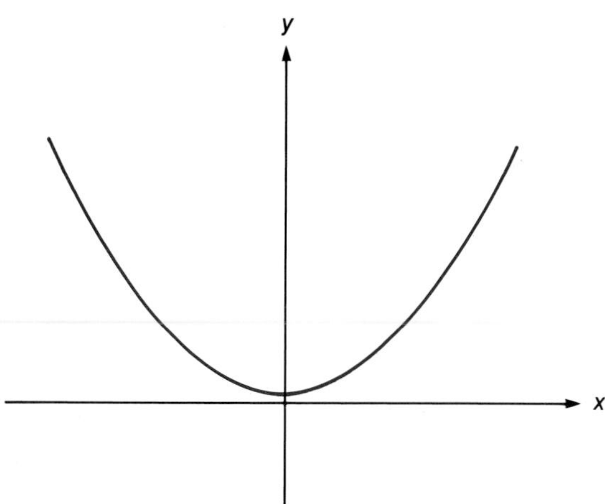

Setting the first derivative equal to zero, we find the one stationary point at $x^* = 2$. Taking the second derivative, we get

$$\begin{aligned} f''(x) &= 6(x - 2)(1) \\ &= 6x - 12 \end{aligned}$$

and

$$\begin{aligned} f''(2) &= 6(2) - 12 \\ &= 0. \end{aligned}$$

Since the value of the second derivative equals zero at the stationary point, the third derivative must be examined.

$$f'''(x) = 6$$

$$f'''(2) = 6.$$

Since the order of this derivative is *odd* ($n = 3$), it is concluded that the function has a stationary inflection point at $x^* = 2$. The function is sketched in Figure B–6.

FOLLOW-UP EXERCISES

For the following functions, identify all stationary points and determine their nature (relative maxima, minima, or stationary inflection point):

16. $y = 5x^2 - 40x + 10.$
17. $y = x^3/3 - 5x^2 + 16x - 100.$
18. $y = x^2 - 10x + 8.$
19. $y = x^4/4 - 9x^2/2.$
20. $y = x^5/5 - x.$
21. $y = x^3/3 + 5x^2/2.$
22. $y = (x^2 - 9)^4.$

FIGURE B–6 Sketch of $y = (x - 2)^3$

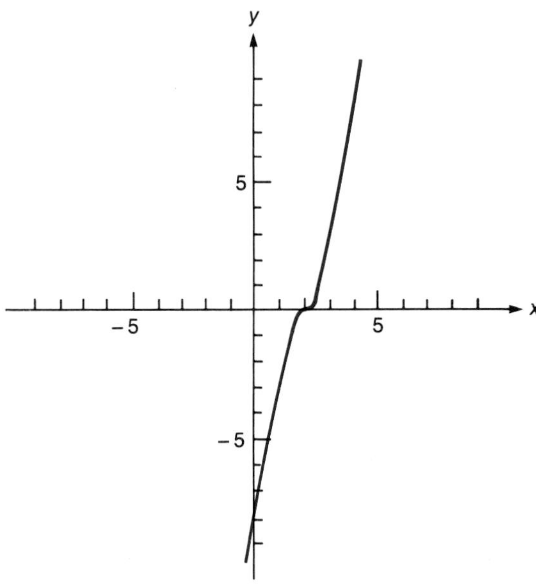

23. $y = e^{3x2+10}$.
24. $y = xe^{-x}$.
25. $y = 1n(30x) - 3x$.
26. $y = 1n(x^2 + 1) - x$.

B.3 TWO-VARIABLE OPTIMIZATION

This section presents the techniques of classical optimization wherein criterion variables are expressed as functions of two independent variables.

The Criterion "Surface"

With one independent variable, an objective function graphs as a curve in two dimensions. If a criterion variable is expressed as a function of two independent variables, then the graphical representation of the relationship is a "surface" in three dimensions. For example, the function

$$z = f(x, y)$$

or

$$z = 9 - x^2 - \frac{y^2}{4}$$

where $z \geq 0$, $x \geq 0$, and $y \geq 0$ is illustrated in Figure B–7. Notice that we focus only on nonnegative values of the three variables. Graphing a function in three dimensions can be accomplished methodically by observing that if a value is assumed for one variable in the function, the three-variable function reduces to a two-variable function, which graphs simply as a curve in two-space.

FIGURE B–7 Graphical Representation of a Surface

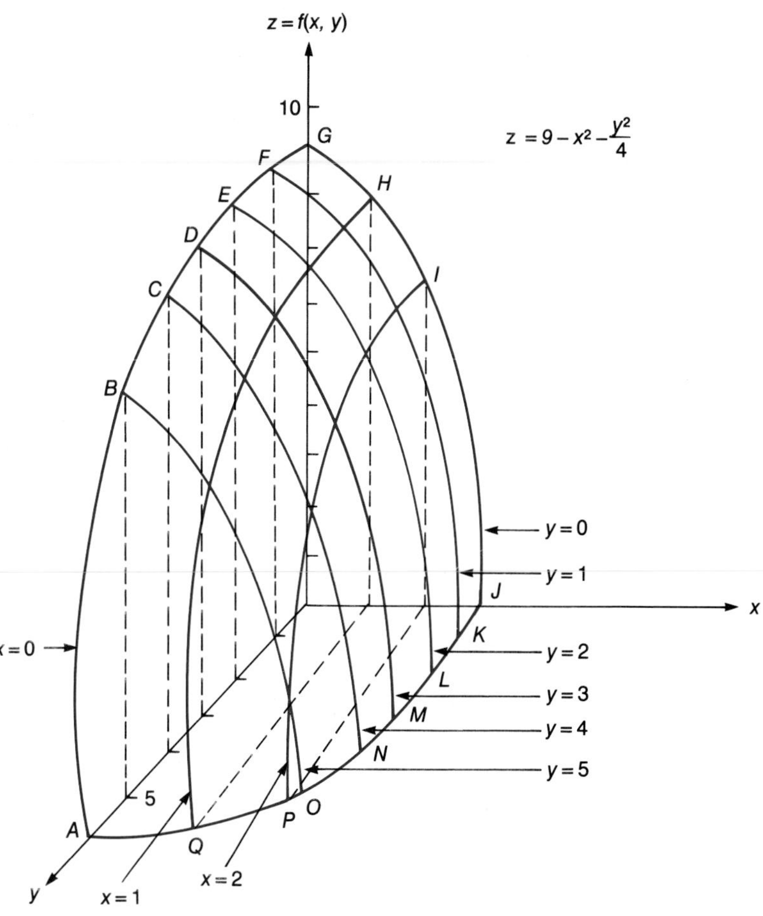

To illustrate how this function was graphed, if x is assumed to equal zero, then the original function becomes

$$z = 9 - (0)^2 - \frac{y^2}{4}$$

$$= 9 - \frac{y^2}{4}.$$

This can be graphed in the zy-plane as a parabola by simply assuming values for y and finding the corresponding values for z. The graphic representation of such a function where one variable is assumed constant is called a **trace**. The trace representing the original function where $x = 0$ is the curve AG in Figure B–7. If x is assumed equal to one, the original function reduces to

$$z = 9 - (1)^2 - \frac{y^2}{4}$$

$$= 8 - \frac{y^2}{4}.$$

Graphically, the trace representing this function is the curve QH, which is parallel to the zy-plane and intersects the x-axis at $x = 1$. One can easily see that if an infinite number of values are assumed for the variable x, the set of associated traces would collectively define the **surface** of the function. Each tract is effectively a "rib," and the composite of all traces forms the shell that represents the function.

Similarly, if values are assumed for the variable y, traces can be graphed parallel to the zx-plane. For example, if $y = 0$, the original function becomes

$$z = 9 - x^2.$$

Graphically, this trace forms parabola GJ, which is parallel to the zx-plane and cuts through the y-axis at $y = 0$. Traces FK, EL, DM, CN, and BO can be defined in the same manner by assuming values of 1, 2, 3, 4, and 5, respectively, for the variable y.

Partial Derivatives and Their Meaning

The calculus of multivariate functions, although more involved, is surprisingly similar to that of single-variable functions. The derivative of a single-variable function represents the instantaneous rate of change of the criterion variable with respect to a change in the independent variable. The derivative of a multivariate function also represents the instantaneous rate of change in the criterion variable, but with respect to changes in each of the variables, separately.

The derivative of a multivariate function is termed a **partial derivative.** Partial derivatives can be found with respect to each of the independent variables of a function. For example, given a function of the form

$$z = f(x, y)$$

derivatives can be taken with respect to both x and y. The partial derivative taken with respect to x is denoted as $\partial z/\partial x$, or sometimes as f_x; that taken with respect to y is denoted as $\partial z/\partial y$, or f_y.

The partial derivative taken with respect to x reflects the instantaneous rate of change in z with respect to a change in x only. To determine this effect, other independent variables *cannot* be allowed to fluctuate. If they are allowed to change, the change in z attributable solely to the variable x is difficult to determine. Thus all other independent variables are assumed constant. The resulting derivative effectively provides a general expression for the instantaneous slope of the family of traces parallel to the zx-plane.

In finding $\partial z/\partial y$, x is assumed to be constant. The resulting partial derivative represents the instantaneous rate of change in z with respect to a change in y. Another interpretation is that it gives a general expression for the instantaneous slope of the family of traces parallel to the *zy*-plane.

The rules for finding partial derivatives are the same as for single-variable functions. The only exception is that the other independent variables must be assumed constant when finding the derivatives. As an illustration, the partial derivative, taken with respect to x of the previously graphed function, is

$$f_x = \frac{\partial z}{\partial x} = -2x .$$

In finding this derivative, the variable y is assumed to be constant and is treated accordingly in applying the derivative rules. As indicated, this represents a general expression for the slope of any trace parallel to the *zx*-plane. Try verifying this expression by rewriting the equations for traces *GJ*, *FK*, *EL*, *DM*, *CN*, or *BO* and taking the derivatives of these with respect to x.

The partial derivative with respect to y is

$$f_y = \frac{\partial z}{\partial y} = -\frac{y}{2} .$$

In finding this derivative, x is assumed constant and is treated accordingly. This derivative represents a general expression for the slope of the family of traces parallel to the *zy*-plane. You can verify this by taking the derivatives of any of the equations representing traces *AG*, *QH*, or *PI*.

Example B.9

Given the function $z = 3x^2 - 2xy + 4y^2 + 100$, the partial derivatives are:

$$f_x = 6x - 2y$$

$$f_y = -2x + 8y .$$

FOLLOW-UP EXERCISES

27. Find f_x and f_y for $z = 4x^2 - 3y^2 + 75$.
28. Find f_x and f_y for $z = x^2 - 2x^2y + xy - 5y^2$.
29. Find f_x and f_y for $z = 3(x^2 - y)^5$.
30. Find f_x and f_y for $z = x^2/y^2$.

Example B.10 Two-Variable Marketing Problem

Assume that annual profits for a television manufacturer can be estimated by the function

$$P(x,y) = 300x + 400y - x^2 - 2y^2 - 2xy$$

where P = Profit in \$100s; x = Number of franchised retail outlets; and y = Advertising expenditures (\$1,000s).

Currently, the firm uses 50 retailers and is spending \$60,000 on advertising. The marginal effect on profits of adding an additional retailer can be approximated by evaluating

$$f_x = 300 - 2x - 2y.$$

If the partial derivative is evaluated at $x = 50$ and $y = 60$,

$$\begin{aligned} f_x(50, 60) &= 300 - 2(50) - 2(60) \\ &= 80, \end{aligned}$$

or profits will increase by approximately \$8,000 with the increase of one retailer—holding advertising expenditures the same. We say "approximately" because the partial derivatives represent tangent slopes to the criterion surface at a particular point. And, as was observed in two dimensions, tangent slopes are continually changing on nonlinear functions.

Similarly, the marginal effect of increasing advertising expenditures by \$1,000 can be estimated by evaluating

$$\begin{aligned} f_y &= 400 - 4y - 2x \\ &= 400 - 4(60) - 2(50) \\ &= 60, \end{aligned}$$

or profits will increase by approximately \$6,000 with an increase of \$1,000 in advertising expenditures.

FOLLOW-UP EXERCISES

31. Compute total profit when $x = 50$ and $y = 60$. Then compute total profit when $x = 51$ and $y = 60$ and compare with the increase in profits expected in Example B.10. Also compute total profit at $x = 50$ and $y = 61$ and compare. Can you explain discrepancies?

Higher-Ordered Partial Derivatives

As with single-variable functions, higher-ordered derivatives can be found for multivariate functions. The interpretation of these derivatives is similar to that for single-variable functions; their importance, as with single-variable functions, is in identifying extreme points.

Second derivatives for a function of the from $z = f(x, y)$ can be of two types: **pure partial derivatives** and **mixed, or cross, partial derivatives.** $\partial^2 z/\partial x^2$ or f_{xx} represents the pure second partial derivative with respect to x. It is found by first determining f_x and then differentiating again with respect to x. From an intuitive standpoint, this derivative offers information about the concavity of traces parallel to the zx-plane. $\partial^2 z/\partial y^2$ or f_{yy} is the second pure partial derivative with respect to y. It is found by first solving for f_y and then differentiating with respect to y. This derivative offers information about the concavity of traces parallel to the zy-plane.

In addition to the two pure second partials, two cross partial derivatives can be found. $\partial^2 z/\partial x\,\partial y$ or f_{yx} is determined by first finding f_y.[1] This partial derivative is then

[1] In the notation f_{yx} the first subscript represents the base with regard to which the first partial derivative was taken and the second subscript is the base of the second derivative.

differentiated with respect to x in order to find the cross partial derivative. The interpretation of this derivative is less intuitive than the pure second derivatives. It represents the rate of change in the slope of traces which are parallel to the zy-plane as the plane shifts incrementally in the x direction.

The other cross partial derivative is found in a similar manner, but by reversing the order of taking the derivatives. In other words, to find $\partial^2 z/\partial y\,\partial x$ of f_{xy}, f_x is found and is then differentiated with respect to y. The interpretation of this cross partial derivative is that it describes the rate of change in the slope of traces parallel to the zx-plane as the plane shifts incrementally in the y direction.

The cross partial derivatives are always equal to one another. In other words, $f_{yx} = f_{xy}$.

▶ Example B.11

Find all first and second derivatives for the function

$$z = f(x, y) = 5x^3 - 2x^2y + 2y^3 - xy + 100.$$

Solution:

$$f_x = 15x^2 - 4xy - y.$$

$$f_y = -2x^2 + 6y^2 - x.$$

$$f_{xx} = 30x - 4y.$$

$$f_{yy} = 12y.$$

$$f_{yx} = -4x - 1.$$

$$f_{xy} = -4x - 1.$$

FOLLOW-UP EXERCISES

32. Find all second derivatives for the function in Exercise 27.
33. Find all second derivatives for the function in Exercise 28.
34. Find all second derivatives for the function in Exercise 29.
35. Find all second derivatives for the function in Exercise 30.

Conditions for Optimality in Three Dimensions

The process of finding optimum values for functions involving two independent variables is similar to that for single-variable functions. It must be remembered that functions of the form $z = f(x, y)$ are graphically represented by a surface in three dimensions. Relative maximum and relative minimum points can be visualized as the tops of "mounds" or the bottoms of "valleys" on the surface. Figures B–8 and B–9 illustrate relative maximum and minimum points, respectively.

If one examines the conditions at the top of a mound or at the bottom of a valley, it would be found that the slope is zero in all directions. This leads to the **necessary condition** for the existence of a relative maximum or minimum. The first partial derivatives of the criterion function must equal zero:

$$f_x = 0 \quad \text{and} \quad f_y = 0. \tag{B.3}$$

FIGURE B–8 Relative Maximum for a Surface

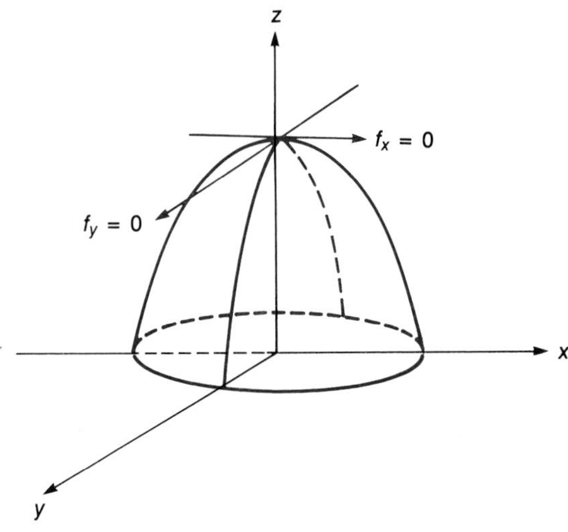

FIGURE B–9 Relative Minimum for a Surface

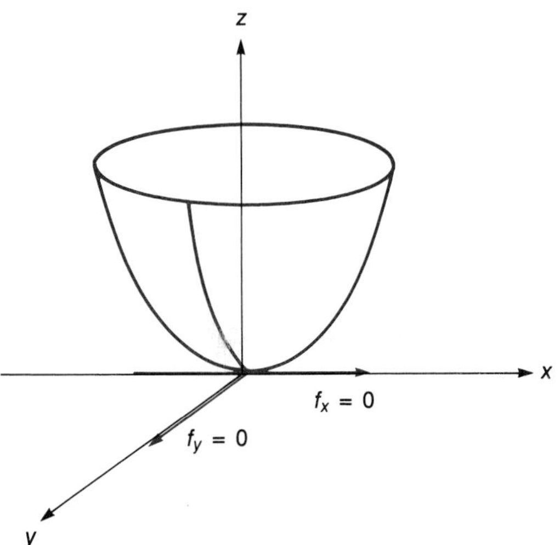

This seems logical if one recalls that the first partial derivatives represent expressions for the instantaneous slope of traces parallel to the *zx*-plane and *zy*-plane. This condition implies that the slopes in both directions must equal zero at a relative maximum or minimum. Any points that satisfy the necessary conditions are termed **stationary points,** as before. These stationary points should have coordinates, or locations, specified for *both* of the independent variables.

Once stationary points have been identified, their nature is determined by way of a second derivative test, which intuitively investigates the **sufficiency (concavity) con-**

ditions at the stationary point. The conditions for determining the nature of a stationary point located at the point (x^*, y^*, z) require the evaluation of

$$D(x^*, y^*) = f_{xx} \cdot f_{yy} - (f_{xy})^2. \tag{B.4}$$

1. If $D(x^*, y^*) > 0$, then
   a. The stationary point is a relative maximum if *both* $f_{xx}(x^*, y^*)$ and $f_{yy}(x^*, y^*)$ are less than zero.
   b. The stationary point is a relative minimum if *both* $f_{xx}(x^*, y^*)$ and $f_{yy}(x^*, y^*)$ are greater than zero.
2. If $D(x^*, y^*) < 0$, the stationary point is what is referred to as a **saddle-point.** A saddle-point is neither a maximum nor a minimum. It satisfies the necessary conditions for a maximum or a minimum, but the concavity conditions are not satisfied. Figure B–10 illustrates a saddle-point.
3. If $D(x^*, y^*) = 0$, other techniques are required to determine the nature of the stationary point.[2]

FIGURE B–10 Saddle-Point

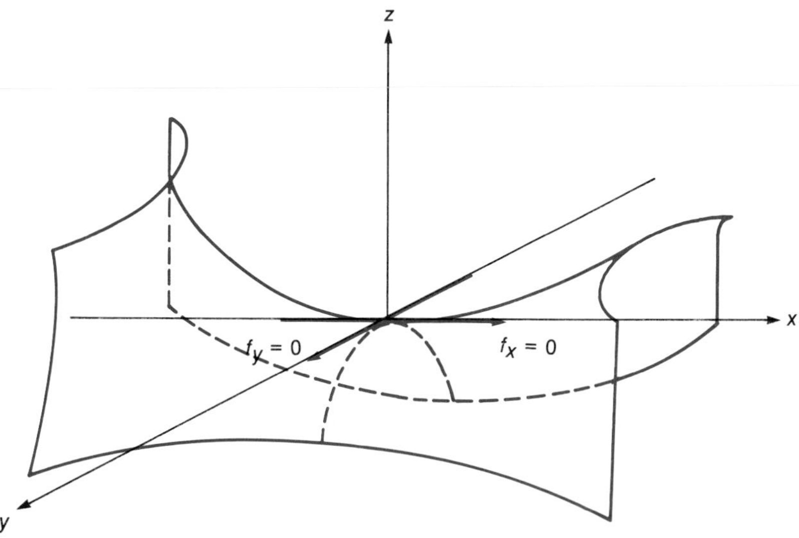

▶ Example B.12

Given

$$z = 4x^2 + 2y^2 - 8x - 2y + 1,$$

[2]For example, see D. Teichroew, *An Introduction to Management Science, Deterministic Models* (New York: John Wiley & Sons, 1964), pp. 270–72.

find all stationary points and determine their nature.

The first partial derivatives are expressed as $f_x = 8x - 8$ and $f_y = 4y - 2$. It follows that $f_x = 0$ when $x^* = 1$ and $f_y = 0$ when $y^* = 1/2$. Thus the only stationary point on the function occurs when $x = 1$ and $y = 1/2$. Finding all second derivatives, we get

$$f_{xx} = 8$$
$$f_{yy} = 4$$
$$f_{xy} = 0$$
$$f_{yx} = 0,$$

and computing $D(x^*, y^*)$, we find that

$$D(1, 1/2) = 8(4) - (0)^2$$
$$= 32.$$

Since $D(x^*, y^*) > 0$, the stationary point is either a relative maximum or a relative minimum. Evaluating the two pure partial derivatives at the stationary point, we find that both are greater than zero, or

$$f_{xx}(1, 1/2) = 8$$

and

$$f_{yy}(1, 1/2) = 4;$$

hence the stationary point is a relative minimum. The value for z at this point is

$$z = 4(1)^2 + 2(1/2)^2 - 8(1) - 2(1/2) + 1$$
$$= -3.5.$$

▶ Example B.13

To locate all stationary points and determine their nature if

$$z = \frac{x^3}{3} - \frac{5x^2}{2} + 3y^2 - 12y,$$

we first determine the first partial derivatives

$$f_x = x^2 - 5x$$
$$f_y = 6y - 12.$$

Setting these equal to zero,

$$f_x = x^2 - 5x = 0 \quad \text{when } x = 0 \text{ and } x = 5$$
$$f_y = 6y - 12 = 0 \quad \text{when } y = 2.$$

Thus there are two stationary points on the function; one occurs when $x^* = 0$ and $y^* = 2$ and the other when $x^* = 5$ and $y^* = 2$.

In order to test the nature of these two stationary points, we first find the second partial derivatives:

$$f_{xx} = 2x - 5$$

$$f_{yy} = 6$$
$$f_{xy} = 0$$
$$f_{yx} = 0.$$

Testing the first stationary point,

$$D(0, 2) = [2(0) - 5](6) - (0)^2$$
$$= -30 < 0.$$

Since $D(0, 2) < 0$, we conclude that the stationary point is a saddle point.

Testing the second stationary point,

$$D(5, 2) = [2(5) - 5](6) - (0)^2$$
$$= 30 > 0.$$

Because $D > 0$ and $f_{xx}(5, 2) = 5 > 0$ and $f_{yy}(5, 2) = 6 > 0$, we conclude that the stationary point is a relative minimum.

FOLLOW-UP EXERCISES

In the following exercises, locate any stationary points and determine their nature.

36. $y = x_1^2 - x_1 + 2x_2^2 - 2x_2$.
37. $y = x_1^2 - 3x_1x_2 + 5x_1 + 2x_2^2 - 6x_2$.
38. $y = 10x_1^2 - 10x_1x_2 - 30x_1 + 8x_2^2 + 37x_2$.
39. $y = -x_1^3 + 24x_1^2 - 4x_2^2 + 100$.

SELECTED REFERENCES

See Chapter 2 references.

ADDITIONAL EXERCISES

40. Find the first and second derivatives for the following functions:
    - a. $y = 3x^6$.
    - b. $y = 6x^2 - 4x + 10$.
    - c. $y = (5x^2 - 1)(x^3 + 3)$.
    - d. $y = (1 - x)/x^2$.
    - e. $y = (x + 2)^3$.
    - f. $y = e^{(5-x2)}$.
    - g. $y = \ln(x^2 - 5x)$.
    - h. $y = (6)^{3x}$.
    - i. $y = 12x^4 - 5x^3 + 100$.
    - j $y = 15x/(1 - x^2)$.
    - k. $y = (x^3 - 1)^4$.
    - l. $y = x^2\sqrt{x}$.
    - m. $y = 5x^3/3 + 2x^2 + 3x - 100$.
    - n. $y = e^{x2-5x}$.

o. $y = ln(5x^5 - 3x^2)$.
p. $y = (9 - x^2)(x + 3)^4$.
q. $y = 7/\sqrt{x - 1}$.
r. $y = [(x^2 + 3)/(4 - x)]^3$.

41. For the following functions, identify all stationary points, and determine their nature (relative maxima, minima, or stationary inflection point).
a. $y = 12x^2 - 6x + 50$.
b. $y = -6x^4$.
c. $y = 2(x - 3)^3$.
d. $y = e^{-5x} - 4x$.
e. $y = x^3 - 9x^2 - 100$.
f. $y = 2x^2 - 5x + 3$.
g. $y = -x^2/2 + 6x - 7$.
h. $y = x^4 - 9x^2/2$.
i. $y = x^3 - 2x^2 + 4$.
j. $y = 3x^4 - 16x^3 + 24x^2 + 10$.
k. $y = x^4 - 20x^3 + 100x^2 + 80$.
l. $y = 50x - e^x$.
m. $y = e^{(x-.2x2)}$.
n. $y = 20x - e^{0.1x} + 50$.

42. For the following functions, find *all* first and second partial derivatives.
a. $y = 5x_1^3 - 2x_1^2x_2 + 4x_2^2$.
b. $y = 4x_1^2 - 2x_1x_2 + 8x_2^2$.
c. $y = -2x_1^2 - 5x_1 + 6x_2^2 + 6x_2 - 10x_1x_2$.
d. $y = 10e^{x_1x_2}$.
e. $y = e^{-x_1^2 + x_2^2}$.
f. $y = 6x_1^2 - 2x_1x_2 + x_2^2 - 6x_2x_3 + 2x_3^2$.
g. $y = 10x_1^2 - 5x_2^2 + 8x_3^2$.
h. $y = 2x_1^2 + 3x_1x_2 - x_1x_2^2 + 3x_2^4$.
i. $y = 10x_1x_2^4 - 20x_1 + 30x_2^3$.
j. $y = e^{x_1x_2}$.
k. $y = e^{(2x_1 - x_1x_2)}$.

43. For each of the following functions, identify any stationary points and determine their nature.
a. $y = 2x_1^2 - 2x_1 + x_2^2 - x_2$.
b. $y = -x_1^2 - 2x_2^2 + x_1 + 4x_2 - 2x_1x_2$.
c. $y = 5x_1^2 + 20x_1 - 8x_2^2 + 40x_2$
d. $y = x_1^2 - 2x_1x_2^2 + 4x_2^2$.
e. $y = 4x_1^2 - x_2^2 + 80x_1 + 20x_2 - 10$.
f. $y = x_1^2 + x_1x_2 - 5x_1 - 2x_2^2 + 2x_2$.
g. $y = x_1^3 + x_2^3 - 3x_1x_2$.
h. $y = x_1^2 - 2x_1x_2 + 3x_2^2 + 4x_1 - 16x_2 + 22$.

Appendix C
Matrix Concepts

A matrix is a rectangular array of numbers. It is described as being of dimension $m \times n$ if it has m rows and n columns. In the generalized matrix below, the elements are denoted by a_{ij} where i is the row and j is the column in which the element is located.

$$\mathbf{A} = \begin{pmatrix} a_{11} & a_{12} & a_{13} & \cdots & a_{1n} \\ a_{21} & a_{22} & a_{23} & \cdots & a_{2n} \\ \vdots & \vdots & \vdots & \ddots & \vdots \\ a_{m1} & a_{m2} & a_{m3} & \cdots & a_{mn} \end{pmatrix}$$

Matrices provide a powerful, practical, and efficient vehicle for both representing and manipulating data. They are compact in their representation and lend themselves well to computer applications. In fact, the manipulation of matrices for an important class of linear models in mathematics and statistics has become so central that the field of **linear** (or **matrix**) **algebra** has evolved.

C.1 THE DETERMINANT

Any **square matrix** (that is, a matrix with $m = n$) has an associated scalar value called the **determinant** of the matrix. If a matrix is denoted by the symbol **A**, then the determinant of the matrix is represented as $|\mathbf{A}|$. Although the determinant can be defined rigorously in terms of permutations of the elements in the matrix and its importance in mathematics can be illustrated, we will devote our present efforts to calculating the value of the determinant. An appreciation of its usefulness will be deferred to other sections of this textbook.

If a matrix is 1×1 in dimension, then the determinant is equal to the element in the matrix. For example, if

$$\mathbf{A} = (-6)$$

then

$$|\mathbf{A}| = -6\,.$$

If a matrix is of dimension (2×2) and has the general form

$$\mathbf{A} = \begin{pmatrix} a & b \\ c & d \end{pmatrix},$$

then

$$|\mathbf{A}| = a \cdot d - c \cdot b\,.$$

For example, if

$$\mathbf{A} = \begin{pmatrix} 2 & -5 \\ 6 & 3 \end{pmatrix},$$

then

$$\begin{aligned} |\mathbf{A}| &= (2)(3) - (6)(-5) \\ &= 36\,. \end{aligned}$$

The most generalized approach for finding a determinant is the **method of cofactors.** For this method, the determinant can be found by expanding along *any* row or column. The expansion is performed by selecting any row or column, multiplying each element in the row or column by its cofactor, and algebraically summing. For any row, i, of an $m \times m$ matrix,

$$|\mathbf{A}| = \sum_{j=1}^{m} a_{ij} \cdot c_{ij} = a_{i1} \cdot c_{i1} + a_{i2} \cdot c_{i2} + \cdots + a_{im} \cdot c_{im}$$

where c_{ij} = The cofactor associated with matrix element a_{ij}. For any column, j, of an $m \times m$ matrix,

$$|\mathbf{A}| = \sum_{i=1}^{m} a_{ij} \cdot c_{ij} = a_{1j} \cdot c_{1j} + a_{2j} \cdot c_{2j} + \cdots + a_{mj} \cdot c_{mj} .$$

A cofactor can be defined for each element of a square matrix. If a_{ij} represents the element contained in row i and column j of the original matrix, c_{ij} is used to represent the cofactor associated with a_{ij}. To find the cofactor, c_{ij}:

1. Eliminate row i and column j of the original matrix.
2. Calculate the **minor**, which is the determinant of the remaining submatrix $\mathbf{S}_{ij}$.
3. Find the cofactor by multiplying the minor by either plus or minus one, depending upon the position of the original element in the matrix. Specifically,

$$c_{ij} = (-1)^{i+j} \cdot |\mathbf{S}_{ij}|$$

where $|\mathbf{S}_{ij}|$ is the minor associated with element a_{ij}; that is, the determinant of the submatrix $\mathbf{S}_{ij}$.

Example C.1

Find the cofactor for the element a_{11} in the 3×3 matrix

$$\mathbf{A} = \begin{pmatrix} 5 & 2 & 4 \\ 1 & 0 & 6 \\ 2 & 3 & 2 \end{pmatrix} .$$

Crossing off row 1 and column 1 leaves the 2×2 submatrix

$$\mathbf{S}_{11} = \begin{pmatrix} 0 & 6 \\ 3 & 2 \end{pmatrix} .$$

The determinant of the submatrix equals -18 and is the minor. The cofactor, c_{11}, is found as

$$\begin{aligned} c_{11} &= (-1)^{1+1}(-18) \\ &= -18 . \end{aligned}$$

You should verify that the matrix below contains the cofactors for all elements in the original matrix.

$$\mathbf{C} = \begin{pmatrix} -18 & 10 & 3 \\ 8 & 2 & -11 \\ 12 & -26 & -2 \end{pmatrix}.$$

You should also verify that by expanding along any row or column, the determinant is found to have a value of −58. For example, expanding down column 3,

$$\begin{aligned} |\mathbf{A}| &= a_{13} \cdot C_{13} + a_{23} \cdot C_{23} + a_{33} \cdot C_{33} \\ &= 4(3) + 6(-11) + 2(-2) \\ &= -58. \end{aligned}$$

Do you see any advantages to expanding along either row 2 or down column 2? Computational efficiencies are introduced if you expand along any row or column containing zeros in the original matrix. For such elements, it is unnecessary to compute the cofactor.

The method of cofactors is valid for matrices larger than 3 × 3. In a 4 × 4 matrix, the computation of cofactors requires finding the determinant of 3 × 3 submatrices. For 5 × 5 matrices, it is necessary to find the determinants of 4 × 4 matrices, and so forth. Obviously, the process of finding determinants for matrices larger than 3 × 3 becomes tedious by hand calculations. Those of us regularly requiring determinants need not despair, however; computer packages for evaluating determinants are common.

C.2 MATRIX MULTIPLICATION

Matrix algebra facilitates the manipulation of data stored in matrix form. In this section we present a brief discussion of matrix multiplication, an understanding of which is useful in Chapter 15.

Let us define a matrix, **A**, as having dimension (rows and columns) m_1 by n_1, or $m_1 \times n_1$. Another matrix, **B**, has dimension $m_2 \times n_2$. Two matrices may be multiplied if and only if the number of columns in the first matrix equals the number of rows in the second matrix. As an example, the multiplication of matrix **A** times matrix **B**, defined by **AB**, is possible if and only if $n_1 = m_2$. Similarly, the product **BA** is possible if and only if $n_2 = m_1$.

If it is determined that matrix multiplication is possible, then the resulting matrix will have dimension $m \times n$ where m equals the number of rows contained in the first matrix and n equals the number of columns in the second matrix. Referring to the matrices **A** and **B**, we see that if **AB** is possible and

$$\mathbf{AB} = \mathbf{C},$$

then the product matrix, **C**, will have dimension $m_1 \times n_2$. Similarly, if **BA** is possible and

$$\mathbf{BA} = \mathbf{D},$$

then **D** will have dimension $m_2 \times n_1$.

To actually compute the product matrix, consider the product

$$\mathbf{AB} = \mathbf{C}.$$

Let c_{ij} be a generalized element located in row i and column j of the product matrix. To compute any c_{ij}, the elements in row i of matrix **A** are multiplied times the respective elements in column j of matrix **B** and are algebraically summed. This operation is often called a **vector** or **inner product.** This rule will be illustrated by the following examples.

▶ Example C.2

If

$$\mathbf{A} = \begin{pmatrix} 1 & 4 \\ 5 & -3 \end{pmatrix}$$

and

$$\mathbf{B} = \begin{pmatrix} 1 \\ 4 \end{pmatrix},$$

then **A** is a 2×2 matrix and **B** is a 2×1 matrix. If we desire to find the product **AB**, then we must first examine the dimensions of the matrices. The product **AB** involves multiplying matrices with dimensions

Inner Dimensions

$$(2 \times 2) \text{ times } (2 \times 1).$$

Outer Dimensions

This product is defined because the "inner" dimensions are equal; that is, the number of columns of **A** equals the number of rows of **B**. The product matrix **C** will have dimension equal to the "outer" dimensions indicated above, that is, 2×1. Thus the product will be of the form

$$\mathbf{AB} = \mathbf{C}$$

or

$$\begin{pmatrix} 1 & 4 \\ 5 & -3 \end{pmatrix} \begin{pmatrix} 1 \\ 4 \end{pmatrix} = \begin{pmatrix} c_{11} \\ c_{21} \end{pmatrix}.$$

To compute the elements of **C**,

$$c_{11} = (1 \quad 4)\begin{pmatrix} 1 \\ 4 \end{pmatrix} = (1)(1) + (4)(4)$$

$$= 17$$

and

$$c_{21} = (5 \quad -3)\begin{pmatrix}1\\4\end{pmatrix} = (5)(1) + (-3)(4)$$

$$= -7,$$

or

$$\mathbf{C} = \begin{pmatrix}17\\-7\end{pmatrix}.$$

The product, **BA**, is not defined because the inner dimensions do not match; that is, it involves multiplying a 2×1 matrix times a 2×2 matrix, and the number of columns of **B** *does not equal* the number of rows of **A** ($1 \neq 2$).

▶ Example C.3

If

$$\mathbf{A} = \begin{pmatrix}1 & 0 & 6\\2 & -3 & 1\end{pmatrix}$$

and

$$\mathbf{B} = \begin{pmatrix}1 & 0 & 0\\0 & 1 & 0\\0 & 0 & 1\end{pmatrix},$$

then **AB** is defined because inner dimensions match. In this case **C** will have dimensions 2×3:

$$\mathbf{AB} = \mathbf{C}$$

or

$$\begin{pmatrix}1 & 0 & 6\\2 & -3 & 1\end{pmatrix}\begin{pmatrix}1 & 0 & 0\\0 & 1 & 0\\0 & 0 & 1\end{pmatrix} = \begin{pmatrix}c_{11} & c_{12} & c_{13}\\c_{21} & c_{22} & c_{23}\end{pmatrix}.$$

The elements of **C** are computed as follows:

$$c_{11} = (1 \quad 0 \quad 6)\begin{pmatrix}1\\0\\0\end{pmatrix} = (1)(1) + (0)(0) + (6)(0)$$

$$= 1,$$

$$c_{12} = (1 \quad 0 \quad 6)\begin{pmatrix}0\\1\\0\end{pmatrix} = (1)(0) + (0)(1) + (6)(0)$$

$$= 0,$$

$$c_{13} = (1 \quad 0 \quad 6)\begin{pmatrix}0\\0\\1\end{pmatrix} = (1)(0) + (0)(0) + (6)(1)$$

$$= 6,$$

$$c_{21} = (2 \quad -3 \quad 1)\begin{pmatrix}1\\0\\0\end{pmatrix} = (2)(1) + (-3)(0) + (1)(0)$$

$$= 2,$$

$$c_{22} = (2 \quad -3 \quad 1)\begin{pmatrix}0\\1\\0\end{pmatrix} = (2)(0) + (-3)(1) + (1)(0)$$

$$= -3,$$

and

$$c_{23} = (2 \quad -3 \quad 1)\begin{pmatrix}0\\0\\1\end{pmatrix} = (2)(0) + (-3)(0) + (1)(1)$$

$$= 1,$$

or

$$\mathbf{C} = \begin{pmatrix}1 & 0 & 6\\2 & -3 & 1\end{pmatrix}.$$

Notice anything peculiar about the preceding example? Matrix **B** is called a 3×3 **identity matrix.** By definition, an identity matrix is a square matrix with 1s along the main diagonal and 0s elsewhere. If the product of an identity matrix, **I**, and another matrix, **A**, is defined, then the resultant product matrix will simply equal matrix **A**, or

$$\mathbf{AI} = \mathbf{A}$$

In effect, **I** is to matrix multiplication what the number 1 is to scalar multiplication. For this reason, $\mathbf{A} \equiv \mathbf{C}$ in Example C.3. Note, however, that the product **BA** or **IA** is not defined in Example C.3. Why?

Appendix D
Selected Tables

TABLE D–1 Exponential Functions

x	e^x	e^{-x}	x	e^x	e^{-x}	x	e^x	e^{-x}
0.010	1.0101	0.9901	0.610	1.8404	0.5434	2.050	7.7678	0.1287
0.020	1.0202	0.9802	0.620	1.8589	0.5379	2.100	8.1660	0.1225
0.030	1.0305	0.9704	0.630	1.8776	0.5326	2.150	8.5847	0.1165
0.040	1.0408	0.9608	0.640	1.8965	0.5273	2.200	9.0250	0.1108
0.050	1.0513	0.9512	0.650	1.9155	0.5220	2.250	9.4875	0.1054
0.060	1.0618	0.9418	0.660	1.9348	0.5169	2.300	9.9740	0.1003
0.070	1.0725	0.9324	0.670	1.9542	0.5117	2.350	10.486	0.0954
0.080	1.0833	0.9231	0.680	1.9739	0.5066	2.400	11.023	0.0907
0.090	1.0942	0.9139	0.690	1.9937	0.5016	2.450	11.588	0.0863
0.100	1.1052	0.9048	0.700	2.0138	0.4966	2.500	12.182	0.0821
0.110	1.1163	0.8958	0.710	2.0340	0.4916	2.550	12.807	0.0781
0.120	1.1275	0.8869	0.720	2.0544	0.4868	2.600	13.464	0.0743
0.130	1.1388	0.8781	0.730	2.0751	0.4819	2.650	14.154	0.0707
0.140	1.1503	0.8694	0.740	2.0959	0.4771	2.700	14.880	0.0672
0.150	1.1618	0.8607	0.750	2.1170	0.4724	2.750	15.643	0.0639
0.160	1.1735	0.8521	0.760	2.1383	0.4677	2.800	16.445	0.0608
0.170	1.1853	0.8437	0.770	2.1598	0.4630	2.850	17.287	0.0578
0.180	1.1972	0.8353	0.780	2.1815	0.4584	2.900	18.174	0.0550
0.190	1.2092	0.8270	0.790	2.2034	0.4538	2.950	19.106	0.0523
0.200	1.2214	0.8187	0.800	2.2255	0.4493	3.000	20.086	0.0498
0.210	1.2337	0.8106	0.810	2.2479	0.4449	3.050	21.115	0.0474
0.220	1.2461	0.8025	0.820	2.2705	0.4404	3.100	22.198	0.0451
0.230	1.2586	0.7945	0.830	2.2933	0.4360	3.150	23.336	0.0429
0.240	1.2712	0.7866	0.840	2.3164	0.4317	3.200	24.533	0.0408
0.250	1.2840	0.7788	0.850	2.3396	0.4274	3.250	25.790	0.0388
0.260	1.2969	0.7711	0.860	2.3632	0.4232	3.300	27.113	0.0369
0.270	1.3100	0.7634	0.870	2.3869	0.4190	3.350	28.503	0.0351
0.280	1.3231	0.7558	0.880	2.4109	0.4148	3.400	29.964	0.0334
0.290	1.3364	0.7483	0.890	2.4351	0.4107	3.450	31.500	0.0317
0.300	1.3499	0.7408	0.900	2.4596	0.4066	3.500	33.115	0.0302
0.310	1.3634	0.7334	0.910	2.4843	0.4025	3.550	34.813	0.0287
0.320	1.3771	0.7261	0.920	2.5093	0.3985	3.600	36.598	0.0273
0.330	1.3910	0.7189	0.930	2.5345	0.3946	3.650	38.475	0.0260
0.340	1.4049	0.7118	0.940	2.5600	0.3906	3.700	40.447	0.0247
0.350	1.4191	0.7047	0.950	2.5857	0.3867	3.750	42.521	0.0235
0.360	1.4333	0.6977	0.960	2.6117	0.3829	3.800	44.701	0.0224
0.370	1.4477	0.6907	0.970	2.6379	0.3791	3.850	46.993	0.0213
0.380	1.4623	0.6839	0.980	2.6645	0.3753	3.900	49.402	0.0202
0.390	1.4770	0.6771	0.990	2.6912	0.3716	3.950	51.935	0.0193
0.400	1.4918	0.6703	1.000	2.7183	0.3679	4.000	54.598	0.0183
0.410	1.5068	0.6637	1.050	2.8576	0.3499	4.050	57.397	0.0174
0.420	1.5220	0.6570	1.100	3.0042	0.3329	4.100	60.340	0.0166
0.430	1.5373	0.6505	1.150	3.1582	0.3166	4.150	63.434	0.0158
0.440	1.5527	0.6440	1.200	3.3201	0.3012	4.200	66.686	0.0150
0.450	1.5683	0.6376	1.250	3.4903	0.2865	4.250	70.105	0.0143
0.460	1.5841	0.6313	1.300	3.6693	0.2725	4.300	73.700	0.0136
0.470	1.6000	0.6250	1.350	3.8574	0.2592	4.350	77.478	0.0129
0.480	1.6161	0.6188	1.400	4.0552	0.2466	4.400	81.451	0.0123
0.490	1.6323	0.6126	1.450	4.2631	0.2346	4.450	85.627	0.0117
0.500	1.6487	0.6065	1.500	4.4817	0.2231	4.500	90.017	0.0111
0.510	1.6653	0.6005	1.550	4.7114	0.2122	4.550	94.637	0.0106
0.520	1.6820	0.5945	1.600	4.9530	0.2019	4.600	99.484	0.0101
0.530	1.6989	0.5886	1.650	5.2069	0.1921	4.650	104.58	0.0096
0.540	1.7160	0.5827	1.700	5.4739	0.1827	4.700	109.95	0.0091
0.550	1.7333	0.5770	1.750	5.7545	0.1738	4.750	115.58	0.0087
0.560	1.7507	0.5712	1.800	6.0496	0.1653	4.800	121.51	0.0082
0.570	1.7683	0.5655	1.850	6.3597	0.1572	4.850	127.74	0.0078
0.580	1.7860	0.5599	1.900	6.6858	0.1496			
0.590	1.8040	0.5543	1.950	7.0286	0.1423			
0.600	1.8221	0.5488	2.000	7.3891	0.1353			

x	e^x	e^{-x}	x	e^x	e^{-x}	x	e^x	e^{-x}
4.900	134.29	0.0074	6.650	772.78	0.0013	8.400	4447.1	0.0002
4.950	141.17	0.0071	6.700	812.41	0.0012	8.450	4675.1	0.0002
5.000	148.41	0.0067	6.750	854.06	0.0012	8.500	4914.8	0.0002
5.050	156.02	0.0064	6.800	897.85	0.0011	8.550	5166.8	0.0002
5.100	164.02	0.0061	6.850	943.88	0.0011	8.600	5431.7	0.0002
5.150	172.43	0.0058	6.900	992.27	0.0010	8.650	5710.1	0.0002
5.200	181.27	0.0055	6.950	1043.1	0.0010	8.700	6002.9	0.0002
5.250	190.57	0.0052	7.000	1096.6	0.0009	8.750	6310.7	0.0002
5.300	200.34	0.0050	7.050	1152.9	0.0009	8.800	6634.2	0.0002
5.350	210.61	0.0047	7.100	1212.0	0.0008	8.850	6974.4	0.0001
5.400	221.41	0.0045	7.150	1274.1	0.0008	8.900	7332.0	0.0001
5.450	232.76	0.0043	7.200	1339.4	0.0007	8.950	7707.9	0.0001
5.500	244.69	0.0041	7.250	1408.1	0.0007	9.000	8103.1	0.0001
5.550	257.24	0.0039	7.300	1480.3	0.0007	9.050	8518.5	0.0001
5.600	270.43	0.0037	7.350	1556.2	0.0006	9.100	8955.3	0.0001
5.650	284.29	0.0035	7.400	1636.0	0.0006	9.150	9414.4	0.0001
5.700	298.87	0.0033	7.450	1719.9	0.0006	9.200	9897.1	0.0001
5.750	314.19	0.0032	7.500	1808.0	0.0006	9.250	10405.	0.0001
5.800	330.30	0.0030	7.550	1900.7	0.0005	9.300	10938.	0.0001
5.850	347.23	0.0029	7.600	1998.8	0.0005	9.350	11499.	0.0001
5.900	365.04	0.0027	7.650	2100.6	0.0005	9.400	12088.	0.0001
5.950	383.75	0.0026	7.700	2208.3	0.0005	9.450	12708.	0.0001
6.000	403.43	0.0025	7.750	2321.6	0.0004	9.500	13360.	0.0001
6.050	424.11	0.0024	7.800	2440.6	0.0004	9.550	14045.	0.0001
6.100	445.86	0.0022	7.850	2565.7	0.0004	9.600	14765.	0.0001
6.150	468.72	0.0021	7.900	2697.3	0.0004	9.650	15522.	0.0001
6.200	492.75	0.0020	7.950	2835.6	0.0004	9.700	16318.	0.0001
6.250	518.01	0.0019	8.000	2981.0	0.0003	9.750	17154.	0.0001
6.300	544.57	0.0018	8.050	3133.8	0.0003	9.800	18034.	0.0001
6.350	572.49	0.0017	8.100	3294.5	0.0003	9.850	18958.	0.0001
6.400	601.85	0.0017	8.150	3463.4	0.0003	9.900	19930.	0.0001
6.450	632.70	0.0016	8.200	3641.0	0.0003	9.950	20952.	0.0000
6.500	665.14	0.0015	8.250	3827.6	0.0003	10.000	22026.	0.0000
6.550	699.24	0.0014	8.300	4023.9	0.0002			
6.600	735.10	0.0014	8.350	4230.2	0.0002			

TABLE D–2 Natural Logarithms

x	ln x	x	ln x	x	ln x	x	ln x
0.050	−2.9957	0.900	−0.1054	1.750	0.5596	2.600	0.9555
0.100	−2.3026	0.950	−0.0513	1.800	0.5878	2.650	0.9745
0.150	−1.8971	1.000	−0.0000	1.850	0.6152	2.700	0.9932
0.200	−1.6094	1.050	0.0488	1.900	0.6418	2.750	1.0116
0.250	−1.3863	1.100	0.0953	1.950	0.6678	2.800	1.0296
0.300	−1.2040	1.150	0.1398	2.000	0.6932	2.850	1.0473
0.350	−1.0498	1.200	0.1823	2.050	0.7178	2.900	1.0647
0.400	−0.9163	1.250	0.2231	2.100	0.7419	2.950	1.0818
0.450	−0.7985	1.300	0.2624	2.150	0.7655	3.000	1.0986
0.500	−0.6932	1.350	0.3001	2.200	0.7884	3.050	1.1151
0.550	−0.5978	1.400	0.3365	2.250	0.8109	3.100	1.1314
0.600	−0.5108	1.450	0.3716	2.300	0.8329	3.150	1.1474
0.650	−0.4308	1.500	0.4055	2.350	0.8544	3.200	1.1631
0.700	−0.3567	1.550	0.4382	2.400	0.8755	3.250	1.1786
0.750	−0.2877	1.600	0.4700	2.450	0.8961	3.300	1.1939
0.800	−0.2231	1.650	0.5008	2.500	0.9163	3.350	1.2089
0.850	−0.1625	1.700	0.5306	2.550	0.9361	3.400	1.2238

FIGURE D–1 Normal Probability Distribution

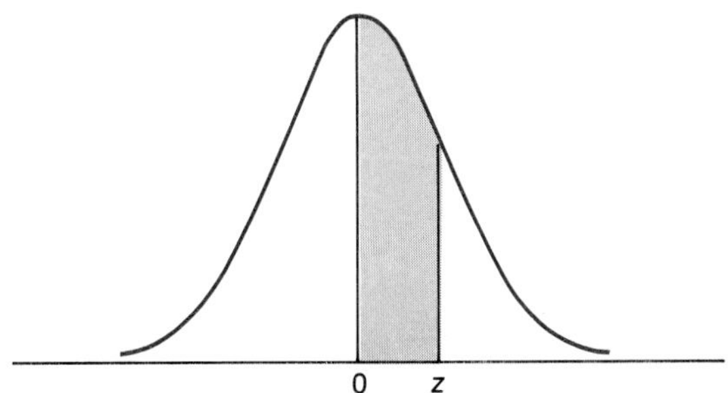

TABLE D–3 Area under the Standard Normal Curve

x	00	01	.02	.03	.04	.05	.06	.07	.08	.09
0.0	.0000	.0040	.0080	.0120	.0160	.0199	.0239	.0279	.0319	.0359
0.1	.0398	.0438	.0478	.0517	.0557	.0596	.0636	.0675	.0714	.0753
0.2	.0793	.0832	.0871	.0910	.0948	.0987	.1026	.1064	.1103	.1141
0.3	.1179	.1217	.1255	.1293	.1331	.1368	.1406	.1443	.1480	.1517
0.4	.1554	.1591	.1628	.1664	.1700	.1736	.1772	.1808	.1844	.1879
0.5	.1915	.1950	.1985	.2019	.2054	.2088	.2123	.2157	.2190	.2224
0.6	.2257	.2291	.2324	.2357	.2389	.2422	.2454	.2486	.2518	.2549
0.7	.2580	.2612	.2642	.2673	.2704	.2734	.2764	.2794	.2823	.2852
0.8	.2881	.2910	.2939	.2967	.2995	.3023	.3051	.3078	.3106	.3133
0.9	.3159	.3186	.3212	.3238	.3264	.3289	.3315	.3340	.3365	.3389
1.0	.3413	.3438	.3461	.3485	.3508	.3531	.3554	.3577	.3599	.3621
1.1	.3643	.3665	.3686	.3708	.3729	.3749	.3770	.3790	.3810	.3830
1.2	.3849	.3869	.3888	.3907	.3925	.3944	.3962	.3980	.3997	.4015
1.3	.4032	.4049	.4066	.4082	.4099	.4115	.4131	.4147	.4162	.4177
1.4	.4192	.4207	.4222	.4236	.4251	.4265	.4279	.4292	.4306	.4319
1.5	.4332	.4345	.4357	.4370	.4382	.4394	.4406	.4418	.4429	.4441
1.6	.4452	.4463	.4474	.4484	.4495	.4505	.4515	.4525	.4535	.4545
1.7	.4554	.4564	.4573	.4582	.4591	.4599	.4608	.4616	.4625	.4633
1.8	.4641	.4649	.4656	.4664	.4671	.4678	.4686	.4693	.4699	.4706
1.9	.4713	.4719	.4726	.4732	.4738	.4744	.4750	.4756	.4761	.4767
2.0	.4772	.4778	.4783	.4788	.4793	.4798	.4803	.4808	.4812	.4817
2.1	.4821	.4826	.4830	.4834	.4838	.4842	.4846	.4850	.4854	.4857
2.2	.4861	.4864	.4868	.4871	.4875	.4878	.4881	.4884	.4887	.4890
2.3	.4893	.4896	.4898	.4901	.4904	.4906	.4909	.4911	.4913	.4916
2.4	.4918	.4920	.4922	.4925	.4927	.4929	.4931	.4932	.4934	.4936
2.5	.4938	.4940	.4941	.4943	.4945	.4946	.4948	.4949	.4951	.4952
2.6	.4953	.4955	.4956	.4957	.4959	.4960	.4961	.4962	.4963	.4964
2.7	.4965	.4966	.4967	.4968	.4969	.4970	.4971	.4972	.4973	.4974
2.8	.4974	.4975	.4976	.4977	.4977	.4978	.4979	.4979	.4980	.4981
2.9	.4881	.4982	.4982	.4983	.4984	.4984	.4985	.4985	.4986	.4986
3.0	.49865	.4987	.4987	.4988	.4988	.4989	.4989	.4989	.4990	.4990

Answers to Selected Odd-Numbered Exercises

CHAPTER 2

3. $t^* = 35$ days, $P(35) = \$28{,}182.94$.
5. $t^* = 0$, $P(0) = -2{,}500$.
9. *a)* $x^* = 2$, $y^* = 4$, $t^* = .1333$ hrs.
   b) $x^* = 3.133$, $y^* = 3.133$, $t^* = .2088$ hrs.

11.

a	t*	C(t*)
1,000	8.94	\$18,888.50
3,000	8.94	20,888.50
7,000	8.94	24,888.50
9,000	8.94	26,888.50

13. *b)* $t^* = \left(\dfrac{P - S}{ab}\right)^{1/(b+1)}$. *c)* For $b = 1.2$, t^*=3.25 yrs. For $b = .8$, $t^* = 5.28$ yrs.
19. $\dfrac{R'(t^*)}{R(t^*)} = \dfrac{1}{t^*} \cdot \ln[R(t^*)/C]$.
21. $q_1^* = 15$, $q_2^* = 50$, $C(15, 50) = 7{,}050$.
23. $x^* = -7.9$, $y^* = 12.63$.
25. $x_1^* = 3$, $x_2^* = -3$, $x_3^* = 4$.
29. Relative min. when $x_1^* = 3$, $x_2^* = -3$, and $x_3^* = 4$.
37. *a)* $q^* = 25$. *b)* $C(25) = 70{,}000$.
39. $p^* = 10$, $q^* = 3678.8$, $R(10) = \$36{,}788$.
41. $x_1^* = 89.2$, $x_2^* = 110.8$, revenue maximized at \$2,382,150.
43. *a)* $r^* = 22.50$. *b)* \$20,312,500.
    c) \$20,000,000. *d)* \$312,500 less.
45. *a)* 109,544.51 miles. *c)*\$1.2477226/mile.
    d) \$136,681.16. *e)*\$176,182.20.
47. $x^* = 21.84$.
49. *a)* 191.34 km down river.
    b) $C = \$9{,}039{,}200$.
    c) 17.32 kilometers.
51. $y = -3x + 63\frac{1}{3}$.
53. $y = -3x^2 + 2x + 10$.
55. $x^* = -2\frac{1}{3}$, $y^* = 5\frac{1}{3}$.
57. *a)* $p_1^* = 9{,}666.67$, $p_2^* = 7{,}500$, $p_3^* = 9{,}833.33$.
    b) $q_1 = 2{,}000$, $q_2 = 3{,}000$, $q_3 = 2{,}500$.
    c) \$66,416,665.
59. *a)* $x^* = 100$, $y^* = 400$, $f_{max} = 1.048576 \cdot 10^{31}$.
    b) $x^* = .549$, $y^* = .110$, $z^* = -2.198$, $f_{min} = 5.494506$. *c)* $x^* = y^* = z^* = 0$, $f_{min} = 0$.
61. $x_A^* = 96$, $x_B^* = 80$, $R = \$4{,}000$, weekly profit = \$1,000.

CHAPTER 3

1. $3C + F \leq 100$.

9. min. $z = x_1 + x_2 + \cdots + x_8$
   s.t.

$$\begin{array}{ll} x_1 + x_8 \geq 30 & x_4 + x_5 \geq 60 \\ x_1 + x_2 \geq 20 & x_5 + x_6 \geq 50 \\ x_2 + x_3 \geq 40 & x_6 + x_7 \geq 40 \\ x_3 + x_4 \geq 50 & x_7 + x_8 \geq 40 \\ x_t \geq 0 & \end{array}$$

11. New objective function:

$$\text{max. } z = 72(x_1 + x_2 + \cdots + x_8)$$

13. Overtime constraint:

$$\sum_{j=1}^{8} y_j \geq .10\left[\sum_{j=1}^{8} (x_j + y_j)\right]$$

or

$$.9\sum_{j=1}^{8} y_j - .1\left[\sum_{j=1}^{8} x_j\right] \geq 0$$

15. $\sum_{j=1}^{3} x_{1_j} \leq 60{,}000$ $\quad \sum_{j=1}^{3} x_{3_j} \leq 50{,}000$

$\sum_{j=1}^{3} x_{2_j} \leq 25{,}000$ $\quad \sum_{i=1}^{3}\sum_{j=1}^{3} x_{i_j} \leq 125{,}000$

$\sum_{j=1}^{3} x_{i_1} \geq 40{,}000$

25. Revised objective function:

$$\begin{aligned} z &= 4x_1 + 3x_2 - .05x_3 - .03(10x_1 + 8x_2 - x_3) \\ &= 3.7x_1 + 2.76x_2 - .02x_3 \end{aligned}$$

27. x_{15} = Number of pounds of material 1 used in product D.
    Resulting changes:
    $r = 3(0.9x_1 + 0.8x_4 + 0.6x_7) + \ldots + 0.1(x_6 + x_{12} + x_{13} + x_{14} + x_{15})$
    $c = 2.1(x_1 + x_2 + x_3 + x_{15}) + \ldots$

$$x_1 + x_2 + x_3 + x_{15} \geq 2{,}000 \quad (1)$$

$$x_1 + x_2 + x_3 + x_{15} \leq 6{,}000 \quad (2)$$

$$x_6 = 0.3(x_6 + x_{12} + x_{13} + x_{14} + x_{15}) \quad (19)$$

New constraint:

$$x_{15} = .2(x_6 + x_{12} + x_{13} + x_{14} + x_{15})$$

29. The following constaints must be added:

$$x_{15} = .9x_1 + .8x_4 + .6x_7$$

$$x_{16} = .8x_2 + .8x_5 + .5x_8$$

$$x_{17} = x_3 + x_9 + x_{10} + x_{11}$$

$$x_{18} = x_6 + x_{12} + x_{13} + x_{14}$$

Constraints (7)–(11), (18), and (19) may be modified to become

$$.9x_1 \geq .2x_{15}$$

or

$$.9x_1 - .2x_{15} \geq 0 \quad (7)$$

$$.8x_4 \geq .4x_{15}$$

or

$$.8x_4 - .4x_{15} \geq 0 \quad (8)$$

$$.6x_7 \leq .1x_{15}$$

or

$$.6x_7 - .1x_{15} \leq 0 \quad (9)$$

$$.8x_2 \geq .1x_{16}$$

or

$$.8x_2 - .1x_{16} \geq 0 \quad (10)$$

$$.5x_8 \leq .3x_{16}$$

or

$$.5x_8 - .3x_{16} \leq 0 \quad (11)$$

$$x_3 = .2x_{17}$$

or

$$x_3 - .2x_{17} = 0 \quad (18)$$

$$x_6 = .3x_{18}$$

or

$$x_6 - .3x_{18} = 0 \quad (19)$$

The revenue component of the objective function, r, would be modified to become

$$r = 3x_{15} + 2.5x_{16} + .6x_{17} + .1x_{18}$$

31. Let $x_2 = -x_2'$, $x_3 = x_3' - x_3''$
min. $z = 6x_1 - 2x_2' - 3(x_3' - x_3'')$
s.t.

$$\begin{aligned} x_1 - \quad\quad 2x_3' + x_3'' &\leq 20 \\ 2x_1 - 3x_2' + 5x_3' - 5x_3'' &\geq 40.001 \\ x_1 + x_2' + x_3' - x_3'' &\leq 24.999 \\ x_1, x_2', x_3', x_3'' &\geq 0 \end{aligned}$$

33. max.
$z = 2{,}000L + 1{,}000P + 1{,}000T + 180S - 2{,}300$
s.t.

$$\begin{aligned} L + P + T + S &\leq 20 \\ 20{,}000L &\leq 48{,}000 \\ 20{,}000P &\leq 110{,}000 \\ 5{,}000T &\leq 55{,}000 \\ 20{,}000L &\geq 8{,}000 \\ 20{,}000P &\geq 10{,}000 \\ 5{,}000T &\geq 5{,}000 \\ L, P, T, S &\geq 0 \end{aligned}$$

35. x_1 = Number of AC models produced
x_2 = Number of battery models produced
x_3 = Number of AC models purchased
x_4 = Number of battery models purchased
max. $z = 2.00x_1 + 3.75x_2 + 1.50x_3 + 3.25x_4$
s.t.

$$\begin{aligned} .15x_1 + .10x_2 &\leq 1{,}000 & x_1 + x_3 &\geq 10{,}000 \\ .20x_1 + .20x_2 &\leq 1{,}800 & x_2 + x_4 &\geq 8{,}000 \\ .10x_1 + .15x_2 &\leq 1{,}200 & x_1, x_2, x_3, x_4 &\geq 0 \\ x_3 + x_4 &\leq 15{,}000 \\ x_3 + x_4 &\geq 2{,}500 \\ x_3 &\leq 6{,}000 \end{aligned}$$

37. x_j = Dollars invested in alternative j
max. $z = .3x_1 + .34x_2 + .35x_3 + .37x_4 + .38x_5 + .45x_6$
s.t.

$$\begin{aligned} x_5 &\leq 40{,}000 \\ x_4 + x_6 &\leq 75{,}000 \\ x_1 + x_2 + x_3 + x_4 + x_5 + x_6 &= 300{,}000 \\ x_2 &\geq 50{,}000 \\ x_1, x_2, \ldots, x_6 &\geq 0 \end{aligned}$$

39. min. $z = 1{,}100x_1 + 400x_2 + 1{,}250x_3 + 500x_4 + 1{,}000x_5 + 400x_6 + 1{,}250x_7 + 500x_8$
s.t.

$$\begin{aligned} x_1 + x_3 + x_5 + x_7 &= 2{,}500 \\ x_2 + x_4 + x_6 + x_8 &= 800 \\ x_1 + x_3 &\geq 1{,}250 \\ x_2 + x_4 &\geq 400 \\ x_3 + x_7 &\geq 1{,}000 \\ x_4 + x_8 &\geq 320 \\ x_7 + x_8 &\geq x_5 + x_6 \\ x_j &\geq 0 \end{aligned}$$

41. min. $z = 30x_{11} + 4x_{12} + 8x_{13} + 5x_{21} + 10x_{22} + 20x_{23}$
s.t.

$$\begin{aligned} x_{11} + x_{12} + x_{13} &\leq 50 \\ x_{21} + x_{22} + x_{23} &\leq 70 \\ x_{11} + x_{21} &= 40 \\ x_{12} + x_{22} &= 60 \\ x_{13} + x_{23} &= 20 \\ x_{ij} &\geq 0 \end{aligned}$$

43. max. $z = 3.7375x_1 + 4.70x_2 + 4.10x_3$
s.t.

$$\begin{aligned} .2x_1 + .1x_2 + .3x_3 &\leq 50{,}000 \\ .15x_1 + .4x_2 + .1x_3 &\leq 40{,}000 \\ .3x_1 + .2x_2 + .1x_3 &\leq 30{,}000 \end{aligned}$$

$$
\begin{aligned}
.1x_1 + .1x_2 + .2x_3 &\le 10{,}000 \\
.25x_1 + .2x_2 + .3x_3 &\le 20{,}000 \\
x_1 + x_2 + x_3 &\le 125{,}000 \\
x_1 &\ge 20{,}000 \\
x_2 &\ge 20{,}000 \\
x_3 &\ge 10{,}000 \\
x_1, x_2, x_3 &\ge 0
\end{aligned}
$$

45. max. $z = 10.40x_1 + 13.50x_2 + 17x_3 + 14.90x_4 + 16.25x_5 + 30.00x_6$

s.t.

$$
\begin{aligned}
80x_1 + 100x_2 + 160x_3 + 120x_4 + 150x_5 + 200x_6 &\le 2{,}500{,}000 \\
200x_6 &\le 250{,}000 \\
80x_1 + 100x_2 &\le 500{,}000 \\
x_1 &\ge 100 \\
x_2 &\ge 100 \\
x_3 &\ge 100 \\
x_4 &\ge 100 \\
x_5 &\ge 100 \\
x_6 &\ge 100 \\
72x_1 + 90x_2 - 16x_3 - 12x_4 - 15x_5 - 20x_6 &\ge 0 \\
4x_1 + 6.5x_2 + 1.0x_3 + 0.5x_4 + 2.75x_5 &\ge 10{,}000 \\
-4x_1 - 7x_2 + 12x_4 - 6x_5 + 4x_6 &\le 0 \\
x_1, x_2, x_3, x_4, x_5, x_6 &\ge 0
\end{aligned}
$$

47.

	Pattern																
Width	1	2	3	4	5	6	7	8	9	10	11	12	13	14	15	16	17
12	5	3	3	2	2	2	2	1	1	1	1	0	0	0	0	0	0
15	0	1	0	2	1	0	0	3	2	1	0	4	2	1	1	0	0
18	0	0	1	0	1	2	0	0	1	0	1	0	0	2	1	3	0
25	0	0	0	0	0	0	1	0	0	1	1	0	1	0	1	0	2
Trim loss	0	9	6	6	3	0	11	3	0	8	5	0	5	9	2	6	10

Let x_j = Number of reels slit using pattern j

min. $z = 9x_2 + 6x_3 + 6x_4 + 3x_5 + 11x_7 + 3x_8 + 8x_{10} + 5x_{11} + 5x_{13} + 9x_{14} + 2x_{15} + 6x_{16} + 10x_{17} + 12E_1 + 15E_2 + 18E_3 + 25E_4$

s.t.

$$
\begin{aligned}
5x_1 + 3x_2 + 3x_3 + 2x_4 + 2x_5 + 2x_6 + 2x_7 + x_8 + x_9 + x_{10} + x_{11} - E_1 &= 300 \\
x_2 + 2x_4 + x_5 + 3x_8 + 2x_9 + x_{10} + 4x_{12} + 2x_{13} + x_{14} + x_{15} - E_2 &= 250 \\
x_3 + x_5 + 2x_6 + x_9 + x_{11} + 2x_{14} + x_{15} + 3x_{16} - E_3 &= 200 \\
x_7 + x_{10} + x_{11} + x_{13} + x_{15} + 2x_{17} - E_4 &= 150 \\
x_j, E_i \ge 0 \qquad j &= 1, \ldots, 17 \\
i &= 1, \ldots, 4
\end{aligned}
$$

CHAPTER 4

1. *a*) No; insufficient weight capacity.
   b) Yes; sufficient weight and volume capacity.
   c) (4, 1); quantities which result in utilization of full weight and volume capacities.
   d) b: Ship 2.6 containers of pork only. Weight capacity fully utilized; additional volume capacity available.
   c: See part *c*.
   d: Ship 4.8 containers of beef only. Volume capacity fully utilized; additional weight capacity available.
3. Profit maximized at 33 ($100s) when 2.33 containers of beef and 1.66 containers of pork are shipped.
5. *a*) $x_1 = 4.5$, $x_2 = 1$, $z = 48$
   b) No feasible solution.
9. z maximized at value of 72. Alternative optima along line segment connecting (3⅓, 7) and (8, 0).
11. *a*) z maximized at 340 along line segment connecting (20, 30) and (42.5, 0).
13. $n = 15$, $m = 8$, 6,435.
15. Because S_2 positive, constraint 2 inactive. Since $S_1 = 0$, constraint 1 active. Yes, since point *d* lies on constraint 1 but below constraint 2.
17. $S_1 = 0$, $S_2 = 0$; there is no slack or unused weight or volume capacity. $E_3 = 1$ indicates that we are shipping one container above the minimum combined shipment requirement of four.
19.
$$
\begin{aligned}
5x_1 - 3x_2 + 4x_3 - E_1 + A_1 &= 10 \\
x_1 + 2x_2 + A_2 &= 15 \\
x_2 + x_3 + S_3 &= 20
\end{aligned}
$$
21. *a*) Corner point c.
    b) $x_1 = 4$, $x_2 = 1$, $E_3 = 0$. Basic variable $E_3 = 0$.
23. Total costs are minimized at value of $5,144.75 ($5,084.75 + $60) when 500 units of product A are made in quarter 1, 75 units of product B are made in quarter 1, 625 units of product B are made in quarter 2, 40 unused labor hours remain in quarter 1, 475 unused kilos of raw materials remain in quarter 1, 100 unused kilos of raw materials remain in quarter 2. All labor hours used in quarter 1. Production requirements met in both periods.
27. *a*) $z_{max} = 61$ at (7.5, 2)
    b) $z_{max} = 63$ at (2, 5⅔) and at (7.5, 2).
    c) No feasible solution.
    d) $z_{max} = 96$ at (8, 6)
    e) Unbounded solution.
    f) $z_{max} = 28$ at (2, 2).
29. *a*) $z_{min} = 60.6$ at (2.8, 3).
    b) $z_{min} = 33.5$ at (0.8, 8).
    c) No feasible solution.
    d) Same as part *a*.
    e) Unbounded solution.

31. *a*) max. $z = 225x_1 + 230x_2 + 240x_3 - 20{,}000$
s.t.

$x_1 \geq 20$ condition (*a*)
$x_2 \geq 70$ condition (*b*)
$x_2 \leq 140$ condition (*b*)
$x_3 \geq 60$ condition (*c*)
$x_1 \leq 60$ condition (*d*)
$x_1 + x_2 \geq 120$ condition (*e*)
$x_1, x_2, x_3 \geq 0$

b) $x_3 = 200 - x_1 - x_2$
max $z = -15x_1 - 10x_2 + 28{,}000$
s.t.

$x_1 \geq 20$ condition (*a*)
$x_2 \geq 70$ condition (*b*)
$x_2 \leq 140$ condition (*b*)
$x_1 + x_2 \leq 140$ condition (*c*)
$x_1 \leq 60$ condition (*d*)
$x_1 + x_2 \geq 120$ condition (*e*)
$x_1, x_2 \geq 0$

c) Profit maximized at $26,700.
When $x_1 = 20$, $x_2 = 100$, and $x_3 = 80$, 20 deluxe, 100 standard, and 80 economy tours.

33. *a*) 3 (≤) constraints.
b) 3 slack variables.
c) 3.
d) S_1, S_2, S_3.
e) x_2, S_1, S_2 at point A. x_1, x_2, S_3 at point C.

35. 20 slack, 25 surplus, and 35 artificial variables. 55 basic variables.

37. Profit maximized at $61,250 when 4,000 AC units and 4,000 battery models are produced by Sniffy and 6,000 AC units and 9,000 battery units are purchased from the subcontractor. The production department (constraint1) is used to capacity, while the assembly department has 200 hours (constraint 2) and the packaging department 200 hours (constraint 3) of unused time. The total capacity of the subcontractor (constraint 4) is utilized as is the sub's capacity for AC models (constraint 5). The minimum order requirement by the subcontractor (constraint 6) is exceeded by 12,500 units. Seer's minimum order requirement of 10,000 AC units (constraint 7) is satisfied exactly, while their minimum order for battery units (constraint 8) is exceeded by 5,000 units.

39. Profit maximized at $397,750 when 20,000 gallons of blend 1, 60,000 of blend 2, and 10,000 of blend 3 are produced. Components 1, 2, and 3 will have 37,000, 12,000, and 11,000 additional gallons available, while the complete supply of components 4 and 5 is utilized. There is remaining plant capacity equal to 35,000 gallons. The minimum production requirement of blend 1 is satisfied exactly, as is the same for blend 3. Production of blend 2 exceeds the minimum requirement by 40,000 gallons.

		Blend		
		1	**2**	**3**
Component	1	4,000	6,000	3,000
	2	3,000	24,000	1,000
	3	6,000	12,000	1,000
	4	2,000	6,000	2,000

Blend	Revenue	Cost	Profit
1	$130,000	$ 55,250	$ 74,750
2	450,000	168,000	282,000
3	70,000	29,000	41,000
	$670,000	$252,250	$397,750

41. *a*) (Hospital Administration Model: Example 3.5) Number of nurses minimized at 170 when number hired to work each shift are

Shift	Number
1	30
2	0
3	40
4	10
5	50
6	0
7	40
8	0

b) (Blending Model: Example 3.6) Weekly profit maximized at $90,833.33 when 12,000 pounds of component 1 used in final blend 1, 6,666.67 pounds of component 1 used in final blend 2, 41,333.33 pounds of component 1 used in final blend 3, 14,666.67 pounds of component 2 used in final blend 2, 10,333.33 pounds of component 2 used in final blend 3, 28,000.00 pounds of component 3 used in final blend 1, 12,000.00 pounds of component 3 used in final blend 2.

c) (Financial Mix Model: Example 3.8) Total weekly profit maximized at $4,272.73 when 727.27 units of product 1 and 454.55 units of product 2 are produced. No loan is taken.

CHAPTER 5

3. Yes; an increase of 6 implies a 60 percent increase on the original coefficient of 10.
5. *a*) $4 < c_1 < 12.5$. *b*) $c_1 = 4$. *c*) $c_1 = 12.5$. *d*) $c_1 < 4$.
7. *a*) $x_1 = 4.8, x_2 = 0, z = 15(4.8) = 72$.
   b) $\Delta z^* = \Delta c_j$ times x_j if $L_j < c_j + \Delta c_j < U_j$; $\Delta x_j = 0$.
   c) Yes; if x_j nonbasic, its value is zero and $\Delta z^* = 0$.
   d) Alternative optimal solutions would exist; Δz^* is at its maximum absolute value for the current basis.
9. $x_1 = 5$, and $z^* = 100$. *b*) $x_1 = 4.8$ and $z^* = 96$.
11. *a*) $\Delta z^* = z^* + \Delta b_i(y_i)$.
    b) $L_i \leq b_i + \Delta b_i \leq U_i$.
    c) $\Delta z^* = 96 + \Delta b_i(4)$.
    d) A basic variable would become zero. For example, both weight and volume slack would be zero in the air cargo problem, and x_2 would be zero, leaving $x_1 = 4.8$ as the only nonzero variable.
13. *a*) Increase b_1, decrease b_2, no change in b_3.
    b) Increase b_1, decrease b_2, no change in b_3.
17. Alternative optimal solutions would exist with decreased production quantities for product B in the second quarter. Would be indifferent about producing 625 units of B in second quarter versus reducing this quantity and producing more during first quarter.
19. This should lower optimal costs by \$56.50.
27. max. $z = -250y_1 + 125y_2 - 30y_3 + 30y_4$
    s.t.

$$\begin{aligned}
-2y_1 + 4y_2 - y_3 + y_4 &\leq 5 \\
-3y_1 - 2y_2 &\leq 4 \\
-y_1 + 2y_2 - y_3 + y_4 &\leq 8 \\
-2y_1 + y_2 + y_3 - y_4 &= 7 \\
y_1, y_2, y_3, y_4 &\geq 0
\end{aligned}$$

39. *a*) z maximized at value of 400 when $x_1 = 40$, $x_2 = 0$.
    c) $(40, 0)$ remains uniquely optimal as long as $c_1 > 6$ and $c_2 = 6$ or $c_2 < 10$ and $c_1 = 10$.
41. *a*) z minimized at value of 30 when $x_1 = 10$ and $x_2 = 0$.
    c) $0 \leq c_1 < 6$, $c_2 > 3$.
49. max. $z = 20y_1 + 75y_2 + 10y_3 + 125y_4 + 8y_5$
    s.t.

$$\begin{aligned}
y_1 + 6y_2 \qquad + 2y_4 + 2y_5 &\leq 10 \\
y_1 - y_2 + y_3 + 4y_4 - 3y_5 &= 5 \\
y_1, y_3 &\geq 0 \\
y_2, y_4 &\leq 0 \\
y_5 &\text{ unrestricted}
\end{aligned}$$

CHAPTER 6

1. $x_1 = 5, x_2 = -2$.
3. $x_1 = 0, x_2 = 26/4, x_3 = 14/4$.
5. max. $z = 6x_1 + 7x_2 - 3x_3 + 0S_1 + 0S_2 + 0S_3$
   s.t.

$$\begin{aligned}
x_1 + x_2 + x_3 + S_1 \qquad\qquad &= 300 \\
2x_1 + x_2 + 8x_3 \qquad + S_2 \qquad &= 450 \\
2x_1 - 3x_2 - 6x_3 \qquad\qquad + S_3 &= 100 \\
x_1, x_2, x_3, S_1, S_2, S_3 &\geq 0
\end{aligned}$$

7. $z_{max} = 19, x_1 = 50, x_2 = 20, S_2 = 30$.
9. Final tableau

Basis	z	x_1	x_2	E_2	S_1	A_2	A_3	b_i	Row Number
—	1	0	−2	0	0	$-M$	$2-M$	20	(0)
S_1	0	0	4	0	1	0	−1	70	(1)
x_1	0	1	1	0	0	0	1	10	(2)
E_2	0	0	2	1	0	−1	4	20	(3)

11. z_{min} at 20 when $x_1' = 5, x_1'' = 0, x_2 = 0$, and $x_3 = 0$, or $x_1 = 5, x_2 = 0, x_3 = 0$.
13. Basic alternative optima occur at: $(8, 0)$ with $z = 24$, $(0, 12)$ with $z = 24$, $X_{a1} = 8w_1 + 0w_2$, $X_{a2} = 0w_1 + 12w_2$.
15. $z_{min} = -45$ at $x_1 = 5$ and $x_2 = 5$.
17. *a*) $z = -5$ at $(5, 5)$
    b) Unbounded solution.
    c) z minimized at value of -10 at $(5, 0)$.
19. z maximized at value of 3 when $x_1 = 0, x_2 = 0$, and $x_3 = 1$.
21. Nothing changes: $x_1^* = 24/5, x_2^* = 0, z^* = 96$. Alternative optimal solutions exist if $\Delta_2 = 6$ ($c_2 = 16$) by introducing x_2 into the basis.
23. *a*) $x_1^* = 24/5, x_2^* = 0, z^* = 72$.
    b) Alternative optimal solutions would exist by introducing x_2 into basis with $z^* = 60$.
    c) If x_j is basic, z^* changes by $x_j(\Delta j)$; if x_j is nonbasic, z^* does not change.
25. $0 < c_2 < 12$ and $c_4 > 5$.
27. $8 \leq b_1 \leq 50\tfrac{10}{11}$, $-50 \leq b_2 \leq 50$, $b_3 \geq 147.5$.
37. *a*) z maximized at $83\tfrac{1}{3}$ when $x_1 = 0$ and $x_2 = 16\tfrac{2}{3}$.
    c) If *RHS* constant for constraint 1 is increased by 1 unit, z will increase by $5/3$. If the *RHS* constant in constraint 2 is increased by 1 unit, z will not change.
    d) $z_{max} = 85$ at $(0, 17)$.
    e) $c_1 \leq 8.333$, $c_2 \geq 4.2000$, $b_1 \geq 0$, $b_2 \geq -33.333$.

39. *a*) Unbounded solution.
d) $z_{min} = 12$ when $x_1 = 4$ and $x_2 = 0$.

41. *a*) $z = 200/9$, $x_1 = 0$, $x_2 = 35/9$, $x_3 = 95/9$.
b) Shadow price for constraint 1 = $10/9$. Shadow price for constraint 2 = $2/3$.

43. *a*) $b_1 \geq 4$, $b_2 \geq 0$, $0 \leq b_3 \leq 8$.
b) Shadow prices equal zero for constraints 1 and 2 and $3/2$ for constraint 3.
c) Valid over ranges given in part (*a*).
d) 1. New basis will be created.
2. New basis will be created.
3. $z = 9$, $x_4 = 3$, $S_1 = 1$, $S_2 = 3/2$.

45. *a*) $c_1 \leq 6$, $5 \leq c_2 \leq 7$, $c_3 \geq 6$.

47. *a*) max. $z = 1{,}000y_1 + 300y_2 + 150y_3 + 200y_4$
s.t.

$$\begin{aligned} y_1 + y_2 \quad\quad & \leq 5 \\ y_1 \quad + y_3 \quad & \leq 6 \\ y_1 \quad\quad + y_4 & \leq 7 \end{aligned}$$

y_1 unrestricted, y_2 nonpositive
$y_3, y_4 \geq 0$

b) $y_1 = 6$, $y_2 = -1$, $y_3 = 0$, $y_4 = 1$, $z_d = 5{,}900$.

CHAPTER 7

1. *a*) x_{ij} = Number of thousands of gallons shipped from plant *i* and to depot *j*.
min. $z = 30x_{11} + 4x_{12} + 8x_{13} + 5x_{21} + 10x_{22} + 20x_{23}$
s.t.

$$\begin{aligned} x_{11} + x_{12} + x_{13} &= 50 \\ x_{21} + x_{22} + x_{23} &= 70 \\ x_{11} + x_{21} &= 40 \\ x_{12} + x_{22} &= 60 \\ x_{13} + x_{23} &= 20 \\ x_{ij} &\geq 0 \end{aligned}$$

3. *a*) $z_{min} = \$67{,}000$ when $x_{12} = 110$, $x_{21} = 80$, $x_{23} = 80$, $x_{31} = 60$, $x_{32} = 90$.
b) $z_{min} = \$780$ when $x_{12} = 30$, $x_{13} = 20$, $x_{21} = 40$, $x_{22} = 30$.

5. *a*) $z_{max} = 88{,}500$ when $x_{11} = 110$, $x_{31} = 30$, $x_{22} = 160$, $x_{32} = 40$, $x_{33} = 80$.
b) $z = 88{,}500$ when $x_{11} = 110$, $x_{21} = 30$, $x_{22} = 130$, $x_{32} = 70$, $x_{33} = 80$.
c) $z = 88{,}500$.

11. *a*) $z = 67{,}000 + 75(50) = \$70{,}750$, $x_{11} = 75$, $x_{12} = 35$, $x_{21} = 65$, $x_{22} = 15$, $x_{13} = 80$, $x_{32} = 150$.
b) $z = 72{,}000$ when $x_{11} = 110$, $x_{22} = 80$, $x_{23} = 80$, $x_{31} = 30$, $x_{32} = 120$.

13. min. $z = 4x_{12} + 8x_{13} + 5x_{21} + 10x_{22} + 20x_{23}$
s.t.

$$\begin{aligned} x_{12} + x_{13} \quad\quad &\leq 75 \\ x_{21} + x_{22} + x_{23} &\leq 70 \\ x_{12} + x_{22} \quad\quad &= 60 \\ x_{13} + x_{23} \quad\quad &= 40 \\ x_{12} \quad\quad &\geq 30 \\ x_{ij} &\geq 0 \end{aligned}$$

15. *a*) Make exact allocation adjusting corresponding supply/demand parameters; cost the cell as undesirable and proceed on.
b)

		Destination 1	Destination 2	Destination 3	
Origin	1	M	100	100	10
	2	M	300	200	120
	3	100	200	300	150
		0	200	80	

with $x_{11} = 100$ and $x_{21} = 40$, or eliminate destination 1 from the table.
c) $x_{11} = 100$, $x_{21} = 40$, $x_{12} = 10$, $x_{22} = 40$, $x_{23} = 80$, $x_{32} = 150$, $z = 72{,}000$.
d) $z = 72{,}000$ when $x_{11} = 100$, $x_{21} = 40$, $x_{12} = 10$, $x_{22} = 40$, $x_{23} = 80$, $x_{32} = 150$.

17. *a*) $z = 2{,}627.50$ when $x_{13} = 200$, $x_{23} = 50$, $x_{24} = 175$, $x_{25} = 25$, $x_{35} = 150$, $x_{41} = 50$, $x_{42} = 200$, $x_{43} = 50$, $x_{51} = 100$.
b) $z = 2847.50$ when $x_{11} = 150$, $x_{13} = 50$, $x_{23} = 75$, $x_{24} = 175$, $x_{35} = 150$, $x_{42} = 200$, $x_{43} = 100$, $x_{53} = 75$, $x_{55} = 25$.

19. *a*) $z = 1{,}445{,}000$ when $x_{15} = 500{,}000$, $x_{22} = 600{,}000$, $x_{34} = 750{,}000$, $x_{41} = 250{,}000$, $x_{43} = 500{,}000$, $x_{44} = 50{,}000$.
b) Same as part (*a*).

21. *a*) *z* minimized at $1,032.50 with following production schedule.

	Period 1	Period 2	Period 3	Period 4
Units produced, reg.	50	50	50	50
Units produced, O. T.	0	5	20	10
Ending inventory	10	5	0	0

b)

Costs	Period 1	2	3	4	Total
Regular time	$150	$150	$150	$150	$ 600.00
Overtime	—	25	100	50	175.00
Raw material	50	55	70	60	235.00
Inventory	15	7.50	—	—	22.50
Excess capacity	—	—	—	—	—
	$215	$237.50	$320	$260	$1,032.50

25.a) $x_{ij} = \begin{cases} 1 \text{ if team } i \text{ assigned to tournament } j \\ 0 \text{ if team } i \text{ not assigned to tournament } j \end{cases}$

min. $z = 2{,}600x_{11} + 3200x_{12} + 2{,}750x_{13} + \ldots + 3{,}000x_{44}$

s.t.

$x_{11} + x_{12} + x_{13} + x_{14} = 1$
$x_{21} + x_{22} + x_{23} + x_{24} = 1$
$x_{31} + x_{32} + x_{33} + x_{34} = 1$
$x_{41} + x_{42} + x_{43} + x_{44} = 1$
$x_{11} + x_{21} + x_{31} + x_{41} = 1$
$x_{12} + x_{22} + x_{32} + x_{42} = 1$
$x_{13} + x_{23} + x_{33} + x_{43} = 1$
$x_{14} + x_{24} + x_{34} + x_{44} = 1$

27. $x_{12} = 110$, $x_{22} = 80$, $x_{23} = 80$, $x_{31} = 140$, $x_{32} = 10$. There are 80 *all-integer* alternative optimal solutions.

29. $z = 780$, $x_{12} = 30$, $x_{13} = 20$, $x_{21} = 40$, $x_{22} = 30$.

31. $z = \$70{,}750$ when $x_{11} = 75$, $x_{12} = 35$, $x_{21} = 65$, $x_{22} = 15$, $x_{23} = 80$, $x_{32} = 150$.

33. $z = 1{,}032.50$ when

Production Period	Type	Demand Period	Number of Units
1	Reg.	1	40
1	Reg.	2	10
2	Reg.	2	50
2	O. T.	3	5
3	Reg.	3	50
3	O. T.	3	20
4	Reg.	4	50
4	O. T.	4	10

39. $z = 2{,}375$ when $x_{11} = 25$, $x_{12} = 50$, $x_{21} = 125$, $x_{34} = 100$ (greedy algorithm identifies optimal solution).

41. Net dollar returns maximized at $1,445,000 when

Year	Investment	Amount
1	5	$500,000
2	2	600,000
3	4	750,000
4	1	250,000
4	3	500,000
4	4	50,000

43. z minimized at 6,625 when $x_{12} = 200$, $x_{23} = 325$, $x_{31} = 150$, $x_{33} = 150$.

45. z minimized at 5,125 when $x_{12} = 200$, $x_{23} = 325$, $x_{31} = 150$.

47. $c_{13} > 5.5$, $c_{14} > 10.5$, $c_{21} > -2$, $c_{23} > 2.5$, $c_{31} > -3.5$, $c_{32} > 3$.

49. $c_{12} < 150$, $c_{23} < 300$, $100 < c_{31} < 150$, $150 < c_{32} < 200$.

51. $9 < c_{11} < 15$, $8 < c_{13}$, $9 < c_{21} < 13$, $17 < c_{22}$, $8 < c_{41} < 12$.

53. a) $\Delta z = 6$, x_{12} decreases to 29, and x_{22} increases to 31.
b) $\Delta z = 5$, x_{22} increases to 31, and x_{21} decreases to 39.
c) $\Delta z = 5$, x_{21} increases to 41.
d) $\Delta z = -5$, x_{21} decreases to 39.
e) $\Delta z = 0$, no change in basic variables.
f) $\Delta z = -4$, x_{13} decreases to 19, x_{12} increases to 31.
g) $\Delta z = -14$, x_{13} decreases to 19, x_{12} increases to 31, x_{22} decreases to 31.
h) $\Delta z = -10$, x_{22} decreases to 29.

55. z minimized at 73 when

Person	Assigned to	Job
1		4
2		3
3		1
4		2
5		5

57. z maximized at 35,500 when $x_{13} = 400$, $x_{22} = 600$, $x_{31} = 500$.

59. a) With M assigned to restricted routes and dummy destination added with demand of 150, $x_{11} = 800$, $x_{21} = 200$, $x_{22} = 800$, $x_{33} = 1{,}200$, $x_{34} = 300$, $x_{44} = 450$, $x_{4D} = 150$, and $z = 173{,}000 + 450M$.
b) $z = \$118{,}500$ when $x_{12} = 800$, $x_{23} = 100$, $x_{24} = 750$, $x_{31} = 400$, $x_{33} = 1{,}100$, and $x_{41} = 600$.

61. *a)* z = \$7.1 million when $x_{12} = 25$, $x_{14} = 10$, $x_{21} = 30$, $x_{33} = 15$ (all in millions).
b) z = \$7.18 million when $x_{11} = 4$, $x_{12} = 25$, $x_{14} = 10$, $x_{21} = 26$, and $x_{33} = 15$ (all in millions).
63. *b)* z minimized at \$4,035 with following assignments:

Social Worker	Type of Application	Number Assigned
1	1	80
2	1	45
2	2	55
3	2	45
3	3	75
4	1	20
5	1	55
5	3	75

65. *b)* Expected number of crimes minimized at 1,512 or maximum number deterred at 788 when

Team	Assigned to District
1	3
2	1
3	5
4	2
5	4

67. *b)* $c_{12} > 68$, $c_{21} > 62$.
c) $c_{11} < 68$, $56 < c_{13} < 84$, $66 < c_{22} < 90$, $46 < c_{23} < 70$, $c_{32} < 4$.
d)

	Change in Optimal Cost
Case 1	−70.0
Case 2	−4.0
Case 3	0
Case 4	0
Case 5	−70.0
Case 6	0
Case 7	0
Case 8	−70.0

71. *b)* Total cost minimized at \$48,000, 400 original provided for college B, 700 purchased for college A, 200 purchases for college B, 700 Friday night sets cleaned for college C, 500 Saturday morning sets provided for college D.

CHAPTER 8

1. *a)* $y = 0$ implies purchase of machine 1, $y = 1$ implies purchase of machine 2.
b) Yes; add constraint $y_1 + y_2 = 1$, $y_i = 0$ implies purchase of machine i, $y_i = 1$ implies nonpurchase of machine i.
5. $x_1 + x_2 + x_3 \leq 40 + My_1$, $2x_1 - x_2 + x_3 \geq 20 - My_2$, $x_1 - x_3 \geq 15 - My_3$, $y_1 + y_2 + y_3 = 2$.
7. $x_j \geq L_j - My$, $x_j \leq 0 + M(1 - y)$.
9. $2x_1 + 4x_2 + x_3 \leq 200 + My_1$, $x_1 + x_2 + x_3 \geq 50 - My_2$, $3x_1 - x_2 + 5x_3 \geq 35 - My_3$, $3x_1 - x_2 + 5x_3 \leq 35 + My_3$, $y_1 + y_2 + y_3 = 1$.
15. Add constraints: $x_{ij} \leq My_{ij}$ for all i,j where $y_{ij} = 0$ or 1. Objective function becomes:

$$z = \sum_{i=1}^{m} \sum_{j=1}^{n} [c_{ij}x_{ij} + F_{ij}y_{ij}]$$

27. City 1 to city 4, city 4 to city 5, city 5 to city 3, city 3 to city 2, city 2 to city 1.
29. *a)* max. $z = \sum_{j=1}^{n} c_j x_j$
s.t.

$$\sum_{j=1}^{n} w_j x_j \leq W$$

$$\sum_{j=1}^{n} v_j x_j \leq V$$

x_j = nonnegative integer

31. *a)* $x_1 = x_3$ or $x_1 - x_3 = 0$.
b) $x_1 + x_2 + x_3 + x_4 + x_5 \leq 4$.
c) $x_4 + x_5 \leq 1$.
d) $x_4 \leq x_2$ or $-x_2 + x_4 \leq 0$.
33. $z = 351.4$ when $x_1 = 4.285$ and $x_2 = 2.000$.
37. z maximized at value of 178 when $x_1 = 21$, $x_2 = 3$, and $x_3 = 5$.
39. (0, 0, 0, 0) not feasible, (0, 0, 0, 1) $z = 4$, (0, 0, 1, 0) not feasible, (0, 0, 1, 1) not feasible, (0, 1, 0, 0) $z = 5$, (0, 1, 0, 1) $z = 9$, (0, 1, 1, 0) not feasible, (0, 1, 1, 1) $z = 12$, (1, 0, 0, 0) not feasible, (1, 0, 0, 1) not feasible, (1, 0, 1, 0) not feasible, (1, 0, 1, 1) not feasible, (1, 1, 0, 0) not feasible, (1, 1, 0, 1) not feasible, (1, 1, 1, 0) not feasible, (1, 1, 1, 1) not feasible.
41. *a)* z maximized at 1,050 when $x_2 = x_3 = 1$ and $x_1 = x_4 = x_5 = 0$.
b) z maximized at 1,000 when $x_1 = x_4 = x_5 = 1$ and $x_2 = x_3 = 0$.
c) z maximized at 10 when $x_1 = x_2 = x_3 = x_5 = 1$ and $x_4 = 0$.
43. $z = 340$ when $x_1 = 4$ and $x_2 = 2$.

47. *a*) Let x_{ij} = Number of hearings of type *i* scheduled in court *j*.

$$\max. z = 20x_{11} + 18x_{12} + 22x_{13} + 2x_{21} + 3x_{22} + 2x_{23} + 12x_{31} + 13x_{32} + 10x_{33} + 5x_{41} + 6x_{42} + 7x_{43}$$

s.t.

$$\begin{aligned}
x_{11} + x_{21} + x_{31} + x_{41} &\leq 1{,}400 \\
x_{12} + x_{22} + x_{32} + x_{42} &\leq 800 \\
x_{13} + x_{23} + x_{33} + x_{43} &\leq 600 \\
x_{11} + x_{12} + x_{13} &\geq 20 \\
x_{21} + x_{22} + x_{23} &\geq 10 \\
x_{31} + x_{32} + x_{33} &\geq 25 \\
x_{41} + x_{42} + x_{43} &\geq 30 \\
20x_{11} &\geq 280 \\
18x_{12} &\geq 160 \\
22x_{13} &\geq 120 \\
x_{21} + x_{22} + x_{23} &\leq .6(x_{11} + x_{12} + x_{13} + \dots + x_{43})
\end{aligned}$$

b) *z* maximized at 54,965 when x_{11} = 1,400, x_{12} = 735, x_{13} = 600, x_{22} = 10, x_{32} = 25, x_{42} = 30.

49. *c*) Main offices should be built in cities 1, 4, 9, and 15.

53. Let x_{ij} = Number of commuters assigned from suburb *i* to site *j*

$$y_j = \begin{cases} 1 \text{ if site } j \text{ selected} \\ 0 \text{ if site } j \text{ not selected} \end{cases}$$

$$\min. z = 105.6x_{11} + 91.2x_{12} + 74.4x_{13} + 86.8x_{15} + 98.4x_{21} + 82.8x_{25} + 97.6x_{32} + 114x_{33} + \dots + 93.4x_{85}$$

s.t.

$$\begin{aligned}
x_{11} + x_{12} + x_{13} + x_{15} &= 600 \\
x_{21} + x_{25} &= 750 \\
x_{32} + x_{33} + x_{35} &= 1{,}500 \\
x_{41} + x_{42} + x_{44} &= 800 \\
x_{52} + x_{53} + x_{54} + x_{55} &= 700 \\
x_{62} + x_{63} + x_{64} &= 550 \\
x_{71} + x_{72} + x_{75} &= 1{,}000 \\
x_{83} + x_{84} + x_{85} &= 400 \\
x_{11} + x_{21} + x_{41} + x_{71} &\leq 3{,}000y_1 \\
x_{12} + x_{32} + x_{42} + x_{52} + x_{62} + x_{72} &\leq 4{,}000y_2 \\
x_{13} + x_{33} + x_{53} + x_{63} + x_{83} &\leq 3{,}500y_3 \\
x_{44} + x_{54} + x_{64} + x_{84} &\leq 2{,}800y_4 \\
x_{15} + x_{25} + x_{35} + x_{55} + x_{75} + x_{85} &\leq 3{,}750y_5 \\
y_1 + y_2 + y_3 + y_4 + y_5 &\leq 3
\end{aligned}$$

b) Sites 2, 3, and 5 chosen. Fuel consumption minimized at 549,230 liters: x_{42} = 800, x_{52} = 700, x_{62} = 550, x_{13} = 600, x_{83} = 400, x_{25} = 750, x_{35} = 1,500, x_{75} = 1,000.

55. *a*) x_j = Number of controllers beginning a regular day with shift *j*

y_j = Number of controllers beginning a regular *plus* overtime day with shift *j*.

$$\min. z = 96x_1 + 88x_2 + 96x_3 + 96x_4 + 80x_5 + 80x_6 + 80x_7 + 88x_8 + 168y_1 + 154y_2 + 168y_3 + 168y_4 + 140y_5 + 140y_6 + 140y_7 + 154y_8$$

s.t.

$$\begin{aligned}
x_1 + x_8 + y_1 + y_8 &\geq 3 \\
x_1 + y_1 + y_2 &\geq 2 \\
x_8 + y_8 + y_2 &\geq 2 \\
x_1 + x_8 + y_1 + y_8 &\geq 2 \\
x_1 + x_3 + y_1 + y_3 &\geq 2 \\
x_3 + y_3 + y_8 &\geq 3 \\
x_1 + x_4 + y_1 + y_4 + y_8 &\geq 6 \\
x_1 + x_3 + x_4 + x_5 + y_1 + y_3 + y_4 + y_5 &\geq 10 \\
x_3 + x_5 + y_3 + y_5 &\geq 12 \\
x_4 + y_4 + y_1 &\geq 8 \\
x_3 + x_4 + x_5 + y_3 + y_4 + y_5 + y_1 &\geq 6 \\
x_3 + x_5 + x_6 + y_3 + y_5 + y_6 &\geq 8 \\
x_4 + x_6 + y_4 + y_6 &\geq 8 \\
x_4 + x_5 + x_7 + y_4 + y_5 + y_7 + y_3 &\geq 6 \\
x_5 + x_6 + x_7 + y_5 + y_6 + y_7 + y_3 &\geq 7 \\
x_6 + y_6 + y_4 &\geq 10 \\
x_2 + x_7 + y_2 + y_7 + y_4 + y_5 &\geq 12 \\
x_2 + x_6 + x_7 + y_2 + y_6 + y_7 + y_5 &\geq 14 \\
x_6 + y_6 &\geq 12 \\
x_2 + x_7 + y_2 + y_7 &\geq 8 \\
x_2 + x_7 + x_8 + y_2 + y_7 + y_8 + y_6 &\geq 6 \\
x_8 + y_8 + y_6 &\geq 5 \\
x_2 + y_2 + y_7 &\geq 4 \\
x_2 + x_8 + y_2 + y_8 + y_7 &\geq 3 \\
x_j, y_j &= \text{Nonnegative integers}
\end{aligned}$$

b) x_3 = 3, x_4 = 7, x_5 = 5, x_6 = 9, x_7 = 7, x_8 = 2, y_1 = 1, y_2 = 1, y_5 = 4, y_6 = 3. Total cost minimized at $4,118.

CHAPTER 9

3. $\min. z = d^- + d^+$

s.t.

$$\begin{aligned}
10{,}000x_1 + 7{,}500x_2 &\geq 1{,}200{,}000 \\
x_1 + x_2 + d^- - d^+ &= 100 \\
x_1 &\leq 70 \\
x_1, x_2, d^-, d^+ &\geq 0
\end{aligned}$$

5. *a*) $\min. z = P_1d_1^- + P_2d_2^+ + P_3d_3^+ + P_4d_4^-$

s.t.

$$\begin{aligned}
10{,}000x_1 + 7{,}500x_2 + d_1^- - d_1^+ &= 1{,}000{,}000 \\
x_1 + d_2^- - d_2^+ &= 70 \\
x_1 + x_2 + d_3^- - d_3^+ &= 100 \\
10{,}000x_1 + 7{,}500x_2 + d_4^- - d_4^+ &= 750{,}000 \\
x_j, d_j^-, d_j^+ &\geq 0 \text{ for all } j
\end{aligned}$$

b) $\min. z = P_1d_4^- + P_2d_3^+ + P_3d_2^+ + P_4d_1^-$.

7. Both d_5^- and d_6^- are assigned priority P_5 with no differential weight.

11. a) min. $z = P_1d_1^- + P_2d_7^+ + P_3d_2^+ + P_4d_3^+ + P_5d_4^- + P_6d_5^- + 2P_6d_6^-$.

b) $$d_2^+ + d_7^- - d_7^+ = 5$$

where

d_7^- = Amount by which the budget overrun falls short of $5,000

d_7^+ = Amount by which budget overrun exceeds $5,000.

c) $$x_1 + x_2 + d_7^- - d_7^+ = 105$$

13. d_7^- = Amount by which the underachievement of the $1,200,000 award is less than $200,000.
d_7^+ = Amount by which the underachievement of the $1,200,000 award is greater than $200,000.

15. Add four new goal constraints:

$$25x_{11} + 30x_{31} + 40x_{41} + d_8^- - d_8^+ = 1{,}500{,}000 \quad (16)$$

$$28x_{12} + 80x_{22} + 28x_{32} + d_9^- - d_9^+ = 1{,}500{,}000 \quad (17)$$

$$75x_{23} + 33x_{33} + d_{10}^- - d_{10}^+ = 1{,}500{,}000 \quad (18)$$

$$30x_{14} + 82x_{24} + 42x_{44} + d_{11}^- - d_{11}^+ = 1{,}500{,}000 \quad (19)$$

or

$$d_3^+ + d_8^- - d_8^+ = 300{,}000 \quad (16)$$

$$d_4^+ + d_9^- - d_9^+ = 300{,}000 \quad (17)$$

$$d_5^+ + d_{10}^- - d_{10}^+ = 300{,}000 \quad (18)$$

$$d_6^+ + d_{11}^- - d_{11}^+ = 300{,}000 \quad (19)$$

In either case, objective function has the added term

$$P_5(d_8^+ + d_9^+ + d_{10}^+ + d_{11}^+)$$

17. Objective function would change to
min. $z = P_1(d_1^- + d_1^+) + P_2(d_3^- + d_3^+) + P_3(d_4^- + d_4^+) + P_4(d_2^- + d_2^+) + P_5(d_5^-) + P_6d_6^+ + P_7d_7^- + P_8d_8^- + P_9d_9^+$.

23. System constraints (8–11) would be replaced with four goal constraints. Deviational variables $d_6^{-,+}$, $d_7^{-,+}$, $d_8^{-,+}$ and $d_9^{-,+}$ would be included. The objective function would include the term

$$P_6(d_6^- + d_7^- + d_8^- + d_9^-)$$

25. Second priority goal becomes $P_2(d_2^- + d_2^+)$.

29. Point A of (0, 10) satisfies the new set of goals best. New goal constraint:
$2x_1 + 5x_2 + d_3^- - d_3^+ = 60$.
New objective function:
$z = P_1d_1^- + P_2d_2^- + P_3(d_3^- + d_3^+)$.

31. Spend $70,000 on TV advertising, $30,000 for radio. Total exposures are 925,000 resulting in underachievement of the goal of 1 million by 75,000. One million exposures could be realized if all the budget could be allocated to TV. Otherwise, to achieve this level while spending no more than 70 percent of the budget on TV would require an increase in the budget beyond $100,000.
Point B does not do well in minimizing d_4^-; it results in 750,000 exposures.

33. a) (70, 30). b) (70, 30).

35. a) Alternative optimal solutions exist along the line segment connecting (8, 6) and (13, 6).
b) (16,0). c) (8, 3⅓).

37. a) Optimal solutions exist at (8, 6), (9, 6), (10, 6), (11, 6), (12, 6), and (13, 6).
b) (16, 0). c) (12, 0).

39. a) $x_1 = 9, x_2 = 0, E_1 = 28, S_2 = 9$,
$d_1^- = d_1^+ + d_2^+ = d_3^+ = 0, d_2^- = 1, d_3^- = 6$.
b) $x_1 = 4, x_2 = 6, E_1 = 20, S_2 = 0$,
$d_1^- = d_2^+ = d_3^+ = d_3^- = 0, d_2^- = 6, d_1^+ = 8$.

41. a) min. $z = P_1(d_1^- + d_1^+) + P_2(d_2^- + d_2^+) + P_3(d_3^+)$
s.t.

$$\begin{aligned}
.5x_1 \quad\quad + .8x_3 \quad\quad &\le 350 \\
.5x_2 \quad\quad + .8x_4 &\le 500 \\
10x_1 \quad\quad + 7x_3 \quad\quad &\le 6{,}000 \\
10x_1 + 10x_2 + 7x_3 + 7x_4 &\le 10{,}000 \\
x_1 + x_2 + d_1^- - d_1^+ &= 500 \\
x_3 + x_4 + d_2^- - d_2^+ &= 700 \\
3x_1 + 4x_2 + 6.13x_3 + 5x_4 + d_3^- - d_3^+ &= 4{,}940
\end{aligned}$$

$$x_j, d_j^-, d_j^+ \ge 0 \quad \text{for all } j$$

43. a) Let x_1 = Number of acres allocated for backpacking
x_2 = Number of acres allocated for hunting
x_3 = Number of acres allocated for timber wolves
x_4 = Number of acres allocated for timber cutting

min. $z = P_1d_1^+ + P_2d_2^- + P_3(d_3^- + d_3^+) + P_4d_4^+$
s.t.

$$240x_4 - 15x_1 - 20x_2 - 5x_3 - 4x_4 \ge 0$$

or

$$-15x_1 - 20x_2 - 5x_3 + 236x_4 \ge 0 \quad (1)$$

$$x_1 + x_2 + x_3 + x_4 = 20{,}000 \quad (2)$$

$$12{,}000x_4 + d_1^- - d_1^+ = 6{,}000{,}000 \quad (3)$$

$$100x_2 + d_2^- - d_2^+ = 700{,}000 \quad (4)$$

$$2x_3 + d_3^- - d_3^+ = 20{,}000 \quad (5)$$

$$1{,}000x_1 \qquad + d_4^- - d_4^+ = 5{,}000{,}000 \qquad (6)$$
$$x_j, d_j^-, d_j^+ \geq 0 \quad \text{for all } j$$

47. *a*) Defining variables as in exercise 39 (Chapter 3)

$$\text{min. } z = P_1 d_1^+ + P_2(d_2^- + d_3^-) + P_3(d_4^- + d_5^-) + P_4 d_6^+$$

s.t.

$$\begin{aligned}
&1{,}100x_1 + 440x_2 + 1{,}250x_3 + 500x_4 + 1{,}000x_5 + 400x_6 + 1{,}250x_7 + 500x_8 + d_1^- - d_1^+ = 2{,}500{,}000\\
&x_1 + x_3 + d_2^- - d_2^+ = 1{,}250\\
&x_2 + x_4 + d_3^- - d_3^+ = 400\\
&x_3 + x_7 + d_4^- - d_4^+ = 1{,}000\\
&x_4 + x_8 + d_5^- - d_5^+ = 320\\
&d_1^+ + d_6^- - d_6^+ = 250{,}000\\
&x_1 + x_3 + x_5 + x_7 = 2{,}500\\
&x_2 + x_4 + x_6 + x_8 = 800\\
&x_7 + x_8 \geq x_5 + x_6\\
&x_j, d_j^-, d_j^+ \geq 0
\end{aligned}$$

CHAPTER 10

1. *a*) $\text{min. } z = 5.00x_{13} + 4.50x_{14} + 6.00x_{15} + 3.90x_{23} + 6.20x_{24} + 4.75x_{25}$

s.t.

$$\begin{aligned}
x_{13} + x_{14} + x_{15} &= 8{,}000\\
x_{23} + x_{24} + x_{25} &= 6{,}000\\
-x_{13} - x_{23} &= -4{,}500\\
-x_{14} - x_{24} &= -3{,}700\\
-x_{15} - x_{25} &= -5{,}800\\
x_{ij} &\geq 0
\end{aligned}$$

b)

Node	1–3	1–4	1–5	2–3	2–4	2–5	*RHS*
1	1	1	1	0	0	0	8,000
2	0	0	0	1	1	1	6,000
3	−1	0	0	−1	0	0	−4,500
4	0	−1	0	0	−1	0	−3,700
5	0	0	−1	0	0	−1	−5,800

3. *a*) $\text{min. } z = 5x_{12} + 3x_{13} + 6x_{23} + 8x_{24} + 7x_{25} + 6x_{35} + 8x_{36} + 5x_{47} + 8x_{54} + 12x_{57} + 9x_{65} + 10x_{67} + 4x_{74}$

s.t.

$$\begin{aligned}
x_{12} + x_{13} &= 20{,}000\\
-x_{12} + x_{24} + x_{25} + x_{23} &= 0\\
-x_{13} - x_{23} + x_{35} + x_{36} &= 0\\
-x_{24} - x_{54} - x_{74} + x_{47} &= -4{,}000\\
-x_{25} - x_{35} - x_{65} + x_{54} + x_{57} &= 0\\
-x_{36} + x_{65} + x_{67} &= 0\\
-x_{47} - x_{57} - x_{67} + x_{74} &= -16{,}000\\
x_{ij} &\geq 0
\end{aligned}$$

See Table below

5. *a*)

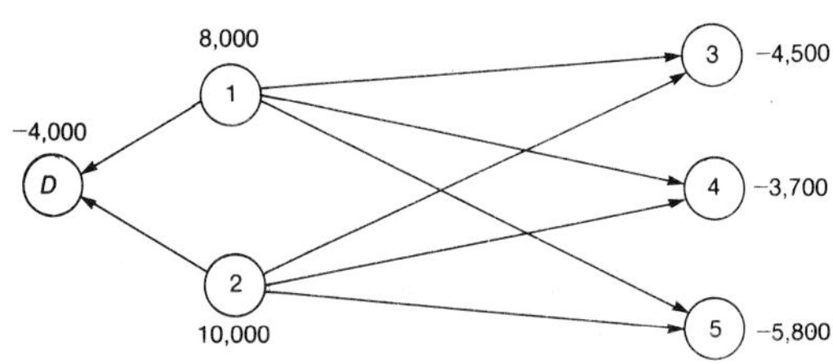

b) In objective function *add terms* $c_{1D}x_{1D} + c_{2D}x_{2D}$

Constraints:

$$\begin{aligned}
x_{13} + x_{14} + x_{15} + x_{1D} &= 10{,}000\\
x_{23} + x_{24} + x_{25} + x_{2D} &= 6{,}000\\
-x_{13} - x_{23} &= -4{,}500\\
-x_{14} - x_{24} &= -3{,}700\\
-x_{15} - x_{25} &= -5{,}800\\
-x_{1D} - x_{2D} &= -4{,}000
\end{aligned}$$

c) Add new row for node *D*; add 2 columns for the arcs 1–*D* and 2–*D*.

d) If surplus supply costs nothing (units not produced and factors of production not compensated). Units produced and held in inventory might incur holding costs which should be reflected in objective function.

See Exercise 3a.

Node	1–2	1–3	2–3	2–4	2–5	3–5	3–6	4–7	5–4	5–7	6–5	6–7	7–4	*RHS*
1	1	1	0	0	0	0	0	0	0	0	0	0	0	20,000
2	−1	0	1	1	1	0	0	0	0	0	0	0	0	0
3	0	−1	−1	0	0	1	1	0	0	0	0	0	0	0
4	0	0	0	−1	0	0	0	1	−1	0	0	0	−1	−4,000
5	0	0	0	0	−1	−1	0	0	1	1	−1	0	0	0
6	0	0	0	0	0	0	−1	0	0	0	1	1	0	0
7	0	0	0	0	0	0	0	−1	0	−1	0	−1	1	−16,000

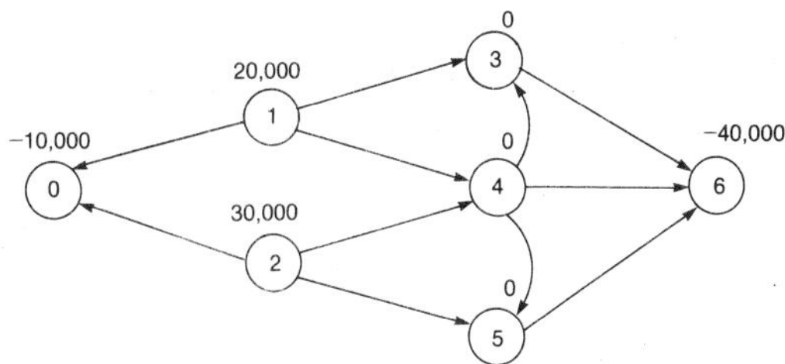

Minimal spanning tree

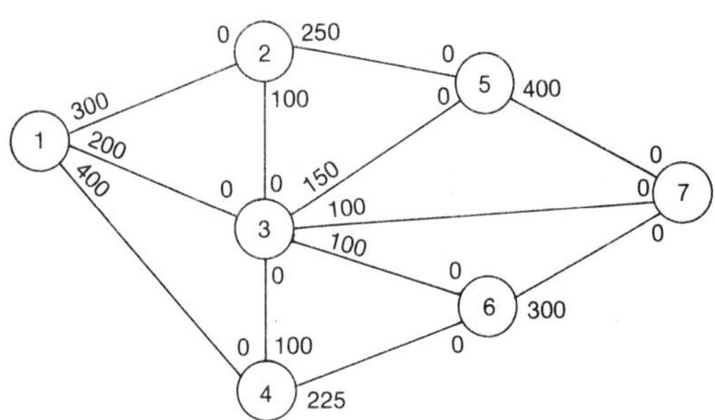

17. 1–2, 2–7, 2–3, 3–4, 4–5, 2–6, 6–8, 6–9; minimum distance = 88.
19. 1–3–4 (distance = 25), 1–3–5 (distance = 24), 1–3–5–6 (distance = 27).

21.

Shortest Route	Distance
1–5–4	15
1–5	8
1–5–6	13
1–5–6–7	17
1–5–8	17
1–5–9	14
1–5–9–10	21

23. Buy in year 1, replace at beginning of year 2, and hold until end of year 5.

25.

Allocation	Path	Quantity
1	1–2′–2″–3	4
2	1–2′–3	12
3	1–2‴–3	21
4	1–2″–2′–3	7
5	1–2‴–2′–3	3

27. Maximal flow = 800

Allocations	Quantity
1–2–5–7	250
1–4–6–7	225
1–2–3–5–7	50
1–3–5–7	100
1–3–7	100
1–4–3–6–7	75

Allocations across each arc:

1–2	300	3–5	150
1–3	200	3–7	100
1–4	300	3–6	75
2–5	250	4–6	225
2–3	50	5–7	400
4–3	75	6–7	300

31. Minimum cost = 85($10,000s). Connect 1–2, 1–3, 2–5, 3–5, 5–8, 6–7, 4–9, 8–9, 8–11, 7–11, 11–12, 10–11, 10–14, 11–15, 9–13.

33.

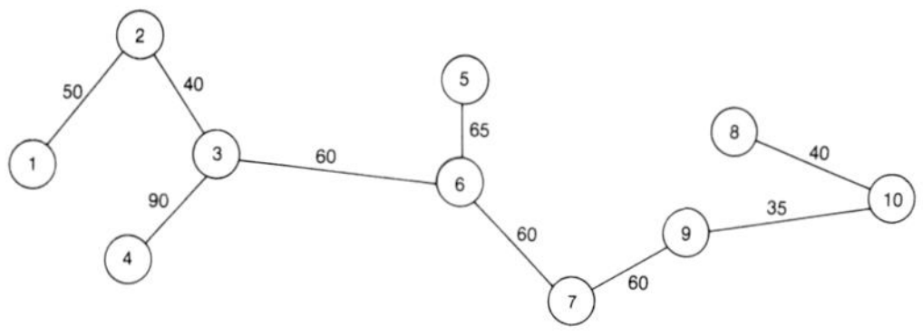

39. *a*) Maximal flow = 16,000 vehicles/hour

Path	Quantity
1–2–7	5
1–3–5–7	3
1–4–6–7	5
1–3–7	2
1–4–6–5–2–7	1
	16

CHAPTER 11

3. The second part of the network requires a new node and new dummies:

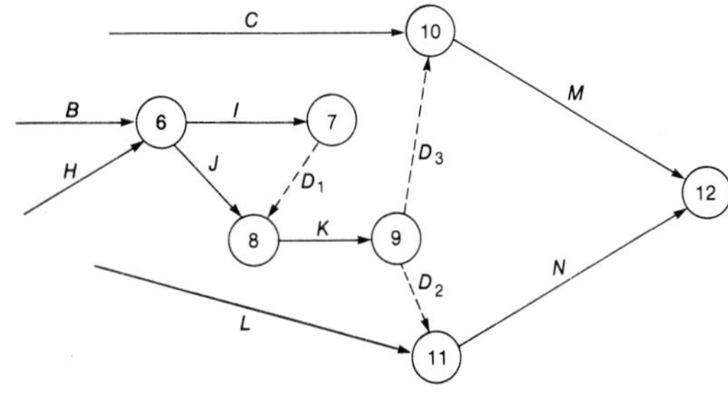

7. Now activity 5–10 becomes critical on a second critical path given by 1–2–3–4–5–10–11.
9. Same as Figure 11.7 except:
   (1) Activity J can begin as early as the end of day 21 (as before) but can end as late as the end of day 31 (which is 6 more days than before). Its latest starting time is the end of day 28.
   (2) Activity M can begin as early as the end of day 31 (which is 6 more days than before) and can end as late as the end of day 38 (as before). Its latest starting time is still the end of day 34.
11. Part *a*: Activity J is scheduled as before for days 22–24, but now M and its 2 personnel are scheduled for days 32–35 instead of days 26–29. Looking at the data in exercise 10*d*, under part *a*, this means that 3 personnel will be required in days 26–29 and 4 personnel will be required in days 32–35.

$$\bar{x} = 4.26 \qquad \hat{\sigma}_x^2 = 3.60 \qquad \hat{\sigma}_x = 1.90$$

Part *b*: Activity M is scheduled as before, but J is now scheduled on days 29–31 instead of days 23–25. Since J requires 2 personnel, the schedule in part *b* of exercise 10*d* changes as follows: 5 personnel for days 23–25 and 6 personnel for days 29–31.

$$\bar{x} = 4.37 \qquad \hat{\sigma}_x^2 = 2.94 \qquad \hat{\sigma}_x = 1.72$$

The schedule in part *a* requires slightly less personnel per day on the average but also has a higher variance in personnel requirements.

17. $P(e_i \leq L_i) = 0.5$ whenever event i is critical.
19. See table on page 971.
21.

Activity	$\bar{d}_{ij}$*	v_{ij}*
A	13	46
B	3	3
C	1	0
D	3	6
E	8	14
F	3	2
G	4	3
H	6	19
I	4	2
J	3	0
K	7	9
L	3	0
M	5	6
N	6	6

*To nearest day.

i	$E(e_i)$	$V(e_i)$	S_i	z_i	$P(e_i \le S_i)$
2	3	6	2	−0.41	0.34
3	11	20	10	−0.22	0.41
4	14	22	11	−0.64	0.26
5	18	25	20	0.40	0.66
6	24	44	24	0.00	0.50
7	28	46	34	0.88	0.81
8	28	46	27	−0.15	0.44
9	28	46	28	0.00	0.50
10	35	54	32	−0.41	0.34
11	41	60	40	−0.13	0.45

27. *a*) and *b*)

Activity	i–j	$\bar{d}_{ij}$	v_{ij}	E_i	L_j	TS_{ij}	FS_{ij}
A	1–2	2.8	0.25	0	12.4	9.6	0
B	1–5	1.2	0.03	0	13.4	12.2	12.2
C	1–3	5.5	0.69	0	5.5	0.0	0
D	2–5	1.0	0.00	2.8	13.4	9.6	9.6
E	3–4	6.7	1.78	5.5	12.2	0.0	0
F	4–5	1.2	0.03	12.2	13.4	0.0	0
G	5–6	2.0	0.11	13.4	15.4	0.0	0
H	6–7	8.0	0.44	15.4	23.4	0.0	0

d) $E(e_7) = 23.4$

$V(e_7) = 3.05$

1. $P(e_7 \le 22) = P(Z_7 \le -0.80) = 0.21$
2. $P(e_7 \le 23.4) = 0.5.$
3. $P(e_7 > 30) = 1 - P(e_7 \le 30) = 1 - P(Z_7 \le 3.78) = 1 - 1.0 = 0.$

29. *a*)

Step	Action	Critical Path(s)	Direct Cost, Duration
Normal	—	C–E–F–G–H	(140.9, 22)
All crash	—	Same	(244.0, 13.5)
1	Crash F	Same	(141.7, 21.5)
2	Compress C	Same	(146.2, 20.5)
3	Crash C	Same	(150.7, 19.5)
4	Crash G	Same	(155.7, 18.5)
5	Compress E	Same	(165.7, 17.5)
6	Compress E	Same	(175.7, 16.5)
7	Crash E	Same	(185.7, 15.5)
8	Compress H	Same	(210.7, 14.5)
9	Crash H	Same	(235.7, 13.5)

	Costs			
t	Direct	Indirect	Opportunity	Total
22.0	140.9	27.5	11.0	179.4
21.5	141.7	26.5	9.0	177.2
20.5	146.2	25.5	7.0	178.7
19.5	150.7	24.5	5.0	180.2
18.5	155.7	23.5	3.0	182.2
17.5	165.7	22.5	1.0	189.2
16.5	175.7	21.5	0	197.2
15.5	185.7	20.5	0	206.2
14.5	210.7	19.5	0	230.2
13.5	235.7	18.5	0	254.2

Note: Duration for minimum total cost is 21.5 weeks.

See Exercise 19.

i	Longest Path	$E(e_i)$	$V(e_i)$	S_i	z_i	$P(e_i \le S_i)$
2	1–2	2	2	2.4	0.28	0.61
3	1–2–3	9	6	10.8	0.73	0.77
4	1–2–3–4	12	6	14.4	0.98	0.84
5	1–2–3–4–5	17	7	20.4	1.29	0.90
6	1–2–3–4–5–6	21	12	25.2	1.21	0.89
7	1–2–3–4–5–6–8–9–7	31	15	40.8	2.53	0.99
8	1–2–3–4–5–6–8	25	12	30.0	1.44	0.93
9	1–2–3–4–5–6–8–9	31	15	37.2	1.60	0.95
10	1–2–3–4–5–6–8–9–10	31	15	37.2	1.60	0.95
11	1–2–3–4–5–6–8–9–10–11	38	17	45.6	1.84	0.97

31. *a*) and *b*)

Activity	*i–j*	$\bar{d}_{ij}$	v_{ij}	E_i	L_j	TS_{ij}	FS_{ij}
A	1–2	31.7	11.1	0	32.1	0.4	0.0
B	1–3	15.0	2.8	0	32.3	17.3	0.0
C	1–4	25.8	6.2	0	25.8	0.0	0.0
D	2–5	3.3	0.1	31.7	35.4	0.4	0.0
E	4–7	7.5	1.4	25.8	33.3	0.0	0.0
F	3–6	1.0	0.0	15.0	33.3	17.3	0.0
D_1	6–7	0.0	0.0	16.0	33.3	17.3	17.3
D_2	6–5	0.0	0.0	16.0	35.4	19.4	19.0
G	5–9	5.2	0.2	35.0	47.9	7.7	7.7
H	5–8	2.2	0.0	35.0	37.6	0.4	0.4
I	7–8	4.3	0.1	33.3	37.6	0.0	0.0
J	8–9	10.3	1.0	37.6	47.9	0.0	0.0
K	9–10	8.8	2.2	47.9	56.7	0.0	0.0

c) No.

d) $E(e_{10}) = 56.7, \quad V(e_{10}) = 10.9$

1. $P(e_{10} \leq 54) = P(Z_{10} \leq -0.82) = 0.21$
2. $P(e_{10} \leq 56.7) = 0.5$
3. $P(e_{10} > 70) = 1 - P(e_{10} \leq 70) = 1 - P(Z_{10} \leq 4.0) = 1 - 1 = 0.$

33. Critical path: A–B–D–E–G–K or 1–2–4–6–8–12–13. Earliest completion time: 38 person-days.

35. min. $z = E_{11}$
s.t.

$$
\begin{aligned}
E_2 &\geq 2 && (1)\\
-E_2 + E_3 &\geq 7 && (2)\\
-E_3 + E_4 &\geq 3 && (3)\\
E_4 &\geq 10 && (4)\\
-E_4 + E_5 &\geq 5 && (5)\\
-E_5 + E_6 &\geq 4 && (6)\\
E_6 &\geq 3 && (7)\\
E_7 &\geq 1 && (8)\\
-E_8 + E_7 &\geq 0 && (9)\\
-E_6 + E_8 &\geq 4 && (10)\\
-E_8 + E_9 &\geq 0 && (11)\\
-E_6 + E_9 &\geq 3 && (12)\\
-E_5 + E_{10} &\geq 3 && (13)\\
-E_9 + E_{10} &\geq 6 && (14)\\
-E_7 + E_{11} &\geq 4 && (15)\\
-E_{10} + E_{11} &\geq 7 && (16)\\
E_j &\geq 0 \quad \text{all } j
\end{aligned}
$$

37. min. $z = E_6$
s.t.

$$
\begin{aligned}
E_2 &\geq 2 && (1)\\
E_3 &\geq 8 && (2)\\
-E_2 + E_4 &\geq 4 && (3)\\
-E_3 + E_4 &\geq 1 && (4)\\
-E_3 + E_5 &\geq 2 && (5)\\
-E_4 + E_6 &\geq 5 && (6)\\
-E_5 + E_6 &\geq 6 && (7)\\
E_j &\geq 0 \quad \text{all } j
\end{aligned}
$$

Computer solution: z minimized at 16; $E_2 = 7$, $E_3 = 8$, $E_4 = 11$, $E_5 = 10$, $E_6 = 16$. Shadow prices: 0, 1, 0, 0, 1, 0, 1 for constraints 1–7, respectively. Thus, the critical path is associated with constraints 2, 5, and 7, which identifies (1, 3), (3, 5), and (5, 6) as the critical activities.

CHAPTER 12

3. The longest route is I–II–V–VII with a distance of 15.
7. Select projects I, E, and B with a net present value of $5 million. Same solution with a $4 million budget. Recommendation then is to select I, E, and B and to either reconsider the constraint of only one project per division or else to invest the extra $1 million elsewhere when given a $4 million budget.
9. Optimal solution: $z = 6$, $A2 = 1$, $B2 = 1$, $C2 = 1$, all others 0;
or $z = 6$, $A1 = 1$, $B2 = 1$, $C3 = 1$, all others 0.
11. The longest route is still I–II–V–VII with a distance of 15.
15. *b*) Backward stage transformations: See chart below.

c) Method 1:

t	BI	Production	Demand	EI
1	0	4	2	2
2	2	0	2	0
3	0	4	3	1
4	1	5	3	3

See Exercise 15b.

$s_4 = 3$ → [$x_4^* = 5$, $d_4 = 3$] → $s_3 = 3 - 5 + 3 = 1$ → [$x_3^* = 4$, $d_3 = 3$] → $s_2 = 1 - 4 + 3 = 0$ → [$x_2^* = 0$, $d_2 = 2$] → $s_1 = 0 - 0 + 2 = 2$ → [$x_1^* = 4$, $d_1 = 2$] → $s_0 = 2 - 4 + 2 = 0$

Method 2: See stages in part *b*.

d)

t	x_t	s_t	Production Cost in t	Inventory Cost in t	Total Cost in t	Cumulative Cost
1	4	2	5	2	7	7
2	0	0	0	0	0	7
3	4	1	7	2	9	16
4	5	3	11	6	17	33

17. Stage 5: $f_5 = r_5 + f_4^* = C_5(x_5) + 2 \cdot s_5 + f_4^*$

s_5 \ x_5	0	1	2	3	4	5	x_5^*	f_5^*
0			9 + 0 + 33 = 42	8 + 0 + 28 = 36	9 + 0 + 23 = 32	12 + 0 + 20 = 32	4, 5	32

Alternative optimal solutions. Two possible schedules:

	x_1	x_2	x_3	x_4	x_5
1.	4	0	3	3	5
2.	4	0	3	4	4

19. The *r*-function must be changed to reflect a zero carrying cost and a penalty cost whenever ending inventory is negative.

$$r_i = C_i(x_i) + h_i \cdot \max[0, s_i] + b_i \cdot |\min[0, s_i]|$$

where b_i is the backorder (penalty) cost in Stage *i*.
Now, as before, $f_i = r_i + f_{i-1}^*$.
Backward stage transformations:

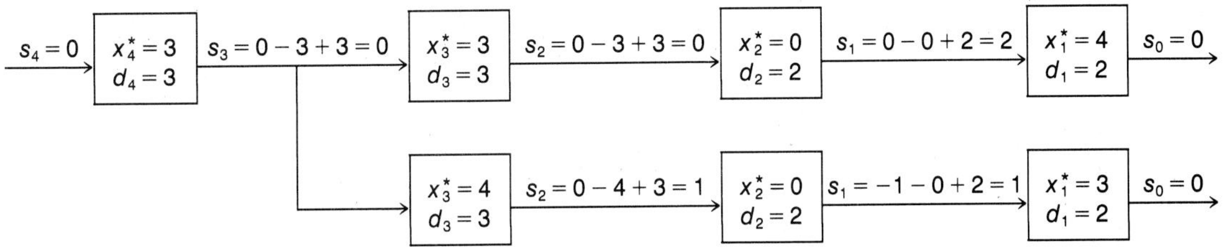

$s_4 = 0$ → [$x_4^* = 3$, $d_4 = 3$] → $s_3 = 0 - 3 + 3 = 0$ → [$x_3^* = 3$, $d_3 = 3$] → $s_2 = 0 - 3 + 3 = 0$ → [$x_2^* = 0$, $d_2 = 2$] → $s_1 = 0 - 0 + 2 = 2$ → [$x_1^* = 4$, $d_1 = 2$] → $s_0 = 0$

$s_3 = 0$ → [$x_3^* = 4$, $d_3 = 3$] → $s_2 = 0 - 4 + 3 = 1$ → [$x_2^* = 0$, $d_2 = 2$] → $s_1 = -1 - 0 + 2 = 1$ → [$x_1^* = 3$, $d_1 = 2$] → $s_0 = 0$

21. Stage 4: $f_4 = r_4 \cdot f_3^*$

s_4 \ x_4	1	2	3	x_4^*	f_4^*
7	(.7)(.24) = .168			1	.168
8	(.7)(.36) = .252	(.91)(.24) = .218	(.97)(.24) = .233	1	.252
9	(.7)(.432) = .302	(.91)(.36) = .328	(.97)(.36) = .349	3	.349
10	(.7)(.507) = .355	(.91)(.432) = .393	(.97)(.432) = .419	3*	.419

Optimal design: 2, 2, 1, 3 units for components 1, 2, 3, 4 respectively.

23. $s_4 = 40{,}000$, $x_4^* = -150$, $x_3^* = 150$, $x_2^* = 4{,}850$, $x_1^* = 5{,}150$, $f_4 = 859{,}550$, $s_4 = 50{,}000$, $x_4^* = -5{,}150$, $x_3^* = -4{,}850$, $x_2^* = 4{,}850$, $x_1^* = 5{,}150$, $f_4^* = 1{,}149{,}550$.

25. *b*) Stage 3:

s_3 \ x_3	0	1	2	3	x_3^*	f_3^*
3	1.5 + 0.6 = 2.1	1.0 + 0.8 = 1.8	0.7 + 1.4 = 2.1	0.3 + 2.5 = 2.8	1	1.8
4	1.5 + 0.5 = 2.0	1.0 + 0.6 = 1.6	0.7 + 0.8 = 1.5	0.3 + 1.4 = 1.7	2	1.5
5	1.5 + 0.4 = 1.9	1.0 + 0.5 = 1.5	0.7 + 0.6 = 1.3	0.3 + 0.8 = 1.1	3	1.1

Optimal solution when 5 stations allocated: $x_3^* = 3$, $x_2^* = 0$, $x_1^* = 2$, with expected total damages of $1.1 million.

c) If 4 stations allocated, then $x_3^* = 2$, $x_2^* = 0$, $x_1^* = 2$ with damages of $1.5 million.

29. Use backward recursions and match stage *i* with product *i*.
Stage 5:

Possible Decisions

s_5 \ x_5	0	1	2	3	4	x_5^*	f_5^*
12	43.4	40.7	41.0	41.7	42.1	0	43.4

Optimal decisions are: product 5, $0; product 4, $3 million; product 3, $4 million; product 2, $3 million; and product 1, $2 million.

31. *b*) Stage 3:

s_3 \ x_3	0	1	2	3	4	5	6	x_3^*	f_3^*
4	36	39	40	40	45			4	45
5	51	45	44	45	50	50		0	51
6	71	60	50	49	55	55	60	0	71

If $s_3 = 6$, then 71 million lives saved when all funds go to clinic 1.

c) All $5 million goes to clinic 1, with 51 million lives saved. Note radical change in decision if only $4 million is disbursed; clinic 3 gets all funds.

33. *b*) Stage 3:

s_3 \ x_3	150	200	250	x_3^*	f_3^*
700	20 + 1.50 + 67.20 = 88.70	30 + 2.10 + 56.80 = 88.90	35 + 2.40 + 51.70 = 89.10	150	88.70

Optimal decision: $x_3^* = 150$, $x_2^* = 200$, $x_1^* = 250$.

35. *a*)

i \ j	2	3	4	5
1	0.48	0.886	1.2348	1.53984
2		0.510	0.9420	1.31360
3			0.5400	0.99800
4				0.57000

b) Buy the asset at the beginning of period 1 and keep it until the end of the planning horizon ($x_1^* = j = 5$) at a total cost of $1.53984 million.

CHAPTER 13

1.

	θ_1	θ_2	θ_3	θ_4
D_1	9.500	9.500	11.000	11.000
D_2	9.250	10.750	10.000	11.500
D_3	9.000	12.000	9.000	12.000
D_4	9.125	11.375	9.500	11.750
D_5	9.375	10.125	10.500	11.250

3.

Rates for B

Rates for A	−0.10	0.20
−0.05	θ_1	θ_2
0.00	θ_3	θ_4
0.10	θ_5	θ_6

	θ_1	θ_2	θ_3	θ_4	θ_5	θ_6
D_1	9.50	9.50	10.00	10.00	11.00	11.00
D_2	9.25	10.75	9.50	11.00	10.00	11.50
D_3	9.00	12.00	9.00	12.00	9.00	12.00

5. D_3, expected value = 10.8
7. D_2, min-max regret = 1.25.
9. $f(\theta_1) = 1.0$, $f(\theta_2) = 0$, $f(\theta_3) = 0$,
$EV(D_1) = 1.0(-2) + 0(1) + 0(1) = -2.0$
$EV(D_2) = 1.0(0) + 0(0) + 0(0) = 0.0$
Maximum occurs with D_2 and $EV(D_2) = 0.0$, but this is the same as max-min. These probability assignments make sense for the pessimist who assigns a probability of 1.0 to the worst happening.
11. For D_1: $f(\theta_1 \text{ or } \theta_2) = 0$, $f(\theta_3 \text{ or } \theta_4) = 1$, $E(R) = 11.00$. For D_2: $f(\theta_1 \text{ or } \theta_2 \text{ or } \theta_3) = 0$, $f(\theta_4) = 1$, $E(R) = 11.50$. For D_3: $f(\theta_1 \text{ or } \theta_3) = 0$, $f(\theta_2 \text{ or } \theta_4) = 1$, $E(R) = 12.00$. Thus $D^* = D_3$, which is identical to the max-max rule.
13.

θ	$f(\theta)$	$f(3\|\theta)$	$f(\theta) \cdot f(3\|\theta)$	$f(\theta\|3)$
$p = 0.05$	0.4	0.0596	0.02384	0.1606
$p = 0.10$	0.4	0.1901	0.07604	0.5123
$p = 0.15$	0.2	0.2428	0.04856	0.3271
			$f(3) = 0.14844$	1.0000

	$E'(R)$
D_1	1.8266 ← D_B^*
D_2	0

Note: The result 3 out of 20 consumers is consistent with θ_3 and favors D_1.

15. *a*)

	$E'(R)$
D_1	9.875
D_2	10.000
D_3	10.185 ← D_B^*

b)

	$E'(R)$
D_1	10.679 ← D_B^*
D_2	10.161
D_3	9.643

25. $EVPI$ = 0.2 million, $EVSI$ = 0.04 million, $ENVSI$ = 0.03 million.
31. $U(R) = (1-p) \cdot U(R_{min}) + p \cdot U(R_{max})$
$= (1-p) \cdot (0) + p \cdot (1)$
$= p$
33. *a*) A_3. *b*) A_1. *c*) A_1. *d*) A_1.
35. *a*) A_4, 378.60. *b*) 445.40. *c*) 66.80.
37. *a*) A_4, 378.60 *b*) 445.40 *c*) 66.80.
39. D^* = 2,000 containers and $E(R^*)$ = \$390/week, compared with current return of \$295/week.
41. $EVPI$ = 165, so room for improvement, EPE = 444.50 − 50 = \$394.50/week, EVE = \$394.50 − 390 = \$4.50/week. As long as forecasting service costs under \$54.50/week, its use is economically attractive.
43. *a*) Stock four parts (D^* = 4).
b) As long as $43.85 < C_p < 540.06$, and all other parameters remain fixed, then D^* = 4.
47. 1. *Max-min* rule reflects a risk-averse decision maker. Select D_2.
2. *Max-max* rule reflects risk affinity if it can be argued that this is implicit in an optimist. Select D_1.
3. *Min-max regret* rule reflects risk aversion. Select D_1. Note the behavioral conflict with rule 2 or the decision conflict with rule 1.
4. *Maximize expected payoff* rule reflects risk neutrality. Select D_1.

CHAPTER 14

1. $P(X_{11} = 0 | X_1 = 0, \ldots, X_{10} = 0) = P(X_{11} = 0 | X_{10} = 0)$.
5. $P = \begin{pmatrix} 3/6 & 3/6 \\ 2/4 & 2/4 \end{pmatrix}$
7. *a*) Holding power probabilities.
b) Brand 3, since $p_{23} > p_{21}$.
c) Brand 1, since $p_{11} > p_{22} > p_{33}$.
d) Brand 3, since $p_{33} < p_{22} < p_{11}$.
9. Ten possible states.

Number of Purchases	Brand Mix
0	(0, 0, 0)
1	(1, 0, 0)
	(0, 1, 0)
	(0, 0, 1)
2	(1, 1, 0)
	(1, 0, 1)
	(0, 1, 1)
	(2, 0, 0)
	(0, 2, 0)
	(0, 0, 2)

11. *b*) $\begin{pmatrix} 0.933 & 0.053 & 0.014 \\ 0.037 & 0.780 & 0.183 \\ 0.200 & 0.120 & 0.680 \end{pmatrix}$.
13. The Markovian property would not be satisfied, but we still have a stochastic process.
15. $\begin{pmatrix} 5/10 & 1/10 & 4/10 \\ 0/1 & 0/1 & 1/1 \\ 4/8 & 0/8 & 4/8 \end{pmatrix}$.
17. $P(X_{11} = 1 | X_{10} = 0) = 0.04$, $P(X_{12} = 1 | X_{10} = 0) = (0.6)(0.4) + (0.4)(0.5) = 0.44$, $P(X_{13} = 1 | X_{10} = 0) = (0.6)(0.6)(0.4) + (0.6)(0.4)(0.5) + (0.4)(0.5) \cdot (0.4) + (0.4)(0.5)(0.5) = 0.444$.
19. $P(X_1 = 1 | X_0 = 3) = 0.20$, $P(X_2 = 1 | X_0 = 3) = 0.3184$, $P(X_3 = 1 | X_0 = 3) = 0.38796$
21. $P(X_2 = 1 | X_0 = 3) = (0.5)(0.5) + (0)(0) + (0.5) \cdot (0.5) = 0.50$, $P(X_2 = 2 | X_0 = 3) = (0.5)(0.1) + (0)(0) + (0.5)(0) = 0.05$, $P(X_2 = 3 | X_0 = 3) = (0.5)(0.4) + (0)(1) + (0.5)(0.5) = 0.45$.
23. $P^4 = \begin{pmatrix} 0.5556 & 0.4444 \\ 0.5555 & 0.4445 \end{pmatrix}$, $P_{11}^{(4)} = 0.5556$.
25. The probability that a brand 1 customer in week 27 will be a brand 1 customer in week 29 equals 0.8174. The probability that a brand 2 customer in week 27 will be a brand 1 customer in week 29 equals 0.0664. The probability that a brand 3 customer in week 27 will be a brand 1 customer in week 29 equals 0.3184.
29. $u^{(2)} = (0.2321 \quad 0.4014 \quad 0.2486 \quad 0.1179)$.
31. $u_1^* = 5/9$, $u_2^* = 4/9$.
37. Q_3; expected cost equals \$172.22.
39. $u^* = (0.3259 \quad 0.5148 \quad 0.1593)$.
41. $\overline{Z}(Q_4) = (0.515)(50{,}000{,}000)(0.50) - 900{,}000$
$= \$11{,}975{,}000$ per week.
Undertake both promotion campaigns.
43. *a*) $\begin{pmatrix} 0.6760 & 0.2822 & 0.0418 \\ 0.3100 & 0.6065 & 0.0835 \\ 0.0320 & 0.2544 & 0.7136 \end{pmatrix}$
b) Poor = 41,025.6, good = 41,025.6, excellent = 17,948.8.
45. *a*) $\begin{pmatrix} 0.8 & 0.1 & 0.1 \\ 0.04 & 0.95 & 0.01 \\ 0.15 & 0.15 & 0.70 \end{pmatrix}$.
b) (0.46 0.39 0.15).
c) (0.4061 0.4390 0.1549), (0.365675 0.480895 0.15343).
e) $u_1^* = 0.2093023$, $u_2^* = 0.6976744$, $u_3^* = 0.0930233$.
47. *c*) (570 220 0 0 210), (343.32 132 0 0 524.68).
d) $u_1^* = 0$, $u_2^* = 0$, $u_3^* = 0$, $u_4^* = 0$, $u_5^* = 1{,}000$.
51. *a*) Not ergodic.
b) Once in an absorbing state, other states may not be achieved. State D is also ergodic.

CHAPTER 15

7. *a*) $Q^* = 273.86$. *b*) $Q^* = 353.55$.
   c) $Q^* = 316.23$.

9. $Q^* = \sqrt{\dfrac{2DC_o}{(C_h + 2C_s)}}$.

11. *EOQ* from 10 is 146,103.

13. *a*) $\dfrac{dEPQ}{dC_o/C_h} = 2D(1 - d/p)$.

15. $Q^* = 5{,}164.03$.

17. $Q^* = \sqrt[3]{\dfrac{2DC_o}{C_h}}$. Annual holding cost equals annual carrying cost.

25. *EOQ* total cost = \$12,005,163.98. Under discount, total cost = \$11,987,711.10. $Q = 100{,}000$, $S = 11{,}111.11$.

31. *b*) $TC(5{,}000, 29.70) = \$749.175$, $TC(10{,}000, 29.55) = \$751{,}300$. Buy in lots of 5,000.
    c) $TC(507.67, 97) = \$489{,}924.43$, $TC(1{,}000, 96) = \$486{,}050$, $TC(2{,}000, 95) = \$485{,}125$. Buy in lots of 2,000.
    d) Cost minimized at \$19,447,250 when ordered in lot sizes of 10,000.

33. When salvage value is 7, order 103 units. When salvage value is 12, order 111 units. More willing to risk stockout when salvage value is higher.

35. Equation 15.17 assumes $R > d_L$. If $R < d_L$, then $R - d_L < 0$ and $C_h(R - d_L)$ would make no sense because money would be received for holding negative inventory.

37. $P(d_L > R^*) = .02$, $R^* = 960$.

39. *a*) $Q^* = 3{,}000$, $R^* = 960$, $R^* - d_L = 80$.
    b) $Q^* = 3{,}000$, $R^* = 940$, $R^* - d_L = 60$.
    c) $Q^* = 3{,}000$, $R^* = 900$, $R^* - d_L = 20$.
    d) $Q^* = 3{,}000$, $R^* = 940$, $R^* - d_L = 60$.

41. $D = 4{,}964$, $d_L = 68$, $Q^* = 249.1$, $R^* = 72$, safety stock = 4 units.

43. $Q = 821.2916$, $R = 510$.

45. 45 to 60 percent of items make up 5 percent of dollar volume. Percentages do not need to work out exactly.

47. $EOQ_1 + EOQ_2 = 400{,}000$.

49. No; this could not be done because 1,098 units of the gozinto subassembly would not be ready on time. Expediting to cut down the gozinto lead time might make it possible.

51. Widgets:

	Week			
	5	**6**	**7**	**8**
MPS		300		300

Widgets:

	Week				
	4	**5**	**6**	**7**	**8**
GR			300		300
OH	50	50	0	0	0
POR	250		300		

Gadget subassembly:

	Week				
	2	**3**	**4**	**5**	**6**
GR			250		300
OH	3	3			
POR	247				

Gozinto subassembly:

	Week					
	1	**2**	**3**	**4**	**5**	**6**
GR				500		600
OH	2	2	2			
POR	498		600			

CHAPTER 16

11.

n	P_n	ΣP_n
0	0.160	0.160
1	0.134	0.294
2	0.113	0.407
3	0.095	0.502
4	0.080	0.582
5	0.067	0.649
6	0.056	0.705
7	0.047	0.752

13. $2.625 < \mu < 2.8$

15. $\mu > 9.39$

17. $\lambda = 0.9/2 = 0.45$ and $\rho = 0.45/0.4 > 1$. Steady state not achievable.

19. $0.45 < \mu < 0.5$

21. The use of 5 windows yields $W_b = 4.54 < 5$; 45 percent; $5 \cdot L_s = 5(0.818) = 4.09$ customers in system which compares to 9 when three windows used.

25. $R = 0.42$.

27. $N = 5$

N	P_o	L_s	L_q	L_b	W_s	W_q	W_b
2	0.4324	0.8108	0.2432	0.4286	3.57	1.07	1.89
5	0.3041	1.7009	1.0050	1.4443	6.11	3.61	5.19

Significant increases in all L and W.

29. $R = 2.5$, $E_1 = 0.875$, $E_2 = 0.0016$.

33. $P(n < 3) = 0.432242$.

37.

N	L_s	L_q	L_b	W_s	W_q	W_b
∞	3.95	1.70	2.98	4.39	1.89	3.31
5	2.40	0.46	1.88	3.10	0.60	2.42

$P_5 = 0.1391$. Expected number of rejections = $\lambda P_5 = 7.5114$ cars/hour.

41. Realized revenue = \$23.55, lost revenue = \$76.40, implicit revenue = −\$52.85.

43. a)

c	P(wait)	L_s	L_q	L_b	W_s	W_q	W_b
1	0.9984	3.50	2.50	2.50	140	100	100
2	0.9302	3.03	1.12	1.12	63	23	23

Total cost per day = \$351.45, compared to \$448.37 with one terminal.

47. a) $W_s = 4.39$, $L_s = 3.95$, $L_q = 1.70$
    b) $\lambda_e = 0.228$, $W_s = 3.50$, $L_s = 0.80$, $L_q = 0.23$.
    c) $\lambda_e = 0.025$, $W_s = 140$, $L_s = 3.5$, $L_q = 2.5$.

49.

	Each L_s	Overall L_s	W_s	W_q	L_q
Example 16.8	21.15	84.6	1.175	1.125	20.25
With 5 facilities	5.76	29.8	0.400	0.350	5.04

Significant improvement occurs.

51.

	Each L_s	Overall L_s	W_s	W_q	L_q
M/G/1	21.15	84.6	1.175	1.125	20.25
M/D/1	4.95	19.8	0.275	0.225	4.05

67. M/M/1 finite population model with $\lambda = 0.2$, $\mu = 4$, $\rho = 0.05$:

m	P_o	$P(n > 0)$
10	0.538	0.462
9	0.582	0.418
8	0.627	0.373
7	0.672	0.328
6	0.718	0.282

Assign six terminals to each service rep.

69. M/G/1 model with $\lambda = 0.0667$ products/min. and $\rho = 0.8$:
    a) $L_s = 6.4$ products/subsystem = 19.2 products for overall system, $W_s = 96$ minutes/product, $W_q = 84$ minutes/product, $L_q = 5.6$ products/queue.
    b) $L_s = 2.8$/subsystem; 8.4 overall, $W_s = 42$, $W_q = 30$, $L_q = 2$.
    c) $L_s = 2.4$/subsystem; 7.2 overall, $W_s = 36$, $W_q = 24$, $L_q = 1.6$.

CHAPTER 17

1. Expected weekly profit; robot 1—\$8,600, robot 2—\$10,200, robot 3—\$8,650.
3. Expected weekly profit: robot 1—\$8,500, robot 2—\$9,675, robot 3—\$7,675.
7. a) Experimental objectives: Determine which of the two systems provides the best system performance.
   b) Design alternatives: aside from express tellers, the number of each type might be varied along with the definition of the function of express tellers.
   c) Initialization: Number of tellers of each type, number of customers in bank at beginning of simulation (zero or a typical number), day of week, time of day.
   d) Parameters: Arrival rates, service rates, and variations in these subject to day of week and time of day considerations.
   e) Criteria for length of run: Specified number of customers, specified time period (hours or days).
9. a) Experimental objectives; predict outcome of fight.
   b) Design alternatives: Ages of fighters, number of rounds, scoring methods, definition of events for example, (how does fight simulation advance?).
   c) Initialization: Round number, scoring, clock.
   d) Parameters: Condition of fighters, ability of fighters to land different types of punches,

damage inflicted by different types of punches, probability of fighter using particular punch, blocking ability, and so forth.

e) Criteria for length of run: Number of rounds, occurrence of some type of knockout, number of punches landed against one fighter.

11. Experimental objectives: Determine comparative ability of existing and proposed dining halls to serve needs of students.
    b) Design alternative: Different configurations for two new serving lines and five existing lines, different service station arrangements.
    c) Initialization: Number of students in the system, number of employees and their functions, day of week and meal being served.
    d) Parameters; Arrival rates, service time rates.
    e) Criteria for length of run: Number of meals served, number of students served, number of days or hours simulated.
15. *a*) $W_q = 9/10 = 0.9$ minute.
    b) $W_b = 9/6 = 1.5$ minutes.
    c) $1/10 = 0.1$ unit.
    d) $L_q = 0.21$ unit.
    e) $L_b = 0.38$ unit.
    f) $Ws = 3.3$ minutes.
    g) $P(\text{idle}) = 19/43 = 0.44$.
19. *a*) Overall utilization = 0.784.
    b) Total entries (arrivals) are 25,000 in each part. Mean time in queue (8.011 minutes) the same. Of the 25,000 arrivals, 48.7 percent entered immediately.
    c) 0, 0.71, $1 - 0.933 = 0.067$, $1 - 0.487 = 0.513$.
21. $c = 5$, $\lambda = 1/6$, $\mu = 1/20 = 0.05$, $\rho = 3.334 < 5$, $P_o = 0.0317$, $P(n > c) = 0.3269$, $L_s = 3.988$, $L_q = 0.654$, $W_q = 3.924$, $W_b = 12.005$.
23. *a*) $S = \$2,000$, $C = \$5,720$, $\overline{C} = \$286$ (21 percent increase in $\overline{C}$ for 100 percent increase in C_s.).
    b) $O = \$500$, $C = \$5,120$, $\overline{C} = \$256$ (8 percent increase in $\overline{C}$ for 400 percent increase in C_o).
    c) $H = \$5,430$, $C = \$6,530$, $\overline{C} = 326.50$ (38 percent increase in $\overline{C}$ for 50 percent increase in C_h.).
    d) $H = \$10,920$, $O = \$60$, $S = \$0$, $C = \$10,980$, $\overline{C} = \$549$.
25. *a*)

	Physical Units of B_1	Physical Units of E_1	H	O	S	C
Total	6,940	6,940	6,940	60	600	7,600
Average	347	347	347	3	30	380
b)						
Total	6,340	6,120	6,120	100	0	6,220
Average	317	306	306	5	0	311

29. *a*) $W_q = 504/20 = 25.2$ hours, $W_b = 504/12 = 42.0$ hours, mean queue length at entry = 0.95 freighter, $L_q = 504/510 = 0.99$ freighter, $L_b = 504/336 = 1.5$ freighters, $W_s = 840/20 = 42$ hours, $P(\text{idle}) = 174/510 = 0.34$.
    b) $E(\text{service time}) = 21.36$ hours; $\mu = 1/21.36 = 0.0468$, $E(\text{interarrival time}) = 25.0$ hours, $\lambda = 1/25.0 = 0.04$, $\rho = 0.04/0.0468 = 0.8547 < 1$. See table below.
    c) $W_q = 882/20 = 44.1$ hours, $W_b = 882/16 = 55.1$ hours, mean queue length at entry = 2.35 freighters, $L_q = 1,152/502 = 2.29$ freighters, $L_b = 1,152/468 = 2.46$ freighters, $W_s = 1,278/20 = 63.9$ hours, $P(\text{idle}) = 34/502 = 0.068$.
31. $E(\text{gain}) = 8 - E$ (number of flips in game)
    $= 8 - 9$ (based on over 1,000 games)
    $= -\$1/\text{game}$.
33. *a*) Based on columns 1 and 2 of Table 17–10:

	Design 1	Design 2
Average amortized cost/day	\$1.00	\$1.50
Average heating cost/day	2.37	1.70
Total cost/day	\$3.37	\$3.20

APPENDIX A

1. 0.4, 0.65, 0.35, 0.25, 0.5, $P(E_1'$ *and* E_1' and $E_1') = (40/100)(39/99)(38/98) = 0.061$.

See Exercise 29.

	P_o	ρ	L_s	L_q	L_b	W_s	W_q	W_b
Theoretical	0.1453	0.8547	5.88	5.03	5.88	147.1	125.7	147.1
Simulation	0.3400	0.6600	1.65	0.99	1.50	42.0	25.2	42.0

11.

	$N = 20$ $P = 0.5$	$N = 100$ $P = 0.1$
$P(X \leq 10)$	0.5881	0.5832
$P(X = 10)$	0.1762	0.1319
$E(X)$	10.0	10.0
$V(X)$	5.0	9.0

13. $f(x) = 1$, $F(x) = x$, $E(X) = 1/2$, $V(X) = 1/12$.

25. y_c = expected total cost, x = number of orders, $y_c = 496.94 + 31.11x$.

27.

Source	SS	dF	MS	F
Regression	34,844	1	34,844	189
Residual	1,106	6	184	
Total	35,950	7		

$t = 13.752$, $r = 0.985$, $r^2 = 0.97$. For $\alpha = .01$, reject null hypothesis that $B = 0$.

29. $y_c = 683.60$, expected $y_i = 683.60 \pm 19.67$, individual $y_i = 683.60 \pm 59.35$.

APPENDIX B

9. *a)* $y'' = -4(7 + 4x + x^2)^{-3} + (48 + 24x) \cdot (7 + 4x + x^2)^{-4}$.
   b) $y'' = 540x^4 - 720x^2 + 100$.
   c) $y'' = \dfrac{-12x^4 + 48x}{x^6 + 4x^3 + 4}$.

11. $x^* = 0$ and $x^* = -4/15$.
13. min. at $x^* = 0$; max. at $x^* = -4/15$.
15. max. at $x^* = 10$.
17. max. at $(2, -85\frac{1}{3})$ and min. at $(8, -121\frac{1}{3})$.
19. max. at $(0, 0)$, min. at $(-3, -81/4)$, min. at $(3, -81/4)$.
21. min. at $(0, 0)$ and max at $(-5, 125/6)$.
23. min. at $(0, 22026)$.
25. max. at $(1/3, 1.3026)$.
27. $f_x = 8x$, $f_y = -6y$.
29. $f_x = 30x(x^2 - y)^4$, $f_y = -15(x^2 - y)^4$.
33. $f_{xx} = 2 - 4y$, $f_{yy} = -10$, $f_{xy} = -4x + 1$, $f_{yx} = -4x + 1$.
35. $f_{xx} = 2/y^2$, $f_{yy} = 6x^2/y^4$, $f_{xy} = -4x/y^3$, $f_{yx} = -4x/y^3$.
37. Saddle point at $(2, 3, -4)$.
39. Saddle point at $(0, 0, 100)$, and relative max. at $(16, 0, 2, 148)$.
41. *a)* max. at $x^* = 1/4$.
    c) Stationary inflection point at $x^* = 3$.
    e) max. at $x^* = 0$; min. at $x^* = 6$.
    g) max. at $x^* = 6$.
    i) max. at $x^* = 0$; min. at $x^* = 4/3$.
    k) min. at $x^* = 0$; max. at $x^* = 5$; min. at $x^* = 10$.
    m) max. at $x^* = 2.5$.
43. *a)* min when $x_1^* = 1/2$ and $x_2^* = 1/2$.
    c) Saddle point when $x_1^* = -1$ and $x_2^* = 3/2$.
    e) Saddle point when $x_1^* = -10$ and $x_2^* = 10$.
    g) Saddle point when $x_1^* = x_2^* = 0$ and min. when $x_1^* = x_2^* = 1$.

INDEX

T

U

V–Z